CALCULUS
and its Applications

First Edition

Angelo B. Mingarelli
Carleton University

www.math.carleton.ca/~amingare/calculus/cal104.html

For your Free Plotter, visit the author's **Mathzone** at
http://www.math.carleton.ca/~amingare/calculus/cal104.html

August 26, 2002

This book is dedicated
to the immutable memory of my father,
Giosafat Mingarelli,
and
to my mother, Oliviana Lopez Mingarelli,
who showed a young child of 10
how to perform long division ...

Preface to the First Edition

This text is a combined form of two previous modules by the author entitled *Differential Calculus* and *Integral Calculus* each part of the Millennium Series in Calculus, an ongoing series of calculus texts intended to treat the Calculus sequence as a whole.

The present book is a major revision of both modules. Many typographical and other errors have been identified and corrected and some exercises (even some proofs!) have been added to complement the text. Among the major additions in this volume we cite: The compilation of a section on *Improper Integrals*, one on *Measuring the Length of an Arc*, and a section on *Moments and Centers of Mass*. The Solution Manual has been updated and expanded. The following sections are in preparation: Applied Problems in Calculus, Differentials, Related Rates, Life and Neutron Stars (really!).

Angelo Mingarelli, July 28, 1999

The August 14, 2000 edition includes a preliminary working chapter on Multivariable Calculus and optimization techniques as well as two new appendices on Radicals and Straight Lines. Typographical errors have been corrected and the material expanded in various places. Applications to Business and Economics are also included throughout. A complete Solutions Manual is fused with this Edition.

Angelo Mingarelli, August 14, 2000

The August 2001 edition, dubbed the first edition, is to be considered the definite edition as it takes into account typographical and other corrections from the Aug. 14, 2000 edition and student comments from the past three years. In addition, there is a new section on single variable optimization problems as well as a section on relating rates of change. Many thanks to each one of the students whose names were reported to me (all of whom are mentioned in the Credits at the end of this book) and who drew my attention to discrepancies and improvements, and countless thanks to all those who chose to remain anonymous. This edition has a full Solutions Manual available on the website.

The author, August 2001

The August 2002 edition, takes into account further typographical and other corrections from the Aug. 27, 2001 edition and student comments from the past four years. The main difference is the addition of computer assisted problems (technology) at the end of each chapter and a complete set of solutions. The chapter on Advanced Topics has been left out of this custom edition and the same is true of the chapter on Multivariable Optimization Problems.

The author, August, 2002

Preface to the Earlier Modules

This book is about learning to work out Calculus problems and understanding some of the underlying mathematics. It is written primarily for students wishing to learn and be proficient in the subject. It is assumed that every Instructor will have a personal approach to the delivery of this material and that this approach may be independent of this author's vision of the same. Nevertheless, this manual is directed at the students and it can be used to complement most classroom presentations.

The basic philosophy underlying its content lies in leaving out complicated looking proofs of theorems and moving these either to the author's Website (a location on the Internet's World Wide Web) or to the Exercises where many hints are given. In this way we may simplify the visual impact of this text and concentrate on those points which one deems important. In the author's opinion, there is a need to review basic material while working towards a common goal which includes the fostering of a feeling for what Calculus is and how to solve problems correctly in the field. The choice and ordering of the subject matter is based upon a purely personal view into the perceived skills acquired by students as they embark upon the first-year experience.

Chapters usually begin with a section entitled *The Big Picture* where a basic introduction to the material is given in reference to what is already known, and what one may expect later. This is usually followed by a box entitled *Review* where it becomes clear that some skills are more necessary than others for mastery of the subject matter at hand. In some cases we present the material in an odd mix of combined verbal, theoretical, practical, numerical, and geometrical approaches in an attempt to satisfy as many learning styles as possible. The presentation is very personal and it is based upon the author's delivery of the material in a large classroom setting (normally comprised of around 200 students).

At various times in the text, *Shortcuts* are introduced in an attempt to simplify the solution of a given exercise, or class of exercises. Most chapters have individual breaks at a box entitled *Snapshots*. These snapshots consist of *more* examples where we leave out many of the details and outline the rest. We have made a conscious attempt at being repetitive as, in many cases, this is a key to remembering material. Each chapter and its sections concludes with many routine and not so routine exercises that complement the examples. The matter of specific *applications* is treated in a very limited form in this preliminary edition. In many cases, notably in the early chapters, we leave in the most simple of details in order to reinforce those skills which students may find nebulous at times. The student will find it useful to know that the Tables listed under the heading *List of Tables* comprise most of the material and definitions necessary for proficiency in the subject.

The material presented here is used at a first-year level in a standard one-term course in Calculus for Engineers or Scientists at Carleton University. The book will eventually evolve into a full-fledged Calculus text, complete with web site references and use of computer technology. The manual can be used in a High-School setting with students having mastered the basics of Algebra, Geometry and Trigonometry. The normal part of Differential Calculus includes Chapters 1-5. An optional section entitled *Advanced Topics* introduces the interested student to the real core of Calculus, with rigorous definitions, limit results and *epsilon-delta* arguments, although this is usually left out of the standard Calculus sequence. This text may be used as an introductory (including Honours) one-term course in Calculus. The choice of topics may be left to the Instructor but the main breakdown of this presentation may be found on the author's website.

Finally, we point out that the author's web site is a source of information with multiple-choice quizzes that will reinforce the material presented in the text along with links to other websites. The quizzes are graded *on the fly* by means of a cgi-script running on our servers and answers are delivered within seconds of submission along with a score. Since websites are always 'under construction' our web site will evolve along with this series. Comments and suggestions are encouraged.

Angelo B. Mingarelli
Ottawa, Canada
October 12, 1998 and August 18, 2002.
http://www.math.carleton.ca/~amingare/
e-mail: amingare@math.carleton.ca

ISBN 0-9698889-3-7

Acknowledgments

This manual is the combined effort of about twenty volunteer typesetters. Most of them were former students in first-year or upper-level Calculus courses that I taught. They spent many, many hours of long arduous work learning the new environment which LaTeX brings with it and began and submitted their work during the summer of 1998. My most sincere thanks goes to each one of them as I remember them here:

Among those who went *beyond the call of duty* and who have made an outstanding contribution, I cite: Genevieve Hay, M.Sc., M.B.A., (LaTeX guru *extraordinaire*), David Willis, Fu Keong Gary (Bomberman) Chan, Stephen Knox, and Rosemary Takac. I am also very grateful to Jean-Luc Cooke, Caroline Lam, Carson Tsang, Marsha Bissessarsingh, and Alan Speer for typesetting many parts of the chapters in this text. I also wish to thank Ela Beres, Pedram Sodouri, and Selvakumar Krishnathasan for their contributions. I am particularly indebted to my colleague Dr. C. K. Fong, of the School of Mathematics and Statistics, for his careful proofreading and his suggestions during the final reading of the original manuscript. As well, I must acknowledge with thanks the availability of the excellent original course notes by Kristy Townshend, notes which were derived from a Pre-Calculus course that I taught in 1997. Many thanks are also due to Ms. Ann Woodside for her assistance.

These dedicated individuals made the production of this manual possible in a mere three months. As well, I am grateful to Carleton University, Ottawa, for their generous support in the form of a Teaching Achievement Award for 1998-1999, thereby providing me with teaching release during the Winter of 1999. I extend many thanks to the Faculty of Science for its recognition of my contributions in the form of two further awards for Excellence in Teaching within the Faculty.

On a more personal note, I am most grateful to my children and to my partner, Karen, for believing in me and for believing in this project, and for their unusual patience and understanding during my long absences in the Summer of 1998. This work is as much theirs as it is mine: I may not have embarked upon so great an enterprise had I not been given all this moral support.

Additonal acknowledgments will be given in the Credits section at the end of the text as revisions appear.

Angelo B. Mingarelli

Contents

List of Tables

Chapter 1

Functions and Their Properties

Gottfried Wilhelm Leibniz
1646 - 1716

The Big Picture

This chapter deals with the definition and properties of things we call *functions*. They are used all the time in the world around us although we don't recognize them right away. Functions are a mathematical device for describing an inter-dependence between things or objects, whether real or imaginary. With this notion, the original creators of Calculus, namely, the English mathematician and physicist, Sir Isaac Newton, and the German philosopher and mathematician, Gottfried Wilhelm Leibniz (see inset), were able to quantify and express relationships between real things in a mathematical way. Most of you will have seen the famous Einstein equation

$$E = mc^2.$$

This expression defines a dependence of the quantity, E, called the *energy* on m, called the *mass*. The number c is the *speed of light* in a vacuum, some 300,000 kilometers per second. In this simple example, E is a *function* of m. Almost all naturally occuring phenomena in the universe may be quantified in terms of functions and their relationships to each other. A complete understanding of the material in this chapter will enable you to gain a foothold into the fundamental vocabulary of Calculus.

Review

You'll need to remember or learn the following material before you get a thorough understanding of this chapter. Look over your notes on functions and be familiar with all the **basic algebra** and **geometry** you learned and also don't forget to review your **basic trigonometry**. Although this seems like a lot, it is necessary as mathematics is a sort of language, and before you learn any language you need to be familiar with its vocabulary and its grammar and so it is with mathematics. Okay, let's start ...

1.1 The Meaning of a Function

You realize how important it is to know your account number when you step into a bank! That's because the bank associates you with your account number. This is

You can think of a function f as an I/O device, much like a computer CPU; it takes input, x, works on x, and produces only one output, which we call $f(x)$.

what a **function** does ... a function is a rule that associates to each element in some set that we like to call the **domain** (in our case, people who have a bank account at the bank) only one element of another set, called the **range** (in our case, the set of all their bank account numbers).

Example 1. *Two people can share a common bank account number (in the case of a joint account) but in general, no one person can have, say, two driving permit numbers from the same locality. You can see this depicted graphically in Figure 2, where the rule wants to assign to A the two values a,b, which would contradict the definition of a function. On the other hand, in Figure 1, both C and D share bank account number b and this is alright, and it is easy to see that every one in the domain of this function has exactly one account.*

This association between the domain and the range is depicted graphically in Figure 1 using arrows, called an **arrow diagram**. Such arrows are useful because they start in the domain and point to the corresponding element of the range.

Example 2. *Let's say that Jennifer Black has account number 234124. The arrow would start at a point which we label "Jennifer Black" (in the domain) and end at a point labeled "234124" (in the range).*

Okay, so here's the formal definition of a function ...

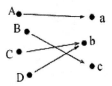

Figure 1.

NOTATION

Dom (f) = Domain of f

Ran (f) = Range of f

Objects in the domain of f are referred to as independent variables, while objects in the range are dependent variables.

> **Definition 1.** *A function f is a rule which associates with each object (say, x) from one set named the domain, a single object (say, $f(x)$) from a second set called the range. (See Figure 1)*

Rather than replace every person by their photograph, the objects of the domain of a function are replaced by **symbols** and mathematicians like to use the symbol "x" to mark some unknown quantity in the domain (this symbol is also called an **independent variable**), because it can be *any* object in the domain. If you don't like this symbol, you can use any other symbol and this won't change the function. The symbol, $f(x)$, is also called a **dependent variable** because its value generally *depends* on the value of x. Below, we'll use the "box" symbol, $\Box$, in many cases instead of the more standard symbol, x.

Example 3. *Let f be the (name of the) function which associates a person with their height. Using a little shorthand we can write this rule as $h = f(p)$ where p is a particular person, (p is the independent variable) and h is that person's height (h is the dependent variable). The domain of this function f is the set of all persons, right? Moreover, the range of this function is a set of numbers (their height, with some units of measurement attached to each one). Once again, let's notice that many people can have the same height, and this is okay for a function, but clearly there is no one having two different heights (otherwise this rule would not be a function, see Figure 2, where the arrow starting at A splits and meets a and b at the same time.)*

> **LOOK OUT!** When an arrow "splits" in an arrow diagram (Figure 2) the resulting rule is *never* a function.

In applications of calculus to the physical and natural sciences the domain and the range of a function are both sets of real numbers. The symbols used to represent objects within these sets may vary though ... E may denote energy, p the price of a commodity, x distance, t time, etc. The domain and the range of a function may be the same set or they may be totally unrelated sets of numbers, people, aardvarks,

A rule which is NOT a function

Figure 2.

aliens, etc. Now, functions have to be identified somehow, so rules have been devised to *name them.* Usually, we use the lower case letters $f, g, h, k, \ldots$ to name the function itself, but you are allowed to use any other symbols too, but try not to use x as this might cause some confusion ... we already decided to name objects of the domain of the function by this symbol, x, remember?.

Quick Summary Let's recapitulate. A function has a *name*, a *domain* and a *range*. It also has a *rule* which associates to every object of its domain only one object in its range. So the rule (whose name is) g which associates to a given number its square as a number, can be denoted quickly by $g(x) = x^2$ (Figure 3). You can also represent this rule by using $g(\square) = \square^2$ where $\square$ is a "box"... something that has nothing to do with its shape. It's just as good a symbol as "x" and both equations represent the *same* function.

> You need to think beyond the *shape* of an independent variable and just keep your mind on a generic "variable", something that has nothing to do with its shape.

Remember... x is just a symbol for what we call an independent variable, that's all. We can read off a rule like $g(x) = x^2$ in many ways: The purist would say "The value of g at x is x^2" while some might say, "g of x is x^2". What's really important though is that you *understand the rule...* in this case we would say that the function associates a symbol with its square *regardless of the shape of the symbol itself*, whether it be an x, $\square$, $\triangle$, $\heartsuit$, t, etc.

Example 4.   *Generally speaking,*

- The association between a one-dollar bill and its serial number is a function (unless the bill is counterfeit!) whose domain is the collection of all one-dollar bills and whose range is a subset of the natural numbers along with 26 letters of the alphabet.

- The association between a CD-ROM and its own serial number is also a function (unless the CD was copied!).

- Associating a fingerprint with a specific human being is another example of a function, as is

- Associating a human being with the person-specific DNA.

- The association between the value of a stock, say, x, at time t is also function but this time it is a function of *two* variables, namely, x, t. It could be denoted by $f(x, t)$ meaning that this symbol describes the value of the stock x at time t.

- The correspondence between a patent number and a given (patented) invention is a function

- The difference between two functions is also a function. For example, if $R(x) = px$ denotes the *total revenue* function, that is, the product of the number of units, x, sold at price p, and $C(x)$ denotes the total cost of producing these x units, then the difference, $P(x) = R(x) - C(x)$ is the *profit* acquired after the sale of these x units.

1.2   Function Values and the Box Method

The function $g(x) = x^2$ and some of its values.

x	$g(x)$
-2	4
-1	1
0.5	0.25
1.5	2.25
3	9
0.1	0.01
-2.5	6.25
5	25
10	100
-3	9

Figure 3.

NOTATION for Intervals.

$(a, b) = \{x : a < x < b\}$, and this is called an **open interval**. $[a, b]$ $= \{x : a \le x \le b\}$, is called a **closed interval**. $(a, b], [a, b)$ each denote the sets $\{x : a < x \le b\}$ and $\{x : a \le x < b\}$, respectively (either one of these is called a **semi-open**

Now look at our function g defined above by the rule $g(x) = x^2$. Let's say we want to know the value of the mysterious looking symbols, $g(3x + 4)$.

How do we get this?

The Box Method

To find the value of $g(3x+4)$ when $g(x) = x^2$: We place all the symbols "$3x+4$" (all the stuff between the parentheses in the symbol "$g(...)$") inside a box, say, $\Box$, and let the function g take the box $\Box$ to $\Box^2$ (because this is what a function *does* to a symbol, regardless of what it looks like, right?). Then we "remove the box" , replace its sides by parentheses, and there you are ... what's left is the value of $g(3x + 4)$.

We call this procedure the **Box Method**.

Example 5.   *So, if $g(x) = x^2$, then $g(\Box) = \Box^2$. So, according to our rule, $g(3x + 4) = g(\boxed{3x+4}) = \boxed{3x+4}^2 = (3x+4)^2$. This last quantity, when simplified, gives us $9x^2 + 24x + 16$. We have found that $g(3x + 4) = 9x^2 + 24x + 16$.*

Example 6.   *If f is a new function defined by the rule $f(x) = x^3 - 4$ then $f(\Box) = \Box^3 - 4$ (regardless of what's in the box!), and*

$$f(a + h) = f(\boxed{a+h}) = \boxed{a+h}^3 - 4 = (a+h)^3 - 4 = a^3 + 3a^2h + 3ah^2 + h^3 - 4.$$

Also,

$$f(2) = 2^3 - 4 = 4,$$

and

$$f(-1) = (-1)^3 - 4 = -5,$$
$$f(a) = a^3 - 4,$$

where a is another symbol for any object in the domain of f.

Example 7.   *Let $f(x) = \dfrac{1.24x^2}{\sqrt{2.63x - 1}}$. Find the value of $f(n + 6)$ where n is a positive integer.*

Solution The Box Method gives

$$f(x) = \frac{1.24x^2}{\sqrt{2.63x - 1}}$$

$$f(\Box) = \frac{1.24\Box^2}{\sqrt{2.63\Box - 1}}$$

$$f(\boxed{n+6}) = \frac{1.24\boxed{n+6}^2}{\sqrt{2.63\boxed{n+6} - 1}}$$

$$f(n + 6) = \frac{1.24(n + 6)^2}{\sqrt{2.63(n + 6) - 1}}$$

$$= \frac{1.24(n^2 + 12n + 36)}{\sqrt{2.63n + 15.78 - 1}}$$

$$= \frac{1.24n^2 + 14.88n + 44.64}{\sqrt{2.63n + 14.78}}.$$

Example 8. *On the other hand, if $f(x) = 2x^2 - x + 1$, and $h \neq 0$ is some real number, how do we find the value of the quotient*

$$\frac{f(x + h) - f(x)}{h} ?$$

Solution Well, we know that $f(\square) = 2\square^2 - \square + 1$. So, the idea is to put the symbols $x + h$ inside the box, use the rule for f on the *box* symbol, then expand the whole thing and subtract the quantity $f(x)$ (and, finally, divide this result by h). Now, the value of f evaluated at $x + h$, that is, $f(x + h)$, is given by

$$\begin{aligned} f(\boxed{x + h}) &= 2\boxed{x + h}^2 - \boxed{x + h} + 1, \\ &= 2(x + h)^2 - (x + h) + 1 \\ &= 2(x^2 + 2xh + h^2) - x - h + 1 \\ &= 2x^2 + 4xh + 2h^2 - x - h + 1. \end{aligned}$$

From this we get,

$$\begin{aligned} \frac{f(x + h) - f(x)}{h} &= \frac{2x^2 + 4xh + 2h^2 - x - h + 1 - (2x^2 - x + 1)}{h} \\ &= \frac{4xh + 2h^2 - h}{h} \\ &= \frac{h(4x + 2h - 1)}{h} \\ &= 4x + 2h - 1. \end{aligned}$$

provided $h \neq 0$.

> **Don't forget** that, in Calculus, we always assume that angles are described in **radians** and not degrees. The conversion is given by
>
> $$Radians = \frac{(Degrees) \times (\pi)}{180}$$
>
> For example, 45 degrees $= 45\,\pi/180 = \pi/4 \approx 0.7853981633974$ radians.

Example 9. *Let $f(x) = 6x^2 - 0.5x$. Write the values of f at an integer by $f(n)$, where the symbol "n" is used to denote an integer. Thus $f(1) = 5.5$. Now write $f(n) = a_n$. Calculate the quantity $\frac{a_{n+1}}{a_n}$.*

Solution The Box method tells us that since $f(n) = a_n$, we must have $f(\square) = a_\square$. Thus, $a_{n+1} = f(n + 1)$. Furthermore, another application of the Box Method gives $a_{n+1} = f(n + 1) = f(\boxed{n+1}) = 6\boxed{n+1}^2 - 0.5\boxed{n+1}$. So,

$$\frac{a_{n+1}}{a_n} = \frac{6(n + 1)^2 - 0.5(n + 1)}{6n^2 - 0.5n} = \frac{6n^2 + 11.5n + 5.5}{6n^2 - 0.5n}.$$

"Formerly, when one invented a new function, it was to further some practical purpose; today one invents them in order to make incorrect the reasoning of our fathers, and nothing more will ever be accomplished by these inventions."

Henri Poincaré, 1854 - 1912
French mathematician

Some useful angles expressed in radians

degrees	radians
0	0
30°	$\pi/6$
45°	$\pi/4$
60°	$\pi/3$
90°	$\pi/2$
180°	π
270°	$3\pi/2$
360°	2π

Figure 4.

EXAMPLES

Example 10.   *Given that*

$$f(x) = \frac{3x + 2}{3x - 2}$$

determine $f(x - 2)$.

Solution Here, $f(\Box) = \frac{3\Box + 2}{3\Box - 2}$. Placing the symbol "$x - 2$" into the box, collecting terms and simplifying, we get,

$$f(x - 2) = f(\boxed{x\text{-}2}) = \frac{3\boxed{x\text{-}2} + 2}{3\boxed{x\text{-}2} - 2} = \frac{3(x - 2) + 2}{3(x - 2) - 2} = \frac{3x - 4}{3x - 8}.$$

Example 11.   *If* $g(x) = x^2 + 1$ *find the value of* $g(\sqrt{x - 1})$.

Solution Since $g(\Box) = \Box^2 + 1$ it follows that

$$g(\sqrt{x - 1}) = [\sqrt{x - 1}]^2 + 1 = [x - 1] + 1 = x$$

on account of the fact that $\sqrt[2]{\Box}^2 = \Box$, regardless of "what's in the box".

Example 12.   *Let* f *be defined by*

$$f(x) = \begin{cases} x + 1, & \text{if} \quad -1 \leq x \leq 0, \\ x^2, & \text{if} \quad 0 < x \leq 3, \end{cases}$$

a) What is $f(-1)$?

b) Evaluate $f(0.70714)$.

c) Given that $0 < x < 1$ *evaluate* $f(2x + 1)$.

Solution a) Since $f(x) = x + 1$ for any x in the interval $-1 \leq x \leq 0$ and $x = -1$ is in this interval, it follows that $f(-1) = (-1) + 1 = 0$.

b) Since $f(x) = x^2$ for any x in the interval $0 < x \leq 3$ and $x = 0.70714$ is in this interval, it follows that $f(0.70714) = (0.70714)^2 = 0.50005$

c) For $0 < x < 1$ we know that $0 < 2x < 2$ and so once we add 1 to each of the terms in the inequality we see that $1 = 0 + 1 < 2x + 1 < 2 + 1 = 3$. In other words, whenever $0 < x < 1$, the values of the expression $2x + 1$ must lie in the interval $1 < 2x + 1 < 3$. We now use the Box method: Since $f(x) = x^2$ we have, by definition, $f(\Box) = \Box^2$ whenever $0 < \Box \leq 3$. Putting $2x + 1$ in the box, (and using the fact that $1 < \boxed{2x\text{+}1} < 3$) we find that $f(\boxed{2x\text{+}1}) = \boxed{2x\text{+}1}^2$ from which we deduce $f(2x + 1) = (2x + 1)^2$ for $0 < x < 1$.

NOTES:

> **SNAPSHOTS**

Example 13. *This example requires knowledge of trigonometry. Given that* $h(t) = t^2 \cos(t)$ *and* $Dom(h) = (-\infty, \infty)$. *Determine the value of* $h(\sin x)$.

Solution We know that $h(\square) = \square^2 \cos(\square)$. So, $h(\boxed{\sin x}) = \boxed{\sin x}^2 \cos(\boxed{\sin x})$. Removing the box we get, $h(\sin x) = (\sin x)^2 \cos(\sin x)$, or, equivalently, $h(\sin x) = (\sin x)^2 \cos(\sin x) = \sin^2(x) \cos(\sin x)$.

Example 14. *Let* f *be defined by the rule* $f(x) = \sin x$. *Then the function whose values are defined by* $f(x - vt) = \sin(x - vt)$ *can be thought of as representing a travelling wave moving to the right with velocity* $v \geq 0$. *Here* t *represents time and we take it that* $t \geq 0$. *You can get a feel for this motion from the graph below where we assume that* $v = 0$ *and use three increasing times to simulate the motion of the wave to the right.*

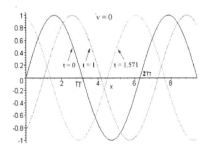

The function $f(x) = \sin x$ and some of its values.

x (in radians)	$\sin x$
0	0
$\pi/6$	$1/2 = 0.5$
$-\pi/6$	$-1/2 = -0.5$
$\pi/3$	$\sqrt{3}/2 \approx 0.8660$
$-\pi/3$	$-\sqrt{3}/2 \approx -0.8660$
$\pi/2$	1
$-\pi/2$	-1
$\pi/4$	$\sqrt{2}/2 \approx 0.7071$
$-\pi/4$	$-\sqrt{2}/2 \approx -0.7071$
$3\pi/2$	-1
$-3\pi/2$	1
2π	0

Figure 5.

Example 15. *On the surface of our moon, an object* P *falling from rest will fall a distance,* $f(t)$, *of approximately* $5.3t^2$ *feet in* t *seconds. Let's take it for granted that its, so-called,* **instantaneous velocity***, denoted by the symbol* $f'(t)$, *at time* $t = t_0 \geq 0$ *is given by the expression*

$$\text{Instantaneous velocity at time } t = f'(t) = 10.6\,t.$$

Determine its (instantaneous) velocity after 1 second (at $t = 1$) *and after* 2.6 *seconds* ($t = 2.6$).

Solution We calculate its instantaneous velocity, at $t = t_0 = 1$ second. Since, in this case, $f(t) = 5.3t^2$, it follows that its instantaneous velocity at $t = 1$ second is given by $10.6(1) = 10.6$ feet per second, obtained by setting $t = 1$ in the formula for $f'(t)$. Similarly, $f'(2.6) = 10.6(2.6) = 27.56$ feet per second. The observation here is that one can conclude that an object falling from rest on the surface of the moon will fall at approximately *one-third* the rate it does on earth (neglecting air resistance, here).

Example 16. *Now let's say that* f *is defined by*

$$f(x) = \begin{cases} x^2 + 1, & \text{if } -1 \leq x \leq 0, \\ \cos x, & \text{if } 0 < x \leq \pi, \\ x - \pi, & \text{if } \pi < x \leq 2\pi. \end{cases}$$

Find an expression for $f(x + 1)$.

Solution This function is defined *in pieces* ... In other words, **it is defined differently depending on where** x **is** ... Its domain is obtained by taking the union of all the intervals on the right side making up one big interval, which, in our case is the interval

$-1 \leq x \leq 2\pi$. So, we see that $f(2) = \cos(2)$ because the number 2 is in the interval $0 < x \leq \pi$. On the other hand, $f(8)$ is not defined because 8 is not within the domain of definition of our function, since $2\pi \approx 6.28$.

Now, the value of $f(x+1)$, say, will be different depending on where the symbol "$x+1$" is. We can still use the "box" principle to write down the values $f(x + 1)$. In fact, we replace every occurence of the symbol x by our standard "box", insert the symbols "$x + 1$" inside the box, and then remove the boxes... We'll find

$$f(\boxed{x+1}) = \begin{cases} \boxed{x+1}^2 + 1, & \text{if} \quad -1 \leq \boxed{x+1} \leq 0, \\ \cos\boxed{x+1}, & \text{if} \quad 0 < \boxed{x+1} \leq \pi, \\ \boxed{x+1} - \pi, & \text{if} \quad \pi < \boxed{x+1} \leq 2\pi. \end{cases}$$

or

$$f(x+1) = \begin{cases} (x+1)^2 + 1, & \text{if} \quad -1 \leq x + 1 \leq 0, \\ \cos(x+1), & \text{if} \quad 0 < x + 1 \leq \pi, \\ (x+1) - \pi, & \text{if} \quad \pi < x + 1 \leq 2\pi. \end{cases}$$

We now solve the inequalities on the right for the symbol x (by subtracting 1 from each side of the inequality). This gives us the values

$$f(x+1) = \begin{cases} x^2 + 2x + 2, & \text{if} \quad -2 \leq x \leq -1, \\ \cos(x+1), & \text{if} \quad -1 < x \leq \pi - 1, \\ x + 1 - \pi, & \text{if} \quad \pi - 1 < x \leq 2\pi - 1. \end{cases}$$

Exercise Set 1.

Use the method of this section to evaluate the following functions at the indicated point(s) or symbol.

1. $f(x) = x^2 + 2x - 1$. What is $f(-1)$? $f(0)$? $f(+1)$? $f(1/2)$?

2. $g(t) = t^3 \sin t$. What is the value of $g(x + 1)$?

3. $h(z) = z + 2 \sin z - \cos(z + 2)$. Evaluate $h(z - 2)$.

4. $k(x) = -2 \cos(x - ct)$. Evaluate $k(x + 2ct)$.

5. $f(x) = \sin(\cos x)$. Find the value of $f(\pi/2)$. [*Hint*: $\cos(\pi/2) = 0$]

6. $f(x) = x^2 + 1$. Find the value of

$$\frac{f(x + h) - f(x)}{h}$$

whenever $h \neq 0$. Simplify this expression as much as you can!

7. $g(t) = \sin(t + 3)$. Evaluate

$$\frac{g(t + h) - g(t)}{h}$$

whenever $h \neq 0$ and simplify this as much as possible.
Hint: Use the trigonometric identity

$$\sin(A + B) = \sin A \, \cos B + \cos A \, \sin B$$

valid for any two angles A, B where we can set $A = t + 3$ and $B = h$ (just two more **symbols**, right?)

8. Let x_0, x_1 denote two symbols which refer to real numbers. In addition, let $f(x) = 2\,x^2\,\cos x$.

   a) If $x_0 = 0$ and $x_1 = \pi$, evaluate the expression

   $$\frac{f(x_0) + f(x_1)}{2}.$$

   Hint: $\cos(\pi) = -1$

   b) What is the value of the expression

   $$f(x_0) + 2\,f(x_1) + f(x_2)$$

   if we are given that $x_0 = 0$, $x_1 = \pi$, and $x_2 = 2\,\pi$.?

   Hint: $\cos(2\pi) = 1$

9. Let f be defined by

   $$f(x) = \begin{cases} x + 1, & \text{if} \quad -1 \le x \le 0, \\ -x + 1, & \text{if} \quad 0 < x \le 2, \\ x^2, & \text{if} \quad 2 < x \le 6. \end{cases}$$

   a) What is $f(0)$?
   b) Evaluate $f(0.142857)$.
   c) Given that $0 < x < 1$ evaluate $f(3x + 2)$.

   Hint Use the ideas in Example 16.

10. Let $f(x) = 2\,x^2 - 2$ and $F(x) = \sqrt{\frac{x}{2} + 1}$. Calculate the values $f(F(x))$ and $F(f(x))$ using the *box method* of this section. Don't forget to expand completely and simplify your answers as much as possible.

Suggested Homework Set 1. *Go into a library or the World Wide Web and come up with five (5) functions which appear in the literature. Maybe they have names associated with them? Are they useful in science, engineering or in commerce? Once you have your functions, identify the dependent and independent variables and try to evaluate those functions at various points in their domain.*

If you want to use your calculator for this question (you don't have to...) don't forget to change your angle settings to **radians**!

The **Binomial Theorem** states that, in particular,

$$(\square + \triangle)^2 = \square^2 + 2\,\square\triangle + \triangle^2$$

for any two symbols $\square, \triangle$ representing real numbers, functions, etc. **Don't forget the middle terms**, namely, " $2\,\square\triangle$ " in this formula.

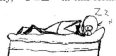

Great! Now that you have a good grasp of what a function *is* and what it *does*, let's keep going!

NOTES

1.3 The Natural Domain of a Function

You must have noticed that we didn't put too much emphasis on the actual *domain* of a function in Section 1.2. This is because, most of the time, the domain of the given function is sort of "clear" from the rule which defines that function. Remember that we always want the value of the function to be a real number, because we are dealing with real-valued functions in this book. This condition defines the natural domain of the function. In other words, If the value $f(x)$ of a function f at x is an actual, *trueblue, real number ...* something like -1, 1.035246946, 1.6, $1/4$, $-355/113$, π, ... then **we say that f is defined at x** and, as a result, x belongs to the **natural domain** of f (See the text in Figure 6). Remember that the natural domain of a function f is *actually a set of real numbers*, indeed, it is the largest set of numbers for which the function values $f(x)$ are defined.

In Table 1.1 below you'll find the natural domain of real valued functions which occur frequently in Calculus.

$f(x)$	Natural domain of $f(x)$	Remarks (See Figure 6)
$x, x^2, x^3, \ldots$	$(-\infty, +\infty)$	Power functions are defined for any real x
$\dfrac{1}{x}, \dfrac{1}{x^2}, \ldots$	Every real $x \neq 0$	Division by 0 NOT allowed!
$\sqrt{x}$	$[0, +\infty)$	Square roots of negatives not allowed !
$\sqrt[n]{x}$	If n is **odd**: $(-\infty, +\infty)$	If $x < 0$ then $\sqrt[n]{x} < 0$
$\sqrt[n]{x}$	If n is **even**: $[0, +\infty)$	Even roots of negatives NOT allowed !
$\sqrt{g(x)}$	x with $g(x) \geq 0$	Can't allow $g(x) < 0$
$\sin x, \cos x$	$(-\infty, +\infty)$	x always in RADIANS not degrees
$\tan x, \sec x$	$x \neq \pm\pi/2, \pm 3\pi/2, \ldots$	Equality gives infinite values
$\cot x, \csc x$	$x \neq 0, \pm\pi, \pm 2\pi, \ldots$	Equality gives infinite values

Table 1.1: The Natural Domain of Some Basic Functions

You should remember this table ... In fact, if you refer to this table you'll see that

Example 17. *The function defined by $f(x) = x^3 \cos x$, made up of the product of the two rules x^3 and $\cos x$, is defined for each x in the interval $(-\infty, +\infty)$ and so this is its natural domain (this is a consequence of the fact that the natural domain of the product of two or more functions is the (set-theoretic) intersection of the natural domains of all the functions under consideration).*

Of course, this function can have any subset of $(-\infty, +\infty)$ as its **domain**, *in which case that set would be given ahead of time.* **The thing to remember here is that the domain and the natural domain of a function may be different!**

For example, we could be asking a question about the function $f(x) = (2x^2+1)\sin x$ for x in the interval $0 < x < 1$ only. This interval, $0 < x < 1$, then becomes its domain (but its natural domain is still $(-\infty, +\infty)$).

Example 18. *The function f defined by*

$$f(x) = \frac{\sin x}{x}$$

is defined for every real number x except when $x = 0$ (because we are dividing by 0). Hence its natural domain is the set of all real numbers excluding the number $x = 0$.

Example 19. *The function g defined by the rule $g(x) = x \cot x$ is not defined at zero and at every odd integer multiple of π (see Table 1.1 above) but it is defined everywhere else! Hence its natural domain is the set of all numbers $\{x : x \neq 0, \pm\pi, \pm3\pi, \pm5\pi, \ldots\}$.*

Example 20. *Let's say that we define a function f by the rule by $f(x) = \sin x$ and say nothing about its domain. Then we take it that x can be any angle whatsoever right? And this angle is in radians, right? OK, good. The point is that this function f **is** defined for any angle x whatsoever (by trigonometry) and so x can be any real number. This means that the natural domain of f is given by the open interval $(-\infty, +\infty)$.*

Note that it is very common that when we study a field called **differential equations** we are asked to consider functions on a subset of the natural domain of the unknown function. In our case, for instance, we may be asked to consider the rule $f(x) = x^3 \cos x$ on the interval $(0, \pi)$, or $(-1.2\,,\, \infty)$, and so on, instead of its natural domain which is $(-\infty, +\infty)$. We'll be learning about differential equations later on so **don't worry** if the symbols in Figure 7 don't make any sense to you right now. Just remember that such equations are very useful, for instance, the motion of a satellite around the earth is given by a solution to a differential equation.

Example 21. *Find the natural domain of the function defined by the rule*

$$f(x) = \frac{1}{x^2 - 4}.$$

Solution Okay, first notice that this function is of the type "one over something". The only time there can be a problem is if the something is zero (since we would be dividing by zero, see Figure 6), because if it isn't zero, the quotient is defined as a real number and this is good! Now, the denominator is zero only when $x^2 - 4 = 0$. Factoring this expression gives, $x^2 - 4 = (x - 2)(x + 2)$ and for this to be zero it is necessary that either $x = 2$ or $x = -2$. But these points are NOT ALLOWED in the natural domain of f! Thus the natural domain of our function is the set of all real numbers except the numbers ± 2.

Example 22. *What is the natural domain of the function f defined by*

$$f(x) = \sqrt{1 - x^2} \ ?$$

Solution We refer to Table 1.1 where we put $g(x) = 1 - x^2$ in the expression for $\sqrt{g(x)}$. Using the result there (and Figure 6) we see that we must be looking for x such that $g(x) \geq 0$, right? OK, this means that $1 - x^2 \geq 0$ or, adding x^2 to both

TYPICAL DIFFERENTIAL EQUATIONS

- Schrödinger's equation

$$-\frac{h^2}{2\pi m}\frac{d^2\psi}{dx^2} + V(x)\psi = E\psi$$

where x is in $(-\infty, +\infty)$. It appears in Quantum Mechanics.

- The Logistic equation

$$\frac{dN}{dt} = \alpha N(1 - \beta N)$$

where t is in $(0, +\infty)$, and α, β are two fixed real numbers. This one shows up in Chaos Theory.

Figure 7.

sides, we find $1 \geq x^2$. Now, solving for x using the **square root of the square rule** (see Figures 8 and 9), we get $1 \geq |x|$ where $|x|$ represents the function which associates to each symbol x its **absolute value** (see Definition 2 above). So, the natural domain of this function is the closed interval $[-1, +1]$ or, the set of all points x for which $|x| \leq 1$, which is the same thing.

| **Example 23.** | *Find the natural domain of the function f defined by* |

$$f(x) = \frac{x - 2}{2x^2 - 1}.$$

Solution OK, this function is a quotient of two functions, namely, "$(x - 2)$" and "$2x^2 - 1$". It's alright for the numerator to be zero but it's not alright for the denominator to be zero (Figure 6), because f is not defined at those points where $2x^2 - 1 = 0$. There are no "square roots" to worry about and any "infinities" can only arise when the denominator is actually equal to zero. So the natural domain consists of the set of all real numbers x where $2x^2 - 1 \neq 0$ or, what comes to the same thing, those x for which $x^2 \neq 1/2$. Finally, taking the square root of both sides, we get that if $x \neq \pm\sqrt{1/2}$ then such an x is in the natural domain of f. That is, the natural domain of our f is the set of all real numbers x such that $x \neq \pm\sqrt{1/2} = \pm 1/\sqrt{2} \approx \pm\, 0.707....$

| **Example 24.** | *What is the natural domain of the function g defined by $g(t) =$* |

$\sqrt{(t + 2)^{-1}}$.

Solution This one has a square root in it so we can expect some trouble ... (remember Figure 6). But don't worry, it's not that bad. Let's recall that we can't take the square root of a negative number, so, if there are $t's$ such that $(t + 2)^{-1} < 0$ then these $t's$ are NOT in the natural domain, right? But $(t+2)^{-1} = \frac{1}{t+2}$, so, if $t + 2 < 0$ then t is NOT in the natural domain, i.e., if $t < -2$ then t is not in the natural domain. Are there any other points NOT in the natural domain ? We can't divide by zero either, ... but if $t = -2$ then we ARE dividing by zero, because when $t = -2$, $(t + 2)^{-1} = \frac{1}{t+2} = 1/0$. So this value of t is NOT in the natural domain either! After this there are no other numbers NOT in the natural domain other than the ones we found. Thus, the natural domain consists of all real numbers t with the property that $t > -2$ (because all the others, those with $t \leq -2$, are not in the natural domain).

Definition 2. *The function whose rule is defined by setting*

$$|x| = \begin{cases} x, & \text{if } x \geq 0, \\ -x, & \text{if } x < 0. \end{cases}$$

is called the **absolute value** *function. For example,$| - 5| = -(-5) = +5$, and $|6.1| = 6.1$*

You see from this Definition that the absolute value of a number is either that same number (if it is positive) or the original *unsigned* number (dropping the minus sign completely). Thus, $| - 5| = -(-5) = 5$, since $-5 < 0$ while $|3.45| = 3.45$ since $3.45 > 0$. Now the inequality

$$0 \leq \quad |\, \square \, | \leq \triangle \tag{1.1}$$

is exactly the same as the inequality

$$-\triangle \leq \square \leq \triangle. \tag{1.2}$$

The Square Root of the Square Rule !!

For any real number x,

$$\sqrt{x^2} = |\, x \, |.$$

More generally,

$$\sqrt{\square^{\,2}} = |\, \square \, |$$

where $\square$ is any symbolic expression involving x or any other variable.

Figure 8.

Definition of the absolute value function

where $\square$ and $\triangle$ are any two symbols whatsoever (x, t, or any function of x, etc). For example, $|x - a| < 1$ means that *the distance from x to a is at most* 1 and, in terms of an inequality, this can be written as $-1 < x - a < +1$.

Why? Well, put $x - a$ in the box of (1.1) and the number 1 in the triangle. Move these symbols to (1.2) and remove the box and triangle, then what's left is what you want. That's all. Now, adding a to both ends and the middle term of this latest inequality we find the equivalent statement $a - 1 < x < a + 1$.

This business of passing from Equation (1.1) to Equation (1.2) is **really important in Calculus** and you should be able to do this without thinking (after lots of practice you will, don't worry).

| **Example 25.** | *Write down the values of the function f defined by the rule $f(x) = |1 - x^2|$ and describe its natural domain.*

Solution Looks tough? Those absolute values can be very frustrating sometimes! Just use the Box Method of Section 1.2. That is, use Definition 2 and replace all the symbols between the vertical bars replaced by a $\square$. This really makes life easy, let's try it out. Put the symbols between the vertical bars, namely, the "$1 - x^2$" inside a box, $\square$. Since

$$|\square| = \begin{cases} \square, & \text{if } \square \geq 0, \\ -\square, & \text{if } \square < 0, \end{cases} \qquad (1.3)$$

we also have

$$|1 - x^2| = |\boxed{1 - x^2}| = \begin{cases} \boxed{1 - x^2}, & \text{if } \boxed{1 - x^2} \geq 0, \\ -\boxed{1 - x^2}, & \text{if } \boxed{1 - x^2} < 0. \end{cases}$$

Removing the boxes and replacing them by parentheses we find

$$|1 - x^2| = |(1 - x^2)| = \begin{cases} (1 - x^2), & \text{if } (1 - x^2) \geq 0, \\ -(1 - x^2), & \text{if } (1 - x^2) < 0. \end{cases}$$

Adding x^2 to both sides of the inequality on the right we see that this last display is the same as saying that

$$|1 - x^2| = \begin{cases} (1 - x^2), & \text{if } 1 \geq x^2, \\ -(1 - x^2), & \text{if } 1 < x^2. \end{cases}$$

Almost done! We just need to solve for x on the right, above. To do this, we're going to use the results in Figure 9 with $A = 1$. So, if $x^2 \leq 1$ then $|x| \leq 1$ too. Similarly, if $1 < x^2$ then $1 < |x|$, too. Finally, we find

$$|1 - x^2| = \begin{cases} (1 - x^2), & \text{if } 1 \geq |x|, \\ -(1 - x^2), & \text{if } 1 < |x|. \end{cases}$$

This last display for $|1 - x^2|$ may be rewritten as

Solving a square root inequality!

If for some real numbers A and x, we have

$$x^2 < A,$$

then, it follows that

$$|x| < \sqrt{A}$$

More generally, this result is true if x is replaced by any other symbol (including functions!), say, $\square$. That is, if for some real numbers A and $\square$, we have

$$\square^2 < A,$$

then, it follows that

$$|\square| < \sqrt{A}$$

These results are still true if we replace "$<$" by "$\leq$" or if we reverse the inequality and $A > 0$.

Figure 9.

$$| \, 1 - x^2 \, | = \begin{cases} 1 - x^2, & \text{if } -1 \le x \le +1, \\ x^2 - 1, & \text{if } x > 1 \text{ or } x < -1. \end{cases}$$

Steps in removing absolute values in a function f

- Look at that part of f with the absolute values,

- Put all the stuff between the vertical bars in a $\boxed{\text{box}}$,

- Use the definition of the absolute value, equation 1.3.

- Remove the boxes, and replace them by parentheses,

- Solve the inequalities involving $x's$ for the symbol x.

- Rewrite f *in pieces*

(See Examples 25 and 27)

Figure 10.

Sir Isaac Newton
1642 - 1727

A glance at this latest result shows that the natural domain of f as defined here is the set of all real numbers.

> **NOTE** The procedure described in Example 25 will be referred to as the process of **removing the absolute value**. You just can't leave out those vertical bars because you feel like it! Other functions defined by absolute values are handled in the same way.

Example 26. *Remove the absolute value in the expression $f(x) = \left| x^2 + 2x \right|$ where the domain of f is its natural domain.*

Solution We note that since $x^2 + 2x$ is a polynomial, its natural domain is the set of all real numbers, $(-\infty, +\infty)$. We use the Box Method. Since for any symbol, say, $\square$, we have by definition,

$$| \, \square \, | = \begin{cases} \square, & \text{if } \square \ge 0, \\ -\square, & \text{if } \square < 0. \end{cases}$$

we see that, upon inserting the symbols $x^2 + 2x$ inside the box and then removing its sides, we get

$$\left| \, \boxed{x^2 + 2x} \, \right| = \begin{cases} \boxed{x^2 + 2x}, & \text{if } \boxed{x^2 + 2x} \ge 0, \\ -(\boxed{x^2 + 2x}), & \text{if } \boxed{x^2 + 2x} < 0. \end{cases}$$

So the required function *defined in pieces* is given by

$$| \, x^2 + 2x \, | = \begin{cases} x^2 + 2x, & \text{if } x^2 + 2x \ge 0, \\ -(x^2 + 2x), & \text{if } x^2 + 2x < 0. \end{cases}$$

where we need to solve the inequalities $x^2 + 2x \ge 0$ and $x^2 + 2x < 0$, for x. But $x^2 + 2x = x(x + 2)$. Since we want $x(x + 2) \ge 0$, there are now *two cases*. Either *both* quantities $x, x + 2$ must be greater than or equal to zero, OR *both* quantities $x, x + 2$ must be less than zero (but not *equal* to zero, why?).

Solving $x^2 + 2x \ge 0$:

Case 1: $x \ge 0$, $(x + 2) \ge 0$. In this case, it is clear that $x \ge 0$ (since if $x \ge 0$ then $x + 2 \ge 0$ too). This means that the polynomial inequality $x^2 + 2x \ge 0$ has among its solutions the set of real numbers $\{x : x \ge 0\}$.

Case 2: $x \le 0$, $(x + 2) \le 0$. In this case, we see that $x + 2 \le 0$ implies that $x \le -2$. On the other hand, for such x we also have $x \le 0$, (since if $x \le -2$ then $x \le 0$ too). This means that the polynomial inequality $x^2 + 2x \ge 0$ has for its *solution* the set of real numbers $\{x : x \le -2 \text{ or } x \ge 0\}$.

A similar argument applies to the case where we need to solve $x(x + 2) < 0$. Once again there are two cases, namely, the case where $x > 0$ and $x + 2 < 0$ and the separate case where $x < 0$ and $x + 2 > 0$. Hence,

Solving $x^2 + 2x < 0$:

Case 1: $x > 0$ and $(x+2) < 0$. This case is impossible since, if $x > 0$ then $x + 2 > 2$ and so $x + 2 < 0$ is impossible. This means that there are no such x satisfying this case.

Case 2: $x < 0$ and $(x + 2) > 0$. This implies that $x < 0$ and $x > -2$, which gives the inequality $x^2 + 2x < 0$. So, the the solution set is $\{x : -2 < x < 0\}$.

Combining the conclusions of each of these cases, our function takes the form,

$$| \, x^2 + 2x \, | = \begin{cases} x^2 + 2x, & \text{if} \quad x \leq -2 \text{ or } x \geq 0, \\ -(x^2 + 2x), & \text{if} \quad -2 < x < 0. \end{cases}$$

Its graph appears in the margin.

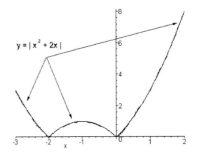

The graph of $f(x) = |x^2 + 2x|$.

Example 27. *Remove the absolute value in the function f defined by the rule* $f(x) = \sqrt{|\cos x|}$, *for $-\infty < x < +\infty$.*

Solution First, we notice that $|\cos x| \geq 0$ regardless of the value of x, right? So, the square root of this absolute value is defined for every value of x too, and this explains the fact that its natural domain is the open interval $-\infty < x < +\infty$. We use the method in Figure 10.

- Let's look at that part of f which has the absolute value signs in it...
  In this case, it's the part with the $|\cos x|$ term in it.

- Then, take all the stuff between the vertical bars of the absolute value and stick them in a box ...
  Using Definition 2 in disguise namely, Equation 1.3, we see that

$$| \cos x \, | = | \, \boxed{\cos x} \, | = \begin{cases} \boxed{\cos x}, & \text{if} \quad \boxed{\cos x} \geq 0, \\ -\boxed{\cos x}, & \text{if} \quad \boxed{\cos x} < 0. \end{cases}$$

- Now, remove the boxes, and replace them by parentheses if need be ...

$$| \cos x \, | = \begin{cases} \cos x, & \text{if} \quad \cos x \geq 0, \\ -\cos x, & \text{if} \quad \cos x < 0. \end{cases}$$

- Next, solve the inequalities on the right of the last display above for x.
  In this case, this means that we have to figure out when $\cos x \geq 0$ and when $\cos x < 0$, okay? There's a few ways of doing this... One way is to look at the graphs of each one of these functions and just find those intervals where the graph lies above the x-axis.

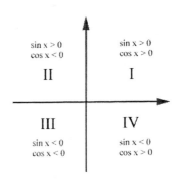

Another way involves remembering the trigonometric fact that the cosine function is positive in Quadrants I and IV (see the margin for a quick recall). Turning this last statement into symbols means that if x is between $-\pi/2$ and $\pi/2$, then $\cos x \geq 0$. Putting it another way, if x is in the interval $[-\pi/2, +\pi/2]$ then $\cos x \geq 0$.

But we can always add positive and negative multiples of 2π to this and get more and more intervals where the cosine function is positive ... why?. Either way, we get that $\cos x \geq 0$ whenever x is in the closed intervals $[-\pi/2, +\pi/2]$, $[3\pi/2, +5\pi/2]$, $[7\pi/2, +9\pi/2], \ldots$ or if x is in the closed intervals $[-5\pi/2, -3\pi/2]$, $[-9\pi/2, -7\pi/2], \ldots$ (Each one of these intervals is obtained by adding multiples of 2π to the endpoints of the basic interval $[-\pi/2, +\pi/2]$ and rearranging the

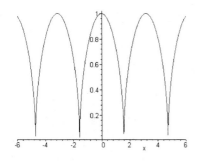

The graph of $y = \sqrt{|\cos x|}$

Figure 11.

numbers in increasing order).

Combining these results we can write

$$
|\cos x| = \begin{cases} \cos x, & \text{if } x \text{ is in } [-\pi/2, +\pi/2], [3\pi/2, +5\pi/2], \\ & [7\pi/2, +9\pi/2], \ldots, \text{ or if } x \text{ is in } \\ & [-5\pi/2, -3\pi/2], [-9\pi/2, -7\pi/2], \ldots, \\ \\ -\cos x, & \text{if } x \text{ is NOT IN ANY ONE} \\ & \text{of the above intervals.} \end{cases}
$$

• Feed all this information back into the original function to get it "in pieces" Taking the square root of all the cosine terms above we get

$$
\sqrt{|\cos x|} = \begin{cases} \sqrt{\cos x}, & \text{if } x \text{ is in } [-\pi/2, +\pi/2], [3\pi/2, +5\pi/2], \\ & [7\pi/2, +9\pi/2], \ldots, \text{ or if } x \text{ is in } \\ & [-5\pi/2, -3\pi/2], [-9\pi/2, -7\pi/2], \ldots, \\ \\ \sqrt{-\cos x}, & \text{if } x \text{ is NOT IN ANY ONE} \\ & \text{of the above intervals.} \end{cases}
$$

Phew, that's it! Look at Fig. 11 to see what this function looks like.

You shouldn't worry about the minus sign appearing inside the square root sign above because, inside those intervals, the cosine is negative, so the negative of the cosine is positive, and so we can take its square root without any problem! Try to understand this example completely; then you'll be on your way to mastering one of the most useful concepts in Calculus, handling absolute values!

EXAMPLES

SNAPSHOTS

Example 28. *The natural domain of the function h defined by $h(x) = \sqrt{x^2 - 9}$ is the set of all real numbers x such that $x^2 - 9 \geq 0$ or, equivalently, $|x| \geq 3$ (See Table 1.1 and Figure 9).*

Example 29. *The function f defined by $f(x) = x^{2/3} - 9$ has its natural domain given by the set of all real numbers, $(-\infty, \infty)$! No exceptions! All of them...why?*

Solution Look at Table 1.1 and notice that, by algebra, $x^{2/3} = \left(\sqrt[3]{x}\right)^2$. Since the natural domain of the "cube root" function is $(-\infty, \infty)$, the same is true of its "square". Subtracting "9" doesn't change the domain, that's all!

Example 30. *Find the natural domain of the the function f defined by*

$$f(x) = \frac{x}{\sin x \, \cos x}.$$

Solution The natural domain of f is given by the set of all real numbers with the property that $\sin x \, \cos x \neq 0$, (cf., Table 1.1), that is, the set of all real numbers x with $x \neq \pm \pi/2, \pm 3\pi/2, \pm 5\pi/2, \pm 7\pi/2, \ldots, 0, \pm \pi, \pm 2\pi, \pm 3\pi, \pm 4\pi, \ldots$ (as these are the values where the denominator is zero).

Example 31. *The natural domain of the function f given by*

$$f(x) = \frac{|\sin x|}{\sqrt{1 - x^2}}$$

is given by the set of all real numbers x with the property that $1 - x^2 > 0$ or, equivalently, the open interval $|x| < 1$, or, $-1 < x < +1$ (See Equations 1.1 and 1.2).

Example 32. *Find the natural domain of the function f defined by $f(x) = \sqrt{|\sin x|}$*

Solution The natural domain is given by the set of all real numbers x in the interval $(-\infty, \infty)$, that's right, *all* real numbers! Looks weird right, because of the square root business! But the absolute value will turn any negative number inside the root into a positive one (or zero), so the square root is always defined, and, as a consequence, f is defined everywhere too.

List of Important Trigonometric Identities

Recall that an **identity** is an equation which is true for any value of the variable for which the expressions are defined. So, this means that the identities are true regardless of whether or not the variable looks like an x, y, $[]$, $\diamond$, $f(x)$, etc.

YOU'VE GOT TO KNOW THESE!

Odd-even identities

$$\begin{aligned} \sin(-x) &= -\sin x, \\ \cos(-x) &= \cos x. \end{aligned}$$

Pythagorean identities

$$\begin{aligned} \sin^2 x + \cos^2 x &= 1, \\ \sec^2 x - \tan^2 x &= 1. \\ \csc^2 x - \cot^2 x &= 1, \end{aligned}$$

Addition identities

$$\begin{aligned} \sin(x + y) &= \sin x \cos y + \cos x \sin y, \\ \cos(x + y) &= \cos x \cos y - \sin x \sin y. \end{aligned}$$

Double-angle identities

$$\begin{aligned} \sin(2x) &= 2\sin x \cos x, \\ \cos(2x) &= \cos^2 x - \sin^2 x, \\ \sin^2 x &= \frac{1 - \cos(2x)}{2}, \\ \cos^2 x &= \frac{1 + \cos(2x)}{2}. \end{aligned}$$

You can derive the identities below from the ones above, or ... you'll have to memorize them! Well, it's best if you know how to get to them from the ones above using some basic algebra.

Sofya Kovalevskaya (1850 - 1891)

Celebrated immortal mathematician, writer, and revolutionary, she was appointed Professor of Mathematics at the University of Stockholm, in Sweden, in 1889, the first woman ever to be so honored in her time and the second such in Europe (Sophie Germain, being the other one). At one point, she was apparently courted by Alfred Nobel and brothers (of Nobel Prize fame). Author of slightly more than 10 mathematical papers, she proved what is now known as the **Cauchy-Kovalevski Theorem**, one of the first deep results in a field called *Partial Differential Equations*, an area used in the study of airplane wings, satellite motion, wavefronts, fluid flow, among many other applications. A. L. Cauchy's name appears because he had proved a more basic version of this result earlier.

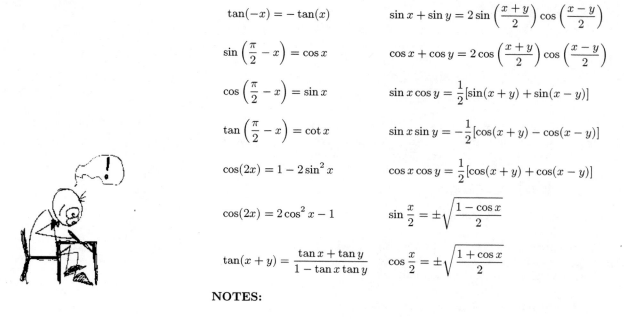

$$\tan(-x) = -\tan(x)$$

$$\sin x + \sin y = 2\sin\left(\frac{x+y}{2}\right)\cos\left(\frac{x-y}{2}\right)$$

$$\sin\left(\frac{\pi}{2} - x\right) = \cos x$$

$$\cos x + \cos y = 2\cos\left(\frac{x+y}{2}\right)\cos\left(\frac{x-y}{2}\right)$$

$$\cos\left(\frac{\pi}{2} - x\right) = \sin x$$

$$\sin x \cos y = \frac{1}{2}[\sin(x+y) + \sin(x-y)]$$

$$\tan\left(\frac{\pi}{2} - x\right) = \cot x$$

$$\sin x \sin y = -\frac{1}{2}[\cos(x+y) - \cos(x-y)]$$

$$\cos(2x) = 1 - 2\sin^2 x$$

$$\cos x \cos y = \frac{1}{2}[\cos(x+y) + \cos(x-y)]$$

$$\cos(2x) = 2\cos^2 x - 1$$

$$\sin\frac{x}{2} = \pm\sqrt{\frac{1-\cos x}{2}}$$

$$\tan(x+y) = \frac{\tan x + \tan y}{1 - \tan x \tan y}$$

$$\cos\frac{x}{2} = \pm\sqrt{\frac{1+\cos x}{2}}$$

NOTES:

Exercise Set 2.

Use the methods of this section and Table 1.1 to find the natural domain of the functions defined by the following rules.

1. $f(x) = 3x^2 + 2x - 1$.

2. $g(t) = t^3 \ \tan t$.

3. $h(z) = \sqrt{3z + 2}$.

4. $k(x) = \dfrac{-2}{\sqrt{4 - x^2}}$.

5. $f(x) = x \ \cot x$.

6. $f(x) = 16.345$

7. $g(x) = \sqrt{|\cos x|}$

8. $f(t) = 3 \ t^{4/5} \ \sin t$

9. $h(x) = \dfrac{x^2 + 2x + 1}{x^3 - 1}$ *Hint:* $x^3 - 1 = (x - 1)(x^2 + x + 1)$

10. $h(z + 3)$ where h is given above by $h(z) = \sqrt{3z + 2}$.

11. $f(x) = \dfrac{1}{x\sqrt{x^2 - 1}}$

12. $g(\square) = -\sqrt{1 - \square^2}$

13. $f(\triangle) = \dfrac{1}{1 + \triangle^2}$

14. $f(\heartsuit) = 3\heartsuit^{1/4} - 2$

15. $k(x) = \dfrac{1}{\sqrt{1 - x^2}}$

Use the method of Example 25, Example 27, and the discussion following Definition 2 to **remove the absolute value** appearing in the values of the functions defined below. Note that, once the absolute value is removed, the function will be defined *in pieces*.

16. $f(x) = |x^2 - 1|$, for $-\infty < x < +\infty$.

17. $g(x) = |3x + 4|$, for $-\infty < x < +\infty$.
     Hint: Put the symbols $3x + 4$ in a box and use the idea in Example 25

18. $h(x) = x|x|$, for $-\infty < x < +\infty$.

19. $f(t) = 1 - |t|$, for $-\infty < t < +\infty$.

20. $g(w) = |\sin w|$, for $-\infty < w < +\infty$.
     Hint: $\sin w \geq 0$ when w is in Quadrants I and II, or, equivalently, when w is between 0 and π radians, 2π and 3π radians, etc.

21.
$$f(x) = \frac{1}{|x|\sqrt{x^2 - 1}}$$

for $|x| > 1$.

22. The *signum* function, whose name is simply *sgn* (and pronounced *the sign of x*) where
$$sgn(x) = \frac{x}{|x|}$$

for $x \neq 0$. The motivation for the name comes from the fact that the values of this function correspond to the *sign* of x (whether it is positive or negative).

1. $\sin(A + B) = \sin A \cos(B) + \cos A \sin B$
2. $\cos(A + B) = \cos A \cos(B) - \sin A \sin B$
3. $\sin^2 x + \cos^2 x = 1$
4. $\sec^2 x - \tan^2 x = 1$
5. $\csc^2 x - \cot^2 x = 1$
6. $\cos 2x = \cos^2 x - \sin^2 x$
7. $\sin 2x = 2 \sin x \cos x$
8. $\cos^2 x = \dfrac{1 + \cos 2x}{2}$
9. $\sin^2 x = \dfrac{1 - \cos 2x}{2}$

Table 1.2: Useful Trigonometric Identities

23. $f(x) = x + |x|$, for $-\infty < x < +\infty$.
24. $f(x) = x - \sqrt{x^2}$, for $-\infty < x < +\infty$.

Suggested Homework Set 2. *Do problems* $2, 4, 6, 8, 10, 17, 23$, *above.*

WHAT'S WRONG WITH THIS ??

$$-1 = -1$$
$$\sqrt{\frac{1}{-1}} = \sqrt{\frac{-1}{1}}$$
$$\frac{\sqrt{1}}{\sqrt{-1}} = \frac{\sqrt{-1}}{\sqrt{1}}$$
$$\sqrt{1}\,\sqrt{1} = \sqrt{-1}\,\sqrt{-1}$$
$$(\sqrt{1})^2 = (\sqrt{-1})^2$$
$$1 = -1$$

Crazy, right?

A Basic Inequality

If
$$0 < \square \leq \triangle,$$

then
$$\frac{1}{\square} \geq \frac{1}{\triangle},$$

regardless of the meaning of the box or the triangle or what's in them!

OR

You reverse the inequality when you take reciprocals !

Table 1.3: Reciprocal Inequalities Among Positive Quantities

Inequalities among reciprocals

If
$$0 < \frac{1}{\square} \leq \frac{1}{\triangle},$$

then
$$\square \geq \triangle,$$

regardless of the meaning of the box or the triangle or what's in them!

OR

You <u>still</u> reverse the inequality when you take reciprocals !

Table 1.4: Another Reciprocal Inequality Among Positive Quantities

1.4   A Quick Review of Inequalities

In this section we will review basic inequalities because they are really important in Calculus. Knowing how to manipulate basic inequalities will come in handy when we look at how graphs of functions are sketched, in our examination of the monotonicity of functions, their convexity and many other areas. We leave the subject of reviewing the solution of basic and polynomial inequalities to Chapter 5. So, this is one section you should know well!

In this section, as in previous ones, we make heavy use of the generic symbols $\square$ and $\triangle$, that is, our box and triangle. Just remember that variables *don't have to be* called x, and any other symbol will do as well.

Recall that the **reciprocal** of a number is simply the number 1 divided by the number. Table 1.3 shows what happens when you **take the reciprocal** of each term in an inequality involving two **positive** terms. You see, you need to **reverse the sign!**. The same result is true had we started out with an inequality among reciprocals of positive quantities, see Table 1.4.

The results mentioned in these tables are really useful! For example,

Example 33.   *Show that given any number $x \neq 0$,*

$$\frac{1}{x^2} > \frac{1}{x^2 + 1}.$$

Solution We know that $0 < x^2 < x^2 + 1$, and this is true regardless of the value of x, so long as $x \neq 0$, which we have assumed anyhow. So, if we put x^2 in the box in Table 1.3 and (make the triangle big enough so that we can) put $x^2 + 1$ in the triangle, then we'll find, as a conclusion, that

$$\frac{1}{x^2} > \frac{1}{x^2 + 1},$$

and this is true for any value of $x \neq 0$, whether x be positive or negative.

Example 34.   *Solve the inequality $|2x - 1| < 3$ for x.*

Solution Recall that $|\square| < \triangle$ is equivalent to $-\triangle < \square < \triangle$ for any two symbols (which we denote by $\square$ and $\triangle$). In this case, putting $2x - 1$ in the box and 3 in the triangle, we see that we are looking for x's such that $-3 < 2x - 1 < 3$. Adding 1 to all the terms gives $-2 < 2x < 4$. Finally, dividing by 2 right across the inequality we get $-1 < x < 2$ and this is our answer.

Example 35.   *Solve the inequality*

$$\left| \frac{x + 1}{2x + 3} \right| < 2$$

for x.

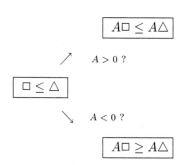

Solution Once again, by definition of the absolute value, this means we are looking for x's such that

$$-2 < \frac{x + 1}{2x + 3} < 2.$$

There now two main cases: **Case 1** where $2x + 3 > 0$ OR **Case 2** where $2x + 3 < 0$. Of course, when $2x + 3 = 0$, the fraction is undefined (actually infinite) and so this is not a solution of our inequality. We consider the cases in turn:

Case 1: $2x + 3 > 0$ In this case we multiply the last display throughout by $2x + 3$ and keep the inequalities as they are (by the rules in Figure 12). In other words, we must now have

$$-2(2x + 3) < x + 1 < 2(2x + 3).$$

Grouping all the x's in the "middle" and all the constants "on the ends" we find the two inequalities $-4x - 6 < x + 1$ and $x + 1 < 4x + 6$. Solving for x in both instances we get $5x > -7$ or $x > -\frac{7}{5}$ and $3x > -5$ or $x > -\frac{5}{3}$. Now what?

Well, let's recapitulate. We have shown that if $2x + 3 > 0$ then we must have $x > -\frac{7}{5} = -1.4$ and $x > -\frac{5}{3} \approx -1.667$. On the one hand if $x > -1.4$ then $x > -1.667$ for sure and so the two inequalities together imply that $x > -1.4$, or $x > -\frac{7}{5}$. But this is not all! You see, we still need to guarantee that $2x + 3 > 0$ (by the main assumption of this case)! That is, we need to make sure that we have BOTH $2x + 3 > 0$ AND $x > -\frac{7}{5}$, *i.e.*, we need $x > -\frac{3}{2}$ and $x > -\frac{7}{5}$. These last two inequalities together imply that

$$x > -\frac{7}{5}.$$

Case 2: $2x + 3 < 0$ In this case we still multiply the last display throughout by $2x + 3$ but now we must REVERSE the inequalities (by the rules in Figure 12, since

Figure 12.

now $A = 2x + 3 < 0$). In other words, we must now have

$$-2(2x + 3) > x + 1 > 2(2x + 3).$$

As before we can derive the two inequalities $-4x - 6 > x + 1$ and $x + 1 > 4x + 6$. Solving for x in both instances we get $5x < -7$ or $x < -\frac{7}{5}$ and $3x < -5$ or $x < -\frac{5}{3}$. But now, these two inequalities together imply that $x < -\frac{5}{3} \approx -1.667$. This result, combined with the basic assumption that $2x + 3 < 0$ or $x < -\frac{3}{2} = -1.5$, gives us that $x < -\frac{5}{3}$ (since $-1.667 < -1.4$). The solution in this case is therefore given by the inequality

$$x < -\frac{5}{3}.$$

Combining the two cases we get the final solution as (see the margin)

$$-1.4 = -\frac{7}{5} < x \quad \text{OR} \quad x < -\frac{5}{3} \approx -1.667.$$

In terms of intervals the answer is the set of points x such that

$$-\infty < x < -\frac{5}{3} \quad OR \quad -\frac{7}{5} < x < \infty.$$

| **Example 36.** | *Show that if x is any number , $x \geq 1$, then* |

$$\frac{1}{\sqrt{x}} \geq \frac{1}{|x|}.$$

Solution If $x = 1$ the result is clear. Now, everyone believes that, if $x > 1$, then $x < x^2$. OK, well, we can take the square root of both sides and use Figure 9 to get $\sqrt{x} < \sqrt{x^2} = |x|$. From this we get,

$$\text{If } x > 1, \quad \frac{1}{\sqrt{x}} > \frac{1}{|x|}.$$

On the other hand, one has to be careful with the opposite inequality $x > x^2$ if $x < 1 \ldots$ This is *true*, even though it doesn't seem right!

| **Example 37.** | *Show that if x is any number, $0 < x \leq 1$, then* |

$$\frac{1}{\sqrt{x}} \leq \frac{1}{x}.$$

Solution Once again, if $x = 1$ the result is clear. Using Figure 9 again, we now find that if $x < 1$, then $\sqrt{x} > \sqrt{x^2} = |x|$, and so,

$$\text{If } 0 < x < 1, \quad \frac{1}{\sqrt{x}} < \frac{1}{|x|} = \frac{1}{x}.$$

| **Example 38.** | *We know that $\square < \square + 1$ for any $\square$ representing a positive number. The box can even be a function! In other words, we can put a function of x inside the box, apply the reciprocal inequality of Table 1.3, (where we put the symbols $\square + 1$ inside the triangle) and get a new inequality, as follows. Since $\square < \square + 1$, then* |

$$\frac{1}{\square} > \frac{1}{\square + 1}.$$

Now, put the function f defined by $f(x) = x^2 + 3x^4 + |x| + 1$ inside the box. Note that $f(x) > 0$ (this is really important!). It follows that, for example,

$$\frac{1}{x^2 + 3x^4 + |x| + 1} > \frac{1}{x^2 + 3x^4 + |x| + 1 + 1} = \frac{1}{x^2 + 3x^4 + |x| + 2}.$$

There are 2 other really important inequalities called the **Triangle Inequalities**: If $\square, \triangle$ are any 2 symbols representing real numbers, functions, etc. then

$$|\square + \triangle| \leq |\square| + |\triangle|,$$

and

$$|\square - \triangle| \geq |\,|\square| - |\triangle|\,|.$$

These inequalities can allow us to estimate how big or how small functions can be!

Multiplying inequalities by an unknown quantity

- If $A > 0$, is any symbol (variable, function, number, fraction, ...) and

$$\square \leq \triangle,$$

then

$$A\square \leq A\triangle,$$

- If $A < 0$, is any symbol (variable, function, number, fraction, ...) and

$$\square \leq \triangle,$$

then

$$A\square \geq A\triangle,$$

Don't forget to **reverse the inequality sign when** $A < 0$!

Table 1.5: Multiplying Inequalities Together

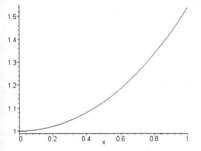

Figure 13.

Example 39.   *How "big" is the function f defined by $f(x) = x^2 + \cos x$ if x is in the interval $[0,1]$?*

Solution The best way to figure out how big f is, is to try and estimate each term which makes it up. Let's leave x^2 alone for the time being and concentrate on the $\cos x$ term. We know from trigonometry that $|\cos x| \leq 1$ for any value of x. OK, since $\pm \cos x \leq |\cos x|$ by definition of the absolute value, and $|\cos x| \leq 1$ it follows that

$$\pm \cos x \leq 1$$

for any value of x. Choosing the plus sign, because that's what we want, we add x^2 to both sides and this gives

$$f(x) \ = \ x^2 + \cos x \leq x^2 + 1$$

and this is true for any value of x. But we're only given that x is between 0 and 1. So, we take the right-most term, the $x^2 + 1$, and *replace it by something "larger"*. The simplest way to do this is to notice that, since $x \leq 1$ (then $x^2 \leq 1$ too) and $x^2 + 1 \leq 1^2 + 1 = 2$. Okay, now we combine the inequalities above to find that, if $0 \leq x \leq 1$,

$$f(x) = x^2 + \cos x \leq x^2 + 1 \leq 2.$$

This shows that $f(x) \leq 2$ for such $x's$ and yet we never had to calculate the range of f to get this ... We just used inequalities! You can see this too by plotting its graph as in Figure 13.

NOTE: We have just shown that the so-called **maximum value of the function** f **over the interval** $[0,1]$ denoted mathematically by the symbols

$$\max_{x \ in \ [0,1]} \ f(x)$$

is not greater than 2, that is,

$$\max_{x \ in \ [0,1]} \ f(x) \leq \ 2.$$

For a 'flowchart interpretation' of Table 1.5 see Figure 12 in the margin.

Example 40.   *Show that if x is any real number, then $-x^3 \geq -x^2(x+1)$.*

Solution We know that, for any value of x, $x < x+1$ so, by Table 1.5, with $A = -2$ we find that $-2x > -2(x+1)$. You see that we reversed the inequality since we multiplied the original inequality by a negative number! We could also have multiplied the original inequality by $A = -x^2 \leq 0$, in which case we find, $-x^3 \geq -x^2(x+1)$ for any value of x, as being true too.

Example 41.   *Show that if $p \geq 1$, and $x \geq 1$, then*

$$\frac{1}{x^p} \leq \frac{1}{x}.$$

Solution Let $p \geq 1$ be any number, (e.g, $p = 1.657, p = 2, \dots$). Then you'll believe that if $p - 1 \geq 0$ and if $x \geq 1$ then $x^{p-1} \geq 1$ (for example, if $x = 2$ and $p = 1.5$, then $2^{1.5-1} = 2^{0.5} = 2^{1/2} = \sqrt{2} = 1.414\ldots > 1$). Since $x^{p-1} \geq 1$ we can multiply both sides of this inequality by $x > 1$, which is positive, and find, by Figure 12 with $A = x$, that $x^p \geq x$. From this and Table 1.3 we obtain the result

$$\frac{1}{x^p} \leq \frac{1}{x}, \quad \text{if } p \geq 1, \text{ and } x \geq 1$$

Example 42.   *Show that if $p > 1$, and $0 < x \leq 1$, then*

$$\frac{1}{x^p} \geq \frac{1}{x}.$$

Solution In this example we change the preceding example slightly by requiring that $0 < x \leq 1$. In this case we get the opposite inequality, namely, if $p > 1$ then $x^{p-1} \leq 1$ (e.g., if $x = 1/2, p = 1.5$, then $(1/2)^{1.5-1} = (1/2)^{0.5} = (1/2)^{1/2} = 1/\sqrt{2} = 0.707\ldots < 1$). Since $x^{p-1} \leq 1$ we can multiply both sides of this inequality by $x > 0$, and find, by Figure 12 with $A = x$, again, that $x^p \leq x$. From this and Table 1.3 we obtain the result (see Fig. 14)

$$\frac{1}{x^p} \geq \frac{1}{x}, \quad \text{if } p \geq 1, \text{ and } 0 < x \leq 1$$

Example 43.   *Show that if $0 < p \leq 1$, and $x \geq 1$, then*

$$\frac{1}{x^p} \geq \frac{1}{x}.$$

Solution In this final example of this type we look at what happens if we change the p values of the preceding two examples and keep the x-values larger than 1. Okay, let's say that $0 < p \leq 1$ and $x \geq 1$. Then you'll believe that, since $p - 1 \leq 0$, $0 < x^{p-1} \leq 1$, (try $x = 2, p = 1/2$, say). Multiplying both sides by x and taking reciprocals we get the important inequality (see Fig. 15),

$$\frac{1}{x^p} \geq \frac{1}{x}, \quad \text{if } 0 < p \leq 1, \text{ and } x \geq 1 \tag{1.4}$$

NOTES:

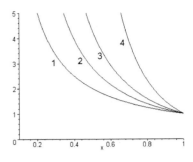

1. The graph of $1/x$

2. The graph of $1/x^{1.5}$

3. The graph of $1/x^{2.1}$

4. The graph of $1/x^{3.8}$

Figure 14.

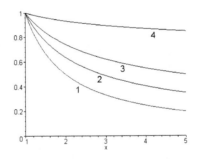

1. The graph of $1/x$

2. The graph of $1/x^{0.65}$

3. The graph of $1/x^{0.43}$

4. The graph of $1/x^{0.1}$

Figure 15.

Remember, if

$$\square^2 \leq \triangle^2,$$

then

$$|\square| \leq |\triangle|,$$

regardless of the values of the variables or symbols involved. If $\square > 0$, this is also true for positive powers, p, other than 2. So, if, for example, $\square > 0$, and

$$\square^p \leq \triangle^p,$$

then

$$|\square| \leq |\triangle|.$$

This result is not true if $\square < 0$ since, for example, $(-2)^3 < 1^3$ but $|-2| > |1|$.

Figure 16.

SNAPSHOTS

Example 44.   *We know that* $\sin x \geq 0$ *in Quadrants I and II, by trigonometry. Combining this with Equation (1.4), we find that: If x is an angle expressed in radians and $1 \leq x \leq \pi$ then*

$$\frac{\sin x}{x^p} \geq \frac{\sin x}{x}, \qquad 0 < p \leq 1$$

Think about why we had to have some restriction like $x \leq \pi$ here.

Example 45.   *On the other hand,* $\cos x \leq 0$ *if* $\pi/2 \leq x \leq \pi$ *(notice that $x > 1$ automatically in this case, since $\pi/2 = 1.57... > 1$). So this, combined with Equation (1.4), gives*

$$\frac{\cos x}{x^p} \leq \frac{\cos x}{x} \qquad 0 < p \leq 1$$

where we had to "reverse" the inequality (1.4) as $\cos x \leq 0$.

Example 46.   *There is this really cool (and old) inequality called the AG- inequality, (meaning the Arithmetic-Geometric Inequality). It is an inequality between the "arithmetic mean" of two positive numbers, $\square$ and $\triangle$, and their "geometric mean". By definition, the **arithmetic mean** of $\square$ and $\triangle$, is $(\square + \triangle)/2$, or more simply, their "average". The **geometric mean** of $\square$ and $\triangle$, is, by definition, $\sqrt{\square \triangle}$. The inequality states that if $\square \geq 0$, $\triangle \geq 0$, then*

$$\frac{\square + \triangle}{2} \geq \sqrt{\square \triangle}$$

Do you see why this is true? Just start out with the inequality $(\sqrt{\square} - \sqrt{\triangle})^2 \geq 0$, expand the terms, rearrange them, and then divide by 2.

Example 47.   *For example, if we set x^2 in the box and x^4 in the triangle and apply the AG-inequality (Example 46) to these two positive numbers we get the "new" inequality*

$$\frac{x^2 + x^4}{2} \geq x^3$$

valid for any value of x, something that is not easy to see if we don't use the AG-inequality.

We recall the **general form of the Binomial Theorem**. It states that if n is any positive integer, and $\square$ is any symbol (a function, the variable x, or a positive number, or negative, or even zero) then

$$(1+\square)^n = 1 + n\square + \frac{n(n-1)}{2!}\square^2 + \frac{n(n-1)(n-2)}{3!}\square^3 + \ldots + \frac{n(n-1)\cdots(2)(1)}{n!}\square^n \tag{1.5}$$

where the symbols that look like 3!, or n!, called **factorials**, mean that we multiply all the integers from 1 to n together. For example, $2! = (1)(2) = 2$, $3! = (1)(2)(3) = 6$, $4! = (1)(2)(3)(4) = 24$ and, generally, "n factorial" is defined by

$$n! = (1)(2)(3) \cdots (n-1)(n) \tag{1.6}$$

When $n = 0$ we all agree that $0! = 1 \ldots$ Don't worry about why this is true right now, but it has something to do with a function called the **Gamma Function**, which will be defined later when we study things called **improper integrals**. Using this we can arrive at identities like:

$$(1-x)^n = 1 - nx + \frac{n(n-1)}{2!}x^2 \pm \ldots + (-1)^n \frac{n(n-1)\cdots(2)(1)}{n!}x^n,$$

obtained by setting $\square = -x$ in (1.5) or even

$$2^n \;=\; 1 + n + \frac{n(n-1)}{2!} + \frac{n(n-1)(n-2)}{3!} + \ldots + \frac{n(n-1)\cdots(2)(1)}{n!}$$

(just let $\square = 1$ in the Binomial Theorem), and finally,

$$(2x-3)^n \;=\; (-1)^n 3^n \left(1 - \frac{2nx}{3} + \frac{4n(n-1)x^2}{9 \cdot 2!} + \ldots + (-1)^n \frac{2^n x^n}{3^n} \right),$$

found by noting that

$$(2x-3)^n = \left(-3(1 - \frac{2x}{3}) \right)^n = (-3)^n \left(1 - \frac{2x}{3} \right)^n = (-1)^n 3^n \left(1 - \frac{2x}{3} \right)^n$$

and then using the boxed formula (1.5) above with $\square = -\frac{2x}{3}$. In the above formulae note that

$$\frac{n(n-1)\cdots(2)(1)}{n!} = 1$$

by definition of the factorial symbol.

If you already know something about improper integrals then the Gamma Function can be written as,

$$\Gamma(p) = \int_0^\infty x^{p-1}\, e^{-x}\, dx$$

where $p \geq 1$. One can actually prove that $\Gamma(n+1) = n!$ if n is a positive integer. The study of this function dates back to Euler.

Exercise Set 3.

Determine which of the following 7 statements is true, if any. If the statement is false give an example that shows this. Give reasons either way.

1. If $-A < B$ then $-\frac{1}{A} > \frac{1}{B}$

2. If $-\frac{1}{A} < B$ then $-A > -B$

3. If $A < B$ then $A^2 < B^2$

4. If $A > B$ then $1/A < 1/B$

5. If $A < B$ then $-A < -B$

6. If $A^2 < B^2$ and $A > 0$, then $A < B$

7. If $A^2 > B^2$ and $A > 0$, then $|B| < A$

8. Start with the obvious $\sin x < \sin x + 1$ and find an interval of $x's$ in which we can conclude that

$$\csc x > \frac{1}{\sin x + 1}$$

9. How big is the function f defined by $f(x) = x^2 + 2\sin x$ if x is in the interval $[0,2]$?

10. How big is the function g defined by $g(x) = 1/x$ if x is in the interval $[-1, 4]$?

11. Start with the inequality $x > x - 1$ and conclude that for $x > 1$, we have $x^2 > (x-1)^2$.

12. If x is an angle expressed in radians and $1 \leq x \leq \pi$ show that

$$\frac{\sin x}{x^{p-1}} \geq \sin x, \qquad p \leq 1.$$

13. Use the AG-inequality to show that if $x \geq 0$ then $x + x^2 \geq \sqrt{x^3}$. Be careful here, you'll need to use the fact that $2 > 1$! Are you allowed to "square both sides" of this inequality to find that, if $x \geq 0$, $(x + x^2)^2 \geq x^3$? Justify your answer.

14. Can you replace the $x's$ in the inequality $x^2 \geq 2x - 1$ by an arbitrary symbol, like □ ? Under what conditions on the symbol?

15. Use the ideas surrounding Equation (1.4) to show that, if $p \leq 1$ and $|x| \geq 1$, then

$$\frac{1}{|x|^p} \geq \frac{1}{|x|}$$

Hint: Note that if $|x| \geq 1$ then $|x|^{1-p} \geq 1$.

16. In the theory of relativity developed by A. Einstein, H. Lorentz and others at the turn of this century, there appears the quantity γ, read as "gamma", defined as a function of the velocity, v, of an object by

$$\gamma = \frac{1}{\sqrt{1 - \frac{v^2}{c^2}}}$$

where c is the speed of light. Determine the conditions on v which give us that the quantity γ is a real number. In other words, find the natural domain of γ. Hint: This involves an inequality and an absolute value.

17. Show that for any integer $n \geq 1$ there holds the inequalities

$$2 \leq \left(1 + \frac{1}{n}\right)^n < 3.$$

Hint: This is a really hard problem! Use the Binomial Theorem, (1.5), with □ $= \frac{1}{n}$. But first of all, get a *feel* for this result by using your calculator and setting $n = 2, 3, 4, \ldots, 10$ and seeing that this works!

Suggested Homework Set 3. *Work out problems* $3, 6, 11, 12, 14$

Web Links

Additional information on Functions may be found at:
http://www.coolmath.com/func1.htm

For more on inequalities see:
http://math.usask.ca/readin/ineq.html

More on the AG- inequality at:
http://www.cut-the-knot.com/pythagoras/corollary.html

Mathematics is not always done by mathematicians. For example, **Giordano Bruno**, 1543-1600, Renaissance Philosopher, once a Dominican monk, was burned at the stake in the year 1600 for heresy. He wrote around 20 books in many of which he upheld the view that Copernicus held, i.e., that of a sun centered solar system (called *heliocentric*). A statue has been erected in his honor in the *Campo dei Fiori*, in Rome. Awesome. The rest is history...What really impresses me about Bruno is his steadfastness in the face of criticism and ultimate torture and execution. It is said that he died without uttering a groan. Few would drive on this narrow road...not even **Galileo Galilei**, 1564 - 1642, physicist, who came shortly after him. On the advice of a Franciscan, Galileo retracted his support for the heliocentric theory when called before the Inquisition. As a result, he stayed under house arrest until his death, in 1642. The theories of Copernicus and Galileo would eventually be absorbed into Newton and Leibniz's Calculus as a consequence of the basic laws of motion. All this falls under the heading of *differential equations*.

1.5 Chapter Exercises

Use the methods of this Chapter to evaluate the following functions at the indicated point(s) or symbol.

1. $f(x) = 3x^2 - 2x + 1$. What is $f(-1)$? $f(0)$? $f(+1)$? $f(-1/2)$?

2. $g(t) = t^3 \, \cos t$. What is the value of $g(x^2 + 1)$?

3. $h(z) = z + 2 \, \sin z - \cos(z + 2)$. Evaluate $h(z + 3)$.

4. $f(x) = \cos x$. Find the value of

$$\frac{f(x + h) - f(x)}{h}$$

whenever $h \neq 0$. Simplify this expression as much as you can!
   - Use a trigonometric identity for $\cos(A + B)$ with $A = x$, $B = h$.

Solve the following inequalities for the stated variable.

5. $\dfrac{3}{x} > 6, \quad x$

6. $3x + 4 \geq 0, \quad x$

7. $\dfrac{3}{2x - 1} \leq 0, \quad x$

8. $x^2 > 5, \quad x$

9. $t^2 < \sqrt{5}, \quad t$

10. $\sin^2 x \leq 1, \quad x$

11. $z^p \geq 2, \quad z$, if $p > 0$

12. $x^2 - 9 \leq 0, \quad x$

Remove the absolute value (see Section 1.3 and Equation 1.3).

13. $f(x) = |x + 3|$

14. $g(t) = |t - 0.5|$

15. $g(t) = |1 - t|$

16. $f(x) = |2x - 1|$

17. $f(x) = |1 - 6x|$

18. $f(x) = |x^2 - 4|$

19. $f(x) = |3 - x^3|$

20. $f(x) = |x^2 - 2x + 1|$

21. $f(x) = |2x - x^2|$

22. $f(x) = |x^2 + 2|$

23. If x is an angle expressed in radians and $1 \leq x \leq \pi/2$ show that

$$\frac{\cos x}{x^{p-1}} \geq \cos x, \qquad p \leq 1$$

24. Use your calculator to tabulate the values of the quantity

$$\left(1 + \frac{1}{n}\right)^n$$

for $n = 1, 2, 3, \ldots, 10$ (See Exercise 17 of Exercise Set 3). Do the numbers you get seem to be getting close to something?

25. Use the AG-inequality to show that if $0 \leq x \leq \pi/2$, then

$$\frac{\sin x + \cos x}{\sqrt{2}} \geq \sqrt{\sin 2x}.$$

Suggested Homework Set 4. *Work out problems* $2, 4, 12, 17, 19, 21, 24$

1.6   Using Computer Algebra Systems (CAS),

Use your favorite Computer Algebra System (CAS), like Maple, MatLab, etc., or even a graphing calculator to answer the following questions:

Evaluate the functions at the following points:

1. $f(x) = \sqrt{x}$, for $x = -2, -1, 0, 1.23, 1.414, 2.7$. What happens when $x < 0$? Conclude that the natural domain of f is $[0, +\infty)$.

2. $g(x) = \sin(x\sqrt{2}) + \cos(x\sqrt{3})$, for $x = -4.37, -1.7, 0, 3.1415, 12.154, 16.2$. Are there any values of x for which $g(x)$ is not defined as a real number? Explain.

3. $f(t) = \sqrt[3]{t}$, for $t = -2.1, 0, 1.2, -4.1, 9$. Most CAS define power functions only when the base is positive, which is not the case if $t < 0$. In this case the natural domain of f is $(-\infty, +\infty)$ even though the CAS wants us to believe that it is $[0, \infty)$. So, be careful when reading off results using a CAS.

4. $g(x) = \dfrac{x+1}{x-1}$. Evaluate $g(-1), g(0), g(0.125), g(1), g(1.001), g(20), g(1000)$. Determine the behavior of g near $x = 1$. To do this use values of x just less than 1 and then values of x just larger than 1.

5. Define a function f by

$$f(t) = \begin{cases} \dfrac{t + \sqrt{t}}{\sqrt{t}}, & \text{if } t > 0, \\ 1, & \text{if } t = 0. \end{cases}$$

Evaluate $f(1)$, $f(0)$, $f(2.3)$, $f(100.21)$. Show that $f(t) = \sqrt{t} + 1$ for every value of $t \geq 0$.

6. Let $f(x) = 1 + 2\cos^2(\sqrt{x+2}) + 2\sin^2(\sqrt{x+2})$.

   a) Evaluate $f(-2)$, $f(0.12)$, $f(-1.6)$, $f(3.2)$, $f(7)$.
   b) Explain your results.
   c) What is the natural domain of f?
   d) Can you conclude something simple about this function? Is it a constant function? Why?

7. To solve the inequality $|2x - 1| < 3$ use your CAS to
   a) Plot the graphs of $y = |2x - 1|$ and $y = 3$ and superimpose them on one another
   b) Find their points of intersection, and
   c) Solve the inequality (see the figure below)

The answer is: $-1 < x < 2$.

Evaluate the following inequalities graphically using a CAS:

a) $|3x - 2| < 5$
b) $|2x - 2| < 4.2$
c) $|(1.2)x - 3| > 2.61$
d) $|1.3 - (2.5)x| = 0.5$
e) $|1.5 - (5.14)x| > 2.1$

8. Find an interval of x's such that
   a) $|\cos x| < \dfrac{1}{2}$
   b) $\sin x + 2 \cos x < 1$
   c) $\sin(x\sqrt{2}) - \cos x > -\dfrac{1}{2}$.

   Hint: Plot the functions on each side of the inequality separately, superimpose their graphs, estimate their points of intersection visually, and solve the inequality.

9. Plot the values of
$$f(x) = x \, \sin\left(\frac{1}{x}\right)$$
   for small x's such as $x = 0.1, \ 0.001, \ -0.00001, 0.000001, -0.00000001$ etc. Guess what happens to the values of $f(x)$ as x gets closer and closer to zero (regardless of the direction, *i.e.*, regardless of whether $x > 0$ or $x < 0$.)

10. Let $f(x) = 4x - 4x^2$, for $0 \leq x \leq 1$. Use the Box method to evaluate the following terms, called the *iterates* of f for $x = x_0 = 0.5$:
$$f(0.5), \ f(f(0.5)), \ f(f(f(0.5))), \ f(f(f(f(0.5)))), \ldots$$
   where each term is the image of the preceding term under f. Are these values approaching any specific value? Can you find values of $x = x_0$ (*e.g.*, $x_0 = 0.231, 0.64, \ldots$) for which these iterations actually seem to be approaching some specific number? This is an example of a *chaotic sequence* and is part of an exciting area of mathematics called "Chaos".

11. Plot the graphs of $y = x^2, \ (1.2)x^2, \ 4x^2, \ (10.6)x^2$ and compare these graphs with those of
$$y = x^{\frac{1}{2}}, \ (1.2)x^{\frac{1}{2}}, \ 4x^{\frac{1}{2}}, \ (10.6)x^{\frac{1}{2}}.$$
   Use this graphical information to guess the general shape of graphs of the form $y = x^p$ for $p > 1$ and for $0 < p < 1$. Guess what happens if $p < 0$?

12. Plot the graphs of the family of functions $f(x) = \sin(ax)$ for $a = 1, 10, 20, 40, 50$.

   a) Estimate the value of those points in the interval $0 \leq x \leq \pi$ where $f(x) = 0$ (these x's are called "zeros" of f).
   b) How many are there in each case?
   c) Now find the position and the number of exact zeros of f inside this interval $0 \leq x \leq \pi$.

NOTES:

Chapter 2

Limits and Continuity

The Big Picture

The notion of a 'limit' permeates the universe around us. In the simplest cases, the *speed of light*, denoted by 'c', in a vacuum is the upper *limit* for the velocities of any object. Photons always travel with speed c but electrons can never reach this speed exactly no matter how much energy they are given. That's life! In another vein, let's look at the speed barrier for the $100m$ dash in Track & Field. World records rebound and are broken in this, the most illustrious of all races. But there *must be a limit* to the time in which one can run the $100m$ dash, right? For example, it is clear that none will ever run this in a record time of, say, 3.00 seconds! On the other hand, it *has* been run in a record time of 9.79 seconds. So, there must be a *limiting time* that no one will ever be able to reach but the records will get closer and closer to! It is the author's guess that this limiting time is around 9.70 seconds. In a sense, this time interval of 9.70 seconds between the start of the race and its end, may be considered a *limit* of human locomotion. We just can't seem to run at a constant speed of $100/9.70 = 10.3$ meters per second. Of course, the actual 'speed limit' of any human may sometimes be slightly higher than 10.3 m/sec, but, not over the whole race. If you look at the Records Table below, you can see why we *could* consider this number, 9.70, a limit.

0. Maurice Greene	USA	9.79	99/06/16	Athens, Invitational
1. Donovan Bailey	CAN	9.84	96/07/26	Atlanta, Olympics
2. Leroy Burrell	USA	9.85	94/07/06	Lausanne
3. Carl Lewis	USA	9.86	91/08/25	Tokyo, Worlds
4. Frank Fredericks	NAM	9.86	96/07/03	Lausanne
5. Linford Christie	GBR	9.87	93/08/15	Stuttgart, Worlds
6. Ato Boldon	TRI	9.89	97/05/10	Modesto
7. Maurice Green	USA	9.90	97/06/13	Indianapolis
8. Dennis Mitchell	USA	9.91	96/09/07	Milan
9. Andre Cason	USA	9.92	93/08/15	Stuttgart, Worlds
10. Tim Montgomery	USA	9.92	97/06/13	Indianapolis

On the other hand, in the world of temperature we have another 'limit', namely, something called *absolute zero* equal to -273^oC, or, by definition, $0K$ where K stands for Kelvin. This temperature is a lower *limit* for the temperature of any object under normal conditions. Normally, we may remove as much heat as we want from an object but we'll never be able to remove all of it, so to speak, so the object will never attain this limiting temperature of $0\ K$.

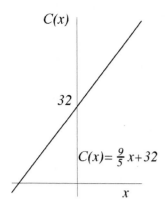

Figure 17.

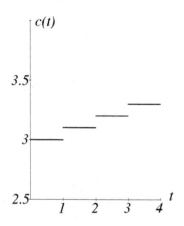

Figure 18.

These are physical examples of limits and long ago some guy called **Karl Weierstrass** (1815-1897), decided he would try to make sense out of all this limit stuff mathematically. So he worked really hard and created this method which we now call the *epsilon-delta* method which most mathematicians today use to prove that such and such a number is, in fact, the limit of some given function. We don't always have to prove it when we're dealing with applications, but if you want to know how to use this method you can look at the *Advanced Topics* later on. Basically, Karl's idea was that you could call some number L a 'limit' of a given function if the values of the function managed to get close, really close, always closer and closer to this number L but never really reach L. He just made this last statement meaningful using symbols.

In many practical situations functions may be given in different formats: that is, their graphs may be unbroken curves or even broken curves. For example, the function C which converts the temperature from degrees Centigrade, x, to degrees Fahrenheit, $C(x)$, is given by the straight line $C(x) = \frac{9}{5}x + 32$ depicted in Fig. 17.

This function's graph is an unbroken curve and we call such graphs the **graph of a continuous function** (as the name describes).

| **Example 48.** | If a taxi charges you \$3 as a flat fee for stepping in and 10 cents for every minute travelled, then the graph of the cost $c(t)$, as a function of time t (in minutes), is shown in Fig. 18.

When written out symbolically this function, c, in Fig. 18 is given by

$$c(t) = \begin{cases} 3, & 0 \le t < 1 \\ 3.1, & 1 \le t < 2 \\ 3.2, & 2 \le t < 3 \\ 3.3, & 3 \le t < 4 \\ \dots & \dots \end{cases}$$

or, more generally, as:

$$c(t) = 3 + \frac{n}{10}, \text{ if } n \le t \le n+1$$

where $n = 0, 1, 2, \dots$.

In this case, the graph of c is a broken curve and this is an example of a **discontinuous function** (because of the 'breaks' it cannot be continuous). It is also called a **step-function** for obvious reasons.

These two examples serve to motivate the notion of continuity. Sometimes functions describing real phenomena are not continuous but we "turn" them into continuous functions as they are easier to visualize graphically.

| **Example 49.** | For instance, in Table 2.1 above we show the plot of the frequency of Hard X-rays versus time during a Solar Flare of 6th March, 1989:

The actual X-ray count per centimeter per second is an integer and so the plot should consist of points of the form $(t, c(t))$ where t is in seconds and $c(t)$ is the X-ray count, which is an *integer*. These points are grouped tightly together over small time intervals in the graph and "consecutive" points are joined by a line segment (which is quite short, though). The point is that even though these signals are *discrete* we tend to *interpolate* between these data points by using these small line segments. It's a fair thing to do but is it the *right* thing to do? Maybe nature doesn't like straight lines! The resulting graph of $c(t)$ is now the graph of a **continuous** function (there are no "breaks").

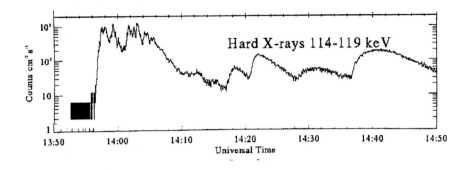

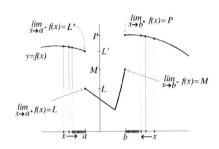

Figure 19.

Table 2.1: The Mathematics of Solar Flares

As you can gather from Fig. 18, the size of the **break in the graph of $c(t)$** is given by **subtracting neighbouring values of the function c around $t = a$**.

To make this idea more precise we define the **limit from the left** and the **limit from the right** of function f at the point $x = a$, see Tables 2.2 & 2.3 (and an optional chapter for the rigorous definitions).

2.1   One-Sided Limits of Functions

Limits from the Right

We say that the function f **has a limit from the right at $x = a$** (or the right-hand limit of f exists at $x = a$) whose value is L and denote this symbolically by

$$f(a + 0) = \lim_{x \to a^+} f(x) = L$$

if BOTH of the following statements are satisfied:

1. Let $x > a$ and x be very close to $x = a$.

2. As x approaches a ("from the right" because "$x > a$"), the values of $f(x)$ approach the value L.

(For a more rigorous definition see the **Advanced Topics**, later on.)

Table 2.2: One-Sided Limits From the Right

For example, the function H defined by

$$H(x) = \begin{cases} 1, & for \ x \geq 0 \\ 0, & for \ x < 0 \end{cases}$$

called the **Heaviside Function** (named after *Oliver Heaviside*, (1850 - 1925) an electrical engineer) has the property that

$$\lim_{x \to 0^+} H(x) = 1$$

Why? This is because we can set $a = 0$ and $f(x) = H(x)$ in the definition (or in Table 2.2) and apply it as follows:

a) Let $x > 0$ and x be very close to 0;

b) As x approaches 0 we need to ask the question: "What are the values, $H(x)$, doing?"

Well, we know that $H(x) = 1$ for **any** $x > 0$, so, as long as $x \neq 0$, the values $H(x) = 1$, (see Fig. 20), so this will be true "in the limit" as x approaches 0.

Limits from the Left

We say that the function $\boldsymbol{f}$ **has a limit from the left at $\boldsymbol{x = a}$** (or the left-hand limit of f exists at $x = a$) and is equal to L and denote this symbolically by

$$f(a - 0) = \lim_{x \to a^-} f(x) = L$$

if BOTH of the following statements are satisfied:

1. Let $x < a$ and x be very close to $x = a$.

2. As x approaches a ("from the left" because "$x < a$"), the values of $f(x)$ approach the value L.

Table 2.3: One-Sided Limits From the Left

Returning to our Heaviside function, $H(x)$, (see Fig. 20), defined earlier we see that

$$\lim_{x \to 0^-} H(x) = 0$$

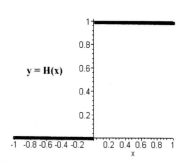

y = H(x)

The graph of the Heaviside Function, $H(x)$.

Figure 20.

Why? In this case we set $a = 0$, $f(x) = H(x)$ in the definition (or Table 2.3), as before:

a) Let $x < 0$ and x very close to 0;

b) As x approaches 0 the values $H(x) = 0$, right? (This is because $x < 0$, and by definition, $H(x) = 0$ for such x). The same must be true of the "limit" and so we have

$$\lim_{x \to 0^-} H(x) = 0$$

OK, but how do you find these limits?

In practice, the idea is to choose some specific values of x near a (to the 'right' or to the 'left' of a) and, using your calculator, find the corresponding values of the function near a.

Example 50.   Returning to the Taxi problem, Example 48 above, find the values of $c(1 + 0)$, $c(2 - 0)$ and $c(4 - 0)$, (See Fig. 18).

Solution By definition, $c(1 + 0) = \lim_{t \to 1^+} c(t)$. But this means that we want the values of $c(t)$ as $t \to 1$ from the right, *i.e.*, the values of $c(t)$ for $t > 1$ (just slightly bigger than 1) and $t \to 1$. Referring to Fig. 18 and Example 48 we see that $c(t) = 3.1$ for such t's and so $c(1 + 0) = 3.1$. In the same way we see that $c(2 - 0) = \lim_{t \to 2^-} c(t) = 3.1$ while $c(4 - 0) = \lim_{t \to 4^-} c(t) = 3.3$.

Example 51.

The function f is defined by:

$$f(x) = \begin{cases} x+1, & x < -1 \\ -2x, & -1 \le x \le +1 \\ x^2, & x > +1 \end{cases}$$

Evaluate the following limits whenever they exist and justify your answers.

i) $\lim_{x \to -1^-} f(x)$; ii) $\lim_{x \to 0^+} f(x)$; iii) $\lim_{x \to 1^+} f(x)$

Solution i) We want a left-hand limit, right? This means that $x < -1$ and x should be very close to -1 (according to the definition in Table 2.3).

Now as x approaches -1 (from the 'left', i.e., with x always less than -1) we see that $x+1$ approaches 0, that is, $f(x)$ approaches 0. Thus,

$$\lim_{x \to -1^-} f(x) = 0.$$

ii) We want a right-hand limit here. This means that $x > 0$ and x must be very close to 0 (according to the definition in Table 2.2). Now for values of $x > 0$ and close to 0 the value of $f(x)$ is $-2x$ ... OK, this means that as x approaches 0 then $-2x$ approaches 0, or, equivalently $f(x)$ approaches 0. So

$$\lim_{x \to 0^+} f(x) = 0$$

iii) In this case we need $x > 1$ and x very close to 1. But for such values, $f(x) = x^2$ and so if we let x approach 1 we see that $f(x)$ approaches $(1)^2 = 1$. So,

$$\lim_{x \to 1^+} f(x) = 1.$$

See Figure 21, in the margin, where you can 'see' the values of our function, f, in the second column of the table while the x's which are approaching one (from the right) are in the first column. Note how the numbers in the second column get closer and closer to 1. This table is **not a proof** but it does make the limit we found believable.

Numerical evidence for Example 51, (iii). You can think of 'x' as being the name of an athlete and '$f(x)$' as being their record at running the 100 m. dash.

x	$f(x)$
1.5000	2.2500
1.2500	1.5625
1.1000	1.2100
1.0500	1.1025
1.0033	1.0067
1.0020	1.0040
1.0012	1.0025
1.0010	1.0020
1.0001	1.0002
...	...

Figure 21.

Example 52. Evaluate the following limits and explain your answers.

$$f(x) = \begin{cases} x+4 & x \le 3 \\ 6 & x > 3 \end{cases}$$

i) $\lim_{x \to 3^+} f(x)$ and ii) $\lim_{x \to 3^-} f(x)$

Solution i) We set $x > 3$ and x very close to 3. Then the values are all $f(x) = 6$, by definition, and these don't change with respect to x. So

$$\lim_{x \to 3^+} f(x) = 6$$

ii) We set $x < 3$ and x very close to 3. Then the values $f(x) = x+4$, by definition, and as x approaches 3, we see that $x+4$ approaches $3+4 = 7$. So

$$\lim_{x \to 3^-} f(x) = 7$$

Example 53.   Evaluate the following limits, if they exist.

$$f(x) = \begin{cases} x^2 & x > 0 \\ -x^2 & x \leq 0 \end{cases}$$

i) $\lim_{x \to 0^-} f(x)$; ii) $\lim_{x \to 0^+} f(x)$

Solution **i)** Let $x < 0$ and x very close to 0. Since $x < 0$, $f(x) = -x^2$ and $f(x)$ is very close to $-0^2 = 0$ since x is. Thus

$$\lim_{x \to 0^-} f(x) = 0$$

ii) Let $x > 0$ and x very close to 0. Since $x > 0$, $f(x) = x^2$ and $f(x)$ is very close to 0 too! Thus

$$\lim_{x \to 0^+} f(x) = 0$$

NOTE: In this example the graph of f has no breaks whatsoever since $f(0) = 0$.. In this case we say that the function f is **continuous** at $x = 0$. Had there been a 'break' or some points 'missing' from the graph we would describe f as **discontinuous** whenever those 'breaks' or 'missing points' occurred.

$f(x)$

12

6

$(18,12)$

3 18 x

Figure 22.

Example 54.   Use the graph in Figure 22 to determine the value of the required limits.

i) $\lim_{x \to 3^-} f(x)$; ii) $\lim_{x \to 3^+} f(x)$; iii) $\lim_{x \to 18^+} f(x)$

Solution **i)** Let $x < 3$ and let x be very close to 3. The point $(x, f(x))$ which is **on** the curve $y = f(x)$ now approaches a definite point as x approaches 3. Which point? The graph indicates that this point is $(3, 6)$. Thus

$$\lim_{x \to 3^-} f(x) = 6$$

ii) Let $x > 3$ and let x be very close to 3. In this case, as x approaches 3, the points $(x, f(x))$ travel down towards the point $(3, 12)$. Thus

$$\lim_{x \to 3^+} f(x) = 12$$

iii) Here we let $x > 18$ and let x be very close to 18. Now as x approaches 18 the points $(x, f(x))$ on the curve are approaching the point $(18, 12)$. Thus

$$\lim_{x \to 18^+} f(x) = 12$$

<hr>

Exercise Set 4.

Evaluate the following limits and justify your conclusions.

1. $\lim\limits_{x \to 2^+} (x + 2)$

7. $\lim\limits_{x \to 0^+} x \sin x$

2. $\lim\limits_{x \to 0^+} (x^2 + 1)$

8. $\lim\limits_{x \to \pi^+} \left(\dfrac{\cos x}{x} \right)$

3. $\lim\limits_{x \to 1^-} (1 - x^2)$

9. $\lim\limits_{x \to 2^+} \left(\dfrac{x - 2}{x + 2} \right)$

4. $\lim\limits_{t \to 2^+} \left(\dfrac{1}{t - 2} \right)$

10. $\lim\limits_{x \to 1^-} \dfrac{x}{|x - 1|}$

5. $\lim\limits_{x \to 0^+} (x|x|)$

11. $\lim\limits_{x \to 1^-} \left(\dfrac{x - 1}{x + 2} \right)$

6. $\lim\limits_{x \to 0^-} \dfrac{x}{|x|}$

12. $\lim\limits_{x \to 3^+} \left(\dfrac{x - 3}{x^2 - 9} \right)$
(Hint: Factor the denominator)

13. Let the function f be defined as follows:

$$f(x) = \begin{cases} 1 - |x| & x < 1 \\ x & x \geq 1 \end{cases}$$

Evaluate i) $\lim\limits_{x \to 1^-} f(x)$; ii) $\lim\limits_{x \to 1^+} f(x)$

Conclude that the graph of $f(x)$ must have a 'break' at $x = 1$.

14. Let g be defined by

$$g(x) = \begin{cases} x^2 + 1 & x < 0 \\ 1 - x^2 & 0 \leq x \leq 1 \\ x & x > 1 \end{cases}$$

Evaluate

i). $\lim\limits_{x \to 0^-} g(x)$ ii). $\lim\limits_{x \to 0^+} g(x)$

iii). $\lim\limits_{x \to 1^-} g(x)$ iv). $\lim\limits_{x \to 1^+} g(x)$

v) Conclude that the graph of g has no breaks at $x = 0$ but it does have a break at $x = 1$.

15. Use the graph in Figure 23 to determine the value of the required limits. (The function f is composed of parts of 2 functions).

Evaluate

i). $\lim\limits_{x \to -1^+} f(x)$ ii). $\lim\limits_{x \to -1^-} f(x)$

iii). $\lim\limits_{x \to 1^-} f(x)$ iv). $\lim\limits_{x \to 1^+} f(x)$

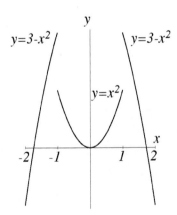

Figure 23.

2.2   Two-Sided Limits and Continuity

At this point we know how to determine the values of the limit from the left (or right) of a given function f at a point $x = a$. We have also seen that whenever

$$\lim_{x \to a^+} f(x) \neq \lim_{x \to a^-} f(x)$$

then there is a 'break' in the graph of f at $x = a$. The **absence of breaks or holes in the graph** of a function is what the notion of **continuity** is all about.

Definition of the limit of a function at $x = a$.

We say that **a function f has the (two-sided) limit L as x approaches a** if

$$\lim_{x \to a^+} f(x) = \lim_{x \to a^-} f(x) = L$$

When this happens, we write (for brevity)

$$\lim_{x \to a} f(x) = L$$

and read this as: the limit of $f(x)$ as x approaches a is L (L may be infinite here).

One of the key mathematical figures during the first millennium was a monk called **Alcuin of York** (735 - 804) who was Charlemagne's scribe and general advisor. He wrote a very influential book in Latin which contained many mathematical problems passed on from antiquity. In this book of his you'll find the following (paraphrased) problem:

A dog chases a rabbit who has a head-start of 150 feet. All you know is that every time the dog leaps 9 feet, the rabbit leaps 7 feet. How many leaps will it take for the dog to pass the rabbit?

NOTE: So, in order for a limit to exist both the right- and left-hand limits must exist and be equal. Using this notion we can now define the 'continuity of a function f at a point $x = a$.'

We say that f is **continuous** at $x = a$ if all the following conditions are satisfied:

1. f is defined at $x = a$ (i.e., $f(a)$ is finite)
2. $\lim\limits_{x \to a^+} f(x) = \lim\limits_{x \to a^-} f(x)$ (= L, their common value) and
3. $L = f(a)$.

NOTE: These three conditions must be satisfied in order for a function f to be continuous at a given point $x = a$. If any one or more of these conditions is not satisfied we say that f is **discontinuous** at $x = a$. In other words, we see from the Definition above (or in Table 2.7) that the one-sided limits from the left and right must be equal in order for f to be continuous at $x = a$ but that this equality, in itself, is **not enough to guarantee continuity** as there are 2 other conditions that need to be satisfied as well.

Example 55.   Show that the given function is continuous at the given points, $x = 1$ and $x = 2$, where f is defined by

$$f(x) = \begin{cases} x + 1 & 0 \leq x \leq 1 \\ 2x & 1 < x \leq 2 \\ x^2 & x > 2 \end{cases}$$

Solution To show that f is continuous at $x = 1$ we need to verify 3 conditions (according to Table 2.7):

1. **Is f defined at $x = 1$?** Yes, its value is $f(1) = 1 + 1 = 2$ by definition.

2. **Are the one-sided limits equal?** Let's check this: (See Fig. 24)

$$\lim_{x \to 1^-} f(x) = \underbrace{\lim_{x \to 1^-} (x + 1)}_{\text{because } f(x) = x+1 \text{ for } x \le 1} = 1 + 1 = 2$$

Moreover,

$$\lim_{x \to 1^+} f(x) = \underbrace{\lim_{x \to 1^+} (2x)}_{\text{because } f(x) = 2x \text{ for } x > 1, \text{ and close to } 1} = 2 \cdot 1 = 2$$

The one-sided limits are equal to each other and their common value is $L = 2$.

3. **Is $L = f(1)$?** By definition $f(1) = 1 + 1 = 2$, so OK, this is true, because $L = 2$.

Thus, by definition f is continuous at $x = 1$.

We proceed in the same fashion for $x = 2$. Remember, we still have to verify 3 conditions ...

EXAMPLES

1. **Is f defined at $x = 2$?** Yes, because its value is $f(2) = 2 \cdot 2 = 4$.

2. **Are the one-sided limits equal?** Let's see:

$$\lim_{x \to 2^+} f(x) = \underbrace{\lim_{x \to 2^+} x^2}_{\text{because } f(x) = x^2 \text{ for } x > 2} = 2^2 = 4$$

and

$$\lim_{x \to 2^-} f(x) = \underbrace{\lim_{x \to 2^-} (2x)}_{\text{because } f(x) = 2x \text{ for } x \le 2 \text{ and close to } 2} = 2 \cdot 2 = 4$$

So they are both equal and their common value, $L = 4$.

3. **Is $L = f(2)$?** We know that $L = 4$ and $f(2) = 2 \cdot 2 = 4$ by definition so, OK.

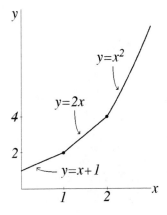

Figure 24.

Thus, by definition (Table 2.7), f is continuous at $x = 2$.

Remarks:

1. The **existence of the limit of a function f at $x = a$ is equivalent to requiring that both one-sided limits be equal (to each other)**.

2. The existence of the limit of a function f at $x = a$ doesn't imply that f is continuous at $x = a$.
   Why? Because the value of this limit may be different from $f(a)$, or, worse still, $f(a)$ may be infinite.

3. It follows from (1) that

$$\text{If } \lim_{x \to a^+} f(x) \neq \lim_{x \to a^-} f(x), \text{ then } \lim_{x \to a} f(x) \text{ does not exist,}$$

so, in particular, f cannot be continuous at $x = a$.

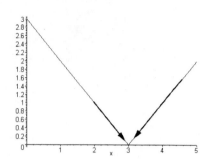

The function $f(x) = |x - 3|$

Figure 25.

Example 56. Show that the function f defined by $f(x) = |x-3|$ is continuous at $x = 3$ (see Figure 25).

Solution By definition of the absolute value we know that

$$f(x) = |x - 3| = \begin{cases} x - 3 & x \geq 3 \\ 3 - x & x < 3 \end{cases}$$

(Remember: $|symbol| = symbol$ if $symbol \geq 0$ and $|symbol| = -symbol$ if $symbol < 0$ where '*symbol*' is any expression involving some variable...) OK, now

$$\lim_{x \to 3^+} f(x) = \lim_{x \to 3^+} (x - 3) = 3 - 3 = 0$$

and

$$\lim_{x \to 3^-} f(x) = \lim_{x \to 3^-} (3 - x) = 3 - 3 = 0$$

so $\lim_{x \to 3} f(x)$ exists and is equal to 0 (by definition).

Is $0 = f(3)$? Yes (because $f(3) = |3 - 3| = |0| = 0$). Of course $f(3)$ is defined. We conclude that f is continuous at $x = 3$.

Remark: In practice it is easier to remember the statement:

$$\boxed{\begin{array}{c} \boldsymbol{f} \textbf{ is continuous at } \boldsymbol{x = a} \textbf{ if} \\ \lim_{x \to a} \boldsymbol{f(x) = f(a)} \end{array}}$$

whenever all the 'symbols' here have meaning (*i.e.* the limit exists, $f(a)$ exists etc.).

Example 57. Determine whether or not the following functions have a limit at the indicated point.

a) $f(x) = x^2 + 1$ at $x = 0$

b) $f(x) = 1 + |x - 1|$ at $x = 1$

c) $f(t) = \begin{cases} 1 & \text{for } t \geq 0 \\ 0 & \text{for } t < 0 \end{cases}$ at $t = 0$

d) $f(x) = \dfrac{1}{x}$ at $x = 0$

e) $g(t) = \dfrac{t}{t + 1}$ at $t = 0$

The **Arabic numerals** or those 10 basic symbols we use today in the world of mathematics seem to have been accepted in Europe and subsequently in the West, sometime during the period 1482-1494, as can be evidenced from old merchant records from the era (also known as the *High Renaissance* in art). Prior to this, merchants and others used Roman numerals (X=10, IX=9, III = 3, etc.) in their dealings.

Solution **a)**
$$\begin{aligned} \lim_{x \to 0^+} f(x) &= \lim_{x \to 0^+} (x^2 + 1) = 0^2 + 1 = 1 \\ \lim_{x \to 0^-} f(x) &= \lim_{x \to 0^-} (x^2 + 1) = 0^2 + 1 = 1 \end{aligned}$$

Thus $\lim_{x \to 0} f(x)$ exists and is equal to 1. *i.e.* $\lim_{x \to 0} f(x) = 1$.

b)
$$\lim_{x \to 1^+} f(x) = \lim_{x \to 1^+} (1 + |x - 1|)$$
$$= \lim_{x \to 1^+} (1 + (x - 1)) \quad \text{(because } |x - 1| = x - 1 \text{ as } x > 1)$$
$$= \lim_{x \to 1^+} x$$
$$= 1$$

$$\lim_{x \to 1^-} f(x) = \lim_{x \to 1^-} (1 + |x - 1|)$$
$$= \lim_{x \to 1^-} (1 + (1 - x) \quad \text{(because } |x - 1| = 1 - x \text{ as } x < 1)$$
$$= \lim_{x \to 1^-} (2 - x)$$
$$= 2 - 1$$
$$= 1$$

Thus $\lim_{x \to 1} f(x)$ exists and is equal to 1, *i.e.* $\lim_{x \to 1} f(x) = 1$.

c)
$$\lim_{t \to 0^+} f(t) = \lim_{t \to 0^+} (1) \quad \text{(as } f(t) = 1 \text{ for } t > 0)$$
$$= 1$$
$$\lim_{t \to 0^-} f(t) = \lim_{t \to 0^-} (0) \quad \text{(as } f(t) = 0 \text{ for } t < 0)$$
$$= 0$$

Since $\lim_{t \to 0^+} f(t) \neq \lim_{t \to 0^-} f(t)$, it follows that $\lim_{t \to 0} f(t)$ does not exist. (In particular, f cannot be continuous at $t = 0$.)

d)
$$\lim_{x \to 0^+} f(x) = \lim_{x \to 0^+} \frac{1}{x} = +\infty$$

because "division by zero" does not produce a real number, in general. On the other hand

$$\lim_{x \to 0^-} f(x) = \lim_{x \to 0^-} \frac{1}{x} = -\infty \quad \text{(since } x < 0)$$

Since $\lim_{x \to 0^+} f(x) \neq \lim_{x \to 0^-} f(x)$ the limit does not exist at $x = 0$.

e)
$$\lim_{t \to 0^+} g(t) = \lim_{t \to 0^+} \frac{t}{t + 1} = \frac{0}{0 + 1} = 0$$
$$\lim_{t \to 0^-} g(t) = \lim_{t \to 0^-} \frac{t}{t + 1} = \frac{0}{0 + 1} = 0$$

and so $\lim_{t \to 0} g(t)$ exists and is equal to 0, *i.e.* $\lim_{t \to 0} g(t) = 0$.

> The rigorous method of handling these examples is presented in an optional Chapter, **Advanced Topics**. Use of your calculator will be helpful in determining some limits but cannot substitute a theoretical proof. The reader is encouraged to consult the *Advanced Topics* for more details.

Remark:

It follows from Table 2.4 that continuous functions themselves have similar properties, being based upon the notion of limits. For example it is true that:

1. The sum or difference of two continuous functions (at $x = a$) is again continuous (at $x = a$).

The **Sandwich Theorem** states that, if

$$g(x) \leq f(x) \leq h(x)$$

for all (sufficiently) large x and for some (extended) real number A, and

$$\lim_{x \to a} g(x) = A, \qquad \lim_{x \to a} h(x) = A$$

then f also has a limit at $x = a$ and

$$\lim_{x \to a} f(x) = A$$

In other words, f is "sandwiched" between two values that are ultimately the same and so f must also have the same limit.

2. The product or quotient of two continuous functions (at $x = a$) is also continuous (provided the quotient has a non-zero denominator at $x = a$).

3. A multiple of two continuous functions (at $x = a$) is again a continuous function (at $x = a$).

Properties of Limits of Functions

Let f, g be two given functions, $x = a$ be some (finite) point. The following statements hold (but will not be proved here):

Assume $\lim_{x \to a} f(x)$ and $\lim_{x \to a} g(x)$ both exist and are **finite**.

Then

a) **The limit of a sum is the sum of the limits.**
$$\lim_{x \to a} (f(x) + g(x)) = \lim_{x \to a} f(x) + \lim_{x \to a} g(x)$$

b) **The limit of a difference is the difference of the limits.**
$$\lim_{x \to a} (f(x) - g(x)) = \lim_{x \to a} f(x) - \lim_{x \to a} g(x)$$

c) **The limit of a multiple is the multiple of the limit.**
If c is any number, then $\lim_{x \to a} cf(x) = c \lim_{x \to a} f(x)$

d) **The limit of a quotient is the quotient of the limits.**
If $\lim_{x \to a} g(x) \neq 0$ then $\lim_{x \to a} \dfrac{f(x)}{g(x)} = \dfrac{\lim_{x \to a} f(x)}{\lim_{x \to a} g(x)}$

e) **The limit of a product is the product of the limits.**
$$\lim_{x \to a} f(x)g(x) = \left(\lim_{x \to a} f(x) \right) \left(\lim_{x \to a} g(x) \right)$$

f) If $f(x) \leq g(x)$ then $\lim_{x \to a} f(x) \leq \lim_{x \to a} g(x)$

Table 2.4: Properties of Limits of Functions

Now, the Properties in Table 2.4 and the following Remark allow us to make some very important observations about some classes of functions, such as polynomials.

How? Well, let's take the simplest polynomial $f(x) = x$. It is easy to see that for some given number $x = a$ and setting $g(x) = x$, Table 2.4 Property (e), implies that the function $h(x) = f(x)g(x) = x \cdot x = x^2$ is also continuous at $x = a$. In the same way we can show that $k(x) = f(x)h(x) = x \cdot x^2 = x^3$ is also continuous at $x = a$, and so on.

In this way we can prove (using, in addition, Property (a)), that **any polynomial whatsoever is continuous at $x = a$, where a is any real number.** We summarize this and other such consequences in Table 2.8.

SUMMARY: One-Sided Limits from the Right

We say that the function f **has a limit from the right at $x = a$** (or the right-hand limit of f exists at $x = a$) whose value is L and denote this symbolically by

$$\lim_{x \to a^+} f(x) = L$$

if BOTH the following statements are satisfied:

1. Let $x > a$ and x be very close to $x = a$.

2. As x approaches a ("from the right" because "$x > a$"), the values of $f(x)$ approach the value L.

(For a more rigorous definition see the **Advanced Topics**)

Table 2.5: SUMMARY: One-Sided Limits From the Right

SUMMARY: One-Sided Limits from the Left

We say that the function f **has a limit from the left at $x = a$** (or the left-hand limit of f exists at $x = a$) and is equal to L and denote this symbolically by

$$\lim_{x \to a^-} f(x) = L$$

if BOTH the following statements are satisfied:

1. Let $x < a$ and x be very close to $x = a$.

2. As x approaches a ("from the left" because "$x < a$"), the values of $f(x)$ approach the value L.

Table 2.6: SUMMARY: One-Sided Limits From the Left

Exercise Set 5.

Determine whether the following limits exist. Give reasons.

1. $\lim_{x \to 0} f(x)$ where $f(x) = \begin{cases} x + 2 & x \leq 0 \\ x & x > 0 \end{cases}$

2. $\lim_{x \to 1} (x + 3)$

3. $\lim_{x \to -2} \left(\dfrac{x + 2}{x} \right)$

4. $\lim_{x \to 0} x \sin x$

5. $\lim_{x \to 1} f(x)$ where $f(x) = \begin{cases} \sin(x - 1) & 0 \leq x \leq 1 \\ |x - 1| & x > 1 \end{cases}$

6. $\lim_{x \to 0} \left(\dfrac{x + 1}{x} \right)$

7. $\lim_{x \to 0} \left(\dfrac{2}{x} \right)$

Nicola Oresme, (1323-1382), Bishop of Lisieux, in Normandy, wrote a tract in 1360 (this is before the printing press) where, for the first time, we find the introduction of perpendicular xy-axes drawn on a plane. His work is likely to have influenced **René Descartes** (1596-1650), the founder of modern *Analytic Geometry*.

SUMMARY: Continuity of f at $x = a$.

We say that f is **continuous** at $x = a$ if all the following conditions are satisfied:

1. f is defined at $x = a$ (i.e., $f(a)$ is finite)

2. $\displaystyle\lim_{x \to a^+} f(x) = \lim_{x \to a^-} f(x)$ (= L, their common value) and

3. $L = f(a)$.

These three conditions must be satisfied in order for a function f to be continuous at a given point $x = a$. If any one or more of these conditions is not satisfied we say that f is **discontinuous** at $x = a$.

Table 2.7: SUMMARY: Continuity of a Function f at a Point $x = a$

8. $\displaystyle\lim_{x \to 1} \left(\frac{x}{x+1} \right)$

9. $\displaystyle\lim_{x \to 2} \left(2 + |x - 2| \right)$

10. $\displaystyle\lim_{x \to 0} f(x)$ where $f(x) = \begin{cases} 3 & x \leq 0 \\ 2 & x > 0 \end{cases}$

11. Are the following functions continuous at 0? Give reasons.

    a) $f(x) = |x|$

    b) $g(t) = t^2 + 3t + 2$

    c) $h(x) = 3 + 2|x|$

    d) $f(x) = \dfrac{2}{x+1}$

    e) $f(x) = \dfrac{x^2 + 1}{x^2 - 2}$

12. **Hard** Let f be defined by

$$f(x) = \begin{cases} x \sin\left(\frac{1}{x}\right) & x \neq 0 \\ 0 & x = 0 \end{cases}$$

Show that f is continuous at $x = 0$.

(*Hint*: Do this in the following steps:

    a) Show that for $x \neq 0$, $\left| x \sin\left(\frac{1}{x}\right) \right| \leq |x|$.

    b) Use (a) and the Sandwich Theorem to show that

$$0 \leq \lim_{x \to 0} \left| x \sin\left(\frac{1}{x}\right) \right| \leq 0$$

    and so

$$\lim_{x \to 0} \left| x \sin\left(\frac{1}{x}\right) \right| = 0$$

    c) Conclude that $\displaystyle\lim_{x \to 0} x \sin\left(\frac{1}{x}\right) = 0$.

    d) Verify the other conditions of continuity.)

Some Continuous Functions

Let $x = a$ be a given point.

a) The polynomial p of degree n, with fixed coefficients, given by

$$p(x) = a_n x^n + a_{n-1} x^{n-1} + \ldots + a_0$$

is continuous at any real number $x = a$.

b) The rational function, r, where $r(x) = \frac{p(x)}{q(x)}$ where p, q are both polynomials is continuous at $x = a$ provided $q(a) \neq 0$ or equivalently, provided $x = a$ is not a root of $q(x)$. Thus

$$r(x) = \frac{a_n x^n + a_{n-1} x^{n-1} + \ldots + a_0}{b_m x^m + b_{m-1} x^{m-1} + \ldots + b_0}$$

is continuous at $x = a$ provided the denominator is not equal to zero at $x = a$.

c) If f is a continuous function, so is its **absolute value** function, $|f|$, and if

$$\lim_{x \to a} |f(x)| = 0, \quad \text{then}$$

$$\lim_{x \to a} f(x) = 0$$

(The proof of (c) uses the ideas in the Advanced Topics chapter.)

Table 2.8: Some Continuous Functions

What about discontinuous functions?

In order to show that a function is discontinuous somewhere we need to show that at least one of the three conditions in the definition of continuity (Table 2.7) is not satisfied.

Remember, to show that f is continuous requires the verification of all three conditions in Table 2.7 whereas to show some function is discontinuous only requires that **one** of the three conditions for continuity is not satisfied.

Example 58. Determine which of the following functions are discontinuous somewhere. Give reasons.

a) $f(x) = \begin{cases} x & x \leq 0 \\ 3x + 1 & x > 0 \end{cases}$

b) $f(x) = \dfrac{x}{|x|}$, $f(0) = 1$

c) $f(x) = \begin{cases} x^2 & x \neq 0 \\ 1 & x = 0 \end{cases}$

d) $f(x) = \dfrac{1}{|x|}$, $x \neq 0$

Solution **a)**   Note that $\displaystyle\lim_{x\to 0^-} f(x) = \lim_{x\to 0^-} (x) = 0$

while $\displaystyle\lim_{x\to 0^+} f(x) = \lim_{x\to 0^+} (3x+1) = 1$

Thus the $\displaystyle\lim_{x\to 0} f(x)$ does not exist and so f cannot be continuous at $x = 0$, or, equivalently, f is discontinuous at $x = 0$.

What about the other points, $x \neq 0$?

Well, if $x \neq 0$, and $x < 0$, then $f(x) = x$ is a polynomial, right? Thus f is continuous at each point x where $x < 0$. On the other hand, if $x \neq 0$ and $x > 0$ then $f(x) = 3x + 1$ is also a polynomial. Once again f is continuous at each point x where $x > 0$.

Conclusion: f is continuous at every point x except at $x = 0$.

b) Since $f(0) = 1$ is defined, let's check for the existence of the limit at $x = 0$. (You've noticed, of course, that at $x = 0$ the function is of the form $\frac{0}{0}$ **which is not defined as a real number** and this is why an additional condition was added there to make the function defined for **all** x and not just those $x \neq 0$.)

Now,

$$\lim_{x\to 0^+} f(x) = \lim_{x\to 0^+} \frac{x}{|x|} = \underbrace{\lim_{x\to 0^+} \frac{x}{x} = \lim_{x\to 0^+} (1)}_{\text{(because } x\neq 0)}$$

$$= 1$$

$$\lim_{x\to 0^-} f(x) = \lim_{x\to 0^-} \frac{x}{|x|} = \lim_{x\to 0^-} \frac{x}{(-x)} = \lim_{x\to 0^-} (-1)$$
$$= -1$$

(since $|x| = -x$ if $x < 0$ by definition). Since the one-sided limits are different it follows that

$$\lim_{x\to 0} f(x) \text{ does not exist.}$$

Thus f is discontinuous at $x = 0$.

What about the other points? Well, for $x \neq 0$, f is nice enough. For instance, if $x > 0$ then

$$f(x) = \frac{x}{|x|} = \frac{x}{x} = +1$$

for each such $x > 0$. Since f is a constant it follows that f is continuous for $x > 0$. On the other hand, if $x < 0$, then $|x| = -x$ so that

$$f(x) = \frac{x}{|x|} = \frac{x}{(-x)} = -1$$

and once again f is continuous for such $x < 0$.

Conclusion: f is continuous for each $x \neq 0$ and at $x = 0$, f is discontinuous.

The graph of this function is shown in Figure 26.

c) Let's look at f for $x \neq 0$ first, (it doesn't really matter how we start). For $x \neq 0$, $f(x) = x^2$ is a polynomial and so f is continuous for each such $x \neq 0$, (Table 2.8).

How can a function f be discontinuous at $x = a$? If any one (or more) of the following occurs ...

1. $f(a)$ is not defined (*e.g.*, it is infinite, or we are dividing by 0, or extracting the root of a negative number, ...) (See Example 58 (d))

2. If either one of the left- and right-limits of f at $x = a$ is infinite (See Example 58 (d))

3. $f(a)$ is defined but the left- and right-limits at $x = a$ are *unequal* (See Example 58 (a), (b))

4. $f(a)$ is defined, the left- and right-limits are *equal* to L but $L = \pm\infty$

5. $f(a)$ is defined, the left- and right-limits are *equal* to L but $L \neq f(a)$ (See Example 58 (c))

Then f is discontinuous at $x = a$.

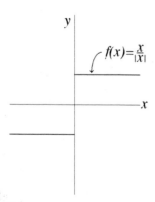

Figure   26.

What about $x = 0$? We are given that $f(0) = 1$ so f is defined there. What about the limit of f as x approaches $x = 0$. Does this limit exist?

Let's see

$$\lim_{x \to 0^+} f(x) = \lim_{x \to 0^+} x^2 = 0^2 = 0$$

and

$$\lim_{x \to 0^-} f(x) = \lim_{x \to 0^-} x^2 = 0^2 = 0$$

OK, so $\lim\limits_{x \to 0} f(x)$ exists and is equal to 0. But note that

$$\lim_{x \to 0} f(x) = 0 \neq f(0) = 1$$

So, in this case, f is discontinuous at $x = 0$, (because even though conditions (1) and (2) of Table 2.7 are satisfied the final condition (3) is not!)

d) In this case we see that

$$\lim_{x \to 0^+} f(x) = \lim_{x \to 0^-} f(x) = +\infty$$

and $f(0) = +\infty$ as well! Ah, but now $f(0)$ is not defined as a real number (thus violating condition (1)). Thus f is discontinuous at $x = 0$ ... and the other points? Well, for $x < 0$, $f(x) = -\frac{1}{x}$ is a quotient of two polynomials and any x (since $x \neq 0$) is not a root of the denominator. Thus f is a continuous function for such $x < 0$. A similar argument applies if $x > 0$.

Conclusion: f is continuous everywhere except at $x = 0$ where it is discontinuous.

We show the graph of the functions defined in (c), (d) in Figure 27.

The graph of Example 58(c)

Exercise Set 6.

Determine the points of discontinuity of each of the following functions.

1. $f(x) = \dfrac{|x|}{x} + 1$ for $x \neq 0$ and $f(0) = 2$

2. $g(x) = \begin{cases} x & x < 0 \\ 1 + x^2 & x \geq 0 \end{cases}$

3. $f(x) = \dfrac{x^2 + 3x + 3}{x^2 - 1}$
   (*Hint*: Find the zeros of the denominator.)

4. $f(x) = \begin{cases} x^3 + 1 & x \neq 0 \\ 2 & x = 0 \end{cases}$

5. $f(x) = \dfrac{1}{x} + \dfrac{1}{x^2}$ for $x \neq 0$, $f(0) = +1$

6. $f(x) = \begin{cases} 1.62 & x < 0 \\ 2x & x \geq 0 \end{cases}$

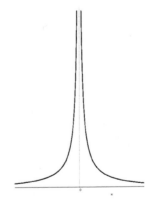

The graph of Example 58(d)

Figure 27.

Before proceeding with a study of some trigonometric limits let's recall some fundamental notions about trigonometry.

Recall that the measure of angle called the **radian** is equal to $\frac{360^o}{2\pi} \approx 57^o$. It is also that angle whose arc is numerically equal to the radius of the given circle. (So 2π

Continuity of various trigonometric functions
(**Recall**: Angles x are in **radians**)   1. The functions f, g defined by $f(x) = \sin x$, $g(x) = \cos x$ are continuous everywhere (i.e., for each real number x).   2. The functions $h(x) = \tan x$ and $k(x) = \sec x$ are continuous at every point which is not an odd multiple of $\frac{\pi}{2}$. At such points h, k are discontinuous. (*i.e.* at $-\frac{\pi}{2}$, $\frac{3\pi}{2}$, $-\frac{3\pi}{2}$, $\frac{5\pi}{2}$, ...)   3. The functions 'csc' and 'cot' are continuous whenever x is not a multiple of π, and discontinuous whenever x is a multiple of π. (*i.e.* at $x = \pi$, $-\pi$, 2π, -5π, etc.)

Table 2.9: Continuity of Various Trigonometric Functions

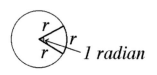

Figure 28.

radians correspond to 360°, π radians correspond to 180°, 1 radian corresponds to $\approx 57^{\circ}$, etc.) Now, to find the area of a sector of a circle of radius r subtending an angle θ at the center we note that the area is proportional to this central angle so that

$$\frac{2\pi}{\text{Area of circle}} = \frac{\theta}{\text{Area of sector}}$$

$$\text{Area of sector} = \frac{\theta}{2\pi}(\pi r^2)$$

$$= \frac{r^2 \theta}{2}$$

We conclude that the area of a sector subtending an angle θ at the center is given by $\frac{r^2\theta}{2}$ where θ is in radians and summarize this in Table 2.10.

The area of a sector subtending an angle θ (in radians) at the center of a circle of radius r is given by
$$\text{Area of a sector} = \frac{r^2\theta}{2}$$

Table 2.10: Area of a Sector of a Circle

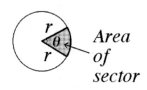

Figure 29.

Next we **find some relationships between triangles in order to deduce a very important limit in the study of calculus.**

We begin with a circle $\mathcal{C}$ of radius 1 and a sector subtending an angle, $x < \frac{\pi}{2}$ in radians at its center, labelled O. Label the extremities of the sector along the arc by A and B as in the adjoining figure, Fig. 30.

At A produce an altitude which meets OB extended to C. Join AB by a line segment. The figure now looks like Figure 31.

We call the 'triangle' whose side is the arc AB and having sides AO, OB a "**curvilinear triangle**" for brevity. (It is also a "sector"!)

Figure 30.

Let's compare areas. Note that

$$\text{Area of } \triangle ACO \quad > \quad \text{Area of curvilinear triangle}$$
$$> \quad \text{Area of } \triangle ABO$$

Now the area of $\triangle ACO \quad = \quad \frac{1}{2}(1)|AC| = \frac{1}{2}\tan x$

Area of curvilinear triangle $\quad = \quad$ Area of the sector with central angle x

$$= \quad \frac{1}{2}(1^2) \cdot x \text{ (because of Table 2.10 above)}$$

$$= \quad \frac{x}{2}$$

Finally, from Figure 31,

Area of triangle $ABO \quad = \quad \frac{1}{2}$(altitude from base AO)(base length)

$$= \quad \frac{1}{2}(\text{length of BD}) \cdot (1) = \frac{1}{2}(\sin x) \cdot (1)$$

$$= \quad \frac{\sin x}{2}$$

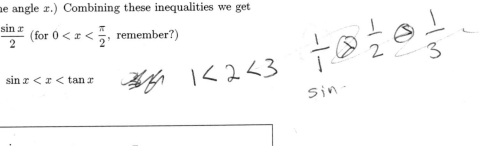

Figure 31.

(by definition of the sine of the angle x.) Combining these inequalities we get

$$\frac{1}{2}\tan x > \frac{x}{2} > \frac{\sin x}{2} \text{ (for } 0 < x < \frac{\pi}{2}, \text{ remember?)}$$

or

$$\sin x < x < \tan x$$

from which we can derive

$$\boxed{\cos x < \frac{\sin x}{x} < 1 \quad \text{for } 0 < x \le \frac{\pi}{2}}$$

since all quantities are positive. This is a fundamental inequality in trigonometry.

We now apply Table 2.4(f) to this inequality to show that

$$\underbrace{\lim_{x\to 0^+}\cos x}_{1} \;\le\; \lim_{x\to 0^+}\frac{\sin x}{x} \;\le\; \underbrace{\lim_{x\to 0^+}1}_{1}$$

and we conclude that

$$\boxed{\lim_{x\to 0^+}\frac{\sin x}{x} = 1}$$

If, on the other hand, $-\frac{\pi}{2} < x < 0$ (or x is a negative angle) then, writing $x = -x_0$, we have $\frac{\pi}{2} > x_0 > 0$. Next

$$\frac{\sin x}{x} = \frac{\sin(-x_0)}{-x_0} = \frac{-\sin(x_0)}{-x_0} = \frac{\sin x_0}{x_0}$$

where we have used the relation $\sin(-x_0) = -\sin x_0$ valid for any angle x_0 (in radians, as usual). Hence

$$\lim_{x\to 0^-}\left(\frac{\sin x}{x}\right) \quad = \quad \lim_{x\to 0^-}\frac{\sin x_0}{x_0}$$

$$= \quad \lim_{-x_0\to 0^-}\frac{\sin x_0}{x_0}$$

$$= \quad \lim_{x_0\to 0^+}\frac{\sin x_0}{x_0} \quad \text{(because if } -x_0 < 0 \text{ then } x_0 > 0 \text{ and } x_0 \text{ approaches } 0^+\text{)}$$

$$= \quad 1.$$

Since both one-sided limits are equal it follows that

$$\lim_{x \to 0} \frac{\sin x}{x} = 1$$

Another important limit like the one in Table 2.11 is obtained by using the basic

---

If the symbol $\square$ represents any continuous function then, so long as we can let $\square \to 0$, we have

$$\lim_{\square \to 0} \frac{\sin \square}{\square} = 1$$

Table 2.11: Limit of $(\sin \square)/\square$ as $\square \to 0$

identity

$$1 - \cos\theta = \frac{1 - \cos^2 \theta}{1 + \cos\theta} = \frac{\sin^2 \theta}{1 + \cos\theta}$$

Dividing both sides by θ and rearranging terms we find

$$\frac{1 - \cos\theta}{\theta} = \frac{\sin\theta}{\theta} \cdot \frac{\sin\theta}{1 + \cos\theta}$$

Now, we know that

$$\lim_{\theta \to 0} \frac{\sin\theta}{\theta} = 1$$

and

$$\lim_{\theta \to 0} \left(\frac{\sin\theta}{1 + \cos\theta} \right)$$

exists (because it is the limit of the quotient of 2 continuous functions, the denominator not being 0 as $\theta \to 0$). Furthermore it is easy to see that

$$\lim_{\theta \to 0} \left(\frac{\sin\theta}{1 + \cos\theta} \right) = \frac{\sin 0}{1 + \cos 0} = \frac{0}{1 + 1} = 0$$

It now follows from Table 2.4(e) that

$$\lim_{\theta \to 0} \frac{1 - \cos\theta}{\theta} = \left(\lim_{\theta \to 0} \frac{\sin\theta}{\theta} \right) \left(\lim_{\theta \to 0} \frac{\sin\theta}{1 + \cos\theta} \right) = 1 \cdot 0$$
$$= 0$$

and we conclude that

$$\lim_{\theta \to 0} \frac{1 - \cos\theta}{\theta} = 0$$

If you want, you can replace 'θ' by 'x' in the above formula or any other '*symbol*' as in Table 2.11. Hence, we obtain Table 2.12,

---

$$\lim_{\square \to 0} \frac{1 - \cos \square}{\square} = 0.$$

Table 2.12: Limit of $(1 - \cos \square)/\square$ as $\square \to 0$

| Example 59. | Evaluate the following limits. |

a) $\displaystyle\lim_{x\to 0}\frac{\sin(3x)}{x}$

b) $\displaystyle\lim_{x\to 0}\frac{1-\cos(2x)}{x}$

c) $\displaystyle\lim_{x\to 0}\frac{\sin(2x)}{\sin(3x)}$

d) $\displaystyle\lim_{x\to 0^+}\frac{\sin(\sqrt{x})}{\sqrt{x}}$

One of the first complete introductions to *Trigonometry* was written by one **Johannes Müller of Königsberg**, (1436 - 1476), also known as *Regiomontanus*. The work, written in Latin, is entitled *De Triangulis omnimodus* first appeared in 1464.

Solution **a)** We use Table 2.11. If we let $\square = 3x$, we also need the symbol $\square$ in the denominator, right? In other words, $x = \frac{\square}{3}$ and so

$$\frac{\sin 3x}{x} = \frac{\sin(\square)}{(\frac{\square}{3})} = 3 \cdot \frac{\sin(\square)}{\square}$$

Now, as $x \to 0$ it is clear that, since $\square = 3x$, $\square \to 0$ as well. Thus

$$\lim_{x\to 0}\frac{\sin(3x)}{x} = \lim_{\square \to 0} 3 \cdot \frac{\sin(\square)}{\square}$$

$$= 3 \lim_{\square \to 0}\frac{\sin(\square)}{\square} \quad \text{(by Table 2.4(c))}$$

$$= 3 \cdot 1 \quad \text{(by Table 2.11)}$$

$$= 3$$

b) We use Table 2.12 because of the form of the problem for $\square = 2x$ then $x = \frac{\square}{2}$. So

$$\frac{1-\cos(2x)}{x} = \frac{1-\cos\square}{\frac{\square}{2}} = 2 \cdot \frac{1-\cos\square}{\square}$$

As $x \to 0$, we see that $\square \to 0$ too! So

$$\lim_{x\to 0}\frac{1-\cos(2x)}{x} = \lim_{\square \to 0}(2 \cdot \frac{1-\cos(\square)}{\square})$$

$$= 2 \lim_{\square \to 0}(\frac{1-\cos(\square)}{\square}) = 2 \cdot 0 = 0$$

c) This type of problem is not familiar at this point and all we have is Table 2.11 as reference ... The idea is to rewrite the quotient as something that is *more familiar*. For instance, using plain algebra, we see that

$$\frac{\sin 2x}{\sin 3x} = (\frac{\sin 2x}{2x})(\frac{2x}{3x})(\frac{3x}{\sin 3x}),$$

so that some of the $2x$'s and $3x$-cross-terms **cancel out** leaving us with the original expression.

OK, now as $x \to 0$ it is clear that $2x \to 0$ and $3x \to 0$ too! So,

$$\lim_{x\to 0}\frac{\sin 2x}{\sin 3x} = (\lim_{x\to 0}\frac{\sin 2x}{2x})(\lim_{x\to 0}\frac{2x}{3x})(\lim_{3x\to 0}\frac{3x}{\sin 3x})$$

(because "the limit of a product is the product of the limits" cf., Table 2.4.) Therefore

$$\lim_{x\to 0}\frac{\sin 2x}{\sin 3x} = (\lim_{x\to 0}\frac{\sin 2x}{2x})\lim_{x\to 0}\frac{2x}{3x}(\lim_{3x\to 0}\frac{3x}{\sin 3x})$$

$$= 1 \cdot \frac{2}{3} \cdot 1 = \frac{2}{3}$$

(by Tables 2.11& 2.4). Note that the middle-term, $\frac{2x}{3x} = \frac{2}{3}$ since $x \neq 0$.

Using the 'Box' method we can rewrite this argument more briefly as follows: We have **two** symbols, namely '$2x$' and '$3x$', so if we are going to use Table 2.11 we need to introduce these symbols into the expression as follows: (**Remember**, $\square$ and $\triangle$ are just '*symbols*'...).

Let $\square = 2x$ and $\triangle = 3x$. Then

$$\frac{\sin 2x}{\sin 3x} = \frac{\sin \square}{\sin \triangle} = \left(\frac{\sin \square}{\square}\right)\left(\frac{\square}{\triangle}\right)\left(\frac{\triangle}{\sin \triangle}\right)$$

So that $\square$'s and $\triangle$'s **cancel out** leaving the original expression.

OK, now as $x \to 0$ it is clear that $\square \to 0$ and $\triangle \to 0$ too! So

$$\lim_{x \to 0} \frac{\sin 2x}{\sin 3x} = \left(\lim_{\square \to 0} \frac{\sin \square}{\square}\right)\left(\lim_{x \to 0} \frac{\square}{\triangle}\right)\left(\lim_{\triangle \to 0} \frac{\triangle}{\sin \triangle}\right)$$

(because "the limit of a product is the product of the limits", cf., Table 2.4.) Therefore

$$\lim_{x \to 0} \frac{\sin 2x}{\sin 3x} = \left(\lim_{\square \to 0} \frac{\sin \square}{\square}\right)\lim_{x \to 0}\frac{2x}{3x}\left(\lim_{\triangle \to 0} \frac{\triangle}{\sin \triangle}\right)$$
$$= 1 \cdot \frac{2}{3} \cdot 1 = \frac{2}{3}$$

(by Tables 2.11& 2.4).

d) In this problem we let $\square = \sqrt{x}$. As $x \to 0^+$ we know that $\sqrt{x} \to 0^+$ as well. Thus

$$\lim_{x \to 0^+} \frac{\sin \sqrt{x}}{\sqrt{x}} = \lim_{\square \to 0^+} \frac{\sin \square}{\square} = 1$$

(by Table 2.11).

Philosophy:

Learning mathematics has a lot to do with learning the rules of the interaction between symbols, some recognizable (such as 1, 2, $\sin x$, ...) and others not (such as $\square$, $\triangle$, etc.) Ultimately these are all 'symbols' and we need to recall **how** they interact with one another.

Sometimes it is helpful to replace the commonly used symbols 'y', 'z', etc. for variables, by other, not so commonly used ones, like $\square$, $\triangle$ or '*squiggle*' etc. It doesn't matter **how** we denote something, what's important is **how it interacts** with other symbols.

NOTES:

Limit questions can be approached in the following way.

You want to find

$$\lim_{x \to a} f(x).$$

Option 1 **Take the value to which x tends, *i.e.* $x = a$, and evaluate the expression (function) at that value, *i.e.* $f(a)$.**

Three possibilities arise:

a) You obtain a number like $\frac{B}{A}$, with $A \neq 0$ and the question is answered (if the function is continuous at $x = a$), the answer being $\frac{B}{A}$.

b) You get $\frac{B}{0}$, with $B \neq 0$ which implies that the limit exists and is plus infinity $(+\infty)$ if $B > 0$ and minus infinity $(-\infty)$ if $B < 0$.

c) You obtain something like $\frac{0}{0}$ which means that the limit being sought may be "in disguise" and we need to move onto Option 2 below.

Option 2 If the limit is of the form $\frac{0}{0}$ proceed as follows:
We need to **play around** with the expression, that is you may have to factor some terms, use trigonometric identities, substitutions, simplify, rationalize the denominator, multiply and divide by the same symbol, etc. until you can return to Option 1 and repeat the procedure there.

Option 3 If 1 and 2 fail, then check the left and right limits.

a) If they are equal, the limit exists and go to Option 1.

b) If they are unequal, the limit does not exist. Stop here, that's your answer.

Table 2.13: Three Options to Solving Limit Questions

EXAMPLES

Exercise Set 7.

Determine the following limits if they exist. Explain.

1. $\lim\limits_{x \to \pi} \dfrac{\sin x}{x - \pi}$
   (*Hint:* Write $\square = x - \pi$. Note that $x = \square + \pi$ and as $x \to \pi$, $\square \to 0$.)

2. $\lim\limits_{x \to \frac{\pi}{2}} (x - \dfrac{\pi}{2}) \tan x$
   (*Hint:* $(x - \dfrac{\pi}{2}) \tan x = \dfrac{(x - \frac{\pi}{2})}{\cos x} \sin x$. Now set $\square = x - \frac{\pi}{2}$, so that $x = \square + \frac{\pi}{2}$ and note that, as $x \to \frac{\pi}{2}$, $\square \to 0$.)

3. $\lim\limits_{x \to 0} \dfrac{\sin (4x)}{2x}$

4. $\lim\limits_{x \to 0} \dfrac{1 - \cos(3x)}{4x}$

5. $\lim\limits_{x \to 0} \dfrac{\sin(4x)}{\sin(2x)}$

6. $\lim\limits_{x \to 1^+} \dfrac{\sin \sqrt{x-1}}{\sqrt{x-1}}$

Web Links

For a very basic introduction to Limits see:
www.coolmath.com/frm_calculus_1.htm

Section 2.1:   For one-sided limits and quizzes see:

www.math.montana.edu/~frankw/ccp/calculus/estlimit/onesided/learn.htm
www.npac.syr.edu/REU/reu94/williams/ch2/subsection3_1_4.html

More theory about limits can be found at:

www.shu.edu/html/teaching/math/reals/gloss/index.html
www.math.montana.edu/~frankw/ccp/calculus/topic.htm#estimation   and
limits
www.ping.be/~ping1339/limth.htm

The proofs of the results in Table 2.4 can be found at:

www.math.montana.edu/~frankw/ccp/calculus/estlimit/addition/learn.htm
www.math.montana.edu/~frankw/ccp/calculus/estlimit/conmult/learn.htm
www.math.montana.edu/~frankw/ccp/calculus/estlimit/divide/learn.htm
www.math.montana.edu/~frankw/ccp/calculus/estlimit/multiply/learn.htm

---

Exercise Set 8.

Find the following limits whenever they exist. Explain.

1. $\lim\limits_{x \to 2} \dfrac{x-2}{x}$

6. $\lim\limits_{x \to 2^-} \sin(\pi x)$

2. $\lim\limits_{x \to 0^+} \sqrt{x} \cos x$

7. $\lim\limits_{x \to 0} \dfrac{\sin(3x)}{x}$

3. $\lim\limits_{x \to 3} \left(\dfrac{x-3}{x^2-9} \right)$

8. $\lim\limits_{x \to \pi^+} \left(\dfrac{\cos x}{x - \pi} \right)$

4. $\lim\limits_{x \to \frac{\pi}{2}} \left(x - \dfrac{\pi}{2} \right) \sec x$

9. $\lim\limits_{x \to \pi^-} \left(\dfrac{\cos x}{x - \pi} \right)$

5. $\lim\limits_{x \to \frac{\pi}{2}} \left(\dfrac{2x - \pi}{\cos x} \right)$

10. $\lim\limits_{x \to 0^+} x \, | \, x \, |$

Hints:
3) Factor the denominator (Table 2.13, Option 2).

4) Write $\Box = x - \frac{\pi}{2}$, $x = \Box + \frac{\pi}{2}$ and simplify (Table 2.13, Option 2).

5) Let $\Box = x - \frac{\pi}{2}$, $x = \Box + \frac{\pi}{2}$ and use a formula for the cosine of the sum of two angles.

9) See Table 2.13, Option 1(b).

Find the points of discontinuity, if any, of the following functions f:

11. $f(x) = \dfrac{\cos x}{x - \pi}$

12. $f(x) = \begin{cases} \dfrac{\sin x}{x} & x \neq 0 \\[2mm] -1 & x = 0 \end{cases}$

13. $f(x) = x^3 + x^2 - 1$

14. $f(x) = \dfrac{x^2 + 1}{x^2 - 1}$

15. $f(x) = \dfrac{x - 2}{|\, x^2 - 4 \,|}$

Evaluate the following limits, whenever they exist. Explain.

16. $\displaystyle \lim_{x \to 0} \frac{\cos x - \cos 2x}{x^2}$

(*Hint:* Use the trigonometric identity

$$\cos A - \cos B = -2 \sin \left(\frac{A + B}{2} \right) \sin \left(\frac{A - B}{2} \right)$$

along with Table 2.11.)

17. $\displaystyle \lim_{x \to 0} \frac{\tan x - \sin x}{x^2}$

(*Hint:* Factor the term 'tan x' out of the numerator and use Tables 2.11 & 2.12.)

18. $\displaystyle \lim_{x \to 1} \frac{x^2 + 1}{(x - 1)^2}$

19. Find values of a and b such that

$$\lim_{x \to \pi} \frac{ax + b}{2 \sin x} = \frac{\pi}{4}$$

(*Hint:* It is necessary that $a\pi + b = 0$, why? Next, use the idea of Exercise Set 9 #1.)

20. $\displaystyle \lim_{x \to 0^+} \frac{1}{\sqrt{x + 1} - \sqrt{x}}$

2.3   Important Theorems About Continuous Functions

There are two main results (one being a consequence of the other) in the basic study of continuous functions. These are based on the property that the graph of a continuous function on a given interval has no 'breaks' in it.

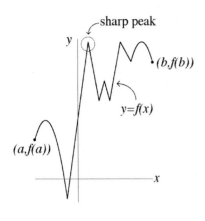

Basically one can think of such a graph as a string which joins 2 points, say $(a, f(a))$ to $(b, f(b))$ (see Figure 32).

In Figure 32(a), the graph may have "sharp peaks" and may also look "smooth" and still be the graph of a continuous function (as is Figure 32(b)).

The **Intermediate Value Theorem** basically says that if you are climbing a mountain and you stop at 1000 meters and you want to reach 5000 meters, then at some future time you will pass, say the 3751 meter mark! This is obvious, isn't it? But this basic observation allows you to understand this deep result about continuous functions.

(a)

For instance, the following graph may represent the fluctuations of your local Stock Exchange over a period of 1 year.

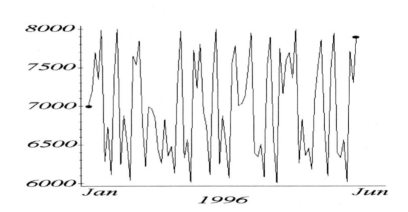

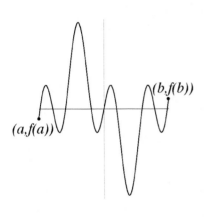

(b)

Figure 32.

Assume that the index was 7000 points on Jan. 1, 1996 and that on June 30 it was 7900 points. Then sometime during the year the index passed the 7513 point mark at least once . . .

OK, so what does this theorem say mathematically?

Intermediate Value Theorem (IVT)

Let f be continuous at each point of a closed interval $[a, b]$. Assume
1. $f(a) \neq f(b)$;
2. Let z be a point between $f(a)$ and $f(b)$.
Then there is at least one value of c between a and b such that

$$f(c) = z$$

The idea behind this Theorem is that **any** horizontal line that intersects the graph of a continuous function must intersect it at a point of its domain! This sounds and looks obvious (see Figure 33), but it's NOT true if the graph is NOT that of a continuous function (see Example 34). One of the most important **consequences** of this Intermediate Value Theorem (IVT) is sometimes called **Bolzano's Theorem** (after *Bernhard Bolzano (1781-1848)* mathematician, priest and philosopher).

Theorem 2.3.1. *Let* f *be* **continuous on a closed interval** $[a, b]$ *(i.e., at each point* x *in* $[a, b]$*). If* $f(a)f(b) < 0$*, then there is at least one point* c *between* a *and* b *such that* $f(c) = 0$.

Bolzano's Theorem is especially useful in determining the **location of roots** of polynomials or general (continuous) functions. Better still, it is also helpful in determining **where the graphs of functions intersect** each other.

For example, at which point(s) do the graphs of the functions given by $y = \sin x$ and $y = x^2$ intersect? In order to find this out you need to equate their values, so that $\sin x = x^2$ which then means that $x^2 - \sin x = 0$ so the points of intersection are roots of the function whose values are given by $y = x^2 - \sin x$.

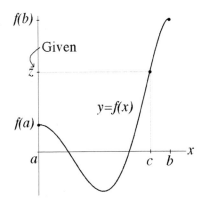

Figure 33.

| **Example 60.** | Show that there is one root of the polynomial $p(x) = x^3 + 2$ in

the interval $-2 \le x \le -1$.

Solution We note that $p(-2) = -6$ and $p(-1) = 1$. So let $a = -2$, $b = -1$ in Bolzano's Theorem. Since $p(-2) < 0$ and $p(-1) > 0$ it follows that $p(x_0) = 0$ for some x_0 in $[-2, -1]$ which is what we needed to show.

Remark:

If you're not given the interval where the root of the function may be you need to find it! Basically **you look for points** a **and** b **where** $f(a) < 0$ **and** $f(b) > 0$ and then you can refine your estimate of the root by "narrowing down" your interval.

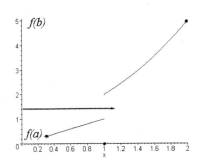

Figure 34.

| **Example 61.** | The distance between 2 cities A and B is 270 km. You're driving along the superhighway between A and B with speed limit 100 km/h hoping to get to your destination as soon as possible. You quickly realize that after one and one-half hours of driving you've travelled 200 km so you decide to stop at a rest area to relax. All of a sudden a police car pulls up to yours and the officer hands you a speeding ticket! Why?

Solution Well, the officer didn't actually **see** you speeding but saw you leaving A. Had you been travelling at the speed limit of 100 km/h it should have taken you 2 hours to get to the rest area. The officer quickly realized that somewhere along the highway you must have travelled at speeds of around 133 km/hr $\left(= \left(\dfrac{200 \text{ km}}{90 \text{min}} \right) 60 \text{min} \right)$. As a check notice that if you were travelling at a constant speed of say 130 km/h then you would have travelled a distance of only $130 \times 1.5 = 195$ km short of your mark.

A typical graph of your journey appears in Figure 35. Note that your "speed" must be related to the amount of "steepness" of the graph. The faster you go, the "steeper" the graph. This motivates the notion of a **derivative** which you'll see in

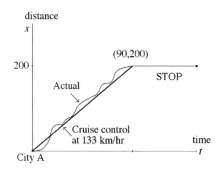

Figure 35.

Another result which you know about continuous functions is this: **If f is continuous on a closed interval $[a, b]$, then it has a maximum value and a minimum value, and these values are attained by some points in $[a, b]$.**

the next chapter.

Philosophy

Actually one uses a form of the Intermediate Value Theorem almost daily. For instance, do you find yourself asking: "Well, based on this and that, such and such must happen somewhere between 'this' and 'that'?"

When you're driving along in your car you make decisions based on your speed, right? Will you get to school or work on time? Will you get to the store on time? You're always assuming (correctly) that your **speed is a continuous function of time** (of course you're not really **thinking** about this) and you make these quick mental calculations which will verify whether or not you'll get "there" on time. Basically you know what time you started your trip and you have an idea about when it should end and then figure out where you have to be in between...

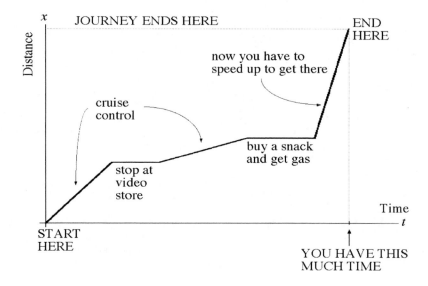

Since total distance travelled is a continuous function of time it follows that there exists at least one time t at which you were at the video store (this is true) and some other time t at which you were "speeding" on your way to your destination (also true!)... all applications of the IVT.

Finally, we should mention that since the definition of a continuous function depends on the notion of a limit it is immediate that many of the properties of limits should reflect themselves in similar properties of continuous functions. For example, from Table 2.4 we see that sums, differences, and products of continuous functions are continuous functions. The same is true of quotients of continuous functions provided the denominator is not zero at the point in question!

Web Links

For an application of the IVT to Economics see :

http://hadm.sph.sc.edu/Courses/Econ/irr/irr.html

For proofs of the main theorems here see:

www.cut-the-knot.com/Generalization/ivt.html
www.netsrq.com/~hahn/ivtproof.html
www.cut-the-knot.com/fta/brodie.html

NOTES:

2.4 Evaluating Limits at Infinity

In this section we introduce some basic ideas as to when the variable tends to **plus infinity** ($+\infty$) or **minus infinity** ($-\infty$). Note that limits at infinity are always one-sided limits, (why?). This section is intended to be a prelude to a later section on **L'Hospital's Rule** which will allow you to evaluate many of these limits by a neat trick involving the function's **derivatives**.

For the purposes of evaluating limits at infinity, the symbol '∞' has the following properties:

PROPERTIES

1. It is an 'extended' real number (same for '$-\infty$').

2. For any real number c (including 0), and $r > 0$,

$$\lim_{x \to \infty} \frac{c}{x^r} = 0$$

(Think of this as saying that $\frac{c}{\infty^r} = 0$ and $\infty^r = \infty$ for $r > 0$.)

3. The symbol $\frac{\infty}{\infty}$ is undefined and **can only be defined in the limiting sense** using the procedure in Table 2.13, Stage 2, some insight and maybe a little help from your calculator. We'll be using this procedure a little later when we attempt to evaluate limits at $\pm\infty$ using extended real numbers.

Table 2.14: Properties of $\pm\infty$

Basically, the limit symbol "$x \to \infty$" means that the real variable x can be made "larger" than any real number!

A similar definition applies to the symbol "$x \to -\infty$" except that now the real variable x may be made "smaller" than any real number. The next result is very useful in evaluating limits involving oscillating functions where it may not be easy to find the limit.

The **Sandwich Theorem** (mentioned earlier) is also valid for **limits at infinity**, that is, if

$$g(x) \leq f(x) \leq h(x)$$

for all (sufficiently) large x and for some (extended) real number A,

$$\lim_{x \to \infty} g(x) = A, \qquad \lim_{x \to \infty} h(x) = A$$

then f has a limit at infinity and

$$\lim_{x \to \infty} f(x) = A$$

Table 2.15: The Sandwich Theorem

Example 62.   Evaluate the following limits at infinity.

a) $\displaystyle \lim_{x \to \infty} \frac{\sin(2x)}{x}$

b) $\displaystyle\lim_{x\to\infty} \frac{3x^2 - 2x + 1}{x^2 + 2}$

c) $\displaystyle\lim_{x\to-\infty} \frac{1}{x^3 + 1}$

d) $\displaystyle\lim_{x\to\infty} (\sqrt{x^2 + x + 1} - x)$

Solution **a)** Let $f(x) = \dfrac{\sin(2x)}{x}$. Then $|f(x)| = \dfrac{|\sin(2x)|}{x}$ and $|f(x)| \le \dfrac{1}{x}$ since $|\sin(2x)| \le 1$ for every real number x. Thus

$$0 \le \lim_{x\to\infty} |f(x)| \le \lim_{x\to\infty} \frac{1}{x} = 0$$

(where we have set $g(x) = 0$ and $h(x) = \dfrac{1}{x}$ in the statement of the Sandwich Theorem.) Thus,

$$\lim_{x\to\infty} |f(x)| = 0$$

which means that

$$\lim_{x\to\infty} f(x) = 0$$

(See Table 2.8 (c)).

b) Factor the term 'x^2' out of both numerator and denominator. Thus

$$\frac{3x^2 - 2x + 1}{x^2 + 2} = \frac{x^2(3 - \frac{2}{x} + \frac{1}{x^2})}{x^2(1 + \frac{2}{x^2})}$$
$$= \frac{(3 - \frac{2}{x} + \frac{1}{x^2})}{(1 + \frac{2}{x^2})}$$

Now

$$\lim_{x\to\infty} \frac{3x^2 - 2x + 1}{x^2 + 2} = \frac{\lim_{x\to\infty}\left(3 - \frac{2}{x} + \frac{1}{x^2}\right)}{\lim_{x\to\infty}\left(1 + \frac{2}{x^2}\right)}$$

(because the limit of a quotient is the quotient of the limits)

$$= \frac{3 - 0 + 0}{1 + 0}$$
$$= 3$$

where we have used the Property 2 of limits at infinity, Table 2.14.

c) Let $f(x) = \dfrac{1}{x^3 + 1}$. We claim $\displaystyle\lim_{x\to-\infty} f(x) = 0 \ldots$ Why?

Well, as $x \to -\infty$, $x^3 \to -\infty$ too, right? Adding 1 won't make any difference, so $x^3 + 1 \to -\infty$ too (remember, this is true because $x \to -\infty$). OK, now $x^3 + 1 \to -\infty$ which means $(x^3 + 1)^{-1} \to 0$ as $x \to -\infty$.

d) As it stands, letting $x \to \infty$ in the expression $x^2 + x + 1$ also gives ∞. So $\sqrt{x^2 + x + 1} \to \infty$ as $x \to \infty$. So we have to calculate a "difference of two infinities" *i.e.*,

$$f(x) = \sqrt{x^2 + x + 1} - x$$
$$\swarrow \qquad\qquad \searrow$$
$$\infty \text{ as } x \to \infty \qquad \infty \text{ as } x \to \infty$$

There is no way of doing this so we have to simplify the expression (see Table 2.13, Stage 2) by rationalizing the expression ... So,

$$\begin{aligned}
\sqrt{x^2+x+1}-x &= \frac{(\sqrt{x^2+x+1}-x)(\sqrt{x^2+x+1}+x)}{\sqrt{x^2+x+1}+x} \\
&= \frac{(x^2+x+1)-x^2}{\sqrt{x^2+x+1}+x} \\
&= \frac{x+1}{\sqrt{x^2+x+1}+x}
\end{aligned}$$

The form still isn't good enough to evaluate the limit directly. (We would be getting a form similar to $\frac{\infty}{\infty}$ if we took limits in the numerator and denominator separately.)

OK, so we keep simplifying by factoring out 'x's from both numerator and denominator ... Now,

$$\begin{aligned}
\sqrt{x^2+x+1}-x &= \frac{x+1}{\sqrt{x^2+x+1}+x} \\
&= \frac{x(1+\frac{1}{x})}{x\left(\sqrt{1+\frac{1}{x}+\frac{1}{x^2}}+1\right)} \\
&= \frac{1+\frac{1}{x}}{\sqrt{1+\frac{1}{x}+\frac{1}{x^2}}+1}
\end{aligned}$$

OK, now we can let $x \to \infty$ and we see that

$$\begin{aligned}
\lim_{x\to\infty}(\sqrt{x^2+x+1}-x) &= \lim_{x\to\infty}\frac{1+\frac{1}{x}}{\sqrt{1+\frac{1}{x}+\frac{1}{x^2}}+1} \\
&= \frac{1+0}{\sqrt{1+0+0}+1} \\
&= \frac{1}{2}
\end{aligned}$$

As a **quick check** let's use a calculator and some large values of x: e.g. $x = 10$, 100, 1000, 10000, ... This gives the values: $f(10) = 0.53565$, $f(100) = 0.50373$, $f(1000) = 0.50037$, $f(10000) = 0.500037$, ... which gives a sequence whose limit appears to be 0.500... $= \frac{1}{2}$, which is our theoretical result.

Exercise Set 9.

Evaluate the following limits (a) numerically and (b) theoretically.

1. $\displaystyle\lim_{x\to\infty}\frac{\sin(3x)}{2x}$ (Remember: x is in **radians** here.)

2. $\displaystyle\lim_{x\to-\infty}\frac{x}{x^3+2}$

3. $\displaystyle\lim_{x\to\infty}\frac{x^3+3x-1}{x^3+1}$

4. $\displaystyle\lim_{x\to\infty}\sqrt{x}(\sqrt{x+1}-\sqrt{x})$

5. $\displaystyle\lim_{x\to-\infty}\frac{\cos x}{x^2}$

6. **Hard** Show that

$$\lim_{x \to \infty} \sin x$$

does **not** exist by giving a **graphical** argument.
(*Hint:* Use the ideas developed in the Advanced Topics to **prove this theoretically**.)

2.5 How to Guess a Limit

We waited for this part until you learned about limits in general. Here we'll show you a quick and quite reliable way of *guessing* or *calculating* some limits at infinity (or "minus" infinity). Strictly speaking, you still need to 'prove' that your guess *is* right, even though it *looks* right. See Table 2.16. Later on, in Section 3.12, we will see a method called *L'Hospital's Rule* that can be used effectively, under some mild conditions, to evaluate limits involving *indeterminate forms*.

OK, now just a few words of caution before you start manipulating infinities. If an operation between infinities and reals (or another infinity) is not among those listed in Table 2.16, it is called an **indeterminate form**.

The most common indeterminate forms are:

$$0 \cdot (\pm\infty), \quad \pm\frac{\infty}{\infty}, \quad \infty - \infty, \quad (\pm\infty)^0, \quad 1^{\pm\infty}, \quad \frac{0}{0}, \quad 0^0$$

When you meet these forms in a limit you can't do much except simplify, rationalize, factor, etc. and then see if the form becomes "determinate".

FAQ about Indeterminate Forms

Let's have a closer look at these *indeterminate* forms: They are called indeterminate because we cannot assign a single real number (once and for all) to any one of those expressions. For example,

Question 1: Why can't we define $\frac{\infty}{\infty} = 1$? After all, this looks okay ...

Answer 1: If that were true then,

$$\lim_{x \to \infty} \frac{2x}{x} = 1,$$

but this is impossible because, for any real number x no matter how large,

$$\frac{2x}{x} = 2,$$

and so, in fact,

$$\lim_{x \to \infty} \frac{2x}{x} = 2,$$

and so we can't define $\frac{\infty}{\infty} = 1$. Of course, we can easily modify this example to show that if r is any real number, then

$$\lim_{x \to \infty} \frac{rx}{x} = r,$$

which seems to imply that $\frac{\infty}{\infty} = r$. But r is also arbitrary, and so these numbers r can't all be equal because we can choose the r's to be different! This shows that we cannot define the quotient $\frac{\infty}{\infty}$. Similar reasoning shows that we cannot define the quotient $-\frac{\infty}{\infty}$.

Question 2: All right, but surely $1^{\infty} = 1$, since $1 \times 1 \times 1 \times ... = 1$?

Answer 2: No. The reason for this is that there is an infinite number of 1's here and this statement about multiplying 1's together is only true if there is a *finite* number of 1's. Here, we'll give some **numerical evidence** indicating that $1^{\infty} \neq 1$, necessarily.

Let $n \geq 1$ be a positive integer and look at some of the values of the expression

$$\left(1 + \frac{1}{n}\right)^n, \quad n = 1, 2, 3, ..., 10,000$$

These values are summarized below:

n	$\left(1+\frac{1}{n}\right)^n$	$value$
$n = 1$	$\left(1+\frac{1}{1}\right)^1$	2
$n = 2$	$\left(1+\frac{1}{2}\right)^2$	2.25
$n = 3$	$\left(1+\frac{1}{3}\right)^3$	2.37
$n = 4$	$\left(1+\frac{1}{4}\right)^4$	2.44
$n = 5$	$\left(1+\frac{1}{5}\right)^5$	2.48
$n = 10$	$\left(1+\frac{1}{10}\right)^{10}$	2.59
$n = 50$	$\left(1+\frac{1}{50}\right)^{50}$	2.69
$n = 100$	$\left(1+\frac{1}{100}\right)^{100}$	2.7048
$n = 1,000$	$\left(1+\frac{1}{1000}\right)^{1000}$	2.7169
$n = 10,000$	$\left(1+\frac{1}{10000}\right)^{10000}$	2.71814
...	...	...

Well, you can see that the values do not appear to be approaching 1! In fact, they seem to be getting closer to some number whose value is around 2.718. More on this special number later, in Chapter 4. Furthermore, we saw in Exercise 17, of Exercise Set 3, that these values must always lie between 2 and 3 and so, once again cannot converge to 1. This shows that, generally speaking, $1^{\infty} \neq 1$. In this case one can show that, in fact,

$$\lim_{n \to \infty} \left(1 + \frac{1}{n}\right)^n = 2.7182818284590...$$

is a special number called *Euler's Number*, (see Chapter 4).

Question 3: What about $\infty - \infty = 0$?

Answer 3: No. This isn't true either since, to be precise, ∞ is NOT a real number, and so we cannot apply real number properties to it. The simplest example that shows that this difference between two infinities is not zero is the following. Let n be an integer (not infinity), for simplicity. Then

$$\infty - \infty = \lim_{n \to \infty} [n - (n-1)]$$

$$= \lim_{n \to \infty} [n - n + 1]$$
$$= \lim_{n \to \infty} 1$$
$$= 1.$$

The same argument can be used to find examples where $\infty - \infty = r$, where r is any given real number. It follows that we cannot assign a real number to the expression $\infty - \infty$ and so this is an indeterminate form.

Question 4: Isn't it true that $\frac{0}{0} = 0$?

Answer 4: No, this isn't true either. See the example in Table 2.11 and the discussion preceding it. The results there show that

$$\frac{0}{0} = \frac{\sin 0}{0}$$
$$= \lim_{x \to 0} \frac{\sin x}{x}$$
$$= 1$$

in this case. So we cannot assign a real number to the quotient "zero over zero".

Question 5: Okay, but it must be true that $\infty^0 = 1!$?

Answer 5: Not generally. An example here is harder to construct but it can be done using the methods in Chapter 4.

The Numerical Estimation of a Limit

At this point we'll be guessing limits of indeterminate forms by performing numerical calculations. See Example 65, below for their *theoretical*, rather than *numerical* calculation.

| **Example 63.** | Guess the value of each of the following limits at infinity:

a) $\displaystyle \lim_{x \to \infty} \frac{\sin(2x)}{x}$

b) $\displaystyle \lim_{x \to -\infty} \frac{x^2}{x^2 + 1}$

c) $\displaystyle \lim_{x \to \infty} \left(\sqrt{x+1} - \sqrt{x} \right)$

Solution **a)** Since $x \to \infty$, we only need to try out **really large values** of x. So, just set up a table such as the one below and look for a pattern ...

Some values of x	The values of $f(x) = \dfrac{\sin 2x}{x}$
10	.0913
100	$-.00873$
1,000	0.000930
10,000	0.0000582
100,000	-0.000000715
1,000,000	-0.000000655
...	...

EXAMPLES

We note that even though the values of $f(x)$ here alternate in sign, they are always getting smaller. In fact, they seem to be approaching $f(x) = 0$, as $x \to \infty$. This is our guess and, on this basis, we can claim that

$$\lim_{x \to \infty} \frac{\sin 2x}{x} = 0.$$

See Example 65 a), for another way of seeing this.

Below you'll see a graphical depiction (made by using your favorite software package or the Plotter included with this book), of the function $f(x)$ over the interval $[10, 100]$.

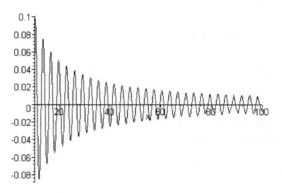

Note that the *oscillations* appear to be dying out, that is, they are getting smaller and smaller, just like the oscillations of your car as you pass over a bump! We guess that the value of this limit is 0.

b) Now, since $x \to -\infty$, we only need to try out really *small* (and negative) values of x. So, we set up a table like the one above and look for a pattern in the values.

Some values of x	The values of $f(x) = \dfrac{x^2}{x^2 + 1}$
-10	0.9900990099
-100	0.9999000100
$-1,000$	0.9999990000
$-10,000$	0.9999999900
$-100,000$	0.9999999999
$-1,000,000$	1.0000000000
$\ldots$	$\ldots$

In this case the values of $f(x)$ all have the same sign, they are always *positive*. Furthermore, they seem to be approaching $f(x) = 1$, as $x \to \infty$. This is our guess and, on this numerical basis, we can claim that

$$\lim_{x \to -\infty} \frac{x^2}{x^2 + 1} = 1.$$

See Example 65 b), for another way of seeing this.

A graphical depiction of this function $f(x)$ over the interval $[-100, -10]$ appears below.

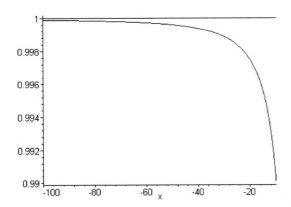

In this example, the values of the function appear to increase steadily towards the line whose equation is $y = 1$. So, we guess that the value of this limit is 1.

c) Once again $x \to +\infty$, we only need to try out really *large* (and positive) values of x. Our table looks like:

Some values of x	The values of $f(x) = \sqrt{x+1} - \sqrt{x}$
10	0.15434713
100	0.04987562
1,000	0.01580744
10,000	0.00499999
100,000	0.00158120
1,000,000	0.00050000
...	...

In this case the values of $f(x)$ all have the same sign, they are always *positive*. Furthermore, they seem to be approaching $f(x) = 0$, as $x \to \infty$. We can claim that

$$\lim_{x \to \infty} \left(\sqrt{x+1} - \sqrt{x} \right) = 0.$$

See Example 65 d), for another way of seeing this. A graphical depiction of this function $f(x)$ over the interval $[10, 100]$ appears below.

Note that larger values of x are not necessary since we have a *feeling* that they'll just be closer to our limit. We can believe that the values of $f(x)$ are always getting closer to 0 as x gets larger. So 0 should be the value of this limit. In the graph below we see that the function is getting smaller and smaller as x increases but it always stays positive. Nevertheless, its values never reach the number 0 exactly, but only in the *limiting sense* we described in this section.

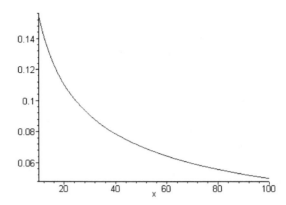

Watch out!

This numerical way of "guessing" limits **doesn't always work!** It works well when the function *has* a limit, but it doesn't work if the limit doesn't exist (see the previous sections).

For example, the function $f(x) = \sin x$ has NO limit as $x \to \infty$. But how do you know this? The table could give us a hint;

Some values of x	The values of $f(x) = \sin x$
10	-0.5440211109
100	-0.5063656411
1,000	$+0.8268795405$
10,000	-0.3056143889
100,000	$+0.0357487980$
1,000,000	-0.3499935022
...	...

As you can see, these values do not seem to have a pattern to them. They don't seem to "converge" to any particular value. We should be suspicious at this point and claim that the limit doesn't exist. But remember: **Nothing can replace a rigorous (theoretical) argument for the existence or non-existence of a limit!** Our guess may not coincide with the reality of the situation as the next example will show!

Now, we'll manufacture a function **with the property that, based on our numerical calculations,** *it seems to have a limit* **(actually $= 0$) as $x \to \infty$, but, in reality, its limit is SOME OTHER NUMBER!**

Example 64.   Evaluate the following limit using your calculator,

$$\lim_{x \to \infty} \left(\frac{1}{x} + 10^{-12} \right).$$

Solution Setting up the table gives us:

Some values of x	The values of $f(x) = \left(\dfrac{1}{x} + 10^{-12}\right)$
10	0.100000000
100	0.010000000
1,000	0.001000000
10,000	0.000100000
100,000	0.000001000
999,999,999	0.000000001
. . .	. . .

Well, if we didn't know any better we would think that this limit should be 0. But this is **only because we are limited by the number of digits displayed upon our calculator!** The answer, based upon our knowledge of limits, should be the number 10^{-12} (but this number would display as 0 on most hand-held calculators). That's the real problem with using calculators for finding limits. You must be careful!!

Web Links

More (solved) examples on limits at infinity at:

www.npac.syr.edu/REU/reu94/williams/ch2/section3_2.html
math.ucdavis.edu/~kouba/CalcOneDIRECTORY/
liminfdirectory/LimitInfinity.html
www-math.cudenver.edu/~rbyrne/online/140w4.htm

Finding Limits using Extended Real Numbers (Optional)

At this point we'll be guessing limits of indeterminate forms by performing a new arithmetic among *infinite quantities*! In other words, we'll define addition and multiplication of infinities and then use these ideas to actually *find* limits at (plus or minus) infinity. This material is not standard in Calculus Texts and so can be omitted if so desired. However, it does offer an alternate method for actually guessing limits correctly every time!

If you think that adding and multiplying 'infinity' is nuts, you should look at the work of **Georg Cantor** (1845-1918), who actually developed an arithmetic of *transfinite cardinal numbers*, (or numbers that are infinite). He showed that 'different infinities' exist and actually set up rules of arithmetic for them. His work appeared in 1833.

As an example, the totality of all the integers (one type of infinite number), is different from the totality of all the numbers in the interval $[0, 1]$ (another 'larger' infinity). In a very specific sense, there are more "real numbers" than "integers".

Operations on the Extended Real Number Line

The **extended real number line** is the collection of all (usual) real numbers plus **two new symbols**, namely, $\pm\infty$ (**called extended real numbers**) which have the following properties:

Let x be any real number. Then

a) $x + (+\infty) = (+\infty) + x = +\infty$

b) $x + (-\infty) = (-\infty) + x = -\infty$

c) $x \cdot (+\infty) = (+\infty) \cdot x = +\infty$ if $x > 0$

d) $x \cdot (-\infty) = (-\infty) \cdot x = -\infty$ if $x > 0$

e) $x \cdot (+\infty) = (+\infty) \cdot x = -\infty$ if $x < 0$

f) $x \cdot (-\infty) = (-\infty) \cdot x = +\infty$ if $x < 0$

The operation $0 \cdot (\pm\infty)$ is undefined and requires further investigation.

Operations between $+\infty$ and $-\infty$

g) $(+\infty) + (+\infty) = +\infty$

h) $(-\infty) + (-\infty) = -\infty$

i) $(+\infty) \cdot (+\infty) = +\infty = (-\infty) \cdot (-\infty)$

j) $(+\infty) \cdot (-\infty) = -\infty = (-\infty) \cdot (+\infty)$

Quotients and powers involving $\pm\infty$

k) $\dfrac{x}{\pm\infty} = 0$ for **any** real x

l) $\infty^r = \begin{cases} \infty & r > 0 \\ 0 & r < 0 \end{cases}$

m) $a^\infty = \begin{cases} \infty & a > 1 \\ 0 & 0 \le a < 1 \end{cases}$

Table 2.16: Properties of Extended Real Numbers

The **extended real number line** is, by definition, the ordinary (positive and negative) real numbers with the addition of two idealized points denoted by $\pm\infty$ (and called the points at infinity). The way in which infinite quantities interact with each other and with real numbers is summarized briefly in Table 2.16 above.

It is important to note that any basic operation that is not explicitly mentioned in Table 2.16 is to be considered an *indeterminate form*, unless it can be derived from one or more of the basic axioms mentioned there.

Evaluating Limits of Indeterminate Forms

OK, now what? Well, you want

$$\lim_{x \to \pm\infty} f(x)$$

Basically, you look at $f(\pm\infty)$ respectively.

This is an expression involving "infinities" which you simplify (if you can) using the rules of arithmetic of the extended real number system listed in Table 2.16. If you get an indeterminate form you need to factor, rationalize, simplify, separate terms etc. until you get something more manageable.

> **Example 65.** Evaluate the following limits involving indeterminate forms:

a) $\displaystyle \lim_{x \to \infty} \frac{\sin 2x}{x}$

b) $\displaystyle \lim_{x \to \infty} \frac{x^2}{x^2 + 1}$

c) $\displaystyle \lim_{x \to -\infty} \frac{x^3 + 1}{x^3 - 1}$

d) $\displaystyle \lim_{x \to \infty} \sqrt{x + 1} - \sqrt{x}$

e) $\displaystyle \lim_{x \to 0^+} \frac{x}{\sin x}$

Solution **a)** Let $f(x) = \dfrac{\sin(2x)}{x}$, then $f(\infty) = \dfrac{\sin(2\infty)}{\infty}$. Now use Table 2.16 on the next page. Even though $\sin(2\infty)$ doesn't really have a meaning, we can safely take it that the "$\sin(2\infty)$ is something less than or equal to 1", because the sine of any *finite* angle has this property. So $f(\infty) = \dfrac{\text{something}}{\infty} = 0$, by property (k), in Table 2.16.

We conclude our guess which is:

$$\lim_{x \to \infty} \frac{\sin 2x}{x} = 0$$

> **Remember:** This is just an educated guess; you really have to *prove* this to be sure. This method of guessing is far better than the numerical approach of the previous subsection since it gives the right answer in case of Example 64, where the numerical approach failed!

b) Let $f(x) = \frac{x^2}{x^2+1}$. Then $f(\infty) = \frac{\infty}{\infty}$ by properties (l) and (a) in Table 2.16. So we have to simplify, etc. There is no other recourse ... Note that

$$
\begin{aligned}
f(x) &= \frac{x^2}{x^2 + 1} = 1 - \frac{1}{x^2 + 1} \\
\text{So } \lim_{x \to \infty} f(x) &= \lim_{x \to \infty} 1 - \frac{1}{x^2 + 1} \\
&= 1 - \frac{1}{\infty} \quad \text{(by property (l) and (a))} \\
&= 1 - 0 \quad \text{(by property (k))} \\
&= 1
\end{aligned}
$$

c) Let $f(x) = \dfrac{x^3 + 1}{x^3 - 1}$. Then

$$f(-\infty) = \frac{(-\infty)^3 + 1}{(-\infty)^3 - 1} = \frac{-\infty^3 + 1}{-\infty^3 - 1} = \frac{-\infty + 1}{-\infty - 1} = \frac{-\infty}{-\infty} = \frac{\infty}{\infty}$$

is an indeterminate form! So we have to simplify ... Dividing the numerator by the denominator using long division, we get

$$\frac{x^3 + 1}{x^3 - 1} = 1 + \frac{2}{x^3 - 1}$$

$$\text{Hence } \lim_{x \to -\infty} \frac{x^3 + 1}{x^3 - 1} = \lim_{x \to \infty} \left(1 + \frac{2}{x^3 - 1}\right)$$

$$= 1 + \frac{2}{\infty} \quad \text{(by property (e) and (a))}$$

$$= 1 + 0 \quad \text{(by property (k), in Table 2.16)}$$

$$= 1$$

d) Let $f(x) = \sqrt{x + 1} - \sqrt{x}$. Then

$$f(\infty) = \sqrt{\infty + 1} - \sqrt{\infty}$$

$$= \sqrt{\infty} - \sqrt{\infty} \quad \text{(by property (a))}$$

$$= \infty - \infty \quad \text{(by property (k), in Table 2.16)}$$

It follows that $f(\infty)$ is an indeterminate form. Let's simplify ... By rationalizing the numerator we know that

$$\sqrt{x + 1} - \sqrt{x} = \frac{(x + 1) - x}{\sqrt{x + 1} + \sqrt{x}}$$

$$= \frac{1}{\sqrt{x + 1} + \sqrt{x}}.$$

So,

$$\lim_{x \to \infty} f(x) = \lim_{x \to \infty} \frac{1}{\sqrt{x + 1} + \sqrt{x}}$$

$$= \frac{1}{\sqrt{\infty + 1} + \sqrt{\infty}}$$

$$= \frac{1}{\sqrt{\infty} + \sqrt{\infty}} \quad \text{(by property (a))}$$

$$= \frac{1}{\infty + \infty} \quad \text{(by property (h))}$$

$$= \frac{1}{\infty} \quad \text{(by property (g))}$$

$$= 0 \quad \text{(by property (k))}$$

d) In this case the function can be seen to be of *more than one indeterminate form*: For example,

$$0 \cdot \frac{1}{\sin 0} = 0 \cdot \frac{1}{0} = 0 \cdot \infty,$$

which is indeterminate (by definition), or

$$\frac{0}{\sin 0} = \frac{0}{0},$$

which is also indeterminate. But we have already seen in Table 2.11 that when this indeterminate form is interpreted as a limit, it is equal to 1.

2.6 Chapter Exercises

Use the methods of this Chapter to decide the continuity of the following functions at the indicated point(s).

1. $f(x) = 3x^2 - 2x + 1$, at $x = 1$

2. $g(t) = t^3 \cos(t)$, at $t = 0$

3. $h(z) = z + 2 \sin(z) - \cos(z + 2)$ at $z = 0$

4. $f(x) = 2 \cos(x)$ at $x = \pi$

5. $f(x) = |x + 1|$ at $x = -1$

Evaluate the limits of the functions from Exercises 1-5 above and justify your conclusions.

6. $\lim\limits_{x \to 1} (3x^2 - 2x + 1)$

7. $\lim\limits_{t \to 0} t^3 \cos(t)$

8. $\lim\limits_{z \to 0} (z + 2 \sin(z) - \cos(z + 2))$

9. $\lim\limits_{x \to \pi} 2 \cos(x)$

10. $\lim\limits_{x \to -1} |x + 1|$

Evaluate the following limits

11. $\lim\limits_{t \to 2^+} \left(\dfrac{t - 2}{t + 2} \right)$

12. $\lim\limits_{x \to 4^+} \left(\dfrac{x - 4}{x^2 - 16} \right)$

13. $\lim\limits_{t \to 2^+} \left(\dfrac{1}{t - 2} \right)$

14. $\lim\limits_{x \to 1^+} \left(\dfrac{x - 1}{|x - 1|} \right)$

15. $\lim\limits_{x \to 0^+} \left(1 + \dfrac{1}{x^3} \right)$

16. Let g be defined as

$$g(x) = \begin{cases} x^2 + 1 & x < 0 \\ 1 - |x| & 0 \le x \le 1 \\ x & x > 1 \end{cases}$$

Evaluate

i). $\lim\limits_{x \to 0^-} g(x)$ ii). $\lim\limits_{x \to 0^+} g(x)$

iii). $\lim\limits_{x \to 1^-} g(x)$ iv). $\lim\limits_{x \to 1^+} g(x)$

v) Conclude that the graph of g has no breaks at $x = 0$ but it does have a break at $x = 1$.

Determine whether the following limits exist. Give reasons

17. $\lim\limits_{x \to 0} f(x)$ where $f(x) = \begin{cases} 2 - x & x \le 0 \\ x + 1 & x > 0 \end{cases}$

18. $\lim\limits_{x \to 1} |x - 3|$

19. $\lim\limits_{x \to -2} \left(\dfrac{x + 2}{x + 1} \right)$

20. $\lim\limits_{x \to 0} x^2 \sin x$

21. $\lim\limits_{x \to 1} f(x)$ where $f(x) = \begin{cases} \frac{\sin (x-1)}{x-1}, & 0 \le x < 1 \\ 1, & x = 1 \\ |x - 1| & x > 1 \end{cases}$

Determine the points of discontinuity of each of the following functions.

22. $f(x) = \dfrac{|x|}{x} - 1$ for $x \ne 0$ and $f(0) = 1$

23. $g(x) = \begin{cases} \frac{x}{|x|} & x < 0 \\ 1 + x^2 & x \ge 0 \end{cases}$

24. $f(x) = \dfrac{x^2 - 3x + 2}{x^3 - 1}, \ for \ x \ne 1; f(1) = -1/3.$

25. $f(x) = \begin{cases} x^4 - 1 & x \ne 0 \\ -0.99 & x = 0 \end{cases}$

26. $f(x) = 1.65 + \dfrac{1}{x^2}$ for $x \ne 0$, $f(0) = +1$

Determine whether the following limits exist. If the limits exist, find their values in the extended real numbers.

27. $\lim\limits_{x \to 0} \dfrac{\sin (ax)}{bx}$,   where $a \ne 0, b \ne 0$

28. $\lim\limits_{x \to 0} \dfrac{\cos (2x)}{|x|}$

29. $\lim\limits_{x \to 0} \dfrac{x \sin (x)}{\sin (2x)}$

30. $\lim\limits_{x \to 3^-} \dfrac{\sin \sqrt{3 - x}}{\sqrt{3 - x}}$

31. $\lim\limits_{x \to 0} \dfrac{bx}{\sin (ax)}$,   where $a \ne 0, b \ne 0$

32. $\lim\limits_{x \to \infty} \dfrac{\cos 3x}{4x}$

33. $\lim\limits_{x \to -\infty} x \sin x$

34. $\lim\limits_{x \to \infty} \sqrt{x^2 + 1} - x$

35. Use Bolzano's Theorem and your pocket calculator to prove that the function f defined by $f(x) = x \sin x + \cos x$ has a root in the interval $[-5, 1]$.

36. Use Bolzano's Theorem and your pocket calculator to prove that the function f defined by $f(x) = x^3 - 3x + 2$ has a root in the interval $[-3, 0]$. Can you find it?

Are there any others? (Idea: Find smaller and smaller intervals and keep applying Bolzano's Theorem)

37. Find an interval of $x's$ containing the $x-$coordinates of the point of intersection of the curves $y = x^2$ and $y = \sin x$. Later on, when we study **Newton's Method** you'll see how to calculate these intersection points very accurately.

Hint: Use Bolzano's Theorem on the function $y = x^2 - \sin x$ over an appropriate interval (you need to find it).

Suggested Homework Set 5. *Problems* $1, 9, 12, 17, 22, 27, 34, 36$

2.7   Using Computer Algebra Systems

Use your favorite Computer Algebra System (CAS), like Maple, MatLab, etc., or even a graphing calculator to answer the following questions:

1. Define a function f by

$$f(x) = \begin{cases} x \sin\left(\dfrac{1}{x^2}\right), & \text{if } x \neq 0, \\ 0, & \text{if } x = 0. \end{cases}$$

Calculate $f(10.6)$, $f(1001)$, $f(10^4)$, $f(30,000)$, $f(10^{10})$.

a) Guess the value of the limit

$$\lim_{x \to \infty} x \sin\left(\frac{1}{x^2}\right)$$

based on your calculations.

b) Now plot the function f over the interval $[0, 1001]$. Do the values of f appear top be approaching some specific number? Which one?

c) Use the Box method of Chapter 1 to give a more reliable justification for your answer in (a), above by noting that

$$\lim_{\square \to 0} \frac{\sin \square}{\square} = 1,$$

and then setting $\square = \frac{1}{x^2}$, realizing that when $x \to \infty$, we must have $\square \to 0$.

2. Evaluate the limit of the function f defined by

$$f(x) = \frac{x}{x+1} + 10^{-20}$$

as $x \to \infty$. If you use a hand calculator, then you'll likely get the value 1 for an answer. But thast isn't really the answer, right? Is your answer equal to $1 + 10^{-20}$? If so, great! If not, that shows you the limit of computer assisted technology in doing Calculus. In many cases, such as this one, computers can only give you *approximations* to the real answers...

3. Plot the graphs of the family of functions defined by

$$f(x) = \frac{\sin ax}{x},$$

for $a = -1, -5, 14, 18, 34$, over the common interval $0 \le x \le 20$. Determine the value of the limit,

$$\lim_{x \to 0} \frac{\sin ax}{x},$$

in terms of a.

4. Plot the graph of the function whose values are given by

$$y = \frac{x}{|x|}$$

for $x \ne 0$. Find both one-sided limits at $x = 0$, that is, calculate

$$\lim_{x \to 0^\pm} \frac{x}{|x|}.$$

5. Plot the graph of the function whose values are given by

$$y = 2 + \frac{1}{|x-1|}$$

for $x \ne 1$. Find both one-sided limits at $x = 1$, that is, calculate

$$\lim_{x \to 1^\pm} \left(2 + \frac{1}{|x-1|} \right).$$

6. Use the "limit" command to approximate (or calculate) the following limit,

$$\lim_{x \to 3} \frac{x^3 - 27}{x^2 - 9},$$

and compare your answer with the theoretical answer you would obtain by "guessing" this limit (that is, by factoring the expression and simplifying).

7. Use the "limit" command to approximate (or calculate) the following limit,

$$\lim_{x \to 0} \frac{1 - \cos(x^2)}{x^2},$$

and compare your answer with the theoretical answer you would obtain by "guessing" this limit (that is, by using the Box method with $\Box = x^2$).

8. Use the "limit" command to approximate (or calculate) the following limit,

$$\lim_{x \to 0} \frac{\sin(3x \tan x)}{x \tan x},$$

and compare your answer with the theoretical answer you would obtain by "guessing" this limit (that is, by using the Box method with $\Box = 3x \tan x$).

9. Let

$$f(x) = \begin{cases} \dfrac{\sin\left(x^2\right)}{x^2}, & \text{if } x \ne 0, \\ L, & \text{if } x = 0. \end{cases}$$

For what value(s) of L is f continuous at $x = 0$?

10. Give an example of a function f such that

$$\lim_{x \to 0} |f(x)|$$

exists yet

$$\lim_{x \to 0} f(x)$$

does not exist.

Hint: Consider the Heaviside function.

11. By examining the graph of the function defined by

$$f(x) = \sin \frac{1}{x}$$

for $-1 \leq x \leq 1$ decide whether or not f can be made continuous at $x = 0$ by defining it appropriately there.

Hint: Define $f(0) = L$. Show that you can make $x \to 0$ in such a way that $f(x) = 0$ all the time. So, if f is continuous at $x = 0$ then L must be zero. On the other hand, show that you can make $x \to 0$ in such a way that $f(x) = 1$ all the time, and now conclude that $L = 1$. Since the limit must be unique if it exists, conclude that L cannot exist.

12. Evaluate the limit

$$\lim_{x \to +\infty} (x^2 - 1) \sin \left(\frac{1}{x^2 - 1} \right)$$

by examining its graph. Can you justify your guess?

Chapter 3

The Derivative of a Function

The Big Picture

This chapter contains material which is fundamental to the further study of Calculus. Its basis dates back to the great Greek scientist Archimedes (287-212 B.C.) who first considered the problem of the *tangent line*. Much later, attempts by the key historical figures Kepler (1571-1630), Galileo (1564-1642), and Newton (1642-1727) among others, to understand the motion of the planets in the solar system and thus the speed of a moving body, led them to the problem of *instantaneous velocity* which translated into the mathematical idea of a *derivative*. Through the geometric notion of a tangent line we will introduce the concept of the **ordinary derivative of a function**, itself another function with certain properties. Its interpretations in the physical world are so many that this book would not be sufficient to contain them all. Once we know what a derivative is and how it is used we can formulate many problems in terms of these, and the natural concept of an **ordinary differential equation** arises, a concept which is central to most applications of Calculus to the sciences and engineering. For example, the motion of every asteroid, planet, star, comet, or other celestial object is governed by a differential equation. Once we can solve these equations we can describe the motion. Of course, this is hard in general, and if we can't solve them exactly we can always approximate the solutions which give the orbits by means of some, so-called, **numerical approximations**. This is the way it's done these days ... We can send probes to Mars because we have a very good idea of where they should be going in the first place, because we know the mass of Mars (itself an amazing fact) with a high degree of accuracy.

Most of the time we realize that things are in motion and this means that certain physical quantities are changing. These changes are best understood through the derivative of some underlying function. For example, when a car is moving its distance from a given point is changing, right? The "rate at which the distance changes" is the derivative of the distance function. This brings us to the notion of "instantaneous velocity". Furthermore, when a balloon is inflated, its volume is changing and the "rate" at which this volume is changing is approximately given by the derivative of the original volume function (its units would be $meters^3/sec$). In a different vein, the stock markets of the world are full of investors who delve into **stock options** as a means of furthering their investments. Central to all this business is the **Black-Sholes equation**, a complicated differential equation, which won their discoverer(s) a Nobel Prize in Economics a few years ago.

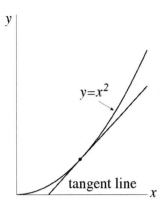

Figure 36.

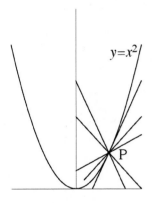

Figure 37.

3.1   Motivation

We begin this chapter by motivating the notation of the **derivative of a function,** itself another function with certain properties.

First, we'll define the notion of a **tangent to a curve.** In the phrase that describes it, a tangent at a given point P on the graph of the curve $y = f(x)$ is a straight line segment which intersects the curve $y = f(x)$ at P and is 'tangent' to it (think of the ordinary tangents to a circle, see Figure 36).

Example 66.   Find the equation of the line tangent to the curve $y = x^2$ at the point $(1, 1)$.

Solution Because of the shape of this curve we can see from its graph that every straight line crossing this curve will do so in at most two points, and we'll actually show this below. Let's choose a point P, say, $(1, 1)$ on this curve for ease of exposition. We'll **find the equation of the tangent line to P** and we'll do this in the following steps:

1. Find the equation of all the straight lines through P.
2. Show that there exists, among this set of lines, a **unique** line which is tangent to P.

OK, the equation of every line through $P(1, 1)$ has the form

$$y = m(x - 1) + 1$$

where m is its slope, right? (Figure 37).

Since we want the straight line to intersect the curve $y = x^2$, we must set $y = x^2$ in the preceding equation to find

$$x^2 = m(x - 1) + 1$$

or the quadratic

$$x^2 - mx + (m - 1) = 0$$

Finding its roots gives 2 solutions (the two x-coordinates of the point of intersection we spoke of earlier), namely,

$$x = m - 1 \text{ and } x = 1$$

The second root $x = 1$ is clear to see as all these straight lines go through $P(1, 1)$. The first root $x = m - 1$ gives a new root which is related to the **slope** of the straight line through $P(1, 1)$.

OK, we want only **one point of intersection,** right? (Remember, we're looking for a **tangent**). This means that the two roots must coincide! So we set $m - 1 = 1$ (as the two roots are equal) and this gives $m = 2$.

Thus the line whose slope is 2 and whose equation is

$$y \;=\; 2(x-1)+1 = 2x-1$$

is the equation of the line tangent to $P(1,1)$ for the curve $y = x^2$. Remember that at the point $(1,1)$ this line has slope $m = 2$. This will be useful later.

OK, but this is only an example of a tangent line to a curve .... How do you define this in general?

Well, let's take a function f, look at its graph and choose some point $P(x_0, y_0)$ on its graph where $y_0 = f(x_0)$. Look at a nearby point $Q(x_0 + h, f(x_0 + h))$. **What is the equation of the line** joining P to Q? Its form is

$$y - y_0 = m(x - x_0)$$

But $y_0 = f(x_0)$ and m, the slope, is equal to the quotient of the difference between the y-coordinates and the x-coordinates (of Q and P), that is,

$$m = \frac{f(x_0 + h) - f(x_0)}{(x_0 + h) - x_0} = \frac{f(x_0 + h) - f(x_0)}{h}.$$

OK, so the equation of this line is

$$y = \{\frac{f(x_0 + h) - f(x_0)}{h}\}(x - x_0) + f(x_0)$$

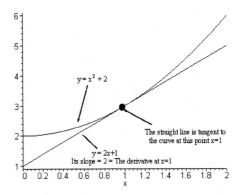

From this equation you can see that the slope of this line must change with "h". So, if we let h approach 0 as a limit, this line may approach a "limiting line" and it is this limiting line that we call the **tangent line to the curve $y = f(x)$ at $P(x_0, y_0)$** (see the figure in the margin on the right). The **slope** of this "tangent line" to the curve $y = f(x)$ at (x_0, y_0) defined by

$$m = \lim_{h \to 0} \frac{f(x_0 + h) - f(x_0)}{h}$$

(whenever this limit exists and is finite) is called the **derivative of f at x_0.** It is a number!!

Notation for Derivatives The following notations are all adopted universally for the derivatives of f at x_0:

$$f'(x_0), \; \frac{df}{dx}(x_0), \; D_x f(x_0), \; Df(x_0)$$

All of these have the same meaning.

Consequences!

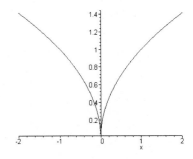

This graph has a vertical tangent line, namely $x = 0$, at the origin.

1. If the limit as $h \to 0$ does not exist as a two-sided limit or it is infinite we say that the **derivative does not exist.** This is equivalent to saying that there is no uniquely defined tangent line at $(x_0, f(x_0))$, (Example 69).

2. The derivative, $f'(x_0)$ when it exists, is **the slope of the tangent line** at $(x_0, f(x_0))$ on the graph of f.

3. There's nothing special about these tangent lines to a curve in the sense that **the same line can be tangent to other points on the same curve.** (The simplest example occurs when $f(x) = ax + b$ is a straight line. Why?)

In this book we will use the symbols '$f'(x_0)$, $Df(x_0)$' to mean the derivative of f at x_0 where

$$
\begin{aligned}
f'(x_0) &= \lim_{h \to 0} \frac{f(x_0 + h) - f(x_0)}{h} \\
&= \text{The slope of the tangent line at } x = x_0 \\
&= \text{The instantaneous rate of change of } f \text{ at } x = x_0.
\end{aligned}
$$

whenever this (two-sided) limit exists and is finite.

Table 3.1: Definition of the Derivative as a Limit

4. If either one or both one-sided limits defined by $f'_{\pm}(x_0)$ is infinite, the tangent line at that point P$(x_0, f(x_0))$ is **vertical** and given by the equation $x = x_0$, (See the margin).

The key idea in finding the derivative using Table 3.1, here, is always to

SIMPLIFY first, THEN pass to the LIMIT

The concept of a left and right-derivative of f at $x = x_0$ is defined by the left and right limits of the expression on the right in Table 3.1. So, for example,

$$
\begin{aligned}
f'_-(x_0) &= \lim_{h \to 0^-} \frac{f(x_0 + h) - f(x_0)}{h}, \\
f'_+(x_0) &= \lim_{h \to 0^+} \frac{f(x_0 + h) - f(x_0)}{h},
\end{aligned}
$$

define the left and right-derivative of f at $x = x_0$ respectively, whenever these limits exist and are finite.

Example 67.   In Example 66 we showed that the slope of the tangent line to the curve $y = x^2$ at $(1,1)$ is equal to 2. Show that the derivative of f where $f(x) = x^2$ at $x = 1$ is also equal to 2 (using the limit definition of the derivative, Table 3.1).

Solution By definition, the derivative of f at $x = 1$ is given by

$$
f'(x) = \lim_{h \to 0} \frac{f(1 + h) - f(1)}{h}
$$

provided this limit exists and is finite. OK, then calculate

$$
\begin{aligned}
\frac{f(1 + h) - f(1)}{h} &= \frac{(1 + h)^2 - 1^2}{h} \\
&= \frac{1 + 2h + h^2 - 1}{h} \\
&= 2 + h
\end{aligned}
$$

Since this is true for each value of $h \neq 0$ we can let $h \to 0$ and find

$$
\begin{aligned}
\lim_{h \to 0} \frac{f(1 + h) - f(1)}{h} &= \lim_{h \to 0} (2 + h) \\
&= 2
\end{aligned}
$$

and so $f'(1) = 2$, as well. Remember, this also means that the slope of the tangent line at $x = 1$ is equal to 2, which is what we found earlier.

Example 68.   Find the slope of the tangent line at $x = 2$ for the curve whose equation is $y = 1/x$.

Solution OK, we set $f(x) = 1/x$. As we have seen above, the slope's value, m_{tan}, is given by

$$
m_{tan} = \lim_{h \to 0} \frac{f(2 + h) - f(2)}{h}.
$$

Remember to simplify this ratio as much as possible (without the "lim" symbol). For $h \neq 0$ we have,

$$
\begin{aligned}
\frac{f(2+h) - f(2)}{h} &= \frac{\frac{1}{(2+h)} - \frac{1}{2}}{h} \\
&= \frac{\frac{2}{2(2+h)} - \frac{(2+h)}{2(2+h)}}{h} \\
&= \frac{2 - (2+h)}{2h(2+h)} \\
&= \frac{-h}{2h(2+h)} \\
&= \frac{-1}{2(2+h)}, \quad \text{since } h \neq 0.
\end{aligned}
$$

Since this is true for each $h \neq 0$, we can pass to the limit to find,

$$
\begin{aligned}
m_{tan} &= \lim_{h \to 0} \frac{f(2+h) - f(2)}{h} \\
&= \lim_{h \to 0} \frac{-1}{2(2+h)} \\
&= -\frac{1}{4}.
\end{aligned}
$$

Example 69.   We give examples of the following:

a) A function f whose derivative does not exist (as a two-sided limit).

b) A function f with a vertical tangent line to its graph $y = f(x)$ at $x = 0$, ('infinite' derivative at $x = 0$, i.e., both one-sided limits of the derivative exist but are infinite).

c) A function f with a horizontal tangent line to its graph $y = f(x)$ at $x = 0$, (the derivative is equal to zero in this case).

Solution a) Let

$$
f(x) = \begin{cases} x & \text{if } x \geq 0 \\ -x & \text{if } x < 0 \end{cases}
$$

This function is the same as $f(x) = |x|$, the absolute value of x, right? The idea is that in order for the two-sided (or ordinary) limit of the "derivative" to exist at some point, it is necessary that both one-sided limits (from the right and the left) each exist and both be equal, remember? The point is that **this function's derivative has both one-sided limits existing at $x = 0$ but unequal.** Why? Let's use Table 3.1 and try to find its "limit from the right" at x = 0.

For this we suspect that we need $h > 0$, as we want the limit from the **right**, and we're using the same notions of right and left limits drawn from the theory of continuous functions.

$$
\begin{aligned}
\frac{f(0+h) - f(0)}{h} &= \frac{f(h) - f(0)}{h} \\
&= \frac{h - 0}{h} \quad (\text{because } f(h) = h \text{ if } h > 0) \\
&= 1, \quad (\text{since } h \neq 0).
\end{aligned}
$$

Leonardo da Vinci, 1452-1519, who has appeared in a recent film on Cinderella, is the ideal of the Italian *Risorgimento*, the Renaissance: Painter, inventor, scientist, engineer, mathematician, pathologist etc., he is widely accepted as a universal genius, perhaps the greatest ever. What impresses me the most about this extremely versatile man is his ability to assimilate nature into a quantifiable whole, his towering mind, and his insatiable appetite for knowledge. He drew the regular polytopes (three-dimensional equivalents of the regular polygons) for his friend **Fra Luca Pacioli**, priest and mathematician, who included the hand-drawn sketches at the end of the original manuscript of his book on the golden number entitled *De divina proportione*, published in 1509, and now in Torino, Italy.

This is true for each possible value of $h > 0$. So,

$$\lim_{h \to 0+} \frac{f(h) - f(0)}{h} = 1,$$

and so this limit from the right, also called the **right derivative of f at $x = 0$**, exists and is equal to 1. This also means that as $h \to 0$, the slope of the tangent line to the graph of $y = |x|$ approaches the value 1.

OK, now let's find its limit from the **left** at $x = 0$. For this we want $h < 0$, right? Now

$$
\begin{aligned}
\frac{f(0 + h) - f(0)}{h} &= \frac{f(h) - f(0)}{h} \\
&= \frac{-h - 0}{h} \quad \text{(because } f(h) = -h \text{ if } h < 0) \\
&= -1 \quad \text{(since } h \neq 0)
\end{aligned}
$$

This is true for each possible value of $h < 0$. So,

$$\lim_{h \to 0-} \frac{f(h) - f(0)}{h} = -1.$$

This, so-called, **left derivative of f at $x = 0$** exists and its value is -1, a different value than 1 (which is the value of the right derivative of our f at $x = 0$). Thus

$$\lim_{h \to 0} \frac{f(0 + h) - f(0)}{h}$$

does not exist as a two-sided limit. The graph of this function is shown in Figure 38. Note the cusp/ sharp point/v-shape at the origin of this graph. This graphical phenomenon guarantees that the derivative does not exist there.

Note that there is **no uniquely defined tangent line** at $x = 0$ (as **both** $y = x$ and $y = -x$ should qualify, so there is no actual "tangent line").

Solution b) We give an example of a function whose derivative is infinite at $x = 0$, say, so that its tangent line is $x = 0$ (if its derivative is infinite at $x = x_0$, then its tangent line is the vertical line $x = x_0$).

Define f by

$$f(x) = \begin{cases} \sqrt{x}, & x \geq 0, \\ -\sqrt{-x}, & x < 0. \end{cases}$$

The graph of f is shown in Figure 39.

Let's calculate its left- and right-derivative at $x = 0$. For $h < 0$, at $x_0 = 0$,

$$
\begin{aligned}
\frac{f(0 + h) - f(0)}{h} &= \frac{f(h) - f(0)}{h} \\
&= \frac{-\sqrt{-h} - 0}{h} \quad (\text{ because } f(h) = -\sqrt{-h} \text{ if } h < 0) \\
&= \frac{-\sqrt{-h}}{-(-h)} \\
&= \frac{1}{\sqrt{-h}}.
\end{aligned}
$$

So we obtain,

$$
\begin{aligned}
\lim_{h \to 0-} \frac{f(0 + h) - f(0)}{h} &= \lim_{h \to 0-} \frac{1}{\sqrt{-h}} \\
&= +\infty,
\end{aligned}
$$

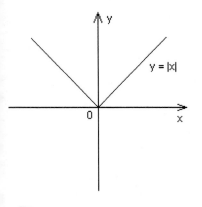

Figure 38.

SIMPLIFY first, then
GO to the LIMIT

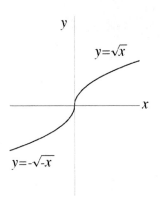

Figure 39.

$f'(x_0)$	Tangent Line Direction	Remarks
$+$	↙ ↗	"rises", bigger means steeper up
$-$	↖ ↘	"falls", smaller means steeper down
0	⟷	horizontal tangent line
$\pm\infty$	↕	vertical tangent line

Table 3.2: Geometrical Properties of the Derivative

and, similarly, for $h > 0$,

$$\lim_{h \to 0^+} \frac{f(0+h) - f(0)}{h} = \lim_{h \to 0^+} \frac{1}{\sqrt{h}}$$
$$= +\infty.$$

Finally, we see that

$$\lim_{h \to 0^-} \frac{f(0+h) - f(0)}{h} = \lim_{h \to 0^+} \frac{f(0+h) - f(0)}{h}$$

both exist and are equal to $+\infty$.

Note: The line $x = 0$ acts as the 'tangent line' to the graph of f at $x = 0$.

Solution c) For an example of a function with a horizontal tangent line at some point (*i.e.* $f'(x) = 0$ at, say, $x = 0$) consider f defined by $f(x) = x^2$ at $x = 0$, see Figure 40. Its derivative $f'(0)$ is given by

$$f'(0) = \lim_{h \to 0} \frac{f(0+h) - f(0)}{h} = 0$$

and since the derivative of f at $x = 0$ is equal to the slope of the tangent line there, it follows that the tangent line is horizontal, and given by $y = 0$.

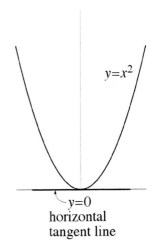

horizontal
tangent line

Figure 40.

Example 70. On the surface of our moon, an object P falling from rest will fall a distance of approximately $5.3t^2$ feet in t seconds. Find its instantaneous velocity at $t = a$ sec, $t = 1$ sec, and at $t = 2.6$ seconds.

Solution We'll need to calculate its instantaneous velocity, let's call it, "v", at $t = a$ seconds. Since, in this case, $f(t) = 5.3t^2$, we have, by definition,

$$v = \lim_{h \to 0} \frac{f(a+h) - f(a)}{h}.$$

Now, for $h \neq 0$,

$$\frac{f(a+h) - f(a)}{h} = \frac{5.3(a+h)^2 - 5.3a^2}{h}$$
$$= \frac{5.3a^2 + 10.6ah + 5.3h^2 - 5.3a^2}{h}$$
$$= 10.6a + 5.3h$$

So,

$$v = \lim_{h \to 0} (10.6a + 5.3h) = 10.6a$$

$f'(x_0)$ does not exist (right and left derivatives not equal)

$f'(x_1) = 0$, (horizontal tangent line).

$f'(x_2)$ does not exist (left derivative at $x = x_2$ is infinite).

$f'(x_3) < 0$, (tangent line "falls")

$f'(x_4) = 0$, (horizontal tangent line)

$f'(x_5) > 0$, (tangent line "rises").

Table 3.3: Different Derivatives in Action: See Figure 41

Different derivatives in action.

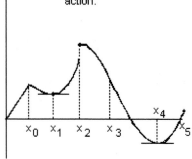

Figure 41.

feet per second. It follows that its instantaneous velocity at $t = 1$ second is given by $(10.6) \cdot (1) = 10.6$ feet per second, obtained by setting $a = 1$ in the formula for v. Similarly, $v = (10.6) \cdot (2.6) = 27.56$ feet per second. From this and the preceding discussion, you can conclude that an object falling from rest on the surface of the moon will fall at approximately *one-third* the rate it does on earth (neglecting air resistance, here).

| **Example 71.** | How long will it take the falling object of Example 70 to reach an instantaneous velocity of 50 feet per second?

Solution We know from Example 70 that $v = 10.6a$, at $t = a$ seconds. Since, we want $10.6a = 50$ we get $a = \frac{50}{10.6} = 4.72$ seconds.

| **Example 72.** | Different derivatives in action, see Figure 41, and Table 3.3.

| **Example 73.** | Evaluate the derivative of the function f **defined** by $f(x) = \sqrt{5x + 1}$ at $x = 3$.

Solution By definition,

$$f'(3) = \lim_{h \to 0} \frac{f(3 + h) - f(3)}{h}.$$

Now, we **try to simplify as much as possible before passing to the limit.** For $h \neq 0$,

$$\frac{f(3 + h) - f(3)}{h} = \frac{\sqrt{5(3 + h) + 1} - \sqrt{5(3) + 1}}{h}$$
$$= \frac{\sqrt{16 + 5h} - 4}{h}.$$

Think BIG here: Remember that rationalization gives

$$\sqrt{\square} - \sqrt{\triangle} = \frac{\square - \triangle}{\sqrt{\square} + \sqrt{\triangle}}$$

for any two positive symbols, $\square, \triangle$.

Now, to simplify this last expression, we *rationalize* the numerator (by multiplying both the numerator *and* denominator by $\sqrt{16 + 5h} + 4$). Then we'll find,

$$\frac{\sqrt{16 + 5h} - 4}{h} = \{\frac{\sqrt{16 + 5h} - 4}{h}\}\{\frac{\sqrt{16 + 5h} + 4}{\sqrt{16 + 5h} + 4}\}$$
$$= \frac{16 + 5h - 16}{h(\sqrt{16 + 5h} + 4)}$$
$$= \frac{5}{\sqrt{16 + 5h} + 4}, \quad since \ h \neq 0.$$

We can't simplify this any more, and now the expression "looks good" if we set $h = 0$ in it, so we can pass to the limit as $h \to 0$, to find,

$$
\begin{aligned}
f'(3) &= \lim_{h \to 0} \frac{f(3 + h) - f(3)}{h} \\
&= \lim_{h \to 0} \frac{5}{\sqrt{16 + 5h} + 4} \\
&= \frac{5}{\sqrt{16} + 4} \\
&= \frac{5}{8}.
\end{aligned}
$$

Summary

The derivative of a function f at a point $x = a$, (or $x = x_0$), denoted by $f'(a)$, or $\frac{df}{dx}(a)$, or $Df(a)$, is defined by the two equivalent definitions

$$
\begin{aligned}
f'(a) &= \lim_{h \to 0} \frac{f(a + h) - f(a)}{h} \\
&= \lim_{x \to a} \frac{f(x) - f(a)}{x - a}.
\end{aligned}
$$

whenever either limit exists (in which case so does the other). You get the second definition from the first by setting $h = x - a$, so that the statement "$h \to 0$" is the same as "$x \to a$".

The **right-derivative** (resp. **left-derivative**) is defined by the right- (resp. left-) hand) limits

$$
\begin{aligned}
f'_+(a) &= \lim_{h \to 0+} \frac{f(a + h) - f(a)}{h} \\
&= \lim_{x \to a+} \frac{f(x) - f(a)}{x - a},
\end{aligned}
$$

and

$$
\begin{aligned}
f'_-(a) &= \lim_{h \to 0-} \frac{f(a + h) - f(a)}{h} \\
&= \lim_{x \to a-} \frac{f(x) - f(a)}{x - a}.
\end{aligned}
$$

SIMPLIFY first, then
GO to the LIMIT

Exercise Set 10.

Evaluate the following limits

1. $\displaystyle \lim_{h \to 0} \frac{f(2 + h) - f(2)}{h}$ where $f(x) = x^2$

2. $\displaystyle \lim_{h \to 0} \frac{f(-1 + h) - f(-1)}{h}$ where $f(x) = |x|$

3. $\displaystyle \lim_{h \to 0} \frac{f(0 + h) - f(0)}{h}$ where $f(x) = \begin{cases} 0 & x = 0 \\ \dfrac{1}{x} & x \neq 0 \end{cases}$

4.a) $\displaystyle \lim_{h \to 0^-} \frac{f(1 + h) - f(1)}{h}$

b) $\displaystyle\lim_{h\to 0^+} \frac{f(1+h)-f(1)}{h}$ where $f(x) = \begin{cases} x+1 & x \geq 1 \\ x & 0 \leq x < 1 \end{cases}$

5. $\displaystyle\lim_{h\to 0} \frac{f(2+h)-f(2)}{h}$ where $f(x) = \sqrt{x}$

    HINT : Rationalize the numerator and simplify.

6. $\displaystyle\lim_{h\to 0} \frac{f(-2+h)-f(-2)}{h}$ where $f(x) = -x^2$

Find the slope of the tangent line to the graph of f at the given point.

7. $f(x) = 3x + 2$ at $x = 1$

8. $f(x) = 3 - 4x$ at $x = -2$

9. $f(x) = x^2$ at $x = 3$

10. $f(x) = |x|$ at $x = 1$

11. $f(x) = x|x|$ at $x = 0$

    HINT: Consider the left and right derivatives separately.

12. $f(x) = \begin{cases} 1 & x \geq 0 \\ 0 & x < 0 \end{cases}$ (Remember Heaviside's function?)

Determine whether or not the following functions have a derivative at the indicated point. Explain.

13. $f(x) = \begin{cases} 1 & x \geq 0 \\ -1 & x < 0 \end{cases}$ at $x = 0$

14. $f(x) = \sqrt{x+1}$ at $x = -1$

    HINT: Graphing this function may help.

15. $f(x) = |x^2|$ at $x = 0$

16. $f(x) = \sqrt{6 - 2x}$ at $x = 1$

17. $f(x) = \frac{1}{x^2}$ at $x = 1$

18. A function f is defined by

$$f(x) = \begin{cases} x & 0 \leq x < 1 \\ x+2 & 1 \leq x < 2 \\ 8 - x^2 & 2 \leq x < 3. \end{cases}$$

a) What is $f'(1)$? Explain.

b) Does $f'(2)$ exist? Explain.

c) Evaluate $f'(\frac{5}{2})$.

NOTES:

3.2 Working with Derivatives

By now you know how to find the derivative of a given function (and you can actually check to see whether or not it **has** a derivative at a given point). You also understand the relationship between the derivative and the slope of a tangent line to a given curve (otherwise go to Section 3.1).

Sometimes it is useful to define the derivative $f'(a)$ of a given function at $x = a$ as

$$f'(a) = \lim_{x \to a} \frac{f(x) - f(a)}{x - a} \tag{3.1}$$

provided the (two-sided) limit exists and is finite. Do you see why this definition is equivalent to

$$f'(a) = \lim_{h \to 0} \frac{f(a + h) - f(a)}{h}?$$

Simply replace the symbol "h" by "$x - a$" and simplify. As $h \to 0$ it is necessary that $x - a \to 0$ or $x \to a$.

Notation
When a given function f has a derivative at $x = a$ we say that "f is differentiable at $x = a$" or briefly "f is differentiable at a."

If f is differentiable at every point x of a given interval, **I**, we say that "f is differentiable on **I**."

Example 74. The function f defined by $f(x) = x^2$ is differentiable everywhere on the real line (i.e., at each real number) and its derivative at x is given by $f'(x) = 2x$.

Example 75. **The Power Rule**. The function g defined by $g(x) = x^n$ where $n \geq 0$ is any given integer is differentiable at every point x. If $n < 0$ then it is differentiable everywhere except at $x = 0$. Show that its derivative is given by

$$\frac{d}{dx} x^n = nx^{n-1}.$$

Solution We need to recall the *Binomial Theorem:* This says that

$$(x + h)^n = x^n + nx^{n-1}h + \frac{n(n-1)}{2}x^{n-2}h^2 + \ldots + nxh^{n-1} + h^n$$

for some integer n whenever $n \geq 1$, (there are $(n+1)$ terms in total). From this we get the well-known formulae

$$\begin{aligned}
(x + h)^2 &= x^2 + 2xh + h^2, \\
(x + h)^3 &= x^3 + 3x^2h + 3xh^2 + h^3, \\
(x + h)^4 &= x^4 + 4x^3h + 6x^2h^2 + 4xh^3 + h^4.
\end{aligned}$$

OK, by definition (and the Binomial Theorem), for $h \neq 0$,

$$\begin{aligned}
\frac{g(x + h) - g(x)}{h} &= \frac{nx^{n-1}h + \frac{n(n-1)}{2}x^{n-2}h^2 + \ldots + nxh^{n-1} + h^n}{h} \\
&= nx^{n-1} + \frac{n(n-1)}{2}x^{n-2}h + \ldots + nxh^{n-2} + h^{n-1}.
\end{aligned}$$

Since $n \geq 1$ it follows that (because the limit of a sum is the sum of the limits),

$$
\begin{aligned}
\lim_{h \to 0} \frac{g(x+h) - g(x)}{h} &= \lim_{h \to 0}\left(nx^{n-1} + \frac{n(n-1)}{2}x^{n-2}h + \ldots + h^{n-1}\right) \\
&= nx^{n-1} + \lim_{h \to 0}\left(\frac{n(n-1)}{2}x^{n-2}h + \ldots + h^{n-1}\right) \\
&= nx^{n-1} + 0 \\
&= nx^{n-1}.
\end{aligned}
$$

Thus $g'(x)$ exists and $g'(x) = nx^{n-1}$.

Remark! Actually, more is true here. It is the case that **for every number** 'a' (integer or not), but a is NOT a variable like 'x, $\sin x$, ...',

$$
\frac{d}{dx}x^a = ax^{a-1} \text{ if } x > 0.
$$

This formula is useful as it gives a simple expression for the derivative of any power of the independent variable, in this case, 'x'.

QUICKIES

a) $f(x) = x^3$; $f'(x) = 3x^{3-1} = 3x^2$

b) $f(t) = \frac{1}{t} = t^{-1}$, so $f'(t) = (-1)t^{-2} = -\frac{1}{t^2}$

c) $g(z) = \frac{1}{z^2} = z^{-2}$, so $g'(z) = (-2)z^{-3} = -\frac{2}{z^3}$

d) $f(x) = \sqrt{x} = x^{\frac{1}{2}}$, so $f'(x) = \frac{1}{2}x^{-\frac{1}{2}} = \frac{1}{2\sqrt{x}}$

e) $f(x) = x^{-\frac{2}{3}}$; $f'(x) = -\frac{2}{3}x^{-\frac{5}{3}}$

f) $f(x) = $ constant, $f'(x) = 0$

Quick summary

Notation:

1. By cf we mean the function whose values are given by

$$(cf)(x) = cf(x)$$

where c is a constant.

2. By the symbols $f + g$ we mean the function whose values are given by

$$(f + g)(x) = f(x) + g(x)$$

A function f is said to be **differentiable at the point a** if its derivative $f'(a)$ exists there. This is equivalent to saying that both the left- and right-hand derivatives exist at a and are equal. A function f is said to be **differentiable everywhere** if it is differentiable at every point a of the real line.

For example, the function f defined by the absolute value of x, namely, $f(x) = |x|$, is differentiable at every point except at $x = 0$ where $f'_-(0) = -1$ and $f'_+(0) = 1$. On the other hand, the function g defined by $g(x) = x|x|$ is differentiable everywhere. Can you show this ?

Properties of the Derivative

Let f, g be two differentiable functions at x and let c be a constant. Then cf, $f \pm g$, fg are all differentiable at x and

a)

$$\frac{d}{dx}(cf) = c\frac{df}{dx} = cf'(x)$$

b)

$$\frac{d}{dx}(f \pm g) = \frac{df}{dx} \pm \frac{dg}{dx}, \qquad \textbf{Sum/Difference Rule}$$
$$= f'(x) \pm g'(x)$$

c)

$$\frac{d}{dx}(fg) = f'(x)\, g(x) + f(x)\, g'(x), \qquad \textbf{Product Rule}$$

d) If for some x, the value $g(x) \neq 0$ then $\frac{f}{g}$ is differentiable at x and

$$\frac{d}{dx}\left(\frac{f}{g}\right) = \frac{f'(x)\, g(x) - f(x)\, g'(x)}{g^2(x)}, \qquad \textbf{Quotient Rule}$$

where all the derivatives are evaluated at the point 'x'. Hints to the *proofs* or *verification* of these basic Rules may be found at the end of this section. They are left to the reader as a Group Project.

Note that the formula

$$\frac{d}{dx}(fg) = \frac{df}{dx}\frac{dg}{dx}$$

is **NOT TRUE** in general. For example, if $f(x) = x, g(x) = 1$, then $f(x)g(x) = x$ and so $(fg)'(x) = 1$. On the other hand, $f'(x)g'(x) = 0$, and so this formula cannot be true.

Example 76.   Find the derivative, $f'(x)$ of the function f defined by $f(x) = 2x^3 - 5x + 1$. What is its value at $x = 1$?

Solution We use Example 75 and Properties (a) and (b) to see that

$$\begin{aligned}
f'(x) &= \frac{d}{dx}(2x^3) + \frac{d}{dx}(-5x) + \frac{d}{dx}(1) = 2\frac{d}{dx}(x^3) + (-5)\cdot\frac{d}{dx}(x) + 0 \\
&= 2\cdot 3x^2 + (-5)\cdot 1 \\
&= 6x^2 - 5.
\end{aligned}$$

So, $f'(x) = 6x^2 - 5$ and thus the derivative evaluated at $x = 1$ is given by $f'(1) = 6\cdot(1)^2 - 5 = 6 - 5 = 1$.

Example 77.   Given that $f(x) = \sqrt[3]{x} + \sqrt[3]{2} - 1$ find $f'(x)$ at $x = -1$.

Solution We rewrite all "roots" as powers and then use the Power Rule. So,

$$\begin{aligned}
f'(x) &= \frac{d}{dx}\left(\sqrt[3]{x} + \sqrt[3]{2} - 1\right) \\
&= \frac{d}{dx}\left(x^{1/3} + 2^{1/3} - 1\right) = \frac{d}{dx}\left(x^{1/3}\right) + \frac{d}{dx}\left(2^{1/3} - 1\right) \\
&= \frac{1}{3}x^{\frac{1}{3}-1} + 0 - 0 \\
&= \frac{1}{3}x^{-\frac{2}{3}}.
\end{aligned}$$

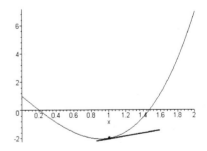

The tangent line at $x = 1$ to the curve $f(x)$ defined in Example 76.

Figure 42.

Finally, $f'(-1) = \frac{1}{3}(-1)^{-\frac{2}{3}} = \frac{1}{3}\left(\sqrt[3]{-1}\right)^{-2} = \frac{1}{3}(-1)^{-2} = -\frac{1}{3}$.

Example 78. Find the slope of the tangent line to the curve defined by the function $h(x) = (x^2 + 1)(x - 1)$ at the point $(1, 0)$ on its graph.

Solution Using the geometrical interpretation of the derivative (cf., Table 3.1), we know that this slope is equal to $h'(1)$. So, we need to calculate the derivative of h and then evaluate it at $x = 1$. Since h is made up of two functions we can use the Product Rule (Property (c), above). To this end we write $f(x) = (x^2 + 1)$ and $g(x) = x - 1$. Then $h(x) = f(x)g(x)$ and we want $h'(x)$. So, using the Product Rule we see that

$$
\begin{aligned}
h'(x) &= \frac{d}{dx}f(x)g(x) = f'(x)\ g(x) + f(x)\ g'(x) \\
&= \frac{d}{dx}\left(x^2 + 1\right)\cdot(x - 1) + (x^2 + 1)\cdot\frac{d}{dx}(x - 1) \\
&= (2x + 0)\cdot(x - 1) + (x^2 + 1)\cdot(1 - 0) = 2x(x - 1) + x^2 + 1 \\
&= 3x^2 - 2x + 1.
\end{aligned}
$$

The required slope is now given by $h'(1) = 3 - 2 + 1 = 2$. See Figure 43.

Example 79. Find the equation of the tangent line to the curve defined by

$$
h(t) = \frac{t}{t^2 + 1}
$$

at the point $(0, 0)$ on its graph.

Solution Since the function h is a quotient of two functions we may use the Quotient Rule, (d). To this end, let $f(t) = t$ and $g(t) = t^2 + 1$. The idea is that we have to find $h'(t)$ at $t = 0$ since this will give the slope of the tangent line at $t = 0$, and then use the general equation of a line in the form $y = mx + b$ in order to get the actual equation of our tangent line passing through $(0, 0)$. OK, now

$$
\begin{aligned}
h'(t) &= \frac{f'(t)\ g(t) - f(t)\ g'(t)}{g^2(t)} \\
&= \frac{(1)\cdot(t^2 + 1) - (t)\cdot(2t)}{(t^2 + 1)^2} \\
&= \frac{1 - t^2}{(t^2 + 1)^2}.
\end{aligned}
$$

Next, it is clear that $h'(0) = 1$ and so the tangent line must have the equation $y = x + b$ for an appropriate point (x, y) on it. But $(x, y) = (0, 0)$ is on it, by hypothesis. So, we set $x = 0, y = 0$ in the general form, solve for b, and conclude that $b = 0$. Thus, the required equation is $y = x + 0 = x$, i.e., $y = x$, see Figure 44.

Example 80. At which points on the graph of $y = x^3 + 3x$ does the tangent line have slope equal to 9?

Solution This question is not as direct as the others, above. The idea here is to find the expression for the derivative of y and then set this expression equal to 9 and then solve for x. Now, $y'(x) = 3x^2 + 3$ and so $9 = y'(x) = 3x^2 + 3$ implies that $3x^2 = 6$ or $x = \pm\sqrt{2}$. Note the *two* roots here. So there are two points on the required graph where the slope is equal to 9. The y−coordinates are then given by setting $x = \pm\sqrt{2}$ into the expression for y. We find the points $(\sqrt{2}, 5\sqrt{2})$ and $(-\sqrt{2}, -5\sqrt{2})$, since $(\sqrt{2})^3 = 2\sqrt{2}$.

Example 81. If $f(x) = (x^2 - x + 1)(x^2 + x + 1)$ find $f'(0)$ and $f'(1)$.

Solution Instead of using the Product Rule we can simply expand the product noting that $f(x) = (x^2 - x + 1)(x^2 + x + 1) = x^4 + x^2 + 1$. So, $f'(x) = 4x^3 + 2x$ by the Power Rule, and thus, $f'(0) = 0$, $f'(1) = 6$.

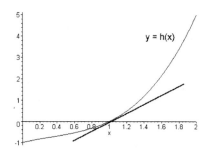

The graph of the function h and its tangent line at $x = 1$. The slope of this straight line is equal to 2

Figure 43.

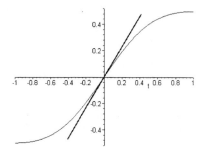

The tangent line $y = x$ through $(0, 0)$ for the function h in Example 79.

Figure 44.

Exercise Set 11.

Find the derivative of each of the following functions using any one of the Rules above: Show specifically which Rules you are using at each step. There is no need to simplify your final answer.

Example: If $f(x) = \dfrac{x^{0.3}}{x+1}$, then

$$
\begin{aligned}
f'(x) &= \frac{D(x^{0.3})(x+1) - x^{0.3}D(x+1)}{(x+1)^2}, \quad \text{by the Quotient Rule,} \\
&= \frac{(0.3)x^{-0.7}(x+1) - x^{0.3}(1)}{(x+1)^2}, \quad \text{by the Power Rule with } a = 2/3 \\
&= \frac{(0.3)x^{-0.7}(x+1) - x^{0.3}}{(x+1)^2}.
\end{aligned}
$$

1. $f(x) = x^{1.5}$
2. $f(t) = t^{-2}$
3. $g(x) = 6$
4. $h(x) = x^{\frac{2}{3}}$
5. $k(t) = t^{\frac{1}{5}}$
6. $f(x) = 4.52$
7. $f(t) = t^4$
8. $g(x) = x^{-3}$
9. $f(x) = x^{-1}$
10. $f(x) = x^{\pi}$
11. $f(t) = t^2 - 6$
12. $f(x) = 3x^2 + 2x - 1$
13. $f(t) = (t-1)(t^2 + 4)$
14. $f(x) = \sqrt{x}\left(3x^2 + 1\right)$
15. $f(x) = \dfrac{x^{0.5}}{2x+1}$
16. $f(x) = \dfrac{x-1}{x+1}$
17. $f(x) = \dfrac{x^3 - 1}{x^2 + x - 1}$
18. $f(x) = \dfrac{x^{\frac{2}{3}}}{\sqrt{x} + 3x^{\frac{3}{4}}}$

Group Project on Differentiation

Prove the Differentiation Rules in Section 3.2 using the definition of the derivative as a limit, the limit properties in Table 2.4, and some basic algebra. Assume throughout that f and g are differentiable at x and $g(x) \neq 0$. In order to prove the Properties proceed as follows using the hints given:

1. **Property a)**

   Show that for any real number c, and $h \neq 0$, we have

   $$(cf)'(x) = c \times \lim_{h \to 0} \frac{f(x+h) - f(x)}{h},$$

   and complete the argument.

2. **Property b) The Sum/Difference Rule:** Show that for a given x and $h \neq 0$,

   $$\frac{(f+g)(x+h) - (f+g)(x)}{h} = \frac{f(x+h) - f(x)}{h} + \frac{g(x+h) - g(x)}{h}.$$

   Then use Table 2.4, a) and the definition of the derivatives.

3. **Property c) The Product Rule:** Show that for a given x and $h \neq 0$,

   $$\frac{(fg)(x+h) - (fg)(x)}{h} = g(x)\frac{f(x+h) - f(x)}{h} + f(x+h)\frac{g(x+h) - g(x)}{h}.$$

   Then use Table 2.4 e),the definition of the derivatives, and the continuity of f at x.

4. **Property d) The Quotient Rule:** First, show that for a given x and any h,

   $$\left(\frac{f}{g}\right)(x+h) - \left(\frac{f}{g}\right)(x) = \frac{f(x+h)}{g(x+h)} - \frac{f(x)}{g(x)}.$$

   Next, rewrite the previous expression as

   $$\frac{f(x+h)}{g(x+h)} - \frac{f(x)}{g(x)} = \frac{f(x+h)g(x) - f(x)g(x+h)}{g(x+h)g(x)},$$

   and then rewrite it as,

   $$\frac{f(x+h)g(x) - f(x)g(x+h)}{g(x+h)g(x)} =$$

   $$\frac{(f(x+h) - f(x))g(x) - f(x)(g(x+h) - g(x))}{g(x+h)g(x)}.$$

   Now, let $h \to 0$ and use Table 2.4, d) and e), the continuity of g at x, and the definition of the derivatives.

Suggested Homework Set 6. *Problems 1, 3, 6, 8, 18*

3.3   The Chain Rule

This section is about a method that will enable you to find the derivative of complicated looking expressions, with some speed and simplicity. After a few examples you'll be using it without much thought ... It will become very natural. Many examples in nature involve variables which depend upon other variables. For example, the speed of a car depends on the amount of gas being injected into the carburator, and this, in turn depends on the diameter of the injectors, etc. In this case we could ask the question: "How does the speeed change if we vary the size of the injectors only ?" and leave all the other variables the same. We are then led naturally to a study of the *composition* (not the same as the product), of various functions and their derivatives.

We recall the **composition of two functions**, (see Chapter 1), and the **limit-definition of the derivative** of a given function from Section 3.2. First, let's see if we can discover the form of the Rule that finds the derivative of the composition of two functions in terms of the individual derivatives. That is, we want an explicit Rule for finding

$$\frac{d}{dx}(f \circ g)(x) = \frac{d}{dx}f(g(x)),$$

in terms of f and $g(x)$.

We assume that f and g are both differentiable at some point that we call x_0 (and so g is also *continuous* there). Furthermore, we must assume that the range of g is contained in the domain of f (so that the composition *makes sense*). Now look at the quantity

$$k(x) = f(g(x)),$$

which is just shorthand for this composition. We want to calculate $k'(x_0)$. So, we need to examine the expression

$$\frac{k(x_0 + h) - k(x_0)}{h} = \frac{f(g(x_0 + h)) - f(g(x_0))}{h},$$

and see what happens when we let $h \to 0$. Okay, now let's **assume that g is not identically a constant function near $x = x_0$**. This means that $g(x) \neq g(x_0)$ for any x in a small interval around x_0. Now,

$$\frac{k(x_0 + h) - k(x_0)}{h} = \frac{f(g(x_0 + h)) - f(g(x_0))}{h}$$

$$= \frac{f(g(x_0 + h)) - f(g(x_0))}{g(x_0 + h) - g(x_0)} \cdot \frac{g(x_0 + h) - g(x_0)}{h}.$$

As $h \to 0$, $g(x_0 + h) \to g(x_0)$ because g is continuous at $x = x_0$. Furthermore,

$$\frac{g(x_0 + h) - g(x_0)}{h} \to g'(x_0),$$

since g is differentiable at the point $x = x_0$. Lastly,

$$\frac{f(g(x_0 + h)) - f(g(x_0))}{g(x_0 + h) - g(x_0)} \to f'(g(x_0))$$

since f is differentiable at $x = g(x_0)$ (use definition 3.1 with $x = g(x_0 + h)$ and $a = g(x_0)$ to see this). It now follows by the theory of limits that

$$\lim_{h \to 0} \frac{k(x_0 + h) - k(x_0)}{h} = \lim_{h \to 0} \frac{f(g(x_0 + h)) - f(g(x_0))}{g(x_0 + h) - g(x_0)} \cdot \frac{g(x_0 + h) - g(x_0)}{h},$$

$$= \lim_{h \to 0} \left(\frac{f(g(x_0 + h)) - f(g(x_0))}{g(x_0 + h) - g(x_0)} \right) \times$$

$$\times \cdot \lim_{h \to 0} \left(\frac{g(x_0 + h) - g(x_0)}{h} \right),$$
$$= \quad f'(g(x_0)) \cdot g'(x_0),$$
$$= \quad k'(x_0).$$

In other words we can believe that

$$k'(x_0) = f'(g(x_0)) \cdot g'(x_0),$$

and this is the formula we wanted. It's called the **Chain Rule**.

The Chain Rule also says

$$\boxed{Df(\Box) = f'(\Box)\ D\Box}\,,$$

where "Df = df/dx = f'(x). You can read this as: "Dee of f of box is f prime box dee box". We call this the **Box formulation of the Chain Rule.**

> **The Chain Rule: Summary**
>
> Let f, g be two differentiable functions with g differentiable at x and $g(x)$ in the domain of f'. Then $y = f \circ g$ is differentiable at x and
>
> $$\frac{d}{dx}(f \circ g)(x) = \frac{d}{dx}f(g(x)) = f'(g(x)) \cdot g'(x)$$

Let's see what this means. When the composition $(f \circ g)$ is defined (and the range of g is contained in the domain of f') then $(f \circ g)'$ exists and

$$\frac{d}{dx}(f \circ g)(x) \quad = \quad \frac{df}{dx}(g(x)) \cdot g'(x)$$

$$\underbrace{\frac{d}{dx}f(g(x))}_{\text{derivative of composition}} \quad = \quad \underbrace{f'(g(x)) \cdot g'(x)}_{\text{derivative of } f \text{ at } g(x)\ \cdot\ \text{derivative of } g \text{ at } x}$$

In other words, the derivative of a composition is found by differentiating the *outside* function first, (here, f), evaluating its derivative, (here f'), at the *inside* function, (here, $g(x)$), and finally multiplying this number, $f'(g(x))$, by the derivative of g at x.

The **Chain Rule** is one of the most useful and important rules in the theory of differentiation of functions as it will allow us to find the derivative of very complicated-looking expressions with ease. For example, using the Chain Rule we'll be able to show that

$$\frac{d}{dx}(x + 1)^3 = 3(x + 1)^2.$$

Without using the Chain Rule, the alternative is that we have to expand

$$(x + 1)^3 = x^3 + 3x^2 + 3x + 1$$

using the Binomial Theorem and then use the Sum Rule along with the Power Rule to get the result which, incidentally, is identical to the stated one since

$$\frac{d}{dx}(x^3 + 3x^2 + 3x + 1) = 3x^2 + 6x + 3 = 3(x + 1)^2.$$

> An easy way to remember the Chain Rule is as follows:

Replace the symbol "$g(x)$" by our box symbol, $\Box$. Then the Chain Rule says that

$$\underbrace{\frac{d}{dx}f(\Box)}_{\text{derivative of a composition}} \quad = \quad \underbrace{f'(\Box) \cdot \Box\,'}_{\text{derivative of } f \text{ at } \Box\ \cdot\ \text{derivative of } \Box \text{ at } x}$$

Symbolically, it can be shortened by writing that

$$Df(\Box) = f'(\Box)\,D\Box\,, \qquad \text{The Chain Rule}$$

where the $\Box$ may represent (or even *contain*) any other function(s) you wish. In words, it can be remembered by saying that the

> Derivative of f of Box is f prime Box dee-Box

like a famous brand name for "sneakers", (*i.e.* 'dee-Box').

Consequences of the Chain Rule!

Let g be a differentiable function with $g(x) \neq 0$. Then $\frac{1}{g}$ is differentiable and by the Quotient Rule,

1. $\dfrac{d}{dx}\left(\dfrac{1}{g(x)}\right) = \dfrac{-1}{(g(x))^2}\cdot g'(x)$, or,

2. $\dfrac{d}{dx}(g(x))^a = a(g(x))^{a-1}\cdot g'(x)$ \quad The Generalized Power Rule

whenever a is a real number and $g(x) > 0$. This Generalized Power Rule follows easily from the Chain Rule, above, since we can let $f(x) = x^a$, $g(x) = \Box$. Then the composition $(f \circ g)(x) = g(x)^a = \Box^{\,a}$. According to the Chain Rule,

$$\frac{d}{dx}f(\Box) \;=\; f'(\Box)\cdot\Box'.$$

But, by the ordinary Power Rule, Example 75, we know that $f'(x) = ax^{a-1}$. Okay, now since $f'(\Box) = a\Box^{\,a-1}$, and $\Box' = g'(x)$, the Chain Rule gives us the result.

An easy way to remember these formulae, once and for all, is by writing

$$
\begin{array}{rll}
D\,\Box^{\,power} &=& power\cdot\Box^{\,(power)-1}\cdot D\,\Box \qquad \textbf{Generalized Power Rule}\\[2mm]
D\left(\dfrac{1}{\Box}\right) &=& \dfrac{-1}{(\Box)^2}\cdot D\,\Box\,, \qquad\qquad \textbf{Reciprocal Rule}
\end{array}
$$

where $\Box$ may be some differentiable function of x, and we have used the modern notation "D" for the derivative with respect to x. Recall that the **reciprocal** of *something* is, by definition, " 1 divided by that something".

The Chain Rule can take on different forms. For example, let $y = f(u)$ and assume that the variable u is itself a function of another variable, say x, and we write this as $u = g(x)$. So $y = f(u)$ and $u = g(x)$. So y must be a function of x and it is reasonable to expect that y is a *differentiable* function of x if certain additional conditions on f and g are imposed. Indeed, let y be a differentiable function of u and let u be a differentiable function of x. Then y is, in fact, a differentiable function of x. Now the question is:

"How does y vary with x?" The result looks like this ...

$$\frac{dy}{dx} \;=\; \frac{dy}{du}\cdot\frac{du}{dx}$$

$$\text{or}$$

$$y'(x) \;=\; f'(u)\cdot g'(x)$$

It's **NOT TRUE** that

$$Df(g(x)) = f'(x)\,g'(x),$$

where **we must replace all occurrences of the symbol 'u' in the above by the symbol '$g(x)$' after the differentiations are made.**

Sophie Germain, 1776-1831, was the second of three children of a middle-class Parisian family. Somewhat withdrawn, she never married, and by all accounts lived at home where she worked on mathematical problems with a passion. Of the many stories which surround this gifted mathematician, there is this one ... Upon the establishment of the *École Polytechnique* in 1795, women were not allowed to attend the lectures so Sophie managed to get the lecture notes in mathematics by befriending students. She then had some great ideas and wrote this big essay called a *memoire* and then submitted it (under a male name) to one of the great French mathematcians of the time, **Joseph Lagrange**, 1736-1813, for his advice and opinion. Lagrange found much merit in the work and wished to meet its creator. When he did finally meet her he was delighted that the work had been written by a woman, and went on to introduce her to the great mathematicians of the time. She won a prize in 1816 dealing with the solution of a problem in two-dimensional harmonic motion, yet remained a lone genius all of her life.

Example 82.   Let f be defined by $f(x) = 6x^{\frac{1}{2}} + 3$. Find $f'(x)$.

Solution We know $f(x) = 6x^{\frac{1}{2}} + 3$. So, if we let $x = \square$ we get

$$
\begin{aligned}
f'(x) &= 6\frac{d}{dx}\square^{1/2} + \frac{d}{dx}3 \text{ (by Properties (a) and (b))}, \\
&= 6 \cdot \frac{1}{2}\square^{-1/2} + 0, \\
&= 3x^{-1/2} \\
&= \frac{3}{\sqrt{x}}.
\end{aligned}
$$

Example 83.   Let g be defined by $g(t) = t^5 - 4t^3 - 2$. What is $g'(0)$, the derivative of g evaluated at $t = 0$?

Solution

$$
\begin{aligned}
g'(t) &= \frac{d}{dt}(t^5) - 4\frac{d}{dt}(t^3) - \frac{d}{dt}2 \quad \text{(by Property (b))} \\
&= 5t^4 - 4(3)t^2 - 0 \quad \text{(Power Rule)} \\
&= 5t^4 - 12t^2.
\end{aligned}
$$

But $g'(0)$ is $g'(t)$ with $t = 0$, right? So, $g'(0) = 5(0)^4 - 12(0)^2 = 0$.

Example 84.   Let y be defined by $y(x) = (x^2 - 3x + 1)(2x + 1)$. Evaluate $y'(1)$.

Solution Let $f(x) = x^2 - 3x + 1$, $g(x) = 2x + 1$. Then $y(x) = f(x)g(x)$ and we want $y'(x)$... So, we can use the **Product Rule** (or you can multiply the polynomials out, collect terms and then differentiate each term). Now,

$$
\begin{aligned}
y'(x) &= f'(x)g(x) + f(x)g'(x) \\
&= (2x - 3 + 0)(2x + 1) + (x^2 - 3x + 1)(2 + 0) \\
&= (2x - 3)(2x + 1) + 2(x^2 - 3x + 1), \quad \text{so,}
\end{aligned}
$$

$$
\begin{aligned}
y'(1) &= (2(1) - 3)(2(1) + 1) + 2((1)^2 - 3(1) + 1) \\
&= -5.
\end{aligned}
$$

Example 85.   Let y be defined by $y(x) = \dfrac{x^2 + 4}{x^3 - 4}$. Find the slope of the tangent line to the curve $y = y(x)$ at $x = 2$.

Solution We write $y(x) = \dfrac{f(x)}{g(x)}$ where $f(x) = x^2 + 4$, $g(x) = x^3 - 4$. We also need $f'(x)$ and $g'(x)$, since the Quotient Rule will come in handy here.

The next Table may be useful as we always need these 4 quantities when using the Quotient Rule:

$f(x)$	$f'(x)$	$g(x)$	$g'(x)$
$x^2 + 4$	$2x$	$x^3 - 4$	$3x^2$

Now, by the Quotient Rule,

$$y'(x) = \frac{f'(x)g(x) - f(x)g'(x)}{(g(x))^2}$$

$$= \frac{2x(x^3 - 4) - (x^2 + 4)(3x^2)}{(x^3 - 4)^2}.$$

No need to simplify here. We're really asking for $y'(2)$, right? Why? Think "slope of tangent line $\Rightarrow$ derivative". Thus,

$$y'(2) = \frac{4(4) - 8(12)}{16}$$

$$= -5$$

and the required slope has value -5.

Example 86. Let $y(x) = x^2 - \dfrac{6}{x - 4}$. Evaluate $y'(0)$.

Solution Now

$$y'(x) = \frac{d}{dx}(x^2) - 6\frac{d}{dx}(\frac{1}{x - 4})$$

(where we used Property (a), the Power Rule, and Consequence 1.)

$$= 2x - 6\left[\frac{-1}{(x - 4)^2}\frac{d}{dx}(x - 4)\right]$$

since $\dfrac{d}{dx}(\dfrac{1}{\boxed{x\text{-}4}}) = \dfrac{d}{dx}\left(\dfrac{1}{\square}\right) = \left(\dfrac{-1}{\square^2}\right)\square'$

where $\square = (x - 4)$.

All right, now

$$y'(x) = 2x + \frac{6}{(x - 4)^2},$$

and so

$$y'(0) = 2(0) + \frac{6}{(-4)^2},$$

$$= \frac{3}{8}.$$

Example 87. Let y be defined by $y(x) = \dfrac{4 - x^2}{x^2 - 2x - 3}$. Evaluate $y'(x)$ at $x = 1$.

Solution Write $y(x) = \dfrac{f(x)}{g(x)}$. We need $y'(1)$, right? OK, now we have the table …

$f(x)$	$f'(x)$	$g(x)$	$g'(x)$
$4 - x^2$	$-2x$	$x^2 - 2x - 3$	$2x - 2$

$$y'(1) = \frac{f'(1)g(1) - f(1)g'(1)}{(g(1))^2}$$

$$= \frac{(-2)(1 - 2 - 3) - (3)(2 - 2)}{(1 - 2 - 3)^2}$$

$$= \frac{8 - 0}{16}$$

$$= \frac{1}{2}.$$

EXAMPLES

Example 88.   Let y be defined by $y(x) = \dfrac{1.6}{(x+1)^{100}}$. Evaluate $y'(0)$.

Solution Write $y(x) = (1.6)(x+1)^{-100} = 1.6f(x)^{-100}$ where $f(x) = x+1$ (or, replace $f(x)$ by $\square$). Now use Property (a) and Consequence (2) to find that

$$
\begin{aligned}
y'(x) &= (1.6)(-100)f(x)^{-101} \cdot f'(x) \\
&= -160(x+1)^{-101} \cdot (1) \\
&= \frac{-160}{(x+1)^{101}},
\end{aligned}
$$

so $y'(0) = -160$.

On the other hand, you could have used Consequence (1) to get the result... For example, write $y(x)$ as $y(x) = \dfrac{1.6}{f(x)}$ where $f(x) = (x+1)^{100}$. Then

$$
\begin{aligned}
y'(x) &= \frac{-1.6}{(f(x))^2} \cdot f'(x) \qquad \text{(by Consequence(1))} \\
&= \frac{-1.6}{(x+1)^{200}}\left(100(x+1)^{99}(1)\right) \qquad \text{(by Consequence(2))} \\
&= \frac{-160}{(x+1)^{200}}(x+1)^{99} \\
&= \frac{-160}{(x+1)^{101}}
\end{aligned}
$$

and so $y'(0) = -160$, as before.

Example 89.   Let $y = u^5$ and $u = x^2 - 4$. Find $y'(x)$ at $x = 1$.

Solution Here $f(u) = u^5$ and $g(x) = x^2 - 4$. Now $f'(u) = 5u^4$ by the Power Rule and $g'(x) = 2x$... So,

$$
\begin{aligned}
y'(x) &= f'(u) \cdot g'(x) \\
&= 5u^4 \cdot 2x \\
&= 10xu^4 \\
&= 10x(x^2-4)^4, \quad \text{since } u = x^2 - 4.
\end{aligned}
$$

At $x = 1$ we get

$$
\begin{aligned}
y'(1) &= 10(1)(-3)^4 \\
&= 810.
\end{aligned}
$$

Since this value is 'large' for a slope the actual tangent line is very 'steep', close to 'vertical' at $x = 1$.

SHORTCUT

Write $y = \square^{\,5}$, then $y' = 5\,\square^{\,4}\,\square\,'$, by the Generalized Power Rule. Replacing the $\square$ by $x^2 - 4$ we find, $y' = 5\,(x^2-4)^4\,2x = 10x(x^2-4)^4$, as before.

The point is, you don't have to memorize another formula. The "Box" formula basically gives all the different variations of the Chain Rule.

Example 90.   Let $y = u^3$ and $u = (x^2 + 3x + 2)$. Evaluate $y'(x)$ at $x = 0$ and interpret your result geometrically.

Solution The Rule of Thumb is:

> Whenever you see a function raised to the power of some number (NOT a variable), then put everything "between the outermost parentheses", so to speak, in a box, $\square$. The whole thing then looks like just a box raised to some power, and you can use the box formulation of the Chain Rule on it.

Chain Rule approach: Write $y = u^3$ where $u = x^2 + 3x + 2$. OK, now $y = f(u)$ and $u = g(x)$ where $f(u) = u^3$ and $g(x) = x^2 + 3x + 2$. Then the Chain Rule gives

$$
\begin{aligned}
y'(x) &= f'(u)g'(x) \\
&= 3u^2 \cdot (2x + 3) \\
&= 3(x^2 + 3x + 2)^2 \, (2x + 3).
\end{aligned}
$$

Since $u = x^2 + 3x + 2$, we have to replace each u by the original $x^2 + 3x + 2$. Don't worry, you don't have to simplify this. Finally,

$$
\begin{aligned}
y'(0) &= 3(3)(2)^2 \\
&= 36
\end{aligned}
$$

and this is the slope of the tangent line to the curve $y = y(x)$ at $x = 0$.

Power Rule/Box approach: Write $y = \square^3$ where $\square = x^2 + 3x + 2$ and $a = 3$. Then

$$
\begin{aligned}
y'(x) &= 3\square^2 \cdot \square' \\
&= 3(x^2 + 3x + 2)^2(2x + 3)
\end{aligned}
$$

and so $y'(0) = 36$, as before.

Example 91. Let y be defined by $y(x) = (x + 2)^2(2x - 1)^4$. Evaluate $y'(-2)$.

Solution We have a product and some powers here. So we expect to use a combination of the Product Rule and the Power Rule. OK, we let $f(x) = (x + 2)^2$ and $g(x) = (2x - 1)^4$, use the Power Rule on f, g, and make the table:

$f(x)$	$f'(x)$	$g(x)$	$g'(x)$
$(x + 2)^2$	$2(x + 2)$	$(2x - 1)^4$	$4(2x - 1)^3(2)$.

Using the Product Rule,

$$
\begin{aligned}
y'(x) &= f'(x)g(x) + f(x)g'(x) \\
&= 2(x + 2)(2x - 1)^4 + 8(x + 2)^2(2x - 1)^3
\end{aligned}
$$

Finally, it is easy to see that $y'(-2) = 0$.

Example 92. Find an expression for the derivative of $y = \sqrt{f(x)}$ where $f(x) > 0$ is differentiable.

Solution OK, this 'square root' is really a power so we think "Power Rule". We can speed things up by using boxes, so write $\square = f(x)$. Then, the Generalized Power Rule gives us,

$$
y'(x) = \frac{d}{dx}\square^{\frac{1}{2}}
$$

$$= \frac{1}{2} \square^{\frac{1}{2}-1} \cdot \square' \quad \text{(PowerRule)}$$

$$= \frac{1}{2} \square^{-\frac{1}{2}} \square'$$

$$= \frac{1}{2\square^{\frac{1}{2}}} \square'$$

$$= \frac{\square'}{2\sqrt{\square}}$$

$$= \frac{f'(x)}{2\sqrt{f(x)}}$$

SNAPSHOTS

Example 93. $f(x) = (x^{2/3}+1)^2$, $f'(x)$?

Solution Let $\square = (x^{2/3}+1) = x^{2/3}+1$. So, $f(x) = \square^2$ and

$$f'(x) = \overbrace{(2) \cdot (x^{2/3}+1)^1}^{D(\square^2)} \cdot \overbrace{(2/3) \cdot x^{-1/3}}^{D(\square)}$$

$$= \frac{4}{3} \cdot (x^{2/3}+1) \cdot x^{-1/3}$$

$$= \frac{4}{3} \cdot (x^{1/3}+x^{-1/3}).$$

Example 94. $f(x) = \sqrt{\sqrt{x}+1}$. Evaluate $f'(x)$.

Solution Let $\square = (\sqrt{x}+1) = x^{1/2}+1$. Then $f(x) = \sqrt{\square}$ so

$$f'(x) = \overbrace{(1/2) \cdot (x^{1/2}+1)^{-1/2}}^{D(\sqrt{\square})} \cdot \overbrace{(1/2) \cdot x^{-1/2}}^{D(\square)}$$

$$= \frac{1}{4} \cdot (x^{1/2}+1)^{-1/2} \cdot x^{-1/2}$$

$$= \frac{1}{4\sqrt{x \cdot (1+\sqrt{x})}}$$

Example 95. $f(x) = \dfrac{\sqrt{x}}{\sqrt{1+x^2}}$. Find $f'(1)$.

Solution Simplify this first. Note that

$$\frac{\sqrt{x}}{\sqrt{1+x^2}} = \sqrt{\frac{x}{1+x^2}} = \square^{1/2}$$

where $\square = \dfrac{x}{1+x^2}$. So $f(x) = \sqrt{\square}$, and

$$f'(x) = \overbrace{(1/2) \cdot (\frac{x}{1+x^2})^{-1/2}}^{D(\sqrt{\square})} \cdot \overbrace{\frac{(x^2+1) \cdot 1 - (x) \cdot (2x)}{(1+x^2)^2}}^{D(\square)}$$

$$= (1/2) \cdot (\frac{x}{1+x^2})^{-1/2} \cdot \frac{1-x^2}{(1+x^2)^2}$$

$$= \frac{x^{-1/2} \cdot (1-x^2)}{2 (1+x^2)^{3/2}},$$

where we used the Generalized Power Rule to get $D(\sqrt{\square})$ and the Quotient Rule to evaluate $D(\square)$. So, $f'(1) = 0$.

Example 96. $f(x) = \pi \cdot \left(\dfrac{1}{x}\right)^{-2.718}$, where $\pi = 3.14159...$. Find $f'(1)$.

Solution Simplify this first, in the sense that you can turn negative exponents into positive ones by taking the reciprocal of the expression, right? In this case, note that $(1/x)^{-2.718} = x^{2.718}$. So the question now asks us to find the derivative of $f(x) = \pi \cdot x^{2.718}$. The Power Rule gives us $f'(x) = (2.718) \cdot \pi \cdot x^{1.718}$. So, $f'(1) = (2.718) \cdot \pi = 8.53882$.

Example 97. Find an expression for the derivative of $y = f(x^3)$ where f is differentiable.

Solution This looks mysterious but it really isn't. If you don't see an 'x' for the variable, replace all the symbols between the outermost parentheses by '$\square$'. Then $y = f(\square)$ and you realize quickly that you need to differentiate a composition of two functions. This is where the Chain Rule comes into play. So,

$$
\begin{aligned}
y'(x) &= Df(\square) \\
&= f'(\square) \cdot D\square \\
&= f'(x^3) \cdot \frac{d}{dx}(x^3) \text{ (because } \square = x^3) \\
&= f'(x^3) \cdot 3x^2
\end{aligned}
$$

> The Generalized Power Rule takes the form
> $$\frac{d}{dx}\square^r = r\,\square^{r-1}\frac{d}{dx}\square,$$
> where the box symbol, $\square$, is just another symbol for some differentiable function of x.

So, we have shown that any function f for which $y = f(x^3)$ has a derivative $y'(x) = 3x^2 f'(x^3)$ which is the desired expression. Remember that $f'(x^3)$ means that you find the derivative of f, and every time you see an x you replace it by x^3.

OK, but what does this $f'(x^3)$ really mean?

Let's look at the function f, say, defined by $f(x) = (x^2 + 1)^{10}$. Since $f(\square) = (\square^2 + 1)^{10}$ it follows that $f(x^3) = ((x^3)^2 + 1)^{10} = (x^6 + 1)^{10}$, where we replaced $\square$ by x^3 (or you put x^3 IN the box, remember the *Box method*?).

The point is that this new function $y = f(x^3)$ has a derivative given by

$$y'(x) = 3x^2 \cdot f'(x^3),$$

which means that we find $f'(x)$, replace each one of the x's by x^3, and simplify (as much as possible) to get $y'(x)$. Now, we write $f(\square) = \square^{10}$, where $\square = x^2 + 1$. The Generalized Power Rule gives us

$$
\begin{aligned}
f'(x) &= D(\square^{10}) = (10)\square^9\,(d\square) = (10)(x^2+1)^9\,(2x), \\
&= (20x)(x^2+1)^9. \text{ So,} \\
y'(x) &= 3x^2 \cdot f'(x^3) = (3x^2)\,(20\,x^3)\,(x^6+1)^9 \\
&= 60\,x^5(x^6+1)^9.
\end{aligned}
$$

Example 97 represents a, so-called, **transformation of the independent variable** (since the original 'x' is replaced by 'x^3') and such transformations appear within the context of **differential equations** where they can be used to simplify very difficult looking differential equations to simpler ones.

EXAMPLES

A Short Note on Differential Equations

More importantly though, examples like the last one appear in the study of **differential equations** which are equations which, in some cases called **linear**, look like polynomial equations

$$a_n x^n + a_{n-1}x^{n-1} + \ldots + a_1 x^1 + a_0 = 0$$

and each x is replaced by a symbol '$D = \frac{d}{dx}$' where the related symbol $D^n = \frac{d^n}{dx^n}$ means the operation of taking the nth derivative. This symbol, $D = \frac{d}{dx}$, has a special name: it's called a **differential operator** and its domain is a collection of functions while it range is also a collection of functions. In this sense, the concept of an operator is more general than that of a function. Now, the symbol D^2 is the derivative of the derivative and it is called the **second derivative**; the derivative of the second derivative is called the **third derivative** and denoted by D^3, and so on. The coefficients a_m above are usually given functions of the independent variable, x.

Symbolically, we write these **higher-order derivatives** using Leibniz's notation:

$$\frac{d^2 y}{dx^2} = \frac{d}{dx}\frac{dy}{dx} = y''(x)$$

for the **second derivative of y**,

$$\frac{d^3 y}{dx^3} = \frac{d}{dx}\frac{d^2 y}{dx^2} = y'''(x)$$

for the **third derivative of y**, and so on. These higher order derivatives are very useful in determining the graphs of functions and in studying a 'function's behavior'. We'll be seeing them soon when we deal with **curve sketching**.

Example 98.   Let f be a function with the property that $f'(x) + f(x) = 0$ for every x. We'll meet such functions later when we discuss Euler's constant, $e \approx 2.71828...$, and the corresponding exponential function.

Show that the new function y defined by $y(x) = f(x^3)$ satisfies the differential equation $y'(x) + 3x^2 y(x) = 0$.

Solution We use Example 97. We already know that, by the Chain Rule, $y(x) = f(x^3)$ has its derivative given by $y'(x) = 3x^2 \cdot f'(x^3)$. So,

$$y'(x) + 3x^2 y(x) = 3x^2 \cdot f'(x^3) + 3x^2 f(x^3)$$
$$= 3x^2(f'(x^3) + f(x^3))$$

But $f'(x) + f(x) = 0$ means that $f'(\triangle) + f(\triangle) = 0$, right? (Since it is true for any 'x' and so for any symbol '$\triangle$'). Replacing $\triangle$ by x^3 gives $f'(x^3) + f(x^3) = 0$ as a consequence, and the conclusion now follows ...

The function y defined by $y(x) = f(x^3)$, where f is any function with $f'(x) + f(x) = 0$, satisfies the equation $y'(x) + 3x^2 y(x) = 0$.

Example 99.   Find the second derivative $f''(x)$ given that $f(x) = (2x+1)^{101}$. Evaluate $f''(-1)$.

Solution We can just use the Generalized Power Rule here. Let $\square = 2x + 1$. Then $\square' = 2$ and so $f'(x) = 101 \cdot \square^{100} \cdot \square' = 101 \cdot \square^{100} \cdot 2 = 202 \cdot \square^{100}$. Doing this one more time, we find $f''(x) = (202) \cdot (100) \cdot 2 \cdot \square^{99} = 40,400 \cdot \square^{99} = 40,400 \cdot (2x+1)^{99}$.

Finally, since $(-1)^{\text{odd number}} = -1$, we see that $f''(-1) = 40,400 \cdot (-1)^{99} = -40,400$.

Example 100. Find the second derivative $f''(x)$ of the function defined by $f(x) = (1 + x^3)^{-1}$. Evaluate $f''(0)$.

Solution Use the Generalized Power Rule again. Let $\square = x^3 + 1$. Then $\square' = 3x^2$ and so $f'(x) = (-1) \cdot \square^{-2} \cdot \square' = (-1) \cdot \square^{-2} \cdot (3x^2) = -(3x^2) \cdot \square^{-2} = -(3x^2) \cdot (1 + x^3)^{-2}$. To find the derivative of THIS function we can use the Quotient Rule. So,

$$f''(x) = -\left\{ \frac{(1 + x^3)^2 \cdot (6x) - (3x^2) \cdot (2)(1 + x^3)^1 (3x^2)}{(1 + x^3)^4} \right\}$$

$$= \frac{-6x}{(1 + x^3)^2} + \frac{18x^4}{(1 + x^3)^3}$$

$$= \frac{6x \cdot (3x^3 - 1)}{(1 + x^3)^3}$$

It follows that $f''(0) = 0$.

Exercise Set 12.

Find the indicated derivatives.

1. $f(x) = \pi$, $f'(x) =$?

2. $f(t) = 3t - 2$, $f'(0) =$?

3. $g(x) = x^{\frac{2}{3}}$, $g'(x) =$? at $x = 1$

4. $y(x) = \sqrt{(x - 4)^3}$, $y'(x) =$?

5. $f(x) = \dfrac{1}{\sqrt{x^5}}$, $f'(x) =$?

6. $g(t) = \sqrt[3]{t^2 + t - 2}$, $g'(t) =$?

7. $f(x) = 3x^2$, $\dfrac{d^2 f}{dx^2} =$?

8. $f(x) = x(x + 1)^4$, $f'(x) =$?

9. $y(x) = \dfrac{x^2 - x + 3}{\sqrt{x}}$, $y'(1) =$?

10. $y(t) = (t + 2)^2 (t - 1)$, $y'(t) =$?

11. $f(x) = 16x^2 (x - 1)^{\frac{2}{3}}$, $f'(x) =$?

12. $y(x) = (2x + 3)^{105}$, $y'(x) =$?

13. $f(x) = \sqrt{x} + 6$, $f'(x) =$?

14. $f(x) = x^3 - 3x^2 + 3x - 1$, $f'(x) =$?

15. $y(x) = \dfrac{1}{x} + \sqrt{x^2 - 1}$, $y'(x) =$?

16. $f(x) = \dfrac{1}{1 + \sqrt{x}}$, $f''(x) =$?

17. $f(x) = (x - 1)^2 + (x - 2)^3$, $f''(0) =$?

18. $y(x) = (x + 0.5)^{-1.324}$, $y''(x) =$?

19. Let f be a differentiable function for every real number x. Show that $\dfrac{d}{dx} f(x^2) = 2x f'(x^2)$.

20. Let g be a differentiable function for every x with $g(x) > 0$. Show that
$$\frac{d}{dx}\sqrt[3]{g(x)} = \frac{g'(x)}{3\sqrt[3]{g(x)^2}}.$$

21. Let f be a function with the property that f is differentiable and
$$f'(x) + f(x) = 0.$$
Show that $y = f(x^2)$ satisfies the differential equation
$$y'(x) + 2xy(x) = 0.$$

22. Let $y = f(x)$ and assume f is differentiable for each x in $(0,1)$. Assume that f has an inverse function, F, defined on its range, so that $f(F(x)) = x$ for every $x, 0 < x < 1$. Show that F has a derivative satisfying the equation $F'(x) = \frac{1}{f'(F(x))}$ at each $x, 0 < x < 1$.
   (**Hint:** Differentiate both sides of $f(F(x)) = x$.)

23. Let $y = t^3$ and $t = \sqrt{u} + 6$. Find $\frac{dy}{du}$ when $u = 9$.

24. Find the equation of the tangent line to the curve $y = (x^2 - 3)^8$ at the point $(x, y) = (2, 1)$.

25. Given $y(x) = f(g(x))$ and that $g'(2) = 1, g(2) = 0$ and $f'(0) = 1$. What is the value of $y'(2)$?

26. Let $y = r + \frac{2}{r}$ and $r = 3t - 2\sqrt{t}$. Use the Chain Rule to find an expression for $\frac{dy}{dt}$.

27. **Hard.** Let $f(x) = \sqrt{x + \sqrt{x}}$. Evaluate $f'(9)$. If $x = t^2$, what is $\frac{df}{dt}$?

28. Use the definition of $\sqrt{x^2}$ as $\sqrt{x^2} = |x|$ for each x, to show that the function $y = |x|$ has a derivative whenever $x \neq 0$ and $y'(x) = \frac{x}{|x|}$ for $x \neq 0$.

29. **Hard** Show that if f is a differentiable at the point $x = x_0$ then f is continuous at $x = x_0$. (Hint: You can try a proof by 'contradiction', that is you assume the conclusion is false and, using a sequence of logically correct arguments, you deduce that the original claim is false as well. Since, generally speaking, a statement in mathematics cannot be both true **and** false, (aside from **undecidable statements**) it follows that the conclusion has to be true. So, assume f is not continuous at $x = x_0$, and look at each case where f is discontinuous (unequal one-sided limits, function value is infinite, etc.) and, **in each case**, derive a contradiction.)

   Alternately, you can prove this directly using the methods in the *Advanced Topics* chapter. See the Solution Manual for yet another method of showing this.

Suggested Homework Set 7. *Do problems 4, 10, 16, 23, 25, 27*

Web Links

For more information and applications of the Chain Rule see:

www.bacad.bridgton.me.us/banet/faculty/peterh/calculus/ch3/3_5.htm
www.hofstra.edu/~matscw/tutorials3/unit4_2.html
www.math.hmc.edu/calculus/tutorials/chainrule/
www.math.arizona.edu/~vector/Block2/der_rev/node3.html
gamba.ugrad.math.ubc.ca/coursedoc/math100/notes/derivative/chainap.html
math.ucdavis.edu/~kouba/CalcOneDIRECTORY/chainrulesoldirectory/
ChainRuleSol.html   (contains more than 20 solved examples)
albert.math.uiuc.edu/deriv4/deriv4.htm
www.npac.syr.edu/REU/reu94/williams/ch3/subsection3_5_1.html

For more information on the Power Rule see :

www.npac.syr.edu/REU/reu94/williams/ch3/subsection3_5_2.html
www.math.arizona.edu/~vector/Block2/der_rev/node2.html

NOTES:

3.4   Implicit Functions and Their Derivatives

You can imagine the variety of different functions in mathematics. So far, all the functions we've encountered had this one thing in common: You could write them as $y = f(x)$ (or $x = F(y)$) in which case you know that x is the independent variable and y is the dependent variable. We know which variable is which. Sometimes it is not so easy to see "which variable is which" especially if the function is written as, say,

$$x^2 - 2xy + tan(xy) - 2 = 0.$$

What do we do? Can we solve for either one of these variables at all? And if we can, do we solve for x in terms of y, or y in terms of x? Well, we don't always "have to" solve for any variable here, and we'll still be able to find the derivative so long as we agree on which variable x, or y is the independent one. Actually, Newton was the first person to perform an *implicit differentiation*. Implicit functions appear very often in the study of **general solutions** of differential equations. We'll see later on that the general solution of a *separable* differential equation is usually given by an implicit function. Other examples of implicit functions include the equation of closed curves in the xy-plane (circles, squares, ellipses, etc. to mention a few of the common ones).

In his *Method of Fluxions*, (1736), Isaac Newton was one of the first to use the procedure of this section, namely, *implicit differentiation*. He used his brand of derivatives though, things he called *fluxions* and he got into big trouble because they weren't well defined. In England, one famous philosopher by the name of **Bishop Berkeley** criticized Newton severely for his inability to actually explain what these fluxions really were. Neverthless, Newton obtained the right answers (according to our calculations). *What about Leibniz?* Well, even Leibniz got into trouble with his, so-called, *differentials* because he really couldn't explain this stuff well, either! His nemesis in this case was one **Bernard Nieuwentijt** of Amsterdam (1694). Apparently, neither Berkeley nor Nieuwentijt could put the Calculus on a rigorous foundation either, so, eventually the matter was dropped. It would take another 150 years until Weierstrass and others like him would come along and make sense out of all this Calculus business with rigorous definitions (like those in the Advanced Topics chapter).

Review

You should review the **Chain Rule** and the **Generalized Power Rule** in the preceding section. A mastery of these concepts and the usual rules for differentiation will make this section much easier to learn.

We can call our usual functions **explicit** because their values are given explicitly (i.e., we can write them down) by solving one of the variables in terms of the other. This means that for each value of x there is only one value of y. But this is the same as saying that y is a function of x, right? An equation involving two variables, say, x, y, is said to be an **explicit relation** if one can solve for y (or x) uniquely in terms of x (or y).

Example 101.   For example, the equation $2y = 2x^6 - 4x$ is an explicit relation because we can easily solve for y in terms of x. In fact, it reduces to the rule $y = x^6 - 2$ which defines a function $y = f(x)$ where $f(x) = x^6 - 2$. Another example is given by the function y whose values are given by $y(x) = x + \sqrt{x}$ whose values are easily calculated: Each value of x gives a value of $y = x + \sqrt{x}$ and so on, and y can be found directly using a calculator. Finally, $3x + 6 - 9y^2 = 0$ also defines an explicit relation because now we can solve for x in terms of y and find $x = 3y^2 - 2$.

In the same spirit we say that an equation involving two variables, say, x, y, is said to be an **implicit relation** if it is *not explicit*.

Example 102.   For example, the relation defined by the rule $y^5 + 7y = x^3 \cos x$ is implicit. Okay, you can isolate the y, but what's left still involves y and x, right? The equation defined by $x^2 y^2 + 4 \sin(xy) = 0$ also defines an implicit relation.

Such implicit relations are useful because they usually define a *curve* in the xy-plane, a curve which is not, generally speaking, the graph of a function. In fact, you can probably believe the statement that a "closed curve" (like a circle, ellipse, etc.) cannot be the graph of a function. Can you show why? For example, the circle defined by the implicit relation $x^2 + y^2 = 4$ is not the graph of a unique function, (think of the, so-called, Vertical Line Test for functions).

So, if y is 'obscured' by some complicated expression as in, say, $x^2 - 2xy + tan(xy) - 2 = 0$, then it is not easy to solve for 'y' given a value of 'x'; in other words, it would be very difficult to isolate the y's on one side of the equation and group the x's together on the other side. In this case y is said to be defined implicitly or y is an **implicit function** of x. By the same token, x may be considered an implicit function of y and it would equally difficult to solve for x as a function of y. Still, it is possible to draw its graph by looking for those points x, y that satisfy the equation, see Figure 45.

Other examples of functions defined implicitly are given by:

$$(x - 1)^2 + y^2 = 16 \qquad \text{A circle of radius 4 and center at } (1, 0).$$

$$\frac{(x-2)^2}{9} + \frac{(y-6)^2}{16} = 1 \qquad \text{An ellipse 'centered' at } (2, 6).$$

$$(x - 3)^2 - (y - 4)^2 = 5 \qquad \text{A hyperbola.}$$

OK, so how do we find the derivative of such 'functions' defined implicitly?

1. Assume, say y, is a differentiable function of x, (or x is a differentiable function of y).

2. Write $y = y(x)$ (or $x = x(y)$) to show the dependence of y on x, (even though we really don't know what it 'looks like').

3. Differentiate the relation/expression which defines y **implicitly** with respect to x (or y - *this expression is a curve in the xy-plane.*)

4. *Solve for the derivative $\frac{dy}{dx}$* **explicitly**, *yes, explicitly!*

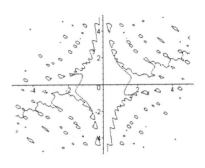

An approximate plot of the implicit relation

$x^2 - 2xy + tan(xy) - 2 = 0$.

This plot fails the "vertical line test" and so it cannot be the graph of a function.

Figure 45.

Note: It can be shown that the 4 steps above always **produce an expression for $\frac{dy}{dx}$ which can be solved explicitly**. In other words, even though y is given implicitly, the function $\frac{dy}{dx}$ is explicit, that is, given a point P(x, y) on the defining curve described in (3) *we can actually solve* for the term $\frac{dy}{dx}$.

This note is based on the assumption that we already know that y *can* be written as a differentiable function of x. This assumption isn't obvious, and involves an important result called the *Implicit Function Theorem* which we won't study here but which can be found in books on *Advanced Calculus*. One of the neat things about this implicit function theorem business is that it tells us that, under certain conditions, *we can always solve for the derivative dy/dx* even though we can't solve for y! Amazing, isn't it?

Example 103. Find the derivative of y with respect to x, that is, $\frac{dy}{dx}$, when x, y are related by the expression $xy - y^2 = 6$.

Solution We assume that y is a differentiable function of x so that we can write $y = y(x)$ and y is differentiable. Then the relation between x, y above really says that

$$xy(x) - y(x)^2 = 6.$$

OK, since this is true for all x under consideration (the x's were not specified, so don't worry) it follows that we can take the derivative of both sides and still get equality, *i.e.*

$$\frac{d}{dx}(xy(x) - y(x)^2) = \frac{d}{dx}(6).$$

Now, $\frac{d}{dx}(6) = 0$ since the derivative of a constant is always 0 and

$$\begin{aligned}\frac{d}{dx}(xy(x) - y(x)^2) &= \frac{d}{dx}\,xy(x) - \frac{d}{dx}\,y(x)^2 \\ &= \left[x\frac{dy}{dx} + y(x)\frac{d(x)}{dx}\right] - 2y(x)\frac{dy}{dx} \\ &= [x - 2y(x)]\frac{dy}{dx} + y(x)\end{aligned}$$

where we used a combination of the Product Rule and the Generalized Power Rule (see Example 92 for a similar argument). So, we have

$$[x - 2y(x)]\frac{dy}{dx} + y(x) = \frac{d}{dx}(6) = 0,$$

and solving for $\frac{dy}{dx}$ we get

$$\begin{aligned}\frac{dy}{dx} &= \frac{-y(x)}{x - 2y(x)}. \\ &= \frac{y(x)}{2y(x) - x}.\end{aligned}$$

OK, so we have found $\frac{dy}{dx}$ in terms of x and $y(x)$ that is, since $y = y(x)$,

$$\frac{dy}{dx} = \frac{y}{2y - x}$$

provided x and y are related by the original expression $xy - y^2 = 6$ which describes a curve in the xy-plane. This last display then describes the values of the derivative $y'(x)$ along this curve for a given point P(x,y) on it.

To find the slope of the tangent line to a point $P(x_0, y_0)$ on this curve we calculate

$$\frac{dy}{dx} = \frac{y_0}{2y_0 - x_0}$$

where $x_0 y_0 - y_0^2 = 6$, that's all. So, for example the point $(7, 1)$ is on this curve because $x_0 = 7, y_0 = 1$ satisfies $x_0 y_0 - y_0^2 = 6$. You see that the derivative at this point $(7, 1)$ is given by

$$\frac{dy}{dx} = \frac{1}{2(1) - 7} = -\frac{1}{5}$$

Example 104. Let $x^3 + 7x = y^3$ define an implicit relation for x in terms of y. Find $x'(1)$.

Solution We'll assume that x can be written as a differentiable function of y. We take the derivative of both sides (with respect to y this time!). We see that

$$3x^2\frac{dx}{dy} + 7\frac{dx}{dy} = 3y^2,$$

since

$$\frac{d}{dy}x^3 = 3x^2\frac{dx}{dy}$$

by the Generalized Power Rule. We can now solve for the expression dx/dy and find a formula for the derivative, namely,

$$\frac{dx}{dy} = \frac{3y^2}{3x^2 + 7}.$$

Now we can find the derivative easily at any point (x, y) on the curve $x^3 + 7x = y^3$. For instance, the derivative at the point $(1, 2)$ on this curve is given by substituting the values $x = 1, y = 2$ in the formula for the derivative just found, so that

$$\frac{dx}{dy} = \frac{(3)(2)^2}{(3)(1)^2 + 7} = \frac{12}{10} = \frac{6}{5}.$$

For a geometrical interpretation of this derivative, see Figure 46 on the next page.

> **Example 105.** Find the slope of the tangent line to the curve $y = y(x)$ given implicitly by the relation $x^2 + 4y^2 = 5$ at the point $(-1, 1)$.

Solution First, you should always check that the given point $(-1, 1)$ is **on** this curve, otherwise, there is nothing to do! Let $x_0 = -1, y_0 = 1$ and $P(x_0, y_0) = P(-1, 1)$. We see that $(-1)^2 + 4(1)^2 = 5$ and so the point $P(-1, 1)$ is on the curve.

Since we want the slope of a tangent line to the curve $y = y(x)$ at $x = x_0$, we need to find it's derivative $y'(x)$ and evaluate it at $x = x_0$.

OK, now

$$\frac{d}{dx}(x^2 + 4y(x)^2) = \frac{d}{dx}(5)$$

$$2x + 4\underbrace{\frac{d}{dx}(y(x)^2)}_{} = 0$$

$$2x + 4 \cdot 2y(x) \cdot y'(x) = 0$$

$$y'(x) = -\frac{2x}{8y(x)} = -\frac{x}{4y(x)}, \quad (\text{if } y(x) \neq 0)$$

and this gives the value of the derivative, $y'(x)$ at any point (x, y) on the curve, that is $y' = -\frac{x}{4y}$ where (x, y) is on the curve (remember $y = y(x)$). It follows that at $(-1, 1)$, this derivative is equal to

$$y'(-1) = (-1)\frac{(-1)}{4(1)} = \frac{1}{4}.$$

> **Example 106.** A curve in the xy-plane is given by the set of all points (x, y) satisfying the equation $y^5 + x^2y^3 = 10$. Find $\frac{dx}{dy}$ at the point $(x, y) = (-3, 1)$.

Solution Verify that $(-3, 1)$ is, indeed, on the curve. This is true since $1^5 + (-3)^2(1)^3 = 10$, as required. Next, we assume that $x = x(y)$ is a differentiable function of y. Then

$$\frac{d}{dy}(y^5 + x^2y^3) = \frac{d}{dy}(10)$$

$$5y^4 + 2x(y)\, x'(y)\, y^3 + x(y)^2(3y^2) = 0,$$

(where we used the Power Rule and the Product Rule). Isolating the term $x'(y) = \frac{dx}{dy}$ gives us the required derivative,

$$\frac{dx}{dy} = \frac{-3x^2y^2 - 5y^4}{2xy^3}.$$

When $x = -3, y = 1$ so,

$$\frac{dx}{dy} = \frac{-27 - 5}{-6} = \frac{16}{3}.$$

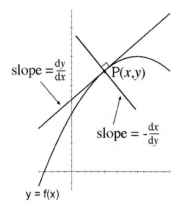

slope $= \frac{dy}{dx}$

$P(x,y)$

slope $= -\frac{dx}{dy}$

$y = f(x)$

Figure 46. *Geometric meaning of $\frac{dx}{dy}$*

Remark If we were to find $\frac{dy}{dx}$ at $(-3, 1)$ we would obtain $\frac{3}{16}$; the **reciprocal** of $\frac{dx}{dy}$. Is this a coincidence? No. It turns out that if y is a differentiable function of x and x is a differentiable function of y then their derivatives are related by the relation

$$\frac{dy}{dx} = \frac{1}{\frac{dx}{dy}}.$$

if $\frac{dx}{dy} \neq 0$, at the point P(x, y) under investigation. This is another consequence of the Implicit Function Theorem and a result on Inverse Functions.

O.K., we know what $\frac{dy}{dx}$ means geometrically, right ? Is there some geometric meaning for $\frac{dx}{dy}$? Yes, the value of $\frac{dx}{dy}$ at P(x, y) on the given curve is equal to the **negative of the slope of the line perpendicular to the tangent line through P.** For example, the equation of the tangent line through P$(-3, 1)$ in Example 106 is given by $y = (3x + 25)/16$, while the equation of the line perpendicular to this tangent line and through P is given by $y = (16x + 51)/3$. This last (perpendicular) line is called the **normal line** through P. See Figure 46.

Exercise Set 13.

Use implicit differentiation to find the required derivative.

1. $x^2 + xy + y^2 = 1$, $\frac{dy}{dx}$ at $(1, 0)$

2. $2xy^2 - y^4 = x^3$, $\frac{dy}{dx}$ and $\frac{dx}{dy}$

3. $\sqrt{x + y} + xy = 4$, $\frac{dy}{dx}$ at $(16, 0)$

4. $x - y^2 = 4$, $\frac{dy}{dx}$

5. $x^2 + y^2 = 9$, $\frac{dy}{dx}$ at $(0, 3)$

Find the equation of the tangent line to the given curve at the given point.

6. $2y^2 - x^2 = 1$,   at $(-1, -1)$

7. $2x = xy + y^2$,   at $(1, 1)$

8. $x^2 + 2x + y^2 - 4y - 24 = 0$,   at $(4, 0)$

9. $(x + y)^3 - x^3 - y^3 = 0$,   at $(1, -1)$

Suggested Homework Set 8. *Problems 1, 2, 4, 7, 9*

Web Links

For more examples on implicit differentiation see:

math.ucdavis.edu/~kouba/CalcOneDIRECTORY/implicitdiffdirectory/
gamba.ugrad.math.ubc.ca/coursedoc/math100/notes/derivative/implicit.html
(the above site requires a Java-enabled browser)

NOTES:

3.5 Derivatives of Trigonometric Functions

An integrated circuits board

Our modern world runs on electricity. In these days of computers, space travel and robots we need to have a secure understanding of the basic laws of electricity and its uses. In this realm, electric currents both alternating (as in households), and direct (as in a flashlight battery), lead one to the study of sine and cosine functions and their interaction. For example, how does an electric current vary over time? We need its 'rate of change' with respect to time, and this can be modeled using its derivative.

In another vein, so far we've encountered the derivatives of many different types of functions; polynomials, rational functions, roots of every kind, and combinations of such functions. In many applications of mathematics to physics and other physical and natural sciences we need to study combinations of trigonometric functions and other 'changes', the shapes of their graphs and other relevant data. In the simplest of these applications we can mention the study of **wave phenomena**. In this area we model incoming or outgoing waves in a fluid (such as a lake, tea, coffee, etc.) as a combination of sine and cosine waves, and then study how these waves change over time. Well, to study how these waves change over time we need to study their derivatives, right? This, in turn, means that we need to be able to find the derivatives of the sine and cosine functions and that's what this section is all about.

There are two fundamental limits that we need to recall here from an earlier chapter, namely

$$\lim_{x \to 0} \frac{\sin x}{x} = 1, \tag{3.2}$$

$$\lim_{x \to 0} \frac{1 - \cos x}{x} = 0, \tag{3.3}$$

Let's also recall some fundamental trigonometric identities in Table 3.4.

All angles, A, B and x are in **radians** in the Table above, and this is customary in calculus.

Recall that $1 \text{ } radian = \frac{180}{\pi} \text{ } degrees$.

> I1 $\sin(A + B) = \sin(A)\cos(B) + \cos(A)\sin(B)$
> I2 $\cos(A + B) = \cos(A)\cos(B) - \sin(A)\sin(B)$
> I3 $\sin^2 x + \cos^2 x = 1$
> I4 $\sec^2 x - \tan^2 x = 1$
> I5 $\csc^2 x - \cot^2 x = 1$
> I6 $\cos 2x = \cos^2 x - \sin^2 x$
> I7 $\sin 2x = 2\sin x \cos x$
> I8 $\cos^2 x = \frac{1 + \cos 2x}{2}$
> I9 $\sin^2 x = \frac{1 - \cos 2x}{2}$

Table 3.4: Useful Trigonometric Identities

The first result is that the derivative of the sine function is the cosine function, that is,

$$\frac{d}{dx}\sin x = \cos x.$$

This is not too hard to show; for example, assume that $h \neq 0$. Then

$$\frac{\sin(x+h) - \sin x}{h} = \frac{\sin x \cos h + \cos x \sin h - \sin x}{h}, \quad \text{(by I1)}$$

$$= \sin x \frac{\cos h - 1}{h} + \cos x \frac{\sin h}{h}, \text{(re-arranging terms)}$$

Now we use a limit theorem from Chapter 2: Since the last equation is valid for each $h \neq 0$ we can pass to the limit and find

$$\lim_{h\to 0} \frac{\sin(x+h) - \sin x}{h} = \sin x \lim_{h\to 0}(\frac{\cos h - 1}{h}) + \cos x \lim_{h\to 0}(\frac{\sin h}{h})$$

$$= (\sin x) \cdot (0) + (\cos x) \cdot (1), \quad \text{(by (3.3) and (3.2))}$$

$$= \cos x.$$

A similar derivation applies to the next result;

$$\frac{d}{dx}\cos x = -\sin x$$

For example,

$$\frac{\cos(x+h) - \cos x}{h} = \frac{\cos x \cos h - \sin x \sin h - \cos x}{h}, \quad \text{(by I2)}$$

$$= \cos x \frac{\cos h - 1}{h} - \sin x \frac{\sin h}{h}, \quad \text{(re} - \text{arranging terms)}$$

As before, since this last equation is valid for each $h \neq 0$ we can pass to the limit and find

$$\lim_{h\to 0} \frac{\cos(x+h) - \cos x}{h} = \cos x \lim_{h\to 0}(\frac{\cos h - 1}{h}) - \sin x \lim_{h\to 0}(\frac{\sin h}{h})$$

$$= (\cos x) \cdot (0) - (\sin x)(1), \quad \text{(by (3.3) and (3.2))}$$

$$= -\sin x.$$

Since these two limits define the derivative of each trigonometric function we get the boxed results, above.

OK, now that we know these two fundamental derivative formulae for the sine and cosine functions we can derive all the other such formulae (for $\tan, \cot, \sec,$ and $\csc$) using basic properties of derivatives.

For example, let's show that

$$\frac{d}{dx}\tan x = \frac{1}{\cos^2 x}$$

or, since $\frac{1}{\cos^2 x} = \sec^2 x$, we get

$$\frac{d}{dx}\tan x = \sec^2 x$$

as well. To see this we use the Quotient Rule and recall that since $\tan x = \frac{\sin x}{\cos x}$,

$$
\begin{aligned}
\frac{d}{dx} \tan x &= \frac{d}{dx}\left(\frac{\sin x}{\cos x}\right) \quad \text{(by definition)} \\
&= \frac{\cos x \frac{d}{dx}(\sin x) - (\frac{d}{dx}\cos x)\sin x}{\cos^2 x} \quad \text{(Quotient Rule)} \\
&= \frac{\cos^2 x + \sin^2 x}{\cos^2 x} \quad \text{(just derived above)} \\
&= \frac{1}{\cos^2 x} \quad \text{(by I3).}
\end{aligned}
$$

By imitating this argument it's not hard to show that

$$
\boxed{\frac{d}{dx}\cot x = -\frac{1}{\sin^2 x},}
$$

or, equivalently,

$$
\boxed{\frac{d}{dx}\cot x = -\csc^2 x}
$$

a formula which we leave to the reader as an **exercise**, as well.

There are two more formulae which need to be addressed, namely, those involving the derivative of the secant and cosecant functions. These are:

$$
\boxed{\begin{aligned}
\frac{d}{dx}\sec x &= \sec x \tan x \\
\frac{d}{dx}\csc x &= -\csc x \cot x
\end{aligned}}
$$

Each can be derived using the Quotient Rule. Now armed with these formulae and the Chain Rule we can derive formulae for derivatives of very complicated looking functions, see Table 3.5.

Example 107. Find the derivative of f where $f(x) = \sin^2 x + 6x$.

Solution The derivative of a sum is the sum of the derivatives. So

$$
\begin{aligned}
f'(x) &= \frac{d}{dx}(\sin x)^2 + \frac{d}{dx}(6x) \\
&= \frac{d}{dx}(\sin x)^2 + 6
\end{aligned}
$$

Now let $\square = \sin x$. We want $\frac{d}{dx}\square^2$ so we'll need to use the Generalized Power Rule here... So,

$$
\begin{aligned}
\frac{d}{dx}(\sin x)^2 &= \frac{d}{dx}\square^2 \\
&= 2\square^1 \frac{d\square}{dx} \quad \text{(Power Rule)} \\
&= 2\square\,\square' \\
&= 2(\sin x)(\cos x), \quad \text{(since } \square' = \cos x\text{)} \\
&= \sin 2x, \quad \text{(by I7)}
\end{aligned}
$$

The final result is $f'(x) = 6 + \sin 2x$.

Example 108. Evaluate $\dfrac{d}{dx}\sqrt{1+\cos x}$ at $x = 0$.

Solution We write $f(x) = \sqrt{1 + \cos x}$ and convert the root to a power (always do this so you can use the Generalized Power Rule).

We get $f(x) = (1 + \cos x)^{\frac{1}{2}} = \square^{\frac{1}{2}}$ if we set $\square = 1 + \cos x$ so that we can put the original function into a more recognizable form. So far we know that

$$f(x) = \sqrt{1 + \cos x} = \square^{\frac{1}{2}}$$

So, by the Power Rule, we get

$$f'(x) = \frac{1}{2}\square^{-\frac{1}{2}}\square'$$

where $\square'$ is the derivative of $1 + \cos x$ (**without** the root), *i.e.*

$$
\begin{aligned}
\square' &= \frac{d}{dx}(1 + \cos x) \\
&= \frac{d}{dx}(1) + \frac{d}{dx}(\cos x) \\
&= 0 - \sin x \\
&= -\sin x
\end{aligned}
$$

Combining these results we find

$$
\begin{aligned}
f'(x) &= \frac{1}{2}(1 + \cos x)^{-\frac{1}{2}}(-\sin x) \\
&= -\frac{\sin x}{2\sqrt{1 + \cos x}}
\end{aligned}
$$

after simplification. At $x = 0$ we see that

$$
\begin{aligned}
f'(0) &= -\frac{\sin 0}{2\sqrt{1 + \cos 0}} = -\frac{0}{2\sqrt{2}} \\
&= 0
\end{aligned}
$$

which is what we are looking for.

Example 109. Evaluate $\dfrac{d}{dx}\left(\dfrac{\cos x}{1 + \sin x}\right)$.

Solution Write $f(x) = \cos x$, $g(x) = 1 + \sin x$. We need to find the derivative of the quotient $\frac{f}{g}$ and so we can think about using the Quotient Rule.

Now, recall that

$$\frac{d}{dx}(f(g(x)) = \frac{f'(x)g(x) - f(x)g'(x)}{g(x)^2}$$

In our case,

$f(x)$	$f'(x)$	$g(x)$	$g'(x)$
$\cos x$	$-\sin x$	$1 + \sin x$	$\cos x$

Combining these results we find, (provided $1 + \sin x \neq 0$),

$$\frac{d}{dx}\left(\frac{\cos x}{1 + \sin x}\right) = \frac{(-\sin x)(1 + \sin x) - (\cos x)(\cos x)}{(1 + \sin x)^2}$$

Joseph Louis (Comte de) Lagrange, 1736 -1813, was born in Torino, Italy and died in Paris, France. His main contributions to mathematics were in the fields of analysis where he studied analytical and celestial mechanics, although he excelled in everything that he studied. In 1766, Lagrange became the successor of Euler in the Berlin Academy of Science, and during the next year he was awarded the first of his many prizes for his studies on the irregularities of the motion of the moon. He helped to found the Academy of Science in Torino in 1757, and the École Polytechnique in 1795. He also helped to create the first commission on *Weights and Measures* and was named to the *Legion d'Honneur* by Napoleon and elevated to Count in 1808.

$$= \frac{-\sin x - (\sin^2 x + \cos^2 x)}{(1 + \sin x)^2}$$

$$= -\frac{1 + \sin x}{(1 + \sin x)^2} \quad \text{(by I3)}$$

$$= -\frac{1}{1 + \sin x}.$$

Example 110. Let the function be defined by $f(t) = \dfrac{3}{\sin(t)}$. Evaluate $f'(\frac{\pi}{4})$.

Solution OK, we have a constant divided by a function so it looks like we should use the Power Rule (or the Quotient Rule, either way you'll get the same answer). So, let's write $f(t) = 3\square^{-1}$ where $\square = \sin(t)$ then

$$f'(t) = (-1) \cdot 3 \cdot \square^{-2} \square'$$

by the Generalized Power Rule. But we still need $\square'$, right? Now $\square = \sin(t)$, so $\square' = \cos t$. Combining these results we find

$$\begin{aligned} f'(t) &= -3(\sin t)^{-2}(\cos t) \\ &= -3\frac{\cos t}{(\sin t)^2}. \end{aligned}$$

Note that this last expression is also equal to $-3 \csc t \cot t$. At $t = (\frac{\pi}{4})$, (which is 45 degrees expressed in radians), $\cos(\frac{\pi}{4}) = \sin(\frac{\pi}{4}) = \frac{1}{\sqrt{2}}$ and so

$$\begin{aligned} f'(\tfrac{\pi}{4}) &= -3\frac{(\frac{1}{\sqrt{2}})}{(\frac{1}{\sqrt{2}})^2} = -3\frac{1}{\sqrt{2}} \cdot \frac{(\sqrt{2})^2}{1}, \\ &= -3\sqrt{2}. \end{aligned}$$

Note: Notice that we could have written $f(t) = \frac{3}{\sin(t)}$ as $f(t) = 3 \csc t$ and use the derivative formula for $\csc t$ mentioned above. This would give $f'(t) = -3 \csc t \cot t$ and we could then continue as we did above.

Example 111. Let's look at an example which can be solved in two different ways. Consider the implicit relation

$$y + sin^2 y + cos^2 y = x.$$

We want $y'(x)$.

The easy way to do this is to note that, by trigonometry (I3), $sin^2 y + cos^2 y = 1$ regardless of the value of y. So, the original relation is really identical to $y + 1 = x$. From this we observe that $dy/dx = 1$.

But what if you didn't notice this identity? Well, we differentiate both sides as is the case whenever we use implicit differentiation. The original equation really means

$$y + \{sin(y)\}^2 + \{cos(y)\}^2 = x.$$

Use of the Generalized Power Rule then gives us,

$$\frac{dy}{dx} + 2\{sin(y)\}^1 \frac{d}{dx} sin(y) + 2\{cos(y)\}^1 \frac{d}{dx} cos(y) = 1,$$

or

$$\frac{dy}{dx} + 2\{sin(y)\}^1 \cos(y)\frac{dy}{dx} + 2\{cos(y)\}^1(-sin(y))\frac{dy}{dx} = 1.$$

Derivatives of Trigonometric Functions: Summary

Let $\square$ denote any differentiable function, and D denote the operation of differentiation. Then

$$D \sin \square = cos\square \cdot D\square \qquad D\cos\square = -sin\square \cdot D\square$$
$$Dtan\square = \sec^2\square \cdot D\square \qquad D\cot\square = -csc^2\square \cdot D\square$$
$$D\sec\square = \sec\square \cdot \tan\square \cdot D\square \qquad D\csc\square = -\csc\square \cdot \cot\square \cdot D\square$$

Table 3.5: Derivatives of Trigonometric Functions

But the second and third terms cancel out, and we are left with

$$\frac{dy}{dx} = 1,$$

as before. Both methods do give the same answer as they should.

Example 112. Evaluate the following derivatives using the rules of this Chapter and Table 3.5.

     a) $f(x) = \sin(2x^2 + 1)$

     b) $f(x) = \cos 3x \sin \sqrt{x}$

     c) $f(t) = (\cos 2t)^2$, at $t = 0$

     d) $f(x) = \cos(\sin x)$ at $x = 0$

     e) $h(t) = \frac{t}{\sin 2t}$ at $t = \pi/4$

Solution   **a)** Replace the stuff between the outermost brackets by a box, $\square$. We want $D \sin \square$, right? Now, since $\square = 2x^2 + 1$, we know that $D\square = 4x$, and so Table 3.5 gives

$$\begin{aligned} D\sin\square &= \cos\square \cdot D\square \\ &= \cos(2x^2 + 1) \cdot 4x \\ &= 4x\cos(2x^2 + 1). \end{aligned}$$

b) We use a combination of the Product Rule and Table 3.5. So,

$$\begin{aligned} f'(x) &= D(\cos 3x) \cdot \sin \sqrt{x} + \cos(3x) \cdot D \sin \sqrt{x} \\ &= (-3 \cdot \sin(3x)) \cdot (\sin \sqrt{x}) + \cos(3x) \cdot \frac{\cos(\sqrt{x})}{2\sqrt{x}}, \end{aligned}$$

since $D \sin \sqrt{x} = \cos(\sqrt{x}) \cdot D(\sqrt{x}) = \cos(\sqrt{x}) \cdot ((1/2)\, x^{-1/2}) = \cos(\sqrt{x})/(2\sqrt{x})$.

c) Let $\square = \cos 2t$. The Generalized Power Rule comes to mind, so, use of Table 3.5 shows that

$$\begin{aligned} f'(t) &= 2\square \cdot D\square, \\ &= (2 \cdot \cos 2t) \cdot (-2 \cdot \sin 2t) \\ &= -4\cos 2t \sin 2t \\ &= -2\sin 4t, \qquad \text{(where we use Table 3.4, (I7), with } x = 2t). \end{aligned}$$

So $f'(0) = -2\sin(0) = 0$.

d) We need to find the derivative of something that looks like $\cos \square$. So, let $\square = \sin x$. We know that $D\square = D\sin x = \cos x$, and once again, Table 3.5 shows that

$$
\begin{aligned}
f'(x) &= -\sin \square \cdot D\square, \\
&= -\sin(\sin x) \cdot \cos x, \\
&= -\cos x \cdot \sin(\sin x).
\end{aligned}
$$

So $f'(0) = -\cos(0) \cdot \sin(\sin(0)) = -1 \cdot sin(0) = 0$.

e) We see something that looks like a quotient so we should be using the Quotient Rule, right? Write $f(t) = t$, $g(t) = \sin 2t$. We need to find the derivative of the quotient $\frac{f}{g}$. Now, recall that this Rule says that (replace the x's by t's)

$$
\frac{d}{dt}(f(g(t))) = \frac{f'(t)g(t) - f(t)g'(t)}{g(t)^2}.
$$

In our case,

$f(t)$	$f'(t)$	$g(t)$	$g'(t)$
t	1	$\sin 2t$	$2\cos 2t$

Substituting these values into the Quotient Rule we get

$$
\begin{aligned}
\frac{d}{dt}(f(g(t))) &= \frac{1 \cdot \sin 2t - t \cdot 2\cos 2t}{(\sin 2t)^2}, \\
&= \frac{\sin 2t - 2t\cos 2t}{(\sin 2t)^2}.
\end{aligned}
$$

At $\pi/4$, $\sin(\pi/4) = \sqrt{2}/2$, so, $\sin(2 \cdot \pi/4) = 1$, $\cos(2 \cdot \pi/4) = 0$, and the required derivative is equal to 1.

Exercise Set 14.

Evaluate the derivative of the functions whose values are given below, at the indicated point.

1. $\sin \sqrt{x}$, *at* $x = 1$

2. $\sec(2x) \cdot \sin x$

3. $\sin x \cos x$, *at* $x = 0$

4. $\dfrac{\cos x}{1 - \sin x}$

5. $\sqrt{1 + \sin t}$, *at* $t = 0$

6. $\sin(\cos(x^2))$

7. $x^2 \cdot \cos 3x$

8. $x^{2/3} \cdot \tan(x^{1/3})$

9. $\cot(2 + x + \sin x)$

10. $(\sin 3x)^{-1}$

11. $\dfrac{x + 1}{\sin x}$, *at* $x = \pi/2$

12. $\sin(2x^2)$

13. $\sin^2 x$, *at* $x = \pi/4$

14. $\cot(3x - 2)$

15. $\dfrac{2x + 3}{\sin x}$

16. $\cos(x \cdot \sin x)$

17. $\sqrt{x} \cdot sec(\sqrt{x})$

18. $\csc(x^2 - 2) \cdot \sin(x^2 - 2)$

19. $\cos^2(x - 6) + \csc(2x)$

20. $(\cos 2x)^{-2}$

21. Let y be defined by

$$y(x) = \begin{cases} \frac{\sin x}{\tan x} & x \neq 0 \\ 1 & x = 0 \end{cases},$$

a) Show that y is continuous at $x = 0$,

b) Show that y is differentiable at $x = 0$ and,

c) Conclude that $y'(0) = 0$.

Suggested Homework Set 9. *Do problems 1, 4, 6, 13, 20*

3.6   Important Results About Derivatives

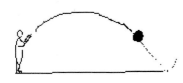

Figure 47.

This section is about things we call **theorems**. Theorems are truths about things mathematical ... They are statements which can be substantiated (or proved) using the language of mathematics and its underlying logic. It's not always easy to prove something, whether it be mathematical or not. The point of a 'proof' is that it makes everything you've learned 'come together', so to speak, in a more logical, coherent fashion.

The results here form part of the cornerstones of basic Calculus. One of them, the **Mean Value Theorem** will be used later when we define the, so-called, **antiderivative** of a function and the **Riemann integral**.

We will motivate this first theorem by looking at a sample real life situation.

A ball is thrown upwards by an outfielder during a baseball game. It is clear to everyone that the ball will reach a maximum height and then begin to fall again, hopefully in the hands of an infielder. Since the motion of the ball is 'smooth' (not 'jerky') we expect the trajectory produced by the ball to be that of a differentiable function (remember, there are no 'sharp corners' on this flight path). OK, now since the trajectory is differentiable (as a function's graph) there must be a (two-sided) derivative at the point where the ball reaches its maximum, right? What do you think is the value of this derivative? Well, look at an idealized trajectory... it has to be mainly 'parabolic' (because of gravity) and it looks like the path in the margin.

Tangent lines to the left (respectively, right) of the point where the maximum height is reached have positive (respectively, negative) slope and so we expect the tangent line to be horizontal at M (the point where the maximum value is reached). This is the key point, **a horizontal tangent line means a 'zero derivative' mathematically**. Why? Well, you recall that the derivative of f at a point x is the slope of the tangent line at the point $P(x, f(x))$ on the graph of f. Since a horizontal line has zero slope, it follows that the derivative is also zero.

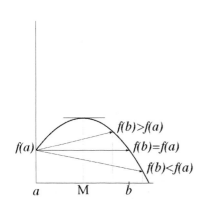

Figure 48.

OK, now let's translate all this into the language of mathematics. The curve has an equation $y = f(x)$ and the ball leaves the hand of the outfielder at a point a with a height of $f(a)$ (meters, feet, ... we won't worry about units here). Let's say that the ball needs to reach 'b' at a height $f(b)$, where $f(b) = f(a)$, above the ground. The fastest way of doing this, of course, is by throwing the ball in a straight line path from point to point (see Figure 48), but this is not realistic! If it were, the tangent line along this flight path would still be horizontal since $f(a) = f(b)$, right!?

So, the ball can't really travel in a 'straight line' from a to b, and will always reach a 'maximum' in our case, a maximum where necessarily $y'(M) = 0$, as there is a horizontal tangent line there, see Figure 48. OK, now let's look at all possible (differentiable) curves from $x = a$ to $x = b$, starting at height $f(a)$ and ending at height $f(b) = f(a)$, (as in Figure 49). We want to know "Is there always a point between a and b at which the curve reaches its maximum value ?"

A straight line from $(a, f(a))$ to $(b, f(b))$, where $f(b) = f(a)$, is one curve whose maximum value is the same everywhere, okay? And, as we said above, this is necessarily horizontal, so this line is the same as its tangent line (for each point x between a and b). As can be seen in Figure 49, all the 'other' curves seem to have a maximum value at some point between a and b and, when that happens, there is a horizontal tangent line there.

It looks like we have discovered something here: If f is a differentiable function on an interval $I = (a, b)$ (recall $(a, b) = \{x : a < x < b\}$) and $f(a) = f(b)$ then $f'(c) = 0$ for some c between a and b; *at least one* c, but there may be more than one. Actually, this mathematical statement is true! The result is called **Rolle's Theorem** and it is named after **Michel Rolle**, (1652-1719), a French mathematician.

Of course we haven't 'proved' this theorem of Rolle but it is believable! Its proof can be found in more advanced books in **Analysis**, a field of mathematics which includes Calculus.)

We will state it here for future reference, though:

Rolle's Theorem (1691)

Let f be a continuous function on $[a, b]$ and let f be differentiable at each point in (a, b). If $f(a) = f(b)$, then there is at least one point c between a and b at which $f'(c) = 0$.

Remark

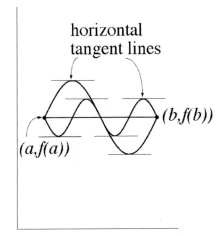

1. Remember that the point c, whose existence is guaranteed by the theorem, is not necessarily unique. There may be lots of them... but there is always **at least** one. Unfortunately, **the theorem doesn't tell us where it is** so we need to rely on graphs and other techniques to find it.

2. Note that whenever the derivative is zero it seems that the graph of the function has a 'peak' or a 'sink' at that point. In other words, such points appear to be related to where the graph of the function has a **maximum** or **minimum** value. This observation is very important and will be very useful later when we study the general problem of sketching the graph of a general function.

Figure 49.

| **Example 113.** | Show that the function whose values are given by $f(x) = \sin(x)$ |

on the interval $[0, \pi]$ satisfies the assumptions of Rolle's Theorem. Find the required value of c explicitly.

Solution We know that 'sin' as well as its derivative, 'cos', are continuous everywhere. Also, $\sin(0) = 0 = \sin(\pi)$. So, if we let $a = 0, b = \pi$, we see that we can apply Rolle's Theorem and find that $y'(c) = 0$ where c is somewhere in between 0 and π. So, this means that $\cos c = 0$ for some value of c. This is true! We can choose $c = \pi/2$ and see this c exactly.

We have seen Rolle's Theorem in action. Now, let's return to the case where the baseball goes from $(a, f(a))$ to $(b, f(b))$ but where $f(a) \neq f(b)$ (players of different heights!). **What can we say in this case?**

Well, we know that there is the straight line path from $(a, f(a))$ to $(b, f(b))$ which, unfortunately, does not have a zero derivative *anywhere* as a curve (see Figure 50). But look at all possible curves going from $(a, f(a))$ to $(b, f(b))$. This is only a thought experiment, OK? They are differentiable (let's assume this) and they bend this way and that as they proceed from their point of origin to their destination. Look at **how** they turn and compare this to the straight line joining the origin and destination. It looks like **you can always find a tangent line** to any one of these curves **which is parallel to the line joining $(a, f(a))$ to $(b, f(b))$**! (see Figure 51). It's *almost* like Rolle's Theorem (graphically) but it is **not** Rolle's Theorem because $f(a) \neq f(b)$. Actually, if you think about it a little, you'll see that it's more general than Rolle's Theorem. It has a different name ... and it too is a

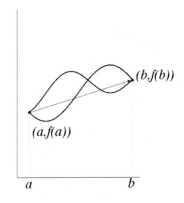

Figure 50.

true mathematical statement! We call it the **Mean Value Theorem** and it says the following:

Mean Value Theorem

Let f be continuous on the interval $a \leq x \leq b$ and differentiable on the interval $a < x < b$. Then there is a point c between a and b at which

$$\frac{f(b) - f(a)}{b - a} = f'(c).$$

Remark The number on the left of the equation, namely, $\frac{f(b)-f(a)}{b-a}$ is really the slope of the line pointing from $(a, f(a))$ to $(b, f(b))$. Moreover, $f'(c)$ is the slope of the tangent line through some point $(c, f(c))$ on the graph of f. Since **these slopes are equal**, the corresponding lines must be parallel, which is what we noticed above.

Example 114. Show that the function whose values are given by $f(x) = \cos 2x$ on the interval $[0, \pi/2]$ satisfies the assumptions of the Mean Value Theorem. Show that there is a value of c such that $\sin 2c = 2/\pi$.

Solution Here, '$\cos 2x$' as well as its derivative, '$-2\sin 2x$', are continuous everywhere. Also, $\cos(0) = 1$ and $\cos(\pi) = -1$. So, if we let $a = 0, b = \pi/2$, we see that we can apply Mean Value Theorem and find that $y'(c) = 0$ where c is somewhere in between 0 and $\pi/2$. This means that $-2\sin 2c = -4/\pi$, or for some value of c, we must have $\sin 2c = 2/\pi$. We may not know what this value of c is,

exactly, but it does exist! In fact, in the next section we'll show you how to find this value of c using **inverse trigonometric functions**.

Applications

Example 115. Let y be continuous in the interval $a \leq x \leq b$ and a differentiable function on an interval (a, b) whose derivative is equal to zero at each point x, $a < x < b$. Show that $y(x) = constant$ for each x, $a < x < b$. *i.e.* If $y'(x) = 0$ for all x then the values $y(x)$ are equal to one and the same number (or, y is said to be a **constant function**).

Solution This is one very nice application of the Mean Value Theorem. OK, let t be any point in (a, b). Since y is continuous at $x = a$, $y(a)$ is finite. Re-reading the statement of this example shows that all the assumptions of the Mean Value Theorem are satisfied. So, the quotient

$$\frac{y(t) - y(a)}{t - a} = y'(c)$$

where $a < c < t$ is the conclusion. But whatever c is, we know that $y'(c) = 0$ (by hypothesis, *i.e.* at each point x the derivative at x is equal to 0). It follows that $y'(c) = 0$ and this gives $y(t) = y(a)$. But now look, t can be changed to some **other** number, say, t^*. We do the same calculation once again and we get

$$\frac{y(t^*) - y(a)}{t^* - a} = y'(c^*)$$

where now $a < c^* < t^*$, and c^* is generally different from c. Since $y'(c^*) = 0$ (again, by hypothesis) it follows that $y(t^*) = y(a)$ as well. OK, but all this means that $y(t) = y(t^*) = y(a)$. So, we can continue like this and repeat this argument for every possible value of t in (a, b), and every time we do this we get that $y(t) = y(a)$. It follows that for **any** choice of t, $a < t < b$, we must have $y(t) = y(a)$. In other words, we have actually proved that $y(t) = constant \ (= y(a))$, for t in $a < t < b$. Since y is continuous at each endpoint a, b, it follows that $y(b)$ must also be equal to $y(a)$. Finally, we see that $y(x) = y(a)$ for every x in $[a, b]$.

Example 116. The function defined by $y = |x|$ has $y(-1) = y(1)$ but yet $y'(c) \neq 0$ for any value of c. **Explain why this doesn't contradict Rolle's Theorem.**

Solution **All** the assumptions of a theorem need to be verified **before** using the theorem's conclusion. In this case, the function f defined by $f(x) = |x|$ has no derivative at $x = 0$ as we saw earlier, and so the assumption that f *be differentiable over* $(-1, 1)$ is not true since it is not differentiable at $x = 0$. So, we can't use the Theorem at all. This just happens to be one of the many functions that doesn't satisfy the conclusion of this theorem. You can see that there's no contradiction to Rolle's Theorem since it doesn't apply.

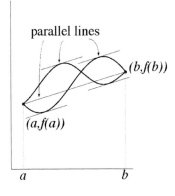

Figure 51.

Example 117. The function f is defined by

$$f(x) = \begin{cases} -x, & -2 \leq x \leq 0 \\ 1 - x, & 0 < x \leq 3. \end{cases}$$

In this example, the function f is defined on $[-2, 3]$ by the 2 curves in the graph and $\frac{f(3) - f(-2)}{3 - (-2)} = -\frac{4}{5}$ but there is no value of c, $-2 < c < 3$ such that $f'(c) = -\frac{4}{5}$, because $f'(c) = -1$ at every c except $c = 0$ where $f'(0)$ is not defined. **Does this contradict the Mean Value Theorem?**

Solution No, there is no contradiction here. Once again, all the assumptions of the Mean Value Theorem must be verified before proceeding to its conclusion. In this example, the function f defined above is not continuous at $x = 0$ because its left-hand limit at $x = 0$ is $f_-(0) = 0$, while its right-hand limit, $f_+(0) = 1$. Since these limits are different f is not continuous at $x = 0$. Since f is not continuous at $x = 0$, it cannot be continuous on **all** of $[-2, 3]$. So, we can't apply the conclusion. So, there's nothing wrong with this function or Rolle's Theorem.

Example 118. Another very useful application of the Mean Value Theorem/Rolle's Theorem is in the theory of differential equations which we spoke of earlier.

Let y be a differentiable function for each x in $(a, b) = \{x : a < x < b\}$ and continuous in $[a, b] = \{x : a \leq x \leq b\}$. Assume that y has the property that for every number x in (a, b),

$$\frac{dy}{dx} + y(x)^2 + 1 = 0.$$

Show that this function y cannot have two zeros (or roots) in the interval $[a, b]$.

Solution Use Rolle's Theorem and show this result by assuming the contrary. This is called a **a proof by contradiction**, remember? Assume that, if possible, there are two points A, B in the interval $[a, b]$ where $y(A) = y(B) = 0$. Then, by Rolle's Theorem, there exists a point c in (A, B) with $y'(c) = 0$. Use this value of c in the equation above. This means that

$$\frac{dy}{dx}(c) + y(c)^2 + 1 = 0,$$

Summary

Rolle's Theorem

Let f be continuous at each point of a closed interval $[a, b]$ and differentiable at each point of (a, b). If $f(a) = f(b)$, then there is a point c between a and b at which $f'(c) = 0$.

Remark Don't confuse this result with Bolzano's Theorem (Chapter 2). Bolzano's Theorem deals with the existence of a **root** of a continuous function f while Rolle's Theorem deals with the existence of a root of the *derivative* of a function.

Mean Value Theorem

Let f be continuous on the interval $a \leq x \leq b$ and differentiable on the interval $a < x < b$. Then there is a point c between a and b at which $\frac{f(b)-f(a)}{b-a} = f'(c)$.

Table 3.6: Rolle's Theorem and the Mean Value Theorem

right? Now, since $y'(c) = 0$, it follows that $y(c)^2 + 1 = 0$. But $y(c)^2 \geq 0$. So, this is an impossibility, it can never happen. This last statement is the contradiction. The original assumption that *there are two points A, B in the interval $[a, b]$ where $y(A) = y(B) = 0$* must be false. So, there can't be 'two' such points. It follows that y cannot have two zeros in $a \leq x \leq b$.

Remark This is a really interesting aspect of most differential equations: We **really don't know what '$y(x)$' looks like** either explicitly or implicitly but still, we can get some information about its graph! In the preceding example we showed that $y(x)$ could not have two zeros, for example. This sort of analysis is part of an area of differential equations called **"qualitative analysis"**.

Note The function y defined by $y(x) = \tan(c - x)$ where c is any fixed number, has the property that $\frac{dy}{dx} + y(x)^2 + 1 = 0$. If $c = \pi$, say, then $y(x) = \tan(\pi - x)$ is such a function whose graph is reproduced in Figure 52.

Note that this function has 'lots' of zeros! Why does this graph not contradict the result of Example 118? It's because on this interval, $[0, \pi]$ the function f is not defined at $x = \pi/2$ (so it not continuous on $[0, \pi]$), and so Example 118 does not apply.

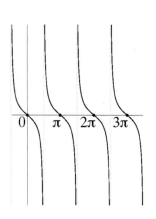

Figure 52.

Example 119. In a previous example we saw that if y is a differentiable function on $[a, b]$ and $y'(x) = 0$ for all x in (a, b) then $y(x)$ must be a constant function.

The same ideas may be employed to show that if y is a twice differentiable function on (a, b) (*i.e.* the derivative itself has a derivative), y and y' are each continuous on $[a, b]$ and if $y''(x) = 0$ for each x in (a, b) then $y(x) = mx + b$, for each $a < x < b$, for some constants m and b. That is, y must be a linear function.

Solution We apply the Mean Value Theorem to the function y' first. Look at the interval $[a, x]$. Then $\frac{y'(x)-y'(a)}{x-a} = y''(c)$ where $a < c < x$. But $y''(c) = 0$ (regardless of the value of c) so this means $y'(x) = y'(a) = constant$. Since x can be any

---

Intermediate Value Theorem

Let f be continuous at each point of a closed interval $[a, b] = \{x : a \leq x \leq b\}$. Assume,

    1. $f(a) \neq f(b)$

    2. z is a point between the numbers $f(a)$ and $f(b)$.

Then there is at least one value of c between a and b such that $f(c) = z$

Remark This result is very useful in finding the **root** of certain equations, or the points of intersection of two or more curves in the plane.

Bolzano's Theorem

Let f be **continuous on a closed interval** $[a, b]$ (i.e., at each point x in $[a, b]$).

If $f(a)f(b) < 0$, then there is at least one point c between a and b such that $f(c) = 0$. In other words there is at least one root of f in the interval (a, b).

Table 3.7: Main Theorems about Continuous Functions

number, $x > a$, and the *constant* above does not 'change' (it is equal to $y'(a)$), it follows that $y'(x) = y'(a)$ for **any** x in (a, b).

Now, apply the Mean Value Theorem to y, NOT y' ... Then

$$\frac{y(x) - y(a)}{x - a} = y'(c)$$

where $a < c < x$ (**not** the same c as before, though). But we know that $y'(c) = y'(a)$ (from what we just proved) so this means that $y(x) - y(a) = y'(a)(x - a)$ or

$$\begin{aligned} y(x) &= y'(a)(x - a) + y(a) \\ &= mx + b \end{aligned}$$

if we chose $m = y'(a)$ and $b = y(a) - ay'(a)$. That's all!

Two other big theorems of elementary Calculus are the Intermediate Value Theorem and a special case of it called Bolzano's Theorem, both of which we saw in our chapter on Limits and Continuity. We recall them here.

Example 120.   Show that there is a root of the equation $f(x) = 0$ in the interval $[0, \pi]$, where $f(x) = x \sin x + \cos x$.

Solution OK, what's this question about? The key words are 'root' and 'function' and at this point, basing ourselves on the big theorems above, we must be dealing with an application of **Bolzano's Theorem**, you see? (Since it deals with roots of functions, see Table 3.7.) So, let $[a, b] = [0, \pi]$ which means that $a = 0$ and $b = \pi$. Now the function whose values are given by $x \sin x$ is continuous (as it is the product of two continuous functions) and since '$\cos x$' is continuous it follows that $x \sin x + \cos x$ is continuous (as the sum of continuous functions is, once again continuous). Thus f is continuous on $[a, b] = [0, \pi]$.

What about $f(0)$? Well, $f(0) = 1$ (since $0 \sin 0 + \cos 0 = 0 + (+1) = +1$).

Bernhard Bolzano, 1781-1848, Czechoslovakian priest and mathematician who specialized in Analysis where he made many contributions to the areas of limits and continuity and, like Weierstrass, he produced a method (1850) for constructing a continuous function which has no derivative anywhere! He helped to establish the tenet that mathematical truth should rest on rigorous proofs rather than intuition.

And $f(\pi)$? Here $f(\pi) = -1$ (since $\pi \sin \pi + \cos \pi = 0 + (-1) = -1$).

So, $f(\pi) = -1 < 0 < f(0) = 1$ which means that $f(a) \cdot f(b) = f(0) \cdot f(\pi) < 0$. So, **all** the hypotheses of Bolzano's theorem are satisfied. This means that the conclusion follows, that is, there is a point c between 0 and π so that $f(c) = 0$.

> **Remark** Okay, but 'where' is the root of the last example?

Well, we need more techniques to solve this problem, and there is one, very useful method, called **Newton's method** which we'll see soon, (named after the same Newton mentioned in Chapter 1, one of its discoverers.)

Exercise Set 15.

Use Bolzano's theorem to show that each of the given functions has a root in the given interval. **Don't forget to verify the assumption of continuity in each case.** You may want to use your calculator.

In the first few exercises show 1) that the function is continuous, and 2) that there are two points a, b inside the given interval with $f(a)f(b) < 0$. Then use Bolzano's Theorem.

1. $y(x) = 3x - 2,\ 0 \le x \le 2$
2. $y(x) = x^2 - 1,\ -2 \le x \le 0$
3. $y(x) = 2x^2 - 3x - 2,\ 0 \le x \le 3$
4. $y(x) = \sin x + \cos x,\ 0 \le x \le \pi$
5. $y(x) = x \cos x + \sin x,\ 0 \le x \le \pi$
6. The function y has the property that y is three-times differentiable in (a, b) and continuous in $[a, b]$. If $y'''(x) = 0$ for all x in (a, b) show that $y(x)$ is of the form $y(x) = Ax^2 + Bx + C$ for a suitable choice of A, B, and C.
7. The following function y has the property that $\frac{dy}{dx} + y(x)^4 + 2 = 0$ for x in (a, b). Show that $y(x)$ cannot have two zeros in the interval $[a, b]$.
8. Use the Mean Value Theorem to show that $\sin x \le x$ for any x in the interval $[0, \pi]$.
9. Use Rolle's Theorem applied to the sine function on $[0, \pi]$ to show that the cosine function must have a root in this interval.
10. Apply the Mean Value Theorem to the sine function on $[0, \pi/2]$ to show that $x - \sin x \le \frac{\pi}{2} - 1$. Conclude that if $0 \le x \le \frac{\pi}{2}$, then $0 \le x - \sin x \le \frac{\pi}{2} - 1$.
11. Use a calculator to find that value c in the conclusion of the Mean Value Theorem for the following two functions:

    a) $f(x) = x^2 + x - 1,\ [a, b] = [0, 2]$

    b) $g(x) = x^2 + 3,\ [a, b] = [0, 1]$

    Hint In (a) calculate the number $\frac{f(b)-f(a)}{b-a}$ explicitly. Then find $f'(c)$ as a function of c, and, finally, solve for c.

12. An electron is shot through a 1 meter wide plasma field and its time of travel is recorded at 0.3×10^{-8} seconds on a timer at its destination. Show, using the Mean Value Theorem, that its velocity at some point in time had to **exceed the speed of light** in that field given approximately by 2.19×10^8 m/sec. (**Note** This effect is actually observed in nature!)

Suggested Homework Set 10. *Do problems 1, 3, 6, 8, 11*

3.7   Inverse Functions

One of the most important topics in the theory of functions is that of the **inverse of a function**, a function which is NOT the same as the reciprocal (or 1 divided by the function). Using this new notion of an inverse we are able to 'back-track' in a sense, the idea being that we interchange the domain and the range of a function when defining its inverse and points in the range get associated with the point in the domain from which they arose. These inverse functions are used everywhere in Calculus especially in the topic of finding the **area between two curves**, or calculating the **volume of a solid of revolution** two topics which we will address later. The two main topics in Calculus namely, differentiation and integration of functions, are actually related. In the more general sense of an **inverse of an operator**, these operations on functions are *almost* inverses of one another. Knowing how to manipulate and find inverse functions is a necessity for a thorough understanding of the methods in Calculus. In this section we will learn what they are, how to find them, and how to sketch them.

Review

You should be completely familiar with Chapter 1, and especially how to find the composition of two functions using the 'box' method or any other method.

We recall the notion of the **composition of two functions** here: Given two functions, f, g where the range of g is contained in the domain of f, (i.e., R=Ran(g) $\subseteq$ Dom(f)=D) we define the **composition of f and g**, denoted by the symbol $f \circ g$, a new function whose values are given by $(f \circ g)(x) = f(g(x))$ where x is in the domain of g (denoted briefly by D).

Example 121. Let $f(x) = x^2 + 1$, $g(x) = x - 1$. Find $(f \circ g)(x)$ and $(g \circ f)(x)$.

Solution Recall the box methods of Chapter 1. By definition, since $f(x) = x^2 + 1$ we know that $f(\square) = \square^2 + 1$. So,

$$f(\boxed{g(x)}) = \boxed{g(x)}^2 + 1 = \boxed{(x\text{-}1)}^2 + 1 = (x-1)^2 + 1 = x^2 - 2x + 2.$$

On the other hand, when the same idea is applied to $(g \circ f)(x)$, we get $(g \circ f)(x) = x^2$.

Note: This shows that the operation of **composition is not commutative**, that is, $(g \circ f)(x) \neq (f \circ g)(x)$, in general. The point is that **composition is not the same as multiplication**.

Let f be a given function with domain, D=Dom(f), and range, R=Ran(f). We say that the function **F is the inverse of f** if all these four conditions hold:

$$Dom(F) = Ran(f)$$
$$Dom(f) = Ran(F)$$
$$(F \circ f)(x) = x, \quad \text{for every x in Dom(f)}$$
$$(f \circ F)(x) = x, \quad \text{for every x in Dom(F)}$$

Thus, the inverse function's domain is R. The inverse function of f is usually written f^{-1} whereas the reciprocal function of f is written as $\frac{1}{f}$ so that $(\frac{1}{f})(x) = \frac{1}{f(x)} \neq f^{-1}(x)$. This is the source of much confusion!

Example 122. Find the composition of the functions f, g where $f(x) = 2x + 3$, $g(x) = x^2$, and show that $(f \circ g)(x) \neq (g \circ f)(x)$.

Solution Using the box method or any other method we find

$$(f \circ g)(x) = f(g(x)) = 2g(x) + 3 = 2x^2 + 3$$

while

$$(g \circ f)(x) = g(f(x)) = (f(x))^2 = (2x + 3)^2 = 4x^2 + 12x + 9$$

So we see that

$$(f \circ g)(x) \neq (g \circ f)(x)$$

as the two expressions need to be exactly the same for equality.

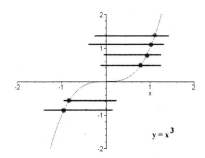

Figure 53.

Example 123. Show that the functions f, F defined by $f(x) = 2x + 3$ and $F(x) = \frac{x-3}{2}$ are inverse of one another. That is, show that F is the inverse of f and f is the inverse of F.

Solution As a check we note that $\text{Dom}(F) = \text{Ran}(f) = (-\infty, \infty)$ and

$$f(F(x)) = 2F(x) + 3 = 2(\frac{x-3}{2}) + 3 = x,$$

which means that $(f \circ F)(x) = x$. On the other hand, $\text{Dom}(f) = \text{Ran}(F) = (-\infty, \infty)$ and

$$F(f(x)) = \frac{f(x) - 3}{2} = \frac{(2x + 3) - 3}{2} = x,$$

which now means that $(F \circ f)(x) = x$. So, by definition, these two functions are inverse functions of one another.

EXAMPLES

How can we tell if a given function has an inverse function?. In order that two functions f, F be inverses of one another it is necessary that each function be **one-to-one** on their respective domains. This means that the **only** solution of the equation $f(x) = f(y)$ (resp. $F(x) = F(y)$) is the solution $x = y$, whenever x, y are in $\text{Dom}(f)$, (resp. $\text{Dom}(F)$). The simplest geometrical test for deciding whether a given function is one-to-one is the so-called *Horizontal Line Test*. Basically, one looks at the graph of the given function on the xy-plane, and if every horizontal line through the range of the function intersects the graph at only one point, then the function is one-to-one and so it has an inverse function, see Figure 53. The moral here is "Not every function has an inverse function, only those that are one-to-one!"

Example 124. Show that the function $f(x) = x^2$ has no inverse function if we take its domain to be the interval $[-1, 1]$.

Solution This is because the Horizontal Line Test shows that every horizontal line through the range of f intersects the curve at two points (except at $(0,0)$, see Figure 54). Since the Test fails, f is not one-to-one and this means that f cannot have an inverse. Can you show that this function **does have an inverse** if its domain is restricted to the smaller interval $[0, 1]$?

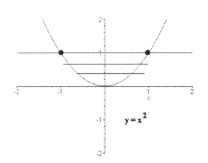

Figure 54.

Example 125. Find the form of the inverse function of the function f defined by $f(x) = 2x + 3$, where x is real.

> **How to find the inverse of a function**
>
> 1. • Write $y = f(x)$
>
>   • Solve for x in terms of y
>
>   • Then $x = F(y)$ where F is the inverse.
>
> 2. Interchange the x's and y's.
>
>   Solve for the symbol y in terms of x.
>
>   • This gives $y = F(x)$ where F is the inverse.
>
> It follows that the graph of the inverse function, F, is obtained by reflecting the graph of f about the line $y = x$. More on this later.

Table 3.8: How to Find the Inverse of a Function

Solution Use Table 3.8. Write $y = f(x) = 2x + 3$. We solve for x in terms of y. Then

$$y = 2x + 3 \; means \; x = \frac{y-3}{2} = F(y).$$

Now interchange x and y. So the inverse of f is given by F where $F(x) = \dfrac{x-3}{2}$.

Example 126. $f(x) = x^4$, $x \geq 0$, what is its inverse function $F(x)$ (also denoted by $f^{-1}(x)$) ?

Solution Let's use Table 3.8, once again. Write $y = x^4$. From the graph of f (Figure 55) we see that it is one-to-one if $x \geq 0$. Solving for x in terms of y, we get $x = \sqrt[4]{y}$ since x is real, and $y \geq 0$. So $f^{-1}(y) = F(y) = \sqrt[4]{y}$ or $f^{-1}(x) = F(x) = \sqrt[4]{x}$ is the inverse function of f.

Example 127. If $f(x) = x^3 + 1$, what is its inverse function, $f^{-1}(x)$?

Solution We solve for x in terms of y, as usual. Since $y = x^3 + 1$ we know $y - 1 = x^3$ or $x = \sqrt[3]{y-1}$ (and y can be *any* real number here). Interchanging x and y we get $y = \sqrt[3]{x-1}$, or $f^{-1}(x) = \sqrt[3]{x-1}$, or $F(x) = \sqrt[3]{x-1}$

The **derivative of the inverse function** f^{-1} of a given function f is related to the derivative of f by means of the next formula

$$\frac{dF}{dx}(x) = \frac{df^{-1}}{dx}(x) = \frac{1}{f'(f^{-1}(x))} = \frac{1}{f'(F(x))} \qquad (3.4)$$

where the symbol $f'(f^{-1}(x))$ means that the derivative of f is evaluated at the point $f^{-1}(x)$, where x is given. **Why?**

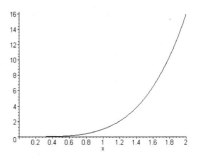

The graph of $f(x) = x^4$. If $x \geq 0$ this function is one-to-one. It is not true that f is one-to-one if the domain of f contains negative points, since in this case there are horizontal lines that intersect the graph in TWO points.

Figure 55.

The simplest reason is that the Chain Rule tells us that since $f(F(x)) = x$ we can differentiate the composition on the left using the Box Method (with $F(x)$ in the box...). By the Chain Rule we know that

$$Df(\Box) = f'(\Box) \cdot D(\Box).$$

Applying this to our definition of the inverse of f we get

$$\begin{aligned} x &= f(F(x)) \\ Dx &= Df(F(x)) = Df(\Box) \\ 1 &= f'(\Box) \cdot D(\Box) \\ &= f'(F(x)) \cdot F'(x). \end{aligned}$$

Now solving for the symbol $F'(x)$ in the last display (because this is what we want) we obtain

$$F'(x) = \frac{1}{f'(F(x))},$$

where $F(x) = f^{-1}(x)$ is the inverse of the original function $f(x)$. This proves our claim.

Another, more geometrical, argument proceeds like this: Referring to Figure 56 in the margin let (x, y) be a point on the graph of $y = f^{-1}(x)$. We can see that the tangent line to the graph of f has equation $y = mx + b$ where m, its slope, is also the derivative of f at the point in question (*i.e.*, $f'(y)$). On the other hand, its reflection is obtained by interchanging x, y, and so the equation of its counterpart (on the other side of $y = x$) is $x = my + b$. Solving for y in terms of x in this one we get $y = \frac{x}{m} - \frac{b}{m}$. This means that *it* has slope equal to the reciprocal of the first one. Since these slopes are actually derivatives this means that

$$(f^{-1})'(x) = \frac{1}{f'(y)} = \frac{1}{f'(f^{-1}(x))}$$

since our point (x, y) lies on the graph of the inverse function, $y = f^{-1}(x)$.

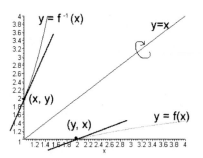

The two tangents are reflections of one another, and so their slopes must be the reciprocal of one another (see the text).

Figure 56.

Example 128. For Example 126 above, what is $\dfrac{df^{-1}}{dx}(16)$? i.e., the derivative of the inverse function of f at $x = 16$?

Solution Using Equation 3.4, we have

$$(f^{-1})'(16) = \frac{1}{f'(f^{-1}(16))}$$

But $f^{-1}(x) = \sqrt[4]{x}$ means that $f^{-1}(16) = \sqrt[4]{16} = 2$. So, $(f^{-1})'(16) = \frac{1}{f'(2)}$ and now we need $f'(2)$. But $f(x) = x^4$, so $f'(2) = 4(2)^3 = 32$. Finally, we find that $(f^{-1})'(16) = \frac{1}{32}$.

Example 129. A function f with an inverse function denoted by F has the property that $F(0) = 1$ and $f'(1) = 0.2$. Calculate the value of $F'(0)$.

Solution We don't have much given here but yet we can actually find the answer as follows: Since

$$F'(0) = \frac{1}{f'(F(0))}$$

by (3.4) with $x = 0$, we set $F(0) = 1$, and note that $f'(F(0)) = f'(1)$. But since $f'(1) = 0.2$ we see that

$$F'(0) = \frac{1}{f'(F(0))} = \frac{1}{f'(1)} = \frac{1}{0.2} = 5.$$

Example 130. Let g be a function defined by

$$g(x) = \frac{x+2}{x-2}$$

with $Dom(g) = \{x : x \neq 2\}$. Show that g has an inverse function, G, find its form, and describe its Domain and Range.

Solution Let's denote its inverse function by G. The first question you should be asking yourself is: "How do we know that there *is* an inverse function at all?" In other words, we have to show that the graph of g satisfies the *Horizontal Line Test* mentioned above (see Fig. 53), or, in other words, g is one-to-one. To do this we can do one of two things: We can either draw the graph as in Fig. 57 (if you have that much patience), or check the condition algebraically by showing that if $g(x) = g(y)$ then $x = y$ must be true (for any points x, y in the domain of g). Since the graph is already given in the margin we are done, but let's look at this using the algebraic test mentioned here.

In order to prove that g is one-to-one algebraically, we have to show that if $g(x) = g(y)$ then $x = y$. Basically, we use the definitions, perform some algebra, simplify and see if we get $x = y$ at the end. If we do, we're done. Let's see.

We assume that $g(x) = g(y)$ (here y is thought of as an independent variable, just like x). Then, by definition, this means that

$$\frac{x+2}{x-2} = \frac{y+2}{y-2}$$

for $x, y \neq 2$. Multiplying both sides by $(x-2)(y-2)$ we get $(x+2)(y-2) = (y+2)(x-2)$. Expanding these expressions we get

$$xy + 2y - 2x - 4 = yx + 2x - 2y - 4$$

from which we easily see that $x = y$. That's all. So g is one-to-one. Thus, its inverse function G exists.

Next, to find its values, $G(x)$, we replace all the x's by y's and solve for y in terms of x, (cf., Table 3.8). Replacing all the x's by y's (and the only y by x) we get

$$x = \frac{y+2}{y-2}.$$

Multiplying both sides by $(y-2)$ and simplifying we get

$$y = \frac{2x+2}{x-1}.$$

This is $G(x)$. Its domain is $Dom(G) = \{x : x \neq 1\} = Ran(g)$ while its range is given by $Ran(G) = Dom(g) = \{x : x \neq 2\}$ by definition of the inverse.

Now that **we know how to find the form of the inverse** of a given (one-to-one) function, the natural question is: "What does it look like?". Of course, it is simply another one of those graphs whose shape may be predicted by means of existing computer software or by the old and labor intensive method of finding the critical points of the function, the asymptotes, etc. So, *why worry about the graph of an inverse function?* Well, one reason is that the **graph of an inverse function is related to the graph of the original function** (that is, the one for which it is the inverse). How? Let's have a look at an example.

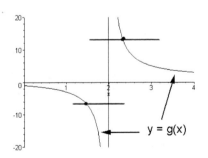

The graph of the function g in Example 130. Note that any horizontal line intersects the graph of g in only one point! This means that g is one-to-one on its domain. The vertical line across the point $x = 2$ is called a vertical asymptote (a line on which the function becomes infinite). More on this in Chapter 5.

Figure 57.

Example 131.   Let's look at the graph of the function $f(x) = \sqrt{x}$, for x in $(0,4)$, and its inverse, the function, $F(x) = x^2$, for x in $(0,2)$, Figure 58.

When we study these graphs carefully, we note, by definition of the inverse function, that the **domain and the range are interchanged.** So, this means that if we interchanged the x-axis (on which lies the domain of f) and the y-axis, (on which we find the range of f) we would be in a position to graph the inverse function of f. This graph of the inverse function is simply the reflection of the graph for $y = \sqrt{x}$, about the line $y = x$. Try it out ! Better still, check out the following experiment!

EXPERIMENT:

1. Make a copy of the graph of $f(x) = \sqrt{x}$, below, by tracing it onto some **tracing paper** (so that you can see the graph from both sides). Label the axes, and fill in the domain and the range of f by thickening or thinning the line segment containing them, or, if you prefer, by colouring them in.

2. Now, **turn the traced image around, clockwise, by 90 degrees** so that the x-axis is vertical (but pointing down) and the y-axis is horizontal (and pointing to the right).

3. Next, **flip the paper over onto its back** without rotating the paper! **What do you see? The graph of the inverse function** of $f(x) = \sqrt{x}$, that is, $F(x) = x^2$.

REMARK This technique of making the graph of the inverse function by rotating the original graph clockwise by 90 degrees and then flipping it over always works! You will **always** get the graph of the inverse function on the back side (verso), as if it had been sketched on the x and y axes as usual (once you interchange x and y). Here's a visual summary of the construction ...

The graph of a function and its inverse

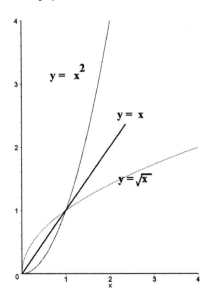

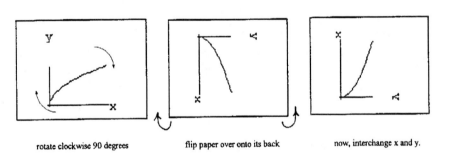

rotate clockwise 90 degrees   flip paper over onto its back   now, interchange x and y.

Why does this work? Well, there's some *Linear Algebra* involved. (The author's module entitled *The ABC's of Calculus: Module on Inverse Functions* has a thorough explanation!)

We summarize the above in this

Figure 58. *The graphs of $y = x^2$ and its inverse, $y = \sqrt{x}$ superimposed on one another*

> **RULE OF THUMB.** We can always find the graph of the inverse function by applying the above construction to the original graph
>
> or, equivalently,
>
> by reflecting the original graph of f about the line $y = x$ and eliminating the original graph.

Example 132. We sketch the graphs of the function f, and its inverse, F, given by $f(x) = 7x + 4$ and $F(x) = \frac{x-4}{7}$, where $Dom(f) = \Re$, where $\Re = (-\infty, +\infty)$. The graphs of f and its inverse superimposed on the same axes are shown in Figure 59.

NOTE THAT if you are **given the graph of the inverse function**, $F(x)$, of a function $f(x)$, you can **find the graph of** $f(x)$ by applying the preceding "rule of thumb" with f and F interchanged. Furthermore, the inverse of the inverse function of a function f (so, we're looking for the inverse) is f itself. Why? Use the definition of the inverse! We know that $F(f(x)) = x$, for each x in $Dom(f)$, and $x = f(F(x))$ for each x in $Dom(F)$; together, these relations say that "F is the inverse of f". If we interchange the symbols 'F' and 'f' in this equation we get the **same** equation with the interpretation "f is the inverse of F", which is what we wanted!

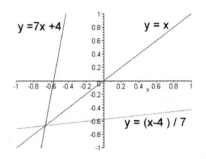

Figure 59. *The graphs of* $f(x) = 7x + 4$ *and its inverse* $F(x) = \frac{x-4}{7}$ *superimposed on one another.*

Exercise Set 16.

Sketch the graphs of the following functions and their inverses. Don't forget to indicate the domain and the range of each function.

1. $f(x) = 4 - x^2$, $0 \le x \le 2$

2. $g(x) = (x - 1)^{-1}$, $1 < x < \infty$

3. $f(z) = 2 - x^3$, $-\infty < x < \infty$

4. $h(x) = \sqrt{5 + 2x}$, $-\frac{5}{2} \le x < \infty$

5. $f(y) = (2 + y)^{\frac{1}{3}}$, $-2 < y < \infty$

6. Let f be a function with domain $D = \Re$. Assume that f has an inverse function, F, defined on $\Re$ (another symbol for the real line) also.

   (i) Given that $f(2) = 0$, what is $F(0)$?

   (ii) If $F(6) = -1$, what is $f(-1)$?

   (iii) Conclude that the only solution of $f(x) = 0$ is $x = 2$.

   (iv) Given that $f(-2) = 8$, what is the solution y, of $F(y) = -2$? Are there any other solutions ??

   (v) We know that $f(-1) = 6$. Are there any other points, x, such that $f(x) = 6$?

7. Given that f is such that its inverse F exists, $f'(-2.1) = 4$, $F(-1) = -2.1$, find the value of the derivative of F at $x = -1$.

Find the form of the inverse of the given functions on the given domain and determine the Domain and the Range of the inverse function. Don't forget to show that each is one-to-one first.

8. $f(x) = x, \quad -\infty < x < +\infty$

9. $f(x) = \dfrac{1}{x}, \quad x \neq 0$

10. $f(x) = x^3, \quad -\infty < x < +\infty$

11. $f(t) = 7t + 4, \quad 0 \leq t \leq 1$

12. $g(x) = \sqrt{2x+1}, \quad x \geq -\dfrac{1}{2}$

13. $g(t) = \sqrt{1 - 4t^2}, \quad 0 \leq t \leq \dfrac{1}{2}$

14. $f(x) = \dfrac{2 + 3x}{3 - 2x}, \quad x \neq \dfrac{3}{2}$

15. $g(y) = y^2 + y, \quad -\dfrac{1}{2} \leq y < +\infty$

Suggested Homework Set 11. *Work out problems 3, 5, 6, 8, 12, 15.*

Web Links

More on Inverse Functions at:

library.thinkquest.org/2647/algebra/ftinvers.htm
(requires a Java-enabled browser)
www.sosmath.com/algebra/invfunc/fnc1.html
linux11.ma.utexas.edu/users/lane/305/handouts/inverse/node1.html
www.math.wpi.edu/Course_Materials/MA1022B95/lab3/node5.html
(The above site uses the software "Maple")
www.math.duke.edu/education/ccp/materials/intcalc/inverse/index.html
www.math.armstrong.edu/MathTutorial/exerciseStatements/
Inverse%20Functions/Inverse%20Functions.html
www.aae.wisc.edu/aae421/421week9/sld007.htm
www.mathstat.uoguelph.ca/courses/offerings/math108/modules/module5.html

NOTES:

3.8 Inverse Trigonometric Functions

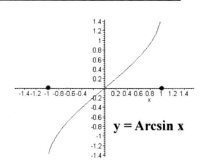

y = Arcsin x

When you think of the graph of a trigonometric function you may have the general feeling that it's very *wavy*. In this case, the Horizontal Line Test should fail as horizontal lines through the range will intersect the graph quite a lot! So, how can they have an inverse? The only way this can happen is by making the domain 'small enough'. It shouldn't be surprising if it has an inverse on a suitable interval. So, every trigonometric function has an inverse on a suitably defined interval.

At this point we introduce the notion of the **inverse of a trigonometric function**. The graphical properties of the sine function indicate that it has an inverse when $\text{Dom}(\sin) = [-\pi/2, \pi/2]$. Its inverse is called the **Arcsine function** and it is defined for $-1 \leq x \leq 1$ by the rule that

$$y = \underline{Arcsin}(\underline{x}) \text{ means that } y \text{ is an \underline{an}gle whose \underline{sine} is } \underline{x}.$$

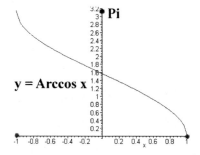

y = Arccos x

Since $\sin(\pi/2) = 1$, it follows that $Arcsin(1) = \pi/2$. The cosine function with $\text{Dom}(\cos) = [0, \pi]$ also has an inverse and it's called the **Arccosine function**, This Arccosine function is defined for $-1 \leq x \leq 1$, and its rule is given by $y = Arccos(x)$ which means that y is an angle whose cosine is x. Thus, $Arccos(1) = 0$, since $\cos(0) = 1$. Finally, the tangent function defined on $(-\pi/2, \pi/2)$ has an inverse called the **Arctangent function** and it's defined on the interval $(-\infty, +\infty)$ by the statement that $y = Arctan(x)$ only when y is an angle in $(-\pi/2, \pi/2)$ whose tangent is x. In particular, since $\tan(\pi/4) = 1$, $Arctan(1) = \pi/4$.

The remaining inverse trigonometric functions can be defined by the relations $y = Arccot(x)$, the **Arccotangent function**, which is defined only when y is an angle in $(0, \pi)$ whose cotangent is x (and x is in $(-\infty, +\infty)$). In particular, since $\cot(\pi/2) = 0$, we see that $Arccot(0) = \pi/2$. Furthermore, $y = Arcsec(x)$, the **Arcsecant function**, only when y is an angle in $[0, \pi]$, different from $\pi/2$, whose secant is x (and x is outside the open interval $(-1, 1)$). In particular, $Arcsec(1) = 0$, since $\sec(0) = 1$. Finally, $y = Arccsc(x)$, the **Arccosecant function**, only when y is an angle in $[-\pi/2, \pi/2]$, different from 0, whose cosecant is x (and x is outside the open interval $(-1, 1)$). In particular, since $\csc(\pi/2) = 1$, $Arccsc(1) = \pi/2$.

NOTE: sin, cos are defined for all x (**in radians**) but this is **not true** for their 'inverses', arcsin (or *Arcsin*), arccos (or *Arccos*). Remember that the inverse of a function is always defined on the **range** of the original function.

Example 133. Evaluate $Arctan(1)$.

Solution By definition, we are looking for an angle <u>in radians</u> whose tangent is 1. So $y = Arctan(1)$ means $\tan y = 1$ or $y = \dfrac{\pi}{4}$.

Function	Domain	Range
$y = \text{Arcsin } x$	$-1 \leq x \leq +1$	$-\frac{\pi}{2} \leq y \leq +\frac{\pi}{2}$
$y = \text{Arccos } x$	$-1 \leq x \leq +1$	$0 \leq y \leq \pi$
$y = \text{Arctan } x$	$-\infty < x < +\infty$	$-\frac{\pi}{2} < y < +\frac{\pi}{2}$
$y = \text{Arccot } x$	$-\infty < x < +\infty$	$0 < y < \pi$
$y = \text{Arcsec } x$	$\mid x \mid \geq 1$	$0 \leq y \leq \pi,\ y \neq \frac{\pi}{2}$
$y = \text{Arccsc } x$	$\mid x \mid \geq 1$	$-\frac{\pi}{2} \leq y \leq +\frac{\pi}{2},\ y \neq 0$

Table 3.9: The Inverse Trigonometric Functions

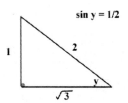

sin y = 1/2

Figure 60.

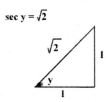

sec y = √2

Figure 61.

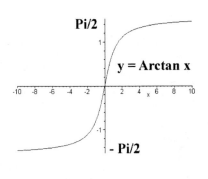

Pi/2

y = Arctan x

- Pi/2

Example 134. Evaluate $Arcsin(\frac{1}{2})$.

Solution By definition, we are looking for an angle in <u>radians</u> whose sine is $\frac{1}{2}$. So $y = Arcsin(\frac{1}{2})$ means $\sin y = \frac{1}{2}$ or $y = \frac{\pi}{6}$ (see Figure 60).

Example 135. Evaluate $Arccos(\frac{1}{\sqrt{2}})$.

Solution By definition, we seek an angle in <u>radians</u> whose cosine is $\frac{1}{\sqrt{2}}$. So $y = Arccos(\frac{1}{\sqrt{2}})$ means $\cos y = \frac{1}{\sqrt{2}}$ or $y = \frac{\pi}{4}$.

Example 136. Evaluate $Arcsec(\sqrt{2})$.

Solution By definition, we are looking for an angle in radians whose secant is $\sqrt{2}$. So $y = Arcsec(\sqrt{2})$ means $\sec y = \sqrt{2}$ $(= \frac{\sqrt{2}}{1})$. The other side has length $s^2 = (\sqrt{2})^2 - 1^2 = 2 - 1 = 1$. So $s = 1$. Therefore, the $\triangle$ is isosceles and $y = \frac{\pi}{4}$ (see Figure 61).

Example 137. Find the value of $\sin(Arccos(\frac{\sqrt{2}}{2}))$.

Solution Let $y = Arccos(\frac{\sqrt{2}}{2})$ then $\cos y = \frac{\sqrt{2}}{2}$. But we want $\sin y$. So, since $\cos^2 y + \sin^2 y = 1$, we get

$$\sin y = \pm\sqrt{1 - \cos^2 y} = \pm\sqrt{1 - \frac{1}{2}} = \pm\frac{1}{\sqrt{2}}.$$

Hence

$$\sin(Arccos(\frac{\sqrt{2}}{2})) = \frac{1}{\sqrt{2}} \ (= \frac{\sqrt{2}}{2}).$$

Example 138. Find $\sec(Arctan(-\frac{1}{2}))$.

Solution Now $y = Arctan(-\frac{1}{2})$ means $\tan y = -\frac{1}{2}$ but we want $\sec y$. Since $\sec^2 y - \tan^2 y = 1$ this means $\sec y = \pm\sqrt{1 + \tan^2 y} = \pm\sqrt{1 + \frac{1}{4}} = \pm\sqrt{\frac{5}{4}} = \pm\frac{\sqrt{5}}{2}$. Now we use Table 3.10, above.

Now, if we have an angle whose tangent is $-\frac{1}{2}$ then the angle is either in II or IV. But the angle must be in the interval $(-\frac{\pi}{2}, 0)$ of the domain of definition $(-\frac{\pi}{2}, \frac{\pi}{2})$ of tangent. Hence it is in IV and so its secant is > 0. Thus, $\sec y = \sqrt{5}/2$ and we're done.

Example 139. Find the sign of $\sec(Arccos(\frac{1}{2}))$.

Solution Let $y = Arccos(\frac{1}{2}) \Rightarrow \cos y = \frac{1}{2} > 0$, therefore y is in I or IV. By definition,

Other Method: Signs of Trigonometric Functions

Quadrant	sin	cos	tan	cot	sec	csc
I	+	+	+	+	+	+
II	+	-	-	-	-	+
III	-	-	+	+	-	-
IV	-	+	-	-	+	-

Table 3.10: Signs of Trigonometric Functions

$Arccos(\frac{1}{2})$ is in $[0, \pi]$. Therefore y is in I or II, but this means that y must be in I. So, $\sec y > 0$ by Table 3.10, and this forces $\sec\left(Arccos\left(\frac{1}{2}\right)\right) = \sec y > 0$.

Example 140. Determine the sign of the number $\csc(Arcsec(2))$.

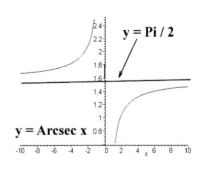

Solution Let $y = Arcsec(2)$. Then $\sec y = 2 > 0$. Therefore y is in I or IV. By definition, $Arcsec(2)$ is in I or II. Therefore y is in I, and from the cosecant property, $\csc y > 0$ if y is in $[0, \frac{\pi}{2})$. So, $\csc(Arcsec(2)) = \csc y > 0$.

Example 141. Find the sign of $\tan(Arcsin(-\frac{1}{2}))$.

Solution Let $y = Arcsin(-\frac{1}{2})$. Then $\sin y = -\frac{1}{2} \Rightarrow y$ in III or IV. By definition of $Arcsin$; But, $y = Arcsin(-\frac{1}{2})$ must be in I or IV. Therefore y is in IV. So $\tan(Arcsin(-\frac{1}{2})) < 0$ (because $\tan < 0$ in IV).

CAREFUL!!

Many authors of Calculus books use the following notations for the inverse trigonometric functions:

$$Arcsin\ x \iff \sin^{-1} x$$
$$Arccos\ x \iff \cos^{-1} x$$
$$Arctan\ x \iff \tan^{-1} x$$
$$Arccot\ x \iff \cot^{-1} x$$
$$Arcsec\ x \iff \sec^{-1} x$$
$$Arccsc\ x \iff \csc^{-1} x$$

The reason we try to avoid this notation is because it makes too many readers associate it with the reciprocal of those trigonometric functions and not their inverses. The reciprocal and the inverse are really different! Still, **you should be able to use both notations interchangeably**. It's best to know what the notation means, first.

NOTE: The inverse trigonometric functions we defined here in Table 3.9, are called the **principal branch** of the inverse trigonometric function, and we use the notation with an upper case letter '**A**' for **Arcsin**, etc. to emphasize this. Just about everything you ever wanted know about the basic theory of principal and non-principal branches of the inverse trigonometric functions may be found in the author's *Module on Inverse Functions* in the series *The ABC's of Calculus*, The Nolan Company, Ottawa, 1994.

Finally, we emphasize that since these functions are *inverses* then for any symbol, $\Box$, representing some point in the domain of the corresponding inverse function (see Table 3.9), we always have

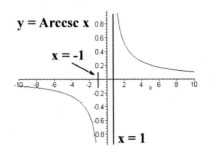

$$\sin(Arcsin \,\Box\,) = \Box \qquad \cos(Arccos \,\Box\,) = \Box$$
$$\tan(Arctan \,\Box\,) = \Box \qquad \cot(Arccot \,\Box\,) = \Box$$
$$\sec(Arcsec \,\Box\,) = \Box \qquad \csc(Arccsc \,\Box\,) = \Box$$

Exercise Set 17.

Evaluate the following expressions.

1. $\sin(Arccos(0.5))$ 2. $\cos(Arcsin(0))$ 3. $\sec(\sin^{-1}(\frac{1}{2}))$

4. $\csc(\tan^{-1}(-\frac{1}{2}))$ 5. $\sec(\sin^{-1}\frac{\sqrt{3}}{2})$ 6. $Arcsin(\tan(-\pi/4))$

NOTES:

3.9 Derivatives of Inverse Trigonometric Functions

Now that we know what these inverse trigonometric functions are, how do we find the derivative of the inverse of, say, the Arcsine (sin^{-1}) function? Well, we know from equation 3.4 that

$$\frac{dF}{dx}(x) = \frac{1}{f'(F(x))}$$

where $F(x) = f^{-1}(x)$ is the more convenient notation for the inverse of f. Now let $f(x) = \sin x$, and $F(x) = \text{Arcsin}\,x$ be its inverse function. Since $f'(x) = \cos x$, we see that

$$
\begin{aligned}
\frac{d}{dx}\text{Arcsin}\,x &= \frac{dF}{dx}(x) \\
&= \frac{1}{f'(F(x))} \\
&= \frac{1}{\cos(F(x))} \\
&= \frac{1}{\cos(\text{Arcsin}\,x)}
\end{aligned}
$$

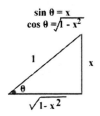

$\sin \theta = x$
$\cos \theta = \sqrt{1 - x^2}$

Figure 62.

Now, let $\theta = \text{Arcsin}\,x$, where θ is a lowercase Greek letter pronounced 'thay-ta'. It is used to denote angles. Then, by definition, $\sin \theta = x$, and we're looking for the value of $\cos \theta$, right? But since $\sin^2(\theta) + \cos^2(\theta) = 1$, this means that $\cos \theta = \pm\sqrt{1 - x^2}$. So, which is it? There are two choices, here.

Look at the definition of the Arcsin function in Table 3.9. You'll see that this function is defined only when the domain of the original sin function is restricted to $[-\pi/2, \pi/2]$. But, by definition, $Ran(\text{Arcsin}) = Dom(\sin) = [-\pi/2, \pi/2]$. So, $\cos \theta = \cos \text{Arcsin}\,x \geq 0$ because $\text{Arcsin}\,x$ is in the interval $[-\pi/2, \pi/2]$ and the cos function is either 0 or positive in there. So we must choose the '+' sign. Good. So,

$$\cos(\text{Arcsin}\,x) = \sqrt{1 - x^2}.$$

For another argument, see Figure 62. Finally, we see that

$$
\begin{aligned}
\frac{d}{dx}\text{Arcsin}\,x &= \frac{1}{\cos(\text{Arcsin}\,x)} \\
&= \frac{1}{\sqrt{1 - x^2}}.
\end{aligned}
$$

The other derivatives are found using a similar approach.

$$
\begin{array}{ll}
\dfrac{d}{dx}\sin^{-1}(u) = \dfrac{1}{\sqrt{1 - u^2}}\dfrac{du}{dx} & \dfrac{d}{dx}\cos^{-1}(u) = \dfrac{-1}{\sqrt{1 - u^2}}\dfrac{du}{dx}, \quad |u| < 1, \\[2ex]
\dfrac{d}{dx}\tan^{-1}(u) = \dfrac{1}{1 + u^2}\dfrac{du}{dx} & \dfrac{d}{dx}\cot^{-1}(u) = \dfrac{-1}{1 + u^2}\dfrac{du}{dx} \\[2ex]
\dfrac{d}{dx}\sec^{-1}(u) = \dfrac{1}{|u|\sqrt{u^2 - 1}}\dfrac{du}{dx}, & \dfrac{d}{dx}\csc^{-1}(u) = \dfrac{-1}{|u|\sqrt{u^2 - 1}}\dfrac{du}{dx}, \quad |u| > 1
\end{array}
$$

Table 3.11: Derivatives of Inverse Trigonometric Functions

If we let $u = u(x) = \square$ be any differentiable function, then we can use the basic derivative formulae and derive very general ones using the Chain Rule. In this way we can obtain Table 3.11.

Example 142. Evaluate the derivative of $y = \cos^{-1}(\frac{1}{x})$, (or $Arccos(\frac{1}{x})$).

Solution You can use any method here, but it always comes down to the Chain Rule. Let $u = \frac{1}{x}$, *then* $\frac{du}{dx} = -\frac{1}{x^2}$. By Table 3.11,

$$
\begin{aligned}
\frac{dy}{dx} &= \frac{d}{dx}\cos^{-1}u = -\frac{1}{\sqrt{1-u^2}}\frac{du}{dx} \\
&= -\frac{1}{\sqrt{1-(\frac{1}{x})^2}}(-\frac{1}{x^2}) = \frac{\frac{1}{x^2}}{\sqrt{1-\frac{1}{x^2}}} \\
&= \frac{1}{x^2\sqrt{1-\frac{1}{x^2}}} = \frac{\sqrt{x^2}}{|x|^2\sqrt{x^2-1}} \\
&= \frac{|x|}{|x|^2\sqrt{x^2-1}} \\
&= \frac{1}{|x|\sqrt{x^2-1}}, \quad (|x|>1).
\end{aligned}
$$

Example 143. Evaluate the derivative of $y = \cot^{-1}(\sqrt{x})$.

Solution Let $u = \sqrt{x}$, *then* $\frac{du}{dx} = \frac{1}{2\sqrt{x}}$. So,

$$
\begin{aligned}
\frac{dy}{dx} &= \frac{d}{dx}\cot^{-1}u = -\frac{1}{1+u^2}\frac{du}{dx} \\
&= -\frac{1}{1+(\sqrt{x})^2}\cdot\frac{1}{2\sqrt{x}} = -\frac{1}{2\sqrt{x}(1+x)}.
\end{aligned}
$$

Example 144. If $y = \csc^{-1}(\sqrt{x+1})$, what is $y'(x)$?

Solution Let $u = \sqrt{x+1}$, *then* $\frac{du}{dx} = \frac{1}{2\sqrt{x+1}}$. So,

$$
\begin{aligned}
\frac{dy}{dx} &= \frac{d}{dx}\csc^{-1}u = \frac{-1}{|u|\sqrt{u^2-1}}\frac{du}{dx} \\
&= \frac{-1}{\sqrt{x+1}(\sqrt{x+1-1})}\cdot\frac{1}{2\sqrt{x+1}} \\
&= \frac{-1}{2(x+1)\sqrt{x}}.
\end{aligned}
$$

NOTES:

Exercise Set 18.

Use Table 3.11 and the Chain Rule to find the derivatives of the functions whose values are given here.

1. $Arcsin(x^2)$, at $x = 0$ 6. $\sqrt{\sec^{-1} x}$

2. $x^2 \, Arccos(x)$ 7. $\sin(2Arcsinx)$, at $x = 0$

3. $\tan^{-1}(\sqrt{x})$ 8. $\cos(\sin^{-1}(4x))$

4. $Arcsin(\cos x)$ 9. $\dfrac{1}{Arctanx}$

5. $\dfrac{\sin^{-1} x}{\sin x}$ 10. $x^3 \, Arcsec(x^3)$

Suggested Homework Set 12. *Do problems 1, 4, 5, 7, 9*

Web Links

On the topic of Inverse Trigonometric Functions see:

www.math.ubc.ca/~maxwell/calculus_online/notes/zoo/invtrig.html
gamba.ugrad.math.ubc.ca/coursedoc/math100/notes/zoo/invtrig.html
(the above two sites require a Java enabled browser)
www.math.ucdavis.edu/~kouba/CalcOneDIRECTORY/
invtrigderivdirectory/InvTrigDeriv.html

NOTES:

3.10   Relating Rates of Change

There are many situations in life where things depend on other things which in turn depend upon time. For example, the rate at which a balloon grows depends upon the rate at which we blow into it, among other things. Similarly, the rate at which we can stop an automobile by braking depends upon our reaction rate; these rates are clearly related although it may be difficult to quantify them. In order to get an understanding on how to model such situations we need to develop some basic knowledge about how to model it first! Let's start with an example.

Example 145.   As a spherical balloon is being inflated with Helium gas it is noted that its radius is increasing at the rate of $1\,in./sec.$ How fast is its volume changing when its radius is $5\,in.$?

Solution In order to model this and come up with a solution we need to relate the quantities given (it's the whole point of this section!). For example, we are talking about a spherical balloon, that is one shaped like a sphere, at all times! We are asking a question about its volume; so this means that we need to first know what its volume is, in general. We recall that the volume of a sphere is $V = \frac{4}{3}\pi r^3$, where r is its radius. The question asked is about the quantity $\frac{dV}{dt}$, in other words, we want to know how *fast* the volume is changing.

Okay, now another part of the question deals with the fact that the *radius is increasing at the rate ....* This tells us that we know something about the derivative, $\frac{dr}{dt}$, too! Let's put all this together. We know the volume V is a function of time t and so r is a function of time too. Since both V and r are functions of t we can differentiate both sides of the volume formula with respect to t! Let's see... From

$$V = \frac{4}{3}\pi r^3$$

we find by *implicit differentiation* that

$$\frac{dV}{dt} = \frac{4}{3}\pi\,3\,r^2\,\frac{dr}{dt} = 4\,\pi\,r^2\,\frac{dr}{dt},$$

since the implicit derivative of r^3 is really $3r^2\frac{dr}{dt}$ and NOT just $3r^2$. Watch out for this, it's just the Chain Rule, remember?

Now, let's see if we can get any further. Let's look at the expression

$$\frac{dV}{dt} = 4\,\pi\,r^2\,\frac{dr}{dt}.$$

We are given that the quantity $\frac{dr}{dt} = 1$ (inch per second) and we need to find the rate of change of the volume. This means we still need the quantity r, but this is given too! You see, we are asking for these rates of change at the time t when $r = 5$ (inches). So, that's about it. We just insert $r = 5$ and $\frac{dr}{dt} = 1$ into the last display and we get the required volume rate ... that is,

$$\frac{dV}{dt} = 4\,\pi\,(5)^2\,1 = 100\pi \approx 314\ \text{in}^3/sec.$$

Note The neat thing about this previous example is that we could have replaced the word *balloon* by a "red giant" and determine the rate of expansion of such a dying star at times t in the future! An example of such a star is Betelgeuse (one of the stars at the corner of the Orion constellation; it even *looks* red, check it out!).

In working on problems involving such rates of change we need to think about how **to relate the quantities and rates given.** To do this we need to be able to recall some basic formulae about geometry, or just have some common sense. Ultimately though, all we do is **we relate what we want to what is given, use some formulae, then usually an application of the Chain Rule, then use some logic, and finally the ideas in this section.**

Example 146.   A swimming pool is being drained through an opening at its deepest end and it is noticed that it will take about 960 minutes to drain the pool if its volume is 10,000 gallons. Now, the volume V of water left in the pool after t minutes is given by Torricelli's Law:

$$V = 10,000 \left(1 - \frac{t}{960}\right)^2.$$

How fast is the water draining from the pool after 30 minutes?

Solution This one isn't hard. The point is that we are asking the question, "How fast is the water draining from the pool ...". This is really a question about how the *volume of water* is changing, you see? That is, these words at the end of the problem are really asking us to compute the derivative $\frac{dV}{dt}$ at time $t = 30$ minutes, that's all. In our case,

$$\frac{dV}{dt} = -2\,(10,000)\left(1 - \frac{t}{960}\right)\left(\frac{1}{960}\right).$$

So, after $t = 30$ minutes, the volume is changing at the rate of

$$
\begin{aligned}
\frac{dV}{dt} &= -2\,(10,000)\left(1 - \frac{30}{960}\right)\left(\frac{1}{960}\right), \\
&= -20,000\,\frac{31}{32}\frac{1}{960} \\
&= 20.182 \quad \text{gallons per minute.}
\end{aligned}
$$

Example 147.   A sunbather is lying on a tropical beach, with her head 1 m away from a palm tree whose height is 4 m. The sun is rising behind the tree as it casts a shadow on the sunbather (see the figure in the margin). Experience indicates that the angle α between the beach surface and the tip of the shadow is changing at the rate of $\frac{\pi}{36}$ rads/hr. At what rate is the shadow of the palm tree moving across the sunbather when $\alpha = \frac{\pi}{6}$?

Solution Now, let's analyze this problem carefully. You can see that this question is about a *triangle*, right? Actually, we are really asking how the angle α of the triangle is changing with time. We are given the height (call it y, so that $y = 4$) of the palm tree (or, the length of the opposite side of the triangle), and we need to know the distance of the tip of the shadow from the base of the tree (we call this x, and we know it varies with t). We also know that the required angle is called α. So, we have to relate x, the height of the palm tree and α. How? Use trigonometry. We know that $y = x \tan\alpha$ or equivalently,

$$x = y \cot\alpha = 4 \cot\alpha.$$

From this we see that we require some information about the rate dx/dt, since this gives information on the rate of the motion of the shadow. So, using implicit differentiation and the Chain Rule we get,

$$\frac{dx}{dt} = -4 \csc^2 \alpha \, \frac{d\alpha}{dt}.$$

But we know that $d\alpha/dt = \pi/36$ and we want information about dx/dt when $\alpha = \pi/6$. Feeding this information into the last display we get

$$\frac{dx}{dt} = -4\left(\csc^2 \frac{\pi}{6}\right)\left(\frac{\pi}{36}\right) = -4(4)\,\frac{\pi}{36} = -\frac{4\pi}{9} \approx -1.4\,\text{m/hr.}$$

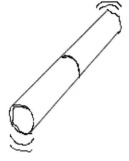

Example 148. A strip of hard bristle board is rolled up into a cylinder and held together temporarily by means of a rubber band. Once released, the bristle board expands and the rubber band flexes in a circular fashion. Determine how fast the length of the band is changing when its length is 30 cm and the rate of change of the cross sectional area of the bristle board cylinder is 60 cm^2.

Solution Now this problem looks tough because there are so many words and so few formulae, or even numbers for that matter! Let's analyze the data carefully and see if we can work this through logically.

A picture like the one in the margin (or a similar experiment that is also easy to perform) will help us understand the event. Basically, we roll up some board, try to hold it together using a rubber band but it doesn't work well because the rubber band isn't strong enough to hold it together. So, it starts to unravel forcing the band to expand in a circular fashion. OK, this makes sense and we can imagine this.

What are we given and what are we asked to find?

We note that we are given that the length of the band (or its perimeter) at some time t (unknown to us) is equal to 30. We can write this mathematically using the formula $P = 30$, where P stands for the perimeter of the band at that particular time. Furthermore, we are given that the cross-sectional area of the cylindrical board is *changing* at the rate of 60. Mathematically, this is saying that

$$\frac{dA}{dt} = 60,$$

where A is approximately equal to the area of the circle outlined by the rubber band. Now what? We have to find *how fast the length of the band is changing*, that is, what is the quantity

$$\frac{dP}{dt} \text{ equal to, when } P = 30 \text{ and } \frac{dA}{dt} = 60?$$

This means **we have to relate all these quantities somehow**.... That is, we need to find some formula that relates the perimeter of a circle to its area when each one of these in turn depends upon time. Well, the only formulae we can think of right now are the obvious ones that relate P and A but in terms of the radius! In other words, we know that $A = \pi r^2$ and $P = 2\pi r$. Now we need to write A in terms of P (we *relate A to P*). We can do this if we **eliminate the variable** r from these two simple equations! It's easy to see that this elimination of the usual variable r gives us the new relation

$$A = \frac{P^2}{4\pi}.$$

Of course, you see that this isn't a formula we usually learn in school, but it can be found using formulae we already know!

Now both A and P depend upon t so we can find the derivative of both sides of the last display with respect to t (using implicit differentiation). We then find,

$$\frac{dA}{dt} = \frac{1}{4\pi} \frac{d}{dt} \left(P^2\right) = \frac{P}{2\pi} \frac{dP}{dt}.$$

That's it!! We have found a relation between the three main quantities in this problem, $P, dP/dt, dA/dt$! All we have to do now is feed in what is known, and solve for what is unknown. Solving for dP/dt (the unknown) we get

$$\frac{dP}{dt} = \frac{2\pi}{P} \frac{dA}{dt}.$$

But $P = 30$ and $dA/dt = 60$, so the required rate of change of the perimeter (at that unspecified moment in time t) is equal to $4\pi \approx 12.57$ cm/sec.

Example 149. An economic concept called the **Earnback Period** was introduced by Reijo Ruuhela back in 1987. Basically, this is the number of years required for a company with a constant growth rate to earn back its share price. Now, this quantity, let's call it R, is a function of E, its expected earnings; P, the price of a stock at some specific time, usually $t = 0$; and G, its expected growth rate (usually given by a quantity called the ROE: its return on equity). The relationship between these variables is given by

$$R = \frac{\ln\left(1 + g\frac{P}{E}\right)}{\ln(1+g)}.$$

Let's assume that the P/E ratio varies with time (it usually does). Then R is essentially a function of the one variable P/E (since g is assumed constant in the model).

Determine the rate at which the Earnback Period changes when $g = 38\%$, $P/E = 27.3$ and the rate of change of $P/E = 0.6$ (This is *actual data* drawn from a famous cellular telephone manufacturer).

Solution Since R is given explicitly, all we need to do is differentiate that expression implicitly with respect to t. This gives

$$\begin{aligned}
\frac{dR}{dt} &= \frac{g}{\left(1 + g\frac{P}{E}\right)\ln(1+g)} \frac{d\left(\frac{P}{E}\right)}{dt} \\
&= \frac{(0.38)}{(1 + (0.38)(27.3))\ln(1+0.38)} (0.6) \\
&= 0.57608
\end{aligned}$$

This quantity, being positive, means it will take longer for the company to earnback its original share price under these conditions.

NOTE: For this company, the actual earnback ratio for the given data above, was equal to 7.54. This means that it would take about seven and one-half years for it to earn back its stock price (assuming this expected constant growth rate).

A matter/antimatter collision will occur in a laboratory when a particle and an antiparticle collide. One such attempt was undertaken by the Nobel Prize-winning physicist, Carlo Rubbia. His experimental work verified the theoretically predicted particles called the Z and W particles predicted by others. the unification of the electromagnetic force with the weak nuclear force, the first step towards a grand unification of the fundamental forces of nature.

Example 150.   An electron and a positron (a positively charged electron) are approaching a common target along straight line paths that are perpendicular to each other. If the electron is 1000 meters away from the target and is travelling at a speed of $299,000,000$ meters/sec while the positron is 900 meters away and travelling at a speed of $272,727,000$ meters/sec, determine how fast the distance between them is changing as they approach the target.

Solution Let's think about this: We are given that the two particles are travelling along the sides of a right-angled triangle towards the vertex containing the right angle (see the figure). Their distance from each other is simply the length of the hypotenuse of this imaginary triangle and we want to find out how fast this distance is changing. Let's call y the vertical distance and x the horizontal distance from the target. Let's also denote by D, the length of the hypotenuse of the triangle formed by the two particles and their common target. In other words, we are given x, the speed $x' = dx/dt$, the distance y and the speed $y' = dy/dt$. We really want dD/dt. This means we have to relate this time derivative of D to x and y and their derivatives.

Let's see. We have a right triangle, we have its two sides and we want its hypotenuse. This must have something to do with Pythagoras' Theorem! Let's try it. The relation

$$D^2 = x^2 + y^2$$

must hold for all time t, by hypothesis, since the particles are assumed to be moving in a straight line. But now, each one of these quantities is varying with t, so we can takwe the implict derivative of each side to find:

$$2D \frac{dD}{dt} = 2x \frac{dx}{dt} + 2y \frac{dy}{dt},$$

or, solving for dD/dt we find

$$\frac{dD}{dt} = \frac{x \frac{dx}{dt} + y \frac{dy}{dt}}{D}.$$

Substituting the values given above should do it. But wait! We're missing D here. Anyhow, this isn't bad because we know (from Pythagoras) that $D = \sqrt{x^2 + y^2} = \sqrt{(1000)^2 + (900)^2} = 1345.36$ meters at the given moment of our calculation. Finally, we get

$$\frac{dD}{dt} = \frac{(900)\,(272,727,000) + (1000)\,(299,000,000)}{1345.36} = 4.047 \times 10^8 \text{ meters/sec.}$$

Example 151.   We recall the *Ideal Gas Law* from chemistry texts. It says that for an ideal gas,

$$PV = nRT$$

where R is the ideal gas constant (0.08206 liter-atmospheres/mole/degree Kelvin, and T is the temperature in Kelvins), P is the pressure (in atmospheres), V is its volume (in liters), and n is the number of moles of the gas. Generally, all these variables, P, V, n, T, can vary with time with the exception of R. If there is a constant 2 moles of gas; the pressure is 5 atmospheres and is increasing at the rate of 0.02 atmospheres per hour; the volume is decreasing at the rate of 0.05 liters per hour; the temperature is given to be $300K$ and is decreasing at the rate of $1.5K$ per hour, find the volume V of gas at this time.

Solution You can see that there's a lot of data here. The rates being discussed are all rates of change with respect to time (given in hours). This tells us that we should be looking at our Law and differentiate it with respect to time so that we can use the information given. You can't use the original Law ($PV = nRT$) to find V because this is a *dynamic* problem; all the quantities are generally changing with time (except for n, R in this case). Okay, so let's differentiate everything in the basic Law to find

$$P'V + PV' = nRT'.$$

Solving for the volume, V, we get a formula like

$$V = \frac{nRT' - PV'}{P'}.$$

Now we just substitute in all the given information, but be careful with the rate of change of temperature and volume: $T' = -1.5$ (note the negative sign!) and $V' = -0.05$. In the end we find,

$$V = \frac{2\,(0.08206)\,(-1.5) - 5\,(-0.05)}{0.02} \approx 0.191 \text{ liters.}$$

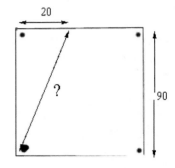

Example 152. A senior league baseball field is in the form of a square whose sides are 90 ft long. During a game a player attempts to steal third base by sprinting at a constant speed of 9.2 ft/sec. At what rate is the player's distance from home plate changing when the player is 20 ft from third base?

Solution A picture will be helpful here (see the margin). Let y denote the distance from the second base (denoted by the point A) to the player (denoted by the point B) at a given time and x be the distance from the player to home plate (denoted by the point O). We are given that $y' = 9.2$ and that the player is $90 - 20 = 70$ ft from second base so that $y = 70$. Now we want some information about x'. This means that we have to relate x and its derivative to y and its derivative. Looks like we'll have to use some basic trigonometry in order to relate x to y. To do this, we draw the diagonal from second base to home plate and look at $\triangle$ABO. Since angle $BAO = \pi/4$ and $AO = \sqrt{16,200} \approx 127.28$ (by Pythagoras) we can use the *Cosine Law* to find x. How? Recall that the Cosine Law is a more general form of the theorem of Pythagoras. When the Law is applied to $\triangle$ABO we get

$$x^2 = (AO)^2 + y^2 - 2\,(AO)\,y\,\cos(\pi/4),$$

or

$$\begin{aligned}
x^2 &= 16,200 + y^2 - 2\,(127.28)\,y\,\frac{\sqrt{2}}{2} \\
&= 16,200 + y^2 - 180y.
\end{aligned}$$

We have just derived the basic formula relating x to y. Now we can find the derivative of both sides:

$$2\,x\,x' = 2\,y\,y' - 180y',$$

and solve for x'. This gives

$$x' = \frac{(y - 90)\,y'}{x}.$$

But we know $y = 70$ and $y' = 9.2$ so all we need is to find x. But this is easy because of Pythagoras again. In other words, it is easy to see that $x^2 = (20)^2 + (90)^2$. Thus, $x \approx 92.2$ ft. It follows that $x' = \frac{(70-90)\,(9.2)}{92.2} \approx -2$ ft/sec..

Special Exercise Set

---

1. As a spherical snowball is melting its radius is changing at the rate of $2\,\mathrm{mm/min}$. How fast is its volume changing when the radius is $2\,\mathrm{cm}$?

2. A large cubical room in an old pyramid is being compressed uniformly from all sides in such a way that its volume is changing at the rate of $6\,\mathrm{m^3/min}$. How fast is the length of one of its walls changing when it is equal to $2\,\mathrm{m}$.?

3. A rectangular screen saver is changing, while maintaining its shape, in such a way that, at all times, the ratio of its sides is equal to the *Golden number*,

$$\tau = \frac{\sqrt{5} - 1}{2}.$$

   How fast is its area changing when one of its sides varies at the rate of $2.1\,\mathrm{cm/sec}$ and that same side's length is $6.2\,\mathrm{cm}$?

4. Two *Formula 1* racing cars are at rest and facing away from each other at a cross-shaped intersection on a desert highway. As the race begins they quickly reach top speeds of 281 and $274\,\mathrm{km/hr}$, respectively. How fast is the distance between them changing when they are 4 and $6.7\,\mathrm{km}$ away from the intersection, respectively?

5. The area of a plane circular region is changing at the rate of $25\,\mathrm{cm^2/sec}$. How fast is its circumference changing when it is equal to $67\,\mathrm{cm}$?

6. A rotating star (or our own planet) can be more accurately modelled by means of a solid object called an *oblate spheroid*. This solid can be thought of as a tangible sphere compressed from its poles thus forcing its equatorial section "out". In the case of a rotating sar (or the Earth) this *bulging out* at the equator is caused by its rapid rotation rate and the inherent tidal forces.

   The resulting object has an *equatorial radius* given by a and a *polar radius*, c. It follows that $a > c$ (since the sphere is compressed at the poles).

   Now, the volume of an oblate spheroid with polar radius c and equatorial radius a is given by

$$V = \frac{4}{3}\pi a^2 c.$$

   If a star rotates in such a way that its polar radius is a constant $50,000\,\mathrm{km}$ while its equatorial radius is changing at the rate of $1300\,\mathrm{km/hr}$, determine the rate at which its volume is changing when $a = 50,500\,\mathrm{km}$.

7. Two airplanes at the same altitude are moving towards an airport along straight line flight paths at a constant angle of $120^o = \frac{2\pi}{3}$ rads and at speeds of 790 and 770 mph respectively. How fast is the distance between them changing when they are respectively, 30 and 46 miles away from the airport?

8. A computer manufacturer found the cost of manufacturing x computers to be given approximately by the function

$$C(x) = (3.2 \times 10^{-5})\,x^3 - 0.002\,x^2 - (2.1)\,x + 2000 \text{ dollars.}$$

   Find the rate of change in cost over time given that $dx/dt = 10\,\mathrm{PC's/wk}$ and $x = 100\,PC's$.

9. **PROJECT**.

   In the gravitational $3-$body problem in Celestial Mechanics there is a concept known as a *central configuration*. It is clear that any three point masses (such as spherical planets, or stars) form a triangle.

   When this triangle (or system of three bodies) has the property that if the three masses are released with zero initial velocity subject only to Newton's Laws of motion, then they all collide at the *center of mass* simultaneously, we call such a triangle a **central configuration in the problem of three bodies**. Of course, this is bad news if you happen to live on one of them!

a) Look up the subject of central configurations on the Web and determine who discovered the fact that any three point masses at the vertices of an equilateral triangle is necessarily a central configuration. When was this discovered?

b) At a fixed time t, three massive spherical bodies are positioned at the vertices of a large equilateral triangle in space. Given that the area enclosed by this celestial triangle is decreasing at the rate of $237,100 \, \text{km}^2/\text{sec}$, determine the rate at which their mutual distances is changing when the enclosed area is $500,000 \, \text{km}^2$.

3.11   Newton's Method for Calculating Roots

The Big Picture

In many applications of Calculus to mathematics and the real world we'll need to find out where things are: For instance, if we have two curves which may be describing some complicated trajectory for a system of two particles, we may want to know at which point they will meet (if ever). If they do meet, where do they meet? It's not always possible to do this theoretically meaning that we need to resort to some sort of numerical procedure (using a computer or a calculator) to estimate their location. Recently, many Hollywood movies have been produced whose subject matter deals with an imminent collision of an asteroid with the earth. That's just one such example. Each one of these celestial bodies moves according to Newton's Laws of Motion and their trajectories are usually well known to astronomers. If there is a collision then it must happen at some point along their mutual trajectories and this means that their 'curves' will intersect!

The method which we'll be studying below is due to Sir Isaac Newton and is dated 1669 in an unpublished work of his where he applied the technique to finding the roots of a cubic equation (by hand, no calculator!). In fact, if the polynomial is of degree greater than or equal to 5 then there is **no general formula** for finding its roots. Newton's method, however, *can* be used to estimate its real roots. Another application of this method can be found in the study of populations. The decline of the species *Amospitza Maritima Nigrescens*, known as the Seaside Dusky Sparrow can be modelled, in hindsight, by a power function P where $P(t)$, the total world population of Duskies at time t, is given by

$$P(t) = 1000 \cdot \frac{\sin(10t) + 3}{(1 + 3^{2t})},$$

so that, in 1955, there were, let's say, approximately 3000 Duskies. The Dusky Sparrow was a local species of sparrows which thrived near St. John's River close to Cape Canaveral, the cradle of the U.S. Space Program. This species became extinct with the the passing of Orange Band (whose name was inspired by a distinctive marking around one of its legs), the last remaining Dusky Sparrow, in 1986, at Disney World, Florida, alone, behind a cage. If the model were right and you needed to predict the extinction date you would need to solve an equation like $P(t) = 0.99$ or, equivalently, you would need to find a root of the equation $P(t) - 0.99 = 0$. Models like this one can be used to make predictions about the future development of populations of any kind and this is where the method we will study will lead to some numerical results with hopefully less disastrous consequences.

The finding of the roots of a polynomial equation is a very old problem. Everyone knows the quadratic formula for a quadratic (or polynomial of degree two), but few know or can remember the formula for the roots of a cubic equation! The formula for the roots of some special cases of the cubic had been found by Omar Khayyam (ca. 1079) and obtained generally by Nicolo Tartaglia (ca. 1543) and Hieronimo Cardano (1501-1576). The formula for the roots of a quartic (polynomial of degree 4) was discovered by Ludovico Ferrari (1522-1565) and Raffaello Bombelli (ca. 1530 - 1572?) while the *impossibility* of finding a formula for the roots of the general quintic is due to Evariste Galois (1811-1832) and Niels Abel (1802-1829). In this case we have to use **Newton's Method** or something similar in order to find the actual real roots.

Review

Review the methods for finding a derivative and **Bolzano's Theorem** (in Chapter 2) and check your calculator battery's charge, you'll really need to use it in this section! **Think BIG**, in the sense that you'll be making many numerical calculations but only the *last one*, is the one you care about. It is helpful if you can develop a 'feel' for what the answer should be, and we'll point out some ways of doing this.

The idea behind this method is that it uses our knowledge of a function and its derivative in order to estimate the value of a so-called **zero (or root) of the function**, that is, a point x where $f(x) = 0$. So, the first thing to remember is that this method **applies only to differentiable functions** and won't work for functions that are only continuous (but not differentiable).

Remark Newton's method is based on the simple geometrical fact that if the graph of a differentiable function has a zero at $x = a$ (i.e., $f(a) = 0$), then its tangent line at the point $\text{P}(a, f(a))$ must cross the x−axis at $x = a$ too! In other words, the tangent line must also have a zero at $x = a$. If the tangent line happens to be horizontal at a zero, then it must coincide with the x-axis itself! (see Figure 63).

OK, so let's see what this simple remark tells us about the graph and about the root, itself. We know that the equation of this tangent line at a generic point $\text{P}(x_m, y_m) = P(x_m, f(x_m))$ along the graph of f is given by

$$
\begin{aligned}
y &= y_m + (slope) \cdot (x - x_m), \\
&= f(x_m) + f'(x_m) \cdot (x - x_m),
\end{aligned}
$$

since the slope of the tangent line to the graph of f at the point x_m is equal to the derivative of f at x_m. Now, for this tangent line to cross the x−axis we must set $y = 0$, (because the point in question must look like $(a, 0)$ there). Setting $y = 0$ in the last display and solving for x, the root we're looking for, we find $x = x_m - \frac{f(x_m)}{f'(x_m)}$, or, since $x = a$ is our root,

$$
a = x_m - \frac{f(x_m)}{f'(x_m)}, \quad (\text{if } f'(x_m) \neq 0)
$$

is the value of the root we need. The problem with this is we don't know the value of x_m. The way this is resolved is by **starting with some arbitrary value which we call x_0.** Ideally, you should choose x_0 close to the root $x = a$, that you're trying to approximate.

Next, you **use this value of x_0 to define a new value**, which we call x_1, (and which depends on x_0). This new value of x_1 is defined explicitly by

$$
x_1 = x_0 - \frac{f(x_0)}{f'(x_0)},
$$

so you'll need your calculator to find it. OK, once you've done this, you now realize you have two values, namely, x_0, x_1. Now, using our calculator once again, we'll generate a new value, which we'll call x_2, by setting

$$
x_2 = x_1 - \frac{f(x_1)}{f'(x_1)}.
$$

Since you just found x_1, you'll be able to find x_2. Alright, now you found three values, x_0, x_1, x_2. You're probably getting the general idea, here. So, we continue this method by defining another value x_3 by

$$
x_3 = x_2 - \frac{f(x_2)}{f'(x_2)}.
$$

This now gives us the four values x_0, x_1, x_2, x_3. We just keep doing this until the numbers in the **sequence** $x_0, x_1, x_2, x_3, x_4, \ldots$ seem to 'level off', i.e., the last ones in this list are very close together numerically. Of course, we can only do this a finite number of times and this is OK, since an approximation which is accurate to 15 decimal places is accurate enough for the most precise applications. In general, the $(m + 1)^{st}$ number we generated using this technique called an **iteration** is defined by using the previous m numbers by, you guessed it, Table 3.12, above.

Now, **if the sequence $\{x_m\} = \{x_0, x_1, x_2, x_3, x_4, \ldots\}$ converges** to a value say, L, (see the *Advanced Topics* chapter for a precise meaning to this), then we can use some Limit Theorems from Chapter 2 and see that

$$
L = \lim_{m \to \infty} x_{m+1} = \lim_{m \to \infty} \left\{ x_m - \frac{f(x_m)}{f'(x_m)} \right\},
$$

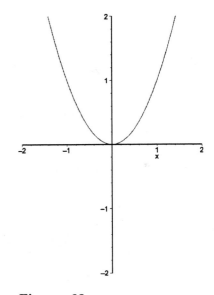

Figure 63. *The graph of $y = x^2$ showing its tangent at $x = 0$*

$$x_{m+1} \;=\; x_m - \frac{f(x_m)}{f'(x_m)},$$

where $m = 0, 1, 2, 3, 4, \dots$. This formula gives every term in the *whole sequence*, which is denoted by $\{x_m\}$, for brevity.

Table 3.12: Netwon's Method: Definition of the Iteration

$$= \lim_{m \to \infty} x_m - \frac{\lim_{m \to \infty} f(x_m)}{\lim_{m \to \infty} f'(x_m)}$$

$$= L - \frac{f(L)}{f'(L)},$$

since both f, f' are continuous everywhere in their domain, and so at $x = L$.

Remark 1. This last equation shows that if

$$\lim_{m \to \infty} x_m = L,$$

then L is a root of f, that is, $f(L) = 0$. But it doesn't have to be the root we are actually looking for! This is one of the problems with this method: When the sequence $\{x_m\}$, defined in Table 3.12, converges to a value (i.e., it has a finite limit as $m \to \infty$) that value is not necessarily equal to a, UNLESS we know something more about the root $x = a$. We'll see some examples below.

Remark 2. If you think about this preamble carefully and you remember the stuff we learned in Chapter 2, then you'll realize that the *above arguments should work on functions that have a derivative which is continuous over some interval I containing the root.* In addition, we should require that the root be a so-called, **simple root**. This means that the derivative of f evaluated at the root is not zero. The reason for this is to avoid those crazy results which occur when you try to divide by 0 in the formula for some iterate x_m.

What do the Newton iterates mean geometrically?

For this we refer to Figure 64 in the margin. There we have sketched the graph of the function $y = x^4 - 1$ over the interval $[0, 5]$ in an attempt to understand the nature of the *iterates*, or the points $x_0, x_1, x_2, x_3 \dots$ defined by the process outlined in Table 3.12, above. Now we know that the zero of this function is at $x = 1$, so it must be the case that $x_n \to 1$ as $n \to \infty$.

We choose the starting point $x_0 = 5$ so that x_1, defined by Table 3.12 with $m = 0$, falls near 3.75 as in the graph. Why 3.75? Because

$$\begin{aligned}
x_1 &= x_0 - \frac{f(x_0)}{f'(x_0)} \\
&= 5 - \frac{f(5)}{f'(5)} \\
&= 5 - \frac{624}{500} \\
&\approx 3.75.
\end{aligned}$$

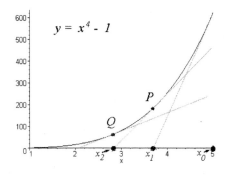

Figure 64.

Now, at this point $x_1 = 3.75$ we draw a perpendicular which intersects the graph at $P : (x_1, f(x_1))$. Draw the tangent line at P. We claim that this line now intersects the x−axis at x_2. It must, really! This is because the equation of the tangent line at P is given by

$$
\begin{aligned}
y - f(x_1) &= (slope)(x - x_1) \\
&= f'(x_1)(x - x_1) \\
y &= f(x_1) + f'(x_1)(x - x_1).
\end{aligned}
$$

This tangent line intersects the x−axis when $y = 0$, and so, solving for x, we find that

$$
x = x_1 - \frac{f(x_1)}{f'(x_1)} = x_2,
$$

by definition. So x_2 is the zero of this tangent line and it's value is given by

$$
\begin{aligned}
x_2 &= x_1 - \frac{f(x_1)}{f'(x_1)} \\
&= 3.75 - \frac{f(3.75)}{f'(3.75)} \\
&= 3.75 - \frac{196.7}{210.9} \\
&\approx 2.82.
\end{aligned}
$$

Now we just keep doing this over and over again. At this point $x_2 = 2.82$ we draw a perpendicular which intersects the graph at $Q : (x_2, f(x_2))$. Draw the tangent line at Q and we claim that this line intersects the x−axis at x_3. Use the same argument as the one above to convince yourself of this. So, you see, the string of iterates $x_0, x_1, x_2, x_3, \ldots$ is really a string of roots of a collection of tangent lines to the graph of f. When this sequence converges, it converges to a root of the original function, f.

Now let's look at some examples.

Example 153. Find an approximation to the root of the polynomial given by $f(x) = 2x^2 - 3x + 1$ in the interval $[0.75, 2]$.

Solution Why the interval $[0.75, 2]$? We chose this one because $f(0.75) \cdot f(2) = (-0.125) \cdot 3 = -0.375 < 0$ and so by Bolzano's Theorem (Chapter 2), it follows that f has a root in this interval. For a starting value, x_0, we'll choose the point half-way between the end-points of our interval, namely the point $x_0 = (0.75 + 2)/2 = 1.375$.

m	x_m	$f(x_m)$	$f'(x_m)$	x_{m+1}
0	1.375	0.656	2.5	1.1125
1	1.1125	0.1378	1.45	1.0175
2	1.0175	0.0181	1.0698	1.0006
3	1.0006	0.0006	1.0023	1.0000
4	1.0000	.0000	1.0000	1.0000
...	...	...	...	...
		Column 3		*Column 5*

Use your calculator or software to verify the numbers in this Table!

Let's look at how this table was generated in the first place. The rest of the examples follow a similar procedure. In this case, $f(x) = 2x^2 - 3x + 1$, while $f'(x) = 4x - 3$.

Substituting these values into Table 3.12 and expanding the terms on the right we'll find,

$$x_{m+1} = x_m - \frac{f(x_m)}{f'(x_m)} = x_m - \frac{2\,x_m{}^2 - 3\,x_m + 1}{4x_m - 3}, \quad for \ m \geq 0.$$

So we let $m = 0$ and find x_1 by using the iteration just derived (Note that the right-hand side depends only on terms of the form x_0 when $m = 0$).

$$\begin{aligned}
x_1 &= x_0 - \frac{f(x_0)}{f'(x_0)}, \quad m = 0 \text{ here,} \\
&= \boxed{1.375} - \frac{2 \cdot (\boxed{1.375})^2 - 3 \cdot (\boxed{1.375}) + 1}{4 \cdot (\boxed{1.375}) - 3} \\
&= 1.375 - \frac{0.656}{2.5} \\
&= 1.1125.
\end{aligned}$$

The number we just found, this number 1.1125, goes in the Table above as the first term in Column 5. It is boxed in for convenience. The starting value, 1.375 is also boxed in for convenience. The other boxed terms in this calculation emphasize the fact that *we're always using the previous term in Column 5 in our calculations.* Let's work out another iteration. Now we know that $x_0 = 1.375, x_1 = 1.1125$. Let's find the next term, x_2, in the approximation to the root. Using the same idea as in the previous display we have

$$\begin{aligned}
x_2 &= x_1 - \frac{f(x_1)}{f'(x_1)}, \quad m = 1 \text{ here,} \\
&= \boxed{1.1125} - \frac{2 \cdot (\boxed{1.1125})^2 - 3 \cdot (\boxed{1.1125}) + 1}{4 \cdot (\boxed{1.1125}) - 3} \\
&= 1.1125 - \frac{0.1378}{1.0698} \\
&= 1.0175,
\end{aligned}$$

and this number x_2 is then inserted in the Table's Column 5 as the second entry.

Let's work out one more iteration just so can get the 'feel' for what's happening. So far we know that $x_0 = 1.375, x_1 = 1.1125,$ *and* $x_2 = 1.0175$. Let's find the next term, x_3, in the approximation to the root. Using the same idea over again,

$$\begin{aligned}
x_3 &= x_2 - \frac{f(x_2)}{f'(x_2)}, \quad m = 2 \text{ here,} \\
&= \boxed{1.0175} - \frac{2 \cdot (\boxed{1.0175})^2 - 3 \cdot (\boxed{1.0175}) + 1}{4 \cdot (\boxed{1.0175}) - 3} \\
&= 1.0175 - \frac{0.0181}{1.45} \\
&= 1.0006,
\end{aligned}$$

and this number x_3 is then inserted in the Table's Column 5 as the third entry.

You should check the remaining calculations in this Table with your calculator/computer. On the other hand, you may want to write a short program in C or C++ which will do the trick too!

This table shows that the sequence $\{x_m\}$ appears to be converging to the value 1.00000 or, just 1, as you can gather from Column 5. In Column 3, we see the values of the function f evaluated at the various points x_m generated by Newton's iteration in Table 3.12. These are the important Columns, namely, **Column 3 and**

5. Note that we managed to obtain a fair estimate of the root after only 8 steps. It may or may not take more steps depending on the problem.

As a check, we note that the polynomial f can be factored as

$$f(x) = 2\,x^2 - 3\,x + 1 = (2x - 1) \cdot (x - 1).$$

Right away we see that $x = 1$ is indeed a root, and so is $x = 1/2 = 0.5$.

> **NOTE:** Actually, if f is continuous and you want to generate a starting value, x_0, you look for an interval $[a, b]$ where $f(a) \cdot f(b) < 0$ and then you can let x_0 be its midpoint, say, $x_0 = (a+b)/2$. There has to be a root in this interval $[a, b]$ by Bolzano's Theorem.
>
> Remember that you can't guarantee that you'll find the 'right root' though.

| **Example   154.** | Find an approximation to the root of the function given by

$f(x) = x \cdot \sin x + \cos x$ in the interval $[0, \pi]$.

Solution   Why the interval $[0, \pi]$? We chose this one because $f(0) \cdot f(\pi) = (1)(-1) = -1 < 0$ and so by Bolzano's Theorem (Chapter 2), it follows that f has a root in this interval. Let's choose $x_0 = \pi$ as a starting value.

| **WATCH OUT!** | This is one of those examples where you could be dividing by 0 if you're not careful. In this case, if we choose our starting value as $x = \pi/2$, the preferred value, we are actually dividing by zero as soon as we calculate x_1 (because $f'(\pi/2) = 0$). So don't use this starting value, try another one. So, we chose $x = \pi$. You could have chosen any other value so long as the denominator is not zero there. In a way **you're always hoping that you won't run into zeros of the denominator, $f'(x_m)$.**

m	x_m	$f(x_m)$	$f'(x_m)$	x_{m+1}
0	3.141592653	-1.0000000	-3.141592653	2.82328
1	2.82328	$-.0661786486$	-2.681452104	2.79860
2	2.79860	$-.0005638521$	-2.635588362	2.79839
3	2.79839	$-.0000104201$	-2.635192901	2.79839
4	2.79839	$-.0000104201$	-2.635192901	2.79839
5	2.79839	$-.0000104201$	-2.635192901	2.79839
6	2.79839	$-.0000104201$	-2.635192901	2.79839
...	...	...	...	...
		Column 3		*Column 5*

What's happening? You gather from Column 3 that the numbers seem to be 'stuck' at $x \approx -0.0000104201$. What went wrong? Nothing, really. Well, you see, we (secretly) declared '5 decimal place accuracy' prior to doing this calculation on the computer. What you get as a result is not more than the first few decimals of the right answer for the root, some number around 2.79839.

But if this makes you nervous, you should try declaring , say, '10 decimal place accuracy'. Then you'll get the next table.

m	x_m	$f(x_m)$	$f'(x_m)$	x_{m+1}
0	3.1415926536	-1.0000000	-3.141592653	2.8232827674
1	2.8232827674	$-.0661860695$	-2.681457177	2.7985998935
2	2.7985998935	$-.0005635713$	-2.635588162	2.7983860621
3	2.7983860621	$-.0000000429$	-2.635185484	2.7983860458
4	2.7983860458	0.000000000	-2.635185454	2.7983860458
5	2.7983860458	0.000000000	-2.635185454	2.7983860458
6	2.7983860458	0.000000000	-2.635185454	2.7983860458
...	...	... *Column 3*	...	... *Column 5*

This time the sequence sems to be leveling off around the value 2.7983860458, with an accuracy of at least 9 decimal places. Not bad. So, you see that the **more you demand out of your calculations the more you'll get as a result.** The required root is given approximately by 2.798386.

| **Example 155.** | Determine whether or not the function defined by |

$$f(x) = x^{-1} - 2x^{-2}$$

has a root, and if so, find it.

Solution Well, this one isn't so bad. It 'looks' bad because we are dividing by x a few times but let's simplify it first. Now, $f(x) = 0$ means that $1/x = 2/x^2$, right? But if $x \neq 0$, then $x = 2$ is the only solution! On the other hand, $x = 0$ doesn't give a root because we get the **indeterminate form** $\infty - \infty$ at $x = 0$. So, $x = 2$ is the only root. That' all.

| OK, but what if you didn't think about simplifying? | In this case, use Newton's method. Let's use it in combination with Bolzano's Theorem, as we did above. It's also suggested that you should find the 'graph' of this function, just to see where the root may be. Draw the graph as an exercise. You'll see that the root will satisfy $x > 0$. So, let's start with $a = 1$, $b = 3$. Then $f(1) \cdot f(3) = -1/9 < 0$. Since f is continuous in the interval $[1, 3]$ (no problem in here), Bolzano's Theorem guarantees the existence of a root in this interval. In this case the derivative of f is given by $f'(x) = -x^{-2} + 4x^{-3}$. We set up the iterations as in Table 3.12, and use the starting value $x_0 = 1$.

Meaningless Newton iterates for
$f(x) = x^{-1} - 2x^{-2}$ and $x_0 = 3$

m	x_m
0	3.0
1	0.111
2	-153.000
3	$-.0066$
4	-45768.61
5	$-.0000218$
6	-4189211739.2
7	......

Figure 65.

m	x_m	$f(x_m)$	$f'(x_m)$	x_{m+1}
0	1.0000000000	-1.0000000	3.0000000000	1.33333333333
1	1.3333333333	$-.3750000000$	1.125000000	1.6666666667
2	1.6666666667	$-.1200000000$	.5040000000	1.9047619048
3	1.9047619048	$-.0262500000$	.3031875000	1.9913419914
4	1.9913419914	$-.0021833648$	.2543714967	1.9999253620
5	1.9999253620	$-.0000186608$	.2500373223	1.9999999945
6	1.9999999945	$-.0000000014$	.2500000030	2.0000000000
7	2.0000000000	$-.0000000000$	.2500000000	2.0000000000
...	...	... *Column 3*	...	... *Column 5*

A quick glance at Columns 3 and 5 shows that the sequence of iterates appears to converge to 2, with accuracy up to 10 decimal places, and this after only 7 iterations.

NOTE: What if we had chosen a different starting value, say, $x_0 = 3$? This is not a good value to start with as there doesn't appear to be any convergence whatsoever, and the numbers would be meaningless, see Figure 65!

Example 156. Find the points of intersection of the curves whose equations are given by $y = x^2$ and $y = \sin x$, in the interval $(0, \infty)$.

Solution You can sketch these graphs and that will give you an idea of where to look for a starting value. OK, now look at the function f defined by $f(x) = x^2 - \sin x$. Then *the required points of intersection coincide with the roots of the equation $f(x) = x^2 - \sin x = 0$.*

Now this function f is a nice continuous function with a continuous first derivative (namely, $f'(x) = 2x - \cos x$). We see immediately that $x = 0$ is a root, just by inspection. Are there any other roots? If we look at its graph we'll see that there appears to be just one more root and it is somewhere near $x = 1$. To confirm this we use Bolzano's Theorem. Note that if we choose $[a, b]$ to be the inteval $[0.5, 1.5]$, (which contains our proposed guess for a starting value, namely, $x_0 = 1$) then $f(a) \cdot f(b) = -0.28735 < 0$ and so we know there is a root in here. OK, so let's choose $x_0 = 1$ and hope for the best. We get the following table (see Figure 66) where we've included only Columns 3 and 5 for brevity.

From this table we gather that the other root has a value equal to approximately 0.876726, which agrees with our predictions about it. OK, so we found the roots of f in the interval $(0, \infty)$.

Now, let's go back to the points of intersection: These points of intersection are given approximately by setting $x = 0$ and $x = 0.8767$ into either one of the expressions x^2 or $\sin x$. Once this is done we find the points P$(0, 0)$ and P$(0.8767, 0.76865)$, where $(0.8767)^2 \approx 0.76865 \approx \sin(0.8767)$.

Example 157. Show that the polynomial equation $f(x) = x^3 - 3x^2 + 6x - 1 = 0$ has a simple root in the interval $(0, 1)$. Find the root to within an accuracy of 0.001.

Solution First we show that a typical root, let's call it a, is simple. Remember that this means that $f(a) = 0$ and $f'(a) \neq 0$. Now, $f'(x) = 3x^2 - 6x + 6 = 3 \cdot (x^2 - 2x + 2)$. But note that the discriminant of this polynomial is negative (actually equal to -4) and so it can't have any other (real) root. So, if the root were not simple, then $f'(a) = 0$ but this means that a is a root of the derivative, which, as we have just seen, is not possible. So any root must be simple.

Next, we have to show that there is a root in the interval $(0, 1)$. So, let's use Bolzano's Theorem once again. OK, f is continuous since it is a polynomial, and if we set $a = 0, b = 1$ then $f(0) \cdot f(1) = (-1) \cdot (3) = -3 < 0$ and so f *does* have a root in this interval. Now let's use the starting value $x_0 = 0$. We get the table (see Figure 67):

You see from this table that the root is given by $a \approx 0.182268$ with an accuracy much greater than asked. In fact, it would have been sufficient to stop at $m = 1$ to obtain the desired accuracy. Why?

Example 158. Show that the equation $x^2 \text{Arctan} \, x = 1$ has one positive real root. Approximate its value to within an accuracy of 0.0001.

Newton iterates for
$f(x) = x^2 - \sin x$ and $x_0 = 1$

m	$f(x_m)$	x_{m+1}
0	.158529	.8913960
1	.016637	.8769848
2	.000288	.8767263
3	.000000	.8767262
4	.000000	.8767262
5	.000000	.8767262
$\cdots$	$\cdots$	$\cdots$

Figure 66.

Newton iterates for
$f(x) = x^3 - 3x^2 + 6x - 1$ and $x_0 = 0$

m	$f(x_m)$	x_{m+1}
0	-1.00000	.1666667
1	$-.078704$	.182149
2	$-.000596$	.182268
3	$-.000000$	.182268
$\cdots$	$\cdots$	$\cdots$

Figure 67.

Solution   We let $f(x) = x^2 \text{Arctan}\, x - 1$. Then $f(0) = -1$ and $f(2) = 3.4285949$. So, $f(0) \cdot f(2) = -3.4286 < 0$, and so by Bolzano's Theorem, $f(x) = 0$ somewhere in the interval $(0, 2)$. Furthermore,

$$f'(x) = x^2 \cdot \frac{1}{1 + x^2} + \text{Arctan}\, x \cdot (2x),$$

which shows that the derivative is continuous on $(0, 2)$ since all the functions involved are continuous and the denominator '$1 + x^2$' is never equal to zero. So, we can apply Newton's method with, say, $x_0 = 1$ (which is the midpoint between 0 and 2). This generates the table (Figure 68):

From this adjoining table we see that the root is given approximately by the value 1.09667 with an accuracy to 6 decimal places, well within the accuracy of 0.0001 as required. Had we stopped at $m = 2$ we would still be within the required accuracy, but this wouldn't be the case if we had stopped at $m = 1$.

Newton iterates for
$f(x) = x^2 \text{Arctan}\, x - 1$ and $x_0 = 1$

m	$f(x_m)$	x_{m+1}
0	$-.214602$	1.103632
1	.0165735	1.096702
2	.000075	1.096670
3	.000000	1.096670
...	...	...

Figure 68.

SNAPSHOTS

Example 159.   Find the value of the root of the function defined by $f(x) = x^3 - 2x - 1$ near the point 1.5.

Solution   Here $f(x) = x^3 - 2x - 1$. So we set $x_0 = 1.5$, and find that Table 3.12 becomes in this case,

$$x_{m+1} = x_m - \frac{f(x_m)}{f'(x_m)} = x_m - \frac{x_m^3 - 2x_m - 1}{3x_m^2 - 2}, \quad \text{for } m \geq 0$$

As seen in Figure 69, the root is given approximately by the value 1.61803.

Iterations for $f(x) = x^3 - 2x - 1$
with $x_0 = 1.5$.

m	x_m
0	1.5
1	1.63158
2	1.61818
3	1.61803
4	1.61803
5	1.61803

Figure 69.

Example 160.   Find the approximate value of solution of the equation $x^3 \sin x = 2$ near the point $x = 1$.

Solution   Here $f(x) = x^3 \sin x - 2$, and $f'(x) = 3x^2 \sin x + x^3 \cos x$. So we set $x_0 = 1.0$, and find that Table 3.12 becomes in this case,

$$x_{m+1} = x_m - \frac{f(x_m)}{f'(x_m)} = x_m - \frac{x_m^3 \sin x_m - 2}{3x^2 \sin x_m + x_m^3 \cos x_m}, \quad \text{for } m \geq 0$$

From Figure 70, we see that the root of f is given approximately by the value 1.27828. It follows that the solution of the equation is given by the same value, 1.27828 to six **significant digits** which means 'you're right on the number' so far.

Iterations for $f(x) = x^3 \sin x - 2$
with $x_0 = 1$.

m	x_m
0	1.37802
1	1.28474
2	1.27831
3	1.27828
4	1.27828

Figure 70.

Exercise Set 19.

Remember to set your calculator/computer software to RADIAN mode.

1. Approximate the value of the root of the equation $x - \cos x = 0$ to three significant digits using $x_0 = 0$, or equivalently, to within an accuracy of 0.001.

2. Show that **Kepler's equation** $x = 0.52 \sin x + 1$ has a root using the starting value $x_0 = 0$. Find its value to four significant digits, or equivalently, to within an accuracy of 0.0001.

3. Use the method of this section to approximate the value of the cube root of 2, $\sqrt[3]{2}$, to three significant digits.
   - Solve the equation $x^3 - 2 = 0$ with a suitable starting value.

4. Find the root of the equation $x^5 + 5x + 1 = 0$ in the interval $(-1, 0)$ and find the root to within an accuracy of 0.001.

5. Determine the points of intersection of the curves $y = \sin x$ and $y = \cos 2x$ in the interval $[-2, -1]$. Use a starting value $x_0 = -1.5$.

6. Find the point of intersection of the curves defined by $y = x^3$ and $y = \sqrt{x} + 1$ where $x \geq 0$.

7. The function defined by $f(x) = 2\sin(x \cdot \sqrt{2}) + \cos x$ is called a **quasi-periodic function**. It is known that it has an infinite number of roots in the interval $(-\infty, \infty)$. Find one of these roots in the interval $[1, 3]$ to three significant digits. Use $x_0 = 1.5$. What happens if you use $x_0 = 0$?
   - You may assume that $\sqrt{2} \approx 1.41421$.

Suggested Homework Set 13. *Do problems 1, 2, 4, 6*

NOTES:

3.12   L'Hospital's Rule

The Big Picture

In Chapter 2 we saw various methods for evaluating limits; from using their properties as continuous functions to possibly applying *extended real numbers* (see the web-site for this one). They all give the same answer, of course. Now that we've mastered the machinery of the derivative we can derive yet another method for handling limits involving the so-called **indeterminate forms**. This method was described by one **Marquis de L'Hospital** (1661-1704), and pronounced 'Lo-pit-al', who in fact wrote the first book ever on Calculus back in 1696. L'Hospital was a student of the famous mathematician **Johann Bernoulli** (1667-1748), who absorbed the methods of Leibniz from the master himself. This 'rule' was likely due to Bernoulli who discovered things faster than he could print them! So, it became known as L'Hospital's Rule because it first appeared in L'Hospital's Calculus book. Actually, most of what you're learning in this book is more than 300 years old so it must be really important in order to survive this long, right?

Review

You should review all the material on limits from Chapter 2. You should be really good in finding derivatives too! The section on **Indeterminate Forms** is particularly important as this method allows you yet another way of evaluating such mysterious looking limits involving '0/0', '∞/∞', etc. Also remember the basic steps in evaluating a limit: Rewrite or simplify or rationalize, and finally evaluate using whatever method (this Rule, extended real numbers, continuity, numerically by using your calculator, and finally, incantations).

We begin by recalling the notion of an indeterminate form. A limit problem of the form

$$\lim_{x \to a} \frac{f(x)}{g(x)}$$

is called an **indeterminate form** if the expression $f(a)/g(a)$ is one of the following types:

$$\frac{\infty}{\pm\infty}, \quad \infty - \infty, \quad (\pm\infty)^0, \quad 1^{\pm\infty}, \quad \frac{0}{0}, \quad 0^0$$

Up until now, when you met these forms in a limit you couldn't do much except simplify, rationalize, factor, etc. and then see if the form becomes "determinate". If the numerator and denominator are both differentiable functions with some nice properties, then it is sometimes possible to determine the limit by appealing to **L'Hospital's Rule**. Before we explore this Rule, a few words of caution ...

CAUTION

1. The Rule is about LIMITS

2. The Rule always involves a QUOTIENT of two functions

So, what this means is **"If your limit doesn't involve a quotient of two functions then you can't use the Rule!"** So, if you can't use the Rule, you'll have to **convert your problem** into one where you can use it.

Before describing this Rule, we define the simple notions of a **neighborhood of a point** a. Briefly stated, if a is finite, a neighborhood of a consists of an open interval (see Chapter 1) containing a.

Example 161. The interval $(-1, 0.5)$ is a neighborhood of 0, as is the interval $(-0.02, 0.3)$.

In the same vein, a **left-neighborhood** of $x = a$ consists of an open interval with a as its right endpoint.

Example 162. The interval $(-1, 0)$ is a left-neighborhood of 0, so is $(-3, 0)$, or $(-2.7, 0)$, etc.

Similarly, a **right-neighborhood** of $x = a$ consists of an open interval with a has its left endpoint

Example 163. The interval $(1, 4)$ is a right-neighborhood of 1, so is $(1, 1.00003)$, or $(1, 1000)$, etc

Finally, a **punctured neighborhood of** a is an open interval around a without the point a itself. Just think of it as an *open interval with one point missing.*

Example 164. The interval $(-0.5, 0.2)$ without the point 0, is a punctured neighborhood of 0. Also, the interval $(-1, 6)$ without the point 0, is a punctured neighborhood of 0. The statement of L'Hospital's Rule is in Table 3.13.

> **L'Hospital's Rule**
>
> Let f, g be two functions defined and differentiable in a punctured neighborhood of a, where a is finite. If $g'(x) \neq 0$ in this punctured neighborhood of a and $f(a)/g(a)$ is one of $\pm\infty/\infty$, *or* $0/0$, then
>
> $$\lim_{x \to a} \frac{f(x)}{g(x)} = \lim_{x \to a} \frac{f'(x)}{g'(x)}$$
>
> provided the limit on the right exists (it may be $\pm\infty$).
>
> The Rule also holds if a is replaced by $\pm\infty$, or even if the limits are *one-sided limits* (i.e., limit as x approaches a from the right or left).

Table 3.13: L'Hospital's Rule for Indeterminate Forms of Type $0/0$.

Table showing the likelihood that $\sin x / x \to 1$ as $x \to 0$. **Note that x can be positive or negative so long as $x \to 0$.**

x	$f(x)/g(x)$
.50000	.95885
−.33333	.98158
.25000	.98961
−.20000	.99334
−.12500	.99740
.10000	.99833
.01000	.99998
.00826	.99998
.00250	.99998
−.00111	.99999
−.00010	.99999
.00008	.99999
.00002	.99999
−.00001	.99999
.00001	.99999
...	...
0	1.00000

Figure 71.

Example 165. Use L'Hospital's Rule (Table 3.13) to show that

$$\lim_{x \to 0} \frac{\sin x}{x} = 1.$$

Solution Here $a = 0$, $f(x) = \sin x$, $g(x) = x$. The first thing to do is to **check the form!** Is it really an indeterminate form? Yes, because $(\sin 0)/0 = 0/0$.

The next thing to do is to **check the assumptions on the functions**. Both these functions are differentiable around $x = 0$, $f'(x) = \cos x$, and $g'(x) = 1 \neq 0$ in any neighborhood of $x = 0$. So we can go to the next step.. The next step is to **see if**

the the limit of the quotient of the derivatives exists!? Now,

$$\lim_{x \to 0} \frac{f'(x)}{g'(x)} = \lim_{x \to 0} \frac{\cos x}{1}$$
$$= \lim_{x \to 0} \cos x$$
$$= \cos 0 = 1, \quad \text{since the cosine function is continuous at } x = 0.$$

So, it *does* exist and consequently so does the original limit (by the Rule) and we have

$$\lim_{x \to 0} \frac{\sin x}{x} = 1.$$

Remember the geometric derivation of this limit in Chapter 2? This is much easier, no?

Three Steps to Solving Limit Problems using L'Hospital's Rule.

- What is the 'form'? ($\infty/\infty, 0/0$?)

- Check the assumptions on the quotient.

- Investigate the existence of the limit

$$\lim_{x \to a} \frac{f'(x)}{g'(x)}.$$

If this limit exists, then so does the original one and they must be equal!

Example 166.

Show that if α is any given real number, then

$$\lim_{x \to 0} \frac{\tan(\alpha x)}{x} = \alpha.$$

Solution

1. What is the form? The form is $\tan(\alpha \cdot 0)/0 = \tan(0)/0 = 0/0$, which is indeterminate.

2. Check the assumptions on the functions. Here $a = 0$ and we have a quotient of the form $f(x)/g(x) = \tan(\alpha x)/x$, where $f(x) = \tan(\alpha x)$ and $g(x) = x$. Then, by the Chain Rule, $f'(x) = \alpha \sec^2(\alpha x)$, while $g'(x) = 1$, which is not zero near $x = 0$. Both functions are differentiable near 0, so there's no problem, we can go to Step 3.

3. Check the existence of the limit of the quotient of the derivatives.

$$\lim_{x \to 0} \frac{f'(x)}{g'(x)} = \lim_{x \to 0} \frac{\alpha \sec^2(\alpha x)}{1}$$
$$= \alpha \cdot \lim_{x \to 0} \sec^2(\alpha x)$$
$$= \alpha \cdot \sec^2(0), \quad \text{since the secant function is continuous at } x = 0.$$
$$= \alpha \cdot 1 = \alpha.$$

So, this limit *does* exist and consequently so does the original limit (by the Rule) and we have

$$\lim_{x \to 0} \frac{\tan(\alpha x)}{x} = \alpha.$$

Example 167.

Evaluate

$$\lim_{x \to -1} \frac{x^2 + 6x + 5}{x^2 - x - 2}$$

Solution

1. What is the form? The form is $((-1)^2 + 6(-1) + 5)/((-1)^2 - (-1) - 2) = 0/0$, which is indeterminate.

2. Check the assumptions on the functions. Here $a = -1$ and we have a quotient of the form $f(x)/g(x) = (x^2 + 6x + 5)/(x^2 - x - 2)$, where $f(x) = x^2 + 6x + 5$ and $g(x) = x^2 - x - 2$. A simple calculation gives $f'(x) = 2x + 6$, while $g'(x) = 2x - 1 \neq 0$, near $x = -1$. Both functions are differentiable near -1, so we go to Step 3.

3. Check the existence of the limit of the quotient of the derivatives.

$$\lim_{x \to -1} \frac{f'(x)}{g'(x)} = \lim_{x \to -1} \frac{2x + 6}{2x - 1}$$
$$= (-2 + 6)/(-2 - 1), \quad \text{continuity at } x = -1.$$
$$= 4/(-3) = -4/3.$$

So, this limit *does* exist and consequently so does the original limit (by the Rule) and

$$\lim_{x \to -1} \frac{x^2 + 6x + 5}{x^2 - x - 2} = -\frac{4}{3}.$$

We check this out numerically in Figure 72. Note that $-4/3 \approx -1.333333...$

This rule of L'Hospital is not all powerful, you can't use it all the time! Now we look at an example where everything *looks good* at first but you still can't apply the Rule.

> **Example 168.** Evaluate
>
> $$\lim_{x \to 0} \frac{\sqrt{x + 1} - 1}{x^2}$$

Solution

1. What is the form? The form is $(\sqrt{1} - 1)/0 = 0/0$, which is indeterminate.

2. Check the assumptions on the functions. Here $a = 0$ and we have a quotient of the form $f(x)/g(x) = (\sqrt{x + 1} - 1)/(x^2)$, where $f(x) = \sqrt{x + 1} - 1$ and $g(x) = x^2$. A simple calculation gives $f'(x) = (2 \cdot \sqrt{x + 1})^{-1}$, while $g'(x) = 2x \neq 0$, near $x = 0$. Both functions are differentiable near 0, so we can go to Step 3.

3. Check the existence of the limit of the quotient of the derivatives.

$$\lim_{x \to 0} \frac{f'(x)}{g'(x)} = \lim_{x \to 0} \frac{\frac{1}{2 \cdot \sqrt{x + 1}}}{2x}$$
$$= \lim_{x \to 0} \frac{1}{4x \cdot \sqrt{x + 1}},$$

But this limit *does not exist* because the left and right-hand limits are not equal. In fact,

$$\lim_{x \to 0^-} \frac{1}{4x \cdot \sqrt{x + 1}} = -\infty, \quad (see \ Figure \ 73)$$
$$\lim_{x \to 0^+} \frac{1}{4x \cdot \sqrt{x + 1}} = +\infty, \quad (see \ Figure \ 74)$$

Table showing the likelihood that $f(x)/g(x) \to -4/3$ as $x \to -1$. **Note that x can be greater than or less than 1 so long as $x \to -1$.**

x	$f(x)/g(x)$
$-.990000$	-1.413793
$-.999917$	-1.340425
$-.999989$	-1.335845
$-.999997$	-1.334609
$-.999999$	-1.334188
...	...
-1	-1.333333
...	...
-1.00003	-1.333307
-1.00250	-1.331391
-1.00500	-1.329451
-1.02000	-1.317881

Figure 72.

Table showing the likelihood that $f(x)/g(x) \to -\infty$ as $x \to 0^-$.

x	$f(x)/g(x)$
$-.0050000$	-99.87532
$-.0033333$	-149.87520
$-.0016667$	-299.8751
$-.0014290$	-349.8751
$-.0010000$	-499.875
$-.0001000$	-4999.9
$-.0000010$	-500000

Figure 73.

Since the limit condition is not verified, we can't use the Rule.

So, it seems like we're back to where we started. What do we do? Back to the original ideas. We see a square root so we should be rationalizing the numerator, so as to simplify it. So, let $x \neq 0$. Then

$$
\begin{aligned}
\frac{\sqrt{x+1}-1}{x^2} &= \frac{(\sqrt{x+1}-1) \cdot (\sqrt{x+1}+1)}{x^2(\sqrt{x+1}+1)} \\
&= \frac{(x+1)-1}{x^2(\sqrt{x+1}+1)} \\
&= \frac{x}{x^2\,(\sqrt{x+1}+1)} \\
&= \frac{1}{x\,(\sqrt{x+1}+1)}.
\end{aligned}
$$

Table showing the likelihood that $f(x)/g(x) \to +\infty$ as $x \to 0^+$.

x	$f(x)/g(x)$
.0050000	99.87532
.0033333	149.87520
.0016667	299.8751
.0014290	349.8751
.0010000	499.875
.0001000	4999.9
.0000010	500000

But this quotient *does not have a limit at* 0 because the left and right-hand limits are not equal there. In fact,

$$
\lim_{x \to 0^+} \frac{1}{x\,(\sqrt{x+1}+1)} = +\infty, \quad while
$$

$$
\lim_{x \to 0^-} \frac{1}{x\,(\sqrt{x+1}+1)} = -\infty.
$$

The conclusion is that the **original limit does not exist**.

Figure 74.

Table showing the likelihood that $f(x)/g(x) \to -1/9$ as $x \to 1$. Note that $-1/9 \approx -0.111111...$

x	$f(x)/g(x)$
1.00333	−.11089
1.00250	−.1109
1.001667	−.1110
1.001250	−.1111
1.001000	−.111
...	...
1	−.11111...
...	...
.9990000	−.1112
.9950000	−.11143
.9750000	−.11268
.9000000	−.11772

Example 169. Evaluate the limit

$$
\lim_{x \to 1} \frac{3\sqrt[3]{x} - x - 2}{3(x-1)^2}.
$$

using any method. Verify your guess numerically.

Solution **1. What is the form?** At $x = 1$, the form is $(3-3)/0 = 0/0$, which is indeterminate.

2. Check the assumptions on the functions. Here $a = 1$ and we have a quotient of the form $f(x)/g(x) = (3\sqrt[3]{x} - x - 2)/3(x-1)^2$, where $f(x) = 3\sqrt[3]{x} - x - 2$ and $g(x) = 3(x-1)^2$. A simple calculation gives $f'(x) = x^{-2/3} - 1$, while $g'(x) = 6(x-1) \neq 0$, near $x = 1$. Both functions are differentiable near 1, so we can go to Step 3.

3. Check the existence of the limit of the quotient of the derivatives. Note that, in this case,

$$
\lim_{x \to 1} \frac{f'(x)}{g'(x)} = \lim_{x \to 1} \frac{x^{-2/3} - 1}{6(x-1)}.
$$

which is **still indeterminate** and of the form '0/0'. So we want to apply the Rule to it! This means that we have to check the conditions of the Rule for these functions, too. Well, let's assume you did this already. You'll see that, eventually, this part gets easier the more you do.

So, differentiating the (new) numerator and denominator gives

$$
\begin{aligned}
\lim_{x \to 1} \frac{x^{-2/3} - 1}{6(x-1)} &= \lim_{x \to 1} \frac{-\frac{2}{3}x^{-5/3}}{6} = -\frac{2}{18} \\
&= -\frac{1}{9}.
\end{aligned}
$$

Figure 75.

Sometimes you have to use L'Hospital's Rule more than once in the same problem!

This is really nice! Why? Because the existence of **this** limit means that we can apply the Rule to guarantee that

$$\lim_{x \to 1} \frac{f'(x)}{g'(x)} = -\frac{1}{9},$$

and since **this** limit exists, the Rule can be applied again to get that

$$\lim_{x \to 1} \frac{3\sqrt[3]{x} - x - 2}{3(x-1)^2} = -\frac{1}{9}.$$

See Figure 75 for the numerical evidence supporting this answer. Keep that battery charged!

Example 170. Evaluate

$$\lim_{x \to 0} \frac{\tan 2x - 2x}{x - \sin x}.$$

Solution The form is $0/0$ and all the conditions on the functions are satisfied. Next, the limit of the **quotient of the derivatives** is given by (remember the Chain Rule and the universal symbol 'D' for a derivative),

$$\lim_{x \to 0} \frac{D(\tan 2x - 2x)}{D(x - \sin x)} = \lim_{x \to 0} \frac{2 \cdot sec^2 2x - 2}{1 - \cos x},$$

which is also an indeterminate form of the type $0/0$. The conditions required by the Rule about these functions are also satisfied, so we need to check the limit of the **quotient of these derivatives**. This means that we need to check the existence of the limit

$$\lim_{x \to 0} \frac{D\left(2 \cdot sec^2 2x - 2\right)}{D\left(1 - \cos x\right)} = \lim_{x \to 0} \frac{8 \cdot sec^2(2x) \cdot \tan(2x)}{\sin x},$$

which is yet another indeterminate form of the type $0/0$ (because $\tan 0 = 0, \sin 0 = 0$). The conditions required by the Rule about these functions are also satisfied, so we need to check the limit of the **quotient of these new derivatives**. We do the same thing all over again, and we find

$$\begin{aligned}
\lim_{x \to 0} \frac{D(8 \cdot sec^2(2x) \cdot \tan(2x))}{D(\sin x)} &= (8) \cdot \lim_{x \to 0} \frac{2 \cdot sec^4 2x + 4 \cdot sec^2 2x \cdot \tan^2(2x)}{\cos x}, \\
&= \frac{(8) \cdot (2+0)}{1} \\
&= 16.
\end{aligned}$$

Phew, this was a lot of work! See Figure 76 for an idea of how this limit is reached. Here's a shortcut in writing this down:

SHORTCUT

We can write

$$\begin{aligned}
\lim_{x \to 0} \frac{\tan 2x - 2x}{x - \sin x} &= \lim_{x \to 0} \frac{D(\tan 2x - 2x)}{D(x - \sin x)}, \\
&= \lim_{x \to 0} \frac{2 \cdot sec^2 2x - 2}{1 - \cos x}, \\
&= \lim_{x \to 0} \frac{D\left(2 \cdot sec^2 2x - 2\right)}{D\left(1 - \cos x\right)},
\end{aligned}$$

Table showing the likelihood that $f(x)/g(x) \to 16$ as $x \to 0$.

x	$f(x)/g(x)$
.100000	16.26835
.033333	16.02938
.016667	16.00743
.010101	15.97674
.010000	15.99880
.001042	16.03191
.001031	15.96721
.001020	16.05640
...	...
0.00000	16.00000..
...	...
−.00100	15.99880
−.01000	16.00260
−.05000	16.06627
−.10000	16.26835

Figure 76.

$$= \lim_{x \to 0} \frac{8 \cdot sec^2(2x) \cdot \tan(2x)}{\sin x},$$

$$= \lim_{x \to 0} \frac{D(8 \cdot sec^2(2x) \cdot \tan(2x))}{D(\sin x)},$$

$$= (8) \cdot \lim_{x \to 0} \frac{2 \cdot sec^4 2x + 2 \cdot sec^2 2x \cdot \tan^2(2x)}{\cos x},$$

$$= \frac{(8) \cdot (2 + 0)}{1},$$

$$= 16,$$

if all the limits on the right exist!

WATCH OUT!

Even if ONE of these limits ON THE RIGHT of an equation fails to exist, then we have to STOP and TRY SOMETHING ELSE. If they ALL exist then you have your answer.

NOTES:

SNAPSHOTS

Example 171.   Evaluate

$$\lim_{x \to 3} \frac{x^2 - 4x + 3}{x^2 + x - 12}$$

Solution The form is $0/0$ and all the conditions on the functions are satisfied. Next, the limit of the **quotient of the derivatives** exists and is given by

$$\lim_{x \to 3} \frac{2x - 4}{2x + 1} = \frac{((2)(3) - 4)}{((2)(3) + 1)} = \frac{2}{7}.$$

So, by the Rule, the original limit also exists and

$$\lim_{x \to 3} \frac{x^2 - 4x + 3}{x^2 + x - 12} = \lim_{x \to 3} \frac{2x - 4}{2x + 1} = \frac{2}{7}.$$

Example 172.   Evaluate

$$\lim_{x \to 1} \frac{x^2 - 2x + 1}{x^3 - x}.$$

Sometimes L'Hospital's Rule gives NO information even though the actual limit may exist! For example, the Sandwich Theorem shows that

$$\lim_{x \to 0+} x \sin\left(\frac{1}{x}\right) = 0.$$

However, if we apply the Rule to

$$\lim_{x \to 0+} x \sin\left(\frac{1}{x}\right) = \lim_{x \to 0+} \frac{\sin\left(\frac{1}{x}\right)}{\frac{1}{x}},$$

we get

$$\lim_{x \to 0+} \frac{-\frac{1}{x^2} \cos\left(\frac{1}{x}\right)}{-\frac{1}{x^2}} = \lim_{x \to 0+} \cos\left(\frac{1}{x}\right)$$

and this last limit DOES NOT EXIST! So, L'Hospital's Rule would be claiming that the limit does not exist even though the original limit DOES exist!

Solution The form is $0/0$ and all the conditions on the functions are satisfied. The limit of the **quotient of the derivatives** exists and is given by

$$\lim_{x \to 1} \frac{2x - 2}{3x^2 - 1} = \frac{0}{2} = 0.$$

So, by the Rule, the original limit also exists and

$$\lim_{x \to 1} \frac{x^2 - 2x + 1}{x^3 - x} = \lim_{x \to 1} \frac{2x - 2}{3x^2 - 1} = 0.$$

Example 173.   Evaluate

$$\lim_{x \to 1} \frac{\sin \pi x}{x^2 - 1}$$

Solution The form is $(\sin 0)/0 = 0/0$ and all the conditions on the functions are satisfied. The limit of the **quotient of the derivatives** exists and is given by

$$\lim_{x \to 1} \frac{\pi \cdot \cos(\pi x)}{2x} = \frac{\pi \cdot \cos(\pi)}{2}$$
$$= -\frac{\pi}{2}.$$

So, by the Rule, the original limit also exists and

$$\lim_{x \to 1} \frac{\sin \pi x}{x^2 - 1} = \lim_{x \to 1} \frac{\pi \cdot \cos(\pi x)}{2x}$$
$$= -\frac{\pi}{2}.$$

L'Hospital's Rule for Limits at Infinity

Suppose that f and g are each differentiable in some interval of the form $M < x < \infty$, $f'(x) \neq 0$ in $M < x < \infty$, and the next two limits exist and

$$\lim_{x \to \infty} f(x) = 0 \qquad and \qquad \lim_{x \to \infty} g(x) = 0.$$

Then

$$\lim_{x \to \infty} \frac{f(x)}{g(x)} = \lim_{x \to \infty} \frac{f'(x)}{g'(x)}$$

whenever the latter limit (the one on the right) exists. A similar result is true if we replace ∞ by $-\infty$.

Table 3.14: L'Hospital's Rule for Indeterminate Forms of Type 0/0.

Example 174. Evaluate

$$\lim_{x \to 0} \frac{\sin 4x}{\sin 7x}.$$

Solution The form is $(\sin 0)/(\sin 0) = 0/0$ and all the conditions on the functions are satisfied. The limit of the **quotient of the derivatives** exists and is given by

$$\lim_{x \to 0} \frac{4 \cdot \cos 4x}{7 \cdot \cos 7x} \quad = \quad \frac{4 \cdot 1}{7 \cdot 1}$$
$$= \quad \frac{4}{7}.$$

So, by the Rule, the original limit exists and

$$\lim_{x \to 0} \frac{\sin 4x}{\sin 7x} \quad = \quad \lim_{x \to 0} \frac{4 \cdot \cos 4x}{7 \cdot \cos 7x}$$
$$= \quad \frac{4}{7}.$$

At this point we move on to the study of *limits at infinity*. In these cases the Rule still applies as can be shown in theory: Refer to Table 3.14 above for the result. The Rule is used in exactly the same way, although we must be more careful in handling these limits, because they are at '$\pm\infty$', so it may be helpful to review your section on *Extended Real Number Arithmetic*, in Chapter 2, in order to cook up your guesses.

Sometimes these limit problems may be '*in disguise*' so you may have to move things around and get them in the right form (i.e., a quotient) BEFORE you apply the Rule.

Example 175. Compute

$$\lim_{x \to \infty} \frac{1}{x \, \sin(\frac{\pi}{x})}.$$

Solution **Check the form** In this case we have '$1/(\infty \cdot 0)$', which is indeterminate because '$0 \cdot \infty$' is itself indeterminate. So, we can't even *think* about using the Rule. But, if we rewrite the expression as

$$\lim_{x \to \infty} \frac{1/x}{\sin(\frac{\pi}{x})},$$

then the form is of the type '$0/0$', right? (because $1/\infty = 0$).

Check the assumptions on the functions. This is OK because the only thing that can go wrong with the derivative of $f(x) = 1/x$ is at $x = 0$, so if we choose $M = 1$, say, in Table 3.14, then we're OK. The same argument applies for g.

Check the limit of the quotient of the derivatives. We differentiate the numerator and the denominator to find,

$$\lim_{x \to \infty} \frac{1/x}{sin(\pi/x)} = \lim_{x \to \infty} \frac{-1/x^2}{(-\pi/x^2) \cdot cos(\pi/x)} = \lim_{x \to \infty} \frac{1}{\pi cos(\pi/x)} = \frac{1}{\pi},$$

since all the limits exist, and $\pi/x \to 0$, *as* $x \to \infty$ (which means $\cos(\pi/x) \to \cos 0 = 1$ as $x \to \infty$).

Don't like to tangle with infinity?

No problem. Whenever you see '$x \to \infty$ just let $x = 1/t$ everywhere in the expressions and then let $t \to 0^+$. Suddenly, the limit at ∞ is converted to a one-sided limit at 0. In fact, what happens is this:

$$\lim_{x \to +\infty} \frac{f(x)}{g(x)} = \lim_{t \to 0+} \frac{f'(1/t)}{g'(1/t)}$$
$$= \lim_{x \to 0+} \frac{f'(1/x)}{g'(1/x)}$$

In this way you can find limits at infinity by transforming them to limits at 0.

Example 176.	Compute

$$\lim_{x \to -\infty} \frac{x^2 - 1}{x^2 + 1}.$$

Table showing the likelihood that $(x^2 - 1)/(x^2 + 1) \to 1$ as $x \to -\infty$.

x	$f(x)/g(x)$
-20	.99501
-50	.99920
-200	.99995
-300	.99997
$-1,000$	.99998
$-10,000$	.99999
...	...
$-\infty$	1.00000...

Figure 77.

Solution **Without the Rule** In this case we have ∞/∞, which is indeterminate. Now let's convert this to a problem where the symbol $-\infty$ is converted to 0^-. We let $x = 1/t$. Then,

$$\lim_{x \to -\infty} \frac{x^2 - 1}{x^2 + 1} = \lim_{t \to 0-} \frac{(1/t)^2 - 1}{(1/t)^2 + 1},$$
$$= \lim_{t \to 0-} \frac{1 - t^2}{1 + t^2},$$
$$= 1,$$

since both the numerator and denominator are continuous there. Did you notice we didn't use the Rule at all? (see Figure 77 to convince yourself of this limit). This is because the last limit you see here is **not an indeterminate form** at all.

With the Rule The original form is ∞/∞, which is indeterminate. We can also use the Rule because it applies and all the conditions on the functions are met. This means that, provided all the following limits exist,

$$\lim_{x\to-\infty} \frac{x^2-1}{x^2+1} = \lim_{x\to-\infty} \frac{2x}{2x},$$
$$= \lim_{x\to-\infty} 1,$$
$$= 1,$$

as before.

Example 177. Compute

$$\lim_{x\to+\infty} \sqrt{x+1} - \sqrt{x}.$$

Solution **Check the form** In this case we have $\infty - \infty$, which is indeterminate. You can't use the Rule at all here because the form is not right, we're not dealing with a quotient, but a difference. So, let's convert this to a problem where the symbol $+\infty$ is converted to 0^+. We let $x = 1/t$. Then, (see the margin),

$$\lim_{x\to+\infty} \sqrt{x+1} - \sqrt{x} = \lim_{t\to0^+} \sqrt{(1/t)+1} - \sqrt{1/t},$$
$$= \lim_{t\to0^+} \frac{(\sqrt{(1/t)+1} - \sqrt{1/t}) \cdot (\sqrt{(1/t)+1} + \sqrt{1/t})}{\sqrt{(1/t)+1} + \sqrt{1/t}},$$
$$= \lim_{t\to0^+} \frac{(1/t+1) - (1/t)}{\sqrt{(1/t)+1} + \sqrt{1/t}},$$
$$= \lim_{t\to0^+} \frac{1}{\sqrt{(1/t)+1} + \sqrt{1/t}},$$
$$= 0,$$

This is a standard trick; for any two positive symbols, $\square, \triangle$ we have

$$\sqrt{\square} - \sqrt{\triangle} = \frac{\square - \triangle}{\sqrt{\square} + \sqrt{\triangle}}.$$

Here $\square = (1/t) + 1, \triangle = 1/t$.

since the denominator is infinite at this point and so its reciprocal is zero.

Once again, did you notice we didn't use the Rule at all? This is because the last limit you see here is **not an indeterminate form** either.

Example 178. Evaluate

$$\lim_{x\to+\infty} x^2 \cdot \sin\frac{1}{x}.$$

Solution **Check the form** In this case we have $(\infty) \cdot (0)$, which is indeterminate. You can't use the Rule at all here because the form is not right again, we're not dealing with a quotient, but a product. So, once again we convert this to a problem where the symbol $+\infty$ is converted to 0^+. We let $x = 1/t$. Then,

$$\lim_{x\to+\infty} x^2 \cdot \sin\frac{1}{x} = \lim_{x\to+\infty} \frac{\sin\frac{1}{x}}{\frac{1}{x^2}},$$
$$= \lim_{t\to0^+} \frac{\sin t}{t^2},$$

and this last form *is* indeterminate. So we can use the Rule on it (we checked all the assumptions, right?). Then,

$$\lim_{x\to+\infty} x^2 \cdot \sin\frac{1}{x} = \lim_{t\to0^+} \frac{\sin t}{t^2},$$
$$= \lim_{t\to0^+} \frac{\cos t}{2t},$$
$$= +\infty,$$

Table showing the likelihood that $f(x)/g(x) \to +\infty$ as $x \to +\infty$.

x	$x^2 \cdot \sin(1/x)$
20	19.99167
60	59.99722
200	199.99917
300	299.99944
2000	1999.99992
10,000	9999.9
...	...
$+\infty$	$+\infty$

Figure 78.

since this last form is of the type $\cos 0/\infty = 0$. So, the limit exists and

$$\lim_{x \to +\infty} x^2 \cdot \sin \frac{1}{x} = +\infty,$$

see Figure 78.

Exercise Set 20.

Determine the limits of the following quotients if they exist, using any method. Try to check your answer numerically with your calculator too.

1. $\displaystyle\lim_{x \to 0} \frac{-\sin x}{2x}$

2. $\displaystyle\lim_{t \to 0} \frac{\sin t}{t}$

3. $\displaystyle\lim_{x \to 0} \frac{1 - \cos x}{x}$

4. $\displaystyle\lim_{x \to -1} \frac{x^2 - 1}{x + 1}$

5. $\displaystyle\lim_{x \to 1} \frac{x^4 - 1}{x^2 - 1}$

6. $\displaystyle\lim_{x \to \pi} \frac{\tan 2x}{x - \pi}$

7. $\displaystyle\lim_{x \to \pi} \frac{1 + \cos x}{\sin 2x}$

8. $\displaystyle\lim_{t \to 0} \frac{\sin^2 t - \sin t^2}{t^2}$

9. $\displaystyle\lim_{x \to 1} \frac{x^3 - 3x + 1}{x^4 - x^2 - 2x}$

10. $\displaystyle\lim_{x \to 0} \frac{\text{Arctan } x}{x^2}$

11. $\displaystyle\lim_{x \to 0} \frac{\text{Arcsin } x}{\text{Arctan } x}$

12. $\displaystyle\lim_{x \to 0} \frac{2 \cdot \sin 3x}{\sin 5x}$

13. $\displaystyle\lim_{x \to 1} \frac{x^2 - 1}{x^6 - 1}$

14. $\displaystyle\lim_{x \to 0} \frac{2 \cos x - 2 + x^2}{3x^4}$

15. $\displaystyle\lim_{x \to 0} \frac{x \sin(\sin x)}{1 - \cos(\sin x)}$

Suggested Homework Set 14. *Do problems 3, 5, 8, 12, 14*

NOTES:

3.13   Chapter Exercises

Use any method to find the derivative of the indicated function. There is no need to simplify your answers.

1. $(x+1)^{27}$ 6. $\sqrt{2x-5}$ 11. $\dfrac{1}{\sin 3x}$

2. $\cos^3(x)$ 7. $\sin 2x$ 12. $\dfrac{x+2}{\cos 2x}$

3. $\dfrac{x+1}{\sin 2x}$ 8. $\cos(\sin 4x)$ 13. $\dfrac{x^2+1}{2x+3}$

4. $\sin\left((x+5)^2\right)$ 9. $\dfrac{1}{(\cos 2x)^3}$ 14. $(\sin 3x)\cdot(x^{1/5}+1)$

5. $\dfrac{1}{\sin x+\cos x}$ 10. $\dfrac{x^2+1}{\cos 2x}$ 15. $\sin(x^2+6x-2)$

Find the derivative of the following functions at the given point

16. $\dfrac{-1.4}{2x+1}$, *at* $x=0$ 19. $(2x+3)^{105}$, *at* $x=1$

17. $(x+1)^{\frac{2}{3}}$, *at* $x=1$ 20. $x\cdot\sin 2x$, *at* $x=0$

18. $\dfrac{1}{x+\sqrt{x^2-1}}$, *at* $x=2$ 21. $\sin(\sin 4x)$, *at* $x=\pi$

Evaluate the following limits directly using any method

22. $\displaystyle\lim_{h\to 0}\dfrac{f(2+h)-f(2)}{h}$ where $f(x)=(x-1)^2$

23. $\displaystyle\lim_{h\to 0}\dfrac{f(-1+h)-f(-1)}{h}$ where $f(x)=|x+2|$

24. $\displaystyle\lim_{h\to 0}\dfrac{f(1+h)-f(1)}{h}$ where $f(x)=\sqrt{x+1}$,
   • Rationalize the numerator and simplify.

25. Find the second derivative $f''(x)$ given that $f(x)=(3x-2)^{99}$. Evaluate $f''(+1)$.

26. Let f be a differentiable function for every real number x. Show that $\frac{d}{dx}f(3x^2)=6x\cdot f'(3x^2)$. Verify this formula for the particular case where $f(x)=x^3$.

27. Find the equation of the tangent line to the curve $y=(x^2-3)^6$ at the point $(x,y)=(2,1)$.

28. Let $y=t^3+\cos t$ and $t=\sqrt{u}+6$. Find $\frac{dy}{du}$ when $u=9$.

29. Let $y=r^{1/2}-\frac{3}{r}$ and $r=3t-2\sqrt{t}$. Use the Chain Rule to find an expression for $\frac{dy}{dt}$.

30. Use the definition of the derivative to show that the function $y=x\cdot|x|$ has a derivative at $x=0$ but $y''(0)$ does not exist.

Use implicit differentiation to find the required derivative.

31. $x^3 + 2xy + y^2 = 1$, $\quad \dfrac{dy}{dx}$ at $(1,0)$

32. $2xy^2 - y^4 = x^3$, $\quad \dfrac{dy}{dx}$ and $\dfrac{dx}{dy}$

33. $\sqrt{x+y} + x^2 y^2 = 4$, $\quad \dfrac{dy}{dx}$ at $(0,16)$

34. $y^5 - 3y^2 x - yx = 2$, $\quad \dfrac{dy}{dx}$

35. $x^2 + y^2 = 16$, $\quad \dfrac{dy}{dx}$ at $(4,0)$

Find the equation of the tangent line to the given curve at the given point.

36. $2x^2 - y^2 = 1$, $\quad$ at $(-1,-1)$
37. $2x + xy + y^2 = 0$, $\quad$ at $(0,0)$
38. $x^2 + 2x + y^2 - 4y - 24 = 0$, $\quad$ at $(4,0)$
39. $(x-y)^3 - x^3 + y^3 = 0$, $\quad$ at $(1,1)$
40. $\sin x + \sin y - 3y^2 = 0$, $\quad$ at $(\pi, 0)$

Evaluate the following limits at infinity.

41. $\displaystyle \lim_{x \to +\infty} \frac{x^2 - 1}{2x^2 - 1}$

42. $\displaystyle \lim_{x \to +\infty} \frac{x}{x - 1}$

43. $\displaystyle \lim_{x \to +\infty} \left(\frac{x^3}{x^2 + 1} - x \right)$

44. $\displaystyle \lim_{x \to -\infty} \frac{x^2}{x^3 - 1}$

45. $\displaystyle \lim_{x \to -\infty} x^2 \cdot \left(\frac{\pi}{2} + \operatorname{Arctan} x \right)$

Suggested Homework Set 15. *Work out problems* $14, 20, 21, 24, 28, 33, 37$

3.14 Using Computer Algebra Systems

Use your favorite Computer Algebra System (CAS), like Maple, MatLab, etc., or even a graphing calculator to answer the following questions:

1. Two functions f, g have the property that $f'(9.657463) = -2.34197$, and $g(1.2) = 9.657463$. If $g'(1.2) = -6.549738$ calculate the value of the derivative of their composition, $D(f \circ g)(1.2)$.

2. Let $f(x) = x(x+1)(x-2)$ be defined on the interval $[-3, 3]$. Sketch the graph of $f(x)$ and then, on the same axes, sketch the graph of its derivative $f'(x)$. Can you tell them apart? If we hadn't told you what the function f was but only gave you their graphs, would you be able to distinguish f from its derivative, f'? Explain.

3. Find the equations of the tangent lines to the curve

$$y = \frac{x+1}{x^2+1}$$

through the points $x = 0$, $x = -1.2$, $x = 1.67$ and $x = 3.241$.

4. Remove the absolute value in the function f defined by $f(x) = |x^3 - x|$. Next, remove the absolute value in the function $g(x) = |x - 2|$. Now write down the values of the function h defined by the difference $h(x) = f(x) - 3g(x)$ where $-\infty < x < +\infty$. Finally, determine the points (if any) where the function h fails to be differentiable (*i.e.*, has no derivative). Is there a point x where $f'(x) = 0$?

5. Use implicit differentiation to find the first and second derivative of y with respect to x given that
$$x^2 + y^2x + 3xy = 3.$$

6. Find a pattern for the first eight derivatives of the function f defined by $f(x) = (3x + 2)^5 2$. Can you guess what the 25th derivative of f looks like?

7. Use Newton's method to find the positive solution of the equation $x + \sin x = 2$ where $0 \le x \le \frac{\pi}{2}$. (Use Bolzano's theorem first to obtain an initial guess.)

8. Use repeated applications of the **Product Rule** to find a formula for the derivative of the product of *three* functions f, g, h. Can you find such a formula given *four* given functions? More generally, find a formula for the derivative of the product of n such functions, $f_1, f_2, \ldots, f_n$ where $n \ge 2$ is any given integer.

9. Use repeated applications of the **Chain Rule** to find a formula for the derivative of the composition of *three* functions f, g, h. Can you find such a formula given *four* given functions? More generally, find a formula for the derivative of the composition of n such functions, $f_1, f_2, \ldots, f_n$ where $n \ge 2$ is any given integer.

Chapter 4

Exponentials and Logarithms

The Big Picture

This Chapter is about exponential functions and their properties. Whenever you write down the expression $2^3 = 8$ you are really writing down the value (i.e., 8) of an exponential function at the point $x = 3$. Which function? The function f defined by $f(x) = 2^x$ has the property that $f(3) = 8$ as we claimed. So f is an example of such an exponential function. It's okay to think about 2^x when x is an integer, but what what happens if the '2' is replaced by an arbitrary number? Even worse, what happens if the *power, or, exponent*, x is an **irrational number**? (not an ordinary fraction). We will explore these definitions in this chapter. We will also study one very important function called **Euler's Exponential Function**, sometimes referred to by mathematicians as *The Exponential Function* a name which describes its importance in Calculus. **Leonhard Euler**, (pronounced 'oiler'), 1707-1783, is one of the great mathematicians. As a teenager he was tutored by Johann Bernoulli (the one who was L'Hospital's teacher) and quickly turned to mathematics instead of his anticipated study of Philosophy. His life work (much of which is lost) fills around 80 volumes and he is responsible for opening up many areas in mathematics and producing important trendsetting work in Physics in such areas as Optics, Mechanics, and Planetary Motion.

This exponential function of Euler will be denoted by e^x. It turns out that all other exponential functions (like $2^x, (0.5)^x, \dots$) can be written in terms of it too! So, we really only need to study this one function, e^x. Part of the importance of this function of Euler lies in its applications to growth and decay problems in population biology or nuclear physics to mention only a few areas outside of mathematics *per se*. We will study these topics later when we begin solving differential equations. The most remarkable property of this function is that it is its own derivative! In other words, $D(e^x) = e^x$ where D is the derivative. Because of this property of its derivative we can solve equations which at one time seemed impossible to solve.

Review

You should review Chapter 1 and especially Exercise Set 3, Number 17 where the inequalities will serve to pin down Euler's number, denoted by 'e' and whose value is approximately $e = 2.7182818284590....$

4.1 Exponential Functions and Their Logarithms

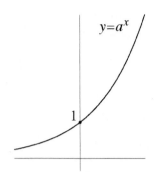

$a>1$

Figure 79.

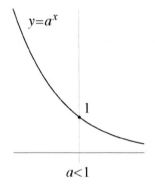

$a<1$

Figure 80.

Exponentials or **power functions** are functions defined by expressions which look like:

$$f(x) = a^x$$

where a is the base and x is the **power** or **exponent**. In this section we will be reviewing the basic properties of exponents first, leaving the formal definition of the exponential function until later. We will always assume that $a > 0$. It can be shown that such power functions have an **inverse** function. This inverse function will be called the **logarithm** (a quantity which must depend on the base) and the symbol used to denote the logarithm is:

$$F(x) = \boxed{\log_a(x)}$$

which is read as "the logarithm with base a of x". Since this is an inverse function in its own right, it follows by definition of the inverse that:

$$\begin{aligned} x &= f(F(x)) \\ &= a^{F(x)} \\ &= a^{\log_a(x)} \end{aligned}$$

and, more generally:

$$\boxed{\square = a^{\log_a(\square)}}$$

for any '*symbol*' denoted by $\square$ for which $\square > 0$. Furthermore:

$$\begin{aligned} x &= F(f(x)) \\ &= \log_a(f(x)) \\ &= \log_a(a^x) \end{aligned}$$

and, once again,

$$\boxed{\square = \log_a(a^{\square})}$$

for any symbol $\square$ where now $-\infty < \square < \infty$.

Typical graphs of such functions are given in Figures 79, 80 in the adjoining margin along with their inverses (or logarithms) whose graphs appear in Figures 81, 82.

Example 179. Let, $f(x) = 3^x$. Then $F(x) = \log_3(x)$ is its inverse function and

$$\begin{aligned} 3^{\log_3(x)} &= x, & x > 0 \\ \log_3(3^x) &= x, & -\infty < x < \infty. \end{aligned}$$

Example 180. $3^2 = 9$ means the same as:

$$\log_3(9) = 2.$$

Now notice the following pattern: In words this is saying that,

$$\boxed{\log_{base}(result) = power}$$

or,

$$\boxed{base^{power} = result}$$

Example 181. Write the following expression as a logarithm.

$$2^{-\frac{1}{2}} = \frac{1}{2^{\frac{1}{2}}} = \frac{\sqrt{2}}{2}$$

Solution In terms of logarithms, we can rewrite the equation

$$2^{-\frac{1}{2}} = \frac{\sqrt{2}}{2}$$

as,

$$\log_2\left(\frac{\sqrt{2}}{2}\right) = -\frac{1}{2}$$

because here the *base* = 2, the *power* is $-\frac{1}{2}$ and the *result* is $\frac{\sqrt{2}}{2}$

Example 182. Write the following expression as a logarithm.

$$4^{\sqrt{2}} \approx 7.10299$$

means we set the *base* = 4, *power* = $\sqrt{2}$ and *result* = 7.10299. So,

$$\log_4(7.10299) = \sqrt{2}$$

Example 183. Write the following expression as a logarithm.

$$\sqrt[3]{2}^{\sqrt{3}} \approx 1.38646$$

Solution This means that we set the *base* = $\sqrt[3]{2}$, the *power* = $\sqrt{3}$ and the result:

$$\log_{\sqrt[3]{2}}(1.38646) = \sqrt{3}$$

Remember that the base does not have to be an integer, it can be any irrational or rational (positive) number.

Example 184. Sketch the graph of the following functions by using a calculator: use the same axes (compare your results with Figure 83).

    a. $f(x) = 3^x$

    b. $f(x) = \dfrac{1}{2^x}$

    c. $f(x) = (\sqrt{2})^x$

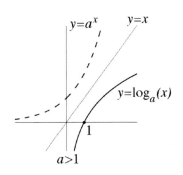

Figure 81.

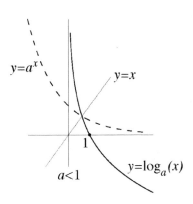

Figure 82.

Properties of the Logarithm

1. $\log_a(\square^{\triangle}) = \triangle \log_a(\square)$
2. $\log_a(\square\triangle) = \log_a(\square) + \log_a(\triangle)$
3. $\log_a(\dfrac{\triangle}{\square}) = \log_a(\triangle) - \log_a(\square)$

Table 4.1: Properties of the Logarithm

x	-2	-1	0	1	2
3^x	0.12	0.33	1	3	9

x	-2	-1	0	1	2
$\frac{1}{2^x}$	4	2	1	0.5	0.25

x	-2	-1	0	1	2
$(\sqrt{2})^x$	0.5	0.71	1	1.4	2

Remarks: Note that as 'a' increases past 1 the graph of $y = a^x$ gets 'steeper' as you proceed from left to right (harder to climb).

If $0 < a < 1$ and 'a' is small but positive, the graph of $y = a^x$ also becomes steeper, but in proceeding from right to left.

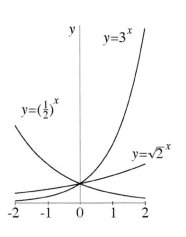

Figure 83.

From these graphs and the definitions of the exponential and logarithm functions we get the following important properties:

$$a^{\triangle} = \square \quad \text{means} \quad \log_a(\square) = \triangle$$

and

$$
\begin{aligned}
a^0 &= 1 \\
\log_a(a) &= 1 \\
\log_a(1) &= 0
\end{aligned}
$$

along with the very practical properties:

where, as usual, $\triangle, \square$ are any two '*symbols*' (usually involving x but not necessarily so).

Example 185. Show that for $\triangle > 0$ and $\square > 0$ we have the equality:

Solution

$$\log_a(\square \, \triangle) = \log_a(\square) + \log_a(\triangle)$$

(**Hint:** Let $A = \log_a(\triangle), B = \log_a(\square)$. Show that $a^{A+B} = \triangle\square$, by using the definition of the logarithm. Conclude that $A + B = \log_a(\triangle\square)$.)

Example 186. Calculate the value of $\log_{\sqrt{2}}(4)$ exactly!

Let's show that $\log_a(\square^{\triangle}) = \triangle \log_a(\square)$.

Write $y = \log_a(\square)$. Then, by definition of the logarithm, this really means,

$$a^y = \square$$

raising both sides to the power $\triangle$ we get,

$$(a^y)^{\triangle} = \square^{\triangle}$$

or, by the usual Power Laws,

$$a^{y\triangle} = \square^{\triangle}.$$

Using the definition of a logarithm once again we find,

$$\log_a(\square^{\triangle}) = y\triangle$$

(as '$y\triangle$' and '$\square^{\triangle}$' are just two 'new' symbols). But $y\triangle = \triangle \log_a(\square)$, and so the result is true, namely that,

$$\log_a(\square^{\triangle}) = \triangle \log_a(\square)$$

The other properties may be shown using similar arguments.

Table 4.2: Why is $\log_a(\square^{\triangle}) = \triangle \log_a(\square)$?

Solution Write the definition down...Here the *base* $= \sqrt{2}$, the *result* is 4 so the *power* =? Well,

$$(\sqrt{2})^{power} = 4$$

means *power* $= 4$, by inspection (i.e., $\sqrt{2} \cdot \sqrt{2} \cdot \sqrt{2} \cdot \sqrt{2} = 4$). So,

$$\log_{\sqrt{2}}(4) = 4$$

Example 187. Solve for x if $\log_2(x) = -3$

Solution By definition of this inverse function we know that $2^{-3} = x$ or $x = \frac{1}{8}$.

Example 188. If $\log_a(9) = 2$ find the *base* a.

Solution By definition, $a^2 = 9$, and so $a = +3$ or $a = -3$. Since $a > 0$ by definition, it follows that $a = 3$ is the *base*.

Example 189. Evaluate $\log_3(\sqrt{3})$ exactly.

Solution We use the rule $\log_a(\square^{\triangle}) = \triangle \log_a(\square)$ with $a = 3$. Note that

$$\log_3(\sqrt{3}) = \log_3(3^{\frac{1}{2}})$$

So we can set $\square = 3, \triangle = \frac{1}{2}$. Then

$$\log_3(\sqrt{3}) = \log_3(3^{\frac{1}{2}})$$

$$= \frac{1}{2}\log_3(3), \quad \text{by Table 4.2,}$$
$$= \frac{1}{2}(1) \quad (\text{because } \log_a(a) = 1)$$
$$= \frac{1}{2}$$

Example 190. Simplify the following expression for $f(x)$ using the properties above:

$$f(x) = \log_2(\sqrt{x}\sin x), \text{ if } 0 < x < \frac{\pi}{2}.$$

Solution:

$$\begin{aligned}
f(x) &= \log_2(\sqrt{x}\sin x), \\
&= \log_2(\sqrt{x}) + \log_2(\sin x), \quad \text{by Table 4.1, (2)} \\
&= \log_2(x^{\frac{1}{2}}) + \log_2(\sin x) \\
&= \frac{1}{2}\log_2(x) + \log_2(\sin x), \quad \text{by Table 4.1, (1)}
\end{aligned}$$

Example 191. Simplify the following expression for $f(x)$ using the properties above:

$$f(x) = \log_4(4^x 8^{x^2+1}), \ x \geq 0$$

Solution: All references refer to Table 4.1. OK, now

$$\begin{aligned}
f(x) &= \log_4(4^x) + \log_4(8^{x^2+1}) \quad \text{(by Property 2)} \\
&= x\log_4(4) + (x^2+1)\log_4(8) \quad \text{(by Property 1)} \\
&= x(1) + (x^2+1)\log_4(2^3) \quad (\text{because } \log_a(a) = 1 \text{ and } 8 = 2^3) \\
&= x + (x^2+1)\cdot 3\log_4(2) \quad \text{(by Property 1.)}
\end{aligned}$$

Now if $\log_4(2) = z$, say, then, by definition, $4^z = 2$, but this means that $(2^2)^z = 2$ or $2^{2z} = 2$ or $2z = 1$, that is, $z = \frac{1}{2}$. Good, this means

$$\log_4(2) = \frac{1}{2}$$

and so,

$$f(x) = x + \frac{3}{2}(x^2+1),$$

hard to believe isn't it?

NOTES:

> **Exercise Set 21.**

Simplify as much as you can:

1. $2^{\log_2(x^2+1)}$
2. $\left(\dfrac{1}{2}\right)^{\log_{\frac{1}{2}}(x)}$ $\left(\text{Hint}:\ \text{Let } a = \dfrac{1}{2}\right)$
3. $\log_4(2^x 16^{-x^2})$
4. $\log_3\left(\dfrac{3}{4}\right)$ (Hint : Use Property 3)
5. $\log_a(2^x 2^{-x})$

Sketch the graphs of the following functions using your calculator:

6. $f(x) = 4^x$
7. $f(x) = \dfrac{1}{4^x}$
8. $(\sqrt{3})^x$

Write the following equations in logarithmic form (e.g. $2^3 = 8$ means $\log_2(8) = 3$):

9. $\sqrt{2}^{\sqrt{2}} \approx 1.6325$
10. $2^{-4} = \dfrac{1}{16}$
11. $3^{-2} = \dfrac{1}{9}$

Write the following equations as power functions (e.g. $\log_2(8) = 3$ means $2^3 = 8$).

12. $\log_2(f(x)) = x$
13. $\log_3(81) = 4$
14. $\log_{\frac{1}{2}}(4) = -2$
15. $\log_{\frac{1}{3}}(27) = -3$
16. $\log_a(1) = 0$
17. $\log_{\sqrt{2}}(1.6325) = \sqrt{2}$

Solve the following equations for x:

18. $\log_2(x) + \log_2(3) = 4$, (**Hint:** Use property 2)
19. $\log_3\left(\dfrac{x}{x+1}\right) = 1$
20. $\log_{\sqrt{2}}(x^2 - 1) = 0$
21. $\log_{\frac{1}{2}}(x) = -1$
22. Sketch the graph of the function y defined by $y(x) = \log_2(2^{x^2})$
     (**Hint:** Let $\square = x^2$)

4.2   Euler's Number, e = 2.718281828 ...

Now that we know how to handle various exponential functions and their logarithms we'll define one very special but really important exponential function. We'll introduce Euler's number, denoted by 'e', after Euler, whose value is approximately $e \approx 2.718281828459$. Using this number as a 'base', we'll define the special exponential function, e^x, and its inverse function, called the **natural logarithm**. We'll then look at the various formulae for the derivative of exponential and logarithmic functions. The most striking property of e lies in that $y = e^x$ has the property that $y\prime = y$ (*a really neat property!*).

Before we move on to the definition of this number 'e' which is the cornerstone of differential and integral calculus, we need to look at **sequences**, or strings of numbers separated by commas. Well, more precisley, a sequence is the range of a function, denoted by 'a', whose domain is a subset of the integers. So, its values are given by $a(n) = a_n$, where a_n is just shorthand for this value and it can be thought of as representing the nth term of the sequence, the term in the nth position. For example, if $a(n) = 2n - 1$, then $a(6) = 2 \cdot 6 - 1 = 11$, and so we write $a_6 = 11$; $a(15) = 29$ and so we write $a_{15} = 29$, and so on. The whole sequence looks like

$$1, 3, 5, 7, 9, \underbrace{11}, 13, 15, 17, \ldots$$

the 6th term is a_6

Before we jump into this business of exponentials, we need to describe one central result. A sequence of numbers is said to be **monotone increasing** if consecutive terms get bigger as you go along the sequence. For example,

$$1, 2, 3, 4, 5, 6, \ldots$$

is an increasing sequence. So is

$$\frac{1}{2}, 1, \frac{3}{2}, 2, \frac{5}{2}, \ldots$$

or even,

$$1.6, 1.61, 1.612, 1.6123, 1.61234, \ldots$$

and so on. Mathematically we write this property of a sequence $\{a_n\}$ by the inequality,

$$\boxed{a_n < a_{n+1},}\quad n = 1, 2, 3, \ldots$$

which means that the nth term, denoted by a_n, has the property that a_n *is smaller than the next one, namely,* a_{n+1}; makes sense right?!

Well, the next result makes sense if you think about it, and it is *believable* but we won't prove it here. At this point we should recall the main results on limits in Chapter 2. When we speak of the **convergence of an infinite sequence** we mean it in the sense of Chapter 2, that is, in the sense that

$$\lim_{n \to +\infty} a_n = \lim_{n \to +\infty} a(n)$$

or, if you prefer, replace all the symbols n by x above, so that we are really looking at the limit of a function as $x \to +\infty$ but x is always an integer, that's all.

Convergence of Increasing Sequences

Let $\{a_n\}$ be an increasing sequence. Then,

$$\lim_{n \to \infty} a_n$$

exists in the extended real numbers.

In other words; *either*

$$\lim_{n \to \infty} a_n = L < \infty$$

or,

$$\lim_{n \to \infty} a_n = +\infty$$

For *example*, the sequence $\{a_n\}$ where $a_n = n$ is increasing and $a_n \to \infty$ as $n \to \infty$.

On the other hand, the sequence $\{b_n\}$ where

$$b_n = \frac{n}{n+1}$$

is increasing and

$$\lim_{n \to \infty} b_n = 1$$

(Why? The simplest proof uses L'Hospital's Rule on the quotient $x/(x+1)$. Try it.)

The practical use of this result on the convergence of increasing sequences is shown in this section. We summarize this as:

The Increasing Sequence Theorem

Let $\{a_n\}$ be an increasing sequence.

1. If the a_n are smaller than some fixed number M, then

$$\lim_{n \to \infty} a_n = L$$

  where $L \leq M$.

2. If there is no such number M, then

$$\lim_{n \to \infty} a_n = +\infty$$

Example 192. What is $\displaystyle\lim_{n \to \infty} \sqrt{\frac{n}{n+1}}$?

Solution Here $a_n = \sqrt{\dfrac{n}{n+1}}$ and $a_{n+1} = \sqrt{\dfrac{n+1}{n+2}}$. (Remember, just replace the subscript/symbol 'n' by '$n+1$'.) Compare the first few terms using your calculator,

$$a_1 = 0.7071$$
$$a_2 = 0.8165$$

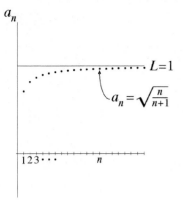

Figure 84.

$$a_3 = 0.8660$$
$$a_4 = 0.8944$$
$$a_5 = 0.9129$$

and since $a_1 < a_2 < a_3 < a_4 < a_5 < \ldots$ it is *conceivable* that the sequence $\{a_n\}$ is increasing, right? Well, the proof of this is not too hard. You can get a proof as follows. For example, the statement

$$a_n < a_{n+1}$$

is equivalent to the statement

$$\sqrt{\frac{n}{n+1}} < \sqrt{\frac{n+1}{n+2}},$$

which, in turn is equivalent to the statement

$$\frac{n}{n+1} < \frac{n+1}{n+2},$$

and this is equivalent to the statement

$$n(n+2) < (n+1)^2,$$

Now this last statement is equivalent to the statement (after rearrangement)

$$n^2 + 2n < n^2 + 2n + 1$$

which is equivalent to the statement

$$0 < 1,$$

which is clearly true! Since all these statements are equivalent, you can 'go backwards' from the last statement that '0 < 1 to the first staement which is that '$a_n < a_{n+1}$' which is what we wanted to show, (see Figure 84 for a graph of the sequence $\{a_n\}$).

This is basically how these arguments go insofar as proving that a sequence is increasing: A whole bunch of inequalities which need to be solved and give another set of equivalent inequalities.

OK, so it has a limit (*by the Increasing Sequence Theorem*) and

$$\lim_{n \to \infty} \sqrt{\frac{n}{n+1}} = \lim_{n \to \infty} \sqrt{1 - \frac{1}{n+1}}$$
$$= \sqrt{1 - 0}$$
$$= 1$$

That's all. You could also have used L'Hospital's Rule to get this answer (replacing n by x and using this Rule on the corresponding function).

Now we proceed to define Euler's number, *e*.

Definition of Euler's number *e*.

We define e as

$$e = \lim_{n \to \infty} \left(1 + \frac{1}{n}\right)^n$$

It's value is approximately $e \approx 2.7182818284590 \ldots$.

Why does this limit exist? Well, in Exercise 17 of Exercise Set 3, we proved that if n is any integer with $n \geq 2$, then

$$2 < \left(1 + \frac{1}{n}\right)^n < 3.$$

OK, in that same Exercise we also found that the nth term of the sequence $\{a_n\}$ defined by

$$a_n = \left(1 + \frac{1}{n}\right)^n$$

can be rewritten as

$$a_n = \left(1 + \frac{1}{n}\right)^n = 1 + 1 + \left(1 - \frac{1}{n}\right)\frac{1}{2!} + \left(1 - \frac{1}{n}\right)\left(1 - \frac{2}{n}\right)\frac{1}{3!}$$
$$+ \ldots + \left(1 - \frac{1}{n}\right)\left(1 - \frac{2}{n}\right)\left(1 - \frac{3}{n}\right)\cdots\left(1 - \frac{n-1}{n}\right)\frac{1}{n!}$$

(where there are $(n + 1)$ terms on the right side).

Now notice that $\{a_n\}$ is increasing because if we replace 'n' by '$n+1$' in the expression for a_n above, we note that every factor of the form $\left(1 - \frac{i}{n}\right)$, $i \geq 1$, 'increases' (because every such term is replaced by $\left(1 - \frac{i}{n+1}\right)$ which is **larger** than the preceding one. So a_{n+1} is larger than a_n, in general for $n > 1$ and $\{a_n\}$ is increasing.

That's it! Using the Increasing Sequence Theorem we know that

$$\lim_{n \to \infty} a_n$$

exists and is not greater than 3. The first few terms of this sequence are given in Figure 85 in the margin.

The value of this limit, e, is given approximately by

$$\boxed{e \approx 2.7182818284590\ldots}$$

It was shown long ago that e is not a *rational number*, that is, it is not the quotient of two integers, (so it is said to be *irrational*) and so we know that its decimal expansion given above cannot repeat.

Remark Reasoning similar to the one above shows that

$$\lim_{x \to \infty}\left(1 + \frac{1}{x}\right)^x = e$$

so that x **does not have to converge** to infinity along integers only!

Example 193. Evaluate $\lim_{n \to \infty}\left(1 + \frac{2}{n}\right)^n$.

Solution There is no need to use the *Binomial Theorem* as in Example 17, but you can if you really want to! Observe that

$$\left(1 + \frac{2}{n}\right)^n = \left(1 + \frac{1}{\left(\frac{n}{2}\right)}\right)^{\frac{n}{2}\cdot 2}$$

n	$\left(1 + \dfrac{0.02}{n}\right)^n$
1	1.02
10	1.02018 ...
100	1.020199 ...
1,000	1.020201 ...
10,000	1.020201 ...
100,000	1.020201 ...

In monetary terms, the numbers on the right can be thought of as the bank balance at the end of 1 year for an initial deposit of 1.00 at an interest rate of 2% that is compounded n times per year. The limit of this expression as the number of compounding period approaches infinity, that is, when we continuously compound the interest, gives the number $e^{0.02}$, where e is Euler's number. Use your calculator to check that the value of $e^{0.02} \approx 1.020201340$ in very good agreement with the numbers above, on the right.

Figure 85.

$$= \left(1 + \frac{1}{m}\right)^{m \cdot 2} \quad \left(\text{if we set } m = \frac{n}{2}\right)$$

$$= \left[\left(1 + \frac{1}{m}\right)^{m}\right]^{2}.$$

Now, as $n \to +\infty$ we also have $m \to +\infty$, right? Taking the limit we get that

$$\lim_{n \to +\infty} \left(1 + \frac{2}{n}\right)^{n} = \lim_{m \to +\infty} \left[\left(1 + \frac{1}{m}\right)^{m}\right]^{2}$$

$$= \left(\lim_{m \to +\infty} \left(1 + \frac{1}{m}\right)^{m}\right)^{2}$$

$$= e^{2},$$

where $e = 2.718...$ is Euler's number.

Exercise Set 22.

---

1. Calculate the first few terms of the sequence $\{b_n\}$ whose n^{th} term, b_n, is given by

$$b_n = \left(1 - \frac{1}{n}\right)^{n}, \qquad 1 \le n$$

Find $b_1, b_2, b_3, \ldots, b_{10}$.

2. Can you guess $\lim_{n \to \infty} b_n$ where the sequence is as in Exercise 1?
   (**Hint:** It is a simple power (negative power) of e.)

3. Show that

$$\lim_{n \to \infty} \left(1 + \frac{a}{n}\right)^{n} = e^{a}$$

where a is any given number.

Known Facts About *e*.

---

1. $\boxed{e^{i\pi} + 1 = 0}$ where $i = \sqrt{-1}$, $\pi = 3.14159\ldots$ [L. Euler (1707-1783)]

2. If you think (1) is nuts, what about $\boxed{e^{2\pi i} = 1}$, (this is really nuts!)
   This follows from (1) by squaring both sides.

3. $\boxed{e^{\pi} = (-1)^{-i}}$, (what?), where $i = \sqrt{-1}$ [Benjamin Peirce (1809-1880)]

4. $\boxed{e = \lim_{n \to \infty} \left(1 + \frac{1}{2!} + \frac{1}{3!} + \ldots + \frac{1}{n!}\right)}$ [Leonard Euler (above)]

5. $\boxed{e = \lim_{x \to 0} (1 + x)^{\frac{1}{x}}}$

6. $\boxed{i^{i} = e^{-\frac{\pi}{2}}}$, (this is completely nuts!) [Leonard Euler (1746)]

7. The number e is also that number such that the area under the graph of the curve $y = \frac{1}{x}$ (between the lines $x = 1, x = e$ and the x-axis) is equal to 1, (see Figure 86).

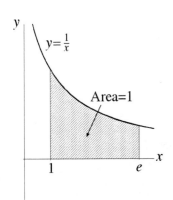

Figure 86.

4.3 Euler's Exponential Function and the Natural Logarithm

At this point we can introduce the **exponential function, e^x,** whose basic property is that if $y(x) = e^x$, then **its derivative equals itself,** that is,

$$y'(x) = y(x) \text{ for all } x$$

One way of doing this is as follows. Let's recall that the rational numbers are *dense* in the set of real numbers. What does this mean? Well, *given any real number, we can find a rational number (fraction) arbitrarily close to it!*

For example, the number 'e' is well-defined and

$$e \approx \frac{2718}{1000}$$

is a fair approximation correct to 3 decimal places (or 4 significant digits). The approximation

$$e \approx \frac{27182818284}{10000000000}$$

is better still and so on. Another example is

$$\pi \approx \frac{355}{113}$$

which gives the correct digits of π to 6 decimal places! It is much better than the classical $\pi \approx \frac{22}{7}$ which is only valid to 2 decimal places.

In this way we can *believe* that **every real number can be approximated by a rational number.** The actual proof of this result is beyond the scope of this book and the reader is encouraged to look at books on *Real Analysis* for a proof.

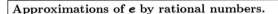

Approximations of e by rational numbers.

$$e = 2.71828182849504523536\ldots$$

Fraction	Value
$\frac{1957}{720}$	$2.7180555\ldots$
$\frac{685}{252}$	$2.7182539\ldots$
$\frac{9864101}{3628800}$	$2.718281801\ldots$
$\frac{47395032961}{17435658240}$	$2.71828182845822\ldots$ *etc.*

Better and better rational approximations to e may be obtained by adding up more and more terms of the **infinite series** for e, namely,

$$e = 1 + 1 + \frac{1}{2!} + \frac{1}{3!} + \frac{1}{4!} + \frac{1}{5!} + \cdots$$

The last term in this table was obtained by adding the first 15 terms of this series!

Exercise Find a rational number which approximates e to 9 decimal places.

Armed with this knowledge we can define the exponential function (or **Euler's exponential function** as follows:

If $x = p$ **is an integer** then

$$
\begin{aligned}
e^x &= e^p \\
&= \underbrace{e \cdot e \cdot e \cdots e}_{p \text{ times}}
\end{aligned}
$$

If $x = \frac{p}{q}$ **is a rational number,** with $q > 0$, say, then

$$
\begin{aligned}
e^x &= e^{\frac{p}{q}} \\
&= \sqrt[q]{e^p}
\end{aligned}
$$

If x is irrational, let $x_n = \frac{p_n}{q_n}$ be an infinite sequence of rational numbers converging to x. From what we said above, such a sequence always exists. Then

$$
\begin{aligned}
e^x &= \lim_{n \to \infty} e^{x_n} \\
&= \lim_{n \to \infty} e^{\frac{p_n}{q_n}}
\end{aligned}
$$

That's all! This defines Euler's exponential function, or THE exponential function, e^x, which is often denoted by $\mathrm{Exp}(x)$ or $\exp(x)$.

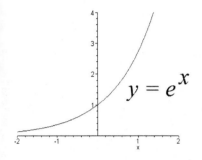

Figure 87. *Euler's exponential function*

Properties of e^x

1. $e^{x+y} = e^x e^y$ for any numbers x, y

2. $e^0 = 1$

3. $e^{x-y} = e^x e^{-y} = \dfrac{e^x}{e^y}$

4. $\displaystyle\lim_{x \to +\infty} e^x = +\infty$

5. $\displaystyle\lim_{x \to -\infty} e^x = 0$

6. One of the neatest properties of this exponential function is that

$$
\boxed{\frac{d}{dx} e^x = e^x}.
$$

Table 4.3: Properties of e^x

Let's look at that cool derivative property, Property (6) in Table 4.3. You'll need Exercise 3 from the previous Exercise Set, with $a = h$. OK, here's the idea: For $h \neq 0$,

$$
\begin{aligned}
\frac{e^{x+h} - e^x}{h} &= \frac{e^x (e^h - 1)}{h} \\
&= e^x \cdot \frac{(e^h - 1)}{h} \\
&= e^x \cdot \frac{1}{h} \left\{ \left[1 + h + \frac{h^2}{2!} + \frac{h^3}{3!} + \cdots \right] - 1 \right\}
\end{aligned}
$$

$$\begin{aligned}
&= e^x \cdot \frac{1}{h}\left\{h + \frac{h^2}{2!} + \frac{h^3}{3!} + \dots\right\} \\
&= e^x \cdot \left\{1 + \frac{h}{2!} + \frac{h^2}{3!} + \dots\right\} \quad \text{so, passing to the limit,} \\
\frac{d}{dx}e^x &= e^x \lim_{h \to 0}\left\{1 + \frac{h}{2!} + \frac{h^2}{3!} + \dots\right\} \\
&= e^x(1 + 0 + 0 + \dots) \\
&= e^x(1) \\
&= e^x.
\end{aligned}$$

That's the idea!

Now the inverse of the exponential function is called the **natural logarithm** and there are a few symbols in use for the natural logarithm:

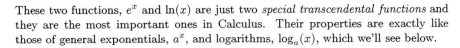

Natural logarithm of x: $\ln(x)$, $\log_e(x)$, $\log(x)$

These two functions, e^x and $\ln(x)$ are just two *special transcendental functions* and they are the most important ones in Calculus. Their properties are exactly like those of general exponentials, a^x, and logarithms, $\log_a(x)$, which we'll see below.

Properties of the Special Transcendental Functions

1. $e^{\ln \square} = \square$, if $\square > 0$
2. $\ln e^{\square} = \square$, for any '*symbol*', $\square$
3. $\ln(e) = 1$
4. $\ln(1) = 0$
5. $\ln \square^{\triangle} = \triangle \ln \square$, if $\square > 0$
6. $\ln(\triangle\square) = \ln \triangle + \ln \square$, $\triangle, \square > 0$
7. $\ln\left(\frac{\triangle}{\square}\right) = \ln(\triangle) - \ln(\square)$, $\triangle, \square > 0$

Table 4.4: Properties of the Special Transcendental Functions

Application

Find the derivative of the following function at the indicated point:

$$f(x) = \frac{e^x + e^{-x}}{2}, \text{ at } x = 2$$

This is called the **hyperbolic cosine of x** and is very important in applications to engineering. For example, the function defined by $g(x) = f(ax)$ where

$$g(x) = \frac{e^{ax} + e^{-ax}}{2}, \ a > 0$$

represents the shape of a hanging chain under the influence of gravity. the resulting curve is called a **catenary**. Another example of a catenary is the *Gateway Arch* in St. Louis, Missouri, in a well known architectural monument by Finnish architect **Eero Saarinen** (1910-1961).

Now that we've defined the Euler exponential function we can define the **general exponential function** $f(x) = a^x$, $a > 0$, by

$$a^x = e^{x \ln a}, \text{ for any real x}$$

Figure 88. *A catenary curve: It is the result of gravitational effects upon a wire hanging between two telephone posts, for instance.*

Most pocket calculators actually work this way when evaluating expressions of the form a^x, if this key is present.

Remember: The term '$\ln a$' is a number which can be positive (or negative) depending on whether a is bigger than 1 or less than 1.

It makes sense to define a^x as we did above because we know that:

$$e^{\ln \square} = \square$$

so we can replace the symbol $\square$ by a^x and use Property (1), Table 4.1, of the logarithm, namely, $\ln(a^x) = x \ln a$ to get at the definition. Using the *change of base formula* (see the margin) for a logarithm we can then define the inverse function of the general exponential function by

The Change of Base Formula for Logarithms is easy to show: Let $\square = a^x$. Then, by definition, $x = \log_a \square$. But $\ln \square = \ln(a^x) = x \ln a$. Solving for x in both expressions and equating we get the formula.

$$\boxed{\log_a(\square) = \frac{\ln(\square)}{\ln a}}.$$

where $\square > 0$.

Example 194.   Evaluate or rewrite the following quantities using the Euler exponential function.

1. $(2.3)^{1.2}$

   Solution: Here $a = 2.3$ and $x = 1.2$. Since $a^x = e^{x \cdot \ln a}$, it follows that $(2.3)^{1.2} = e^{(1.2)\ln(2.3)}$. We look up $\ln(2.3)$ on our (scientific) calculator which gives us 0.83291. Thus,

$$
\begin{aligned}
(2.3)^{1.2} &= e^{0.99949} \\
&= 2.71690.
\end{aligned}
$$

2. $f(x) = 2^{\sin x}$

   Solution: By Table 4.1, Property 1, $2^{\sin x} = e^{\ln 2 \cdot (\sin x)} = e^{0.693 \cdot (\sin x)}$ where $\ln 2 = 0.693 \ldots$

3. $g(x) = x^x, \ (x > 0)$

   Solution: The right way of defining this, is by using Euler's exponential function. So,

$$x^x = e^{x \ln x}$$

   where now $\ln x$ is another function multiplying the x in the *exponent*. Thus we have reduced the problem of evaluating a complicated expression like x^x with a 'variable' *base* to one with a 'constant' *base*, that is,

$$x^x = e^{h(x)}, \qquad \text{and } h(x) = x \ln x.$$

   variable base   constant base

Historical Note: Leonard Euler, mentioned earlier, proved that if

$$f(x) = x^{x^{x^{x^{\cdot^{\cdot^{\cdot}}}}}}$$

where the number of exponents tends to infinity then

$$\lim_{x \to a} f(x) = L < \infty$$

if $e^{-e} < a < e^{\frac{1}{e}}$ (or if $0.06599 < a < 1.44467$). What is L? *This is hard!*

4.4   Derivative of the Natural Logarithm

Let f, F be differentiable inverse functions of one another so that $x = f(F(x))$ and $x = F(f(x))$. Then

$$\frac{d}{dx}(x) = \frac{d}{dx}f(F(x))$$

or

$$1 = f'(F(x)) \cdot F'(x), \qquad \text{(by the Chain Rule)}.$$

Solving for $F'(x)$ we get

$$F'(x) = \frac{1}{f'(F(x))}$$

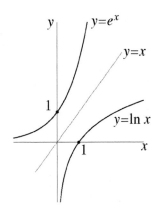

Now we can set $f(x) = e^x$ and $F(x) = \ln x$. You can believe that F is differentiable for $x > 0$ since f is, right? The graph of $\ln x$ is simply a reflection of the graph of e^x about the line $y = x$ and this graph is 'smooth' so the graph of '$\ln x$' will also be 'smooth'. Actually, one proves that the natural logarithm function is differentiable by appealing to a result called the **Inverse Function Theorem** which we won't see here. It's basically a theorem which guarantees that an inverse function will have some nice properties (like being differentiable) if the original function is differentiable.

Figure 89.

Exercise: Show that F defined by $F(x) = \ln x$ is differentiable at $x = a$ for $a > 0$ using the following steps:

a) The derivative of '$\ln$' at $x = a > 0$ is, by definition, given by

$$F'(x) = \lim_{x \to a} \frac{\ln(x) - \ln(a)}{x - a}$$

provided this limit exists.

b) Let $x = e^z$. Show that

$$F'(x) = \lim_{z \to \ln a} \left(\frac{z - \ln(a)}{e^z - a} \right)$$

provided this limit exists.

c) But note that $F'(a) = \dfrac{1}{\frac{d}{dz}(e^z)}$ evaluated at $z = \ln a$

d) Conclude that both limits in (b) and (a) exist.

OK, knowing that the natural logarithm function 'ln' is differentiable we can find it's derivative using the argument below:

$$
\begin{aligned}
F'(x) = \frac{d}{dx} \ln x &= \frac{1}{f'(F(x))} \\
&= \frac{1}{e^{F(x)}} \\
&= \frac{1}{e^{\ln x}} \\
&= \frac{1}{x}
\end{aligned}
$$

More generally (using Chain Rule) we can show that

$$
\begin{aligned}
\frac{d}{dx} \ln u(x) &= \frac{1}{u(x)} \left(\frac{du}{dx} \right) \\
&= \frac{u'(x)}{u(x)}
\end{aligned}
$$

and, in particular

$$
\boxed{ \frac{d}{dx} \ln x = \frac{1}{x} }
$$

In general it is best to remember that

$$
\boxed{ \frac{d}{dx} \ln \square = \frac{1}{\square} \frac{d}{dx} (\square), \ \square > 0 }
$$

where $\square$ is any function of x which is positive and differentiable (but see the margin for something more general!)

If $\square < 0$, then $-\square > 0$ and so by the Chain Rule,

$$
\frac{d}{dx} \ln(-\square) = \frac{1}{-\square} \frac{d}{dx}(-\square)
$$

$$
= -\frac{1}{\square}(-1)\frac{d}{dx}(\square) = \frac{1}{\square} \frac{d}{dx}(\square).
$$

This means that so long as $\square \neq 0$ then

$$
\frac{d}{dx} \ln |\square| = \frac{1}{\square} \frac{d}{dx}(\square)
$$

a formula that will become very useful later on when dealing with the *antiderivative* of the exponential function.

Example 195. Find the derivatives of the following functions at the indicated point (if any).

a) $\ln(x^2 + 2)$, at $x = 0$
b) $e^x \log(x)$ (remember $\log x = \ln x$)
c) $\ln(x^2 + 2x + 1)$
d) $3\ln(x + 1)$, at $x = 1$
e) $e^{2x} \log(x^2 + 1)$

Solution:

a) Let $\square = x^2 + 2$. Then

$$
\begin{aligned}
\frac{d}{dx} \ln(x^2 + 2) &= \frac{d}{dx} \ln(\square) \\
&= \frac{1}{\square} \frac{d}{dx}(\square) \\
&= \frac{1}{x^2 + 2} \frac{d}{dx}(x^2 + 2) \\
&= \frac{1}{x^2 + 2}(2x)
\end{aligned}
$$

so that when evaluated at $x = 0$ this derivative is equal to 0.

b) We have a product of two functions here so we can use the Product Rule.

$$
\begin{aligned}
\frac{d}{dx}(e^x \log x) &= \frac{d}{dx}(e^x)\log x + e^x \frac{d}{dx}\log x \\
&= e^x \log x + e^x \left(\frac{1}{x}\right) \\
&= e^x \left(\log x + \frac{1}{x}\right)
\end{aligned}
$$

c) Let $u(x) = x^2 + 2x + 1$. We want the derivative of $\ln u(x)$. Now

$$
\begin{aligned}
\frac{d}{dx}\ln u(x) &= \frac{1}{u(x)}u'(x) \\
&= \frac{1}{x^2 + 2x + 1}\frac{d}{dx}(x^2 + 2x + 1) \\
&= \frac{1}{x^2 + 2x + 1}(2x + 2) \\
&= \frac{2x + 2}{x^2 + 2x + 1}
\end{aligned}
$$

d) Let $u(x) = x + 1$. Then $u'(x) = 1$. Furthermore,

$$
\begin{aligned}
\frac{d}{dx}3\ln(x + 1) &= 3\frac{d}{dx}\ln(x + 1) \\
&= 3\frac{d}{dx}\ln u(x) \\
&= 3 \cdot \frac{1}{u(x)} \cdot u'(x) \\
&= 3\frac{1}{x + 1} \cdot 1 \\
&= \frac{3}{x + 1}
\end{aligned}
$$

EXAMPLES

So, at $x = 1$, we get that the derivative is equal to $\frac{3}{2}$.

e) Once again, this is a product of two functions, say, f and g, where

$$
\begin{aligned}
f(x) &= e^{2x} \\
g(x) &= \log(x^2 + 1)
\end{aligned}
$$

By the Product Rule we get $\frac{d}{dx}\left(e^{2x}\log(x^2 + 1)\right) = \frac{df}{dx}g(x) + f(x)\frac{dg}{dx}$. But

$$
\frac{df}{dx} = \frac{d}{dx}(e^{2x}) = e^{2x}\frac{d}{dx}(2x) = 2e^{2x}
$$

and

$$
\begin{aligned}
\frac{dg}{dx} &= \frac{d}{dx}\log(x^2 + 1) \\
&= \frac{d}{dx}\log(\square) \ (\text{where } \square = x^2 + 1) \\
&= \frac{1}{\square}\frac{d}{dx}(\square) \\
&= \frac{1}{x^2 + 1}\frac{d}{dx}(x^2 + 1) \\
&= \frac{1}{x^2 + 1}(2x)
\end{aligned}
$$

Combining these results for $f'(x)$, $g'(x)$ we find

$$
\frac{d}{dx}e^{2x}\log(x^2 + 1) = (2e^{2x})\log(x^2 + 1) + e^{2x}\left(\frac{2x}{x^2 + 1}\right)
$$

Exercise Set 23.

Find the derivative of each of the following functions at the indicated point (if any).

1. $\ln(x^3 + 3)$, at $x = 1$

2. $e^{3x} \log x$

3. $\dfrac{e^x}{\log x}$, (**Hint:** Use the Quotient Rule)

4. $\ln(e^{2x}) + \ln(x + 6)$, at $x = 0$

5. $\ln(x + \sqrt{x^2 + 3})$
   (**Hint:** Let $\square = x + \sqrt{x^2 + 3}$ and use the Chain Rule on the second term.)

6. $4\ln(x + 2)$

7. $\ln(\sqrt{x^2 + 4})$ (**Hint:** Simplify the 'log' first using one of its properties.)

4.5 Differentiation Formulae for General Exponential Functions

In this section we derive formulae for the general exponential function f defined by

$$f(x) = a^x, \qquad \text{where } a > 0,$$

and its logarithm,

$$F(x) = \log_a x,$$

and then use the Chain Rule in order to find the derivative of more general functions like

$$g(x) \;=\; a^{h(x)}$$
$$\text{and}$$
$$G(x) \;=\; \log_a h(x)$$

where $h(x)$ is some given function. Applications of such formulae are widespread in scientific literature from the rate of decay of radioactive compounds to population biology and interest rates on loans.

OK, we have seen that, by definition of the general exponential function, if h is some function then

$$a^{h(x)} = e^{h(x) \cdot \ln a}.$$

Now the power '$h(x) \cdot \ln a$' is just another function, right? Let's write it as $k(x)$, so that

$$k(x) = h(x) \cdot \ln a.$$

Then

$$a^{h(x)} \;=\; e^{k(x)}$$
$$\;=\; f(k(x))$$

where $f(x) = e^x$ and $k(x) = \ln a \cdot h(x)$, right? Good. Now, since $f'(x) = f(x)$, ($f'(\square) = f(\square) = e^{\square}$),

$$
\begin{aligned}
\frac{d}{dx} a^{h(x)} &= \frac{d}{dx} f(k(x)) \\
&= f'(k(x)) \cdot k'(x) \quad \text{(by the Chain Rule)} \\
&= e^{k(x)} \cdot k'(x) \quad \left(\text{because } \frac{d}{dx} e^x = e^x\right) \\
&= e^{h(x) \cdot \ln a} \cdot \left(\frac{d}{dx} h(x) \cdot \ln a\right) \\
&= e^{\ln(a^{h(x)})} \left(\ln a \, \frac{d}{dx} h(x)\right) \\
&= a^{h(x)} (\ln a) \, h'(x)
\end{aligned}
$$

and we have discovered the general formula

$$
\frac{d}{dx} a^{h(x)} = a^{h(x)} \underbrace{(\ln a) h'(x)}_{\text{multiply original exponential by these two terms}}
$$

In the special case of $h(x) = x$, we have $h'(x) = 1$ so that

$$
\frac{d}{dx} a^x = a^x \ln a
$$

just a little more general than Euler's exponential function's derivative, because of the presence of the natural logarithm of a, on the right.

Example 196. Find the derivative of the exponential functions at the indicated points (if any).

1. $f(x) = e^{3x}$
2. $g(x) = e^{-(1.6)x}$, at $x = 0$
3. $f(x) = 2^{\sin x}$
4. $g(x) = (e^x)^{-2}$, at $x = 1$
5. $k(x) = (1.3)^{x^2} \cos x$

Solutions:

1. Set $a = e$, $h(x) = 3x$ in the boxed formula above. Then

$$
\begin{aligned}
\frac{d}{dx} e^{3x} &= \frac{d}{dx} a^{h(x)} \\
&= a^{h(x)} (\ln a) \, h'(x) \\
&= e^{3x} (\ln e)(3) \quad \left(\text{since } \frac{d}{dx} 3x = 3\right) \\
&= e^{3x} \cdot 1 \cdot 3 \quad (\text{since } \ln e = 1) \\
&= 3e^{3x}.
\end{aligned}
$$

2. Set $a = e$, $\ln x = -(1.6)x$. Then

$$\begin{aligned}
\frac{d}{dx}e^{-(1.6)x} &= \frac{d}{dx}a^{h(x)} \\
&= a^{h(x)}(\ln a)h'(x) \\
&= e^{-(1.6)x}(\ln e)\frac{d}{dx}((-1.6)x) \\
&= e^{-(1.6)x}(1)\cdot(-1.6) \\
&= -(1.6)e^{-(1.6)x}
\end{aligned}$$

and at $x = 0$ its derivative is equal to -1.6.

3. Set $a = 2$ and $h(x) = \sin x$. Then

$$\begin{aligned}
\frac{d}{dx}2^{\sin x} &= 2^{\sin x}(\ln 2)\frac{d}{dx}(\sin x) \\
&= 2^{\sin x}(\ln 2)\cdot(\cos x)
\end{aligned}$$

4. Simplify first: $(e^x)^{-2} = (e^x)^{(-2)} = e^{(x)(-2)} = e^{-2x}$. So now we can set $a = e$, $h(x) = -2x$. Then

$$\begin{aligned}
\frac{d}{dx}(e^x)^{-2} &= \frac{d}{dx}e^{-2x} \\
&= e^{-2x}(\ln e)(-2) \\
&= -2e^{-2x}
\end{aligned}$$

So at $x = 1$ this derivative is equal to $-2e^{-2}$.

5. We have a **product of two functions** here so we have to use the Product Rule. Let $f(x) = (1.3)^{x^2}$ and $g(x) = \cos x$. We know that $k'(x) = f'(x)g(x) + f(x)g'(x)$ (by the Product Rule) and

$$\begin{aligned}
f'(x) &= \frac{d}{dx}(1.3)^{x^2} \\
g'(x) &= (\cos x)' = -\sin x
\end{aligned}$$

So, we only need to find $f'(x)$ as we know all the other quantities f, g, g'. Finally, we set $a = 1.3$ and $h(x) = x^2$. Then

$$\begin{aligned}
\frac{d}{dx}(1.3)^{x^2} &= \frac{d}{dx}a^{h(x)} \\
&= a^{h(x)}(\ln a)h'(x) \\
&= (1.3)^{x^2}\cdot(\ln 1.3)\cdot(2x) \\
&= 2\cdot(\ln 1.3)x\cdot(1.3)^{x^2}
\end{aligned}$$

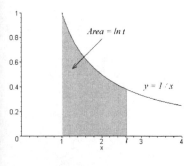

Figure 90.

Historical Note

Long ago **Grégoire de Saint Vincent** (1584 - 1667) showed that the area (Fig. 90) under the curve

$$y = \frac{1}{x}$$

between the lines $x = 1$ and $x = t$ (where $t > 1$) and the x-axis is given by $\log t$ (and this was *before* Euler came on the scene!).

Exercise Set 24.

Show that the following sequences are increasing and find their limits in the extended real numbers.

1. $a_n = n + 2$, $n \geq 1$

2. $a_n = \dfrac{n-1}{n}$, $n \geq 1$

3. $a_n = \dfrac{n(n-2)}{n^2}$, $n \geq 1$

4. $a_n = \dfrac{n}{n+3}$, $n \geq 1$

5. $a_n = \dfrac{n-1}{n+1}$, $n \geq 1$

6. Sketch the graph of the sequence $\{a_n\}$ given by

$$a_n = \sqrt{\frac{n-1}{n}}$$

for $n = 1, 2, \ldots, 15$, and find it's limit.

7. Evaluate

$$\lim_{n \to \infty} \left(1 - \frac{2}{n}\right)^n$$

(**Hint:** See Example 193.)

8. Show that

$$\lim_{x \to 0} (1 + x^2)^{\frac{1}{x^2}} = e$$

(**Hint:** Assume you know Fact #5 about e.)

9. Find a rational approximation to e not given in the text.

10. Use your present knowledge of dilations and translations to sketch the graph of the function y defined by

$$y(x) = e^{2(x-1)}$$

using the graph of $y = e^x$.

11. Evaluate the following expressions and simplify as much as possible.

    a) $e^{3\ln x}$, at $x = 1$

    b) $\dfrac{e^{3\ln x} - e^{\ln(x^3)}}{2}$

    c) $\ln(e^{3x+2})$, at $x = 1$

    d) $\ln(e^{2x}) - 2x + 1$

    e) $\ln(\sin^2 x + \cos^2 x)$

    f) $\ln\left(\dfrac{1}{\sin\left(\frac{\pi}{2}\right)}\right)$

    g) $e^{(2x+1)\ln(2)} - 2^{2x}$

    h) $\ln\left(\dfrac{x^2 - 1}{x + 1}\right)$, for $x > 1$

    i) $\ln\left(\dfrac{e^{3x}}{e^{2x+1}}\right)$

j) $e^{x^2} - \ln\left(e^{e^{x^2}}\right)$

12. Evaluate

$$\lim_{x \to \infty} \left(\frac{x^2}{e^x}\right)$$

Hint Use L'Hospital's Rule.

13. Evaluate the following expressions using

   i) your calculator only and

   ii) writing them in terms Euler's exponential function and then using your calculator:

$$
\begin{aligned}
\text{Example}: \quad &\text{i) } (2.3)^{1.2} &=& \quad 2.71690 \\
&\text{ii) } (2.3)^{1.2} &=& \quad e^{(1.2)\ln(2.3)} \\
& &=& \quad e^{0.99949} \\
& &=& \quad 2.71690
\end{aligned}
$$

   a) $(1.2)^{2.1}$

   b) $\left(\frac{1}{2}\right)^2$

   c) $2^{6.25}$

   d) $3^{-2.61}$

   e) $\left(\frac{1}{3}\right)^{-2.21}$

14. Write the function f defined by

$$f(x) = x^{\sin x}, \ x > 0$$

   as an exponential function with base e.
   (**Hint:** See Example 194, (3)).

15. Find the derivative of each of the following functions at the indicated points (if any).

   a) $f(x) = 2e^{2x}$

   b) $g(x) = e^{-(3.4)x+2}$, at $x = 0$

   c) $f(x) = 3^{\cos x}$

   d) $g(x) = (e^{3x})^{-2}$, at $x = 1$

   e) $k(x) = e^{x^2} \sin x$, at $x = 0$

   f) $f(x) = e^x \cos x$

   g) $g(x) = -e^{-x} x^2$, at $x = 0$

   h) $f(x) = x^2 e^{2x}$

   i) $g(x) = \dfrac{e^{-2x}}{x^2}$

   j) $f(x) = (1.2)^x$

   k) $g(x) = x^{1.6} e^{-x}$

NOTES:

4.6 Differentiation Formulae for General Logarithmic Functions

Finally, the situation for the general logarithm is similar to the one for the natural logarithm except for an **additional factor** in the expression for its derivative.

OK. We know that for $a > 0$,

$$a^x = e^{x \ln a}$$

by definition, so that if we write $f(x) = a^x$ and let F denote its inverse function, then

$$F'(x) = \frac{1}{f'(F(x))}$$

as we saw earlier, but $f'(x) = a^x \ln a$ and so

$$
\begin{aligned}
\frac{d}{dx} \log_a(x) &= \frac{1}{f'(F(x))} \\
&= \frac{1}{a^{F(x)} \ln a} \\
&= \frac{1}{a^{\log_a(x)} \ln a} \\
&= \frac{1}{x \ln a}, \ (\text{if } a > 0, \ x > 0)
\end{aligned}
$$

More generally we can see that (using the Chain Rule)

$$\boxed{\frac{d}{dx} \log_a(\square) = \frac{1}{\ln a} \cdot \frac{1}{\square} \cdot \frac{d}{dx}(\square)}$$

where $\square > 0$, $a > 0$ (see the margin).

Actually, more can be said: If $\square \neq 0$, then

$$\boxed{\frac{d}{dx} \log_a(|\square|) = \frac{1}{\ln a} \cdot \frac{1}{\square} \cdot \frac{d}{dx}(\square)}$$

so that you can replace the $\square$ term by its *absolute value*. To show this just *remove the absolute value* and use the Chain Rule.

Exercise: Show the following **change of base** formula for logarithms:

$$\boxed{\log_a(\square) = \frac{\ln(\square)}{\ln a}}$$

This formula **allows one to convert from logarithms with *base a* to natural logarithms,** (those with base e).

Use the following steps.

1. Let $a^{\triangle} = \square$ where $\triangle$, $\square$ are symbols denoting numbers, functions, etc. Show that $\triangle = \log_a(\square)$.
2. Show that $\ln(\square) = \triangle \ln(a)$.
3. Show the formula by solving for $\triangle$.

Example 197. Find the derivatives of the following functions at the indicated point.

a) $\log_a(x^2 + 1)$, at $x = 0$

b) $\log_2(3^x)$

c) $\log_4(2x + 1)$, at $x = 0$

d) $\log_{0.5}(e^{2x})$

e) $2^x \log_3(3x)$

f) $(\sin x)^x$ using any logarithm.

Solutions

a) Let $\square = x^2 + 1$. Then $\frac{d\square}{dx} = 2x$, and

$$\frac{d}{dx}\log_a(\square) = \frac{1}{\ln a} \cdot \frac{1}{\square} \cdot \frac{d\square}{dx}$$
$$= \frac{1}{\ln a} \cdot \frac{1}{x^2 + 1} \cdot 2x$$
$$= \frac{2x}{(x^2 + 1)\ln a}$$

So, at $x = 0$, its value is equal to 0.

b) Note that $\log_2(3^x) = x \log_2(3)$ by the property of logarithms. Thus,

$$\frac{d}{dx}\log_2(3^x) = \frac{d}{dx} x \log_2(3)$$
$$= \log_2(3)\frac{d}{dx}(x) \text{ (since } \log_2(3) \text{ is a constant)}$$
$$= \log_2(3)$$

You don't need to evaluate $\log_2(3)$.

c) Let $\square = 2x + 1$. Then $\frac{d\square}{dx} = 2$ and

$$\frac{d}{dx}\log_4(2x + 1) = \frac{d}{dx}\log_4(\square)$$
$$= \frac{1}{\ln 4} \cdot \frac{1}{\square} \cdot \frac{d\square}{dx}$$
$$= \frac{1}{\ln 4} \cdot \frac{1}{2x + 1} \cdot 2$$
$$= \frac{2}{(2x + 1)\ln 4}, \left(\text{for each } x > -\frac{1}{2}\right)$$
$$= \frac{2}{\ln 4} \text{ (at } x = 0)$$

d) Let $a = 0.5$, $\square = e^{2x}$. Then $\frac{d\square}{dx} = 2e^{2x}$ and

$$\frac{d}{dx}\log_a\square = \frac{1}{\ln a} \cdot \frac{1}{\square} \cdot \frac{d\square}{dx}$$
$$= \frac{1}{\ln(0.5)} \cdot \frac{1}{e^{2x}} \cdot 2e^{2x}$$
$$= \frac{2}{\ln(0.5)}$$
$$= \frac{2}{\ln(\frac{1}{2})}$$
$$= -\frac{2}{\ln(2)} \text{ (since } \ln(\frac{1}{2}) = \ln 1 - \ln 2)$$

Thus, $\frac{d}{dx}\log_{0.5}(e^{2x}) = -\frac{2}{\ln 2}$ at $x = 0$.

NOTE: We could arrive at the answer more simply by noticing that

$$
\begin{aligned}
\log_{0.5} e^{2x} &= 2x \log_{0.5}(e) \\
&= x \underbrace{(2 \log_{0.5}(e))}_{\text{constant}}
\end{aligned}
$$

So its derivative is equal to $2 \log_{0.5}(e) = -\frac{2}{\ln(2)}$ (by the change of base formula with $a = \frac{1}{2}$, $\square = e$).

e) Use the Product Rule here. Then

$$
\begin{aligned}
\frac{d}{dx}(2^x \log_3(3x)) &= \frac{d}{dx}(2^x) \log_3(3x) + 2^x \frac{d}{dx}(\log_3(3x)) \\
&= (2^x \ln 2) \log_3(3x) + 2^x \left(\frac{1}{\ln 3} \cdot \frac{1}{3x} \cdot 3 \right) \\
&= 2^x (\ln 2)(\log_3(3x)) + \frac{3 \cdot 2^x}{3x(\ln 3)}
\end{aligned}
$$

f) Let $y = (\sin x)^x$. Then, $\ln y = \ln((\sin x)^x) = x \ln \sin x$. Now use *implicit differentiation* on the left, and the Product Rule on the right!

$$
\begin{aligned}
\frac{1}{y}\frac{dy}{dx} &= \frac{d}{dx}(x \ln \sin x), \\
&= x \frac{1}{\sin x} \cos x + \ln \sin x, \\
&= x \cot x + \ln \sin x, \quad \text{and solving for the derivative we find,} \\
\frac{dy}{dx} &= y(x \cot x + \ln \sin x), \\
&= (\sin x)^x (x \cot x + \ln \sin x).
\end{aligned}
$$

Exercise Set 25.

Find the derivative of each of the following functions.

a) $\log_a(x^3 + x + 1)$

b) $\log_3(x^x)$,
   (**Hint:** Use a property of logarithms and the Product Rule.)

c) x^x, (**Hint:** Rewrite this as a function with a constant base.)

d) $\log_3(4x - 3)$

e) $\log_{1/3}(e^{4x})$

f) $3^x \log_2(x^2 + 1)$

g) $x \ln(x)$

h) $e^x \log_2(e^x)$

i) $\log_2(3x + 1)$

j) $\log_2(\sqrt{x + 1})$, (**Hint:** Simplify first.)

4.7   Applications

The exponential function occurs naturally in physics and the use of nuclear reactors. Let $N(t)$ denote the amount of radioactive substance at time t (whose units may be seconds, minutes, hours or years depending on the substance involved). The **half-life** of a substance is, by definition, the time, **T**, that it takes for one-half of the substance to remain (on account of radioactive decay).

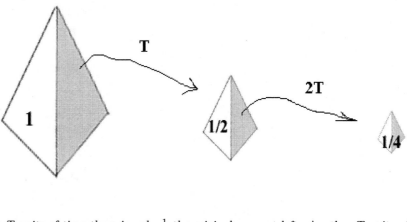

After T units of time there is only $\frac{1}{2}$ the original amount left. Another T units of time results in only $\frac{1}{4}$. The original amount, and so on.

It is known that *the rate of decay $\frac{dN}{dt}$ is proportional to the amount of material present at time t, namely, $N(t)$.* This means that

$$\frac{dN}{dt} \quad = \quad kN$$

rate of decay   amount present at time t

proportionality constant

This differential equation for $N(t)$ has solutions of the form (we'll see why later, in the chapter on Differential Equations)

$$\boxed{N(t) = Ce^{kt}}$$

where C and k are constants. The number $\tau = k$ is called the **decay constant** which is a measure of the rate at which the nuclide releases radioactive emissions. At $t = 0$ we have a quantity $N(0)$ of material present, so $C = N(0)$. Since $N(T) = \frac{N(0)}{2}$ if T is the half-life of a radionuclide, it follows that

$$\frac{N(0)}{2} \quad = \quad N(T)$$
$$= \quad N(O)e^{kT} \text{ (since } C = N(0))$$
$$\text{or } \frac{1}{2} \quad = \quad e^{kT}$$

which, when we solve for T gives

$$kT \quad = \quad \ln(\frac{1}{2})$$
$$= \quad -\ln 2$$

or

$$T = -\frac{\ln 2}{k}$$

So if we know the decay constant we can get the half-life and vice-versa. The formula for radioactive decay now becomes

$$
\begin{aligned}
N(t) &= N(0)e^{kt} \\
&= N(0)e^{-\frac{\ln 2}{T}t} \\
&= N(0)\left(e^{-\ln 2}\right)^{\frac{t}{T}} \\
&= N(0)\left(\frac{1}{2}\right)^{\frac{t}{T}}
\end{aligned}
$$

i.e.

$$N(t) = \frac{N(0)}{2^{t/T}}$$

Half-Life of Radioisotopes

Isotope	Half − Life
Kr87	1.27 hours
Sr89	50.5 days
Sr90	29.1 years
Pu240	6,500 years
Pu239	24,100 years

Table 4.5: Half-Life of Radioisotopes

Example 198. Plutonium 240 has a half-life of 6500 years. This radionuclide is extremely toxic and is a byproduct of nuclear activity. How long will it take for a 1 gram sample of Pu240 to decay to 1 microgram?

Solution We know that $N(t)$, the amount of material at time t satisfies the equation

$$N(t) = \frac{N(0)}{2^{t/T}}$$

where T is the half-life and $N(0)$ is the initial amount. In our case, $T = 6500$ (and all time units will be measured in years). Furthermore, $N(0) = 1$g. We want a time t where $N(t) = 1$ microgram $= 10^{-6}$g, right? So

$$10^{-6} = \frac{1}{2^{t/6500}}$$

initial amount =1 here

amount left

or

$$2^{t/6500} = 10^6$$

or, by taking the natural logarithm of both sides we have

$$\frac{t}{6500} \ln(2) = \ln(10^6)$$

or, solving for t,

$$
\begin{aligned}
t &= \frac{6500 \ln(10^6)}{\ln(2)} \text{ (years)} \\
&= \frac{6500 \cdot 6 \ln 10}{\ln 2} \\
&= \frac{6500(6)(2.3026)}{(0.6931)} \\
&= 129564 \text{ years}
\end{aligned}
$$

Figure 91.

approximately!

Exercise Strontium 90 has a half-life of 29.1 years. How long will it take for a 5 gram sample of Sr90 to decay to 90% of its original amount?

The equation of motion of a body moving in free-fall through the air (Fig. 91) is given by

$$m\frac{dv}{dt} = mg - kv^2$$

where $v = v(t)$ is the velocity of the body in its descent, g is the acceleration due to gravity and m is its mass. Here k is a constant which reflects air resistance.

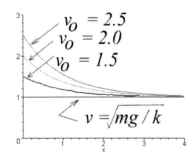

Figure 92.

We can learn to 'solve' this equation for the unknown velocity '$v(t)$' using methods from a later Chapter on Integration. At this point we can mention that this 'solution' is given by

$$v(t) = \sqrt{\frac{mg}{k}} \tanh\left(t\sqrt{\frac{gk}{m}} + \operatorname{arctanh}\left(v_0\sqrt{\frac{k}{mg}}\right)\right)$$

where v_0 is its 'initial velocity'. For example, if one is dropping out of an airplane in a parachute we take it that $v_0 = 0$.

As $t \to \infty$ we see that $v(t) \to \sqrt{\frac{mg}{k}} = v_\infty$ (because the *hyperbolic tangent* term on the right approaches 1 as $t \to \infty$).

This quantity 'v_∞' called the limiting velocity is the 'final' or 'maximum' velocity of the body just before it reaches the ground. As you can see by taking the limit as $t \to \infty$, v_∞ *depends on the mass and the air resistance but does not depend upon the initial velocity!* See Figure 92.

Other Applications

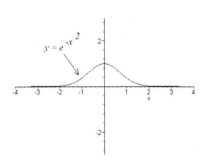

Figure 93.

1. The function f defined by $\boxed{f(x) = (2\pi)^{-1/2} e^{\frac{-x^2}{2}}}$ for $-\infty < x < \infty$, appears in probability theory, statistical mechanics, quantum physics, etc. It is referred to as a **normal distribution**, (see Fig. 93). It is also used by some teachers to 'curve' the grades of unsuccessful students!

2. The **entropy**, S, of a physical system is, by definition, an expression of the form

$$S = k \ln \Omega$$

where k is a physical constant and Ω is a measure of the number of states accessible to the system [Statistical Mechanics, Berkeley Physics (Vol 5). p. 143]. This notation is central to the study of Statistical Mechanics and Thermodynamics.

3. According to Newton, the temperature $T(t)$ of a cooling object drops at a rate proportional to the difference $T(t) - T_0$ where T_0 is the temperature of the surrounding space. This is represented analytically by a differential equation of the form

$$\frac{dT}{dt} = -k(T(t) - T_0)$$

where k is a constant.

It can be shown that the general solution if this equation looks like

$$T(t) = ae^{-kt} + T_0$$

where a is a constant. This law is called **Newton's Law of Cooling** as it represents the temperature of a heat radiating body (for example, coffee), as it cools in its surrounding space. Using this law, we can determine, for example, the temperature of a cup of coffee 10 minutes after it was poured, or determine the temperature of a hot pan, say, 5 minutes after it is removed from a heat source.

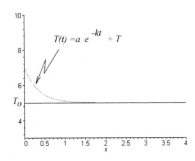

Figure 94.

There are many other natural phenomena for which the rate of change of a quantity $y(t)$ at time t is proportional to the amount present at time t. That is, for which

$$\frac{dy}{dt} = ky \quad \text{with solution} \quad y(t) = Ce^{kt} \quad \text{where} \quad C = y(0).$$

Such a model is often called an **exponential decay** model if $k < 0$, and an **exponential growth** model if $k > 0$.

Example 199.

If an amount of money P is deposited in an account at an annual interest rate, r, compounded continuously, then the balance $A(t)$ after t years is given by the exponential growth model

$$A = Pe^{rt} \quad \text{(note that } P = A(0))$$

How long will it take for an investment of \$1000 to double if the interest rate is 10 % compounded continuously?

Solution   Here $P = 1000$ and $r = .10$, so at any time t, $A = 1000e^{0.1t}$. We want to find the value of t for which $A = 2000$, so

$$2000 = 1000e^{0.1t}$$

so

$$2 = e^{0.1t}$$

and taking the natural logarithm of both sides

$$\ln 2 = \ln e^{0.1t} = 0.1t.$$

Thus

$$t = 10\ln 2 \approx 6.9 \text{years.}$$

Example 200.

A startup company that began in 1997 has found that its gross revenue follows an exponential growth model. The gross revenue was \$10,000 in 1997 and \$200,000 in 1999. If the exponential growth model continues to hold, what will be the gross revenue in 2000?

Solution   Let $y(t)$ be the amount of the gross revenue in year t, so $y(t) = y(0)e^{kt}$. Taking 1997 as $t = 0$, $y(0) = 10,000$ so $y(t) = 10,000e^{kt}$. In 1999, $t = 2$, so

$$200,000 = 10,000e^{2k}$$

$$20.5 = e^{2k}$$

$$ln(20.5) = 2k$$

$$k = \frac{1}{2}ln(20.5) = 1.51$$

and hence,

$$y(t) = 10,000e^{1.51t}.$$

Thus, in the year 2000, the gross revenue will be

$$y(3) = 10,000e^{1.51 \times 3} \approx \$927586.$$

NOTES:

Summary of the Chapter

$$e^x = 1 + x + \frac{x^2}{2!} + \frac{x^3}{3!} + \frac{x^4}{4!} + \cdots$$

$$e = \lim_{n \to \infty} \left(1 + \frac{1}{n}\right)^n$$

$$a^x = e^{x \log a} = e^{x \ln a}, \quad \ln = \log$$

$$\frac{d}{dx} a^x = a^x \ln a, \ a > 0$$

$$\frac{d}{dx} a^{\square} = a^{\square} \ln a \, \frac{d\square}{dx}$$

$$\frac{d}{dx} \log_a(\square) = \frac{1}{\square} \cdot \frac{1}{\ln a} \cdot \frac{d\square}{dx}$$

$$\frac{d}{dx} e^{\square} = e^{\square} \frac{d\square}{dx}$$

$$\frac{d}{dx} \ln \square = \frac{1}{\square} \frac{d\square}{dx}$$

($\square$ any 'symbol' involving x, $\square > 0$, and differentiable)

The **exponential** and **logarithm** have the following properties:

(a) $a^0 = 1, \ a > 0$

(b) $\lim\limits_{x \to +\infty} a^x = +\infty$

(c) $\lim\limits_{x \to -\infty} a^x = 0$

(d) $a^{\triangle + \square} = a^{\triangle} a^{\square}$

(e) $a^{\triangle - \square} = \dfrac{a^{\triangle}}{a^{\square}}$

(f) $\log_a(1) = 0, \ a > 0$

(g) $\log_a(a) = 1$

(h) $\lim\limits_{x \to +\infty} \log_a(x) = \begin{cases} +\infty & \text{if } a > 1 \\ -\infty & \text{if } 0 < a < 1 \end{cases}$

9. $\log_a(\triangle\square) = \log_a(\triangle) + \log_a(\square)$

10. $\log_a\left(\dfrac{\triangle}{\square}\right) = \log_a(\triangle) - \log_a(\square)$

where $\triangle > 0$, $\square > 0$ are any 'symbols' (numbers, functions, ...)

Table 4.6: Summary of the Chapter

4.8   Chapter Exercises

Show that the following sequences are increasing and find their limits in the extended real numbers.

1. $a_n = n + 3$, $n \geq 1$

2. $a_n = \dfrac{n - 3}{n}$, $n \geq 1$

3. $a_n = \dfrac{n(n - 1)}{n^2}$, $n \geq 1$

4. $a_n = \dfrac{n}{n + 4}$, $n \geq 1$

5. Sketch the graph of the sequence $\{a_n\}$ given by

$$a_n = \sqrt{\frac{n - 1}{2n}}$$

   for $n = 1, 2, \ldots, 15$, and find it's limit.

6. Evaluate the following expressions and simplify as much as possible.

   a) $e^{x \ln x}$

   b) $\ln(e^{\sqrt{x}})$,

7. Evaluate the following expressions using

   i) your calculator only and

   ii) writing them in terms Euler's exponential function and then using your calculator:

$$
\begin{aligned}
\text{Example}: \quad &\text{i)} \ (2.3)^{1.2} &=& \quad 2.71690 \\
&\text{ii)} \ (2.3)^{1.2} &=& \quad e^{(1.2)\ln(2.3)} \\
&&=& \quad e^{0.99949} \\
&&=& \quad 2.71690
\end{aligned}
$$

   a) $(2.1)^{1.2}$

   b) $(0.465)^2$

   c) $(0.5)^{-0.25}$

8. Find the derivative of each of the following functions at the indicated points (if any).

   a) $f(x) = 3e^{5x}$

   b) $g(x) = 2e^{3x+2}$, at $x = 0$

   c) $f(x) = \cos(x\,e^x)$

   d) $g(x) = (e^{4x})^{-2}$, at $x = 1$

   e) $k(x) = e^{x^2}\sin(x^2)$, at $x = 0$

   f) $f(x) = e^x \ln(\sin x)$

   g) $g(x) = xe^{-x}$, at $x = 0$

   h) $f(x) = x^2 e^{-2x}$

   i) $g(x) = e^{-2x}\operatorname{Arctan} x$

   j) $f(x) = (x^2)^x$, at $x = 1$.

   k) $g(x) = \sqrt{x}\ln(\sqrt{x})$

   l) $f(x) = 2^x \log_{1.6}(x^3)$

m) $g(x) = 3^{-x} \log_{0.5}(\sec x)$

9. If \$500 is deposited in an account with an annual interest rate of 10 % , compounded continuously,

   (a) What amount will be in the account after 5 years?

   (b) How long will it be until the amount has tripled?

10. An annuity pays 12 % compounded continuously. What amount of money deposited today, will have grown to \$2400 in 8 years?

11. Four months after discontinuing advertising in Mcleans' Magazine, a manufacturer notices that sales have dropped from 10,000 units per month to 8,000 units per month. If the sales can be modelled by an exponential decay model, what will they be after another 2 months?

12. The revenue for a certain company was \$486.8 million in 1990 and \$1005.8 million in 1999.

    (a) Use an exponential growth model to estimate the revenue in 2001. (Hint: $t = 0$ in 1990.)

    (b) In what year will the revenue have reached \$1400.0 million?

13. The cumulative sales S (in thousands of units), of a new product after it has been on the market for t years is modelled by

$$S = Ce^{\frac{k}{t}}.$$

During the first year 5000 units were sold. The saturation point for the market is 30,000 units. That is, the limit of S as $t \to \infty$ is 30,000.

    (a) Solve for C and k in the model.

    (b) How many units will be sold after 5 years?

Suggested Homework Set 16. *Work out problems* $6, 8c, 8d, f8f, 8j, 8l$

4.9   Using Computer Algebra Systems

Use your favorite Computer Algebra System (CAS), like Maple, MatLab, etc., or even a graphing calculator to answer the following questions:

1. Let $x > 0$. Calculate the quotient $\frac{\log x}{\log_3 x}$. What is the value of this quotient as a natural logarithm?

2. Find a formula for the first 10 derivatives of the function $f(x) = \log x$. What is the natural domain of each of these derivatives? Can you find a formula for ALL the derivatives of f?

3. Evaluate

$$\lim_{n \to \infty} n \log \left(1 + \frac{a}{n}\right)^n$$

by starting with various values of a, say, $a = 0.1, 2.6, 5.2, 8.4, 10$ and then guessing the answer for any given value of a. Can you prove your guess using L'Hospital's Rule?

4. Let n be a given positive integer and $a_0, a_1, \ldots, a_n$ any given real numbers. Show that

$$\lim_{x \to \infty} \frac{a_n x^n + a_{n-1} x^{n-1} + \cdots + a_1 x + a_0}{e^x} = 0.$$

Roughly, this says that the **exponential function grows to infinity faster than any polynomial regardless of its degree**. For example, plot the graphs of the functions $f(x) = e^x$ and $g(x) = x^{1}0 + 3x^8 - 6$ on the same axes.

Even though this quotient is a very big number for $10 \leq x \leq 30$, it's easy to see that if $x = 40$ or above then the quotient is less than 1 (in fact, we know that it has to approach zero, so this inequality must be eventually true).

5. Show that

$$\lim_{x \to \infty} \frac{\log x}{x^a} = 0$$

regardless of the value of the exponent a so long as $a > 0$. Roughly, this says that the **logarithmic function grows to infinity more slowly than any polynomial regardless of its degree**.

6. Use a precise plot to show that

$$\left| \log_{10} x - 0.86304 \frac{x-1}{x+1} - 0.36415 \left(\frac{x-1}{x+1} \right)^3 \right| \leq 0.0006$$

provided

$$\frac{1}{\sqrt{10}} \leq x \leq \sqrt{10}.$$

7. Using a graphical plotter prove the inequality

$$\frac{x}{1+x} < \log 1 + x < x$$

whenever $x > -1$ but $x \neq 0$. Can you prove this inequality using the Mean Value Theorem?

8. Calculate all the derivatives of the function $f(x) = e^{-x^2}$ at $x = 0$ and show that $f^{(}n)(0) = 0$ for any ODD integer n.

9. Compare the values $f(x) = e^x$ with the values of

$$g(x) = 1 + x + \frac{x^2}{2!} + \frac{x^3}{3!} + \frac{x^4}{4!} + \frac{x^5}{5!}.$$

Can you guess what happens if we continue to add more terms of the same type to the polynomial on the right ?

Chapter 5

Curve Sketching

The Big Picture

In this Chapter much of what you will have learned so far in differential calculus will be used in helping you draw the graph of a given function. Curve sketching is one of the big applications of elementary calculus. You will see that the various types of limits and the methods used in finding them (e.g., L'Hospital's Rule) will show up again under the guise of **vertical asymptotes** or **horizontal asymptotes** to a graph. In addition, your knowledge of differentiation will help you determine whether a function is **increasing** or **decreasing** and whether or nor it is **concave up** or **concave down**. Furthermore, **Newton's method** for locating the roots of functions will come in handy in finding so-called **critical points** along with the various **intercepts**. All these ideas can be generalized to functions of two or even three variables, so a sound grasp of this chapter is needed to help you visualize the graphs of functions in the plane. We outline here the basic steps required in sketching a given planar curve defined by a function.

Review

Look over all the various **methods of differentiation**. A thorough review of Chapters 2 and 3 is needed here as all that material gets to be used in this chapter (at least do the Chapter Exercises at the end). The material in the first two sections of this chapter is also very important so don't skip over this unless you've already seen it before.

5.1 Solving Polynomial Inequalities (Optional)

The subject of this section is the development of a technique used in solving inequalities involving polynomials or **rational functions** (quotients of polynomials) and some slightly more general functions which look like polynomials or rational functions. One of the main reasons for doing this in Calculus is so that we can use this idea to help us sketch the graph of a function. Recall that a polynomial in x is an expression involving x and multiples of its powers only. For example, $2x^2 - 3x + 1$, $x - 1$, -1.6, $0.5x^3 + 1.72x - 5$, ... are all polynomials. Yes, even ordinary numbers are polynomials (of degree zero).

We'll learn how to solve a polynomial inequality of the form

$$(x-1)(x-\tfrac{1}{2})(x+2) < 0$$

for all possible values of x, or a rational function inequality of the form

$$\frac{(x-2)(x+4)}{x^2-9} > 0$$

for every possible value of x! For example, the inequality $x^2 - 1 < 0$ has the set of numbers which is the open interval $(-1, 1)$ as the set of all of its solutions. Once we know how to solve such inequalities, we'll be able to find those intervals where the graph of a given (differentiable) function has certain properties. All this can be done without the help of a plotter or computer hardware of any kind, but a hand-held calculator would come in handy to speed up simple operations.

Why polynomials? It turns out that many, many functions can be approximated by polynomials, and so, if we know something about this polynomial approximation then we will know something about the original function (with some small errors!). So it is natural to study polynomials. Among the many approximations available, we find one very common one, the so-called **Taylor polynomial approximation** which is used widely in the sciences and engineering and in your pocket calculator, as well.

For example, the trigonometric function $y = \sin x$ can be approximated by this Taylor polynomial of degree $2n - 1$, namely,

x	Actual $\sin(x)$	Est. $p_5(x)$	Est. $p_{13}(x)$
-2	-0.9093	-0.9333	-0.9093
-1	-0.8415	-0.8417	-0.8415
0	0	0	0
1	0.8415	0.8417	0.8415
2	0.9093	0.9333	0.9093
3	0.1411	0.5250	0.1411
4	-0.7568	1.8667	-0.7560

$$p_{2n-1}(x) = x - \frac{x^3}{3!} + \frac{x^5}{5!} - \frac{x^7}{7!} + \ldots + \frac{(-1)^{n-1}x^{2n-1}}{(2n-1)!}$$

The **larger the degree, the better the approximation** is a generally true statement in this business of Taylor polynomials and their related 'series', (see the margin for comparison). You don't have to worry about this now because we'll see all this in a forthcoming chapter on **Taylor series**.

The first step in solving polynomial inequalities is the factoring of the polynomial $p(x)$. Since all our polynomials have real coefficients it can be shown (but we won't do this here) that its factors are of exactly two types:

Either a polynomial, $p(x)$, has a factor that looks like

- A **Type I (or Linear) Factor**:

$$a_1 x - a_2,$$

or it has a factor that looks like,

- A **Type II (Quadratic Irreducible) Factor**:

$$ax^2 + bx + c, \text{ where } b^2 - 4ac < 0$$

---

where a_1, a_2, a, b, c are all real numbers. All the factors of $p(x)$ must look like either Type I or Type II. This isn't obvious at all and it is an old and important result from Algebra. In other words, **every polynomial (with real coefficients) can be factored into a product of Type I and/or Type II factors and their powers**.

Example 201.

$$x^2 + 3x + 2 = \underbrace{(x+1)(x+2)}_{Type\ I\ factors}$$

Example 202.

$$\begin{aligned} x^2 + 2x + 1 &= (x+1)^2 \\ &= \underbrace{(x+1)(x+1)}_{Type\ I\ factors} \end{aligned}$$

Example 203.

$$2x^2 - 3x - 2 = \underbrace{(2x+1)(x-2)}_{Type\ I\ factors}$$

Example 204.

$$\begin{aligned} x^4 - 1 &= (x^2 - 1)(x^2 + 1) \\ &= \underbrace{(x-1)(x+1)}_{Type\ I}\underbrace{(x^2+1)}_{Type\ II} \end{aligned}$$

In this example, $x^2 + 1$ is a quadratic irreducible factor as $b^2 - 4ac = 0^2 - 4 \cdot 1 \cdot 1 = -4 < 0$.

Example 205. $2x^4 + 19x^2 + 9 = (x^2 + 9)(2x^2 + 1)$. *Notice that there are* **no** **Type I** *factors at all in this example. Don't worry, this is OK, it can happen!*

Example 206. $x^2 + x + 1 = x^2 + x + 1$. *We cannot simplify this one further because $b^2 - 4ac = 1^2 - 4 \cdot 1 \cdot 1 = -3 < 0$. So the polynomial is identical with its Type II factor, and we leave it as it is!*

Example 207.

$$\begin{aligned} x^6 - 1 &= (x^3 - 1)(x^3 + 1) \\ &= (x-1)(x^2 + x + 1) \cdot (x+1)(x^2 - x + 1) \\ &= \underbrace{(x-1)(x+1)}_{Type\ I}\underbrace{(x^2 - x + 1)}_{Type\ II}\underbrace{(x^2 + x + 1)}_{Type\ II} \end{aligned}$$

Example 208.

$$(x^2 - 2x + 1)(x^2 - 4x + 4) = \underbrace{(x-1)^2(x-2)^2}_{All\ Type\ I\ factors}$$

Don't worry about the powers which may appear in a linear factor (Type I factor), sometimes they show up, just use them.

Exercise Set 26.

Factor the following polynomials into Type I and Type II factors and identify each one as in the examples above.

1. $x^2 - 1$
2. $x^3 - x^2 + x - 1$ (Hint: x = 1 is a root)
3. $x^2 + x - 6$
4. $x^3 - x^2 - x + 1$
5. $x^4 - 16$
6. $2x^2 + x - 1$
7. $x^4 - 2x^2 + 1$ (Hint: $x = 1$ and $x = -1$ are both roots.)
8. $x^3 + x^2 + x + 1$ (Hint: $x = -1$ is a root.)

For the purposes of solving inequalities we will call real points x where $p(x) = 0$, **break-points** (or real roots, or zeros, is more common). Thus,

$$x^2 - 1 = (x - 1)(x + 1)$$

has $x = \pm 1$ as break-points, while

$$x^4 - 16 = (x - 2)(x + 2)(x^2 + 4)$$

has $x = \pm 2$ as break-points, but no other such points (since $x^2 + 4 \neq 0$ for any x).

Remember: Quadratic irreducible factors (Type II factors) have no break-points. Break-points come from linear factors (Type I factors) **only**.

The Sign Decomposition Table of a Polynomial

The next step in our guide to solving polynomial inequalities is the creation of the so-called Sign Decomposition Table (SDT, for short) of a polynomial, $p(x)$. Once we have filled in this SDT with the correct '+' and '−' signs, we can **essentially read off the solution of our inequality**. In Table 5.1, we present an example of a SDT for the polynomial $p(x) = x^4 - 1$.

Look at the SDT, Table 5.1, of $x^4 - 1$. The solution of the inequality

$$x^4 - 1 < 0$$

can be "read off" the SDT by looking at the last column of its SDT and choosing the intervals with the '−' sign in its last column. In this case we see the row

$$\mid (-1, 1) \parallel + \mid - \mid + \parallel - \parallel$$

which translates into the statement

"If $-1 < x < 1$ then $x^4 - 1 < 0$."

The Sign Decomposition Table of $x^4 - 1$

	$x + 1$	$x - 1$	$x^2 + 1$	sign of $p(x)$
$(-\infty, -1)$	$-$	$-$	$+$	$+$
$(-1, 1)$	$+$	$-$	$+$	$-$
$(1, \infty)$	$+$	$+$	$+$	$+$

The SDT is made up of *rows containing intervals whose end-points are break-points of $p(x)$ and columns are the factors of $p(x)$* and various $+/-$ signs. We'll explain all this below and show you how it works!

Table 5.1: The Sign Decomposition Table of $x^4 - 1$

Size of SDT $= (r + 1)$ **by** $(s + 1)$

(rows by columns, excluding the margin and headers) where

r = the total number of **different** break-points of $p(x)$, and

s = (the total number of different break-points of $p(x)$) + (the total number of **different** Type II factors of $p(x)$).

Table 5.2: Size of SDT

The same kind of argument works if we are looking for all the solutions of $x^4 - 1 > 0$. In this case, there are **2** rows whose last column have a '$+$' sign namely,

$(-\infty, -1)$	$-$	$-$	$+$	$+$
$(1, \infty)$	$+$	$+$	$+$	$+$

The Size of a Sign Decomposition Table

This last piece of information tells us that,

"If $-\infty < x < -1$ **or** $1 < x < \infty$ then $x^4 - 1 > 0$"

So, all the information we need in order to solve the inequality $p(x) > 0$ can be found in its Sign Decomposition Table!

OK, so what is this SDT and how do we fill it in?

First, we need to decide on **the size of a SDT**. Let's say it has $r + 1$ rows and $s + 1$ columns (the ones containing the $+/-$ signs).

Example 209. What is the size of the STD of $p(x) = x^4 - 1$?

Solution The first step is to factor $p(x)$ into its linear (or Type I) and quadratic irreducible (or Type II) factors. So,

$$x^4 - 1 = (x^2 - 1)(x^2 + 1)$$

$$= (x+1)(x-1)(x^2+1)$$

The next step is to determine r and s. Now the break-points are ± 1 and so $r = 2$. There is only one quadratic irreducible factor , so $s = r + 1 = 2 + 1 = 3$, by Table 5.2. So the SDT has size $(r + 1)$ by $(s + 1)$ which is $(2 + 1)$ by $(3 + 1)$ or 3 by 4. The SDT has 3 rows and 4 columns.

| **Example 210.** | Find the size of the SDT of the polynomial |

$$p(x) = (x-1)(x-2)(x-3)(x^2+1)(x^2+4)$$

Solution The polynomial $p(x)$ is already in its desired factored form because it is a product of 3 Type I factors and 2 Type II factors! Its break-points are $x = 1, x = 2, x = 3$ and so $r = 3$, since there are 3 break-points. Next, there are only 2 distinct Type II factors, right? So, by Table 5.2, $s = r + 2 = 3 + 2 = 5$. The SDT of $p(x)$ has size $(3 + 1)$ by $(5 + 1)$ or 4 by 6.

How to fill in a SDT?

OK, now that we know how big a SDT can be, what do we do with it?

Now **write down all the Type I and Type II factors and their powers** so that, for example,

$$p(x) = (x - a_1)^{p_1}(x - a_2)^{p_2} \ldots (x - a_r)^{p_r}(A_1 x^2 + B_1 x + C_1)^{q_1} \ldots$$

Rearrange the break-points $a_1, a_2, \ldots, a_r$ in increasing order, you may have to relabel them though, that is, let

$$(-\infty <) \quad a_1 < a_2 < a_3 < \ldots < a_r \quad (< +\infty)$$

Form the following open intervals: $I_1, I_2, \ldots, I_{r+1}$ where

$$\begin{aligned}
I_1 : \quad & (-\infty, a_1) = \{x : -\infty < x < a_1\} \\
I_2 : \quad & (a_1, a_2) \\
I_3 : \quad & (a_2, a_3) \\
I_4 : \quad & (a_3, a_4) \\
& \cdots \\
I_r : \quad & (a_{r-1}, a_r) \\
I_{r+1} : \quad & (a_r, +\infty)
\end{aligned}$$

and put them in the **margin** of our SDT.

At the top of each column place every factor (Type I and Type II) along with their 'power':

	$(x - a_1)^{p_1}$	...	$(x - a_r)^{p_r}$	$(A_1 x^2 + B_1 x + C_1)^{q_1}$	...
$(-\infty, a_1)$					
(a_1, a_2)					
(a_2, a_3)					
$\cdots$					..
(a_{r-1}, a_r)					
$(a_r, +\infty)$					

Finally we "fill in" our SDT with the symbols '+' (for plus) and '−' (for minus).

So far, so good, but *how do we choose the sign?*

Filling in a SDT

1. Choose **any** point in the interval $I_i = (a_{i-1}, a_i)$.

2. Evaluate the factor (at the very top of column j along with its power) at the point you chose in (1), above.

3. The sign of the number in (2) is the sign we put in this box at row i and column j.

4. The sign in the **last column** of row i is just the product of all the signs in that row.

Table 5.3: Filling in an Sign Decomposition Table

Actually, this is not hard to do. Let's say you want to know what sign $(+/-)$ goes into the ith row and j^{th} column.

NOTE: For item (1) in Table 5.3, if the interval is *finite*, we can **choose the midpoint** of the interval $(a_{i-1}, a_i) = I_i$ or,

$$\text{midpoint} = \frac{a_i + a_{i-1}}{2}$$

Here's a few examples drawn from Table 5.1.

Example 211. In Table 5.1 we choose $x = -2$ inside the interval $(-\infty, -1)$, evaluate the factor $(x-1)$ at $x = -2$, look at its sign, (it is negative) and then place the plus or minus sign in the corresponding cell.

You have complete freedom in your choice of number in the given interval. The method is summarized in the diagram below:

$$\boxed{(x-1)}$$

Choose $x = -2$ ↗ ↓ Sign of $(-2-1)$

$$\boxed{(-\infty, -1)} \qquad \boxed{-}$$

Example 212. In Table 5.1 we choose $x = 0$ inside the interval $(-1, 1)$, evaluate the factor $(x+1)$ at $x = 0$, look at its sign, and then place the plus or minus sign in the corresponding cell.

$$\boxed{(x+1)}$$

Choose $x = 0$ ↗ ↓ Sign of $(0+1)$

$$\boxed{(-1, 1)} \qquad \boxed{+}$$

Example 213. In Table 5.1 we choose $x = 1.6$ inside the interval $(1, \infty)$, evaluate the factor $(x^2 + 1)$ at $x = 1.6$, look at its sign, and then place the plus or minus sign in the corresponding cell.

$$\boxed{(x^2 + 1)}$$

Choose $x = 1.6$ ↗   ↓ Sign of $(2.56 + 1)$

$$\boxed{(1, \infty)} \qquad \boxed{+}$$

Example 214. In Table 5.1 we choose $x = -0.8$ inside the interval $(-1, 1)$, evaluate the factor $(x - 1)$ at $x = -0.8$, look at its sign, and then place the plus or minus sign in the corresponding cell.

$$\boxed{(x - 1)}$$

Choose $x = -0.8$ ↗   ↓ Sign of $(-0.8 - 1)$

$$\boxed{(-1, 1)} \qquad \boxed{-}$$

OK, now we are in a position to create the SDT of a given polynomial.

Example 215. Find the SDT of the polynomial

$$p(x) = (x - 1)(x - 2)^2(x^2 + 1)$$

Solution The first question is: What is the complete factorization of $p(x)$ into Type I and II factors? In this case we have nothing to do as $p(x)$ is already in this special form. Why?

Next, we must decide on the size of the SDT. Its size, according to our definition, is 3 by 4 (excluding the margin and headers).

We can produce the SDT: Note that its break-points are at $x = 1$ and $x = 2$.

	$(x-1)$	$(x-2)^2$	(x^2+1)	Sign of $p(x)$
$(-\infty, 1)$				
$(1, 2)$				
$(2, \infty)$				

We fill in the $3 \times 4 = 12$ cells with $+/-$ signs according to the procedure in Table 5.3. We find the table,

	$(x-1)$	$(x-2)^2$	(x^2+1)	Sign of $p(x)$
$(-\infty, 1)$	-	+	+	-
$(1, 2)$	+	+	+	+
$(2, \infty)$	+	+	+	+

as its SDT, since the product of all the signs in the first row is negative (as $(-1)(+1)(+1) = -1$) while the product of the signs in each of the other rows is positive.

Example 216. Find the SDT of the polynomial

$$p(x) = (x + 1)^2(x - 1)(x + 3)^3$$

Solution The break-points are given by $x = -3, -1, 1$. These give rise to some intervals, namely $(-\infty, -3), (-3, -1), (-1, 1), (1, \infty)$. The table now looks like

Such SDT tables will be used later to help us find the properties of graphs of polynomials and rational functions!

	$(x+3)^3$	$(x+1)^2$	$(x-1)$	Sign of $p(x)$
$(-\infty, -3)$				
$(-3, -1)$				
$(-1, 1)$				
$(1, \infty)$				

OK, now we have to fill in this SDT with $+/-$ signs, right? So choose some points in each one of the intervals in the left, find the sign of the corresponding number in the columns and continue this procedure. (See the previous Example). We will get the table,

	$(x+3)^3$	$(x+1)^2$	$(x-1)$	Sign of $p(x)$
$(-\infty, -3)$	$-$	$+$	$-$	$+$
$(-3, -1)$	$+$	$+$	$-$	$-$
$(-1, 1)$	$+$	$+$	$-$	$-$
$(1, \infty)$	$+$	$+$	$+$	$+$

That's all!

Example 217. Find the SDT of the polynomial

$$p(x) = \left(x - \frac{1}{2}\right)(x + 2.6)(x - 1)^2(x^2 + x + 1)$$

Solution OK, first of all, do not worry about the type of numbers that show up here, namely, $\frac{1}{2}, 2.6$ etc. It doesn't matter what kind of numbers these are; they do not have to to be integers! The break-points are $-2.6, \frac{1}{2}, 1$ and $\boxed{?}$. Well, there is no other because $x^2 + x + 1$ is a quadratic irreducible (remember that such a polynomial has no real roots, or equivalently its discriminant is negative).

The SDT looks like (convince yourself):

SDT	$(x+2.6)$	$(x-\frac{1}{2})$	$(x-1)^2$	(x^2+x+1)	Sign of $p(x)$
$(-\infty, -2.6)$	$-$	$-$	$+$	$+$	$+$
$(-2.6, \frac{1}{2})$	$+$	$-$	$+$	$+$	$-$
$(\frac{1}{2}, 1)$	$+$	$+$	$+$	$+$	$+$
$(1, \infty)$	$+$	$+$	$+$	$+$	$+$

Example 218. Find the SDT of the polynomial

$$p(x) = 3(x^2 - 4)(9 - x^2)$$

Solution Let's factor this completely first. Do not worry about the number '3' appearing as the leading coefficient there, it doesn't affect the 'sign' of $p(x)$ as it is positive.

In this example the break-points are, $x = -3, -2, 2, 3$, in increasing order, because the factors of $p(x)$ are $(x - 2)(x + 2)(3 - x)(3 + x)$. (Notice that the '$x$' does not come first in the third and fourth factors ... that's OK!). We produce the SDT as usual.

SDT	$(x+3)$	$(x+2)$	$(x-2)$	$(3-x)$	Sign of $p(x)$
$(-\infty, -3)$	–	–	–	+	–
$(-3, -2)$	+	–	–	+	+
$(-2, 2)$	+	+	–	+	–
$(2, 3)$	+	+	+	+	+
$(3, \infty)$	+	+	+	–	–

The $+/-$ signs in the graph indicate the region(s) where the function is positive/negative, (see Figure 95).

How to solve polynomial inequalities?

Okay, now that you know how to find the SDT of a given polynomial it's going to be really easy to find the solution of a polynomial inequality involving that polynomial! All the information you need is in the SDT! Let's backtrack on a few examples to see how it's done.

Example 219. Solve the inequality $(x-1)(x-2)^2(x^2+1) < 0$

Solution The polynomial here is $p(x) = (x-1)(x-2)^2(x^2+1)$ and we need to solve the inequality $p(x) < 0$, right? Refer to Example 215 for its SDT. Just go to the last column of its SDT under the header 'Sign of $p(x)$' and look for *minus signs* only. There is only one of them, see it? It also happens to be in the row which corresponds to the interval $(-\infty, 1)$. There's your solution! That is, the solution of the inequality

$$(x-1)(x-2)^2(x^2+1) < 0,$$

is given by the set of all points x inside the interval $(-\infty, 1)$.

Example 220. Solve the inequality $p(x) = (x+1)^2(x-1)(x+3)^3 > 0$

Solution The polynomial is $p(x) = (x+1)^2(x-1)(x+3)^3$ and we need to solve the inequality $p(x) > 0$. Look at Example 216 for its SDT. Once again, go to the last column of its SDT under the header 'Sign of $p(x)$' and look for *plus signs* only. Now there are *two* of them, right? The rows they are in correspond to the two intervals $(-\infty, -3)$ and $(1, \infty)$. So the solution of the inequality is the *union* of these two intervals, that is, the solution of the inequality

$$(x+1)^2(x-1)(x+3)^3 > 0,$$

is given by the set of all points x where x is **either** in the interval $(-\infty, -3)$, **or**, in the interval $(1, \infty)$.

Example 221. Solve the inequality

$$p(x) = \left(x - \frac{1}{2}\right)(x+2.6)(x-1)^2(x^2+x+1) < 0.$$

Solution Now the polynomial is $p(x) = (x-(1/2))(x+2.6)(x-1)^2(x^2+x+1)$ and we need to solve the inequality $p(x) < 0$. Look at Example 217 for its SDT. Once again, go to the last column of its SDT under the header 'Sign of $p(x)$' and look for *minus signs* only. This time there is only one of them. The row it is in corresponds to the interval $(-2.6, 1/2)$. So the solution of the inequality

$$\left(x - \frac{1}{2}\right)(x+2.6)(x-1)^2(x^2+x+1) < 0$$

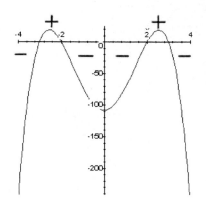

Figure 95.

is given by the set of all points x in the interval $(-2.6, 0.5)$.

In case the polynomial inequality is of the form $p(x) \geq 0$ (or $p(x) \leq 0$), we simply

1. Solve the 'strict' inequality $p(x) > 0$ (or $p(x) < 0$) and

2. Add **all** the break-points to the solution set.

Let's look at an example.

Example 222. Solve the inequality $p(x) = 3(x^2 - 4)(9 - x^2) \leq 0$

Solution The polynomial is $p(x) = 3(x^2 - 4)(9 - x^2)$ and we need to solve the inequality $p(x) < 0$ and add all the break-points of p to the solution set, right? Look at Example 218 for its SDT. Once again, go to the last column of its SDT under the header 'Sign of $p(x)$' and look for *minus signs* only. This time there are three rows with minus signs in their last column. The rows correspond to the intervals $(-\infty, -3)$, $(-2, 2)$, and $(3, \infty)$. So the solution of the inequality

$$3(x^2 - 4)(9 - x^2) \leq 0,$$

is given by the union of all these intervals along with all the break-points of p. That is the solution set is given by the set of all points x where x is **either** in the interval $(-\infty, -3)$, **or**, in the interval $(-2, 2)$, **or**, in the interval $(3, \infty)$, along with the points $\{-2, 2, -3, 3\}$.

This can be also be written briefly as: $(-\infty, -3] \cup [-2, 2] \cup [3, \infty)$, where, as usual, the symbol '$\cup$' means the union.

Exercise Set 27.

---

1. Find all the break-points (or roots) of the following polynomials.

   a) $p(x) = (9x^2 - 1)(x + 1)$

   b) $q(x) = (x^4 - 1)(x + 3)$

   c) $r(x) = (x^2 + x - 2)(x^2 + x + 1)$

   d) $p(t) = t^3 - 1$ ($t - 1$ is a factor)

   e) $q(w) = w^6 - 1$ ($w - 1$ and $w + 1$ are factors)

2. Find the Sign Decomposition Table of each one of the polynomials in Exercise 1 above.

3. Find the Sign Decomposition Table of the function

$$p(x) = 2(x^2 - 9)(16 - x^2)$$

(Hint: See Example 218).

4. What are the break-points of the function

$$p(x) = (2 + \sin(x))\,(x^2 + 1)(x - 2)?$$

(Hint: $|\sin(x)| \leq 1$ for every value of x.)

5. Determine the SDT of the function

$$q(x) = (x^4 - 1)\,(3 + \cos(x))$$

(Hint: Use the ideas in the previous exercise and show that $3 + \cos(x) > 0$ for every value of x.)

6. Solve the polynomial inequality $x(x^2 + x + 1)(x^2 - 1) < 0$

7. Solve the inequality $(x^4 - 1)(x + 3) > 0$

8. Solve the polynomial inequality $(x + 1)(x - 2)(x - 3)(x + 4) \leq 0$

9. Solve the inequality $(x - 1)^3(x^2 + 1)(4 - x^2) \geq 0$

10. Solve the polynomial inequality $(9x^2 - 1)(x + 1) \geq 0$

NOTES:

5.2 Solving Rational Function Inequalities (Optional)

Recall that a rational function is, by definition, the quotient of two polynomials, so that, for example,

$$r(x) = \frac{x^3 - 3x^2 + 1}{x - 6}$$

is a rational function. When we study functions called **derivatives** we see that the way in which the graph of a rational function 'curves' around depends upon the need to solve inequalities of the form $r(x) > 0$ for certain values of x, or $r(x) < 0$, where r is some rational function. In this case we can extend the ideas of the previous sections and define an **SDT** for a given rational function. Let's see how this is done:

The idea is to extend the notion of a **break-point** for a polynomial to that for a rational function. Since a break-point is by definition a root of a polynomial, it is natural to define a break-point of a rational function to be a root of either its numerator or its denominator, and this is what we will do!

A **break-point** of a rational function r is any real root of either its numerator or its denominator but not a root of both.

This means that in the event that the numerator and denominator have a *common factor of the same multiplicity*, then we agree that there is *no break point there*. For instance, the rational function

$$r(x) = (x^2 - 9)/(x - 3)$$

has its only break-point at $x = -3$, because $x - 3$ is a factor in both the numerator and denominator! However, the slightly modified function

$$r(x) = (x^2 - 9)^2/(x - 3)$$

does have a break point at $x = 3$ since $x = 3$ is a double root of the numerator but only a simple root of the denominator. Since the multiplicities are different, we must include $x = 3$ as a break-point.

On the other hand, the break-points of the rational function

$$r(x) = \frac{x^2 - 4}{x^2 - 1}$$

are given by $x = \pm 2$ and $x = \pm 1$. Now we can build the SDT of a rational function by using the ideas in the polynomial case, which we just covered.

Example 223. Find the break-points of the following rational functions:

1) $r(x) = \dfrac{x^2 + 1}{x}$ 2) $R(x) = \dfrac{x^3 - 1}{x + 1}$ 3) $r(t) = \dfrac{3 - t^2}{t^3 + 1}$

4) $R(t) = \dfrac{4t}{t^2 + 9}$ 5) $r(x) = x + 1 + \dfrac{2}{x - 1}$

Solution

1. Let's write

$$r(x) = \frac{p(x)}{q(x)}$$

where $p(x) = x^2 + 1$ and $q(x) = x$. The break-points of the $r(x)$ are by definition the same as the break-points of $p(x)$ and $q(x)$. But $p(x)$ is a quadratic irreducible (as its discriminant is negative) and so it has *no* break points, right? On the other hand, the break-point of the denominator $q(x)$ is given by $x = 0$ (it's the only root!). The collection of break points is given by $\{x = 0\}$.

2. Write $R(x) = \frac{p(x)}{q(x)}$, as before, where $p(x) = x^3 - 1$, $q(x) = x + 1$. We factor $R(x)$ completely to find

$$p(x) = x^3 - 1 = (x - 1)(x^2 + x + 1)$$

and

$$q(x) = x + 1$$

Now $x^2 + x + 1$ is an irreducible quadratic factor and so it has no break-points. The break-points of $p(x)$ are simply given by the single point $x = 1$ while $q(x)$ has $x = -1$ as its only break-point. The collection of break-points of $R(x)$ is now the set $\{x = 1,\ x = -1\}$.

3. Write $r(t) = \frac{p(t)}{q(t)}$ where $p(t) = 3 - t^2$ and $q(t) = t^3 + 1$. The factors of $p(t)$ are $(\sqrt{3} - t)(\sqrt{3} + t)$, right? The factors of $q(t)$ are $(t + 1)(t^2 - t + 1)$, so the break points are given by $t = -\sqrt{3}, -1, +\sqrt{3}$, since $t^2 - t + 1$ is an irreducible quadratic (no break-points).

4. In this example, the numerator $p(t) = 4t$ has only one break point, at $t = 0$. The denominator, $q(t) = t^2 + 9$ is an irreducible quadratic, right? Thus, the collection of break-points of $R(t)$ consists of only one point, $\{t = 0\}$.

5. This example looks mysterious, but all we need to do is find a common denominator, that is, we can rewrite $r(x)$ as

$$\begin{aligned} r(x) &= \frac{(x+1)(x-1)}{x-1} + \frac{2}{x-1} \\ &= \frac{(x+1)(x-1) + 2}{x-1} \\ &= \frac{x^2 + x - x - 1 + 2}{x-1} \\ &= \frac{x^2 + 1}{x-1} \end{aligned}$$

From this equivalent representation we see that its break-points consist of the single point $\{x = 1\}$, since the numerator is irreducible.

Connections

Later on we'll see that the **break-points/roots of the denominator** of a rational function coincide with a vertical line that we call a **vertical asymptote**, a line around which the graph "peaks sharply" or "drops sharply", towards infinity.

For example, the two graphs in the adjoining margin indicate the presence of vertical asymptotes (v.a.) at $x = 0$ and $x = 1$.

> The SDT of a rational function is found in exactly the same way as the SDT for a polynomial. The only difference is that we have to **include all the break-points** of the numerator and denominator which make it up. Remember that we never consider 'common roots'.

Example 224. Find the SDT of the rational function whose values are given by

$$\frac{(x-2)(x+4)}{x^2-9}$$

Solution From the SDT

	$(x+4)$	$(x+3)$	$(x-2)$	$(x-3)$	Sign of $r(x)$
$(-\infty, -4)$	$-$	$-$	$-$	$-$	$+$
$(-4, -3)$	$+$	$-$	$-$	$-$	$-$
$(-3, 2)$	$+$	$+$	$-$	$-$	$+$
$(2, 3)$	$+$	$+$	$+$	$-$	$-$
$(3, \infty)$	$+$	$+$	$+$	$+$	$+$

we see immediately that the solution of the inequality

$$\frac{(x-2)(x+4)}{x^2-9} < 0$$

is given by combining the intervals in rows 2 and 4 (as their last entry is negative). We get the set of points which is the union of the 2 intervals $(-4, -3)$ and $(2, 3)$. Check it out with specific values, say, $x = -3.5$ or $x = 2.5$ and see that it really works! On the other hand, if one wants the set of points for which

$$\frac{(x-2)(x+4)}{x^2-9} \leq 0$$

then one must add the break points $x = 2$ and $x = -4$ to the two intervals already mentioned, (note that $x = \pm 3$ are not in the domain).

Example 225. Solve the inequality

$$\frac{x^2-3x+1}{x^3-1} \geq 0$$

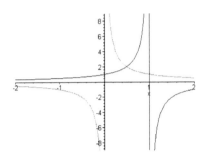

The graphs of Example 225 and $y = 1/x$ showing their vertical asymptotes at $x = 1$ and $x = 0$ respectively.

Solution The break points of the values of this rational function, call them $r(x)$, are given by finding the roots of the quadratic in the numerator and the cubic in the denominator. Using the quadratic equation we get that the two roots of $x^2 - 3x + 1 = 0$ are $x = (3 + \sqrt{5})/2$ and $x = (3 - \sqrt{5})/2$. Let's approximate these values by the numbers 2.618 and 0.382 in order to simplify the display of the SDT. The roots of the cubic $x^3 - 1 = 0$ are given by $x = 1$ only, as its other factor, namely, the polynomial $x^2 + x + 1$ is irreducible, and so has no real roots, and consequently, no break-points.

Writing these break-points in increasing order we get: $0.382, 1, 2.618$. The SDT of this rational function is now

	$(x-0.382)$	$(x-1)$	$(x-2.618)$	Sign of $r(x)$
$(-\infty, 0.382)$	$-$	$-$	$-$	$-$
$(0.382, 1)$	$+$	$-$	$-$	$+$
$(1, 2.618)$	$+$	$+$	$-$	$-$
$(2.618, \infty)$	$+$	$+$	$+$	$+$

The solution can be read off easily using the last column as the intervals corresponding to the '+' signs. This gives the union of the two intervals $(0.382, 1), (2.618, \infty)$ *along* with the two break-points $x = 0.382, 2.618$, (why?).

Example 226. Solve the inequality

$$\frac{x}{3x-6} + \frac{2x}{x-2} < 0$$

Solution Looks strange because it's not in the 'usual' form, right? No problem, just put it in the usual form (i.e., a polynomial divided by another polynomial) by finding a common denominator, in this case, $3(x-2)$. We see that

$$\frac{x}{3x-6} + \frac{2x}{x-2} = \frac{x}{3x-6} + \frac{(3)(2x)}{3(x-2)} = \frac{7x}{3x-6}$$

The break points of the values of this rational function are given by setting $7x = 0$ and $3x - 6 = 0$. Solving these two equations is easy and this gives us the two break-points $x = 0$ and $x = 2$. Writing these break-points in increasing order we find: $0, 2$. The SDT of this rational function is then

	$(x-0)$	$(x-2)$	Sign of $r(x)$
$(-\infty, 0)$	$-$	$-$	$+$
$(0, 2)$	$+$	$-$	$-$
$(2, \infty)$	$+$	$+$	$+$

The solution can be read off easily using the last column, by looking at the intervals corresponding to the '$-$' signs. This gives only *one* interval $(0, 2)$, and nothing else.

Example 227. Solve the inequality

$$\frac{x^2 - 9}{(x^2 - 4)^2} \le 0$$

Solution The 4 break-points are given in increasing order by $x = -3, -2, 2, 3$. The corresponding factors are then $(x + 3)$, $(x + 2)^2$, and $(x - 2)^2$, $(x - 3)$. (Don't forget the squares, because the denominator is squared !). Okay, now its SDT is then given by

	$(x+3)$	$(x+2)^2$	$(x-2)^2$	$(x-3)$	Sign of $r(x)$
$(-\infty, -3)$	$-$	$+$	$+$	$-$	$+$
$(-3, -2)$	$+$	$+$	$+$	$-$	$-$
$(-2, 2)$	$+$	$+$	$+$	$-$	$-$
$(2, 3)$	$+$	$+$	$+$	$-$	$-$
$(3, \infty)$	$+$	$+$	$+$	$+$	$+$

You could include the points $x = \pm 2$ in the solution if you allow *extended real numbers* as solutions. But, strictly speaking, we don't allow them as solutions.

In this case, the solution set is the closed interval $[-3, 3]$ **without** the points $x = \pm 2$ (why?). This answer could have been arrived at more simply by noticing that, since the denominator is always positive (or zero) the negative sign on the right (or zero) can only occur if the numerator is negative (or zero), and the denominator is non-zero. This means that $x^2 - 9 \le 0$ and $x^2 - 4 \ne 0$ which together imply that $|x| \le 3$, and $x \ne \pm 2$ as before.

SNAPSHOTS

Example 228. Find the solution of the inequality

$$\frac{4 - x^2}{x - 2} \le 0.$$

Solution The solution of the inequality

$$\frac{4 - x^2}{x - 2} \leq 0$$

is given by the interval $[-2, \infty)$, excluding the point $x = 2$. This is because the given rational function is essentially a polynomial "in disguise". Factoring the difference of squares and simplifying what's left under the assumption that $x \neq 2$, we'll find the expression $-(x + 2) \leq 0$ from which the solution $x \geq -2$ follows. Note that we must include the break-point $x = -2$ to the solution set because we have a '$\leq$' sign. On the other hand, we can't ever divide by '0' right? So, we have to forget about $x = 2$.

Example 229. | Find the solution of the inequality

$$\frac{1}{x^2 - 4} \geq 0.$$

Solution The solution of the inequality

$$\frac{1}{x^2 - 4} \geq 0$$

is given by the set of points x with $|x| > 2$ (think about this). Notice that this rational function is never equal to zero, but that's OK. The points $x = \pm 2$ are not allowed since we are dividing by '0' if we decide to use them. No go! Its solution set is the set of points x where $|x| > 2$ and its SDT is

	$(x + 2)$	$(x - 2)$	Sign of $r(x)$
$(-\infty, -2)$	$-$	$-$	$+$
$(-2, 2)$	$+$	$-$	$-$
$(2, \infty)$	$+$	$+$	$+$

In some cases, another function may be multiplying a rational function. When this happens, it is still possible to use the methods in this section to solve an inequality associated with that function. Here's an example.

Example 230. | Solve the inequality

$$\frac{x|\sin(x)|}{1 + x} \geq 0.$$

Solution Now here, $|\sin(x)| \geq 0$ for **any** x so all we should think about is "what's left"? Well, what's left is the rational function $r(x) = x/(1 + x)$. Its 2 break-points are $x = -1, 0$ and the corresponding factors are now $(x + 1)$, x. Its SDT is then given by

	$(x + 1)$	x	Sign of $r(x)$
$(-\infty, -1)$	$-$	$-$	$+$
$(-1, 0)$	$+$	$-$	$-$
$(0, \infty)$	$+$	$+$	$+$

and the solution set is the union of the intervals $(-\infty, -1)$ and $[0, \infty)$ with the break-point $x = 0$ included, but without $x = -1$ (division by zero, remember?), along with all the zeros of the sin function (namely $x = \pm\pi, \pm 2\pi, ...$). These extra points are already included in the union of the two intervals given above, so there's nothing more to do.

Exercise Set 28.

1. Find all the break-points of the following rational functions.

a) $\dfrac{1+x^2}{x-2}$ b) $\dfrac{3t-2}{t^3-1}$ c) $\dfrac{x+2}{1}-\dfrac{1}{x-1}$

d) $\dfrac{x^3+1}{x^3-1}$ e) $\dfrac{x^2-2x+1}{x^2-1}$ f) $\dfrac{4-x^2}{1-x^2}$

2. Find the Sign Decomposition Table (SDT) of each one of the following functions from above.

a) $\dfrac{1+t^2}{t-2}$ b) $\dfrac{3t-2}{t^3-1}$ c) $\dfrac{t+2}{1}-\dfrac{1}{t-1}$

d) $\dfrac{t^3+1}{t^3-1}$ e) $\dfrac{t^2-2t+1}{t^2-1}$ f) $\dfrac{4-t^2}{1-t^2}$

3. Use the results of the previous exercises to solve the following inequalities involving rational functions.

a) $\dfrac{1+t^2}{t-2}\le 0$ b) $\dfrac{3t-2}{t^3-1}\ge 0$ c) $\dfrac{t+2}{1}-\dfrac{1}{t-1}>0$

d) $\dfrac{t^3+1}{t^3-1}<0$ e) $\dfrac{t^2-2t+1}{t^2-1}\ge 0$ f) $\dfrac{4-t^2}{1-t^2}<0$

4. Find the break-points and SDT of the given rational functions, and solve the inequalities.

a) $\dfrac{x^2-16}{x-4}>0$ b) $3x+\dfrac{5}{x}<0$ c) $\dfrac{x^2-5}{x-5}>0$

d) $\dfrac{3x^2+4x+5}{x^2+8x-20}<0$ e) $\dfrac{x^3+x^2}{x^4-1}\ge 0$ f) $\dfrac{x^2\,|\cos x|}{x-2}<0$

5. Find the break-points and SDT of the given rational functions, and solve the inequalities.

a) $\dfrac{x^2-1}{x^2+4}>0$ b) $\dfrac{x^2+1}{x^4+1}>0$ c) $\dfrac{x^2-9}{x^2+x+1}<0$

d) $\dfrac{2x-3}{(x-4)^2}<0$ e) $\dfrac{x+1}{(x+2)(x+3)}>0$ f) $\dfrac{x^3-1}{x+1}<0$

Hint: 5b) $x^4+1=(x^2+\sqrt{2}x+1)(x^2-\sqrt{2}x+1)$ is the product of two irreducible quadratic polynomials, or Type II factors. Don't worry, this isn't obvious!

Suggested Homework Set 17. *Work out problems* $4a, 4f, 5c, 5e, 5f$.

Group Project

Get together with some of your classmates and try to extend the ideas in this section to a more general mathematical setting. By this we mean, for example, try to find a general method for making a SDT for a function of the form $f(x)r(x)$ where f is not necessarily either a polynomial or a rational function while $r(x)$ *is* a rational function. For instance, think of a way of making the SDT of the function

$$\frac{x}{x^2 - 1} \sin x$$

or more generally, a function whose values look like

    (rational function) (any single trig. function here) .

5.3   Graphing Techniques

The first thing you should do in this business of sketching the graph of a function is to just **plot a few points** to get a feel for what's happening to the graph, what you think it looks like. It's not going to be the best you can do, and there may be some missing data but still you'll get the basic idea. See Figure 96 for such an instance for the function f defined by $f(x) = sin(\frac{1}{x})$, where x is in radians. But **watch out**, this isn't enough as you'll see below!

The next thing you may want to do is to find out where the function has a **zero**, that is, a point where the function is actually equal to zero. Another name for this is a **root**. Now, you've seen **Newton's Method** in action in the last chapter, and this is really all you need in case you get stuck and the roots are not obvious. For instance, in the case of Figure 96, there seems to be only a few roots in the interval $[0, 0.3]$, right? But actually there is an *infinite number* of them (see Figure 97); you just can't see them because they are really close to $x = 0$. This is one of the reasons you shouldn't rely on *just* plotting a few points. What this means is you'll need *additional* tools for analyzing the data you've plotted and this is where the derivative comes in handy.

One of the objects we're looking for has a name which describes it nicely. At these special points of the domain (or at its endpoints), a typical graph will have a 'peak' or a 'valley'. These last two words are only another way of describing the notions of a *maximum* and a *minimum*. These special points are called 'critical' because something really important happens there ... the function may 'blow up to $\pm\infty$' or the graph may reach its 'peak' or hit 'rockbottom'.

A point c in the domain (or one of its end-points) of a differentiable function f is called a **critical point** if either

1. $f'(c) = 0$ or

2. $f'(c)$ does not exist,

either as a finite number, or as a (two-sided) derivative. It follows from this definition that **if c is an end-point of the domain of f, then c is a critical point of** f (since there cannot exist a two-sided derivative there!). At a critical point $x = c$ defined by $f'(c) = 0$ the graph of the function looks like a 'rest area' for the graph of the function because its tangent line is horizontal at this special point.

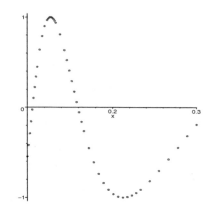

A few points of $y = \sin\frac{1}{x}$

Figure 96.

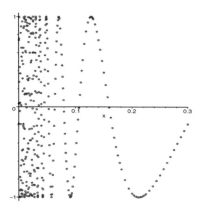

More points of $y = \sin\frac{1}{x}$

Figure 97.

Example 231.

Show that the functions $f(x) = 1/x$, $g(x) = x^{\frac{2}{3}}$ have a critical point at $x = 0$.

Solution Here, $x = 0$ is an end-point of the domain of f (being $(0, \infty)$). So, by definition, f has a critical point there (see Figure 98; guess which graph corresponds to this function). On the other hand, $x = 0$ belongs to the natural domain of g but now $g'(0)$ is undefined, since $g'_+(0) = +\infty$. Thus, once again, $x = 0$ is a critical point but for a different reason.

Example 232.

Show that $f(x) = x^2$ has a critical point at $x = 0$.

Solution In this case $f'(x) = 2x$ and this derivative is equal to zero when $x = 0$, i.e., $f'(0) = 0$. So, by definition, f has a critical point there (see Figure 98).

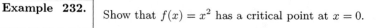

Example 233. Show that $f(x) = |x|$ has a critical point at $x = 0$.

Solution In this case we have to 'remove the absolute value'. Now, by definition of the absolute value, if $x \geq 0$, then $f(x) = x$. On the other hand, if $x \leq 0$, then $f(x) = -x$. It follows that $f'_+(0) = 1$ while $f'_-(0) = -1$. So, f is not differentiable at $x = 0$ since the right-and left-derivatives are not equal there. So, again by definition, f has a critical point there (see Figure 98, the 'V' shaped curve).

The next tool that we can use has to do with how 'inclined' (up or down) a graph can be. For this study of its inclination we use the ordinary derivative of the function and see when it's positive or negative. This motivates the next definition.

A function f defined on an interval, I, is said to be **increasing** (resp. **decreasing**) if given any pair of points x_1, x_2 in I with $x_1 < x_2$, then we have $f(x_1) < f(x_2)$, (resp. $f(x_1) > f(x_2)$).

When does this happen? Let f be differentiable over (a, b).

  (i) If $f'(x) > 0$ for all x in (a, b) then f is increasing on $[a, b]$

  (ii) If $f'(x) < 0$ for all x in (a, b) then f is decreasing on $[a, b]$

  In each of these cases, the slope of the tangent line is positive (resp. negative) at any point on the graph of $y = f(x)$.

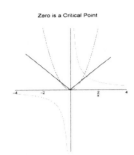

Zero is a Critical Point

Three curves $y = |x|, y = x^2, y = \frac{1}{x}$

Figure 98.

Example 234. The function $f(x) = x$ is increasing on I (where I can be **any** interval that you wish to choose as its domain), because, obviously, the statement $x < y$ is equivalent to $f(x) < f(y)$, for x, y in I, on account of the definition of f. Alternately, since f is differentiable and $f'(x) = 1 > 0$, for any x the result in the table above shows that f is increasing.

Example 235. The function $g(s) = 3s + 9$, with domain $\boldsymbol{R}$, the set of all real numbers, is increasing there (use the definition) whereas the function $g(s) = -3s + 9$ is decreasing on $\boldsymbol{R}$ (again, by definition).

Example 236. The function $f(x) = 4$ is *neither increasing nor decreasing* on a given domain, it is **constant** there. Of course, **every** constant function is neither increasing nor decreasing.

Example 237. The function $g(x) = x + \sin x$ is increasing on the *closed* interval $I = [3\pi/2, 5\pi/2]$ because its derivative, $g'(x) = 1 + \cos x > 0$ for these values of the independent variable x in I, by trigonometry (see Figure 99).

Example 238. Similarly, the function $h(z) = cos(z)$ is decreasing on $I = (2\pi, 3\pi)$ because its derivative $h'(z) = -\sin z < 0$ on this interval.

SNAPSHOTS

Example 239. The function $f(x) = x^4$ is increasing on $(0, \infty)$ and decreasing on $(-\infty, 0)$. Just check its derivative.

Example 240. The function $g(z) = z^3$ is increasing on all of **R**. If you sketch the graph of a typical polynomial (with real coefficients) you will notice that the graph is generally ondulatory (i.e., wave-like). This phenomenon is a particular case of the general property that the **graph of a non-constant polynomial consists of intervals on each of which the function is either increasing or decreasing**.

Example 241. The polynomial $p(x) = (x - 2)^2$ is increasing on $(2, \infty)$ and decreasing on $(-\infty, 2)$.

Example 242. On the other hand, the polynomial function $q(x) = (x - 1)(x - 3)(x - 4)$ with domain **R** is increasing on $(4, \infty)$ and its graph has one "bump" (or peak) and one "valley" (think of it as a point on the 'seafloor') between $x = 1$ and $x = 4$, (see Figure 100).

Here's a few more sophisticated examples:

Example 243. Determine the intervals on which the polynomial p defined by $p(x) = x(x^4 - 5)$ is increasing and decreasing.

Solution We use its Sign Decomposition Table, SDT, as defined in the previous sections. In this case, since every polynomial is differentiable, we have $p'(x) = D(x^5 - 5x) = 5x^4 - 5 = 5(x^4 - 1)$. This means that, aside from the constant factor of 5, the SDT for this p is identical to the SDT in Table 5.1! So, the SDT for $p'(x)$ looks like

	$x + 1$	$x - 1$	$x^2 + 1$	sign of $p'(x)$
$(-\infty, -1)$	$-$	$-$	$+$	$+$
$(-1, 1)$	$+$	$-$	$+$	$-$
$(1, \infty)$	$+$	$+$	$+$	$+$

It follows that $p'(x) > 0$ if x is in either $(-\infty, -1)$ or $(1, \infty)$, that is if $|x| > 1$. Similarly, p is decreasing when $p'(x) < 0$, which in this case means that x is in the interval $(-1, 1)$, or equivalently, $|x| < 1$.

Example 244. Determine the intervals on which the function f defined on its *natural domain* (see Chapter 1) by

$$f(x) = x + \frac{5}{6} \ln |x - 3| - \frac{5}{6} \ln |x + 3|$$

is increasing and decreasing.

Solution Now, this is pretty weird looking, right? Especially those absolute values! No, problem. Just remember that whenever $\Box \neq 0$, (see Chapter 4),

$$\boxed{D \ln |\Box| = \tfrac{1}{\Box} \, D\Box}\,,$$

so that, ultimately, we really don't have to worry about these absolute values.

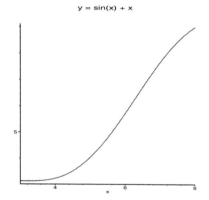

y = sin(x) + x

Figure 99.

y = (x−1)(x−3)(x−4)

Figure 100.

Let's find its derivative $f'(x)$ and then solve the inequalities. Now, the derivative of f is easily found using the methods of Chapters 3 and 4. We get

$$
\begin{aligned}
f'(x) &= 1 + \frac{5}{6}\frac{1}{x-3} - \frac{5}{6}\frac{1}{x+3} \\
&= \frac{(x^2-4)}{(x-3)(x+3)} \\
&= \frac{x^2-4}{x^2-9}
\end{aligned}
$$

which is a rational function ! Okay, so we can use the SDT method of the previous section to solve the inequalities $f'(x) > 0$ and $f'(x) < 0$. The break-points of f' are given by $-3, -2, 2, 3$ in increasing order. Its SDT is found to be

	$(x+3)$	$(x+2)$	$(x-2)$	$(x-3)$	Sign of $f'(x)$
$(-\infty,-3)$	$-$	$-$	$-$	$-$	$+$
$(-3,-2)$	$+$	$-$	$-$	$-$	$-$
$(-2,2)$	$+$	$+$	$-$	$-$	$+$
$(2,3)$	$+$	$+$	$+$	$-$	$-$
$(3,\infty)$	$+$	$+$	$+$	$+$	$+$

Now we can just read off the intervals where f is increasing and decreasing. We see that f is increasing when x is in either $(-\infty,-3)$, $(-2,2)$, or $(3,\infty)$. It is decreasing when x is in either $(-3,-2)$, or $(2,3)$, (see Figure 101).

OK, now we know when a function is increasing or decreasing, what its zeros are and we know how to find its critical points. What else do these critical points tell us?

A function f is said to have a **local maximum at a point $\boldsymbol{x = a}$** if there is a neighborhood of $x = a$ in which $f(x) \leq f(a)$, or there is a 'peak' or a 'big bump' in the graph of f at $x = a$. In this case, the value of $f(a)$ is called the **local maximum value**. It is said to have a **global maximum at $\boldsymbol{x = a}$** if $f(x) \leq f(a)$ for every x in the domain of f. This means that the 'tallest peak' or the 'Everest' or the 'biggest bump' occurs when $x = a$. In this case, the value of $f(a)$ is called the **global maximum value of $\boldsymbol{f}$**. We can define similar concepts for the notion of a *minimum* too.

So, a function f is said to have a **local minimum at a point $\boldsymbol{x = a}$** if there is a neighborhood of $x = a$ in which $f(x) \geq f(a)$, or there is a 'valley' in the graph of f at $x = a$, or the graph 'hits rockbottom'. In this case, the value of $f(a)$ is called the **local minimum value**. It is said to have a **global minimum at $\boldsymbol{x = a}$** if $f(x) \geq f(a)$ for every x in the domain of f. This means that the 'deepest valley' or the 'seafloor' or the 'biggest of all drops' occurs when $x = a$. In this case, the value of $f(a)$ is called the **global minimum value of $\boldsymbol{f}$**. As you can gather, these are nice geometrical notions which are intuitively true.

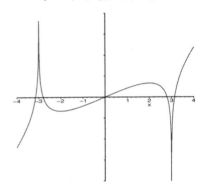

$y = x + (5/6)\log[(x-3)/(x+3)]$

$y = x + \frac{5}{6}\ln|x-3| - \frac{5}{6}\ln|x+3|$

Figure 101.

First Derivative Test: Let $f'(c) = 0$ with f a differentiable function.

(i) If $f'(x) > 0$ in a left-neighbourhood of c **and** $f'(x) < 0$ in a right-neighbourhood of c then $f(c)$ is a **local maximum value** of f.

(ii) If $f'(x) < 0$ in a left-neighbourhood of c **and** $f'(x) > 0$ in a right-neighbourhood of c then $f(c)$ is a **local minimum value** of f.

Example 245. | Refer to Example 244. Show that $x = -2$ gives rise to a local

A point is called an **extreme point** of f if it is either a local maximum or a local minimum for the given function, f

minimum value of f, while $x = +2$ gives rise to a local maximum value of f. Find the global maximum value and global minimum value of f. *Solution* Look at Example 244 above and Figure 101. From the SDT in that example, we gather that $f'(x) < 0$ just to the left of $x = -2$ and $f'(x) > 0$ just to the right of $x = -2$. So, according to the First Derivative Test, the value $f(-2)$ is a *local minimum value* of f, or we say that **a local minimum occurs at** $x = -2$. The value of this minimum is $f(-2) \approx -0.6588$.

On the other hand, from the same SDT we see that $f'(x) > 0$ just to the left of $x = 2$ and $f'(x) < 0$ just to the right of $x = 2$. So, according to the First Derivative Test again, the number, $f(2)$, is a *local maximum value* of f, or we say that *a local maximum occurs at* $x = 2$. The value of this maximum is $f(2) \approx +0.6588$.

Notice from the graph, Figure 101, that there is NO global maximum value of f, since the point where it should be, namely, $x = -3$, is NOT a point in the domain of f. Similarly, there is no global minimum value of f, (because $x = 3$ in not in the domain of f).

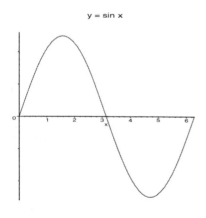

The graph of $y = -x^2$

Figure 102.

QUICKIES

If you look at Figure 100 you'll see that the function f defined there has a local maximum somewhere near $x = 2$ and a local minimum in between $x = 3$ and $x = 4$. If the domain of f is defined to be the interval $[0, 4]$ only, then these two special points would represent **global extrema**, just a fancy word for saying that there is either a global maximum or global minimum. On the other hand, if you refer to Figure 98, then you see that the function with $f(x) = x^2$ has a local (actually global) minimum at $x = 0$ and so does the function with $f(x) = |x|$. Finally, you would probably believe that, in the case of Figure 96, there is an *infinite* number of local and global extrema.

Now, so far we have seen that a study of the points where a given function is increasing and decreasing, the position of its critical points, its zeros, and a few points on its graph tells us a lot about the curve it defines. But still, the picture is not complete. We need to know how the graph 'bends' this way and that, or 'how it curves around'. For this we need one more derivative, the **second derivative** of f which, we assume, exists. Then we need to define a new notion called **concavity**, which some authors prefer to call *convexity*. This has something to do with whether a graph is 'concave up' or 'concave down'. The graph of a twice differentiable function is said to be **concave up** on an interval I, or 'U - shaped' if $f''(x) > 0$ for every x in I. Similarly, the graph of a twice differentiable function is said to be **concave down** on an interval I, or 'hill-shaped' if $f''(x) < 0$ for every x in I.

Example 246. A simple example of these concepts is seen in Figure 98 for the function f defined by $f(x) = x^2$. It's easy to see that $f'(x) = 2x$, so $f''(x) = 2 > 0$ which, by definition means that the graph of this f is *concave up*. As you can see, this means that the graph is sort of U-shaped (or bowl-shaped).

On the other hand, if f is defined by $f(x) = -x^2$. then $f''(x) = -2 < 0$ which, by definition, means that the graph of this f is *concave down*. This means that the graph is similar to a smooth mountain or hill, see Figure 102.

Example 247. Show that the sine function, sin, is concave up on the interval

$y = \sin x$

Figure 103.

$(\pi, 2\pi)$ and concave down on $(0, \pi)$.

Solution Let $f(x) = \sin x$. Then $f'(x) = \cos x$, and $f''(x) = -\sin x > 0$, since when $\pi < x < 2\pi$, we know from trigonometry that $\sin x < 0$. So, by definition, the graph is concave up. On the other hand, if $0 < x < \pi$, then $\sin x > 0$ which means that $f''(x) = -\sin x < 0$ and the graph is concave down, (see Figure 103).

We mimic what we did earlier in the case of the 'first derivative' and so we define a new kind of point, a point around which the function changes its **concavity**. Basically, this means that the graph changes from concave up (or down) to concave down (or up) around that point. Such a point is called a *point of inflection* and we define it formally below.

A point P with coordinates $(c, f(c))$ on the graph of a *twice differentiable* function f is called a **point of inflection** or *inflection point* if either:

(i) $f''(x) > 0$ in a left-neighbourhood of c **and** $f''(x) < 0$ in a right-neighbourhood of c, OR,

(ii) $f''(x) < 0$ in a left-neighbourhood of c **and** $f''(x) > 0$ in a right-neighbourhood of c

---

Example 248. Show that the polynomial function of Example 243 has an inflection point at $x = 0$.

Solution We need to find the SDT of its *second derivative*, right? We have only found the SDT of its (first) derivative so we have a little more work to do. We know that $p(x) = x^5 - 5x$ and $p'(x) = 5x^4 - 5$. So, $p''(x) = 20x^3$. Well, this is really easy to handle since p'' has only one root, namely, $x = 0$. So, we don't really have to display this SDT since we can just read off any information we need from the expression for p''. We see from the definitions that when $x < 0$ then $p''(x) = 20x^3 < 0$ and so the graph is concave down, while for $x > 0$, $p''(x) = 20x^3 > 0$ and so the graph is concave up. So, by definition, $x = 0$ is an inflection point (since the graph changes its concavity around that point).

In practice, when you're looking for points of inflection you look for the roots of $f''(x) = 0$. Check these first.

Example 249. Show that the polynomial function of Figure 100 above has an inflection point at $x = \frac{8}{3}$.

Solution We do a few calculations. First, $q(x) = (x-1)(x-3)(x-4)$ means that $q'(x) = (x-3)(x-4) + (x-1)(x-4) + (x-1)(x-3)$ and that $q''(x) = 6x - 16$. All the candidates for 'point of inflection' solve the equation $q''(x) = 0$. This means that $6x - 16 = 0$ or $x = 8/3$. This is the only candidate! Note that to the just to the left of $x = 8/3$, we have $q''(x) = 6x - 16 < 0$ while just to the right of $x = 8/3$ we have $q''(x) = 6x - 16 > 0$. By definition, this means that $x = 8/3$ is a point of inflection. You can see from the graph of q, Figure 100, that there is indeed a change in the concavity of q around $x = 8/3$, although it appears to be closer to 3, because of plotting errors.

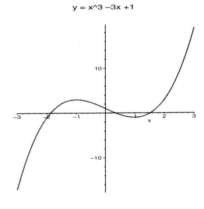

$y = x^3 - 3x + 1$

Figure 104.

LOOK OUT! The statement "$f''(c) = 0$ implies c is a point of inflection" is generally <u>FALSE</u>. Look at $f(x) = x^4$ which has the property that $f''(c) = 0$ when $c = 0$ only, but yet there is no point of inflection at $x = 0$ (because its graph is *always* concave up), so there is no change in concavity. Its graph is similar to Fig. 98, for $f(x) = x^2$ but it is flatter.

Some General Terminology

The graph of a twice differentiable function f is said to be **concave up (down) on an interval** if it is concave up (down) at every point of the interval, *i.e.* $f''(x) \geq 0$ (or $f''(x) \leq 0$) for all x in the interval.

Now, we're lucky that there is *another* test which can handle the question of whether or not a function has a maximum or a minimum value at a point $x = c$. It is easier to apply than the First Derivative Test but the disadvantage is that you have to compute one more derivative ... This is how it sounds: Let c be a critical point of a twice differentiable function f, then there is the

The Second Derivative Test: Let $f'(c) = 0$ (c is a critical point)

(i) If $f''(c) < 0$ then c is a local maximum of f.

(ii) If $f''(c) > 0$ then c is a local minimum of f.

(iii) If $f''(c) = 0$ more information is needed. We don't know.

Example 250. Find all the critical points of the function defined by $f(x) = x^3 - 3x + 1$ on the interval $[-3, 3]$ and determine the **nature of these critical points** (i.e., local maximum/local minimum). Find its points of inflection, if any.

Solution We know that since f is a polynomial, it is differentiable and $f'(x) = 3x^2 - 3$. If c is a critical point, then, by definition, $f'(c) = 0$ which is equivalent to saying that $3c^2 - 3 = 0$ which is equivalent to $c = \pm 1$ and there cannot be any other critical points (as the derivative of f always exists and is finite).

Now, we use the Second Derivative Test to determine their nature. Here $f''(x) = 6x$. Now, when $x = +1$, $f''(+1) = 6 > 0$ which means that there must be a local minimum at $x = 1$. On the other hand, when $x = -1$, then $f''(-1) = -6 < 0$ which means that there must be a local maximum at $x = -1$. The values of f at these extrema are $f(1) = -1$, (the local minimum value) and $f(-1) = 1$, (the local maximum value). See Figure 104 for its graph.

The only *candidate* for a point of inflection is when $f''(c) = 6c = 0$, that is, when $c = 0$, right? Now, just to the left of 0, (i.e, $x < 0$) we have $f''(x) = 6x < 0$ while just to the right of $x = 0$ (i.e. $x > 0$) we have $f''(x) = 6x > 0$. So there is a change in concavity (from concave down to concave up) as you move from $x < 0$ to $x > 0$ through the point $x = 0$. So, by definition, this is a point of inflection. It is the only one since there are no other roots of $f''(x) = 0$.

NOTE: Notice that the global maximum and the global minimum values of this polynomial on the given interval, $[-3, 3]$ occur at the endpoints, and not, as you might think, at the critical points. This is why we call these things 'local', meaning that this property only holds just around the point but not everywhere in the interval.

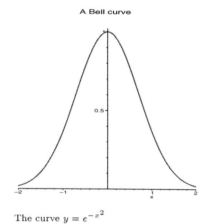

A Bell curve

The curve $y = e^{-x^2}$

Figure 105.

Example 251. Find all the critical points of the function defined by $f(x) = e^{-x^2}$ on the interval $(-\infty, \infty)$ and determine the nature of these critical points (i.e., local maximum/local minimum). Determine any points of inflection, if any.

Solution We see that f is a nice exponential, and by the Chain Rule we see that it is differentiable as well and $f'(x) = -2xe^{-x^2}$. If c is a critical point, then, by definition, $f'(x) = 0$ and this is equivalent to saying that $-2xe^{-x^2} = 0$. This, in turn, is equivalent to $x = 0$ and there cannot be any other critical points (because an exponential function is never zero).

We apply the Second Derivative Test to this f. Since $f''(x) = (4x^2 - 2) \cdot e^{-x^2}$, at the critical point $x = 0$ we have $f''(0) = -2 < 0$ which means that $x = 0$ is a local maximum of f.

For (candidates for) points of inflection we set $f''(x) = 0$. This occurs only when $(4x^2 - 2) \cdot e^{-x^2} = 0$, and this is equivalent to saying that $4x^2 - 2 = 0$, that is,

$$x = \pm \frac{1}{\sqrt{2}} \approx \pm 0.7071.$$

We observe that around these points there is a change of concavity since, for example, $f''(x) < 0$ just to the left of $x = 1/\sqrt{2}$ while $f''(x) > 0$ just to the right of $x = 1/\sqrt{2}$. The same argument works for the other candidate, $x = -1/\sqrt{2}$. See Figure 105 for its graph.

Inflection Point at x=0

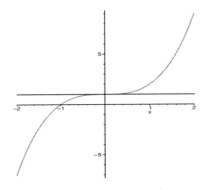

The curve $y = x^3 + 1$

Figure 106.

But, geometrically, what is a point of inflection?

Look at the graph of $y = x^3 + 1$, Figure 106. The tangent line at the inflection point, $x = 0$ here, *divides the curve into two parts*, one below the line and one above the line. More generally the tangent line at an inflection point divides a small portion of the curve into two parts, one part of the curve is on one side of the tangent line, while the other part of the curve is on the other side.

Horizontal and Vertical Asymptotes:

Another calculation which is helpful in drawing the graph of a given function involves the finding of *special straight lines called asymptotes*. We already referred to these in Chapter 2, in our study of limits, so it will be an easy matter for us to review what we saw then and apply it here.

The horizontal lines $y = L$, $y = M$ on the xy-plane are called **horizontal asymptotes for the graph of f** if

$$\lim_{x \to +\infty} f(x) = L$$

or

$$\lim_{x \to -\infty} f(x) = M,$$

or both these limits exist (and may or may not be equal).

Remark: In other words, a horizontal asymptote is a horizontal line, $y = L$, with the property that the graph of f gets closer and closer to it, and may even cross this line, looking more and more like this line at infinity. Remember that the value of L is a number which is equal to a limiting value of f at either $\pm\infty$.

The vertical line $x = a$ is called a **vertical asymptote** for the graph of f provided either

$$\lim_{x \to a} f(x) = \infty, \quad (\text{or } -\infty)$$

or

$$\lim_{x \to a^+} f(x) = \infty, \quad (\text{or } -\infty)$$

or

$$\lim_{x \to a^-} f(x) = \infty, \quad (\text{or } -\infty)$$

Example 252. We refer to Figure 107. In this graph we see that the lines $y = \pm 1$ are both horizontal asymptotes for the graph of the function f defined on its natural domain, by

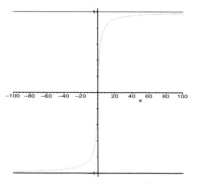

Some horizontal asymptotes

Two asymptotes in $y = \frac{x}{|x|+2}$

Figure 107.

$$f(x) = \frac{x}{|x| + 2}.$$

Why? We simply calculate the required limits ... Since $|x| = x$ when $x > 0$ we see that,

$$
\begin{aligned}
\lim_{x \to +\infty} f(x) &= \lim_{x \to +\infty} \frac{x}{|x| + 2}, \\
&= \lim_{x \to +\infty} \frac{x}{x + 2} \\
&= \lim_{x \to +\infty} \frac{D(x)}{D(x+2)}, \quad \text{by L'Hospital's Rule,} \\
&= \lim_{x \to +\infty} \frac{1}{1} \\
&= 1.
\end{aligned}
$$

So, $L = 1$ here. In the same way we can show that

$$
\begin{aligned}
\lim_{x \to -\infty} f(x) &= \lim_{x \to -\infty} \frac{x}{|x| + 2}, \\
&= \lim_{x \to -\infty} \frac{x}{-x + 2}, \quad \text{since } |x| = -x \text{ when } x < 0, \\
&= \lim_{x \to +\infty} \frac{1}{-1} \\
&= -1,
\end{aligned}
$$

once again, by L'Hospital's Rule. In this case, $M = -1$ and these two limits are different.

NOTE: These two limiting values, when they exist as finite numbers, may also be the same number. For example, the function $f(x) = x^{-1}$ has $L = M = 0$, (see Figure 98).

Example 253. Determine the vertical and horizontal asymptotes of the function f defined by

$$f(x) = \frac{2x^2}{x^2 + 3x - 4}.$$

Solution The horizontal asymptotes are easily found using L'Hospital's Rule (because the values of f at infinity are 'indeterminate', of the form ∞/∞). In this case,

$$
\begin{aligned}
\lim_{x \to +\infty} f(x) &= \lim_{x \to +\infty} \frac{2x^2}{x^2 + 3x - 4}, \\
&= \lim_{x \to +\infty} \frac{4x}{2x + 3}, \quad \text{by L'Hospital's Rule,} \\
&= \lim_{x \to +\infty} \frac{4}{2}, \quad \text{once again, by L'Hospital's Rule,} \\
&= 2.
\end{aligned}
$$

So, $L = 2$ and the line $y = 2$ is a horizontal asymptote, (see Figure 108).

In order to find a vertical asymptote, we simply have to look for points where the graph 'takes off' and the best place for this is the zeros of the denominator of our function. When we factor the denominator $x^2 + 3x - 4$ completely, we get $x^2 + 3x - 4 = (x + 4)(x - 1)$. So, its roots are $x = -4$ and $x = 1$. These are merely candidates for vertical asymptotes, right? Let's check the values of the limits as required by the definition. In case of doubt, always use one-sided limits, first.

$$
\begin{aligned}
\lim_{x \to -4^+} f(x) &= \lim_{x \to -4^+} \frac{2x^2}{x^2 + 3x - 4}, \\
&= \lim_{x \to -4^+} \frac{2x^2}{(x + 4)(x - 1)}, \\
&= -\infty,
\end{aligned}
$$

since $x \to -4^+$ implies that $x > -4$, or $x + 4 > 0$, so $(x + 4)(x - 1) < 0$. A very similar calculation shows that

$$
\begin{aligned}
\lim_{x \to -4^-} f(x) &= \lim_{x \to -4^-} \frac{2x^2}{x^2 + 3x - 4}, \\
&= \lim_{x \to -4^-} \frac{2x^2}{(x + 4)(x - 1)}, \\
&= +\infty,
\end{aligned}
$$

since $x \to -4^-$ implies that $x < -4$, or $x + 4 < 0$, so $(x + 4)(x - 1) > 0$. So, it follows by the definition that the vertical line $x = -4$ is a vertical asymptote. In the same way we can show that

$$
\begin{aligned}
\lim_{x \to 1^+} f(x) &= \lim_{x \to 1^+} \frac{2x^2}{x^2 + 3x - 4}, \\
&= \lim_{x \to 1^+} \frac{2x^2}{(x + 4)(x - 1)}, \\
&= +\infty,
\end{aligned}
$$

since $x \to 1^+$ implies that $x > 1$, or $x + 1 > 0$, so $(x + 4)(x - 1) > 0$. Furthermore,

$$
\begin{aligned}
\lim_{x \to 1^-} f(x) &= \lim_{x \to 1^-} \frac{2x^2}{x^2 + 3x - 4}, \\
&= \lim_{x \to 1^-} \frac{2x^2}{(x + 4)(x - 1)}, \\
&= -\infty,
\end{aligned}
$$

since $x \to 1^-$ implies that $x < 1$, or $x + 1 < 0$, so $(x + 4)(x - 1) < 0$. Part of the graph of this function showing both vertical asymptotes and the one horizontal asymptote can be seen in Figure 108.

Vertical and Horizontal Asymptotes

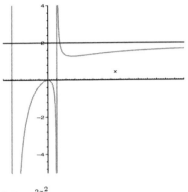

$y = \frac{2x^2}{x^2 + 3x - 4}$

Figure 108.

The concept of **Left and right continuity** is defined like Continuity except that we take the limit from the left or the limit from the right in the definition of continuity (instead of a two-sided limit); see Chapter 2.

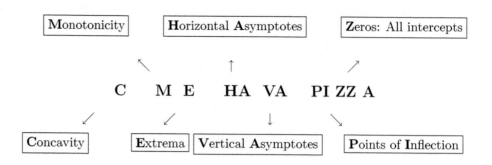

Table 5.4: The 'C Me Hava Pizza' Rule

> The graph of a function f is said to have a **vertical tangent line** at a point $P(a, f(a))$ if f is (left- or right-) continuous at $x = a$ and if either its left- or right- derivative is infinite there, that is, if
>
> $$\lim_{x \to a^{\pm}} |f'(x)| = \infty.$$

NOTE: This business of a 'vertical tangent line' is not the same as a vertical asymptote. Why? You see, a function cannot be continuous at a point where an asymptote occurs because, by definition, we are looking at the values of the function at infinity, and the function can't be continuous there. But, in the case of a vertical tangent line, the function *is* continuous (from the left or right) at the point on its graph where this line is tangent, so the graph actually touches that value, $f(a)$. So, even though it *looks* like a vertical asymptote, it certainly isn't! Let's look at an example.

Example 254. Show that $y = \sqrt{x}$ has a vertical tangent line at $x = 0$.

Solution Its graph appears in Figure 109. We calculate the derivative $y'(x)$ using the Power Rule and find that,

$$D(\sqrt{x}) = y'(x) = \frac{1}{2\sqrt{x}}.$$

For the tangent line to be vertical the derivative there must be 'infinite' and so this leaves only $x = 0$ as a candidate. We easily see that

$$\lim_{x \to 0^+} \left| \frac{1}{2\sqrt{x}} \right| = \lim_{x \to 0^+} \frac{1}{2\sqrt{x}} = +\infty,$$

so, by definition, this graph has a vertical tangent at $x = 0$, namely, the $y-$axis (or the line $x = 0$). Note that the (two-sided) limit cannot exist in this case because the square root function is only defined for $x \geq 0$. So, we had to take a one-sided limit from the right.

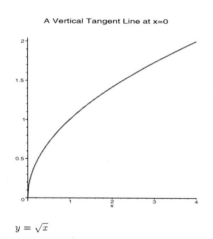

$y = \sqrt{x}$

Figure 109.

Phew! That's about it! But how are you going to remember all this stuff? Well, let's look at the following jingle or *mnemonic device*, that is, something to help you remember what you have to do. It goes like this: We call it the *C me Hava Pizza* Rule... See Table 5.4 for an explanation.

The boxed words in the 'C Me Hava Pizza' Rule describe the following instructions:

Let the graph of the function f be represented on the $xy-$plane, where, as usual, we assume that $y = f(x)$.

1. $\boxed{\text{Monotonicity}} \Longleftrightarrow$ Look for intervals where the graph is **Increasing** and **Decreasing**,

2. $\boxed{\text{Horizontal Asymptotes}} \Longleftrightarrow$ Look for all the **horizontal asymptotes**, if any.

3. $\boxed{\text{Zeros: All intercepts}} \Longleftrightarrow$ Look for all the points where the **graph crosses the $x-$axis** (set $y = 0$ and solve), AND look for all the points where the **graph crosses the $y-$axis** (set $x = 0$ and solve).

4. $\boxed{\text{Concavity}} \Longleftrightarrow$ Look for all the intervals where the graph is **concave up** or **concave down**.

5. $\boxed{\text{Extrema}} \Longleftrightarrow$ Look for all the **critical points**, and classify them as local maximum, and local minimum.

6. $\boxed{\text{Vertical Asymptotes}} \Longleftrightarrow$ Look for all the **vertical asymptotes**, if any.

7. $\boxed{\text{Points of Inflection}} \Longleftrightarrow$ Look for all the **points of inflection** to see how the graph bends this way and that.

OK, good, all we have to do now is put this Rule into action. Let's try a few examples.

$\boxed{\textbf{Example 255.}}$ Sketch the graph of $f(x) = \dfrac{4}{9 + x^2}$.

Solution These are the questions you should be thinking about ...

Questions to Ask:

1. What are the zeros of f and the $y-$intercepts? (*i.e.* When is $f(x) = 0$?)

2. What are the critical points of f, and what is their nature?

3. Where is f increasing/decreasing?

4. Where is the graph of f concave up/concave down?

5. What are the points of inflection?

6. Where are the asymptotes of f, if any, and identify them (horizontal asymptotes, vertical asymptotes)?

7. Take a deep breath, assimilate all this, and finally, sketch the graph of f.

Solution (continued)

1. $\boxed{\text{Zeros: All intercepts}}$ Well, we see that $y = 0$ is impossible since

$$f(x) = \frac{4}{9 + x^2} \neq 0,$$

for any x. It just can't be zero, so there are NO $x-$intercepts. So, $f(x) > 0$ and its graph lies in the first two quadrants (think trig. here). Setting $x = 0$ we get the one and only y-intercept value, namely, $y = 4/9$. We note that the natural domain of f is $-\infty < x < \infty$, (*i.e.* the real line).

2. $\boxed{\text{Extrema}}$ Next, let's look for the critical points of f ...

$$f'(x) = \frac{(9 + x^2) \cdot 0 - 4(2x)}{(9 + x^2)^2} = -\frac{8x}{(9 + x^2)^2}.$$

Since the denominator is never 0, the derivative always exists, and so the critical points are given by solving the equation $f'(c) = 0$. So,

$$f'(c) = -\frac{8c}{(9 + c^2)^2} = 0 \Rightarrow c = 0.$$

Therefore, **$c = 0$ is the only critical point.** Let's classify this point as to whether a local maximum or local minimum occurs here. We know that $f'(0) = 0$ so we can apply the Second Derivative Test. Now,

$$\begin{aligned} f''(x) &= \frac{d}{dx}\left\{ \frac{-8x}{(9 + x^2)^2} \right\} = \frac{(9 + x^2)^2(-8) - (-8x)(4x(9 + x^2))}{(9 + x^2)^4} \\ &= \frac{(-8)(9 + x^2)^2 + 32x^2(9 + x^2)}{(9 + x^2)^4} = \frac{(9 + x^2)[-8(9 + x^2) + 32x^2]}{(9 + x^2)^4} \\ &= \frac{24x^2 - 72}{(9 + x^2)^3} = 24\frac{x^2 - 3}{(9 + x^2)^3}. \end{aligned}$$

So,

$$f''(0) = \frac{-72}{9^3} = -\frac{8}{81} < 0,$$

which means that there is a **local maximum** at $x = 0$ and so the *graph bends down and away from its local maximum value* there. Since there are no other critical points it follows that there is NO local minimum value. So, **$f(0) = \frac{4}{9} \approx 0.444$ is a local maximum value of f.**

At this point the only information we have about this graph is that it looks like Figure 110. Don't worry, this is already quite a lot.

3. $\boxed{\text{Monotonicity}}$ To find where f is increasing (decreasing) we look for those x such that $f'(x) > 0$ ($f'(x) < 0$), respectively. Note that we have already calculated the derivative in item (2). Now,

$$\begin{aligned} f'(x) &= -\frac{8x}{(9 + x^2)^2} > 0 \quad \text{only when } x < 0 \text{ and,} \\ f'(x) &< 0 \text{ only when } x > 0. \end{aligned}$$

Therefore, **f is increasing on $(-\infty, 0)$ and f is decreasing on $(0, \infty)$.** This says something about the values of the function, right? In other words, its values, $f(x)$, are getting 'smaller' as $x \to -\infty$ and the same is true as $x \to +\infty$. But still, $f(x) > 0$, so you think "they must be getting closer and closer to the x-axis".

4. $\boxed{\text{Concavity}}$ We know that f is concave up if $f''(x) > 0$, f is concave down if $f''(x) < 0$. But

$$f''(x) > 0 \quad \text{only when } 24\frac{x^2 - 3}{(9 + x^2)^3} > 0 \text{ } i.e. \text{ when } x^2 - 3 > 0,$$

and

$$f''(x) < 0 \quad \text{only when } 24\frac{x^2 - 3}{(9 + x^2)^3} < 0 \text{ } i.e. \text{ when } x^2 - 3 < 0.$$

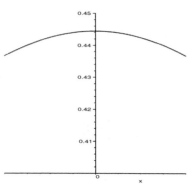

Around a local maximum

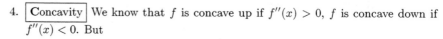

A first guess at $y = \frac{4}{9 + x^2}$

Figure 110.

Now, $x^2 - 3 > 0$ when $x^2 > 3$, which is equivalent to $|x| > \sqrt{3}$. Therefore, $x^2 - 3 < 0$ whenever $|x| < \sqrt{3}$. Hence f **is concave up** on the interval $|x| > \sqrt{3}$, *i.e.* on each of the intervals

$$(-\infty, -\sqrt{3}) \quad \text{and} \quad (\sqrt{3}, \infty),$$

and **concave down** on the interval $|x| < \sqrt{3}$, *i.e.* on the interval

$$(-\sqrt{3}, \sqrt{3})$$

Now, let's re-evaluate the information we have about this graph. It should look like Figure 111, because the graph is concave down on the interval $(-\sqrt{3}, \sqrt{3}) = (-0.732, +0.732)$. It must be *bell-shaped* here. On the other hand, we know that it becomes concave up after we pass the two points $x = \pm\sqrt{3}$, which we must suspect are points of inflection! Furthermore, the function is decreasing whenever $x > 0$, from item (3), which means that it's always getting smaller, too! So, we already have a pretty good idea about what will happen here. Let's see.

5. Points of Inflection This is almost obvious. We know, from item (4) above, and by definition that

$$f''(x) = 0 \quad \text{only when} \quad 24\frac{x^2 - 3}{(9 + x^2)^3} = 0 \ \ \textit{i.e. when} \ \ x^2 - 3 = 0,$$

and this forces

$$|x| = \sqrt{3}.$$

These two points, $x = \pm\sqrt{3}$, are the candidates for being such points of inflection. But we already showed in passing that there *is* a change in concavity around these points (from item (4)). So, they are, in fact, the two points of inflection. There can be no other.

6. Horizontal Asymptotes The horizontal asymptotes are given by evaluating the $\lim_{x\to\infty} f(x)$, if it exists. Now,

$$\lim_{x\to\infty} f(x) \ = \ \lim_{x\to\infty} \frac{4}{9 + x^2} = 4 \lim_{x\to\infty} \frac{1}{9 + x^2}$$

$$= \ 4 \cdot 0 = 0.$$

This one was really easy, because it was not an indeterminate form, right? Therefore $\lim_{x\to\infty} f(x) = 0$ means that the horizontal line $\boldsymbol{y = 0}$ **is a horizontal asymptote**. Note also that

$$\lim_{x\to-\infty} f(x) = 0$$

therefore the graph of f tends to the x-axis (*i.e.* $y = 0$) at both ends of the real line. Since $f(x) > 0$, this information along with the above data indicates that the graph of f at the "extremities" of the real line will look like Figure 112, in the sense that the curve is approaching the $x-$axis *asymptotically*.

Vertical Asymptotes The graph has **no vertical asymptotes** since $\lim_{x\to a} f(x)$ is always finite, for any value of the number a. In fact,

$$\lim_{x\to a} f(x) = \frac{4}{9 + a^2}, \quad \text{for any real } a.$$

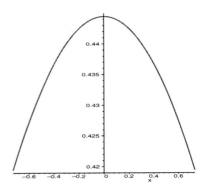

The curve is concave down

A better guess at $y = \frac{4}{9+x^2}$

Figure 111.

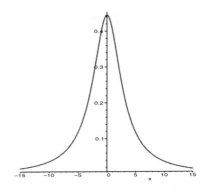

The curve looks bell-shaped

A final analysis of $y = \frac{4}{9+x^2}$

Figure 112.

7. Note that f has no absolute minimum on $(-\infty, \infty)$, since it is always positive and approaching the value 0 at infinity. Because of the shape of the graph of f, we see that $f(0) = 4/9$ is the **absolute maximum value** of f, and this means the values of f are never larger than this number, $4/9$. The final graph of f appears in Figure 112.

Example 256. Sketch the graph of the function $f(x) = x \ln x$ on its natural domain, the interval $I = (0, \infty)$.

Solution Now we can start accelerating the process initiated in the previous example. The zeros of this function are given by setting either $x = 0$, which is not allowed since this number is not in the natural domain, or by setting $\ln x = 0$.

But $\ln x = 0$ only when $x = 1$. So, the only zero is at $x = 1$. The critical points are found by solving $f'(c) = 0$ for c or by finding any points where the derivative does not exist. Let's see.

$$
\begin{aligned}
f'(x) &= \frac{d}{dx}\, x \ln x, \\
&= 1 \cdot \ln x + x \cdot \frac{1}{x}, \\
&= 1 + \ln x.
\end{aligned}
$$

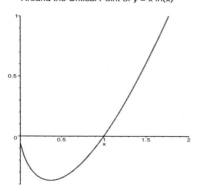

Around the Critical Point of $y = x \ln(x)$

Figure 113.

The derivative fails to exist only when $x = 0$, right? Note that this point is NOT in the domain of our function, though. No problem, it is on the 'edge', at the left end-point of our interval, and strange things can happen there, you'll see. Anyways, the only critical point inside our interval is obtained by setting $f'(x) = 0$. This means that $1 + \ln x = 0$, which is equivalent to $\ln x = -1$. But, by definition of the logarithm, this means that $x = e^{-1}$, where 'e' is Euler's number, right? OK, so the only critical point inside I is $x = e^{-1} \approx 0.3679$. What is its nature? Let's use the Second Derivative Test to determine this. Here $c = 1/e$ and $f'(c) = 0$. Next,

$$
\begin{aligned}
f''(x) &= \frac{d}{dx}\, (1 + \ln x), \\
&= 0 + \frac{1}{x}, \\
&= \frac{1}{x}.
\end{aligned}
$$

So, $f''(c) = 1/c = e > 0$ which indicates that $x = 1/e$ is local minimum of f. The value of f at our critical point is $f(1/e) = (1/e)\ln(1/e) = (1/e)(\ln 1 - \ln e) = (1/e)(0 - 1) = -1/e < 0$. So, up to now we're sure that the graph looks like a small U-shaped bowl around the value $-1/e = -0.3679$ at its bottom. We also see that the requirement that $f'(x) = 1 + \ln x > 0$ is equivalent to $\ln x > -1$, or solving this inequality by taking the exponential of both sides, we get, $x > 1/e$. This means that f is increasing for $x > 1/e$. Similarly, we can show that f is decreasing when $x < 1/e$.

Next, since we have already found the second derivative of f, we see that $f''(x) = 1/x > 0$ only when $x > 0$. This means that the graph of f is concave up when $x > 0$. Since x is never less than 0 (because these negative points are not in the domain of f), it follows that the graph of f is *always* concave up on its domain. Furthermore, there can't be any points of inflection, because $f''(x) \neq 0$, never, for any x!

OK, now you *assimilate all this information.* You know that there is a zero at $x = 1$, the graph is always concave up and the graph is increasing to the right of the local minimum at $x = 1/e$. It is also 'decreasing' to the left of the local minimum. So, the graph should look like Figure 113 ... the only problem is, we don't know what's happening near $x = 0$. We said earlier that strange things may be going on near this point because the derivative does not exist there. So let's take the limit

$$\lim_{x \to 0^+} f(x) = \lim_{x \to 0^+} x \ln x \quad \text{(Indeterminate Form: } (0) \cdot (-\infty))$$

$$= \lim_{x \to 0^+} \frac{\ln x}{\frac{1}{x}} \quad \text{(Indeterminate Form: } (\infty)/(\infty))$$

$$= \lim_{x \to 0^+} \frac{\frac{1}{x}}{\frac{-1}{x^2}} \quad \text{(by L'Hospital's Rule)}$$

$$= \lim_{x \to 0^+} -x \quad \text{(after simplifying the fraction)}$$

$$= 0.$$

So, amazingly enough, the graph is trying to reach the point $(0, 0)$ as $x \to 0^+$, but never quite makes it! But the definition of a vertical asymptote requires us to have an infinite limit as we approach zero, right? So, what's happening here? Well, we know that f is not defined at $x = 0$. But we CAN define $f(0)$ to be this limit, that is, let's agree to define $f(0)$ by

The graph of $y = x \ln(x)$

$$f(0) = \lim_{x \to 0^+} f(x) = \lim_{x \to 0^+} x \ln x = 0.$$

In this case we can prove, using the methods of Chapter 2, that f is actually right-continuous at $x = 0$ (because we can never define f for negative values so we can't expect more). So, $x = 0$ is actually a *vertical tangent line* because

$$\lim_{x \to 0^+} |f'(x)| = \lim_{x \to 0^+} |1 + \ln x|,$$

$$= |-\infty|, \quad \text{(since } \lim_{x \to 0^+} \ln x = -\infty),$$

$$= \infty.$$

Figure 114.

What about horizontal asymptotes? In this case,

$$\lim_{x \to +\infty} f(x) = \lim_{x \to \infty} x \ln x \quad \text{(Form: } (+\infty) \cdot (\infty))$$

$$= +\infty$$

since the form of the product of x with $\ln x$ is NOT indeterminate at $+\infty$ (so you can't use L'Hospital's Rule!). Since this limit is infinite there are no horizontal asymptotes. Our guess that Figure 113 is the graph of this f is a good one, except that it should look more like Figure 114, because of the additional information we gathered from the vertical tangent, above.

Let's work out one more example, but this time of a trigonometric function-polynomial combo. This long example uses *a lot* of what we have studied.

Example 257. Sketch the graph of the function f defined by

$$f(x) = \frac{\sin x}{x}$$

on the open interval $I = (0, 6)$, and determine what happens near $x = 0$ by taking a limit.

Solution In this example we will be using many of the ideas we learned so far about Differential Calculus. This is the kind of example that shows up in real world applications, and where you need to use Newton's method to find roots and make other estimates. You'll see that it's no too bad. Ok, so let's start off by looking for the zeros of f.

In this case the zeros of f are the same as the zeros of the sin function right? Now, the positive zeros of the sin function are given by the roots of $\sin x = 0$. These occur at $x = 0, \pi, 2\pi, 3\pi, \ldots$. But notice that $x = 0$ is excluded because $x = 0$ isn't in I. Next, $x = \pi$ is in I, because $\pi \approx 3.14 < 6$. So that's one zero. The next zero is at $2\pi \approx 6.28 > 6$. So this zero is NOT in I. So, there's only ONE zero in I, and it is at $x = \pi$. So, the only x−intercept is $x = \pi$. Since $x = 0$ is not in I, we're not allowed to plug-in the value $x = 0$ into the expression for $f(x)$. So, there are no y−intercepts.

Next, we'll look for the critical points of f in I. Note that f is differentiable for every value of x in I (because 0 is excluded). So, the critical points are given by the solution(s) of $f'(c) = 0$, for c in I. Now, its derivative is given by (use the Quotient Rule),

$$f'(x) = \frac{x \cos x - \sin x}{x^2}.$$

The critical points are given by solving for c in the equation

$$f'(c) = \frac{c \cos c - \sin c}{c^2} = 0.$$

or, equivalently, we need to find the solution(s) of the equation

$$c \cos c - \sin c = 0, \qquad \text{since } c \neq 0.$$

So, we're really looking for the zero(s) in I of the function, let's call it g, defined by

$$g(x) = x \cos x - \sin x.$$

This is where Newton's Method comes in (see Chapter 3). Before we use it though, it would be nice to know *how many zeros there are*, right? Otherwise, we don't know if we'll 'get them all' using the Newton iterations. How do we do this? We simplify the expression for the zero of g. For example, let c be any one of its zeros. Note that $\cos c \neq 0$ (think about this). So, dividing $g(c)$ by $\cos c$, we get, since $\cos c \neq 0$,

$$c - \tan c = 0.$$

The graphs of y =tan(x) and y=x

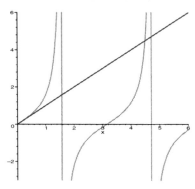

Figure 115.

Newton iterates for

$g(x) = x \cos x - \sin x$ and $x_0 = 4$

m	$g(x_m)$	x_{m+1}
0	-1.857772	4.613691
1	0.540511	4.495964
2	0.011213	4.493411
3	0.000063	4.493409
4	0.000000	4.493409
$\ldots$	$\ldots$	$\ldots$

Figure 116.

This means that these zeros of g (i.e., the critical points of f) coincide with the *points of intersection of the graph of the function $y = \tan x$ with the graph of $y = x$.* Furthermore, we only want those points of intersection whose x−coordinates are in I. But these two graphs are easy to draw, see Figure 115. You see from this Figure that there are only *two points of intersection*, one at $x = 0$ (which is not in I, so we forget about it) and another one near $x = 4$. That's the one! It looks like there's only ONE ROOT of $x - \tan x = 0$ in I, and so only one root of $g(x) = 0$ in I and so only one root of $f'(x) = 0$ in I. The conclusion is that there is **only one critical point** of f in I.

Now, recall that the approximations to this root of $g(x) = 0$ are given by x_m where the **larger the subscript m the better the approximation** and,

$$x_{m+1} = x_m - \frac{g(x_m)}{g'(x_m)} = x_m + \frac{x_m \cos x_m - \sin x_m}{x_m \sin x_m}, \quad for\ m \geq 0.$$

Let's use $x_0 = 4$ as our initial guess from Figure 115. Then $x_1 \approx 4.6137$ (check this using your calculator). The remaining better estimates are given in Figure 116. So, the one and only critical point of f in I is given by the boxed entry in Figure 116, that is,

$$f'(c) = 0 \quad \Rightarrow \quad c \approx 4.4934.$$

What is the nature of this critical point? Is it a $\boxed{\text{local maximum, local minimum?}}$. The best thing to do here is to use the Second Derivative Test. Now,

$$f''(x) \quad = \quad \frac{-x^2 \sin x - 2x \cos x + 2 \sin x}{x^3},$$

so, evaluating this expression at our critical point, $x = 4.4934$, we see that

$$f''(4.4934) \approx 0.2172 > 0,$$

which means that our critical point $c = 4.4934$, is a *local minimum* with a local minimum value equal to $f(c) = f(4.4934) \approx -0.2172$. Actually, it can be shown that $f(c) = -f''(c)$, and not only to five significant digits. Can you show why?

Now, let's $\boxed{\text{look for the intervals where } f \text{ is increasing or decreasing.}}$ We can rewrite $f'(x)$ for x in I as

$$f'(x) = \begin{cases} (x - \tan x) \cdot \frac{\cos x}{x^2}, & \text{if } \ x \neq \frac{\pi}{2}, \\ \frac{-4}{\pi^2}, & \text{if } \ x = \frac{\pi}{2}, \end{cases}$$

because $x = \pi/2$ is the only place in I where $\tan x$ is undefined. Now, look at Figure 115. Note that the graph of $y = x$ lies *above* the graph of $y = \tan x$ if $\pi/2 < x < 4.4934$. This means that $x - \tan x > 0$ for such values of x, right? Furthermore, for these same values of x, $\cos x < 0$, so,

$$f \text{ is decreasing if } \pi/2 < x < 4.4934 \quad i.e., \quad f'(x) < 0.$$

Similarly, if $0 < x < \pi/2$, $\cos x > 0$ but now the graph of $y = x$ is *under* the graph of $y = \tan x$. This means that $x - \tan x < 0$ and so,

$$f \text{ is decreasing if } 0 < x < \pi/2 \quad i.e., \quad f'(x) < 0.$$

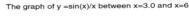
The graph of y = sin(x)/x between x=3.0 and x=6

We already know that $f'(\pi/2) = -4/\pi^2 < 0$, so all this information tells us that f is decreasing on the interval $(0, 4.4934)$. A similar argument shows that f is increasing on the interval $(4.4934, 6)$, (you should convince yourself of this).

Let's recap. Up to now we have a graph that looks like a shallow bowl, because the minimum value is so small (≈ -0.2172). This is because we know that f has a local minimum at $x \approx 4.4934$ and that f is increasing to the right of this point and decreasing to the left of this point. We also know that $f(\pi) = 0$. So, the picture so far is similar to Figure 117.

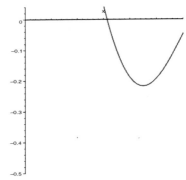

Figure 117.

Now, our intuition tells us that the graph is concave up on the interval $(\pi, 6)$, based on the rough figure we sketched in the margin. What happens near $x = 0$? Is there going to be a change in concavity? Is it going to be concave down anywhere near $x = 0$? Before we go on finding out the concavity of our graph let's look at what's happening near $x = 0$. First, we take the limit of $f(x)$ as $x \to 0$ and then we'll look at its right-derivative there. So,

$$\lim_{x \to 0^+} f(x) = \lim_{x \to 0^+} \frac{\sin x}{x},$$
$$= \lim_{x \to 0^+} \frac{\cos x}{1}, \qquad \text{(by L'Hospital's Rule; Form is 0/0)}$$
$$= 1.$$

Next,

$$\lim_{x \to 0^+} f'(x) = \lim_{x \to 0^+} \frac{x \cos x - \sin x}{x^2},$$
$$= \lim_{x \to 0^+} \frac{-x \sin x}{2x}, \qquad \text{(by L'Hospital's Rule; Form is 0/0)}$$
$$= \lim_{x \to 0^+} \frac{-\sin x}{2},$$
$$= 0.$$

So the derivative is 'leveling off' at $x = 0$ (the tangent line becomes horizontal) and the function itself tends to a finite value of 1 at $x = 0$. But then, we reason like this: The derivative is positive near $x = 3$ and it's 0 at $x = 0$ which means, we think, that maybe it's always getting *smaller* as $x \to 0$. But this is the same as saying that f' is decreasing, i.e., the graph of f is concave down (or, $f''(x) < 0$) in that inteval! But wait! The graph is known to be concave up in $(3, 6)$. So, there should be a point of inflection, c, with $0 < c < 3$. Let's see if our intuition is right...

Well, let's spare us the details in using Newton's Method one more time to find the roots of $f''(c) = 0$, whose solution(s) define the inflection point, c. We use the starting value, $x_0 = 2$, and define the function h to be the numerator of $f''(x)$. So,

$$h(x) = -x^2 \sin x - 2x \cos x + 2 \sin x,$$

and the iterations converge to the root whose value is $c \approx 2.081576$, see Figure 118. This value of c is indeed a point of inflection since, just to the left of c you can calculate that $f''(x) < 0$ while just to the right of c we have $f''(x) > 0$.

Finally, we can now infer almost without a doubt that the graph of f is concave up in $(2.0816, 6)$ and concave down in $(0, 2.0816)$.

As for asymptotes, there are no horizontal asymptotes since the interval is finite, and there cannot be any vertical asymptotes since the only candidate, $x = 0$, is *neither* a vertical asymptote or a vertical tangent line. The complete graph of this function appears in Figure 119.

NOTE: What is really nice here is the graph of the function $f(x) = \sin x/x$, we just described on the interval $(0, \infty)$. Unfortunately, this would likely take us years (really!) to do with just a calculator, and it could never be done entirely (since the interval is infinite), but its general form could be described using arguments which are very similar to the one just presented. You'll then get the graph in Table 5.5. In this case the graph *does* have a horizontal asymptote at $y = 0$, since

$$\lim_{x \to \infty} \frac{\sin x}{x} = 0,$$

by the Sandwich Theorem for Limits (Chapter 2), and NOT by L'Hospital's Rule, because $\sin(\infty)$ is meaningless in the limiting sense.

Newton iterates for

$$h(x) = -x^2 \sin(x) - 2x \cos(x) + 2\sin(x)$$

and $x_0 = 2$

m	$h(x_m)$	x_{m+1}
0	-0.154007	2.092520
1	0.023531	2.081737
2	0.000340	2.081576
3	0.000000	2.081576
...	...	...

Figure 118.

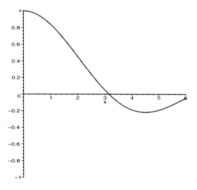

The graph of y =sin(x)/x between x=0 and x=6

Figure 119.

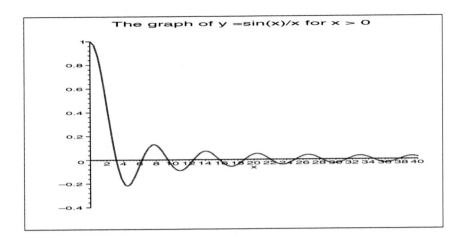

Table 5.5: The Graph of $\frac{\sin x}{x}$ on the Interval $(0, \infty)$.

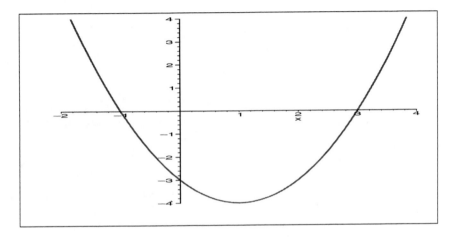

Table 5.6: The Graph of $x^2 - 2x - 3$ on the Interval $(-\infty, \infty)$.

SNAPSHOTS

Example 258. Sketch the graph of the function f defined by $f(x) = x^2 - 2x - 3$.

Solution The function is a polynomial which factors easily as $f(x) = (x-3)(x+1)$, so its zeros are at $x = 3$ and $x = -1$. So, its x-intercepts are at these points $x = 3, -1$. Its y-intercept is $y = -3$. Furthermore, since $f'(x) = 2x - 2$ and $f''(x) = 2 > 0$ the graph is a function which is *always concave up*, (so has no inflection points) and has one critical point c where $f'(c) = 2c - 2 = 0$, i.e., when $c = 1$. This point $x = 1$ is a local minimum (by the Second Derivative Test). A few extra points plotted for convenience generate the graph, Table 5.6.

Example 259. Sketch the graph of the function f defined by

$$f(x) = \frac{1}{x^2 - 1}.$$

Solution This function is a rational function whose denominator factors easily as $x^2 - 1 = (x-1)(x+1)$, so its zeros are at $x = 1$ and $x = -1$. This means that f is undefined at these points, $x = \pm 1$, so the lines $x = \pm 1$ qualify as vertical asymptotes. Since $f(x) \neq 0$, the graph has no x−intercepts. Its y−intercept (set $x = 0$) is $y = -1$. Next,

$$f'(x) = \frac{-2x}{(x^2 - 1)^2}, \quad and$$

$$f''(x) = \frac{2(3x^2 + 1)}{(x^2 - 1)^3}.$$

The only critical point in the domain of f is when $x = 0$. There cannot be *any* inflection points since, for any x, $f''(x) \neq 0$. The point $x = 0$ is a local maximum (by the Second Derivative Test) and $f(0) = -1$. In order to find the intervals of increase and decrease and the intervals where the graph of f is concave up or down, we use the SDT's of each rational function $f'(x), f''(x)$.

Intervals	$(x+1)^2$	$-x$	$(x-1)^2$	sign of $f'(x)$
$(-\infty, -1)$	+	+	+	+
$(-1, 0)$	+	+	+	+
$(0, 1)$	+	−	+	−
$(1, \infty)$	+	−	+	−

NOTE: We've included the '− sign' in front of the function f', into the 'x column' in our Table, just so we don't forget it. The SDT for $f''(x)$ is (since its numerator is irreducible),

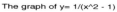
The graph of y= 1/(x^2 - 1)

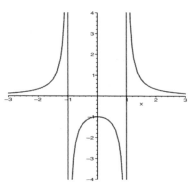

Figure 120.

Intervals	$(x+1)^3$	$(x-1)^3$	sign of $f''(x)$
$(-\infty, -1)$	−	−	+
$(-1, 1)$	+	−	−
$(1, \infty)$	+	+	+

Assimilating all this we see that f is increasing on $(-\infty, 0)$, decreasing on $(0, \infty)$, concave up on $(-\infty, -1), (1, \infty)$, and concave down on $(-1, 1)$. Lastly, there is a horizontal asymptote at both 'ends' of the real line given by $y = 0$, since

$$\lim_{x \to \pm\infty} \frac{1}{x^2 - 1} = 0,$$

and two vertical asymptotes given by the lines $x = \pm 1$ (as mentioned above). Combining all this data and adding a few extra points using our calculator, we get the graph in Figure 120.

Example 260. Sketch the graph of the function f defined by $f(x) = x^3 - 3x + 2$.

Solution By inspection we note that $x = 1$ is a zero of f $(f(1) = 0)$. To find the remaining factors we need to divide $(x - 1)$ into $f(x)$. We do this using **long division**, (a quick review of this procedure is given elsewhere in this book). So, we see that

$$\frac{x^3 - 3x + 2}{(x - 1)} = x^2 + x - 2,$$
$$= (x + 2)(x - 1).$$

We see that the factors of f are given by $f(x) = (x-1)^2(x+2)$. From this we see that f has a **double root** at $x = +1$ (i.e., $f(1) = 0$ and $f'(1) = 0$). Its x−intercepts are at these points $x = 1, -2$. Its y−intercept is $y = 2$.

Next, $f'(x) = 3x^2 - 3 = 3(x^2 - 1) = 3(x-1)(x+1)$ and $f''(x) = 6x$. The only critical points are at $x = \pm 1$ and the Second Derivative Test shows that $x = +1$ is a local minimum while $x = -1$ is a local maximum. The graph is a function which is concave up when $x > 0$ and concave down when $x < 0$. Since $f''(x) = 0$, it follows that $x = 0$ is a point of inflection. Using the SDT of f', or, more simply this time, by solving the inequalities $x^2 - 1 > 0, x^2 - 1 < 0$, we see that if $|x| > 1$, then f is increasing , while if $|x| < 1$, then f is decreasing. Since f is a polynomial, there are **no vertical or horizontal asymptotes**, (can you show this?). A few extra points added to the graph for convenience generate Figure 121.

NOTES:

POSSIBLE SHORTCUTS

The graph of a cubic with a double root

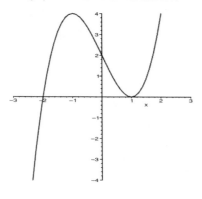

Figure 121.

A slant asymptote

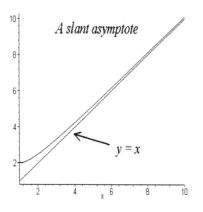

The curve $y = \frac{x^2+1}{x}$

Figure 122.

1. **EVEN SYMMETRY**. There is an additonal tool that one can use to help draw the graph of a function. This tool is not always useful in practice, but it *can* be useful in some cases. The tool involves some *symmetry* and depending on whether or not the given f has this or that property we can cut down the amount of time needed to draw the graph. It works like this.

If the given function is an **even function**, then the graph of f is symmetric with respect to the $y-$axis. This means that you can fold the graph of f for $x > 0$ along the $y-$axis and obtain the same graph on the other side, $x < 0$. In other words, if a mirror is placed along the $y-$axis, then the graph is its own mirror image. OK, so what's an even function? A function is said to be *even* if it satisfies

$$f(-x) = f(x), \quad \text{for every value of } x \text{ in its domain.}$$

You can use the Box principle (Chapter 1) to check this. For example, the function $f(x) = x^2$ is even, since $f(-x) = (-x)^2 = x^2 = f(x)$. Another example is $f(x) = x^2 \cos(x)$, since the cosine function is, itself an even function, that is, $\cos(-x) = \cos x$. Other examples include the functions f defined in Examples 251, 255, and 259. In each of these Examples, the graph is 'symmetric' with respect to the $y-$axis.

2. **ODD SYMMETRY**. On the other hand, if the given function is an **odd function**, then the graph of f is symmetric with respect to the origin, $(0,0)$, (the fancy word for this is a **central reflection**). This means that the graph of f can be found by folding the graph of f for $x > 0$ about the $y-$axis, and then folding *that graph* along the $x-$axis.

But what's an odd function? A function is said to be *odd* if it satisfies

$$f(-x) = -f(x), \quad \text{for every value of } x \text{ in its domain.}$$

For example, the function $f(x) = x^3$ is odd, since $f(-x) = (-x)^3 = -x^3 = -f(x)$. Another example is $f(x) = \sin(x)$, which declares that the sine function is, itself an odd function. Another such example includes the functions f defined in Example 252. In each of these Examples, the graph is 'symmetric' with respect to the origin, $(0,0)$. However, in the remaining examples the functions are **neither even nor odd.**

Why these odd names, even and odd? Well, because someone, somewhere, ages ago figured that if you associate an even function with a *plus sign* and an odd function with a *minus sign*, then the 'product of two such functions' behaves much like the product of the corresponding *plus and minus signs*. So, one can show without much difficulty that

$$
\begin{aligned}
(Even\ function) \cdot (Even\ function) &\implies Even\ function, \\
(Even\ function) \cdot (Odd\ function) &\implies Odd\ function, \\
(Odd\ function) \cdot (Even\ function) &\implies Odd\ function, \\
(Odd\ function) \cdot (Odd\ function) &\implies Even\ function,
\end{aligned}
$$

For example, let's show that if f is an odd function and g is an even function, their product is an odd function. let f be odd and g be even.Writing $h = fg$, their product, (not their *composition*), we know that $h(x) = f(x)g(x)$, by definition, and so,

$$h(-x) \quad = \quad f(-x)g(-x),$$

$$\begin{aligned}
&= \quad (-f(x))(g(x)), \quad \text{(since f is odd and g is even),} \\
&= \quad -f(x)g(x), \\
&= \quad -h(x), \quad \text{(which means that f is odd, by definition.)}
\end{aligned}$$

3. **SLANT ASYMPTOTES** These are lines which are neither vertical nor horizontal asymptotes. They are 'slanted' or 'tilted' at an arbitrary angle. If the function f has the property that there are two real numbers, m and b with

$$\lim_{x \to \infty} (f(x) - (mx + b)) \quad = \quad 0,$$

then we say that the line $y = mx + b$ is a **slant asymptote** of the graph of f. For example, the function f defined by

$$f(x) \quad = \quad \frac{x^2 + 1}{x},$$

has the property that

$$\lim_{x \to \infty} \left(\frac{x^2 + 1}{x} - x \right) \quad = \quad 0,$$

because $1/x \to 0$ as $x \to \infty$. Its graph can be seen in Figure 122.

4. **WHAT IF YOU CAN'T USE THE SECOND DERIVATIVE TEST** because $f'(c) = 0$ and $f''(c) = 0$? What do you do?

We use the following neat result which is more general than the Second Derivative Test. Its proof requires something called **Taylor's Formula** which we will see in a later Chapter. So here is

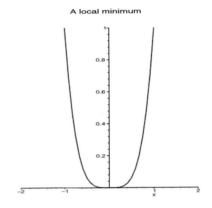

A local minimum

The curve $y = x^4$

Figure 123.

THE GENERAL EXTREMUM TEST

Let f be $n-$times differentiable over an interval I. Assume that for $x = c$ we have,

$$f'(c) = 0, \quad f''(c) = 0, \quad f'''(c) = 0, \ldots, \quad f^{(n-1)}(c) = 0, \quad f^{(n)}(c) \neq 0.$$

(a) If n is even and $f^{(n)}(c) > 0$, $\implies$ c is a local minimum

(b) If n is even and $f^{(n)}(c) < 0$, $\implies$ c is a local maximum

(c) If n is odd, $\implies$ c is a point of inflection

The classic examples here are these: Let f be defined by $f(x) = x^4$. Then $f'(0) = 0, f''(0) = 0, f'''(0) = 0, f^{(4)}(0) = 24 > 0$. So, $n = 4$, and the General Extremum Test tells us that $x = 0$ is a local minimum (see Figure 123).

On the other hand, if we let $f(x) = x^3$, then $f'(0) = 0, f''(0) = 0, f'''(0) = 6$. Now, $n = 3$ is an odd number, so regardless of the sign of the third derivative we know that $x = 0$ is a point of inflection (see Figure 124).

NOTES:

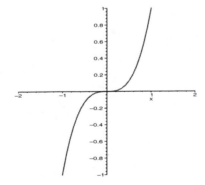

A point of inflection

The graph of $y = x^3$

Figure 124.

5.4   Application of Derivatives to Business and Economics

Another important use of rates of change is in the optimization of economic and business functions such as revenue, cost, profit, and demand functions.

Notation and Definitions

$x =$ Number of items of a product produced (or sold) by a firm or industry.

$p =$ Price per unit

$R(x) =$ Total revenue from selling x units $= xp$

$C(x) =$ Total cost of producing x units

$P(x) =$ Total profit $= R(x) - C(x)$

Demand Equation: an equation relating the price of a product and the number of units sold

Marginal Revenue Function: $\dfrac{dR}{dx}$

Marginal Cost Function: $\dfrac{dC}{dx}$

Marginal Profit Function: $\dfrac{dP}{dx}$

Example 261.

A company has found that the demand for one of its products can be modelled by the demand function $p = 1200 - x$ dollars, where x is the number of units sold per year. The annual cost of producing x units is $C(x) = 30,000 - 100x$ dollars, and the annual production capacity is 800 units.

1. Determine the annual revenue function $R(x)$

2. How many units should be produced (assume number sold = number produced) to maximize the profit?

3. What is the maximum profit?

4. What price per unit maximizes the profit?

5. If the annual production capacity is 400 units, how many units should be produced to produce the maximum profit?

6. Find the value of the marginal revenue when $x = 200$.

Solution

1. $R(x) = xp = x(1200 - x) = 1200x - x^2$, where $0 \le x \le 800$.

2. Profit is

$$P(x) = R(x) - C(x) = 1200x - x^2 - (30,000 + 100x) = 1100x - x^2 - 30,000.$$

The maximum profit will occur at a critical point or at an end-point of the interval (0, 800).

$$\frac{dP}{dx} = 1100 - 2x = 0 \quad \text{for a critical point.}$$

Thus $x = 550$ gives a local maximum (since $P(x)$ is a parabola opening downwards, or since $\frac{d^2 P}{dx^2} = -2 < 0$).

$$P(550) = 1100(550) - (550)^2 - 30,000 = 272,500.$$

Now check the endpoints. $P(0) < 0$, and

$$P(800) = 1100(800) - 800^2 - 30,000 = 210,000$$

Thus, 550 units should be produced to maximize the profit.

3. From above the maximum profit is \$272,500.

4. The demand equation is $p = 1200 - x$, so the price per unit that maximizes the profit is $p = 1200 - 550 = \$650$.

5. If the maximum production capacity is only 400 units then $x = 550$ is outside the domain of the functions so the maximum profit occurs when $x = 400$ and is \$250,000.

6. The marginal revenue function is

$$\frac{dR}{dx} = \frac{d(1200x - x^2)}{dx} = 1200 - 2x.$$

Therefore when $x = 200$, the marginal revenue is $1200 - 2(200) = \$800$. That is, the rate of increase of the revenue with respect to the number of units produced is \$800 when the number of units is 200.

NOTES:

5.5 Single variable optimization problems

Base Angle

a

b

h

1. Find two positive numbers whose sum is 60 and whose product is a maximum

2. Find two numbers whose difference is 60 and whose product is a minimum

3. Find the dimensions of that rectangle of largest area whose perimeter is 400m. **Note:** Recall that the *perimeter* is the sum of the lengths of all the sides

4. What are the dimensions of that rectangular plot of land of largest area having a perimeter of 160m.?

5. A rectangular swimming pool with a perimeter equal to 60 ft and having a uniform depth equal to 10ft is to be excavated in a garden. What are the dimensions of the pool that will utilize the largest amount of water when filled right up to the top?

6. An isosceles trapezoid is a closed four-sided figure (a quadrilateral) with two parallel sides and and two equal sides. The cross-section of a camping tent is in the form of an isosceles trapezoid of height h, base angle θ, and base length b. The width of its *living space* is given by a (see the figure in the margin) because outside this space you hit the slanted wall with your head. Show that its *perimeter* (the sum of the lengths of all its sides) is given by

$$P = a + b + 2h \csc \theta,$$

and that this perimeter is as small as possible when $\theta = \frac{\pi}{2}$, that is, when the cross-section is actually a square!

7. Refer to Example 6. Given that $\theta = \frac{\pi}{4}$ and $a = 3$ meters find that height h where $2 \leq h \leq 3$ that (a), will maximize and (b), will minimize the cross-sectional area of the trapezoid.

8. The volume of a circular cylinder of radius R and height h is given by $V = \pi R^2 h$. If a closed tin of canned fish in the form of such a cylinder is to contain 3.5 oz. (fluid ounces), find those dimensions that will minimize the amount of tin used in its construction.

9. When superimposed on a Cartesian coordinate system we find that the contour of a beach may be modeled by the curve $y = x^2 + 1$ where x is in kilometers. Find the closest distance of a scuba diver at the point $(3, 1)$ from the beach.

10. A shoe manufacturer sells sneakers to a wholesaler at a cost of $20 per pair provided less than 100 pairs are ordered. If more than 100 pairs are ordered (up to 700) the cost per pair falls at a rate equal to $0.02 times the number of pairs ordered. What size order will result in a maximum revenue to the manufacturer?

11. A rectangular piece of museum board having an area 140 in^2 needs to be cut into a mat for framing purposes so as to allow for a picture window whose margins are 3 in. from the top and 3 in. from each of its sides and 3.5 in. from the bottom. Find the dimensions of the picture window of maximum area that can be cut from this piece of board.

12. A teepee in the form of a right circular cone is made out of canvas. Its radius is given to be 5 ft and its height is 12 ft. Find the dimensions of the largest possible rectangle (having one side along the base of the teepee) that can be inscribed within one of its triangular cross sections (this will give you an idea of the maximum standing space within the teepee). **Hint:** Position the rectangle so that it and the triangle have a common bisector. Then use similar triangles!

13. The Best Paper Company has found that the revenue obtained from the sale of x boxes of laser printer paper can be approximated by the function $R(x) = 40x - 1.2x^2$ dollars whenever an order does not exceed 25 boxes. Now, the cost of producing these x boxes of paper is given by $C(x) = 5 + 1.6x$ dollars. How many boxes should the company try to be selling so that it maximizes its profits for a given order?

5.6 Chapter Exercises

Sketch the graphs of the following functions using your CAS or a graphing calculator or failing this, your hand calculator and a few points. Then sketch the graphs using the methods in this Chapter. Compare your results.

1. $y = (x + 1)^2$

2. $y = 4 - x^2$

3. $y - 3x^2 - 3x = 0$

4. $y = x^2 - 2x + 1$

5. $y = x\sqrt{x}$

6. $y = x^3 - 27$

7. $y = \sin 2x$

8. $y = x^2 - 5x + 6$

9. $y = \cos 2x$

10. $y(x - 2) = 1$

11. $y = (x - 1)(x + 1)^3$

12. $y + x^2 y = 4x$

13. $y = \dfrac{x^2 + 1}{2x + 3}$

14. $y = x^3 + x$

15. $y = \sin(2x + 1)$

Use the Sign Decomposition Table (SDT) to help you sketch the following graphs.

16. $y = \dfrac{x + 1}{x^2 + 1}$

17. $y = \dfrac{x - 2}{x^2 - 2x + 1}$

18. $y = \dfrac{x + 1}{x^3 - 1}$

19. $y = \dfrac{x^2 - 1}{(x - 1)(x + 2)^2}$

   - Simplify this expression first!

20. $y = \dfrac{x^3}{1 + x^2}$

Sketch the graphs of the following functions

21. $y = xe^{-x}$

22. $y = |x - 4|$

23. $y = x^2 \ln x, \ x > 0$

24. $y = \ln(x^2)$

25. $y = e^{2\ln x}$

26. $y = x \sin x$

27. $y = (x - 1)^2(x + 1)$

28. $y + x^2 y = 4$

29. $y = x^2 e^{-x}, x \geq 0$

30. **Challenge Problem:** Sketch the graph of the function f defined by

$$f(x) = \frac{1 - \cos(2x)}{x}$$

for $0 < x < 4\pi$.

31. A company that makes and sells stereos has found that its daily cost function and revenue function, respectively, are given by

$$C(x) = 5 + 35x - 1.65x^2 + 0.1x^3 \qquad R(x) = 32x.$$

If the company can produce at most 20 stereos per day, what production level x will yield the maximum profit and what is the maximum profit?

32. A company has determined that it can sell x units per day of a particular small item if the price per item is set at $p = 4 - 0.002x$ dollars, with $0 \leq x \leq 1200$.

(a) What production level x and price p will maximize daily revenue?

(b) If the corresponding cost function is $C(x) = 200 + 1.5x$ dollars, what production level will maximize daily profit?

(c) What is the maximum daily profit?

(d) Find the marginal cost and marginal revenue functions.

(e) Equate the marginal cost and marginal revenue functions and solve for x. Notice that this is the same value of x that maximized the profit. Can you explain why this is true?

33. A manufacturer of cabinets estimates that the cost of producing x cabinets can be modelled by
$$C(x) = 800 + 0.04x + 0.0002x^2.$$

How many cabinets should be produced to minimize the **average cost** per cabinet, $C(x)/x$?

34. In economics, a **demand equation** is an equation which gives the relationship between the price of a product, p, and the number of units sold, x. A small company thinks that the demand equation for its new product can be modelled by
$$p = Ce^{kx}.$$

It is known that when $p = \$45$, $x = 1000$ units, and when $p = \$40$, $x = 1200$ units.

(a) Solve for C and k.

(b) Find the values of x and p that will miximize the revenue for this new product.

Suggested Homework Set 18. *Do problems 2, 6, 11, 18, 23*

NOTES:

Chapter 6

Integration

The Big Picture

This Chapter is about the subject of *Integration*. One can argue that the reason for the existence of this subject of integration is intimately tied with the existence of the derivative. With the notion of the *derivative* we have seen that we can model the world around us. The integral allows to go 'backwards', so to speak. In other words, let's say that you know the speed of a particle moving in a straight line in some fixed direction and you want to know where it is... Mmm, not enough information, right? You only know its speed, so you can't know where it *is* unless you ask a question like: "Where was it, say, 5 seconds ago?". Then we can tell you where it is now and where it will be later (assuming its speed remains the same). Well, this whole business of finding out where a body is given its speed is part of the subject of integration. You can imagine that Newton and Leibniz and Bernoulli and all the early discoverers of Calculus had to wrestle with this concept so that they could actually make calculations about where planetary bodies were and where they would be, given their present position and Newton's own Laws. They also solved other problems of practical interest and needed to find the solution of a *differential equation* using the *integral*.

Sometimes this mathematical subject called *integration* is not classified correctly by librarians and one may find it in some libraries under the heading of *Social Studies*, or *Sociology*. Anyways, this topic of integration together with the topic of *Differentiation* which we saw in Chapters 3 and 4, comprise the main tools used in the study of Calculus of functions of one variable. These two topics really go hand-in-hand through an important result called the **Fundamental Theorem of Calculus**, called by some authors, the *Fundamental Theorem of Integral Calculus*. The statement of this Fundamental Theorem says something like 'The operation of taking the derivative of a function and the operation of *taking the integral of a function*' are basically "inverse operations" to one another. The word 'inverse' here is meant in a sense analogous to *inverse functions*, a topic which we saw in Chapter 3.

So, one thinks that this last statement about inverses should mean: "The derivative of the integral of a function is the function itself" while "the integral of the derivative of a function is *almost* the function, itself, because there is a constant missing". This explains why we said " ... *basically* inverses of one another", above. Among the applications of the integral we'll see that it is used to find the area under a curve, or the **area between two curves**, or even for finding the volume of a region called a **solid of revolution**. It is also used to calculate **centers of mass** in engineering, or to find the probability that an electron is in such and such a place (in quantum mechanics). Since most physical dynamical phenomena are modeled using differential equations it becomes reasonable that their *solutions* will be given by the integral of something or other. There are many, many more applications of the integral that we could give but these will suffice for our purposes. This chapter is part of the heart of Calculus, its importance cannot be underestimated.

Review

Review all the Tables involving **derivatives of exponential and trigonometric functions and their inverses**. Soon enough you'll see that you don't really have to memorize any more formulae so long as you've committed to memory those Tables from Chapters 3 and 4.

6.1 Antiderivatives and the Indefinite Integral

The procedure of finding the **antiderivative** of a given function is the **inverse operation** to that of differentiation or the "taking of a derivative". Basically, given a function f continuous over an interval $[a, b]$, its *antiderivative* is a differentiable function, $\mathcal{F}$, (read this as 'script F') whose derivative, $\mathcal{F}'$, satisfies

$$\mathcal{F}'(x) = f(x), \quad a < x < b,$$

i.e. the *derivative of an antiderivative of a function is the function itself.* We will use the symbol, script F, or $\mathcal{F}(x)$ for an antiderivative of a given function f, script G, or $\mathcal{G}(x)$ for an antiderivative of g, etc.

Example 262.   Find an antiderivative, $\mathcal{F}(x)$, of the function whose values are
$f(x) = 2x$.

Solution We want to find a function $\mathcal{F}$ such that $\mathcal{F}'(x) = 2x$, right? Let's try a function like $\mathcal{F}(x) = x^r$, where we have to find r. Why this type? Because we know that the derivative of such a power function is another such power function (by the Power Rule for Derivatives in Chapter 3). Now,

$$\begin{aligned} \mathcal{F}'(x) &= rx^{r-1}, \quad \textit{in general,} \\ &= 2x, \quad \textit{in particular,} \end{aligned}$$

when we choose (by inspection) $r = 2$, right? This means that if we choose $\mathcal{F}(x) = x^2$, then $\mathcal{F}'(x) = 2x$, which, by definition, means that $\mathcal{F}$ is an antiderivative of f. On the other hand, the function whose values are $\mathcal{F}(x) = x^2 + 4.123$ is **also** an antiderivative of f (because the derivative of a constant, like 4.123, is zero). The moral of all this is in Table 6.1, below.

The final result in Table 6.1 is not hard to show. We need to show that the difference between any two antiderivatives of a given function is always a constant. This is because if $\mathcal{F}_1, \mathcal{F}_2$ are each antiderivatives of f, then

$$\begin{aligned} D(\mathcal{F}_1 - \mathcal{F}_2) &= D(\mathcal{F}_1) - D(\mathcal{F}_2), \\ &= f - f, \\ &= 0, \end{aligned}$$

> When it exists, the derivative f' of a given function f is always unique, in the sense that it is the only function with the name "derivative of f". On the other hand, the *antiderivative*, $\mathcal{F}$, of a given function f is *not unique*. This means that if $\mathcal{F}$ is an antiderivative of f then the function $\mathcal{F} + C$, where C is a constant, is a NEW antiderivative of f.
>
> Mathematicians summarize this property of an antiderivative by saying that: **"an antiderivative of a function is defined up to the addition of an arbitrary constant"**.
>
> Mathematically, this means that if $\mathcal{F}_1, \mathcal{F}_2$ are each antiderivatives of f then, their difference, $\mathcal{F}_1 - \mathcal{F}_2 = C$ where C is some constant (number).

Table 6.1: The Basic Property of an Antiderivative

since $D(\mathcal{F}_i) = f$, by assumption, for $i = 1, 2$. This means that the function $\mathcal{F} = \mathcal{F}_1 - \mathcal{F}_2$ has a derivative which is equal to zero everywhere and so, by Example 97, $\mathcal{F}(x) = constant$, that is, $\mathcal{F}_1 - \mathcal{F}_2 = constant$, which is what we wanted to show.

Another notation (symbol) for an antiderivative of a given function f is given by Leibniz's own 'elongated S' notation, which is called the **indefinite integral** of f, that is,

$$\mathcal{F}(x) = \int^x f(t) \, dt, \qquad (6.1)$$

where the variable t appearing on the right is sometimes called a *free variable*, the older term being a *dummy variable*. The shape of the symbol defining a free variable is not important, so, for instance, (6.1) can be rewritten as

$$\mathcal{F}(x) = \int^x f(u) \, du$$

also defines an antiderivative of f, or even $\int^x f(\square) \, d\square$. Combining the above results and notation we can write

$$\mathcal{F}'(x) = \frac{d}{dx} \int^x f(t) \, dt = f(x), \qquad (6.2)$$

for $a < x < b$, whenever $\mathcal{F}$ is an antiderivative of f over $[a, b]$.

Example 263. Show that every antiderivative of the function f defined by $f(x) = cx^r$, where c is a given constant and $r \neq -1$, looks like

$$\int^x ct^r \, dt = \frac{cx^{r+1}}{r+1} + C \qquad (6.3)$$

where C is a constant, called a **constant of integration**.

Solution Here, $f(x) = cx^r$, or $f(t) = ct^r$. Notice that the function $\mathcal{F}$ whose values are $\mathcal{F}(x)$ where

$$\mathcal{F}(x) = \frac{cx^{r+1}}{r+1} + C$$

has the property that $\mathcal{F}'(x) = cx^r = f(x)$, by the Power Rule for derivatives. It follows that this function is an antiderivative, and every other antiderivative of f differs from this one by a constant, by Table 6.1. So,

$$\mathcal{F}(x) = \int^x ct^r \, dt,$$

$$= \frac{cx^{r+1}}{r+1} + C.$$

Equation (6.3) is very useful when combined with the next result, because it will allow us to find the most general antiderivative (or indefinite integral) of a general polynomial of degree n.

Example 264. If $\mathcal{F}, \mathcal{G}$ are antiderivatives of f, g, respectively, and c is any constant (positive or negative), then the function $\mathcal{F} + c \cdot \mathcal{G}$ is an antiderivative of $f + c \cdot g$, that is,

$$\int^x (f(t) + c \cdot g(t)) \, dt = \int^x f(t) \, dt + c \int^x g(t) \, dt$$

This result is sometimes stated as: **an antiderivative of a sum of two or more functions is the sum of the antiderivatives of each of the functions**, and the antiderivative of a scalar multiplication of a function is the antiderivative of this function multiplied by the same scalar.

Solution We use the definition of an antiderivative. All we have to do is to find the derivative of the function $\mathcal{F} + c \cdot \mathcal{G}$ and show that it is the same as $f + c \cdot g$. So,

$$\frac{d}{dx}(\mathcal{F} + c \cdot \mathcal{G}) = \mathcal{F}'(x) + c \cdot \mathcal{G}'(x),$$

$$= f(x) + c \cdot g(x),$$

by the usual properties of the derivative.

Let's use the result in Example 264 in the next few Examples.

Example 265. Find $\displaystyle\int (2x + 3) \, dx$.

Solution In order to find an antiderivative of $2x + 3$ we find an antiderivative of $2x$ and 3 and use the results of Example 264 and Equation (6.3). So, we let $f(x) = 2x$, $g(x) = 3$. Then, $\mathcal{F}(x) = x^2 + C_1$ and $\mathcal{G}(x) = 3x + C_2$ (by Equation (6.3) with $r = 0, c = 3$). So,

$$\int^x (2t + 3) \, dt = \int^x 2t \, dt + \int^x 3 \, dt,$$

$$= (x^2 + C_1) + (3x + C_2),$$

$$= x^2 + 3x + \underbrace{C_1 + C_2},$$

$$= x^2 + 3x + \quad C,$$

where $C = C_1 + C_2$ is a new constant of integration.

Example 266. Find $\int (x^3 - 3x^2) \; dx$.

Solution We use the results of Example 264 and Equation (6.3). In this case, we let $f(x) = x^3$, $g(x) = -3x^2$. Then, $\mathcal{F}(x) = \frac{x^4}{4} + C_1$ and $\mathcal{G}(x) = -x^3 + C_2$ (by Equation (6.3) with $r = 2, c = -3$). So,

$$
\begin{aligned}
\int^x (t^3 - 3t^2) \; dt &= \int^x t^3 \; dt + \int^x -3t^2 \; dt, \\
&= (\frac{x^4}{4} + C_1) + (-x^3 + C_2), \\
&= \frac{x^4}{4} - x^3 + \underbrace{C_1 + C_2}, \\
&= \frac{x^4}{4} - x^3 + \quad C,
\end{aligned}
$$

where $C = C_1 + C_2$ is, once again, a new constant of integration.

> Many authors will use the following notation for an indefinite integral, that is,
>
> $$\int f(x) \; dx = \int^x f(t) \; dt.$$
>
> Both symbols mean the same thing: They represent an antiderivative of f.

Now, repeated applications of Example 264 shows that we can find an antiderivative of the sum of three, or four, or more functions by finding an antiderivative of each one in turn and then adding them. So, for example,

Example 267. Evaluate $\int (3x^2 - 2x + (1.3)x^5) \; dx$.

Solution In this case,

$$
\begin{aligned}
\int (3x^2 - 2x + (1.3)x^5) \; dx &= \int 3x^2 \; dx + \int (-2x) \; dx + \int (1.3)x^5 \; dx, \\
&= (x^3 + C_1) + (-x^2 + C_2) + ((1.3)\frac{x^6}{6} + C_3), \\
&= x^3 - x^2 + (1.3)\frac{x^6}{6} + \underbrace{C_1 + C_2 + C_3}, \\
&= x^3 - x^2 + \frac{13x^6}{60} + \quad C,
\end{aligned}
$$

where now $C = C_1 + C_2 + C_3$ is, once again, a NEW constant of integration. All the other constants add up to make another constant, and we just don't know what it is, so we label it by this generic symbol, C.

So, **why are these 'constants of integration' always floating around?** The reason for this is that these 'constants' allow you to distinguish one antiderivative from another. Let's see ...

Example 268. Find that antiderivative $\mathcal{F}$ of the function f defined by $f(x) = 4x^3 - 2$ whose value at $x = 0$ is given by $\mathcal{F}(0) = -1$.

Solution First, we find the most general antiderivative of f. This is given by

$$\mathcal{F}(x) = \int (4x^3 - 2) \; dx = x^4 - 2x + C,$$

where C is just a constant of integration. Now, all we have to do is use the given information on $\mathcal{F}$ in order to evaluate C. Since we want $\mathcal{F}(0) = -1$, this means that $\mathcal{F}(0) = 0 - 0 + C = -1$, which gives $C = -1$. So, the antiderivative that we want is given by $\mathcal{F}(x) = x^4 - 2x + (-1) = x^4 - 2x - 1$.

Now, let's recall the **Generalized Power Rule**, from Chapter 3. To this end, let u denote any differentiable function and let r be any real number. We know that

$$\frac{d}{dx}\underbrace{u(x)^r}_{\mathcal{F}(x)} = \underbrace{r\,u(x)^{r-1}\,\frac{du}{dx}}_{f(x)},$$

so, if we denote all the stuff on the right by $f(x)$, and the function being differentiated on the left by $\mathcal{F}(x)$, then we just wrote that $\mathcal{F}'(x) = f(x)$, or, by definition, that $\mathcal{F}(x)$ is an antiderivative of $f(x)$. In other words, the Generalized Power Rule for derivatives tells us that

$$\int r\,u(x)^{r-1}\,\frac{du}{dx}\,dx = u(x)^r + C,$$

or, rewriting this in another way by replacing r by $r+1$, dividing both sides by $r+1$ and simplifying, we see that,

$$\boxed{\int u(x)^r\,\frac{du}{dx}\,dx = \frac{u(x)^{r+1}}{r+1} + C, \qquad r \neq -1,} \qquad (6.4)$$

where now, the 'new' C is the 'old' C divided by $r+1$. Still, we replace this 'old' symbol by a generic symbol, C, always understood to denote an arbitrary constant. As is usual in this book, we may simplify the 'look' of (6.4) by replacing every occurrence of the symbols '$u(x)$' by our generic symbol, $\Box$. In this case, (6.4) becomes

$$\int \Box^{\,r}\,\frac{d\Box}{dx}\,dx = \frac{\Box^{\,r+1}}{r+1} + C, \qquad r \neq -1, \qquad (6.5)$$

Let's see how this works in practice:

Example 269. Evaluate the (most general) antiderivative of f where $f(x) = \sqrt{5x+1}$, that is, find

$$\int \sqrt{5x+1}\,dx$$

Solution The first thing to do is to bring this into a more recognizable form. We want to try and use either one of (6.4) or (6.5). The square root symbol makes us think of a *power*, so we let $\Box = 5x+1$. The whole thing now looks like

$$\int \sqrt{\Box}\,dx = \int \Box^{\frac{1}{2}}\,dx.$$

but, don't forget, in order to use (6.5) there should be the symbol $\frac{d\Box}{dx}$ on the left. It's not there, right? So, what do we do? We'll have to **put it in there and also divide by it!** OK, so we need to calculate the derivative of $\Box$, right? (because it has to be part of the left-hand side of the formula). We find $\Box\,'(x) = \frac{d\Box}{dx} = 5$. Now, let's see what happens...

$$\int \sqrt{5x+1}\, dx \;=\; \int \square^{\frac{1}{2}}\, dx$$

$$=\; \int \square^{\frac{1}{2}} \cdot 5 \cdot \frac{1}{5}\, dx, \quad \text{(Multiply and divide by } \square'(x) \text{ here)}$$

$$=\; \frac{1}{5} \int \square^{\frac{1}{2}} \frac{d\square}{dx}\, dx, \quad \text{(now it looks like (6.5) with } r = 1/2\text{),}$$

$$=\; \frac{1}{5} \left(\frac{\square^{\frac{1}{2}+1}}{\frac{1}{2}+1} \right) + C, \quad \text{(by (6.5)),}$$

$$=\; \frac{1}{5} \left(\frac{2}{3} \square^{\frac{3}{2}} \right) + C,$$

$$=\; \frac{2}{15} (5x+1)^{\frac{3}{2}} + C.$$

Okay, **but how do we know we have the right answer!?** Well, by definition of an antiderivative, *if we find the derivative of this antiderivative then we have to get the original result*, right? A simple check shows that this is true once we use the Generalized Power Rule, that is,

$$\frac{d}{dx}\mathcal{F}(x) \;=\; \frac{d}{dx}\left(\frac{2}{15}(5x+1)^{\frac{3}{2}} + C \right),$$

$$=\; \frac{2}{15} \cdot \frac{3}{2}(5x+1)^{\frac{1}{2}} \cdot 5,$$

$$=\; f(x).$$

EXAMPLES

The method just outlined in the previous example is the basis for one of many methods of integration, namely the **method of substitution**, a method which we'll see in the next chapter. The anatomy of an indefinite integral is described here:

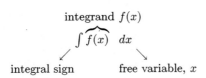

integrand $f(x)$

$\int f(x)\ dx$

integral sign   free variable, x

Example 270. Evaluate $\displaystyle\int (2x^3 + 1)x^2\, dx$.

Solution Inspect this one closely. There are 'two ways' of doing this one! The first one involves recognizing the fact that the integrand is really a polynomial *in disguise* (when you multiply everything out). If you don't see this, then you can try to use (6.5). The first way of doing it is the easiest.

Method 1 We note that $(2x^3 + 1)x^2 = 2x^5 + x^2$. So,

$$\int (2x^3 + 1)x^2\, dx \;=\; \int (2x^5 + x^2)\, dx,$$

$$=\; \frac{2x^6}{6} + \frac{x^3}{3} + C_1,$$

$$=\; \frac{x^6 + x^3}{3} + C_1,$$

$$=\; \mathcal{F}_1(x).$$

Method 2 We set $u(x) = 2x^3 + 1$, and find $\frac{du}{dx} = 6x^2$, which, aside from the number 6, is similar to the "other" term appearing in the integrand. So,

$$
\begin{aligned}
\int (2x^3 + 1)x^2 \, dx &= \int \frac{1}{6}(2x^3 + 1)(6x^2) \, dx, \\
&= \frac{1}{6} \int u(x)\frac{du}{dx} \, dx, \\
&= \frac{1}{6}\left(\frac{u(x)^2}{2}\right) + C_2, \quad \text{(by (6.4) with } r = 1\text{)}, \\
&= \frac{1}{12}u(x)^2 + C_2, \\
&= \frac{1}{12}(2x^3 + 1)^2 + C_2, \quad \text{where } C \text{ is some constant,} \\
&= \mathcal{F}_2(x).
\end{aligned}
$$

Now you look at these two answers, $\mathcal{F}_1(x), \mathcal{F}_2(x)$ and you probably think: "This is nuts! These two answers don't *look* the same", and ... you're right! But, *believe it or not* they each represent the *same* general antiderivative. Let's have a closer look...

$$
\begin{aligned}
\mathcal{F}_1(x) - \mathcal{F}_2(x) &= \left(\frac{x^6 + x^3}{3} + C_1\right) - \left(\frac{1}{12}(2x^3 + 1)^2 + C_2\right), \\
&= \frac{x^6 + x^3}{3} + C_1 - \left(\frac{1}{12}(4x^6 + 4x^3 + 1) + C_2\right), \\
&= \frac{x^6}{3} + \frac{x^3}{3} + C_1 - \left(\frac{x^6}{3} + \frac{x^3}{3} + \frac{1}{12} + C_2\right), \\
&= C_1 - \frac{1}{12} - C_2, \\
&= C \qquad \text{where } C \text{ is some NEW constant.}
\end{aligned}
$$

We just showed something that we knew for a while now, namely, that any two antiderivatives always differ by a constant, (Table 6.1)! So, these two answers define the *same general antiderivative*.

Still not convinced? Let's see what happens if we were asked to find the antiderivative such that $\mathcal{F}_1(1) = -2$, say. We know that there is *only one answer* to this question, right? (no constants floating around!). OK, so we set $x = 1$ into the expression for $\mathcal{F}_1(x)$ and find $\mathcal{F}_1(1) = \frac{2}{3} + C_1$. But $\mathcal{F}_1(1) = -2$, because this is given. So, $\frac{2}{3} + C_1 = -2$, which says that $C_1 = -\frac{8}{3}$. So, the claim is that

$$
\begin{aligned}
\mathcal{F}_1(x) &= \frac{x^6 + x^3}{3} - \frac{8}{3}, \\
&= \frac{x^6 + x^3 - 8}{3},
\end{aligned}
$$

is the required antiderivative. We use exactly the same idea with $\mathcal{F}_2(x)$. We set $\mathcal{F}_2(1) = -2$ into the expression for $\mathcal{F}_2(x)$ and find that $C_2 = -2 - \frac{9}{12} = -\frac{11}{4}$. The expression for $\mathcal{F}_2(x)$ now looks like,

$$
\begin{aligned}
\mathcal{F}_2(x) &= \frac{1}{12}(2x^3 + 1)^2 - \frac{11}{4}, \\
&= \frac{x^6 + x^3}{3} + \frac{1}{12} - \frac{11}{4}, \\
&= \frac{x^6 + x^3 - 8}{3},
\end{aligned}
$$

just like before. So, even though the constants differ, the answer is the same. That's all.

SNAPSHOTS

Example 271. Evaluate $\displaystyle\int \sin^2 x \, \cos x \, dx$.

Solution We see a power, so we can start by trying $\square = \sin x$, so that we have a term that looks like $\square^2$. But we also need $\square'(x)$, right? From Chapter 3, we know that $\square'(x) = \cos x$ which is just the term we have! Okay, we were lucky. Using (6.5) with $r = 2$, we find

$$
\begin{aligned}
\int \sin^2 x \, \cos x \, dx &= \int \square^2 \frac{d\square}{dx} \, dx, \\
&= \frac{\square^3}{3} + C, \\
&= \frac{(\sin x)^3}{3} + C, \\
&= \frac{\sin^3 x}{3} + C.
\end{aligned}
$$

As a check we note that, using the Generalized Power Rule,

$$
\begin{aligned}
\frac{d}{dx}\left(\frac{\sin^3 x}{3} + C \right) &= \frac{3\sin^2 x}{3} D(\sin x) + 0, \\
&= \sin^2 x \cos x,
\end{aligned}
$$

so we found the correct form of the most general antiderivative (the one with the C in it).

Example 272. Let k be a real number (or constant). Find the most general antiderivative of f where $f(x) = e^{kx}$ where e is **Euler's number**, (Chapter 4).

Solution We want $\int e^{kx} \, dx$, right? There is a power here, but it's not easy to see what to do. How about we let $\square = e^x$? Then we can write the integrand as $\square^k$, so maybe there's some hope that we can use (6.5). But we also need $\square' = e^x$, remember (see Chapter 4)? So,

$$
\begin{aligned}
\int e^{kx} \, dx &= \int \square^k \frac{e^x}{e^x} \, dx, \quad \text{(because we need a } \square' \text{ in here)} \\
&= \int \square^k \frac{\square'}{\square} \, dx, \\
&= \int \square^{k-1} \frac{d\square}{dx} \, dx, \\
&= \frac{\square^k}{k} + C, \quad \text{(by (6.5) with } r = k-1), \\
&= \frac{(e^x)^k}{k} + C, \\
&= \frac{e^{kx}}{k} + C,
\end{aligned}
$$

and this is the required antiderivative.

If $\mathcal{F}, \mathcal{G}$ are antiderivatives of f, g, respectively, and c is any constant (positive or negative), then the function $\mathcal{F} + c \cdot \mathcal{G}$ is an antiderivative of $f + c \cdot g$, that is,

$$\int^x (f(t) + c \cdot g(t))\, dt \;=\; \int^x f(t)\, dt + c \int^x g(t)\, dt.$$

If $\square, f$ represent any two differentiable functions, then

$$\int \square^r \frac{d\square}{dx}\, dx \;=\; \frac{\square^{r+1}}{r+1} + C, \qquad r \neq -1,$$

$$\int \frac{d\square}{dx}\, dx \;=\; \square + C,$$

$$\frac{d}{dx} \int^x f(t)\, dt \;=\; f(x) + C,$$

Table 6.2: Summary of Basic Formulae Regarding Antiderivatives

Example 273. Evaluate

$$\int x(1 + x^2)^{\frac{3}{2}}\, dx.$$

Solution We want $\int x(1 + x^2)^{3/2}\, dx$, right? Once again, there is a power here, and we can write the integrand as $x \,\square^{\,3/2}$, where $\square = 1 + x^2$, so that we can recognize it as being of the form (6.5). What about the x? Well, this should be part of the $\square' = 2x$ - term, right? But we don't have the factor of '2' in the integrand ... no problem, because we can rewrite this as

$$\int (1 + x^2)^{3/2}\, x\, dx \;=\; \int \square^{\,3/2} \frac{2x}{2}\, dx, \quad \text{(because we need a } \square'\text{ in here)}$$

$$=\; \frac{1}{2} \int \square^{\,3/2} \square'\, dx,$$

$$=\; \frac{1}{2} \int \square^{\,3/2} \frac{d\square}{dx}\, dx,$$

$$=\; \frac{1}{2} \left(\frac{2}{5} \square^{\,5/2} \right) + C, \quad \text{(by (6.5) with } r = 3/2\text{)},$$

$$=\; \frac{1}{5} \square^{\,5/2} + C,$$

$$=\; \frac{1}{5}(1 + x^2)^{5/2} + C,$$

which is the required antiderivative or indefinite integral. We recap the main results of this section in Table 6.2, above.

Some simple applications

We recall that a **differential equation** is basically an equation which relates the derivatives of some unknown function, a function that we seek. If we can find it, and it is sufficiently differentiable, we call it a **solution** of the differential equation. One of the earliest uses of the indefinite integral was in solving simple (and not so simple) differential equations, like the one in the next example ...

Example 274. Solve the equation $\dfrac{dy}{dx} = \dfrac{x}{y}$, $y > 0$.

Solution This means we seek a differentiable function $y(x)$ whose derivative at x is equal to $\frac{x}{y(x)}$, if $y(x) > 0$. To do this we "separate variables" *i.e.* put all the "y's" on one side (usually the left) and the "x's" on the other (the right side), a very old idea which can be traced right down to Johann (John) Bernoulli, 300 years ago! Thus, this unknown function $y = y(x)$ has the property that

$$y(x)\frac{dy}{dx} = x$$

and so these functions must have the same antiderivative (up to a constant), *i.e.*

$$\text{antiderivative of } \left(y\frac{dy}{dx}\right) \quad = \quad \text{antiderivative of } (x), \text{ or,}$$

$$\int y\frac{dy}{dx}\ dx \quad = \quad \int x\ dx.$$

But, on the left-hand-side we have by (6.4) with $r = 1$, and $y = u$,

$$\int y\frac{dy}{dx}\ dx = \frac{y(x)^2}{2} + c_1,$$

where c_1 is a constant, while on the right-hand-side,

$$\int x\,dx = \frac{x^2}{2} + c_2,$$

where c_2 is another constant. Combining the last two equalities gives

$$\frac{y(x)^2}{2} + c_1 \quad = \quad \frac{x^2}{2} + c_2$$

$$\frac{y(x)^2}{2} \quad = \quad \frac{x^2}{2} + c_3, \quad \text{(where } c_3 = c_2 - c_1)$$

$$y(x)^2 \quad = \quad x^2 + C, \quad (C = 2c_3)$$

$$y(x) \quad = \quad \sqrt{x^2 + C}, \quad \text{(since } y(x) > 0\text{, we choose the '+' square root).}$$

As usual, we can **check this answer** by *substituting back into the equation.* We want $\frac{dy}{dx} = \frac{x}{y}$. Now, our candidate '$y(x)$' has the following property, that,

$$\frac{dy}{dx} \quad = \quad \frac{1}{2}(2x)(x^2 + C)^{-\frac{1}{2}},$$

$$= \quad x(x^2 + C)^{-\frac{1}{2}},$$

$$= \quad \frac{x}{\sqrt{x^2 + C}} = \frac{x}{y(x)},$$

$$= \quad \frac{x}{y},$$

which is what is required.

Notice that constant of integration, C, which is still 'floating around'. As we pointed out when we studied *Laws of Growth and Decay* in Chapter 4.7, (where it looked like

THE CONSTANT C IS DE-TERMINED BY AN INITIAL CONDITION!! That is, if we are given the value of y somewhere, then we can determine C. For example, the solution of $\frac{dy}{dx} = \frac{x}{y}$ such that $y(0) = 1$ is given by $y(x) = \sqrt{x^2 + 1}$ (because $1 = y(0) = \sqrt{x^2 + C}\Big|_{x=0} = \sqrt{C}$ so $C = 1$ and the results follows.)

$N(0)$ there), this constant of integration C is necessary in order to solve so-called **initial value problems**. Let's recall how this is done.

Example 275. On the moon, acceleration due to gravity is 1.6 m/sec^2. If a rock is dropped into a crevasse, how fast will it be going just before it hits the bottom 30 seconds later? How far down the crevasse is the rock after 30 seconds?

Solution From basic Physics we know $\frac{d^2 s}{dt^2} = 1.6$ m/sec^2 where $s(t)$ is the distance of the rock at time t from its "original" position. We want its <u>speed</u> after 30 seconds, *i.e.*

$$\frac{ds}{dt}(30) = ?$$

Now,

$$\frac{d^2 s}{dt^2} = \frac{d}{dt}\left(\frac{ds}{dt}\right) = 1.6, \quad \text{(where we forget about units here.)}$$

Taking the antiderivative of both sides gives,

$$\int \frac{d}{dt}\left(\frac{ds}{dt}\right) \, dt = \int (1.6) \, dt, \quad \text{(we'll put the } C \text{ in later ...)}$$

$$\int \frac{d}{dt}\left(\Box\right) \, dt = \int (1.6) \, dt, \quad (\Box = \frac{ds}{dt} \text{ here)}$$

$$\Box = \int (1.6) \, dt, \quad \text{(by (6.5) with } r = 0, \text{ since } \Box^0 = 1, \text{ yes! ...)}$$

$$\frac{ds}{dt} = (1.6)t + C,$$

is the <u>speed</u> of the rock at any time t! Since the rock is merely "dropped", its initial <u>velocity</u> is zero, and mathematically this means

$$\frac{ds}{dt}(0) = 0.$$

Now, this 'initial condition' determines C, since

$$0 = \frac{ds}{dt}(0) = (1.6) \cdot 0 + C = C$$

so $C = 0$. Thus, in general,

$$\frac{ds}{dt} = (1.6)t$$

gives the speed of the rock at any time t, while after 30 seconds its speed is obtained by setting $t = 30$ into the expression for the speed, that is,

$$\frac{ds}{dt}(30) = 1.6 \text{ m/sec}^2 \cdot 30 \text{ sec} = 48 \text{ m/sec}.$$

NOTE:

We only need *ONE* initial condition in order to determine C in the above.

How far down the crevasse is the rock after 30 seconds? Well, we need *another* initial condition in order to get this, because even though we know its speed, we don't know where the rock is *initially*! So, let's say that

$$s(0) = 0,$$

i.e., its initial position is 0 units, which is the location of some arbitrary point which we decide upon before hand (e.g., the height of our outstretched horizontal arm above the lunar surface could be defined to be $s = 0$). Then

$$\frac{ds}{dt} = (1.6)t,$$

$$\int \frac{ds}{dt}\, dt = \int (1.6)t\, dt,$$

$$s(t) = (1.6)\frac{t^2}{2} + C, \quad \text{(by (6.4) with } r = 0,\ s = u,\ t = x)$$

is the "distance" at time t. Since $s(0) = 0$, we have $C = 0$ again, (just set $t = 0$, here). Thus, after 30 seconds,

$$s(30) = (1.6) \cdot \frac{900}{2} = (1.6) \cdot (450),$$

$$= 720\text{ m},$$

a "deep" crevasse!

MORAL: We needed 2 "initial" conditions to determine the unknown function in this "second order" differential equation and, as we have seen earlier, only *one* condition is needed for determining the antiderivative of a function explicitly. The general result says that *we need n initial conditions to explicitly determine the unknown function of a differential equation of order n.*

Example 276. The escape velocity v_0 at the surface of a star of radius R, and mass M (assumed constant) is given by

$$v_0 = \sqrt{\frac{2GM}{R}}.$$

Given that the star is "collapsing" according to the formula

$$R(t) = \frac{1}{t^2},$$

how long will it take the star to become a "black hole"!? Show that the rate of change of its 'escape velocity' is a constant for all t. [You're given that $M = 10^{31}$, (10 solar masses), $G = 6.7 \times 10^{-11}$, and that the speed of light, $c = 3 \times 10^8$, all in MKS units.]

Solution Since R is a function of t, the initial velocity also becomes a function of t, right? We're assuming that its mass remains constant for simplicity. It's easy to calculate $\sqrt{2GM} \approx 3.7 \times 10^{10}$ so $v_0(t) = (3.7 \times 10^{10})\, t$. Now, we want $v_0(t) > c$, because then, by definition, the *photons* inside can't escape through the surface. This means that we need to solve the inequality $v_0(t) > c = 3 \times 10^8$ which holds only if $(3.7 \times 10^{10})\, t > 3 \times 10^8$ or, solving for t, we find $t > 10^{-2}$ or $t > 0.01$ seconds! This means that after $t = 0.01$ sec. light will no longer be able to escape from its surface, and so it will appear 'black'.

In this case, $v_0(t) = \sqrt{2GM/R} = \sqrt{2GM}\, t$, because of the assumption on $R(t)$, so $v_0'(t) = D(v_0(t)) = \sqrt{2GM}$ is a constant.

A **black hole** is the remnant of a collapsed star. The gravitational field around a black hole is so intense that even light cannot escape from it. Thus, it appears "black" to the human eye.

Example 277. Solve the equation

$$\frac{d^3 y}{dx^3} = 6$$

given that $y = 5$, $\frac{dy}{dx} = 0$ and $\frac{d^2y}{dx^2} = -8$ when $x = 0$.

Solution The initial conditions here are given by $y(0) = 5$, $\frac{dy}{dx}(0) = 0$ and $\frac{d^2y}{dx^2}(0) = -8$. Note that there are 3 initial conditions and the equation is of "order" 3 (because the highest order derivative which appears there is of order 3). Now,

$$
\begin{aligned}
\frac{d^3y}{dx^3} &= \frac{d}{dx}\left(\frac{d^2y}{dx^2}\right) = 6, \quad \text{(is given, so)} \\
\int \frac{d}{dx}\left(\frac{d^2y}{dx^2}\right) \, dx &= \int 6 \, dx, \\
&= 6x + C, \quad \text{or, if we set } \square = y'' \text{ and use Table 6.2 ... ,} \\
\frac{d^2y}{dx^2} &= 6x + C,
\end{aligned}
$$

where we've "reduced" the order of the differential equation by 1 after the integration .... We determine C using the "initial condition" $\frac{d^2y}{dx^2}(0) = -8$.

So, we set $x = 0$ in the formula $\frac{d^2y}{dx^2} = 6x + C$ to find

$$
\begin{aligned}
-8 &= 6 \cdot 0 + C = C, \quad \text{and so,} \\
\frac{d^2y}{dx^2} &= 6x + C, \\
&= 6x - 8.
\end{aligned}
$$

"Integrating" this latest formula for $y''(x)$ once again we find

$$
\frac{dy}{dx} = 6\frac{x^2}{2} - 8x + C
$$

where C is some generic constant (not related to the previous one). To determine C we set $x = 0$ in preceding formula and find

$$
0 = y'(0) = 3 \cdot 0^2 - (8 \cdot 0) + C = C.
$$

Now, $C = 0$ and so because of this,

$$
\begin{aligned}
\frac{dy}{dx} &= 3x^2 - 8x + C, \\
&= 3x^2 - 8x.
\end{aligned}
$$

Finally, one last integration (our third such integration...) gives us

$$
y(x) = 3\frac{x^3}{3} - 8\frac{x^2}{2} + C
$$

where C is a generic constant again. Setting $x = 0$ here, gives us $C = 5$, (since $y(0) = 5$) and so,

$$
\begin{aligned}
y(x) &= x^3 - 4x^2 + C, \\
&= x^3 - 4x^2 + 5,
\end{aligned}
$$

is the required answer. *Check this by differentiating and using initial conditions.*

NOTES:

Exercise Set 29.

Find the required antiderivatives or indefinite integrals. Don't forget to add a generic constant C at the end.

1. $\int -5 \, dx$

2. $\int 1 \, dx$

3. $\int 0 \, dx$

4. $\int x^{0.6} \, dx$

5. $\int^x 3t \, dt$

6. $\int (x-1) \, dx$

7. $\int (x^2+1) \, dx$

8. $\int (2x^2+x-1) \, dx$

9. $\int^x 3u \, du$

10. $\int (4x^3 + 2x - 1.314) \, dx$

11. $\int \sqrt{2x-2} \, dx$

12. $\int \sqrt{3x+4} \, dx$

13. $\int \sqrt{1-x} \, dx$,   careful here: Look out for the minus sign!

14. $\int x\sqrt{4x^2+1} \, dx$

15. $\int x\sqrt{1-2x^2} \, dx$

16. $\int x(1+x^2)^{0.75} \, dx$

17. $\int x^2(2+x^3)^{2/3} \, dx$

18. $\int -x^3\sqrt{4+9x^4} \, dx$

19. $\int x^{1.4}\sqrt{1+x^{2.4}} \, dx$

Evaluate the following antiderivatives, $\mathcal{F}$, under the given initial condition. No generic constant should appear in your final answer.

20. $\int \sin^3 x \cos x \, dx$ given that $\mathcal{F}(0) = -1$.

21. $\int \cos^2 x \sin x \, dx$ given that $\mathcal{F}(0) = 0$.

22. $\int e^{-2x} \, dx$ given that $\mathcal{F}(1) = 0$.

Find the solution of the following differential equations subject to the indicated initial condition(s).

23.
$$\frac{dy}{dx} = \frac{x^2}{y^3}, \quad y(0) = 1.$$

• Leave your solution in *implicit form*, that is, don't solve for y explicitly.

24.
$$\frac{d^2y}{dx^2} = 12x^2, \quad y(0) = -1, \quad y'(0) = 0.$$

25.

$$\frac{d^3y}{dx^3} = 24x, \quad y(0) = -1, \quad y'(0) = 0, \quad y''(0) = 0.$$

Suggested Homework Set 19. *Do problems 4, 8, 13, 15, 18, 22, 23.*

6.2 Definite Integrals

You'll remember that the principal geometric interpretation of the **derivative** of a function, f, is its representation as the slope of the tangent line to the graph of the given function. So far, our presentation of the **antiderivative** has focussed upon the actual finding of antiderivatives of given functions. In this section, we develop the machinery necessary to arrive at a **geometric interpretation of the antiderivative** of a function. For example, let $\mathcal{F}$ be any given antiderivative of f on an interval I containing the points a, b, where we assume that $f(x) \geq 0$ there. The number $\mathcal{F}(b) - \mathcal{F}(a)$, will be called the **definite integral** of f between the limits $x = a$ and $x = b$, and it will be denoted generally by the symbol on the left of (6.6),

$$\int_a^b f(x)\, dx = \mathcal{F}(b) - \mathcal{F}(a). \tag{6.6}$$

This number turns out to be the **area** of the closed region under the graph of the given function and between the lines $x = a$, $x = b$ and the x−axis, (see Figure 125). Even if f is not positive in the interval, there is still some area-related interpretation of this definite integral, and we'll explore this below. In order to arrive at this area interpretation of the definite integral of f, we'll use the so-called **Riemann Integral** which will define the *area* concept once and for all, along with the Mean Value Theorem of Chapter 3, which will relate this area to the difference $\mathcal{F}(b) - \mathcal{F}(a)$ of any one of its antiderivatives, $\mathcal{F}$. This will result in the Fundamental Theorem of Calculus which is the source of many applications of the integral. Let's see how this works...

Let $[a, b]$ be a given interval, f a given function with domain $[a, b]$, assumed **continuous** on its domain. The **definite integral of f over** $[a, b]$ is, by definition, an expression of the form

$$\int_a^b f(x)\, dx = \mathcal{F}(b) - \mathcal{F}(a),$$

where $\mathcal{F}' = f$, *i.e.*, $\mathcal{F}$ is some antiderivative of f. Well, the right-hand side should be some number, right? And, this number *shouldn't change* with the choice of the antiderivative (because it is a number, not a variable). So, you may be wondering why this definition involves *any* antiderivative of f! This is okay. The idea behind this is the fact that antiderivatives differ from one another by a constant, C, (see Table 6.1). So, if we let $\mathcal{F}_1, \mathcal{F}_2$ be any two antiderivatives of f, then, by the discussion following Table 6.1, there is a constant C such that $\mathcal{F}_1 - \mathcal{F}_2 = C$, and so,

$$\begin{aligned}
\mathcal{F}_1(b) - \mathcal{F}_1(a) &= (\mathcal{F}_2(b) + C) - (\mathcal{F}_2(a) + C), \\
&= \mathcal{F}_2(b) - \mathcal{F}_2(a),
\end{aligned}$$

and the constant C cancels out! Because of this, it follows that we can put **any** antiderivative in the right side of (6.6). Let's look at a few examples.

Example 278. Evaluate $\displaystyle\int_0^1 (2x + 1)\, dx$.

Solution Using the methods of the preceding section, *one* antiderivative of $2x + 1$ is given by

$$\int (2x + 1)\, dx = x^2 + x,$$

where we have chosen $C = 0$ here because we want *one* antiderivative, not the most general one (so we can leave out the C). Thus $\mathcal{F}(x) = x^2 + x$. Hence, by definition,

$$\int_0^1 (2x + 1)\, dx = \mathcal{F}(1) - \mathcal{F}(0)$$

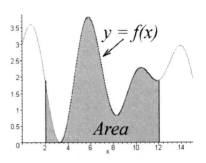

The shaded area is given by $\mathcal{F}(12) - \mathcal{F}(2)$, where $\mathcal{F}$ is any antiderivative of f.

Figure 125.

$$= (1^2 + 1) - (0^2 + 0)$$
$$= 2.$$

Example 279. Evaluate $\int_0^\pi \sin^2 x \cos x \; dx$.

Solution Refer to Example 271. Using this Example we see that *one* antiderivative of this integrand is given by

$$\int \sin^2 x \cos x \; dx = \frac{\sin^3 x}{3},$$

where, once again, we have chosen $C = 0$ here because we want *one* antiderivative, not the most general one (so we can leave out the C). Thus,

$$\mathcal{F}(x) = \frac{\sin^3 x}{3}.$$

Hence, by definition,

$$\int_0^\pi \sin^2 x \cos x \; dx = \mathcal{F}(\pi) - \mathcal{F}(0),$$
$$= (\frac{\sin^3 \pi}{3}) - (\frac{\sin^3 0}{3}),$$
$$= 0 - 0, \quad (\text{because } \sin \pi = 0 = \sin 0),$$
$$= 0.$$

It's okay for a definite integral to be equal to zero because, the 'areas' we spoke of above 'cancel out', see Figure 126.

Example 280. Evaluate $\int_{-1}^{+1} x^2 \; dx$.

Solution In this example we can choose

$$\mathcal{F}(x) = \int x^2 \; dx = \frac{x^3}{3}.$$
$$\text{Thus,} \quad \int_{-1}^{+1} x^2 \; dx = \mathcal{F}(+1) - \mathcal{F}(-1),$$
$$= \left(\frac{1^3}{3}\right) - \left(\frac{(-1)^3}{3}\right),$$
$$= \left(\frac{1}{3}\right) - \left(\frac{-1}{3}\right),$$
$$= \frac{2}{3}.$$

In this case, the 'area' we spoke of earlier is *double* the area of the region under the graph of f between the lines $x = 0$, $x = 1$, and the x−axis, (see Figure 127).

The main properties of the definite integral of an arbitrary function are listed in Table 6.3. These properties can be verified by using the definition of an antiderivative, $\mathcal{F}$, of f, and the methods in Chapters 3 and 5.

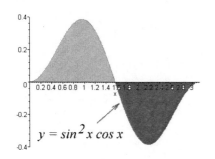

$y = \sin^2 x \cos x$

The two areas in the shaded regions 'cancel out' because they are equal but opposite in sign. The general idea is that the area of the region above the x−axis is positive, while the area of the region below the x−axis is negative.

Figure 126.

For example, in order to verify item 5 in Table 6.3, we proceed as follows: We let $\mathcal{F}(x) = \int f(x)\,dx$ and assume that $f(x) > 0$. Using the definition of the definite integral we must show that $\mathcal{F}(b) - \mathcal{F}(a) > 0$, right? But, by definition of an antiderivative, we know that $\mathcal{F}'(x) = f(x)$ and that $f(x) > 0$, (because this is given). This means that $\mathcal{F}'(x) > 0$ which implies that $\mathcal{F}$ is an increasing function over $[a, b]$. But this last conclusion means that if $a < b$ then $\mathcal{F}(a) < \mathcal{F}(b)$, which, in turn, means that $\mathcal{F}(b) - \mathcal{F}(a) > 0$. Now, if $f(x)$ is equal to zero somewhere, the argument is a little more complicated. If you're interested, see the margin on the right for the idea ...

Let $f(x) \geq 0$. We define a new function f_ε by setting its values $f_\varepsilon(x) = f(x) + \varepsilon$, where $\varepsilon > 0$ is an arbitrary small but positive number. This new function, $f_\varepsilon(x) > 0$, right? It also has an antiderivative, $\mathcal{F}_\varepsilon$, given by $\mathcal{F}_\varepsilon(x) = \mathcal{F}(x) + \varepsilon \cdot x$. We can apply the argument of the paragraph to $\mathcal{F}_\varepsilon$ instead of $\mathcal{F}$, and obtain the conclusion that $\mathcal{F}_\varepsilon(b) - \mathcal{F}_\varepsilon(a) = (\mathcal{F}(b) - \mathcal{F}(a)) + \varepsilon \cdot (b - a) > 0$. But this is true for each $\varepsilon > 0$. So, we can take the limit as $\varepsilon \to 0$ and find that $\mathcal{F}(b) - \mathcal{F}(a) \geq 0$.

Properties of the Definite Integral

1. $\displaystyle \int_a^a f(x)\,dx = 0$

2. $\displaystyle \int_a^b f(x)\,dx = -\int_b^a f(x)\,dx$

3. If k is a constant, then $\displaystyle \int_a^b k f(x)\,dx = k \int_a^b f(x)\,dx$

4. $\displaystyle \int_a^b (f(x) \pm g(x))\,dx = \int_a^b f(x)\,dx \pm \int_a^b g(x)\,dx$

5. If $f(x) \geq 0$ and $a \leq b$, then $\displaystyle \int_a^b f(x)\,dx \geq 0$

6. If $f(x) \leq g(x)$, for each x in $[a, b]$, then $\displaystyle \int_a^b f(x)\,dx \leq \int_a^b g(x)\,dx$

7. $\displaystyle \left(\min_{[a,b]} f(x) \right)(b - a) \leq \int_a^b f(x)\,dx \leq \left(\max_{[a,b]} f(x) \right)(b - a),$

   where the symbols on the left (resp. right) denote the (global) minimum and maximum values of f over $[a, b]$, (see Chapter 5).

8. If c is any number (or variable) for which $\mathcal{F}(c)$ is defined, then
   $$\int_a^b f(x)\,dx = \int_a^c f(x)\,dx + \int_c^b f(x)\,dx$$

Table 6.3: Properties of the Definite Integral

Example 281. Evaluate $\displaystyle \int_0^1 \frac{1}{1 + x^2}\,dx$.

Solution From Chapter 3, we know that

$$\frac{d}{dx} \operatorname{Arctan} x = \frac{1}{1 + x^2}.$$

But, by definition of the antiderivative, this means that $\mathcal{F}(x) = \operatorname{Arctan} x$ is the antiderivative of $(1 + x^2)^{-1}$, right? That is, we can infer that

$$\int \frac{1}{1 + x^2}\,dx = \operatorname{Arctan} x + C,$$

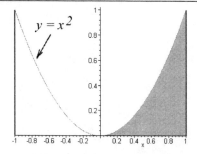

The area of the shaded region is one-half the area under the curve $y = x^2$ between the points -1 and $+1$.

Figure 127.

where C is a constant. Now, by definition of the definite integral, we can set $C = 0$ for convenience, and find

$$\int_0^1 \frac{1}{1+x^2}\, dx \;=\; \mathcal{F}(1) - \mathcal{F}(0),$$

$$= \text{Arctan}\, 1 - \text{Arctan}\, 0,$$

$$= \frac{\pi}{4}, \quad \text{(since } \tan(\pi/4) = 1 \text{ and } \tan 0 = 0\text{).}$$

Example 282. Evaluate $\int_0^1 xe^{-x^2}\, dx$.

Solution This one is a little tricky. We have the product of a function, x, and an exponential of a function, e^{-x^2}, which makes us think about a composition of two functions. Next, we're asking for an antiderivative of such a combination of functions. So, we should be thinking about the Chain Rule for derivatives (because it deals with compositions) applied to exponentials. This brings to mind the following formula from Chapter 4, namely, if u (or $\square$), is a differentiable function then

$$\frac{d}{dx} e^{u(x)} = e^{u(x)} \frac{du}{dx}.$$

In terms of antiderivatives this is really saying,

$$\int e^{u(x)} \frac{du}{dx}\, dx = e^{u(x)} + C, \tag{6.7}$$

or the term on the right of (6.7) is the antiderivative of the integrand on the left. Now, let's apply this formula to the problem at hand. We have little choice but to use the identification $u(x) = -x^2$ so that our preceding integral in (6.7) will even remotely look like the one we want to evaluate, right? What about the $u'(x)$-term? Well, in this case, $u'(x) = -2x$ and we 'almost' have this term in our integrand (we're just missing the constant, -2). So, we use the ideas of the preceding Section and write,

$$\int xe^{-x^2}\, dx \;=\; \int (-2x)\left(-\frac{1}{2}\right)e^{-x^2}\, dx,$$

$$= -\frac{1}{2} \int (-2x)e^{-x^2}\, dx,$$

$$= -\frac{1}{2} \int e^{u(x)} \frac{du}{dx}\, dx, \quad \text{(since } u(x) = -x^2, \text{ here),}$$

$$= -\frac{1}{2} e^{u(x)} + C, \quad \text{(by (6.7)),}$$

$$= -\frac{1}{2} e^{-x^2} + C,$$

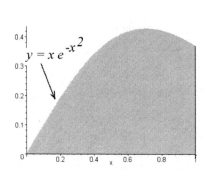

Figure 128.

and this is the most general antiderivative, $\mathcal{F}(x)$. The required definite integral is therefore given by (let's choose $C = 0$ again)

$$\int_0^1 xe^{-x^2}\, dx \;=\; \mathcal{F}(1) - \mathcal{F}(0),$$

$$= -\frac{1}{2} e^{-1^2} - \left(-\frac{1}{2}\right) e^{-0^2},$$

$$= -\frac{1}{2}\left(e^{-1} - 1\right), \quad \text{(since } e^0 = 1\text{),}$$

$$= \frac{1}{2}\left(1 - \frac{1}{e}\right),$$

$$= \frac{e-1}{2e}.$$

Summary

In order to evaluate the definite integral

$$\int_a^b f(x)\ dx,$$

we must

1. Find an antiderivative, $\mathcal{F}$, (*any* antiderivative will do), and

2. Evaluate the quantity $\mathcal{F}(b) - \mathcal{F}(a)$.

Table 6.4: How to Evaluate a Definite Integral

This last number is the area of the shaded region in Figure 128.

NOTATION

There is a universal convention for writing down the results of a definite integral. Let $\mathcal{F}$ denote any antiderivative of f. Instead of writing

$$\int_a^b f(x)\ dx = \mathcal{F}(b) - \mathcal{F}(a), \quad \text{we can write this briefly as,}$$

$$= \mathcal{F}(x)\big|_{x=a}^{x=b}, \quad \text{or,}$$

$$= \mathcal{F}(x)\big|_a^b$$

Next, we summarize in Tables 6.5, 6.6, 6.7 those basic formulae regarding antiderivatives which are most useful in Calculus.

NOTES:

Derivatives   **Antiderivatives**

$$D(\square^{r+1}) = (r+1)\square^r D\square, \quad r \neq -1. \qquad \int \square^r \frac{d\square}{dx}\, dx = \frac{\square^{r+1}}{r+1} + C$$

$$D(e^\square) = e^\square D\square \qquad\qquad\qquad \int e^\square \frac{d\square}{dx}\, dx = e^\square + C$$

$$D(a^\square) = a^\square \ln a\, D\square, \quad a > 0. \qquad \int a^\square \frac{d\square}{dx}\, dx = \frac{a^\square}{\ln a} + C$$

$$D(\ln|\square|) = \frac{1}{\square} D\square, \quad \square \neq 0. \qquad \int \frac{1}{\square} \frac{d\square}{dx}\, dx = \ln|\square| + C$$

$$D(\log_a |\square|) = \frac{1}{\ln a}\, \frac{1}{\square} D\square, \quad \square \neq 0,\; a > 0. \quad \text{Not needed.}$$

Table 6.5: Antiderivatives of Power and Exponential Functions

NOTES:

Derivatives	Antiderivatives
$D(\sin \square) = \cos \square \ D\square$	$\displaystyle\int \cos \square \ \frac{d\square}{dx} \ dx = \sin \square \ + C,$
$D(\cos \square) = -\sin \square \ D\square$	$\displaystyle\int \sin \square \ \frac{d\square}{dx} \ dx = -\cos \square \ + C,$
$D(\tan \square) = \sec^2 \square \ D\square$	$\displaystyle\int \sec^2 \square \ \frac{d\square}{dx} \ dx = \tan \square \ + C,$
$D(\cot \square) = -\csc^2 \square \ D\square$	$\displaystyle\int \csc^2 \square \ \frac{d\square}{dx} \ dx = -\cot \square \ + C,$
$D(\sec \square) = \sec \square \ \tan \square \ D\square$	$\displaystyle\int \sec \square \ \tan \square \ \frac{d\square}{dx} \ dx = \sec \square \ + C,$
$D(\csc \square) = -\csc \square \ \cot \square \ D\square$	$\displaystyle\int \csc \square \ \cot \square \ \frac{d\square}{dx} \ dx = -\csc \square \ + C,$

Table 6.6: Antiderivatives of Trigonometric Functions

Derivatives	Antiderivatives
$D(\text{Arcsin} \ \square) = \dfrac{1}{\sqrt{1 - \square^2}} \ D\square$	$\displaystyle\int \frac{1}{\sqrt{1 - \square^2}} \ \frac{d\square}{dx} \ dx = \text{Arcsin} \ \square \ + C$
$D(\text{Arccos} \ \square) = -\dfrac{1}{\sqrt{1 - \square^2}} \ D\square$	Not needed, use one above.
$D(\text{Arctan} \ \square) = \dfrac{1}{1 + \square^2} \ D\square$	$\displaystyle\int \frac{1}{1 + \square^2} \ \frac{d\square}{dx} \ dx = \text{Arctan} \ \square \ + C$
$D(\text{Arccot} \ \square) = -\dfrac{1}{1 + \square^2} \ D\square$	Not needed, use one above.
$D(\text{Arcsec} \ \square) = \dfrac{1}{|\square|\sqrt{\square^2 - 1}} \ D\square$	$\displaystyle\int \frac{1}{|\square|\sqrt{\square^2 - 1}} \ \frac{d\square}{dx} \ dx = \text{Arcsec} \ \square$ $+ C$
$D(\text{Arccsc} \ \square) = -\dfrac{1}{|\square|\sqrt{\square^2 - 1}} \ D\square$	Not needed, use one above.

Table 6.7: Antiderivatives Related to Inverse Trigonometric Functions

---

Exercise Set 30.

Evaluate the following definite integrals.

1. $\displaystyle\int_0^1 3x \, dx$

2. $\displaystyle\int_{-1}^0 x \, dx$

3. $\displaystyle\int_{-1}^1 x^3 \, dx$

4. $\displaystyle\int_0^2 (x^2 - 2x) \, dx$

5. $\displaystyle\int_{-2}^2 (4 - 4x^3) \, dx$

6. $\displaystyle\int_0^{\frac{\pi}{2}} \sin x \cos x \, dx$

7. $\displaystyle\int_0^{\pi} \cos^2 x \sin x \, dx$

8. $\displaystyle\int_{-\pi}^{\frac{\pi}{2}} \sin^3 x \cos x \, dx$

9. $\displaystyle\int_{1.5}^{1.2} (2x - x^2) \, dx$
   - *Hint:* Use Table 6.3, (2).

10. $\displaystyle\int_0^1 \frac{1}{\sqrt{1-x^2}} \, dx$
    - *Hint:* Think about the Arcsine function. Notice that the integrand approaches $+\infty$ as $x \to 1^-$. Thus the value of this integral is the area of an *unbounded region*, (*i.e.*, a region which is *infinite* in extent, see Figure 129)!

11. $\displaystyle\int_0^1 xe^{x^2} \, dx$

12. $\displaystyle\int_0^2 4xe^{-x^2} \, dx$

13. $\displaystyle\int_0^1 3^x \, dx$
    - *Hint:* Think about the derivative of the power function, 3^x, then guess its antiderivative.

14. $\displaystyle\int_{\square}^{\triangle} e^{3x} \, dx$

15. $\displaystyle\int_0^{0.5} \frac{x}{\sqrt{1-x^2}} \, dx$
    - *Hint:* Rewrite the integrand as $x(1-x^2)^{-1/2}$. Now, let $\square = 1 - x^2$, find $D\square$, and use equation (6.5).

16. $\displaystyle\int_0^1 x \, 2^{x^2+1} \, dx$
    - *Hint:* Find the derivative of a general power function.

17. $\displaystyle\int_0^{\frac{\sqrt{\pi}}{2}} x \ \sec(x^2) \ \tan(x^2) \ dx$

    • *Hint:* What is the derivative of the secant function?

18. $\displaystyle\int_{-1}^1 \frac{x}{1+x^4} \ dx$

    • *Hint:* Let $\square = x^2$ and think 'Arctangent'.

19. Show that $\dfrac{d}{dx} \displaystyle\int_0^{x^2} e^t \ dt = 2x \ e^{x^2}$ in the following steps:

    • a) Let $\mathcal{F}(t) = e^t$ be an antiderivative of f where $f(t) = e^t$. Show that the definite integral, by itself, is given by

    $$\int_0^{x^2} e^t \ dt \ = \ \mathcal{F}(x^2) - \mathcal{F}(0).$$

    • b) Next, use the Chain Rule for derivatives and the definition of $\mathcal{F}$ to show that

    $$\frac{d}{dx}\left(\mathcal{F}(x^2) - \mathcal{F}(0)\right) \ = \ 2x \ f(x^2) - 0,$$
    $$= \ 2x \ f(x^2).$$

    • c) Conclude that $\dfrac{d}{dx} \displaystyle\int_0^{x^2} e^t \ dt = 2x \ e^{x^2}$.

    This result is special case of a more general result called **Leibniz's Rule**.

20. Recall the definitions of an *odd* and an *even* function (see Chapter 5). Use a geometrical argument and the ideas in Figures 126, 127 to convince yourself that on a given **symmetric interval**, $[-a, a]$, where $a > 0$, we have:

    • If f is even, then $\displaystyle\int_{-a}^a f(x) \ dx = 2\int_0^a f(x) \ dx$,

    • If f is odd, then $\displaystyle\int_{-a}^a f(x) \ dx = 0$. (See Example 18 above with $a = 1$.)

Suggested Homework Set 20. *Suggested problems: 7, 11, 13, 15, 17, 18*

NOTES:

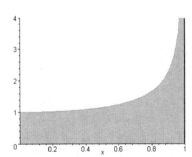

The shaded area is actually infinite (towards the top of the page) in its extent. The area under the graph of the Arcsine function is, however, finite.

Figure 129.

6.3   The Summation Convention

This section summarizes the basic material and notation used in the theory of the integral. The "*summation*" sign Σ (upper case Greek letter and corresponding to our "s" and read as "sigma") is defined by the symbols

$$\sum_{i=1}^{n} a_i = a_1 + a_2 + \ldots + a_n, \tag{6.8}$$

where the a_i are all real numbers. This last display is read as "The sum of the numbers a_i as i runs from 1 to n is equal to ..." (whatever). Okay, what this means is that the group of symbols on the left of this equation are *shorthand* for the sum of the n numbers on the right. Here, the numbers $\{a_n\}$ represent a *finite sequence* of numbers (see Chapter 2 for more details on sequences). For example, if we are asked to find the sum of the first 15 whole numbers and obtain 120, the equivalent statement

$$120 = 1 + 2 + 3 + 4 + 5 + 6 + 7 + 8 + 9 + 10 + 11 + 12 + 13 + 14 + 15, \tag{6.9}$$

would be rewritten more simply as

$$\sum_{i=1}^{15} i = 120, \tag{6.10}$$

because it takes up less room when you write it down. Here, the sequence $\{a_n\}$ is characterized by setting its nth-term equal to n, that is, $a_n = n$, where $n \geq 1$. Replacing n by i we get $a_i = i$ (because i is just another symbol for an integer) and so we find that the right-side of (6.8) becomes the right-side of (6.9) which can be rewritten more briefly as (6.10).

The formula for the sum of the first n squares of the integers is given by:

$$\sum_{i=1}^{n} i^2 = \frac{n(n+1)(2n+1)}{6}.$$

See Example 283, with $n = 5$. This formula is shown by using the *Principle of Mathematical Induction*. Briefly stated, a demonstration using this Principle goes like this: Let S_n be the nth statement of a string of (mathematical) statements. Let's say that we can prove that S_1 is a true statement. Next, we assume that S_n is a 'true' statement and *on this basis* we prove that S_{n+1} is also a true statement. Then, the Principle says that each statement S_n must be a true (mathematical) statement.

Figure 130.

| **Example 283.** | Evaluate $\sum_{i=1}^{5} i^2$. |

Solution By definition, this statement means that we want to find the sum of numbers of the form $a_i = i^2$ as i runs from 1 to 5. In other words, we want the value of the quantity

$$\begin{aligned}
\sum_{i=1}^{5} i^2 &= 1^2 + 2^2 + 3^2 + 4^2 + 5^2, \\
&= 1 + 4 + 9 + 16 + 25, \\
&= 55, \quad (\textit{see Fig. 130.})
\end{aligned}$$

There may be 'other symbols' appearing in the a_i (like $x, y, \ldots$),and that's OK, don't worry. This is one reason that we have to specify which symbol, or variable, is the one that is being used in the summation (in our case it is 'i').

| **Example 284.** | Let $n \geq 1$ be any integer. The quantity |

$$p(x) = \sum_{i=1}^{n} \frac{\sin ix}{i}$$

is called a **finite trigonometric polynomial**, and these are of central importance in areas of mathematics and engineering which deal with **Fourier Series**. What is this symbol shorthand for? What is the value of $p(0)$?

Solution By definition, this string of symbols is shorthand for

$$\sum_{i=1}^{n} a_i = \sum_{i=1}^{n} \frac{\sin ix}{i},$$

$$= \frac{\sin 1x}{1} + \frac{\sin 2x}{2} + \frac{\sin 3x}{3} + ... + \frac{\sin nx}{n},$$

$$= \sin x + \frac{\sin 2x}{2} + \frac{\sin 3x}{3} + ... + \frac{\sin nx}{n},$$

so, you just leave the $x's$ alone. But if you want the value of $p(0)$, say, then substitute $x = 0$ in each term of the last display. Then $p(0) = 0 + 0 + 0 + ... + 0 = 0$. Sometimes, you may have these long sums of numbers or functions that you want to write more compactly, using this shorthand notation. In this case you have to *guess* the general term of the sequence of numbers whose sum you're taking and then use the summation convention, above. Let's look at such an example.

Example 285. Rewrite the sum

$$f(t_1)\Delta t_1 + f(t_2)\Delta t_2 + f(t_3)\Delta t_3 + f(t_4)\Delta t_4,$$

using the summation convention. Don't worry about what the symbols mean, right now, just concentrate on the form.

Solution We see that we're adding four terms and they can be identified by their relative position. For example the *second term* is $f(t_2)\Delta t_2$, the fourth term is $f(t_4)\Delta t_4$. If we denote the first term by the symbol a_1, the second term by the symbol a_2, etc. then we see that

$$f(t_1)\Delta t_1 + f(t_2)\Delta t_2 + f(t_3)\Delta t_3 + f(t_4)\Delta t_4 = a_1 + a_2 + a_3 + a_4,$$

$$= \sum_{i=1}^{4} a_i,$$

$$= \sum_{i=1}^{4} f(t_i)\Delta t_i,$$

because the term in the ith position is $f(t_i)\Delta t_i$, that's all.

Occasionally, we use the summation convention to define functions too. Maybe the function is a sum of a finite number of other, simpler looking functions, (we call this sum a **finite series**) or it may be the sum of an infinite number of different functions (and we then call this sum an **infinite series**).

Example 286. A function ζ_n (read this as 'zeta sub n'; zeta is the Greek letter for our 'z') is defined by the sum

$$\zeta_n(s) = \sum_{i=1}^{n} \frac{1}{i^s}$$

$$= 1 + \frac{1}{2^s} + \frac{1}{3^s} + ... + \frac{1}{n^s},$$

where s is a variable (usually a **complex number**, like $\sqrt{-1}$). It can be shown that, if we take the limit as $n \to \infty$, then the resulting so-called **infinite series** is called **Riemann's Zeta Function**, denoted by $\zeta(s)$, and it is associated with a very old unsolved problem in mathematics called the **Riemann Hypothesis**. This old question asks for the location of all the zeros (see Chapter 5) of this function, whether they be real or complex numbers. Over 100 years ago, Bernhard Riemann

The story goes ... When the famous mathematician **C.F. Gauss**, 1777 - 1855, was ten years young he was asked to add the first one hundred numbers (because he was apparently bored in his mathematics class?). So, he was asked to find the sum $1 + 2 + 3 + ... + 100$, or, using our shorthand notation,

$$\sum_{i=1}^{100} i.$$

Within minutes, it is said, he came up with the answer, ... 5050. How did he do it? Here's the idea ... Let's say you want to add the first 5 numbers (using his method). Write $S = 1 + 2 + 3 + 4 + 5$. Now write S again but the other way around, that is, $S = 5 + 4 + 3 + 2 + 1$. Add these two equalities together ... Then $2S = (1 + 5) + (2 + 4) + (3 + 3) + (4 + 2) + (5 + 1)$. But this gives $2S = 6+6+6+6+6$ and there are as many 6's as there are numbers in the original sum, right? That is, there are 5 of these 6's. So, $2S = 5 \cdot 6 = 30$ and then $S = \frac{5 \cdot 6}{2}$. See if you can do this in general, like Gauss did.

Figure 131.

Let a_i, b_i be any two finite sequences of numbers. Then,

$$(I) \quad \sum_{i=m}^{n} (a_i + b_i) = \sum_{i=m}^{n} a_i + \sum_{i=m}^{n} b_i$$

$$(II) \quad \sum_{i=m}^{n} (a_i - b_i) = \sum_{i=m}^{n} a_i - \sum_{i=m}^{n} b_i$$

If c is any quantity not depending on the index i, then

$$(III) \quad \sum_{i=m}^{n} c \cdot a_i = c \cdot \sum_{i=m}^{n} a_i.$$

Table 6.8: Properties of the Summation Operator

conjectured that *all* the zeros must look like $\frac{1}{2} + \beta\sqrt{-1}$, where β is some real number. So far, no one has been able to prove or disprove this result ... It's one of those unsolved mysteries whose answer would impact on many areas within mathematics.

Anyhow, let's look at the quantity

$$
\begin{aligned}
\zeta_{10}(2) &= \sum_{i=1}^{10} \frac{1}{i^2} \\
&= 1 + \frac{1}{2^2} + \frac{1}{3^2} + ... + \frac{1}{10^2} \\
&= 1 + \frac{1}{4} + \frac{1}{9} + ... + \frac{1}{100} \\
&= 1.54977, \quad approximately.
\end{aligned}
$$

Now, the larger we take n the closer we get to $\zeta(2)$, see Figure 132. We can use the Theory of Fourier Series (mentioned above) and show that $\zeta(2) = \frac{\pi^2}{6}$, an amazing result, considering we have to 'add infinitely many terms' to get this!

Since 'sums' consist of sums (or differences) of numbers, we can permute them (move them around) and not change their values, right? So, we would expect the results in Table 6.8 to hold. We can refer to the Greek letter, Σ as a **summation operator**, much like the symbol D is referred to a *differential operator* in Chapter 3. Furthermore, you don't always *have* to start with $i = 1$, you can start with any other number, too, for example $i = m$, where $m \geq 2$.

Approximating the value of $\zeta(2) = \frac{\pi^2}{6} \approx 1.644934068$ using a finite sum (or finite series) consisting of 1 term, 5 terms, 10 terms, 100 terms, etc.

n	$\zeta_n(2)$
1	1.0
5	1.463611
10	1.549768
100	1.634984
1000	1.643935
10000	1.644834
100000	1.644924
...	...

Figure 132.

Example 287. Show that Table 6.8 (III) holds whenever c is any quantity not depending on the index i.

Solution The point is that c can be factored out of the whole expression. Now, by definition,

$$
\begin{aligned}
\sum_{i=m}^{n} c \cdot a_i &= c \cdot a_m + c \cdot a_{m+1} + c \cdot a_{m+2} + ... + c \cdot a_n, \\
&= c \cdot (a_m + a_{m+1} + a_{m+2} + ... + a_n),
\end{aligned}
$$

$$= c \cdot \sum_{i=m}^{n} a_i.$$

Example 288. Find an approximate value of

$$\sum_{k=2}^{5} \frac{(-1)^k}{k^2}.$$

Solution Refer to Table 6.8. Watch out, but $m = 2$ here, right ? And we have replaced the symbol i by a new symbol, k. This is OK. By definition, we are looking for the value of a sum of numbers given by

$$\sum_{k=2}^{5} \frac{(-1)^k}{k^2} = \frac{(-1)^2}{2^2} + \frac{(-1)^3}{3^2} + \frac{(-1)^4}{4^2} + \frac{(-1)^5}{5^2},$$

$$= \frac{1}{2^2} - \frac{1}{3^2} + \frac{1}{4^2} - \frac{1}{5^2},$$

$$= \frac{1}{4} - \frac{1}{9} + \frac{1}{16} - \frac{1}{25},$$

$$= 0.161389, \ approx.$$

NOTE: You can't factor out the $(-1)^k$ term out of the original expression because it is raised to a power which depends on the index, k. However, since $(-1)^k = (-1) \cdot (-1)^{k-1}$, we can write (using Table 6.8, (III), with $c = -1$),

$$\sum_{k=m}^{n} \frac{(-1)^k}{k^2} = (-1) \cdot \sum_{k=m}^{n} \frac{(-1)^{k-1}}{k^2}$$

because now, the extra (-1) does not involve k. More results on Bernoulli numbers may be found in books on **Number Theory**, see also Figure 133. In fact, the main result in Figure 130 involves Bernoulli numbers too! The exact formula for the sum of the kth powers of the first n integers is also known and involves Bernoulli numbers.

Finally, we note that, as a consequence of Table 6.8, (III), if $n \geq m$, then we must have

$$\boxed{\sum_{k=m}^{n} c = c \cdot (n - m + 1),}$$

because there are $n - m + 1$ symbols 'c' appearing on the right.

Exercise Set 31.

Write the following sums in terms of the summation operator, Σ, and some index, i.

Approximating the value of $\zeta(3) \approx 1.202056903$ using a finite sum (or finite series) consisting of 1 term, 5 terms, 10 terms, 100 terms, etc. There is **no known 'nice' explicit formula for the values of $\zeta(odd\ number)$**, compare this with Example 286. On the other hand, there *is* an explicit formula for $\zeta(even\ number)$ which involves mysterious numbers called **Bernoulli numbers**.

n	$\zeta(3)$
1	1.0
5	1.185662
10	1.197532
100	1.202007
1000	1.202056
...	...

Indeed, if we denote the $2n^{th}$ Bernoulli number by B_{2n}, then the value of the zeta function evaluated at an even number, $2n$, is given by

$$\zeta(2n) = \frac{(2\pi)^{2n} |B_{2n}|}{2(2n)!}$$

Figure 133.

1. $1 + 2 + 3 + 4 + 5 + 6 + 7 + 8 + 9 + 10$

2. $1 - 1 + 1 - 1 + 1 - 1 + 1 - 1 + 1$

3. $\sin \pi + \sin 2\pi + \sin 3\pi + \sin 4\pi + \sin 5\pi$

4. $\dfrac{1}{n} + \dfrac{2}{n} + \dfrac{3}{n} + \dfrac{4}{n} + ... + \dfrac{n}{n}$

Expand and find the value of each of the following sums (using a calculator, if you wish).

5. $\displaystyle\sum_{k=1}^{5} \dfrac{(-1)^k}{k^2}$

6. $\displaystyle\sum_{k=2}^{6} \dfrac{1}{k^3}$

7. $p(x) = \displaystyle\sum_{k=1}^{3} \dfrac{\sin(k\pi x)}{k^2}$, at $x = 1$

8. $\displaystyle\sum_{i=1}^{50} i$

   • See Figure 131.

9. $\displaystyle\sum_{i=1}^{100} i^2$

   • See Figure 130.

10. $\displaystyle\sum_{i=1}^{n} \dfrac{i}{n}$

    • See the method outlined in Figure 131, and factor out the $\frac{1}{n}$ term because it doesn't depend on the index i.

11. $\displaystyle\sum_{i=1}^{n} 6 \left(\dfrac{i}{n}\right)^2$

    • See Figure 130.

12. Show that $\displaystyle\sum_{i=1}^{6} (a_i - a_{i-1}) = a_6 - a_0$ for any 7 numbers, $\{a_0, a_1, a_2, a_3, ..., a_6\}$.

13. Use the idea in the previous Exercise to conclude that

$$\sum_{i=1}^{n} (a_i - a_{i-1}) = a_n - a_0,$$

for any finite sequence of numbers $\{a_i\}$. This is called a **telescoping sum**.

14. Use Figure 130 and your knowledge of limits to show that

$$\lim_{n \to \infty} \sum_{i=1}^{n} \dfrac{1}{n} \left(\dfrac{i}{n}\right)^2 = \dfrac{1}{3}.$$

15. This problem is **Really, really, hard**, but not impossible! A **prime number** is a positive integer whose only proper divisors are 1 and itself. For example, 2, 3, 5, 11, are primes while $4, 8, 9$ are not primes. It was proved by **Euclid of Alexandria** over 2000 years ago, that there is an infinite number of such primes. Let's label them by $\{p_1, p_2, p_3, ...\}$ where, for the purpose of this Exercise, we

take it that $p_1 = 1, p_2 = 2, p_3 = 3, p_4 = 5, p_5 = 7, p_6 = 11, p_7 = 13, p_8 = 17,$ *etc.*
Show that

$$\lim_{n \to \infty} \sum_{i=0}^{n-1} \frac{n^3}{n^4 + in^3 + p_n} = \ln 2.$$

Hint: Use the fact the nth-prime can be estimated by $p_n < 36n \ln n$, for every $n \geq 2$. This estimate on the nth-prime number is called **Sierpinski's Estimate**. Then see Example 298 in the next section.

NOTES:

6.4 Area and the Riemann Integral

In this section we produce the construction of the so-called **Riemann Integral** developed by Gauss' own *protégé*, G. F. Bernhard Riemann, 1826-1866, over 100 years ago. When this integral is combined with our own definition of the 'definite integral' we'll be able to calculate areas under curves, areas between curves, and even areas of arbitrary closed regions, etc. This will identify the antiderivative and the subsequent definite integral with the notion of area, thus giving to the definite integral this powerful geometric interpretation.

Let $[a, b]$ be a closed interval of real numbers i.e., $[a, b] = \{x : a \leq x \leq b\}$. By a **partition $\mathcal{P}$ of $[a, b]$** we mean a subdivision (or splitting, or breaking up) of the interval by a finite number of points $a = x_0, x_1, x_2, ..., x_{n-1}, x_n = b$, into a finite number of smaller intervals, where these points are arranged in ascending order as

$$a = x_0 < x_1 < x_2 < ... < x_{n-1} < x_n = b. \tag{6.11}$$

Example 289. For example, the points $a = 3 < 3.1 < 3.2 < 3.3 < 4.0 < 4.2 < b = 5$ define a partition of the closed interval $[3, 5]$ where the points are given by $x_0 = 3, x_1 = 3.1, x_2 = 3.2, x_3 = 3.3, x_4 = 4.0, x_5 = 4.2$ and $x_6 = 5$. Note that these points **do not have to be equally spaced** along the interval $[3, 5]$.

Example 290. Another example of a partition is given by selecting any finite sequence of numbers in the interval $[0, 1]$, say. Let's choose

$$a = x_0 = 0,$$
$$x_1 = \frac{1}{19}, \quad x_2 = \frac{1}{17},$$
$$x_3 = \frac{1}{13}, \quad x_4 = \frac{1}{11},$$
$$x_5 = \frac{1}{7}, \quad x_6 = \frac{1}{5},$$
$$x_7 = \frac{1}{3}, \quad x_8 = \frac{1}{2},$$
$$x_9 = b = 1.$$

Can you guess where these numbers come from? Well, this is a partition of the interval $[0, 1]$ into 9 subintervals and the partition consists of 10 points (because we include the end-points).

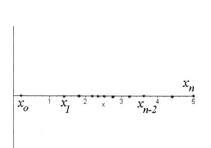

A typical partition of the interval $[0.2, 5]$ by $(n+1)$ points, $0.2 = x_0 < x_1 < ... < x_n = 5$.

Figure 134.

Now you can see that **any** partition of $[a, b]$ breaks up the interval into a finite number of subintervals so that $[a, b]$ is the union of all these subintervals $[a, x_1]$, $[x_1, x_2]$, $[x_2, x_3]$,..., $[x_{n-1}, b]$, right? O.K., now the **length** of each subinterval of the form $[x_i, x_{i+1}]$ is, of course, equal to $x_{i+1} - x_i$. We use the notation "Δx_i" (read this symbol Δx_i, as "**delta-x-eye**") to represent this length, so, for any subscript i, $i = 0, 1, 2, 3, ..., n-1$,

$$\Delta x_i = x_{i+1} - x_i. \tag{6.12}$$

The symbol, Δ, just defined is also called a **forward difference operator**, and it is used extensively in applications of Calculus in order to estimate the size of a derivative, when we're not given the actual function, but we just have some of its values. For the partition in Example 289, $\Delta x_0 = x_1 - x_0 = 3.1 - 3 = 0.1$, $\Delta x_1 = x_2 - x_1 = 3.2 - 3.1 = 0.1$, $\Delta x_4 = x_5 - x_4 = 4.2 - 4.0 = 0.2$, etc.

Finally, for a **given** partition $\mathcal{P}$ of an interval $[a, b]$ we define its **norm** by the symbol $|\mathcal{P}|$, to be the **length of the largest subinterval making it up.** The norm of a partition is used to measure the *size* or *fineness* of a partition.

> **Example 291.** For example, the norm of our partition $\mathcal{P}$, in Example 289, is

by definition, the length of the largest subinterval, which, in this case, is the largest of all the numbers

$$
\begin{aligned}
\Delta x_0 &= 0.1, \\
\Delta x_1 &= 0.1, \\
\Delta x_2 &= 0.1, \\
\Delta x_3 &= 0.7, \\
\Delta x_4 &= 0.2, \\
\Delta x_5 &= 0.8, \quad \longleftarrow \text{largest length!}
\end{aligned}
$$

which, of course, is 0.8. So $|\mathcal{P}| = 0.8$, by definition.

> **Example 292.** We let $I = [0, 1]$ and define $\mathcal{P}$ to be the partition defined by the

subintervals $[0, 1/5], [1/5, 1/3], [1/3, 1/2], [1/2, 7/8], [7/8, 1]$. Then the norm, $|\mathcal{P}|$, of this partition is equal to $7/8 - 1/2 = 3/8 = 0.375$, which is the length of the largest subinterval contained within $\mathcal{P}$.

Now, let f be some function with domain, $Dom(f) = [a, b]$. For a given partition $\mathcal{P}$ of an interval $[a, b]$, we define a quantity of the form

$$
\sum_{i=0}^{n-1} f(t_i)\Delta x_i = f(t_0)\,(x_1 - x_0) + f(t_1)\,(x_2 - x_1) + \ldots + f(t_{n-1})\,(x_n - x_{n-1}). \quad (6.13)
$$

where t_i is some number between x_i and x_{i+1}. This quantity is called a **Riemann sum** (pronounced **Ree-man**), and it is used in order to approximate the 'area under the curve $y = f(x)$' between the lines $x = a$ and $x = b$, see Figures 134, 135, 136, 137.

Now, we define another type of limit. The string of symbols

$$
\lim_{|\mathcal{P}| \to 0} \sum_{i=0}^{n-1} f(t_i)\Delta x_i = L \quad (6.14)
$$

means the following: Let's say we are given some small number $\varepsilon > 0$, (called 'epsilon'), and we have this guess, L, and for a given partition, $\mathcal{P}$, we can make

$$
\left| \sum_{i=0}^{n-1} f(t_i)\,\Delta x_i - L \right| < \varepsilon. \quad (6.15)
$$

but **only if** our partition is 'small enough', that is, if $|\mathcal{P}| < \delta$, where the choice of this new number δ will depend on the original ε.

If we can do this calculation (6.15) for **every possible $\varepsilon > 0$**, provided the partition is small enough, then we say that **limit of the Riemann sum as the norm of the partition $\mathcal{P}$ approaches 0 is L**. These ideas involving these curious numbers ε, δ are akin to those presented in an optional chapter on rigorous methods. The limit definition included here is for completeness, and not intended to cause any stress.

Generally speaking, this inequality (6.15) depends upon the function f, the partition, $\mathcal{P}$, and the actual points t_i chosen from the partition, in the sense that if we change any one of these quantities, then we expect the value of L to change too, right? This is natural. But now comes the definition of the **Riemann Integral**.

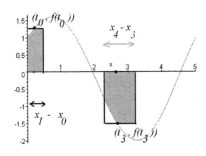

The area of the rectangle with base-length $x_1 - x_0$ and height $f(t_0)$ approximates the actual shaded area 'under the graph' on the interval $[x_0, x_1]$. The same thing can be said for the rectangle $x_4 - x_3$ and height $f(t_3)$.

Figure 135.

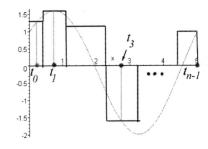

A typical Riemann sum consists of the sum of the areas of each rectangle in the figure, with due regard taken for rectangles which lie below the x-axis. For such rectangles, the area is interpreted as being **negative**. Note that in this Figure, the point $t_{n-1} = x_n = 5$, is the endpoint of the interval. This is OK.

Figure 136.

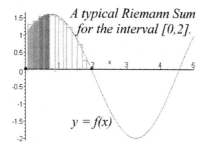

A typical Riemann Sum for the interval [0,2].

$y = f(x)$

This Riemann sum shows that the smaller the rectangles, (or the closer together the x_i), the better is this sum's approximation to the area 'under the curve'. Remember that if the curve is below the x−axis, its area is negative in that portion.

Figure 137.

Let's assume that f is a function defined on $[a, b]$ with the property that the limit, L, in (6.14) exists and the number L so obtained is **independent** of the choice of the partition (so long as its norm approaches zero), and L is also independent of the choice of the interior points, t_i, ... In this case, we say that f is **Riemann Integrable** over the interval $[a, b]$ and L is the **value of the Riemann Integral of f over $[a, b]$**. We will denote this value of L by the quick and descriptive notation,

$$L = \mathcal{R} \int_a^b f(x)\ dx = \lim_{|\mathcal{P}| \to 0} \sum_{i=0}^{n-1} f(t_i) \Delta x_i$$

where the symbols on the right make up what we'll call the Riemann integral, or equivalently, the **$\mathcal{R}$-integral** of f over $[a, b]$.

Seems hard to believe that this integral will exist at all, right? Well, lucky for us this Riemann integral does exist when f is continuous over $[a, b]$ and even if f is continuous over a finite number of pieces whose union is the whole of the interval $[a, b]$, see Figure 138. We then call f **piecewise continuous**.

At this point in the discussion we will relate the definite integral of a function (assumed to have an antiderivative) with its Riemann integral (assumed to exist). We will then be in a position to define the area under the graph of a given continuous or piecewise continuous function and so we will have related the definite integral with the notion of 'area', its principal geometric interpretation. Thus, the concepts of a derivative and an antiderivative will each have a suitable and wonderful geometric interpretation.

In order to arrive at this geometric result, we'll make use of the **Mean Value Theorem** which we will recall here (see Chapter 3). If f is continuous on $[a, b]$ and differentiable on (a, b), then there is at least one c between a and b at which

$$\frac{f(b) - f(a)}{b - a} = f'(c).$$

Let $\mathcal{P}$ denote an arbitrary partition of the interval $[a, b]$, so that (6.11) holds. Let $\mathcal{F}$ denote an antiderivative of f. Note that for any increasing sequence of points $x_0 = a, x_1, x_2, \ldots, x_{n-1}, x_n = b$, in $[a, b]$ we have,

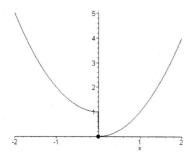

The graph of a piecewise continuous function. Note that the function is continuous at every point except at a finite number of points where its graph makes a 'jump!' In this case, its only jump is at $x = 0$.

Figure 138.

$$
\begin{aligned}
\mathcal{F}(b) - \mathcal{F}(a) &= \mathcal{F}(x_n) - \mathcal{F}(x_0) \\
&= \mathcal{F}(x_n) - \mathcal{F}(x_{n-1}) + \mathcal{F}(x_{n-1}) - \mathcal{F}(x_{n-2}) + \ldots \\
&\quad + \mathcal{F}(x_2) - \mathcal{F}(x_1) + \mathcal{F}(x_1) - \mathcal{F}(x_0) \\
&= \left(\frac{\mathcal{F}(x_n) - \mathcal{F}(x_{n-1})}{x_n - x_{n-1}} \right)(x_n - x_{n-1}) \\
&\quad + \left(\frac{\mathcal{F}(x_{n-1}) - \mathcal{F}(x_{n-2})}{x_{n-1} - x_{n-2}} \right)(x_{n-1} - x_{n-2}) + \ldots \\
&\quad + \left(\frac{\mathcal{F}(x_1) - \mathcal{F}(x_0)}{x_1 - x_0} \right)(x_1 - x_0).
\end{aligned}
$$

Now, we apply the Mean Value Theorem to $\mathcal{F}$ over each interval of the form $[x_i, x_{i+1}]$,

For $f(x) \geq 0$,

$$\text{Area under } f \text{ between the two lines at } a \text{ and } b \ = \ \int_a^b f(x) \, dx,$$
$$= \ \mathcal{F}(b) - \mathcal{F}(a),$$
$$= \ \mathcal{F}(x) \big|_a^b .$$

Table 6.9: The Area Formula for a Positive Integrable Function

$(i = 0, 1, 2, ..., n - 1)$ to find that,

$$\frac{\mathcal{F}(x_{i+1}) - \mathcal{F}(x_i)}{x_{i+1} - x_i} \ = \ \mathcal{F}'(c_i) \text{ where } c_i \text{ is in } (x_i, x_{i+1})$$
$$= \ f(c_i) \quad (\text{because } \mathcal{F}' = f),$$

where the existence of the $c_i's$ is guaranteed by the Mean Value Theorem. Note that these depend on the initial partition (or on the choice of the points $x_0, x_1, \ldots, x_n$). So, we just keep doing this construction every time, for every interval of the form (x_i, x_{i+1}), $i = 0, 1, ..., n - 1$, until we've found the particular string of numbers, $c_0, c_1, ..., c_{n-2}, c_{n-1}$, and we'll see that

$$\mathcal{F}(b) - \mathcal{F}(a) \ = \ \sum_{i=0}^{n-1} \frac{\mathcal{F}(x_{i+1}) - \mathcal{F}(x_i)}{x_{i+1} - x_i} \Delta x_i,$$
$$= \ \sum_{i=0}^{n-1} \mathcal{F}'(c_i) \Delta x_i,$$
$$= \ \sum_{i=0}^{n-1} f(c_i) \Delta x_i.$$

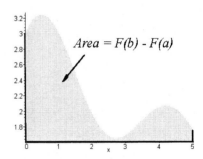

The shaded area under the graph of this positive function is given by its definite integral from $x = 0$ to $x = 5$, that is,

$$Area = \int_0^5 f(x) \, dx$$

Figure 139.

Now, the left-hand side, namely the number $\mathcal{F}(b) - \mathcal{F}(a)$, is just a constant, right? But the sum on the right is a Riemann sum for the given partition, and the given partition is *arbitrary*. So, we can make it as fine as we like by choosing $|\mathcal{P}|$ as small as we want, and then finding the $c_i's$. Then we can pass to the limit as $|\mathcal{P}| \to 0$ and find (since f is continuous and its Riemann integral exists),

$$\mathcal{F}(b) - \mathcal{F}(a) \ = \ \lim_{|\mathcal{P}| \to 0} \sum_{i=0}^{n-1} f(c_i) \Delta x_i,$$
$$= \ \mathcal{R} \int_a^b f(x) \, dx, \quad (\text{by definition of the } \mathcal{R}-\text{integral}),$$
$$= \ \int_a^b f(x) \, dx \quad (\text{by definition of the definite integral}).$$

So, we have just shown that the $\mathcal{R}-$integral and the definite integral coincide. This means that we can use antiderivatives to evaluate Riemann integrals! Okay, but because of the nice geometric interpretation of the Riemann integral as some sort of area (see Figure 137), we can use this notion to **define the area under a curve whose equation is given by $y = f(x) \geq 0$ and between the vertical lines $x = a, x = b$ and the $x-$axis**, by Table 6.9 if, say, f is continuous (or even piecewise continuous) on $[a, b]$.

Recall that we had already done area calculations earlier, in the section on *Definite integrals*. The results from Table 6.9 and the $\mathcal{R}$−integral above justify what we were doing then, (see Figure 139).

Let's recap. (... contraction of the word *recapitulate*). If f has an antiderivative $\mathcal{F}$ over $[a, b]$, then for x in (a, b), we will have

$$
\begin{aligned}
\frac{d}{dx} \int_a^x f(t)\, dt &= \frac{d}{dx}\left(\mathcal{F}(x) - \mathcal{F}(a)\right), \\
&= \mathcal{F}'(x) - 0, \quad \text{(since } \mathcal{F}(a) \text{ is a constant)}, \\
&= f(x), \quad \text{(by definition of the antiderivative)}.
\end{aligned}
$$

This means that we can consider an indefinite integral as a function in its own right, a function defined on the *same* domain as the original integrand from where it was defined. Now, let f be a continuous function over $[a, b]$ and differentiable over (a, b). Let's also assume that this derivative function is itself continuous over $[a, b]$. Then the function f is an antiderivative of the function f', right? But this means that we can set $\mathcal{F} = f$ in the expression for the definite integral of f', and find,

$$
\begin{aligned}
\int_a^b f'(x)\, dx &= \mathcal{F}(b) - \mathcal{F}(a), \\
&= f(b) - f(a), \quad \text{(since } f = \mathcal{F} \text{ here)}.
\end{aligned}
$$

This is one of the many versions of the **Fundamental Theorem of Calculus**. Summarizing all this we get,

---

The Fundamental Theorem of Calculus

If f' is continuous over $[a, b]$, then

$$
\int_a^b f'(x)\, dx = f(b) - f(a),
$$

while if f is continuous over $[a, b]$, then

$$
\frac{d}{dx} \int_a^x f(t)\, dt = f(x).
$$

One of the important consequences of the Fundamental Theorem of Calculus is **Leibniz's Rule** which is used for differentiating an integral with variable limits of integration. For example, if we assume that a, b are differentiable functions whose ranges are contained within the domain of f, then we can believe the next formula, namely that

$$
\int_{a(x)}^{b(x)} f(t)\, dt = \mathcal{F}(b(x)) - \mathcal{F}(a(x)),
$$

and from this formula, if we differentiate both sides and use the Chain Rule on the right, we find

The notion of **area** as introduced here is only ONE possible definition of this concept. It is the most natural at this point in your studies in mathematics. This *area* topic has been defined by mathematicians for functions which do not have the property of continuity stated here. Words like **Lebesgue measure, Jordan content** are more general in their description of area for much wider classes of functions. The interested reader may consult any book on **Real Analysis** for further details.

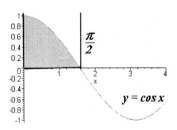

The area of the shaded region under the graph of the cosine function is given by its definite integral from $x = 0$ to $x = \frac{\pi}{2}$, that is,

$$
\text{Shaded Area} = \int_0^{\frac{\pi}{2}} \cos x\, dx
$$

Figure 140.

$$\frac{d}{dx} \int_{a(x)}^{b(x)} f(t) \ dt = f(b(x))\frac{db}{dx} - f(a(x))\frac{da}{dx}.$$

Table 6.10: Leibniz's Rule for Differentiating a Definite Integral

$$\begin{aligned}
\frac{d}{dx} \int_{a(x)}^{b(x)} f(t) \ dt &= \frac{d}{dx}(\mathcal{F}(b(x)) - \mathcal{F}(a(x))), \\
&= \mathcal{F}'(b(x))b'(x) - \mathcal{F}'(a(x))a'(x), \\
&= f(b(x))\frac{db}{dx} - f(a(x))\frac{da}{dx},
\end{aligned}$$

which is Leibniz's Rule, see Table 6.10.

Example 293. Show that the area under the curve defined by $f(x) = \cos x$ on the interval $[0, \pi/2]$ is given by the definite integral (see Figure 140),

EXAMPLES

$$\int_0^{\frac{\pi}{2}} \cos x \ dx = 1,$$

Solution First we must check that the given function is positive on the given interval. But this is true by trigonometry, right? (or you can see this from its graph too, Figure 140). Now, we see that the area *under the curve* defined by $f(x) = \cos x$ on the interval $[0, \pi/2]$ is (by definition) the same as the area of the region bounded by the vertical lines $x = 0$, $x = \frac{\pi}{2}$, the x−axis, and the curve $y = \cos x$. Using Table 6.9, we see that the required area is given by

$$\begin{aligned}
\int_0^{\frac{\pi}{2}} \cos x \ dx &= \sin x \Big|_0^{\pi/2}, \\
&= \sin \frac{\pi}{2} - \sin 0 = 1.
\end{aligned}$$

In the next example we'll explore what happens if the region whose area we want to find lies above and below the x−axis.

Example 294. Evaluate $\int_0^6 (\sin(x\sqrt{2}) + \cos x) \ dx$, and interpret your result geometrically.

Solution The integration is straightforward using the techniques of the previous sections. Thus,

$$\int_0^6 (\sin(x\sqrt{2}) + \cos x) \ dx = \int_0^6 \sin(x\sqrt{2}) \ dx + \int_0^6 \cos x \ dx.$$

In order to evaluate the first of these integrals, we use the fact that if $\square = x\sqrt{2}$, then $\square'(x) = \sqrt{2}$, and so

$$
\begin{aligned}
\int \sin(x\sqrt{2})\, dx &= \int \sin(\square)\frac{d\square}{dx}\frac{1}{\sqrt{2}}\, dx, \\
&= \frac{1}{\sqrt{2}}\int \sin(\square)\frac{d\square}{dx}\, dx, \\
&= \frac{1}{\sqrt{2}}(-\cos\square) + C, \quad \text{(by Table 6.6)}, \\
&= -\frac{1}{\sqrt{2}}\cos(x\sqrt{2}) + C, \\
&= -\frac{\cos(x\sqrt{2})}{\sqrt{2}} + C.
\end{aligned}
$$

So, [remember to switch to radian mode on your calculator], we find

$$
\begin{aligned}
\int_0^6 \sin(x\sqrt{2})\, dx + \int_0^6 \cos x\, dx &= \left(-\frac{\cos(x\sqrt{2})}{\sqrt{2}} + \sin x\right)\Bigg|_0^6, \\
&= \left(-\frac{\cos(6\sqrt{2})}{\sqrt{2}} + \sin 6\right) - \left(-\frac{1}{\sqrt{2}} + \sin 0\right), \\
&= \frac{1 - \cos(6\sqrt{2})}{\sqrt{2}} + \sin 6, \\
&= .84502.
\end{aligned}
$$

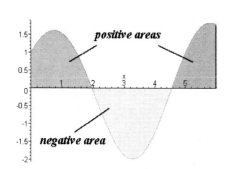

positive areas

negative area

The value of the definite integral is the sum of the areas of the three shaded regions above, where the region under the $x-$axis is taken to have a negative area. Even though we don't know the area of each region individually, we can still find their area sum, which is the number 0.84502.

Figure 141.

For a geometric interpretation see the graph of the integrand in Figure 141. Notice that if we had found the zeros of this function (using *Newton's method*, Chapter 3) then we could have obtained the areas of *each one* of the shaded regions in Figure 141 by integrating over each interval separately. But we don't have to find these zeros to get the answer!

Example 295. Evaluate $\dfrac{d}{dx}\displaystyle\int_a^x e^{-t^2}\, dt.$

Solution We set $f(t) = e^{-t^2}$ in the Fundamental Theorem of Calculus (FTC). Then,

$$
\begin{aligned}
\frac{d}{dx}\int_a^x f(t)\, dt &= f(x), \\
&= e^{-x^2}.
\end{aligned}
$$

Amazingly enough, we don't have to compute the antiderivative first and *then* find the derivative, as this would be almost impossible for this type of exponential function. This, so-called, **Gaussian function** is a common occurrence in **Probability Theory** and, although it *does* have an antiderivative, we can't write it down with a finite number of symbols (this is a known fact). Reams of reference tables abound where the definite integral of this function is calculated numerically using sophisticated methods (such as one called **Simpson's Rule**) a few of which we'll see later.

Example 296. Evaluate $\dfrac{d}{dx}\displaystyle\int_{-x^2+1}^4 \cos(t^2 \ln t)\, dt.$

Solution Because of the variable limit $-x^2 + 1$, we think about using Leibniz's Rule, Table 6.10, on the *function* defined by the definite integral. Next, we set $f(t) = \cos(t^2 \ln t)$, $a(x) = -x^2 + 1$, $b(x) = 4$ into the expression for the Rule. Then,

$a'(x) = -2x$, $b'(x) = 0$ and so,

$$\frac{d}{dx} \int_{-x^2+1}^{4} \cos(t^2 \ln t) \, dt \;=\; \frac{d}{dx} \int_{a(x)}^{b(x)} f(t) \, dt,$$
$$=\; f(b(x))\frac{db}{dx} - f(a(x))\frac{da}{dx},$$
$$=\; f(4)(0) - f(-x^2 + 1)(-2x),$$
$$=\; 2x \cos\left((-x^2 + 1)^2 \ln(-x^2 + 1)\right),$$

where we could have used the 'Box' method of Chapter 1 to evaluate $f(-x^2 + 1)$ explicitly.

Example 297. Evaluate

$$\frac{d}{dx} \int_{x^2}^{\sin x} 3t^2 \, dt$$

in *two* different ways, first by integrating and then finding the derivative, and secondly by using Leibniz's Rule. Compare your answers.

Solution First, an antiderivative of the integrand $3t^2$ is easily seen to be $\mathcal{F}(t) = t^3$. Thus,

$$\int_{x^2}^{\sin x} 3t^2 \, dt \;=\; \mathcal{F}(\sin x) - \mathcal{F}(x^2),$$
$$=\; (\sin x)^3 - (x^2)^3,$$
$$=\; \sin^3 x - x^6.$$

So,

$$\frac{d}{dx} \int_{x^2}^{\sin x} 3t^2 \, dt \;=\; \frac{d}{dx}\left(\sin^3 x - x^6\right),$$
$$=\; 3\left(\sin x\right)^2 \cos x - 6(x^5),$$
$$=\; 3 \sin^2 x \cos x - 6x^5.$$

Next, we use Leibniz's Rule, as in Table 6.10. We set $f(t) = 3t^2$, $a(x) = x^2$, and $b(x) = \sin x$, to find $a'(x) = 2x$, $b'(x) = \cos x$. So,

$$\frac{d}{dx} \int_{x^2}^{\sin x} 3t^2 \, dt \;=\; f(\sin x) \cos x - f(x^2)2x,$$
$$=\; 3(\sin x)^2 \cos x - (3x^4)(2x),$$
$$=\; 3 \sin^2 x \cos x - 6x^5.$$

We get the same answer, as expected (but Leibniz's Rule is definitely less tedious!).

The next example shows another powerful application of the Riemann integral. It will be used to find a very difficult looking limit!

Example 298. Show that

$$\lim_{n \to +\infty} \sum_{i=0}^{n-1} \frac{1}{n + i} = \ln 2.$$

Solution This is not obvious! First we check the numerical evidence supporting this claim, For example, let's note that $\boxed{\ln 2 \approx 0.693147}$ to 7 significant digits.

For $n = 100$,

$$\sum_{i=0}^{99} \frac{1}{100+i} = \frac{1}{100} + \frac{1}{101} + \frac{1}{102} + ... + \frac{1}{199},$$

$$\approx \boxed{0.69565}.$$

0   0.1   0.2   0.3   0.4   0.5   0.6   0.7   0.8   0.9   1

This figure shows a regular partition, $\mathcal{P}$, of the interval $[0,1]$ into $n = 10$ pieces where the x_i's are numbered. Each subinterval has length 0.1 or, equivalently, the distance between successive points $x_i = i/n = i/10$, where $i = 0, 1, 2, ..., 10$, is 0.1. As the integer $n \to +\infty$ the partition gets smaller and smaller, and its norm (*i.e.*, the length of the largest subinterval), approaches zero. The converse is also true, that is if the norm of the partition approaches zero, then $n \to \infty$, too. In this way we can use definite integrals to approximate or even evaluate complicated looking sums inlvolving limits at infinity.

Figure 142.

For $n = 10,000$,

$$\sum_{i=0}^{9999} \frac{1}{10000+i} = \frac{1}{10000} + \frac{1}{10001} + \frac{1}{10002} + ... + \frac{1}{19999},$$

$$\approx \boxed{0.693172}.$$

For $n = 100,000$,

$$\sum_{i=0}^{99999} \frac{1}{100000+i} = \frac{1}{100000} + \frac{1}{100001} + \frac{1}{100002} + ... + \frac{1}{199999},$$

$$\approx \boxed{0.6931497},$$

so the result is believable. We are only off by about 0.000002 in the latest estimate of the required limit. But how do we show that this limit *must* converge to this number, $\ln 2$? The idea is that sums of this type should remind us of Riemann sums for a particular function f, a given interval, and a corresponding partition. But which ones? We make a few standard assumptions...

Let's assume that the partition is *regular*, that is all the numbers Δx_i appearing in a typical Riemann sum are *equal*! This means that the points x_i subdivide the given interval into an equal number of subintervals, right? Let's also assume that the interval is $[0,1]$. In this case we get $x_i = \frac{i}{n}$, (see Figure 142). We want to convert the original sum into a Riemann sum so we'll have to untangle and re-interpret the terms in the original sum somehow!? Note that $\Delta x_i = 1/n$. Now, here's the idea ...

$$\frac{1}{n+i} = \Delta x_i \cdot (something\ else),$$

$$= \left(\frac{1}{n}\right)\left(\frac{n}{n+i}\right),$$

$$= \left(\frac{1}{n}\right)\left(\frac{1}{1+\frac{i}{n}}\right),$$

$$= \left(\frac{1}{1+c_i}\right)\left(\frac{1}{n}\right),$$

$$= f(c_i)\Delta x_i,$$

if we define f by $f(t) = \dfrac{1}{1+t}$, and the c_i are chosen by setting $c_i = x_i = \frac{i}{n}$, for $i = 0, 1, 2, ..., n-1$.

Now, we simply take the limit as the norm (*i.e.*, the length of the largest subinterval), of our regular partition approaches zero to find,

$$\sum_{i=0}^{n-1} \frac{1}{n+i} = \sum_{i=0}^{n-1} f(c_i)\Delta x_i,$$

$$\lim_{|\mathcal{P}| \to 0} \sum_{i=0}^{n-1} \frac{1}{n+i} = \lim_{|\mathcal{P}| \to 0} \sum_{i=0}^{n-1} f(c_i) \Delta x_i,$$

$$\lim_{n \to \infty} \sum_{i=0}^{n-1} \frac{1}{n+i} = \int_0^1 \frac{1}{1+t} \, dt, \quad \text{(because } |\mathcal{P}| = 1/n \to 0 \text{ means } n \to \infty\text{)},$$

$$= \ln(1+t) \Big|_0^1, \quad \text{(see the second of Table 6.5 with } \square = 1+t\text{)},$$

$$= \ln 2 - \ln 1,$$

$$= \ln 2.$$

Example 299. Let

$$\mathcal{F}(x) = \int_0^x f(t) \, dt$$

where $f(1) = 0$ and $f'(x) > 0$ for every value of x (see the margin). Which of the following statements is true?

a) $\mathcal{F}$ is a differentiable function of x?

b) $\mathcal{F}$ is a continuous function of x?

c) The graph of $\mathcal{F}$ has a horizontal tangent at $x = 1$?

d) $\mathcal{F}$ has a local maximum at $x = 1$?

e) $\mathcal{F}$ has a local minimum at $x = 1$?

f) The graph of $\mathcal{F}$ has an inflection point at $x = 1$?

g) The graph of $\frac{d\mathcal{F}}{dx}$ crosses the x-axis at $x = 1$?

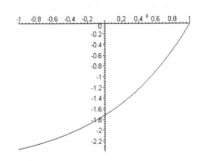

Solution a) Yes, by the FTC.

b) Yes, because $\mathcal{F}$ is differentiable by the FTC, so it must be continuous too!

c) Yes, since $\mathcal{F}$ is differentiable and $\mathcal{F}'(x) = f(x)$ by the FTC, we see that $\mathcal{F}'(1) = f(1) = 0$, by the given assumption on f. Since $\mathcal{F}'(1) = 0$ this means that the graph of $\mathcal{F}$ has a horizontal tangent at $x = 1$.

d) No, since the Second Derivative Test applied to $\mathcal{F}$ gives us $\mathcal{F}''(1) = f'(1) > 0$, by the given assumption on the derivative of f. For a local maximum at $x = 1$ we ought to have $\mathcal{F}''(1) < 0$.

e) Yes, see the reason in (d), above.

f) No, since $\mathcal{F}''(x)$ must change its sign around $x = 1$. In this case, $\mathcal{F}''(x) = f'(x) > 0$, for each x including those near $x = 1$. So, there is no change in concavity around $x = 1$ and so $x = 1$ cannot be a point of inflection.

g) Yes, since $\mathcal{F}'(1) = f(1) = 0$, and so, by definition, $\mathcal{F}'(x) = 0$ at $x = 1$ and its graph must touch the $x-$axis there. That the graph of $\mathcal{F}'$ *crosses* the $x-$axis at $x = 1$ follows since $f'(x) > 0$ for any x, and so $x = 1$ cannot be a **double root** of f. Recall that a root $x = c$ of f is called a double root of f if $f(c) = 0$ and $f'(c) = 0$.

Example 300. Evaluate $\displaystyle\int_0^{\frac{\pi}{6}} \frac{\sin 2x}{\cos^2 2x}\, dx$. Interpret your result geometrically.

Solution First we need an antiderivative $\mathcal{F}(x) = \displaystyle\int f(x)\, dx = \int \frac{\sin 2x}{\cos^2 2x}\, dx$. We really want to use one of the Tables 6.5 6.6, or 6.7. We *do* have a power here, and it's in the denominator. So, let $\square = \cos 2x$, then $\square'(x) = -2\sin 2x$ from Table 6.6. Now, an antiderivative looks like

$$
\begin{aligned}
\mathcal{F}(x) &= -\frac{1}{2}\int \frac{1}{\square^2}\frac{d\square}{dx}\, dx, \\
&= -\frac{1}{2}\int \square^{-2}\frac{d\square}{dx}\, dx, \\
&= -\frac{1}{2}\left(-\frac{1}{\square}\right) + C, \\
&= \frac{1}{2\cos 2x} + C,
\end{aligned}
$$

where we have used the first of Table 6.5 with $r = -2$ in the second equation, above. Choosing $C = 0$ as usual, we see that

$$
\begin{aligned}
\int_0^{\frac{\pi}{6}} \frac{\sin 2x}{\cos^2 2x}\, dx &= \mathcal{F}\left(\frac{\pi}{6}\right) - \mathcal{F}(0) = \mathcal{F}(x)\Big|_0^{\frac{\pi}{6}}, \\
&= \frac{1}{2\cos\frac{\pi}{3}} - \frac{1}{2\cos 0} = 1 - \frac{1}{2}, \\
&= \frac{1}{2}.
\end{aligned}
$$

We note that the integrand $f(x) \geq 0$ for $0 \leq x \leq \frac{\pi}{6}$, because the denominator is the square of something while the numerator $\sin 2x \geq 0$ on this interval. Thus, the value of $1/2$ represents the area of the closed region bounded by the curve $y = f(x)$, the x-axis, and the vertical lines $x = 0$ and $x = \pi/6$, see Figure 143.

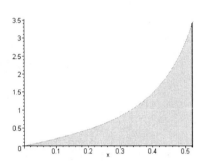

The area (equal to 1/2) under the curve $y = f(x)$, the x-axis, and the vertical lines $x = 0$ and $x = \pi/6$, is the area of the shaded region where

$$f(x) = \frac{\sin 2x}{\cos^2 2x}.$$

Figure 143.

Example 301. Given that

$$I(x) = \int_1^{x^2} \frac{1}{1 + \sqrt{1 - t}}\, dt,$$

find $I'(x)$ using any method.

Solution Integrating directly and then finding the derivative looks difficult, so we use Leibniz's Rule, Table 6.10 where we set $a(x) = 1$, $b(x) = x^2$, and

$$f(t) = \frac{1}{1 + \sqrt{1 - t}}.$$

Then,

$$
\begin{aligned}
I'(x) &= \frac{d}{dx}\int_1^{x^2} \frac{1}{1 + \sqrt{1 - t}}\, dt, \\
&= f(b(x))b'(x) - f(a(x))a'(x), \\
&= \frac{2x}{1 + \sqrt{1 - x^2}},
\end{aligned}
$$

and we didn't have to find the antiderivative first!

Example 302. Find the area under the curve $y = f(t)$ over the interval $[0, 1]$, where $f(t) = t\sqrt{1 - t^2}$.

Solution Hopefully, the given function satisfies $f(t) \geq 0$ on the given interval, otherwise we will have to draw a graph (using the methods of Chapter 5, see Figure 144). However, we see directly (without using the graph) that $f(t) \geq 0$ on the interval $0 \leq t \leq 1$. OK, now we need an antiderivative. Since we see a square root, we think of a power, and so we try to use the first of Table 6.5, with $r = 1/2$. Then with $\Box = 1 - t^2$, $\Box'(t) = -2t$, we find

$$
\begin{aligned}
\mathcal{F}(t) &= \int t\sqrt{1 - t^2} \, dt = -\frac{1}{2} \int \frac{d\Box}{dt} \Box^{\frac{1}{2}} \, dt, \\
&= -\frac{1}{3} \Box^{3/2} + C, \\
&= -\frac{1}{3}(1 - t^2)^{3/2} + C.
\end{aligned}
$$

So we can choose $C = 0$ as usual and then the required area is simply given by the definite integral in Table 6.9, or

$$
\begin{aligned}
Area &= \left. -\frac{1}{3}(1 - t^2)^{3/2} \right|_0^1, \\
&= \frac{1}{3}.
\end{aligned}
$$

Example 303. Evaluate

$$
\int_{-\frac{\pi}{4}}^{\frac{\pi}{4}} \tan^2 x \sec^2 x \, dx,
$$

and interpret your result geometrically.

Solution The given function satisfies $f(x) \geq 0$ on the given interval, because both the trigonometric terms in the integrand are 'squared'. So, the natural interpretation of our result will be as an area under the curve, etc. Now we need an antiderivative. Since we see powers, we think about using the first of Table 6.5, with $r = 2$. OK, but what is $\Box$? If we let $\Box = \tan x$, then $\Box'(x) = \sec^2 x$, (table 6.6). This is really good because now

$$
\begin{aligned}
\mathcal{F}(x) &= \int \tan^2 x \sec^2 x \, dx = \int \Box^2 \frac{d\Box}{dx} \, dx, \\
&= \frac{1}{3} \Box^3 + C, \\
&= \frac{1}{3}(\tan x)^3 + C.
\end{aligned}
$$

Choosing $C = 0$ as usual the required area is again simply given by the definite integral in Table 6.9, or (see Figure 145 for the region under consideration),

$$
\begin{aligned}
Area &= \left. \frac{1}{3}(\tan x)^3 \right|_{-\frac{\pi}{4}}^{\frac{\pi}{4}}. \\
&= \frac{2}{3}.
\end{aligned}
$$

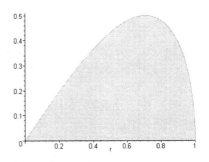

The area (equal to 1/3) under the curve $y = f(t)$, the t-axis, and the vertical lines $t = 0$ and $t = 1$, is the area of the shaded region where

$$f(t) = t\sqrt{1 - t^2}.$$

Figure 144.

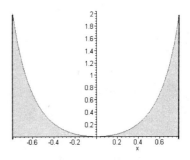

The area (equal to 2/3) under the curve $y = f(x)$, the x-axis, and the vertical lines $x = -\frac{\pi}{4}$ and $x = \frac{\pi}{4}$, is the area of the shaded region where

$$f(x) = \tan^2 x \sec^2 x.$$

In fact, since this function is an *even function*, its area is *double* the area of the single shaded region to the right or left of the y-axis.

Figure 145.

NOTES:

6.5   Chapter Exercises

Find the most general antiderivative of the following functions. Let k be real constant.

1. $(x+1)^{26}$ 6. $\sqrt{5-2x}$ 11. $\csc 3x \, \cot 3x$

2. $\cos 2x$ 7. $\sin 2x$ 12. xe^{-3x^2}

3. $\sqrt{2x+1}$ 8. $x^{1.5} - \sin(1.6x)$ 13. e^{-kx}

4. $x\sqrt{1-4x^2}$ 9. $3\sec^2 x$ 14. $\cos kx, \ \ k \neq 0$

5. $\sin x + \cos x$ 10. $x(x^2+1)^{99}$ 15. $\sin kx, \ \ k \neq 0$

Evaluate the following definite integrals using any method.

16. $\displaystyle\int_0^1 (2x+1) \, dx,$

17. $\displaystyle\int_{-1}^1 x^3 \, dx,$

18. $\displaystyle\int_0^2 (3x^2 + 2x - 1) \, dx,$

19. $\displaystyle\int_0^{\pi/2} \sin^4 x \, \cos x \, dx,$

20. $\displaystyle\int_0^1 x 3^{x^2} \, dx,$

21. $\displaystyle\int_0^1 2^{-x} \, dx,$

22. $\displaystyle\int_0^{\pi} \cos^2 x \, \sin x \, dx,$

23. $\displaystyle\int_{-2}^2 (x^2 + 1) \, dx,$

24. $\displaystyle\int_0^{0.5} \frac{1}{\sqrt{1-x^2}} \, dx,$

25. $\displaystyle\int_0^2 xe^{x^2} \, dx,$

26. Expand and find the value of the following sum, $\displaystyle\sum_{i=i}^n 12\left(\frac{i}{n}\right)^2$

27. Use the method of Example 298 to show that

$$\lim_{n\to\infty} \sum_{i=0}^{n-1} \frac{1}{n} e^{\frac{i}{n}} = e - 1.$$

- *Hint:* Let $f(x) = e^x$.

28. **Hard.** Show that

$$\lim_{n\to\infty} \left(\frac{n}{n^2 + 0^2} + \frac{n}{n^2 + 1^2} + \frac{n}{n^2 + 2^2} + \ldots + \frac{n}{n^2 + (n-1)^2} \right) = \frac{\pi}{4}.$$

- *Hint:* Factor out n^2 from each denominator and let $f(x) = (1 + x^2)^{-1}$.

29. This problem is **Really, really, hard**, but not impossible! A **prime number** is a positive integer whose only proper divisors are 1 and itself. For example, 2, 3, 5, 11, are primes while 4, 8, 9 are not primes. It was proved by **Euclid of Alexandria** over 2000 years ago, that there is an infinite number of such primes. Let's label them by $\{p_1, p_2, p_3, \ldots\}$ where, for the purpose of this Exercise, we take it that $p_1 = 1, p_2 = 2, p_3 = 3, p_4 = 5, p_5 = 7, p_6 = 11, p_7 = 13, p_8 = 17$, *etc.* Show that

$$\lim_{n\to\infty} \sum_{i=0}^{n-1} \frac{n^3}{\sqrt{n^8 - i^2 n^6 - 2i p_n - p_n^2}} = \frac{\pi}{2}.$$

Hint: Use the fact the nth–prime can be estimated by $p_n < 36n \ln n$, for every $n \geq 2$. This estimate on the nth–prime number is called **Sierpinski's Estimate**.

This crazy-looking limit can be verified theoretically using the Riemann integral and the fundamental idea of Example 298. You can actually verify the stated convergence using your calculator (or a simple C++ program) and you'll realize that the convergence is very slow, that is, even after $n = 20,000$ you may only get 4 or 5 significant digits!

Show that the integrand is positive, calculate the following definite integrals, and interpret your result as an area.

30. $\displaystyle\int_0^\pi \sin x \, dx$

31. $\displaystyle\int_0^{\frac{\pi}{2}} |\cos x - \sin x| \, dx$

32. $\displaystyle\int_{\frac{\pi}{12}}^{\frac{\pi}{8}} \frac{\cos 2x}{\sin^2 2x} \, dx$

33. $\displaystyle\int_0^1 t^2 \sqrt{1 + t^3} \, dt$

34. $\displaystyle\int_0^1 \frac{x}{1 + x^4} \, dx$

Use Leibniz's Rule and/or L'Hospital's Rule to justify the values of the following limits

35. Show that $\displaystyle\lim_{x\to 0+} \frac{d}{dx} \int_1^{x^2} \frac{\sin t}{t^{3/2}} \, dt = 2.$

36. Show that $\displaystyle\lim_{x\to\infty} \frac{d}{dx} \int_{\sqrt{3}}^{\sqrt{x}} \frac{r^3}{(r+1)(r-1)} \, dr = \frac{1}{2}.$

37. Show that $\displaystyle\lim_{x\to\infty} \frac{d}{dx} \int_x^{x^2} e^{-t^2} \, dt = 0.$

38. Show that $\displaystyle\lim_{x\to 0} \frac{d}{dx} \int_1^{\sqrt{x}} \frac{\sin(y^2)}{2y} \, dy = \frac{1}{4}.$

39. Show that $\displaystyle\lim_{x\to 0+} \frac{d}{dx} \int_{1}^{\sin x} \frac{\ln t}{\ln(\text{Arcsin } t)} \, dt = 1$.

40. If c is a constant, show that $\displaystyle\lim_{t\to 0+} \frac{d}{dt} \int_{2\pi-ct}^{2\pi+ct} \frac{\sin x}{cx} \, dx = 0$.

41. Show that $\displaystyle\lim_{h\to 0+} \frac{d}{dx} \left(\frac{1}{h} \int_{x-h}^{x+h} \sqrt{t} \, dt \right) = \frac{1}{\sqrt{x}}$.

42. Show that $\displaystyle\lim_{x\to 0} \frac{1}{2x} \int_{-x}^{x} \cos t \, dt = 1$.

Find the solution of the following differential equations subject to the given initial condition. Leave your solutions in implicit form.

43. $\dfrac{dy}{dx} = \dfrac{x^3}{y^4}, \quad y(0) = 1$.

44. $\dfrac{dy}{dx} = \dfrac{\sin x}{\cos y}, \quad y(0) = \dfrac{\pi}{2}$.

45. $\dfrac{dy}{dx} = (1+y^2) \, e^{2x}, \quad y(0) = 1$.

46. $\dfrac{d^2y}{dx^2} = 24x^2 + 8x, \quad y(0) = 0, y'(0) = 1$.

47. $\dfrac{d^3y}{dx^3} = -24x, \quad y(0) = 0, y'(0) = 0, y''(0) = -1$.

48. $\dfrac{d^2y}{dx^2} = e^x, \quad y(0) = 0, y'(0) = 0$.

49. $\dfrac{d^4y}{dx^4} = 2, \quad y(0) = 0, y'(0) = 0, y''(0) = 0, y'''(0) = 2$.

50. A company producing hand held computers has a marginal cost per computer of
$$MC(x) = 60 + \frac{40}{x+10}$$
dollars per computer at production level x per week.

   (a) Find the increase in total costs resulting from an increase in production from $x = 20$ to $x = 40$ computers per week.

   (b) If fixed costs of production are $C(0) = 5000$ dollars per week, find the total cost of producing $x = 20$ hand held computers per week.

51. An investment is growing at the rate of $\frac{500e^{\sqrt{t}}}{\sqrt{t}}$ dollars per year. Find the value of the investment after 4 years if its initial value was $1000 (**Hint:** Let $\square = \sqrt{t}$ and Table 6.5.)

Suggested Homework Set 21. *Do problems 19, 25, 27, 34, 38, 45*

6.6 Using Computer Algebra Systems

Use your favorite Computer Algebra System (CAS), like Maple, MatLab, etc., or even a graphing calculator to answer the following questions:

1. Estimate the value of the definite integral $\displaystyle\int_0^1 e^{x^2}\, dx$ to six significant digits.

2. Show by differentiating that $\displaystyle\int e^{x^2}\, dx \neq \frac{e^{x^2}}{2x}$ as many would like to believe!

3. Let n be a given integer, $n \geq 1$. Calculate the value of the sum

$$\sum_{k=1}^{n} k^2 = 1^2 + 2^2 + 3^2 + 4^2 + \cdots + n^2.$$

Verify that for any given integer $n \geq 1$ we actually get

$$\sum_{k=1}^{n} k^2 = \frac{n(n+1)(2n+1)}{6}.$$

Can you prove this formula using the method of mathematical induction?

4. Find a formula for the sum $\displaystyle\sum_{k=1}^{n} 3k + 2k^2$.

5. Let $n \geq 1$ be an integer. Prove the trigonometric identity

$$\sec((n+1)x)\, \sec(nx) = \frac{\tan((n+1)x) - \tan(nx)}{\sin x},$$

for all values of x for which the denominator is defined.

6. Find a formula for the sum $\displaystyle\sum_{k=1}^{n} k^4$. Can you prove it using mathematical induction?

7. Confirm the values of the limits obtained in Exercises 35-42 above using your CAS.

8. Try to verify the result in Exercise 28 above using your CAS.

9. Evaluate $\displaystyle\int \frac{\sin 2x}{1 + \cos x}\, dx$.

Chapter 7

Techniques of Integration

The Big Picture

In this chapter we describe the main techniques used in evaluating an indefinite or definite integral. Many such integrals cannot be evaluated simply by applying a formula so one has to look at the integrand carefully, move terms around, simplify, and ultimately use something more elaborate like a substitution or a, so-called, Integration by Parts, among many other possibilities. However, with the **Substitution Rule** and **Integration by Parts** we can evaluate many integrals. Other techniques for evaluation depend on the actual *form* of the integrand, whether it has any "squared" expressions, trigonometric functions, etc. This Chapter is at the core of *Integral Calculus*. Without it, the Theory of the Integral developed in Chapter 7 would remain just a theory, devoid of any practical use.

Review

Review Chapter 6, especially the examples involving the evaluation of specific definite and indefinite integrals. Also, always keep in mind Tables 6.5, 6.6, and Table 6.7. Many of the integrals can be simplified or transformed to one of the basic forms in these Tables and so, the better you remember them, the faster you'll get to the final answers. You should also review Chapter 3, in particular, the Chain Rule.

7.1 Trigonometric Identities

Before we start this new chapter on *Techniques of Integration* let's review some trigonometric identities, identities which we reproduce here, for convenience. Don't forget, **you should remember this stuff!** It is true that: For any symbols θ, x, y representing real numbers, (or angles in radians),

$$\sin^2 \theta + \cos^2 \theta = 1 \tag{7.1}$$

$$\sec^2 \theta - \tan^2 \theta = 1 \tag{7.2}$$

$$\csc^2 \theta - \cot^2 \theta = 1 \tag{7.3}$$

$$\cos^2 \theta - \sin^2 \theta = \cos 2\theta \tag{7.4}$$

$$2 \sin \theta \cos \theta = \sin 2\theta \tag{7.5}$$

$$\cos^2 \theta = \frac{1 + \cos 2\theta}{2} \tag{7.6}$$

$$\sin^2 \theta = \frac{1 - \cos 2\theta}{2} \tag{7.7}$$

$$\sin(x + y) = \sin x \cos y + \cos x \sin y \tag{7.8}$$

$$\cos(x + y) = \cos x \cos y - \sin x \sin y \tag{7.9}$$

$$\sin(-\theta) = -\sin \theta \tag{7.10}$$

$$\cos(-\theta) = \cos \theta \tag{7.11}$$

If you know these basic formulae you can deduce almost every other basic trigonometric formula that you will need in your study of Calculus. For example, if we let $y = -z$ in (7.9) and use (7.10) and (7.11) with $\theta = z$ we get a "*new*" (7.9) formula (see (7.12) below).

$$\begin{aligned} \cos(x - z) &= \cos x \cos(-z) - \sin x \sin(-z), \\ &= \cos x \cos z + \sin x \sin z. \end{aligned}$$

And since x, z are any two **arbitrary** angles, it doesn't matter what "*symbol*" we use to describe them, so we can also write:

$$\cos(x - y) = \cos x \cos y + \sin x \sin y. \tag{7.12}$$

Similarly, (by setting $y = -z$ in (7.8) and use (7.10) and (7.11), once again) we can show that:

$$\sin(x - y) = \sin x \cos y - \cos x \sin y. \tag{7.13}$$

Combining the expressions (7.8) and (7.13) we get

$$\sin(x + y) + \sin(x - y) = 2\sin(x)\cos(y)$$

(since the other two terms cancel each other out), or

$$\sin x \cos y = \frac{\sin(x + y) + \sin(x - y)}{2}. \tag{7.14}$$

We can use the same idea to show that when (7.9) and (7.12) are combined we get

$$\cos x \cos y = \frac{\cos(x + y) + \cos(x - y)}{2}. \tag{7.15}$$

Of course, once we know (7.14) and (7.15) you don't really have to worry about memorizing the formula for "$\cos x \sin y$" because we can **interchange x and y** in (7.14) to obtain

$$\sin y \cos x = \cos x \sin y = \frac{\sin(x + y) + \sin(y - x)}{2}.$$

Note that from (7.10) we can write $\sin(-\theta) = -\sin \theta$ for $\theta = y - x$, right? (Because this 'θ' is just another angle). This means that $-\sin(y - x) = \sin(x - y)$ or, combining this with the last display, we see that

$$\cos x \sin y = \frac{\sin(x + y) - \sin(x - y)}{2}. \tag{7.16}$$

Finally, if we combine (7.12) and (7.9) we find that

$$\sin x \sin y = \frac{\cos(x - y) - \cos(x + y)}{2} \tag{7.17}$$

(since the other two terms cancel each other out, right?)

Lucky for us, with (7.1) to (7.7) we can perform many simplifications in the *integrands*, which we'll introduce below, and these will result in a simpler method for evaluating the integral!

7.2 The Substitution Rule

The evaluation of indefinite and corresponding definite integrals is of major importance in Calculus. In this section we introduce the method of substitution as a possible rule to be used in the evaluation of indefinite or definite integrals. Actually, we SAW and actually USED this Rule earlier, in Section 6.2 (without knowing its name). In this section we are simply elaborating on what we did earlier. It is based on a *change of variable formula*, cf. (7.19) below, for integrals which we now describe. Given a definite integral of f over $I = [a, b]$ we know that

$$\int_a^b f(x)\ dx = \mathcal{F}(b) - \mathcal{F}(a), \qquad (7.18)$$

where $\mathcal{F}$ is any antiderivative of f. The substitution $u(x) = t$, where we assume that u has a differentiable inverse function $x = u^{-1}(t)$ inside the integral, corresponds to the **change of variable formula**

$$\mathcal{F}(b) - \mathcal{F}(a) = \int_{u(a)}^{u(b)} f(u^{-1}(t)) \left(\frac{d}{dt} u^{-1}(t) \right)\ dt. \qquad (7.19)$$

This formula is a consequence of the following argument: By the Chain Rule of Chapter 3, (setting $u^{-1}(t) = \Box$),

$$\frac{d}{dt}\, \mathcal{F}(u^{-1}(t)) \quad = \quad \mathcal{F}'(u^{-1}(t))\, \frac{d}{dt}\, u^{-1}(t), \qquad (7.20)$$

$$= \quad f(u^{-1}(t))\, \frac{d}{dt}\, u^{-1}(t),\ \text{(since } \mathcal{F}' = f). \qquad (7.21)$$

Integrating both sides of (7.21) over the interval $u(a)$, $u(b)$ and using the Fundamental Theorem of Calculus, we obtain

$$\int_{u(a)}^{u(b)} f(u^{-1}(t))\, \frac{d}{dt}\, u^{-1}(t)\ dt \quad = \quad \int_{u(a)}^{u(b)} \frac{d}{dt}\, \mathcal{F}(u^{-1}(t))\ dt,$$

$$= \quad \mathcal{F}(u^{-1}(u(b))) - \mathcal{F}(u^{-1}(u(a))),$$

$$= \quad \mathcal{F}(b) - \mathcal{F}(a),$$

which is (7.19).

In practice, we proceed as follows.

Example 304. Evaluate $\displaystyle \int_a^b f(x)\ dx = \int_0^2 2x\ e^{x^2}\ dx.$

Solution We see an exponential to a power so we think, $e^{\Box}$, right? That is, we're hoping that we can apply the third formula in Table 6.5 to find an antiderivative. We make the *substitution*

$$u(x) = x^2 = t,$$

whose inverse (that is, whose inverse function) is given by

$$x = \sqrt{t} = u^{-1}(t).$$

Using this substitution we see that the *old* limits, $x = 0$ and $x = 2$, correspond to the *new* limits, $u(0) = 0$, and $u(2) = 4$. Since $f(u^{-1}(t)) = f(\sqrt{t}) = 2\sqrt{t}\ e^t$, and the derivative of $u^{-1}(t)$ is $1/(2\sqrt{t})$, (7.19) becomes, in this case,

$$\int_0^2 2x\ e^{x^2}\ dx \quad = \quad \int_0^4 2\sqrt{t}\ e^t\ \frac{1}{2\sqrt{t}}\ dt,$$

$$= \quad \int_0^4 e^t\ dt,$$

$$= \quad (e^4 - 1).$$

Shortcut

The **shortcut to Integration by Substitution**, which amounts to the same thing as an answer can be summarized, in the case of this example, by setting $t = x^2$, $dt = 2x\,dx$ with the limits being changed according to the rule $t = 0$ when $x = 0$, $t = 4$ when $x = 2$. We then write

$$\int_0^2 2x\,e^{x^2}\,dx = \int_0^4 e^t\,dt$$

as before, but more directly. The point is we can leave out all the details about the inverse function and its derivative.

For convenience, let's recall some of the most basic antiderivatives and results from Tables 6.5, 6.6, 6.7. Let $\square$ represent any differentiable function with its derivative denoted by $\square\,'$. Think of $\square$ as a generic symbol for any other symbol like, u, t, x, etc. Then

$$\int \cos\square \cdot \square\,'\,dx = \sin\square + C, \tag{7.22}$$

where C is our generic *constant of integration* which follows every indefinite integral.

Next, for $r \neq -1$,

$$\int \square^r dx = \frac{\square^{r+1}}{r+1} + C, \tag{7.23}$$

while, if $r = -1$, we get, provided $\square \neq 0$,

$$\int \frac{\square\,'}{\square}\,dx = \ln|\square| + C. \tag{7.24}$$

Formula 7.31 with $\square = x$ is obtained by noticing that $\tan x = \sin x / \cos x$ and then using the substitution $u = \cos x$, $du = -\sin x\,dx$, so that the integral becomes

$$\begin{aligned}
\int \tan x\,dx &= \int \frac{-du}{u}, \\
&= -\ln|u| + C, \\
&= -\ln|\cos x| + C, \\
&= \ln\left(|\cos x|^{-1}\right) + C, \\
&= \ln|\sec x| + C.
\end{aligned}$$

Furthermore, if e is **Euler's number** $e = 2.71828....$, (see Chapter 4),

$$\int e^{\square}\,\square\,'\,dx = e^{\square} + C \tag{7.25}$$

and since $a^{\square} = e^{\ln a^{\square}} = e^{\square\,\ln a}$ we get, if $a \neq 0$,

$$\int a^{\square}\,\square\,'\,dx = \frac{a^{\square}}{\ln a} + C \tag{7.26}$$

Next from our *differentiation* formulae for trigonometric functions we obtain our *integration* formulae,

$$\int \sin\square \quad \square\,'\,dx = -\cos\square + C \tag{7.27}$$

$$\int \cos\square \quad \square\,'\,dx = \sin\square + C \tag{7.28}$$

$$\int \sec^2 \Box \quad \Box'\, dx = \tan \Box \; + C \qquad\qquad (7.29)$$

$$\int \csc^2 \Box \quad \Box'\, dx = -\cot \Box \; + C \qquad\qquad (7.30)$$

$$\int \tan \Box \quad \Box'\, dx \;\; = \;\; -\ln|\cos \Box| + C, \qquad (7.31)$$
$$= \;\; \ln|\sec \Box| + C. \qquad (7.32)$$

$$\int \cot \Box \quad \Box'\, dx = \ln|\sin \Box| + C \qquad\qquad (7.33)$$

In some applications you may see functions called **hyperbolic functions**. These functions are denoted by $\sinh x, \cosh x$, etc. in agreement with convention. These hyperbolic functions, analogous to the usual **circular functions** or *trigonometric functions*, are defined by

$$\sinh x = \frac{e^x - e^{-x}}{2},$$
$$\cosh x = \frac{e^x + e^{-x}}{2},$$
$$\tanh x = \frac{\sinh x}{\cosh x}, \; etc,$$

just as one would expect them to be defined. For these functions it's not hard to see that,

$$\int \sinh \Box \quad \Box'\, dx = \cosh \Box \; + C, \qquad\qquad (7.34)$$

$$\int \cosh \Box \quad \Box'\, dx = \sinh \Box \; + C, \qquad\qquad (7.35)$$

where we don't have to worry about that "minus sign" in front of the sine integral!

Finally, you should remember that

$$\int \sec \Box \; \tan \Box \quad \Box'\, dx = \sec \Box \; + C, \qquad\qquad (7.36)$$

$$\int \csc \Box \; \cot \Box \quad \Box'\, dx = -\csc \Box \; + C, \qquad\qquad (7.37)$$

Let $a \neq 0$ be any number (NOT a variable), and let $\Box$ represent some differentiable function. Then the following two formulae may be verified by finding the derivative of the corresponding right-hand sides along with the Chain Rule:

$$\int \frac{\Box'}{\Box^2 + a^2} \; dx = \frac{1}{a}\operatorname{Arctan} \frac{\Box}{a} + C \qquad\qquad (7.38)$$

$$\int \frac{\Box'}{\sqrt{a^2 - \Box^2}} \; dx = \operatorname{Arcsin} \frac{\Box}{a} + C \qquad\qquad (7.39)$$

The study of these hyperbolic functions began when someone noticed that the area under a hyperbola was given by an integral of the form

$$\int \sqrt{x^2 - a^2}\; dx$$

whereas the area under a circle was given by an integral of the form

$$\int \sqrt{a^2 - x^2}\; dx.$$

Since the two expressions differ by a factor of $\sqrt{-1}$ and the first integral can be evaluated using the substitution $x = a\sin\theta$, and the area under the hyperbola is related to the natural logarithm, it was guessed that there should be a relation between the logarithm and the circular functions. This led to the birth of these hyperbolic functions whose first comprehensive treatment was given by J.H. Lambert in 1768. Note that, for example, $\sin(\theta\sqrt{-1}) = \sqrt{-1}\sinh\theta$ is one of the fundamental relationships.

Example 305. Evaluate the definite integral, $\int_0^{\sqrt{\pi}} x \sin x^2 \, dx$.

Solution

Method 1 We need an antiderivative $\mathcal{F}(x)$, first, right? We see the sine of "something", so we try *something* $= \square$, and hope that this will lead to one of the formulae above, like, maybe, (7.27).

O.K., this is where we use the substitution $\square = x^2$. Well, if $\square = x^2$, then $\square' = 2x$. So, rewriting the integrand in terms of $\square$ and $\square'$ we get

$$\int x \sin x^2 \, dx = \int \frac{\square'}{2} \cdot \sin \square \, dx,$$

because $x = \frac{\square'}{2}$ and $\sin(x^2) = \sin(\square)$. So,

$$
\begin{aligned}
\mathcal{F}(x) &= \int x \sin(x^2) dx, \\
&= \frac{1}{2} \int \sin \square \ \square' \, dx, \\
&= \frac{1}{2} \left(-\cos \square \right) + C, \quad \text{(by (7.27))}, \\
&= -\frac{1}{2} \left(\cos \square \right) + C, \\
&= -\frac{1}{2} \cos(x^2) + C, \quad \text{(by \textbf{back substitution}, i.e., setting } \square = x^2).
\end{aligned}
$$

Next, it follows that

$$
\begin{aligned}
\int_0^{\sqrt{\pi}} x \sin x^2 \, dx &= \left. -\frac{1}{2} \cos(x^2) \right|_0^{\sqrt{\pi}}, \\
&= -\frac{1}{2} \cos \pi + \frac{1}{2} \cos(0), \\
&= 1.
\end{aligned}
$$

WATCH OUT! When evaluating an indefinite integral you must always *back-substitute* after a change of variable, i.e., always replace your "Box terms" or your "last variable" by the variable in the original integral.

This means that you *start and end your integration with the same symbol!*.

Method 2 This amounts up to the same reasoning as Method 1, above, but it is somewhat shorter to write down. You can use it in case you don't like boxes. Let $t = x^2$. Now think of t as a differentiable function of x. Then we have $\frac{dt}{dx} = 2x$ from which we write the symbolic relation $dt = 2x \, dx$. Don't worry about what this means, right now. Now, let's see "what's left over" after we substitute this t into the integral (and forget about the limits of integration for now).

$$
\begin{aligned}
\int x \sin x^2 \, dx &= \int \sin x^2 \, (x \, dx), \\
&= \int \sin t \, (x \, dx),
\end{aligned}
$$

where we have to write the stuff inside the parentheses (i.e., the stuff that is "left-over") in terms of dt. But there is only the term $x \, dx$ that is "left over". So, we need to solve for the symbol, $x \, dx$ in the expression for dt. Since $dt = 2x \, dx$, this gives us

$$x \, dx = \frac{dt}{2}.$$

The right-hand side of the previous formula depends only on the new variable t and this is good. There shouldn't be any x's floating around on the right-side, just t's. Using this, we see that

$$
\begin{aligned}
\int x \sin x^2 \, dx &= \int \sin t \, (x \, dx), \\
&= \int \sin t \, \left(\frac{dt}{2}\right), \\
&= \frac{1}{2} \int \sin t \, dt.
\end{aligned}
$$

Now, we put the *limits of integration* back in on the left. The ones on the right are to be found using the substitution formula, $t = x^2$. When $x = 0$, $t = 0$ (because $t = x^2$). Next, when $x = \sqrt{\pi}$, $t = x^2 = (\sqrt{\pi})^2 = \pi$. So, according to our *Change of Variable* formula we get,

$$
\begin{aligned}
\int_0^{\sqrt{\pi}} x \sin x^2 \, dx &= \frac{1}{2} \int_0^{\pi} \sin t \, dt, \\
&= \left. -\frac{1}{2} \cos t \right|_0^{\pi}, \\
&= 1,
\end{aligned}
$$

as before.

NOTE: If this Example seems long it is because *we put in all the details*. Normally, you can skip many of these details and get to the answer faster. See the *Snapshots* later on for such examples.

Example 306. Evaluate $\mathcal{G}(y) = \int e^y \sec e^y \tan e^y \, dy$.

Solution We want an antiderivative, $\mathcal{G}(y)$, right? We see a bunch of trig. functions acting on *the same* symbol, namely, e^y. So, let's just replace this symbol by $\square$ or t, or "whatever" and see what happens ... Maybe we'll get lucky and this will look like maybe, (7.36), with something in the Box, (x or t or whatever.)

So, let $x = e^y$. Then, proceeding as above, $dx = e^y \, dy$ and now, (do you see it?),

$$
\begin{aligned}
\mathcal{G}(y) &= \int \sec e^y \, \tan e^y \, (e^y \, dy), \\
&= \int \sec x \, \tan x \, dx,
\end{aligned}
$$

which is (7.36) with $\square$ **replaced by** x. So, we get

$$
\begin{aligned}
\mathcal{G}(y) &= \sec x \ + C, \\
&= \sec (e^y) \ + C, \quad \text{(after the \textbf{back-substitution}).}
\end{aligned}
$$

Example 307. Evaluate $\int \dfrac{\tan (\ln x)}{x} \, dx$.

Solution Here we see the tangent of *something* and an x in the denominator. Remember that we really don't know what to do when we're starting out, so we have to make "good guesses". What do we do? Let's try $t = \ln x$ and hope that this will lead to an easier integral involving $\tan t$, hopefully something like (7.31), with $\square = t$. By substituting $t = \ln x$, we get $dt = \frac{1}{x}\, dx$ so, now what? Well,

$$
\begin{aligned}
\int \frac{\tan(\ln x)}{x}\, dx &= \int \tan(\ln x) \cdot \left(\frac{1}{x}\, dx\right), \\
&= \int \tan t\, dt, \\
&= -\ln|\cos t| + C, \quad \text{(by (7.31) with } \square = t), \\
&= -\ln|\cos(\ln x)| + C, \quad \text{(since } t = \ln x),
\end{aligned}
$$

and this is the answer.

Note that $\ln(A^{-1}) = -\ln A$ for any $A > 0$, by a property of logarithms. So, replacing A by $\cos(\ln x)$ and using the fact that the reciprocal of the cosine function, cos, is the secant function, sec, we can also write this answer as

$$
\int \frac{\tan(\ln x)}{x}\, dx = \ln|\sec(\ln x)| + C.
$$

Example 308. Evaluate $\int \frac{\sinh \sqrt{z}}{\sqrt{z}}\, dz$.

Solution Recall the definition of the sinh function from before and its basic property in (7.34). We see a "square root" in both the numerator and denominator so, what if we try to replace the square root by a new variable, like, x, or box, $\square$? Will this simplify the integrand? Let's see if we can get this integral into the more familiar form, (7.34), if possible. So, we set $x = \sqrt{z}$. Then, $dx = \frac{1}{2\sqrt{z}}\, dz$. Let's see "what's left over" after we substitute this $x = \sqrt{z}$ into the integral.

$$
\int \frac{\sinh \sqrt{z}}{\sqrt{z}}\, dz = \int \sinh x \left(\frac{1}{\sqrt{z}}\, dz\right),
$$

where we have to write the stuff inside the parentheses in terms of dx. Now there is only $\frac{1}{\sqrt{z}}\, dz$ that's "left over". So, we need to solve for the symbol, $\frac{1}{\sqrt{z}}\, dz$ in the expression for dx. This gives us

$$
\frac{1}{\sqrt{z}}\, dz = 2\, dx.
$$

The right-hand side of the previous formula depends only on the new variable x and this is good. There shouldn't be any z's floating around on the right-side, just x's. Now,

$$
\begin{aligned}
\int \frac{\sinh \sqrt{z}}{\sqrt{z}}\, dz &= \int \sinh \sqrt{z} \left(\frac{1}{\sqrt{z}}\, dz\right), \\
&= \int \sinh x \cdot (2\, dx) \quad \text{(since } 2\, dx = \frac{1}{\sqrt{z}}\, dz), \\
&= 2 \int \sinh x\, dx, \\
&= 2 \cosh x + C, \quad \text{(by (7.34) with } \square = x), \\
&= 2 \cosh \sqrt{z} + C, \quad \text{(since } x = \sqrt{z} \text{ to begin with)},
\end{aligned}
$$

and we're done!

Example 309. Evaluate $\int_0^1 x^2 \sec^2 x^3\, dx$.

Solution This complicated-looking expression involves a $\sec^2$, right? So, we set $u = x^3$, and hope that this will make the integrand look like, say, (7.29), with $\square = u$. In this case, $u = x^3$ means that $du = 3x^2 \, dx$. Now, let's see "what's left over" after we substitute this into the integral.

$$\int x^2 \sec^2 x^3 \, dx = \int \sec^2 x^3 \left(x^2 \, dx \right),$$
$$= \int \sec^2 u \left(x^2 \, dx \right),$$

where we have to write the stuff inside the parentheses in terms of du. But there is only $x^2 \, dx$ that's "left over". So, we need to solve for the symbol, $x^2 \, dx$ in the expression for du, namely $du = 3x^2 \, dx$. This gives us

$$x^2 \, dx = \frac{du}{3}.$$

The right-hand side of the previous formula depends only on the new variable u and this is good. There shouldn't be any x's floating around on the right-side, just u's. Now,

$$\int x^2 \sec^2 x^3 \, dx = \int \sec^2 u \left(x^2 \, dx \right),$$
$$= \int \sec^2 u \left(\frac{du}{3} \right),$$
$$= \frac{1}{3} \int \sec^2 u \, du.$$

When $x = 0$ we have $u = 0$, while if $x = 1$ we have $u = x^3 = (1)^3 = 1$. So, the new limits of integration for u are the same as the old limits for x. OK, we were just *lucky*, that's all. It follows that

$$\int_0^1 x^2 \sec^2 x^3 \, dx = \frac{1}{3} \int_0^1 \sec^2 u \, du,$$
$$= \frac{1}{3} \tan u \Big|_0^1, \quad (\text{ from (7.29), with } \square = u),$$
$$= \frac{1}{3} \tan 1 - 0,$$
$$\approx 0.5191.$$

NOTE: These example serve to reinforce the technique of **substitution** which is used in cases where we feel that a particular substitution might simplify the **look** of an integrand, thereby allowing easy evaluation of the integral by means of formulae like those in (7.22 - 7.35) and the ones in Tables 6.5, 6.6, 6.7.

As a check: You can always check your answer by *differentiating* it, and this is easy when you know the Chain Rule really well (Chapter 3.5).

SNAPSHOTS

Example 310. Evaluate $\int x^2 \sqrt{1 + x^3} \, dx$.

Solution Let $\boxed{u = 1 + x^3}$. Then $du = 3x^2 \, dx$ and

$$x^2 \, dx = \frac{du}{3}.$$

So,

$$\int x^2 \sqrt{1+x^3} \, dx = \int \sqrt{1+x^3} \left(x^2 \, dx \right),$$

$$= \frac{1}{3} \int \sqrt{u} \, du,$$

$$= \left(\frac{1}{3} \right) \left(\frac{2}{3} \right) u^{\frac{3}{2}} + C,$$

$$= \frac{2}{9} (1+x^3)^{\frac{3}{2}} + C.$$

Check your answer by differentiation!

Example 311. Evaluate $\displaystyle\int_{-1}^{0} \frac{x^3 \, dx}{\sqrt[4]{1+x^4}}$.

Solution

Let $\boxed{u = 1 + x^4}$. Then $du = 4x^3 \, dx$, or, solving for the symbols $x^3 \, dx$ (which appear in the numerator of the integrand) we get

$$x^3 \, dx = du/4.$$

Substituting this information back into the integral we get

$$\int \frac{x^3 \, dx}{\sqrt[4]{1+x^4}} = \frac{1}{4} \int \frac{du}{\sqrt[4]{u}},$$

$$= \frac{1}{4} \int u^{-\frac{1}{4}} \, du,$$

$$= \frac{1}{4} \cdot \frac{4}{3} u^{\frac{3}{4}} + C,$$

or,

$$\int \frac{x^3 \, dx}{\sqrt[4]{1+x^4}} = \frac{1}{3} (1+x^4)^{\frac{3}{4}} + C.$$

It follows that

$$\int_{-1}^{0} \frac{x^3 \, dx}{\sqrt[4]{1+x^4}} = \frac{1}{3} (1+x^4)^{\frac{3}{4}} \Big|_{-1}^{0},$$

$$= \frac{1}{3} - \frac{1}{3} 2^{\frac{3}{4}},$$

$$= \frac{1}{3} \left(1 - \sqrt[4]{8} \right).$$

Equivalently, we could use the *Change of Variable* formula, and find (since $u = 2$ when $x = -1$ and $u = 1$ when $x = 0$),

$$\int_{-1}^{0} \frac{x^3 \, dx}{\sqrt[4]{1+x^4}} = \frac{1}{4} \int_{2}^{1} u^{-\frac{1}{4}} \, du,$$

$$= \frac{1}{3} u^{\frac{3}{4}} \Big|_{2}^{1},$$

$$= \frac{1}{3} \left(1 - \sqrt[4]{8} \right),$$

as before.

Example 312. Evaluate $\displaystyle\int \frac{x+1}{2\sqrt{x+1}} \, dx$.

Solution Always try to simplify the integrand whenever possible! In this case we don't really have to use a complicated substitution since

$$\frac{x+1}{2\sqrt{x+1}} = \frac{\sqrt{x+1}}{2},$$

so, all we really want to do is to evaluate

$$
\begin{aligned}
\int \frac{\sqrt{x+1}}{2}\, dx &= \frac{1}{2}\int \sqrt{x+1}\, dx, \\
&= \frac{1}{2}\cdot\frac{2}{3}(x+1)^{\frac{3}{2}} + C, \\
&= \frac{1}{3}(x+1)^{\frac{3}{2}} + C,
\end{aligned}
$$

by the Generalized Power Rule for integrals, (Table 6.5 with $r = 1/2$, $\square = x+1$).

Example 313. Evaluate $\displaystyle\int \frac{y^2+1}{y^3+3y+1}\, dy.$

Solution Let $u = y^3+3y+1$. Then $du = (3y^2+3)\, dy = 3(y^2+1)\, dy$, and it contains the term, $(y^2+1)\, dy$, which also appears in the numerator of the integrand. Solving for this quantity and rewriting we get

$$\frac{(y^2+1)\, dy}{y^3+3y+1} = \left(\frac{du}{3}\right)\frac{1}{u},$$

right? This means that the integral looks like

$$
\begin{aligned}
\int \frac{y^2+1}{y^3+3y+1}\, dy &= \int \frac{du}{3u}, \\
&= \frac{1}{3}\int \frac{du}{u}, \\
&= \frac{1}{3}\ln|u| + C, \text{ (by the second entry in Table 6.5, } \square = u\text{)}, \\
&= \frac{1}{3}\ln\left|y^3+3y+1\right| + C.
\end{aligned}
$$

Example 314. Evaluate $\displaystyle\int_1^2 x\sqrt{x-1}\, dx.$

Solution The *square root sign* makes us think of the substitution $u = x - 1$. Then $du = 1\, dx = dx$. Okay, now solve for x (which we need as it appears in "what's left over" after we substitute in $u = x-1$). So, $x = u+1$. When $x = 1$, $u = 0$ and when $x = 2$, $u = 1$. These give the new limits of integration and the integral becomes,

$$
\begin{aligned}
\int_1^2 x\sqrt{x-1}\, dx &= \int_0^1 (u+1)\sqrt{u}\, du, \\
&= \int_0^1 \left(u^{3/2}+u^{1/2}\right)\, du, \\
&= \left.\left(\frac{2}{5}u^{\frac{5}{2}} + \frac{2}{3}u^{\frac{3}{2}}\right)\right|_0^1, \\
&= \frac{2}{5}+\frac{2}{3}, \\
&= \frac{16}{15}.
\end{aligned}
$$

Notice that the opening equation in the last display had only u's on the right: You always try to do this, so you may have to solve for the "original" variable (in this case, x, in terms of u), sometimes.

Example 315. Evaluate $\int (\ln x)^3 \dfrac{dx}{x}$.

Solution We see a power so we let $u = \ln x$ and see... In this case, $du = \frac{dx}{x}$ which is precisely the term we need! So,

$$
\begin{aligned}
\int (\ln x)^3 \frac{dx}{x} &= \int u^3 \, du \\
&= \frac{u^4}{4} + C \\
&= \frac{(\ln x)^4}{4} + C,
\end{aligned}
$$

because of the "back substitution", $u = \ln x$.

Example 316. Evaluate $\int \dfrac{e^{-x}}{1 + e^{-x}} \, dx$.

Solution Trying $u = e^{-x}$ gives $du = -e^{-x} \, dx$, which we have to write in terms of u. This means that $du = -u \, dx$ or $dx = -du/u$. The integral now looks like,

$$
\begin{aligned}
\int \frac{e^{-x}}{1 + e^{-x}} \, dx &= -\int \frac{u \, du}{(1 + u)u}, \\
&= -\int \frac{1}{1 + u} \, du, \\
&= -\ln|1 + u| + C, \\
&= \ln|1 + e^{-x}| + C, \\
&= \ln(1 + e^{-x}) + C.
\end{aligned}
$$

Example 317. Evaluate $\displaystyle\int_0^{\frac{1}{3}} \dfrac{dx}{1 + 9x^2}$.

Solution The natural guess $u = 9x^2$ leads nowhere, since $du = 18x \, dx$ and we can't solve for dx easily, (just in terms of u and du). The denominator does have a square term in it, though, and so this term looks like $1 + (something)^2$, which reminds us of an Arctan integral, (third item in Table 6.7, with $\square = 3x$). Okay, this is our clue. If we let $something = u = 3x$, then the denominator looks like $1 + u^2$ and the subsequent expression $du = 3 \, dx$ is not a problem, as we can easily solve for dx in terms of du. Indeed, $dx = du/3$. This looks good so we try it and find,

$$
\begin{aligned}
\int \frac{dx}{1 + 9x^2} &= \int \frac{du}{3(1 + u^2)}, \\
&= \frac{1}{3} \int \frac{du}{1 + u^2}, \\
&= \frac{1}{3} \operatorname{Arctan} u + C, \\
&= \frac{1}{3} \operatorname{Arctan} 3x + C.
\end{aligned}
$$

It follows that

$$
\begin{aligned}
\int_0^{\frac{1}{3}} \frac{dx}{1 + 9x^2} &= \frac{1}{3} \operatorname{Arctan} 3x \Big|_0^{\frac{1}{3}}, \\
&= \frac{1}{3} \operatorname{Arctan} 1 - \frac{1}{3} \operatorname{Arctan} 0, \\
&= \frac{1}{3} \cdot \frac{\pi}{4} - 0, \\
&= \frac{\pi}{12}.
\end{aligned}
$$

Exercise Set 32.

Evaluate the following integrals

1. $\displaystyle\int (2x - 1)^{99} \, dx$

2. $\displaystyle\int 3(1 + x)^{5.1} \, dx$

3. $\displaystyle\int_0^1 \frac{1}{(3x + 1)^5} \, dx$

4. $\displaystyle\int \frac{dx}{(x - 1)^2}$

5. $\displaystyle\int x(1 - x^2)^{100} \, dx$

6. $\displaystyle\int x \, 2^{x^2} \, dx$
   - *Hint:* See Table 6.5.

7. $\displaystyle\int_0^{\frac{\pi}{4}} \tan x \, dx$

8. $\displaystyle\int z^2 \, e^{z^3} \, dz$

9. $\displaystyle\int \sqrt[3]{2 - x} \, dx$

10. $\displaystyle\int_{-2}^2 \cos(2x + 4) \, dx$

11. $\displaystyle\int \frac{\cos t \, dt}{1 + \sin t}$

12. $\displaystyle\int \frac{x}{\sqrt{1 - x^2}} \, dx$

13. $\displaystyle\int \frac{y + 1}{y^2 + 2y} \, dy$

14. $\displaystyle\int \frac{dx}{\cos^2 x \sqrt{1 + \tan x}}$

15. $\displaystyle\int_0^{\frac{\pi}{4}} \frac{\sin x}{\cos^2 x} \, dx$

16. $\displaystyle\int \sec x \, dx$
    - *Hint:* Multiply the numerator and denominator by the same expression, namely, $\sec x + \tan x$, use some identity, and then a substitution.

17. $\displaystyle\int (z^4 + z)^4 \cdot (4z^3 + 1) \, dz$

18. $\displaystyle\int \frac{\sin x}{1 + \cos^2 x} \, dx$

19. $\displaystyle\int_0^1 \frac{t}{t^4 + 1} \, dt$

20. $\displaystyle\int x \, \sin^3(x^2 + 1) \cos(x^2 + 1) \, dx$
    - *Hint:* This one requires *two* substitutions.

21. $\displaystyle \int \frac{3x-1}{x^2+1}\,dx$

    • *Hint:* Separate this integral into two parts and apply appropriate substitutions to each one, separately.

22. $\displaystyle \int_e^{e^2} \frac{dx}{x\ln x}$, where $e = 2.71828...$ is Euler's constant.

23. $\displaystyle \int \frac{(\text{Arctan}\,x)^2}{1+x^2}\,dx$

24. $\displaystyle \int \frac{\cosh(e^t)}{e^{-t}}\,dt$

25. $\displaystyle \int \frac{ds}{\sqrt{1-25s^2}}$

26. $\displaystyle \int_{\pi^2}^{4\pi^2} \frac{\cos\sqrt{x}}{\sqrt{x}}\,dx$

27. $\displaystyle \int x\,e^{x^2}\,dx$

28. $\displaystyle \int \frac{1+y}{\sqrt{1-y^2}}\,dy$

29. $\displaystyle \int \sec(\ln x)\tan(\ln x)\,\frac{dx}{x}$

30. $\displaystyle \int \frac{\cos x}{\sqrt[3]{\sin^2 x}}\,dx$

31. $\displaystyle \int_0^1 e^t e^{e^t}\,dt$

32. $\displaystyle \int x\,(1.5^{x^2+1})\,dx$

Suggested Homework Set 22. *Work out problems 1, 5, 7, 12, 15, 19, 21, 26, 29*

NOTES:

7.3 Integration by Parts

When you you've tried everything in the evaluation of a given integral using the Substitution Rule, you should resort to **Integration by Parts**. This procedure for the possible evaluation of a given integral (it doesn't always work, though) is the "reverse operation" of the Product Rule for derivatives (see Chapter 3). Recall that the Product Rule states that if u, v are each differentiable functions, then

$$\frac{d}{dx}(uv) = \frac{du}{dx} \cdot v + u \cdot \frac{dv}{dx},$$

where the "·" represents the usual product of two functions. Use of the Fundamental Theorem of Calculus (Chapter 7), tells us that, on integrating both sides and re-arranging terms, we find

$$\int \left(u\frac{dv}{dx} \right) \, dx \;=\; u(x)v(x) - \int \left(v\frac{du}{dx} \right) \, dx + C, \qquad (7.40)$$

where C is a constant of integration. This technique is useful when "nothing else seems to work". In fact, there is this old saying in Calculus, that says, "If you don't know what to do, try *integrating by parts*".

This formula is more commonly written as:

$$\int u \, dv = uv - \int v \, du, \qquad (7.41)$$

where u, v are functions with the property that the symbols $u \, dv$ make up all the terms appearing to the right of the integral sign, but we have to determine what these u, v actually look like!

| **Example 318.** | Evaluate $\int x \sin x \, dx$. |

Solution This business of integration can be time consuming. First, we'll do it the *long* way. It is completely justifiable but it has the disadvantage of just being long. After this we'll do it the *normal way* and, finally, we'll show you the *lightning fast* way of doing it.

The long way

We need to rewrite the integrand as a product of two functions, u and $\frac{dv}{dx}$ and so WE have to decide how to break up the terms inside the integrand! For example, here, we let

$$u = x, \quad \frac{dv}{dx} = \sin x.$$

Then, in accordance with (7.40), we need to find $\frac{du}{dx}$ and $v(x)$, right? But it is easy to see that

$$\frac{du}{dx} = 1, \quad v(x) = -\cos x,$$

since we are being asked to provide the antiderivative of $\sin x$ and the derivative of x. Combining these quantities into the general formula (7.40), we obtain

$$\int x \sin x \, dx \;=\; \int (u\frac{dv}{dx}) \, dx,$$

$$= u(x)v(x) - \int \left(v\frac{du}{dx}\right) dx + C,$$

$$= x(-\cos x) - \int (-\cos x)\cdot 1\ dx + C,$$

$$= -x\cos x + \int \cos x\ dx + C,$$

$$= -x\cos x + \sin x + C,$$

where C is our usual constant of integration. This answer can be checked as usual by differentiating it and showing that it can be brought into the form of "$x\ \sin x$". But this merely involves a simple application of the Product Rule. So, we have shown that,

$$\int x\sin x\ dx = -x\cos x + \sin x + C.$$

The normal way

For decades integrals involving the use of Integrations by Parts have been evaluated using this slighly faster and more convenient method. Let's apply it to the problem at hand. As before, we write

$$u = x,\ \ dv = \sin x\ dx.$$

We'll be using the modified version of the formula, namely, (7.41). The principle is the same, we just write

$$du = 1\ dx,\ \ v = -\cos x,$$

and now use (7.41) directly. This gives,

$$\int u\ dv = uv - \int v\ du,$$

$$= -x\cos x - \int (-\cos x)\ dx$$

$$= -x\cos x + \sin x + C,$$

just like before.

The Table Method

The answer follows by just "**looking**" at the Table below:

x	$\sin x$
1	$-\cos x$
0	$-\sin x$

This last method is essentially **a more rapid way of setting up the Integration by Parts environment** and it is completely justifiable (and also much faster, in most cases). This is how it works: Let's say that we want to evaluate

$$\int u\frac{dv}{dx}\ dx.$$

We set up a special table whose cells contain the entries as described:

The Table Method

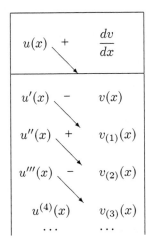

$u(x)$	$+$	$\dfrac{dv}{dx}$
$u'(x)$	$-$	$v(x)$
$u''(x)$	$+$	$v_{(1)}(x)$
$u'''(x)$	$-$	$v_{(2)}(x)$
$u^{(4)}(x)$		$v_{(3)}(x)$
$\ldots$		$\ldots$

The arrows indicate that the entries connected by such arrows are multiplied together and their product is preceded by the '+' or '−' sign directly above the arrow, in an alternating fashion as we move down the Table.

Table 7.1: Schematic Description of the Table Method

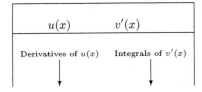

$u(x)$	$v'(x)$
Derivatives of $u(x)$	Integrals of $v'(x)$

so that the **first column (on the left) contains the successive derivatives of u** while the **second column (on the right) contains the successive antiderivatives (or integrals) of v**, (see Table 7.1). Here, u', u'', u''' denote the successive derivatives of u (they appear in the *first column*) and $v_{(1)}(x), v_{(2)}(x), \ldots$ the successive antiderivatives of v' (without the constants of integration), so that

$$v_{(1)}(x) = \int v(x)\, dx$$

$$v_{(2)}(x) = \int v_{(1)}(x)\, dx$$

$$v_{(3)}(x) = \int v_{(2)}(x)\, dx$$
$$\ldots$$

In Table 7.1, the arrows indicate that the entries connected by such arrows are multiplied together and their product is preceded by the '+' or '−' sign directly above the arrow, in an alternating fashion as we move down the Table. Don't worry, many examples will clarify this technique. Remember that this technique we call the Table Method must give the *correct answer* to any integration by parts problem as it is simply a re-interpretation of the normal method outlined at the beginning of this Section.

So, when do we stop calculating the entries in the Table?

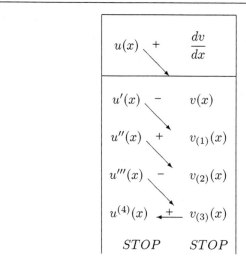

$$\int u \frac{dv}{dx} dx = u(x)v(x) - u'(x)v_{(1)}(x) + u''(x)v_{(2)}(x) - u'''v_{(3)}(x) + \int u^{(4)}v_{(3)} dx$$

where the last integral is obtained by taking the antiderivative of the product of the two entries in the given row (here, $v_{(3)}u^{(4)}$), producing an arrow from right to left, and multiplying the product by either "+1" (if the row number is ODD) or "−1" (if the row number is EVEN).

Here, the row number is 5 so we multiply the product by +1 which means that the product stays unchanged. We show this by placing a "+" sign above the last arrow to remind us.

Table 7.2: Example of the Table Method: Stopping at the 5th Row

Normally, we try to stop when one of the two columns contains a zero entry (normally the one on the left). In fact, this is the general idea in using this Method. But the general rule of thumb is this:

Remember: Functions in the **left column are differentiated** while those in the **right column are integrated!**

Look at every row of the table and see if any of the products of the two quantities in that row can be integrated without much effort. If you find such a row, stop filling in the table and proceed as follows:

Let's say you decide to stop at row "n". Then the **last term in your answer must be the integral of the PRODUCT of the two functions in that row, multiplied by the constant $(-1)^{n-1}$ (which is either ± 1 depending on the whether n is even or odd). We can stop anytime and read a result such as the one in Table 7.2.**

Example 319. Evaluate $I = \int x \sin^{-1}(\frac{1}{x}) \, dx$

Solution We can see that it if we place the Arcsine term on the right column of our Table, it will be very difficult to integrate, so we can't get to the second row! OK, just forget about it and place it on the left!

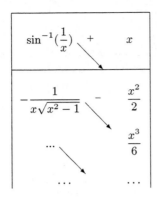

Okay, now you're looking at this table and you're probably starting to worry!? Things are not getting any easier and there is the calculation of the derivative to go in row three (on the left) which will be a nightmare ... But wait! find the product of the two functions in row 2. This gives us

$$\frac{-x}{2\sqrt{x^2-1}},$$

which is a function which we CAN integrate easily (if we use the substitution $u = x^2 - 1$). Okay, this is really good so we can STOP at row 2 and use Table 7.2 to get the modified table,

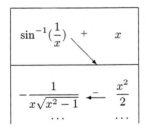

The answer is easily read off as:

$$\int x \sin^{-1}(\frac{1}{x})\, dx = \frac{x^2}{2} \sin^{-1}(\frac{1}{x}) - \int \frac{x^2}{2} \left(-\frac{1}{x\sqrt{x^2-1}}\right)\, dx,$$
$$= \frac{x^2}{2} \sin^{-1}(\frac{1}{x}) + \int \frac{x}{2\sqrt{x^2-1}}\, dx,$$
$$= \frac{x^2}{2} \sin^{-1}(\frac{1}{x}) + \frac{1}{4} \int \frac{du}{\sqrt{u}},\ (u = x^2 - 1,\ du = 2x\, dx,\ \text{etc.}),$$
$$= \frac{x^2}{2} \sin^{-1}(\frac{1}{x}) + \frac{1}{4}(2u^{\frac{1}{2}}),$$
$$= \frac{x^2}{2} \sin^{-1}(\frac{1}{x}) + \frac{(x^2-1)^{\frac{1}{2}}}{2} + C.$$

7.3.1   The Product of a Polynomial and a Sine or Cosine

The previous method can be used directly to evaluate any integrals of the form

$\int (polynomial\ in\ x)\ (sine/cosine\ function\ in\ x)\, dx$

SUMMARY We put all the successive derivatives on the left and all the successive antiderivatives (or indefinite integrals) on the right until we reach a "zero term" on the left, or until we decide we want to stop!

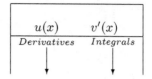

Now, find the product of the terms joined by arrows, with the sign in front of that product being the sign appearing over that arrow. Add up all such products to get the answer! In other words, terms connected by arrows are multiplied together and their product is preceded by the '+' or '−' sign directly above the arrow, in an alternating fashion as we move down the Table.

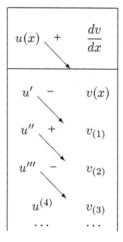

If you decide to STOP then you must use SOMETHING LIKE the NEXT formulae (for example) to get your answer:

$$\int u \frac{dv}{dx} dx = u(x)v(x) - u'(x)v_{(1)}(x) + \int u'' v_{(1)} \ dx, \qquad (7.42)$$

or,

$$\int u \frac{dv}{dx} dx = u(x)v(x) - u'(x)v_{(1)}(x) + u''(x)v_{(2)}(x) - \int u''' v_{(2)} \ dx,$$

or,

$$\int u \frac{dv}{dx} dx = u(x)v(x) - u'(x)v_{(1)}(x) + u''(x)v_{(2)}(x) - u'''(x)v_{(3)}(x) + \int u^{(4)} v_{(3)} dx,$$

and so on.

Table 7.3: Efficient Integration by Parts Setup

where the integrand is a product of a polynomial and either a sine or a cosine function.

Example 320. Evaluate $\int x \sin x \; dx$, using the method outlined above or summarized in Table 7.3.

Solution We apply the technique in Table 7.3 to our original question, Example 318. Using the rules described we find the table,

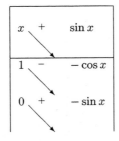

and the answer is read off as follows:

JUST remember to STOP when you see a zero in the LEFT column

$$(+1) \cdot x \cdot (-\cos x) + (-1) \cdot (1) \cdot (-\sin x) \quad = \quad -x \cos x + \sin x,$$

to which we add our constant of integration, C, at the very end!

Example 321. Evaluate $\int 2x^3 \cos 2x \; dx$.

Solution If done the "long way", this example would require a few coffees. Using the method in Table 7.3, however, we can obtain the answer fairly quickly. All that needs to be observed is that, if $a \neq 0$ is a number, then an antiderivative of $\cos ax$ is given by

$$\int \cos ax \; dx \quad = \quad \frac{\sin ax}{a},$$

(from the Substitution Rule) while, if $a \neq 0$, an antiderivative of $\sin ax$ is given by

$$\int \sin ax \; dx \quad = \quad -\frac{\cos ax}{a}.$$

The Table now takes the form,

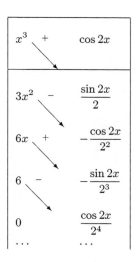

EXAMPLES

We conclude with the answer in the form,

$$\int 2x^3 \cos 2x \, dx = 2 \int x^3 \cos 2x \, dx,$$

$$= 2\left\{ \frac{x^3 \sin 2x}{2} - (-1)\frac{3x^2 \cos 2x}{2^2} + (-6x)\frac{\sin 2x}{2^3} - 6\frac{\cos 2x}{2^4} \right\},$$

$$= x^3 \sin 2x + \frac{3}{2} \cdot x^2 \cos 2x - \frac{3}{2} \cdot x \sin 2x - \frac{3}{4} \cdot \cos 2x + C.$$

Example 322.   Evaluate $\int (x^3 + 2x^2 - x + 3) \, \sin(3x + 4) \, dx$.

Solution We proceed as in Example 321. The Table now takes the form,

We can conclude with the answer in the form,

$$\int (x^3 + 2x^2 - x + 3) \, \sin(3x + 4) \, dx = -\frac{(x^3 + 2x^2 - x + 3) \, \cos(3x + 4)}{3} +$$

$$+ \frac{(3x^2 + 4x - 1) \, \sin(3x + 4)}{3^2} +$$

$$\frac{(6x+4)\,\cos(3x+4)}{3^3} - \frac{6\sin(3x+4)}{3^4}$$
$$+C.$$

7.3.2 The Product of a Polynomial and an Exponential

The same idea is used to evaluate an inteegral involving the product of a polynomial and an exponential term. We set the tables up as before and place the polynomial on the left and differentiate it until we get the "0" function while, on the right, we keep integrating the exponentials only to STOP when the corresponding entry on the left is the 0 function.

| Example 323. | Evaluate $\int xe^x\,dx$. |

Solution In this case, the Table is

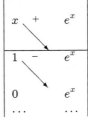

and the final answer can be written as,

$$\int xe^x\,dx \;=\; xe^x - e^x + C.$$

Observe that, if $a \neq 0$ is any number (positive or negative), then an antiderivative of e^{ax} is given by

$$\int e^{ax}\,dx \;=\; \frac{e^{ax}}{a},$$

(from the Substitution Rule).

| Example 324. | Evaluate $\int x^2 e^{-2x}\,dx$. |

Solution In this case, the Table is

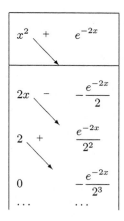

and the final answer can be written as,

$$\int x^2 e^{-2x} \, dx \;=\; -\frac{x^2 e^{-2x}}{2} - \frac{2x e^{-2x}}{2^2} - \frac{2 e^{-2x}}{2^3},$$

$$=\; -\frac{e^{-2x}}{2}\left\{x^2 + x + \frac{1}{2}\right\} + C.$$

Example 325.   Evaluate $\displaystyle\int x^2 e^{3x} \, dx$.

Solution We use the method in Table 7.3. The Table now takes the form,

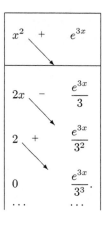

EXAMPLES

and the final answer can be written as,

$$\int x^2 e^{3x} \, dx \;=\; \frac{e^{3x}}{3}\left\{x^2 - \frac{2x}{3} + \frac{2}{9}\right\} + C.$$

Example 326.   Evaluate $\displaystyle\int_0^1 x^3 \, 2^{-2x} \, dx$.

Solution This one looks mysterious but we can bring it down to a more recognizable form. For example, let's recall (from Chapter 4) that

$$\begin{aligned}
2^{-2x} &= e^{\ln 2^{-2x}}, \\
&= e^{(-2\ln 2)x}, \\
&= e^{-(ln4)x}, \\
&= e^{ax},
\end{aligned}$$

if we set $a = -\ln 4$. So, we can set up the Table

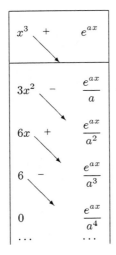

from which the answer can be read off as (remember that $a = -\ln 4$, and so $e^a = \frac{1}{4}$),

$$
\begin{aligned}
\int_0^1 x^3\, 2^{-2x}\, dx &= \int_0^1 x^3\, e^{ax}\, dx, \\
&= \left\{ \frac{x^3\, e^{ax}}{a} - \frac{3x^2\, e^{ax}}{a^2} + \frac{6x\, e^{ax}}{a^3} - \frac{6e^{ax}}{a^4} \right\}\Bigg|_0^1, \\
&= \left\{ \frac{e^a}{a} - \frac{3e^a}{a^2} + \frac{6e^a}{a^3} - \frac{6e^a}{a^4} \right\} - \left\{ -\frac{6}{a^4} \right\}, \\
&= \frac{1}{4a} - \frac{3}{4a^2} + \frac{3}{2a^3} - \frac{3}{2a^4} + \frac{6}{a^4}, \quad \left(\text{as } e^a = \frac{1}{4} \right), \\
&= \frac{a^3 - 3a^2 + 6a + 18}{4a^4}, \\
&\approx 0.08479
\end{aligned}
$$

since $a = -\ln 4 \approx -1.3863$.

As one can see, this method is very efficient for evaluating general integrals of the form

$$\int (polynomial\ in\ x)\ (exponential\ in\ x)\ dx.$$

Basically, we set up a table with the *polynomial function on the left* and then find all its derivatives until we reach the "zero" function and this is where we STOP. See the previous examples.

7.3.3 The Product of a Polynomial and a Logarithm

The case where the integrand is a product of a poynomial and a logarithmic function can be handled by means of a *simple substitution* which effectively replaces the integrand involving a logarithmic term by an integrand with an exponential term so that we can use the table method of Section 7.3.2. Let's look at a few examples.

Example 327. Evaluate $\int \ln x\ dx$.

Solution In this example, the presence of the "logarithmic term" complicates the situation and it turns out to be *easier to integrate the polynomial and differentiate the logarithm* than the other way around. Note that "1" is a polynomial (of degree 0).

The Table method as used in Example 319 gives us easily

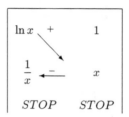

EXAMPLES

and from this we can write down the answer as,

$$\int \ln x \ dx \ = \ x \ \ln x - \int x \ \left(\frac{1}{x}\right) \ dx,$$
$$= \ x \ \ln x - x + C.$$

Example 328. Evaluate $\int x^2 \ln x \ dx$.

Solution Let's write this one out using both the Table Method and the *normal way.* Note that an application of the Table method to the first two rows of Table 7.3 just gives the ordinary Integration by Parts Formula. In other words, using the method described in Example 319 we find the table

From this we see that

$$\int x^2 \ln x \ dx \ = \ \frac{x^3 \ln x}{3} - \int \frac{x^3}{3} \frac{1}{x} \ dx,$$
$$= \ \frac{x^3 \ln x}{3} - \frac{1}{3} \int x^2 \ dx,$$
$$= \ \frac{x^3 \ln x}{3} - \frac{x^3}{9} + C.$$

Had we done this using the *normal way*, we would set $u = \ln x$, $dv = x^2 \ dx$ which means that $du = \frac{1}{x} \ dx$, and $v = \frac{x^3}{3}$. Thus,

$$\int x^2 \ln x \ dx \ = \ \frac{x^3 \ln x}{3} - \int \frac{x^3}{3} \frac{1}{x} \ dx,$$
$$= \ \frac{x^3 \ln x}{3} - \frac{1}{3} \int x^2 \ dx,$$
$$= \ \frac{x^3 \ln x}{3} - \frac{x^3}{9} + C.$$

OK, so the moral is: " If you see a logarithm by itself (not a power of such) then try putting it on the left of the Table ...", so that you can differentiate it. The situation where the logarithm has a power attached to it is more delicate. Sometimes, there are examples where this idea of differentiating the logarithmic term just doesn't work easily, but our Table idea *does* work!

Example 329. Evaluate $\int x^4 (\ln x)^3 \, dx$.

Solution This is a problem involving the power of a logarithm. Any "normal method" will be lengthy. The basic idea here is to **transform out** the logarithmic term by a **substitution which converts the integrand to a product of a polynomial and an exponential** (so we can use Section 7.3.2). This is best accomplished by the *inverse function* of the logarithm (the exponential function). We let

$$x = e^t, \quad \ln x = t, \quad dx = e^t \, dt,$$

which will convert the given integral to one of the types that we have seen ... that is,

$$\int x^4 (\ln x)^3 \, dx = \int e^{4t} t^3 (e^t \, dt),$$
$$= \int t^3 e^{5t} \, dt.$$

Setting up the table we find,

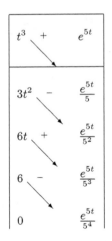

which gives the answer in terms of the "t" variable, that is,

$$\int x^4 (\ln x)^3 \, dx = \int t^3 e^{5t} \, dt,$$
$$= \frac{t^3 e^{5t}}{5} - \frac{3t^2 e^{5t}}{5^2} + \frac{6t e^{5t}}{5^3} - \frac{6 e^{5t}}{5^4} + C,$$
$$= \frac{e^{5t}}{5} \left\{ t^3 - \frac{3t^2}{5} + \frac{6t}{5^2} - \frac{6}{5^3} \right\} + C,$$
$$= \frac{x^5}{5} \left\{ (\ln x)^3 - \frac{3(\ln x)^2}{5} + \frac{6(\ln x)}{5^2} - \frac{6}{5^3} \right\} + C,$$

after our final *back substitution*.

7.3.4 The Product of an Exponential and a Sine or Cosine

The next technique involves the product of an exponential with a sine or cosine function. These integrals are common in the scientific literature so we'll present another method based on Table 7.3 for adapting to this situation.

Example 330. Evaluate $I = \int e^{2x} \sin 3x \; dx$.

Solution We set up a table based on our usual Table 7.3.

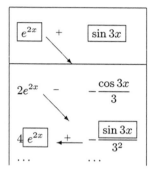

In this case we note that the **the functions appearing in the third row are the same as the first** (aside from the coefficients and their signs). So, we **STOP at the third row**, (this is the rule), and realize that according to Table 7.3, equation (7.42),

$$I = \frac{-e^{2x}\cos 3x}{3} + \frac{2e^{2x}\sin 3x}{3^2} - \frac{4}{9}I$$

or, solving for I, we find

$$\frac{13}{9}I = \frac{e^{2x}}{3}\left(\frac{2\sin 3x}{3} - \cos 3x\right)$$

or

$$I = \frac{3e^{2x}}{13}\left(\frac{2\sin 3x}{3} - \cos 3x\right),$$

i.e., the most general antiderivative is given by

$$I \;=\; \frac{e^{2x}}{13}(2\sin 3x - 3\cos 3x) + C, \tag{7.43}$$

The MyCar Method

where C is a constant.

NOTE: OK, OK, but is there a way of getting from our Table right down to the answer without having to calculate the I symbol like we did? YES! Here's the **MyCar** ... method:

• Use the usual method of Table 7.3 and STOP at the third row. Now, refer to Figure 146 in the adjoining margin. Then write down the following expression

$$I \;=\; \square \left(\frac{-e^{2x}\cos 3x}{3} + \frac{2e^{2x}\sin 3x}{3^2} \right), \qquad (7.44)$$

where **the "number" in the box**, $\square$, is given explicitly by:

- **a) Multiplying,** "My" (for short), the coefficients in the third row (with their signs!)

  Here: $(4)(-\frac{1}{9}) = -\frac{4}{9}$

- **b) Changing,** "C" (for short), the sign of the number in a)

  Here: $+\frac{4}{9}$

- **c) Adding,** "A" for short, the number "**1**" to b)

  Here: $1 + \frac{4}{9} = \frac{13}{9}$

- **d) Finding the Reciprocal,** "R" for short, of the number in c)

  Here: $\frac{9}{13}$

- **e) Inserting the number in d) into the BOX in equation (7.44), above.** This is your answer! (aside from the usual constant of integration). Here:

$$I \;=\; \boxed{\tfrac{9}{13}} \left(\frac{-e^{2x}\cos 3x}{3} + \frac{2e^{2x}\sin 3x}{3^2} \right),$$

which gives the SAME answer as before, see equation (7.43).

This process of finding the number in the box, $\square$, can be remembered through the steps, see Figure 146,

<u>M</u>ULTIPLY, <u>C</u>HANGE SIGN, <u>A</u>DD 1, find the <u>R</u>ECIPROCAL

Example 331. Evaluate $I = \displaystyle\int e^{3x} \cos 4x \, dx$.

Solution We proceed as per Figure 146. We set up our table as usual,

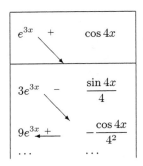

The asnwer is of the form:

$$I \;=\; \square \left\{ \frac{e^{3x}\sin 4x}{4} + \frac{3e^{3x}\cos 4x}{4^2} \right\} + C,$$

where the number in the box is found easily if you ...

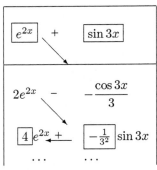

Briefly said, you

- MULTIPLY,
- CHANGE SIGN,
- ADD 1 and find the,
- RECIPROCAL

Figure 146.

- **MULTIPLY:** $-\frac{9}{16}$

- **CHANGE SIGN:** $\frac{9}{16}$

- **ADD** 1: $\frac{25}{16}$

- **find theRECIPROCAL:** $\frac{16}{25}$.

MULTIPLY,
CHANGE SIGN,
ADD 1, find the
RECIPROCAL

The answer is

$$
I = \frac{16}{25}\left\{\frac{e^{3x}\sin 4x}{4} + \frac{3e^{3x}\cos 4x}{4^2}\right\} + C,
$$
$$
= \frac{1}{25}\left\{4e^{3x}\sin 4x + 3e^{3x}\cos 4x\right\} + C.
$$

The same method can be used for other such **three-row problems**. We give them this name because our table only requires *three* rows!

Example 332.	Evaluate $I = \int \sin 3x\ \cos 4x\ dx$.

Solution **Normal method** This is *normally done* using a trigonometric identity, namely,

$$
\sin A\cos B = \frac{\sin(A+B) + \sin(A-B)}{2},
$$

where we set $A = 3x$ and $B = 4x$. This gives,

$$
\int \sin 3x\ \cos 4x\ dx = \int \frac{\sin 7x + \sin(-x)}{2}\ dx, \tag{7.45}
$$
$$
= \int \frac{\sin 7x}{2}\ dx - \int \frac{\sin x}{2}\ dx, \tag{7.46}
$$
$$
= -\frac{\cos 7x}{14} + \frac{\cos x}{2} + C, \tag{7.47}
$$

where we used the basic fact that the sine function is an odd function (see Chapter 5), that is, $\sin(-x) = -\sin(x)$, an identity which is valid for any x.

Table method Refer to the preceding examples. We set up the table,

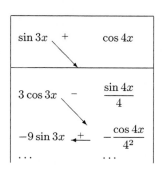

to find that

$$
I = \square\left\{\frac{\sin 3x\sin 4x}{4} + \frac{3\cos 3x\cos 4x}{16}\right\} + C,
$$

where the factor in the box, $\square$, is given by

- **MULTIPLY:** $\frac{9}{16}$

- **CHANGE SIGN:** $-\frac{9}{16}$

- **ADD 1:** $\frac{7}{16}$

- **find the RECIPROCAL:** $\frac{16}{7}$,

and so, we put $\frac{16}{7}$ in the Box, as the factor. The final answer is,

$$I \;=\; \frac{16}{7} \left\{ \frac{\sin 3x \sin 4x}{4} + \frac{3 \cos 3x \cos 4x}{16} \right\} + C, \qquad (7.48)$$

$$=\; \frac{1}{7} \left\{ 4 \sin 3x \sin 4x + 3 \cos 3x \cos 4x \right\} + C. \qquad (7.49)$$

NOTE: Although this answer appears to be VERY different from the one given in (7.47) they must be the same *up to a constant*, right? This means that their difference must be a constant! In fact, repeated use of trigonometric identities show that **equations (7.47), (7.49) are equal**.

As a final example we emphasize that it is "generally" easier to convert an integral containing a natural logarithm to one involving an exponential for reasons that were described above.

Example 333. Evaluate $I = \displaystyle\int \sin(\ln x)\, dx$.

Solution Let $x = e^u$, $u = \ln x$ and $dx = e^u\, du$. This is the substitution which "takes out" the natural logarithm and replaces it by an exponential term. Then

$$I \;=\; \int \sin(\ln x)\, dx,$$

$$=\; \int e^u \sin u\, du.$$

Now use the idea in Figure 146. We get the table,

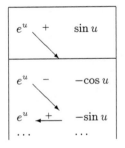

The answer now takes the form,

$$I \;=\; \frac{1}{2} \left\{ e^u \sin u - e^u \cos u \right\} + C,$$

$$=\; \frac{1}{2} \left\{ x \sin(\ln x) - x \cos(\ln x) \right\} + C,$$

after the usual 'back-substitution'.

SNAPSHOTS

Example 334. Evaluate $\int_0^1 x^2 e^{-4x}\ dx$.

Solution The table looks like,

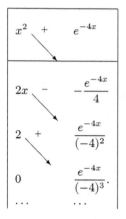

and the indefinite integral can be written as

$$\int x^2 e^{-4x}\ dx\ =\ -\frac{x^2 e^{-4x}}{4} - \frac{xe^{-4x}}{8} - \frac{e^{-4x}}{32} + C,$$

from which we obtain the definite integral

$$\int_0^1 x^2 e^{-4x}\ dx\ =\ -\frac{x^2 e^{-4x}}{4} - \frac{xe^{-4x}}{8} - \frac{e^{-4x}}{32}\bigg|_0^1,$$

$$=\ \left\{ -\frac{e^{-4}}{4} - \frac{e^{-4}}{8} - \frac{e^{-4}}{32} \right\} - \left\{ -\frac{1}{32} \right\},$$

$$=\ -\frac{13}{32}e^{-4} + \frac{1}{32},$$

$$\approx\ 0.02381.$$

Example 335. Evaluate $I = \int_0^{\frac{\pi}{2}} t^2 \cos(2t)\ dt$

Solution We set up our table,

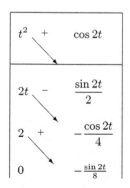

From this we find,

$$I = \frac{t^2 \sin 2t}{2} + \frac{2t \cos 2t}{4} - \frac{2 \sin 2t}{8} + C$$

$$= \frac{t^2 \sin 2t}{2} + \frac{t \cos 2t}{2} - \frac{\sin 2t}{4} + C,$$

and so the definite integral is given by,

$$I = \left\{ \frac{t^2 \sin 2t}{2} + \frac{t \cos 2t}{2} - \frac{\sin 2t}{4} \right\} \Bigg|_0^{\frac{\pi}{2}},$$

$$= -\frac{\pi}{4}.$$

Example 336. Evaluate $I = \int x^3 (\ln x)^2 \, dx$.

Solution Let $x = e^t$, $\ln x = t$, $dx = e^t \, dt$. Then

$$I = \int e^{3t} t^2 e^t \, dt = \int t^2 e^{4t} \, dt,$$

and we obtain the table,

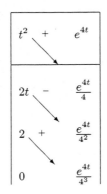

from which we find,

$$I = \frac{t^2 e^{4t}}{4} - \frac{2t e^{4t}}{4^2} + \frac{2 e^{4t}}{4^3} + C,$$

$$= \frac{x^4 (\ln x)^2}{4} - \frac{2 x^4 \ln x}{4^2} + \frac{2 x^4}{4^3} + C,$$

$$= \frac{x^4 (\ln x)^2}{4} - \frac{x^4 \ln x}{8} + \frac{x^4}{32} + C.$$

Example 337. Evaluate $I = \int \cos(3x) \cos(5x) \, dx$, *a "three-row problem"*.

Solution We set it up according to Figure 146. In this example, it doesn't matter which term goes on the right or left, as both can be easily differentiated or integrated. The table is,

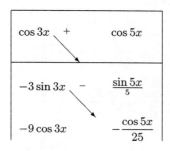

So,

$$I = \square \left(\frac{\cos 3x \sin 5x}{5} - \frac{3 \sin 3x \cos 5x}{25} \right),$$

where the factor in $\square$ is obtained by the **MyCar** method:

a) $\frac{9}{25}$

b) $-\frac{9}{25}$

c) $\frac{16}{25}$

d) $\frac{25}{16}$, in the Box, above.

Finally,

$$
\begin{aligned}
I &= \frac{25}{16} \left(\frac{\cos 3x \sin 5x}{5} - \frac{3 \sin 3x \cos 5x}{25} \right), \\
&= \frac{1}{16} \left(5 \cos 3x \sin 5x - 3 \sin 3x \cos 5x \right).
\end{aligned}
$$

NOTES:

Exercise Set 33.

Evaluate the following integrals.

1. $\int x \cos x \, dx$

2. $\int x \sin x \, dx$

3. $\int_0^{\frac{\pi}{2}} x \cos 2x \, dx$

4. $\int x^2 \sin x \, dx$

5. $\int x \sec^2 x \, dx$

6. $\int x \sec x \tan x \, dx$

7. $\int x^2 e^x \, dx$

8. $\int_0^{+\infty} x^2 e^{-3x} \, dx$

9. $\int x^4 \ln x \, dx$

10. $\int x^3 e^{-3x} \, dx$

11. $\int \sin^{-1} x \, dx$

12. $\int \tan^{-1} x \, dx$

13. $\int x^2 (\ln x)^5 \, dx$

14. $\int x \sec^{-1} x \, dx$, for $x > 1$.

15. $\int (x-1)^2 \sin x \, dx$

16. $\int e^{-2x} \sin 3x \, dx$

17. $\int e^x \cos 4x \, dx$

18. $\int \sin 3x \cos 2x \, dx$

19. $\int \sin 2x \cos 4x \, dx$

20. $\int \cos 3x \cos 4x \, dx$

21. $\int x^5 e^{2x} \, dx$

22. $\int \cos \ln x \, dx$

Suggested Homework Set 23. *Problems 4, 8, 9, 13, 16, 19, 21, 22*

NOTES:

7.4 Partial Fractions

In this section we study a method for integrating rational functions, that is, functions which are the quotient of two polynomials, (see Chapter 5.2). For example,

$$3, \quad x - 1, \quad \frac{x^2 - 1}{x + 2}, \quad \frac{x^3 + 2x - 1}{x^4 + 2x + 6}$$

are all rational functions. Of course, polynomials are rational functions as we can always take the denominator to be equal to the polynomial, 1. On the other hand, polynomials are easy to integrate so we'll look at those rational functions whose denominator is not a constant function.

Review

Study the procedure of long division (next section) very carefully if you've not seen it before. Look over Chapter 5.1-2, in particular, the definition of quadratic irreducible polynomials (Type II factors).

The study of polynomials is an important area of Calculus due to their widespread applications to mathematics and the pure and applied sciences and engineering. In this section we're going to review the method for dividing one polynomial by another of the same or lower degree (and you'll get a *rational function!*). The method is called **long division**. This technique of dividing polynomials is especially useful in dealing with the **method of partial fractions** which occurs when we consider the problem of integrating a given rational function.

Specifically, let $p(x), q(x)$ be two polynomials in x with real coefficients and assume that the degree of $p(x)$, denoted by *deg* $p(x)$, satisfies

$$deg \ p(x) \geq deg \ q(x).$$

For example, $p(x) = x^2 - 1$ and $q(x) = -2x^2 + 2x - 1$ have the same degree, namely, 2. On the other hand, $p(x) = x^3$ and $q(x) = x^2 + 1$ have different degrees and $3 = deg \ p(x) > deg \ q(x) = 2$. If $deg \ p(x) < deg \ q(x)$ we can't apply long division, as such, but we can do our best at factoring both and this situation leads naturally to the subject of **partial fractions**. A partial fraction consists of a special representation of a rational function. We just rewrite the function in another way. For example, the right-side of

$$\frac{5x - 7}{x^2 - 3x + 2} \quad = \quad \frac{3}{x - 2} + \frac{2}{x - 1},$$

is the partial fraction decomposition of the function on the left. The function on the right is the *same* function, it just looks different. This difference, however, will make it very convenient when it comes to integrating the function on the left because the antiderivative of anyone of the two functions on the right gives a natural logarithm. In other words,

$$\begin{aligned}
\int \frac{5x - 7}{x^2 - 3x + 2} \ dx \quad &= \quad \int \frac{3}{x - 2} \ dx + \int \frac{2}{x - 1} \ dx, \\
&= \quad 3 \ln |x - 2| + 2 \ln |x - 1| + C, \\
&= \quad \ln \left| (x - 2)^3 (x - 1)^2 \right| + C.
\end{aligned}$$

We start this section by studying (or reviewing) the method of long division.

7.4.1 Review of Long Division of Polynomials

The study of polynomials is an important area of Calculus due to their widespread applications to mathematics and the pure and applied sciences and engineering. In this section we're going to review the method for dividing one polynomial by another of the same or lower degree (and you'll get a *rational function!*). This technique is especially useful in dealing with the **method of partial fractions** which occurs when we consider **methods of integration**...which we'll see later.

Specifically, let $p(x), q(x)$ be two polynomials in x with real coefficients and assume that the degree of $p(x)$, denoted by *deg* $p(x)$, satisfies

$$deg\ p(x) \geq deg\ q(x).$$

For example, $p(x) = x^2 - 1$ and $q(x) = -2x^2 + 2x - 1$ have the same degree, namely, 2. On the other hand, $p(x) = x^3$ and $q(x) = x^2 + 1$ have different degrees and $3 = deg\ p(x) > deg\ q(x) = 2$. If $deg\ p(x) < deg\ q(x)$ there is no need to apply long division, as such, but we do our best at factoring the denominator.

The method for dividing polynomials of equal or different degrees by one another is similar to the procedure of dividing integers by one another, but the *long way*, that is, without a calculator. Let's start off with an example to set the ideas straight.

Example 338. Simplify the following rational function using long division:

$$\frac{x^3 + x - 1}{x^3 - 2}$$

.

Solution In this example, $deg\ p(x) = 3 = deg\ q(x)$, where $p(x)$ is the numerator, and $q(x)$ is the denominator. The result of long division is given in Figure 147 and is written as

$$\frac{x^3 + x - 1}{x^3 - 2} = 1 + \frac{x + 1}{x^3 - 2}.$$

The polynomial quantity "$x + 1$" left over at the bottom, whose degree is **smaller** than the degree of the denominator, is called the **remainder** of the long division procedure, and, after all is said and done, we can write the answer in the form

$$\frac{p(x)}{q(x)} = (new\ polynomial) + \frac{(remainder)}{(denominator)}.$$

We can summarize the procedure here:

Example 339. Use long division to simplify the rational function

$$\frac{x^4 + 3x^2 - 2x + 1}{x + 1}.$$

Solution Okay, we know from Table 7.4 that the answer will have a remainder whose degree is less than 1, and so it must be 0 (a constant polynomial), and the "new polynomial" part will have degree equal to $deg\ p(x) - deg\ q(x) = 4 - 1 = 3$. The procedure is shown in Figure 148 in the margin.

So we see from this that the remainder is just the number (constant polynomial), 7, and the answer is

$$\frac{x^4 + 3x^2 - 2x + 1}{x + 1} = x^3 - x^2 + 4x - 6 + \frac{7}{x + 1}$$

$$
\begin{array}{r}
1 \qquad\qquad\quad \\
x^3 - 2 \overline{\smash{\big)}\ x^3\ + x\ - 1} \\
\underline{x^3\qquad\ -2} \\
x\ + 1
\end{array}
$$

Figure 147.

$$
\begin{array}{r}
x^3 - x^2 + 4x - 6 \\
x + 1 \overline{\smash{\big)}\ x^4\qquad + 3x^2 - 2x + 1} \\
\underline{x^4 + x^3} \\
-x^3 + 3x^2 - 2x + 1 \\
\underline{-x^3 - x^2} \\
+4x^2 - 2x + 1 \\
\underline{4x^2 + 4x} \\
-6x + 1 \\
\underline{-6x - 6} \\
+ 7
\end{array}
$$

Figure 148.

> Let $deg\ p(x) \geq deg\ q(x)$. The result of a long division of $p(x)$ by $q(x)$ looks like
> $$\frac{p(x)}{q(x)} = (new\ polynomial) + \frac{(remainder)}{q(x)}$$
> where the degree of the remainder is smaller than the degree of the denominator, $q(x)$, and where the degree of the new polynomial is equal to the degree of the numerator *minus* the degree of the denominator. Mathematically, this can be summarized by saying that,
> $$deg\ (remainder) < deg\ (denominator)$$
> $$deg\ (new\ polynomial) = deg\ (numerator) - deg\ (denominator)$$

Table 7.4: The Result of a Long Division

a result which can be easily verified by finding a common denominator for the expression on the right and expanding the result.

Example 340. Use long division and simplify
$$\frac{p(x)}{q(x)} = \frac{x^4 + x^3 + x^2 + x + 1}{2x^2 + 1}.$$

$$2x^2 + 1 \begin{array}{|l} \dfrac{x^2 + x + \frac{1}{2}}{2x^4 + 2x^3 + 2x^2 + 2x + 2} \\ \underline{2x^4 \qquad\quad + x^2} \\ \quad 2x^3 + x^2 + 2x + 2 \\ \quad \underline{2x^3 + \qquad +x} \\ \qquad\quad x^2 + x + 2 \\ \qquad\quad \underline{x^2 \qquad + 1/2} \\ \qquad\qquad\quad x + 3/2 \end{array}$$

Figure 149.

Solution As before, Table 7.4 tells us that the answer will have a remainder whose degree is less than 2, and so it must be 1 *or* 0 (either a linear or a constant polynomial), and the "new polynomial" will have degree equal to $deg\ p(x) - deg\ q(x) = 4 - 2 = 2$. Now, **in order to try and avoid fractions in our calculations as much as possible** we'll multiply both $p(x), q(x)$ by "2", the leading coefficient of the polynomial, $q(x)$. You can always do this and you'll still be OK in your answer. Then, **we'll forget about the "extra 1/2" until the end** because ...

$$\frac{x^4 + x^3 + x^2 + x + 1}{2x^2 + 1} = \boxed{\tfrac{1}{2}} \left(\frac{2x^4 + 2x^3 + 2x^2 + 2x + 2}{2x^2 + 1} \right).$$

This procedure is shown in Figure 149 in the margin. So, we see from this that the remainder is the linear polynomial $x + 3/2$, and

$$\frac{x^4 + x^3 + x^2 + x + 1}{2x^2 + 1} = \boxed{\tfrac{1}{2}} \left(x^2 + x + \frac{1}{2} + \frac{x + 3/2}{2x^2 + 1} \right).$$

or

$$\frac{p(x)}{q(x)} = \frac{x^2}{2} + \frac{x}{2} + \frac{1}{4} + \left(\frac{2x + 3}{8x^2 + 4} \right).$$

Example 341. Simplify the rational function
$$\frac{p(x)}{q(x)} = \frac{3x^3 + 3x^2 + 3x + 2}{x^2(x + 1)}.$$

$$x^2(x + 1) \begin{array}{|l} \dfrac{3}{3x^3 + 3x^2 + 3x + 2} \\ \underline{3x^3 + 3x^2} \\ \qquad\qquad\quad 3x + 2 \end{array}$$

Figure 150.

Solution In this case, $deg\ q(x) = 3$, $deg\ p(x) = 3$ and $deg\ (remainder) = 1 < deg\ q(x)$. It follows from Figure 150 that
$$\frac{3x^3 + 3x^2 + 3x + 2}{x^2(x + 1)} = 3 + \frac{3x + 2}{x^3 + x^2},$$

and we can't do any better than this. Sometimes you can look for patterns ... For example, in this case we could notice that

$$\frac{3x^3 + 3x^2 + 3x + 2}{x^2(x+1)} \;=\; \frac{3x^3 + 3x^2}{x^3 + x^2} + \frac{3x + 2}{x^3 + x^2}$$
$$=\; 3 \;+\; \frac{3x+2}{x^3+x^2},$$

in which case you wouldn't have to use long division!

Example 342. Simplify

$$\frac{p(x)}{q(x)} = \frac{3x^4 - 8x^3 + 20x^2 - 11x + 8}{x^2 - 2x + 5}.$$

Solution Here, *deg q(x)* = 2, *deg p(x)* = 4 and *deg (remainder)* = 1 < *deg q(x)*. Figure 151 shows that

$$\frac{3x^4 - 8x^3 + 20x^2 - 11x + 8}{x^2 - 2x + 5} = 3x^2 - 2x + 1 \;+\; \frac{x+3}{x^2 - 2x + 5}.$$

$$
\begin{array}{r}
3x^2 - 2x + 1 \\
x^2 - 2x + 5 \,\overline{\big)\; 3x^4 - 8x^3 + 20x^2 - 11x + 8} \\
\underline{3x^4 - 6x^3 + 15x^2} \\
-2x^3 + 5x^2 - 11x + 8 \\
\underline{-2x^3 + 4x^2 - 10x} \\
x^2 - x \;+ 8 \\
\underline{x^2 - 2x + 5} \\
x \;+ 3
\end{array}
$$

Figure 151.

Exercise Set 34.

Use long division to simplify the following rational functions.

1. $\dfrac{x^2 - 2x + 1}{x + 1}$

2. $\dfrac{2x^3 - 3x^2 + 3x - 1}{x^3 + 2x + 1}$

3. $\dfrac{x^4 - x^2 + 1}{3x^2 - 1}$

4. $\dfrac{x^4 + 1}{x^2 + 1}$

5. $\dfrac{x^5 + x^3 + 1}{x - 1}$

6. $\dfrac{3x^3 + 5x + 6}{2x^2 + 2x + 1}$

NOTES:

7.4.2 The Integration of Partial Fractions

The method of *partial fractions* applies to the case where the integrand is a *rational function* with real coefficients. It is known from Algebra that every polynomial with real coefficients can be factored into a product of linear factors (e.g., products of factors of the form $(x-r)^p$, or Type I factors), and a product of quadratic factors called **quadratic irreducibles** or Type II factors, (e.g., $ax^2 + bx + c$ where $b^2 - 4ac < 0$, i.e., a quadratic with no real roots). For example, $x^4 - 1 = (x^2 + 1)(x - 1)(x + 1)$, is the product of two Type I factors $((x-1), (x+1))$ and one Type II factor $(x^2 + 1)$. Since the numerator and denominator of every rational function is a polynomial, it follows that the numerator and denominator of every rational function can also be factored in this way. In order to factor a given polynomial in this way one can use Newton's method (Chapter 3.11) in order to find all its real roots successively.

Now, in order to evaluate an expression of the form

$$\int \frac{a_n x^n + a_{n-1} x^{n-1} + \cdots + a_1 x + a_0}{b_m x^m + b_{m-1} x^{m-1} + \cdots + b_1 x + b_0} \, dx,$$

where m, n are integers and the coefficients are assumed real, there are two basic cases:

- **$n \geq m$.**

  In this case we apply the *method of long division*, see Section 7.4. So, we divide the numerator by the denominator and this results in a **polynomial plus a remainder term**. This remainder term is a rational function whose numerator has degree less than the degree of the denominator.

  For example, long division gives us that

  $$\frac{x^4}{x^2 - 1} = x^2 + 1 + \frac{1}{x^2 - 1}.$$

  Here, the remainder is the rational function on the right of the last display (whose numerator, the function 1, has degree 0 and whose denominator, the function $x^2 - 1$, has degree 2).

  Since the leading term after long division is a polynomial it is easily integrated. OK, but how do we integrate the remainder term? The remainder term may be integrated either by *completing the square* (as in the preceding section), or by using the idea in the next item.

- **$n < m$.**

  We **factor the denominator completely into a product of linear and irreducible factors and their powers.** Next, we **decompose this quotient into partial fractions** in the following sense:

  If the denominator has a linear factor of the form $(x - r)^p$ where p is the highest such power, there corresponds a sum of terms of the form

  $$\frac{A_1}{x - r} + \frac{A_2}{(x - r)^2} + \frac{A_3}{(x - r)^3} + \cdots + \frac{A_p}{(x - r)^p}$$

  where the constants, A's, are to be found. If the denominator has a quadratic irreducible factor (*i.e.*, $b^2 - 4ac < 0$) of the form $(ax^2 + bx + c)^q$, where q is the highest such power, there corresponds in its *partial fraction decomposition*, a sum of terms of the form

  $$\frac{B_1 x + C_1}{ax^2 + bx + c} + \frac{B_2 x + C_2}{(ax^2 + bx + c)^2} + \cdots + \frac{B_q x + C_q}{(ax^2 + bx + c)^q}$$

Idea Behind Integrating a Rational Function

1. Break up the denominator into its factors (so find all its roots or zeros).

e.g.: $x^2 - 2x + 1 = (x-1)^2 \leftarrow$ linear (or Type I) factors.
$x^2 + 1$ cannot be factored into "linear" factors (it is a Type II factor).

2. Use these factors to decompose the rational function into a **sum of reciprocals of these factors**.

3. Integrate each term in item 2 separately using the methods of this Chapter.

Table 7.5: Idea Behind Integrating a Rational Function

where the constants, B's and C's, are to be found, as well. The method for finding the A's, B's, and C's is best described using various examples, see Table 7.5 for a quick summary of the procedure.

In the following examples we assume that the degree, n, of the numerator satisfies $n < m$, where m is the degree of the denominator. Otherwise, we have to use *long division* BEFORE we proceed. These problems involving partial fractions can be quite long because of this additional long division which must be performed in some cases.

Example 343. Find the form of the partial fraction decomposition of the following functions:

1. $f(x) = \dfrac{2x}{(x-1)(x+3)}$

2. $f(x) = \dfrac{x-4}{x(x-1)^2}$

3. $f(x) = \dfrac{3x+2}{x^4-1}$

4. $f(x) = \dfrac{x^3 + 2x^2 - 1}{(x-1)^3(x^3-1)}$

5. $f(x) = \dfrac{x^5+1}{(x+1)(x-2)^2(x^4+1)^2}$

Solution 1). The factors of the denominator are $(x-1)$ and $(x+3)$, and each one is linear and simple (the highest power for each one is 1). So, the partial fraction decomposition has one term corresponding to $(x-1)$ and one term corresponding to $(x+3)$. Thus,

$$\frac{2x}{(x-1)(x+3)} = \frac{A}{x-1} + \frac{B}{x+3},$$

where A, B are constants to be determined using the methods of this section.

2). In this case, the factors of the denominator are $x, (x-1)$ where the factor x is simple and linear. The factor $(x-1)$ occurs with a (highest) power of 2, so it is NOT simple. In this case, there are two terms in the partial fraction decomposition of f which correspond to this factor. That is,

$$\frac{x-4}{x(x-1)^2} = \frac{A}{x} + \frac{B}{x-1} + \frac{C}{(x-1)^2},$$

where the constants A, B, C, are to be determined.

3). The factors of the denominator are given by $x^4 - 1 = (x^2-1)(x^2+1) = (x-1)(x+1)(x^2+1)$ where the last factor, namely, x^2+1 is irreducible (or Type II). Each factor appears with a highest power of 1 so,

$$\frac{3x+2}{x^4-1} = \frac{A}{x-1} + \frac{B}{x+1} + \frac{Cx+D}{x^2+1},$$

since, according to the theory of partial fractions, to every Type II factor there corresponds a term of the form $mx+b$ in its partial fraction decomposition.

4). In this example, the denominator needs to be factored completely BEFORE we apply the method of partial fractions (because of the cubic term, $x^3 - 1$). The factors of $x^3 - 1$ are given by $x^3 - 1 = (x-1)(x^2+x+1)$, where $x-1$ is linear and x^2+x+1 is irreducible (Type II). So the denominator's factors are given by $(x-1)^3(x^3-1) = (x-1)^4(x^2+x+1)$. This list of factors contains the terms $x-1$, with a highest power of 4 (not 3, as it seems), and x^2+x+1 (with a highest power of 1). So, the decomposition looks like,

$$\frac{x^3+2x^2-1}{(x-1)^3(x^3-1)} = \frac{A}{x-1} + \frac{B}{(x-1)^2} + \frac{C}{(x-1)^3} + \frac{D}{(x-1)^4} + \frac{Ex+F}{x^2+x+1},$$

where $A, B, C, ..., F$ are to be determined, (of course, it might take quite a few coffees to actually find them!).

5). In this final example we see the need to factor the polynomial $x^4 + 1$ into Type I and Type II factors. This isn't easy, but it can be done. The idea is to write its factors as $x^4 + 1 = (x^2+ax+b)(x^2-ax+b)$ where the right-side is expanded and coefficients are compared to those on the left to give the values $a = \sqrt{2}$ and $b = 1$. So, the factors of the denominator are given by

$$(x+1)(x-2)^2(x^4+1)^2 = (x+1)(x-2)^2(x^2-\sqrt{2}x+1)^2(x^2+\sqrt{2}x+1)^2.$$

The factor $x+1$ appears with a highest power of 1, the factor $x-2$ appears with a highest power of 2 and each Type II factor $x^2+\sqrt{2}x+1$, $x^2-\sqrt{2}x+1$ appears with a highest power of 2. So, the partial fraction decomposition looks like,

$$\frac{x^5+1}{(x+1)(x-2)^2(x^4+1)^2} = \frac{A_1}{x+1} + \frac{A_2}{x-2} + \frac{A_3}{(x-2)^2} +$$

$$+ \frac{B_1x+C_1}{x^2-\sqrt{2}x+1} + \frac{B_2x+C_2}{(x^2-\sqrt{2}x+1)^2} +$$

$$+ \frac{B_3x+C_3}{x^2+\sqrt{2}x+1} + \frac{B_4x+C_4}{(x^2+\sqrt{2}x+1)^2},$$

where the 11 constants $A_i, i = 1, 2, 3$, $B_i, i = 1, 2, 3, 4$ and $C_i, i = 1, 2, 3, 4$ are all to be found !! Don't worry, this doesn't happen much in practice. This example was included to reinforce the actual finding of the FORM of the decomposition, not the actual constants.

Okay, now that we know how to find the FORM of a partial fraction decomposition, we can proceed further to find the constants that appear in it, and finally integrate some rational functions. The next examples show how this is done.

Example 344. Evaluate $\int \dfrac{5x - 7}{x^2 - 3x + 2}\, dx$

Solution **Step 1. Find the form of the partial fraction decomposition.** We are in the case where $n = 1$ and $m = 2$, so $n < m$. In this case, we factor the denominator completely and find $x^2 - 3x + 2 = (x - 1)(x - 2)$. Since each one of its factors $(x - 1)$, $(x - 2)$ is a linear factor, the partial fraction decomposition of this function looks like,

$$
\begin{aligned}
\frac{5x - 7}{x^2 - 3x + 2} &= \frac{5x - 7}{(x - 2)(x - 1)} \\
&= \frac{A}{x - 2} + \frac{B}{x - 1},
\end{aligned}
$$

where A, B are to be found!

Step 2. Find the constants $A, B, ...$ Multiplying both sides by the denominator, $(x - 1)(x - 2)$, we find that

$$5x - 7 = A(x - 1) + B(x - 2),$$

must hold for all x. At this point, one may proceed in many different ways. All we need to do is to find the value of A, B, right? The basic idea is to plug in certain values of x and then obtain a system of two equations in the two unknowns A, B, which we can solve. For example,

Method 1: The "Plug-in" Method. If we set $x = 1$, then $5x - 7 = A(x - 1) + B(x - 2)$ means that $5 \cdot 1 - 7 = -2 = 0 + B(-1)$, and so $B = 2$.

On the other hand, if we set $x = 2$, then $5x - 7 = A(x - 1) + B(x - 2)$ means that $5 \cdot 2 - 7 = 3 = A(1) + 0 = A$, and so $A = 3$. So, $A = 3, B = 2$.

Method 2: Comparing Coefficients. Since $5x - 7 = A(x - 1) + B(x - 2)$ must hold for every value of x the two polynomials (represented by the left-side and by the right-side) are equal and so their coefficients must be equal, as well. So,

$$
\begin{aligned}
5x - 7 &= A(x - 1) + B(x - 2), \\
&= (A + B)x - A - 2B, \\
&= (A + B)x - (A + 2B).
\end{aligned}
$$

Comparing the coefficients we find

$$A + B = 5 \quad and \quad A + 2B = 7,$$

which represents a simple system of two equations in the two unknowns A, B whose solution is given by $A = 3, B = 2$.

Method 3: The Derivative Method. Since $5x - 7 = A(x - 1) + B(x - 2)$ must hold for every value of x the same must be true of its derivative(s) and so,

$$
\begin{aligned}
5x - 7 &= A(x - 1) + B(x - 2), \\
\frac{d}{dx}(5x - 7) &= \frac{d}{dx}(A(x - 1) + B(x - 2)), \\
5 &= A + B,
\end{aligned}
$$

and so we can write A, say, in terms of B. In this case, we get $A = 5 - B$. We substitute this back into the relation $5x - 7 = A(x - 1) + B(x - 2)$ to find

$5x - 7 = (5 - B)(x - 1) + B(x - 2) = 5x - B - 5$, and so $B = 2$. Since $A + B = 5$ it follows that $A = 3$.

Regardless of which method we use to find A, B (each one has its advantages and disadvantages), we will obtain the partial fraction decomposition

$$\frac{5x - 7}{x^2 - 3x + 2} = \frac{3}{x - 2} + \frac{2}{x - 1}.$$

The right-hand side is easily integrated in terms of natural logarithms and so

$$\begin{aligned}
\int \frac{5x - 7}{x^2 - 3x + 2} \, dx &= \int \frac{3}{x - 2} \, dx + \int \frac{2}{x - 1} \, dx, \\
&= 3 \ln |x - 2| + 2 \ln |x - 1| + C, \\
&= \ln \left| (x - 2)^3 (x - 1)^2 \right| + C,
\end{aligned}$$

after using the basic properties of the logarithm and the absolute value, namely, $\triangle \ln \square = \ln \left(\square^{\triangle} \right)$ and $|\square \, \triangle| = |\square| \, |\triangle|$.

NOTE: Normally, Method 1 outlined in Example 344 is the most efficient method in finding the values of $A, B, \ldots$.

Example 345. Evaluate $\displaystyle \int \frac{x}{(x - 1)(x - 2)(x + 3)} \, dx$

Solution We can use Table 7.6 since the factors of the denominator are all linear and simple (there are no powers). We write

$$\frac{x}{(x - 1)(x - 2)(x + 3)} = \frac{A}{x - 1} + \frac{B}{x - 2} + \frac{C}{x + 3}.$$

Then, using the Shortcut in Table 7.6, since $(x - \boxed{1})$ is the factor which is associated with A, we find the value of A as

$$A = \frac{\boxed{1}}{(covered)(\boxed{1} - 2)(\boxed{1} + 3)} = \frac{1}{(-1)(4)} = -\frac{1}{4},$$

and, since $(x - \boxed{2})$ is the factor which is associated with B, its value is given by

$$B = \frac{\boxed{2}}{(\boxed{2} - 1)(covered)(\boxed{2} + 3)} = \frac{2}{(1)(5)} = \frac{2}{5},$$

and finally, since $(x - (-3)) = (x + 3)$ is the factor which is associated with C, the value of C is,

$$C = \frac{\boxed{(-3)}}{(\boxed{-3} - 1)(\boxed{-3} - 2)(covered)} = \frac{(-3)}{(-4)(-5)} = -\frac{3}{20}.$$

Okay, now we can integrate the function readily since

$$\begin{aligned}
\int \frac{x}{(x - 1)(x - 2)(x + 3)} \, dx &= \int \left(\frac{-\frac{1}{4}}{x - 1} + \frac{\frac{2}{5}}{x - 2} + \frac{-\frac{3}{20}}{x + 3} \right) dx, \\
&= -\frac{1}{4} \int \frac{dx}{x - 1} + \frac{2}{5} \int \frac{dx}{x - 2} - \frac{3}{20} \int \frac{dx}{x + 3}, \\
&= -\frac{1}{4} \ln |x - 1| + \frac{2}{5} \ln |x - 2| - \frac{3}{20} \ln |x + 3| + C.
\end{aligned}$$

We can also get the value of B using the same method (even though it is not a simple factor!), but we can't get the value of A. The point is that the method of Table 7.6 even works for *powers* of linear factors **but only for the highest such power!**. For example, we can get B in Example 346 (because it corresponds to the highest power of the linear factor $(x - 1)$, which is 2), but we can't get the value of A using this approach. So, if you cover the $(x - 1)^2$-term and plug in the value $x = 1$ in "what's left over", you'll see that $B = \frac{2}{3}$.

Shortcut: The Cover-up Method

If the **denominator of the rational function f has simple linear factors** (Type I factors, see Chapter 5), then we can find its partial fraction decomposition fairly rapidly as follows.

For example, if

$$f(x) = \frac{A}{x - x_1} + \frac{B}{x - x_2} + \frac{C}{x - x_3} + \ldots,$$

then

$$\lim_{x \to x_1} (x - x_1) f(x) = A,$$

$$\lim_{x \to x_2} (x - x_2) f(x) = B,$$

$$\lim_{x \to x_3} (x - x_3) f(x) = C,$$

and so on.

In practice, if we have the three unknowns A, B, C, we find their values like this:

Write $f(x)$ as

$$f(x) = \frac{p(x)}{(x - x_1)(x - x_2)(x - x_3)}.$$

1. With your finger cover the factor $(x - x_1)$ only!

2. Plug in the value $x = x_1$ in "what's left over" (*i.e.*, the part that's not covered).

3. The number you get in (2) is the value of A.

The other values, B, C, are obtained in the same way, except that we cover the factor $(x - x_2)$ only (in the case of B) and $(x - x_3)$ only (in the case of C), and continue as above.

Table 7.6: Finding a Partial Fraction Decomposition in the Case of Simple Linear Factors

Example 346. Evaluate $\int \dfrac{x+1}{(x-1)^2(x+2)}\,dx$.

Solution Now the denominator has only one simple linear factor, namely, $(x+2) = (x-(-2))$. Notice that the root is "-2" and NOT "2". The other factor is NOT SIMPLE because there is a term of the form $(x-1)^2$. The partial fraction decomposition of this rational function now looks like,

$$\frac{x+1}{(x-1)^2(x+2)} = \frac{A}{x-1} + \frac{B}{(x-1)^2} + \frac{C}{x+2}.$$

Since $x+2$ is a simple linear factor we can use Table 7.6 to find the value of C corresponding to that factor. We get (see the margin),

$$C = \frac{\boxed{-2}+1}{(\boxed{-2}-1)^2(covered)} = -\frac{1}{9}.$$

We're missing A, B, right? The easiest way to get these values is simply to **substitute two arbitrary values of x**, as in the **Plug-in Method** of Example 344. For example, we know that

$$\frac{x+1}{(x-1)^2(x+2)} = \frac{A}{x-1} + \frac{B}{(x-1)^2} - \frac{\frac{1}{9}}{x+2}, \tag{7.50}$$

so, setting $x = 2$ say, we must have,

$$\begin{aligned}
\frac{2+1}{(2-1)^2(2+2)} &= \frac{A}{2-1} + \frac{B}{(2-1)^2} - \frac{\frac{1}{9}}{2+2}, \\
\frac{3}{4} &= A + B - \frac{1}{36}, \\
\frac{7}{9} &= A + B.
\end{aligned}$$

Our first equation for the unknowns A, B is then

$$A + B = \frac{7}{9}. \tag{7.51}$$

We only need another such equation. Let's put $x = -1$ into (7.50), above (because it makes its left-hand side equal to zero!) Then,

$$\begin{aligned}
0 &= \frac{A}{(-1-1)} + \frac{B}{(-1-1)^2} - \frac{\frac{1}{9}}{(-1+2)}, \\
0 &= -\frac{A}{2} + \frac{B}{4} - \frac{1}{9}, \\
\frac{1}{9} &= -\frac{A}{2} + \frac{B}{4}.
\end{aligned}$$

Our second and final equation for the unknowns A, B is now

$$-\frac{A}{2} + \frac{B}{4} = \frac{1}{9}. \tag{7.52}$$

Solving equations 7.53, 7.52 simultaneously, we get the values

$$A = \frac{1}{9}, \quad B = \frac{2}{3}.$$

Feeding these values back into equation 7.50 we get the decomposition

$$\frac{x+1}{(x-1)^2(x+2)} = \frac{\frac{1}{9}}{x-1} + \frac{\frac{2}{3}}{(x-1)^2} - \frac{\frac{1}{9}}{x+2}.$$

It follows that

$$
\begin{aligned}
\int \frac{x+1}{(x-1)^2(x+2)} \, dx &= \int \left(\frac{\frac{1}{9}}{x-1} + \frac{\frac{2}{3}}{(x-1)^2} - \frac{\frac{1}{9}}{x+2} \right) dx, \\
&= \frac{1}{9} \int \frac{1}{x-1} \, dx + \frac{2}{3} \int \frac{1}{(x-1)^2} \, dx - \frac{1}{9} \int \frac{1}{x+2} \, dx, \\
&= \frac{1}{9} \ln|x-1| - \frac{2}{3} \frac{1}{x-1} - \frac{1}{9} \ln|x+2| + C, \\
&= \frac{\ln|x-1|}{9} - \frac{2}{3(x-1)} - \frac{\ln|x+2|}{9} + C,
\end{aligned}
$$

where we used the *Power Rule for Integrals* in the evaluation of the second integral, (*i.e.,* the first of Table 6.5).

The moral is this:

Try to use Table 7.6 as much as possible in your evaluation of the constants $A, B, C, \dots$ in the partial fraction decomposition of the given rational function.

If there are powers of linear factors present (as in Example 346), you can still use the same method provided you are looking for that constant which corresponds to the linear factor with the highest power!

In the following example we introduce a Type II factor into the denominator and we evaluate an integral involving such a factor.

Example 347.   Evaluate

$$
\int \frac{x}{x^4 - 1} \, dx.
$$

Solution Since $x^4 - 1 = (x^2 - 1)(x^2 + 1) = (x-1)(x+1)(x^2+1)$ the partial fraction decomposition of this integrand looks like

$$
\frac{x}{x^4 - 1} = \frac{A_1}{x-1} + \frac{A_2}{x+1} + \frac{B_1 x + C_1}{x^2+1},
$$

since the factors of the denominator are simple and each one occurs with highest power 1, (*i.e.,* $p = 1$, $q = 1$). Notice that we are using the symbols A_1, A_2, B_1, C_1 instead of A, B, C, D. This doesn't change anything. Now, we can proceed as in Table 7.6 and find A_1, A_2 using the method outlined there. We find,

$$
\frac{x}{(x-1)(x+1)(x^2+1)} = \frac{A_1}{x-1} + \frac{A_2}{x+1} + \frac{B_1 x + C_1}{x^2+1},
$$

so covering the $(x-1)$ term on the left and setting $x = 1$ in *what's left over* we find $A_1 = \frac{1}{4}$. Next, covering the $(x+1) = (x-(-1))$ term on the left and setting $x = -1$ there, gives us $A_2 = \frac{1}{4}$, as well. The constants B_1, C_1 are found using the *Plug-in Method*. So we plug-in some two other values of x, say, $x = 0, 2$ in order to **get a system of equations** (two of them) in the two given unknowns, B_1, C_1 (because WE KNOW the values of A_1, A_2). Solving this system, we get $B_1 = -\frac{1}{2}, C_1 = 0$ so that the partial fraction decomposition takes the form

$$
\frac{x}{x^4 - 1} = \frac{\frac{1}{4}}{x-1} + \frac{\frac{1}{4}}{x+1} - \frac{\frac{1}{2}x}{x^2+1}.
$$

It follows that

$$
\begin{aligned}
\int \frac{x}{x^4 - 1} \, dx &= \frac{1}{4} \int \frac{dx}{x-1} + \frac{1}{4} \int \frac{dx}{x+1} - \frac{1}{2} \int \frac{x \, dx}{x^2+1}, \\
&= \frac{1}{4} \ln|x-1| + \frac{1}{4} \ln|x+1| - \frac{1}{4} \ln(x^2+1) + C,
\end{aligned}
$$

where the last integral on the right was evaluated using the substitution $u = x^2 + 1$, $du = 2x\,dx$, etc.

> **Example 348.** Evaluate $\displaystyle\int \frac{3\,dx}{x^2(x^2+9)}$.

Solution The partial fraction decomposition looks like

$$\frac{3}{x^2(x^2+9)} = \frac{A}{x} + \frac{B}{x^2} + \frac{Cx+D}{x^2+9} \quad \swarrow \text{ Type II factor.}$$

$$\underset{\text{non-simple root, highest power}=2}{\vee\nearrow}$$

We shall use a combination of the *Plug-in Method* and the method of comparing coefficients, see Example 344.

We multiply both sides by the denominator to find,

$$3 = Ax(x^2+9) + B(x^2+9) + (Cx+D)(x^2). \tag{7.53}$$

Next, we set $x = 0 \Rightarrow 3 = 0 + 9B + 0 = 9B \Rightarrow B = \frac{1}{3}$ (by the Plug-in Method).

Now, we expand the right-hand side of equation (7.53) completely and collect like terms. This gives the equivalent equation

$$3 = (A+C)x^3 + (B+D)x^2 + (9A)x + 3,$$

(since we already know that $B = \frac{1}{3}$), or,

$$(A+C)x^3 + (B+D)x^2 + (9A)x = 0.$$

Since this last relation must be true for every value of x, we may compare the coefficients and obtain (recall that we already know B),

$$\left\{\begin{array}{ll} A + C = 0 & (\text{coefficient of } x^3 = 0) \\ B + D = 0 & (\text{coefficient of } x^2 = 0) \\ 9A = 0 & (\text{coefficient of } x = 0) \end{array}\right.$$

Solving this last system of three equations in the three unknowns A, C, D, simultaneously gives $A = 0$, $C = 0$ and $B = -D = \frac{1}{3} \Rightarrow D = -\frac{1}{3}$, *i.e.*,

$$\begin{aligned} \frac{3}{x^2(x^2+9)} &= \frac{1/3}{x^2} + \frac{-1/3}{x^2+9}, \\ &= \frac{1}{3}\left(\frac{1}{x^2} - \frac{1}{x^2+9}\right). \end{aligned}$$

It follows that

$$\begin{aligned} \int \frac{3}{x^2(x^2+9)}\,dx &= \frac{1}{3}\int \left(\frac{1}{x^2} - \frac{1}{x^2+9}\right)\,dx \\ &= \frac{1}{3}\int \frac{dx}{x^2} - \frac{1}{3}\int \frac{dx}{x^2+9} \\ &= -\frac{1}{3x} - \frac{1}{3}\int \frac{dx}{9\left(\frac{x^2}{9}+1\right)} \\ &= -\frac{1}{3x} - \frac{1}{27}\int \frac{dx}{\left(\frac{x}{3}\right)^2+1} \\ &= -\frac{1}{3x} - \frac{1}{27}\int \frac{3\,du}{u^2+1} \quad \left\{ \begin{array}{l} Set\ u = \frac{x}{3}, du = \frac{dx}{3}, \\ so,\ dx = 3\,du, \end{array} \right. \end{aligned}$$

$$= -\frac{1}{3x} - \frac{1}{9}\text{Arctan}\, u + C$$

$$= -\frac{1}{3x} - \frac{1}{9}\text{Arctan}\left(\frac{x}{3}\right) + C.$$

Example 349. Evaluate $\displaystyle\int \frac{x^3}{x^2 - 2x + 1}\, dx$.

Solution The numerator has degree $n = 3$ while the denominator has degree $m = 2$. **Since $n > m$ we must divide the numerator by the denominator** using *long division*.

$$
\begin{array}{r}
x + 2 \\
x^2 - 2x + 1\,\big|\,x^3 \\
\underline{x^3 - 2x^2 + x} \\
2x^2 - x \\
\underline{2x^2 - 4x + 2} \\
\text{Remainder} \longrightarrow \boxed{3x - 2}
\end{array}
$$

The result is

$$\frac{x^3}{x^2 - 2x + 1} = x + 2 + \frac{3x - 2}{x^2 - 2x + 1}$$

Use partial fractions here!

Since $n < m$ for the rational function on the right, its partial fraction decomposition is

$$\frac{3x - 2}{x^2 - 2x + 1} = \frac{3x - 2}{(x - 1)^2} = \frac{A}{x - 1} + \frac{B}{(x - 1)^2}$$

We use the Plug-in Method: Remember to multiply both sides of the equation by the denominator so that

$$3x - 2 = A(x - 1) + B.$$

Set $x = 1 \Rightarrow 1 = B$.

Set $x = 0 \Rightarrow -2 = -A + B = -A + 1$ which means that $A = 3$.

So, the decomposition looks like

$$\frac{3x - 2}{(x - 1)^2} = \frac{3}{x - 1} + \frac{1}{(x - 1)^2},$$

where, as a summary, we obtained

$$\frac{x^3}{x^2 - 2x + 1} = \underbrace{x + 2}_{\text{found by division}} + \underbrace{\frac{3}{x - 1} + \frac{1}{(x - 1)^2}}_{\text{found by partial fractions}}$$

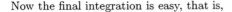

found by division   found by partial fractions

EXAMPLES

Now the final integration is easy, that is,

$$\int \frac{x^3}{x^2 - 2x + 1}\, dx = \int \left(x + 2 + \frac{3x - 2}{x^2 - 2x + 1}\right)\, dx$$

$$= \frac{x^2}{2} + 2x + \int \frac{3x - 2}{x^2 - 2x + 1}\, dx$$

$$= \frac{x^2}{2} + 2x + \int \left(\frac{3}{x-1} + \frac{1}{(x-1)^2} \right) dx$$

$$= \frac{x^2}{2} + 2x + \int \frac{3 \, dx}{x-1} + \int \frac{1 \, dx}{(x-1)^2}$$

$$= \frac{x^2}{2} + 2x + 3 \ln |x-1| - \frac{1}{x-1} + C.$$

Example 350. Evaluate $I = \int_0^1 \frac{3x^2}{x^2 + 2x + 1} \, dx$

Solution In this example we see that $n = m$ or that the degree of the nominator equals the degree of the denominator. So we must divide the two polynomials using the method of *long division*. Then,

$$x^2 + 2x + 1 \, \overline{\big| 3x^3 } \qquad \begin{array}{c} 3 \\ \hline \end{array}$$

$$\begin{array}{c} \underline{3x^2 + 6x + 3} \\ -6x - 3, \end{array}$$

after which we find

$$\frac{3x^2}{x^2 + 2x + 1} = 3 + \frac{(-6x - 3)}{x^2 + 2x + 1}$$

$$= 3 - \frac{(6x + 3)}{x^2 + 2x + 1}.$$

We now see that

$$I = \int_0^1 \frac{3x^2}{x^2 + 2x + 1} \, dx = \int_0^1 \left(3 - \frac{6x + 3}{x^2 + 2x + 1} \right) \, dx$$

$$= \int_0^1 3 \, dx - \int_0^1 \frac{6x + 3}{x^2 + 2x + 1} \, dx$$

$$\uparrow$$

Use partial fractions here!

The partial fraction decomposition of the rational function on the right has the form

$$\frac{6x + 3}{x^2 + 2x + 1} = \frac{6x + 3}{(x+1)^2} = \frac{A}{x+1} + \frac{B}{(x+1)^2}$$

where we can use the method of *comparing coefficients* (remember to multiply both sides by the denominator),

$$6x + 3 = A(x + 1) + B$$
$$= Ax + (A + B)$$

So, $A = 6$ and $A + B = 3 \Rightarrow B = -3$. It follows that

$$I = \int_0^1 \frac{3x^2}{x^2 + 2x + 1} \, dx$$

$$= \int_0^1 3 \, dx - \int_0^1 \frac{6x + 3}{x^2 + 2x + 1} \, dx$$

$$= 3 - \int_0^1 \left(\frac{6}{x+1} - \frac{3}{(x+1)^2} \right) \, dx$$

$$= 3 - 6\ln(x+1)\Big|_0^1 + 3\int_0^1 (x+1)^{-2}\,dx$$

$$= 3 - 6\ln 2 + 3\left(\frac{(x+1)^{-1}}{(-1)}\right)\Big|_0^1$$

$$= 3 - 6\ln 2 + 3\left(-\frac{1}{2} + 1\right)$$

$$= 3 - 6\ln 2 + \frac{3}{2}$$

$$= \frac{9}{2} - 6\ln 2.$$

Example 351. Evaluate $\displaystyle\int \frac{x^5 + 2x - 2}{x^4 - 1}\,dx$.

Solution In this example we have $n > m$ since the numerator has the higher degree. Using long division we find,

$$x^4 - 1\,|\overline{\begin{array}{l} x \\ x^5 + 2x - 2 \\ \underline{x^5 - x} \\ 3x - 2. \end{array}}$$

From this we see that,

$$\frac{x^5 + 2x - 2}{x^4 - 1} = x + \frac{3x - 2}{x^4 - 1}$$

$$= x + \frac{3x - 2}{(x-1)(x+1)(x^2+1)}.$$

EXAMPLES

Now, the partial fraction decomposition of the rational function above, on the right, looks like

$$\frac{3x - 2}{(x-1)(x+1)(x^2+1)} = \frac{A}{x-1} + \frac{B}{x+1} + \frac{Cx + D}{x^2+1} \qquad (7.54)$$

where A, B may be found using the method of Table 7.6 while C, D may be found using the Plug-in Method. Covering the factors $(x - 1)$, $(x + 1)$ respectively we obtain $A = \frac{1}{4}$ and $B = \frac{5}{4}$. Okay, this means that (7.54) is the same as

$$\frac{3x - 2}{(x-1)(x+1)(x^2+1)} = \frac{\frac{1}{4}}{x-1} + \frac{\frac{5}{4}}{x+1} + \frac{Cx + D}{x^2+1} \qquad (7.55)$$

where all we need to find now is C, D. So, let's use the Plug-in Method.

Setting $x = 0$ in (7.55) gives

$$2 = -\frac{1}{4} + \frac{5}{4} + \frac{D}{1}, \quad \text{or, solving for } D,$$

$$D = 2 + \frac{1}{4} - \frac{5}{4}$$

$$= 1.$$

So, (7.54) now looks like,

$$\frac{3x - 2}{(x-1)(x+1)(x^2+1)} = \frac{\frac{1}{4}}{x-1} + \frac{\frac{5}{4}}{x+1} + \frac{Cx + 1}{x^2+1}, \qquad (7.56)$$

and all that's missing is the value of C, right? For this last value, we can substitute *any* value of x other than one of the roots of the denominator. For example, we can set $x = 2$. Then,

$$\frac{4}{15} = \frac{1}{4} + \frac{5}{12} + \frac{2C+1}{5}, \quad \text{or, solving for } C,$$
$$C = -\frac{3}{2}.$$

So,

$$\frac{3x - 2}{(x - 1)(x + 1)(x^2 + 1)} = \frac{\frac{1}{4}}{x - 1} + \frac{\frac{5}{4}}{x + 1} + \frac{-\frac{3}{2}x + 1}{x^2 + 1},$$

is the partial fraction decomposition of the rational function on the left. We now proceed to the integral.

$$\begin{aligned}
\int \frac{x^5 + 2x - 2}{x^4 - 1}\, dx &= \int \left(x + \frac{3x - 2}{(x - 1)(x + 1)(x^2 + 1)} \right) dx \\
&= \frac{x^2}{2} + \int \left(\frac{\frac{1}{4}}{x - 1} + \frac{\frac{5}{4}}{x + 1} + \frac{-\frac{3}{2}x + 1}{x^2 + 1} \right) dx \\
&= \frac{x^2}{2} + \frac{1}{4} \int \frac{dx}{x - 1} + \frac{5}{4} \int \frac{dx}{x + 1} - \frac{3}{2} \int \frac{x\, dx}{x^2 + 1} + \\
&\quad + \int \frac{dx}{x^2 + 1}, \\
&= \frac{x^2}{2} + \frac{1}{4} \ln|x - 1| + \frac{5}{4} \ln|x + 1| - \frac{3}{4} \int \frac{du}{u} + \\
&\quad + \text{Arctan}\, x \\
&\quad \left(\text{where we used the substitution } u = x^2 + 1, du = 2x\, dx\right) \\
&= \frac{x^2}{2} + \frac{1}{4} \ln|x - 1| + \frac{5}{4} \ln|x + 1| - \frac{3}{4} \ln\left(x^2 + 1\right) + \\
&\quad + \text{Arctan}\, x + C.
\end{aligned}$$

SNAPSHOTS

Example 352. | Evaluate $I = \displaystyle\int \frac{x + 4}{x^2 + 5x - 6}\, dx$

Solution The partial fraction decomposition has the form,

$$\frac{x + 4}{x^2 + 5x - 6} = \frac{x + 4}{(x - 1)(x + 6)} = \frac{A}{x - 1} + \frac{B}{x + 6},$$

and so, either the Plug-in Method or the method of Table 7.6, gives the values of A, B. In this case, $x + 4 = A(x + 6) + B(x - 1)$ which means that if we set

$$x = 1 \Rightarrow 5 = 7A \Rightarrow A = \tfrac{5}{7},$$

or $\quad x = -6 \Rightarrow -2 = -7B \Rightarrow B = \tfrac{2}{7}.$

Finally,

$$\begin{aligned}
I &= \int \left(\frac{5/7}{x - 1} + \frac{2/7}{x + 6} \right) dx \\
&= \frac{5}{7} \ln|x - 1| + \frac{2}{7} \ln|x + 6| + C.
\end{aligned}$$

Example 353. Evaluate $I = \int \dfrac{dx}{1 + \sqrt{x}}$

Solution We start with a substitution, $u = \sqrt{x}$, $du = \dfrac{dx}{2\sqrt{x}}$ or $dx = 2u\, du$. Then,

$$
\begin{aligned}
I &= \int \frac{dx}{1 + \sqrt{x}} \\
&= \int \frac{2u\, du}{1 + u} \\
&= 2 \int \frac{u}{1 + u}\, du \quad \text{(rational function in u, $n = m = 1$)}, \\
&= 2 \int \left(1 - \frac{1}{1 + u}\right) du \quad \text{(after using long division)}, \\
&= 2u - 2 \int \frac{du}{1 + u} \\
&= 2u - 2\ln|1 + u| + C \\
&= 2\sqrt{x} - 2\ln|1 + \sqrt{x}| + C.
\end{aligned}
$$

Example 354. Evaluate $I = \displaystyle\int_0^1 \ln(x^2 + 1)\, dx$

Solution We use Integration by Parts.

$$
\text{Set} \begin{cases}
u = \ln(x^2 + 1) & dv = 1\, dx \\
du = \dfrac{2x\, dx}{x^2 + 1} & v = x.
\end{cases}
$$

Then,

$$
\begin{aligned}
I &= uv - \int v\, du \\
&= x\ln(x^2 + 1)\Big|_0^1 - \int_0^1 x\left(\frac{2x}{x^2 + 1}\right) dx \\
&= \ln 2 - 0 - 2\int_0^1 \frac{x^2}{1 + x^2}\, dx \quad \text{(rational function, $n = m = 2$)}, \\
&= \ln 2 - 2\int_0^1 \left(1 - \frac{1}{1 + x^2}\right) dx \quad \text{(after long division)}, \\
&= \ln 2 - 2 + 2\int_0^1 \frac{dx}{1 + x^2} \\
&= \ln 2 - 2 + 2\tan^{-1} x\Big|_0^1 \quad \text{(by Table 6.7)}, \\
&= \ln 2 - 2 + 2(\tan^{-1}(1) - 0) \\
&= \ln 2 - 2 + 2 \cdot \frac{\pi}{4} \\
&= \ln 2 - 2 + \frac{\pi}{2}.
\end{aligned}
$$

Exercise Set 35.

1. $\int \dfrac{x}{x-1}\,dx$

2. $\int \dfrac{x+1}{x}\,dx$

3. $\int \dfrac{x^2}{x+2}\,dx$

4. $\int \dfrac{x^2}{x^2+1}\,dx$

5. $\int \dfrac{x^2}{(x-1)(x+1)}\,dx$

6. $\int \dfrac{2x}{(x-1)(x-3)}\,dx$

7. $\int \dfrac{3x^2}{(x-1)(x-2)(x-3)}\,dx$

8. $\int_0^1 \dfrac{x^3-1}{x+1}\,dx$

9. $\int \dfrac{3x}{(x-1)^2}\,dx$

10. $\int \dfrac{2x-1}{(x-2)^2(x+1)}\,dx$

11. $\int \dfrac{x^4+1}{x^2+1}\,dx$

12. $\int \dfrac{1}{(x^2+1)(x^2+4)}\,dx$

13. $\int \dfrac{1}{x^2(x-1)(x+2)}\,dx$

14. $\int \dfrac{x^5+1}{(x^2-2x)(x^4-1)}\,dx$

15. $\int \dfrac{2}{x(x-1)^2(x^2+1)}\,dx$

Suggested Homework Set 24. *Do problems 1, 3, 5, 7, 10, 14*

NOTES:

7.5 Products of Trigonometric Functions

7.5.1 Products of Sines and Cosines

In this section we provide some insight into the integration of products and powers of trigonometric functions. For example, we will be considering integrals of the form

$$\int \cos^2 x \sin^3 x \; dx, \quad \int \sin^5 x \; dx, \quad \int \cos^4 x \; dx.$$

In almost all the cases under consideration extensive use will be made of some fundamental trigonometric identities, such as those presented in the display below. Furthermore you should recall you angle-sum/angle-difference identities (see Section 1.3) or the text below.

A **trigonometric integral** is an integral whose integrand contains only trigonometric functions and their powers. These are best handled with the repeated use of *trigonometric identities*. Among those which are most commonly used we find (here u or x is in radians):

$$\cos^2 u = \frac{1 + \cos 2u}{2}, \quad \sin^2 u = \frac{1 - \cos 2u}{2}, \tag{7.57}$$

$$\cos^2 u + \sin^2 u = 1, \tag{7.58}$$

$$\sec^2 u - \tan^2 u = 1, \tag{7.59}$$

$$\csc^2 u - \cot^2 u = 1, \tag{7.60}$$

$$\sin 2u = 2 \sin u \; \cos u. \tag{7.61}$$

Of these identities, **(7.57) is used to reduce the power in a trigonometric integral by 1.** As you can see, the left-side is a square while the right-side is not.

Example 355. Evaluate $\int \cos^4 x \; dx.$

Solution One always starts a problem like this by applying some *trigonometric identities*. Before you integrate such functions you should be using trigonometric identities to simplify the form of the integrand, first!

This problem is tackled by **writing $\cos^4 x$ as a product of two squares** and then using (7.57) repeatedly as follows:

$$
\begin{aligned}
\cos^4 x &= \cos^2 x \; \cos^2 x \\
&= \left(\frac{1 + \cos 2x}{2} \right) \left(\frac{1 + \cos 2x}{2} \right) \\
&= \frac{1}{4} \left(1 + 2\cos 2x + \cos^2 2x \right) \\
&= \frac{1}{4} \left(1 + 2\cos 2x + \frac{1 + \cos 4x}{2} \right),
\end{aligned}
$$

since we can use (7.57) with $u = 2x$ to find that

$$\cos^2 2x = \frac{1 + \cos 4x}{2}.$$

Combining the last two identities we find that

$$
\begin{aligned}
\cos^4 x &= \frac{1}{4}\left(\frac{3}{2} + 2\cos 2x + \frac{\cos 4x}{2}\right) \\
&= \frac{3}{8} + \frac{\cos 2x}{2} + \frac{\cos 4x}{8}.
\end{aligned}
$$

Okay, now the last equation is in a form we can integrate just by using simple substitutions (because there are *no powers* left). For example, since we can let $u = 2x, du = 2dx$ in the second integral and $u = 4x, du = 4dx$ in the third integral we see that

$$
\begin{aligned}
\int \cos^4 x\ dx &= \frac{3}{8}\int 1\ dx + \frac{1}{2}\int \cos 2x\ dx + \frac{1}{8}\int \cos 4x\ dx \\
&= \frac{3x}{8} + \frac{1}{4}\sin 2x + \frac{1}{32}\sin 4x + C.
\end{aligned}
$$

The same exact idea may be used to evaluate the integral of its counterpart, $\sin^4 x$.

> **Example 356.** Evaluate $\int \sin^4 x\ dx$.

Solution We write $\sin^4 x$ as a product of two squares and then use (7.57) repeatedly just as before.

$$
\begin{aligned}
\sin^4 x &= \sin^2 x\ \sin^2 x \\
&= \left(\frac{1 - \cos 2x}{2}\right)\left(\frac{1 - \cos 2x}{2}\right) \\
&= \frac{1}{4}\left(1 - 2\cos 2x + \cos^2 2x\right) \\
&= \frac{1}{4}\left(1 - 2\cos 2x + \frac{1 + \cos 4x}{2}\right),
\end{aligned}
$$

just as before. So,

$$
\sin^4 x = \frac{3}{8} - \frac{\cos 2x}{2} + \frac{\cos 4x}{8},
$$

and it follows that

$$
\begin{aligned}
\int \sin^4 x\ dx &= \frac{3}{8}\int 1\ dx - \frac{1}{2}\int \cos 2x\ dx + \frac{1}{8}\int \cos 4x\ dx \\
&= \frac{3x}{8} - \frac{1}{4}\sin 2x + \frac{1}{32}\sin 4x + C.
\end{aligned}
$$

In addition to (7.57)-(7.61) there are a few other identities which may be useful as they help to *untangle* the products. For any two angles, A, B, these are

$$
\sin A\ \sin B = \frac{\cos(A - B) - \cos(A + B)}{2}, \tag{7.63}
$$

$$
\sin A\ \cos B = \frac{\sin(A - B) + \sin(A + B)}{2}, \tag{7.64}
$$

$$
\cos A\ \cos B = \frac{\cos(A - B) + \cos(A + B)}{2}. \tag{7.65}
$$

We present the details for evaluating integrals of the form

$$\int \cos^m x \ \sin^n x \ dx \qquad (7.62)$$

where m, n are positive integers.

- **m is odd, n is even**

Solve (7.58) for $\cos^2 x$. In the integrand, substitute every term of the form $\cos^2 x$ by $1 - \sin^2 x$. Since m is odd, there is always one extra cosine term. Collecting terms we see that we have an integrand involving only sine functions and their powers and only ONE simple cosine factor. Follow this with a substitution of variable, namely, $u = \sin x$, $du = \cos x \ dx$, which now reduces the integrand to a polynomial in u and this is easily integrated.

- **m is odd, n is odd**

Factor out a copy of each of $\sin x$, $\cos x$, leaving behind *even powers* of both $\sin x$, $\cos x$. Convert either one of these even powers in terms of the other using (7.58), and then perform a simple substitution, as before.

- **m is even, n is odd**

Proceed as in the case where m is odd and n is even with the words *sine* and *cosine* interchanged. So, we solve (7.58) for $\sin^2 x$. In the integrand, substitute every term of the form $\sin^2 x$ by $1 - \cos^2 x$. Since n is odd, there is always one extra sine term. Collecting terms we see that we have an integrand involving only cosine functions and their powers and only ONE simple sine term. Follow this with a simple substitution of variable, namely, $u = \cos x$, $du = -\sin x \ dx$, which now reduces the integrand to a polynomial in u which is easily integrated.

- **m is even, n is even**

This is generally the most tedious case. Remove all even powers of the sine and cosine by applying (7.57) repeatedly and reduce the integrand to a more recognizable form after a change of variable. You may then have to apply anyone or more of the three cases, above (see Examples 355, 356).

Table 7.7: Powers and Products of Sine and Cosine Integrals

Example 357. Evaluate $\int \cos^3 x \, dx$.

Solution In this case $m = 3, n = 0$, and so m is odd and n is even (remember that we consider 0 to be an *even* number). Now we solve (7.58) for $\cos^2 x$ and substitute the remaining term into the cosine expression above leaving one cosine term as a factor. Thus,

$$\begin{aligned}
\cos^3 x &= \cos^2 x \cos x \\
&= (1 - \sin^2 x) \cos x.
\end{aligned}$$

Finally,

$$\begin{aligned}
\int \cos^3 x \, dx &= \int (1 - \sin^2 x) \cos x \, dx \\
&= \int (1 - u^2) \, du \ (\text{since we set } u = \sin x, \quad du = \cos x \, dx), \\
&= u - \frac{u^3}{3} + C, \\
&= \sin x - \frac{\sin^3 x}{3} + C, \quad (\text{back-substitution}).
\end{aligned}$$

EXAMPLES

Example 358. Evaluate $\int \sin^3 x \, dx$.

Solution In this case $m = 0, n = 3$, and so m is even and n is odd. So we solve (7.58) for $\sin^2 x$ to find $\sin^2 x = 1 - \cos^2 x$ and substitute this last term into the expression leaving one "sine" term as a factor. Thus,

$$\begin{aligned}
\sin^3 x &= \sin^2 x \sin x \\
&= (1 - \cos^2 x) \sin x.
\end{aligned}$$

Just as before we will find,

$$\begin{aligned}
\int \sin^3 x \, dx &= \int (1 - \cos^2 x) \sin x \, dx \\
&= \int -(1 - u^2) \, du \ (\text{but now we let } u = \cos x, \quad du = -\sin x \, dx), \\
&= -u + \frac{u^3}{3} + C, \\
&= -\cos x + \frac{\cos^3 x}{3} + C, \quad (\text{back-substitution}).
\end{aligned}$$

Example 359. Evaluate $\int \sin^4 x \, \cos^2 x \, dx$.

Solution Here $m = 2, n = 4$, right? Since both m, n are even we remove all even powers of the sine and cosine by applying (7.57) over and over again thereby reducing the powers more and more! Thus,

$$\begin{aligned}
\sin^4 x \, \cos^2 x &= \sin^2 x \sin^2 x \cos^2 x \\
&= \left(\frac{1 - \cos 2x}{2} \right) \left(\frac{1 + \cos 2x}{2} \right) \left(\frac{1 - \cos 2x}{2} \right) \\
&= \frac{1}{8} \left((1 - \cos^2 2x) \ (1 - \cos 2x) \right) \\
&= \frac{1}{8} \left(1 - \cos 2x - \cos^2 2x + \cos^3 2x \right).
\end{aligned}$$

where the first three terms may be integrated without much difficulty. The last term above may be converted to the case of Example 357, with the substitution $u = 2x$, $du = 2dx$, for example. So,

$$
\begin{aligned}
\int \sin^4 x \, \cos^2 x \, dx &= \frac{1}{8} \int \left(1 - \cos 2x - \cos^2 2x + \cos^3 2x \right) \, dx \\
&= \frac{x}{8} - \frac{\sin 2x}{16} - \frac{1}{8} \int \left(\frac{1 + \cos 4x}{2} \right) \, dx + \frac{1}{8} \int \cos^3 2x \, dx \\
&= \frac{x}{8} - \frac{\sin 2x}{16} - \frac{x}{16} - \frac{\sin 4x}{64} + \frac{1}{16} \int \cos^3 u \, du \\
&= \frac{x}{8} - \frac{\sin 2x}{16} - \frac{x}{16} - \frac{\sin 4x}{64} + \frac{1}{16} \left(\sin u - \frac{\sin^3 u}{3} \right) + C \\
&\quad \text{(by the result of Example 357)} \\
&= \frac{x}{8} - \frac{\sin 2x}{16} - \frac{x}{16} - \frac{\sin 4x}{64} + \frac{\sin 2x}{16} - \frac{\sin^3 2x}{48} + C, \\
&\quad \text{(since } u = 2x,\text{)} \\
&= \frac{x}{16} - \frac{\sin 4x}{64} - \frac{\sin^3 2x}{48} + C.
\end{aligned}
$$

Example 360. Evaluate $\int \sin^3 x \cos^3 x \, dx$.

Solution Now, $m = 3, n = 3$ and so both exponents are odd. In accordance with Table 7.7 we **factor out a copy of each of the sine and cosine term** leaving only even powers of the remaining product. Thus,

$$
\sin^3 x \cos^3 x = \left(\sin^2 x \cos^2 x \right) \sin x \, \cos x.
$$

Now we use (7.58) in order to convert either one of the even powers to powers involving the other. For example,

$$
\begin{aligned}
\left(\sin^2 x \cos^2 x \right) \sin x \, \cos x &= \sin^2 x \left(1 - \sin^2 x \right) \sin x \, \cos x \\
&= \left(\sin^2 x - \sin^4 x \right) \sin x \cos x \\
&= \left(\sin^3 x - \sin^5 x \right) \cos x,
\end{aligned}
$$

and this is where we STOP. Now we use the substitution $u = \sin x$, $du = \cos x \, dx$ to transform the integral into a polynomial in u which is easily integrated. The details are,

$$
\begin{aligned}
\int \sin^3 x \cos^3 x \, dx &= \int \left(\sin^3 x - \sin^5 x \right) \cos x \, dx \\
&= \int \left(u^3 - u^5 \right) \, du \\
&= \frac{u^4}{4} - \frac{u^6}{6} + C, \\
&= \frac{\sin^4 x}{4} - \frac{\sin^6 x}{6} + C.
\end{aligned}
$$

Example 361. Evaluate $\int \sin^3 x \cos^2 x \, dx$.

Solution Use Table 7.7 with $m = 2, n = 3$ so that m is even and n is odd. Thus, we solve (7.58) for $\sin^2 x$ to find $\sin^2 x = 1 - \cos^2 x$ and substitute this last term into the expression $\sin^3 x \cos^2 x$ leaving one "sine" term as a factor. Thus,

$$
\begin{aligned}
\sin^3 x \cos^2 x &= \sin^2 x \cos^2 x \sin x \\
&= (1 - \cos^2 x) \cos^2 x \, \sin x, \\
&= \left(\cos^2 x - \cos^4 x \right) \sin x.
\end{aligned}
$$

Finally,

$$
\begin{aligned}
\int \sin^3 x \cos^2 x \, dx &= \int \left(\cos^2 x - \cos^4 x\right) \sin x \, dx \\
&= \int -(u^2 - u^4) \, du, \quad (\text{we let } u = \cos x, \ du = -\sin x \, dx), \\
&= -\frac{u^3}{3} + \frac{u^5}{5} + C, \\
&= -\frac{\cos^3 x}{3} + \frac{\cos^5 x}{5} + C
\end{aligned}
$$

Example 362. Evaluate $\int \sin^5 x \cos^3 x \, dx$.

Solution Now $m = 3, n = 5$ so both m, n are odd. Using Table 7.7 we remember to factor out a copy of each of $\sin x$ and $\cos x$ thereby leaving behind only EVEN exponents. Symbolically,

$$
\begin{aligned}
\sin^5 x \cos^3 x &= \left(\sin^4 x \cos^2 x\right) \sin x \ \cos x \\
&= \sin^4 x \left(1 - \sin^2 x\right) \sin x \ \cos x \\
&= \left(\sin^4 x - \sin^6 x\right) \sin x \cos x \\
&= \left(\sin^5 x - \sin^7 x\right) \cos x,
\end{aligned}
$$

and, once again, this is where we STOP. Use the substitution $u = \sin x, du = \cos x \, dx$ to transform the integral into a polynomial in u so that

$$
\begin{aligned}
\int \sin^5 x \cos^3 x \, dx &= \int \left(\sin^5 x - \sin^7 x\right) \cos x \, dx \\
&= \int (u^5 - u^7) \, du \\
&= \frac{u^6}{6} - \frac{u^8}{8} + C, \\
&= \frac{\sin^6 x}{6} - \frac{\sin^8 x}{8} + C.
\end{aligned}
$$

Example 363. Evaluate $\int \cos^3 x \sin^4 x \, dx$.

Solution In this final problem before the *Snapshots* we note that $m = 3, n = 4$ so that m is odd and n is even. We use Table 7.7 again. We factor out a cosine term out of the integrand leaving us with only even exponents, that is,

$$
\cos^3 x \sin^4 x = \left(\cos^2 x \ \sin^4 x\right) \cos x.
$$

We replace every term in the integrand of the form $\cos^2 x$ by $1 - \sin^2 x$. So,

$$
\begin{aligned}
\cos^3 x \sin^4 x &= \left(\cos^2 x \ \sin^4 x\right) \cos x \\
&= \left(1 - \sin^2 x\right) \sin^4 x \ \cos x \\
&= \left(\sin^4 x - \sin^6 x\right) \ \cos x.
\end{aligned}
$$

This last expression is easily integrated after a simple substitution, *i.e.*,

$$
\begin{aligned}
\int \cos^3 x \ \sin^4 x \, dx &= \int \left(\sin^4 x - \sin^6 x\right) \ \cos x \, dx \\
&= \int (u^4 - u^6) \, du \ (\text{set } u = \sin x, \ du = \cos x \, dx),
\end{aligned}
$$

$$= \frac{u^5}{5} - \frac{u^7}{7} + C,$$

$$= \frac{\sin^5 x}{5} - \frac{\sin^7 x}{7} + C.$$

SNAPSHOTS

Example 364. Evaluate $\int \cos^4 2x \, dx$.

EXAMPLES

Solution We bring the integrand into a *standard form* so that the same symbol appears everywhere in the integral. So we must perform a substitution $u = 2x$, $du = 2dx$. This transforms the integral to

$$\int \cos^4 2x \, dx = \frac{1}{2} \int \cos^4 u \, du.$$

Now $m = 4, n = 0$, so

$$\int \cos^4 2x \, dx = \frac{1}{2} \int \cos^4 u \, du$$

$$= \frac{1}{2} \int \cos^2 u \, \cos^2 u \, du$$

$$= \frac{1}{2} \int \left(\frac{1 + \cos 2u}{2}\right) \left(\frac{1 + \cos 2u}{2}\right) \, du$$

$$= \frac{1}{8} \int (1 + 2\cos 2u + \cos^2 2u) \, du$$

$$= \frac{u}{8} + \frac{\sin 2u}{8} + \frac{1}{16} \int \cos^2 v \, dv \quad (\text{where } v = 2u),$$

$$= \frac{u}{8} + \frac{\sin 2u}{8} + \frac{1}{16} \int \left(\frac{1 + \cos 2v}{2}\right) \, dv$$

$$= \frac{u}{8} + \frac{\sin 2u}{8} + \frac{v}{32} + \frac{1}{32} \int \cos 2v \, dv$$

$$= \frac{u}{8} + \frac{\sin 2u}{8} + \frac{v}{32} + \frac{1}{32} \frac{\sin 2v}{2} + C$$

$$= \frac{u}{8} + \frac{\sin 2u}{8} + \frac{u}{16} + \frac{\sin 4u}{64} + C$$

$$= \frac{x}{4} + \frac{\sin 4x}{8} + \frac{x}{8} + \frac{\sin 8x}{64} + C$$

$$= \frac{3x}{8} + \frac{\sin 4x}{8} + \frac{\sin 8x}{64} + C.$$

NOTES:

Example 365. Evaluate $\int x \cos^2(3x^2 + 1)\ dx$.

Solution Let $u = 3x^2 + 1$, $du = 6x\ dx$. Then

$$\int x \cos^2(3x^2 + 1)\ dx = \frac{1}{6} \int \cos^2 u\ du$$

$$= \frac{1}{6} \int \left(\frac{1 + \cos 2u}{2} \right)\ du$$

$$= \frac{u}{12} + \frac{1}{24} \sin 2u + C$$

$$= \frac{3x^2 + 1}{12} + \frac{1}{24} \sin \left(2(3x^2 + 1) \right) + C$$

$$= \frac{1}{12} + \frac{x^2}{4} + \frac{1}{24} \sin(6x^2 + 2) + C.$$

Example 366. Evaluate $\int_0^{\frac{\pi}{2}} \sin^2 x\ \cos^2 x\ dx$.

Solution Use the identity $\sin 2x = 2 \sin x\ \cos x$ to find

$$\int_0^{\frac{\pi}{2}} \sin^2 x\ \cos^2 x\ dx = \frac{1}{4} \int_0^{\frac{\pi}{2}} \sin^2 2x\ dx$$

$$= \frac{1}{8} \int_0^{\pi} \sin^2 u\ du$$

$$= \frac{1}{8} \int_0^{\pi} \left(\frac{1 - \cos 2u}{2} \right)\ du$$

$$= \frac{\pi}{16} - \frac{1}{16} \int_0^{\pi} \cos 2u\ du$$

$$= \frac{\pi}{16} - \left. \frac{\sin 2u}{32} \right|_0^{\pi}$$

$$= \frac{\pi}{16}.$$

Example 367. Evaluate $\int_0^{\frac{\pi}{2}} \sin^2 x\ \cos^4 x\ dx$.

Solution Use Table 7.7 with $m = 4, n = 2$, so that both m, n are even. Now,

$$\sin^2 x\ \cos^4 x = \sin^2 x\ \cos^2 x\ \cos^2 x$$

$$= \left(\frac{1 - \cos 2x}{2} \right) \left(\frac{1 + \cos 2x}{2} \right) \left(\frac{1 + \cos 2x}{2} \right)$$

$$= \frac{1}{8} \left(1 + \cos 2x - \cos^2 2x - \cos^3 2x \right).$$

We let $u = 2x$, $du = 2dx$, so that when $x = 0$, $u = 0$ and when $x = \frac{\pi}{2}$, $u = \pi$. Now the integral becomes

$$\int_0^{\frac{\pi}{2}} \sin^2 x\ \cos^4 x\ dx = \frac{1}{16} \int_0^{\pi} \left(1 + \cos u - \cos^2 u - \cos^3 u \right)\ du$$

$$= \frac{\pi}{16} + 0 - \frac{1}{32} \int_0^{\pi} \left(1 + \cos 2u \right)\ du - \frac{1}{16} \int_0^{\pi} \cos^3 u\ du$$

$$= \frac{\pi}{16} - \frac{\pi}{32} - 0 - \left. \frac{1}{16} \left(\sin u - \frac{\sin^3 u}{3} \right) \right|_0^{\pi}, \quad \text{(by Example 357)},$$

$$= \frac{\pi}{32}.$$

Exercise Set 36.

Evaluate the following integrals.

1. $\displaystyle\int \sin^3 3x \, dx$

2. $\displaystyle\int \cos^3(2x-1) \, dx$

3. $\displaystyle\int_0^{\frac{\pi}{2}} \sin^2 x \, \cos^3 x \, dx$

4. $\displaystyle\int \cos^2(x-2) \, \sin^3(x-2) \, dx$

5. $\displaystyle\int_{\frac{\pi}{2}}^{\pi} \sin^3 x \, \cos x \, dx$

6. $\displaystyle\int x \, \sin^2(x^2) \, \cos^2(x^2) \, dx$

7. $\displaystyle\int \sin^4 x \, \cos^4 x \, dx$

8. $\displaystyle\int \sin^4 x \, \cos^5 x \, dx$

9. $\displaystyle\int \cos^4 2x \, dx$

10. $\displaystyle\int \sin^5 x \, \cos^3 x \, dx$

11. $\displaystyle\int \sin^5 x \, \cos^4 x \, dx$

12. $\displaystyle\int \sin^6 x \, dx$

13. $\displaystyle\int \cos^7 x \, dx$

Suggested Homework Set 25. *Do problems 1, 3, 4, 6,*

NOTES:

7.5.2 Products of Secants and Tangents

In the previous section we looked at the problem of integrating products of sine and cosine functions and their powers. In this section we provide some additional insight into the integration of products and powers of secant and tangent functions. So, we'll be looking at how to evaluate integrals of the form

$$\int \sec x \tan^2 x \ dx, \quad \int \sec^3 x \ dx, \quad \int \sec^2 x \tan^2 x \ dx.$$

Cases involving the functions Cosecant and Cotangent are handled similarly. In almost all the cases under consideration we will be appealing to the fundamental trigonometric identities of the previous section that is, (7.59) and (7.60). We recall the fundamental identity (7.59) here:

$$\sec^2 u - \tan^2 u = 1,$$

valid for any real number u.

Example 368. Evaluate $I = \displaystyle\int \sec x \ dx$.

Solution This one requires a very clever use of an identity.

$$
\begin{aligned}
\int \sec x \ dx &= \int \frac{\sec x \ (\sec x + \tan x)}{\sec x + \tan x} \ dx \quad \text{(this is the idea!)}, \\
&= \int \frac{\sec^2 x + \sec x \tan x}{\sec x + \tan x} \ dx \\
&= \int \frac{dv}{v} \quad \text{(using the substitution } v = \tan x + \sec x \text{)}, \\
&= \ln |v| + C \\
&= \ln |\sec x + \tan x| + C.
\end{aligned}
$$

Example 369. Evaluate $I = \displaystyle\int \sec^3 x \ dx$.

Solution We rewrite the integrand as $\sec^3 x = \sec^2 x \sec x$ and then use (7.59) in the form $\sec^2 x = \tan^2 x + 1$. This gives us,

$$
\begin{aligned}
\int \sec^3 x \ dx &= \int \sec^2 x \sec x \ dx \\
&= \int (\tan^2 x + 1) \sec x \ dx \\
&= \int \tan^2 x \sec x \ dx + \int \sec x \ dx \\
&= \int \tan^2 x \sec x \ dx + \ln |\sec x + \tan x|, \quad \text{(by Example 368)}.
\end{aligned}
$$

In order to evaluate the first integral on the right, above, we use Integration by Parts. Thus, we write $u = \tan x$, $du = \sec^2 x \ dx$ and $dv = \sec x \tan x \ dx$, $v = \sec x$. Since

$$\int u \ dv = uv - \int v \ du,$$

we get

$$
\begin{aligned}
\int \tan^2 x \ \sec x \ dx &= \int \tan x \cdot \sec x \tan x \ dx \\
&= \tan x \sec x - \int \sec^3 x \ dx.
\end{aligned}
$$

Combining these results with the previous display we find,

$$
\begin{aligned}
\int \sec^3 x \, dx &= \int \tan^2 x \sec x \, dx + \ln|\sec x + \tan x|, \\
&= \tan x \sec x - \int \sec^3 x \, dx + \ln|\sec x + \tan x|, \\
2 \int \sec^3 x \, dx &= \tan x \sec x + \ln|\sec x + \tan x|, \\
\int \sec^3 x \, dx &= \frac{1}{2} \left(\tan x \sec x + \ln|\sec x + \tan x| \right) + C.
\end{aligned}
$$

Example 370. Evaluate $I = \displaystyle\int \sec x \tan^2 x \, dx$.

Solution This is a by-product of Example 369. In the first part of the proof we showed that

$$
\begin{aligned}
\int \tan^2 x \sec x \, dx &= \int \sec^3 x \, dx - \ln|\sec x + \tan x| \\
&= \frac{\tan x \sec x + \ln|\sec x + \tan x|}{2} - \ln|\sec x + \tan x| + C, \\
&= \frac{\tan x \sec x}{2} - \frac{\ln|\sec x + \tan x|}{2} + C.
\end{aligned}
$$

Example 371. Evaluate $I = \displaystyle\int \sec^4 x \, dx$.

Solution We rewrite the integrand as $\sec^4 x = \sec^2 x \sec^2 x$, and we solve for $\sec^2 x$ in 7.58. Now,

$$
\begin{aligned}
\int \sec^4 x \, dx &= \int \sec^2 x \, \sec^2 x \, dx \\
&= \int \sec^2 x \left(1 + \tan^2 x \right) \, dx \\
&= \int \sec^2 x \, dx + \int \sec^2 x \tan^2 x \, dx \\
&\qquad \text{(and let } u = \tan x, \ du = \sec^2 x \, dx \text{ in the second integral)}, \\
&= \tan x + \int u^2 \, du \\
&= \tan x + \frac{u^3}{3} + C \\
&= \tan x + \frac{\tan^3 x}{3} + C.
\end{aligned}
$$

NOTES:

Example 372. Evaluate $I = \int \sec^2 x \tan^3 x \, dx$.

Solution We note that $D(\tan x) = \sec^2 x$ and so the substitution $u = \tan x$, $du = \sec^2 x \, dx$ reduces the integral to

$$
\begin{aligned}
\int \tan^3 x \, \sec^2 x \, dx &= \int u^3 \, du \\
&= \frac{u^4}{4} + C \\
&= \frac{\tan^4 x}{4} + C.
\end{aligned}
$$

Example 373. For k an EVEN integer, $k \geq 2$, evaluate $I = \int \sec^k x \, dx$, and show that it can be written as

$$
\int \sec^k x \, dx = \int \left(1 + u^2\right)^{\frac{k}{2} - 1} \, du,
$$

where $u = \tan x$.

Solution Since k is even we can write it in the form $k = 2p$ where p is some integer. So, replace k by $2p$. We factor out ONE term of the form $\sec^2 x$. Next, we use the fact that $\sec^2 x = 1 + \tan^2 x$ in order to remove all the other terms of the form $\sec^2 x$ from the integrand. This leaves us with only terms of the form $\tan^2 x$ and only one term of the form $\sec^2 x$. Thus,

$$
\begin{aligned}
\int \sec^{2p} x \, dx &= \int \sec^{2p-2} x \, \sec^2 x \, dx \\
&= \int \left(\sec^2 x\right)^{p-1} \sec^2 x \, dx \\
&= \int \left(1 + \tan^2 x\right)^{p-1} \sec^2 x \, dx \text{ (we set } u = \tan x, \ du = \sec^2 x \, dx\text{)}, \\
&= \int \left(1 + u^2\right)^{p-1} \, du,
\end{aligned}
$$

and this last integral is just a polynomial in u of degree $2p - 2$. As a result, it can be integrated easily using term-by-term integration.

NOTE: If we set $p = 2$ so that $k = 4$, then

$$
\begin{aligned}
\int \sec^4 x \, dx &= \int \left(1 + u^2\right)^{2-1} \, du, \\
&= \int (1 + u^2) \, du, \\
&= u + \frac{u^3}{3} + C, \\
&= \tan x + \frac{\tan^3 x}{3} + C,
\end{aligned}
$$

which agrees with the result we obtained in Example 370, above.

Example 374. For k an ODD integer, $k \geq 3$, evaluate $I = \int \sec^k x \, dx$. Show that

$$\int \sec^k x \, dx = \frac{\sec^{k-2} x \, \tan x}{k-1} + \frac{k-2}{k-1} \int \sec^{k-2} x \, dx, \qquad (7.66)$$

Solution We have already covered the cases $k = 1$ and $k = 3$ in Examples 368, and 369. Since k is an odd number we can write it in the form $k = 2p + 1$. This is because every odd number can be written as 1 plus an even number. Let's assume this done, so $k = 2p + 1$. Now we write the integral as

$$\int \sec^k x \, dx = \int \sec^{2p+1} x \, dx$$
$$= \int \sec^{2p-1} x \, \sec^2 x \, dx.$$

Now we use Integration by Parts on the preceding integral with the following substitutions: Let

$$u = \sec^{2p-1} x, \quad du = (2p-1) \sec^{2p-2} x \cdot (\sec x \tan x) \, dx,$$

and

$$dv = \sec^2 x \, dx, \quad v = \tan x.$$

Then

$$
\begin{aligned}
I &= \int \sec^k x \, dx \\
&= \int \sec^{2p+1} x \, dx \\
&= \int \sec^{2p-1} x \, \sec^2 x \, dx \\
&= \sec^{2p-1} x \, \tan x - \int (\tan x) \cdot (2p-1) \cdot \sec^{2p-2} x \cdot (\sec x \tan x) \, dx \\
&= \sec^{2p-1} x \, \tan x - (2p-1) \int \tan x \cdot \sec^{2p-2} x \cdot (\sec x \tan x) \, dx \\
&= \sec^{2p-1} x \, \tan x - (2p-1) \int \sec^{2p-1} x \, \tan^2 x \, dx \\
&= \sec^{2p-1} x \, \tan x - (2p-1) \int \sec^{2p-1} x \, \left(\sec^2 x - 1\right) \, dx \\
&= \sec^{2p-1} x \, \tan x - (2p-1) \int \sec^{2p+1} x \, dx \\
&\quad + (2p-1) \int \sec^{2p-1} x \, dx. \\
&= \sec^{2p-1} x \, \tan x - (2p-1) \, I + (2p-1) \int \sec^{2p-1} x \, dx.
\end{aligned}
$$

Collecting the terms involving I in the last integral we see that

$$I \left(1 + (2p-1)\right) = \sec^{2p-1} x \, \tan x + (2p-1) \int \sec^{2p-1} x \, dx,$$

or

$$\int \sec^{2p+1} x \, dx = \frac{\sec^{2p-1} x \, \tan x}{2p} + \frac{2p-1}{2p} \int \sec^{2p-1} x \, dx, \qquad (7.67)$$

which is of the SAME FORM as the original one in (7.66) but with $k = 2p + 1$. This last integral is the same as (7.66) once we replace $2p$ by $k - 1$ as required.

We present the details for evaluating integrals of the form

$$\int \sec^m x \ \tan^n x \ dx \qquad (7.68)$$

where m, n are positive integers.

- **m is even, (n is even or odd)**

Assume $m > 2$, otherwise the integral is easy. Solve (7.58) for $\sec^2 x$. In the integrand, substitute every term of the form $\sec^2 x$ by $1 + \tan^2 x$. Since m is even and $m \geq 2$ by hypothesis, there is always one extra term of the form $\sec^2 x$ which we can factor out. Collecting terms we see that we have an integrand involving only tangent functions and their powers and only ONE $\sec^2 x$−term. Follow this with a simple substitution of variable, namely, $u = \tan x$, $du = \sec^2 x \ dx$, which now reduces the integral to an integral with a polynomial in u and this is easily integrated.

- **m is odd, n is odd**

Factor out one term of the form $\sec x \ \tan x$ out of the integrand. This leaves only even powers of each of $\tan x$ and $\sec x$. We solve (7.58) for $\tan^2 x$. In the integrand, substitute every term of the form $\tan^2 x$ by $\sec^2 x - 1$. Now the integrand has been rewritten as a product of secant functions along with an additional factor of $\sec x \ \tan x$. Next, we follow this with a simple substitution of variable, namely, $u = \sec x$, $du = \sec x \ \tan x \ dx$, which now reduces the integral to an integral with a polynomial in u and this is easily integrated.

- **m is odd, n is even**

This is by far the most tedious, but not impossible, case. Since n is even every term of the form $\tan^2 x$ may be replaced by an equivalent term of the form $\sec^2 x - 1$. The integral now takes the form

$$\int \sec^m x \ \tan^n x \ dx = \int \sec^m x \ \left(\sec^2 x - 1\right)^{\frac{n}{2}} \ dx,$$

where $n/2$ is an integer (since n is even). The last integral, when expanded completely, gives a sum of integrals of the form

$$\int sec^k x \ dx,$$

where k is an integer. Depending on whether k is even or odd, as the case may be, we can apply the results of Examples 373, 374 respectively, in order to evaluate it.

Table 7.8: Powers and Products of Secant and Tangent Integrals

NOTE: If we set $k = 2p + 1 = 3$, so that $p = 1$, then equation 7.66 becomes

$$\int \sec^3 x \, dx = \frac{\sec x \, \tan x}{2} + \frac{1}{2} \int \sec x \, dx, \text{ (and by Example 368)},$$

$$= \frac{\sec x \, \tan x}{2} + \frac{1}{2} \ln |\sec x + \tan x| + C,$$

which agrees with the result we obtained in Example 369, below.

The general rules for evaluating such integrals can now be summarized in Table 7.8, above.

Example 375. Evaluate $\int \sec^2 x \tan^4 x \, dx$.

Solution We use Table 7.8. In this example, $m = 2$, and $n = 4$ so m is even and n is odd. We *factor* out the only term of the form $\sec^2 x$, and then substitute $u = \tan x$ in the remaining expression consisting only of "tangents". We see that,

$$\int \sec^2 x \tan^4 x \, dx = \int u^4 \, du$$

$$= \frac{u^5}{5} + C$$

$$= \frac{\tan^5 x}{5} + C.$$

Example 376. Evaluate $\int \sec^3 x \tan^5 x \, dx$.

Solution Now $m = 3, n = 5$ so both m, n are odd. In this case we factor a term of the form $\sec x \tan x$ out of the integrand. Then we must replace every term of the form $\tan^2 x$ by $\sec^2 x - 1$. Finally, we substitute $u = \sec x$ in the remaining integral. So,

$$\int \sec^3 x \tan^5 x \, dx = \int \sec^2 x \tan^4 x \cdot (\sec x \tan x) \, dx$$

$$= \int \sec^2 x \cdot \tan^2 x \cdot \tan^2 x \cdot (\sec x \tan x) \, dx$$

$$= \int \sec^2 x \left(\sec^2 x - 1 \right)^2 \cdot (\sec x \tan x) \, dx \quad \text{(and let } u = \sec x),$$

$$= \int u^2 \left(u^2 - 1 \right)^2 \, du$$

$$= \int \left(u^6 - 2u^4 + u^2 \right) \, du$$

$$= \frac{u^7}{7} - \frac{2u^5}{5} + \frac{u^3}{3} + C$$

$$= \frac{\sec^7 x}{7} - \frac{2 \sec^5 x}{5} + \frac{\sec^3 x}{3} + C.$$

Example 377. Evaluate $I = \int \sec^5 x \, dx$.

Solution We use Example 374 with $k = 5$. We know that

$$\int \sec^k x \, dx = \frac{\sec^{k-2} x \, \tan x}{k - 1} + \frac{k - 2}{k - 1} \int \sec^{k-2} x \, dx,$$

Fundamental Results

$$\int \sec\theta \, d\theta \;\; = \;\; \ln|\sec\theta + \tan\theta| + C,$$

and

$$\int \csc\theta \, d\theta \;\; = \;\; \ln|\csc\theta - \cot\theta| + C.$$

Table 7.9: The Antiderivative of the Secant and Cosecant Functions

in general so, in our case,

$$\int \sec^5 x \, dx = \frac{\sec^3 x \, \tan x}{4} + \frac{3}{4}\int \sec^3 x \, dx.$$

But we know from Example 369 that

$$\int \sec^3 x \, dx = \frac{1}{2}\left(\tan x \sec x + \ln|\sec x + \tan x|\right) + C.$$

This means that

$$\begin{aligned}
\int \sec^5 x \, dx &= \frac{\sec^3 x \, \tan x}{4} + \frac{3}{4}\int \sec^3 x \, dx, \\
&= \frac{\sec^3 x \, \tan x}{4} + \frac{3}{8}\left(\tan x \sec x + \ln|\sec x + \tan x|\right) + C.
\end{aligned}$$

NOTES:

Exercise Set 37.

Evaluate the following integrals using any method.

1. $\int \tan x \, dx$

2. $\int \sec^2(3x + 1) \, dx$

3. $\int \sec x \tan x \, dx$

4. $\int \sec^2 x \tan x \, dx$

5. $\int \sec^2 x \tan^2 x \, dx$

6. $\int \sec^2 x \tan^5 x \, dx$

7. $\int \sec x \tan^3 x \, dx$

8. $\int \sec^4 x \tan^4 x \, dx$

9. $\int \sec^3 x \tan^3 x \, dx$

10. $\int \sec^3(2x) \tan^5(2x) \, dx$

11. $\int \sec^2 2x \tan^5 2x \, dx$

12. $\int \tan^3 x \, dx$

13. $\int \sec^7 x \, dx$

14. $\int \sec x \tan^2 x \, dx$

15. $\int \sec^3 x \tan^2 x \, dx$

Suggested Homework Set 26. *Do problems 4, 5, 7, 11, 13*

NOTES:

7.6   Trigonometric Substitutions

7.6.1   Completing the Square in a Quadratic (Review)

In this section we review briefly the classical method of **completing the square** in a quadratic polynomial. This idea is very useful in evaluating the integral of rational functions whose denominators are quadratics and where, at first sight, the Substitution Rule fails to give any simplification! For example, using this method we can show that

$$\int \frac{dx}{x^2 + 2x + 2} = \int \frac{dx}{(x+1)^2 + 1}.$$

Now, the form of the second integral makes us think of the substitution $u = x + 1$ which converts that integral to the form

$$\int \frac{dx}{(x+1)^2 + 1} = \int \frac{du}{u^2 + 1} = \text{Arctan}\, u + C,$$

and back-substitution gives us the final answer,

$$\int \frac{dx}{(x+1)^2 + 1} = \text{Arctan}\,(x+1) + C.$$

The method in this section is particularly useful when we need to integrate the reciprocal of a quadratic irreducible polynomial (or Type II factor, cf., Chapter 5), that is a polynomial of the form $ax^2 + bx + c$ where $b^2 - 4ac < 0$ (when $b^2 - 4ac \geq 0$, there is no problem since the polynomial has only Type I or linear factors, so one can use the method of Partial Fractions).

Integrands involving quadratics, $ax^2 + bx + c$

If you see the expression $ax^2 + bx + c$ or even $\sqrt{ax^2 + bx + c}$ in an integral, proceed as follows: Write

$$ax^2 + bx + c = a\left(x^2 + \frac{b}{a}x + \frac{c}{a}\right),$$
$$= a\left[\left(x + \frac{b}{2a}\right)^2 + \frac{c}{a} - \frac{b^2}{4a^2}\right],$$

so that the quadratic may be expressed in the form of a **"square"** (the $x + b/(2a)$ part) **plus some extra stuff** (the remaining expression $(c/a) - (b^2/(4a^2))$), or

$$ax^2 + bx + c = a\underbrace{\left[\left(x + \frac{b}{2a}\right)^2 + \left(\frac{4ac - b^2}{4a^2}\right)\right]}_{\text{"completing the square"}}.$$

You have just "completed the square". Next, you use the substitution

$$u = x + \frac{b}{2a}$$

to get the right-hand side into the form $a(u^2 \pm A^2)$, where the sign of A^2 is positive or negative depending on whether $(4ac - b^2)/a^2$ is positive or negative, respectively.

> If a, b, c are any three numbers with $a \neq 0$, then
>
> $$ax^2 + bx + c = a \underbrace{\left[\left(x + \frac{b}{2a} \right)^2 + \left(\frac{4ac - b^2}{4a^2} \right) \right]}_{\text{"Completing the square"}}.$$

Table 7.10: Completing the Square in a Quadratic Polynomial

This will simplify your integral to the point where you can write down the answer almost immediately! We summarize this procedure in Table 7.10.

Example 378. Rewrite the following polynomials by "completing the square".

1. $x^2 - 2x + 2$.
2. $x^2 + 2x + 5$.
3. $x^2 - 4x + 3$.
4. $x^2 - x + 1$.
5. $2x^2 - 4x + 4$.

Solution **1)** Use Table 7.10 with $a = 1$, $b = -2$ and $c = 2$. Then,

$$\begin{aligned}
x^2 - 2x + 2 &= \left(x - \frac{2}{2 \cdot 1} \right)^2 + \left(\frac{4 \cdot 2 - 4}{4 \cdot 1} \right), \\
&= (x - 1)^2 + 1.
\end{aligned}$$

2) We use Table 7.10 with $a = 1$, $b = 2$ and $c = 5$. Then,

$$\begin{aligned}
x^2 + 2x + 5 &= \left(x + \frac{2}{2 \cdot 1} \right)^2 + \left(\frac{4 \cdot 5 - 4}{4 \cdot 1} \right), \\
&= (x + 1)^2 + 4.
\end{aligned}$$

3) Use Table 7.10 with $a = 1$, $b = -4$ and $c = 3$. Then,

$$\begin{aligned}
x^2 - 4x + 3 &= \left(x - \frac{4}{2 \cdot 1} \right)^2 + \left(\frac{4 \cdot 3 - 16}{4 \cdot 1} \right), \\
&= (x - 2)^2 - 1.
\end{aligned}$$

4) We use Table 7.10 with $a = 1$, $b = -1$ and $c = 1$. Then,

$$\begin{aligned}
x^2 - x + 1 &= \left(x - \frac{1}{2} \right)^2 + \left(\frac{4 - 1}{4} \right), \\
&= \left(x - \frac{1}{2} \right)^2 + \frac{3}{4}.
\end{aligned}$$

5) Use Table 7.10 with $a = 2$, $b = -4$ and $c = 4$. Then,

$$\begin{aligned}
2x^2 - 4x + 4 &= 2 \cdot \left(x - \frac{4}{4} \right)^2 + \left(\frac{32 - 16}{16} \right), \\
&= 2 \cdot \left((x - 1)^2 + 1 \right), \\
&= 2(x - 1)^2 + 2.
\end{aligned}$$

Example 379. Evaluate $\displaystyle\int \frac{1}{x^2 + 2x + 2} \, dx$.

Solution If we complete the square in the denominator of this expression we find

$$\int \frac{1}{x^2 + 2x + 2}\, dx \;=\; \int \frac{1}{(x+1)^2 + 1}\, dx.$$

Now, use the substitution $u = x + 1$, $du = dx$. Then, by Table 6.7 with $\square = u$,

$$\begin{aligned}\int \frac{1}{(x+1)^2 + 1}\, dx &= \int \frac{1}{u^2 + 1}\, du, \\ &= \text{Arctan}\, u + C, \\ &= \text{Arctan}\,(x+1) + C.\end{aligned}$$

Example 380. Evaluate $\displaystyle\int_0^1 \frac{1}{4x^2 - 4x + 2}\, dx.$

Solution Completing the square in the denominator gives us

$$\int_0^1 \frac{1}{4x^2 - 4x + 2}\, dx \;=\; \int_0^1 \frac{1}{(2x-1)^2 + 1}\, dx.$$

Next, use the substitution $u = 2x - 1$, $du = 2dx$. Furthermore, when $x = 0$, $u = -1$ while when $x = 1$, $u = 1$. Finally, $dx = du/2$, and by Table 6.7 with $\square = u$,

$$\begin{aligned}\int_0^1 \frac{1}{(2x-1)^2 + 1}\, dx &= \frac{1}{2}\int_{-1}^1 \frac{1}{u^2 + 1}\, du, \\ &= \frac{1}{2}\text{Arctan}\, u \Big|_{-1}^1, \\ &= \frac{1}{2}\left(\text{Arctan}\, 1 - \text{Arctan}\,(-1)\right), \\ &= \frac{1}{2}\left(\frac{\pi}{4} - \left(-\frac{\pi}{4}\right)\right), \\ &= \frac{\pi}{4}.\end{aligned}$$

Example 381. Evaluate $\displaystyle\int \frac{1}{\sqrt{2x - x^2}}\, dx.$

Solution If we complete the square inside the square root we find that $2x - x^2 = -(x^2 - 2x) = -((x-1)^2 - 1) = 1 - (x-1)^2$. So,

$$\int \frac{1}{\sqrt{2x - x^2}}\, dx \;=\; \int \frac{1}{\sqrt{1 - (x-1)^2}}\, dx.$$

This time we use the substitution $u = x - 1$, $du = dx$. Then, by the first of Table 6.7 with $\square = u$,

$$\begin{aligned}\int \frac{1}{\sqrt{1 - (x-1)^2}}\, dx &= \int \frac{1}{\sqrt{1 - u^2}}\, du, \\ &= \text{Arcsin}\, u + C, \\ &= \text{Arcsin}\,(x-1) + C.\end{aligned}$$

Example 382. Evaluate $\displaystyle\int \frac{1}{x^2 - x + 1}\, dx.$

Solution Let's use the result from Example 378, (4). When we complete the square in the denominator of this expression we find

$$\int \frac{1}{x^2 - x + 1}\, dx \;=\; \int \frac{1}{\left(x - \frac{1}{2}\right)^2 + \frac{3}{4}}\, dx.$$

We let $u = x - 1/2$, $du = dx$. Then,

$$\int \frac{1}{\left(x - \frac{1}{2}\right)^2 + \frac{3}{4}}\, dx \;=\; \int \frac{1}{u^2 + \frac{3}{4}}\, du,$$

and we think about Table 6.7, that is, we think about the part of this Table which deals with the Arctan function. But instead of 3/4 we need a 1. So, we factor out that number and see that,

$$\int \frac{1}{u^2 + \frac{3}{4}}\, du \;=\; \int \frac{1}{\frac{3}{4}\left(\frac{4u^2}{3} + 1\right)}\, du,$$

$$=\; \frac{4}{3} \int \frac{1}{\frac{4u^2}{3} + 1}\, du,$$

$$=\; \frac{4}{3} \int \frac{1}{\left(\frac{2u}{\sqrt{3}}\right)^2 + 1}\, du.$$

OK, now we use another subtitution! Why? Because although we have the 1 in the right place we still can't integrate it directly using Table 6.7. So we set

$$v = \frac{2u}{\sqrt{3}}, \;\; dv = \frac{2du}{\sqrt{3}} \;\Rightarrow\; du = \frac{\sqrt{3}dv}{2}.$$

Then

$$\frac{4}{3} \int \frac{1}{\left(\frac{2u}{\sqrt{3}}\right)^2 + 1}\, du \;=\; \frac{4}{3} \cdot \frac{\sqrt{3}}{2} \int \frac{1}{v^2 + 1}\, dv,$$

$$=\; \frac{2}{\sqrt{3}} \text{Arctan}\, v + C,$$

$$=\; \frac{2}{\sqrt{3}} \text{Arctan}\left(\frac{2u}{\sqrt{3}}\right) + C,$$

$$=\; \frac{2}{\sqrt{3}} \text{Arctan}\left(\frac{2(x - \frac{1}{2})}{\sqrt{3}}\right) + C,$$

$$=\; \frac{2}{\sqrt{3}} \text{Arctan}\left(\frac{2x - 1}{\sqrt{3}}\right) + C.$$

Example 383. Evaluate $\displaystyle\int \frac{1}{(x - 1)\sqrt{x^2 - 2x}}\, dx$, provided $x > 2$.

Solution Once again we complete the square inside the square root and we find that $x^2 - 2x = (x - 1)^2 - 1$. So,

$$\int \frac{1}{(x - 1)\sqrt{x^2 - 2x}}\, dx \;=\; \int \frac{1}{(x - 1)\sqrt{(x - 1)^2 - 1}}\, dx,$$

The substitution $u = x - 1$, $du = dx$, works once again. Then, by the Arcsecant formula in Table 6.7 with $\square = u$, we find

$$\int \frac{1}{(x - 1)\sqrt{(x - 1)^2 - 1}}\, dx \;=\; \int \frac{1}{u\sqrt{u^2 - 1}}\, dx$$

$$=\; \text{Arcsec}\, u + C, \;\; (\text{since } u > 0 \Longrightarrow |u| = u),$$

$$=\; \text{Arcsec}\,(x - 1) + C.$$

NOTES:

Exercise Set 38.

Evaluate the following integrals by "completing the square", (if need be).

1. $\displaystyle\int_0^1 \frac{1}{1+x^2}\ dx$.

2. $\displaystyle\int \frac{2}{x^2 - 2x + 2}\ dx$.

3. $\displaystyle\int \frac{1}{x^2 - 2x + 5}\ dx$.

4. $\displaystyle\int \frac{1}{x^2 - 4x + 3}\ dx$.

5. $\displaystyle\int \frac{4}{4x^2 + 4x + 5}\ dx$.

6. $\displaystyle\int \frac{1}{4x - x^2 - 3}\ dx$.

7. $\displaystyle\int \frac{1}{\sqrt{4x - x^2}}\ dx$.

 • Complete the square. Factor out 4 from the square root, and then set $u = \dfrac{x-2}{2}$.

8. $\displaystyle\int_{-1}^0 \frac{1}{4x^2 + 4x + 2}\ dx$.

9. $\displaystyle\int \frac{1}{\sqrt{2x - x^2 + 1}}\ dx$.

10. $\displaystyle\int \frac{1}{x^2 + x + 1}\ dx$.

11. $\displaystyle\int \frac{1}{x^2 + x - 1}\ dx$.

12. $\displaystyle\int \frac{1}{(2x+1)\sqrt{4x^2 + 4x}}\ dx$, for $x > -\frac{1}{2}$.

Suggested Homework Set 27. *Do problems 2, 4, 7, 9, 11*

7.6.2 Trigonometric Substitutions

A **trigonometric substitution** is particularly useful when the integrand has a particular form, namely, if it is, or it can be turned into, the sum or a difference of two squares, one of which is a constant. For example, we will see how to evaluate integrals of the form

$$\int \sqrt{x^2 - 4}\ dx, \quad \int_0^3 \sqrt{9 + x^2}\ dx, \quad \int \frac{1}{\sqrt{3x^2 - 2x + 1}}\ dx,$$

where the last one requires the additional use of the method of *completing the square*. In general, we'll be dealing with the integration of functions containing terms like

$$\sqrt{x^2 - a^2}, \quad \sqrt{x^2 + a^2}, \ or, \quad \sqrt{a^2 - x^2}.$$

In this section many of the techniques that you've learned and used in the preceding sections come together in the evaluation of integrals involving square roots of quadratic functions. For instance, the function $3x^2 - 2x + 1$ can be written as a sum or a difference of two squares once we use the method of *completing the square*, (see section 7.6.1).

Example 384. Write the function underneath the square root sign, $\sqrt{3x^2 - 2x + 1}$, as a sum or a difference of *two squares*.

Solution To see this we note that, according to Table 7.10 in Section 7.6.1,

$$3x^2 - 2x + 1 = 3\left[\left(x - \frac{1}{3}\right)^2 + \frac{2}{9}\right],$$

so that

$$\sqrt{3x^2 - 2x + 1} = \sqrt{3}\sqrt{\left[\left(x - \frac{1}{3}\right)^2 + \frac{2}{9}\right]},$$
$$= \sqrt{3}\sqrt{u^2 + a^2},$$

if we use the substitutions

$$u = x - \frac{1}{3} \quad and \quad a = \frac{\sqrt{2}}{3}.$$

The factor, $\sqrt{3}$, is not a problem as it can be factored out of the integral.

Example 385. Write the expression $\sqrt{x^2 - 2x - 2}$ as the square root of a sum or a difference of *two squares*.

Solution We use Table 7.10 once again. Now,

$$\sqrt{x^2 - 2x - 3} = \sqrt{(x - 1)^2 - 4},$$
$$= \sqrt{u^2 - a^2},$$

provided we choose $u = x - 1$, $a = \sqrt{4} = 2$.

Example 386. Write the expression $\sqrt{2x - x^2}$ as the square root of a sum or a difference of *two squares*.

Solution We use Table 7.10 once again. Now,

$$\sqrt{2x - x^2} = \sqrt{-(x^2 - 2x)},$$
$$= \sqrt{1 - (x^2 - 2x + 1)},$$
$$= \sqrt{1 - (x - 1)^2},$$
$$= \sqrt{a^2 - u^2},$$

provided we choose $u = x - 1$, $a = 1$.

In the same way we can see that the method of *completing the square* can be used generally to write the quadratic $ax^2 + bx + c$ with $a \neq 0$, as a sum or a difference of two squares. Once we have written the general quadratic in this special form, we can use the substitutions in Table 7.11 in order to evaluate integrals involving these sums or differences of squares. Let's not forget that

Let $a \neq 0$ be a constant. If the integrand contains a term of the form:

- $\sqrt{a^2 - u^2}$, substitute

$$u = a \sin \theta, \quad du = a \cos \theta \, d\theta, \quad \sqrt{a^2 - u^2} = a \cos \theta,$$

if $-\pi/2 < \theta < \pi/2$.

- $\sqrt{a^2 + u^2}$, set

$$u = a \tan \theta, \quad du = a \sec^2 \theta \, d\theta, \quad \sqrt{a^2 + u^2} = a \sec \theta,$$

if $-\pi/2 < \theta < \pi/2$.

- $\sqrt{u^2 - a^2}$, set

$$u = a \sec \theta, \quad du = a \sec \theta \tan \theta \, d\theta, \quad \sqrt{u^2 - a^2} = a \tan \theta,$$

if $0 < \theta < \pi/2$.

Table 7.11: Trigonometric Substitutions

$$ax^2 + bx + c = a \left[\underbrace{\left(x + \frac{b}{2a}\right)^2 + \left(\frac{4ac - b^2}{4a^2}\right)}_{\text{``completing the square''}} \right].$$

EXAMPLES

| Example 387. | Evaluate $\int_0^{\frac{1}{4}} \frac{dx}{\sqrt{1 - 4x^2}}$. |

Solution Note that we can evaluate this integral using Table 6.7 with $\square = 2x$ and obtain the value $\frac{\text{Arcsin } 2x}{2}$. But let's see how a trigonometric substitution works. The integrand has a term of the form $\sqrt{a^2 - u^2}$ where $a = 1, u = 2x$. So, in accordance with Table 7.11, we set

$$2x = \sin \theta, \quad 2dx = \cos \theta \, d\theta, \text{ so that } \sqrt{1 - 4x^2} = \cos \theta.$$

It follows that

$$\theta = \text{Arcsin } 2x, \text{ and } dx = \frac{\cos \theta \, d\theta}{2}.$$

When $x = 0$, $\theta = \text{Arcsin }(2 \cdot 0) = \text{Arcsin } 0 = 0$, while when $x = \frac{1}{4}$, $\theta = \text{Arcsin }\left(2 \cdot \frac{1}{4}\right)$ $= \text{Arcsin } \frac{1}{2} = \frac{\pi}{6}$. The integral now becomes

$$\begin{aligned}
\int_0^{\frac{1}{4}} \frac{dx}{\sqrt{1 - 4x^2}} &= \frac{1}{2} \int_0^{\frac{\pi}{6}} \frac{\cos \theta}{\cos \theta} d\theta \\
&= \frac{1}{2} \int_0^{\frac{\pi}{6}} d\theta \\
&= \frac{\pi}{12}.
\end{aligned}$$

Useful Integrals

A simple application of the two identities in (7.57) shows that

$$\int \cos^2 x \; dx \;\; = \;\; \frac{x}{2} + \frac{\sin 2x}{4} + C, \qquad (7.69)$$

and

$$\int \sin^2 x \; dx \;\; = \;\; \frac{x}{2} - \frac{\sin 2x}{4} + C. \qquad (7.70)$$

Table 7.12: Integrating the Square of the Cosine or Sine Function

---

Example 388. Evaluate $\int \dfrac{1}{x\sqrt{x^2 - 16}} \; dx$.

Solution This integrand has a term of the form $\sqrt{u^2 - a^2}$ with $u = x$, $a = 4$. So, we let $x = 4\sec\theta$, which gives $\sqrt{x^2 - 16} = 4\tan\theta$, and $dx = 4\sec\theta \ \tan\theta \ d\theta$. So,

$$\begin{aligned}
I &= \int \frac{4 \ \sec\theta \ \tan\theta \ d\theta}{4\sec\theta \cdot 4\tan\theta} \\
&= \frac{1}{4}\theta + C \\
&= \frac{1}{4}\text{Arcsec}\left(\frac{x}{4}\right) + C
\end{aligned}$$

Example 389. Evaluate $\int \sqrt{2x - x^2} \; dx$.

Solution In this example, it isn't clear that this integrand is a square root of a *difference or sum of two squares*. But the method of *completing the square* can be used to show this (see Section 7.6.1). Remember that every quadratic function can be written as a sum or a difference of squares. We have already discussed this function in Example 386, above. We found by completing the square that

$$2x - x^2 \;\; = \;\; 1 - (x - 1)^2,$$

and so,

$$\sqrt{2x - x^2} \;\; = \;\; \sqrt{1 - (x - 1)^2}.$$

Now $\sqrt{1 - (x - 1)^2}$ is of the form $\sqrt{a^2 - u^2}$ provided we choose $a = 1$, $u = x - 1$. This is our cue for the substitution! In accordance with Table 7.11 we use the substitution $x - 1 = \sin\theta$ so that $dx = \cos\theta \ d\theta$ and $\theta = \text{Arcsin}\,(x - 1)$. In this case,

$$\sqrt{1 - (x - 1)^2} = \cos\theta,$$

and

$$\begin{aligned}
\int \sqrt{2x - x^2} \; dx &= \int \sqrt{1 - (x - 1)^2} \; dx \\
&= \int (\cos\theta) \ \cos\theta \ d\theta \\
&= \int \cos^2\theta \ d\theta \quad \text{(and by (7.69) in Table 7.12),}
\end{aligned}$$

$$= \frac{\theta}{2} + \frac{\sin 2\theta}{4} + C,$$

$$= \frac{\theta}{2} + \frac{(2\sin\theta\,\cos\theta)}{4} + C, \quad \text{(see above for } \cos\theta\text{)},$$

$$= \frac{\theta}{2} + \frac{(x-1)\,\sqrt{1-(x-1)^2}}{2} + C,$$

$$= \frac{1}{2}\text{Arcsin}\,(x-1) + \frac{(x-1)\,\sqrt{1-(x-1)^2}}{2} + C.$$

Example 390.   Evaluate $I = \displaystyle\int \frac{1}{\sqrt{4x^2 + 4x + 17}}\,dx.$

Solution. By completing the square we see that we can write

$$4x^2 + 4x + 17 = (2x+1)^2 + 4^2 = u^2 + a^2,$$

where $u = 2x+1$ and $a = 4$. Using Table 7.11 we substitute

$$\begin{aligned} 2x+1 &= 4\tan\theta \\ \sqrt{(2x+1)^2 + 4^2} &= 4\sec\theta \\ dx &= 2\sec^2\theta\,d\theta. \end{aligned}$$

Now the integral is simplified enough so that

$$\begin{aligned} \int \frac{1}{\sqrt{4x^2+4x+17}}\,dx &= \int \frac{2\sec^2\theta\,d\theta}{4\sec\theta} = \frac{1}{2}\int \sec\theta\,d\theta \\ &= \frac{1}{2}\ln|\sec\theta + \tan\theta| + C \\ &= \frac{1}{2}\ln\left|\frac{\sqrt{(2x+1)^2+4^2} + 2x + 1}{4}\right| + C \\ &= \frac{1}{2}\ln\left|\sqrt{4x^2+4x+17} + 2x + 1\right| + C, \end{aligned}$$

where the factor of 1/4 disappears after noting that

$$\frac{1}{2}\ln\left|\frac{\square}{4}\right| = \frac{1}{2}\left(\ln|\square| - \ln 4\right).$$

The constant $-\frac{\ln 4}{2}$ is then absorbed into the (generic) constant of integration, C, where we use the *same symbol* C to denote this constant (don't worry, it's just a convention; we always denote a generic constant by C). So, for example, the constants $C - 1, C + \ln 2, C - 5^2 + 3.2\pi, \ldots$ are all denoted by the same symbol, C.

Example 391.   Evaluate $\displaystyle\int \frac{x^2}{\sqrt{9-x^2}}\,dx.$

Solution This integrand has a term of the form $\sqrt{a^2 - u^2}$ where $a = 3$, $u = x$. So, an application of Table 7.11 shows that if we use the substitution $x = 3\sin\theta$, then $dx = 3\cos\theta\,d\theta$ and $3\cos\theta = \sqrt{\sqrt{9-x^2}}$, or,

$$\cos\theta = \frac{\sqrt{9-x^2}}{3}.$$

So,

$$\int \frac{x^2}{\sqrt{9-x^2}}\,dx = \int \frac{(3\sin\theta)^2\,3\cos\theta\,d\theta}{3\cos\theta}$$

$$= 9 \int \sin^2 \theta \, d\theta$$

$$= \frac{9}{2}\theta - \frac{9 \sin 2\theta}{4} + C \quad \text{(by 7.70)},$$

$$= \frac{9}{2}\theta - \frac{9 \sin \theta \, \cos \theta}{2} + C$$

$$= \frac{9}{2}\text{Arcsin}\left(\frac{x}{3}\right) - \frac{9}{2} \cdot \left(\frac{x}{3}\right) \cdot \frac{\sqrt{9 - x^2}}{3} + C$$

$$= \frac{9}{2}\text{Arcsin}\left(\frac{x}{3}\right) - \frac{x\sqrt{9 - x^2}}{2} + C,$$

where we have used the identity $\sin 2\theta = 2 \sin \theta \, \cos \theta$ (just as before in Example 389).

Example 392. Evaluate $\int \sqrt{x^2 - 4} \, dx$.

Solution This integrand has the form $\sqrt{u^2 - a^2}$ where $a = 2, u = x$. In accordance with Table 7.11, we set

$$x = 2 \sec \theta, \ dx = 2 \sec \theta \tan \theta \, d\theta, \ \text{so that} \ \sqrt{x^2 - 4} = 2 \tan \theta.$$

It follows that $\theta = \text{Arcsec}\left(\frac{x}{2}\right)$, and

$$\int \sqrt{x^2 - 4} \, dx = \int (2 \tan \theta)(2 \sec \theta \tan \theta) \, d\theta$$

$$= 4 \int \sec \theta \, (\tan \theta)^2 \, d\theta$$

$$= 4 \tan \theta \, \sec \theta - 2 \ln |\sec \theta + \tan \theta| + C,$$

by Example 370. Back-substitution tells us that

$$\tan \theta = \frac{\sqrt{x^2 - 4}}{2},$$

and

$$\sec \theta = \frac{x}{2}.$$

Combining these two relations into the last equality gives

$$\int \sqrt{x^2 - 4} \, dx = x\sqrt{x^2 - 4} - 2 \ln \left| \frac{x + \sqrt{x^2 - 4}}{2} \right| + C,$$

$$= x\sqrt{x^2 - 4} - 2 \ln \left| x + \sqrt{x^2 - 4} \right| + 2 \ln 2 + C,$$

$$= x\sqrt{x^2 - 4} - 2 \ln \left| x + \sqrt{x^2 - 4} \right| + C,$$

where the last C is a generic constant denoted by the same symbol.

NOTES:

Example 393. Evaluate $I = \displaystyle\int \frac{dy}{\sqrt{25 + 9y^2}}$.

Solution The integrand has a term of the form $\sqrt{a^2 + u^2}$ where $a = 5$ and $u = 3y$. This is our cue for the substitution. So, using Table 7.11, we set

$$3y = 5\tan\theta, \quad 3\,dy = 5\sec^2\theta\,d\theta, \quad \sqrt{a^2 + u^2} = 5\sec\theta.$$

Then

$$\theta = \operatorname{Arctan}\left(\frac{3y}{5}\right), \quad dy = \frac{5\sec^2\theta\,d\theta}{3},$$

and

$$
\begin{aligned}
\int \frac{dy}{\sqrt{25 + 9y^2}} &= \frac{1}{3}\int \frac{5\sec^2\theta\,d\theta}{5\sec\theta} \\
&= \frac{1}{3}\int \sec\theta\,d\theta \\
&= \frac{1}{3}\ln|\sec\theta + \tan\theta| + C, \text{ (by Example 368),} \\
&= \frac{1}{3}\ln\left|\frac{\sqrt{25 + 9y^2}}{5} + \frac{3y}{5}\right| + C,
\end{aligned}
$$

and we can simplify this slightly by absorbing the constant $\frac{-\ln 5}{3}$ into the generic constant, C. This gives

$$\int \frac{dy}{\sqrt{25 + 9y^2}} = \frac{1}{3}\ln\left|\sqrt{25 + 9y^2} + 3y\right| + C.$$

Example 394. Evaluate $\displaystyle\int \sqrt{3x^2 - 2x + 1}\,dx$.

Solution We look up this function in Example 384, above. We found by completing the square that

$$\sqrt{3x^2 - 2x + 1} = \sqrt{3}\sqrt{\left(x - \frac{1}{3}\right)^2 + \frac{2}{9}}, \tag{7.71}$$

$$= \sqrt{3}\sqrt{u^2 + a^2}, \tag{7.72}$$

if we choose

$$u = x - \frac{1}{3} \quad \text{and} \quad a = \frac{\sqrt{2}}{3}.$$

So, we have to evaluate an integral of the form

$$\int \sqrt{3x^2 - 2x + 1}\,dx = \sqrt{3}\int \sqrt{u^2 + a^2}\,du.$$

Referring to Table 7.11, we let $u = a\tan\theta$, that is,

$$x - \frac{1}{3} = u = \frac{\sqrt{2}}{3}\tan\theta, \quad dx = du = \frac{\sqrt{2}}{3}\sec^2\theta\,d\theta.$$

But our choice of substitution always gives $\sqrt{a^2 + u^2} = a\sec\theta$. So, in actuality,

$$
\begin{aligned}
\sec\theta &= \frac{\sqrt{a^2 + u^2}}{a} \\
&\quad\text{from equation (7.72),} \\
&= \sqrt{\frac{3}{2}}\sqrt{3x^2 - 2x + 1}
\end{aligned}
$$

So,

$$\int \sqrt{3x^2 - 2x + 1} \, dx = \int \left(\sqrt{\frac{2}{3}} \sec\theta \right) \left(\frac{\sqrt{2}}{3} \sec^2\theta \right) d\theta$$

$$= \frac{2\sqrt{3}}{9} \int \sec^3\theta \, d\theta$$

$$= \frac{2\sqrt{3}}{9} \cdot \frac{1}{2} \left(\tan\theta \sec\theta + \ln|\sec\theta + \tan\theta| \right) + C$$

(by Example 369),

$$= \frac{\sqrt{3}}{9} \left(\tan\theta \sec\theta + \ln|\sec\theta + \tan\theta| \right) + C,$$

where, according to our definition of θ,

$$\tan\theta = \frac{3\sqrt{2}}{2} \left(x - \frac{1}{3} \right),$$

and

$$\sec\theta = \sqrt{1 + \tan^2\theta} = \sqrt{1 + \frac{9}{2} \left(x - \frac{1}{3} \right)^2}.$$

You are invited to write down the complete formulation of the final answer!

EXAMPLES

SNAPSHOTS

Example 395. Evaluate $\displaystyle\int \frac{\sqrt{9x^2 - 1}}{x} \, dx$.

Solution This integrand contains a difference of two squares of the form $\sqrt{u^2 - a^2}$ where $u = 3x$ and $a = 1$. So, we set $3x = \sec\theta$. Then $\sqrt{9x^2 - 1} = \tan\theta$, and $dx = \frac{1}{3}\sec\theta \, \tan\theta \, d\theta$. Hence

$$\int \frac{\sqrt{9x^2 - 1}}{x} \, dx = \int \frac{\tan\theta \left(\frac{1}{3}\sec\theta \, \tan\theta \right) d\theta}{\frac{1}{3}\sec\theta}$$

$$= \int \tan^2\theta \, d\theta$$

$$= \int (\sec^2\theta - 1) \, d\theta$$

$$= \tan(\theta) - \theta + C$$

$$= \sqrt{9x^2 - 1} - \text{Arccos}\left(\frac{1}{3x} \right) + C.$$

Example 396. Evaluate $\displaystyle\int_0^5 \sqrt{25 - x^2} \, dx$.

Solution Let $x = 5\sin\theta$, $\Rightarrow$ $\sqrt{25 - x^2} = 5\cos\theta$, $dx = 5\cos\theta \, d\theta$. When $x = 0$, $\theta = 0$, while when $x = 5$, $\theta = \frac{\pi}{2}$. So,

$$\int_0^5 \sqrt{25 - x^2} \, dx = \int_0^{\frac{\pi}{2}} 5\cos\theta \cdot 5\cos\theta \, d\theta$$

$$= 25 \int_0^{\frac{\pi}{2}} \cos^2\theta \, d\theta \quad \text{(and by 7.69)},$$

$$= 25 \left(\frac{\theta}{2} + \frac{1}{4}\sin 2\theta \right) \Bigg|_0^{\frac{\pi}{2}}$$

$$= 25(\frac{\pi}{4} + \frac{1}{4} \sin \pi - 0 - 0)$$

$$= \frac{25\pi}{4}.$$

Example 397. Evaluate $\int \frac{4x^2 \, dx}{(1 - x^2)^{3/2}}$.

Solution Let $x = \sin\theta$, $dx = \cos\theta \, d\theta$. Then,

$$\cos\theta = \sqrt{1 - x^2}, \quad \tan\theta = \frac{x}{\sqrt{1 - x^2}},$$

and

$$
\begin{aligned}
\int \frac{4x^2 \, dx}{(1 - x^2)^{3/2}} &= \int \frac{4 \cdot \sin^2\theta \cdot \cos\theta \, d\theta}{\cos^3\theta} \\
&= 4 \int \tan^2\theta \, d\theta \\
&= 4 \int (\sec^2\theta - 1) \, d\theta \\
&= 4 \int \sec^2\theta \, d\theta - 4\theta \\
&= 4\tan\theta - 4\theta + C \\
&= \frac{4x}{\sqrt{1 - x^2}} - 4\text{Arcsin}\, x + C
\end{aligned}
$$

Exercise Set 39.

Evaluate the following integrals using any method.

1. $\int \sqrt{4 - x^2} \, dx$.

2. $\int \sqrt{x^2 + 9} \, dx$.

3. $\int \sqrt{x^2 - 1} \, dx$.

4. $\int \sqrt{4x - x^2} \, dx$.

5. $\int \frac{dx}{(4 - x^2)^{3/2}}$.

6. $\int \frac{x^2 \, dx}{(9 - x^2)^{3/2}}$.

7. $\int \frac{dx}{x^2\sqrt{x^2 - 4}}$.

8. $\int \sqrt{4x^2 - 4x + 2} \, dx$.

9. $\int \frac{dx}{(9 + x^2)^2}$.

10. $\int \frac{\sqrt{4 - x^2}}{x} \, dx$.

11. $\displaystyle\int \frac{dx}{(x^2 + 25)^{3/2}}$.

12. $\displaystyle\int \frac{\sqrt{4 - x^2}}{x^2}\, dx$.

13. $\displaystyle\int \frac{dx}{x^4\sqrt{a^2 - x^2}}$, where $a \neq 0$ is a constant.

14. $\displaystyle\int \frac{dx}{x^4\sqrt{x^2 - a^2}}$, where $a \neq 0$ is a constant.

15. $\displaystyle\int \frac{\sqrt{x^2 + 2x - 3}}{x + 1}\, dx$.

16. $\displaystyle\int \frac{2x + 1\, dx}{\sqrt{x^2 + 2x + 5}}$.

Suggested Homework Set 28. *Do problems 2, 4, 5, 7, 8, 12*

NOTES:

7.7   Numerical Integration

The Big Picture

When the evaluation of a definite integral is required and every possible method of finding an antiderivative fails (such as incantations, pleading to Crom, etc.), one resorts to **numerical integration**, that is, the numerical approximation of the value of the definite integral. The point is that it's not always possible to find some trick or substitution which will simplify your integral into something more manageable and find yourself with a nice answer at the end. The problem may be that the function *does* have an antiderivative but you can't write it down with a finite number of symbols (*i.e.,* in *closed form*). Bad news. For example, the antiderivative of the function e^{-x^2} exists but can't be written down explicitly with a finite number of terms; indeed, it looks like

$$\int e^{-x^2}\, dx = x - \frac{x^3}{3} + \frac{x^5}{5 \cdot 2!} - \frac{x^7}{7 \cdot 3!} + \dots,$$

where the "..." on the right mean that there is an *infinite number of terms here*. Actually, the whole thing is called an **infinite series** and we'll be studying this later on.

On the other hand, maybe the technique for finding the antiderivative is beyond the scope of the ones presented here. Either way, your boss, teacher, friend, wants an answer ASAP and so you'll have to come up with something! This is where the estimation of the value of the definite integral becomes important. For instance, if you have to evaluate the definite integral below and you come up with an answer like

$$\int_0^1 e^{-x^2}\, dx \approx 0.74$$

the natural question is "How close is this to the *real* answer?" (You know there is a real answer because this function is integrable over the interval $[0, 1]$, being continuous there). So, how good is your approximation? This leads one to study the concept of **error terms** or **error estimate** or more simply the **error** in approximating the definite integral by a method.

Some methods are better than others because they don't require as much effort on your part (or the calculator/computer) to get a *good* answer. You can't always expect to get the correct answer *right on the nose*, so to speak, but you'll be close enough to it to apply it to whatever problem you're working on, be it in engineering, science, economics, etc.

> ### Review
>
> Chapter 1 on the **evaluation of functions** at a given point, the **definition of a definite integral**, and the charge of your scientific calculator battery.

The two principal techniques or methods for approximating a definite integral here are the **Trapezoidal Rule** and **Simpson's Rule**. They're called *Rules* in the sense that there is a very specific formula for you to use in order to arrive at an answer. Many other methods (Midpoint Rule, Quadrature formulae, ...) exist as well, and the reader may consult any manual in an area called **Numerical Analysis** for further details.

7.7.1 The Trapezoidal Rule

Recall that a **trapezoid** is a closed four-sided figure in the plane having two parallel sides. Also, recall that the definite integral of a given integrable function f, can be approximated by **Riemann sums**, that is, sums of "areas" of certain rectangles formed on a given subdivision of the interval $[a, b]$. The basic idea behind the Trapezoidal Rule applied to a continuous function, f, over the interval $[a, b]$ is the following:

We approximate the value of the definite integral of f over $[a, b]$ by the sums of the areas of trapezoids, each one of which approximates the area of a corresponding rectangle in the Riemann sum. This latter sum of areas of rectangles (i.e., the Riemann sum), is approximately equal to the definite integral, right? So, one could believe that the definite integral can be approximated by a sum of areas of trapezoids. For the remaining part of this section we will assume that f is continuous over $[a, b]$ (but it's not really a problem if we assume that, more generally, f is *piecewise continuous* over $[a, b]$ (Chapter 2)).

> **The Basic Problem:** We wish to evaluate $\int_a^b f(x)\,dx$ numerically.

1. Subdivide $[a, b]$ into n equal parts of length $h = \frac{b-a}{n}$. This subdivision is a **partition** of the interval $[a, b]$ in the sense of the Theory of the Integral, (see Chapter 7).

This gives a sequence of points (x_m) where

$$x_0 = a < x_1 < x_2 < ... < x_{n-1} < x_n = b,$$

and each point x_m is given by the formula

$$x_m = a + mh, \quad m = 0, 1, 2, 3, ..., n.$$

For example, $x_0 = a + 0h = a$, $x_1 = a + 1h = a + (b-a)/n$, $x_2 = a + 2h = a + 2(b-a)/n$, etc. Note that $x_{m+1} - x_m = h$, which **must** be the case since the points are all equally spaced, by construction. See Figure 152.

2. Form the trapezoids $T_1, T_2, T_3, \ldots$ see Figure 154.

3. Calculate the area of each trapezoid $T_1, T_2, T_3 \ldots$.

NOTE: If a trapezoid lies below the x−axis its area is taken to be *negative*, as usual.

For example, the area of each trapezoid T_1, T_2, T_3, is given by (see Figure 153).

$$\begin{aligned}
area\ T_1 &= (area\ of\ rectangle) + (area\ of\ triangle), \\
&= h \cdot f(x_0) + \frac{1}{2}h(f(x_1) - f(x_0)) = \frac{h}{2}(f(x_0) + f(x_1)), \\
area\ T_2 &= (area\ of\ rectangle) + (area\ of\ triangle), \\
&= h \cdot f(x_2) + \frac{1}{2}h(f(x_1) - f(x_2)) = \frac{h}{2}(f(x_1) + f(x_2)), \\
area\ T_3 &= (area\ of\ rectangle) + (area\ of\ triangle), \\
&= h \cdot f(x_2) + \frac{1}{2}h(f(x_3) - f(x_2)) = \frac{h}{2}(f(x_2) + f(x_3)), \\
&\ etc.
\end{aligned}$$

Motivation for the Trapezoidal Rule

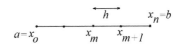

Figure 152.

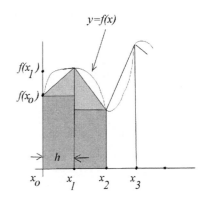

Figure 153.

The Trapezoidal Rule

$$\int_a^b f(x)\ dx \ \approx\ \frac{b-a}{2n}(f(x_0) + 2f(x_1) + 2f(x_2) + ... + 2f(x_{n-1}) + f(x_n)),$$

$$= \frac{b-a}{2n}\left(y_0 + 2y_1 + 2y_2 + ... + 2y_{n-1} + y_n\right),$$

$$= \frac{h}{2}\left(y_0 + 2y_1 + 2y_2 + ... + 2y_{n-1} + y_n\right),$$

$$\equiv\ \mathcal{T}_n, \ \text{by definition,}$$

where, for simplicity, we have set $y_m = f(x_m)$. Furthermore, $x_0 = a$, $x_n = b$ and the interval $[a, b]$ is divided into n subintervals each having length $h = \frac{b-a}{n}$. This gives us the subdivision points

$$x_m\ =\ a + mh,,$$

$$=\ a + \frac{m\,(b-a)}{n}, \quad \text{for}\ \ m = 0, 1, 2, 3, ..., n.$$

Table 7.13: The Trapezoidal Rule for Estimating a Definite Integral

4. Add up all the areas of $T_1, T_2, T_3, ...$ to approximate the Riemann Sum of f for this partition of equally-spaced points. Bear in mind that from the theory of the integral, in the limit as $n \to \infty$, this number is the same as

$$\int_a^b f(x)\ dx.$$

Okay, now summing the areas of each trapezoid $T_1, T_2, T_3, \ldots$, factoring out the number $(b-a)/2n = h/2$ from each term, and collecting the rest, gives us the value of $\mathcal{T}_n$ in Table 7.13.

Now, let's test this Rule on a simple example, in the sense that we can actually **check our answer** independently of the Rule. In this case, by direct integration, using the Power Rule for integrals.

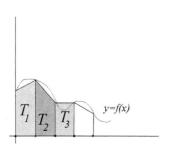

The idea behind this method is that it uses *short line segments* to mimic the *curvature* of the graph of the function f over the given interval.

Figure 154.

| Example 398. | Use the Trapezoidal Rule with $n = 4$ to approximate |

$$\int_0^2 x^2\ dx.$$

Compare your answer with the **exact** value, found by integrating directly.

Solution The problem can be broken down into the following steps. In general, we need to find the quantities a, b, n, from which we get the values $x_0, x_1, x_2, \ldots, x_n$ (see Table 7.13), and then $f(x_0), f(x_1), f(x_2), \ldots, f(x_n)$. Once we have these values we feed them into the formula for the Trapezoidal Rule (see Table 7.13 once again), to find the value of $\mathcal{T}_n$, our approximation.

1. Now,

$$\begin{aligned}
a\ &=0,\\
b\ &=2,\\
n\ &=4,\\
h\ &=\frac{b-a}{n} = \frac{2-0}{4} = \frac{1}{2},\\
f(x)\ &=x^2
\end{aligned}$$

Compute the a, b, n.

2. Next, from Table 7.13,

$$
\begin{aligned}
x_0 &= a = 0, \\
x_1 &= a + 1 \cdot h = 0 + 1 \cdot h = h = \tfrac{1}{2}, \\
x_2 &= a + 2 \cdot h = 0 + 2 \cdot h = 2h = 1, \\
x_3 &= a + 3 \cdot h = 0 + 3 \cdot h = 3h = \tfrac{3}{2}, \\
x_4 &= b = 2.
\end{aligned}
$$

Compute the x_m

3. From these we find,

$$
\begin{aligned}
y_0 &= f(x_0) = x_0^2 = 0, \\
y_1 &= f(x_1) = x_1^2 = \tfrac{1}{4}, \\
y_2 &= x_2^2 = 1^2 = 1, \\
y_3 &= x_3^2 = \tfrac{9}{4}, \\
y_4 &= x_4^2 = 4.
\end{aligned}
$$

Compute the $y_m = f(x_m)$

4. **Use the Trapezoidal Rule** as in Table 7.13 to estimate T_4 (since $n = 4$, here). For $n = 4$,

$$
\begin{aligned}
\int_0^2 x^2 \, dx &\approx T_4, \\
&= \frac{h}{2}(y_0 + 2y_1 + 2y_2 + 2y_3 + y_4), \\
&= \frac{1}{4}(0 + 2(\tfrac{1}{4}) + 2(1) + 2(\tfrac{9}{4}) + 4), \\
&= \frac{1}{4}(\tfrac{1}{2} + \tfrac{9}{2} + 6), \\
&= \frac{11}{4}, \\
&= 2.75.
\end{aligned}
$$

So, the **approximate value of the definite integral** is given by $T_4 = \frac{11}{4} = 2.75$.

5. **The Actual or Exact Value** is given by

$$
\int_0^2 x^2 \, dx = \frac{x^3}{3}\Big|_0^2 = \frac{8}{3} \approx 2.66666666\ldots.
$$

NOTE: The absolute value of the difference between the Actual Value and the approximate value, just found, is very important, as it is a measure of "how good" our approximation is, right? In our case, this difference is equal to

$$
\begin{aligned}
|\,(\text{Actual value}) - (\text{Approximate value})\,| &= |\,(\text{Actual value}) - T_n\,|, \\
&= 2.750 - 2.667, \\
&= 0.083.
\end{aligned}
$$

This calculation motivates the definition of the **Error**, see Table 7.14.

Whenever you know the error, $\mathcal{E}_n(T)$, in estimating the definite integral using the Trapezoidal Rule, you can be sure that the real answer you're looking for, namely, the definite integral itself, satisfies the inequality

$$
T_n - \mathcal{E}_n(T) \leq \int_a^b f(x) \, dx \leq T_n + \mathcal{E}_n(T). \tag{7.74}
$$

Remember that, sometimes, we DON'T KNOW the exact value of an integral regardless how hard we try to evaluate it. So we must ESTIMATE its value. The difference between the estimate and the true (yet unknown) value is a measure of the Error. Our inequality (7.73) gives us an estimate on the size of the error obtained if we use the Trapezoidal Rule in estimating the value of the integral.

Example 399. Refer to Example 398. What value of n is needed so that the error, $\mathcal{E}_n(T)$, obtained in estimating the definite integral using the Trapezoidal Rule with n-steps satisfies $\mathcal{E}_n(T) < 0.01$?

The absolute value of the difference between the Actual Value, given by the definite integral, and the estimated value $\mathcal{T}_n$, given by Table 7.13, is called the **Error**, $\mathcal{E}_n(\mathcal{T})$, in estimating the definite integral of f over $[a, b]$ by the Trapezoidal Rule in n-steps. It is defined mathematically by

$$| \int_a^b f(x) \, dx - \mathcal{T}_n | = \mathcal{E}_n(\mathcal{T}) = Error.$$

If $f''(x)$ is continuous over $[a, b]$, then the error, $\mathcal{E}_n(\mathcal{T})$, is at most

$$\mathcal{E}_n(\mathcal{T}) \leq (\frac{b-a}{12}) \, h^2 \, \left(\max_{x \ in \ [a,b]} |f''(x)| \right) \qquad (7.73)$$

where $h = (b - a)/n$, and the symbol "$\max_{x \ in \ [a,b]} |f''(x)|$" means that we want the *maximum value of* $|f''|$ *over* $[a, b]$, (see Chapter 5).

Table 7.14: The Error Term in Using the Trapezoidal Rule

Solution You know that the larger n is, the better the approximation, right? The more computer time you'll have to use too! So, this question is asking you to find how many points, n, you should define in your subdivision of $[0, 2]$ so that the value of $\mathcal{T}_n$ you get is within 0.01 of the true value. **The answer needed is of the form $n > something$**, because once you've found some n with the required property, all bigger n should give you something "better" and so you'll still satisfy $\mathcal{E}_n(\mathcal{T}) < 0.01$. So, ultimately, we'll be solving an *inequality*, (back to Chapter 1)!

Here $a = 0$, $b = 2$, $f(x) = x^2$ and $f''(x) = 2$. Since f'' is constant, it follows that $\max_{x \ in \ [0,2]} |f''(x)| = 2$.

We're going to solve this problem by making the "right-hand side" of equation (7.73) smaller than 0.01, that is, we need to find an "n" such that

$$(\frac{b-a}{12}) \, h^2 \, (\max_{x \ in \ [a,b]} |f''(x)|) < 0.01, \qquad (7.75)$$

because any such n will also make the "left-hand side", namely, $\mathcal{E}_n(\mathcal{T})$, smaller than 0.01 too! And that's what we want!

Now comes the estimation: We know that $h = \frac{b-a}{n}$, okay? Inserting this into the left-side of equation (7.75) we get the equivalent equation,

$$\frac{(b-a)^3}{12n^2} \cdot \max_{x \ in \ [a,b]} |f''(x)| < 0.01 \ . \qquad (7.76)$$

But $b - a = 2$, and the $\max_{x \ in \ [a,b]} |f''(x)| = 2$. Substituting these values into (7.76) we find

$$\frac{8}{12} \cdot \frac{1}{n^2} \cdot 2 < \frac{1}{100}$$

which means $n^2 > \frac{800}{6} = 133.33...$, or $n > \sqrt{133.33...} \approx 11.547 \ldots$. Since n is an integer, it follows that $n \geq 12$.

Let's recap: If n is any integer with $n \geq 12$, then (7.76) will be satisfied for any such n. It follows that (7.75) will also be satisfied, and consequently we must have $\mathcal{E}_n(\mathcal{T}) < 0.01$ by (7.73).

SHORTCUT

The exposition in Example 398 can be simplified by the creation of Tables such as the ones below: Let $f(x) = x^2, a = 0, b = 2, n = 4$, from which we get $h = 1/2$.

m	x_m	$y_m = f(x_m)$
0	0	0
1	1/2	1/4
2	1	1
3	3/2	9/4
4	2	4

$$\int_0^2 x^2 \, dx \quad \approx \quad T_4 = \frac{h}{2}(y_0 + 2y_1 + 2y_2 + 2y_3 + y_4)$$
$$= \quad \dots$$
$$= \quad 11/4.$$

Example 400. Evaluate

$$\int_0^1 \frac{dx}{(1+x^2)}$$

using the Trapezoidal Rule with $n = 5$. What is the error, $\mathcal{E}_n(T)$, obtained in evaluating this integral with $n = 5$?

Solution Let $f(x) = (1+x^2)^{-1}, a = 0, b = 1, n = 5$ *(given)*, $h = (b-a)/n = 1/5$. Then we see, using Figure 155 in the margin, that

m	x_m	$y_m = f(x_m)$
0	0	1
1	1/5	25/26
2	2/5	25/29
3	3/5	25/34
4	4/5	25/41
5	1	1/2

Figure 155.

$$\int_0^1 \frac{1}{1+x^2} \, dx \quad \approx \quad T_5,$$
$$= \quad \frac{h}{2}(y_0 + 2y_1 + 2y_2 + 2y_3 + 2y_4 + y_5),$$
$$= \quad \frac{1}{10}\left(1 + 2 \cdot \frac{25}{26} + 2 \cdot \frac{25}{29} + 2 \cdot \frac{25}{34} + 2 \cdot \frac{25}{41} + \frac{1}{2}\right),$$
$$= \quad 0.78373152\dots.$$

In order to estimate $\mathcal{E}_5$ we need to find $|f''(x)|$, right? Using the Quotient Rule twice, we see that

$$f''(x) = \frac{2(3x^2 - 1)}{(1+x^2)^3}.$$

But we want the maximum value of the absolute value of this function over $[0, 1]$. Now, we use the methods of Chapter 5 to find the extrema of f'' (e.g., find the first derivative of f'', set it equal to zero, and test for extrema, etc). The critical points of f'' are $x = -1, 0, +1$. Of these critical points, a careful sketch of the **absolute value function** $|f''|$, shows that $x = 0$ gives a local maximum, and, in fact, a global maximum of $|f''|$. Why? The maximum value there is equal to $|f''(0)| = 2$. Since $h = 1/5$, *and* $(b-a) = 1$ we get,

$$\mathcal{E}_5 \quad \leq \quad \left(\frac{b-a}{12}\right) h^2 \left(\max_{x \ in \ [a,b]} |f''(x)|\right)$$
$$\leq \quad \frac{1}{12} \cdot \frac{1}{25} \cdot 2$$
$$\leq \quad 0.00666666\dots$$

Finally, the Actual Value of this definite integral is found easily since

$$\int_0^1 \frac{dx}{(1+x^2)} \;=\; \text{Arctan}\,1 - \text{Arctan}\,0,$$
$$=\; \pi/4,$$
$$=\; 0.785398...$$

Note that this answer is between the two values given by equation (7.74) above, with $n = 5$, that is,

$$0.78373152 - 0.00666666 \leq \; Actual\; Value \;= \pi/4 \leq 0.78373152 + 0.00666666,$$

or

$$0.7770485... \leq \; Actual\; Value \; \leq 0.7903981...,$$

or

$$0.7770485... \leq 0.785398... \leq 0.7903981...,$$

which is clearly true.

Remark: The point here is that if we hadn't known the Actual Value, we could still give it the nice estimate $0.7770485... \leq$ Actual Value $\leq 0.7903981....$ This is what these Rules are good for. They give you estimates about what the answer is ... more or less.

Example 401. Find the area under the graph of the function e^{-x^2} between the lines $x = 0$, $x = 1$ and above the $x-$axis, using the Trapezoidal Rule with $n = 4$.

From the Theory of the Integral (Chapter 7), we know that, since $f(x) \geq 0$, the answer is given by the definite integral $\int_0^1 e^{-x^2}\,dx$. Next, $f(x) = e^{-x^2}, a = 0, b = 1, n = 4$, so $h = 1/4$. Now, pull out your pocket calculator and you'll get Figure 156 in the margin. So,

$$\int_0^1 e^{-x^2}\,dx \;\approx\; \mathcal{T}_4 = \frac{h}{2}(y_0 + 2y_1 + 2y_2 + 2y_3 + y_4)$$
$$=\; \frac{1}{8} \cdot (1 + 2 \cdot e^{-1/16} + 2 \cdot e^{-1/4} + 2 \cdot e^{-9/16} + e^{-1})$$
$$=\; 0.742984098$$

m	x_m	$y_m = f(x_m)$
0	0	1
1	1/4	$e^{-1/16}$
2	1/2	$e^{-1/4}$
3	3/4	$e^{-9/16}$
4	1	e^{-1}

Figure 156.

m	x_m	$y_m = f(x_m)$
0	7	5.00
1	8	7.00
2	9	6.50
3	10	4.00
4	11	4.50
5	12	6.00

Figure 157.

Example 402. The electricity consumed (in Kilowatts, kw) versus time (t in hours) for a typical bachelor apartment is shown below:

Time	7:00 A.M.	8:00	9:00	10:00	11:00	12:00 P.M.
Power	5.00	7.00	6.50	4.00	4.50	6.00

Use the Trapezoidal Rule with $n = 5$ to estimate the total power consumption in Kilowatt-hours over the given time-period (i.e., you need to find the "area" under this graph).

Solution Here, we can choose $a = 0, b = 5, n = 5$, so $h = 1$. Note that we choose $n = 5$ because we are given $6 = 5 + 1$ data points. If you want, you can also start with $a = 7, b = 12, n = 5, h = 1$ but this gives exactly the same answer. Why? We call this "**scaling**". Now, the data is already given in Figure 157. So, just go ahead and use it immediately.

$$Power\ Consumption \approx T_5 = \frac{h}{2}(y_0 + 2y_1 + 2y_2 + 2y_3 + 2y_4 + y_5)$$

$$= \frac{1}{2} \cdot (5.00 + 2 \cdot 7.00 + 2 \cdot 6.50 + 2 \cdot 4.00 + 2 \cdot 4.50 + 6.00)$$

$$= 27.50\ kwh.$$

Example 403. The surface of a small artificial lake is mapped at $30m$ intervals and a reading of its width is taken there using laser/reflector technology. At each such reading the width (in meters) is tabulated in the Table below. Use the following 7 readings to find the approximate area of the Lake.

Distance from Edge	0	30	60	90	120	150	180	210
Width of Lake	0	68	126	143	160	132	110	80

Okay, we'll use the Trapezoidal Rule with $n = 7$ (which is 1 less than the total number of data points), to estimate the total area of the lake (i.e., you need to find another "area").

Here $a = 0, b = 210, n = 7$, so $h = 30$, and once again the data is already given in the Table or in Figure 158.

m	x_m	$y_m = f(x_m)$
0	0	0
1	30	68
2	60	126
3	90	143
4	120	160
5	150	132
6	180	110
7	210	80

Figure 158.

$$Lake\ area \approx T_7,$$

$$= \frac{h}{2}(y_0 + 2y_1 + 2y_2 + 2y_3 + 2y_4 + 2y_5 + 2y_6 + y_7),$$

$$= \frac{30}{2} \cdot (0 + 2 \cdot 68 + 2 \cdot 126 + 2 \cdot 143 + 2 \cdot 160 + 2 \cdot 132 + 2 \cdot 110 + 80),$$

$$= 23,370m^2.$$

Example 404. Approximate the value of $\int_0^1 \frac{\sin x}{x}\ dx$ using the Trapezoidal Rule with $n = 8$.

There is a small problem here in that the function f defined by $f(x) = \sin x/x$ is not defined at $x = 0$. It's only a small problem because we know, by L'Hospital's Rule, that $lim_{x \to 0} f(x) = 1$. So, defining $f(0) = 1$, it can be shown that our f is (right-) continuous over $[0, 1]$.

Now, $a = 0, b = 1, n = 8$, (because there are $9 = 8 + 1$ data points). So, $h = (b - a)/n = 1/8$. Pull out your pocket calculator again, set its angle mode to "radians" and you'll get the results in Figure 159 in the margin. So,

m	x_m	$y_m = f(x_m)$
0	0	1
1	1/8	0.99740
2	1/4	0.98962
3	3/8	0.97673
4	1/2	0.95885
5	5/8	0.93616
6	3/4	0.90885
7	7/8	0.87719
8	1	0.84147

Figure 159.

$$\int_0^1 \frac{\sin x}{x}\ dx \approx T_8,$$

$$= \frac{h}{2}(y_0 + 2y_1 + 2y_2 + 2y_3 + 2y_4 +$$
$$+2y_5 + 2y_6 + 2y_7 + y_8),$$

$$= \frac{1}{16} \cdot (1 + 2 \cdot 0.99740 + 2 \cdot 0.98962 + 2 \cdot 0.97673 +$$
$$+2 \cdot 0.95885 + 2 \cdot 0.93616 + 2 \cdot 0.90885 + 2 \cdot 0.87719$$
$$+0.84147),$$

$$= 0.94559.$$

Simpson's Rule for n Even

$$\int_a^b f(x)\,dx \approx \frac{b-a}{3n}\left(f(x_0) + 4f(x_1) + 2f(x_2) + 4f(x_3) + 2f(x_4) + \right.$$

$$\left. \ldots + 2f(x_{n-2}) + 4f(x_{n-1}) + f(x_n)\right)$$

$$= \frac{h}{3}\left(y_0 + 4y_1 + 2y_2 + 4y_3 + 2y_4 + \ldots + 2y_{n-2} + 4y_{n-1} + y_n\right),$$

$$\equiv \mathcal{S}_n,$$

where the coefficients on the right alternate between $4, 2$ except in the initial and final positions. For simplicity, we have set $y_m = f(x_m)$ as before. Furthermore, $x_0 = a$, $x_n = b$ and the interval $[a, b]$ is divided into n subintervals each having length $h = \frac{b-a}{n}$. As before, this gives us the subdivision points

$$x_m = a + \frac{m\,(b-a)}{n} = a + mh,$$

for $m = 0, 1, 2, 3, ..., n$.

Table 7.15: Simpson's Rule for Estimating a Definite Integral

7.7.2   Simpson's Rule for n Even

The advantage of this method, called **Simpson's Rule**, of no known affiliation to a family of famous cartoon characters, is that the trapezoids of the last section are now "curvilinear trapezoids", *i.e.*, one of its sides is a curve (actually a **parabola**) and not a straight line. If we can choose n to be an even number, this Rule allows for improved accuracy in the approximations to

$$\int_a^b f(x)\,dx.$$

The basic idea behind Simpson's Rule applied to a continuous function, f, over an interval $[a, b]$ is the following:

We **assume that n is even**. This is not a problem as we can always *choose* n to be even. Then we approximate the value of the definite integral of f over $[a, b]$ by the sums of the areas of "curvilinear trapezoids" (four-sided figures with two parallel sides, one straight side and one curved side). Each one of these also approximates a rectangle in the corresponding Riemann sum. As before, this latter sum is approximately equal to the definite integral, so, one could believe that the definite integral can be approximated by a sum of areas of these "curvilinear trapezoids" too. The advantage here, is that the general "curvature" of the graph of f is taken into account by the "curvature of a parabola". Why use a parabola? Because any three non-collinear points (not all on a common line) lie on a unique parabola (do you know why?), so, instead of joining any two points on the graph by a short line segment, as in the Trapezoidal Rule, we join any three of them by such a parabola, see Figure 160.

We won't derive the formula describing Simpson's Rule in this section as it is similar to the one already derived, but just a little more technical. Instead, we'll present the Rule directly in Table 7.15. The important thing here is that the number 'n', which counts the number of subintervals inside the regular partition, must be an **even number**.

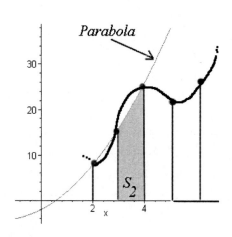

Figure 160.

The idea behind Simpson's Rule is that it uses **parabolic arcs** to mimic the *curvature* of the graph of the function f over the given interval, while the idea behind the Trapezoidal Rule is that it uses **straight line segments** to mimic this curvature. So, you would expect Simpson's Rule to give better answers than the Trapezoidal Rule for a given n and a general f.

The absolute value of the difference between the Actual Value, given by the definite integral, and the estimated value $\mathcal{S}_n$, given by Table 7.15, is called the **Error** in estimating the definite integral of f over $[a, b]$ by Simpson's Rule in n-steps. It is defined mathematically by

$$|\int_a^b f(x)\ dx - \mathcal{S}_n| = \mathcal{E}_n(\mathcal{S}) = Error.$$

If the fourth derivative, $f^{(4)}$, is continuous over $[a, b]$, then the error, $\mathcal{E}_n(\mathcal{S})$, is at most

$$\mathcal{E}_n(\mathcal{S}) \leq (\frac{b-a}{180})\ h^4\ (\max_{x\ in\ [a,b]} |f^{(4)}(x)|) \qquad (7.77)$$

where $h = (b-a)/n$, and the symbol "$\max_{x\ in\ [a,b]} |f^{(4)}(x)|$" means that we want the maximum value of the fourth derivative, $|f^{(4)}|$, over $[a, b]$.

Table 7.16: The Error Term in Using Simpson's Rule

Example 405. Refer to the definite integral of Example 398. What is the minimum value of n needed so that the error, $\mathcal{E}_n(\mathcal{S})$, obtained in estimating the definite integral using Simpson's Rule in n-steps satisfies $\mathcal{E}_n(\mathcal{S}) < 0.01$.

Solution Here $a = 0$, $b = 2$, $f(x) = x^2$. But, in this case, $f^{(4)}(x) = 0$ identically, (i.e., always equal to zero), on $[0, 2]$ giving $\max_{x\ in\ [0,2]} |f^{(4)}(x)| = 0$ and so $\mathcal{E}_n(\mathcal{S}) = 0$ too, right? What does this mean? This means that **Simpson's Rule always gives the right answer (or the Actual Value) if f is a parabola, or even a cubic, for any value of n!** Since n must be an even number, the smallest value that n can assume is $n = 2$.

In fact, **any even value of n will always give you the same answer!** but remember that the graph of f is a parabola. You don't believe it? Check this out ... Let $f(x) = x^2, a = 0$, and $b = 2$.

If $n = 2$, then $h = (b-a)/n = 2/2 = 1$, and so

$$\begin{aligned} \mathcal{S}_2 &= (h/3)(y_0 + 4y_1 + y_2), \\ &= (1/3)(0 + 4 \cdot 1 + 4), \\ &= \boxed{8\ /3}. \end{aligned}$$

If $n = 4$, then $h = (b-a)/4 = 2/4 = 1/2$ so that,

$$\begin{aligned} \mathcal{S}_4 &= \frac{(1/2)}{3}(y_0 + 4y_1 + 2y_2 + 4y_3 + y_4), \\ &= (1/6)(f(0) + 4f(1/2) + 2f(1) + 4f(3/2) + f(2)), \\ &= (1/6)(0 + 4 \cdot 1/4 + 2 \cdot 1 + 4 \cdot 9/4 + 4) = 16/6, \\ &= \boxed{8\ /3}, \textit{ again!} \end{aligned}$$

If $n = 6$, then $h = (b-a)/6 = 2/6 = 1/3$ so that,

$$\begin{aligned} \mathcal{S}_6 &= \frac{(1/3)}{3}(y_0 + 4y_1 + 2y_2 + 4y_3 + 2y_4 + 4y_5 + y_6), \\ &= (1/9)(f(0) + 4f(1/3) + 2f(2/3) + 4f(1) + 2f(4/3) + 4f(5/3) + f(2)), \\ &= (1/9)(0 + 4 \cdot 1/9 + 2 \cdot 4/9 + 4 \cdot 1 + 2 \cdot 16/9 + 4 \cdot 25/9 + 4), \\ &= \boxed{8\ /3}, \textit{ yet again!} \end{aligned}$$

Simpson's Rule always give the right answer (or the Actual Value) if f is a parabola (given by a quadratic), or even a cubic (a polynomial of degree 3), for any value of n! Inspired by these basic rules, other similar formulae were devised to give exact answers for integrands which are general polynomials of degree n, so-called **Gaussian Quadrature Formulae**. Their scope is beyond this book, however, but you can find some information on these in books on Numerical Analysis.

These amazing results are indicative of the general result that we mentioned above, that is, Simpson's Rule always gives the same answer (the Actual Value) if we use it on a quadratic or cubic polynomial! It doesn't give the right answer on other functions though but it does generally give *better* results than the Trapezoidal Rule.

| Example 406. | Look over Examples 398 and 399. Let's ask the same question |

as in Example 399 and try to answer it using Simpson's Rule. Okay, so what value of n is needed so that the error, $\mathcal{E}_n(\mathcal{S})$, in estimating the integral

$$\int_0^2 x^2\, dx$$

using Simpson's Rule with n-steps, satisfies $\mathcal{E}_n(\mathcal{S}) < 0.01$?

Solution Proceed as in Example 399. We still have $a = 0$, $b = 2$, $f(x) = x^2$, $h = 2/n$ and $f''(x) = 2$. But, in this case, we also have that $f^{(4)}(x) = 0$ all the time, so it follows that $\max_{x\ in\ [0,2]} |f^{(4)}(x)| = 0$, and so Simpson's Rule must give the right answer right away! There's nothing more to do. Since Simpson's Rule holds for $n \geq 2$ we can choose $n = 2$ and be certain that $\mathcal{E}_n(\mathcal{S}) = 0$, because of the error estimate for this Rule.

On the other hand, we would have had to use $n \geq 12$ in the Trapezoidal Rule (see Example 399) to get the same error! Of course, we would all want to compute 2 terms instead of 12, right? So, here's one BIG advantage of Simpson's Rule.

| Example 407. | Evaluate $\int_0^1 \dfrac{dx}{1 + x^2}$ using Simpson's Rule with $n = 4$. |

As usual, we let $f(x) = (1 + x^2)^{-1}$, $a = 0$, $b = 1$, $n = 4$ $h = (b - a)/n = 1/4$. Using Figure 161 in the margin, we see that

$$\begin{aligned}
\int_0^1 \frac{1}{1 + x^2}\, dx &\approx \mathcal{S}_4 = \frac{h}{3}(y_0 + 4y_1 + 2y_2 + 4y_3 + y_4) \\
&= (1/12)\cdot(1 + 4 \cdot 16/17 + 2 \cdot 4/5 + 4 \cdot 16/25 + 1/2) \\
&= 0.785392
\end{aligned}$$

It can be shown that the error here is at most 0.0104, (try this as an Exercise using the ideas in Example 400. Notice that you almost get the same degree of precision with fewer steps).

| Example 408. | Find the area under the graph of the function e^{-x^2} between the |

lines $x = 0$, $x = 1$ and above the $x-$axis, using Simpson's Rule with $n = 4$.

We did this one before using the Trapezoidal Rule, (see Example 401). The nice thing is, we don't have to re-do the Table (Figure 162) because we use the same value of n and the "partition points" do not depend on the method, here. We know that $f(x) = e^{-x^2}$, $a = 0$, $b = 1$, $n = 4$, $h = 1/4$. You'll have to pull out your pocket calculator again ... So,

$$\begin{aligned}
\int_0^1 e^{-x^2}\, dx &\approx \mathcal{S}_4 = \frac{h}{3}(y_0 + 4y_1 + 2y_2 + 4y_3 + y_4) \\
&= \frac{1}{12} \cdot (1 + 4 \cdot e^{-1/16} + 2 \cdot e^{-1/4} + 4 \cdot e^{-9/16} + e^{-1}) \\
&= 0.746855
\end{aligned}$$

NOTE: These two sections have provided the basis for most numerical integration packages. Note that we assumed that the integrands f are continuous over some

m	x_m	$y_m = f(x_m)$
0	0	1
1	1/4	16/17
2	1/2	4/5
3	3/4	16/25
4	1	1/2

Figure 161.

m	x_m	$y_m = f(x_m)$
0	0	1
1	1/4	$e^{-1/16}$
2	1/2	$e^{-1/4}$
3	3/4	$e^{-9/16}$
4	1	e^{-1}

Figure 162.

interval $[a, b]$. If these integrands are **piecewise continuous**, that is, continuous except at a finite number of points at each of which the function is finite (see Chapter 2), then we can still use these two methods because "in between" the points of discontinuity the integrand is continuous, and so the methods can be applied on each subinterval separately. Since the integral over the whole interval is the sum of the integrals over each such subinterval (by a property of the integral) the methods work out too. The error terms however, are another story, and should not be used in these cases.

Exercise Set 40.

Use either or both the Trapezoidal and Simpson Rules to estimate the values of the following integrals for the given value of n

1. Compute
$$\ln 10 = \int_1^{10} \frac{dx}{x},$$
$n = 4$. Compare your results with the Actual Value of $\ln 10 \approx 2.30259$.

2. Approximate
$$\int_0^{\frac{\pi}{2}} \sqrt{\cos \phi} \; d\phi$$
with $n = 5$.
   - You can't use Simpson's Rule here, why?

3. Compare both Rules for
$$\int_0^1 e^{x^2} \; dx$$
using $n = 4$.

4. Estimate the integral
$$4 \cdot \int_0^1 \sqrt{1 - x^2} \; dx,$$
with $n = 6$. Work out the Actual Value using a trigonometric substitution.

5. Evaluate
$$\int_0^1 \sqrt{1 + x^4} \; dx$$
with $n = 10$.

Use Simpson's Rule with $n = 6$ to determine the approximate value of the definite integrals defined by each of the following problems

6. Estimate the area under the graph of the function f defined by $f(x) = \sqrt{\sin x}$ between the lines $x = 0$ and $x = \pi/2$.

7. Find the approximate area of the closed figure (loop) bounded by the two curves $y = x$ and $y = x^2$.
   - *Hint:* Sketch the graphs and find the area under the curve $y = x$ and subtract the area under the curve $y = x^2$.

8. Evaluate the integral
$$\int_{1.05}^{1.35} f(x) \; dx$$
given the following table of values for the function f.

x	1.05	1.10	1.15	1.20	1.25	1.30	1.35
$f(x)$	2.32	1.26	1.48	1.60	3.60	2.78	3.02

9. As we know by now, Euclid of Alexandria showed more than $2,000$ years ago that there are infinitely many prime numbers, that is, numbers which have no divisors except 1 and themselves. This subject of primes is a very difficult area within a field called **Number Theory**. The immortal mathematicians C.F. Gauss, A.M. Legendre, among many others made more discoveries concerning **prime numbers**. One quantity that was used at the time was the so-called **logarithmic integral**, denoted by $Li(x)$, the notation being an acronym in Latin for the expression used in English.

If we let $\pi(x)$ denote the number of prime numbers not exceeding x, then this function "π" is a *piecewise continuous* function defined on the real numbers whose values are integers (this function doesn't have much to do with the Greek number $\pi \approx 3.14159$, it is just of historical significance). So, it was shown that

$$\pi(x) = \int_2^x \frac{dt}{\ln t} + R(x)$$

where $R(x)$ is some complicated-looking function which remains finite as $x \to \infty$. The difficulty here is that the definite integral on the right cannot be evaluated using any of the methods we studied here (nothing seems to work)!

Use Simpson's Rule with $n = 10$ to approximate the value of

$$\int_2^{100} \frac{dt}{\ln t}$$

and then find an estimate for the number of primes not exceeding 100 using the estimate

$$\pi(x) \approx Li(x) = \int_2^x \frac{dt}{\ln t}$$

with $x = 100$. Compare this number with the Actual Value of $\pi(100)$ which you can find by inspection. For example, the first few primes are given by $2, 3, 5, 7, 11, 13, 17, 19, 23, \ldots$, so that $\pi(25) = 9$. For comparison purposes note that for larger values of x,

x	$\pi(x)$	$Li(x)$	Error
500,000	41,539	41,606	67
1,000,000	78,499	78,628	129
2,000,000	148,934	149,055	121
5,000,000	348,514	348,638	124
10,000,000	664,580	664,918	338

10. The definite integral

$$L(x) = \int_0^x \ln(\sec \theta) \, d\theta$$

appears in the calculation of the general volume of a tetrahedron in three-dimensional space. (Recall that a tetrahedron is a a four-sided closed figure shaped like a pyramid with a triangular base and triangular sides). The quantity $L(x)$ is named after N. Lobatchewsky, a famous Russian mathematician and one of the founders of the theory of **Non-Euclidean Geometry** a field which is used extensively in association with Einstein's Theory of Relativity, in particular.

Use Simpson's Rule with $n = 6$ to approximate the value of the integral $L(1)$.

11. Occasionally, IQ (Intelligence Quotient) tests are used to measure "intelligence". In theory, these tests compare a person's mental age with a person's chronological (or real) age. The median IQ is set at 100 which means that one-half the population has an IQ less than 100 and the other half has an IQ greater than 100. Now, the proportion of all people having IQ's between A and B is given by the following **Gaussian integral**

$$\frac{1}{15\sqrt{2\pi}} \int_A^B e^{-\frac{1}{2}\{\frac{x-100}{15}\}^2} \, dx.$$

(Why a Gaussian integral? Well, this has a lot to do with a subject called *Statistics*).

Find the proportion of people (as a fraction of the total population) having an IQ between 120 and 140, using the Trapezoidal Rule with $n = 8$.

NOTES:

7.8   Improper Integrals

The Big Picture

In some cases a definite integral may have one or both of its limits infinite. This occurs, for example, when we don't know how big a time or a frequency must be but we know it's BIG so we replace it by ∞ in the hope that we'll get a *sufficiently good* estimate for the problem at hand. For example, in a field of physics called *quantum mechanics* there is a law called the *Wien Distribution Law* which expresses the energy density as a function of frequency. It looks like this ...

$$Energy = \frac{8\pi h}{c^3} \cdot \int_0^\infty \nu^3 \, e^{-\frac{h\nu}{kT}} \, d\nu.$$

Here ν represents the frequency, T the temperature, and all other quantities are physical constants. We know that there is no particle having *infinite* frequency but this Law necessitates that we integrate over *all possible frequencies*, which must be a huge number, but finite nevertheless. We don't know how big it is, so we replace the upper limit by ∞. What else can we do? The answers we get in using this Law are quite accurate indeed. This integral is an example of an **improper integral**.

Such integrals can be grouped into two basic classes:

1. Those with one or both limits being infinite, or
2. Those with both limits being finite but the integrand being infinite somewhere inside the interval (or at the endpoints) of integration.

For example, the integrals

$$\int_0^\infty \frac{dx}{x^2+1}, \quad \int_{-\infty}^\infty e^{-x^2} \, dx,$$

are each of the first class, while the integrals

$$\int_0^2 \frac{dx}{x^2-1}, \quad \int_0^1 \frac{dx}{x}, \quad \int_{-1}^1 \frac{dx}{x+1},$$

are each of the second class (why?).

Review

This subsection deals with the calculation of certain definite integrals and so you should review all the methods of integration in this Chapter.

The natural definition of these symbols involves interpreting the definite integral as a limit of a definite integral with suitable finite limits. In the evaluation of the resulting limit use may be made of L'Hospital's Rule in conjunction with the various techniques presented in this Chapter.

NOTES:

Integrals of the First Class

Let's assume that f is defined and integrable on every finite interval of the real line and let a be *any* fixed number in the domain of definition of f. We define an **improper integral with infinite limit(s)** as follows:

$$\int_a^\infty f(x)\,dx = \lim_{T\to\infty} \int_a^T f(x)\,dx, \qquad \int_{-\infty}^a f(x)\,dx = \lim_{T\to-\infty} \int_T^a f(x)\,dx,$$

whenever either one of these limits exists and is finite, in which case we say that the **improper integral converges**. In the event that the limit does not exist at all, we say the **improper integral diverges**. If the limit exists but its value is $\pm\infty$, we say that the **improper integral converges to $\pm\infty$**, respectively. A similar definition applies when both limits are infinite, *e.g.,* let a be any real number in the domain of f. Then

$$\int_{-\infty}^\infty f(x)\,dx = \int_{-\infty}^a f(x)\,dx + \int_a^\infty f(x)\,dx$$

provided both integrals exist and are finite. In this case, we say that the *improper integral converges*. If either integral does not exist (or is infinite), then the *improper integral diverges* (by definition).

Some authors of Calculus texts prefer to include the case of an improper integral **converging to infinity** as one that is **divergent**. Our definitions are in the traditions of Mathematical Analysis.

Example 409. Determine the values of p for which the improper integral

$$\int_1^\infty \frac{1}{x^p}\,dx$$

converges or diverges.

Solution This is an improper integral since the upper limit is infinite. There are two cases: $p = 1$ which gives a natural logarithm, and $p \neq 1$ which gives a power function. Now, by definition, if $p \neq 1$,

$$\begin{aligned}
\int_1^\infty \frac{1}{x^p}\,dx &= \lim_{T\to\infty} \int_1^T \frac{1}{x^p}\,dx \\
&= \lim_{T\to\infty} \left. \left(\frac{x^{-p+1}}{1-p} \right) \right|_1^T \\
&= \lim_{T\to\infty} \left(\frac{T^{-p+1}}{1-p} - \frac{1}{1-p} \right).
\end{aligned}$$

Now, if $p > 1$, then $p - 1 > 0$ and so,

$$\lim_{T\to\infty} \left(\frac{T^{-p+1}}{1-p} - \frac{1}{1-p} \right) = \lim_{T\to\infty} \left(\frac{1}{T^{p-1}(1-p)} - \frac{1}{1-p} \right) = \frac{1}{p-1}.$$

On the other hand, if $p < 1$, then $1 - p > 0$ and so,

$$\lim_{T\to\infty} \left(\frac{T^{1-p}}{1-p} - \frac{1}{1-p} \right) = \infty - \frac{1}{1-p} = \infty.$$

Finally, if $p = 1$, then

$$\begin{aligned}
\int_1^\infty \frac{1}{x^p}\,dx &= \lim_{T\to\infty} \int_1^T \frac{1}{x}\,dx \\
&= \lim_{T\to\infty} \left. (\ln|x|) \right|_1^T \\
&= \lim_{T\to\infty} (\ln T - 0) \\
&= \infty.
\end{aligned}$$

and so the improper integral converges to ∞. Summarizing these results we find

$$\int_1^\infty \frac{1}{x^p}\ dx = \left\{ \begin{array}{ll} \infty, & \text{if}\quad p \le 1, \\ \frac{1}{p-1} & \text{if}\quad p > 1. \end{array} \right.$$

Example 410. Evaluate $\displaystyle\int_{-\infty}^0 \sin x\ dx$.

Solution We know that

EXAMPLES

$$\begin{aligned} \int_{-\infty}^0 \sin x\ dx &= \lim_{T \to -\infty} \int_T^0 \sin x\ dx \\ &= \lim_{T \to -\infty} (-\cos T + 1) \\ &\quad \text{does not exist at all} \end{aligned}$$

 due to the periodic oscillating nature of the cosine function on the real line. It follows that this improper integral is divergent.

Example 411. Evaluate the improper integral $\displaystyle\int_0^\infty x\ e^{-x}\ dx$.

Solution This is an improper integral since one of the limits of integration is infinite. So, by definition,

$$\int_0^\infty x\ e^{-x}\ dx = \lim_{T \to \infty} \int_0^T x\ e^{-x}\ dx,$$

and this requires Integration by Parts. We set $u = x$, $dv = e^{-x}$, $du = dx$, $v = -e^{-x}$ after which

$$\begin{aligned} \lim_{T \to \infty} \int_0^T x\ e^{-x}\ dx &= \left. \left(-x\ e^{-x} - e^{-x}\right) \right|_0^T \\ &= \lim_{T \to \infty} \left(- (T+1)\ e^{-T} + 1\right) \\ &= \lim_{T \to \infty} \left(-\frac{T+1}{e^T} + 1\right) \\ &= 1, \end{aligned}$$

by L'Hospital's Rule (Don't worry about the "T" here. Think of it as an "x" when using the Rule). If an antiderivative cannot be found using any method, one resorts to Numerical Integration (Section 7.7).

Example 412. Evaluate the improper integral

$$\int_0^\infty x^4\ e^{-x}\ dx = \lim_{T \to \infty} \int_0^T x^4\ e^{-x}\ dx.$$

Solution See Example 323. The Table Method gives

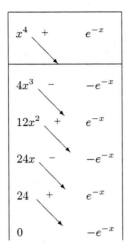

and so the most general antiderivative is given by

$$
\begin{aligned}
I &= -x^4 e^{-x} - 4x^3 e^{-x} - 12x^2 e^{-x} - 24x e^{-x} - 24 e^{-x} + C, \\
&= -e^{-x}(x^4 + 4x^3 + 12x^2 + 24x + 24) + C.
\end{aligned}
$$

Now, we evaluate the definite integral

$$
\begin{aligned}
\int_0^T x^4 e^{-x}\,dx &= \left\{ -e^{-x}(x^4 + 4x^3 + 12x^2 + 24x + 24) \right\} \Big|_0^T, \\
&= \left\{ -e^{-T}(T^4 + 4T^3 + 12T^2 + 24T + 24) \right\} - (-24), \\
&= 24 - \frac{T^4 + 4T^3 + 12T^2 + 24T + 24}{e^T}.
\end{aligned}
$$

Now, we simply take the limit as $T \to \infty$ and use L'Hospital's Rule 5 times on the expression on the right and we'll see that

$$
\begin{aligned}
\int_0^\infty x^4 e^{-x}\,dx &= 24 - \lim_{T \to \infty} \frac{T^4 + 4T^3 + 12T^2 + 24T + 24}{e^T}, \\
&= 24 - 0, \\
&= 24.
\end{aligned}
$$

Example 413. Evaluate $\displaystyle \int_{-\infty}^{\infty} \frac{2x^2}{(1+x^2)^2}\,dx$.

Solution Let's find an antiderivative, first. We set up the following table,

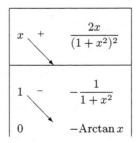

since the second entry on the right is obtained from the first via the simple substitution $u = 1 + x^2$, $du = 2x\,dx$. The third such entry is a basic Arctangent integral.

It follows that,

$$\int_0^T \frac{2x^2}{(1+x^2)^2} \, dx \;=\; \left\{ -\frac{x}{1+x^2} + \text{Arctan}\, x \right\}\Big|_0^T,$$

$$=\; \left\{ -\frac{T}{1+T^2} + \text{Arctan}\, T \right\},$$

and so, for example (we can use ANY number as the lower limit of integration),

$$\int_0^\infty \frac{2x^2}{(1+x^2)^2} \, dx \;=\; \lim_{T \to \infty} \int_0^T \frac{2x^2}{(1+x^2)^2} \, dx,$$

$$=\; \lim_{T \to \infty} \left\{ -\frac{T}{1+T^2} + \text{Arctan}\, T \right\},$$

$$=\; 0 + \frac{\pi}{2},$$

$$=\; \frac{\pi}{2},$$

where we used L'Hospital's Rule (or a more elementary method) in the first limit and a basic property of the Arctangent function (see Chapter 3). A similar argument shows that

$$\int_{-\infty}^0 \frac{2x^2}{(1+x^2)^2} \, dx \;=\; \lim_{T \to -\infty} \int_T^0 \frac{2x^2}{(1+x^2)^2} \, dx,$$

$$=\; \lim_{T \to -\infty} \left\{ -\int_0^T \frac{2x^2}{(1+x^2)^2} \, dx \right\},$$

$$=\; \lim_{T \to -\infty} \left\{ +\frac{T}{1+T^2} - \text{Arctan}\, T \right\},$$

$$=\; 0 + \frac{\pi}{2},$$

$$=\; \frac{\pi}{2},$$

and we conclude that

$$\int_{-\infty}^\infty \frac{2x^2}{(1+x^2)^2} \, dx \;=\; \frac{\pi}{2} + \frac{\pi}{2},$$

$$=\; \pi.$$

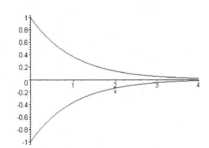

Figure 163.

Example 414. Find the area enclosed by the infinite funnel given by $y^2 = e^{-2x}$, where $x \geq 0$, (see Figure 163).

Solution We use symmetry and realize that the area enclosed by this region is twice the area enclosed by either part lying above or below the $x-$axis. Note that the graph is given by

$$y = \begin{cases} e^{-x}, & \text{if } \; y > 0, \\ -e^{-x} & \text{if } \; y < 0. \end{cases}$$

Let's say that we use that part of the graph lying above the $x-$axis (that is, $y > 0$) in our area calculation. Since the integrand is positive, the total area is given by a definite integral, namely,

$$\text{Area} = 2 \int_0^\infty e^{-x} \, dx.$$

This integral is straightforward since

$$\int_0^\infty e^{-x} \, dx = \lim_{T \to \infty} \int_0^T e^{-x} \, dx = 1.$$

Hence,

$$\text{Area} = 2 \int_0^\infty e^{-x} \, dx = 2,$$

(see the margin for a numerical treatment).

The moral here is that an *infinite region may enclose a finite area!*

| Example 415. | Evaluate the improper integral that defines Wien's Distribution

Law

$$Energy = \frac{8\pi h}{c^3} \cdot \int_0^\infty \nu^3 \, e^{-\frac{h\nu}{kT}} \, d\nu.$$

explicitly.

Solution The first thing to do is to reduce this integral to something more recognizable. This is most readily done by applying a *substitution*, in this case,

$$x = \frac{h\nu}{kT}, \quad dx = \frac{h \, d\nu}{kT}, \Longrightarrow \ d\nu = \frac{kT \, dx}{h}.$$

When $\nu = 0$, $x = 0$ and when $\nu = \infty$, $x = \infty$. Thus,

$$\begin{aligned}
\int_0^\infty \nu^3 \, e^{-\frac{h\nu}{kT}} \, d\nu &= \frac{k^3 T^3}{h^3} \int_0^\infty x^3 \, e^{-x} \, \frac{kT}{h} \, dx \\
&= \frac{k^4 T^4}{h^4} \int_0^\infty x^3 \, e^{-x} \, dx \\
&= \frac{k^4 T^4}{h^4} \lim_{T \to \infty} \int_0^T x^3 \, e^{-x} \, dx.
\end{aligned}$$

But the Table Method applied to the integral on the right gives us

So,

$$\int_0^T x^3 \, e^{-x} \, dx = -\left(\frac{x^3 + 3x^2 + 6x + 6}{e^x} \right) \bigg|_0^T = 6 - \left(\frac{T^3 + 3T^2 + 6T + 6}{e^T} \right).$$

A few applications of L'Hospital's Rule gives us

$$\lim_{T \to \infty} \int_0^T x^3 \, e^{-x} \, dx = 6,$$

and so

$$\begin{aligned}
\int_0^\infty \nu^3 \, e^{-\frac{h\nu}{kT}} \, d\nu &= \frac{k^4 T^4}{h^4} \lim_{T \to \infty} \int_0^T x^3 \, e^{-x} \, dx \\
&= \frac{6k^4 T^4}{h^4}.
\end{aligned}$$

Numerical estimation of the integral in Example 414 as a function of the upper limit, T.

T	Area $\approx 2 \int_0^T e^{-x} \, dx$
5	1.986524106
10	1.999909200
100	1.999999999
1,000	1.999999999
10,000	1.999999999
10^5	1.999999999
...	...

Collecting terms we find an expression for the Energy in terms of the temperature, T:

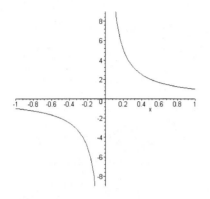

$$
\begin{aligned}
\text{Energy} \quad &= \quad \frac{8\pi h}{c^3} \cdot \int_0^\infty \nu^3 \; e^{-\frac{h\nu}{kT}} \; d\nu \\[2mm]
&= \quad \frac{8\pi h}{c^3} \; \frac{6k^4 T^4}{h^4} \\[2mm]
&= \quad \frac{48\pi k^4 T^4}{h^3 c^3}.
\end{aligned}
$$

The graph of $y = \frac{1}{x}$ over the interval $[-1, 1]$. Note that the area under the curve to the left of 0 equals the negative of the area to the right of 0 but each area is infinite.

Figure 164.

NOTE: In this example we made use of the Susbtitution Rule, Integration by Parts and L'Hospital's Rule!

> **Integrals of the Second Class**

Now we look at the case where the limits of integration are finite but the integrand has an *infinite* discontinuity inside the range of integration. In this case, we need to modify the definition of such an improper integral. The reason we call it *improper* can be gathered from the following examples.

A **common error** in Calculus is the procedure of **integrating across a discontinuity**. This is bad news! You can't normally get away with this! For example,

$$
\int_{-1}^1 f(x) \; dx = \int_{-1}^1 \frac{1}{x} \; dx \neq 0,
$$

yet one would expect this to be equal to zero (by integrating without much thought using the natural logarithm and evaluating it between the limits, -1 and 1). You see, a quick look at the graph, Figure 164, shows that the areas under the graph don't cancel because they are each infinite, and we can't subtract infinities unless we do this in a limiting way. So the answer isn't zero (necessarily).

So, what's going on? The point is that the interval of integration contains an **infinite discontinuity** of f, in this case, at $x = 0$, since (see Figure 164),

$$
\lim_{x \to 0} f(x) = +\infty.
$$

If one *forgets* this, then one can get into trouble as we have seen. What do we do? We simply redefine the notion of an improper integral for functions of this class.

Improper Integrals of functions with an Infinite Discontinuity

Let f be continuous over an interval $[a, b)$ and assume that f has an **infinite discontinuity at $x = b$**. Then we define the improper integral of f over $[a, b)$ by the symbol

$$\int_a^b f(x)\, dx = \lim_{T \to b^-} \int_a^T f(x)\, dx.$$

Note that *this is a one-sided limit*, actually a limit from the left, at $x = b$. In fact, **all the improper integrals of the second class will be defined in terms of one-sided limits!** A similar definition applies in case f has an infinite discontinuity at $x = a$, but not at $x = b$.

Let f be continuous over an interval $(a, b]$ and assume that f has an **infinite discontinuity at $x = a$**. Then we define the improper integral of f over $(a, b]$ by the symbol

$$\int_a^b f(x)\, dx = \lim_{T \to a^+} \int_T^b f(x)\, dx,$$

and this is now a limit from the right at $x = a$.

NOTE: In the event that f has *many infinite discontinuities* inside the interval (see Figure 165) of integration $[a, b]$, then we just break up this interval into those pieces in which f is continuous and apply the definitions above over each piece separately. In the case of Figure 165, the function defined by $y = \csc(\frac{1}{x})$ has *infinitely many infinite discontinuities* in $(0, 1]$! We just showed a few of them here, namely those at $x = \frac{1}{\pi} \approx 0.3$ and at $x = \frac{1}{2\pi} \approx 0.17$

For this function,

$$\int_{0.1}^1 \csc\left(\frac{1}{x}\right)\, dx = \int_{0.1}^{\frac{1}{2\pi}} \csc\left(\frac{1}{x}\right)\, dx + \int_{\frac{1}{2\pi}}^{\frac{1}{\pi}} \csc\left(\frac{1}{x}\right)\, dx + \int_{\frac{1}{\pi}}^1 \csc\left(\frac{1}{x}\right)\, dx.$$

The integral in the middle, on the right of the last display has two discontinuities, one at each end-point, $x = \frac{1}{2\pi}$ and $x = \frac{1}{\pi}$ (Why?). In this case we define the improper integral naturally as follows:

Let f be continuous over an interval (a, b) and assume that f has an **infinite discontinuity at both $x = a$ and $x = b$**. Let c be any point inside (a, b). Then we define the improper integral of f over (a, b) by the symbol

$$\int_a^b f(x)\, dx = \int_a^c f(x)\, dx + \int_c^b f(x)\, dx,$$

where the first integral on the right is defined by a limit from the right, while the second integral is defined by a limit from the left in accordance with our definitions, above.

NOTES:

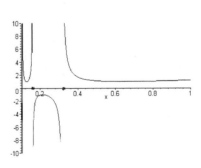

$y = \csc(\frac{1}{x})$ for $0.1 \leq x \leq 1$.

Figure 165.

Example 416. Evaluate the integral $\int_0^1 \dfrac{1}{\sqrt{x}}\,dx$.

Solution Note that is an improper integral since the integrand has an infinite discontinuity at $x = 0$. Using our definitions we see that we can give meaning to the symbol

$$\int_0^1 \frac{1}{\sqrt{x}}\,dx$$

only if we interpret it as a limit, namely,

$$\int_0^1 \frac{1}{\sqrt{x}}\,dx = \lim_{T \to 0^+} \int_T^1 \frac{1}{\sqrt{x}}\,dx.$$

Now,

$$\begin{aligned}
\int_T^1 \frac{1}{\sqrt{x}}\,dx &= \int_T^1 x^{-1/2}\,dx \\
&= 2\left(x^{1/2}\right)\Big|_T^1 \\
&= 2(1 - \sqrt{T}).
\end{aligned}$$

It follows that

$$\int_0^1 \frac{1}{\sqrt{x}}\,dx = \lim_{T \to 0^+} 2(1 - \sqrt{T}) = 2.$$

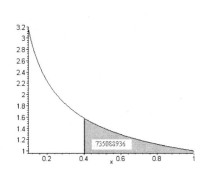

$T = 0.4$

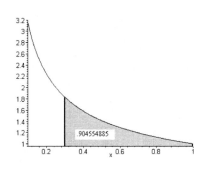

$T = 0.3$

Remark In the margin, we can see the effect of passing to the limit $T \to 0^+$ graphically. The actual values of the corresponding integrals obtained can be interpreted geometrically as the shaded areas seen there. So, for instance,

T	Area $= \displaystyle\int_T^1 \frac{1}{\sqrt{x}}\,dx$
0.4	.735088936
0.3	.904554885
0.001	1.936754447
0.0001	1.980000000
0.000001	1.998000000
...	...
0	2.0000000000

For this example, our answer actually corresponds to a *limiting area*!

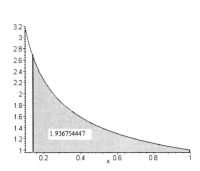

$T = 0.001$

Exercise Convince yourself that if $p > 1$, then

$$\int_0^1 \frac{1}{\sqrt[p]{x}}\,dx = \frac{p}{p-1}.$$

Example 417. Evaluate the integral $\int_0^1 \dfrac{1}{\sqrt{1 - x^2}}\,dx$.

Solution This is an improper integral since the integrand has an infinite discontinuity at $x = 1$. So, we can give meaning to the symbol

$$\int_0^1 \frac{1}{\sqrt{1-x^2}} \, dx$$

only if we interpret it as a limit once again, namely,

$$\int_0^1 \frac{1}{\sqrt{1-x^2}} \, dx = \lim_{T \to 1^-} \int_0^T \frac{1}{\sqrt{1-x^2}} \, dx.$$

But we recall from our chapter on Integration that

$$\begin{aligned}
\int_0^T \frac{1}{\sqrt{1-x^2}} \, dx &= \operatorname{Arcsin} x \Big|_0^T \\
&= \operatorname{Arcsin} T - \operatorname{Arcsin} 0 \\
&= \operatorname{Arcsin} T,
\end{aligned}$$

since $\operatorname{Arcsin} 0 = 0$. Since the Arcsin function is continuous at $x = 1$ we conclude that

$$\int_0^1 \frac{1}{\sqrt{1-x^2}} \, dx = \lim_{T \to 1^-} \operatorname{Arcsin} T = \operatorname{Arcsin} 1 = \frac{\pi}{2}.$$

Thus, the (actually infinite) shaded region in Figure 166 has area equal to $\frac{\pi}{2}$.

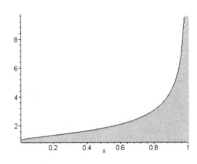

The graph of $y = \dfrac{1}{\sqrt{1-x^2}}$.

Figure 166.

Example 418. Evaluate the integral $\displaystyle\int_0^2 \frac{1}{x^2 - 4x + 3} \, dx$.

Solution At first sight this doesn't look improper. But since we are thinking about using the method of Partial Fractions (what else?), we should factor the denominator and then inspect it for any zeros inside the interval $[0, 2]$. Observe that

$$\int_0^2 \frac{1}{x^2 - 4x + 3} \, dx = \int_0^2 \frac{1}{(x-3)(x-1)} \, dx,$$

and so the point $x = 1$ is an infinite discontinuity of our integrand that is *inside* the interval (not at the endpoints), see Figure 167. According to our definition we can write

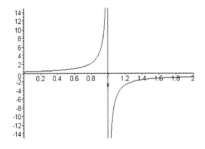

The graph of $y = \dfrac{1}{x^2 - 4x + 3}$ on $[0, 2]$.

Figure 167.

$$\begin{aligned}
\int_0^2 \frac{1}{x^2 - 4x + 3} \, dx &= \int_0^1 \frac{1}{x^2 - 4x + 3} \, dx + \int_1^2 \frac{1}{x^2 - 4x + 3} \, dx \\
&= \lim_{T \to 1^-} \int_0^T \frac{1}{(x-3)(x-1)} \, dx + \\
&\qquad \lim_{T \to 1^+} \int_T^2 \frac{1}{(x-3)(x-1)} \, dx \\
&= \lim_{T \to 1^-} \left(\frac{1}{2} \ln|x-3| - \frac{1}{2} \ln|x-1| \right) \Big|_0^T + \\
&\qquad + \lim_{T \to 1^+} \left(\frac{1}{2} \ln|x-3| - \frac{1}{2} \ln|x-1| \right) \Big|_T^2 \\
&= \lim_{T \to 1^-} \left(\frac{1}{2} \ln \left| \frac{T-3}{T-1} \right| - \frac{\ln 3}{2} \right) + \\
&\qquad \lim_{T \to 1^+} \left(-\frac{1}{2} \ln \left| \frac{T-3}{T-1} \right| \right) \\
&= \infty - \infty,
\end{aligned}$$

so the improper integral diverges (by definition) since each one of these limits actually exists but is infinite (recall that $\ln |1/0| = \infty$).

Example 419. Evaluate the integral $\displaystyle\int_0^1 x \ln x \, dx$.

Solution The integrand is undefined at the left end-point $x = 0$, since we have an indeterminate form of type $0 \cdot (-\infty)$ here. There are no other discontinuities here since $\ln 1 = 0$ and this is fine. So, it is best to treat this integral as an improper integral and take a limiting approach. We integrate by parts: That is, we set

$$u = \ln x, \ du = \frac{1}{x} \, dx, \qquad dv = x \, dx, \ v = \frac{x^2}{2}.$$

Then,

$$
\begin{aligned}
\int_0^1 x \ln x \, dx &= \lim_{T \to 0^+} \int_T^1 x \ln x \, dx \\
&= \lim_{T \to 0^+} \left(\frac{x^2 \ln x}{2} \Big|_T^1 - \int_T^1 \frac{x}{2} \, dx \right) \\
&= \lim_{T \to 0^+} \left(-\frac{T^2 \ln T}{2} - \frac{1 - T^2}{4} \right) \\
&= -\frac{1}{2} \cdot \left(\lim_{T \to 0^+} T^2 \ln T \right) - \frac{1}{4} \\
&\quad \text{provided the first limit exists} \ldots \\
&= -\frac{1}{2} \cdot \left(\lim_{T \to 0^+} \frac{\ln T}{T^{-2}} \right) - \frac{1}{4} \\
&\quad \text{provided this limit exists} \ldots \\
&= -\frac{1}{2} \cdot \left(\lim_{T \to 0^+} \frac{1/T}{-2T^{-3}} \right) - \frac{1}{4} \\
&\quad \text{where we used L'Hospital's Rule,} \\
&= -\frac{1}{2} \cdot \left(\lim_{T \to 0^+} \frac{T^2}{(-2)} \right) - \frac{1}{4} \\
&= -\frac{1}{4}.
\end{aligned}
$$

NOTE: This is an interesting integrand because

$$\lim_{x \to 0^+} x \ln x = 0,$$

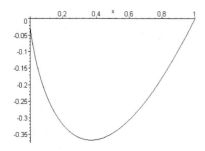

The graph of $y = x \ln x$ on $(0, 1]$.

Figure 168.

as can be gathered from either L'Hospital's Rule (similar to the above calculation) or its graph (see Figure 168). We would have expected the integrand to be infinite but this is not always the case. Indeterminate forms can arise as well at the end-points and the integral should still be treated as improper. The moral is:

> *If an integral looks improper, treat it like an improper integral*

because, even if it isn't, you'll get the *right* answer anyhow, and then you won't have to worry! Here's such an example.

Example 420. Evaluate $\displaystyle\int_{-1}^1 \frac{3x^2 + 2}{\sqrt[3]{x^2}} \, dx$.

Solution The integrand is infinite when $x = 0$ (which is between -1 and 1). So, the integral is improper. Its evaluation is straightforward, however. Let's find an antiderivative, first.

$$\int \frac{3x^2 + 2}{\sqrt[3]{x^2}}\ dx \ = \ \int \left(3x^2 x^{-2/3} + 2x^{-2/3}\right)\ dx$$

$$= \ \int \left(3x^{4/3} + 2x^{-2/3}\right)\ dx$$

$$= \ \frac{9}{7}x^{7/3} + 6x^{1/3}.$$

It follows that

$$\int_{-1}^{1} \frac{3x^2 + 2}{\sqrt[3]{x^2}}\ dx \ = \ \int_{-1}^{0} \frac{3x^2 + 2}{\sqrt[3]{x^2}}\ dx + \int_{0}^{1} \frac{3x^2 + 2}{\sqrt[3]{x^2}}\ dx$$

by definition of the improper integral ...

$$= \ \lim_{T \to 0^-} \int_{-1}^{T} \frac{3x^2 + 2}{\sqrt[3]{x^2}}\ dx + \lim_{T \to 0^+} \int_{T}^{1} \frac{3x^2 + 2}{\sqrt[3]{x^2}}\ dx$$

once again, by definition

$$= \ \lim_{T \to 0^-} \left(\frac{9}{7}x^{7/3} + 6x^{1/3}\right)\Bigg|_{-1}^{T} + \lim_{T \to 0^+} \left(\frac{9}{7}x^{7/3} + 6x^{1/3}\right)\Bigg|_{T}^{1}$$

$$= \ \lim_{T \to 0^-} \left(\frac{9}{7}T^{7/3} + 6T^{1/3} - \left((-1)\frac{9}{7} + (-1)6\right)\right) +$$

$$+ \ \lim_{T \to 0^+} \left(\left(\frac{9}{7} + 6\right) - \left(\frac{9}{7}T^{7/3} + 6T^{1/3}\right)\right)$$

$$= \ \left(\frac{9}{7} + 6\right) + \left(\frac{9}{7} + 6\right)$$

by continuity of our antiderivative at $T = 0$

$$= \ \frac{102}{7} \approx 14.57,$$

NOTE: In this example, the infinite discontinuity at $x = 0$ is "virtual" insofar as the improper integral is concerned, in the sense that we could evaluate the integral directly without resorting to the improper integral definitions and still obtain the right answer! The point is, YOU JUST DON'T KNOW when you're starting out. So, you see, you have nothing to lose (except a few more minutes of your time) in treating such an integral (that is, one that *looks* improper) *as* an improper integral.

NOTES:

Example 421. Evaluate the improper integral $\int_0^\infty x \cos x \, dx$.

Solution This is improper because of the infinite upper limit of integration. Furthermore, Integration by Parts (using the Table Method) gives us

$$\int_0^\infty x \cos x \, dx = \lim_{T \to \infty} \int_0^T x \cos x \, dx$$

$$= \lim_{T \to \infty} (x \sin x + \cos x) \Big|_0^T$$

$$= \lim_{T \to \infty} ((T \sin T + \cos T) - (0 + 1))$$

$$= \lim_{T \to \infty} (T \sin T + \cos T - 1)$$

and this limit does not exist!

It folows that the improper integral diverges (see the margin).

The function "$T \sin T + \cos T - 1$" has no limit at ∞ as you can gather from its erratic behavior as T increases

T	$\int_0^T x \cos x \, dx$
10	−7.279282638
100	−50.77424524
1000	826.4419196
10,000	−3058.096044
10^5	3572.880436
10^6	−349993.5654
...	...

Exercise Set 41.

Determine which of the following integrals is improper and give reasons: Do not evaluate the integrals

1. $\int_{-1}^2 \frac{1}{2x} \, dx$

2. $\int_{-1}^1 \frac{1}{1 + x^2} \, dx$

3. $\int_0^1 \frac{1}{x^p} \, dx$, for $p > 1$

4. $\int_{-1}^\infty \frac{1}{(1 + x)^p} \, dx$, for $p > 1$

5. $\int_{-1}^1 \frac{1}{(1 + x)^p} \, dx$, for $p > 1$

6. $\int_{-1}^1 e^{-x^2} \, dx$

7. $\int_{-\pi}^\pi \csc x \, dx$

8. $\int_{-\infty}^\infty x^2 e^{-2x} \, dx$

9. $\int_0^1 2x^3 \ln 2x \, dx$

10. $\int_{-\infty}^\infty \frac{1}{1 + x^2} \, dx$

Evaluate the following improper integrals using any method

11. $\int_1^\infty \frac{1}{x^{1.5}} \, dx$

12. $\int_2^\infty \frac{1}{\sqrt{x}} \, dx$

13. $\displaystyle\int_0^2 \frac{1}{2x}\,dx$

14. $\displaystyle\int_0^\infty x^2 e^{-x}\,dx$

15. $\displaystyle\int_{-\infty}^\infty \frac{2x}{(1+x^2)^2}\,dx$

16. $\displaystyle\int_{-1}^0 \frac{x}{\sqrt{1-x^2}}\,dx$
    - Use a substitution, first.

17. $\displaystyle\int_0^2 \frac{1}{x^2-1}\,dx$

18. $\displaystyle\int_1^2 \frac{1}{1-x^2}\,dx$

19. $\displaystyle\int_0^\infty e^{-x}\,\sin x\,dx$
    - See Section 7.3.4.

20. $\displaystyle\int_1^2 \frac{dx}{x\ln x}$

21. $\displaystyle\int_{-1}^1 \frac{x+1}{\sqrt[5]{x^3}}\,dx$

22. $\displaystyle\int_{-1}^1 \frac{x-1}{\sqrt[3]{x^5}}\,dx$

23. $\displaystyle\int_{-\infty}^\infty e^{-|x|}\,dx$
    - Consider the cases $x < 0$ and $x > 0$ separately when removing the absolute value; that is, rewrite this integral as a sum of two improper integrals (without absolute values) each having one finite limit of integration (say, $c = 0$).

24. For what values of p does the improper integral

$$\int_2^\infty \frac{dx}{x(\ln x)^p}$$

converge to a finite number?

25. Can you find a value of p such that

$$\int_0^\infty x^p\,dx$$

converges to a finite number?

26. Let f be a continuous function on $(0,\infty)$. Define the improper integral

$$v(\lambda) = \sqrt{\frac{2}{\pi}}\,\int_0^\infty f(t)\,\cos(\lambda t)\,dt$$

This is called the **Fourier Cosine Transform** of f and is of fundamental importance in the study of electromagnetic waves, wavelets, and medical imaging techniques. Evaluate

$$v(\lambda) = \sqrt{\frac{2}{\pi}}\,\int_0^\infty e^{-2t}\,\cos(\lambda t)\,dt.$$

27. **Hard** Let f be a continuous function defined on the interval $[a, \infty)$ and assume that

$$\lim_{x \to \infty} f(x) = 2.$$

Can the improper integral $\int_0^\infty f(x) \, dx$ converge to a *finite* number? Give reasons.

Hint Proceed as follows:

- Show that the hypothesis on the limit forces the existence of a number X such that $f(x) > 1$ for each $x > X$.

- Let T be any number with $T > X$. Show that $\int_X^T f(x) \, dx > T - X$.

- Now let $T \to \infty$ in the last integral and state your conclusion.

28. **Hard** Let f, g each be continuous functions over the interval $[a, \infty)$ where a is some fixed number. Suppose that $0 \le f(x) \le g(x)$ for each x, where $a \le x < \infty$, and that the improper integral

$$\int_a^\infty g(x) \, dx$$

converges to a finite number.
Prove that

$$\int_a^\infty f(x) \, dx$$

also converges to a finite number.

Hints This is called a **Comparison Theorem for improper integrals** as it allows you to test for the convergence of an improper integral by comparing to another one whose convergence you already know! To prove this proceed as follows:

- Since $f(x) \ge 0$ conclude that the integral $\mathcal{F}(x) = \int_a^x f(t) \, dt$ is an increasing function for $x \ge a$ (Use the Fundamental Theorem of Calculus).

- Use the fact that an increasing function must have a limit to deduce that the improper integral $\int_a^\infty f(t) \, dt$ actually exists

- By comparing the definite integrals of f and g, conclude that the *limit* of the improper integral of f must be finite.

29. Use the Comparison Theorem above with $f(x) = e^{-x^2}$ and $g(x) = e^{-x}$ to show that the improper integral

$$\int_0^\infty e^{-x^2} \, dx$$

converges to a finite limit.
- Show that $x^2 \ge x$ if $x \ge 1$ and conclude that $f(x) \le g(x)$ for $x \ge 1$. Now show that the improper integral of g converges and $\int_1^\infty e^{-x} \, dx = 1$. Use the Comparison Theorem to arrive at your conclusion.

30. **Long but not hard** Use Simpson's Rule with $n = 22$ over the interval $[-5, 5]$ to estimate the value of the Gaussian-type integral

$$L = \int_{-\infty}^\infty e^{-x^2} \, dx.$$

Now multiply your numerical result by itself (the result is an estimate of L^2). Do you recognize this number? Now *guess* the value of L.

Suggested Homework Set 29. *Problems 1, 2, 4, 14, 15, 19, 21, 22*

7.9 Chapter Exercises

The exercises in this section are chosen randomly among all the techniques you have seen in this Chapter. Note that levels of difficulty vary from exercise to exercise.

Prove the following trigonometric identities using the basic identities in Section 7.1.

1. $\cos^2 x - \sin^2 x = \cos 2x$

2. $\cos^4 x - \sin^4 x = \cos 2x$

3. $\sec^4 x - \tan^4 x = \sec^2 x + \tan^2 x$

4. $\sqrt{1 + \cos x} = \sqrt{2} \cdot \cos\left(\dfrac{x}{2}\right)$, if $-\pi \leq x \leq \pi$.

5. $\sqrt{1 - \cos x} = \sqrt{2} \cdot \sin\left(\dfrac{x}{2}\right)$, if $0 \leq x \leq 2\pi$

6. $\sqrt{1 + \cos 5x} = \sqrt{2} \cdot \cos\left(\dfrac{5x}{2}\right)$, if $-\pi \leq 5x \leq \pi$.

Use numerical integration to evaluate the following integrals.

7. $\displaystyle\int_0^2 (2x - 1)\, dx$, using the Trapezoidal Rule with $n = 6$. Compare your answer with the exact answer obtained by direct integration.

8. $\displaystyle\int_0^4 (3x^2 - 2x + 6)\, dx$, using Simpson's Rule with $n = 6$. Compare your answer with the exact answer obtained by direct integration.

9. $\displaystyle\int_{-\pi}^{\pi} (\cos^2 x + \sin^2 x)\, dx$, using the Trapezoidal Rule with $n = 6$. Compare your answer with the exact answer obtained by direct integration.

10. $\displaystyle\int_{-\pi}^{\pi} (\cos^2 x - \sin^2 x)\, dx$, using Simpson's Rule with $n = 6$. Compare your answer with the exact answer obtained by direct integration.

11. $\displaystyle\int_0^1 e^{-x^2}\, dx$, using Simpson's Rule with $n = 6$

12. $\displaystyle\int_{-1}^2 \dfrac{1}{1 + x^6}\, dx$, using Simpson's Rule with $n = 4$

13. $\displaystyle\int_{-2}^2 \dfrac{x^2}{1 + x^4}\, dx$, using the Trapezoidal Rule with $n = 6$. Compare your answer with the exact answer obtained by direct integration.

14. $\displaystyle\int_1^2 (\ln x)^3\, dx$, using Simpson's Rule with $n = 6$.

Evaluate the following integrals using any method

15. $\int \sqrt{3x + 2} \; dx$

16. $\int \dfrac{1}{x^2 + 4x + 4} \; dx$

17. $\int \dfrac{dx}{(2x - 3)^2}$

18. $\int \dfrac{dx}{\sqrt{a + bx}}$

19. $\int (\sqrt{a} - \sqrt{x})^2 \; dx$

20. $\int \dfrac{x \; dx}{\sqrt{a^2 - x^2}}$

21. $\int x^2 \sqrt{x^3 + 1} \; dx$

22. $\int \dfrac{(x + 1)}{\sqrt[3]{x^2 + 2x + 2}} \; dx$

23. $\int (x^4 + 4x^2 + 1)^2 (x^3 + 2x) \; dx$

24. $\int x^{-\frac{1}{3}} \sqrt{x^{\frac{2}{3}} - 1} \; dx$

25. $\int \dfrac{2x \; dx}{(3x^2 - 2)^2}$

26. $\int \dfrac{dx}{4x + 3}$

27. $\int \dfrac{x \; dx}{2x^2 - 1}$

28. $\int \dfrac{x^2 \; dx}{1 + x^3}$

29. $\int \dfrac{(2x + 3) \; dx}{x^2 + 3x + 2}$

30. $\int \sin(2x + 4) \; dx$

31. $\int 2 \cos(4x + 1) \; dx$

32. $\int \sqrt{1 - \cos 2x} \; dx$

33. $\int \sin \dfrac{3x - 2}{5} \; dx$

34. $\int x \cos ax^2 \; dx$

35. $\int x \sin(x^2 + 1) \; dx$

36. $\int \sec^2 \dfrac{\theta}{2} \; d\theta$

37. $\int \dfrac{d\theta}{\cos^2 3\theta}$

38. $\int \dfrac{d\theta}{\sin^2 2\theta}$

39. $\int x \csc^2(x^2) \; dx$

40. $\int \tan \dfrac{3x + 4}{5} \; dx$

41. $\int \dfrac{dx}{\tan 2x}$

42. $\int \sqrt{1 + \cos 5x} \; dx$

43. $\int \csc(x + \dfrac{\pi}{2}) \; \cot(x + \dfrac{\pi}{2}) \; dx$

44. $\int \cos 3x \; \cos 4x \; dx$

45. $\int \sec 5\theta \tan 5\theta \; d\theta$

46. $\int \dfrac{\cos x}{\sin^2 x} \; dx$

47. $\int x^2 \cos(x^3 + 1) \; dx$

48. $\int \sec \theta (\sec \theta + \tan \theta) \; d\theta$

49. $\int (\csc \theta - \cot \theta) \csc \theta \; d\theta$

50. $\int \cos^{-4} x \sin(2x) \; dx$

51. $\int \dfrac{\tan^2 \sqrt{x}}{\sqrt{x}} \; dx$

52. $\int \dfrac{1 + \sin 2x}{\cos^2 2x} \; dx$

53. $\int \dfrac{dx}{\cos 3x}$

54. $\int \dfrac{dx}{\sin(3x + 2)}$

55. $\int \dfrac{1 + \sin x}{\cos x} \; dx$

56. $\int (1 + \sec \theta)^2 \; d\theta$

57. $\int \dfrac{\csc^2 x \; dx}{1 + 2 \cot x}$

58. $\int e^x \; \sec e^x \; dx$

59. $\int \dfrac{dx}{x \ln x}$

60. $\int \dfrac{dt}{\sqrt{2 - t^2}}$

61. $\int \dfrac{dx}{\sqrt{3 - 4x^2}}$

62. $\int \dfrac{(2x + 3) \; dx}{\sqrt{4 - x^2}}$

63. $\displaystyle\int \frac{dx}{x^2 + 5}$

64. $\displaystyle\int \frac{dx}{4x^2 + 3}$

65. $\displaystyle\int \frac{dx}{x\sqrt{x^2 - 4}}, \quad x > 0.$

66. $\displaystyle\int \frac{dx}{x\sqrt{4x^2 - 9}}, \quad x > 0$

67. $\displaystyle\int \frac{dx}{\sqrt{x^2 + 4}}$

68. $\displaystyle\int \frac{dx}{\sqrt{4x^2 + 3}}$

69. $\displaystyle\int \frac{dx}{\sqrt{x^2 - 16}}$

70. $\displaystyle\int \frac{e^x}{1 + e^{2x}}\, dx$

71. $\displaystyle\int \frac{1}{x\sqrt{4x^2 - 1}}\, dx$

72. $\displaystyle\int \frac{dx}{\sqrt{4x^2 - 9}}$

73. $\displaystyle\int e^{-3x}\, dx$

74. $\displaystyle\int \frac{dx}{e^{2x}}$

75. $\displaystyle\int (e^x - e^{-x})^2\, dx$

76. $\displaystyle\int xe^{-x^2}\, dx$

77. $\displaystyle\int \frac{\sin\theta\, d\theta}{\sqrt{1 - \cos\theta}}$

78. $\displaystyle\int \frac{\cos\theta\, d\theta}{\sqrt{2 - \sin^2\theta}}$

79. $\displaystyle\int \frac{e^{2x}\, dx}{1 + e^{2x}}$

80. $\displaystyle\int \frac{e^x\, dx}{1 + e^{2x}}$

81. $\displaystyle\int \frac{\cos\theta\, d\theta}{2 + \sin^2\theta}$

82. $\displaystyle\int \sin^3 x \cos x\, dx$

83. $\displaystyle\int \cos^4 5x \sin 5x\, dx$

84. $\displaystyle\int (\cos\theta + \sin\theta)^2\, d\theta$

85. $\displaystyle\int \sin^3 x\, dx$

86. $\displaystyle\int \cos^3 2x\, dx$

87. $\displaystyle\int \sin^3 x \cos^2 x\, dx$

88. $\displaystyle\int \cos^5 x\, dx$

89. $\displaystyle\int \sin^3 4\theta \cos^3 4\theta\, d\theta$

90. $\displaystyle\int \frac{\cos^2 x\, dx}{\sin x}$

91. $\displaystyle\int \frac{\cos^3 x\, dx}{\sin x}$

92. $\displaystyle\int \tan^2 x \sec^2 x\, dx$

93. $\displaystyle\int \sec^2 x \tan^3 x\, dx$

94. $\displaystyle\int \frac{\sin x\, dx}{\cos^3 x}$

95. $\displaystyle\int \frac{\sin^2 x\, dx}{\cos^4 x}$

96. $\displaystyle\int \sec^4 x\, dx$

97. $\displaystyle\int \tan^2 x\, dx$

98. $\displaystyle\int (1 + \cot\theta)^2\, d\theta$

99. $\displaystyle\int \sec^4 x \tan^3 x\, dx$

100. $\displaystyle\int \csc^6 x\, dx$

101. $\displaystyle\int \tan^3 x\, dx$

102. $\displaystyle\int \frac{\cos^2 t\, dt}{\sin^6 t}$

103. $\displaystyle\int \tan\theta \csc\theta\, d\theta$

104. $\displaystyle\int \cos^2 4x\, dx$

105. $\displaystyle\int (1 + \cos\theta)^2\, d\theta$

106. $\displaystyle\int (1 - \sin x)^3\, dx$

107. $\displaystyle\int \sin^4 x\, dx$

108. $\displaystyle\int \sin^2 2x \cos^2 2x\, dx$

109. $\displaystyle\int \sin^4 \theta \cos^2 \theta\, d\theta$

110. $\displaystyle\int \cos^6 x\, dx$

111. $\int \cos x \sin 2x \; dx$

112. $\int \sin x \cos 3x \; dx$

113. $\int \sin 2x \sin 3x \; dx$

114. $\int \cos 2x \cos 4x \; dx$

115. $\int \sin^2 2x \cos 3x \; dx$

116. $\int \sec x \csc x \; dx,$ **hard**

117. $\int \dfrac{dx}{1 - \cos x},$ **hard**

118. $\int \dfrac{dx}{\sqrt{2 + 2x - x^2}}$

119. $\int \dfrac{dx}{\sqrt{1 + 4x - 4x^2}}$

120. $\int \dfrac{dx}{\sqrt{2 + 6x - 3x^2}},$ **hard.**

121. $\int \dfrac{dx}{\sqrt{x^2 + 6x + 13}}$

122. $\int \dfrac{dx}{2x^2 - 4x + 6}$

123. $\int \dfrac{dx}{(1 - x)\sqrt{x^2 - 2x - 3}},$
for $x > 1.$ **hard.**

124. $\int \dfrac{(2x + 3) \; dx}{x^2 + 2x - 3}$

125. $\int \dfrac{(x + 1) \; dx}{x^2 + 2x - 3}$

126. $\int \dfrac{(x - 1) \; dx}{4x^2 - 4x + 2}$

127. $\int \dfrac{x \; dx}{\sqrt{x^2 - 2x + 2}}$

128. $\int \dfrac{(4x + 1) \; dx}{\sqrt{1 + 4x - 4x^2}}$

129. $\int \dfrac{(3x - 2) \; dx}{\sqrt{x^2 + 2x + 3}}$

130. $\int \dfrac{e^x \; dx}{e^{2x} + 2e^x + 3}$

131. $\int \dfrac{x^2 \; dx}{x^2 + x - 6}$

132. $\int \dfrac{(x + 2) \; dx}{x^2 + x}$

133. $\int \dfrac{(x^3 + x^2) \; dx}{x^2 - 3x + 2}$

134. $\int \dfrac{dx}{x^3 - x}$

135. $\int \dfrac{(x - 3) \; dx}{x^3 + 3x^2 + 2x}$

136. $\int \dfrac{(x^3 + 1) \; dx}{x^3 - x^2}$

137. $\int \dfrac{x \; dx}{(x + 1)^2}$

138. $\int \dfrac{(x + 2) \; dx}{x^2 - 4x + 4}$

139. $\int \dfrac{(3x + 2) \; dx}{x^3 - 2x^2 + x}$

140. $\int \dfrac{8 \; dx}{x^4 - 2x^3}$

141. $\int \dfrac{dx}{(x^2 - 1)^2}$

142. $\int \dfrac{(1 - x^3) \; dx}{x(x^2 + 1)}$

143. $\int \dfrac{(x - 1) \; dx}{(x + 1)(x^2 + 1)}$

144. $\int \dfrac{4x \; dx}{x^4 - 1}$

145. $\int \dfrac{3(x + 1) \; dx}{x^3 - 1}$

146. $\int \dfrac{(x^4 + x) \; dx}{x^4 - 4}$

147. $\int \dfrac{x^2 \; dx}{(x^2 + 1)(x^2 + 2)}$

148. $\int \dfrac{3 \; dx}{x^4 + 5x^2 + 4}$

149. $\int \dfrac{(x - 1) \; dx}{(x^2 + 1)(x^2 - 2x + 3)}$

150. $\int \dfrac{x^3 \; dx}{(x^2 + 4)^2}$

151. $\int \dfrac{(x^4 + 1) \; dx}{x(x^2 + 1)^2}$

152. $\int \dfrac{(x^2 + 1) \; dx}{(x^2 - 2x + 3)^2}$

153. $\int \dfrac{x \; dx}{\sqrt{x + 1}}$

154. $\int x\sqrt{x - a} \; dx$

155. $\int \dfrac{\sqrt{x + 2}}{x + 3} \; dx$

156. $\int \dfrac{dx}{x\sqrt{x - 1}}$

157. $\int \dfrac{dx}{x\sqrt{a^2 - x^2}}$

158. $\int \dfrac{dx}{x^2\sqrt{a^2 - x^2}}$

159. $\int x^3 \sqrt{x^2 + a^2} \, dx$

160. $\int \dfrac{dx}{x^2 \sqrt{x^2 + a^2}}$

161. $\int \dfrac{dx}{\sqrt{x^2 + a^2}}$

162. $\int \dfrac{x^2 \, dx}{\sqrt{x^2 + a^2}}$

163. $\int \dfrac{x^2 \, dx}{(x^2 + a^2)^2}$

164. $\int x \cos x \, dx$

165. $\int x \sin x \, dx$

166. $\int x \sec^2 x \, dx$

167. $\int x \sec x \tan x \, dx$

168. $\int x^2 e^x \, dx$

169. $\int x^4 \ln x \, dx$

170. $\int x^3 e^{x^2} \, dx$

171. $\int \sin^{-1} x \, dx$

172. $\int \tan^{-1} x \, dx$

173. $\int (x-1)^2 \sin x \, dx$

174. $\int \sqrt{x^2 - a^2} \, dx$

175. $\int \sqrt{x^2 + a^2} \, dx$

176. $\int \dfrac{x^2 \, dx}{\sqrt{x^2 - a^2}}$

177. $\int e^{2x} \sin 3x \, dx$

178. $\int e^{-x} \cos x \, dx$

179. $\int \sin 3x \cos 2x \, dx$

180. $\int_0^{\frac{\pi}{8}} \cos^3 (2x) \sin(2x) \, dx$

181. $\int_1^4 \dfrac{2^{\sqrt{x}}}{2\sqrt{x}} \, dx$

182. $\int_0^{\infty} x^3 e^{-2x} \, dx$

183. $\int_{-\infty}^{+\infty} e^{-|x|} \, dx$

184. $\int_0^{\infty} \dfrac{4x}{1 + x^4} \, dx$

185. $\int_{-1}^{1} x^2 \cos(n\pi x) \, dx$,
where $n \geq 1$, is an integer.

186. $\dfrac{1}{2} \int_{-2}^{2} x^2 \sin\left(\dfrac{n\pi x}{2}\right) \, dx$,
where $n \geq 1$, is an integer.

187. $\dfrac{1}{L} \int_{-L}^{L} (1 - x) \sin\left(\dfrac{n\pi x}{L}\right) \, dx$,
where $n \geq 1$, is an integer and $L \neq 0$.

188. $\int_0^{2} (x^3 + 1) \cos\left(\dfrac{n\pi x}{2}\right) \, dx$,
where $n \geq 1$, is an integer.

189. $\int_{-1}^{1} (2x + 1) \cos(n\pi x) \, dx$,
where $n \geq 1$, is an integer.

190. $\dfrac{1}{L} \int_{-L}^{L} \sin x \, \cos\left(\dfrac{n\pi x}{L}\right) \, dx$,
where $n \geq 1$, is an integer and $L \neq 0$.

191. A manufacturing company forecasts that the yearly demand x for its product over the next 15 years can be modelled by

$$x = 500(20 + te^{-0.1t}), \quad 0 \leq t \leq 15$$

where x is the number of units produced per year and t is the time in years (see Section 5.4). What is the total demand over the next 10 years?

192. Suppose the time t, in hours, for a bacterial culture to grow to y grams is modelled by the **logistic growth model**

$$t = 25 \int \dfrac{1}{y(10 - y)} \, dy.$$

If one gram of bacterial culture is present at time $t = 0$,

(a) Solve for t

(b) Find the time it takes for the culture to grow to 4 grams

(c) Show that solving for y in terms of t gives

$$y = \dfrac{10}{1 + 9e^{-0.4t}}$$

(d) Find the weight of the culture after 10 hours.

7.10 Using Computer Algebra Systems

Use your favorite Computer Algebra System (CAS), like Maple, MatLab, etc., or even a graphing calculator to answer the following questions:

1. Evaluate $\int_{-2}^{-1} \frac{dx}{x}$ exactly.

2. Show that the value of $\int \sin mt \sin nt \, dt$ where m, n are integers and $m \neq n$ does not depend on the choice of m, n. Do you get the same value if m, n are NOT integers? Explain.

3. Show that the value of $\int \cos mt \cos nt \, dt$ where m, n are integers does not depend on the choice of m, n. Do you get the same value if m, n are NOT integers? Explain.

4. Evaluate $\int_{1}^{3} \sin x^2 \, dx$ using Simpson's Rule with $n = 50$. How close is your answer to the real answer?

5. Compare the values of the integral $\int_{0}^{1} \sqrt{x} \, dx$ with its approximations obatined by using the Trapezoidal Rule with $n = 25$ and Simpson's Rule with $n = 30$.

6. Estimate the value of
$$\int_{0}^{2\pi} \frac{dt}{2 + \cos t}$$
using Simpson's Rule with $n = 20$. Is this an improper integral? Explain.

7. Find the area under the curve $y = x|\sin x|$ between $x = 0$ and $x = 4\pi$.

8. Estimate the improper integral $\int_{0}^{\infty} 2e^{-x^2} \, dx$ using Simpson's Rule with $n = 40$ over the interval $[0, 10]$. Does the number you obtain remind you of a specific relation involving π?

9. Show that $\int_{0}^{1} \frac{\log x}{1 - x} \, dx = -\frac{\pi^2}{6}$. Explain, without actually calculating the value, why this integral must be a negative number.

10. The Gamma function, $\Gamma(x)$, is defined by the improper integral
$$\Gamma(x) = \int_{0}^{\infty} t^{x-1} e^{-t} \, dt$$
for $x > 0$. Show that if $n \geq 1$ is an integer, then $\Gamma(n + 1) = n!$ where $n!$ represents the product of the first n numbers, $n! = 1 \cdot 2 \cdot 3 \cdot 4 \cdots n$.

11. Guess the value of the following limit per referring to the preceding exercise:
$$\lim_{x \to \infty} \frac{e^x \, \Gamma(x)}{x^{x - \frac{1}{2}} \sqrt{2\pi}}.$$

This is called *Stirling's Formula*.

Chapter 8

Applications of the Integral

8.1 Motivation

In this chapter we describe a few of the main applications of the definite integral. You should note that these applications comprise only a minuscule fraction of the totality of applications of this concept. Many Calculus books would have to be written in order to enumerate other such applications to the wealth of human knowledge including the social sciences, the physical sciences, the arts, engineering, architecture, etc.

Review

You should be familiar with each one of the methods of integration desribed in Chapter 7. A thorough knowledge of those principal methods such as the Substitution Rule and Integration by Parts will help you work out many of the problems in this chapter.

Net change in the position and distance travelled by a moving body: The case of rectilinear motion.

Recall that the words "rectilinear motion" mean "motion along a line". If a particle moves with velocity, $v(t)$, in a specified direction along a line, then by physics,

$$v(t) = \frac{d}{dt}s(t)$$

where $s(t)$ is its displacement or distance travelled in time t, from some given point of reference. The *net change in position* as the particle moves from A to B from time $t = a$ to time $t = b$ is given by

$$\text{Net change in position} = \int_a^b v(t)\ dt.$$

Furthermore, the *total distance* that it travels along the line is given by

$$\text{Total distance travelled} = \int_a^b |v(t)|\ dt,$$

where, by definition of the absolute value,

$$|v(t)| = \begin{cases} v(t), & if\ v(t) \geq 0, \\ -v(t), & if\ v(t) < 0. \end{cases}$$

Example 422. A particle starting at the origin of some given coordinate system moves to the right in a straight line with a velocity $v(t) = 4\cos 2t$, for $0 \le t \le \pi$.

a) Sketch the graph of $v(t)$.

b) Sketch the graph of $s(t)$, its distance at time t.

c) Find the total distance travelled.

d) Find the net change in position.

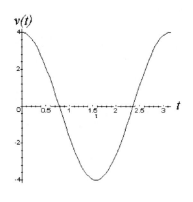

Figure 169.

Solution a) Recall that the velocity is the derivative of the distance, $s(t)$, at time t. So, the velocity is given by $s'(t) = v(t)$. The graph of this motion is given by Figure 169, but this sketch doesn't show what the particle is doing along the line, right? Still, the graph does give us some interesting information. For example, when the velocity is positive (or when the curve is above the x−axis), the particle moves to the right. On the other hand, when the velocity is negative (or when the curve is below the x−axis), the particle moves to the left. When the velocity is zero, the particle stops and may or may not 'reverse' its motion.

b) So, we need to re-interpret the information about the velocity when dealing with the line. The point is that the particle's position is really a plot of the distance, $s(t)$, rather than the velocity, right? But, from the Fundamental Theorem of Calculus, we also know that

$$\begin{aligned}
s(t) &= s(0) + \int_0^t s'(x) \, dx, \\
&= s(0) + \int_0^t 4\cos 2x \, dx, \\
&= 2\sin 2x \big|_0^t, \\
&= 2\sin 2t,
\end{aligned}$$

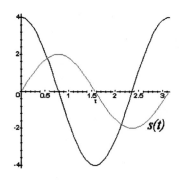

Figure 170.

where $0 \le t \le \pi$. So, the position of this particle along the line segment is given by the graph of $s(t)$ in Figure 170. Note that when $s(t) < 0$ the particle has 'reversed' its motion (*i.e.*, the velocity has changed its sign).

c) Now, the total distance traveled is given by

$$\int_0^\pi |4\cos 2t| \, dt,$$

where

$$|4\cos 2t| = \begin{cases} 4\cos 2t, & \text{if } 0 \le t \le \frac{\pi}{4} \text{ and } \frac{3\pi}{4} \le t \le \pi \\ -4\cos 2t, & \text{if } \frac{\pi}{4} \le t \le \frac{3\pi}{4} \end{cases}$$

You also noticed that the *total distance travelled* is actually equal to the *area* under the curve $y = |4\cos 2t|$ between the lines $t = 0$ and $t = \pi$, because it is given by the definite integral of a positive continuous function. Referring to Figure 169 we see that

$$\begin{aligned}
\int_0^\pi |4\cos 2t| \, dt &= \left(\int_0^{\frac{\pi}{4}} + \int_{\frac{\pi}{4}}^{\frac{3\pi}{4}} + \int_{\frac{3\pi}{4}}^\pi \right) |4\cos 2t| \, dt, \\
&= \int_0^{\frac{\pi}{4}} 4\cos 2t \, dt - \int_{\frac{\pi}{4}}^{\frac{3\pi}{4}} 4\cos 2t \, dt + \int_{\frac{3\pi}{4}}^\pi 4\cos 2t \, dt,
\end{aligned}$$

$$= \quad \frac{4}{2} \sin 2t \Big|_0^{\frac{\pi}{4}} - \frac{4}{2} \sin 2t \Big|_{\frac{\pi}{4}}^{\frac{3\pi}{4}} + \frac{4}{2} \sin 2t \Big|_{\frac{3\pi}{4}}^{\pi} ,$$

$$= \quad \frac{1}{2} [(4 \sin \frac{\pi}{2} - 0) - (4 \sin \frac{3\pi}{2} - 4 \sin \frac{\pi}{2}) + (4 \sin 2\pi - 4 \sin \frac{3\pi}{2})]$$

$$= \quad \frac{1}{2} [4 - 0 - (-4) + 4 + 0 + 4] = 8 \ units$$

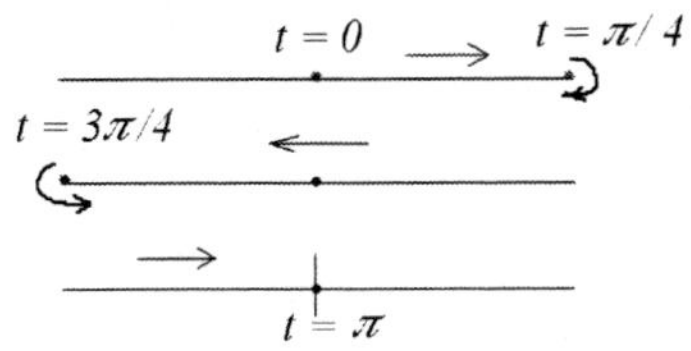

Figure 171.

d) Finally, the net change in position is simply given by $\int_a^b v(t) \, dt$, or

$$\text{Net change in position} \quad = \quad \int_0^{\pi} 4 \cos 2t \, dt,$$

$$= \quad 4 \sin 2t \big|_{t=0}^{t=\pi} = 4 \sin 2\pi - 4 \sin 0$$

$$= \quad 0 - 0 = 0$$

This means that the particle is at the same place (at time $t = \pi$) that it was when it started (at $t = 0$).

Let's recap. Imagine the following argument in your mind but keep your eyes on Figure 170. As t goes from $t = 0$ to $t = \pi/4$, the particle's distance increases and, at the same time, its speed decreases (see Figure 170). When $t = \pi/4$ its speed is zero and its distance is at a maximum (equal to 2 units). As t passes $t = \pi/4$ we see that the speed is negative and the distance is decreasing (so the particle has reversed its motion and is returning to the origin). Next, when $t = \pi/2$ we see that the particle is at the origin (since $s(\pi/2) = 0$), and its speed is -2 units/s. At this point in time the speed picks up again (but it is still negative) and so the particle keeps going left (of the origin) until its speed is zero again (which occurs when $t = 3\pi/4$). Now, at this time, the speed picks up again (it becomes positive), and so the particle reverses its motion once more but it proceeds to the right (towards the origin again) until it stops there when $t = \pi$. This argument is depicted in Figure 171.

NOTES:

8.2   Finding the Area Between Two Curves

The Big Picture

The purpose of this section is to develop machinery which we'll need to correctly formulate the **solution of an area problem using definite integrals**. In other words, we will describe a method for finding the area of an arbitrary closed region in two-dimensional space (or, if you like, the $xy-$plane). For example, what is the area of a given swimming pool? What if you're a contractor and you need to have an estimate on the amount of asphalt that a given stretch of road surface will require? You'll need to know its area first, right? How big should a solar panel be in order to take in a certain amount of solar energy? Many more questions like these can be formulated all over the place and each one requires the knowledge of a certain **area**.

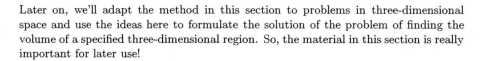

Figure 172.

Later on, we'll adapt the method in this section to problems in three-dimensional space and use the ideas here to formulate the solution of the problem of finding the volume of a specified three-dimensional region. So, the material in this section is really important for later use!

But first, we have to understand how to estimate the area of a given region bounded by two or more curves using vertical or horizontal "slices". Then we need to use this information to set up one or more definite integrals including the limits of integration. Thirdly, we use the methods of the preceding Chapter to evaluate the required integral. Of course, we can always use a formula and we'll write one down in case you prefer this particular method in order to solve the problem.

> # Review
>
> Look over the material dealing with **Curve sketching**, **Inverse functions** and **Absolute values**. In particular, you should know *how to find the form of an inverse function* (when you know there is one) and you should remember the procedure for "removing an absolute value". Finally, a review of **Newton's method for finding the roots of equations** may come in handy in more general situations. This stuff is crucial if you want to know how to solve these area problems! Finally, don't forget to review the techniques of integration (by parts, substitution, etc.) covered earlier .

Figure 173.

Finding an area

You know that decks (the home and garden variety-type) come in all shapes and sizes. What's common to all of them, however, is that they're mostly made up of long cedar slices of different lengths all joined together in a parallel fashion and then fastened down (with nails, glue, etc. see a top-view in Figure 172). So, what's the area of this surface? You get this by finding the area of each cedar slice and adding up all the areas, right? Then *voilà*, you're done! Now, we can apply this principle to a general region in the plane. Given a closed region (a deck) call it $\mathcal{R}$, we can describe it by cutting it up into thin slices of line (you can think of cedar boards) in such a way that the totality of all such lines makes up the region $\mathcal{R}$ (and so its area can be found by adding up the areas of all the boards, see Figure 173). In this section we'll always assume that f, g are two given functions defined and continuous on their common domain of definition, usually denoted by an interval $[a, b]$.

In the following paragraphs, it is helpful to think of a "slice" as a wooden board the totality of which make up some irregularly shaped deck. The first thing we'll do is learn how to **set up the form of the area of a typical slice** of a specified region in the plane. This is really easy if the slice is just a cedar board, right? It's the same idea in this more general setting. The things to remember are that **you need to find the coordinates of the endpoints (or extremities) of a typical slice**, that **areas are always positive numbers**, and that **the area of a rectangle is the product of its height and its width**. The symbol for the width of a "board" will be denoted by dx (or dy), in order to tie this concept of area to the definite integral (see Chapter 6).

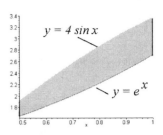

Figure 174.

| Example 423. | The region $\mathcal{R}$ is bounded by the curves $y = e^x$, $y = 4\sin x$, $x = 0.5$

and $x = 1$. Find the area of a typical vertical slice and the area of a typical horizontal slice through $\mathcal{R}$.

Solution A careful sketch (see Figure 174) will convince you that the curve $y = e^x$ lies *below* $y = 4\sin x$ in this range. Don't worry, this isn't obvious and you really have to draw a careful sketch of the graph to see this. The extremities of a typical vertical slice are then given by (x, e^x) and $(x, 4\sin x)$ while its width will be denoted by the more descriptive symbol, dx. So, its area is given by (see Figure 175),

$$
\begin{aligned}
\text{Vertical slice area} \quad &= \quad (\text{height}) \cdot (\text{width}) \\
&= \quad (\text{difference in the y-coordinates}) \cdot (\text{width}) \\
&= \quad (4\sin x - e^x)\, dx
\end{aligned}
$$

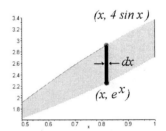

Figure 175.

When describing the *area of a horizontal slice*, the idea is to use the inverse function representation of each one of the curves, defined by some given functions, making up the outline of the region. Now, recall that to get the form of the inverse functions we simply **solve for the $x-$ variable in terms of the $y-$ variable**. The coordinates of the extremities of the slices must then be **expressed as functions of y**, (no " $x's$" allowed at all, okay?).

Now, the extremities of a typical horizontal slice (see Figure 176), are given by

$$(\text{Arcsin}\,(y/4), y) \quad and \quad (\ln y, y),$$

provided that $y \le e$. Why? Because if we solve for x in the expression $y = 4\sin x$ we get $x = \text{Arcsin}\,(y/4)$. Similarly, $y = e^x$ means that $x = \ln y$ so this explains the other point, $(\ln y, y)$. Combining this with the fact that the *height* of such a slice is denoted by the more descriptive symbol, dy, we get

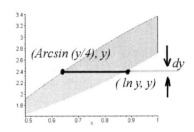

Figure 176.

$$
\begin{aligned}
\text{Horizontal slice area} \quad &= \quad (\text{width}) \cdot (\text{height}) \\
&= \quad (\text{difference in } x-\text{coordinates}) \cdot (\text{height}) \\
&= \quad \left(\ln y - \text{Arcsin}\left(\frac{y}{4}\right)\right)\, dy, \quad \text{if} \ \ y \le e \\
&= \quad \left(1 - \text{Arcsin}\left(\frac{y}{4}\right)\right)\, dy, \quad \text{if} \ \ 1 < y \le 4\sin 1.
\end{aligned}
$$

Example 424. A region in the xy-plane has a vertical slice with coordinates $(x, x^2 e^x)$ and (x, e^{2x}) with $0 \leq x \leq 1$. What is its area?

Solution First, we note that if $0 \leq x \leq 1$, then $x^2 e^x < e^{2x}$ (so that we know which one of the two points is at the top!). You get this inequality by comparing the graph of each function on the interval $0 \leq x \leq 1$, (see Figure 210). By definition, the area of a slice is given by

$$
\begin{aligned}
\text{Vertical slice area} &= (\text{height}) \cdot (\text{width}) \\
&= (\text{difference in the y-coordinates}) \cdot (\text{width}) \\
&= (e^{2x} - x^2 e^x)\, dx
\end{aligned}
$$

NOTE: This is one problem you wouldn't want to convert to horizontal slices because the inverse function of the function with values $x^2 e^x$ is very difficult to write down.

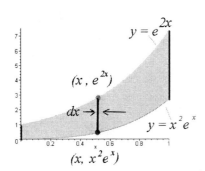

Figure 177.

Example 425. A region in the xy-plane has a horizontal slice whose extremities have coordinates $(-\sqrt{1 - y^2}, y)$ and $(\sqrt{1 - y^2}, y)$, where $0 \leq y \leq 1$. Find the area of a typical slice and determine the shape of the region.

Solution By definition, the area of a typical horizontal slice is given by

$$
\begin{aligned}
\text{Horizontal slice area} &= (\text{width}) \cdot (\text{height}) \\
&= (\text{difference in the } x-\text{coordinates})\ (\text{height}) \\
&= \left(\sqrt{1 - y^2} - (-\sqrt{1 - y^2})\right) dy \\
&= \left(2 \cdot \sqrt{1 - y^2}\right) dy
\end{aligned}
$$

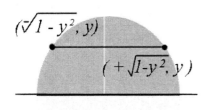

To **find the shape of the region,** just note that the $x-$coordinate of every horizontal slice is of the form $x = \sqrt{1 - y^2}$. Solving for y^2 and rearranging gives the equivalent description, $x^2 + y^2 = 1$. Since $0 \leq y \leq 1$, it follows that the region is the upper half-circle (semi-circle) of radius equal to 1, (see Figure 178).

Figure 178.

In some cases, it's not so easy to see what a typical slice looks like, because there may be more than one of them. Indeed, **there may be two, three, or more of such typical slices.** So, how do you know how many there are? Well, a *rule of thumb* is given in Table 8.1.

Example 426. Find the area of a typical slice(s) for the (closed) region $\mathcal{R}$ bounded by the curves $y = 0$, $x = -2$, $x = 2$ and the curve $y = 3 - x^2/6$.

Solution The graph of this region is shown in Figure 179 and resembles the cross-section of an aircraft hangar. Now refer to Table 8.1. The first step is to find the points of intersection of the curves so that we can "see" the closed region and use this information to find the limits of integration. The required points of intersection are given by setting $x = \pm 2$ into the expression for $y = 3 - x^2/6$. This gives the values $y = 3 - (\pm 2)^2/6 = 7/3$. So, the "roof" of the hangar starts at the point $(-2, 7/3)$ and ends at $(2, 7/3)$.

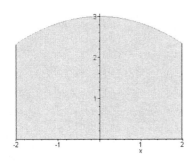

Figure 179.

Now let's take a horizontal slice starting along the line $y = 0$ (the bottom-most portion of $\mathcal{R}$). As we slide this slice "up" along the region $\mathcal{R}$ (see Figure 180), we see that its extremities are points of the form $(-2, y), (2, y)$ at least until we reach the curve where $y = 3 - x^2/6$. We saw above that this happens when $y = 7/3$. Now, as the

> **How many "typical" slices are there?**
>
> 1. **Draw the region** carefully, call it $\mathcal{R}$, and **find all the points of intersection** of the curves making it up.
>
> 2. **Choose a vertical (resp. horizontal) slice** close to the left-most (resp. bottom-most) extremity, say $x = a$ (resp. $y = c$), of $\mathcal{R}$
>
> 3. **Find the coordinates** of its extremities
>
> 4. In your mind's eye (imagine this) ... Slide this slice from left to right (resp. bottom to top) through $\mathcal{R}$ and see if the coordinates of the extremities of the slice change form as you proceed through the whole region. Record the first such change, let's say that it happens when $x = x_0$ (resp. $y = y_0$)
>
> 5. Each time the coordinates of the typical slice change form as you proceed from left to right (resp. bottom to top) you repeat this rule with Item 2, above, and
>
> 6. Continue this procedure until you've reached the right-most (resp. top-most) extremity of $\mathcal{R}$.

Table 8.1: Finding the Number of Typical Slices

slice slides up through this part of the region (past $y = 7/3$), its extremities change and now have coordinates $(-\sqrt{18 - 6y}, y)$ and $(\sqrt{18 - 6y}, y)$. Why? (Just solve the equation $y = 3 - x^2/6$ for x). Eventually, we'll reach the top-most part of the region with such slices and they'll all end when $y = 3$ (the highest peak).

Let's recap. In this case, if we use horizontal slices we get two "typical slices": Those that have endpoints of the form $(-2, y), (2, y)$ (name them Slice 1) and those that have endpoints of the form $(-\sqrt{18 - 6y}, y)$ and $(\sqrt{18 - 6y}, y)$, (call them Slice 2). See Figures 180 and 181 in the margin.

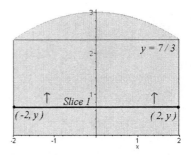

Figure 180.

So, the area of a typical horizontal slice, Slice 1, can be found as follows:

$$\begin{aligned}
\text{Area of Slice 1} &= \text{(width)} \cdot \text{(height)} \\
&= \text{(difference in the } x-\text{coordinates)} \cdot \text{(height)} \\
&= ((2) - (-2))\, dy \\
&= 4\, dy,
\end{aligned}$$

and this formula for a typical Slice 1 is valid whenever $0 \leq y \leq 7/3$.

On the other hand, the area of typical horizontal slice, Slice 2, is

$$\begin{aligned}
\text{Area of Slice 2} &= \text{(width)} \cdot \text{(height)} \\
&= \text{(difference in the } x-\text{coordinates)} \cdot \text{(height)} \\
&= 2\sqrt{18 - 6y}\, dy
\end{aligned}$$

and this formula for a typical Slice 2 is valid whenever $7/3 \leq y \leq 3$.

NOTE: We'll see below that these typical intervals $0 \leq y \leq 7/3$ and $7/3 \leq y \leq 3$ are related to the "limits of the definite integrals" which give the area of the region.

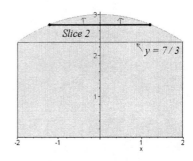

Figure 181.

Find the areas of the following slices of various regions in the plane. It helps to sketch them first.

1. A vertical slice of the closed region bounded by the curves $y = x^2 - 1$ and $y = 0$, between $x = 0$ and $x = 1$.

2. A horizontal slice of the closed region bounded by the curves $y = x^2 - 1$ and $y = 0$, between $x = 0$ and $x = 1$.

3. A vertical slice of the closed region bounded by the curves $y = x^2 + 5x + 6$, $y = e^{2x}$, $x = 0$, and $x = 1$.
   • Find out which one is bigger, first!

4. **Hard**. A horizontal slice of the closed region bounded by the curves $y = x^2 + 5x + 6$, $y = e^{2x}$, and $x = 0$.
   • Be careful here, there are really *two* sets of such slices. Identify each one separately. Furthermore, you'll need to use **Newton's Method** to estimate the points of intersection of the two curves!

5. Refer to the preceding exercise: Now find the area of a typical vertical slice of the region bounded on the top by the curve $y = x^2 + 5x + 6$, on the right by $y = e^{2x}$, below by $y = 5$, and to the left by $x = 0$.
   • Once again, be careful here as there are really *two* sets of such slices. Identify each one separately.

Suggested Homework Set 30. *Work out problems 1, 3, 5*

---

1. Use your knowledge of curve sketching here
2. Vertical or horizontal slices, but which one? See the previous section.
3. Remember that areas are positive numbers, and the area of a rectangle is (base)(height). This part should look like $(f(x) - g(x))\, dx$ or $(F(y) - G(y))\, dy$.
4. This gives you the "limits of integration"
5. This area may be a sum of different definite integrals depending on the number of typical slices within the region.

6. Use the methods of integration of

the previous sections here

Figure 182.

NOTES:

Now that we know how to set up the form of the area of a typical slice we can derive the form of the general area integral as in Table 8.3.

This is basically the way it's done! Let's look at some specific examples which combine all the steps needed in the setup and evaluation of an area integral. In these examples, steps refer to the outline in Table 8.2 at the beginning of this section.

Finding the area of a region $\mathcal{R}$ (see Figure 182)

1. **Sketch the region** $\mathcal{R}$ whose area you want to find.

2. **Divide $\mathcal{R}$ into "typical slices"** (like the cedar boards...)
   - Find the coordinates of each extremity of such a typical slice.

3. Find the **area of one of these typical slices** (think of each one as a very thin rectangle);
   - Its area is equal to the difference between the $y-$ or $x-$ coordinates of the extremities you found above multiplied by the width of the slice (either dx or dy);

4. If the width is dx, find the the **left-most point** $(x = a)$ and the **right-most point** $(x = b)$ of that part of $\mathcal{R}$ corresponding to the chosen slice;
   - Otherwise, the height is dy and you find the the **bottom-most point** $(y = c)$ and the **top-most point** $(y = d)$ of that part of $\mathcal{R}$ corresponding to the chosen slice.

5. **Set up the definite integral** for the area by adding up all the areas of each typical slice making up $\mathcal{R}$ and

6. **Evaluate the integral.**

Table 8.2: Finding the Area of a Region $\mathcal{R}$

Anatomy of an area integral

The area integral for a region with only one typical slice will look like either

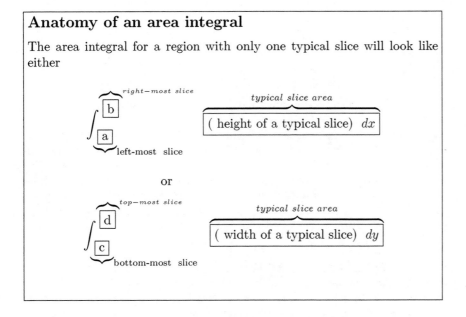

or

Table 8.3: Anatomy of a Definite Integral for the Area Between Two Curves

Example 427.   Find the area of the region $\mathcal{R}$ enclosed by the curves $y = x^2$, $y = 4 - 3x^2$ and the vertical lines $x = -1$ and $x = +1$.

Solution Refer to Table 8.2 for the overall philosophy ...

1. First, we sketch the two parabolic curves (see Figure 183) to obtain a region which looks like an inverted shield.

2. Next, we'll divide our $\mathcal{R}$ into thin *vertical* slices, say. To do this we slice $\mathcal{R}$ with a line segment which begins on the "lower curve" (namely $y = x^2$) and ends on the "upper curve", (namely, $y = 4 - 3x^2$). Now, the coordinates of each extremity of this slice are given by (x, x^2), the lower point, and $(x, 4 - 3x^2)$, the upper point.

3. Now, the area of this slice is given by multiplying its width by its height, right? So, (see Figure 184),

$$
\begin{aligned}
\text{Typical slice area} \quad &= \quad (\text{height}) \cdot (\text{width}) \\
&= \quad (\text{difference in the y-coordinates}) \cdot (\text{width}) \\
&= \quad ((4 - 3x^2) - (x^2))\, dx \\
&= \quad (4 - 4x^2)\, dx
\end{aligned}
$$

4. Next, all these slices start at the left-most $x = a = -1$, right? And they all end at the right-most $x = b = +1$. Note that these two curves intersect at the two points $(-1, 1)$ and $(1, 1)$. Normally, you have to find these points!

5. Since $a = -1$ and $b = 1$, we can set up the integral for the area as

$$
\begin{aligned}
\text{Sum of the areas of all slices} \quad &= \quad \int_{-1}^{1} (4 - 4x^2)\, dx \\
&= \quad 4 \cdot \int_{-1}^{1} (1 - x^2)\, dx \\
&= \quad \frac{16}{3}.
\end{aligned}
$$

Remember that you get the points of intersection by equating the x or y coordinates and then solving the resulting equation. In this case you get $y = 4 - 3x^2 = x^2 = y$ which forces $4 = 4x^2$, or $x^2 = 1$, from which $x = \pm 1$. You get the y-coordinate of these points by setting $y = x^2$ (or $y = 4 - 3x^2$) with $x = \pm 1$.

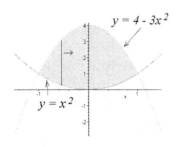

Figure 183.

Example 428.   Find the area enclosed by the triangle bounded by the lines $y = x$, $y = 4 - x$, and the x-axis (or the line $y = 0$, which is the same thing) .

Solution The region is represented as Figure 185 in the margin. Without actually sketching the graph, you could tell that it would be a triangle because the region is bounded by three straight lines. True! Of course, you're probably thinking " Why can't I just find the area of the triangle using the usual formula?". Well, you're right. Let's find its area using geometry: This gives us its area as $(1/2) \cdot (base) \cdot (height) = (1/2) \cdot (4) \cdot (2) = 4$. The area should be equal to 4, but this is only a check, alright? Because we want to know how to find the areas of general regions and not just triangles!

The next step is to find the points of intersection of all these lines, because these points are usually important in our finding the "limits of the definite integral(s)". As before, we equate the y-coordinates and find $4 - x = x$ from which we obtain $x = 2$ and then $y = 4 - 2 = 2$, as well. So the peak of the triangle has coordinates $(2, 2)$. The line $y = 4 - x$ intersects the line $y = 0$ when $4 - x = 0$ or $x = 4$, which now forces $y = 0$. Combining these results we see that the required region is a triangle with vertices at $(0, 0), (2, 2)$ *and* $(4, 0)$.

Next, we need to draw a "typical slice" in our triangle, right? Let's try a vertical slice again, just for practice (we'll look at horizontal slices later). All our vertical slices start on the "lower curve", namely, $y = 0$ and end on the "upper curve" given by ... ? Wait, but there are "2" such "upper curves", that is, $y = x$ and $y = 4 - x$. So, we'll have to divide our typical slice into two classes: 1) Those that end on the curve $y = x$ and 2) Those that end on the curve $y = 4 - x$ (see Figure 186). So, it looks like this problem can be broken down into a problem with "two" typical slices.

Now we need to find the extremities of each of these two sets of slices. Look at the slice, call it "A", which goes from $(x, 0)$ to (x, x) (since $y = x$ on that curve). Its width is dx while its height is equal to the difference between the y−coordinates of its extremities, namely,

$$slice\ height = (x) - (0) = x.$$

Its area is then given by

$$
\begin{aligned}
\text{The area of typical slice, A} \ &= \ \text{(height)} \cdot \text{(width)} \\
&= \ (x) \cdot (dx) \\
&= \ x\ dx
\end{aligned}
$$

Okay, now all such "A-slices" start at the point $(0, 0)$, or the line $x = 0$, and end along the line $x = 2$. This means that $a = 0, b = 2$ for these slices. The area of the triangle, Δ_1, with vertices at $(0, 0), (2, 2), (2, 0)$ is now given by

$$\boxed{\text{Area of } \Delta_1 = \int_0^2 x\ dx.}$$

Now look at the slice, call it "B", which goes from $(x, 0)$ to $(x, 4-x)$ (since, $y = 4-x$ on the other side). Its width is still dx but its height is given by

$$slice\ height = (4 - x) - (0) = 4 - x.$$

The area of a "B-slice" is now given by

$$
\begin{aligned}
\text{The area of typical slice, B} \ &= \ \text{(height)} \cdot \text{(width)} \\
&= \ (4 - x) \cdot (dx) \\
&= \ (4 - x)\ dx
\end{aligned}
$$

In this case, all such "B-slices" start along the line $x = 2$, and end along the line $x = 4$, right? This means that $a = 2, b = 4$ for these slices. The area of the triangle, Δ_2, with vertices at $(2, 2), (2, 0), (4, 0)$ is then given by

$$\boxed{\text{Area of } \Delta_2 = \int_2^4 (4 - x)\ dx.}$$

The total area is now equal to the sum of the areas of the triangles, Δ_1, Δ_2. So, the

$$\text{Area of the region} \ = \ \text{Area of } \Delta_1 + \text{Area of } \Delta_2$$

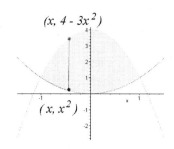

Figure 184.

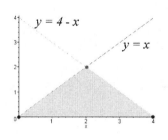

Figure 185.

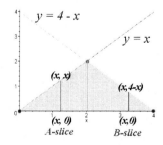

Figure 186.

$$= \int_0^2 x \, dx + \int_2^4 (4 - x) \, dx = \frac{x^2}{2}\Big|_0^2 + \left(4x - \frac{x^2}{2}\right)\Big|_2^4$$

$$= \left(\frac{(2^2)}{2} - 0\right) + \left((4 \cdot 4) - \frac{(4)^2}{2}\right) - \left((4 \cdot 2) - \frac{(2^2)}{2}\right)$$

$$= 2 + 8 - 6 = 4$$

which agrees with our earlier geometrical result!

So, why all the trouble? Because most regions are not triangles, and this example describes the idea behind finding the area of more general regions.

Okay, now what about horizontal slices ?

Well, this is where your knowledge of inverse functions will come in handy. The "rule of thumb" is this ...

We want the area of a region $\mathcal{R}$. There are **always two ways of getting this area**.

If $\mathcal{R}$ is "easily described" using **functions of x only** then **use vertical slices**.

On the other hand, if $\mathcal{R}$ is more "easily described" using **functions of y only** then **use horizontal slices**.

NOTE: By "easily described" we mean that the functions that are obtained are comparatively "easier to integrate" than their counterpart. For example, if the area of a typical vertical slice for a region is given by the expression $(4 - 4x^2) \, dx$ while the corresponding area of its counterpart horizontal slice is given by $(2 \cdot \sqrt{4 - y}/\sqrt{3}) \, dy$ then use the vertical slice to solve the area problem, because that expression is *relatively easier* to integrate.

| Example 429. | Solve the area problem of Example 428 using "horizontal slices". |

Solution The idea here is to use the inverse function representation of each one of the functions making up the outline of the triangle. That is, we need to find the inverse function of each of the functions $y = x$ and $y = 4 - x$. Now, to get these functions we simply **solve for the x−variable in terms of the y−variable**. The coordinates of the extremities of the slices must then be **expressed as functions of y** (no "$x's$" allowed at all!).

Okay, in our case, $y = x$ means that $x = y$ and $y = 4 - x$ implies that $x = 4 - y$. Have a look at Figure 187. You see that the extremities of the horizontal slice are (y, y), on the left, with coordinates as functions of y, and $(4 - y, y)$ on the right. All we did to get these functions of y was to "leave the $y's$ alone" and whenever we see an x we solve for it in terms of y, as we did above.

Now, something really neat happens here! The horizontal slice of Figure 187 is really typical of any such horizontal slice drawn through the triangular region. This means that we only need one integral to describe the area, instead of two, as in Example 428.

Proceeding as before, we can calculate the area of this typical horizontal slice. In fact,

The area of a horizontal slice   =   (height) · (width)

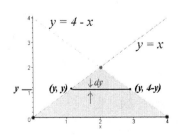

Figure 187.

$$
\begin{aligned}
&= \quad \text{(height)} \cdot \text{(difference in the } x\text{-coordinates)} \\
&= \quad \text{(height)} \cdot (\text{(right } x\text{-coord.)} - \text{(left } x\text{-coord.)}) \\
&= \quad (dy) \cdot ((4 - y) - (y)) \\
&= \quad (4 - 2y)\, dy.
\end{aligned}
$$

Now, all such slices start at the bottom-most point where $y = 0$ and end at the top-most point where $y = 2$. This means that $a = 0, b = 2$. Thus, the area of our region is given by

$$
\begin{aligned}
\text{Area} \quad &= \quad \int_0^2 (4 - 2y)\, dy \\
&= \quad \left(4y - \frac{2y^2}{2}\right)\Bigg|_0^2 \\
&= \quad (8 - 4) - (0 - 0) \\
&= \quad 4.
\end{aligned}
$$

which shows you that either method gives the same answer!

SNAPSHOTS

Example 430. Find an expression for the area of the region bounded by the curves $y = x^2$ and $y = x^2 + 5$ and between the lines $x = -2$ and $x = 1$.

Solution

- Use vertical slices (as y is given nicely as a function of x).
- Area of a typical vertical slice $= ((x^2 + 5) - (x^2))\, dx = 5\, dx$.
- Vertical slices start at $x = -2$ and end at $x = 1$.
- The integral for the area is given by

$$
\begin{aligned}
\text{Area} \quad &= \quad \int_{-2}^1 (\text{Area of a typical vertical slice}) \\
&= \quad \int_{-2}^1 5\, dx.
\end{aligned}
$$

Example 431. Find an expression for the area of the region bounded by the curves $y = 2x - x^2$ and $y = x^3 - x^2 - 6x$ and between the lines $x = -1$ and $x = 0$.

Solution

- Use vertical slices.
- Sketch the graphs carefully, (see Figure 188).
- Area of a typical vertical slice $= ((x^3 - x^2 - 6x) - (2x - x^2))\, dx = (x^3 - 8x)\, dx$.
- Vertical slices start at $x = -1$ and end at $x = 0$.
- The integral for the area is given by

$$
\text{Area} \quad = \quad \int_{-1}^0 (\text{Area of a typical vertical slice})
$$

$$= \int_{-1}^{0} (x^3 - 8x) \, dx.$$

The next example is based on the preceding one...

| **Example 432.** | Find an expression for the area of the region bounded by the |

curves $y = 2x - x^2$ and $y = x^3 - x^2 - 6x$ and between the lines $x = 0$ and $x = 3$, (see Figure 189).

Solution

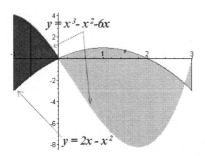

Figure 188.

- Use vertical slices.
- Sketch the graphs carefully on the interval $[0, 3]$.
- Points of intersection in $[0, 3]$: The two curves intersect when $x = \sqrt{8} < 3$.
- Two typical slices here! Slice 1: Those to the left of $x = \sqrt{8}$ and ... Slice 2: Those to the right of $x = \sqrt{8}$.
- Area of a typical vertical Slice 1 $= ((2x - x^2) - (x^3 - x^2 - 6x)) \, dx = (8x - x^3) \, dx$.
- Vertical Slice 1's start at $x = 0$ and end at $x = \sqrt{8}$.
- Area of a typical vertical Slice 2 $= ((x^3 - x^2 - 6x) - (2x - x^2)) \, dx = (x^3 - 8x) \, dx$.
- Vertical Slice 2's start at $x = \sqrt{8}$ and end at $x = 3$.
- The integral for the area is given by a sum of two integrals ...

$$
\begin{aligned}
\text{Area} \;=\; & \int_{0}^{\sqrt{8}} (\text{Area of a typical vertical Slice 1}) + \\
& \int_{\sqrt{8}}^{3} (\text{Area of a typical vertical Slice 2}) \\
=\; & \int_{0}^{\sqrt{8}} (8x - x^3) \, dx + \int_{\sqrt{8}}^{3} (x^3 - 8x) \, dx
\end{aligned}
$$

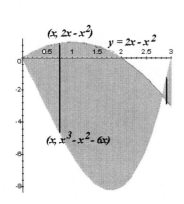

Figure 189.

| **Example 433.** | Find an expression for the area of the region bounded by the |

curves $y^2 = 3 - x$ and $y = x - 1$. Evaluate the integral.

Solution

- Use horizontal slices: It is easier to solve for x in terms of y.
- Sketch the region (see Figure 190).
- Points of intersection: $(2, 1)$ and $(-1, -2)$.
- Area of a typical horizontal slice: $((3 - y^2) - (y + 1)) \, dy = (2 - y^2 - y) \, dy$.
- Horizontal slices start at $y = -2$ and end at $y = 1$.
- The integral for the area is given by

$$
\begin{aligned}
\text{Area} \;=\; & \int_{-2}^{1} (\text{Area of a typical horizontal slice}) \\
=\; & \int_{-2}^{1} (2 - y^2 - y) \, dy = \left(2y - \frac{y^3}{3} - \frac{y^2}{2} \right) \Bigg|_{-2}^{1} \\
=\; & \frac{9}{2}.
\end{aligned}
$$

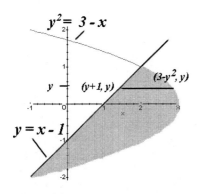

Figure 190.

Example 434. Let $\mathcal{R}$ be the shaded region in Figure 191. It is bounded by the two curves whose equations are $y = f(x)$ and $y = g(x)$ and between the vertical lines $x = a$ and $x = b$ where $a < b$. What is the area of this region $\mathcal{R}$?

Solution Well, the quick formula we spoke of is this:

The area of $\mathcal{R}$ is given by the definite integral of the absolute value of the difference of the two functions in question ...

$$\text{The area of } \mathcal{R} = \int_a^b |f(x) - g(x)|\ dx \qquad (8.1)$$

You know, formulae are just that,– formulae, and you have to "know when and how to use them". So, the moral is, "If you don't want to use slices, you'll have to remember how to remove absolute values "!

If you think about it, this formula is intuitively true, right? Take a vertical slice, find its typical area (which is always a positive number) and add them all up by using the integral.

Now, there is a corresponding formula for "horizontal slices". It's not obvious though and it does need some careful assumptions due to the nature of inverse functions. You can probably believe it because you can use "horizontal slices" instead of vertical ones, etc.

Example 435. Let f, g be continuous functions defined on a common interval $[a, b]$ with the property that $f(a) = g(a)$ and $f(b) = g(b)$, (see Figure 192). If f and g are one-to-one functions on $[a, b]$ then the area of the closed region $\mathcal{R}$ bounded by these two curves is given by

$$\text{The area of } \mathcal{R} = \int_c^d |F(y) - G(y)|\ dy \qquad (8.2)$$

where F, G are the **inverse functions** of f, g respectively and $[c, d]$ is the common range of f and g, that is, $c = f(a) = g(a)$, and $d = f(b) = g(b)$.

Example 436. Use the formula in Example 434 above to find the area of the region bounded by the curves $y = x$ and $y = x^3$ between the lines $x = 0$ and $x = 1$.

Solution By the result above, we know that

$$
\begin{aligned}
\text{The area of } \mathcal{R} &= \int_0^1 |x - x^3|\ dx \\
&= \int_0^1 (x - x^3)\ dx, \text{ (because } x \geq x^3 \text{ on this interval)} \\
&= \left(\frac{x^2}{2} - \frac{x^4}{4} \right) \Big|_0^1 \\
&= (\frac{1}{2} - \frac{1}{4}) - (0 - 0) \\
&= \frac{1}{4}.
\end{aligned}
$$

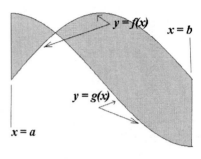

Figure 191.

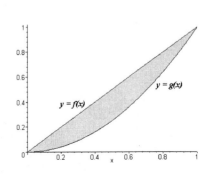

Figure 192.

Even though we didn't have to draw the graphs here, we still have to know "which one is bigger" so that we can remove the absolute value sign in the integrand. A slight variant of the example above is given next. This is an example where we need to think about the "removal of the absolute value" process ...

Example 437. Use the formula in Example 434 above to find the area of the region bounded by the curves $y = x$ and $y = x^3$ between the lines $x = -1$ and $x = 1$.

Solution In this example, we know that (by definition of the absolute value),

$$|x - x^3| = \begin{cases} x - x^3, & \text{if } x \geq x^3, \\ x^3 - x, & \text{if } x \leq x^3, \end{cases}$$

or, since $x \geq x^3$ when $0 \leq x \leq 1$, and $x \leq x^3$ when $-1 \leq x \leq 0$, we get that

$$|x - x^3| = \begin{cases} x - x^3, & \text{if } 0 \leq x \leq 1, \\ x^3 - x, & \text{if } -1 \leq x \leq 0, \end{cases}$$

Now, we break up the domain of integration in order to reflect these different "parts". We find

$$\begin{aligned} \text{The area of } \mathcal{R} &= \int_{-1}^{1} |x - x^3| \, dx \\ &= \int_{-1}^{0} (x^3 - x) \, dx + \int_{0}^{1} (x - x^3) \, dx \\ &= \left(\frac{x^4}{4} - \frac{x^2}{2} \right) \Big|_{-1}^{0} + \left(\frac{x^2}{2} - \frac{x^4}{4} \right) \Big|_{0}^{1} \\ &= \frac{1}{4} + \frac{1}{4} \\ &= \frac{1}{2}. \end{aligned}$$

Sometimes studying the regions for "symmetry" properties (see Chapter 5) can be very useful. In this case, the two regions (the one to the left and the one to the right of the y-axis) really have the same area so, finding the area of one and doubling it, gives the answer we want.

Example 438. Use the formula in Example 435 above to find the area of the region $\mathcal{R}$ bounded by the curves $y = x^2$ and $y = 2x$.

Solution The points of intersection of these graphs occur when $x^2 = 2x$, that is, when $x = 0$ or $x = 2$, see Figure 193. This gives the two points $(0, 0)$ and $(2, 2)$. Note that each of the functions f, g, where $f(x) = 2x$ and $g(x) = x^2$, is one-to-one on the interval $0 \leq x \leq 2$. Furthermore, $f(0) = g(0) = 0$ and $f(2) = g(2) = 4$. Since each one of these is continuous, it follows that the assumptions in Example 435 are all satisfied and so the area of the shaded region $\mathcal{R}$ between these two curves is given by

$$\text{The area of } \mathcal{R} = \int_{0}^{4} |F(y) - G(y)| \, dy$$

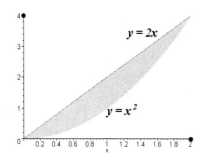

Figure 193.

Let $\mathcal{R}$ be the region bounded by the vertical lines $x = a$, $x = b$ and between the two curves defined by the functions $y = f(x)$ and $y = g(x)$ as in Figure 191. Then the area of this region is given by

$$\text{The area of } \mathcal{R} = \int_a^b |f(x) - g(x)| \, dx. \qquad (8.3)$$

Table 8.4: The Area of a Region Between Two Curves

where F, G are the **inverse functions** of f, g respectively and $[0, 4]$ is the common range of f and g. In this case, the *inverse functions* are given, (see Chapter 3), by the functions $F(y) = y/2$ and $G(y) = \sqrt{y}$. From the theory of Inverse Functions we know that the common domain of these inverses is the common range of the original functions, namely, the interval $[0, 4]$. So, according to formula in Example 435, the area of the shaded region in Figure 193 is given by

$$
\begin{aligned}
\int_0^4 |F(y) - G(y)| \, dy &= \int_0^4 \left| \frac{y}{2} - \sqrt{y} \right| \, dy \\
&= \int_0^4 \left(\sqrt{y} - \frac{y}{2} \right) \, dy, \quad \text{(because } \sqrt{y} \geq \frac{y}{2} \text{ here)}, \\
&= \frac{4}{3}.
\end{aligned}
$$

If we use *vertical slices* we would find that the same area is given by,

$$\int_0^2 \left(2x - x^2 \right) \, dx = \frac{4}{3},$$

which agrees with the one we just found (as it should!).

Example 439. Find the form of the integral for the area of the "curvilinear triangle" in the first quadrant bounded by the $y-$axis and the curves $y = \sin x$, $y = \cos x$, see Figure 194.

Solution The points of intersection of these two curves are given by setting $\cos x = \sin x$ and also finding where $\cos x$, $\sin x$ intersect the $y-$axis. So, from Trigonometry, we know that $x = \frac{\pi}{4}$ is the *first* point of intersection of these two curves in the first quadrant. This, in turn, gives $y = \frac{\sqrt{2}}{2}$. Finally, $x = 0$ gives $y = 1$ and $y = 0$ respectively for $y = \cos x$ and $y = \sin x$. Using Table 8.4 we see that the area of this region is given by

$$
\begin{aligned}
\int_a^b |f(x) - g(x)| \, dx &= \int_0^{\frac{\pi}{4}} |\sin x - \cos x| \, dx, \\
&= \int_0^{\frac{\pi}{4}} (\cos x - \sin x) \, dx, \\
&= \sqrt{2} - 1.
\end{aligned}
$$

Example 440. Find the form of the integral for the area of the region bounded on the right by $y = 6 - x$, on the left by $y = \sqrt{x}$ and below by $y = 1$.

Solution The first thing to do is to sketch the region, see Figure 195, because it involves more than two curves. The points of intersection of all these curves are given

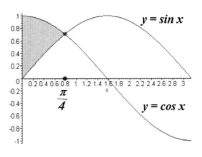

Figure 194.

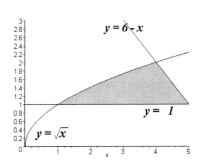

Figure 195.

by $\sqrt{x} = 1 \Rightarrow x = 1$, and $6 - x = 1 \Rightarrow x = 5$, and $6 - x = \sqrt{x} \Rightarrow (\sqrt{x} + 3)(\sqrt{x} - 2) = 0$, $\Rightarrow \sqrt{x} = 2 \Rightarrow x = 4$. The points are therefore $(1, 1), (5, 1),$ and $(4, 2)$.

This region may be split up into two smaller regions, one to the left of the line $x = 4$ and the other one to the right of $x = 4$. We may then use Table 8.4 or, what comes to the same thing, *vertical slices*, to find

$$\text{Area} \quad = \quad \int_1^4 (\sqrt{x} - 1) \ dx + \int_4^5 (5 - x) \ dx,$$
$$= \quad \frac{13}{6},$$

or, if we use *horizontal slices* and take advantage of the shape of the region, we get the simpler formula for the same area, namely,

$$\text{Area} \quad = \quad \int_1^2 \left(6 - y - y^2 \right) \ dy,$$
$$= \quad \frac{13}{6}.$$

Exercise Set 43.

Find an expression for the area of the following closed regions in the plane. It helps to sketch them first; also, you can refer to the first set of exercises in this section for additional help. Evaluate the integrals.

1. The region bounded by the curves $y = x^2 - 1$ and $y = 0$.

2. The region bounded by the curves $y = x^2 - 1$ and $y = 3$.

3. The region bounded by the curves $y = x^2 + 5x + 6$, $y = e^{2x}$, $x = 0$, and $x = 1$.
   • This is a long problem: See which function is bigger, then use Newton's method to find the points of intersection of these two functions on the required interval.

4. The region bounded by the curves $y = x^2 + 5x + 6$, $y = e^{2x}$, and $x = 0$.
   • See the preceding Exercise Set.

5. The region bounded by the curve $x = ye^y$ and the lines $y = 0$ and $y = 1$.
   • Hint: Sketch the curve $y = xe^x$ on the usual xy–axes first, then reflect this curve about the line $y = x$.

6. The region bounded by the curve $y = x^2 \sin x$ between $x = 0$ and $x = \pi$.

7. The region bounded by the curve $y = \cos^2 x \cdot \sin x$ between $x = 0$ and $x = \pi$.
   • Watch out here!

8. The region bounded by the curve $y = \sin 3x \cdot \cos 5x$ between the lines $x = \frac{\pi}{10}$ and $x = \frac{3\pi}{10}$.
   • This region is in the lower half-plane, but your area will still be positive!

9. The region bounded by the curves given by $x + y^2 = 2$ and $x + y = 0$.
   • The easy way is to solve for x in terms of y, sketch the graphs, and use "horizontal slices".

10. The region bounded by the curves $y = 2$, $y = -2$, $y = x + 5$ and $x = y^2$.
    • Use horizontal slices.

11. Find an expression for the area of the region enclosed by $y = \sin |x|$ and the x–axis for $-\pi \le x \le \pi$.
    • This graph is "V"-shaped; take advantage of symmetry.

12. Find an expression for the area of the region enclosed by the curves $y = \cos x$, and $y = \sin x$ for $\frac{\pi}{4} \leq x \leq \frac{9\pi}{4}$.

Suggested Homework Set 31. *Do problems 1, 2, 4, 6, 9*

NOTES:

8.3   The Volume of a Solid of Revolution

The Big Picture

The ideas in the preceding section can be modified slightly to solve the problem of finding the volume of a, so-called, **solid of revolution** obtained by rotating a region in the plane about an axis or even an arbitrary line. For example, if we rotate a region given by a circle of any radius lying in the plane about any line (not intersecting it), we'll get a doughnut-shaped region called a **torus**. This torus is an example of a solid of revolution because it is obtained from the original planar region by *revolving* it about an axis (any axis) by a full 2π radians. Another natural example is obtained by rotating a line segment about an axis parallel to it. This generates a cylinder as in Figure 196 whose axis of rotation is through its center. Another example is furnished by rotating the parabola whose equation is $y = x^2$ about the $y-$axis, a full $2\pi-$radians. This generates the solid in Figure 197, (think of it as full of water).

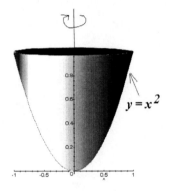

Figure 196.

> ### Review
>
> Review Chapter 7 on Techniques of Integration and the previous section on finding the area between two curves (the geometric way).

The volume of the solid so obtained can be found by slicing up the solid into thin slices much like we did in the previous section, and then rotating the slices themselves about the same axis. The volume of each one of these *thin* slices can be approximated by the volume of a *thin cylinder* and the definite integral for the volume can then be found by *adding up* the volumes of each contribution. Okay, this sounds like a lot, but it's not as difficult as you think.

Figure 197.

The principle for finding the volume of a solid of revolution is simple enough. **We can always reconstruct a solid from all its slices,** much like the collection of all the slices in a loaf of bread can be used to reconstruct the shape of the original loaf! The total volume of bread is approximately equal to the sum of the volumes of each one of the slices, right? Another analogy can be found in a roll of coins. The sum of the volumes of each coin gives the volume of the roll, and so on. The same idea is used here. The world around us is full of solids of revolution; *e.g.,* wheels, car tires, styrofoam cups, most drinking glasses, many lamp shades, eggs, any cylindrical object (pencil, high-lighter, pens, ...), tin cans, buckets, CD-s, records, etc. Of course, we could go on for quite a while and find many, many, more such objects.

Preliminaries

Let's recall the volume of simple cylindrical regions. The volume of a right circular cylinder is, the area of its base times its height, or,

$$\begin{aligned}\text{Volume of Cylinder} \;&=\; \pi \, (radius)^2 \, (height), \\ &=\; \pi r^2 h,\end{aligned}$$

where r is its radius and h is its height, see Figure 198.

Figure 198.

OK, now starting with this simple fact we can derive the volume of a cylinder with a cylindrical hole, as in Figure 199, right? Since the hole is a cylinder in its own right, the resulting volume is given by subtracting the volume of "air" inside the hole from the volume of the cylinder. If we denote the **inner radius**, that is, the radius of the inside hole, by r_{in}, and we denote the radius of the **outer radius** by r_{out}, then the volume, V_{hole}, of the remaining solid which is a *shell*, is given by

$$
\begin{aligned}
V_{hole} &= \pi \, r_{out}{}^2 \, (height) - \pi \, r_{in}{}^2 \, (height), \\
&= \pi \left(r_{out}{}^2 - r_{in}{}^2 \right) \, h, \\
&= \pi (r_{out} + r_{in})(r_{out} - r_{in}) \, h, \\
&= 2\pi \frac{(r_{out} + r_{in})}{2} (r_{out} - r_{in}) \, h, \\
&= 2\pi (\text{average radius}) \, (\text{width of wall}) \, (\text{height}),
\end{aligned}
$$

and this is the key equation, that is,

$$
V_{hole} = 2\pi(\text{average radius}) \, (\text{width of wall}) \, (\text{height}). \qquad (8.4)
$$

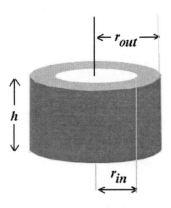

Figure 199.

This formula (8.4) is applicable to cylinders of any orientation, size, or thinness or thickness. It is a basic generic formula which is valid for **any** cylinder with (or even without) a hole in it! See, for example, Figures 200, 201, 202 in the margins to see that this generic formula is verified regardless of the orientation or the size of the cylinder.

Remarks The **width of the wall** of such a cylinder with a hole may be very thin and denoted by dx, (in this case, think of a tin can with a very thin metal wall), or it may be very thick so that the hole is nonexistent (in the case where $r_{in} = 0$).

When the hole is nonexistent the cylinder may look like a coin or a stack of coins. In this case, the outer radius, r_{out}, is just the radius of the cylinder (and $r_{in} = 0$). So its volume is given by the usual formula, $V = \pi r^2 h$. The point is, regardless of how thick or thin the wall is, we still use the same formula (8.4) to find the volume of the remaining cylinder (or shell). Next, the **Average Radius** is, by definition, the average of the two radii, the inner and the outer radii defined above. So, we can write

$$
\text{average radius} \;=\; \frac{r_{out} + r_{in}}{2},
$$

and

$$
\text{wall width} \;=\; r_{out} - r_{in}.
$$

The **height** is a given quantity and has nothing to do with the inner or outer radii (both of which relate together to form the "wall" mentioned above). Let's look at a few examples to see how this formula is used.

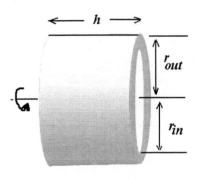

Figure 200.

> **Example 441.** Find the volume of the cylindrical solid (of revolution) obtained
by **rotating the vertical** line segment whose ends are at (x, x^2) and $(x, 1)$, and whose width is defined by the symbol dx, about the $y - axis$. Here we take it that $0 < x < 1$, is some given number.

Solution See Figure 203. The geometry of this situation tells us that

$$
\begin{aligned}
r_{in} &= x - dx, \\
r_{out} &= x,
\end{aligned}
$$

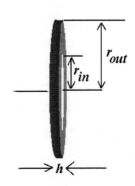

Figure 201.

$$
\begin{aligned}
\text{wall width} \quad &= \quad r_{out} - r_{in}, \\
&= \quad dx, \\
\text{height} \quad &= \quad \text{Difference in the } y-\text{coordinates}, \\
&= \quad 1 - x^2.
\end{aligned}
$$

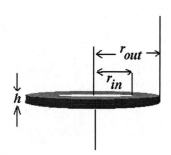

The volume, let's call it dV, of this very thin shell (analogous to the amount of metal making up a tin can) is then equal to

$$
\begin{aligned}
dV \quad &= \quad 2\pi(\text{average radius}) \, (\text{width of wall}) \, (\text{height}), \\
&= \quad 2\pi \frac{(x - dx) + x}{2}(dx) \, (1 - x^2), \\
&= \quad 2\pi x(1 - x^2)dx - \boxed{\pi(1 - x^2)(dx)^2}.
\end{aligned}
$$

Figure 202.

NOTE: Do you see the quadratic term in dx, on the right, the one in the box? This will be very important later, since its contribution is negligible and we'll be able to *forget about it*! We'll just keep the first-order term in dx and using this term we'll be able to write down the definite integral for a solid of revolution. It's really slick and it always works, (this idea of *forgetting* second order terms goes back to Newton and Leibniz).

Example 442.   Find the volume of the cylindrical solid of revolution obtained by **rotating the horizontal line segment** whose ends are at $(0, y)$ and $(\sqrt{y}, y)$, and whose height is defined by the symbol dy, about the $y - axis$. Here we take it that $0 < y \leq 1$, is some given number.

Solution In this case, the geometry tells us that

$$
\begin{aligned}
r_{in} \quad &= \quad 0, \quad (\text{the left end-point is ON the } y-\text{axis}), \\
r_{out} \quad &= \quad \sqrt{y}, \\
\text{wall width} \quad &= \quad r_{out} - r_{in}, \\
&= \quad \sqrt{y}, \\
\text{height} \quad &= \quad dy,
\end{aligned}
$$

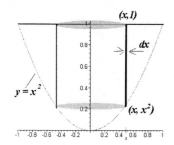

So, the Volume, dV, of this very thin solid of revolution (which looks like a coin) is then equal to

$$
\begin{aligned}
dV \quad &= \quad 2\pi(\text{average radius}) \, (\text{width of wall}) \, (\text{height}), \\
&= \quad 2\pi \frac{\sqrt{y} + 0}{2}(\sqrt{y})(dy), \\
&= \quad \pi(\sqrt{y})^2 dy, \\
&= \quad \pi y \, dy.
\end{aligned}
$$

See Figure 204 for a geometric interpretation of this question.

Figure 203.

Example 443.   Find the volume of the cylindrical solid of revolution obtained by **rotating the vertical line segment** whose ends are at $(x, 0)$ and $(x, 2x - x^2)$, and whose width is defined by the symbol dx, about the y-axis. Here we take it that $0 < x \leq 2$, is some given number.

Solution In this case, the geometry (see Figure 205) tells us that

$$
\begin{aligned}
r_{in} &= x - dx, \quad \text{(as } dx \text{ is the wall width)}, \\
r_{out} &= x, \\
\text{wall width} &= r_{out} - r_{in}, \\
&= dx, \\
\text{height} &= \text{Difference in the } y-\text{coordinates}, \\
&= 2x - x^2.
\end{aligned}
$$

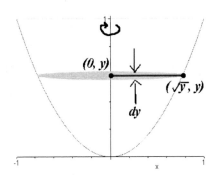

So, the Volume, dV, of this very thin solid of revolution (which looks like an empty tin can) is then equal to

$$
\begin{aligned}
dV &= 2\pi(\text{average radius}) (\text{width of wall}) (\text{height}), \\
&= 2\pi \frac{2x - dx}{2} (2x - x^2)(dx), \\
&= \pi(2x - dx)(2x - x^2)\ dx, \\
&= 2\pi x(2x - x^2)dx - \pi(2x - x^2)(dx)^2.
\end{aligned}
$$

Figure 204. *Note that $r_{in} = 0$ as there is no central "hole" in this example. It follows that the wall width is the same as the radius of the thin coin-like solid generated. The height is small quantity which we denote by dy.*

Example 444. Refer to Example 443 above. Find the volume of the cylindrical solid of revolution obtained by **rotating the vertical line segment** whose ends are at $(x, 0)$ and $(x, 2x - x^2)$, and whose width is defined by the symbol dx, about the x-axis.

Solution Watch out! This same vertical line segment in Figure 205 is now being rotated about the $x-$axis, OK? In this case, draw a picture of the slice rotating about the $x-$axis, and convince yourself that, this time,

$$
\begin{aligned}
r_{in} &= 0, \quad \text{(as there is NO hole now)}, \\
r_{out} &= \text{Difference in the } y-\text{coordinates of ends}, \\
&= (2x - x^2) - (0), \\
&= 2x - x^2, \\
\text{wall width} &= r_{out} - r_{in}, \\
&= 2x - x^2, \\
\text{height} &= dx.
\end{aligned}
$$

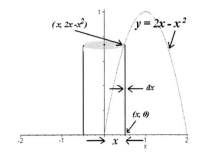

Figure 205.

It follows that the Volume, dV, of this very thin solid of revolution (which looks like a coin on its side) is equal to

$$
\begin{aligned}
dV &= 2\pi(\text{average radius}) (\text{width of wall}) (\text{height}), \\
&= 2\pi \frac{2x - x^2}{2} (2x - x^2)\ (dx), \\
&= \pi(2x - x^2)^2\ dx,
\end{aligned}
$$

and there is NO $(dx)^2-$term this time! This is OK, they don't *always* show up.

Example 445. Once again, refer to Example 443 above. Find the volume of the cylindrical solid of revolution obtained by **rotating the horizontal line segment** whose ends are at $(1 - \sqrt{1-y}, y)$ and $(1 + \sqrt{1-y}, y)$, and whose height is defined by the symbol dy, about the x-axis.

Solution Watch out! Now we are rotating a horizontal line segment about the x−axis, OK? When we do this, **we have to remember to write all the coordinates of the ends in terms of the variable, y**. In this case, draw a picture of the slice rotating about the x−axis, and convince yourself that, this time, you get something that looks like an empty tin can on its side (like Figure 200), above, where

$$
\begin{aligned}
r_{in} &= y - dy, \quad \text{(a really big hole)}, \\
r_{out} &= \text{Distance from slice to } x\text{−axis}, \\
&= y, \\
\text{wall width} &= r_{out} - r_{in}, \\
&= dy, \\
\text{height} &= \text{Difference between the } x\text{−coordinates of ends}, \\
&= \left(1 + \sqrt{1-y}\right) - \left(1 - \sqrt{1-y}\right), \\
&= 2\sqrt{1-y}.
\end{aligned}
$$

So, the Volume, dV, of this very thin solid of revolution (which looks like a tin can on its side) is given by

$$
\begin{aligned}
dV &= 2\pi(\text{average radius})\,(\text{width of wall})\,(\text{height}), \\
&= 2\pi \frac{2y - dy}{2}(dy)(2\sqrt{1-y}), \\
&= \pi(2y - dy)(2\sqrt{1-y})\,dy, \\
&= 4\pi y\sqrt{1-y}\,dy - \boxed{2\pi\sqrt{1-y}\,(dy)^2}
\end{aligned}
$$

and now there is a $(dy)^2$−term! Don't worry, this is OK, we'll forget about it later! Compare your picture of this slice with Figure 206.

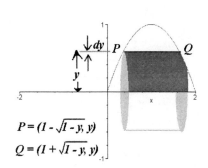

$P = (1 - \sqrt{1-y},\ y)$

$Q = (1 + \sqrt{1-y},\ y)$

Figure 206.

Example 446.   One last time, refer to Example 443 above. Find the volume of the cylindrical solid of revolution obtained by **rotating the horizontal line segment** whose ends are at $(1 - \sqrt{1-y},\ y)$ and $(1 + \sqrt{1-y},\ y)$, and whose height is defined by the symbol dy, about the y-axis.

Solution OK, now we are rotating a horizontal line segment about the **y−axis**! Just like before, **we have to remember to write all the coordinates of the ends in terms of the variable, y**. Once again, we draw a picture of the slice rotating about the y−axis, and you'll note that this time, you get something that looks like a very thin washer, one with a hole in the middle. Now, the calculation is the same but there won't be a $(dy)^2$-term here. We note that the center of the washer is roughly around the point $(0, y)$. So,

$$
\begin{aligned}
r_{in} &= 1 - \sqrt{1-y}, \quad \text{(distance from } (0,y) \text{ to } (1 - \sqrt{1-y},\ y)), \\
r_{out} &= 1 + \sqrt{1-y}, \quad \text{(distance from } (0,y) \text{ to } \textit{outer rim}), \\
\text{wall width} &= r_{out} - r_{in}, \\
&= 2\sqrt{1-y}, \\
\text{height} &= dy,
\end{aligned}
$$

and the Volume, dV, of this very thin solid of revolution (which looks like a very thin washer) is given by

$$
\begin{aligned}
dV &= 2\pi(\text{average radius})\,(\text{width of wall})\,(\text{height}), \\
&= 2\pi \frac{\left(1 - \sqrt{1-y}\right) + \left(1 + \sqrt{1-y}\right)}{2}(2\sqrt{1-y})\,(dy),
\end{aligned}
$$

$$= 2\pi \left(\frac{1+1}{2}\right) 2\sqrt{1-y} \ dy,$$

$$= 4\pi \ \sqrt{1-y} \ dy,$$

and there is no $(dy)^2$-term! Compare your picture of this slice with Figure 207.

Finding the Volume of a Solid of Revolution

Now that we know how to find the volume of a slice when it is rotated about either one of the principal axes (x or y), we can produce the volume of the whole solid of revolution using a definite integral. The neat thing about the method we're using is that **we DON'T have to draw the three-dimensional solid whose volume we want!** All we need is some closed planar region (called a projection or profile) as a starting point. Let's look at how this is done.

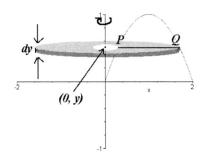

Figure 207.

| **Example 447.** | Find the volume of the solid of revolution obtained by rotating |

the region bounded by the curves $y = x^2$, the y-axis and the line $y = 1$ about the y-axis.

Solution Refer to Example 441 and Figure 203. The region whose volume we wish to find looks roughly like the solid Figure 197, when it is rotated about the y-axis. The procedure for finding this volume is described in the adjoining Table 8.5.

1. **Sketch the region.** This was already done in Figure 203.

2. **Decide on a typical slice.** Let's try a vertical slice as in Example 441.

3. **Find the volume of the slice.** This was done in Example 441. Indeed, its volume is given by the expression

$$dV = 2\pi x(1 - x^2) \ dx - \boxed{\pi(1 - x^2) \ (dx)^2} \qquad (8.5)$$

4. **Find the limits of integration.** Okay, all such slices begin at $x = 0$ and end at $x = 1$ (because we want to describe the whole region). So, the limits of integration are $x = 0$ and $x = 1$.

5. **Write down the definite integral for the volume.** Remember to **DROP** any $(dx)^2$ or $(dy)^2$ terms! In this case we refer to (8.5), drop the square term in the box, and write the definite integral for the volume as

$$Volume \ = \ \int_0^1 2\pi x(1 - x^2) \ dx.$$

6. **Evaluate the definite integral.** This integral is straightforward as it is a polynomial. Its value is found as

$$Volume \ = \ \int_0^1 2\pi x(1 - x^2) \ dx,$$

$$= \ 2\pi \int_0^1 (x - x^3) \ dx,$$

$$= \ \frac{\pi}{2}.$$

This value is the volume of the full (of water, oil ?) solid of revolution which looks like Figure 197.

| **Example 448.** | Find the volume of the solid of revolution obtained by rotating |

the region bounded by the curves $y = x^2$, the y-axis and the line $y = 1$ about the y-axis, using **horizontal slices!**.

Finding the Volume of a Solid of Revolution

(a) **Sketch the region** Use the methods of Chapter 5.

(b) **Decide on a typical slice** The rule of thumb here is just like the one for areas in the previous section: For rotation about either the $x-$ or $y-$axis,

       i. If it easier to describe the region with functions of x, use a vertical slice, see Examples 441, 443, 444, otherwise

      ii. Write all the expressions as functions of y (by finding the inverse functions) and use a horizontal slice. See Examples 442, 445, 446.

(c) **Find the volume of the slice, dV** Use Equation (8.4) and the Examples in this section

(d) **Find the limits of integration** These are obtained by finding the *extremities* of the region, see the Examples.

(e) **Write down the definite integral for the volume** DROP all terms containing the square of either dx or dy from the expression for dV in item 3c.

(f) **Evaluate the definite integral** Use the methods of Chapter 8.

Table 8.5: Setting up the Volume Integral for a Solid of Revolution

Solution We just worked out this one in Example 447 using vertical slices. The nature of the problem makes it clear that it shouldn't matter whether we choose vertical or horizontal slices, right? Both should theoretically give the same answer! The region still looks like the solid Figure 197, when it is rotated about the $y-$axis. This time we use horizontal slices, as required. Fortunately, we found the volume of such a typical horizontal slice in Example 442, namely

$$dV = \pi y \, dy,$$

and, in order for all these slices to cover the whole region, we note that all such horizontal slices start at $y = 0$ and end at $y = 1$. It follows that the definite integral for the volume is given by

$$
\begin{aligned}
Volume &= \int_0^1 \pi y \, dy, \\
&= \pi \int_0^1 y \, dy, \\
&= \frac{\pi}{2},
\end{aligned}
$$

which, of course, *agrees* with the answer we found in the previous problem using vertical slices!.

Example 449.   Find the volume of the cylindrical solid of revolution obtained by rotating the region bounded by the curves $y = 2x - x^2$ and $y = 0$ about the **$y - axis$**, using vertical slices.

Solution We prepared the solution of this problem in Example 443 by finding the volume of a typical vertical slice, dV, where

$$dV = 2\pi x(2x - x^2)\,dx - \pi(2x - x^2)(dx)^2,$$

We drop the $(dx)^2$–term as required and note that all such slices start at $x = 0$ and end at $x = 2$, (see Figure 205). So, the expression for the volume is given by

$$Volume = \int_0^2 2\pi x(2x - x^2)\,dx,$$
$$= 2\pi \int_0^2 (2x^2 - x^3)\,dx,$$
$$= \frac{8\pi}{3}.$$

Example 450. Find the volume of the cylindrical solid of revolution obtained by rotating the region bounded by the curves $y = 2x - x^2$ and $y = 0$ about the ***x − axis***.

Solution Remember that we are rotating about the x−axis! We examined this problem in Example 444 by finding the volume of a typical vertical slice, dV, where

$$dV = \pi(2x - x^2)^2\,dx$$

Note that, in this case, all such slices start at $x = 0$ and end at $x = 2$, (see Figure 205). So, the expression for this volume, is given by

$$Volume = \int_0^2 \pi(2x - x^2)^2\,dx,$$
$$= \pi \int_0^2 (4x^2 - 4x^3 + x^4)\,dx,$$
$$= \frac{16\pi}{15}.$$

This answer differs from that in Example 448 because now we are rotating about the x−axis and not the y−axis! The solids even "look different".

Example 451. Find the volume of the cylindrical solid of revolution obtained by rotating the region bounded by the curves $y = 2x - x^2$ and $y = 0$ about the ***x − axis***, using horizontal slices.

Solution We are still rotating about the x−axis but this time we are using *horizontal* slices! So, our answer must be exactly the same as the one we found in Example 8.3. We examined this problem in Example 445 by finding the volume of a typical horizontal slice, dV, where

$$dV = 4\pi y\sqrt{1 - y}\,dy - \boxed{2\pi\sqrt{1 - y}\,(dy)^2}.$$

We drop the boxed term as usual, and note that, in this case, all such horizontal slices start at $y = 0$ and end at $y = 1$, (see Figure 206). So, the expression for this volume, is given by

$$Volume = \int_0^1 4\pi y\sqrt{1 - y}\,dy,$$
$$= 4\pi \int_0^1 y\sqrt{1 - y}\,dy,$$

EXAMPLES

$$= -4\pi \int_1^0 (1-u)\sqrt{u}\ du, \text{ (use the substitution } 1-y = u, \text{ etc.)},$$

$$= 4\pi \int_0^1 \left(u^{1/2} - u^{3/2}\right)\ du, \text{(and use the Power Rule for Integrals)}$$

$$= 4\pi \left(\frac{2}{3}u^{3/2} - \frac{2}{5}u^{5/2}\right)\Big|_0^1,$$

$$= 8\pi \left(\frac{1}{3} - \frac{1}{5}\right),$$

$$= \boldsymbol{\frac{16\pi}{15}}.$$

Example 452.   Determine the volume of the solid of revolution obtained by rotating the region bounded by the line $y = 0$ and the curve $y = 2x - x^2$ about the $y-$axis.

Solution Let's use a horizontal slice: see Figure 207 for such a typical slice. Its volume is given in Example 446 as

$$dV = 4\pi \sqrt{1-y}\ dy,$$

and the limits of integration are given by noting that all such slices start at $y = 0$ and end at $y = 1$. It follows that the volume of the resulting solid of revolution is given by

$$Volume = 4\pi \int_0^1 \sqrt{1-y}\ dy,$$

$$= -4\pi \int_1^0 \sqrt{u}\ du, \text{ (use the substitution } 1-y = u, \text{ etc.)},$$

$$= 4\pi \int_0^1 u^{1/2}\ du, \text{(and use the Power Rule for Integrals)}$$

$$= 4\pi \left(\frac{2}{3}u^{3/2}\right)\Big|_0^1,$$

$$= 8\pi \left(\frac{2}{3} - 0\right),$$

$$= \boldsymbol{\frac{8\pi}{3}},$$

in accordance with the answer given in Example 449 where we used vertical slices in order to solve the problem.

SNAPSHOTS

Example 453.   A region is bounded by the curves $y = \ln x$, the lines $x = 1$, $x = 2$ and the $x-$axis. Find an expression for the volume of the solid of revolution obtained by revolving this region about the $x-$axis. DO NOT EVALUATE the integral.

Solution A typical vertical slice has the end-points $(x, 0)$ and $(x, \ln x)$. When this slice is rotated about the $x-$axis its volume, dV, is given by

$$dV = \pi(\ln x)^2\ dx.$$

So, the volume of the solid of revolution is given by adding up all the volumes of such slices (which begin at $x = 1$ and end at $x = 2$). This gives rise to the definite integral,

$$Volume \;=\; \pi \int_1^2 (\ln x)^2 \; dx,$$

and this must be integrated using Integration by Parts.

What if we had used a $\boxed{\text{horizontal slice}}$? See Figure 208: In this case we write $x = e^y$ (using the inverse function of the natural logarithm), and so such a typical horizontal slice has end-points (e^y, y) and $(2, y)$. We also have $r_{in} = y - dy$, $r_{out} = y$, wall width $= dy$ and height $= 2 - e^y$, where $0 \le y \le \ln 2$, (since this is the interval which corresponds to the original interval $1 \le x \le 2$, when we set $y = \ln x$). So, the limits of integration are from $y = 0$ to $y = \ln 2$. Neglecting terms in $(dy)^2$ we find the following expression for the volume of the resulting solid:

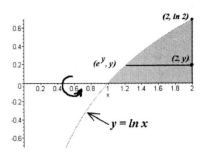

$$Volume \;=\; 2\pi \int_0^{\ln 2} (2y - ye^y) \; dy.$$

In case you want to practice your integration techniques, the common answer to these two integrals is $\pi \left(2(\ln 2)^2 - 4\ln(2) + 2 \right) \approx 0.5916$.

Figure 208.

$\boxed{\textbf{Example 454.}}$ Find the volume of the solid of revolution obtained by rotating the region bounded by the curves $y = x^2$ and $y = 2x$ about the **x—axis**.

Solution Sketch the region and choose a typical vertical slice. Its endpoints have coordinates (x, x^2) and $(x, 2x)$. Note that $y = 2x$ lies above $y = x^2$. Their points of intersection are $x = 0$ and $x = 2$, and these give the limits of integration. In this case, $r_{in} = x^2$, $r_{out} = 2x$, wall width $= 2x - x^2$ and height $= dx$. So, the required volume is given by

$$\begin{aligned} Volume \;&=\; 2\pi \int_0^2 \left(4x^2 - x^4 \right) \; dx, \\ &=\; \frac{128\pi}{15}. \end{aligned}$$

$\boxed{\textbf{Example 455.}}$ A region is bounded by the curves $y = x$, $y = 2 - x$, and the x—axis. Find the volume of the solid of revolution obtained by revolving this region about the y—axis.

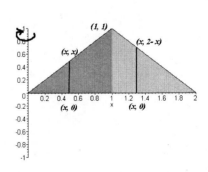

Figure 209.

Solution This region looks like an inverted "v" (it is also similar to the Greek upper case letter, Λ, called *Lambda*) and is, in fact, a triangle with vertices at $(0,0)$, $(1,1)$, and $(2,0)$, (see Figure 209). If you decide to choose a vertical slice you'll need to set up two definite integrals as there are two typical vertical slices, one typical slice lies to the left of $x = 1$ and one lies to the right of $x = 1$. The slices' end-points are respectively, $(x, 0)$, (x, x) and $(x, 0)$, $(x, 2 - x)$. Notice that in both cases, we have $r_{in} = x - dx$, and $r_{out} = x$. The heights change, that's all. The volume of the required solid is given by adding up the two integrals, (remember to drop the $(dx)^2$—terms),

$$Volume \;=\; 2\pi \int_0^1 x^2 \; dx + 2\pi \int_1^2 x(2 - x) \; dx,$$

$$= \frac{2\pi}{3} + \frac{4\pi}{3},$$
$$= 2\pi.$$

The best way to solve this problem is by using a horizontal slice. This is because the geometry of the picture makes it clear that only ONE such slice is needed. Writing all required expressions as functions of y (by solving all $x's$ in terms of y), we find that a typical horizontal slice has end-points (y, y) and $(2 - y, y)$. In this case, $r_{in} = y$, $r_{out} = 2 - y$, $Wall\ width = 2 - 2y$, height $= dy$. So, the required volume is given by

$$Volume = 2\pi \int_0^1 (2 - 2y)\ dy,$$
$$= 2\pi,$$

as we expect (since the answers must be the same).

Example 456.   Find an expression for the volume of the solid of revolution obtained by rotating the region bounded by the curves $y = 4\sin x$, $y = e^x$, $x = 0.5$ and $x = 1$ about the $y-$axis. Evaluate your expression to three significant digits.

Solution Use a vertical slice, see Figure 175. In this case we see that the volume, dV of the small solid of revolution obtained when the slice is rotated about the $y-$axis is

$$dV = 2\pi\ x\ (4\sin x - e^x)\ dx - \pi(4\sin x - e^x)(dx)^2,$$

and so the volume of required the solid of revolution is given by

$$Volume = \int_{0.5}^1 2\pi\ x\ (4\sin x - e^x)\ dx,$$
$$= 8\pi \int_{0.5}^1 x\sin x\ dx - 2\pi \int_{0.5}^1 xe^x\ dx,$$

and two successive "integrations by parts" give

$$Volume = 8\pi \int_{0.5}^1 x\sin x\ dx - 2\pi \int_{0.5}^1 xe^x\ dx,$$
$$= 8\pi(\sin x - x\cos x)\ |_{0.5}^1 - 2\pi(xe^x - e^x)\ |_{0.5}^1,$$
$$= 2.0842\pi - 1.6487\pi,$$
$$= 0.4355\pi = 1.3681.$$

Example 457.   Find an expression for the volume of the solid of revolution obtained by rotating the region bounded by the curves $y = x^2 e^x$, $y = e^{2x}$, $x = 0$ and $x = 1$ about the $x-$axis. DO NOT EVALUATE THE INTEGRAL.

Solution The region is sketched in Figure 210 using a vertical slice. In this case,

$$r_{in} = x^2 e^x$$
$$r_{out} = e^{2x}$$
$$\text{width of wall} = e^{2x} - x^2 e^x,$$
$$\text{height} = dx.$$

So, the volume of the solid of revolution is given by

$$Volume = \pi \int_0^1 \left(e^{4x} - x^4 e^{2x}\right)\ dx,$$

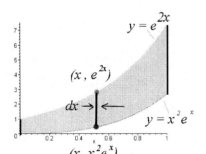

Figure 210.

which, incidentally, can be integrated without much difficulty (the first integral is easy, the second integral is done using integration by parts). If you DO decide you want to integrate this expression your answer should be

$$Volume = \pi \left(\frac{1}{4}e^4 - \frac{1}{4}e^2 + \frac{1}{2} \right).$$

Exercise Set 44.

Find the form (do not evaluate) of the definite integral for the solid of revolution obtained by rotating the following regions about the specified axis.

1. The region bounded by the curve $y = x$, the $x-$axis, and the line $x = 1$. Rotate this about the $x-$axis.

2. The loop enclosed by the curves $y = x^2$ and $y = x$. Rotate this about the $y-$axis.

3. The region bounded by the curves $y = x$, $y = 2x$, and the line $x = 1$ on the right. Rotate this about the $x-$axis.
   - *Hint:* Use a vertical slice.

4. The triangular region bounded by the curve $y = 2x$, the $x-$axis and the lines $x = 0$ and $x = 2$. Rotate this about the $y-$axis.

5. The region bounded by the curves $y = x$, $y = 2x$, and the line $x = 1$ on the right. Rotate this about the $y-$axis.
   - Use both types of slices here: A vertical one first as it is easier to set up, and then use a horizontal slice (dividing the region into two pieces). Base yourself on Example 454.

6. Evaluate the definite integral for the solid of revolution obtained by rotating each one of the previous regions about the specified axis.

Suggested Homework Set 32. *Do problems 1, 3, 5*

NOTES:

8.4 Measuring the length of a curve

The Big Picture

Another important application of the integral consists in finding the length of a curve in the plane (we call these *planar curves*). By the *plane* we usually mean the ordinary $xy-$plane (it is also called the *Cartesian plane*), but it *can* be any *other* two-dimensional plane as well, in that different *coordinate systems* may be used on that plane. There is then a slight change in the formula for the expression of its length (but don't worry about this now, we'll see this much later). Now, all we really need to know in order to handle the material in this section is a working knowledge of how to manipulate a *square root* function and some algebra (see Chapter 1). The reason we may want to calculate the length of a curve is because it may be representing the length of the path of an object (car, satellite, animal, etc) or it may be the length of a strand of DNA. We will motivate the main result in this section with a topic from astronomy.

Long, long ago in a land not far away, Sam Shmidlap discovered an asteroid one evening while observing the night sky. Since Sam had a lot of time on his hands he decided he was going to find out how far this asteroid had travelled over the next few days. Now, Sam thought the orbit of this asteroid was a parabola (it really isn't, but in reality it's pretty close to one). So, all he had to do was to find three reference points to determine this parabola completely, right? (see the Chapter on numerical integration and, in particular, Simpson's Rule, Section 7.7.2). Okay, so he observed the sky, and using a standard Cartesian coordinate system (we'll leave out the details for now) he wrote down its position at three consecutive time intervals. Now that he knew the actual equation of the parabola he called on his friend, Sama, who is a Calculus wiz and asked her to find the length of this celestial parabolic arc that he had just found. She, of course, remembered all the results of this section and provided him with a speedy answer. He then bought her flowers. So the story goes ...

Sounds too theoretical? Let's use some numbers... We'll assume, for simplicity, that Sam's parabola is given by a quadratic equation of the form

$$f(t) = at^2 + bt + c, \quad 0 \le t \le 3,$$

where t is measured in days, say, and a, b, c are some numbers which arise from the observed position of the celestial object. In this case there are three consecutive days, and the interval from $t = 0$ to $t = 1$ represents the time interval corresponding to the first complete day, etc. Now comes Sama who looks at this parabola and writes down the equation of its *length* using the **arc-length formula** (which we'll see below), namely,

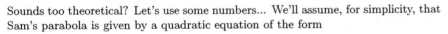

$$\text{The arc length of } f(t) \text{ between } t = a \text{ and } t = b \quad = \quad \int_a^b \sqrt{1 + (f'(t))^2} \, dt$$

where, in this case,

$$\int_0^3 \sqrt{1 + (f'(t))^2} \, dt \quad = \quad \int_0^3 \sqrt{1 + (2at + b)^2} \, dt$$

$$= \quad \frac{1}{2a} \int_b^{6a+b} \sqrt{1 + u^2} \, du,$$

where she used the substitution $u = 2at + b$ (note that a, b are just *numbers*) in the definite integral in order to simplify its form. Since Sama never worries, she then used the *trigonometric substitution* $u = \tan\theta$ to bring the last integral to the form

$$\frac{1}{2a} \int_b^{6a+b} \sqrt{1 + u^2} \, du \quad = \quad \frac{1}{2a} \int_c^d \sec^3\theta \, d\theta,$$

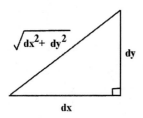

Figure 211.

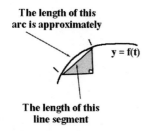

Figure 212.

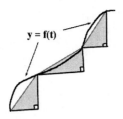

Figure 213.

where now $c = \text{Arctan}\, b$ and $d = \text{Arctan}\,(6a + b)$ (remember these *inverse functions* ?). This last integral in θ was already solved using the methods of Chapter 8, see Example 369.

This simple example shows that the length of the arc of a planar curve has one main interpretation; that is, it represents a physical *length*, such as a distance travelled, or the actual length of a road section, or path, or string, etc. Let's see how we can derive this *simple-to-write-down-but-not-so-easy-to-use* arc length formula. We won't do this rigorously right now, but it should be *believable*.

Review

You'll need to remember the **Theorem of Pythagoras** on the connection between the lengths of the three sides of a right-angled triangle. Next, you'll need to review your techniques of integration, especially **trigonometric substitutions**, (Section 7.6). If these fail to give you some answer then you can use **numerical integration**, which is always good for an approximation to the actual answer.

Let's motivate the derivation of the arc-length formula, the one Sama used in our introduction, above. To see this, all we need to use is the Theorem of Pythagoras applied to a right-angled triangle with sides dx, dy and $\sqrt{dx^2 + dy^2}$, see Figure 211.

We'll be applying this easy formula to the calculation of the sums of the lengths of a sequence of line segments that can be used to approximate the required length of an arc of a given *nice* curve (see Figure 212). The smaller the arc the better the approximation. Since every finite arc of a curve can be thought of as being composed of the union of a finite number of *smaller* arcs (just like a ruler is made up of a finite number of sections), its length is then the sum of the lengths of all these smaller arcs. So its length can be approximated as the sum of the lengths of the line segment approximations to each one of the smaller arcs, see Figure 213. The point is that we just apply the construction in Figure 212 over and over again on every smaller arc until we get something like Figure 213. In this business, remember that *a straight line is also a curve*.

So, a combination of the ideas in Figs. 211, 212 shows that the length of a really small arc in the graph of a differentiable curve is given by the expression

$$
\begin{aligned}
\text{Length of a tiny arc} \;&\approx\; \sqrt{dx^2 + dy^2}, \\[2mm]
&\approx\; \sqrt{dx^2\left(1 + \frac{dy^2}{dx^2}\right)}, \\[2mm]
&\approx\; dx\,\sqrt{\left(1 + \frac{dy^2}{dx^2}\right)}, \\[2mm]
&\approx\; \sqrt{1 + \left(\frac{dy}{dx}\right)^2}\; dx.
\end{aligned}
$$

Now, the amazing thing about Leibniz's notation for the *derivative* of a function is that it allows us to interpret the symbol $\frac{dy}{dx}$ appearing in the last equation as the derivative $y'(x)$ of the function. The point is that even though we started out with dx, dy as being independent numbers (actually *variables*), their quotient can be interpreted as the derivative of the function y.

Since every such arc is a sum of a large number of smaller or *tiny* arcs, the total length of the curve given by $y = f(t)$ between the points $t = a$ and $t = b$ can be thought of as being given by a *definite integral*. This means that the length of a plane curve given by $y = f(t)$ from $t = a$ to $t = b$, provided f is differentiable is denoted by the symbol, $L(f; a, b)$, where this symbol is defined in Equation (8.6) below:

$$L(f; a, b) = \int_a^b \sqrt{1 + (f'(t))^2} \, dt. \qquad (8.6)$$

As usual, it doesn't matter whether we denote the free variables in the definite integral above by t or by x, or by any other symbol as this will always give the same value. For example, it is true that

$$L(f; a, b) = \int_a^b \sqrt{1 + (f'(x))^2} \, dx. \qquad (8.7)$$

Okay, now so far we are convinced that if $y = f(x)$ is a differentiable curve defined on the interval $[a, b]$, then its length is given by (8.7). The actual proof of this result will appear on the web site.

But, you see, whether y is a function of x or x is a function of y doesn't really enter the picture in our explanation of the two basic formulae, (8.6), (8.7) above. We could just interchange the role of these two variables and write x whenever we see y and y whenever we see x. This then gives us the following result.

If $x = F(y)$ is a differentiable curve defined on the interval $[c, d]$, then its length is given by (8.8), This formula is good for finding the length of curves defined by the *inverse*, F, of the function, f, or any other function $x = F(y)$.

$$L(F; c, d) = \int_c^d \sqrt{1 + (F'(y))^2} \, dy. \qquad (8.8)$$

Example 458. Find the length of the line segment whose equation is given by $y = 3x + 2$ where $-2 \le x \le 4$.

Solution Here, $f(x) = 3x + 2$ is a differentiable function whose derivative is given by $f'(x) = 3$. Since y is given in terms of x we use (8.7) for the expression of its length. In this case, $a = -2$ and $b = 4$. This gives us (see Figure 214),

$$\begin{aligned}
L(f; -2, 4) &= \int_{-2}^4 \sqrt{1 + (f'(x))^2} \, dx, \\
&= \int_{-2}^4 \sqrt{1 + 3^2} \, dx, \\
&= \sqrt{10} \int_{-2}^4 dx, \\
&= 6\sqrt{10}.
\end{aligned}$$

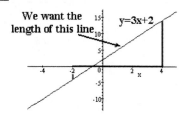

We want the length of this line

Figure 214.

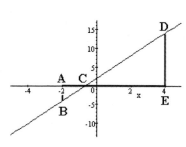

Figure 215.

Check

Let's check this answer using simple geometry. Look at Figure 215 in the margin. The triangles ABC and CDE are each right-angled triangles and so their hypotenuse is given by the Theorem of Pythagoras. Note that the point C coincides with $x = -\frac{2}{3}$. It follows that the length of the hypotenuse CD is given by

$$
\begin{aligned}
CD^2 &= DE^2 + CE^2 \\
&= 14^2 + \left(4 - \left(-\frac{2}{3}\right)\right)^2 \\
&= 14^2 + \left(\frac{14}{3}\right)^2 = 14^2\left(1 + \frac{1}{9}\right) \\
&= \frac{196 \cdot 10}{9}.
\end{aligned}
$$

It follows that

$$
\begin{aligned}
CD &= \sqrt{\frac{196 \cdot 10}{9}} \\
&= \frac{\sqrt{196} \cdot \sqrt{10}}{\sqrt{9}} \\
&= \frac{14 \cdot \sqrt{10}}{3}.
\end{aligned}
$$

A similar calculation shows that the length of the hypotenuse BC of triangle ABC is given by

$$
\begin{aligned}
BC^2 &= AB^2 + AC^2 \\
&= (4)^2 + \left(-\frac{2}{3} - (-2)\right)^2 \\
&= 4^2\left(1 + \frac{1}{9}\right) \\
&= \frac{16 \cdot 10}{9}
\end{aligned}
$$

and so BC has length $4 \cdot \frac{\sqrt{10}}{3}$. Adding up these two lengths, BC and CD, we find $18 \cdot \frac{\sqrt{10}}{3} = \mathbf{6\sqrt{10}}$, as above. Now, which method do you prefer?

Remark We could use the formula defined by (8.8) in order to find the arc length in Example 458. In this case we would need to find the inverse function, F, of f using the methods of Chapter 3.7. In this case we get that $x = F(y) = \frac{y-2}{3}$ (just solve for x in terms of y, remember?). Since the domain of f (which is $[-2, 4]$) must equal the range of F, and the range of f (which is $[-4, 14]$) must equal the domain of F, it follows that $c = -4$, $d = 14$ in equation (8.8). We see that the length of the line segment is also given by

$$
\begin{aligned}
L(F; -4, 14) &= \int_{-4}^{14} \sqrt{1 + \left(\frac{1}{3}\right)^2}\, dy \\
&= \frac{\sqrt{10}}{3} \int_{-4}^{14} dy \\
&= 6\sqrt{10}
\end{aligned}
$$

as before.

Example 459. Find the arc length of the curve whose equation is given by $y = \frac{x^2}{2}$ where $0 \le x \le 1$, (i.e., the length of the shaded arc in Figure 216).

Solution In this example $f(x) = \frac{x^2}{2}$ and $f'(x) = x$, for every x. The length of the required arc is given by (8.7), or

$$
\begin{aligned}
L(f; 0, 1) \;&=\; \int_0^1 \sqrt{1 + x^2}\, dx \\
&\qquad \left(\text{Now let } x = \tan\theta, \; dx = \sec^2\theta\, d\theta, \; \sqrt{1 + x^2} = \sec\theta \ldots \right) \\
&=\; \int_0^{\frac{\pi}{4}} \sec^3\theta\, d\theta \\
&\qquad (\text{and use Example 369, }) \\
&=\; \frac{1}{2}\left(\tan x \sec x + \ln|\sec x + \tan x|\right)\Big|_0^{\frac{\pi}{4}} \\
&=\; \frac{1}{2}\left(1\cdot\sqrt{2} + \ln|\sqrt{2} + 1|\right) - (0\cdot 1 + \ln|1 + 0|) \\
&=\; \frac{1}{2}\left(\sqrt{2} + \ln|\sqrt{2} + 1|\right) \approx 1.1478.
\end{aligned}
$$

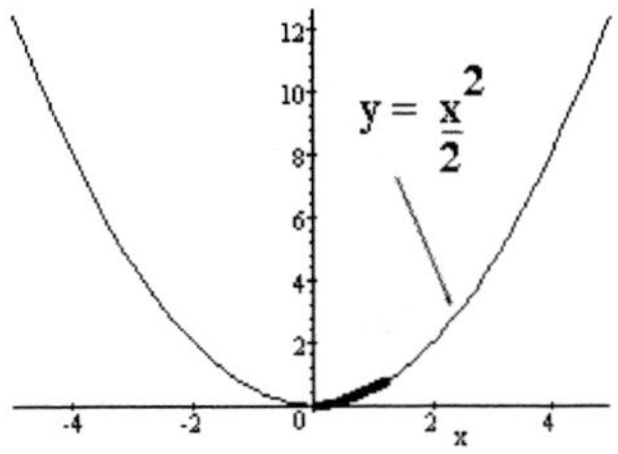

Figure 216.

Example 460. Find the length of the curve whose equation is given by

$$ y = \frac{2}{3} x^{\frac{3}{2}} $$

between $x = 0$ to $x = 3$.

Solution Since the curve is given in the form $y = f(x)$ we can use (8.7) with $a = 0$ and $b = 3$ to find its length. In this case we set $f(x) = \frac{2}{3} x^{\frac{3}{2}}$ so that $f'(x) = \sqrt{x}$, for every x. The length of the required arc is given by (8.7), or

$$
\begin{aligned}
L(f; 0, 3) \;&=\; \int_0^3 \sqrt{1 + f'(x)^2}\, dx \\
&=\; \int_0^3 \sqrt{1 + x}\, dx \\
&\qquad \left(\text{and using the substitution } u = \sqrt{1 + x}, \text{ etc.,}\right) \\
&=\; \int_1^4 \sqrt{u}\, du \\
&=\; \frac{14}{3}.
\end{aligned}
$$

Example 461. Find the length of the curve whose equation is given by

$$ x = g(y) = \frac{y^4}{4} + \frac{1}{8y^2} $$

from $y = 1$ to $y = 2$.

Solution Here x is a given differentiable function of y, so we can use (8.8) with $c = 1$ and $d = 2$. Then

$$
\begin{aligned}
L(g; 1, 2) &= \int_1^2 \sqrt{1 + \left(\frac{dx}{dy}\right)^2}\, dy = \int_1^2 \sqrt{1 + \left(y^3 - \frac{1}{4y^3}\right)^2}\, dy \\
&= \int_1^2 \sqrt{\left(y^3 + \frac{1}{4y^3}\right)^2}\, dy = \int_1^2 \left(y^3 + \frac{1}{4y^3}\right)\, dy \\
&= \frac{123}{32}.
\end{aligned}
$$

> A **parameter** is simply another name for a *variable*. Then, why not just call it a variable? Basically, this is because we want to express our basic x, y variables in terms of it (the parameter). This means that when we see the phrase " t is a parameter ...", we think: "OK, this means that our basic variables (here x, y) are expressed in terms of "t".

For example, if we let t be a variable ($0 \le t < 2\pi$) related to x, y by

$$x = \cos t, \quad y = \sin t.$$

Then t is a parameter (by definition). Now, "eliminating" the parameter shows that x and y are related to each other too, and $x^2 + y^2 = 1$. So, the arc defined by this parametric representation is a *circle* of radius 1, centered at the origin (see figure 217). We call the previous display a **parametric representation** of an arc in the $x, y - plane$ defined by these points with coordinates (x, y) when $0 \le t < 2\pi$.

Thus, the circle $x^2 + y^2 = 1$ may be represented *parametrically* by

$$\left. \begin{aligned} x &= \cos t \\ y &= \sin t \end{aligned} \right\} \quad 0 \le t \le 2\pi,$$

(because $\cos^2 t + \sin^2 t = 1$).

On the other hand, the straight line

$$y = mx + b$$

has the parametric form (representation)

$$
\begin{aligned}
x &= t \\
y &= mt + b.
\end{aligned}
$$

So, the insertion of any number, t, actually gives a point on the curve, a point which changes with t.

Now, it turns out that when a curve C, has the parametric representation

$$(x, y) \ on \ C: \quad \left. \begin{aligned} x &= g(t) \\ y &= h(t) \end{aligned} \right\} \quad a \le t \le b,$$

then

$$\text{Length of } C \text{ between } a \text{ and } b \;=\; \int_a^b \sqrt{\left(\frac{dx}{dt}\right)^2 + \left(\frac{dy}{dt}\right)^2}\, dt \quad (8.9)$$

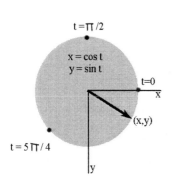

$t = \pi/2$

$x = \cos t$
$y = \sin t$

$t = 0$

x

(x, y)

$t = 5\pi/4$

y

Figure 217.

For a proof of this fact see Exercise 20 at the end of this section.

Example 462. The position of a particle $P(x, y)$ at time t is given by the curve C described by

$$x = \frac{1}{3}(2t + 3)^{3/2}, y = \frac{t^2}{2} + t.$$

Find the distance it travels from time $t = 0$ to $t = 3$.

Solution Note that the curve is described parametrically. We want to know how far the particle travels along the curve C starting from $t = 0$ (corresponding to the point $((x, y) = (\sqrt{3}, 0))$) to $t = 3$, (corresponding to $(x, y) = (9, \frac{15}{2})$), i.e., we need to find the length of the curve C between the points corresponding to $t = 0$ and $t = 3$.

Since C is given parametrically by $x = g(t)$, $y = h(t)$ where g, h are differentiable over $(0, 3)$ we use equation (8.9), that is, the length of C between $t = 0$ and $t = 3$ is given by:

$$Length = \int_0^3 \sqrt{\left(\frac{dx}{dt}\right)^2 + \left(\frac{dy}{dt}\right)^2} \, dt$$

where

$$\frac{dx}{dt} = \frac{d}{dt}\left(\frac{1}{3}(2t + 3)^{3/2}\right) = \frac{1}{2}(2t + 3)^{1/2} \cdot 2 = (2t + 3)^{1/2}$$

and

$$\frac{dy}{dt} = \frac{d}{dt}\left(\frac{t^2}{2} + t\right) = t + 1.$$

So,

$$\sqrt{\left(\frac{dx}{dt}\right)^2 + \left(\frac{dy}{dt}\right)^2} = \sqrt{(2t + 3) + (t + 1)^2} = t + 2.$$

It follows that the length of the curve between the required time values is given by

$$Length = \int_0^3 (t + 2) \, dt = \frac{21}{2}.$$

Example 463. Verify that the length of the arc of a semicircle of radius 1 (*i.e.*, one-half the circumference) is given by the value π.

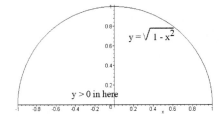

Figure 218.

Solution We'll do this one in *two* ways:

Method 1 First, we can describe this arc by means of the equation $x^2 + y^2 = 1$ where $y > 0$ (see Figure 218). Solving for y we find (note that *positive* square root is used here for the value of y):

$$y = \sqrt{1 - x^2},$$

where $-1 \le x \le 1$. Write $y = f(x)$ and use (8.7) with $a = -1$ and $b = 1$. We find

$$y'(x) = \frac{-x}{\sqrt{1 - x^2}},$$

and after some simplification,

$$\sqrt{1 + (y'(x))^2} = \frac{1}{\sqrt{1 - x^2}}.$$

The required length is given by

$$Length \quad = \quad \int_{-1}^{1} \frac{1}{\sqrt{1-x^2}} \; dx$$

$$= \quad \left. \operatorname{Arcsin} x \; \right|_{-1}^{1} \; = \; \frac{\pi}{2} - \left(\frac{-\pi}{2} \right) = \pi,$$

where we have used the results in Table 6.7 in order to evaluate this integral.

Method 2 We *parametrize* this semicircular arc by setting $x = \cos t, y = \sin t$ where $0 \le t < \pi$ (Why π and not 2π here?). In this case we have that the length of the arc, given by (8.9),

$$\int_{0}^{\pi} \sqrt{\left(\frac{dx}{dt} \right)^2 + \left(\frac{dy}{dt} \right)^2} \; dt \quad = \quad \int_{0}^{\pi} \sqrt{(\sin t)^2 + (\cos t)^2} \; dt$$

$$= \quad \int_{0}^{\pi} \sqrt{1} \; dt$$

$$= \quad \pi,$$

as before.

Example 464. Find the length of the curve $y = f(x)$ where $y = \int_{0}^{x} \sqrt{\cos 2t} \; dt$ from $x = 0$ to $x = \frac{\pi}{4}$.

Solution Since

$$y = \int_{0}^{x} \sqrt{\cos 2t} \; dt$$

it follows that

$$y'(x) \quad = \quad \frac{d}{dx} \int_{0}^{x} \sqrt{\cos 2t} \; dt$$

$$= \quad \sqrt{\cos 2x},$$

by the Fundamental Theorem of Calculus (Section 6.4).

Hence, the length of the curve is given by

$$\int_{0}^{\frac{\pi}{4}} \sqrt{1 + (y'(x))^2} dx \quad = \quad \int_{0}^{\frac{\pi}{4}} \sqrt{1 + \cos 2x} \; dx$$

Now, we need to recall some trigonometry: Note that since $\dfrac{1 + \cos 2x}{2} = \cos^2 x$,

$$1 + \cos 2x \quad = \quad 2\cos^2 x$$

which, when substituted into the previous integral, gives us

$$Length \quad = \quad \int_{0}^{\frac{\pi}{4}} \sqrt{1 + \cos 2x} \; dx$$

$$= \quad \int_{0}^{\frac{\pi}{4}} \sqrt{2 \cos^2 x} \; dx$$

$$= \quad \sqrt{2} \int_{0}^{\frac{\pi}{4}} \cos x \; dx$$

$$= \quad 1,$$

(because $\sqrt{\cos^2 x} = | \cos x |$ by definition and $| \cos x | = \cos x$ on our range $[0, \frac{\pi}{4}]$).

Example 465. A racing track is in the form of an elliptical curve whose equation is given by $x^2 + 4y^2 = 1$, where x is in kilometers (so that it is twice as long as it is wide, see Figure 219). Estimate the distance travelled after completing a full 5 laps.

Solution Using symmetry we see that it is sufficient to estimate the length of "one-half" of the ellipse, then double it (this gives one lap), and finally multiply the last result by 5 in order to obtain the required answer. Solving for y as a function of x we get $y = \dfrac{\sqrt{1-x^2}}{2}$ from which

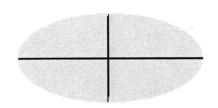

Figure 219. *The elliptical track $x^2 + 4y^2 = 1$.*

$$y'(x) = \frac{-x}{2\sqrt{1-x^2}}.$$

Now compare this example with Example 463, above. The additional multiplicative factor of 2 in the denominator of the last display really complicates things as you will see. We proceed as usual and find, after some simplification, that the length of one-half of the elliptical track is given by

$$\int_{-1}^{1} \sqrt{1 + \left(\frac{dy}{dx}\right)^2} = \int_{-1}^{1} \sqrt{\frac{4-3x^2}{4(1-x^2)}}\ dx.$$

Now, this is NOT an easy integral. We could try a *trigonometric substitution* such as $x = \cos\theta$ and see what happens or, we can estimate it using *Simpson's Rule* (see Section 7.7.2). The last idea is probably the best one. Let's use $n = 6$, say, (larger n's are better but more work is required). In this case, (fill in the details), Simpson's Rule with $n = 6$ applied to the integral

$$\int_{-1}^{1} \sqrt{\frac{4-3x^2}{4(1-x^2)}}\ dx \qquad\qquad (8.10)$$

gives the approximate value, 2.65 km. Doubling this value and multiplying by 5 gives us the required answer which is approximately 26.50 km.

Be careful! The denominator in (8.10) is zero at the endpoints $x \pm 1$. This means that we should replace these values by something like ± 0.99 and *then* use Simpson's Rule. Alternately, you can treat the integral as an *improper integral* first and find an exact answer (but this would be hard in this case).

Exercise Set 45.

Use the methods of this section to find the length of the arcs of the following curves between the specified points.

1. $y = 3, \quad 0 \le x \le 2$

2. $y = x - 1, \quad 0 \le x \le 4$

3. $y = 2x + 1, \quad -1 \le x \le 1$

4. $x = y + 1, \quad 0 \le y \le 2$

5. $2x - 2y + 6 = 0, \quad -2 \le x \le 1$

6. $y = \dfrac{2}{3}x^{3/2}, \quad 0 \le x \le 8$

7. $y = x^2, \quad 0 \le x \le 1$
   - Use the trigonometric substitution $x = \frac{\tan\theta}{2}$ and Example 369.

8. $y = 2x^2 + 1, \quad 0 \le x \le 1$
   - Use a trigonometric substitution.

9. $y = 2x^2, \quad 0 \le x \le 2$
   - Use a trigonometric substitution.

10. $y = \frac{1}{4}x^4 + \frac{1}{8x^2}, \quad 1 \le x \le 3$

11. $x = 2\cos t, \quad y = 2\sin t, \quad 0 \le t < 2\pi$

12. $x = 1 + \cos t, \quad y = 1 - \sin t, \quad 0 \le t < 2\pi$

13. $x = t, \quad y = 2 - t, \quad 0 \le t \le 1$

14. $y = \int_1^x \sqrt{t^2 - 1}\, dt, \quad 1 \le x \le 2$

15. $y = 2 + \int_0^x \sqrt{\cos 2t}\, dt, \quad 0 \le x \le \frac{\pi}{2}$

16. $4x^2 + y^2 = 1, \quad -1 \le y \le 1$
    - Use Simpson's Rule with $n = 6$.

17. $y = \ln x, \quad 1 \le x \le 4$
    - Use a trigonometric substitution.

18. $y = \ln(\sec x), \quad 0 \le x \le \frac{\pi}{4}$

19. Once a meteor penetrates the earth's gravitational field its flight-path (or trajectory, or orbit) is approximately parabolic. Assume that a meteor follows the flight-path given by the parabolic arc $x = 1 - y^2$, where $y > 0$ is its vertical distance from the surface of the earth (in a system of units where 1 unit = 100 km). Thus, when $y = 0$ units the meteor collides with the earth. Find the distance travelled by the meteor from the moment that its vertical distance is calculated to be $y = 1$ to the moment of collision.

    - You need to evaluate an integral of the form $\int_0^1 \sqrt{1 + 4y^2}\, dy$. See Exercise 7 above.

20. Prove formula (8.9) for the length of the arc of a curve represented parametrically over an interval $[c, d]$ in the following steps:

    Let $y = f(x)$ be a given differentiable curve and assume that $x = x(t)$ where x is differentiable, and *increasing* for $c \le t \le d$. Then y is also a function of t.

    a) Use the Chain Rule to show that
    $$y'(t) = f'(x(t)) \cdot x'(t).$$

    b) Next, use the substitution $x = x(t)$ to show that
    $$\int_a^b \sqrt{1 + (f'(x))^2}\, dx = \int_{x^{-1}(a)}^{x^{-1}(b)} \sqrt{1 + (f'(x(t)))^2}\, x'(t)\, dt.$$

    c) Finally, show that
    $$\int_{x^{-1}(a)}^{x^{-1}(b)} \sqrt{1 + (f'(x(t)))^2}\, x'(t)\, dt = \int_c^d \sqrt{\left(\frac{dx}{dt}\right)^2 + \left(\frac{dy}{dt}\right)^2}\, dt$$
    provided we choose $c = x^{-1}(a), d = x^{-1}(b)$.

Suggested Homework Set 33. *Do problems 3, 7, 12, 15, 18*

NOTES:

8.5   Moments and Centers of Mass

The Big Picture

At some point in your life you must have balanced a pencil or a pen on one of your fingers. Usually it was a matter of *trial and error*. You didn't really know where the "balancing point" was until you actually found it by moving the instrument back and forth until it stopped wobbling. By doing so, you actually found out some things about nature! The first thing you found out is that *gravity is uniform*. Basically, this means that the way in which gravity manifests itself on the instrument is the same whether it is acting at the sharp end or at the other end. Furthermore, this balancing point, also called the **center of mass** or **centroid** of the pencil, is a property of every object (or collection of objects) on earth that have *mass*. In sum, for a collection of masses to *balance*, in some sense, they must share a common center of mass. So, yes, even a galaxy has a center of mass! Another example where this notion of a center of mass is used and usually taken for granted includes, but is certainly not restricted to, the teeter-totter or seesaw (found in some parks).

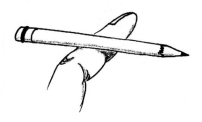

This section is about finding the center of mass of linear objects and (thin) planar regions (like an oddly shaped single sheet of paper, for example). We can assume a *uniform* distribution of mass inside the region whose center of mass we're trying to find, or we can even assume that the distribution of mass is not uniform. For example, the mass distribution along a pencil (with eraser) is not uniform because of the presence of the eraser. It would be approximately uniform if the eraser were absent. The measure of such uniformity of mass along or inside an object is called its **mass density** and denoted by either the symbol $\delta(x)$, or $\delta(x, y)$ (if we are dealing with a two-dimensional region).

Review

This section involves applying the definite integral to the solution of problems involving the center of mass. You should be familiar with all the techniques of integration from Chapter 7 as well as the method of *slices* introduced in Section 8.2.

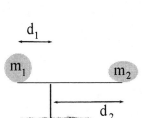

Moments and Centers of Mass

One of the earliest observations about centers of mass is due to the Greek philosopher and mathematician, Archimedes (287-212). Of the many discoveries attributed to him we find the **Principle of the Lever**.

Figure 220.

In its simplest form this principle states that if we take a homogeneous rod of negligible mass and we attach two masses, say m_1 and m_2 at opposite ends, then we can find a point along it that is its center of mass. This center of mass is found by looking for distances d_1 and d_2 from each end, such that

$$m_1 d_1 = m_2 d_2.$$

Experience tells us that there is only *one* such pair of distances, see Figure 220. Why?

Let's actually find the *position* (denoted by $\overline{x}$) of the center of mass given the masses m_1 and m_2 by placing the rod in Figure 220 along the x−axis so that m_1 lies at x_1 and m_2 lies at x_2, see Figure 221. Since $\overline{x}$ is the center of mass, the Principle of the Lever tells us that

$$m_1 \underbrace{(\overline{x} - x_1)}_{d_1} = m_2 \underbrace{(x_2 - \overline{x})}_{d_2}.$$

Now we can isolate the $\overline{x}$ term in the preceding equation by grouping all such terms together . We find $m_1\overline{x} + m_2\overline{x} = m_1x_1 + m_2x_2$. From this we get

$$\overline{x} = \frac{m_1x_1 + m_2x_2}{m_1 + m_2}. \tag{8.11}$$

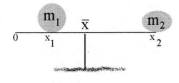

Figure 221.

This result gives us the position of the center of mass, $\overline{x}$, in terms of the positions of the masses and the masses themselves. In other words, once we know *what* the masses are and *where* the masses are, then we know where the center of mass is too! So, there is only one such center of mass just like we expected.

Example 466. Show that you can balance a dune-buggy of mass 500 kg using a 10 m (extremely light!) railroad track. Where is the center of mass? (Assume that your weight is 70 kg.)

Solution Now a railroad track has quite a lot of mass, and so the formulae we developed cannot be used as such as they only apply to the case where the rod has *negligible* mass. Still, we can use them to get an idea, or an approximation to the center of mass. We can refer to Figure 221 where $m_1 = 500$, $m_2 = 70$ and $x_1 = 0$ and $x_2 = 10$ and use equation (8.11) which gives us the location of the center of mass, $\overline{x}$. Thus,

$$\begin{aligned} \overline{x} &= \frac{m_1x_1 + m_2x_2}{m_1 + m_2} \\ &= \frac{500 \cdot 0 + 70 \cdot 10}{500 + 70} \\ &= 1.23m. \end{aligned}$$

As you can see, the center of mass is close to the dune-buggy, at roughly 1.2 meters away from it. At this point $\overline{x}$ you place a *fulcrum* (that part of the track on which it rests) and the system should balance.

Remark Using the notion of the center of mass and Example 466, above, you quickly realize that you can balance just about anything (regardless of its weight!) so long as the rod is *long* enough (and strong enough to hold you both).

Now the products m_1x_1 and m_2x_2 appearing in the expression (8.11) are called the **moments** of the masses m_1, m_2 relative to the origin. So, the center of mass is obtained by adding the two moments and dividing their sum by the total mass of the system. It turns out that *this is true regardless of the number of masses*, that is, the center of mass of a system of n objects all lying on a common line is given by

$$\overline{x} = \frac{m_1x_1 + m_2x_2 + m_3x_3 + \ldots + m_nx_n}{m_1 + m_2 + m_3 + \ldots + m_n} \tag{8.12}$$

$$= \frac{\sum_{i=1}^{n} m_i x_i}{\sum_{i=1}^{n} m_i}, \tag{8.13}$$

where we have used the summation convention of Chapter 6.3.

Example 467.   Three pearls of masses $m_1 = 10$g, $m_2 = 8$g, $m_3 = 4$g are fixed in place along a thin string of very small mass which is then stretched and tied down at both ends. Find the center of mass of this system given that the pearls are all 10cm apart, (see Figure 222).

Solution We place the first pearl at $x_1 = 0$. The second must then be at $x_2 = 10$ while the third must be at $x_3 = 20$, (see Figure 222). It doesn't matter how *long* the string is, since it is assumed to be very light and so its own weight won't displace the system's center of mass by much. Now,

$$
\begin{aligned}
\overline{x} &= \frac{m_1 x_1 + m_2 x_2 + m_3 x_3}{m_1 + m_2 + m_3} \\
&= \frac{0 \cdot 10 + 10 \cdot 8 + 4 \cdot 20}{10 + 8 + 4} \\
&= \frac{160}{22} \\
&= 7.28 cm,
\end{aligned}
$$

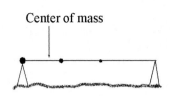

Center of mass

Figure 222.

and so, once again, we notice that the center of mass is closer to the *heavier side* of the system of masses.

If the particles or masses are *not all* on a straight line (see Figure 223) the expressions for the center of mass change slightly but may still be written down using the idea of *moments*, above. It turns out that the center of mass, $(\overline{x}, \overline{y})$, of a system of n bodies with masses $m_1, m_2, \ldots, m_n$ in general position (meaning *anywhere*) on a plane is given by $(\overline{x}, \overline{y})$ where,

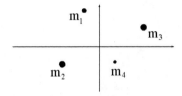

Figure 223.

$$
\overline{x} = \frac{\sum_{i=1}^{n} m_i x_i}{\sum_{i=1}^{n} m_i} = \frac{M_y}{m} \tag{8.14}
$$

and

$$
\overline{y} = \frac{\sum_{i=1}^{n} m_i y_i}{\sum_{i=1}^{n} m_i} = \frac{M_x}{m} \tag{8.15}
$$

where the quantities defined by the symbols M_y, M_x are called **moments**, and m is the **total mass** of the system. Here, (x_i, y_i) denote the coordinates of the mass m_i. Note the similarity of the *form* of these moments to the same notion for the *one-dimensional case* (or the case where the bodies are all on a line, above).

Figure 224.

Specifically, the **moment about the y-axis** is denoted by M_y and is defined by the sum of products of the form

$$
M_y = \sum_{i=1}^{n} m_i x_i.
$$

Similarly, the **moment about the x-axis** is denoted by M_x and is defined by the sum of products of the form

$$
M_x = \sum_{i=1}^{n} m_i y_i.
$$

The quantity M_y, reflects the tendency of a system to rotate about the $y-$axis, while the quantity M_x, reflects a tendency of the system to rotate about the $x-$axis.

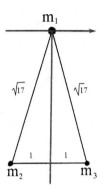

Figure 225.

| Example 468. | Find the center of mass of the isosceles triangle configuration

(see Figure 224) of three bodies with $m_1 = 4, m_2 = 3, m_3 = 3$. Assume that the base has length 2 and that the equal sides have a common length equal to $\sqrt{17}$.

Solution Note that it doesn't matter *where* we place the triangle. So, we position the triangle on a (rectangular) coordinate system with its vertex at the origin, and so that the bisector of the vertex lies along the $y-$axis, see Figure 225. Note that, by the Theorem of Pythagoras, the height of this triangle is 4 units. It follows that the vertices m_1, m_2, m_3 have coordinates $(x_1, y_1) = (0,0), (x_2, y_2) = (-1, -4)$, and $(x_3, y_3) = (1, -4)$ respectively. The total mass is easily seen to be equal to 10 units. We only need to find the moments. Now there are three bodies, so $n = 3$. So,

$$M_x = \sum_{i=1}^{3} m_i y_i = 4 \cdot 0 + 3 \cdot (-4) + 3 \cdot (-4) = -24.$$

This means that $\overline{y} = -24/10 = -2.4$.

Similarly,

$$M_y = \sum_{i=1}^{3} m_i x_i = 4 \cdot 0 + 3 \cdot (-1) + 3 \cdot (1) = 0.$$

On the other hand, this implies that $\overline{x} = 0/10 = 0$. It follows that the center of mass of this system of three bodies is given by the equations (8.14) , (8.15) or

$$(\overline{x}, \overline{y}) = (0, -2.4).$$

Due to the symmetry of the configuration and the base masses, we see that the center of mass lies along the line of symmetry (namely, the $y-$axis). **Remark and Caution:** One can show that if the base masses in Example 468 are unequal, then the center of mass is **not necessarily** along the $y-$axis. Indeed, if we set $m_2 = 5$ (instead of $m_2 = 3$ as in said Example), then $M_y = -32, M_x = -2$ and the new center of mass is calculated to be at the point $(-0.2, -3.2)$. The point is that *even though the configuration of masses is symmetric about a line, this does not force the center of mass to lie along that line of symmetry.* There has to be complete symmetry, between the masses *and* the configuration!

| The Center of Mass of a Region in the Plane |

At this point we have enough information to derive the formula for the center of mass of a (thin) planar region with a mass density $\delta(x)$. Note the dependence of δ on x only! This means that that the mass density, δ, at a point (x, y) in the region is a function of its distance from the $y-$axis only. For example, each picket inside a picket fence around a garden has the same mass density, but here, this density is independent of the picket itself since every picket looks and weighs the same. In this case, $\delta(x)$ is a constant.

We will derive a formula for the center of mass of the region $\mathcal{R}$ having a mass density $\delta(x)$.

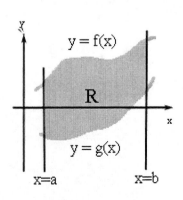

Figure 226.

Let $\mathcal{R}$ denote a region in the $xy-$plane bounded the graphs of two functions $y = f(x)$ and $y = g(x)$ between $x = a$ and $x = b$, where in addition, we assume that $f(x) \geq g(x)$ (see Figure 226). At this point it would be helpful to review the material in Section 8.2.

Fix a point x where $a < x < b$. At x we build a vertical slice of the region $\mathcal{R}$ whose endpoints are given $(x, f(x)), (x, g(x))$ and whose width is dx, (see Figure 227). The mass of this slice is given by the mass density along this slice multiplied by the area of the slice, that is,

$$m_{slice} = \underbrace{(f(x) - g(x)) \; dx}_{Area\; of\; slice:\; dA} \cdot \underbrace{\delta(x)}_{mass\; density\; of\; slice} \qquad .$$

The moment of this slice about the $y-$axis is given by its mass (namely, $\delta \cdot (f(x) - g(x)) \; dx$), multiplied by its distance from the $y-$axis (namely, x). So, the moment of this slice about the $y-$axis is given by

$$M_{y_{slice}} = x \; (f(x) - g(x)) \; \delta(x) \; dx$$

Adding up the moments due to each such slice between a and b we obtain the general formula for the moment, M_y of the region $\mathcal{R}$:

$$\begin{aligned} M_y &= \int_a^b x \; (f(x) - g(x)) \; \delta(x) \; dx \\ &= \int_a^b x \; \delta(x) \; \underbrace{(f(x) - g(x)) \; dx} \\ &= \int_a^b \overline{x}_{slice} \; \delta(x) \; dA. \end{aligned}$$

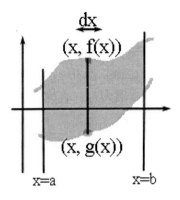

Figure 227.

where $\overline{x} = x$ is the $x-$coordinate of the center of mass of the slice itself. The same method allows us to find the moment M_x of the slice about the $x-$axis. The $y-$coordinate, $\overline{y}$, of the center of mass of the slice is *half-way up the slice* since δ depends on x only! (not on y). This means that

$$\overline{y}_{slice} = \frac{f(x) + g(x)}{2}.$$

So, we find the expression

$$\begin{aligned} M_x &= \int_a^b \overline{y}_{slice} \; \delta(x) \; dA \\ &= \int_a^b \frac{(f(x) + g(x))}{2} \; \delta(x) \; (f(x) - g(x)) \; dx \\ &= \int_a^b \frac{(f^2(x) - g^2(x))}{2} \delta(x) \; dx \end{aligned}$$

Combining these formulae for the moments and the total mass, we obtain that the center of mass $(\overline{x}, \overline{y})$ of the region $\mathcal{R}$, described in Figure 226, is given by

$$\overline{x} = \frac{\int_a^b x \; (f(x) - g(x)) \; \delta(x) \; dx}{\int_a^b (f(x) - g(x)) \; \delta(x) \; dx}. \qquad (8.16)$$

$$\overline{y} = \frac{1}{2} \frac{\int_a^b (f^2(x) - g^2(x)) \; \delta(x) \; dx}{\int_a^b (f(x) - g(x)) \; \delta(x) \; dx} \qquad (8.17)$$

The quantities, M_x, M_y have simple geometrical interpretations: **The system** *balances* **along the line $y = M_x$, if $m = 1$, and the system balances along the line $x = M_y$, if $m = 1$.**

Example 469. Find the approximate value of the center of mass of the earth-moon system at a point where their mutual distance is 3.8×10^5 km. (Data: the mass of the earth is given by 5.97×10^{24} kg, while that of the moon is 7.35×10^{22} kg.)

Solution This is a dynamic (in motion) system of two bodies so the center of mass actually moves around since these astronomical bodies are not generally equidistant from one another for all time. Furthermore, over 300 years ago Newton showed that celestial objects may be treated as *point masses*. This means that one could always assume that *all the mass was concentrated at the center of the object.*

Now, it doesn't matter which one we label m_1 or m_2. Let's say that we set $m_1 = 5.97 \times 10^{24}$ and $m_2 = 7.35 \times 10^{22}$. We can use (8.11) with $x_1 = 0$ and $x_2 = 3.8 \times 10^5$. Then their center of mass at the time where their distance is 3.8×10^5 km is given by

$$
\begin{aligned}
\overline{x} &= \frac{7.35 \times 10^{22} \times 3.8 \times 10^5}{5.9707 \times 10^{24}} \\
&= 4.678 \times 10^3 \\
&= 4678 \; km.
\end{aligned}
$$

The equatorial diameter of the earth is, however, $12,756$ km! So, its equatorial radius is $6,378$ km. This means that their center of mass is *inside the earth!*

Example 470. Find the center of mass of a quarter circle of radius R assuming that the density throughout is uniformly constant (*i.e.,* $\delta(x) = constant$, see Figure 228).

Solution We may always assume that the circle is centered at the origin. In this case, the boundary of the quarter circle is given by points (x, y) where $y = \sqrt{R^2 - x^2}$, and $0 \leq x \leq R$. We can use formulae (8.17, 8.16) for the coordinates of the center of mass. Here we will set

$$
f(x) = \sqrt{R^2 - x^2}, \quad g(x) = 0,
$$

since it is easy to see that the region whose center of mass we seek is bounded by the curves $y = f(x)$, $y = g(x) = 0$, and the vertical lines $x = 0$ and $x = R$. Now $\overline{y}$ is given by (8.17) or

$$
\begin{aligned}
\overline{y} &= \frac{1}{2} \frac{\int_a^b \left(f^2(x) - g^2(x)\right) \delta(x) \, dx}{\int_a^b \left(f(x) - g(x)\right) \delta(x) \, dx} \\
&= \frac{1}{2} \frac{(constant) \cdot \int_0^R \left((R^2 - x^2) - 0\right) \, dx}{(constant) \cdot \int_0^R \sqrt{R^2 - x^2} \, dx} \\
&= \frac{1}{2} \frac{\int_0^R (R^2 - x^2) \, dx}{\int_0^R \sqrt{R^2 - x^2} \, dx} \\
&= \frac{1}{2} \frac{\frac{2R^3}{3}}{\frac{\pi R^2}{4}} \\
&= \frac{4R}{3\pi}.
\end{aligned}
$$

The evaluation of the square-root integral in the denominator is accomplished using the trigonometric substitution $x = R\cos\theta$ and a combination of the methods in Section 7.6 and Section 7.5.

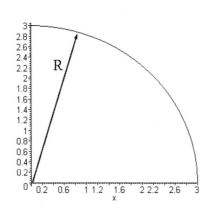

Figure 228.

Similarly, the x−coordinate, $\overline{x}$, of the center of mass is given by

$$\overline{x} = \frac{\int_a^b x \, (f(x) - g(x)) \, \delta(x) \, dx}{\int_a^b (f(x) - g(x)) \, \delta(x) \, dx}$$

$$= \frac{(constant) \cdot \int_0^R x \, \sqrt{R^2 - x^2} \, dx}{(constant) \cdot \int_0^R \sqrt{R^2 - x^2} \, dx}$$

In the numerator use the substitution: $u = R^2 - x^2, \; du = -2x \, dx$

$$= \frac{\frac{R^3}{3}}{\frac{\pi R^2}{4}}$$

$$= \frac{4R}{3\pi}.$$

So, the center of mass

$$(\overline{x}, \overline{y}) = \left(\frac{4R}{3\pi}, \frac{4R}{3\pi} \right)$$

of a quarter plate is located along the *line of symmetry* given by $y = x$ (since the mass density is uniform and the quarter circle is symmetric about this line).

Shortcut It would be easier to evaluate the *total mass integral*

$$m_{quarter \; plate} = \int_0^R \sqrt{R^2 - x^2} \, \delta(x) \, dx$$

on *physical* grounds! For example, the mass of the circular plate is, by definition, its mass density times its surface area. But its mass density is *constant* while its surface area is πR^2. Thus, the mass of the circular plate is $(constant) \cdot \pi R^2$. It follows that the mass of the quarter-plate is given by

$$m_{quarter \; plate} = \frac{(constant) \cdot \pi R^2}{4}.$$

Example 471. Calculate the center of mass of a two-dimensional skateboarding ramp (the shaded region in Figure 229), under the assumption that the mass density, $\delta(x) = const$.

Solution The region is bounded by an arc of the circle with center at (R, R) and radius R, the line segment from $x = 0$ to $x = R$, and the line segment from $y = 0$ to $y = R$. The equation of the circle under consideration is given by $(x-R)^2 + (y-R)^2 = R^2$. It follows that, in (8.17),

$$f(x) = R - \sqrt{R^2 - (x - R)^2}, \;\; g(x) = 0,$$

and $a = 0, b = R$.

Now the total mass, m, of this region can be found (without integrating!) by multiplying its area by the mass-density. In this case, the area of the shaded region can be easily found by noting that it is the difference between the area of a square with side R and vertex at $(0,0)$, and the area of the quarter-circle of radius R, described above. So the total mass of the region is given by

$$m = const. \left(R^2 - \frac{\pi R^2}{4} \right) = const. \left(1 - \frac{\pi}{4} \right) R^2.$$

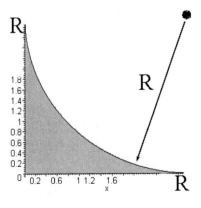

Figure 229.

On the other hand, the region is also symmetric with respect to the line $y = x$. It follows that the center of mass must occur along this line and so it must be the case that for the point $(\overline{x}, \overline{y})$ we must have $\overline{x} = \overline{y}$. It therefore suffices to find either $\overline{x}$ or $\overline{y}$. We choose to find $\overline{x}$ since the required integral for the moment is relatively easier to evaluate. Thus,

$$
\overline{x} = \frac{\int_a^b x \left(f(x) - g(x) \right) \delta(x) \, dx}{\int_a^b (f(x) - g(x)) \delta(x) \, dx}
$$

$$
= \frac{(const.) \cdot \int_0^R x \left(R - \sqrt{R^2 - (x - R)^2} \right) \, dx}{(const.) \cdot \left(1 - \frac{\pi}{4} \right) R^2}.
$$

Now,

$$
\int_0^R x \left(R - \sqrt{R^2 - (x - R)^2} \right) \, dx = R \cdot \frac{x^2}{2} \Big|_0^R - \int_0^R x \sqrt{R^2 - (x - R)^2} \, dx
$$

(Let $x - R = R \sin\theta$, $dx = R\cos\theta \, d\theta$)

$$
= \frac{R^3}{2} - R^3 \cdot \int_{-\frac{\pi}{2}}^0 (1 + \sin\theta) \cos^2\theta \, d\theta
$$

$$
= \frac{R^3}{2} - \left(\frac{R^3 \pi}{4} - \frac{R^3}{3} \right)
$$

$$
= \frac{(10 - 3\pi) R^3}{12}.
$$

It follows that

$$
\overline{x} = \frac{\frac{(10 - 3\pi) R^3}{12}}{\left(1 - \frac{\pi}{4} \right) R^2} = \frac{(10 - 3\pi) R}{(12 - 3\pi)},
$$

and $\overline{x} = \overline{y}$. In this case, the system balances along the line $y = x$, as well as at the point $(\overline{x}, \overline{y})$.

Summary

- For a wire, thin rod or slice along the x-axis from $x = a$ to $x = b$.

  The *Moment about the origin*, $M_0 = \int_a^b x\delta(x) \, dx$, where δ is the mass density (along the wire). The density is said to be *uniform* if $\delta(x) = constant$ inside the region.

  The *total mass*, $m = \int_a^b \delta(x) \, dA$.

  The *Center of Mass*, (or "c.m."), $\overline{x}$, $\overline{x} = \frac{M_0}{M}$.

- For masses m_i at (x_i, y_i): $\overline{x} = \frac{\sum_{i=1}^n m_i x_i}{\sum_{i=1}^n m_i}$, $\overline{y} = \frac{\sum_{i=1}^n m_i y_i}{\sum_{i=1}^n m_i}$ for c.m.

- For a thin plate covering a region in the xy-plane where dA is the area of a thin slice:

  The *Moment about the x−axis*,

$$
M_x = \int \overline{y}_{slice} \, \delta \, dA.
$$

Geometrically, the system *balances* along the line $y = M_x$, if $m = 1$.

The *Moment about the y−axis*,

$$M_y = \int \overline{x}_{slice} \ \delta \ dA$$

Geometrically, the system *balances* along the line $x = M_y$, if $m = 1$.

The total mass, $m = \int_a^b \delta \ dA$.

Its Center of Mass is at $(\overline{x}, \overline{y})$, where $\overline{x} = \frac{M_y}{m}, \overline{y} = \frac{M_x}{m}$.

Here δ is the density per unit area, $(\overline{x}_{slice}, \overline{y}_{slice})$ is the center of mass of a typical thin slice of mass $\delta \ dA$, where dA is the <u>area</u> of our slice.

- The center of mass of a thin slice of uniform density lies halfway between the two ends of the slice (show this using first part: c.m.$= \frac{\delta \int_a^b x \ dx}{\delta (b-a)} = \frac{b+a}{2}$).

We'll work out the next few examples from *first principles* so that you get a feel for the concepts behind the formulae we derived above.

Example 472. Find the center of mass of the region bounded by the parabola $y = h^2 - x^2$ and the x−axis assuming that its mass density is uniform. Here, h is a fixed real constant, (see Figure 230).

Solution We lay out this problem out just like when we calculate areas: But first, note that since the parabola is symmetric about the y−axis (or, equivalently, the line $x = 0$), the center of mass must lie along this line (since δ is uniform) and this forces $\overline{x} = 0$ without having to calculate it directly. Nevertheless, we will calculate it as a check.

- Make a thin slice (horizontal / vertical)
- Find its points of intersection with the curve and the axes
- Now find the center of mass $(\overline{x}_{slice}, \overline{y}_{slice})$ of the thin slice
  Since the density is uniform, $\delta = constant$ and so the center of mass is halfway down the slice. So its coordinates are

$$(\overline{x}_{slice}, \overline{y}_{slice}) = (x, \tfrac{h^2-x^2}{2}), \text{ or } \overline{x}_{slice} = x, \overline{y}_{slice} = \tfrac{h^2-x^2}{2}.$$

Next, the area of our slice,

$$dA = (base) \times (height) = dx \ ((h^2 - x^2) - 0)$$

or,
$$dA = (h^2 - x^2) \ dx.$$
Hence,

$$
\begin{aligned}
M_x &= \int \overline{y}_{slice} \delta \ dA \\
&= \int_{-h}^{h} (\frac{h^2 - x^2}{2}) \delta \ (h^2 - x^2) \ dx \\
&= \frac{\delta}{2} \int_{-h}^{h} (h^2 - x^2)^2 \ dx
\end{aligned}
$$

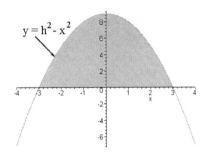

Figure 230.

$$= 2\frac{\delta}{2} \int_0^h (h^2 - x^2)^2 \, dx = \cdots$$

$$= \frac{8h^5\delta}{15}.$$

Remember that h is a <u>constant</u> here.

On the other hand, since $\overline{x} = x$ we have

$$\int_{-h}^h \overline{x}_{slice}\delta \, dA = \delta \int_{-h}^h x \, (h^2 - x^2) \, dx = 0, \leftarrow Why?$$

Finally, the mass of the region $m = \int_{-h}^h \delta dA$ or

$$m = \int_{-h}^h \delta(h^2 - x^2) \, dx = 2\delta \int_0^h (h^2 - x^2) \, dx = \cdots = \tfrac{4}{3}\delta h^3$$

Thus the center of mass $= (\overline{x}, \overline{y}) = (\frac{M_y}{M}, \frac{M_x}{M}) = (0, \frac{\frac{8h^5\delta}{15}}{\frac{4\delta h^3}{3}})$

$$= (0, \tfrac{2h^2}{5})$$

Example 473.

Find the center of mass of a thin homogeneous (*i.e.,* uniform density) plate covering the region bounded by the curves $y = 2x^2 - 4x$ and $y = 2x - x^2$, (see Figure 231).

Solution Recall that the mid-point of the line joining two points (x_1, y_1) and (x_2, y_2) has coordinates $(\frac{x_1+x_2}{2}, \frac{y_1+y_2}{2})$.

Make a thin slice (here, vertical) and find its center of mass. Since $\delta = $ constant, the center of mass of the slice is halfway down slice and so its coordinates are

$$(\overline{x}_{slice}, \overline{y}_{slice}) = (\frac{x + x}{2}, \frac{(2x - x^2) + (2x^2 - 4x)}{2})$$

$$= (x, \frac{x^2 - 2x}{2}).$$

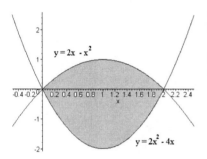

Figure 231.

We see that $\overline{x}_{slice} = x$ and $\overline{y}_{slice} = \frac{x^2 - 2x}{2}$. Now,

$$dA = (base)\,(height)$$
$$= (dx)\,((2x - x^2) - (2x^2 - 4x))$$
$$= (6x - 3x^2)\,dx.$$

Thus

$$M_y = \int_0^2 \overline{x}_{slice}\delta \, dA = \int_0^2 x\delta \, (6x - 3x^2) \, dx = \ldots = 4\delta.$$

Next,

$$M_x = \int_0^2 \overline{y}_{slice}\,\delta \, dA = \delta \int_0^2 (\frac{x^2 - 2x}{2})\,(6x - 3x^2) \, dx$$

$$= \frac{\delta}{2} \cdot 3 \int_0^2 (x^2 - 2x)\,(2x - x^2) \, dx$$

$$= -\frac{3\delta}{2} \int_0^2 (x^2 - 2x)^2 \, dx = -\frac{3\delta}{2} \int_0^2 (x^4 - 4x^3 + 4x^2) \, dx$$

$$= \cdots$$

$$= -\frac{8\delta}{5}.$$

Finally, the mass m of the region is given by $m = \int_0^2 \delta \; dA$, or

$$
\begin{aligned}
m &= \int_0^2 \delta \; (6x - 3x^2) \; dx = \delta \int_0^2 (6x - 3x^2) \; dx = \delta[3x^2 - x^3]_0^2 \\
&= \cdots \\
&= 4\delta.
\end{aligned}
$$

Thus the coordinates of center of mass are given by

$$
\begin{aligned}
(\overline{x}, \overline{y}) &= (\frac{M_y}{M}, \frac{M_x}{M}) = (\frac{4\delta}{4\delta}, \frac{-\frac{8\delta}{5}}{4\delta}) \\
&= (1, -\frac{2}{5}).
\end{aligned}
$$

Remarks: Note that $x = 1$ is a line of symmetry for the region. Since the region is assumed to be of uniform density ("homogeneous") the center of mass <u>must</u> be on this line. Furthermore, since the center of mass generally *"leans on the heavier side of a region"*, in this case, the part of the region below the $x-$axis has more area and so it has more mass. So, the center of mass should be within it, which it is (since $\overline{y} < 0$).

| **Example 474.** |

The density of a thin plate (or "lamina") bounded by the curves $y = x^2$ and $y = x$ in the first quadrant is $\delta(x) = 12x$. Find the plate's center of mass, (see Figure 232).

Solution First we note that the plate is not of uniform density since $\delta(x) \neq constant$ throughout. From this expression for δ we see that the density increases with x, and is lowest when $x = 0$.

Now, the points of intersection are at $(0, 0)$ and $(1, 1)$. The center of mass of a thin (vertical) slice is

$$
(\overline{x}_{slice}, \overline{y}_{slice}) = (x, \frac{x + x^2}{2}).
$$

The density, δ of a slice is $\delta(x) = 12x$ while the area, dA, of a slice is $dA = (x - x^2) \; dx$. Next, the mass of the shaded region in Figure 232 is given by

$$
m = \int_0^1 \delta(x) \; dA = \int_0^1 12x \; (x - x^2) \; dx = \int_0^1 (12x^2 - 12x^3) \; dx = 1.
$$

Now,

$$
\begin{aligned}
M_y &= \int_0^1 \overline{x}_{slice}\delta(x) \; dA = \int_0^1 x \; (12x) \; (x - x^2) \; dx \\
&= \int_0^1 (12x^3 - 12x^4) \; dx = \cdots \\
&= \frac{3}{5}.
\end{aligned}
$$

Finally,

$$
\begin{aligned}
M_x &= \int_0^1 \overline{y}_{slice} \; \delta(x) \; dA = \int_0^1 (\frac{x + x^2}{2}) \; (12x) \; (x - x^2) \; dx \\
&= 6 \int_0^1 x \; (x + x^2) \; (x - x^2) \; dx = 6 \int_0^1 x \; (x^2 - x^4) \; dx \\
&= 6 \int_0^1 (x^3 - x^5) \; dx = 6 \left(\frac{x^4}{4} - \frac{x^6}{6} \right) \Big|_0^1
\end{aligned}
$$

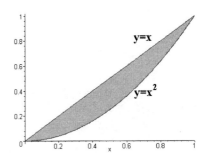

Figure 232.

$$= 6 \left[\frac{1}{4} - \frac{1}{6}\right] = \frac{3}{2} - 1$$

$$= \frac{1}{2}.$$

Combining these moments we get that the region's center of mass coordinates are

$$(\overline{x}, \overline{y}) = (\frac{M_y}{m}, \frac{M_x}{m}) = (\frac{\frac{3}{5}}{1}, \frac{\frac{1}{2}}{1}) = (\frac{3}{5}, \frac{1}{2}).$$

Exercise Set 46.

Find the center of mass of the following systems.

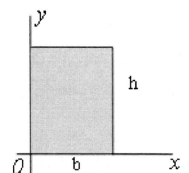

Figure 233.

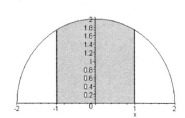

Figure 234.

1. A thin string containing the masses $m_1 = 0.5, m_2 = 1.5$ (in *grams*) separated by a distance of 5 cm.

2. A thin string containing the masses $m_1 = 2, m_2 = 4, m_3 = 6$, each separated by a distance of 1 cm.

3. The system contains 3 masses placed at the points

$$m_1(0,0), m_2(0,1), m_3(1,0)$$

with $m_1 = 3$, $m_2 = 4$, $m_3 = 5$.

4. The system contains 3 masses placed at the points

$$m_1(0,0), m_2(2,0), m_3(1, \sqrt{3})$$

with $m_1 = 3$, $m_2 = 3$, $m_3 = 3$.

5. A semicircle of radius R, centered at the origin and lying in the region $y \geq 0$, having a uniform density, $\delta = constant$.

6. A rectangle of base b and height h having a uniform density, see Figure 233.

7. The V-shaped homogeneous region bounded by the lines $y = x$, $y = -x$ and $y = 1$.

8. The V-shaped region bounded by the lines $y = x$, $y = -x$ and $y = 1$, where $\delta(x) = 1 - x$.

9. The homogeneous region bounded by the x−axis, the line $x = 1$ and $y = \sqrt{x}$.

10. The homogeneous region bounded by the x−axis, the line $x = 2$ and $y = \frac{x^2}{4}$.

11. The homogeneous region bounded by the x−axis and $y = 2\sin(\pi x)$ for $0 \leq x \leq 1$.

12. The region bounded by the x−axis and $y = e^x$ for $0 \leq x \leq 2$, where $\delta(x) = x$.
    • Use Integration by Parts here.

13. The region above the x−axis bounded by an arc of the circle $x^2 + y^2 = 4$ and the vertical lines $x = -1$ and $x = +1$, where $\delta(x) = 2$. This region looks like the doorway of an ancient Roman door (see Figure 234).

14. The region bounded by the curves $y = 2x^2 - 4x$ and $y = 2x - x^2$ where $\delta(x) = 2x$.

Suggested Homework Set 34. *Problems 2, 4, 7, 13, 14*

NOTES:

8.6 Chapter Exercises

In each of the following exercises: a) Sketch the given region, **b)** Choose a typical slice, **c)** Determine the area of the region, and **d)** Find the volume of the solid of revolution obtained when the given region is rotated about the stated axis.

1. The region bounded by the curves $y = x$, $y = 1$, $x = 0$. Rotate this area about the $y-$axis.

2. The region bounded by the curves $y = x$, $x = 1$, $y = 0$. Rotate this area about the $x-$axis.

3. The region bounded by the curves $y = 2x$, $y = 1$, $x = 0$. Rotate this area about the $x-$axis.

4. The region bounded by the curves $y = 2x$, $x = 1$, $y = 0$. Rotate this area about the $y-$axis.

5. The region bounded by the curves $y = x$, $y = 2x$, $x = 2$. Rotate this area about the $y-$axis.

6. The region bounded by the curves $y = x^2$ and $y = 1$. Rotate this area about the $x-$axis.

7. The region bounded by the curve $y = \sin x$ between $x = 0$ and $x = \pi$. Rotate this area about the $x-$axis.

8. The region bounded by the curve $y = \cos x$ between $x = 0$ and $x = \frac{\pi}{2}$. Rotate this area about the $y-$axis.

9. The region bounded by the curve $y = xe^x$ between $x = 0$ and $x = 1$. Rotate this area about the $x-$axis.
   - The graph is that of a nice increasing function. Use a vertical slice and Integration by Parts.

10. The region bounded by the curve $y = xe^{-x}$ between $x = 0$ and $x = 2$. Rotate this area about the $y-$axis.
    - DON'T use a horizontal slice! Apply Integration by Parts.

11. The loop enclosed by the curves $y = x^2$ and $y^2 = x$. Rotate this area about the $x-$axis.
    - Find the two points of intersection and use a vertical slice!

12. The closed region bounded by the curves $y = x^3$, $y = 1$, and $y = x^3 - 3x + 1$. Rotate this area about the $x-$axis.
    - *Hint:* The region looks like a curvilinear triangle. Find all points of intersection. Divide the region into two pieces and then use vertical slices. The integrals are easy to evaluate.

Suggested Homework Set 35. *Do problems 1, 6, 11, 12*

8.7 Using Computer Algebra Systems

Use your favorite Computer Algebra System (CAS), like Maple, MatLab, etc., or even a graphing calculator to answer the following questions. In all the problems it is best to use some form of numerical integration.

1. Approximate the volume of a fruit bowl obtained by rotating the graph of the function $y = e^{-x^2}$ between $x = 0$ and $x = 0.4$ about the x-axis.

2. Find the surface area of an elliptical pool of water whose edge can be approximated by the equation $2x^2 + 9y^2 = 225$ where x and y are measured in meters.

3. A solid steel rivet is made by rotating the region defined by the graph of the function

$$f(x) = \begin{cases} 2, & \text{if } 0 \leq x \leq 2, \\ x - 1, & \text{if } 2 \leq x \leq 2.2. \end{cases}$$

about the x-axis, where x is in centimeters. Find the volume of the rivet.

4. Find the center of mass of the rivet in the preceding example assuming that its density is uniform.

5. Determine the amount of earth required to fill a flower pot to the brim if the pot is defined by rotating the graph of the function $2y = x + 1$ between $x = 10$ and $x = 30$ about the x-axis (where x is in centimeters).

6. Find the volume of the UFO defined by rotating the region described by (careful here!)

$$y = \begin{cases} x^2, & \text{if } 0 \leq y \leq 4, \\ 8 - x^2, & \text{if } 4 \leq y \leq 8. \end{cases}$$

when it is rotated about the y-axis, where y is in meters.

7. Find the center of mass of the saucer-shaped object in the preceding example assuming that its density is uniform.

8. A small glass paper-weight is to be made by revolving the triangular region defined by $y = 1 - 0.4x$, $0 \leq x \leq 2.4$, about the x-axis, where x is in centimeters. Determine the amount of glass required to build such a paper-weight.

9. A spool of thin black thread is wound tightly around a cylindrical drum so as to form a dark region that can be modelled by the set, $\mathcal{D}$, of points bounded by the curves $y = 1$, $y = 2$, $x = 4$ and $y = x + 1$ in the first quadrant.

   - Find the volume of the region $\mathcal{R}$, obtained by rotating $\mathcal{D}$ about the x-axis, where x is in centimeters.

   - If the thread itself is cylindrical and has radius 0.05 millimeters, determine the approximate *length* of thread that is wound up in $\mathcal{R}$.

10. **The jellybean jar problem** An ellipsoid is a three-dimensional analogue of an ordinary ellipse (squashed circle) except that it has three semi-axes instead of two. It is known that if an ellipsoid has semi-axes length given by $x = a$, $y = b$ and $z = c$ then its volume is given by $4\pi abc/3$. These ellipsoids can be used to model ordinary jellybeans. Let's assume that a typical jellybean has $a = 1$, $b = 0.5$ and $c = 0.3$, all units being centimeters. Approximate the number of (essentially identical) jellybeans that can fit in a cylindrical jar of volume 2 liters. (Of course there will be gaps whose volume is hard to estimate. Nevertheless, you can come up with a rough estimate that sometimes can actually clinch the first prize!).

Chapter 9

Simple Differential
Equations

The Big Picture

The essence of most practical physical applications of Calculus includes differential equations. There isn't one comet, asteroid, planet, star, or other heavenly body whose motion is not given by a differential equation. Any physical quantity which involves a rate of change of some function usually includes some differential equation. Most population models in biomathematics are given by such equations as well as more sophisticated models in immunology. Most of Physics relies heavily upon differential equations and most of the physical sciences do so as well. The point is that nature seems to use differential equations as its interface with us, without them it would be very difficult to make accurate predictions about physical events. Indeed, Newton and Leibniz created Calculus so that they could quantify Physics and ultimately, so that they could solve differential equations.

Review

The sections dealing with the derivative and the **Chain Rule** and **Techniques of Integration** are really important here. You should also remember the **Fundamental Theorem of Calculus** in its different formulations. Finally, don't forget to use a generic **constant of integration** when you're finding an antiderivative (or indefinite integral).

9.1   Why Study Differential Equations?

Once he had created the basic rules of Calculus Newton noticed, by simple experimentation, that the rate at which a body cooled (for example, a cup of coffee) was proportional to the difference between the temperature of its environment (for example, the temperature of the room where the coffee is being consumed, also assumed to be at a constant temperature) and the temperature of the body itself (for example, the coffee's temperature as a liquid). You can actually repeat this experiment yourself with any hot liquid in any cup whatsoever so long as you have a high temperature thermometer.

Since he knew about derivatives as rates of change of mathematical quantities he could then write down one of the first differential equations ever to be seen, that is, if $T(t)$ denotes the temperature of the body at time t, then there holds the relation

$$T'(t) = k(T(t) - T_o),$$

where $k > 0$ is a constant that depends on the physical attributes of the body (or the container that holds it, if we are speaking about coffee) and T_o is the temperature of the room itself (assumed constant). Below we will see how to solve this equation, called **Newton's Law of Cooling**, and so be in a position to be able to predict the temperature of the coffee at any time in the future if we know a few basic things about it at some specified time, that we usually denote by $t = t_0$.

Now, note that we can reverse the time variable and make it *negative* because mathematically, nothing stops us from doing this (even though Nature doesn't seem to like negative time!). In this case, the Law becomes one of "heating" and so would govern an event such as the future temperature of a potato being left in an oven at a constant temperature. In other words we could theoretically find out the temeprature of the potato once we know the temperature within the oven itself, the initial temperature of the potato, and some properties about the potato itself.

Another area where differential equations come in handy is in the study of radioactive decay, or in the decay of radioactive elements. Since, over a small time interval, we can assume that the rate at which a given radioactive element disintegrates is the same as the rate as any other element of the same type it follows that if there there are say, $N(t)$ atoms of Plutonium^{239} with a given decay rate (not known at this point) then doubling the quantity should result in twice as much decay, tripling the quantity should result in three times as much decay, etc. This property in reflected in a corresponding differential equation being *linear*. What equation? If we think about it for a minute, we see that we were actually saying was that

$$N'(t) = -kN(t),$$

where k is some constant called the *decay rate* and the *negative sign* was introduced artificially because we want a positive number for $N(t)$ (since this is counting numbers of atoms) and there are *fewer* atoms left after disintegration. In other words, the number $N(t)$ is *decreasing* as a function of time t and so $N'(t) < 0$ (remember Chapter 5?). We will see how this one is solved below, that is, how do we predict the future evolution of $N(t)$ given some basic quantities at the outset?

Basic Concepts in Differential Equations

In this section we will learn how to solve the simplest type of differential equation, that is, a **separable differential equation**. By an **ordinary differential equation of order n** we mean an equation involving some unknown function say, $y(x)$, and its (ordinary) derivatives up to order n. By a **classical solution** of an (ordinary) differential equation of order n we mean a function, y, which has continuous derivatives up to and including that of order n and whose values satisfy the equation at every point x under consideration, except possibly the endpoints. For example, the function $y(x) = e^x$ is a solution of the differential equation of order 1, $y'(x) = y(x)$, because this function has the property that its derivative is equal to itself! Most of the time we're not so lucky in obtaining a nice and quick answer because it is generally difficult to write down the solutions of a given ordinary differential equation. Another simple example is provided by the function whose values are given by $y(x) = \sin x$ which has the property that $y''(x) + y(x) = 0$, which is an equation of order 2. Finally, $y(x) = e^x \sin x$ has the property that $y''(x) - 2y'(x) + 2y(x) = 0$, for any value of x, also an equation of order 2.

| Example 475. | Show that $y(x) = e^x \cos x$ is a solution of the 2nd-order differ-

ential equation $y''(x) - 2y'(x) + 2y(x) = 0$, for any value of x.

Solution Note that y is twice differentiable on any interval (because the exponential function and the cosine function each are). Next, by repeated applications of the Product Rule for derivatives,

$$\begin{aligned}
y(x) &= e^x \cos x \\
y'(x) &= e^x \cos x - e^x \sin x \\
y''(x) &= \{e^x \cos x - e^x \sin x\} - \{e^x \cos x + e^x \sin x\}, \\
&= -2e^x \sin x.
\end{aligned}$$

Combining these three expressions as required by the quantity $y''(x) - 2y'(x) + 2y(x)$ we find that

$$\begin{aligned}
y''(x) - 2y'(x) + 2y(x) &= \{-2e^x \sin x\} - 2\{e^x \cos x - e^x \sin x\} + 2\{e^x \cos x\} \\
&= 0,
\end{aligned}$$

as required.

| Example 476. | Show that $y(x) = ce^{-x}$, where c is a constant, is a solution of

the $n^{th} - order$ differential equation $y^{(n)}(x) = y(x)$ if n is an even integer. What differential equation does y satisfy if n is an odd integer?

Solution As before we must use the Product Rule, but in combination with the Chain Rule here ...

$$\begin{aligned}
y(x) &= ce^{-x} \\
y'(x) &= -ce^{-x} \\
y''(x) &= (-)(-)ce^{-x} = ce^{-x} \\
y'''(x) &= -ce^{-x} \\
y^{(4)}(x) &= (-)(-)ce^{-x} = ce^{-x} \ldots
\end{aligned}$$

From this we see a pattern developing; the plus and minus signs keep "flipping". If the order of the derivative is even, then $y^{(n)}(x) = ce^{-x} = y(x)$, because this is how $y(x)$ is defined here. On the other hand, if n is odd, then $y^{(n)}(x) = -ce^{-x} = -y(x)$. These two equations may be written compactly as one equation, namely,

$$y^{(n)}(x) = (-1)^n y(x)$$

for any integer value of n.

In these two examples we started out with a function and found a differential equation satisfied by it. Normally this can be a hard task in itself, but harder still is the task of working out the "inverse" of this problem.

The Main Problem

We are given a differential equation for some unknown function y and then **we are asked to actually find y explicitly.**

This is the central problem in the field of differential equations, and it is the hardest one! Most of the time we are happy just to be able to *approximate* this unknown function y so that we can infer some of its properties.

By the **general solution** of a differential equation of order n we mean a solution which has the property that it contains every solution of the same equation for particular choices of **parameters** appearing in it. Think of a parameter as just another variable representing some unspecified number. For example, the general solution of the equation $y'(x) = y(x)$ is given by $y(x) = c\,e^x$ where c is an arbitrary constant. every solution of this equation (regardless of how you find it) must agree with a particular choice of the parameter, c, in the general solution just written. For example, $y(x) = 3\,e^x$ is a solution, $y(x) = 0.6721\,e^x$ is another solution, while $y(x) = -\pi\,e^x$ ($\pi = 3.1415926...$) is yet another solution. Each one of these "special looking " solutions is given the name of **particular solution**.

FACT

It is known that the general (classical) solution of an ordinary differential equation of order n must contain n parameters. On the other hand, any solution which contains n arbitrary parameters can be used as the general solution.

This statement is believable because the procedure begins with a derivative of order n of some unkown function and winds up with the an explicit representation of the function we want. So, it looks like we took a whole bunch of antiderivatives, right? (Remember the Fundamental Theorem of Calculus!). But whenever we take the antiderivative of a function, we add a constant of integration, so if we take n antiderivatives then we should have n generic constants lying around. Of course, this is not a proof of the fact but it does make it credible.

Example 477. Show that the expression $y(x) = c_1 \cos x + c_2 \sin x$, where c_1, c_2 are parameters, satisfies the equation $y''(x) + y(x) = 0$.

Solution We know that the derivatives of $y(x) = c_1 \cos x + c_2 \sin x$ are given by

$$
\begin{aligned}
y'(x) &= -c_1 \sin x + c_2 \cos x \\
y''(x) &= -c_1 \cos x - c_2 \sin x = -y(x).
\end{aligned}
$$

The last line tells us that $y''(x) + y(x) = 0$, which is what we wanted to show. Actually, it can be shown that our y, as defined above, is the general solution of the differential equation $y''(x) + y(x) = 0$. This means that no matter how hard you try, you won't be able to find another solution of the equation $y''(x) + y(x) = 0$ which doesn't look like $y(x) = c_1 \cos x + c_2 \sin x$ for some choice of the constants c_1, c_2!

Example 478. Show that $y(x) = c_1 e^{kx}$ where k, c_1 are parameters satisfies the equation $y'(x) = ky(x)$, for any value of x.

Solution This expression for y also represents the general solution of the equation $y'(x) = ky(x)$. For example,

$$
\begin{aligned}
y(x) &= c_1 e^{kx} \\
y'(x) &= kc_1 e^{kx} = ky(x)
\end{aligned}
$$

Now, how important is the interval in which the independent variable x resides? Well, it's very important because **a solution on one interval may not be a solution on a slightly larger interval!**.

Example 479. Show that if $0 < x < \infty$, then $y(x) = x|x|$ (x times its absolute value) is a solution of the differential equation $y''(x) = 2$ but if $-1 < x < \infty$, then y is not a solution.

Solution Recall that a (classical) solution has the property that it must have continuous derivatives up to the order of the equation itself, which, in this case, is 2 (the order of the equation). When $0 < x < \infty$, we know that $|x| = x$ and so $y(x) = x^2$. This function has continuous second order derivatives and $y''(x) = 2$ and this answers the first part of the question.

On the other hand, if $-1 < x < 0$, then $|x| = -x$ so that $y(x) = -x^2$ for such x's. But if $0 < x < \infty$, $|x| = x$ and $y(x) = x^2$. So, we have shown that

$$y(x) = \begin{cases} x^2, & \text{if } 0 \leq x < \infty, \\ -x^2, & \text{if } -1 < x < 0, \end{cases}$$

It follows that $y''_-(0) = -2$ and $y''_+(0) = 2$. This means that $y''(0)$ does not exist and so, by definition, y cannot be a solution of this equation on any interval to the left of $x = 0$.

Let's say a motorcycle is moving at a speed of 30 *mph* and I ask you "Where is it after 10 seconds?" You'd probably say, "Well, I can't tell you" and you would be right! The point is, as you know, that *you need to know where the motorcycle is/was at* the moment I'm asking you the question, right? We call this an **initial condition**. In our case, the initial condition would be something like, "The motorcycle is at the corner of 1st and 2nd and proceeding East ...". Since speed is the derivative of distance we see that the mathematical statement $s'(t) = 30$ reflects the content of the opening paragraph here. But this is also a first-order differential equation for the unknown function $s(t)$, which gives the position at time t! Note that t is the independent variable here. So, let's say we are given, in addition to this, a mathematical condition like $s(0) = 0$ (where the 0 on the right of this equation means we're at the corner of 1st and 2nd), along with some direction, East, say, then we could determine its position at a later time if we assumed that the motorcycle proceeded in a straight line... Good.

> An **initial value problem** or **Cauchy problem**, pronounced "co-shee", is a differential equation along with some specified initial condition(s).

This example tells us something really important about differential equations, in general. We need a specific initial condition (the number of such conditions always depends on the order) in order to even HOPE that there will be a unique solution (or only one solution). It's even a little more complicated than this! Even if we DO have an initial condition, we cannot *guarantee* the uniqueness of the solution, (see the margin for an example). But, if we assume that some kind of Existence Theorem is lurking in the background, then yes, the initial value problem will have a unique solution. These, so-called, Existence Theorems, give us conditions under which we can guarantee that such and such an initial value problem will have a unique solution!

Now, if we don't have an initial condition we'll be in trouble. In other words, there will be an *infinite number* of solutions and, if we are dealing with, say, the position of a satellite around the earth, we're going to have a problem finding out where it really is, unless we are told where it is/was at some specified time! So, physically speaking, **initial conditions go hand-in-hand with differential equations**.

> **Initial value problems always lead to systems of equations** which need to be solved simultaneously for the values of the parameters appearing in the general solution

Example 480. Find the solution of the initial value problem $y(0) = 10$ associated with the equation $y'(x) = ky(x)$ in Example 478.

Solution We know that the general solution is given by $y(x) = ce^{kx}$ where c is a parameter and k is as in the equation. Since we want $y(0) = 10$ it follows that

$10 = y(0) = ce^0 = c$ from which we get $c = 10$. Replacing c in the general solution by 10 we get the desired solution which is $y(x) = 10e^{kx}$.

Example 481. Find the solution of the initial value problem $y(0) = 0, y'(0) = 1$ associated with the equation $y''(x) + y(x) = 0$ in Example 477.

Solution Note that there are two initial conditions (because the equation is of order 2). Furthermore, since the general solution is given by $y(x) = c_1 \cos x + c_2 \sin x$, and this is true for any value of x, we simply have to determine the quantities c_1, c_2. So, we use the initial conditions as follows ...

$$
\begin{aligned}
y(0) &= c_1 \cos(0) + c_2 \sin(0) = 0, \\
y'(0) &= -c_1 \sin(0) + c_2 \cos(0) = 1,
\end{aligned}
$$

which gives us immediately that $c_1 = 0, c_2 = 1$ (since $\cos(0) = 1$ and $\sin(0) = 0$). The required solution is given by setting these values of c_1, c_2 into the general solution. So, we find

$$
\begin{aligned}
y(x) &= c_1 \cos x + c_2 \sin x \\
&= 0 \cdot \cos x + 1 \cdot \sin x \\
&= \sin x.
\end{aligned}
$$

We have shown that the solution satisfying the equation $y''(x) + y(x) = 0$ and the initial conditions $y(0) = 0, y'(0) = 1$ is given by $y(x) = \sin x$.

> **You can always check your answer** by working backwards and differentiating your proposed solution and checking the initial conditions, just like when you checked your solution to an indefinite integral!

For example, the function $y(x) = \sin x$ clearly satisfies the equation $y''(x) + y(x) = 0$ and the initial conditions $y(0) = 0, y'(0) = 1$. Furthermore, it is the *only* solution satisfying this equation and the initial conditions! In other words, the solution of this initial value problem is *unique*.

NOTES:

The fact that **initial value problems have only one solution** is not to be taken for granted, as this fact comes under the heading of a **Uniqueness Theorem** for differential equations. It is necessary that we have unique solutions to initial value problems for physical reasons but remember that there are initial value problems which do not have a unique (or only one) solution. For example, the initial value problem $y(0) = 0$ associated with the equation $y'(t) = \sqrt{y(t)}$ on the interval $0 \leq t < \infty$ has the solutions $y(t) = 0$, the solution which is identically or always zero, and another solution given by $y(t) = t^2/4$. Can you find any more?

Exercise Set 47.

Verify that each given function satisfies the associated differential equation. Treat the c-values as unspecified constants.

1. $y(x) = 3e^x$, $\quad (1-x)y''(x) + xy'(x) - y(x) = 0$
2. $y(x) = 2e^x - 0.652e^{-x}$, $\quad y''(x) - y(x) = 0$
3. $y(x) = 2\sin x$, $\quad y^{(4)}(x) - y(x) = 0$
4. $y(x) = ce^{3x} - e^{2x}$, $\quad y'(x) - 3y(x) = e^{2x}$
5. $y(x) = c_1 x^2 + c_2 x + c_3$, $\quad y'''(x) = 0$,

Determine whether the given functions are solutions of the stated initial value problems. Answer with a Yes or No and give reasons.

6. $y(x) = e^x - e^{-x}$, $\quad y''(x) - y(x) = 0$, $\quad y(0) = 0, y'(0) = 1$
7. $y(x) = e^x + e^{-x}$, $\quad y'(x) = y(x)$, $\quad y(0) = 1$
8. $y(x) = e^{2x} - e^{-2x}$, $\quad y''(x) - 4y(x) = 0$, $\quad y(0) = 0, y'(0) = 2$
9. $y(x) = \sin x + \cos x$, $\quad y''(x) + y(x) = 0$, $\quad y(0) = 0, y'(0) = 1$
10. $y(x) = x^2$, $\quad y'''(x) = 0$, $\quad y(0) = 0, y'(0) = 0, y''(0) = 3$

Find the solution of the following initial value problems given the corresponding general solution. Find the c-values.

11. $y''(x) - 2y'(x) + y(x) = 0$, $\quad y(x) = (c_1 + c_2 x)e^x$, $\quad y(0) = 1, y'(0) = 0$
12. $y'(t) = y(t)^2/t^2$, $\quad y(t) = t/(1+ct)$, $\quad y(1) = -1$
13. $y'''(x) = 24x$, $\quad y(x) = x^4 + c_1 x^2/2 + c_2 x + c_3$, $y(0) = 0, y'(0) = 0, y''(0) = 0$
14. $y'(t) = 4t - 2ty(t)$, $\quad y(t) = ce^{-t^2} + 2$, $\quad y(0) = -2$
15. $y''(x) - xe^{-x} = 0$, $\quad y(x) = c_1 + c_2 x + (x+2)e^{-x}$, $\quad y(1) = 0, y'(1) = 1$

Suggested Homework Set 36. *Do problems 1, 3, 6, 8, 10, 11, 13, 14*

NOTES:

9.2   First-order Separable Equations

The simplest of all differential equations of the first-order is known as a **separable equation**. Its uses are widespread and include the basic **Law of Growth and Decay** (dealt with briefly in Chapter 4), which appear in population biology, radiocarbon dating, etc. We'll have a look at some of these examples in the next section.

A separable equation has the simple form

$$y'(x) \quad = \quad \frac{dy}{dx} = \text{(terms in } x) \text{ (terms in } y), \quad x \text{ in I}, \qquad (9.1)$$

$$y'(x) \quad = \quad f(x)\, g(y), \quad x \text{ in } I, \qquad (9.2)$$

$$y'(x) \quad = \quad f(x)\, g(y(x)), \quad x \text{ in } I, \qquad (9.3)$$

where f, g are both functions of one variable, $g(y(x)) \neq 0$ is a composition of two functions, and x is in some given interval, I. Note that y is a function of x when we find a solution (i.e., y is a dependent variable), but when we write the equation (9.2), g is to be considered a function of y (i.e., so that now y is an independent variable). This interplay between y being a dependent and an independent variable looks mysterious, doesn't it? Don't worry about it. We do it all the time when we work with differential equations even though we know that, strictly speaking, this is wrong (even though we get the right answer ultimately).

An example of a separable equation is given by $y'(x) = y(x)^2/x^2$ because it can be written in the form of equation (9.2). Note that we can choose $f(x) = 1/x^2$ and $g(y) = y^2$ here.

The functions f, g may even be constant so that equations of the form

$$y'(x) = f(x)\, c \quad \text{or} \quad y'(x) = c\, g(y(x)), \qquad (9.4)$$

where c is a parameter (or a constant), are also separable.

Now change the name of the independent variable, x, in equation (9.2) to t, say. We do this a lot in the area of differential equations so that we don't get the $x's$ mixed up. After all, the x appearing in an indefinite integral is a *free variable* and so can be denoted by any symbol. We get,

$$y'(t) = f(t)\, g(y(t)),$$

and so dividing by $g(y(t))$ and integrating over the interval $[a, x]$, where a is given and a, x are some points in the interval I, we find

$$\frac{1}{g(y(t))}\, y'(t) \quad = \quad f(t),$$

$$\int_a^x \frac{1}{g(y(t))}\, y'(t)\, dt \quad = \quad \int_a^x f(t)\, dt.$$

Now we use the Substitution Rule with $u = y(t)$ on the left. Then $t = a$ corresponds to $u = y(a)$ while $t = x$ corresponds to $u = y(x)$ in the new limits of integration. Thus,

$$\int_a^x f(t)\, dt \quad = \quad \int_a^x \frac{1}{g(y(t))}\, y'(t)\, dt,$$

$$= \quad \int_{y(a)}^{y(x)} \frac{1}{g(u)}\, du,$$

and the unknown function $y(x)$ appears in the limit of the integral. So, we have just shown that the **general solution of equation (9.2) is given implicitly by**

$$\int_{y(a)}^{y(x)} \frac{1}{g(u)} \, du = \int_a^x f(t) \, dt \qquad (9.5)$$

because we may not always be able to solve for y in terms of x explicitly! You'll see this in the examples below.

Example 482. Find the general solution of the separable equation

$$\frac{dy}{dx} = \frac{x^2}{y \, e^y},$$

and then find the solution of the initial value problem where $y(0) = 1$.

Solution Here $f(x) = x^2$ while $g(y) = 1/(ye^y)$. Using equation (9.5) we obtain the form of the general solution, that is, since $g(u) = 1/(ue^u)$, and $f(t) = t^2$,

$$
\begin{aligned}
\int_a^x t^2 \, dt &= \int_{y(a)}^{y(x)} ue^u \, du, \\
\left. \frac{t^3}{3} \right|_a^x &= \left. (ue^u - e^u) \right|_{y(a)}^{y(x)}, \\
\frac{x^3}{3} - \frac{a^3}{3} &= \left(y(x) \, e^{y(x)} - e^{y(x)} \right) - \left(y(a) \, e^{y(a)} - e^{y(a)} \right),
\end{aligned}
$$

where we used a simple integration by parts on the right. Combining all the constant terms involving the values $a, y(a)$ into a single quantity which we call C we get the general solution in the form

EXAMPLES

$$
\begin{aligned}
\frac{x^3}{3} &= \left(y(x) \, e^{y(x)} - e^{y(x)} \right) \underbrace{- \left(y(a) \, e^{y(a)} - e^{y(a)} \right) + \frac{a^3}{3}}, \\
\frac{x^3}{3} &= \left(y(x) \, e^{y(x)} - e^{y(x)} \right) + \qquad C.
\end{aligned}
$$

As you can see it isn't easy to solve for the quantity $y(x)$ explicitly in the last equation so this is why we say that this represents the general solution in implicit form. It can also be written more compactly as

$$\frac{x^3}{3} = (y \, e^y - e^y) + C,$$

where the dependence of y on the independent variable x is suppressed. As such it becomes an implicit relation and it defines y as a function of x under some conditions (derived from a general result called the *Implicit Function Theorem*), which we won't study here but which can be found in books on *Advanced Calculus*.

Finally, the solution of the initial value problem is given by setting $y = 1$ when $x = 0$ into the general solution, above (because we are given that $y(0) = 1$), and solving for C. This gives $\frac{0^3}{3} = \left(1 \, e^1 - e^1 \right) + C$, or $0 = e - e + C$ which forces $C = 0$. We now substitute this value of C into the general solution to find that the solution of the required initial value problem is given implicitly by

$$\frac{x^3}{3} = (y \, e^y - e^y).$$

These steps in finding the (general) solution of a separable equation can be summarized in Table 9.1.

1. Identify the functions f, g in equation (9.2) explicitly

2. Set up the general solution in the form of equation (9.5) or

$$\int_{y(a)}^{y(x)} \frac{1}{g(u)} \, du = \int_{a}^{x} f(t) \, dt$$

3. Evaluate the integrals in terms of x and y

4. Write the answer to your evaluation in implicit form

5. Use the initial condition $y(a) = b$ in the form $y = b$ when $x = a$ to find C

6. Substitute C into the general solution to give the solution of the initial value problem.

Table 9.1: Finding the General Solution of a Separable Equation

Example 483. Find the general solution of the equation $\dfrac{dy}{dx} = \dfrac{1+y^2}{1+x^2}$.

Solution We use the steps in Table 9.1, above. A glance at the equation shows that $f(x) = 1/(1+x^2)$ while $g(y) = 1+y^2$. Since the interval is not specified here we will assume that $I = (-\infty, +\infty)$. Next, the general solution can now be set up as

$$\int_{y(a)}^{y(x)} \frac{1}{1+u^2} \, du = \int_{a}^{x} \frac{1}{1+t^2} \, dt,$$

right? Recall that the antiderivatives of each of these functions are 'Arctangents' so we'll get

For any two angles A, B,

$$\tan(A+B) = \frac{\tan(A) + \tan(B)}{1 - \tan(A)\tan(B)}.$$

Now set $A = \text{Arctan}(x), B = C$ and simplify.

Figure 235.

$$
\begin{aligned}
\text{Arctan}(u)\big|_{y(a)}^{y(x)} &= \text{Arctan}(t)\big|_{a}^{x}, \\
\text{or, } \text{Arctan}(y(x)) &= \text{Arctan}(y(a)) + \text{Arctan}(x) - \text{Arctan}(a), \\
&= \text{Arctan}(x) + \underbrace{\text{Arctan}(y(a)) - \text{Arctan}(a)}, \\
&= \text{Arctan}(x) + \qquad C,
\end{aligned}
$$

which we can write as $\text{Arctan}(y) = \text{Arctan}(x) + C$, where C is some unspecified constant or parameter (determined only by an initial condition, as usual). In this case, we can actually solve for y in terms of x using the property "$\tan(\text{Arctan}(\square)) = \square$" of the Arctan function (with $\square = y$), and a "tan-sum" relation from Trigonometry (see Figure 235). We'll find,

$$y = \frac{x + \tan(C)}{1 - x \cdot \tan(C)}$$

where C and so $\tan(C)$, are determined by one initial condition. For example, if we want $y(0) = -1$ then $\tan(C) = -1$, why? It follows that the solution of this initial value problem is given by $y(x) = (x-1)/(x+1)$, an answer which can be checked by differentiation thereby ensuring that it satisfies the original equation of this example.

Example 484. Solve the equation $y' = x^2 y + x^2 + y + 1$.

Solution Sometimes we **have to re-arrange terms and fiddle a little to get things in the right form**. This is one such instance. Factoring y we find $x^2 y + y + x^2 + 1 = y(x^2 + 1) + (x^2 + 1) = (y + 1)(x^2 + 1)$. So, the right-hand side of the equation can be factored into a product of a function of x and a function of y, namely, $f(x) = (x^2 + 1)$ and $g(y) = (y + 1)$. Using Table 9.1 we find

$$\int_{y(a)}^{y(x)} \frac{1}{g(u)}\, du = \int_a^x f(t)\, dt,$$

$$\int_{y(a)}^{y(x)} \frac{1}{u+1}\, du = \int_a^x (t^2 + 1)\, dt,$$

$$\ln\left|\frac{y(x)+1}{y(a)+1}\right| = \frac{x^3}{3} + x - \underbrace{\left(\frac{a^3}{3} + a\right)},$$

$$= \frac{x^3}{3} + x + \quad C.$$

Taking the exponential of both sides of the last equation and re-arranging terms we get

$$|y(x) + 1| = |y(a) + 1|\, e^{\frac{x^3}{3} + x + C},$$

$$= |y(a) + 1| e^C\, e^{\frac{x^3}{3} + x},$$

$$= C_1\, e^{\frac{x^3}{3} + x},$$

where $C_1 = |y(a) + 1|\, e^C = |y(a) + 1|\, e^{-\left(\frac{a^3}{3} + a\right)}$ is another constant. So, the general solution looks like

$$|y + 1| = C_1\, e^{\frac{x^3}{3} + x}$$

where the absolute value is removed in the normal manner (if need be; see Chapter 1).

For example, if we are interested in solutions which have the property that $y(x) \geq 0$ then $|y + 1| = y + 1$ and we can solve for y explicitly. On the other hand, if we want solutions with $y(x) < -1$ then $|y + 1| = -(y + 1)$ and we can again solve for y without difficulty. The quantity C_1 is found as usual (by means of some initial condition).

SNAPSHOTS

Example 485. Solve the initial value problem

$$y'(x) = \frac{\cos(2x)}{3y^2}, \quad y(0) = 1.$$

Solution Let $f(x) = \cos(2x), g(y) = 1/(3y^2)$, and set $a = 0$ because we are given that $y(0) = 1$. Then (cf., Table 9.1), the general solution is given implicitly by the equation (remember to 'flip' the g−term on the left in the integrand),

$$\int_{y(0)}^{y(x)} 3u^2\, du = \int_0^x \cos(2t)\, dt,$$

$$\int_1^{y(x)} 3u^2\, du = \int_0^x \cos(2t)\, dt,$$

$$u^3\Big|_1^{y(x)} = \frac{\sin(2t)}{2}\Big|_0^x,$$

$$y(x)^3 - 1 \;=\; \frac{\sin(2x)}{2},$$

or explicitly by

$$y(x) = \left(1 + \frac{\sin(2x)}{2}\right)^{1/3}.$$

SHORTCUT

When the initial value $y(a)$ is given ahead of time, we can use equation (9.5) directly and "by-pass" the calculation of the constant C in the general solution as it is "built-into" the equation (9.5) itself, as in Example 485.

Checking your answer: When you find an implicit solution you can always check your answer by differentiating it and seeing if the resulting derivatives all satisfy the differential equation. When you check your answer, bear in mind that **you'll be using the Chain Rule** a lot ...

In fact, you should:

• Check the initial condition first, *i.e.*, Make sure that $y(a) = b$ for your candidate function y.

• Check the equation next, *i.e.*, Your function should satisfy the differential equation.

Example 486. Solve the initial value problem

$$y' = x\, e^{y-x}, \quad y(0) = 2.$$

Solution Yet another separable equation *in disguise*! Re-arranging terms we find $y' = x\, e^{y}\, e^{-x} = x\, e^{-x}\, e^{y} = f(x)g(y)$, if we choose $f(x) = x\, e^{-x}$, $g(y) = e^{y}$. So, integration by parts on the right integral gives

$$\begin{aligned}
\int_{y(0)=2}^{y(x)} e^{-u}\, du &= \int_0^x t\, e^{-t}\, dt,\\
-e^{-u}\Big|_2^{y(x)} &= \left(-t\, e^{-t} - e^{-t}\right)\Big|_0^x,\\
-e^{-y(x)} + e^{-2} &= \left(-x\, e^{-x} - e^{-x}\right) - (0-1),\\
e^{-y(x)} &= e^{-2} - \left(-x\, e^{-x} - e^{-x}\right) - 1.
\end{aligned}$$

This last expression can be simplified further through the use of the natural logarithm. Thus, suppressing the x's for clarity we see that

$$y = -\ln\left(e^{-2} + x\, e^{-x} + e^{-x} - 1\right).$$

NOTE: As a check, let's verify that the answer we obtained in Example 486 is the right one! First, the easiest thing to check is the initial condition, if this doesn't work out, there's a mistake somewhere, so stop and review your problem. In this case, $y = 2$ when $x = 0$ should hold, does it? Let's see.

Checking the answer to Example 486.

We figured out that $y = -\ln\left(e^{-2} + x\,e^{-x} + e^{-x} - 1\right)$, or, equivalently, that $e^{-y} = e^{-2} + x\,e^{-x} + e^{-x} - 1$. So, if we set $x = 0$ into this we find $y = -\ln\left(e^{-2} + 0 + 1 - 1\right) = -\ln(e^{-2}) = (-)(-2)\,\ln(e) = 2 \cdot 1 = 2$. Good. This is the first hurdle. Now, what about the equation? Well, it looks like $y = -\ln(\square)$ where $\square = e^{-2} + x\,e^{-x} + e^{-x} - 1$. By the Chain Rule we know that

$$y'(x) = -\frac{d}{dx}\ln(\square) = -\frac{1}{\square}\frac{d\square}{dx}.$$

Now,

$$\frac{d\square}{dx} = 0 - x\,e^{-x} + e^{-x} - e^{-x} - 0 = -x\,e^{-x},$$

so that

$$
\begin{aligned}
y'(x) &= -\frac{1}{\square}\frac{d\square}{dx}, \\
&= \frac{(-)(-)x\,e^{-x}}{e^{-2} + x\,e^{-x} + e^{-x} - 1}, \\
&= \frac{x\,e^{-x}}{e^{-y}}, \\
&= x\,e^{y}\,e^{-x}, \\
&= x\,e^{y-x},
\end{aligned}
$$

and this last equality gives the same equation as the original one. So we have verified that our solution is correct!

Remember that **the derivative of "log box" is "one over box Dee-box"**, like the sneakers!

Example 487. Solve the initial value problem

$$x^2 y'(x) + y(x) = 0, \quad y(1) = 1.$$

Solution This is really a separable equation *in disguise*! Actually, we can re-arrange terms and find that if $x \neq 0$, then $y'(x) = -y/x^2$. So, we can choose $f(x) = 1/x^2, g(y) = -y$ (and don't forget the minus sign here ...). As before, we get

$$
\begin{aligned}
\int_{y(1)}^{y(x)} -\frac{1}{u}\,du &= \int_{1}^{x} \frac{1}{t^2}\,dt, \\
-\int_{1}^{y(x)} \frac{1}{u}\,du &= \int_{1}^{x} t^{-2}\,dt, \\
-\ln|u|\,\Big|_1^{y(x)} &= -\frac{1}{t}\Big|_1^{x}, \\
-\ln|y(x)| &= -\frac{1}{x} + 1, \\
\ln|y(x)| &= \frac{1}{x} - 1, \\
|y(x)| &= e^{\frac{1}{x}-1}.
\end{aligned}
$$

Since $y(1) = 1$, and y is continuous there, it follows that $y(x)$ must be positive near $x = 1$, so we must have $y(x) = e^{\frac{1}{x}-1}$.

We use the special integration (antiderivative) fomula from Chapter 4, namely,

$$\int \frac{d\square}{\square} = \ln|\square| + C.,$$

where $\square \neq 0$.

Example 488. Solve the initial value problem

$$y'(x) - \sin x\, y(x) = 0, \quad y(0) = -1.$$

Solution This is another separable equation *incognito*! Re-arranging terms we find $y' = \sin x \, y(x)$. So, we can choose $f(x) = \sin x$, $g(y) = y$. Then,

$$\int_{y(0)}^{y(x)} \frac{1}{u} \, du = \int_0^x \sin t \, dt,$$

$$\int_{-1}^{y(x)} \frac{1}{u} \, du = -\cos t \big|_0^x,$$

$$\ln|u|\big|_{-1}^{y(x)} = -\cos x + 1,$$

$$\ln|y(x)| - \ln|-1| = 1 - \cos x,$$

$$\ln|y(x)| = 1 - \cos x,$$

$$|y(x)| = e^{1-\cos x}.$$

Now, since $y(0) = -1$, $y(x)$ must be negative near $x = 0$, so we must have $y(x) = -e^{1-\cos x}$.

Exercise Set 48.

Find the solution of the given initial value problems.

1. $y' = (4 + y^2)/(1 - x^2)$, $y(0) = 1$

2. $y' = x^2 e^{x-y}$, $y(0) = -1$

3. $xy' - xy = y$, $y(1) = 1$

4. $y' = (\cos x) \, y^3$, $y(0) = -2$

5. $y' = xy e^{x^2}$, $y(0) = \sqrt{e}$, $e = 2.71828...$

6. $y' = 2y^{2/3}$, $y(0) = 8$

7. $y' = x \, \sin x^2$, $y(\sqrt{\pi}) = 0$, $\pi = 3.14159...$

8. $xy' = 6x$, $y(-1) = -6$

9.3   Laws of Growth and Decay

One of the most important special types of separable equations is one that includes a **Law of Growth and Decay**, (see Chapter 4) for an earlier discussion of this material). These are separable equations of the form

$$\frac{dN(t)}{dt} = kN(t), \tag{9.6}$$

where $t \geq 0$ is the time variable, k is a parameter, and $N(t)$ represents the amount of "something" (population, radioactive material, interest owing on a loan etc) at time t. Think of $N(t)$ as meaning "the Number of something at time t", (N for Number, t for time). Now, the original equation (9.6) is equivalent to $N'(t) = kN(t)$ and so its general solution is given either by dividing throughout by $N(t)$ and then integrating, or setting $N = y$ and $t = x$ in equation (9.2) and solving. Take your pick! We'll stick with the previous concept of **pattern recognition** and reduce our problem to something we can recognize immediately! Note that we can write equation (9.6) in the equivalent form $y'(x) = ky(x)$ or $y' = ky$. Here, $f(x) = k, g(y) = y$ and so the general solution is given by equation (9.5). In this case, it becomes (try it, it's easy) $y(x) = y(0) \, e^{kx}$ or, in terms of the original variables N, t, the general solution of (9.6) looks like

$$N(t) = N(0) \, e^{kt}. \tag{9.7}$$

The interpretation is this: If a quantity grows or decays at an (instantaneous) rate which is proportional to the amount present at any time t, then that quantity satisfies a Law of Growth or a Law of Decay. These assumptions are closely verified for a wide variety of physical phenomena. We'll see some examples below.

Observations:

In a **Law of Growth**, $k > 0$, while in a **Law of Decay**, $k < 0$. Note that the case $k = 0$ is a limiting case where the quantity remains constant. Furthermore,

$$\lim_{t \to \infty} N(t) = \begin{cases} +\infty, & \text{if } k > 0, \\ 0, & \text{if } k < 0, \\ N(0), & \text{if } k = 0. \end{cases}$$

Example 489. The rate at which bacteria multiply is proportional to the instantaneous amount present at any time. If the original number doubles in two hours, in how many hours will it quadruple (or be "four" times the original amount)?

Solution This Law is one of growth: This is because of the statement that "the original number doubles ... ". Thus $N(t)$, where t is in hours, is the amount of bacteria present at time "t" and it is given by equation (9.7) where $N(0), k$ are appropriate constants. If we let $N(0)$ be the original amount (or at time $t = 0$) then we are given that $N(2) = 2 \cdot N(0)$, okay? (Because the amount after $t = 2$ hours is double the amount at $t = 0$). We are being asked to find a value of the time "t" such that $N(t) = 4 \cdot N(0)$, right?

Now, we substitute $t = 2$ into the expression for $N(t)$ and equate this to $2 \cdot N(0)$ to find that $2 = e^{2k}$, or $k = \ln(2)/2$. Using the power properties of the exponential function, we see that this means that

$$\begin{aligned} N(t) &= N(0) \cdot e^{\frac{\ln(2)}{2}t}, \\ &= N(0) \cdot \left(e^{\ln(2)}\right)^{\frac{t}{2}}, \\ &= N(0) \cdot 2^{\frac{t}{2}}. \end{aligned}$$

Finally, we want a value of "t" such that $4 \cdot N(0) = N(t) = N(0) \cdot 2^{t/2}$. Since $N(0) \neq 0$, we find $4 = 2^{t/2}$, which we can solve for t, as follows:

$$\begin{aligned} 4 &= 2^{t/2}, \\ \ln(4) &= \ln(2^{t/2}), \\ &= \frac{t}{2} \cdot \ln(2), \end{aligned}$$

which gives us a quadrupling time of

$$t = 2 \cdot \frac{\ln(4)}{\ln(2)} = 2 \cdot \frac{2 \ln(2)}{\ln(2)} = 4 \text{ hours.}$$

If you think about it, this conclusion is almost obvious from the given data.

In many peaceful (*i.e.*, non-military-related) applications of radioactivity to our daily lives there arises the notion of the **half-life** of a radionuclide (radioactive isotope of something or other). Since radioactivity is a process by which the amount of isotope is reduced, it makes sense to define a measure of this decomposition. This is commonly called the *half-life* of the material. By definition, the half-life of a radionuclide is a unit of time which describes the amount of time required for *exactly* one-half of the original amount to be present after radioactive decay. For example, if a radio-isotope has a half-life of 5000 years, then it will take 5000 years for one gram of this substance to reduce to one-half gram, another 5000 years for this one-half gram to reduce to one-quarter gram, another 5000 years for this one-quarter gram to reduce to one-eighth gram and so on. In sum it would take $15,000$ years for 1 gram of this radioactive compound to become one-eighth gram.

Half-life of Radio-isotopes

Radionuclide	Half-life
Kr^{87}	1.27 hrs
Sr^{89}	50.5 days
Co^{60}	5.27 yrs
Sr^{90}	29.1 yrs
C^{14}	5,700 yrs
Pu^{240}	6,500 yrs
Pu^{239}	24,000 yrs

Radioactive Decay is one process which satisfies a Law of Decay of the type (9.7), with $k < 0$. In this case, k is called the **decay rate**.

Example 490. A radionuclide decays at a rate, N(t), proportional to the instantaneous amount present at any time. If the half-life of radium is T years, determine the amount present after "t" years.

Solution We proceed as in Example 489, above. Let $N(t) = N(0)e^{kt}$. Since $N(T) = N(0)/2$ by assumption, this means that $e^{kT} = 1/2$, right? So, $e^{kt} = e^{kTt/T} = (e^{kT})^{t/T} = (1/2)^{t/T}$. It now follows that after "t" years the amount of material present will be equal to

$$\begin{aligned} N(t) &= N(0)e^{kt}, \\ &= \frac{N(0)}{2^{t/T}}. \end{aligned}$$

As a check, note that this last formula gives us $N(T) = N(0)/2^{(T/T)} = N(0)/2$ which is correct, by definition of the half-life.

Example 491. Find the half-life of a radioactive substance if three-quarters of it is present after 8 hours.

Solution As we are dealing with radioactive decay we can assume a Law of Decay of the form (9.7), with $k < 0$. Furthermore, we are "working backwards", in a sense, as we are looking for the half-life here, and it isn't given.

What we are given is that $N(8) = 3N(0)/4$, right? And we need to find that value of "t" (call it "T", the half-life) such that $N(T) = N(0)/2$, by definition. So, we start, as usual, with $N(t) = N(0) e^{kt}$ and substitute $t = 8$ into the left-side, equate it to $3N(0)/4$ and simplify the result. You'll find $3/4 = e^{8k}$, or, by definition of the logarithm, $k = (1/8) \ln(3/4)$. Thus,

$$\begin{aligned} N(t) &= N(0) e^{kt}, \\ &= N(0) (e^{8k})^{t/8}, \\ &= N(0) \left(\frac{3}{4}\right)^{t/8}, \end{aligned}$$

for any time "t". We have found the Law explicitly but we still don't know the half-life! So, we have to use the definition of the half-life in the the Law we just found. Then we'll get

$$\begin{aligned} N(T) &= \frac{1}{2} N(0), \\ &= N(0) \left(\frac{3}{4}\right)^{T/8}. \end{aligned}$$

Dividing both sides by $N(0)$ and solving for T using "logs", we'll find

$$\begin{aligned} \frac{1}{2} &= \left(\frac{3}{4}\right)^{T/8}, \\ \ln\left(\frac{1}{2}\right) &= \ln\left(\left(\frac{3}{4}\right)^{T/8}\right), \end{aligned}$$

$$= \frac{T}{8} \ln\left(\frac{3}{4}\right),$$

and, finally, solving for T we find,

$$T = \frac{8 \ln(1/2)}{\ln(3/4)},$$

which can be simplified a little by noting that $\ln(1/2) = -\ln(2)$ and $\ln(3/4) = -\ln(4/3)$. Then, the half-life T will be given by

$$T = 8 \frac{\ln(2)}{\ln(4/3)} \approx 19.27 \text{ hours}.$$

Example 492. After two days, 10 grams of a radioactive chemical is present. Three days later there is only 5 grams left. How much of the chemical was present "initially" (*i.e.*, the first day)?

Solution We start with the basic Law of Decay once again, namely, $N(t) = N(0) e^{kt}$, where t is in hours. We know that $N(2) = 10$ from the given information after two days. This means that $10 = N(2) = N(0) e^{2k}$ which gives us the value of k, and this tells us that $10 = N(0) e^{2k}$. Next, we are also given that $N(5) = 5$, because three days "later" than the two already passed, we have 5 grams left. Using the Decay Law again with $t = 5$ means that $5 = N(0) e^{5k}$.

We combine the two equations $10 = N(0) e^{2k}$, and $5 = N(0) e^{5k}$ in the two unknowns, $k, N(0)$ and solve them simultaneously. This can be done in many ways; for example: Dividing the second into the first gives, $2 = e^{2k}e^{-5k} = e^{-3k}$ from which we conclude that

$$k = -\frac{\ln 2}{3}.$$

There is no need to calculate this value of k explicitly using a calculator because this is not what we are asked for. Let's keep going. Now that we have k, let's find $N(0)$ using either equation. For instance,

$$
\begin{aligned}
N(0) &= 10\, e^{-2k}, \\
&= 10\, e^{(-2)(-\frac{\ln 2}{3})}, \\
&= 10\, \left(e^{\ln 2}\right)^{2/3}, \\
&= 10\, 2^{2/3}, \\
&= 10\, \sqrt[3]{4},
\end{aligned}
$$

which gives us the value of $N(0) \approx 15.87$. So, there was approximately 15.87 grams of chemical initially.

Example 493. Cobalt-60 is a radioactive isotope that is used extensively in medical radiology; it has a half-life of 5.27 years. If an initial sample has a mass of $200g$ how many years will it take before 90% of it has decayed?

Solution Let $N(t)$ denote the amount (in grams) of radioactive Cobalt at time t (in years). Then we are given that $N(5.27) = N(0)/2 = 200/2 = 100$, right? The initial sample ($= N(0)$) has a mass of $200g$., and 90% of this is $(0.9)(200) = 180g$.

If there is to be a decay of 90% ($= 180g$) of Cobalt-60 this means that there is only 10% of it "left", i.e., we are looking for a time t where $N(t) = 20$ (as 20 is 10% of 200). We combine our information ... $N(5.27) = 100$, $N(t) = N(0) e^{kt}$, and we want

$$N(t) = \frac{N(0)}{2^{t/T}} \qquad \textbf{The Half-Life Formula}$$

Table 9.2: The Half-Life Formula

$N(t) = 20$ for some time "t". In order to do this, we set $100 = N(5.27) = 200e^{(5.27)k}$ from which we find

$$k = -\frac{\ln 2}{5.27}.$$

Thus, generally,

$$N(t) = \frac{200}{2^{t/5.27}}.$$

Finally, we set $N(t) = 20$ and solve for t as we did many times above, and find that

$$t = \frac{5.27 \ \ln 10}{\ln 2} \approx 17.51 \ \text{years}.$$

Example 494. Plutonium 240 has a half-life of 6500 years. This isotope is extremely toxic (a carcinogen) and is a by-product of nuclear activity. How long would it take for a 1 gram sample of Pu^{240} to decay to 1 microgram?

Solution We know that $N(t)$, the amount of material at time t satisfies the Half-Life Formula, Table 9.2, where T is the half-life and $N(0)$ is the initial amount.

In our case, $T = 6500$ (and all time units will be measured in years). Furthermore, $N(0) = 1$ g. We want a time t when $N(t) = 1$ microgram $= 10^{-6}$ g, right? So, we set

$$
\begin{aligned}
N(t) &= \frac{N(0)}{2^{t/T}}, \quad \text{and so,} \\
10^{-6} &= \frac{1}{2^{t/6500}}, \\
10^{6} &= 2^{t/6500}, \quad \text{(after taking reciprocals),} \\
6 \ \ln 10 &= \frac{t}{6500} \ \ln 2, \quad \text{(after taking ln of both sides),} \\
t &= \frac{6500 \cdot 6 \cdot \ln 10}{\ln 2}, \quad \text{(and where we solved for t),} \\
&= \frac{6500 \cdot 6 \cdot 2.3026}{0.693}, \\
&\approx 129564 \ \text{years.}
\end{aligned}
$$

Exercise Set 49.

Solve the following problems involving rates of growth and decay.

1. The number of viruses in a medium increases from 6000 to 18000 in 2 hours and 30 minutes. Assuming a Law of Growth find a formula for the number of viruses at any time t. What will be the total number of viruses at the end of 5 hours?

2. Find a formula for the amount $N(t)$ of Radium remaining from an initial sample of 50 micrograms (i.e., $50 \times 10^{-6}g$) after t years. How long will it take for the initial sample to be reduced to 20 micrograms? You can assume that the half-life of Radium is about 1600 years.

3. **Newton's Law of Cooling** states that the rate at which an object cools is directly proportional to the difference in temperature between the object and the surrounding medium. Thus, if $T(t)$ is the temperature of the object and T_0 is the temperature (assumed constant) of the surrounding medium, then

$$T'(t) = c\,(T_0 - T(t)), \quad t \geq 0.$$

where c is a constant depending on the composition of the object in question.

a) Show that this equation is separable, and find its general solution.

b) Coffee in a styrofoam cup has been noticed to cool from $90^\circ C$ to $80^\circ C$ in 4 minutes in an auditorium whose temperature is a constant $20^\circ C$. Use Newton's Law of Cooling and the general solution you found in a) to calculate how long it will take for the coffee to reach a temperature of $70^\circ C$ and be drinkable.

- Idea: $T(0) = 90, T(4) = 80, T_0 = 20$. Find c, and then find t such that $T(t) = 70$.

4. **Radiocarbon dating** consists of calculating the amount of $Carbon^{14}$ in a present day sample and determining the age of the sample from the following hypotheses: 1) The amount of $Carbon^{14}$ in the environment has remained constant in the recent past and 2) The rate of radioactive decay of $Carbon^{14}$ is given by a Law of Decay.

a) Given that $Carbon^{14}$ has a half-life of $5,700$ years, find the value of k in equation (9.7) where $N(t)$ is the amount of material after t years and $N(0)$ is the amount of $Carbon^{14}$ in the initial sample (leave your answer in the form of a natural logarithm).

b) What is the age of a sample of Sabertooth Tiger bone in which 90% of the $Carbon^{14}$ has decayed.

- Justify that $N(t) = (0.1) \cdot N(0)$, and solve for t. Note that the "initial amount $N(0)$" cancels out!

5. A bacteria culture consisting of 4000 bacteria triples its size every half-hour. Assuming that the rate of growth of the culture at any time t is proportional to the amount of bacteria present at time t,

a) Find an expression for the number of bacteria present after t hours,

b) Estimate how many bacteria will be present after 20 minutes,

- Careful here. Don't forget to change minutes into hours,

c) When will the global bacteria population reach 50,000?

- You're looking for t such that $N(t) = 50,000$.

6. Let $P(t)$ be the population of the earth at time t, where t is measured in years. Assume that the earth's population changes according to a Law of Growth. If the population of the earth at time $t = 0$ (A.D. 1650) the population was 600 million (i.e., 6×10^8) and that in 1950 its population was 2.8 billion (i.e. 2.8×10^9), in what year will the earth's population reach 25 billion?

- *Hint:* $P(0) = 6 \times 10^8$, $P(300) = 2.8 \times 10^9$, find k and then t such that $P(t) = 25 \times 10^9$.

7. One model of learning asserts that the rate of change of the probability $P(t)$ of mastering a Calculus concept after working out t exercises is roughly proportional to the difference between 1 and $P(t)$, so that,

$$P'(t) = c\,(1 - P(t)).$$

where c is a constant.

a) Show that this equation for $P(t)$ is separable and find its general solution.

b) Assuming that the probability of mastering Calculus is only 0.4 if a student works out only 3 exercises per section of the text, how many exercises must the student work out in order to attain a probability of mastery equal to 0.95?

- *Idea:* You can assume that $P(0) = 0$. Also, $P(3) = 0.4$. Now solve for k and then find t so that $P(t) = 0.95$.

8. The equation of motion of a body moving in free-fall through the air is given by

$$m\frac{dv}{dt} = mg - kv$$

(picture a parachutist here) where $v = v(t)$ is the speed of the body in its descent, g is the acceleration due to gravity and m is its mass. Here k is a constant which reflects air resistance.

Show that if you multiply both sides of the differerential equation for v by $e^{kt/m}$ the new equation is equivalent to a separable equation for the new dependent variable $z(t) = v(t) \cdot e^{kt/m}$. Conclude that its general solution is given by

$$z(t) = \frac{mg}{k}(e^{\frac{kt}{m}} - 1) + v_o,$$

and that the general solution of the original equation is given is given by

$$v(t) = \frac{mg}{k}(1 - e^{\frac{-kt}{m}}) + v_o e^{\frac{-kt}{m}},$$

where v_o is its *initial speed* (is an arbitrary constant). For example, if one is dropping out of an airplane in a parachute we take it that $v_o = 0$. As $t \to \infty$ we see that

$$v(t) \to \frac{mg}{k} = v_\infty,$$

(because $e^{\frac{-kt}{m}} \to 0$ as $t \to \infty$).

This quantity v_∞, called the limiting speed, is the *final* or *maximum* speed of the body just before it reaches the ground. As you can see, v_∞ depends on the mass and the air resistance but does not depend upon the initial speed!

9. Strontium 90 has a half-life of 29.1 years. How long will it take for a 5 gram sample of Sr^{90} to decay to 90% of its original amount?

Suggested Homework Set 37. *Work out numbers 1, 2, 3, 4, 6*

9.4   Using Computer Algebra Systems

Use your favorite Computer Algebra System (CAS), like Maple, MatLab, etc., or even a graphing calculator to answer the following questions.

1. A child drops a rock from rest off a ravine into the creek below. Given that its displacement is given by the relation $y = gt^2/2$ where g, the acceleration due to gravity, is given by $9.8 m/sec^2$, determine how much time it will take for the rock to hit the bottom of the creek $153m$ (meters) below the point of release. (We neglect air resistance here)

2. The equations of motion for a body launched horizontally with an initial vertical velocity, v_{yi}, and an initial horizontal velocity, v_{xi}, are given by

$$x(t) = v_{xi}t, \quad y(t) = v_{yi}t - \frac{1}{2}gt^2$$

where $x(t), y(t)$ denote the coordinates (or the position) (x, y) of the body in the xy-plane at time t. If a rock is thrown with $v_{yi} = 20.4$, $v_{hi} = 34.85$, $g = 9.8$ as before (all units being in meters, sec, etc.), determine the complete trajectory of the rock, *i.e.*,

- How long it takes for the rock to reach its highest point
- The maximum height of the rock
- How far the rock travels
- How long the rock is in the air

As before we neglect air resistance

3. A golf ball is hit at an angle *theta* relative to the ground with a speed v. Neglecting air resistance its motion is described by

$$x(t) = v \cos \theta t, \quad y(t) = v \sin \theta t - \frac{1}{2}gt^2$$

where $x(t), y(t)$ denote the coordinates (or the position) (x, y) of the body in the xy-plane at time t. Here θ is in radians as usual. A golfer drives a golf ball with $\theta = 25^\circ$ and $v = 78 m/sec$. Determine where the ball will land relative to the golfer (neglect any bounces) and how long the ball is in the air.

4. **Virtual golf** may be played in a small room in which there is attached two parallel sensors on the floor a distance d apart. The (real) golf ball hits a canvas screen that (is a really a computer console and) measures its angle of elevation θ (in the preceding exercise) depending on where the ball strikes the screen. The speed of the ball is measured simply by timing the ball's trajectory across the two sensors. The ball's motion can then be recaptured from the preceding exercise. In this way you avoid walking, rain, heat, etc and virtual golf has become a new pass time.

   Show that if θ is known, then the (initial) speed of the ball is given by $v = \sec \theta / T$ where T is the travel time delay between the two sensors (picked up by the computer). If $\theta = 34.65^\circ$ and $T = 0.043sec$, determine the range of the ball on the virtual course.

5. A simplified but effective equation of motion for a rocket of mass $M(t)$ that takes off vertically is given by

$$M(t)\frac{dv}{dt} = -M(t)g - v_{exhaust}\frac{dM}{dt}$$

where g is the acceleration due to gravity and $v_{exhaust}$ is the speed of the exhaust. Find the general solution $v(t)$ of this differential equation as a function of M and the other quantities. At burn-out time (*i.e.,* when the fuel has run out) the mass $M(t) = M_0 - M_{fuel}$ where M_0 is the initial mass of the rocket before lift-off and M_{fuel} is the mass of its fuel. Using this, find a formula for the burn-out velocity. If $v_{exhaust} = 3500m/sec$, $M_0 = 6450kg$ and $M_{fuel} = 3059kg$ find the value of the burn-out velocity.

Chapter 10

Appendix A: Review of Exponents and Radicals

In this section we review the basic laws governing exponents and radicals. This material is truly necessary for a manipulating fundamental expressions in Calculus. We recall that if $a > 0$ is any real number and r is a positive integer, the symbol a^r is shorthand for the product of a with itself r-times. That is, $a^r = a \cdot a \cdot a \cdots a$, where there appears r a's on the right. Thus, $a^3 = a \cdot a \cdot a$ while $a^5 = a \cdot a \cdot a \cdot a \cdot a$, etc. By definition we will always take it that $a^0 = 1$, regardless of the value of a, so long as it is not equal to zero, and $a^1 = a$ for any a.

Generally if $r, s \geq 0$ are any two non-negative real numbers and $a, b > 0$, then the Laws of Exponents say that

$$a^r \cdot a^s = a^{r+s} \tag{10.1}$$

$$(a^r)^s = a^{r \cdot s}, \qquad (a^r)^{-s} = a^{-r \cdot s} \tag{10.2}$$

$$(ab)^r = a^r \cdot b^r \tag{10.3}$$

$$\left(\frac{a}{b}\right)^r = \frac{a^r}{b^r} \tag{10.4}$$

$$\frac{a^r}{a^s} = a^{r-s}. \tag{10.5}$$

The Laws of Radicals are similar. They differ only from the Laws of Exponents in their representation using *radical* symbols rather than powers. For example, if $p, q > 0$ are integers, and we interpret the symbol $a^{\frac{p}{q}}$ as the q-th root of the number a to the power of p, *i.e.*,

$$a^{\frac{p}{q}} = \sqrt[q]{a^p} = \left(\sqrt[q]{a}\right)^p, \tag{10.6}$$

we obtain the Laws of Radicals

$$\sqrt[p]{a^p} = a, \quad \left(\sqrt[p]{a}\right)^p = a$$

$$\sqrt[p]{ab} = \sqrt[p]{a} \cdot \sqrt[p]{b}$$

$$\sqrt[p]{\frac{a}{b}} = \frac{\sqrt[p]{a}}{\sqrt[p]{b}}$$

$$\sqrt[p]{\sqrt[r]{a}} = \sqrt[pr]{a}.$$

Note that we obtain the rule $\sqrt[r]{ab} = \sqrt[r]{a} \cdot \sqrt[r]{b}$ by setting $r = \frac{1}{p}$ in (10.3) above and using the symbol interpreter $a^{\frac{1}{p}} = \sqrt[p]{a}$. For example, by (10.6), we see that $9^{\frac{3}{2}} = \left(\sqrt{9}\right)^3 = 3^3 = 27$, while $(27)^{\frac{2}{3}} = \left(\sqrt[3]{27}\right)^2 = 3^2 = 9$.

We emphasize that these two laws are *completely general* in the sense that the symbols a, b appearing in them need not be single numbers only (like 3 or 1.52) but can be any abstract combination of such numbers or even other symbols and numbers together! For example, it is the case that

$$\left(2x + y\sqrt{x}\right)^{-1} = \frac{1}{2x + y\sqrt{x}}$$

and this follows from the fact that

$$a^{-1} = \frac{1}{a}$$

for any non-zero number a. Incidentally, this latest identity follows from (10.1) with $r = 1, s = -1$ and the defintion $a^0 = 1$. In order to show the power of these formulae we use the Box Method of Section 1.2 to solidify their meaning. Thus, instead of writing the Laws of Exponents and Radicals as above, we rewrite them in the form

$$\Box^r \cdot \Box^s = \Box^{r+s} \tag{10.7}$$

$$(\Box^r)^s = \Box^{r \cdot s}, \qquad (\Box^r)^{-s} = \Box^{-r \cdot s} \tag{10.8}$$

$$(\Box_1 \Box_2)^r = (\Box_1)^r \cdot (\Box_2)^r \tag{10.9}$$

$$\left(\frac{\Box_1}{\Box_2}\right)^r = \frac{(\Box_1)^r}{(\Box_2)^r} \tag{10.10}$$

$$\frac{\Box^r}{\Box^s} = \Box^{r-s}, \tag{10.11}$$

and remember that we can put any abstract combination of numbers or even other symbols and numbers together inside the Boxes in accordance with the techniques described in Section 1.2 for using the Box Method. So, for example, we can easily see that

$$\left(2x + y\sqrt{x}\right)^{-1} = \frac{1}{2x + y\sqrt{x}}$$

alluded to above since we know that

$$\Box^{-1} = \frac{1}{\Box},$$

and we can put the group of symbols $2x + y\sqrt{x}$ *inside* the Box so that we see

$$\left(\boxed{2x + y\sqrt{x}}\right)^{-1} = \frac{1}{\boxed{2x + y\sqrt{x}}}$$

and then remove the sides of the box to get the original identity.

Another example follows: Using (10.9) above, that is,

$$(\Box_1 \Box_2)^r = (\Box_1)^r \cdot (\Box_2)^r$$

we can put the symbol $3y$ inside box 1, *i.e.*, $\Box_1$, and $x + 1$ inside box 2, *i.e.*, $\Box_2$, to find that if $r = 2$ then, once we remove the sides of the boxes,

$$(3y(x+1))^2 = (3y)^2(x+1)^2 = 9y^2(x+1)^2.$$

The Box Method's strength lies in assimilating large masses of symbols into one symbol (the box) for ease of calculation!

Remark Using the same ideas and (10.8) we can show that $\left(3^2\right)^{-3} = 3^{-2\cdot3} = 3^{-6}$ and NOT equal to 3^{2-3} as some might think! You should leave the parentheses alone and not drop them when they are present!

Of course we can put anything we want inside this box so that (if we put $\sqrt{2}x - 16xy^2 + 4.1$ inside) it is still true that (use (10.8))

$$\left(\square^{\,2}\right)^{-3} = \left(\square^{\,-3}\right)^2 = \square^{\,-3\cdot2} = \square^{\,-6}$$

or

$$\left(\left(\sqrt{2}x - 16xy^2 + 4.1\right)^2\right)^{-3} = \left(\sqrt{2}x - 16xy^2 + 4.1\right)^{-6}.$$

Finally, don't forget that

$$\square^{\,0} = 1, \quad \square^{\,1} = \square, \quad \text{and,} \quad \square^{\,-1} = \frac{1}{\square}.$$

Example 495. Simplify the product $2^3 3^2 2^{-1}$, without using your calculator.

Solution We use the Laws of Exponents:

$$\begin{aligned}
2^3 3^2 2^{-1} &= 2^3 2^{-1} 3^2 \\
&= 2^{3-1} 3^2 \qquad \text{by (10.7)} \\
&= 2^2 3^2 \\
&= (2\cdot3)^2 \qquad \text{by (10.9)} \\
&= 6^2 \\
&= 36.
\end{aligned}$$

Example 496. Simplify the expression $(2xy)^{-2} 2^3 (yx)^3$.

Solution Use the Laws (10.7) to (10.11) in various combinations:

$$\begin{aligned}
(2xy)^{-2} 2^3 (yx)^3 &= (2xy)^{-2}(2yx)^3 \qquad \text{by (10.9)} \\
&= (2xy)^{-2+3} \qquad \text{by (10.7)} \\
&= (2xy)^1 \\
&= 2xy.
\end{aligned}$$

Example 497. Simplify $2^8 4^{-2} (2x)^{-4} x^5$.

Solution We use the Laws (10.7) to (10.11) once again.

$$\begin{aligned}
2^8 4^{-2} (2x)^{-4} x^5 &= 2^8 (2^2)^{-2} (2x)^{-4} x^5 \\
&= 2^8 2^{-4} (2x)^{-4} x^5 \qquad \text{by (10.8)} \\
&= 2^{8-4} (2x)^{-4} x^5 \qquad \text{by (10.7)} \\
&= 2^4 2^{-4} x^{-4} x^5 \qquad \text{by (10.9)} \\
&= 2^{4-4} x^{-4+5} \qquad \text{by (10.7)} \\
&= 2^0 x^1 \\
&= x.
\end{aligned}$$

Example 498. Simplify $\dfrac{2^{2^3}\left(2^2\right)^{-3}}{4}$.

Solution Work out the highest powers first so that since $2^3 = 8$ it follows that $2^{2^3} = 2^8$. Thus,

$$
\begin{aligned}
\frac{2^{2^3}\left(2^2\right)^{-3}}{4} &= \frac{2^8 2^{-3\cdot 2}}{4} \qquad \text{by (10.8)} \\
&= \frac{2^8 2^{-6}}{2^2} = \frac{2^{8-6}}{2^2} = \frac{2^2}{2^2} \\
&= 1.
\end{aligned}
$$

Example 499. Write $\left((49)^{-\frac{1}{2}}\right)^3$ as a rational number (ordinary fraction).

Solution $\left((49)^{-\frac{1}{2}}\right)^3 = \left((49)^{\frac{1}{2}}\right)^{-3}$ by (10.8). Next, $(49)^{\frac{1}{2}} = \sqrt{49} = 7$, so, $\left((49)^{\frac{1}{2}}\right)^{-3} = 7^{-3} = \dfrac{1}{7^3} = \dfrac{1}{343}$.

Example 500. Simplify as much as possible: $(16)^{-\frac{1}{6}}4^{\frac{7}{3}}(256)^{-\frac{1}{4}}$.

Solution The idea here is to rewrite the bases $4, 16, 256$, in lowest common terms, if possible. Thus,

$$
\begin{aligned}
(16)^{-\frac{1}{6}}4^{\frac{7}{3}}(256)^{-\frac{1}{4}} &= (4^2)^{-\frac{1}{6}}4^{\frac{7}{3}}(4^4)^{-\frac{1}{4}} \\
&= 4^{-\frac{1}{3}}4^{\frac{7}{3}}4^{-1} \qquad \text{by (10.8)} \\
&= 4^{-\frac{1}{3}+\frac{7}{3}-1} \qquad \text{by (10.7)} \\
&= 4^{\frac{6}{3}-1} \\
&= 4.
\end{aligned}
$$

Example 501. Simplify to an expression with positive exponents: $\dfrac{x^{-\frac{1}{6}}x^{\frac{2}{3}}}{x^{\frac{5}{12}}}$.

Solution Since the bases are all the same, namely, x, we only need to use a combination of (10.7) and (10.11). So,

$$
\begin{aligned}
\frac{x^{-\frac{1}{6}}x^{\frac{2}{3}}}{x^{\frac{5}{12}}} &= \frac{x^{-\frac{1}{6}+\frac{2}{3}}}{x^{\frac{5}{12}}} \qquad \text{by (10.7)} \\
&= \frac{x^{\frac{1}{2}}}{x^{\frac{5}{12}}} \\
&= x^{\frac{1}{2}-\frac{5}{12}} \qquad \text{by (10.11)} \\
&= x^{\frac{7}{12}}.
\end{aligned}
$$

Example 502. Show that if $r \neq 1$ then $1 + r + r^2 = \dfrac{1-r^3}{1-r}$.

Solution It suffices to show that $(1 + r + r^2)(1 - r) = 1 - r^3$ for any value of r. Division by $1 - r$ (only valid when $r \neq 1$) then gives the required result. Now,

$$
\begin{aligned}
(1 + r + r^2)\cdot(1 - r) &= (1 + r + r^2)\cdot(1) + (1 + r + r^2)\cdot(-r) \\
&= (1 + r + r^2) + (1)\cdot(-r) + r\cdot(-r) + r^2\cdot(-r)
\end{aligned}
$$

$$
\begin{aligned}
&= \ 1 + r + r^2 - r - r^2 - r^3 \qquad \text{by (10.7)}\\
&= \ 1 - r^3
\end{aligned}
$$

and that's all.

Example 503. | For what values of a is $x^4 + 1 = (x^2 + ax + 1) \cdot (x^2 - ax + 1)$?

Solution We simply multiply the right side together, compare the coefficients of like powers and then find a. Thus,

$$
\begin{aligned}
x^4 + 1 &= (x^2 + ax + 1) \cdot (x^2 - ax + 1)\\
&= x^2 \cdot (x^2 - ax + 1) + ax \cdot (x^2 - ax + 1) + 1 \cdot (x^2 - ax + 1)\\
&= (x^4 - ax^3 + x^2) + (ax^3 - a^2 x^2 + ax) + (x^2 - ax + 1)\\
&= x^4 - ax^3 + x^2 + ax^3 - a^2 x^2 + ax + x^2 - ax + 1\\
&= x^4 + (2 - a^2) \cdot x^2 + 1.
\end{aligned}
$$

Comparing the coefficients on the left and right side of the last equation we see that $2 - a^2 = 0$ is necessary. This means that $a^2 = 2$ or $a = \pm\sqrt{2}$.

Note Either value of a in Example 503 gives the same factors of the polynomials $x^4 + 1$. More material on such factorization techniques can be found in Chapter 5.

Exercise Set 50.

Simplify as much as you can to an expression with positive exponents.

1. $16^2 \times 8 \div 4^3$
2. $(25^2)^{\frac{1}{2}}$
3. $2^4 4^2 2^{-2}$
4. $\dfrac{3^2 4^2}{12}$
5. $5^3 15^{-2} 3^4$
6. $(2x + y) \cdot (2x - y)$
7. $1 + (x - 1)(x + 1)$
8. $\left((25)^{-\frac{1}{2}}\right)^2 + 5^{-2}$
9. $(4x^2 y)^2 2^{-4} x^{-2} y$
10. $(1 + r + r^2 + r^3) \cdot (1 - r)$
11. $(a^9 b^{15})^{\frac{1}{3}}$
12. $(16 a^{12})^{\frac{3}{4}}$
13. $\dfrac{x^{\frac{1}{4}} x^{-\frac{2}{3}}}{x^{\frac{1}{6}}}$
14. $\left(\dfrac{1}{16}\right)^{-\frac{3}{2}}$
15. $\left(1 + 5^{\frac{1}{3}}\right) \cdot \left(1 - 5^{\frac{1}{3}} + (25)^{\frac{1}{3}}\right)$
16. $\left(9 x^{-8}\right)^{-\frac{3}{2}}$
17. $9^{-\frac{1}{6}} 3^{\frac{7}{3}} (81)^{-\frac{1}{4}}$

18. $\dfrac{(12)^{\frac{3}{2}}\,(16)^{\frac{1}{8}}}{(27)^{\frac{1}{6}}\,(18)^{\frac{1}{2}}}$

19. $\dfrac{3^{n+1}9^{n}}{(27)^{\frac{2n}{3}}}$

20. $\dfrac{\sqrt{xy}\,\,x^{\frac{1}{3}}\,\,2y^{\frac{1}{4}}}{(x^{10}y^{9})^{\frac{1}{12}}}$

21. Show that there is **no** real number a such that $(x^2+1) = (x-a)\cdot(x+a)$.

22. Show that $(1+x^2+x^4)\cdot(1-x^2) = 1-x^6$.

23. Find an expression for the quotient $\dfrac{1-x^8}{1-x}$ as a sum of powers of x only.

24. Show that $(x-1)(x+1)(1+x^2)+1 = x^4$.

25. Show that $3\left(x^2yz\right)^3 \div x^4y^3 - 3x^2z^3 = 0$ for any choice of the variables x, y, z so long as $xy \neq 0$.

26. Using the identities (10.7) and $a^0 = 1$ only, show that $a^{-r} = \dfrac{1}{a^r}$ for any real number r.

27. Show that if r, s are any two integers and $a > 0$, then $(a)^{-rs} = (a^r)^{-s} = (a^s)^{-r}$.

28. Give an example to show that

$$2^{x^y} \neq (2^x)^y.$$

In other words, find two numbers x, y that have this property.

29. Show that for any number $r \neq -1$ we have the identity $1 - r + r^2 = \dfrac{1+r^3}{1+r}$ and use this to deduce that for any value of $x \neq -2$,

$$1 - \frac{x}{2} + \frac{x^2}{4} = \frac{x^3+8}{4(x+2)}.$$

30. If $a > 0$ and $2x = a^{\frac{1}{2}} + a^{-\frac{1}{2}}$ show that

$$\frac{\sqrt{x^2-1}}{x-\sqrt{x^2-1}} = \frac{a-1}{2}.$$

Suggested Homework Set 38. *Do all even-numbered problems from 2 - 28.*

Web Links

Many more exercises may be found on the web site:

http://math.usask.ca/readin/

Chapter 11

Appendix B: The Straight Line

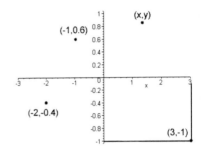

Points in the Euclidean plane

Figure 236.

In this section we review one of the most fundamental topics of analytic geometry, the representation of a **straight line** with respect to a given set of coordinate axes. We recall that a point in the Euclidean plane is denoted by its two coordinates (x, y) where x, y are real numbers either positive, negative or zero, see Figure 236.

Thus, the point $(3, -1)$ is found by moving three positive units to the right along the x-axis and one unit "down" (because of the negative sign) along a line parallel to the y-axis. From the theory of plane Euclidean geometry we know that two given points determine a unique (straight) line. Its *equation* is obtained by describing every point on the straight line in the form $(x, y) = (x, f(x))$ where $y = f(x)$ is the equation of the straight line defined by some function f. To find this equation we appeal to basic Euclidean geometry and, in particular, to the result that states that *any two similar triangles in the Euclidean plane have proportional sides*, see Figure 237. This result will be used to find the equation of a straight line as we'll see.

We start off by considering two given points P and Q having coordinates (x_1, y_1) and (x_2, y_2) respectively. Normally, we'll write this briefly as $P(x_1, y_1)$ etc. Remember that the points P, Q are given ahead of time. Now, we join these two points by means of a straight line $\mathcal{L}$ and, on this line $\mathcal{L}$ we choose some point that we label as $R(x, y)$. For convenience we will assume that R is between P and Q.

Next, see Figure 237, we construct the two similar right-angled triangles $\triangle PQT$ and $\triangle PRS$. Since they are similar the length of their sides are proportional and so,

$$\frac{PS}{SR} = \frac{PT}{TQ}.$$

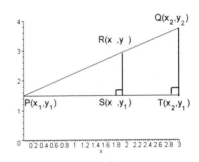

The triangles PRS and PQT have proportional sides as they are similar.

Figure 237.

In terms of the coordinates of the points in question we note that $PS = x - x_1$, $SR = y - y_1$, $PT = x_2 - x_1$, $TQ = y_2 - y_1$. Rewriting the above proportionality relation in terms of these coordinates we get

$$\frac{x - x_1}{y - y_1} = \frac{x_2 - x_1}{y_2 - y_1},$$

or equivalently, solving for y and rewriting the equation, we see that

$$y = mx + b$$

515

where

$$m = \frac{y_2 - y_1}{x_2 - x_1}$$

is called the **slope of the straight line** and the number $b = y_1 - mx_1$ is called the **y-intercept** (*i.e.*, that value of y obtained by setting $x = 0$). The x-intercept is that value of x obtained by setting $y = 0$. In this case, the **x-intercept** is the complicated-looking expression

$$x = \frac{x_1 y_2 - x_2 y_1}{y_2 - y_1}.$$

Let $P(x_1, y_1)$, $Q(x_2, y_2)$ be any two points on a line $\mathcal{L}$. The equation of $\mathcal{L}$ is given by

$$y = mx + b \qquad (11.1)$$

and will be called the **slope-intercept form of a line** where

$$m = \frac{y_2 - y_1}{x_2 - x_1} \qquad (11.2)$$

is called the **slope of the straight line** and the number

$$b = y_1 - mx_1 \qquad (11.3)$$

is the **y-intercept**.

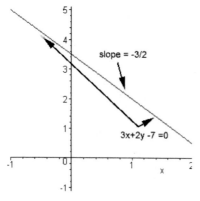

The graph of the line $3x + 2y - 7 = 0$ with a negative slope equal to $-3/2$.

Figure 238.

Example 504. Find the slope of the line whose equation is $3x + 2y - 7 = 0$.

Solution First, let's see if we can rewrite the given equation in "slope-intercept form". To do this, we solve for y and then isolate it (by itself) and then compare the new equation with the given one. So, subtracting $3x - 7$ from both sides of the equation gives $2y = 7 - 3x$. Dividing this by 2 (and so isolating y) gives us $y = \frac{7}{2} - \frac{3}{2}x$. Comparing this last equation with the form $y = mx + b$ shows that $m = -\frac{3}{2}$ and the y-intercept is $\frac{7}{2}$. Its graph is represented in Figure 238.

Example 505. Find the equation of the line passing through the points $(2, -3)$ and $(-1, -1)$.

Solution We use equations (11.1), (11.2) and (11.3). Thus, we label the points as follows: $(x_1, y_1) = (2, -3)$ and $(x_2, y_2) = (-1, -1)$. But the slope m is given by (11.2), *i.e.*,

$$m = \frac{y_2 - y_1}{x_2 - x_1} = \frac{-1 + 3}{-1 - 2} = -\frac{2}{3}.$$

On the other hand the y-intercept is given by

$$b = y_1 - mx_1 = -3 + \frac{2}{3}(2) = -\frac{5}{3}.$$

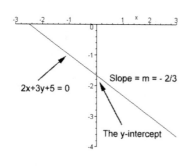

The line $2x + 3y + 5 = 0$ and its y-intercept.

Figure 239.

The equation of the line is therefore $y = -\frac{2}{3}x - \frac{5}{3}$ or, equivalently, $2x + 3y + 5 = 0$, (see Figure 239).

Remark: It doesn't matter *which* point you label with the coordinates (x_1, y_1), you'll still get the same slope value and y-intercept! In other words, if we interchange the roles of (x_1, y_1) and (x_2, y_2) we get the *same* value for the slope, etc. and the *same* equation for the line.

Example 506. Find the equation of the line through $(1, 4)$ having slope equal to 2.

Solution We are given that $m = 2$ in (11.1), so the equation of our line looks like $y = 2x + b$ where b is to be found. But we are given that this line goes thourhg the point $(1, 4)$. This means that we can set $x = 1$ and $y = 4$ in the equation $y = 2x + b$ and use this to find the value of b. In other words, $4 = 2 \cdot 1 + b$ and so $b = 2$. Finally, we see that $y = 2x + 2$ is the desired equation.

Example 507. Find the equation of the line whose x-intercept is equal to -1 and whose y-intercept is equal to -2.

Solution Once again we can use (11.1). Since $y = mx + b$ and the y-intercept is equal to -2 this means that $b = -2$ by definition. Our line now takes the form $y = mx - 2$. We still need to find m though. But by definition the fact that the x-intercept is equal to -1 means that when $y = 0$ then $x = -1$, *i.e.*, $0 = m \cdot (-1) - 2$ and this leads to $m = -2$. Thus, $y = -2x - 2$ is the equation of the line having the required intercepts.

Example 508. Find the point of intersection of the two lines $2x + 3y + 4 = 0$ and $y = 2x - 6$.

Solution The point of intersection is necessarily a point, let's call it (x, y) once again, that belongs to *both* the lines. This means that $2x + 3y + 4 = 0$ AND $y = 2x - 6$. This gives us a system of two equations in the two unknowns (x, y). There are two ways to proceed; (1): We can isolate the y-terms, then equate the two x-terms and finally solve for the x-term, or (2): Use the method of elimination. We use the first of these methods here.

Equating the two y-terms means that we have to solve for y in each equation. But we know that $y = 2x - 6$ and we also know that $3y = -2x - 4$ or $y = -\dfrac{2}{3}x - \dfrac{4}{3}$. So, equating these two y's we get

$$2x - 6 = -\frac{2}{3}x - \frac{4}{3}$$

or, equivalently,

$$6x - 18 = -2x - 4.$$

Isolating the x, gives us $8x = 14$ or $x = \frac{7}{4}$. This says that the x-coordinate of the required point of intersection is given by $x = \frac{7}{4}$. To get the y-coordinate we simply use EITHER one of the two equations, plug in $x = \frac{7}{4}$ and then solve for y. In our case, we set $x = \frac{7}{4}$ in, say, $y = 2x - 6$. This gives us $y = 2 \cdot \left(\frac{7}{4}\right) - 6 = -\frac{5}{2}$. The required point has coordinates $\left(\frac{7}{4}, -\frac{5}{2}\right)$, see Figure 240.

Prior to discussing the *angle between two lines* we need to recall some basic notions from Trigonometry, see Appendix **??**. First we note that the slope m of a line whose equation is $y = mx + b$ is related to the *angle* that the line itself makes with the x-axis. A look at Figure 241 shows that, in fact,

$$m = \frac{y_2 - y_1}{x_2 - x_1} = \frac{\text{opposite}}{\text{adjacent}} = \tan\theta,$$

by definition of the tangent of this angle.

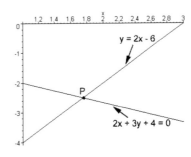

The two lines $2x + 3y + 4 = 0$ and $y = 2x - 6$ and their point of intersection $P(\frac{7}{4}, -\frac{5}{2})$

Figure 240.

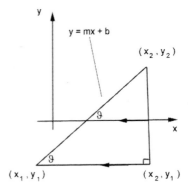

The angle θ between the line $y = mx + b$ and the x-axis is related to the slope m of this line via the relation $m = \tan\theta$.

Figure 241.

So,

$$m = \text{Slope} = \tan\theta$$

where the angle θ is usually expressed in **radians** in accordance with the conventions of Calculus.

Now, if two lines are parallel their corresponding angles are equal (this is from a really old result of Euclid - sometimes called the **corresponding angle theorem**, CAT, for short). This means that the angle that each one makes with the x-axis is the same for each line (see Figure 242), that is $\theta_2 = \theta_1$. But this means that the slopes are equal too, right? Okay, it follows that if two lines are parallel, then their slopes are equal and conversely, if two lines have equal slopes then they must be parallel. If $\theta_2 = \theta_1 = \frac{\pi}{2}$, the lines are still parallel but they are now perpendicular with respect to the x-axis. In this case we say they have no slope or their slope is infinite. Conversely, if two lines have no slopes they are parallel as well (just draw a picture).

We now produce a relation that guarantees the *perpendicularity* of two given lines. For instance, a glance at Figure 243 shows that if θ_1, θ_2 are the angles of inclination of the two given lines and we assume that these two lines are perpendicular, then, by a classical result of Euclidean geometry, we know that

$$\begin{aligned}
\theta_2 &= \theta_1 + \frac{\pi}{2} \\
\tan\theta_2 &= \tan\left(\theta_1 + \frac{\pi}{2}\right) \\
&= -\cot\theta_1 \\
&= -\frac{1}{\tan\theta_1}.
\end{aligned}$$

Since $m_2 = \tan\theta_2, m_1 = \tan\theta_1$, it follows that $m_2 = -\frac{1}{m_1}$. We have just showed that two lines having slopes m_1, m_2 are perpendicular only when

$$m_2 = -\frac{1}{m_1}$$

that is, two lines are perpendicular only when the product of their slopes is the number -1. The converse is also true, that is, if two lines have the product of their slopes equal to -1 then they are perpendicular. This relates the geometrical notion of perpendicularity to the stated relation on the slopes of the lines. It follows from this that if a line has its slope equal to zero, then it must be parallel to the x-axis while if a line has no slope (or its slope is infinite) then it must be parallel to the y-axis.

Example 509. Find the slopes of the sides of the triangle whose vertices are $(6,2),(3,5)$ and $(5,7)$ and show that this is a right-triangle.

Solution Since three distinct points determine a unique triangle on the plane it suffices to find the slopes of the lines making up its sides and then showing that the product of the slopes of two of them is -1. This will prove that the triangle is a right-angled triangle.

Now the line, say $\mathcal{L}_1$, joining the points $(6,2),(3,5)$ has slope $m_1 = \frac{5-2}{3-6} = -1$ while the line, $\mathcal{L}_2$, joining the points $(3,5)$ and $(5,7)$ has slope $m_2 = \frac{7-5}{5-3} = 1$. Finally, the line, $\mathcal{L}_3$, joining $(6,2)$ to $(5,7)$ has slope $m_3 = \frac{7-2}{5-6} = -5$. Since

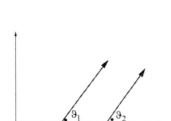

Parallel lines have the same slope and, conversely, if two lines have the same slope they are parallel

Figure 242.

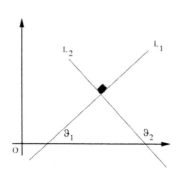

Figure 243.

$m_1 \cdot m_2 = (-1) \cdot (1) = -1$ it follows that those two lines are perpendicular, see Figure 244. Note that we didn't actually have to calculate the *equations* of the lines themselves, just the *slopes!*

Example 510. Find the equation of the straight line through the point $(6, -2)$ that is (a) parallel to the line $4x - 3y - 7 = 0$ and (b) perpendicular to the line $4x - 3y - 7 = 0$.

Solution (a) Since the line passes through $(x_1, y_1) = (6, -2)$ its equation has the form $y - y_1 = m_1(x - x_1)$ or $y = m_1(x - 6) - 2$ where m_1 is its slope. On the other hand, since it is required to be parallel to the $4x - 3y - 7 = 0$ the two must have the *same* slope. But the slope of the given line is $m = \frac{4}{3}$. Thus, $m_1 = \frac{4}{3}$ as well and so the line parallel to $4x - 3y - 7 = 0$ has the equation $y = \frac{4}{3}(x - 6) - 2$ or, equivalently (multiplying everything out by 3), $3y - 4x + 30 = 0$.

(b) In this case the required line must have its slope equal to the negative reciprocal of the first, that is $m_1 = -\frac{3}{4}$ since the slope of the given line is $m = \frac{4}{3}$. Since $y = m_1(x - 6) - 2$, see above, it follows that its equation is $y = -\frac{3}{4}(x - 6) - 2$ or, equivalently, $4y + 3x - 10 = 0$.

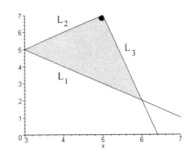

Figure 244.

Exercise Set 51.

1. Find the slope of the line whose equation is $2x - 3y = 8$

2. Find the slope of the line whose equation is $2x - 3y = -8$

3. Find the slope of the line whose equation is $y - 3x = 2$

4. Find the equation of the line passing through the point $(2, -4)$ and $(6, 7)$

5. Find the equation of the line passing through the point $(-4, -5)$ and $(-2, -3)$

6. Find the equation of the line passing through $(-1, -3)$ having slope -2

7. Find the equation of the line passing through $(6, -2)$ having slope $\frac{4}{3}$

8. Write the equation of the line whose $x-$intercept is 2 and whose $y-$intercept is 3

9. Write the equation of the line whose $x-$intercept is $\frac{1}{2}$ and whose $y-$intercept is $\frac{1}{3}$

10. Find the point of intersection of the two lines $y = x + 1$ and $2y + x - 1 = 0$

11. Find the points of intersection of the two lines $2y = 2x + 2$ and $3y - 3x - 3 = 0$. Explain your answer.

12. Find the point of intersection (if any) of the two lines $y - x + 1 = 0$ and $y = x$

13. Recall that the distance between two points whose coordinates are $A(x_1, y_1)$, $B(x_2, y_2)$ is given by

$$AB = \sqrt{(x_2 - x_1)^2 + (y_2 - y_1)^2}.$$

Of course, this quantity AB is also equal to the length of the line segment joining A to B. Use this information to answer the following questions about the triangle formed by the points $A(2, 0)$, $B(6, 4)$ and $C(4, -6)$: (a) Find the equation of the line through AB; (b) Find the length of the altitude from C to AB (*i.e.*, the length of the perpendicular line through C meeting AB); (c) Find the area of this triangle ABC

14. Find the equation of the straight line through $(1, 1)$ and perpendicular to the line $y = -x + 2$

15. Find the equation of the straight line through $(1, 1)$ and parallel to the line $y = -x + 2$

Chapter 1

Complete Solutions

1.1

1.2   Exercise Set 1

1. $-2, -1, 2, \frac{1}{4}$.

2. $(x+1)^3 \sin(x+1)$. Use the Box method.

3. $z - 2 + 2\sin(z-2) - \cos z$.

4. $-2\cos(x + ct)$.

5. $f(\pi/2) = \sin(\cos(\pi/2)) = \sin 0 = 0$.

6. $2x + h$. You get this by dividing by h since $h \neq 0$.

7. $\sin(t+3)\dfrac{\cos h - 1}{h} + \cos(t+3)\dfrac{\sin h}{h}$.

8. (a) $-\pi^2$, (b) $4\pi^2$.

9. (a) $f(0) = 1$, (b) $f(0.142857) = 0.857143$, (c) Since $0 < x < 1$ we see that $2 < 3x + 2 < 5$. So, $f(3x+2) = (3x+2)^2 = 9x^2 + 12x + 4$.

10. $f(F(x)) = x$, $F(f(x)) = |x|$.

1.3   Exercise Set 2

1. $(-\infty, \infty)$.

2. All reals except $\pm\frac{\pi}{2}$, $\pm\frac{3\pi}{2}$, $\pm\frac{5\pi}{2}$, ... (these are the points where $\cos t = 0$.)

3. $z \geq -\frac{2}{3}$.

4. $|x| < 2$. (You can also write this as $-2 < x < 2$.)

5. All reals except 0, $\pm\pi$, $\pm 2\pi$, ... (these are the points where $\sin x = 0$.)

6. $(-\infty, \infty)$.

7. $(-\infty, \infty)$.

8. $(-\infty, \infty)$. Note that $t^{4/5}$ is defined for all values of t.

9. $x \neq 1$.

10. $z \geq -\frac{11}{3}$

11. $|x| > 1$. (That is, either $x > 1$ or $x < -1$.)

12. $\square^2 \leq 1$. (You can also write this as $|\square| \leq 1$, or $-1 \leq \square \leq 1$.)

13. The natural domain of f is $-\infty < \triangle < \infty$.

14. $\heartsuit \geq 0$.

15. $x^2 < 1$. (You can also write this as $|x| < 1$, or $-1 < x < 1$.)

16.
$$f(x) = \begin{cases} x^2 - 1, & x \geq 1 \text{ or } x \leq -1, \\ 1 - x^2, & -1 < x < 1. \end{cases}$$

17.
$$f(x) = \begin{cases} 3x + 4, & \text{if } x \geq -4/3, \\ -3x - 4, & \text{otherwise.} \end{cases}$$

18.
$$h(x) = \begin{cases} x^2, & \text{if } x \geq 0, \\ -x^2, & \text{otherwise.} \end{cases}$$

19.
$$f(x) = \begin{cases} 1 - t, & \text{if } t \geq 0, \\ 1 + t, & \text{if } t < 0. \end{cases}$$

20.
$$g(w) = \begin{cases} \sin w & \text{for } w \text{ in any interval of the form } [2\pi n, 2\pi n + \pi], \\ -\sin w & \text{otherwise,} \end{cases}$$

where n is an integer.

21.
$$f(x) = \begin{cases} \dfrac{1}{x\sqrt{x^2-1}}, & \text{if } x > 1, \\ -\dfrac{1}{x\sqrt{x^2-1}}, & \text{if } x < -1. \end{cases}$$

22.
$$\operatorname{sgn}(x) = \begin{cases} 1, & \text{if } x \geq 0, \\ -1, & \text{if } x < 0. \end{cases}$$

23.
$$f(x) = \begin{cases} 2x, & \text{if } x \geq 0, \\ 0, & \text{if } x < 0. \end{cases}$$

24.
$$f(x) = \begin{cases} 0, & \text{if } x \geq 0, \\ 2x, & \text{if } x < 0. \end{cases}$$

1.4 Exercise Set 3

1. Correction: If $A < 0$, then $-A < B$ implies $-1/A > 1/B$.

2. This is false. To see this, let $A = 1$ and $B = 0$.

3. Correction: $0 \leq A < B$ implies $A^2 < B^2$.

4. Correction: $A > B > 0$ implies $1/A < 1/B$.

5. Correction: $A < B$ implies $-A > -B$.

6. Correction: If $A^2 < B^2$ and $B > 0$, then $A < B$.

7. This statement is correct. There is nothing wrong!

8. $(0, \pi)$. (Note: To complete our argument we need $\sin x > 0$, which is guaranteed by $0 < x < \pi$.)

9. It can be bigger than 4, but not bigger than 6. Actually, its largest value occurs when $x = 2$ in which case $f(2) \approx 5.8186$.

10. g is unbounded: This means that it can be greater than (resp. less than) any given number. The problem occurs at $x = 0$.

11. From $x > 1$ we see that both x and $x - 1$ are positive. Hence we can square both sides of the inequality $x > x - 1$ to arrive at $x^2 > (x-1)^2$. (Alternately, since both x and $x-1$ are positive, $x^2 > x^2 - x - (x-1) = x^2 - 2x + 1 = (x-1)^2$.)

12. From $p \leq 1$ we see that $1 - p \geq 0$. Since $x \geq 1$ (certainly this implies the positivity of x), we have $x^{1-p} \geq 1^{1-p}$, or $x^{1-p} \geq 1$. Now $x^{1-p} = x^{-(p-1)} = \frac{1}{x^{p-1}}$. So the last inequality can be rewritten as $\frac{1}{x^{p-1}} \geq 1$. We can multiply both sides of this inequality by $\sin x$ because $1 \leq x \leq \pi$ guarantees that $\sin x$ is positive.

13. Since both x and x^2 are ≥ 0, we can apply the AG-inequality to get $\frac{x+x^2}{2} \geq \sqrt{x \cdot x^2} = \sqrt{x^3}$. Since $x + x^2 \geq 0$, we have $x + x^2 \geq \frac{x+x^2}{2}$. So $x + x^2 \geq \sqrt{x^3}$. Yes, we can square both sides since $x \geq 0$, and so both terms in the inequality are greater than or equal to 0.

14. Yes. Under no further conditions on the symbol, since it is true that $(\square - 1)^2 \geq 0$ for any symbol, $\square$. Expanding the square and separating terms we get that $\square^2 \geq 2\square - 1$.

15. Since $1 - p \geq 0$ and $|x| \geq 1$, we have $|x|^{1-p} \geq 1^{1-p} = 1$, or $|x|\,|x|^{-p} \geq 1$, which gives $|x| \geq |x|^p$. Taking reciprocals, we get $\frac{1}{|x|} \leq \frac{1}{|x|^p}$. (The last step is legitimate because both $|x|^p$ and $|x|$ are positive.)

16. $|v| < c$. This is because we need $1 - v^2/c^2 > 0$. Now solve this inequality for v.

17. If $n = 2$, the result is clear, because $2 < (1.5)^2 < 3$. So let's assume that $n > 2$, now. We use (1.5) with the quantity "$1/n$" inside the box symbol (or replacing the box by $1/n$, if you like). We'll see that

$$\left(1 + \boxed{\tfrac{1}{n}}\right)^n \quad = 1 + n\boxed{\tfrac{1}{n}} + \frac{n(n-1)}{2!}\boxed{\tfrac{1}{n}}^2 + \ldots + \frac{n(n-1)\cdots(2)(1)}{n!}\boxed{\tfrac{1}{n}}^n$$

$$= 1 + n(\tfrac{1}{n}) + \frac{n(n-1)}{2!}(\tfrac{1}{n})^2 + \ldots + \frac{n(n-1)(n-2)\cdots(2)(1)}{n!}(\tfrac{1}{n})^n.$$

$$= 1 + n(\tfrac{1}{n}) + \frac{n(n-1)}{n^2}(\tfrac{1}{2!}) + \ldots + \frac{n(n-1)(n-2)\cdots(2)(1)}{n^n}(\tfrac{1}{n!}).$$

Now, we regroup all the terms in the above display in the following way .... Note that the following term is not apparent in the display above, but it IS there! See Equation (1.5).

$$\frac{n(n-1)(n-2)}{n^3} \quad = \left(\tfrac{n}{n}\right)\left(\tfrac{n-1}{n}\right)\left(\tfrac{n-2}{n}\right)$$

$$= (1)\left(\tfrac{n-1}{n}\right)\left(\tfrac{n-2}{n}\right)$$

$$= \left(\tfrac{n-1}{n}\right)\left(\tfrac{n-2}{n}\right),$$

$$= \left(1 - \tfrac{1}{n}\right)\left(1 - \tfrac{2}{n}\right).$$

A similar idea is used for the other terms. Okay, so using this rearrangement of terms we can rewrite $(1 + \tfrac{1}{n})^n$ as

$$\left(1 + \tfrac{1}{n}\right)^n \quad = \ldots$$

$$= 1 + 1 + \left(1 - \tfrac{1}{n}\right)\tfrac{1}{2!} + \left(1 - \tfrac{1}{n}\right)\left(1 - \tfrac{2}{n}\right)\tfrac{1}{3!} + \ldots$$

$$+ \left(1 - \tfrac{1}{n}\right)\left(1 - \tfrac{2}{n}\right)\left(1 - \tfrac{3}{n}\right)\cdots\left(1 - \tfrac{n-1}{n}\right)\tfrac{1}{n!}.$$

(where there are $(n + 1)$ terms in the right hand side). Now, notice that for every integer $n > 2$, each term of the form "$1 - (something)/n$" is less than 1 and bigger than zero, because we're subtracting something positive from 1. So,

$$\left(1 - \tfrac{1}{n}\right) \quad < \quad 1$$

$$\left(1 - \tfrac{1}{n}\right)\left(1 - \tfrac{2}{n}\right) \quad < \quad (1)\left(1 - \tfrac{2}{n}\right) < 1, \ldots$$

where we have used Figure 12 with $A = 1 - 2/n$, $\square = 1 - 1/n$ (or with the symbols "$1 - 1/n$" inside the box), and $\triangle = 1$ (or with "1" inside the triangle). Using these estimates we can see that we can replace every term inside the "large brackets" by 1 so that

$$\left(1 + \tfrac{1}{n}\right)^n \quad = \ldots$$

$$= 1 + 1 + \left(1 - \tfrac{1}{n}\right)\tfrac{1}{2!} + \ldots + \left(1 - \tfrac{1}{n}\right)\left(1 - \tfrac{2}{n}\right)\left(1 - \tfrac{3}{n}\right)\cdots\left(1 - \tfrac{n-1}{n}\right)\tfrac{1}{n!} \quad (1.1)$$

$$< \quad 1 + 1 + \tfrac{1}{2!} + \tfrac{1}{3!} + \ldots + \tfrac{1}{n!}$$

We're almost done! Now we use the following inequalities ...

$$3! = 3 \times 2 \times 1 \quad > \quad 2 \times 2 \times 1 = 2^2$$
$$4! = 4 \times 3 \times 2 \times 1 \quad > \quad 2 \times 2 \times 2 \times 1 = 2^3$$
$$5! = 5 \times 4 \times 3 \times 2 \times 1 \quad > \quad 2 \times 2 \times 2 \times 2 \times 1 = 2^4$$
$$\cdots$$
$$n! \quad > \quad 2^{n-1}$$

Now since we must "reverse the inequality when we take reciprocals of positive numbers" (Table 1.3, Table 1.4) we get that for every integer $n > 2$,

$$n! > 2^{n-1} \quad \text{implies} \quad \frac{1}{n!} < \frac{1}{2^{n-1}}$$

Combining this estimate with Equation (1.1) we get a new estimate, namely,

$$\left(1 + \tfrac{1}{n}\right)^n \quad < \quad 1 + 1 + \tfrac{1}{2!} + \tfrac{1}{3!} + \ldots + \tfrac{1}{n!}$$

$$< \quad 1 + 1 + \tfrac{1}{2} + \tfrac{1}{2^2} + \ldots + \tfrac{1}{2^{n-1}}. \quad (1.2)$$

Now, the sum on the right above is a **finite geometric series** and we know that, if $n > 2$,

$$1 + \tfrac{1}{2^1} + \tfrac{1}{2^2} + \ldots + \tfrac{1}{2^n} = \frac{1 - (\tfrac{1}{2})^{n+1}}{1 - \tfrac{1}{2}} < \frac{1}{1 - \tfrac{1}{2}} = 2.$$

Now you can see that, when we combine this latest estimate with (1.2) we find

$$\left(1 + \tfrac{1}{n}\right)^n \quad < \quad 1 + 1 + \tfrac{1}{2} + \tfrac{1}{2^2} + \ldots + \tfrac{1}{2^{n-1}}$$

$$< \quad 1 + 2 = 3$$

which is what we wanted to show. Okay, this looks a bit long, but we did include all the details, right? Eventually, you'll be able to skip many of the details and do them in your head, so to speak, and the whole thing will get shorter and faster, you'll see.

It looks tough, but we'll be using this 200 yr old inequality later on, in Chapter 4, when we define Euler's number, 2.7182818284590.

1.5   Chapter Exercises

1. 6, 1, 2, $2\frac{3}{4} = \frac{11}{4}$.

2. $(x^2 + 1)^3 \cos(x^2 + 1)$.

3. $z + 3 + 2\sin(z + 3) - \cos(z + 5)$.

4. $-\dfrac{\sin h}{h}\sin x + \dfrac{\cos h - 1}{h}\cos x$.

5. From $\frac{3}{x} > 6$ we see that x must be positive: $x > 0$. So we can rewrite it as $3 > 6x$, which gives $x < \frac{1}{2}$. Thus the solution is $0 < x < \frac{1}{2}$.

6. $x \geq -\frac{4}{3}$, since we an subtract 4 from both sides ...

7. $x < \frac{1}{2}$. Note that $2x - 1 < 0$ and so $2x < 1$.

8. $|x| > \sqrt{5}$. In other words, either $x > \sqrt{5}$ or $x < -\sqrt{5}$.

9. $|t| < \sqrt[4]{5}$. That is, $-\sqrt[4]{5} < t < \sqrt[4]{5}$.

10. $-\infty < x < +\infty$. That is, x can be any real number. This is because the stated inequality implies that $\sin x \leq 1$ and this is *always* true!

11. $z \geq 2^{1/p}$. (Note: For general p, z^p is defined only for $z > 0$.)

12. $|x| \leq 3$. Or $-3 \leq x \leq 3$.

13.
$$f(x) = \begin{cases} x + 3, & \text{for } x \geq -3, \\ -x - 3, & \text{for } x < -3. \end{cases}$$

14.
$$g(x) = \begin{cases} t - 0.5, & \text{if } t \geq 0.5, \\ -t + 0.5, & \text{otherwise.} \end{cases}$$

15.
$$g(t) = \begin{cases} 1 - t, & \text{if } t \leq 1, \\ t - 1, & \text{otherwise.} \end{cases}$$

16.
$$f(x) = \begin{cases} 2x - 1, & x \geq \frac{1}{2} \\ 1 - 2x, & x < \frac{1}{2} \end{cases}$$

17.
$$f(x) = \begin{cases} 1 - 6x, & \text{if } x \leq 1/6, \\ 6x - 1, & \text{otherwise.} \end{cases}$$

18.
$$f(x) = \begin{cases} x^2 - 4, & \text{if either } x \geq 2 \text{ or } x \leq -2, \\ 4 - x^2, & \text{if } -2 < x < 2. \end{cases}$$

19.
$$f(x) = \begin{cases} 3 - x^3, & \text{if } x \leq \sqrt[3]{3}, \\ x^3 - 3, & \text{if } x > \sqrt[3]{3}. \end{cases}$$

20. $f(x) = |(x - 1)^2| = (x - 1)^2 = x^2 - 2x + 1$ for all x. (Note that $(x - 1)^2$ is always ≥ 0 for any value of x.)

21.
$$f(x) = |x(2 - x)| = \begin{cases} x(2 - x), & \text{if } 0 \leq x \leq 2, \\ x(x - 2), & \text{otherwise.} \end{cases}$$

22. $f(x) = |x^2 + 2| = x^2 + 2$ for all x, because $f(x) = x^2 + 2 \geq 2 > 0$ to begin with.

23. From $p \leq 1$ we have $1 - p \geq 0$. So $x \geq 1 > 0$ gives $x^{1-p} \geq 1^{1-p} = 1$. Now $x^{1-p} = x^{-(p-1)} = \frac{1}{x^{p-1}}$. Thus $\frac{1}{x^{p-1}} \geq 1$. On the other hand, from $0 \leq x \leq \pi/2$ we have $\cos x \geq 0$. So we can multiply $\frac{1}{x^{p-1}} \geq 1$ throughout by $\cos x$ to arrive at $\frac{\cos x}{x^{p-1}} \geq \cos x$.

24. 2, 2.25, 2.370370, 2.44141, 2.48832, 2.52163, 2.54650, 2.56578, 2.58117, 2.59374. Actually, these numbers approach the value $2.71828\ldots$.

25. From $0 \leq x \leq \frac{\pi}{2}$ we have $\sin x \geq 0$ and $\cos x \geq 0$. Thus we may apply the AG-inequality to get $\frac{\sin x + \cos x}{2} \geq \sqrt{\sin x \cos x}$. Since $\sin 2x = 2\sin x \cos x$, we see that $\sqrt{\sin x \cos x} = \sqrt{\frac{\sin 2x}{2}}$ and so $\frac{\sin x + \cos x}{2} \geq \sqrt{\frac{\sin 2x}{2}}$. Multiplying both sides by $\sqrt{2}$ we get the desired inequality.

Chapter 2

Solutions

2.1   Exercise Set 4

1. 4
2. 1
3. 0
4. $+\infty$, since $t > 2$ and $t \to 2$.
5. 0
6. -1, since $|x| = -x$ for $x < 0$.
7. 0
8. $-\frac{1}{\pi}$
9. 0
10. $+\infty$, since $|x - 1| = 1 - x > 0$ for $x < 1$.
11. 0
12. $\dfrac{1}{6}$
13. i) 0, ii) 1. Since the limits are different the graph must have a break at $x = 1$.
14. i) 1, ii) 1, iii) 0, iv) 1; since the one-sided limits are equal at $x = 0$ and $g(0) = 1$, the graph has no break at $x = 0$. But since these limits are different at $x = 1$, it must have a break at $x = 1$.
15. i) 1, ii) 2, iii) 1, iv) 2.

2.2   Exercise Sets 5, 6, 7, 8

1. No, because the left and right-hand limits at $x = 0$ are different, $(2 \neq 0)$.
2. Yes, the value is 4, because the two one-sided limits are equal (to 4).
3. Yes, the value is 0, because the two one-sided limits are equal (to 0).
4. Yes, the value is 0, because the two one-sided limits are equal (to 0).
5. Yes, the value is 0, because the two one-sided limits are equal; remove the absolute value, first, and note that $\sin 0 = 0$.
6. No, because the left-hand limit at $x = 0$ is $-\infty$ while the right-hand limit there is $+\infty$.
7. No, because the left-hand limit at $x = 0$ is $-\infty$ and the right-hand limit there is $+\infty$.
8. Yes, the answer is 1/2 because the two-one sided limits are equal (to $\frac{1}{2}$).
9. Yes, because the two-one sided limits are equal (to 2).
10. No, because the left-hand limit at $x = 0$ is $+3$ and the right-hand limit there is $+2$ $(3 \neq 2)$.
11. a) Yes, the left and right-hand limits are equal (to 0) and $f(0) = 0$;
    b) Yes, because g is a polynomial;
    c) Yes, because the left and right-limits are equal to 3 and $h(0) = 3$;
    d) Yes, since by Table 2.4d, the left and right-limits exist and are equal and $f(0) = 2$;
    e) Yes, because f is the quotient of two continuous functions with a non-zero denominator at $x = 0$. Use Table 2.4d again.
12. Follow the hints.

Exercise Set 6

1. $x = 0$ only; this is because the right limit is 2 but the left-limit is 0. So, f cannot be continuous at $x = 0$.

2. $x = 0$ only; this is because the right limit is 1 but the left-limit is 0. So, f cannot be continuous at $x = 0$.

3. $x = \pm 1$ because these are the roots of the denominator, so the function is infinite there, and so it cannot be continuous there.

4. $x = 0$ only. In this case the right limit is the same as the left-limit, 1, but the value of $f(0) = 2$ is not equal to this common value, so it cannot be continuous there.

5. $x = 0$ only. This is because the right-limit at $x = 0$ is $+\infty$, so even though $f(0)$ is finite, it doesn't matter, since one of the limits is infinite. So, f cannot be continuous at $x = 0$.

6. $x = 0$ only, because the left-limit there is 1.62 while its right-limit there is 0. There are no other points of discontinuity.

Exercise Set 7

1. -1. Use the trigonometric identity, $\sin(\square + \pi) = -\sin\square$.

2. -1. Use the hint.

3. 2. Multiply the expression by $1 = \frac{2}{2}$ and rearrange terms.

4. 0. Let $\square = 3x$, rearrange terms and simplify.

5. 2. Multiply the whole expression by "1" or $\frac{2x}{4x} \cdot \frac{4x}{2x}$.

6. 1. Let $\square = \sqrt{x-1}$. As $x \to 1$ we have $\square \to 0$ and $\frac{\sin\square}{\square} \to 1$.

Exercise Set 8

1. 0. Continuity of the quotient at $x = 2$.

2. 0. Note that $\cos 0 = 1$.

3. $\frac{1}{6}$. Factor the denominator.

4. -1. Rewrite the secant function as the reciprocal of the cosine function and use the trig. identity $\cos\square = -\sin(\square - \frac{\pi}{2})$.

5. -2. Factor out the 2 from the numerator and then use the idea of Exercise 4, above.

6. 0. The function is continuous at $x = 2$, and $\sin 2\pi = 0$.

7. 3. Multiply and divide the expression by 3 and rewrite it in a more familiar form.

8. $-\infty$. Use your calculator for a test of this limit. The numerator approaches -1 and the denominator approaches 0 through positive values. So the quotient must approach the stated value.

9. $+\infty$. The denominator approaches 0 through negative values, while the numerator approaches -1. Thus, the quotient approaches the stated value.

10. 0. The function is continuous at $x = 0$.

11. $x = \pi$. The denominator is 0 and the numerator isn't.

12. $x \to 0$. Since $\lim_{x \to 0} f(x) = \lim_{x \to 0} \frac{\sin x}{x} = 1 \neq f(0)$, we know that f cannot be continuous there, by definition.

13. None. This is because f is a polynomial and so it is continuous everywhere.

14. $x = \pm 1$, the roots of the denominator.

15. $x = \pm 2$. For $x = 2$ the numerator is of the form $0/0$ and $f(2)$ is not defined at all, so the function is not continuous here (by definition). Next, the denominator is zero for $x = -2$, but the numerator isn't zero here. So the function is of the form $-4/0 = -\infty$ and so once again, f is not continuous here because its value here is $-\infty$.

16. $\frac{3}{2}$. Use the Hint. We know from the Hint (with $A = x$, $B = 2x$) that $\cos x - \cos 2x = -2\sin(3x/2)\sin(-x/2)$. Then

$$\frac{\cos x - \cos 2x}{x^2} = -\frac{2\sin(3x/2)}{x}\frac{\sin(-x/2)}{x},$$
$$= -\frac{2\left(\frac{3}{2}\right)\sin(3x/2)\left(\frac{-1}{2}\right)\sin(-x/2)}{\left(\frac{3x}{2}\right)\left(\frac{-x}{2}\right)},$$
$$= -\left(-\frac{3}{2}\right)\frac{\sin(3x/2)}{\left(\frac{3x}{2}\right)}\frac{\sin(-x/2)}{\left(\frac{-x}{2}\right)}.$$

Now use the hint with $\square = \frac{3x}{2}$ and $\square = -\frac{x}{2}$, as $x \to 0$. Both limits approach 1 and so their product approaches 3/2.

17. 0. Use the Hint. We can rewrite the expression as

$$\frac{\tan x - \sin x}{x^2} = \frac{\tan x\,(1 - \cos x)}{x^2},$$

$$= \frac{\tan x}{x}\left(\frac{1 - \cos x}{x}\right),$$

$$= \left(\frac{\sin x}{x}\right)\left(\frac{1}{\cos x}\right)\left(\frac{1 - \cos x}{x}\right).$$

As $x \to 0$, the first term approaches 1, the second term approaches 1, while the last term approaches 0, by Table 2.12. So, their product approaches 0.

18. $+\infty$. The limit exists and is equal to $+\infty$.

19. $a = -\frac{\pi}{2}$, $b = -\pi a = \frac{\pi^2}{2}$.

20. 1. Rationalize the denominator. Note that the function is continuous at $x = 0$.

2.3

2.4   Exercise Set 9

1. 0. This is a limit as $x \to \infty$, not as $x \to 0$.

2. 0. Divide the numerator and denominator by x and simplify.

3. 1. Divide the numerator and denominator by x and simplify.

4. $\frac{1}{2}$. Rationalize the numerator first, factor out $\sqrt{x}$ out of the quotient, simplify and then take the limit.

5. 0. Use the Sandwich Theorem.

6. The graph of the function $\sin x$ isn't going anywhere definite; it just keeps oscillating between 1 and -1 forever and so it cannot have a limit. This is characteristic of *periodic functions* in general.

2.5

2.6   Chapter Exercises

1. Since f is a polynomial, it is continuous everywhere and so also at $x = 1$.

2. g is the product of two continuous functions (continuous at 0) and so it is itself continuous at $t = 0$.

3. h is the sum of three continuous functions and so it is continuous at $z = 0$.

4. f is a constant multiple of a continuous function and so it is continuous too (at $x = \pi$).

5. The graph of f is 'V'-shaped at $x = -1$ but it is continuous there nevertheless.

6. The limit is $3 - 2 + 1 = 2$ since f is continuous at $x = 1$.

7. The limit is $0 \cdot 1 = 0$ since g is continuous at $t = 0$.

8. The limit is $0 + (2)(0) - \cos 2 = -\cos 2 \approx 0.416$ since h is continuous at $z = 0$.

9. The limit is $2 \cdot \cos \pi = (2)(-1) = -2$ since f is continuous at $x = \pi$.

10. The limit is $|-1 + 1| = |0| = 0$ since f is continuous at $x = -1$.

11. 0. The function is continuous at $t = 2$.

12. $\frac{1}{8}$. Factor the denominator first, then take the limit.

13. $+\infty$. Use extended real numbers.

14. 1. Remove the absolute value first.

15. $+\infty$.

16. i) 1; ii) 1; iii) 0; iv) 1; v) Since (i) and (ii) are equal we see that g is continuous at $x = 0$ as $g(0) = 1$, by definition. Since the left and right limits at $x = 1$ are different (by (iii) and (iv)), we see that g is not continuous at $x = 1$ and so the graph has a break there.

17. The limit from the left is 2 and the limit from the right is 1. So the limit cannot exist.

18. $|-2| = 2$. The absolute value function is continuous there.

19. $0/(-1) = 0$. The quotient is continuous at $x = -2$.

20. 0. The function is continuous at that point.

21. Does not exist. The left-hand limit as $x \to 1$ is 1, but the right-hand limit as $x \to 1$ is $|1 - 1| = 0$, so the limit cannot exist.

22. $x = 0$. This is because the left-and right-hand limits there are not equal. For example, the left limit is -2 while the right-limit is 0. Use the definition of the absolute value, OK?

23. $x = 0$. The left-hand limit is -1 while the right-hand limit is 1.

24. None. The denominator is $x^3 - 1 = (x - 1)(x^2 + x + 1)$ with $x = 1$ as its only real root. Why? By "completing the square", we have $x^2 + x + 1 = \left(x + \frac{1}{2}\right)^2 + \frac{3}{4} \geq \frac{3}{4} > 0$ and hence $x^2 + x + 1$ does not have real roots. The only possible point of discontinuity is $x = 1$. But both the left and right limits at $x = 1$ are $-1/3$, which is also the value of f at $x = 1$. Hence f is continuous at $x = 1$ and so everywhere.

25. $x = 0$. Even though the values of the left and right limits here are 'close' they are not equal, since $-0.99 \neq -1$.

26. $x = 0$. The left and right-hand limits there are both equal to $+\infty$, so f cannot be continuous there.

27. $\frac{a}{b}$. Multiply the expression by $1 = \frac{bx}{ax} \frac{ax}{bx}$, simplify. Then take the limit.

28. $+\infty$. This limit actually exists in the extended reals. Observe that the numerator approaches 1 regardless of the direction (left or right) because it is continuous there, while the denominator approaches 0 regardless of the direction, too, and for the same reason. The quotient must then approach $1/0 = +\infty$ in the extended reals.

29. 0. Break up the expression into three parts, one involving only the term x, another with the term $\sin x / x$ and the remaining one with the term $x / \sin 2x$. The first term approaches 0, the next term approaches 1 while the last term approaches $1/2$, by Exercise 27, with $a = 2, b = 1$ and Table 2.4, (d). So, the product of these three limits must be equal to zero.

30. 1. Let $\square = \sqrt{3 - x}$. As $x \to 3^-$, we have $\square \to 0^+$ and so $\frac{\sin \square}{\square} \to 1$.

31. $\frac{b}{a}$. See Exercise 27 in this Section: Multiply the expression by ax/ax, re-arrange terms and evaluate.

32. 0. This limit actually exists. This is because the numerator oscillates between the values of ± 1 as $x \to \infty$, while the denominator approaches ∞. The quotient must then approach $(something)/\infty = 0$ in the extended reals.

33. Does not exist. There are many reasons that can be given for this answer. The easiest is found by studying its graph and seeing that it's not 'going anywhere'. You can also see that this function is equal to zero infinitely often as $x \to -\infty$ (at the zeros or roots of the sine function). But then it also becomes as large as you want it to when x is chosen to be anyone of the values which makes $\sin x = -1$. So, it oscillates like crazy as $x \to -\infty$, and so its limit doesn't exist.

34. 0. Hard to believe? Rationalize the numerator by multiplying and dividing by the expression $\sqrt{x^2 + 1} + x$.

The numerator will look like $(x^2 + 1) - x^2 = 1$, while the denominator looks like $\sqrt{x^2 + 1} + x$. So, as $x \to +\infty$, the numerator stays at 1 while the denominator tends to ∞. In the end you should get something like $1/\infty = 0$ in the extended reals.

35. Set $a = -5, b = 1$ in Bolzano's Theorem and set your calculator to radians. Now, calculate the values of $f(-5), f(1)$. You should find something like $f(-5) = -4.511$ and $f(1) = 1.382$ so that their product $f(-5) \cdot f(1) < 0$. Since the function is a product of continuous functions, Bolzano's Theorem guarantees that $f(x) = 0$ somewhere inside the interval $[-5, 1]$. So, there is a root there.

36. Set $a = -3, b = 0$. Now, calculate the values of $f(-3), f(0)$. Then $f(-3) = -9$ and $f(0) = 2$ so that their product $f(-3) \cdot f(0) < 0$. Since the function is a polynomial, it is a continuous function, so Bolzano's Theorem guarantees that $f(x) = 0$ somewhere inside the interval $[-3, 0]$. So, there is a root there.

37. Let $f(x) = x^2 - \sin x$. Write $f(a) \cdot f(b)$. Now let a, b with $a < b$ be any two numbers whatsoever. Check that your calculator is in radian mode, and calculate the values $f(a) \cdot f(b)$ like crazy! As soon as you find values of a, b where $f(a) \cdot f(b) < 0$, then STOP. You have an interval $[a, b]$ where $f(x) = 0$ somewhere inside, by Bolzano's Theorem. For example, $f(-0.3) \cdot f(2.5) = 2.179$, $f(0.3) \cdot f(1.5) = -0.257 < 0$. STOP. So we know there is a root in the interval $[0.3, 1.5]$.

Chapter 3

Solutions

3.1 Exercise Set 10

1. 4. Use the binomial theorem to expand and simplify.

2. -1. Note that $f(x) = -x$ for $x < 0$ and so for $x = -1$, too.

3. $+\infty$. The quotient is equal to $1/h^2 \to +\infty$ as $h \to 0$.

4. a) $+\infty$,   b) 1. Note that $f(1 + h) = 1 + h$ for $h < 0$ and $f(1 + h) = 2 + h$ for $h > 0$.

5. $\dfrac{1}{2\sqrt{2}} \approx 0.3536$.

6. 4. Use the binomial theorem to expand and simplify.

7. 3.

8. -4.

9. 6.

10. 1. Note that $f(x) = x$ near $x = 1$.

11. 0. Note that $f(x) = x^2$ for $x > 0$ and $f(x) = -x^2$ for $x < 0$.

12. 0 for all $x \neq 0$, and the slope does not exist when $x = 0$.

13. The derivative does not exist since f is not continuous there.

14. The derivative does not exist because $f(x)$ is undefined for any x slightly less than -1. However, its right-derivative at $x = -1$ is $+\infty$.

15. Yes. The absolute value can be removed so that $f(x) = x^2$. It turns out that $f'(0) = 0$.

16. $f'(1) = -\frac{1}{2}$.

17. $f'(1) = -2$.

18. a) $f'(1)$ does not exist since f is *not continuous* at $x = 1$. Note that the left- and right-derivatives at $x = 1$ are equal: $f'_+(1) = 1$, $f'_-(1) = 1$.

    b) No. In this case f is continuous at $x = 2$ but the one-sided derivatives are unequal: $f'_+(2) = -4$, $f'_-(2) = 1$.

    c) Since $2 < \frac{5}{2} < 3$, we see that $f'(\frac{5}{2}) = -5$.

3.2 Exercise Set 11

1. $\dfrac{3}{2} x^{\frac{1}{2}} = \dfrac{3}{2}\sqrt{x}$.

2. $-2t^{-3} = -\dfrac{2}{t^3}$.

3. 0.

4. $\dfrac{2}{3} x^{-1/3} = \dfrac{2}{3\sqrt[3]{x}}$.

5. $\dfrac{t^{-4/5}}{5} = \dfrac{1}{5\sqrt[5]{t^4}}$.

6. 0.

7. $4t^3$.

8. $-3x^{-4} = -\dfrac{3}{x^4}$.

9. $-x^{-2} = -\dfrac{1}{x^2}$.

10. $\pi x^{\pi-1}$.

11. $2t$. Use the Power Difference Rules

12. $6x + 2$. Use the Power, Sum and Difference Rules

13. $1(t^2 + 4) + 2t(t - 1)$. Use the Product Rule

14. $f(x) = 3x^{5/2} + x^{1/2}$ so $f'(x) = \frac{15}{2}x^{3/2} + \frac{1}{2\sqrt{x}}$, Use the Power Rule

15. $\dfrac{(2x + 1)\,(0.5)x^{-0.5} - 2x^{0.5}}{(2x + 1)^2}$. Use the Quotient Rule

16. $\dfrac{(x + 1) - (x - 1)}{(x + 1)^2} = \dfrac{2}{(x + 1)^2}$. Use the Quotient Rule

17. $\dfrac{(x^2 + x - 1)\,(3x^2) - (x^3 - 1)\,(2x + 1)}{(x^2 + x - 1)^2}$. Use the Quotient Rule

18. $\dfrac{(\sqrt{x} + 3x^{3/4})\,((2/3)x^{-1/3}) - (x^{2/3})\left((1/2)x^{-1/2} + (9/4)x^{-1/4}\right)}{(\sqrt{x} + 3x^{3/4})^2}$. Use the Quotient Rule

3.3   Exercise Set 12

1. 0.

2. 3.

3. $\frac{2}{3}$.

4. $\frac{3}{2}\sqrt{x - 4}$.

5. $-\frac{5}{2}x^{-7/2}$.

6. $\frac{1}{3}(2t + 1)(t^2 + t - 2)^{-2/3}$.

7. $\dfrac{d^2 f}{dx^2} = 6$.

8. $4x(x + 1)^3 + (x + 1)^4 = (x + 1)^3(5x + 1)$.

9. $-\frac{1}{2}$.

10. $(t + 2)^2 + 2(t - 1)(t + 2) = 3t^2 + 6t$.

11. $32(\frac{4}{3}x^2 - x)(x - 1)^{-1/3} = \frac{32}{3}(4x^2 - 3x)(x - 1)^{-1/3}$.

12. $210(2x + 3)^{104}$.

13. $\frac{1}{2}\dfrac{1}{\sqrt{x}} = \dfrac{1}{2\sqrt{x}}$.

14. $3x^2 - 6x + 3$, or $3(x - 1)^2$: Both are identical.

15. $-\dfrac{1}{x^2} + \dfrac{x}{\sqrt{x^2 - 1}}$.

16. $\dfrac{1}{4}\dfrac{1 + 3\sqrt{x}}{x\sqrt{x}(1 + \sqrt{x})^3} = \dfrac{1 + 3\sqrt{x}}{4x^{3/2}(1 + \sqrt{x})^3}$.

17. -10. Note that $f''(x) = 6x - 10$.

18. $3.077(x + 0.5)^{-3.324}$.

19. Use the **Chain Rule**: For instance, let $\square = x^2$, from which we get $\frac{d}{dx}f(\square) = f'(\square)D\square$. Put x^2 in the Box, note that $D\square = 2x$ and simplify. You'll find $\frac{d}{dx}f(x^2) = 2x\,f'(x^2)$.

20. Use another form of the Chian Rule: Putting $u = g(x)$ and $w = \sqrt[3]{u} \equiv u^{1/3}$, we have $w = \sqrt[3]{g(x)}$ and

$$\frac{d}{dx}\sqrt[3]{g(x)} = \frac{dw}{dx} = \frac{dw}{du} \cdot \frac{du}{dx} = \frac{1}{3}u^{-2/3} \cdot g'(x) = \frac{g'(x)}{3\sqrt[3]{g(x)^2}}.$$

21. Let $y(x) = f(x^2)$. By the Chain Rule, we have $y'(x) = f'(x^2) \cdot 2x = 2xf'(x^2)$. Replacing x by x^2 in $f'(x) + f(x) = 0$, we have $f'(x^2) + f(x^2) = 0$, or $f'(x^2) = -f(x^2) = -y(x)$. So $y'(x) = 2xf(x^2)$ can be rewritten as $y'(x) = -2xy(x)$, that is, $y'(x) + 2xy(x) = 0$.

22. Use the Chain Rule once again on both sides of $f(F(x)) = x$. We find $f'(F(x))F'(x) = 1$, which gives $F'(x) = \dfrac{1}{f'(F(x))}$.

23. Use another form of the Chain Rule: $\dfrac{dy}{du} = \dfrac{dy}{dt} \cdot \dfrac{dt}{du} = 3t^2 \cdot \dfrac{1}{2\sqrt{u}}$. At $u = 9$ we have $t = \sqrt{9} + 6 = 9$ and $\dfrac{dy}{du} = 3 \cdot 9^2 \cdot \dfrac{1}{2\sqrt{9}} = \dfrac{81}{2}$.

24. $y = 32(x - 2) + 1$ (or $32x - y - 63 = 0$).

25. Just use the Chain Rule. You don't even have to know f, g explicitly, just their values: So, $y'(2) = f'(g(2)) \cdot g'(2) = f'(0) \cdot 1 = 1$.

26. $\left(1 - \dfrac{2}{(3t - 2\sqrt{t})^2}\right)\left(3 - \dfrac{1}{\sqrt{t}}\right)$. Use the Chain Rule in the form: $\dfrac{dy}{dt} = \dfrac{dy}{dr} \cdot \dfrac{dr}{dt}$. But $\dfrac{dy}{dr}\dfrac{dr}{dt} = \left(1 - 2r^{-2}\right)\left(3 - t^{-1/2}\right)$ Now set $r = 3t - 2\sqrt{t}$.

27. $f'(9) = \frac{7}{24\sqrt{3}}$, since $f'(x) = \frac{1}{2}\frac{1+\frac{1}{2\sqrt{x}}}{\sqrt{x+\sqrt{x}}}$. On the other hand, since $\sqrt{t^2} = |t|$, we see that $\frac{df}{dt} =$

$\frac{2t+1}{2\sqrt{t^2+t}}$, if $t \geq 0$ and $\frac{df}{dt} = \frac{2t-1}{2\sqrt{t^2-t}}$ if $t < 0$.

28. Let $y = |x| = \sqrt{x^2}$. Now, set $g(u) = \sqrt{u}$, $u = u(x) = x^2$. Then, $y = g(u(x))$. Using the Chain Rule we get $y'(x) = g'(u(x)) \cdot u'(x) = \frac{1}{2\sqrt{u}} \cdot (2x) = \frac{x}{\sqrt{x^2}} = \frac{x}{|x|}$, whenever $x \neq 0$.

29. By definition, $\lim_{h \to 0} \frac{f(x_0+h)-f(x_0)}{h} = f'(x_0)$. Look at the limit

$$\lim_{h \to 0}[f(x_0+h)-f(x_0)] = \lim_{h \to 0}\frac{f(x_0+h)-f(x_0)}{h} \cdot h = f'(x_0) \cdot 0 = 0.$$

We have shown that $\lim_{h \to 0} f(x_0+h) - f(x_0) = 0$, which forces

$$\lim_{h \to 0} f(x_0+h) = f(x_0).$$

This, however, is another way of writing

$$\lim_{x \to x_0} f(x) = f(x_0).$$

Hence f is continuous at x_0 (by an equivalent definition of continuity).

3.4   Exercise Set 13

1. -2. Implicit differentiation gives $(2x+y) + y'(x)(x+2y) = 0$. Now set $x = 1$, $y = 0$ and solve for $y'(1)$.

2. $\frac{dy}{dx} = \frac{3x^2-2y^2}{4xy-4y^3}$. $\frac{dx}{dy} = \frac{4xy-4y^3}{3x^2-2y^2}$.

3. $-\frac{1}{129}$. Implicit differentiation gives an expression of the form $\frac{1}{2}(x+y)^{-1/2}(1+y') + xy' + y = 0$. Now solve for y' after setting $x = 16$ and $y = 0$.

4. $\frac{1}{2y}$. Implicit differentiation gives an expression of the form $1 - 2yy'(x) = 0$. Now solve for y'.

5. 0. Implicit differentiation gives an expression of the form $2x + 2yy'(x) = 0$. Now set $x = 0$, $y = 3$. You see that $y'(0) = 0$.

6. $y + 1 = \frac{1}{2}(x+1)$. Note that $y'(x) = \frac{x}{2y}$.

7. $y - 1 = \frac{1}{3}(x-1)$, or $x - 3y + 2 = 0$. Note that $y'(x) = \frac{2-y}{x+2y}$.

8. $y = \frac{5}{2}(x-4)$, or $5x - 2y - 20 = 0$. Note that $y'(x) = \frac{x+1}{2-y}$.

9. $y = -(x-1) - 1$, or $x + y = 0$. Note that $y'(x) = -\frac{y(2x+y)}{x(x+2y)}$.

3.5   Exercise Set 14

1. $\frac{\cos 1}{2}$. The derivative is given by $\frac{\cos\sqrt{x}}{2\sqrt{x}}$.

2. $2\sec(2x) \cdot \tan(2x) \cdot \sin x + \sec(2x) \cdot \cos x$.

3. 1. The derivative is given by $\cos^2 x - \sin^2 x$. Now evaluate this at $x = 0$.

4. $\frac{1}{1-\sin x}$. The derivative is given by $\frac{1+\sin x}{\cos^2 x}$. Now use an identity in the denominator and factor.

5. $\frac{1}{2}$. Note that $y'(t) = \frac{\cos t}{2\sqrt{1+\sin t}}$. Now set $t = 0$.

6. $-2x\sin(x^2)\cos(\cos(x^2))$.

7. $2x\cos 3x - 3x^2\sin 3x$.

8. $\frac{2}{3}x^{-1/3}\tan(x^{1/3}) + \frac{1}{3}\sec^2(x^{1/3})$.

9. $-(1 + \cos x)\csc^2(2 + x + \sin x)$. Don't forget the *minus* sign here!

10. $-3\cot 3x \csc 3x$. The original function is the same as $\csc 3x$.

11. 1. In this case, the derivative is given by $\frac{-\sin x + x\cos x + \cos x}{\cos^2 x - 1}$. Remember that $\cos(\pi/2) = 0$, $\sin(\pi/2) = 1$.

12. $4x\cos(2x^2)$.

13. 1. In this case, the derivative is given by $2\sin x \cos x$. When $x = \frac{\pi}{4}$ we know that $\cos\frac{\pi}{4} = \sin\frac{\pi}{4} = \frac{\sqrt{2}}{2}$.

14. $-3\csc^2(3x - 2)$.

15. $2\csc x - (2x+3)\csc x \cot x$.

16. $-(\sin x + x\cos x)\sin(x\sin x)$.

17. $\dfrac{1}{2\sqrt{x}}\sec\sqrt{x}+\dfrac{1}{2}\sec\sqrt{x}\cdot\tan\sqrt{x}$.

18.   0, except when $x^2 = 2 + 2n\pi$, where $n \geq 0$ is an integer. This is because $\csc\square \cdot \sin\square = 1$ for any symbol, $\square$, by definition, whenever the cosecant is defined.

19. $-\sin 2(x - 6) - 2\csc 2x\cot 2x$. (Use the identity $2\sin u\cos u = \sin 2u$ to simplify.)

20. $4\sec^2 2x\tan 2x$. The given function is equal to $\sec^2(2x)$.

21.   Notice that, for $x \neq 0$, $y(x) = \sin x/\tan x = \sin x\cdot\cot x = \cos x$. On the other hand, at $x = 0$, we have $y(0) = 1$, which coincides with the value of the cosine function at $x = 0$. Therefore, $y(x) = \cos x$ for all x. Now all three parts are clear.

3.6   Exercise Set 15

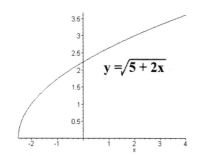

Set 16 # 4:
$f(x) \qquad = \qquad \sqrt{5+2x},$
$x \ in \ [-5/2, \infty).$

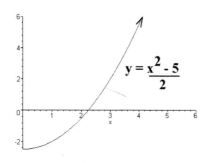

Set 16 # 4:
$f^{-1}(x) = \dfrac{x^2-5}{2}$, $x \ in \ [0,\infty).$

1. $y(x) = 3x - 2$ is continuous on $[0,\ 2]$ and $y(0) = -2 < 0$, $y(2) = 4 > 0$.

2. $y(x) = x^2 - 1$ is continuous, $y(-2) = 3 > 0$ and $y(0) = -1 < 0$.

3. $y(x) = 2x^2 - 3x - 2$ is continuous, $y(0) = -2 < 0$ and $y(3) = 7 > 0$.

4. $y(x) = \sin x + \cos x$ is continuous on $[0,\ \pi]$, $y(0) = 1 > 0$ and $y(\pi) = -1 < 0$.

5. $y(\pi) = -\pi < 0$. But $y(0) = 0$; so 0 is already a root. Try another point instead of 0, say $\frac{\pi}{2}$: $y(\frac{\pi}{2}) = \frac{\pi}{2}\cdot 0 + 1 = 1 > 0$. So there is a root in $[\frac{\pi}{2},\pi]$ and hence in $[0,\pi]$ (besides the root 0.)

6.   (This is hard.) In the proof we use several times the following basic fact in differential calculus: if the derivative of a function is identically zero, then this function must be a constant. Let's begin by applying this fact to the function y'': its derivative $y''' = 0$ implies that y'' is a constant, say $y'' = a$. Let $u = y' - ax$. Then $u' = y'' - a = 0$ and hence u is a constant, say $u = b$, that is, $y' - ax = b$. Let $v = y - \frac{a}{2}x^2 - bx$. Then $v' = y' - \frac{a}{2}\cdot 2x - b = 0$ and hence v is a constant, say $v = c$. Thus $y - \frac{a}{2}x^2 - bx = c$, or $y = \frac{a}{2}x^2 + bx + c$. We can finish the proof by setting $A = \frac{a}{2}$, $B = b$ and $C = c$.

7.   From the assumption that $\frac{dy}{dx} + y(x)^4 + 2 = 0$, we know that $\frac{dy}{dx}$ exists on $(a,\ b)$, and $y(x)$ is continuous on $[a, b]$. Assume the contrary that there are two zeros in $[a, b]$, say x_1, x_2. Using the **Mean Value Theorem,** we see that there exists some c between x_1 and x_2 (*a fortiori*, between a and b) such that $\frac{dy}{dx}(c) = 0$. Thus $y(c)^4 + 2 = 0$. **Impossible!** So there cannot be two zeros for $y(x)$.

8.   Consider the function $y(x) = x - \sin x$. By the Mean Value Theorem we see that, for each $x > 0$, there exists some c between 0 and x such that $y(x) - y(0) = y'(c)(x - 0)$, or $x - \sin x = y'(c)x$; (notice that $y(0) = 0$.) Now $y'(x) = 1 - \cos x$, which is always ≥ 0. So, from $x > 0$ and $y'(c) \geq 0$ we see that $y'(c)x \geq 0$. Thus $x - \sin x \geq 0$, or $\sin x \leq x$.

9.   Use Rolle's Theorem on $[0, \pi]$ applied to the function $f(x) = \sin x$. Since $f(0) = f(\pi) = 0$, we are guaranteed that there exists a point c inside the interval $(0, \pi)$ such that $f'(c) = \cos c = 0$. This point c is the root we seek.

10.   Note that $(\sin x)' = \cos x \leq 1$. For any x in $[0, \frac{\pi}{2}]$, the function $\sin x$ satisfies all the conditions of the **Mean Value Theorem** on $[x,\ \frac{\pi}{2}]$. So, there exists c in $(x,\ \frac{\pi}{2})$ such that

$$\frac{\sin\frac{\pi}{2} - \sin x}{\frac{\pi}{2} - x} = \cos c \leq 1.$$

This stament is equivalent to the stated inequality, since $\sin(\pi/2) = 1$.

11.   (a) $\frac{f(2)-f(0)}{2-0} = \frac{5-(-1)}{2} = 3$ and $f'(c) = 2c + 1 = 3$ give $c = 1$.

(b) $\frac{g(1)-g(0)}{1-0} = \frac{4-3}{1} = 1$ and $g'(c) = 2c = 1$ give $c = \frac{1}{2}$.

12.   Let $x(t)$ denote the distance travelled (in meters) by the electron in time t. We assume that $x(0) = 0$ and we are given that $x(0.3 \times 10^{-8}) = 1$. Now apply the MVT to the time interval $[0, 0.3 \times 10^{-8}]$. Then,

$$\frac{x(0.3 \times 10^{-8}) - x(0)}{0.3 \times 10^{-8} - 0} = x'(c),$$

for some time $t = c$ in between. But this means that the speed of the electron at this time $t = c$ is $\frac{1}{0.3\times 10^{-8}} = 3.3 \times 10^8$ m/sec, which is greater than 2.19×10^8 m/sec, or the speed of light in that medium!

3.7 Exercise Set 16

You can use your Plotter program to sketch the graphs.

1. $f(x) = 4 - x^2$, $0 \le x \le 2$. $f^{-1}(x) = \sqrt{4 - x}$, $0 \le x \le 4$. See the margin.

2. $g(x) = (x - 1)^{-1}$, $1 < x < \infty$. $g^{-1}(x) = x^{-1} + 1$, $0 < x < \infty$.

3. $f(x) = 2 - x^3$, $-\infty < x < \infty$. $f^{-1}(x) = \sqrt[3]{2 - x}$, $-\infty < x < \infty$.

4. $f(x) = \sqrt{5 + 2x}$, $-\frac{5}{2} \le x < \infty$. $f^{-1}(x) = \frac{1}{2}(x^2 - 5)$, $0 \le x < \infty$.

5. $f(y) = (2 + y)^{1/3}$, $-2 < y < \infty$. $f^{-1}(y) = y^3 - 2$, $0 < y < \infty$.

6. (i) $F(0) = 2$, since $f(2) = 0$ forces $2 = F(f(2)) = F(0)$.
   (ii) $f(-1) = 6$, since $F(6) = -1$ means that $6 = f(F(6)) = f(-1)$.
   (iii) Indeed, if $f(x) = 0$ then $x = F(f(x)) = F(0) = 2$, and so this is the only possibility.
   (iv) $y = 8$, because $f(-2) = 8$ means (by definition) that $F(8) = -2$ so $y = 8$ is a solution. No, there are no other solutions since if we set $F(y) = -2$ then $y = f(F(y)) = f(-2) = 8$, so that $y = 8$ is the only such solution.
   (v) No. The reasoning is the same as the preceding exercise. Given that $f(-1) = 6$, the solution x of $f(x) = 6$ must satisfy $x = F(f(x)) = F(6) = -1$, by definition of the inverse function, F.

7. We know that $F'(-1) = \dfrac{1}{f'(F(-1))} = \dfrac{1}{f'(-2.1)} = \dfrac{1}{4}$.

8. $F(x) = x$, $Dom(f) = Ran(F) = (-\infty, +\infty) = \{x : -\infty < x < +\infty\}$, and $Dom(F) = Ran(f) = (-\infty, +\infty)$ too.

9. $F(x) = \dfrac{1}{x}$, $Dom(f) = Ran(F) = \{x : x \ne 0\}$, and $Dom(F) = Ran(f) = \{x : x \ne 0\}$.

10. $F(x) = \sqrt[3]{x}$, $Dom(f) = Ran(F) = \{x : -\infty < x < +\infty\} = Dom(F) = Ran(f)$.

11. $F(t) = \dfrac{t - 4}{7}$, $Dom(f) = Ran(F) = \{x : 0 \le t \le 1\}$ while $Dom(F) = Ran(f) = \{x : -4 \le t \le 11\}$

12. $G(x) = \dfrac{x^2 - 1}{2}$, $Dom(g) = Ran(G) = \{x : -\frac{1}{2} \le x < +\infty\}$ while $Dom(G) = Ran(g) = \{x : 0 \le x < \infty\}$.

13. Note that g is one-to-one on this domain. Its inverse is given by $G(t)$ where $G(t) = \dfrac{\sqrt{1 - t^2}}{2}$, $Dom(g) = Ran(G) = \{t : 0 \le t \le \frac{1}{2}\}$ while $Dom(G) = Ran(g) = \{t : 0 \le t \le 1\}$.

14. This f is also one-to-one on its domain. Its inverse is given by $F(x)$ where $F(x) = \dfrac{3x - 2}{2x + 3}$, $Dom(f) = Ran(F) = \{x : x \ne \frac{3}{2}\}$ while $Dom(F) = Ran(f) = \{x : x \ne -\frac{3}{2}\}$.

15. This g is one-to-one if $y \ge -\frac{1}{2}$ and so it has an inverse, G. Its form is $G(y)$ where $G(y) = \dfrac{-1 + \sqrt{1 + 4y}}{2}$, $Dom(g) = Ran(G) = \{y : -\frac{1}{2} \le y < +\infty\}$ while $Dom(G) = Ran(g) = \{y : -\frac{1}{4} \le y < +\infty\}$.

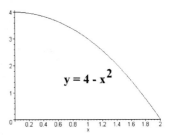

Set 16, # 1:
$f(x) = 4 - x^2$, x in $[0, 2]$.

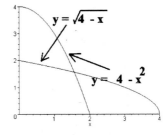

Set 16, # 1:
$f^{-1}(x) = \sqrt{4 - x}$, x in $[0, 4]$.

3.8 Exercise Set 17

1. $\sin(\text{Arccos}(0.5)) = \sin(\frac{\pi}{3}) = \frac{\sqrt{3}}{2}$.

2. $\cos(\text{Arcsin}(0)) = \cos 0 = 1$.

3. $\sec(\sin^{-1}(\frac{1}{2})) = \sec(\frac{\pi}{6}) = \frac{2}{\sqrt{3}}$.

4. $-\sqrt{5}$. (This is hard!) Let $\tan^{-1}(-\frac{1}{2}) = \alpha$. Then $-\frac{\pi}{2} < \alpha < 0$; (see the graph of the Arctangent function in this Section.) Also, $\tan \alpha = -\frac{1}{2}$. Thus

$$\sec^2 \alpha = 1 + \tan^2 \alpha = 1 + (-1/2)^2 = \frac{5}{4}.$$

But $-\frac{\pi}{2} < \alpha < 0$ implies that $\sec \alpha = 1/\cos \alpha > 0$. Therefore

$$\csc \alpha = \frac{1}{\sin \alpha} = \frac{\cos \alpha}{\sin \alpha} \cdot \frac{1}{\cos \alpha} = \frac{1}{\tan \alpha} \cdot \sec \alpha = (-2)\frac{\sqrt{5}}{2} = -\sqrt{5}.$$

5. $\sec(\sin^{-1}(\frac{\sqrt{3}}{2})) = \sec \frac{\pi}{3} = 2$.

6. $\text{Arcsin}(\tan(-\frac{\pi}{4})) = \text{Arcsin}(-1) = -\frac{\pi}{2}$.

3.9   Exercise Set 18

1. $\dfrac{d}{dx}\text{Arcsin}(x^2) = \dfrac{2x}{\sqrt{1-x^4}}$ which is 0 at $x = 0$.

2. $2x\text{Arccos}\,x - \dfrac{x^2}{\sqrt{1-x^2}}$.

3. $\dfrac{1}{2(1+x)\sqrt{x}}$.

4. $-\dfrac{\sin x}{|\sin x|}$. Remember the identity?

5. $\dfrac{\sin x - \sin^{-1}x \cdot \cos x \sqrt{1-x^2}}{\sin^2 x \cdot \sqrt{1-x^2}}$.

6. $\dfrac{1}{2|x|\sqrt{(x^2-1)\sec^{-1}x}}$.

7. 2, because $\cos(2\text{Arcsin}\,x) \cdot \dfrac{2}{\sqrt{1-x^2}}$ which is 2 at $x = 0$.

8. $-\dfrac{16x}{\sqrt{1-16x^2}}$.

9. $-\dfrac{1}{(\text{Arctan}\,x)^2(1+x^2)}$.

10. $3x^2\text{Arc}\sec(x^3) + \dfrac{3|x|^3}{x\sqrt{x^6-1}}$.

3.10   Special Exercise Set

1. $3200\,\pi \approx 10,053.1\,\text{mm}^3/\text{min}$. First, convert all centimeters to millimeters. Then use the volume formulae $V = \frac{4}{3}\pi r^3$ and $\frac{dV}{dt} = 4\pi r^2 \frac{dr}{dt}$. Set $r = 20$ and $r' = 2$.

2. $0.5\,\text{m/sec}$. Let x be the length of one of its walls. Use the volume formulae $V = x^3$ and $\frac{dV}{dt} = 3x^2\frac{dx}{dt}$. Solve for dx/dt and set $x = 2$ and $V' = 6$.

3. $16.1\,\text{cm}^2/\text{sec}$. Let x be the length of one of its sides and y be the other. Use the area formula $A = xy$ and $x = \tau y$. Then $A = \tau y^2$ and $dA/dt = 2\tau y\,dy/dt$. Finally, set $y = 6.2$, $dy/dt = 2.1$.

4. $379.32\,\text{km/hr}$. Use Pythagoras with D, the distance between them, as the hypotenuse. Let x, y be the positions of the cars at a given time. Now use the fact $D^2 = x^2 + y^2$ from which we get

$$\frac{dD}{dt} = \frac{x\frac{dx}{dt} + y\frac{dy}{dt}}{D}.$$

Set $x = 4$, $dx/dt = 281$ and $y = 6.7$, $dy/dt = 274$. From this derive that $D = 7.8$ and then the answer.

5. $\frac{50\pi}{67} \approx 2.34\,\text{cm/sec}$. Let $A = \pi r^2$ be the area and $C = 2\pi r$ its circumference. Relate A to C to find

$$A = \frac{C^2}{4\pi}.$$

Differentiate this formula and solve for dC/dt. Set $C = 67$ and $A' = 25$.

6. $549,988,154.1\,\text{km}^3/\text{hr}$. Let $V = \frac{4}{3}\pi a^2 c$. Differentiate this with respect to t and note that $dc/dt = 0$ by hypothesis. This gives

$$\frac{dV}{dt} = \frac{8\pi a}{3}\frac{da}{dt}.$$

Set $a = 50,500$ and $da/dt = 1300$.

7. Use the Cosine Law to find their mutual distance, D. Note that $\cos(2\pi/3) = -1/2$, so that $D = 1351.04\,\text{mi}$. Now, let A, B denote the distances of each one of the planes from the airport. Since the planes are *approaching* the airport it follows that $A' = dA/dt < 0$ and $B' = dB/dt < 0$. Since, by the Cosine Law, $D^2 = A^2 + B^2 - 2AB\cos(2\pi/3)$ it follows by implicit differentiation that

$$D' = AA' + BB' - \left(A'B + AB'\right)\cos(2\pi/3).$$

Finally, set $A' = -790$, $B' = -770$, $A = 30$, $B = 46$, $D = 1351.04$ to get the answer.

8. $3.5\,\text{dollars/wk}$. Find dC/dt using implicit differentiation and set $x = 100$, $dx/dt = 10$.

9. **Project:** $-254.78\,\text{km/sec}$. Let x be the length of one side. Show that the area of the triangle is given by $A = \frac{\sqrt{3}}{4}x^2$. Find A' and solve for dx/dt. Next, find x in terms of A and derive the formula

$$\frac{dx}{dt} = \frac{1}{\sqrt[4]{3}}\frac{1}{\sqrt{A}}\frac{dA}{dt}.$$

Finally, set $A = 500,000$ and $A' = -237,100$, (note the minus sign).

3.11   Exercise Set 19

1. 0.73909

2. 1.5193. Newton's Method will require 4 iterations.

3. 1.259. This will require 3 iterations.

4. The "answer" may read $-0.20005 < answer < -0.19995$. This root is NOT equal to -0.2!

5. $-1.57079 \approx -\frac{\pi}{2}$. But you only see this approximation after 7 iterations! In fact, note that $-\frac{\pi}{2}$ is the root in this interval as one can check directly.

6. 1.287 after 3 iterations if we start with $x_0 = 1.5$.

7. 2.05 (actually, 2.055255...)

3.12   Exercise Set 20

1. $-\dfrac{1}{2}$.

2. 1.

3. 0.

4. -2. Factor the numerator and simplify.

5. 2. Factor the numerator and simplify.

6. 2. Use L'Hospital's Rule.

7. 0. Use L'Hospital's Rule.

8. 0. Indeed, $\displaystyle\lim_{t \to 0} \frac{\sin^2 t - \sin(t^2)}{t^2} = \lim_{t \to 0}\left[\left(\frac{\sin t}{t}\right)^2 - \frac{\sin(t^2)}{t^2}\right] = 1 - 1 = 0$.

9. $\dfrac{1}{2}$. The quotient is continuous at $x = 1$. Use of L'Hospital's Rule will give nonsense here.

10. This limit does not exist. In fact, applying L'Hospital's rule to the one-sided limits at $x = 0$ shows that
$$\lim_{x \to 0^+} \frac{\text{Arctan } x}{x^2} = \lim_{x \to 0^+} \frac{(1+x^2)^{-1}}{2x} = +\infty \text{ and } \lim_{x \to 0^-} \frac{\text{Arctan } x}{x^2} = \lim_{x \to 0^-} \frac{(1+x^2)^{-1}}{2x} = -\infty. \text{ So}$$
there is NO limit at $x = 0$.

11. 1. By L'Hospital's rule, $\displaystyle\lim_{x \to 0} \frac{(1-x^2)^{-1/2}}{(1+x^2)^{-1}} = 1$.

12. $\dfrac{6}{5}$. Multiply the expression by $1 = \dfrac{5x}{3x} \cdot \dfrac{3x}{5x}$, re-arrange terms and take the limit.

13. $\dfrac{1}{3}$. Use L'Hospital's Rule.

14. $\dfrac{1}{36}$. In this exercise we must apply L'Hospital's rule "three" times before we can see the answer.

15. 2. Indeed,

$$
\begin{aligned}
\lim_{x \to 0} \frac{x \sin(\sin x)}{1 - \cos(\sin x)} &= \lim_{x \to 0} \frac{\sin(\sin x) + x \cos(\sin x) \cdot \cos x}{\sin(\sin x) \cdot \cos x} \\
&= \lim_{x \to 0}\left(\frac{1}{\cos x} + \frac{x \cos(\sin x)}{\sin(\sin x)}\right) \\
&= 1 + \lim_{x \to 0}\left(\frac{x}{\sin(\sin x)} \cdot \cos(\sin x)\right) \\
&= 1 + \lim_{x \to 0}\left(\frac{x}{\sin x} \cdot \frac{\sin x}{\sin(\sin x)} \cdot \cos(\sin x)\right) = 2.
\end{aligned}
$$

3.13   Chapter Exercises

1. $27(x+1)^{26}$.

2. $-3\cos^2 x \sin x$.

3. $\csc 2x - 2(x+1)\csc 2x \cot 2x$. Note that $csc(2x) = \frac{1}{\sin 2x}$.

4. $2(x+5)\cos((x+5)^2)$. You can easily do this one using the "Box" form of the Chain Rule!

5. $\dfrac{\sin x - \cos x}{(\sin x + \cos x)^2}$.

6. $\dfrac{1}{\sqrt{2x-5}}$. Use the Generalized Power Rule.

7. $2\cos 2x$.

8. $-4\cos 4x \cdot \sin(\sin 4x)$.

9. $6\tan 2x \cdot \sec^3 2x$. The two *minus* signs cancel out!

10. $2x \sec 2x + 2(x^2 + 1)\tan 2x \sec 2x$.

11. $-3\csc 3x \cdot \cot 3x$.

12. $\sec 2x + 2(x+2)\tan 2x \sec 2x$.

13. $\dfrac{2x^2 + 6x - 2}{(2x+3)^2}$.

14. $3\cos 3x \cdot (x^{1/5} + 1) + \frac{1}{5}x^{-4/5} \cdot \sin 3x$.

15. $(2x+6)\cos(x^2 + 6x - 2)$.

16. 2.8 .

17. $\dfrac{2}{3\sqrt[3]{2}} = \dfrac{\sqrt[3]{4}}{3}$.

18. $-\dfrac{\sqrt{3}}{3(2+\sqrt{3})}$. Be careful with the square root terms.

19. $210 \times 5^{104} = 42 \times 5^{105}$.

20. 0 .

21. 4 . The derivative is $4\cos(\sin(4x))\cos(4x)$.

22. 2 .

23. 1 . $f(x) = x + 2$ for $x > -2$. In this case, $x = -1 > -2$ so this is our f .

24. $\dfrac{1}{2\sqrt{2}}$.

25. $87{,}318 \cdot (3x-2)^{97}, \quad 87{,}318$.

26. Putting $u = 3x^2$ and $y = f(u)$, we have

$$\frac{d}{dx} f(3x^2) = \frac{dy}{dx} = \frac{dy}{du} \cdot \frac{du}{dx} = f'(u) \cdot 6x = 6x \cdot f'(3x^2).$$

27. $y - 1 = 24(x-2)$, or $24x - y - 47 = 0$.

28. $\dfrac{81}{2} - \dfrac{\sin 9}{6}$. When $u = 9$ we have $t = 9$ also. We know that $\frac{dy}{du} = \frac{dy}{dt} \cdot \frac{dt}{du}$ or, $(3t^2 - \sin t) \cdot \frac{1}{2\sqrt{u}} = \frac{1}{6}(3 \cdot (81) - \sin 9)$.

29.

$$\begin{aligned}
\frac{dy}{dt} &= \frac{dy}{dr} \cdot \frac{dr}{dt} = \left(\frac{1}{2}r^{-1/2} + 3r^{-2}\right)(3 - t^{-1/2}), \\
&= \left(\frac{1}{2}(3t - 2t^{1/2})^{-1/2} + 3(3t - 2t^{1/2})^{-2}\right)(3 - t^{1/2}).
\end{aligned}$$

30. Notice that, for $x > 0$ we have $y(x) = x^2$ and hence y is differentiable at x with $y'(x) = 2x$. Similarly, for $x < 0$ we have $y(x) = -x^2$ and hence $y'(x) = -2x$. Finally, for $x = 0$ we have

$$\frac{y(h) - y(0)}{h} = \frac{h|h|}{h} = |h| \to 0 \quad \text{as } h \to 0$$

and hence y is also differentiable at $x = 0$ with $y'(0) = 0$. From the above argument we see that $y'(x) = 2|x|$ for all x . It is well-known that the absolute value function $|x|$ is not differentiable at $x = 0$. Therefore the derivative of y' at 0 does not exist. In other words, $y''(0)$ does not exist.

31. $-\dfrac{3}{2}$. The derivative is $3x^2 + 2xy' + 2y + 2yy' = 0$. Set $x = 1$, $y = 0$ and solve for y' .

32. $\dfrac{dy}{dx} = \dfrac{3x^2 - 2y^2}{4xy - 4y^3}, \quad \dfrac{dx}{dy} = \dfrac{4xy - 4y^3}{3x^2 - 2y^2}$.

33. Implicit differentiation gives $\dfrac{1+y'}{2\sqrt{x+y}} + 2xy^2 + 2x^2 yy' = 0$. So, at $(0, 16)$, we have $y' = -1$.

34. $\dfrac{dy}{dx} = \dfrac{3y^2 + y}{5y^4 - 6xy - x}$.

35. The tangent line to the curve at $(4, 0)$ is vertical. Here $2x + 2yy' = 0$ and we are dividing by 0 at $x = 4$.

36. $y + 1 = 2(x+1)$, or $2x - y + 1 = 0$.

37. The vertical line through the origin: $x = 0$ (or the y -axis itself.) In this case, $(x + 2y)y' + (2 + y) = 0$. The derivative is undefined (or infinite) at $x = 0$.

38. $y = \frac{5}{2}(x - 4)$, or $5x - 2y - 20 = 0$.

39. $y = x$. At $(1, 1)$ we have $y' = 1$. So $y - 1 = 1(x - 1)$ and the result follows.

40. $y = x - \pi$. The derivative is $\cos x + y'\cos y - 6yy' = 0$. Set $x = \pi$, $y = 0$ and solve for y' .

41. $\dfrac{1}{2}$. Use L'Hospital's Rule.

42. 1

43. 0 . Find a common denominator and use L'Hospital's Rule.

44. 0 . Divide the numerator and denominator by x^2 and let $x \to -\infty$.

45. By L'Hospital's Rule, we have

$$\begin{aligned}
\lim_{x \to -\infty} x^2 \left(\frac{\pi}{2} + \text{Arctan } x\right) &= \lim_{x \to -\infty} \frac{\frac{\pi}{2} + \text{Arctan } x}{x^{-2}} \\
&= \lim_{x \to -\infty} \frac{(1 + x^2)^{-1}}{-2x^{-3}} \\
&= \lim_{x \to -\infty} -\frac{x^3}{2(1 + x^2)} \\
&= +\infty.
\end{aligned}$$

Chapter 4

Solutions

4.1   Exercise Set 21

1. $x^2 + 1$

2. x

3. $\dfrac{x}{2} - 2x^2$. Note that $log_4(2^x) + log_4(16^{-x^2}) = x\, log_4(2) - x^2 log_4(16)$
   $= \dfrac{x}{2} - 2x^2$.

4. $1 - log_3(4)$

5. 0, since $2^x\, 2^{-x} = 1$ for any x.

6. The graph looks like Figure 79. Its values are:

-2	-1	0	1	2
$\frac{1}{16}$	$\frac{1}{4}$	1	4	16

7. The graph looks like Figure 80. Its values are:

-2	-1	0	1	2
16	4	1	$\frac{1}{4}$	$\frac{1}{16}$

8. The graph is similar to $y = \sqrt{2}^x$ in Figure 83. Its values are:

-2	-1	0	1	2
0.333	0.577	1	1.73	3

9. $log_{\sqrt{2}}(1.6325) = \sqrt{2}$

10. $log_2\left(\dfrac{1}{16}\right) = -4$

11. $log_3\left(\dfrac{1}{9}\right) = -2$

12. $f(x) = 2^x$

13. $3^4 = 81$

14. $\left(\dfrac{1}{2}\right)^{-2} = 4$

15. $\left(\dfrac{1}{3}\right)^{-3} = 27$

16. $a^0 = 1$

17. $\sqrt{2}^{\sqrt{2}} = 1.6325$

18. $x = \dfrac{16}{3}$, since $log_2(3x) = 4$ means that $2^4 = 3x$.

19. $x = -\dfrac{3}{2}$, since $3 = \dfrac{x}{x+1}$ forces $3x + 3 = x$, etc.

20. $x = \pm\sqrt{2}$, since $\sqrt{2}^0 = x^2 - 1$, or $x^2 = 2$, etc.

21. $x = 2$, since $\frac{1}{2}^{-1} = x$ is equivalent to $x = 2$.

22. $y = x^2$, since $y = log_2(2^{x^2}) = x^2\, log_2(2) = x^2 \cdot 1 = 2$.

4.2   Exercise Set 22

1. $b_1 = 0$, $b_2 = 0.25$, $b_3 = 0.29630$, $b_4 = 0.31641$, $b_5 = 0.32768$, $b_6 = 0.33490$, $b_7 = 0.33992$, $b_8 = 0.34361$, $b_9 = 0.34644$, $b_{10} = 0.34868$,

2. $e^{-1} = \dfrac{1}{e} \approx 0.3679$. See the following exercise.

3. Let $x = \frac{a}{n}$, so that $n = \frac{a}{x}$ and as $n \to \infty$ we get $x \to 0$, then

$$\lim_{n \to \infty} \left(1 + \frac{a}{n}\right)^n = \lim_{x \to 0} (1 + x)^{\frac{a}{x}}$$

$$= \left[\lim_{x \to 0} (1 + x)^{\frac{1}{x}}\right]^a$$

$$= e^a \text{ by Known Fact\#5}$$

4.3

4.4 Exercise Set 23

1. $\frac{3}{4}$, since $y' = \frac{3x^2}{x^3 + 3}$. Evaluate this at $x = 1$.

2. $3 \cdot e^{3x} \log x + e^{3x} \cdot \frac{1}{x}$

3. $\frac{e^x (x \log x - 1)}{x (\log x)^2}$.

4. $\frac{13}{6}$, since $y = 2x + \ln(x + 6)$ and so $y' = 2 + \frac{1}{x + 6}$. Evaluate this at $x = 0$.

5. $\frac{1}{x + \sqrt{x^2 + 3}} \left(1 + \frac{x}{\sqrt{x^2 + 3}}\right)$.

6. $\frac{4}{x + 2}$.

7. $\frac{x}{x^2 + 4}$, since $\ln(\sqrt{x^2 + 4}) = \frac{1}{2} \ln(x^2 + 4)$.

4.5 Exercise Set 24

1. $a_n = n + 2$ and $a_{n+1} = (n + 1) + 2 = n + 3$. Clearly $n + 3 > n + 2$ and so $\{a_n\}$ is increasing and $\lim\limits_{n \to \infty} a_n = \infty$.

2. $a_n = \frac{n - 1}{n}$ and $a_{n+1} = \frac{(n + 1) - 1}{(n + 1)} = \frac{n}{n + 1}$. Consider $a_{n+1} - a_n$:

$$\frac{n}{n + 1} - \frac{n - 1}{n} = \frac{n^2 - (n - 1)(n + 1)}{n(n + 1)}$$

$$= \frac{n^2 - (n^2 - 1)}{n(n + 1)}$$

$$= \frac{1}{n(n + 1)} > 0 \text{ for all } n \geq 1.$$

Therefore $a_{n+1} > a_n$ and the series increases.
$$\lim_{n \to \infty} a_n = \lim_{n \to \infty} \left(1 - \frac{1}{n}\right) = 1.$$

3. $a_n = \frac{n(n - 2)}{n^2} = \frac{n - 2}{n}$ and $a_{n+1} = \frac{(n + 1)((n + 1) - 2)}{(n + 1)^2} = \frac{n - 1}{n + 1}$

$$a_{n+1} - a_n = \frac{n - 1}{n + 1} - \frac{(n - 2)}{n} = \frac{n(n - 1) - (n + 1)(n - 2)}{n(n + 1)}$$

$$= \frac{n^2 - n - (n^2 - n - 2)}{n(n + 1)}$$

$$= \frac{2}{n(n + 1)} > 0 \text{ for all } n \geq 1.$$

Therefore $a_{n+1} > a_n$ and the series increases. Furthermore,
$$\lim_{n \to \infty} a_n = \lim_{n \to \infty} \left(1 - \frac{2}{n}\right) = 1.$$

4. $a_n = \frac{n}{n + 3}$ and $a_{n+1} = \frac{(n + 1)}{(n + 1) + 3} = \frac{n + 1}{n + 4}$.

$$a_{n+1} - a_n = \frac{n + 1}{n + 4} - \frac{n}{n + 3} = \frac{(n + 1)(n + 3) - n(n + 4)}{(n + 3)(n + 4)}$$

$$= \frac{n^2 + 4n + 3 - (n^2 + 4n)}{(n + 3)(n + 4)}$$

$$= \frac{3}{(n + 3)(n + 4)} > 0 \text{ for all } n \geq 1$$

Thus $\{a_n\}$ is increasing and $\displaystyle\lim_{n\to\infty} a_n = \lim_{n\to\infty}\left(1 - \frac{3}{n+3}\right) = 1$.

5. $a_n = \dfrac{(n-1)}{(n+1)}$ and $a_{n+1} = \dfrac{(n+1)-1}{(n+1)+1} = \dfrac{n}{n+2}$.

$$
\begin{aligned}
a_{n+1} - a_n = \frac{n}{n+2} - \frac{n-1}{n+1} &= \frac{n(n+1) - (n+2)(n-1)}{(n+2)(n+1)} \\[2mm]
&= \frac{n^2 + n - (n^2 + n - 2)}{(n+2)(n+1)} \\[2mm]
&= \frac{2}{(n+2)(n+1)} > 0 \text{ for all } n \ge 1.
\end{aligned}
$$

So $\{a_n\}$ is increasing and $\displaystyle\lim_{n\to\infty} a_n = \lim_{n\to\infty}\left(1 - \frac{2}{n+1}\right) = 1$.

6. For n from 1 to 15, a_n runs like 0, 0.70711, 0.81650, 0.86603, 0.89443, 0.91287, 0.92582, 0.93541, 0.94281, 0.94868, 0.95346, 0.95743, 0.96077, 0.96362, 0.96609. You can guess that the limit must be 1. For the graph, see Figure 84.

7. $\displaystyle\lim_{n\to\infty}\left(1 - \frac{2}{n}\right)^n = e^{-2}$

8. Apply the *Box method* to Fact # 5:

$$
\lim_{x\to 0}(1+x)^{\frac{1}{x}} = e \quad\Rightarrow\quad \lim_{\square\to 0}(1+\square)^{\frac{1}{\square}} = e.
$$

Now let $\square = x^2$. Note that $x^2 \to 0$ as $x \to 0$ and we are done.

9. Use $n = 2000$ in the expression $\left(1 + \dfrac{1}{n}\right)^n \approx 2.7176$. You don't want to write down the rational number, though! The numerator alone has about $11,300$ digits!!

10. The graph of $y(x) = e^{2(x-1)}$ has the same shape as the graph of $y = e^x$ except for three minor differences: first, it is steeper, second, it 'shoots' through $(1,1)$ instead of $(0,1)$, and third, it is a translate of the graph $y = e^{2x}$ by one unit to the right.

11.   a) 1, since $e^{3\ln x} = x^3$.

   b) 0

   c) 5

   d) 1

   e) 0, since $\sin^2 x + \cos^2 x = 1$.

   f) 0, since $\ln 1 = 0$.

   g) $2^{2x} = 4^x$

   h) $\ln(x-1)$

   i) $x - 1$

   j) 0, since $\ln\left(e^{e^{x^2}}\right) = e^{x^2}\ln e = e^{x^2}$.

12. 0. Use L'Hospital's Rule twice.

13.   a) $e^{0.38288} = 1.46650$.

   b) $e^{-1.38629} = 0.250000$.

   c) $e^{4.33217} = 76.1093$.

   d) $e^{-2.86738} = 0.05685$.

   e) $e^{2.42793} = 11.33543$.

14. $f(x) = e^{(\sin x)\ln x}$.

15.   a) $4e^{2x}$.

   b) $-3.4e^2$.

   c) $3^{\cos x}\ln 3 \cdot (-\sin x) = -\ln 3 \cdot \sin x \cdot 3^{\cos x}$.

   d) $-\dfrac{6}{e^6}$. Be careful, $(e^{3x})^{-2} = e^{-6x}$!

   e) 1. The derivative is $e^{x^2}\cos x + 2xe^{x^2}\sin x$.

   f) $e^x(\cos x - \sin x)$.

   g) $(x^2 - 2x)e^{-x}$.

   h) $2x\, e^{2x}\,(1+x)$.

   i) $-2(1+x)x^{-3}e^{-2x}$.

   j) $(1.2)^x\ln(1.2)$.

   k) $x^{0.6}e^{-x}(1.6 - x)$.

4.6 Exercise Set 25

1.   a) $\dfrac{1}{\ln a} \cdot \dfrac{3x^2 + 1}{x^3 + x + 1}$.

b) $\log_3 x + \dfrac{1}{\ln 3} = \dfrac{\ln x}{\ln 3} + \dfrac{1}{\ln 3}$.

c) $x^x(\ln x + 1)$, since $x^x = e^{x \ln x}$.

d) $\dfrac{1}{\ln 3} \cdot \dfrac{1}{4x - 3} \cdot 4 = \dfrac{4}{\ln 3 \cdot (4x - 3)}$.

e) $-\dfrac{4}{\ln 3}$.

f) $(3^x \ln 3) \log_2(x^2 + 1) + 3^x \cdot \dfrac{1}{\ln 2} \cdot \dfrac{2x}{x^2 + 1}$.

g) $1 + \ln x$.

h) $\dfrac{e^x}{\ln 2}(1 + x)$, since $\ln_2(e^x) = \dfrac{\ln(e^x)}{\ln 2} = \dfrac{x}{\ln 2}$.

i) $\dfrac{1}{\ln 2} \cdot \dfrac{1}{3x + 1} \cdot 3 = \dfrac{3}{\ln 2 \cdot (3x + 1)}$.

j) $\dfrac{1}{2}\left(\dfrac{1}{\ln 2} \cdot \dfrac{1}{x + 1} \right) = \dfrac{1}{2 \ln 2 \cdot (x + 1)}$.

4.7

4.8 Chapter Exercises

1. $a_n = n + 3$ and $a_{n+1} = (n + 1) + 3 = n + 4$. Clearly $n + 4 > n + 3$ and so $\{a_n\}$ is increasing and $\lim\limits_{n \to \infty} a_n = \infty$.

2. $a_n = \dfrac{n - 3}{n}$ and $a_{n+1} = \dfrac{(n + 1) - 3}{(n + 1)} = \dfrac{n - 2}{n + 1}$.

$$
\begin{aligned}
a_{n+1} - a_n = \dfrac{n - 2}{n + 1} - \dfrac{n - 3}{n} \quad &= \quad \dfrac{n(n - 2) - (n - 3)(n + 1)}{n(n + 1)} \\
&= \quad \dfrac{n^2 - 2n - (n^2 - 2n - 3)}{n(n + 1)} \\
&= \quad \dfrac{3}{n(n + 1)} > 0 \text{ for all } n \geq 1.
\end{aligned}
$$

Therefore $a_{n+1} > a_n$ and the series increases. Furthermore,

$$\lim_{n \to \infty} a_n = \lim_{n \to \infty} \left(1 - \dfrac{3}{n} \right) = 1.$$

3. $a_n = \dfrac{n(n - 1)}{n^2} = \dfrac{(n - 1)}{n}$ and $a_{n+1} = \dfrac{(n + 1)((n + 1) - 1)}{(n + 1)^2} = \dfrac{n}{(n + 1)}$.

$$
\begin{aligned}
a_{n+1} - a_n = \dfrac{n}{n + 1} - \dfrac{(n - 1)}{n} \quad &= \quad \dfrac{n^2 - (n + 1)(n - 1)}{n(n + 1)} \\
&= \quad \dfrac{n^2 - (n^2 - 1)}{n(n + 1)} \\
&= \quad \dfrac{1}{n(n + 1)} > 0 \text{ for all } n \geq 1.
\end{aligned}
$$

Therefore $a_{n+1} > a_n$ and the series increases. Furthermore,

$$\lim_{n \to \infty} a_n = \lim_{n \to \infty} \left(1 - \dfrac{1}{n} \right) = 1.$$

4. $a_n = \dfrac{n}{n + 4}$ and $a_{n+1} = \dfrac{(n + 1)}{(n + 1) + 4} = \dfrac{n + 1}{n + 5}$.

$$
\begin{aligned}
a_{n+1} - a_n = \dfrac{n + 1}{n + 5} - \dfrac{n}{n + 4} \quad &= \quad \dfrac{(n + 1)(n + 4) - n(n + 5)}{(n + 5)(n + 4)} \\
&= \quad \dfrac{n^2 + 5n + 4 - (n^2 + 5n)}{(n + 5)(n + 4)} \\
&= \quad \dfrac{4}{(n + 5)(n + 4)} > 0 \text{ for all } n \geq 1.
\end{aligned}
$$

Thus $\{a_n\}$ is increasing. Furthermore,

$$\lim_{n \to \infty} a_n = \lim_{n \to \infty} \left(1 - \dfrac{4}{n + 4} \right) = 1.$$

5. Sketch this as in Figure 84. Note that

$$\lim_{n \to \infty} \sqrt{\dfrac{n - 1}{2n}} = \lim_{n \to \infty} \sqrt{\dfrac{n}{2n} - \dfrac{1}{2n}} = \lim_{n \to \infty} \sqrt{\dfrac{1}{2} - \dfrac{1}{2n}} = \dfrac{1}{\sqrt{2}}.$$

6.   a) x^x

     b) $\sqrt{x}$

7.   a) $e^{0.89032} = 2.43592$

     b) $e^{-1.5314} = 0.21623$

     c) $e^{0.17328} = 1.18920$

8.   a) $15e^{5x}$

     b) $6e^2$

     c) $-\sin(xe^x) \cdot e^x(1+x)$

     d) $-8e^{-8}$, since $(e^{4x})^{-2} = e^{-8x}$.

     e) 0

     f) $e^x(\ln(\sin x) + \cot x)$

     g) 1

     h) $2x(1-x)e^{-2x}$

     i) $e^{-2x}\left(-2\operatorname{Arctan} x + \dfrac{1}{1+x^2}\right)$.

     j) 2. Note that $(x^2)^x = x^{2x} = e^{2x\,\ln x}$.

     k) $\dfrac{1}{2\sqrt{x}}(\ln\sqrt{x} + 1)$.

     l) $2^x \cdot \ln 2 \cdot \log_{1.6}(x^3) + 2^x \cdot \dfrac{1}{\ln 1.6} \cdot \dfrac{3}{x}$

     m) $-3^{-x} \cdot \ln 3 \cdot \log_{0.5}(\sec x) + 3^{-x} \cdot \dfrac{1}{\ln 0.5} \cdot \tan x$

9. Amount after t years is: $A(t) = Pe^{rt}$, where $P = \$500$ and $r = 0.10$, so $A(t) = 500e^{0.1t}$

    (a) Thus after 5 years the amount in the account will be $A(5) = 500e^{0.1 \times 5} = \$824.36$

    (b) Want t such that $A = 3P = 1500 = 500e^{0.1t}$, so $3 = e^{0.1t}$ giving $ln(3) = 0.1t$, therefore, $t = 10.986 \approx 11$ years.

10. $A = Pe^{rt}$, where $A = \$2400$ if $r = 0.12$, $t = 8$. So $2400 = Pe^{0.12 \times 8} = 2.6117P$. Thus $P = \dfrac{2400}{2.6117} = \$918.94$

11. Sales after t months: $y(t) = y(0)e^{kt} = 10{,}000e^{kt}$. At $t = 4$, $8{,}000 = 10{,}000e^{4k}$, so $0.8 = e^{4k}$, $ln(.8) = 4k$, and $k = -0.0558$. Thus, $y(t) = 10{,}000e^{-0.0558t}$, and when $t = 6$ (2 more months), sales $= 10{,}000e^{-0.0558 \times 6} = \$7154.81$

12.   (a) Revenue at time t is : $y(t) = y(0)e^{kt} = 486.8e^{kt}$, taking 1990 as $t = 0$. In 1999, $t = 9$, so $y(9) = 1005.8 = 486.8e^{9k}$. Thus $\frac{1005.8}{486.8} = e^{9k}$, so $ln\frac{1005.8}{486.8} = 9k$, giving $k = \frac{1}{9}ln(2.066) \approx 0.08$, so $y(t) = 486.8e^{0.08t}$. In 2001, $t = 11$, so revenue $= 486.8e^{0.08 \times 11} = \$1173.62$ million.

    (b) Want t such that $1400 = 486.8e^{0.08t}$, so $ln\frac{1400}{486.8} = 0.08t$, and $t = 13.2$ years.

13.   (a) $\lim_{t \to \infty} S = 30{,}000 = \lim_{t \to \infty} Ce^{k/t} = C$. Thus, $S = 30{,}000e^{k/t}$. When $t = 1$ $S = 5000$, therefore, $5000 = 30{,}000e^k$, so $\frac{1}{6} = e^k$, and $k = ln\frac{1}{6} = -1.79$. Thus, $S = 30{,}000e^{-1.79/t}$.

    (b) When $t = 5$, number of units sold is $S(5) = 30{,}000e^{-1.79/5} = 30{,}000 \times 0.699 = 20{,}972.19 \approx 20{,}972$ units

Chapter 5

Solutions

Use your **Plotter Software** available on the author's web site to obtain the missing graphs of the functions in the Chapter Exercises, at the end.

5.1 Exercise Sets 26, 27

1. $(x - 1)(x + 1)$,   all Type I.

2. $(x - 1)(x^2 + 1)$. One Type I and one Type II factor.

3. $(x + 3)(x - 2)$,   all Type I.

4. $(x - 1)^2(x + 1)$,   all Type I.

5. $(x - 2)(x + 2)(x^2 + 4)$. Two Type I factors and one Type II factor.

6. $(2x - 1)(x + 1)$,   all Type I.

7. $(x + 1)^2(x - 1)^2$,   all Type I.

8. $(x + 1)(x^2 + 1)$. One Type I and one Type II factor.

hugeExercise Set 27

1.   a). $\pm\frac{1}{3}$, -1. b). ± 1, -3. c). -2, 1. d). 1. e). ± 1.

2. **a)**

	$(x - (1/3))$	$(x + (1/3))$	$(x + 1)$	Sign of $p(x)$
$(-\infty, -1)$	$-$	$-$	$-$	$-$
$(-1, -1/3)$	$-$	$-$	$+$	$+$
$(-1/3, 1/3)$	$-$	$+$	$+$	$-$
$(1/3, \infty)$	$+$	$+$	$+$	$+$

b) Note that $x^2 + 1 > 0$ so it need not be included in the SDT.

	$(x - 1)$	$(x + 1)$	$(x + 3)$	Sign of $q(x)$
$(-\infty, -3)$	$-$	$-$	$-$	$-$
$(-3, -1)$	$-$	$-$	$+$	$+$
$(-1, 1)$	$-$	$+$	$+$	$-$
$(1, \infty)$	$+$	$+$	$+$	$+$

c) Note that $x^2 + x + 1$ is a Type II factor. You may leave it out of the SDT if you want.

	$(x - 1)$	$(x + 2)$	$(x^2 + x + 1)$	Sign of $r(x)$
$(-\infty, -2)$	$-$	$-$	$+$	$+$
$(-2, 1)$	$-$	$+$	$+$	$-$
$(1, \infty)$	$+$	$+$	$+$	$+$

d) Note that $t^3 - 1 = (t - 1)(t^2 + t + 1)$ and the quadratic is a Type II factor.

543

	$(t-1)$	(t^2+t+1)	Sign of $p(t)$
$(-\infty,1)$	$-$	$+$	$-$
$(1,\infty)$	$+$	$+$	$+$

e) Note that
$$w^6 - 1 = (w^3-1)(w^3+1) = (w-1)(w^2+w+1)(w+1)(w^2-w+1).$$

	$w-1$	$w+1$	w^2+w+1	w^2-w+1	Sign $q(w)$
$(-\infty,-1)$	$-$	$-$	$+$	$+$	$+$
$(-1,-1)$	$-$	$+$	$+$	$+$	$-$
$(1,\infty)$	$+$	$+$	$+$	$+$	$+$

3. $p(x) = -(x-3)(x+3)(x-4)(x+4)$. Note the *minus* sign here, since $16-x^2 = -(x^2-16)$!

	$x+4$	$x+3$	$x-3$	$x-4$	Sign of "$-p(x)$"
$(-\infty,-4)$	$-$	$-$	$-$	$-$	$+$
$(-4,-3)$	$+$	$-$	$-$	$-$	$+$
$(-3,3)$	$+$	$+$	$-$	$-$	$+$
$(3,4)$	$+$	$+$	$+$	$-$	$-$
$(4,\infty)$	$+$	$+$	$+$	$+$	$+$

4.   2. This is because $2 + \sin x > 0$ so it doesn't contribute any break-points.

5.   Note that $3 + \cos x \geq 3 - 1 = 2 > 0$, since $\cos x \geq -1$ for any real x. So it doesn't contribute any break-points. On the other hand, $x^4 - 1 = (x^2-1)(x^2+1)$ and so x^2+1 (being a Type II factor) doesn't have any break-points either. Thus the only break points are those of $x^2 - 1 = (x-1)(x+1)$ and so the SDT is equivalent to the SDT of $x^2 - 1$ which is easy to build.

6.   First, we find the SDT of this polynomial, $p(x)$. The only break-points are at $x = -1, 0, 1$ since the quadratic is a Type II factor. So the SDT looks like,

	$(x-1)$	$(x+1)$	x	Sign of $p(x)$
$(-\infty,-1)$	$-$	$-$	$-$	$-$
$(-1,0)$	$-$	$+$	$-$	$+$
$(0,1)$	$-$	$+$	$+$	$-$
$(1,\infty)$	$+$	$+$	$+$	$+$

We can now *read-off* the answer: $p(x) < 0$ whenever $-\infty < x < -1$ or $0 < x < 1$.

7. $-3 < x < -1$, or $x > 1$. Add an extra row and column to the SDT of Table 5.1.

8.   All factors are Type I, so the SDT looks like,

	$x+1$	$x-2$	$x-3$	$x+4$	Sign $p(x)$
$(-\infty,-4)$	$-$	$-$	$-$	$-$	$+$
$(-4,-1)$	$-$	$-$	$-$	$+$	$-$
$(-1,2)$	$+$	$-$	$-$	$+$	$+$
$(2,3)$	$+$	$+$	$-$	$+$	$-$
$(3,\infty)$	$+$	$+$	$+$	$+$	$+$

The solution of the inequality $p(x) \leq 0$ is given by: $-4 \leq x \leq -1$, or $2 \leq x \leq 3$.

9.   Let $p(x) = (x-1)^3(4-x^2)(x^2+1)$. The SDT of $p(x)$ is the same as the SDT of the polynomial $r(x) = (x-1)^3(4-x^2)$. This factors as $(x-1)^3(2-x)(x+2)$. Its SDT is given by:

	$(x-1)^3$	$x+2$	$2-x$	Sign of $r(x)$
$(-\infty,-2)$	$-$	$-$	$+$	$+$
$(-2,1)$	$-$	$+$	$+$	$-$
$(1,2)$	$+$	$+$	$+$	$+$
$(2,\infty)$	$+$	$+$	$-$	$-$

It follows that the solution of the inequality $p(x) \geq 0$ is given by solving $r(x) \geq 0$ since the exra factor in $p(x)$ is positive. Thus, $p(x) \geq 0$ whenever $-\infty < x \leq 2$, or $1 \leq x \leq 2$.

10. $x \geq \frac{1}{3}$, or , $-1 \leq x \leq -\frac{1}{3}$. See Exercise 2 a), above.

5.2   Exercise Set 28

1.   **a)**. 2. **b)**. $1, \frac{2}{3}$. **c)**. $1, -\frac{1+\sqrt{13}}{2}, -\frac{1-\sqrt{13}}{2}$. **d)**. ± 1. **e)**. ± 1. **f)**. $\pm 1, \pm 2$.

2.   **a)** $t = 2$ is the only break-point. Its SDT looks like:

	$(t-2)$	(t^2+1)	Sign of $r(t)$
$(-\infty,2)$	$-$	$+$	$-$
$(2,\infty)$	$+$	$+$	$+$

b) $t = \frac{2}{3}$, $t = 1$ are the only break-points. Note that we factored out the 3 out of the numerator so as to make its leading coefficient equal to a 1. Its SDT now looks like:

	$(t-\frac{2}{3})$	$(t-1)$	Sign of $r(t)$
$(-\infty,\frac{2}{3})$	$-$	$-$	$+$
$(\frac{2}{3},1)$	$+$	$-$	$-$
$(1,\infty)$	$+$	$+$	$+$

c) Write this as a rational function, first. Taking a common denominator we get that

$$t + 2 - \frac{1}{t-1} = \frac{t^2+t-3}{t-1}.$$

Its break-points are given by $t = 1$ and, using the quadratic formula,

$$t = \frac{-1 \pm \sqrt{13}}{2}.$$

The SDT looks like:

	$\left(t - \left(\frac{-1-\sqrt{13}}{2}\right)\right)$	$\left(t - \left(\frac{-1+\sqrt{13}}{2}\right)\right)$	$(t-1)$	Sign $r(t)$
$(-\infty, -2.303)$	$-$	$-$	$-$	$-$
$(-2.303, 1)$	$+$	$-$	$-$	$+$
$(1, 1.303)$	$+$	$-$	$+$	$-$
$(1.303, \infty)$	$+$	$+$	$+$	$+$

where we have used the approximations: $\dfrac{-1 - \sqrt{13}}{2} \approx -2.303$, and

$\dfrac{-1 + \sqrt{13}}{2} \approx +1.303.$

d) Write the rational function as

$$r(t) = \frac{t^3 + 1}{t^3 - 1}.$$

The factors of the numerator and denominator in this quotient are given by: $t^3 + 1 = (t+1)(t^2 - t + 1)$ and $t^3 - 1 = (t-1)(t^2 + t + 1)$, where each quadratic is Type II, and so does not contribute any new sign to its SDT. The SDT looks like the SDT for a polynomial having only the factors $t - 1$ and $t + 1$, that is:

	$(t+1)$	$(t-1)$	Sign of $r(t)$
$(-\infty, -1)$	$-$	$-$	$+$
$(-1, 1)$	$+$	$-$	$-$
$(1, \infty)$	$+$	$+$	$+$

e) This rational function may be rewritten as

$$\frac{t^2 - 2t + 1}{t^2 - 1} = \frac{(t-1)^2}{(t-1)(t+1)} = \frac{t-1}{t+1}.$$

Its SDT is basically the same as the one for a polynomial having only the factors $t - 1$ and $t + 1$. See Exercise 2 d), in this Set.

f) The break-points are easily found to be: $-2, -1, 1, 2$. The corresponding SDT is then

	$t+2$	$t+1$	$t-1$	$t-2$	Sign $r(t)$
$(-\infty, -2)$	$-$	$-$	$-$	$-$	$+$
$(-2, -1)$	$+$	$-$	$-$	$-$	$-$
$(-1, 1)$	$+$	$+$	$-$	$-$	$+$
$(1, 2)$	$+$	$+$	$+$	$-$	$-$
$(2, \infty)$	$+$	$+$	$+$	$+$	$+$

3. Use the SDT's found in Exercise 2 in this Set. From these we see that

a) $\dfrac{1 + t^2}{t - 2} \le 0$ only when $-\infty < t < 2$.

b) $\dfrac{3t - 2}{t^3 - 1} \ge 0$ only when $-\infty < t \le \frac{2}{3}$, or $1 \le t < \infty$.

c) $t + 2 - \dfrac{1}{t + 1} > 0$ only when $\dfrac{-1-\sqrt{13}}{2} < t < 1$, or $\dfrac{-1+\sqrt{13}}{2} < t < \infty$.

d) $\dfrac{t^3 + 1}{t^3 - 1} < 0$ only when $-1 < t < 1$.

e) $\dfrac{t^2 - 2t + 1}{t^2 - 1} \ge 0$ only when $-\infty < t < -1$, or $1 < t < \infty$. You may also allow $t = 1$ in the reduced form of $r(t)$.

f) $\dfrac{4 - t^2}{1 - t^2} < 0$ only when $-2 < t < -1$, or $1 < t < 2$.

4. **a)** Break-points: -4 only. This is because the numerator factors as $x^2 - 16 = (x - 4)(x + 4)$ and one of these cancels out the corresponding one in the denominator. So, its SDT looks like the SDT of the polynomial $x + 4$ only, and this is an easy one to describe.

	$x + 4$	$\dfrac{x^2 - 16}{x - 4} = x + 4$
$(-\infty, -4)$	$-$	$-$
$(-4, +4)$	$+$	$+$
$(+4, +\infty)$	$+$	$+$

The solution of the inequality $\dfrac{x^2 - 16}{x - 4} > 0$ is given by $x > -4$.

b) The only break-point is at $x = 0$, since the other term is a Type II factor. Its SDT looks like:

	x	$3x + \dfrac{5}{x}$
$(-\infty, 0)$	$-$	$-$
$(0, +\infty)$	$+$	$+$

so the solution of the inequality $3x + \dfrac{5}{x} < 0$ is given by $x < 0$.

c) The break-points are at $x = 5$, $\pm\sqrt{5}$; Its SDT looks like:

	$x-5$	$x-\sqrt{5}$	$x+\sqrt{5}$	$\dfrac{x^2-5}{x-5}$
$(-\infty,-\sqrt{5})$	$-$	$-$	$-$	$-$
$(-\sqrt{5},+\sqrt{5})$	$-$	$-$	$+$	$+$
$(+\sqrt{5},5)$	$-$	$+$	$+$	$-$
$(5,+\infty)$	$+$	$+$	$+$	$+$

So, the solution of the inequality $\dfrac{x^2-5}{x-5} > 0$ is given by $x > 5$ or $-\sqrt{5} < x < \sqrt{5}$.

d) The break-points are at $-10, 2$, since the numerator is a Type II factor. Its SDT is the same as the one for

	$x+10$	$x-2$	$3x^2+4x+5$	$\dfrac{3x^2+4x+5}{x^2+8x-20}$
$(-\infty,-10)$	$-$	$-$	$+$	$+$
$(-10,2)$	$+$	$-$	$+$	$-$
$(2,+\infty)$	$+$	$+$	$+$	$+$

So, the solution of the inequality $\dfrac{3x^2+4x+5}{x^2+8x-20} < 0$ is given by
$-10 < x < 2$.

e) The break-points are at $x = 0, 1$ only, since

$$\frac{x^3+x^2}{x^4-1} = \frac{x^2(x+1)}{(x^2+1)(x+1)(x-1)} = \frac{x^2}{(x-1)(x^2+1)},$$

and the only non-Type II factor is x^2+1. Its SDT is basically the same as the one below:

	$x-1$	x^2	x^2+1	$\dfrac{x^2}{(x^2+1)(x-1)}$
$(-\infty,0)$	$-$	$+$	$+$	$-$
$(0,1)$	$-$	$+$	$+$	$-$
$(1,+\infty)$	$+$	$+$	$+$	$+$

So, the solution of the inequality $\dfrac{x^3+x^2}{x^4-1} \geq 0$ is given by
$x > 1$ along with the single point, $x = 0$.

f) The break-points are at $0, 2$.

interval	x^2	$x-2$	$|\cos x|$	$\dfrac{x^2|\cos x|}{x-2}$
$(-\infty,0)$	$+$	$-$	$+$	$-$
$(0,2)$	$+$	$-$	$+$	$-$
$(2,+\infty)$	$+$	$+$	$+$	$+$

The solution of the inequality $\dfrac{x^2|\cos x|}{x-2} < 0$ is given by $x < 2$.

5. **a)** The only break-points are at $x = -1, 1$ and so the SDT is basically like the one in Exercise 2 d), above. Since $x^2 + 4 > 0$ we see that the solution of the inequality $\dfrac{x^2-1}{x^2+4} > 0$, is given by the set $x < -1$ or $x > 1$. This can also be written as $|x| > 1$.

b) There are no break-points here since $x^4 + 1 > 0$ and $x^2 + 1 > 0$ as well, for any value of x. So, no SDT is needed. We see that the solution of the inequality $\dfrac{x^2+1}{x^4+1} > 0$, is given by the set of all real numbers, namely, $-\infty < x < \infty$.

c) The only break-points are at $x = -3, 3$ and so the SDT is basically like the one in Exercise 2 d), above, with 1's replaced by 3's. Since $x^2 + x + 1 > 0$ we see that the solution of the inequality $\dfrac{x^2-9}{x^2+x+1} < 0$, is given by the set $-3 < x < 3$. This can also be written as $|x| < 3$.

d) There are 2 break-points here, namely, at $x = \frac{3}{2}, 4$. Since $(x-4)^2 \geq 0$ for any value of x, this term will not contribute anything to the signs in the SDT. So, the only contributions come from the term $2x - 3 = 2(x - \frac{3}{2})$. It's now a simple matter to see that the solution of the inequality $\dfrac{2x-3}{(x-4)^2} < 0$ is given by the set $x < \frac{3}{2}$.

e) The break-points here are at $x = -3, -2, -1$, as this is easy to see. The SDT looks like:

	$(x+3)$	$(x+2)$	$(x+1)$	Sign of $\dfrac{x+1}{(x+2)(x+3)}$
$(-\infty,-3)$	$-$	$-$	$-$	$-$
$(-3,-2)$	$+$	$-$	$-$	$+$
$(-2,-1)$	$+$	$+$	$-$	$-$
$(-1,\infty)$	$+$	$+$	$+$	$+$

So, the solution of the inequality $\dfrac{x+1}{(x+2)(x+3)} > 0$ is given by
$-3 < x < -2$, or $-1 < x < \infty$.

f) The only break-points here are at $x = -1, 1$. This is because the rational function factors as
$\dfrac{x^3-1}{x+1} = \dfrac{(x-1)(x^2+x+1)}{x+1}$ where the quadratic expression is Type II. So, the SDT looks like the one in Exercise 2 d), above. It follows that the solution of the inequality $\dfrac{x^3-1}{x+1} < 0$ is given by $-1 < x < 1$, or, written more compactly, as $|x| < 1$.

5.3

5.4

5.5   Single variable optimization problems

1. 30 and 30.

2. 30 and -30.

3. A square with side length 200m.

4. A square shaped plot with side length 80ft.

5. A square shaped pool with side length 30ft.

6. Find $P'(\theta)$ and set it equal to zero.

7. The area is maximized when $h = 3$ and minimized when $h = 2$.

8. The smallest amount of tin used is the same as minimizing the surface area. This occurs when $R = (\frac{7}{4\pi})^{1/3} \approx 0.8228$ and $h = 2R$.

9. The distance is minimized when $x = 1$ resulting in a minimum distance of $\sqrt{5}$ km.

10. 500 pairs.

11. $\sqrt{\frac{840}{6.5}} \approx 11.368$ by $\frac{140}{\sqrt{\frac{840}{6.5}}} \approx 12.315$.

12. The base of the rectangle has length 5 ft. and its height is 6 ft.

13. 16 boxes. Use the fact that the profit $P(x) = R(x) - C(x)$ and maximize the function $P(x)$.

5.6 Chapter Exercises: Use Plotter

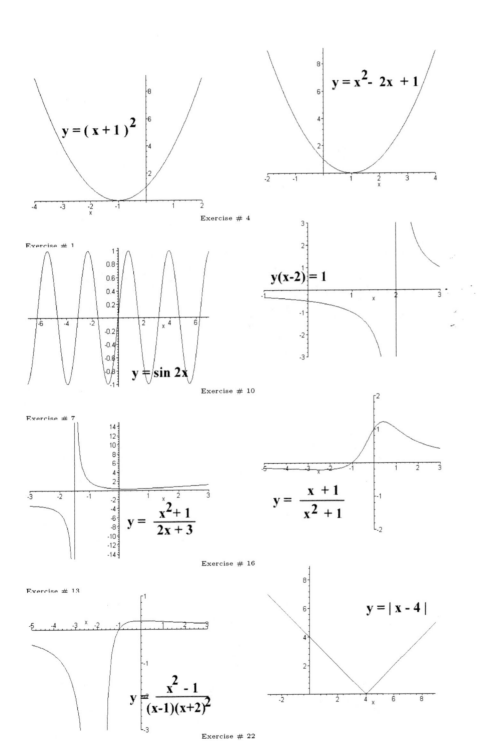

$y = (x+1)^2$

$y = x^2 - 2x + 1$

Exercise # 4

Exercise # 1

$y = \sin 2x$

$y(x-2) = 1$

Exercise # 10

Exercise # 7

$y = \dfrac{x^2 + 1}{2x + 3}$

$y = \dfrac{x + 1}{x^2 + 1}$

Exercise # 16

Exercise # 13

$y = \dfrac{x^2 - 1}{(x-1)(x+2)^2}$

$y = |x - 4|$

Exercise # 22

Exercise # 19

Chapter Exercises: (cont'd.)

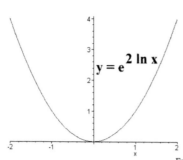

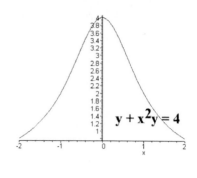

Exercise # 28

Exercise # 25

16. $y = \frac{x+1}{x^2+1}$, $y' = -\frac{x^2+2x-1}{(x^2+1)^2}$, $y'' = \frac{2(x-1)^3}{(x^2+1)^3}$.

interval	$x+1$	$x+1-\sqrt{2}$	$x+1+\sqrt{2}$	$(x-1)^3$	y	y'	y''
$(-\infty, -1-\sqrt{2})$	−	−	−	−	−	−	−
$(-1-\sqrt{2}, -1)$	−	−	+	−	−	+	−
$(-1, -1+\sqrt{2})$	+	−	+	+	+	+	+
$(-1+\sqrt{2}, +\infty)$	+	+	+	+	+	−	+

19. $y = \frac{x^2-1}{(x-1)(x+2)^2}$, $y' = -\frac{x}{(x+2)^3}$, $y'' = \frac{2(x-1)}{(x+2)^4}$,

	interval	$x+1$	$(x+2)^3$	x	y	y'	y''
	$(-\infty, -2)$	−	−	−	−	−	−
SDT:	$(-2, -1)$	−	+	−	+	−	−
	$(-1, 0)$	+	+	−	+	+	−
	$(0, 1)$	+	+	+	+	−	−
	$(1, +\infty)$	+	+	+	−	−	+

32. Profit $P(x) = R(x) - C(x) = 32x - (5 + 35x - 1.65x^2 + 0.1x^3) = -5 - 3x + 1.65x^2 - 0.1x^3$, $0 \leq x \leq 20$.
For a local extremum, $\frac{dP}{dx} = -3 + 3.3x - 0.3x^2 = 0$, so $x^2 - 11x + 10 = 0$, and $(x-10)(x-1) = 0$.
Thus $x = 1$ or $x = 10$. Now $\frac{d^2R}{dx^2} = 3.3 - 0.6x$. This is < 0 when $x = 10$ and > 0 when $x = 1$. So $x = 10$
gives a local maximum of $P(10) = -5 - 30 + 165 - 100 = 30$. Check end points: $P(0) = -5$, $P(20) = -5 - 60 + 660 - 800 < 0$. A production level of $x = 10$ stereos per day yields the maximum profit of $30
per day.

33.   (a) Revenue $R(x) = xp = 4x - 0.002x^2$. For a local maximum, $\frac{dR}{dx} = 4 - 0.004x = 0$, so $x = 1000$.

Checks: $\frac{d^2R}{dx^2} = -0.004$, so $x = 1000$ is a local maximum. Endpoints: $R(0) = 0$, $R(1200) = 1920, $R(1000) = 2000. So a production of $x = 1000$, and hence price of $p = 4 - 0.002(1000) = 2
will maximize revenue.

   (b) Profit $P = R - C = 2.5x - 0.002x^2 - 200$. $\frac{dP}{dx} = 2.5 - 0.004x = 0$ when $x = 625$. $(625, P(625))$,
where $P(625) = 2.5(625) - .002(625)^2 - 200 = 581.25$, is a local maximum since $\frac{d^2P}{dx^2} < 0$. Now
$P(0) = -200$, $P(1200) = 2.5(1200) - .002(1200)^2 - 200 = -80$, so a production level of $x = 625$
maximizes daily profit.

   (c) $581.25 from (b)

   (d) marginal cost $MC = \frac{dC}{dx} = 1.5$. marginal revenue $MR = \frac{dR}{dx} = 4 - 0.004x$

   (e) $4 - .004x = 1.5$, therefore $x = \frac{2.5}{0.004} = 625$ as in (c).

34. Average cost $AC = (800 + .04x + .0002x^2)/x = \frac{800}{x} + .04 + .0002x$, $x \geq 0$. For a local minimum,
$\frac{d(AC)}{dx} = \frac{-800}{x^2} + .0002 = 0$, so $0.0002x^2 = 800$. Thus $x = 2000$ cabinets. (Check: $\frac{d^2(AC)}{dx^2} = \frac{1600}{x^3} > 0$
for $x > 0$, so $x = 2000$ gives a local minimum.)

35.   (a) $45 = Ce^{1000k}$ and $40 = Ce^{1200k}$. Dividing gives $\frac{45}{40} = e^{-200k}$, so $ln \frac{9}{8} = -200k$, and
$k = -.0005889 \approx -.0006$. Thus, $45 = Ce^{-.0006 \times 1000} = Ce^{-.6}$. Thus, $C = 45e^{.6} \approx 82$.

   (b) Revenue, $R = xp$, where $p = 82e^{-.0006x}$ from (a). Thus, $R = 82xe^{-.0006x}$, and $\frac{dR}{dx} = 82e^{-.0006x} - .0006(82)xe^{-.0006x} = 82e^{-.0006x}[1 - .0006x]$. $\frac{dR}{dx} = 0$ for $1 - .0006x = 0$,
so $x = 1666.7$.

	$e^{-.0006x}$	$1 - .0006x$	$R'(x)$
$(-\infty, 1666.7)$	+	+	+
$(1666.7, \infty)$	+	-	-

So maximum revenue occurs when $x \approx 1667$, and hence $p = 82e^{-.0006(1667)} = 30.16.

Chapter 6

Solutions

6.1 Exercise Set 29

1. $-5x + C$. Use Table 6.2 with $r = 1$, $\square = x$, $c = -5$.

2. $x + C$.

3. C. Use Table 6.2 with $r = 1$, $\square = 0$.

4. $\frac{1}{1.6} x^{1.6} + C$. Use Table 6.2 with $r = 0.6$, $\square = x$.

5. $\frac{3}{2} x^2 + C$.

6. $\frac{1}{2} x^2 - x + C$.

7. $\frac{1}{3} x^3 + x + C$. See Example 268.

8. $\frac{2}{3} x^3 + \frac{1}{2} x^2 - x + C$.

9. $\frac{3}{2} x^2 + C$. (Actually, this is the same as Exercise 5 above.)

10. $x^4 + x^2 - 1.314\, x + C$. See Example 268.

11. $\frac{1}{3} (2x - 2)^{3/2} + C$.

12. $\frac{2}{9} (3x + 4)^{3/2} + C$.

13. $-\frac{2}{3} (1 - x)^{3/2} + C$. See Example 269.

14. $\frac{1}{12} (4x^2 + 1)^{3/2} + C$.

15. $-\frac{1}{6} (1 - 2x^2)^{3/2} + C$.

16. $\frac{1}{3.5} (1 + x^2)^{1.75} + C$.

17. $\frac{1}{5} (2 + x^3)^{5/3} + C$.

18. $-\frac{1}{54} (4 + 9x^4)^{3/2} + C$. See Example 273.

19. $\frac{1}{3.6} (1 + x^{2.4})^{3/2} + C$.

20. $\mathcal{F}(x) = \frac{1}{4} \sin^4 x - 1$.

21. $\mathcal{F}(x) = \frac{1}{3} (1 - \cos^3 x)$.

22. $\mathcal{F}(x) = \frac{1}{2} (e^{-2} - e^{-2x})$.

23. $\frac{y^4(x)}{4} = \frac{x^3}{3} + \frac{1}{4}$. See Example 274.

24. $y = x^4 - 1$.

25. $y(x) = x^4 - 1$. See Example 277.

6.2 Exercise Set 30

1. $\frac{3}{2}$. $\displaystyle\int_0^1 3x \; dx = \left. \frac{3x^2}{2} \right|_0^1 = \frac{3(1^2)}{2} - 0 = \frac{3}{2}$.

2. $-\dfrac{1}{2}$. $\displaystyle\int_{-1}^{0} x\,dx = \dfrac{x^2}{2}\,\Big|_{-1}^{0} = -\dfrac{1}{2}$.

3. 0. $\displaystyle\int_{-1}^{1} x^3\,dx = \dfrac{x^4}{4}\,\Big|_{-1}^{0} = 0$; (note: x^3 is an odd function.)

4. $-\dfrac{4}{3}$. $\displaystyle\int_{0}^{2} (x^2 - 2x)\,dx = \dfrac{x^3}{3} - x^2\,\Big|_{0}^{2} = \left(\dfrac{2^3}{3} - 2^2\right) - 0 = -\dfrac{4}{3}$.

5. 16. $\displaystyle\int_{-2}^{2} (4 - 4x^3)\,dx = 4x - x^4\,\Big|_{-2}^{2} = 16$.

6. $\frac{1}{2}$. $\displaystyle\int_{0}^{\pi/2} \sin x \cos x\,dx = \int_{0}^{\pi/2} \sin x\left(\dfrac{d}{dx}\sin x\right)dx = \dfrac{\sin^2 x}{2}\,\Big|_{0}^{\pi/2} = \dfrac{1}{2}$.

7. $\frac{2}{3}$.   Let $\square = \cos x$. Then $D\square = -\sin x$. So, $\mathcal{F}(x) = -\frac{1}{3}\cos^3 x + C$ and, by definition, $\displaystyle\int_{0}^{\pi} \cos^2 x \sin x\,dx =$

$-\dfrac{\cos^3 x}{3}\,\Big|_{0}^{\pi} = \dfrac{1}{3} - \left(-\dfrac{1}{3}\right) = \dfrac{2}{3}$.

8. $\dfrac{1}{4}$. $\displaystyle\int_{-\pi}^{\pi/2} \sin^3 x \cos x\,dx = \dfrac{\sin^4 x}{4}\,\Big|_{-\pi}^{\pi/2} = \dfrac{1}{4}$.

9. -0.26.   (Notice that the upper limit 1.2 of the integral is less than the lower one, namely 1.5; nevertheless we can proceed in the usual way.) $\displaystyle\int_{1.5}^{1.2} (2x - x^2)\,dx = x^2 - \dfrac{x^3}{3}\,\Big|_{1.5}^{1.2} = -0.26$.

10. $\dfrac{\pi}{2}$. $\displaystyle\int_{0}^{1} \dfrac{1}{\sqrt{1 - x^2}}\,dx = \text{Arcsin } x\,\Big|_{0}^{1} = \dfrac{\pi}{2} - 0 = \dfrac{\pi}{2}$.

11. $\dfrac{1}{2}(e - 1)$. $\displaystyle\int_{0}^{1} x e^{x^2}\,dx = \int_{0}^{1} e^{x^2}\dfrac{d}{dx}\left(\dfrac{x^2}{2}\right)dx = \dfrac{1}{2}e^{x^2}\,\Big|_{0}^{1} = \dfrac{1}{2}(e - 1)$.

12. $2(1 - e^{-4})$.

$$\int_{0}^{2} 4x e^{-x^2}\,dx \;=\; \int_{0}^{4} 2e^{-x^2}\left(\dfrac{d}{dx}x^2\right)dx$$

$$=\; -2e^{-x^2}\,\Big|_{0}^{2} = 2(1 - e^{-4}).$$

13. $\dfrac{2}{\ln 3}$.   If we set $f(x) = 3^x$ then $f'(x) = 3^x \ln 3$. So $\displaystyle\int 3^x\,dx = \dfrac{3^x}{\ln 3} + C$. Thus $\displaystyle\int_{0}^{1} 3^x\,dx = \dfrac{3^x}{\ln 3}\,\Big|_{0}^{1} =$

$\dfrac{3}{\ln 3} - \dfrac{1}{\ln 3} = \dfrac{2}{\ln 3}$.

14. $\dfrac{1}{3}\left(e^{3\triangle} - e^{3\square}\right)$.

15. 0.1340. $\displaystyle\int_{0}^{0.5} \dfrac{x}{\sqrt{1 - x^2}}\,dx = -(1 - x^2)^{1/2}\,\Big|_{0}^{0.5} = 1 - \sqrt{0.75} \approx 0.1340$.

16. $\dfrac{1}{\ln 2}$.   We know that $D(a^{\square}) = a^{\square} D(\square) \ln a$, where D as usual denotes the operator of taking derivative.

It follows $\displaystyle\int a^{\square}\dfrac{d\square}{dx}\,dx = \dfrac{a^{\square}}{\ln a} + C$. Now, setting $a = 2$, $\square = x^2 + 1$, and $D\square = 2x$, we see that

$$\int_{0}^{1} x\, 2^{x^2+1}\,dx = \dfrac{1}{2}\dfrac{2^{x^2+1}}{\ln 2}\,\Big|_{0}^{1} = \dfrac{2}{\ln 2} - \dfrac{1}{\ln 2} = \dfrac{1}{\ln 2}.$$

17. $\dfrac{\sqrt{2} - 1}{2}$.

$$I \;\equiv\; \int_{0}^{\sqrt{\pi}/2} x \sec(x^2)\tan(x^2)\,dx$$

$$=\; \int_{0}^{\sqrt{\pi}/2} \dfrac{1}{2}\dfrac{d}{dx}\sec(x^2)\,dx$$

$$=\; \dfrac{1}{2}\sec(x^2)\,\Big|_{0}^{\sqrt{\pi}/2} = \dfrac{1}{2}\left(\sec\dfrac{\pi}{4} - \sec 0\right) = \dfrac{1}{2}(\sqrt{2} - 1).$$

18. 0. Let $\Box = x^2$ So $D\Box = 2x$ and the antiderivative looks like

$$\frac{1}{2} \int \frac{1}{1 + \Box^2} \frac{d\Box}{dx} \, dx,$$

which reminds one of the derivative of the Arctangent function. In fact,

$$\int_{-1}^{1} \frac{x}{1 + x^4} \, dx = \frac{1}{2} \tan^{-1} x^2 \Big|_{-1}^{1} = \frac{1}{2}(\tan^{-1} 1 - \tan^{-1} 1) = 0.$$

(Notice that 0 is the expected answer because the integrand is an odd function.)

19. Following the hint, we have $\dfrac{d}{dx} \displaystyle\int_{0}^{x^2} e^t \, dt = e^{x^2} \dfrac{d}{dx} x^2 = 2x e^{x^2}$.

20. These identities can be seen from the respective symmetry in the graph of f. Here is an analytic argument. Assume that f is even: $f(-x) = f(x)$. Let $\mathcal{F}(x) = \int_{0}^{x} f(t)dt$, $(-\infty < x < \infty)$. Then $\frac{d}{dx}\mathcal{F}(x) = f(x)$ and

$$\int_{-x}^{x} f(t)dt = \int_{-x}^{0} f(t)dt + \int_{0}^{x} f(t)dt$$

$$= -\int_{0}^{-x} f(t)dt + \int_{0}^{x} f(t)dt = -\mathcal{F}(-x) + \mathcal{F}(x).$$

Thus we will have $\int_{-x}^{x} f(t)dt = 2\int_{0}^{x} f(t)dt$ if we can show $-\mathcal{F}(-x) = \mathcal{F}(x)$. Let $\mathcal{G}(x) = -\mathcal{F}(-x)$. We are going to show $\mathcal{G} = \mathcal{F}$. Now

$$\frac{d}{dx}\mathcal{G}(x) = \frac{d}{dx}(-\mathcal{F}(-x)) = -\left(\frac{d}{dx}\mathcal{F}(-x)\right)$$

$$= -\left(\mathcal{F}'(-x) \cdot (-1)\right) = \mathcal{F}'(-x) = f(-x) = f(x).$$

Thus, by the Fundamental Theorem of Calculus, $\mathcal{G}(x) = \int_{0}^{x} f(t) \, dt + C$ for some constant C, or $\mathcal{G}(x) = \mathcal{F}(x) + C$. Now $\mathcal{G}(0) = -\mathcal{F}(-0) = -\mathcal{F}(0) = -0 = 0$, which is the same as $\mathcal{F}(0) \, (= 0)$. So C must be zero. Thus $\mathcal{G} = \mathcal{F}$. Done! (The second part of the exercise which involves an even function f can be dealt with in the same manner.)

6.3   Exercise Set 31

1. $\displaystyle\sum_{i=1}^{10} i$.

2. $\displaystyle\sum_{i=1}^{9} (-1)^{i-1}$,   or $\displaystyle\sum_{i=1}^{9} (-1)^{i+1}$,   or $\displaystyle\sum_{i=0}^{8} (-1)^i$.

3. $\displaystyle\sum_{i=1}^{5} \sin i\pi$.

4. $\displaystyle\sum_{i=1}^{n} \frac{i}{n}$

5. -0.83861

6. 0.19029.

7. 0. Note that $\sin n\pi = 0$ for any integer n.

8. $1 + 2 + 3 + \cdots + 50 = \dfrac{50 \times 51}{2} = 1275$.

9. $1^2 + 2^2 + \cdots + 100^2 = \dfrac{100 \times 101 \times 201}{6} = 338350$.

10. $\displaystyle\sum_{i=1}^{n} \frac{i}{n} = \frac{1}{n} \sum_{i=1}^{n} i = \frac{1}{n} \cdot \frac{n(n+1)}{2} = \frac{n+1}{2}$.

11. $\displaystyle\sum_{i=1}^{n} 6\left(\frac{i}{n}\right)^2 = \frac{6}{n^2} \sum_{i=1}^{n} i^2 = \frac{6}{n^2} \cdot \frac{n(n+1)(2n+1)}{6} = \frac{(n+1)(2n+1)}{n}$.

12.   This is a telescoping sum:

$$\sum_{i=1}^{6}(a_i - a_{i-1}) = (a_1 - a_0) + (a_2 - a_1) + \cdots + (a_6 - a_5) = a_6 - a_0.$$

The final expression stands for what is left after many cancellations.

13.   We prove this identity by induction. For $n = 1$, we have

$$\text{LHS} = \sum_{i=1}^{1}(a_i - a_{i-1}) = a_1 - a_0 = \text{RHS}.$$

Now we assume $\sum_{i=1}^{k}(a_i - a_{i-1}) = a_k - a_0$, that is, the identity holds for $n = k$. Then, for $n = k + 1$, we have

$$\begin{aligned}
\sum_{i=1}^{k+1}(a_i - a_{i-1}) &= \sum_{i=1}^{k}(a_i - a_{i-1}) + (a_{k+1} - a_k)\\
&= (a_k - a_0) - (a_{k+1} - a_k) = a_{k+1} - a_0.
\end{aligned}$$

So the identity is also valid for $n = k + 1$. Done.

14.   Indeed,

$$\begin{aligned}
\sum_{i=1}^{n}\frac{1}{n}\left(\frac{i}{n}\right)^2 &= \left(\frac{1}{n}\right)^3 \sum_{i=1}^{n} i^2 = \left(\frac{1}{n}\right)^3 \frac{n(n+1)(2n+1)}{6}\\
&= \frac{n}{n}\frac{(n+1)}{n}\frac{(2n+1)}{n}\frac{1}{6} = \left(1 + \frac{1}{n}\right)\left(2 + \frac{1}{n}\right)\frac{1}{6}.
\end{aligned}$$

It follows that

$$\lim_{n\to\infty}\sum_{i=1}^{n}\frac{1}{n}\left(\frac{i}{n}\right)^2 = 1\cdot 2\cdot\frac{1}{6} = \frac{1}{3}.$$

15.   For convenience, we write

$$A_n = \sum_{i=1}^{n-1}\frac{n^3}{n^4 + in^3 + p_n}.$$

We have to show that $\lim_{n\to\infty} A_n = \ln 2$. We know that $\int_1^2 \frac{1}{x}\,dx = \ln 2$. Divide the interval $[1, 2]$ into n subintervals of the same length $1/n$ by means of subdivision points $x_i = 1 + \frac{i}{n}$ $(i = 0, 1, 2, \ldots, n - 1)$ and form the corresponding Riemann sum S_n for the function $f(x) = 1/x$:

$$S_n = \sum_{i=0}^{n-1} f(x_i)\cdot\Delta x_i = \sum_{i=0}^{n-1}\frac{1}{x_i}\cdot\Delta x_i = \sum_{i=0}^{n-1}\frac{n}{n+i}\cdot\frac{1}{n} = \sum_{i=0}^{n-1}\frac{1}{n+i}.$$

Since f is continuous on $[1, 2]$, from the theory of Riemann integration we know that $\lim_{n\to\infty} S_n = \ln 2$. It suffices to show that $\lim_{n\to\infty}(S_n - A_n) = 0$. Now

$$\begin{aligned}
S_n - A_n &= \sum_{i=0}^{n-1}\left(\frac{1}{n+i} - \frac{n^3}{n^4 + in^3 + p_n}\right)\\
&= \sum_{i=0}^{n-1}\frac{(n^4 + in^3 + p_n) - n^3(n+i)}{(n^4 + in^3 + p_n)(n+i)} = \sum_{i=0}^{n-1}\frac{p_n}{(n^4 + in^3 + p_n)(n+i)}.
\end{aligned}$$

Thus

$$0 \le S_n - A_n \le \sum_{i=0}^{n-1}\frac{p_n}{n^4\cdot n} = p_n/n^4;$$

(dropping something positive from the denominator of a positive expression would diminish the denominator and hence would increase the size of this expression.) By the *Hint*, we have $p_n < 36n\ln n$. It is well-known that $\ln x \le x$ for all $x > 0$. So $p_n < 36n^2$ for all $n \ge 2$. Thus $0 < S_n - A_n \le p_n/n^4 < 36n^2/n^4 = 36/n^2$ for $n \ge 2$. Now it is clear that $S_n - A_n$ tends to 0 as $n \to \infty$, by the Sandwich Theorem of Chapter 2.

6.4

6.5   Chapter Exercises

1. $\frac{1}{27}(x+1)^{27} + C$. Use Table 6.5, $\Box = x + 1$, $r = 26$.

2. $\frac{1}{2}\sin 2x + C$.

3. $\frac{1}{3}(2x+1)^{3/2} + C$.

4. $-\frac{1}{12}(1 - 4x^2)^{3/2} + C$. Use Table 6.5, $\Box = 1 - 4x^2$, $r = 1/2$.

5. $-\cos x + \sin x + C$.

6. $-\frac{1}{3}(5 - 2x)^{3/2} + C$.

7. $-\frac{1}{2}\cos(2x) + C$. Use Table 6.6, $\Box = 2x$.

8. $0.4\,x^{2.5} + 0.625\,\cos(1.6x) + C$.

9. $3\tan x + C$.

10. $\frac{1}{200}(x^2+1)^{100} + C$. Use Table 6.5, $\Box = x^2 + 1$, $r = 99$.

11. $-\frac{1}{3}\csc 3x + C$.

12. $-\frac{1}{6}e^{-3x^2} + C$. Use Table 6.5, $\Box = -3x^2$.

13. $-\frac{1}{k}e^{-kx} + C$.

14. $\frac{\sin kx}{k} + C$. Use Table 6.6, $\Box = kx$.

15. $-\frac{\cos kx}{k} + C$.

16. 2. $\displaystyle\int_0^1 (2x+1)\,dx = x^2 + x \Big|_0^1 = 2$.

17. 0. Note that $f(x) = x^3$ is an *odd function*.

18. 10. $I = \displaystyle\int_0^2 (3x^2 + 2x - 1)\,dx = x^3 + x^2 - x \Big|_0^2 = 10$.

19. $\frac{1}{5}$. $\displaystyle\int_0^{\pi/2} \sin^4 x \cos x\,dx = \frac{\sin^5 x}{5} \Big|_0^{\pi/2} = \frac{1}{5}$.

20. $\frac{1}{\ln 3}$. $\displaystyle\int_0^1 x \cdot 3^{x^2}\,dx = \frac{1}{2}\frac{3^{x^2}}{\ln 3} \Big|_0^1 = \frac{1}{\ln 3}$. Use Table 6.5, $\Box = x^2$, $a = 3$.

21. $\frac{1}{\ln 4}$. $\displaystyle\int_0^1 2^{-x}\,dx = -\frac{1}{\ln 2}2^{-x} \Big|_0^1 = -\frac{1}{\ln 2}\left(\frac{1}{2} - 1\right) = \frac{1}{2\ln 2} = \frac{1}{\ln 4}$.

22. $\frac{2}{3}$. $\displaystyle\int_0^\pi \cos^2 x \cdot \sin x\,dx = -\frac{\cos^3 x}{3} \Big|_0^\pi = \left(-\frac{(-1)^3}{3}\right) - \left(-\frac{1}{3}\right) = \frac{2}{3}$.

23. $\frac{28}{3}$. Note that $f(x) = x^2 + 1$ is an *even function*.

24. $\frac{\pi}{6}$. $\displaystyle\int_0^{0.5} \frac{1}{\sqrt{1 - x^2}}\,dx = \text{Arcsin } x \Big|_0^{0.5} = \frac{\pi}{6}$.

25. $\frac{1}{2}e^4 - \frac{1}{2}$. Use Table 6.5, $\Box = x^2$.

26. $\displaystyle\sum_{i=1}^n 12\left(\frac{i}{n}\right)^2 = \frac{12}{n^2}\sum_{i=1}^n i^2 = \frac{12}{n^2} \cdot \frac{n(n+1)(2n+1)}{6} = \frac{2(n+1)(2n+1)}{n}$.

27. Consider the partition
$$0 = x_0 < x_1 < x_2 < \cdots < x_n = 1$$
with $x_i = \frac{i}{n}$, which divides $[0,1]$ into n subintervals $[\frac{i}{n}, \frac{i+1}{n}]$ of the same length $1/n$, $(i = 0, 1, 2, \ldots, n-1)$. In each subinterval $[\frac{i}{n}, \frac{i+1}{n}]$ we take c_i to be the left end point $\frac{i}{n}$. Then the corresponding Riemann sum for the function $f(x) = e^x$ is

$$\sum_{i=0}^{n-1} f(c_i)(x_{i+1} - x_i) = \sum_{i=0}^{n-1} e^{i/n}\left(\frac{i+1}{n} - \frac{i}{n}\right) = \sum_{i=0}^{n-1} e^{i/n} \cdot \frac{1}{n}.$$

But we know from the definition of Riemann integration that

$$\lim_{n \to \infty} \sum_{k=1}^{n} f(c_k)(x_k - x_{k-1}) = \int_0^1 f(x)dx = \int_0^1 e^x dx = e - 1.$$

Now the assertion is clear.

28. Indeed,

$$\left(\frac{n}{n^2 + 0^2} + \frac{n}{n^2 + 1^2} + \frac{n}{n^2 + 2^2} + \cdots + \frac{n}{n^2 + (n-1)^2} \right) =$$

$$\left(\frac{n}{n^2(1 + \left(\frac{0}{n}\right)^2)} + \frac{n}{n^2(1 + \left(\frac{1}{n}\right)^2)} + \frac{n}{n^2(1 + \left(\frac{2}{n}\right)^2)} + \cdots + \frac{n}{n^2(1 + \left(\frac{n-1}{n}\right)^2)} \right) =$$

$$\left(\frac{1}{n \left(1 + \left(\frac{0}{n}\right)^2\right)} + \frac{1}{n \left(1 + \left(\frac{1}{n}\right)^2\right)} + \frac{1}{n \left(1 + \left(\frac{2}{n}\right)^2\right)} + \cdots + \frac{1}{n \left(1 + \left(\frac{n-1}{n}\right)^2\right)} \right) =$$

$$\frac{1}{n} \left(\frac{1}{\left(1 + \left(\frac{0}{n}\right)^2\right)} + \frac{1}{\left(1 + \left(\frac{1}{n}\right)^2\right)} + \frac{1}{\left(1 + \left(\frac{2}{n}\right)^2\right)} + \cdots + \frac{1}{\left(1 + \left(\frac{n-1}{n}\right)^2\right)} \right) =$$

$$\sum_{i=0}^{n-1} \frac{1}{\left(1 + \left(\frac{i}{n}\right)^2\right)} \left(\frac{1}{n}\right) = \sum_{i=0}^{n-1} f(c_i) \left(\Delta x_i\right),$$

once we choose the c_i as $c_i = x_i = i/n$ and f as in the Hint. Next, we let $n \to \infty$ so that the norm of this subdivision approaches 0 and, by the results of this Chapter, the Riemann Sum approaches the definite integral

$$\lim_{n \to \infty} \sum_{i=0}^{n-1} f(c_i)\Delta x_i = \int_0^1 \frac{1}{1 + x^2} \, dx,$$

$$= \text{Arctan } 1 - \text{Arctan } 0 = \frac{\pi}{4}.$$

29. **Method 1** First we interpret the integral $\int_0^1 \frac{1}{\sqrt{1-x^2}} \, dx$ (whose value is $\frac{\pi}{2}$) as the limit of a sequence of Riemann sums S_n defined as follows. For fixed n, we divide $[0, 1]$ into n subintervals of length $1/n$ by $x_i \equiv i/n$ $(0 \leq i \leq n)$ and we take c_i to be x_i. Then the corresponding Riemann sum for $f(x) \equiv \frac{1}{\sqrt{1-x^2}}$ is

$$S_n = \sum_{i=0}^{n-1} f(c_i)(x_{i+1} - x_i) = \sum_{i=0}^{n-1} \frac{1}{\sqrt{1 - (i/n)^2}} \cdot \frac{1}{n} = \sum_{i=0}^{n-1} \frac{1}{\sqrt{n^2 - i^2}}.$$

For convenience, let us put $A_{n,i} = n^8 - i^2 n^6 + 2ip_n - p_n^2$. It is enough to show that $S_n - \sum_{i=0}^{n-1} \frac{n^3}{\sqrt{A_{n,i}}} \to$ 0 as $n \to \infty$. Now, for each n and each i,

$$\frac{1}{\sqrt{n^2 - i^2}} - \frac{n^3}{\sqrt{A_{n,i}}} = \frac{\sqrt{A_{n,i}} - n^3 \sqrt{n^2 - i^2}}{\sqrt{n^2 - i^2} \sqrt{A_{n,i}}} = \frac{A_{n,i} - n^6(n^2 - i^2)}{(n^2 - i^2)\sqrt{A_{n,i}} + A_{n,i}\sqrt{n^2 - i^2}}.$$

The denominator is too bulky here and we have to sacrifice some terms to tidy it up. But we have to wait until the numerator is simplified:

$$A_{n,i} - n^6(n^2 - i^2) = (n^8 - i^2 n^6 + 2ip_n - p_n^2) - (n^8 - i^2 n^6) = 2ip_n - p_n^2.$$

Now we drop every thing save $A_{n,i}$ in the denominator. Then within

$$A_{n,i} \equiv n^8 - in^6 + 2ip_n - p_n^2 = n^6(n^2 - i^2) + 2ip_n - p_n^2$$

we drop the positive term $2ip_n$ and the factor $n^2 - i^2$ which is ≥ 1. (We still have to keep the burdensome $-p_n^2$ because it is negative.) Ultimately, the denominator is replaced by a smaller expression, namely $n^6 - p_n^2$. Recall that $p_n < 36n^2$ for $n \geq 2$; (see Exercise 15 in the previous **Exercise Set**.) Using this we see that

$$n^6 - p_n^2 \geq n^6 - 36n^2 = n^2(n^4 - 36).$$

Thus, for $n \geq 2$, $n^2(n^4 - 36)$ is a lower bound of the denominator. Next we get an upper bound for the numerator:

$$|2ip_n - p_n^2| \leq 2ip_n + p_n^2 \leq 2np_n + p_n^2 \leq 2n(36n^2) + (36n^2)^2 = 72n^3 + 1296n^4.$$

Now we can put all things together:

$$\left| S_n - \sum_{i=0}^{n-1} \frac{n^3}{\sqrt{A_{n,i}}} \right| \le \sum_{i=1}^{n-1} \left| \frac{1}{\sqrt{n^2 - i^2}} - \frac{n^3}{\sqrt{A_{n,i}}} \right| \le n \cdot \frac{72n^3 + 1296n^4}{n^2(n^4 - 36)}.$$

The last expression approaches to 0 as n tends to infinity. Done!

Method 2 Let $f(x) = \dfrac{1}{\sqrt{1 - x^2}}$, on $[0, 1)$. Let $\mathcal{P}$ denote the partition with $x_0 = 0$, and $x_i = \frac{i}{n}$, $i = 1, 2, \ldots, n$. It is clear that, as $n \to \infty$, the norm of this partition approaches 0. Next, by Sierpinski's estimate we know that

$$p_n < 36n \ln n.$$

But by L'Hospital's Rule, $\lim\limits_{n \to \infty} \dfrac{\ln n}{n^3} = 0$. This means that

$$\lim_{n \to \infty} \frac{p_n}{n^4} \le \lim_{n \to \infty} \frac{36 \ln n}{n^3} = 0.$$

So

$$\lim_{n \to \infty} \frac{p_n}{n^4} = 0$$

by the Sandwich Theorem of Chapter 2. Okay, now choose our interior points t_i in the interval $(x_i, \ x_{i+1})$, as follows: Let

$$t_i = \frac{i}{n} + \frac{p_n}{n^4}.$$

By what has been said, note that if n is sufficiently large, then t_i lies *indeed in this interval*. By definition of the Riemann integral it follows that this specific Riemann sum given by

$$\lim_{n \to \infty} \sum_{i=0}^{n-1} f(t_i) \, \Delta x_i$$

tends to, as $n \to \infty$, the Riemann integral of f over $[0, 1)$. But

$$
\begin{aligned}
\lim_{n \to \infty} \sum_{i=0}^{n-1} f(t_i) \, \Delta x_i \quad &= \quad \lim_{n \to \infty} \sum_{i=0}^{n-1} \frac{1}{\sqrt{1 - t_i{}^2}} \cdot \frac{1}{n} \\[2mm]
&= \quad \lim_{n \to \infty} \sum_{i=0}^{n-1} \frac{1}{\sqrt{1 - \left(\frac{i}{n} + \frac{p_n}{n^4} \right)^2}} \cdot \frac{1}{n} \\[2mm]
&= \quad \lim_{n \to \infty} \sum_{i=0}^{n-1} \frac{n^3}{\sqrt{n^8 - i^2 n^6 - 2i p_n - p_n{}^2}}.
\end{aligned}
$$

The conclusion follows since the Riemann integral of this function f exists on $[0, 1)$ and

$$\int_0^1 \frac{1}{\sqrt{1 - x^2}} = \text{Arcsin } 1 - \text{Arcsin } 0 = \text{Arcsin } 1 = \frac{\pi}{2}.$$

30. 2. $\displaystyle\int_0^\pi \sin x \, dx = -\cos x \Big|_0^\pi = 2.$

31. $2\sqrt{2} - 2$. Notice that when x runs from 0 to $\pi/2$, the cosine curve drops from 1 to 0 and the sine curve elevates from 0 to 1. Between 0 and $\pi/2$, the sine curve and the cosine curve meet at $x = \frac{\pi}{4}$. Hence

$$|\cos x - \sin x| = \begin{cases} \cos x - \sin x & \text{if } 0 \le x \le \pi/4, \\ \sin x - \cos x & \text{if } \pi/4 \le x \le \pi/2. \end{cases}$$

Thus the required integral is equal to

$$
\begin{aligned}
&\int_0^{\pi/4} (\cos x - \sin x) \, dx + \int_{\pi/4}^{\pi/2} (\sin x - \cos x) \, dx \\[2mm]
= \quad &(\sin x + \cos x)\big|_0^{\pi/4} + (-\cos x - \sin x)\big|_{\pi/4}^{\pi/2} = 2\sqrt{2} - 2.
\end{aligned}
$$

32. $1 - \dfrac{\sqrt{2}}{2}$. $\displaystyle\int_{\pi/12}^{\pi/8} \frac{\cos 2x}{\sin^2 2x} \, dx = \int_{\pi/6}^{\pi/4} \csc 2x \cot 2x \, dx$

$= -\dfrac{1}{2} \csc 2x \Big|_{\pi/12}^{\pi/8} = 1 - \dfrac{\sqrt{2}}{2}.$

33. $\dfrac{4}{9}\sqrt{2} - \dfrac{2}{9}$. $\displaystyle\int_0^1 t^2 \sqrt{1 + t^3} \, dt = \frac{1}{3} \cdot \frac{(1 + t^3)^{3/2}}{3/2} \Big|_0^1 = \frac{4}{9}\sqrt{2} - \frac{2}{9}.$ Use Table 6.5, $\square = 1 + t^3$, $r = 1/2$.

34. $\displaystyle\int_0^1 \frac{x}{1+x^4}\,dx = \frac{1}{2}\,\text{Arctan}\,x^2 \Big|_0^1 = \frac{1}{2}\,(\text{Arctan}\,1 - \text{Arctan}\,0) = \frac{\pi}{8}.$

35. $\displaystyle\frac{d}{dx}\int_1^{x^2}\frac{\sin t}{t^{3/2}}\,dt = \frac{\sin(x^2)}{x^3}\cdot 2x = \frac{2\sin(x^2)}{x^2} \longrightarrow 2 \quad \text{as } x \to 0+.$

36. As $x \to \infty$, we have

$$\frac{d}{dx}\int_{\sqrt{3}}^{\sqrt{x}}\frac{r}{(r+1)(r-1)}\,dr = \frac{x^{3/2}}{(x^{1/2}+1)(x^{1/2}-1)}\cdot\frac{1}{2\sqrt{x}} = \frac{x}{2(x-1)} \longrightarrow \frac{1}{2}.$$

37. $\displaystyle\frac{d}{dx}\int_0^{x^2}e^{-t^2}\,dt = 2xe^{-x^2} = 2\frac{x}{e^{x^2}}$ which is of indefinite form $\frac{\infty}{\infty}$ when $x \to \infty$. By L'Hospital's rule
and the fact that $e^x \to +\infty$ as $x \to +\infty$ we see that $2\frac{x}{e^{x^2}} \to 0$ as $x \to \infty$.

38. $\displaystyle\frac{d}{dx}\int_1^{\sqrt{x}}\frac{\sin(y^2)}{2y}\,dy = \frac{\sin(\sqrt{x}^2)}{2\sqrt{x}}\cdot\frac{1}{2\sqrt{x}} = \frac{\sin x}{4x} \longrightarrow \frac{1}{4} \quad \text{as } x \to 0.$

39.

$$\lim_{x\to 0+}\frac{d}{dx}\int_1^{\sin x}\frac{\ln t}{\ln(\text{Arcsin}\,t)}\,dt$$

$$= \lim_{x\to 0+}\left(\frac{\ln(\sin x)}{\ln(\text{Arcsin}\,(\sin x))}\cdot\cos x - 0\right),$$

$$= \lim_{x\to 0+}\left(\frac{\ln(\sin x)}{\ln x}\cdot\cos x\right)$$

$$= \lim_{x\to 0+}\left(\frac{\ln(\sin x)}{\ln x}\right)\cdot\cos 0$$

$$= \lim_{x\to 0+}\left(\frac{\cot x}{1/x}\right)$$

$$= \lim_{x\to 0+}x\,\cot x = \lim_{x\to 0+}\frac{x}{\sin x}\cos x = (1)(1) = 1.$$

40. Indeed, as $t \to 0$,

$$\frac{d}{dt}\int_{2\pi-ct}^{2\pi+ct}\frac{\sin x}{cx}\,dx = \frac{\sin(2\pi+ct)}{c(2\pi+ct)}\cdot c - \frac{\sin(2\pi-ct)}{c(2\pi-ct)}(-c) \longrightarrow \frac{\sin 2\pi}{\pi} = 0.$$

41.

$$\lim_{h\to 0+}\frac{d}{dx}\left(\frac{1}{h}\int_{x-h}^{x+h}\sqrt{t}\,dt\right) = \lim_{h\to 0+}\frac{\sqrt{x+h}\,(1) - \sqrt{x-h}\,(1)}{h},$$

$$= \lim_{h\to 0+}\frac{\sqrt{x+h}-\sqrt{x-h}}{h} = \lim_{h\to 0+}\frac{2h}{h(\sqrt{x+h}+\sqrt{x-h})},$$

$$= \lim_{h\to 0+}\frac{2}{\sqrt{x+h}+\sqrt{x-h}} = \frac{1}{\sqrt{x}}.$$

42. $\displaystyle\lim_{x\to 0}\frac{1}{2x}\int_{-x}^{x}\cos t\,dt = \lim_{x\to 0}\frac{1}{2x}(\sin x - \sin(-x)) = \lim_{x\to 0}\frac{2\sin x}{2x} = 1.$ [Remark: Actually, for every
continuous function f defined on the real line, we have

$$\lim_{x\to 0+}\frac{1}{2x}\int_{-x}^{x}f(t)\,dt = f(0).$$

Do you know why?]

43. $\displaystyle\frac{y^5}{5} = \frac{x^4}{4} + \frac{1}{5}.$

44. $\sin(y(x)) + \cos x = C$ is the most general antiderivative. But $y = \pi/2$ when $x = 0$. This means that
$\sin(\pi/2) + \cos 0 = C$, or $C = 2$. So, the solution in implicit form is given by $\sin(y(x)) + \cos x = 2$.

45. $\displaystyle y = \tan\left[\frac{1}{2}(e^{2x}-1)+\frac{\pi}{4}\right].$

46. $\displaystyle y = 2x^4 + \frac{4}{3}x^3 + x.$

47. $y(x) = C_1 + C_2\,x + C_3\,x^2 - x^4$ is the most general antiderivative. Now, the initial conditions $y(0) = 0, y'(0) = 0, y''(0) = -1$ imply that $C_1 = 0, C_2 = 0, C_3 = -1/2$. The required solution is given by

$$y(x) = -\frac{1}{2}\,x^2 - x^4.$$

48. $y = e^x - x - 1$.

49. $y = \dfrac{x^4}{12} + \dfrac{x^3}{3}$.

50. Since marginal cost $= \frac{dC}{dx} = 60 + \frac{40}{x+10}$,

    (a) total increase in cost as x goes from 20 to 40 is

$$\int_{20}^{40}\left[60 + \frac{40}{x+10}\right]\,dx = [60x + 40ln|x+40|\,]_{20}^{40}$$

$$= 60 \times 40 + 40\,ln(50) - [60 \times 20 + 40ln(30)] = 1200 + 40(ln\ 50 - ln\ 30) = 1200 + 40ln(5/3) = \$1220.43$$

    (b) Let $I(t)$ be value of investment at time t, t in years. $\frac{dI}{dt} = (500e^{\sqrt{t}})/\sqrt{t}$, thus

$$I(t) = \int \frac{500e^{\sqrt{t}}}{\sqrt{t}}\,dt = 500e^{\sqrt{t}} + C.$$

When $t = 0$, $I = 1000$, so $1000 = 500 + C$, and $C = 500$. Therefore, at $t = 4$, $I = 500e^2 + 500 = \$4194.53$.

Chapter 7

Solutions

7.1

7.2 Exercise Set 32

1. $\frac{1}{200}(2x-1)^{100} + C$.

2. $3 \cdot \dfrac{(x+1)^{6.1}}{6.1} + C$.

3. $I = \displaystyle\int_0^1 (3x+1)^{-5}\,dx = \frac{1}{3} \cdot \frac{(3x+1)^{-4}}{-4}\,\Big|_0^1 \approx 0.0830$.

4. $I = \displaystyle\int (x-1)^{-2}\,dx = -(x-1)^{-1} + C = \dfrac{1}{1-x} + C$.

5. $-\dfrac{1}{202}(1-x^2)^{101} + C = \dfrac{1}{202}(x^2-1)^{101} + C$.

6. $\dfrac{1}{\ln 2}\,2^{x^2-1} + C$. Let $u = x^2$, $du = 2x\,dx$, etc.

7. $\displaystyle\int_0^{\pi/4} \tan x\,dx = -\ln|\cos x| = \ln|\sec x|\,\Big|_0^{\pi/4} = \ln\sqrt{2} - \ln 1 = \dfrac{\ln 2}{2}$.

8. $\dfrac{1}{3}e^{z^3} + C$.

9. $-\dfrac{3}{4}(2-x)^{4/3} + C$.

10. $\frac{1}{2}\sin 8 \approx 0.49468$.

11. $I = \displaystyle\int \frac{1}{1+\sin t} \cdot \frac{d(1+\sin t)}{dt}\,dt = \ln|1+\sin t| + C$.

12. $-\sqrt{1-x^2} + C$.

13. $\frac{1}{2}\ln|y^2+2y| + C$. Let $u = y^2 + 2y$, $du = 2(y+1)\,dy$, etc.

14. $I = \displaystyle\int \frac{\sec^2 x\,dx}{\sqrt{1+\tan x}} = \int \frac{\left(\frac{d}{dx}\tan x\right)\,dx}{\sqrt{1+\tan x}} = 2\sqrt{1+\tan x} + C$.

15. $I = -\displaystyle\int_0^{\pi/4} \frac{1}{\cos^2 x} \cdot \frac{d\cos x}{dx}\,dx = \frac{1}{\cos x}\,\Big|_0^{\pi/4} = \sqrt{2} - 1$. Alternatively,

$$I = \int_0^{\pi/4} \tan x \sec x\,dx = \sec x\,\Big|_0^{\pi/4} = \sqrt{2} - 1.$$

16. **Hard! Very hard!** The function $\sec x + \tan x$ in the hint seems to be extremely tricky and unthinkable; see Example 364 in §8.5.2 for manipulating this integral according to the hint. Here is a slightly more natural way (although just as unthinkable): Try to put everything in terms of sines or cosines. Let's begin. Don't feel bad if you find this still too slick for you.

$$\int \sec x \; dx \;\; = \;\; \int \frac{1}{\cos x} \; dx = \int \frac{\cos x}{\cos^2 x} \; dx = \int \frac{1}{\cos^2 x} \cdot \frac{d \sin x}{dx} \; dx$$

$$= \;\; \int \frac{1}{1 - \sin^2 x} \cdot \frac{d \sin x}{dx} \; dx = \int \frac{1}{1 - u^2} \; du \quad (u = \sin x)$$

$$= \;\; \int \frac{1}{(1-u)(1+u)} \; du = \int \frac{1}{2} \left[\frac{1}{1-u} + \frac{1}{1+u} \right] \; du$$

$$= \;\; \frac{1}{2} \left[-\ln|1-u| + \ln|1+u| \right] + C = \frac{1}{2} \ln \left| \frac{1+u}{1-u} \right| + C$$

$$= \;\; \frac{1}{2} \ln \left| \frac{1 + \sin x}{1 - \sin x} \right| + C$$

$$= \;\; \frac{1}{2} \ln \left| \frac{(1 + \sin x)^2}{(1 - \sin x)(1 + \sin x)} \right| + C$$

$$= \;\; \frac{1}{2} \ln \left| \frac{(1 + \sin x)^2}{\cos^2 x} \right| + C$$

$$= \;\; \ln \left| \frac{1 + \sin x}{\cos x} \right| + C = \ln |\sec x + \tan x| + C.$$

17. One way to do this is to multiply out everything and then integrate term by term. But this way is very messy! Observe that $4z^3 + 1$ is nothing but the derivative of $z^4 + z$. So we have an easy way out:

$$I = \int (z^4 + z)^4 \cdot \frac{d}{dz}(z^4 + z) \; dz = \frac{1}{5}(z^4 + z)^5 + C.$$

18. $-\text{Arctan}(\cos x) + C$. Let $u = \cos x$, $du = -\sin x \; dx$, etc.

19. $I = \left. \frac{1}{2} \text{Arctan}(t^2) \right|_0^1 = \frac{\pi}{8}$.

20. $\frac{1}{8} \sin^4(x^2 + 1) + C$. Let $u = x^2 + 1$ first, then $v = \sin u$ as the next substitution.

21. $\frac{3}{2} \ln(x^2 + 1) - \text{Arctan } x + C$. (Since $x^2 + 1$ is always positive, there is no need to put an absolute value sign around it.)

22. $I = \int_e^{e^2} \frac{1}{\ln x} \cdot \frac{d \ln x}{dx} \; dx = \left. \ln(\ln x) \right|_e^{e^2} = \ln 2 - \ln 1 = \ln 2.$

23. $\frac{1}{3}(\text{Arctan } x)^3 + C$.

24. $I = \int \cosh(e^t) \cdot e^t \; dt = \sinh(e^t) + C$. (Recall that $D \sinh \Box = \cosh \Box \; D\Box$ and $D \cosh \Box = \sinh \Box \; D\Box$.)

25. $\frac{1}{5} \text{Arcsin } 5s + C$.

26. $I = \int_{\pi^2}^{4\pi^2} \cos \sqrt{x} \cdot 2 \frac{d\sqrt{x}}{dx} \; dx = \left. 2 \sin \sqrt{x} \right|_{\pi^2}^{4\pi^2} = 2(\sin 2\pi - \sin \pi) = 0.$

27. $\frac{1}{2} e^{x^2} + C$.

28. $-\sqrt{1 - y^2} + \text{Arcsin } y + C$. Split this integral up into two pieces and let $u = 1 - y^2$, etc.

29. $\sec(\ln x) + C$. Let $u = \ln x$, etc.

30. $I = \int \sin^{-2/3} x \cdot \frac{d}{dx} \sin x \; dx = 3 \sin^{1/3} x + C.$

31. $I = \int_0^1 e^{e^t} \cdot \frac{de^t}{dt} \; dt = \left. e^{e^t} \right|_0^1 = e^e - e.$

32. $\frac{1}{2 \ln(1.5)} 1.5^{x^2+1} + C = 1.23316 \; 1.5^{x^2+1} + C.$

7.3   Exercise Set 33

1. Using the normal method, we have:

$$I = \int x \frac{d}{dx} \sin x \; dx = x \sin x - \int \sin x \; dx = x \sin x + \cos x + C.$$

2. $-x\cos x + \sin x + C$.

3. $-1/2$.

4. Using the normal method, we have:

$$\int x^2 \sin x\ dx = \int x^2 \frac{d}{dx}(-\cos x)dx$$

$$= -x^2 \cos x + \int 2x \cdot \cos x\ dx$$

$$= -x^2 \cos x + \int 2x \frac{d}{dx}\sin x\ dx$$

$$= -x^2 \cos x + 2x \sin x - \int 2 \sin x\ dx$$

$$= -x^2 \cos x + 2x \sin x + 2 \cos x + C.$$

Now you can see the advantage of the Table method over the above normal method: you don't have to copy down some expressions several times and the minus signs are no longer a worry!

5. $x \tan x + \ln|\cos x| + C$.

6. $x \sec x - \ln|\sec x + \tan x| + C$. (Here you have to recall the answer to a very tricky integral: $\int \sec x\ dx = \ln|\sec x + \tan x|$. See Exercise Set 32, Number 16.)

7. $(x^2 - 2x + 2)e^x + C$.

8. $I = -\frac{1}{3}x^2 e^{-3x} + \frac{2}{9}xe^{-3x} - \frac{2}{27}e^{-3x}\ \Big|_0^\infty = \frac{2}{27}$. Notice that here we have used the fact $p(x)e^{-3x} \longrightarrow 0$ as $x \to +\infty$, where $p(x)$ is any polynomial, that is, the exponential growth is faster than the polynomial growth. Alternately, use L'Hospital's Rule for each limit except for the last one.

9. $\frac{1}{5}x^5 \ln x - \frac{1}{25}x^5 + C$.

10. $-\frac{1}{3}\left(x^3 + x^2 + \frac{2}{3}x + \frac{2}{9}\right)e^{-3x} + C$.

11. $x \sin^{-1} x + \sqrt{1 - x^2} + C$.

12. $x \tan^{-1} x - \frac{1}{2}\ln(1 + x^2) + C$.

13. Let $u = \ln x$. Then $x = e^u$ and $dx = e^u du$. Thus the integral can be converted to $\int u^5 e^{2u} e^u\ du = \int u^5 e^{3u}\ du$. Using the Table method to evaluate the last integral, we have

$$\int u^5 e^{3u}\ du = e^{3u}\left(\frac{1}{3}u^5 - \frac{5}{9}u^4 + \frac{20}{27}u^3 - \frac{20}{27}u^2 + \frac{40}{81}u - \frac{40}{243}\right) + C.$$

Substituting $u = \ln x$ back, we get the answer to the original integral $\int x^2 (\ln x)^5\ dx$:

$$x^3 \left(\frac{1}{3}(\ln x)^5 - \frac{5}{9}(\ln x)^4 + \frac{20}{27}(\ln x)^3 - \frac{20}{27}(\ln x)^2 + \frac{40}{81}\ln x - \frac{40}{243}\right) + C.$$

14. $\frac{x^2}{2}\sec^{-1} x - \frac{1}{2}\sqrt{x^2 - 1} + C$, if $x > 0$.

15. Use the Table method for this problem.

$$\int (x-1)^2 \sin x\ dx = -(x-1)^2 \cos x + 2(x-1)\sin x + 2\cos x + C.$$

16. $-\frac{1}{13}(2\sin 3x + 3\cos 3x)e^{-2x} + C$.

17. $\frac{1}{17}(\cos 4x + 4\sin 4x)e^x + C$.

18. $-\frac{1}{10}\cos 5x - \frac{1}{2}\cos x + C$, or $-\frac{1}{5}(2\sin 3x \sin 2x + 3\cos 3x \cos 2x) + C$.
Use the identity $\sin A \cos B = \frac{1}{2}(\sin(A + B) - \sin(A - B))$ with $A = 3x$ and $B = 2x$ and integrate. Alternately, this is also a **three-row problem**: This gives the second equivalent answer.

19. $-\frac{1}{12}\cos 6x + \frac{1}{4}\cos 2x + C$, or $-\frac{1}{3}\cos^3 2x + \frac{1}{4}\cos 2x + C$, or $\frac{1}{12}(4\sin 2x \sin 4x + 2\cos 2x \cos 4x) + C$. This is a **three-row problem** as well. See the preceding exercise.

20. $\frac{1}{14}\sin 7x + \frac{1}{2}\sin x + C$, or $\frac{1}{7}(4\cos 3x \sin 4x - 3\sin 3x \cos 4x) + C$. Use the identity $\cos A \cos B = \frac{1}{2}(\cos(A + B) + \cos(A - B))$ with $A = 4x$ and $B = 3x$ and integrate. Alternately, this is also a **three-row problem**: This gives the second equivalent answer.

21. $e^{2x}\left(\frac{1}{2}x^5 - \frac{5}{4}x^4 + \frac{5}{2}x^3 - \frac{15}{4}x^2 + \frac{15}{4}x - \frac{15}{8}\right) + C$. For this exercise you really should use the Table method, otherwise you will find the amount of work overwhelming!

22. $\frac{x}{2}(\cos \ln x + \sin \ln x) + C$. See Example 333.

7.4

7.4.1 Exercise Set 34

1. $x - 3 + \dfrac{4}{x+1}$

2. $2 - \dfrac{3x^2 + x + 3}{x^3 + 2x + 1}$

3. $\dfrac{1}{3}\left(x^2 - \dfrac{2}{3} + \dfrac{7/3}{3x^2 - 1}\right)$

4. $x^2 - 1 + \dfrac{2}{x^2 + 1}$

5. $x^4 + x^3 + 2x^2 + 2x + 2 + \dfrac{3}{x-1}$

6. $\dfrac{3}{2}\left(x - 1 + \dfrac{13x + 15}{6x^2 + 6x + 3}\right)$

7.4.2 Exercise Set 35

1. $\displaystyle\int \frac{x}{x-1}\, dx = \int \left(1 + \frac{1}{x-1}\right)\, dx = x + \ln|x-1| + C.$

2. $\displaystyle\int \frac{x+1}{x}\, dx = \int \left(1 + \frac{1}{x}\right)\, dx = x + \ln|x| + C.$

3. $\displaystyle\int \frac{x^2\, dx}{x+2} = \int \left(x - 2 + \frac{4}{x+2}\right)\, dx = \frac{x^2}{2} - 2x + 4\ln|x+2| + C.$

4. $\displaystyle\int \frac{x^2\, dx}{x^2+1} = \int \left(1 - \frac{1}{x^2+1}\right)\, dx = x - \operatorname{Arctan} x + C.$

5. Since the denominator and the numerator have the same degree, we have to perform the long division first

$$
\begin{aligned}
I &\equiv \int \frac{x^2}{(x-1)(x+1)}\, dx = \int \frac{x^2}{x^2-1}\, dx = \int \left(1 + \frac{1}{x^2-1}\right)\, dx \\
&= \int \left(1 + \frac{1}{(x+1)(x-1)}\right)\, dx = \int \left(1 + \frac{1}{2}\cdot\frac{1}{x-1} - \frac{1}{2}\cdot\frac{1}{x+1}\right)\, dx \\
&= x + \frac{1}{2}\ln|x-1| - \frac{1}{2}\ln|x+1| + C.
\end{aligned}
$$

6. Put $\dfrac{2x}{(x-1)(x-3)} = \dfrac{A}{x-1} + \dfrac{B}{x-3}$. Then $2x = A(x-3) + B(x-1)$. Setting $x = 1$ we have $A = -1$ and setting $x = 3$ we have $B = 3$. Thus the required integral is

$$
\int \left(\frac{-1}{x-1} + \frac{3}{x-3}\right)\, dx = 3\ln|x-3| - \ln|x-1| + C.
$$

7. Put $\dfrac{3x^2}{(x-1)(x-2)(x-3)} = \dfrac{A}{x-1} + \dfrac{B}{x-2} + \dfrac{C}{x-3}$. Then

$$
3x^2 = A(x-2)(x-3) + B(x-1)(x-3) + C(x-1)(x-2).
$$

Setting $x = 1$, 2, 3 respectively, we have $A = 3/2$, $B = -12$ and $C = 27/2$. Thus

$$
\int \frac{3x^2\, dx}{(x-1)(x-2)(x-3)} = \frac{3}{2}\ln|x-1| - 12\ln|x-2| + \frac{27}{2}\ln|x-3| + C.
$$

8. We start with long division:

$$
\begin{aligned}
I &\equiv \int_0^1 \frac{x^3 - 1}{x+1}\, dx = \int_0^1 \left(x^2 - x + 1 - \frac{2}{x+1}\right)\, dx \\
&= \left.\frac{x^3}{3} - \frac{x^2}{2} + x - 2\ln|x+1|\right|_0^1 = \frac{1}{3} - \frac{1}{2} + 1 - 2\ln 2 - 0 = \frac{5}{6} - \ln 4.
\end{aligned}
$$

9. Here we perform a small trick on the numerator of the integrand:

$$\int \frac{3x}{(x-1)^2}\,dx = \int \frac{3(x-1)+3}{(x-1)^2}\,dx$$

$$= \int \frac{3}{(x-1)^2}\,dx + \int \frac{3}{x-1}\,dx$$

$$= 3(1-x)^{-1} + 3\ln|x-1| + C.$$

10. Put

$$\frac{2x-1}{(x-2)^2(x+1)} = \frac{A}{x+1} + \frac{B}{x-2} + \frac{C}{(x-2)^2}.$$

Then $2x - 1 = A(x-2)^2 + B(x-2)(x+1) + C(x+1)$. Setting $x = -1$, we have $-3 = A(-3)^2$ and hence $A = -1/3$. Setting $x = 2$, we have $3 = 3C$; so $C = 1$. Comparing the coefficients of x^2 on both sides, we get $0 = A + B$, which gives $B = -A = 1/3$. Thus

$$\int \frac{2x\,dx}{(x-2)^2(x+1)} = \int \left(-\frac{1}{3}\cdot\frac{1}{x+1} + \frac{1}{3}\cdot\frac{1}{x-2} + \frac{1}{(x-2)^2} \right)\,dx$$

$$= \frac{1}{2-x} + \frac{1}{3}\ln|x-2| - \frac{1}{3}\ln|x+1| + C.$$

11. By long division, we get $\dfrac{x^4+1}{x^2+1} = x^2 - 1 + \dfrac{2}{x^2+1}$. So

$$\int \frac{x^4+1}{x^2+1}\,dx = \frac{x^3}{3} - x + 2\operatorname{Arctan} x + C.$$

12. Putting $u = x^2$, the integrand becomes
$\dfrac{1}{(u+1)(u+4)} = \dfrac{1}{3}\cdot\dfrac{1}{u+1} - \dfrac{1}{3}\dfrac{1}{u+4}$. So

$$\int \frac{dx}{(x^2+1)(x^2+4)} = \frac{1}{3}\int \frac{dx}{x^2+1} - \frac{1}{3}\int \frac{dx}{x^2+4}$$

$$= \frac{1}{3}\operatorname{Arctan} x - \frac{1}{6}\operatorname{Arctan}\frac{x}{2} + C.$$

13. Put

$$\frac{1}{x^2(x-1)(x+2)} = \frac{A}{x} + \frac{B}{x^2} + \frac{C}{x-1} + \frac{D}{x+2}.$$

The we have

$$1 = Ax(x-1)(x+2) + B(x-1)(x+2) + Cx^2(x+2) + Dx^2(x-1).$$

Setting $x = 1,\ 0,\ -2$ respectively, we have $C = 1/3$, $B = -1/2$ and $D = -1/12$. Comparing coefficients of x^3 on both sides, we have $0 = A + C + D$, or $A + \frac{1}{3} - \frac{1}{12} = 0$ and hence $A = -\frac{1}{4}$. Thus

$$\int \frac{dx}{x^2(x-1)(x+2)} = -\frac{1}{4}\int \frac{dx}{x} - \frac{1}{2}\int \frac{dx}{x^2} + \frac{1}{3}\int \frac{dx}{x-1} - \frac{1}{12}\int \frac{dx}{x+2}$$

$$= -\frac{1}{4}\ln|x| + \frac{1}{2x} + \frac{1}{3}\ln|x-1| - \frac{1}{12}\ln|x+2| + C.$$

14. Put

$$\frac{x^5+1}{x(x-2)(x-1)(x+1)(x^2+1)} = \frac{A}{x} + \frac{B}{x-2} + \frac{C}{x-1} + \frac{D}{x+1} + \frac{Ex+F}{x^2+1}.$$

Using the method of "covering" described in this section, we get $A = 1/2$, $B = 11/10$, $C = -1/2$ and $D = 0$. By using the "plug-in method" described in the present section we have $E = -\frac{1}{10}$ and $F = \frac{3}{10}$. Thus the partial fraction decomposition for the integrand is

$$\frac{1}{2}\cdot\frac{1}{x} + \frac{11}{10}\cdot\frac{1}{x-2} - \frac{1}{2}\cdot\frac{1}{x-1} - \frac{1}{10}\cdot\frac{x}{x^2+1} + \frac{3}{10}\cdot\frac{1}{x^2+1}.$$

Thus the required integral is

$$\frac{1}{2}\ln|x| + \frac{11}{10}\ln|x-2| - \frac{1}{2}\ln|x-1| - \frac{1}{20}\ln(x^2+1) + \frac{3}{10}\operatorname{Arctan} x + C.$$

15. Putting

$$\frac{2}{x(x-1)^2(x^2+1)} = \frac{A}{x} + \frac{B}{x-1} + \frac{C}{(x-1)^2} + \frac{Dx+E}{x^2+1},$$

we have

$$2 = A(x-1)^2(x^2+1) + Bx(x-1)(x^2+1) + Cx(x^2+1) + (Dx+E)x(x-1)^2.$$

Setting $x = 0$, we obtain $A = 2$. Setting $x = 1$, we get $C = 1$. Next we set $x = 2$. This gives us an identity relating the unknowns from A to E. Substituting $A = 2$ and $C = 1$ in this identity and then simplifying, we get a relation

$$5B + 2D + E = -9$$

between B, D and E. Setting $x = 3$ will give us another such a relation:

$$5B + 3D + E = -9.$$

From these two relations we can deduce that $D = 0$ and $5B + E = -9$. Finally, setting $x = -1$ will give us yet another relation among B, D and E:

$$B + D - E = -3.$$

Now it is not hard to solve for B and E: $B = -2$, $E = 1$. (Remark: if you are familiar with complex numbers, you can find D and E efficiently by setting $x = i$ to arrive at $2 = (Di + E)i(i - 1)^2$, which gives $Di + E = 1$ and hence $D = 0$ and $E = 1$, in view of the fact that D and E are real numbers.) We conclude

$$\frac{2}{x(x-1)^2(x^2+1)} = \frac{2}{x} - \frac{2}{x-1} + \frac{1}{(x-1)^2} + \frac{1}{x^2+1}.$$

So the required integral is equal to

$$\int \frac{2\,dx}{x(x-1)^2(x^2+1)} = 2\ln|x| - 2\ln|x-1| - \frac{1}{x-1} + \text{Arctan } x + C.$$

7.5

7.5.1   Exercise Set 36

1. Let $u = \cos 3x$ so that $du = -3\sin 3x\ dx$ and $\sin^2 3x = 1 - u^2$.

$$
\begin{aligned}
\int \sin^3 3x\ dx &= \int \sin^2 3x \cdot \sin 3x\ dx \\
&= \int (1 - u^2) \cdot (-1/3)du = -\frac{u}{3} + \frac{u^3}{9} + C \\
&= -\frac{\cos 3x}{3} + \frac{\cos^3 3x}{9} + C.
\end{aligned}
$$

2. Let $u = \sin(2x - 1)$ so that $du = 2\cos(2x - 1)\ dx$ and $\cos^2(2x - 1) = 1 - u^2$.

$$
\begin{aligned}
\int \cos^3(2x - 1)\ dx &= \int \cos^2(2x - 1) \cdot \cos(2x - 1)\ dx \\
&= \int (1 - u^2) \cdot \frac{1}{2}du = \frac{u}{2} - \frac{u^3}{6} + C \\
&= \frac{\sin(2x - 1)}{2} - \frac{\sin^3(2x - 1)}{6} + C.
\end{aligned}
$$

3. Let $u = \sin x$ so that $du = \cos x\ dx$. Notice that $x = 0 \Rightarrow u = 0$ and $x = \frac{\pi}{2} \Rightarrow u = 1$. Thus

$$
\int_0^{\pi/2} \sin^2 x \cos^3 x\ dx = \int_0^1 u^2(1 - u^2)du = \left(\frac{u^3}{3} - \frac{u^5}{5} \right) \Bigg|_0^1 = \frac{2}{15}.
$$

4. Let $u = \cos(x - 2)$. Then $du = -\sin(x - 2)\ dx$ and

$$
\begin{aligned}
\int \cos^2(x - 2)\sin^3(x - 2)\ dx &= \int u^2(1 - u^2)(-du) = -\frac{u^3}{3} + \frac{u^5}{5} + C \\
&= -\frac{1}{3}\cos^3(x - 2) + \frac{1}{5}\cos^5(x - 2) + C.
\end{aligned}
$$

5. Let $u = \sin x$. Then $du = \cos x\ dx$. Also, $x = \pi/2 \Rightarrow u = 1$ and $x = \pi \Rightarrow u = 0$. So

$$
\int_{\pi/2}^{\pi} \sin^3 x \cos x\ dx = \int_1^0 u^3\ du = \frac{u^4}{4} \Bigg|_1^0 = -\frac{1}{4}.
$$

The negative value in the answer is acceptable because $\cos x$ is negative when $\pi/2 < x < \pi$.

6. Set $u = x^2$. Then $du = 2x\ dx$. So

$$
\begin{aligned}
\int x\sin^2(x^2)\cos^2(x^2)\ dx &= \frac{1}{2}\int \sin^2 u \cos^2 u\ du = \frac{1}{8}\int \sin^2 2u\ du \\
&= \frac{1}{8}\int \left(\frac{1 - \cos 4u}{2} \right) du = \frac{u}{16} - \frac{\sin 4u}{64} + C \\
&= \frac{x^2}{16} - \frac{\sin(4x^2)}{64} + C.
\end{aligned}
$$

7. We use the "double angle" formulae several times:

$$
\begin{aligned}
\int \sin^4 x \cos^4 x\ dx &= \frac{1}{16}\int \sin^4 2x\ dx = \frac{1}{16}\int \sin^2 2x\ \sin^2 2x\ dx \\
&= \frac{1}{16}\int \left(\frac{1 - \cos 4x}{2} \right)^2 dx \\
&= \frac{1}{64}\int (1 - 2\cos 4x + \cos^2 4x)\ dx \\
&= \frac{1}{64}x - \frac{1}{128}\sin 4x + \frac{1}{64}\int \frac{1 + \cos 8x}{2}\ dx \\
&= \frac{3}{128}x - \frac{1}{128}\sin 4x + \frac{1}{1024}\sin 8x + C.
\end{aligned}
$$

8. Let $u = \sin x$. Then $du = \cos x\, dx$ and $\cos^2 x = 1 - u^2$. So

$$
\begin{aligned}
\int \sin^4 x \cos^5 x\, dx &= \int u^4 (1 - u^2)^2\, du = \frac{1}{5} u^5 - \frac{2}{7} u^7 + \frac{1}{9} u^9 + C \\
&= \frac{1}{5} \sin^5 x - \frac{2}{7} \sin^7 x + \frac{1}{9} \sin^9 x + C.
\end{aligned}
$$

9. Use the "double angle formula" twice:

$$
\begin{aligned}
\int \cos^4 2x\, dx &= \int \left(\frac{1 + \cos 4x}{2} \right)^2 dx \\
&= \frac{1}{4} \int (1 + 2 \cos 4x + \cos^2 4x)\, dx \\
&= \frac{x}{4} + \frac{\sin 4x}{8} + \frac{1}{4} \int \frac{1 + \cos 8x}{2}\, dx \\
&= \frac{3x}{8} + \frac{\sin 4x}{8} + \frac{\sin 8x}{64} + C.
\end{aligned}
$$

10. Let $u = \sin x$. Then $du = \cos x\, dx$ and $\cos^2 x = 1 - u^2$. So

$$
\int \sin^5 x \cos^3 x\, dx = \int u^5 (1 - u^2)\, du = \frac{u^6}{6} - \frac{u^8}{8} + C = \frac{\sin^6 x}{6} - \frac{\sin^8 x}{8} + C.
$$

11. Set $u = \cos x$. Then $du = -\sin x\, dx$ and $\sin^2 x = 1 - u^2$. So

$$
\begin{aligned}
\int \sin^5 x \cos^4 x\, dx &= \int \sin^4 x \cos^4 x \cdot \sin x\, dx = \int (1 - u^2)^2 u^4\, (-du) \\
&= \int (-u^4 + 2u^6 - u^8)\, du \\
&= -\frac{1}{5} u^5 + \frac{2}{7} u^7 - \frac{1}{9} u^9 + C \\
&= -\frac{1}{5} \cos^5 x + \frac{2}{7} \cos^7 x - \frac{1}{9} \cos^9 x + C.
\end{aligned}
$$

12. We use the "double angle formula" several times.

$$
\begin{aligned}
\int \sin^6 x\, dx &= \int \left(\frac{1 - \cos 2x}{2} \right)^3 dx \\
&= \frac{1}{8} \int (1 - 3 \cos 2x + 3 \cos^2 2x - \cos^3 2x)\, dx \\
&= \frac{x}{8} - \frac{3}{16} \sin 2x + \frac{3}{8} \int \frac{1 + \cos 4x}{2}\, dx - \\
&\quad \frac{1}{8} \int (1 - \sin^2 2x) \cdot \frac{d}{dx} \left(\frac{\sin 2x}{2} \right) dx \\
&= \frac{5}{16} x - \frac{1}{4} \sin 2x + \frac{1}{48} \sin^3 2x + \frac{3}{64} \sin 4x + C.
\end{aligned}
$$

13. Let $u = \sin x$. Then $du = \cos x\, dx$ and $\cos^6 x = (1 - \sin^2 x)^3 = (1 - u^2)^3$. So

$$
\begin{aligned}
\int \cos^7 x\, dx &= \int (1 - u^2)^3\, du = \int (1 - 3u^2 + 3u^4 - u^6)\, du \\
&= u - u^3 + \frac{3}{5} u^5 - \frac{1}{7} u^7 + C \\
&= \sin x - \sin^3 x + \frac{3}{5} \sin^5 x - \frac{1}{7} \sin^7 x + C.
\end{aligned}
$$

7.5.2   Exercise Set 37

1. $-\ln|\cos x| + C = \ln|\sec x| + C$.   Let $u = \cos x$, $du = -\sin x\, dx$.

2. $\frac{1}{3} \tan(3x + 1) + C$. Let $u = 3x + 1$.

3. $\sec x + C$, since this function's derivative is $\sec x \, \tan x$.

4. $\frac{\tan^2 x}{2} + C$. Let $u = \tan x$, $du = \sec^2 x\, dx$.

5. $\dfrac{\tan^3 x}{3} + C$. Let $u = \tan x$, $du = \sec^2 x\, dx$.

6. $\dfrac{\tan^6 x}{6} + C$. Let $u = \tan x$, $du = \sec^2 x\, dx$.

7. $\dfrac{\sec^3 x}{3} - \sec x + C$. Case m, n both ODD. Use (8.59) then let $u = \sec x$, $du = \sec x \tan x\, dx$.

8. $\dfrac{\tan^5 x}{5} + \dfrac{\tan^7 x}{7} + C$. Case m, n both EVEN. Solve for one copy of $\sec^2 x$ then let $u = \tan x$, $du = \sec^2 x\, dx$, in the remaining.

9. $\dfrac{\sec^5 x}{5} - \dfrac{\sec^3 x}{3} + C$.   Case m, n both ODD. Factor out one copy of $\sec x \ \tan x$, use (8.59), then let $u = \sec x$, $du = \sec x \tan x\, dx$ in the remaining.

10. $\dfrac{\sec^7 2x}{14} - \dfrac{\sec^5 2x}{5} + \dfrac{\sec^3 2x}{6} + C$. Let $u = 2x$ and use Example 376.

11. $\dfrac{\tan^6 2x}{12} + C$. Let $u = 2x$, $du = 2\, dx$, and use Exercise 6, above or, more directly, let $v = \tan 2x$, $dv = 2 \sec^2 2x\, dx$.

12. $\dfrac{\tan^2 x}{2} + \ln |\cos x|$. Solve for $\tan^2 x$ in (8.59), break up the integral into two parts, use the result in Exercise 1 for the first integral, and let $u = \tan x$ in the second integral.

13. $\dfrac{1}{6} \sec^5 x \ \tan x + \dfrac{5}{24} \sec^3 x \ \tan x + \dfrac{5}{16} (\sec x \ \tan x + \ln |\sec x + \tan x|)$. Use Example 374 with $k = 7$, and then apply Example 377.

14. See Example 370.

15. $\dfrac{1}{4} \sec^3 x \ \tan x - \dfrac{1}{8} (\sec x \ \tan x + \ln |\sec x + \tan x|)$. The case where m is ODD and n is EVEN. Solve for $\tan^2 x$ and use Example 374 with $k = 5$ along with Example 369.

7.6

7.6.1   Exercise Set 38

1. $\displaystyle\int_0^1 \dfrac{1}{1 + x^2}\, dx = \text{Arctan } x \ \Big|_0^1 = \dfrac{\pi}{4}$.

2. $\displaystyle\int \dfrac{2\, dx}{x^2 - 2x + 2} = \int \dfrac{2\, dx}{(x-1)^2 + 1} = 2 \text{ Arctan } (x - 1) + C$.

3. $I = \displaystyle\int \dfrac{dx}{(x-1)^2 + 4} = \dfrac{1}{2} \text{Arctan } \dfrac{x-1}{2} + C$.

4. There is no need to complete a square:

$$\int \dfrac{dx}{x^2 - 4x + 3} \quad = \quad \int \dfrac{dx}{(x-1)(x-3)}$$
$$= \quad \int \dfrac{1}{2} \left(\dfrac{1}{x-3} - \dfrac{1}{x-1} \right) dx$$
$$= \quad \dfrac{1}{2} \ln |x-3| - \dfrac{1}{2} \ln |x-1| + C.$$

5. We need to complete the square in the denominator of the integrand:

$$\int \dfrac{4}{4x^2 + 4x + 5}\, dx \quad = \quad \int \dfrac{4\, dx}{(2x+1)^2 + 4}$$
$$= \quad \int \dfrac{dx}{\left(x - \frac{1}{2} \right)^2 + 1} = \text{Arctan } \left(x + \dfrac{1}{2} \right) + C.$$

$$\dfrac{(2x+1)^2}{4} = \dfrac{2x}{2} + \dfrac{1}{2} = x + \dfrac{1}{2}$$

6. The minus sign in front of x^2 should be taken out first.

$$\int \dfrac{dx}{4x - x^2 - 3} \quad = \quad - \int \dfrac{dx}{(x-1)(x-3)}$$
$$= \quad \dfrac{1}{2} \ln |x-1| - \dfrac{1}{2} \ln |x-3| + C.$$

(For the last step, see the answer to Exercise 4 above.)

7. We have

$$\int \frac{1}{\sqrt{4x - x^2}}\, dx = \int \frac{dx}{\sqrt{-(x^2 - 4x + 4 - 4)}} = \int \frac{dx}{\sqrt{4 - (x-2)^2}}$$

$$= \frac{1}{2}\int \frac{dx}{\sqrt{1 - \left(\frac{x-2}{2}\right)^2}} = \text{Arcsin}\ \frac{x-2}{2} + C.$$

8. We have

$$\int_{-1}^{0} \frac{1}{4x^2 + 4x + 2}\, dx = \int_{-1}^{0} \frac{1}{(2x+1)^2 + 1}\, dx$$

$$= \frac{1}{2}\text{Arctan}\ (2x+1)\Big|_{-1}^{0} = \pi/4.$$

9. $\displaystyle \int \frac{dx}{\sqrt{2x - x^2 + 1}} = \int \frac{dx}{\sqrt{2 - (x-1)^2}} = \text{Arcsin}\ \frac{x-1}{\sqrt{2}} + C.$

10. $\displaystyle \int \frac{dx}{x^2 + x + 1} = \int \frac{dx}{(x+1/2)^2 + 3/4} = \frac{2}{\sqrt{3}}\text{Arctan}\ \left(\frac{2x+1}{\sqrt{3}}\right) + C.$

11. The roots of $x^2 + x - 1$ are $(-1 \pm \sqrt{5})/2$; (these interesting numbers are related to the so-called Golden Ratio and the Fibonacci sequence.) We have the following partial fraction decomposition:

$$\frac{1}{x^2 + x - 1} = \frac{1}{\left(x - \frac{(-1+\sqrt{5})}{2}\right)\left(x - \frac{(-1-\sqrt{5})}{2}\right)} = \frac{1}{\sqrt{5}}\left(\frac{1}{x - \frac{(-1+\sqrt{5})}{2}} - \frac{1}{x - \frac{(-1-\sqrt{5})}{2}}\right).$$

So $\displaystyle \int \frac{dx}{x^2 + x - 1} = \frac{1}{\sqrt{5}}\left\{\ln\left|x - \frac{(-1+\sqrt{5})}{2}\right| - \ln\left|x - \frac{(-1-\sqrt{5})}{2}\right|\right\} + C.$

12. $\displaystyle I = \int \frac{dx}{(2x+1)\sqrt{(2x+1)^2 - 1}} = \frac{1}{2}\text{Arcsec}\ (2x+1) + C,$

since $|2x + 1| = 2x + 1$ for $x > -1/2$ (see Table 6.7).

7.6.2   Exercise Set 39

1. Set $x = 2\sin\theta$. Then $dx = 2\cos\theta\, d\theta$ and $\sqrt{4 - x^2} = 2\cos\theta$. So

$$\int \sqrt{4 - x^2}\, dx = \int 2\cos\theta \cdot 2\cos\theta\, d\theta = 4\int \cos^2\theta\, d\theta$$

$$= 2\theta + \sin 2\theta + C = 2\theta + 2\sin\theta\cos\theta + C$$

$$= 2\,\text{Arcsin}\ (x/2) + \frac{1}{2}x\sqrt{4 - x^2} + C.$$

2. Let $x = 3\tan\theta$. Then $\sqrt{x^2 + 9} = 3\sec\theta$ and $dx = 3\sec^2\theta\, d\theta$. Hence

$$\int \sqrt{x^2 + 9}\, dx = \int 3\sec\theta \cdot 3\sec^2\theta\, d\theta = 9\int \sec^3\theta\, d\theta$$

$$= \frac{9}{2}\{(\tan\theta\sec\theta + \ln|\sec\theta + \tan\theta|\} + C$$

$$= \frac{x}{2}\sqrt{x^2 + 9} + \frac{9}{2}\ln\left[\sqrt{x^2 + 9} + x\right] + C.$$

(A constant from the ln term is absorbed by C.)

3. Let $x = \sec\theta$. Then $\sqrt{x^2 - 1} = \tan\theta$ and $dx = \sec\theta \cdot \tan\theta\, d\theta$. Hence

$$\int \sqrt{x^2 - 1}\, dx = \int \sec\theta\ \tan^2\theta\, d\theta$$

$$= \frac{1}{2}\tan\theta\ \sec\theta - \frac{1}{2}\ln|\sec\theta + \tan\theta| + C$$

$$= \frac{1}{2}x\sqrt{x^2 - 1} - \frac{1}{2}\ln\left|x + \sqrt{x^2 - 1}\right| + C.$$

4. Let $x - 2 = 2\sin\theta$. Then $dx = 2\cos\theta\ d\theta$ and

$$\sqrt{4x - x^2} = \sqrt{-(x^2 - 4x + 4 - 4)} = \sqrt{4 - (x-2)^2} = 2\cos\theta.$$

So we have

$$\begin{aligned}
\int \sqrt{4x - x^2}\ dx &= \int 2\cos\theta \cdot 2\cos\theta \cdot d\theta \\
&= 2\theta + \sin 2\theta + C \\
&= 2\theta + 2\sin\theta\cos\theta + C \\
&= 2\sin^{-1}\frac{x-2}{2} + \frac{x-2}{2}\sqrt{4x - x^2} + C.
\end{aligned}$$

5. Let $x = 2\sin u$. Then $dx = 2\cos u\ du$ and $(4 - x^2)^{1/2} = 2\cos u$. Thus

$$\begin{aligned}
\int \frac{dx}{(4 - x^2)^{3/2}} &= \int \frac{2\cos u\ du}{2^3 \cos^3 u} = \frac{1}{4}\int \sec^2 u\ du \\
&= \frac{1}{4}\tan u + C = \frac{1}{4} \cdot \frac{\sin u}{\cos u} + C = \frac{1}{4} \cdot \frac{x}{\sqrt{4 - x^2}} + C.
\end{aligned}$$

6. Let $x = 3\sin u$. Then $dx = 3\cos u\ du$ and $(9 - x^2)^{1/2} = 3\cos u$. Thus

$$\begin{aligned}
\int \frac{x^2\ dx}{(9 - x^2)^{3/2}} &= \int \frac{3^2 \sin^2 u \cdot 3\cos u\ du}{3^3 \cos^3 u} = \int \tan^2 u\ du \\
&= \int (\sec^2 u - 1)\ du = \tan u - u + C = \frac{\sin u}{\cos u} - u + C \\
&= \frac{x}{\sqrt{9 - x^2}} - \text{Arcsin}\ \frac{x}{3} + C.
\end{aligned}$$

7. Let $x = 2\sec\theta$. Then $\sqrt{x^2 - 4} = 2\tan\theta$ and $dx = 2\sec\theta\tan\theta\ d\theta$. Also notice that $\cos\theta = 1/\sec\theta = 2/x$.

$$\begin{aligned}
\int \frac{dx}{x^2\sqrt{x^2 - 4}} &= \int \frac{2\sec\theta \cdot \tan\theta\ d\theta}{4\sec^2\theta \cdot 2\tan\theta} \\
&= \frac{1}{4}\int \cos\theta\ d\theta = \frac{1}{4}\sin\theta + C = \frac{1}{4}\sqrt{1 - \cos^2\theta} + C \\
&= \frac{1}{4}\sqrt{1 - (2/x)^2} + C = \frac{\sqrt{x^2 - 4}}{4x} + C.
\end{aligned}$$

8. Let $2x - 1 = \tan\theta$. Then $2\ dx = \sec^2\theta\ d\theta$ and

$$\sqrt{4x^2 - 4x + 2} = \sqrt{(2x - 1)^2 + 1} = \sqrt{\tan^2\theta + 1} = \sec\theta.$$

Therefore we have

$$\begin{aligned}
\int \sqrt{4x^2 - 4x + 2}\ dx &= \frac{1}{2}\int \sec^3\theta\ d\theta \\
&= \frac{1}{4}(\tan\theta\sec\theta + \ln|\sec\theta + \tan\theta|) + C \\
&= \frac{1}{4}(2x - 1)\sqrt{4x^2 - 4x + 2} + \frac{1}{4}\ln\left|2x - 1 + \sqrt{4x^2 - 4x + 2}\right| + C.
\end{aligned}$$

9. Let $x = 3\tan\theta$. Then $9 + x^2 = 9\sec^2\theta$ and $dx = 3\sec^2\theta\ d\theta$. So

$$\begin{aligned}
\int \frac{dx}{(9 + x^2)^2} &= \int \frac{3\sec^2\theta\ d\theta}{81\sec^4\theta} = \frac{1}{27}\int \cos^2\theta\ d\theta \\
&= \frac{1}{27}\left(\frac{\theta}{2} + \frac{\sin 2\theta}{4}\right) + C \\
&= \frac{1}{27}\left\{\frac{1}{2}\text{Arctan}\ \frac{x}{3} + \frac{1}{4}\sin\left(2\text{Arctan}\ \frac{x}{3}\right)\right\} + C.
\end{aligned}$$

NOTE: It is possible to simplify the expression for $\sin(2\ \text{Arctan}\ x/3) \equiv \sin 2\theta$:

$$\begin{aligned}
\sin 2\theta &= 2\sin\theta\cos\theta = 2\frac{\sin\theta}{\cos\theta} \cdot \cos^2\theta = 2\tan\theta \cdot \frac{1}{\sec^2\theta} \\
&= \frac{2\tan\theta}{1 + \tan^2\theta} = \frac{2 \cdot x/3}{1 + (x/3)^2} = \frac{6x}{9 + x^2}.
\end{aligned}$$

10. The easiest way to solve this exercise is to use the substitution $u = \sqrt{4 - x^2}$. (This is highly nontrivial! At first sight one would try the trigonometric substitution $x = 2\sin\theta$. This method works, but the computation involved is rather tedious and lengthy.) Then $u^2 = 4 - x^2$ and hence $2u\,du = -2x\,dx$, which gives $u\,du = -x\,dx$. Now

$$\frac{dx}{x} = \frac{x\,dx}{x^2} = \frac{-u\,du}{4 - u^2} = \frac{u\,du}{u^2 - 4}$$

and hence

$$
\begin{aligned}
\int \frac{\sqrt{4 - x^2}}{x}\,dx &= \int u \cdot \frac{u\,du}{u^2 - 4} = \int \left(1 + \frac{4}{u^2 - 4}\right)\,du \\
&= u + \int \left(\frac{1}{u - 2} - \frac{1}{u + 2}\right)\,du \\
&= u + \ln|u - 2| - \ln|u + 2| + C \\
&= u + (\ln|2 - u| + \ln|2 + u|) - 2\ln|2 + u| + C \\
&= u + \ln|4 - u^2| - 2\ln|u + 2| + C \\
&= \sqrt{4 - x^2} + 2\ln|x| - 2\ln|2 + \sqrt{4 - x^2}| + C.
\end{aligned}
$$

11. Let $x = 5\tan\theta$. Then we have $dx = 5\sec^2\theta\,d\theta$, $(x^2 + 25)^{1/2} = 5\sec\theta$ and $(x^2 + 25)^{3/2} = 5^3\sec^3\theta$. Hence

$$
\begin{aligned}
\int \frac{dx}{(x^2 + 25)^{3/2}} &= \int \frac{5\sec^2\theta\,d\theta}{5^3\sec^3\theta} \\
&= \frac{1}{25}\int \cos\theta\,d\theta \\
&= \frac{1}{25}\sin\theta + C = \frac{1}{25}\frac{x}{\sqrt{x^2 + 25}} + C.
\end{aligned}
$$

12. Let $x = 2\sin\theta$. Then $\sqrt{4 - x^2} = 2\cos\theta$ and $dx = 2\cos\theta\,d\theta$. So

$$
\begin{aligned}
\int \frac{\sqrt{4 - x^2}}{x^2}\,dx &= \int \frac{2\cos\theta}{4\sin^2\theta} \cdot 2\cos\theta\,d\theta \\
&= \int \cot^2\theta\,d\theta \\
&= \int (\csc^2\theta - 1)\,d\theta = -\cot\theta - \theta + C \\
&= -\frac{\sqrt{4 - x^2}}{x} - \operatorname{Arcsin}\frac{x}{2} + C.
\end{aligned}
$$

13. Let $x = a\sin\theta$. Then $dx = a\cos\theta\,d\theta$ and hence

$$
\begin{aligned}
\int \frac{dx}{x^4\sqrt{a^2 - x^2}} &= \int \frac{a\cos\theta\,d\theta}{a^4\sin^4\theta \cdot a\cos\theta} \\
&= a^{-4}\int \frac{d\theta}{\sin^4\theta} = a^{-4}\int \csc^4\theta\,d\theta \\
&= a^{-4}\int (\csc^2\theta + \csc^2\theta\cot^2\theta)\,d\theta \\
&= a^{-4}\left(-\cot\theta - \frac{\cot^3\theta}{3}\right) + C, \\
&= -\frac{1}{a^4}\cdot \frac{(a^2 - x^2)^{1/2}}{x} - \frac{1}{3a^4}\cdot \frac{(a^2 - x^2)^{3/2}}{x^3} + C.
\end{aligned}
$$

14. Let $x = a\sec\theta$. Then $dx = a\sec\theta\tan\theta$ and hence

$$
\begin{aligned}
\int \frac{dx}{x^4\sqrt{x^2 - a^2}} &= \int \frac{a\sec\theta\tan\theta\,d\theta}{a^4\sec^4\theta \cdot a\tan\theta} \\
&= \frac{1}{a^4}\int \cos^3\theta\,d\theta = \frac{1}{a^4}\int (1 - \sin^2\theta)\cos\theta\,d\theta \\
&= \frac{1}{a^4}\left(\sin\theta - \frac{\sin^3\theta}{3}\right) + C \\
&= \frac{1}{a^4}\left(\frac{(x^2 - a^2)^{1/2}}{x} - \frac{1}{3}\frac{(x^2 - a^2)^{3/2}}{x^3}\right) + C.
\end{aligned}
$$

Notice that

$$\sin \theta = (1 - \cos^2 \theta)^{1/2} = (1 - \sec^{-2} \theta)^{-1/2} = \left(1 - \frac{a^2}{x^2}\right)^{1/2} = \frac{(x^2 - a^2)^{1/2}}{x},$$

for $x > 0$.

15. We have

$$\begin{aligned}
I &\equiv \int \frac{\sqrt{x^2 + 2x - 3}}{x + 1}\, dx \\
&= \int \frac{\sqrt{(x+1)^2 - 4}}{x + 1}\, dx = \int \frac{\sqrt{u^2 - 4}}{u}\, du,
\end{aligned}$$

where $u = x + 1$. Use the tricky substitution similar to the one in Exercise 8 above: $v = \sqrt{u^2 - 4} \equiv \sqrt{x^2 + 2x - 3}$. Then $v^2 = u^2 - 4$ and hence $2v\,dv = 2u\,du$, or $v\,dv = u\,du$. Thus

$$\frac{du}{u} = \frac{u\,du}{u^2} = \frac{v\,dv}{v^2 + 4}.$$

Now we can complete our evaluation as follows:

$$\begin{aligned}
I &= \int \frac{v^2\,dv}{v^2 + 4} = \int \left(1 - \frac{4}{v^2 + 4}\right)\, dv \\
&= v - 2\operatorname{Arctan} \frac{v}{2} + C \\
&= \sqrt{x^2 + 2x - 3} - 2\operatorname{Arctan} \frac{\sqrt{x^2 + 2x - 3}}{2} + C.
\end{aligned}$$

16. Let $u = x^2 + 2x + 5$. Then $du = (2x + 2)dx$ and hence

$$\begin{aligned}
\int \frac{(2x + 1)\, dx}{\sqrt{x^2 + 2x + 5}} &= \int \frac{(2x + 2 - 1)\, dx}{\sqrt{x^2 + 2x + 5}} \\
&= \int \frac{du}{\sqrt{u}} - I = 2\sqrt{u} - I = 2\sqrt{x^2 + 2x + 5} - I,
\end{aligned}$$

where

$$I = \int \frac{dx}{\sqrt{x^2 + 2x + 5}} \equiv \int \frac{dx}{\sqrt{(x+1)^2 + 4}}.$$

Let $x + 1 = 2\tan\theta$. Then $dx = 2\sec^2\theta\, d\theta$ and $\sqrt{x^2 + 2x + 5} = 2\sec\theta$. So

$$\begin{aligned}
I &= \int \frac{2\sec^2\theta\, d\theta}{2\sec\theta} = \int \sec\theta\, d\theta = \ln|\tan\theta + \sec\theta| + C \\
&= \ln\left| x + 1 + \sqrt{x^2 + 2x + 5} \right| + C,
\end{aligned}$$

where a factor of $\frac{1}{2}$ inside the logarithm symbol is absorbed by the integral constant C. Thus our final answer is

$$\int \frac{(2x + 1)\, dx}{\sqrt{x^2 + 2x + 5}} = 2\sqrt{x^2 + 2x + 5} - \ln\left| x + 1 + \sqrt{x^2 + 2x + 5} \right| + C.$$

7.7

7.7.1

7.7.2 Exercise Set 40

1. $\boxed{T_4 = 2.629 \text{ and } S_4 = 2.408}$. Here $n = 4$, $a = 1$, $b = 10$, $f(x) = 1/x$. So, $h = (b - a)/n = 9/4$, $x_i = a + i(b - a)/n = 1 + 9i/n$, and

$$T_4 = \frac{h}{2} \cdot (y_0 + 2y_1 + 2y_2 + 2y_3 + y_4),$$

$$= \frac{9}{8} \cdot \left(1 + 2 \cdot \sum_{i=1}^{3} \frac{1}{1 + \frac{9i}{4}} + \frac{1}{1 + 10} \right),$$

$$= \frac{99}{80} + \frac{9}{4} \cdot \sum_{i=1}^{3} \frac{1}{1 + \frac{9i}{4}},$$

$$\mathcal{T}_4 \approx \boxed{2.629}$$

On the other hand, S_4 is given by,

$$S_4 = \frac{h}{3} \cdot (y_0 + 4y_1 + 2y_2 + 4y_3 + y_4),$$

$$= \frac{1}{12} \cdot \left(1 + 4 \cdot \frac{1}{1 + \frac{9}{4}} + 2 \cdot \frac{1}{1 + \frac{9 \cdot 2}{4}} + 4 \cdot \frac{1}{1 + \frac{9 \cdot 3}{4}} + \frac{1}{1 + \frac{9 \cdot 4}{4}} \right),$$

$$= \frac{9}{12} \cdot \left(1 + \frac{16}{13} + \frac{8}{22} + \frac{16}{31} + \frac{1}{10} \right),$$

$$S_4 \approx \boxed{2.408}$$

The Actual value is given by $\ln 10 \approx 2.302$, so Simpson's Rule is closer to the Actual value.

2. $\boxed{\mathcal{T}_5 = 1.161522}$. You can't use Simpson's Rule because n is ODD. The Actual value is approximately given by $\boxed{1.19814}$ here is given in terms of so-called **elliptic functions** and so it cannot be written down nicely.

3. $\boxed{\mathcal{T}_4 = 1.49067 \text{ and } S_4 = 1.46371}$. The Actual value is found to be around 1.46265.

4. $\boxed{\mathcal{T}_6 = 3.062 \text{ and } S_6 = 3.110}$. Here $n = 6$, $a = 0$, $b = 1$, $f(x) = 4 \cdot \sqrt{1 - x^2}$. So, $h = (b - a)/n = 1/6$, $x_i = a + i(b - a)/n = 0 + i/6 = i/6$, and

$$\mathcal{T}_6 = \frac{h}{2} \cdot (y_0 + 2y_1 + 2y_2 + 2y_3 + 2y_4 + 2y_5 + y_6),$$

$$= \frac{1}{12} \cdot \left(4 + 2 \cdot \sum_{i=1}^{5} 4 \cdot \sqrt{1 - (i/6)^2} + 0 \right),$$

$$= \frac{1}{3} + \frac{1}{6} \cdot \sum_{i=1}^{5} \left(4 \cdot \sqrt{1 - \frac{i^2}{36}} \right),$$

$$\mathcal{T}_6 \approx \boxed{3.062}$$

On the other hand, S_6 is given by,

$$S_6 = \frac{h}{3} \cdot (y_0 + 4y_1 + 2y_2 + 4y_3 + 2y_4 + 4y_5 + y_6),$$

$$\approx \boxed{3.110}.$$

Now, remember to use a trigonometric substitution like $x = \sin \theta$ to convert the integral into an easily solvable trigonometric integral like

$$\int_0^{\frac{\pi}{2}} \cos^2 \theta \, d\theta.$$

The Actual value is then found to be $\pi \approx 3.1416$, so Simpson's Rule is closer to the Actual value.

5. $\boxed{\mathcal{T}_{10} = 1.090607 \text{ and } S_{10} = 1.089429}$. The Actual value is about 1.089429, and so Simpson's Rule gives an extremely good estimate!

6. $\boxed{1.18728}$, by using Simpson's Rule with $n = 6$. The area is given by a definite integral, namely, $\int_0^{\frac{\pi}{2}} \sqrt{\sin x} \, dx$, since the values $\sin x \geq 0$ for every x in this interval. The Actual value is around 1.19814.

7. First, sketch the graphs and find the points of intersection (equate the $y-$values) of these two curves. You will see that they intersect when $x = 0$ and $x = 1$. See the graph in the margin below.

Then we find the area under the curve $y = x$ and subtract from it the area under the curve $y = x^2$, (because the line lies *above* the parabola). So, the area of the closed lop is given by

$$\int_0^1 (x - x^2) \, dx.$$

Let $n = 6$. Applying both Rules with $a = 0$, $b = 1$, $f(x) = x - x^2$, $h = 1/6$, we get the values,

$$\mathcal{T}_6 = 0.1621, \quad S_6 = 0.1667,$$

and the estimate using Simpson's Rule is EXACT (*i.e.* equal to the Actual value) because the curve $y = x - x^2$ is a parabola (or a quadratic, see the margin).

8. $\boxed{\mathcal{T}_6 = 0.6695 \text{ and } \mathcal{S}_6 = 0.5957}$. Here $n = 6$, $a = 1.05$, $b = 1.35$, and the values of $f(x)$ are given in the
Table. So, $h = (b - a)/n = 0.05$, $x_i = a + i(b - a)/n = 1.05 + i(0.05)$, and

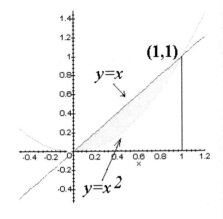

$$
\begin{aligned}
\mathcal{T}_6 &= \frac{h}{2} \cdot (y_0 + 2y_1 + 2y_2 + 2y_3 + 2y_4 + 2y_5 + y_6), \\
&= 0.025 \cdot (2.32 + 2(1.26) + 2(1.48) + 2(1.6) + 2(3.6) + 2(2.78) + (3.02)), \\
&\approx 0.6695 \\
\mathcal{T}_6 &\approx \boxed{0.6695}
\end{aligned}
$$

On the other hand, $\mathcal{S}_6$ is given by,

$$
\begin{aligned}
\mathcal{S}_6 &= \frac{h}{3} \cdot (y_0 + 4y_1 + 2y_2 + 4y_3 + 2y_4 + 4y_5 + y_6), \\
&= \frac{0.05}{3} \cdot (2.32 + 4(1.26) + 2(1.48) + 4(1.6) + 2(3.6) + 4(2.78) + 3.02) \\
\mathcal{S}_6 &\approx \boxed{0.5957}.
\end{aligned}
$$

9. $\boxed{30.7655}$, using Simpson's Rule with $n = 10$. This means that there are roughly 30 primes less than 100.

10. $\boxed{L(6) \approx 0.1876}$. Use $a = 0$, $b = 1$, $n = 6$, and $h = 1/6$ in the expression for $\mathcal{S}_6$.

11. $\boxed{0.087817}$, using the Trapezoidal Rule with $n = 8$. This means that only about 8% of the total population
has an IQ in this range.

7.8   Exercise Set 41

1. Yes, $x = 0$ is an infinite discontinuity.

2. No, the integrand is continuous on $[-1, 1]$.

3. Yes, $x = 0$ is an infinite discontinuity.

4. Yes, $x = 1$ is an infinite discontinuity (and ∞ is an upper limit).

5. Yes, $x = -1$ is an infinite discontinuity.

6. No, the integrand is continuous on $[-1, 1]$.

7. Yes, $x = -\pi, \pi$ are each infinite discontinuities of the cosecant function.

8. Yes, $\pm\infty$ are the limits of integration.

9. Yes, $x = 0$ gives an indeterminate form of the type $0 \cdot \infty$ in the integrand.

10. Yes, $\pm\infty$ are the limits of integration.

11. 2. This is because $\displaystyle \lim_{T \to \infty} \int_0^T x^{-1.5}\, dx = \lim_{T \to \infty} \left(\frac{-2}{\sqrt{T}} + 2 \right) = 2$.

12. $+\infty$. This is because $\displaystyle \lim_{T \to \infty} \int_2^T x^{-1/2}\, dx = \lim_{T \to \infty} \left(2T^{1/2} - 2\sqrt{2} \right) = +\infty$.

13. $+\infty$. Note that $\displaystyle \lim_{T \to 0^+} \frac{1}{2} \int_T^2 \frac{dx}{x} = \lim_{T \to 0^+} \left. \left(\frac{1}{2} \ln|x| \right) \right|_T^2 = \lim_{T \to 0^+} \left(\frac{1}{2} \ln 2 - \frac{1}{2} \ln T \right) = -(-\infty) = +\infty$.

14. 2. Use Integration by Parts (with the Table Method) and L'Hospital's Rule twice.

   This gives $\displaystyle \lim_{T \to \infty} \int_0^T x^2 e^{-x}\, dx = \lim_{T \to \infty} \left(2 - \frac{T^2 + 2T + 2}{e^T} \right) = 2$.

15. 0. Use the substitution $u = 1 + x^2$, $du = 2x\, dx$ to find an antiderivative and note that
$$\int_{-\infty}^{\infty} \frac{2x}{(1 + x^2)^2}\, dx = \int_{-\infty}^0 \frac{2x}{(1 + x^2)^2}\, dx + \int_0^{\infty} \frac{2x}{(1 + x^2)^2}\, dx.$$
$$= \lim_{T \to -\infty} \int_T^0 \frac{2x}{(1 + x^2)^2}\, dx + \lim_{T \to \infty} \int_0^T \frac{2x}{(1 + x^2)^2}\, dx,$$
$$= \lim_{T \to -\infty} \left. \left(-\frac{1}{1 + x^2} \right) \right|_T^0 + \lim_{T \to \infty} \left. \left(-\frac{1}{1 + x^2} \right) \right|_0^T = -1 + 0 + 0 - (-1) = 0.$$

16. -1. Note that the infinite discontinuity is at $x = -1$ only. Now, use the substitution $u = 1 - x^2$, $-\frac{du}{2} = x\, dx$. Then
$$\int_{-1}^0 \frac{x}{\sqrt{1 - x^2}}\, dx = \lim_{T \to -1} \left. \left(-\sqrt{1 - T^2} \right) \right|_T^0 = -1 - 0 = -1.$$

17. Diverges (or does not exist). There is one infinite discontinuity at $x = 1$. First, use partial fractions here to find that
$$\frac{1}{x^2 - 1} = \frac{1}{2} \cdot \frac{1}{x - 1} - \frac{1}{2} \cdot \frac{1}{x + 1}.$$
Next, using the definitions, we see that
$$\int_0^2 \frac{1}{x^2 - 1}\, dx = \int_0^1 \frac{1}{x^2 - 1}\, dx + \int_1^2 \frac{1}{x^2 - 1}\, dx =$$
$$= \lim_{T \to 1^-} \int_0^T \frac{1}{x^2 - 1}\, dx + \lim_{T \to 1^+} \int_T^2 \frac{1}{x^2 - 1}\, dx = \lim_{T \to 1^-} \left. \left(\frac{1}{2} \ln|x - 1| - \frac{1}{2} \ln|x + 1| \right) \right|_0^T +$$
$$+ \lim_{T \to 1^+} \left. \left(\frac{1}{2} \ln|x - 1| - \frac{1}{2} \ln|x + 1| \right) \right|_T^2 =$$
$$= \lim_{T \to 1^-} \left. \left(\frac{1}{2} \ln \left| \frac{x - 1}{x + 1} \right| \right) \right|_0^T + \lim_{T \to 1^+} \left. \left(\frac{1}{2} \ln \left| \frac{x - 1}{x + 1} \right| \right) \right|_T^2 =,$$
$$= \lim_{T \to 1^-} \left(\frac{1}{2} \ln \left| \frac{T - 1}{T + 1} \right| - \frac{1}{2} \ln|-1| \right) + \lim_{T \to 1^+} \left(\frac{1}{2} \ln \left| \frac{1}{3} \right| - \frac{1}{2} \ln \left| \frac{T - 1}{T + 1} \right| \right) = = (-\infty - 0) + (-\frac{1}{2} \ln 3 -$$
$(-\infty) = \infty - \infty$, and so the limit does not exist.
So, the improper integral diverges.

18. $-\infty$. See the (previous) Exercise 17 above for more details. In this case the discontinuity, $x = 1$, is at an end-point. Thus, using partial fractions as before, we find that
$$\int_1^2 \frac{1}{1 - x^2}\, dx = \lim_{T \to 1^+} \int_T^2 \frac{1}{1 - x^2}\, dx = -\lim_{T \to 1^+} \int_T^2 \frac{1}{x^2 - 1}\, dx =$$
$$= -\lim_{T \to 1^+} \left. \left(\frac{1}{2} \ln \left| \frac{x - 1}{x + 1} \right| \right) \right|_T^2 = -\left(-\frac{1}{2} \ln 3 - (-\infty) \right) = -\infty.$$

19. $\frac{1}{2}$. Use Integration by Parts and the Sandwich Theorem to find that

$$\int_0^\infty e^{-x}\sin x\ dx = \lim_{T\to\infty}\int_0^T e^{-x}\sin x\ dx = \lim_{T\to\infty}\frac{1}{2}\left(-e^{-x}\cos x - e^{-x}\sin x\right)\Big|_0^T$$

$$= \lim_{T\to\infty}\left(\frac{1}{2}\left(-\frac{\cos T}{e^T}-\frac{\sin T}{e^T}\right)-\left(-\frac{1}{2}\right)\right)=\frac{1}{2}.$$

Recall that the Sandwich Theorem tells us that, in this case,

$$0\le\lim_{T\to\infty}\left|\frac{\cos T}{e^T}\right|\le\lim_{T\to\infty}\left|\frac{1}{e^T}\right|=0,$$

and so the required limit is also 0. A similar argument applies to the other limit.

20. $+\infty$. The infinite discontinuity is a $x=1$. Use the substitution $u=\ln x$, $du=\frac{dx}{x}$. Then

$$\int_1^2\frac{dx}{x\ln x}=\lim_{T\to1+}\int_T^2\frac{dx}{x\ln x}=\lim_{T\to1+}\ln(\ln x))\Big|_T^2=$$

$$=\lim_{T\to1+}\left(\ln(\ln2)-\ln(\ln T)\right)=-(-\infty)=+\infty.$$

21. $\frac{10}{7}$. The integrand is the same as $\displaystyle\int_{-1}^1\left(x^{2/5}+x^{-3/5}\right)dx$ and so the infinite discontinuity (at $x=0$)

is in the second term only. So, $\displaystyle\int_{-1}^1\left(x^{2/5}+x^{-3/5}\right)dx=\int_{-1}^1 x^{2/5}\ dx+\int_{-1}^1 x^{-3/5}\ dx=\frac{10}{7}+$

$$\int_{-1}^0 x^{-3/5}\ dx+\int_0^1 x^{-3/5}\ dx=\frac{10}{7}+\lim_{T\to0-}\int_{-1}^T x^{-3/5}\ dx+\lim_{T\to0+}\int_T^1 x^{-3/5}\ dx=\frac{10}{7}+$$

$$\lim_{T\to0-}\left(\frac{5T^{2/5}}{2}-\frac{5}{2}\right)+\lim_{T\to0+}\left(\frac{5}{2}-\frac{5T^{2/5}}{2}\right)=\frac{10}{7}-\frac{5}{2}+\frac{5}{2}=\frac{10}{7}.$$

22. Diverges. The integrand is the same as $\displaystyle\int_{-1}^1\left(x^{-2/3}+x^{-5/3}\right)dx$ and so the discontinuity is present in

both terms. Thus, $\displaystyle\int_{-1}^1\left(x^{-2/3}+x^{-5/3}\right)dx=$

$$=\int_{-1}^0\left(x^{-2/3}+x^{-5/3}\right)dx+\int_0^1\left(x^{-2/3}+x^{-5/3}\right)dx$$

$$=\lim_{T\to0-}\int_{-1}^T\left(x^{-2/3}+x^{-5/3}\right)dx+\lim_{T\to0+}\int_T^1\left(x^{-2/3}+x^{-5/3}\right)dx$$

$$=\lim_{T\to0-}\left(3x^{1/3}-\frac{3}{2}x^{-2/3}\right)\Big|_{-1}^T+\lim_{T\to0+}\left(3x^{1/3}-\frac{3}{2}x^{-2/3}\right)\Big|_T^1$$

$$=\lim_{T\to0-}\left(3T^{1/3}-\frac{3}{2}T^{-2/3}\right)-\left(-3-\frac{3}{2}\right)+\left(3-\frac{3}{2}\right)-$$

$$=\lim_{T\to0+}\left(3T^{1/3}-\frac{3}{2}T^{-2/3}\right)=$$

$$-\infty+6+\infty=\infty-\infty,$$

and so the improper integral diverges.

23. 2. Simply rewrite this integral as $\displaystyle\int_{-\infty}^\infty e^{-|x|}\ dx=\int_{-\infty}^0 e^x\ dx+\int_0^\infty e^{-x}\ dx$, since for $x<0$ we have

$|x|=-x$ while for $x>0$ we have $|x|=x$. The integrals are straightforward and so are omitted.

24. Converges for $p>1$ only. Let $u=\ln x$, $du=\frac{dx}{x}$. Then $\displaystyle\int_2^\infty\frac{dx}{x(\ln x)^p}=\int_{\ln2}^\infty\frac{du}{u^p}=\lim_{T\to\infty}\int_{\ln2}^T\frac{du}{u^p}=$

$$\lim_{T\to\infty}\frac{u^{1-p}}{1-p}\Big|_{\ln2}^T=\lim_{T\to\infty}\left(\frac{T^{1-p}}{1-p}\right)-\frac{(\ln2)^{1-p}}{1-p}=$$

$$0-\frac{(\ln2)^{1-p}}{1-p}=\frac{1}{(p-1)(\ln2)^{p-1}},\text{ only for }p>1.\text{ The case }p=1\text{ is treted as in Exercise 20, above,}$$

while the case $p<1$ leads to an integral which converges to $+\infty$.

25. No, this is impossible. There is no real number p such the stated integral converges to a finite number. Basically, this is because the integrand has a "bad" discontinuity at $x=0$ whenever $p<1$ and another discontinuity at $x=\infty$ whenever $p\ge1$. The argument is based on a case-by-case analysis and runs like this:

If $p+1>0$, then $\displaystyle\int_0^\infty x^p\ dx=\lim_{T\to\infty}\int_0^T x^p\ dx=\lim_{T\to\infty}\left(\frac{T^{p+1}}{p+1}-\frac{1}{p+1}\right)=+\infty$. On the

other hand, if $p+1<0$, then $\displaystyle\int_0^\infty x^p\ dx=\int_0^1 x^p\ dx+\int_1^\infty x^p\ dx=\lim_{T\to0+}\left(\frac{1}{p+1}-\frac{T^{p+1}}{p+1}\right)+$

$$\lim_{T\to\infty}\left(\frac{T^{p+1}}{p+1}-\frac{1}{p+1}\right)=$$

$= \left(\dfrac{1}{p+1} - \infty \right) + \left(0 - \dfrac{1}{p+1} \right) = -\infty.$ Finally, if $p = 1$ the integrand reduces to x, by itself and it converges to $+\infty$. Thus, we have shown that for any value of p the improper integral cannot converge to a finite value.

26. $\sqrt{\dfrac{2}{\pi}} \cdot \dfrac{2}{4 + \lambda^2}$. Use the method outlined in Exercise 19, above.

27. No, the integral must converge to $+\infty$. Follow the hints.

28. Follow the hints.

29. Follow the hints.

30. $L = \sqrt{\pi}$. Simpson's Rule with $n = 22$ gives us the value 1.7725 as an estimate for the value of this integral over the interval $[-5, 5]$. Its square is about 3.1416, which is close to $\sqrt{\pi}$.

7.9 Chapter Exercises

Please add a constant of integration, C, after every indefinite integral!

1. $\cos^2 x - \sin^2 x = \cos 2x$. Use the identity $\cos(A + B) = \cos A \cos B - \sin A \sin B$ with $A = B = x$.

2. $\cos^4 x - \sin^4 x = \cos 2x$. This is because
   $\cos^4 x - \sin^4 x = (\cos^2 x - \sin^2 x)(\cos^2 x + \sin^2 x) = (\cos^2 x - \sin^2 x)(1) = \cos 2x.$

3. $\sec^4 x - \tan^4 x = \sec^2 x + \tan^2 x$. Use the same idea as the preceding one except that now, $\sec^2 x - \tan^2 x = 1$.

4. $\sqrt{1 + \cos x} = \sqrt{2} \cdot \cos \left(\dfrac{x}{2} \right)$, if $-\pi \le x \le \pi$. Replace x by $x/2$ in the identity $\dfrac{1 + \cos 2x}{2} = \cos^2 x$, and then extract the square root. Note that whenever $-\pi/2 \le \theta \le \pi/2$, we have $\cos \theta \ge 0$. Consequently, if $-\pi \le \theta \le \pi$, then $\cos \dfrac{\theta}{2} \ge 0$. This explains that the positive square root of $\cos^2 \dfrac{\theta}{2}$ is $\cos \dfrac{\theta}{2}$.

5. $\sqrt{1 - \cos x} = \sqrt{2} \cdot \sin \left(\dfrac{x}{2} \right)$, if $0 \le x \le 2\pi$. Replace x by $x/2$ in the identity $\dfrac{1 - \cos 2x}{2} = \sin^2 x$.

6. $\sqrt{1 + \cos 5x} = \sqrt{2} \cdot \cos \left(\dfrac{5x}{2} \right)$, if $-\pi \le 5x \le \pi$. Replace x by $5x/2$ in the identity $\dfrac{1 + \cos x}{2} = \cos^2 x$.

7. $\displaystyle\int_0^2 (2x - 1)\, dx = 2$, since the function is linear (a polynomial of degree 1). In this case, the Trapezoidal Rule always gives the Actual value.

8. $\displaystyle\int_0^4 (3x^2 - 2x + 6)\, dx = 72$, using Simpson's Rule with $n = 6$. Once again, since the integrand is a quadratic function, Simpson's Rule is exact and always gives the Actual value.

9. $\displaystyle\int_{-\pi}^{\pi} (\cos^2 x + \sin^2 x)\, dx = 2\pi$. The Trapezoidal Rule with $n = 6$ and the Actual value agree exactly, since the integrand is equal to 1.

10. $\displaystyle\int_{-\pi}^{\pi} (\cos^2 x - \sin^2 x)\, dx = 0$, using Simpson's Rule with $n = 6$. The exact answer, obtained by direct integration, is 0, since the integrand is equal to $\cos 2x$. Note that the two values agree!

11. $\displaystyle\int_0^1 e^{-x^2}\, dx \approx 1.4628$, using Simpson's Rule with $n = 6$. The Actual value is 1.462651746

12. $\displaystyle\int_{-1}^2 \dfrac{1}{1 + x^6}\, dx \approx 1.82860$, using Simpson's Rule with $n = 4$. The Actual value is ≈ 1.94476. Don't try to work it out!

13. $\displaystyle\int_{-2}^2 \dfrac{x^2}{1 + x^4}\, dx \approx 1.221441$, using the Trapezoidal Rule with $n = 6$. The exact answer obtained by direct integration is 1.23352.

14. $\displaystyle\int_1^2 (\ln x)^3\, dx \approx 0.10107$, using Simpson's Rule with $n = 6$. The Actual value is $2 \ln^3 2 - 6 \ln^2 2 + 12 \ln 2 - 6 \approx 0.101097387$.

15. $\displaystyle\int \sqrt{3x + 2}\, dx = \dfrac{2}{9} \left(\sqrt{3x + 2} \right)^3$.

   Let $u = 3x + 2$.

16. $\int \dfrac{1}{x^2 + 4x + 4} \; dx = -\dfrac{1}{x+2}$.

Note that $x^2 + 4x + 4 = (x+2)^2$.
Then let $u = x + 2$, $du = dx$.

17. $\int \dfrac{dx}{(2x-3)^2} = -\dfrac{1}{2\,(2x-3)}$.

Let $u = 2x - 3$, $du = 2dx$, and so $dx = du/2$.

18. $\int \dfrac{dx}{\sqrt{a+bx}} = 2\dfrac{\sqrt{a+bx}}{b}$.

Let $u = a + bx$, $du = bdx$, and $dx = du/b$, if $b \neq 0$.

19. $\int (\sqrt{a} - \sqrt{x})^2 \; dx = ax - \dfrac{4\sqrt{a}}{3} \left(\sqrt{x}\right)^3 + \dfrac{1}{2}x^2$.

Expand the integrand and integrate term-by-term.

20. $\int \dfrac{x \; dx}{\sqrt{a^2 - x^2}} = -\sqrt{a^2 - x^2}$.

Let $u = a^2 - x^2$. Then $du = -2xdx$ and $x \; dx = -du/2$.

21. $\int x^2 \sqrt{x^3 + 1} \; dx = \dfrac{2}{9} \left(\sqrt{x^3 + 1} \right)^3$.

Let $u = x^3 + 1$, $du = 3x^2 \; dx$, so that $x^2 \; dx = du/3$.

22. $\int \dfrac{(x+1)}{\sqrt[3]{x^2 + 2x + 2}} \; dx = \dfrac{3}{4} \left(\sqrt[3]{\left(x^2 + 2x + 2\right)} \right)^2$.

Let $u = x^2 + 2x + 2$, $du = (2x+2) \; dx = 2(x+1) \; dx$. So, $(x+1) \; dx = du/2$.

23. $\int (x^4 + 4x^2 + 1)^2 (x^3 + 2x) \; dx = \dfrac{1}{12}(x^4 + 4x^2 + 1)^3$

Let $u = x^4 + 4x^2 + 1$, $du = (4x^3 + 8x) \; dx = 4(x^3 + 2x) \; dx$ and so, $(x^3 + 2x) \; dx = du/4$.

24. $\int x^{-1/3} \sqrt{x^{2/3} - 1} \; dx = \left(\sqrt{x^{2/3} - 1} \right)^3$.

Let $u = x^{2/3} - 1$. Then $du = (2/3)x^{-1/3} \; dx$, or $x^{-1/3} \; dx = 3 \; du/2$.

25. $\int \dfrac{2x \; dx}{(3x^2 - 2)^2} = -\dfrac{1}{3\left(3x^2 - 2\right)}$

Let $u = 3x^2 - 2$, $du = 6x \; dx$ and so $2x \; dx = du/3$.

26. $\int \dfrac{dx}{4x + 3} = \dfrac{1}{4} \ln|4x + 3|$

Let $u = 4x + 3$, $du = 4dx$ so that $dx = du/4$.

27. $\int \dfrac{x \; dx}{2x^2 - 1} = \dfrac{1}{4} \ln\left|2x^2 - 1\right|$

Let $u = 2x^2 - 1$, $du = 4x \; dx$ so that $x \; dx = du/4$.

28. $\int \dfrac{x^2 \; dx}{1 + x^3} = \dfrac{1}{3} \ln\left|1 + x^3\right|$

Let $u = 1 + x^3$, $du = 3x^2 \; dx$ so that $x^2 \; dx = du/3$.

29. $\int \dfrac{(2x + 3) \; dx}{x^2 + 3x + 2} = \ln\left|x^2 + 3x + 2\right|$

Let $u = x^2 + 3x + 2$, $du = (2x + 3) \; dx$.

30. $\int \sin(2x + 4) \; dx = -\dfrac{1}{2} \cos(2x + 4)$

Let $u = 2x + 4$, $du = 2 \; dx$, and $dx = du/2$.

31. $\int 2 \cos(4x + 1) \; dx = \dfrac{1}{2} \sin(4x + 1)$

Let $u = 4x + 1$, $du = 4 \; dx$, and $dx = du/4$.

32. $\int \sqrt{1 - \cos 2x} \; dx = \sqrt{2} \cos x$.

Note that $\dfrac{1 - \cos 2x}{2} = \sin^2 x$. The result follows upon the extraction of a square root. In actuality, we are

assuming that $\sqrt{\sin^2 x} = |\sin x| = \sin x$, here (or that $\sin x \geq 0$ over the region of integration).

33. $\displaystyle\int \sin \frac{3x-2}{5}\, dx = -\frac{5}{3}\cos\left(\frac{3x-2}{5}\right)$

Let $u = \frac{3x-2}{5}$, $du = \frac{3dx}{5}$. Then $dx = \frac{5du}{3}$.

34. $\displaystyle\int x\cos ax^2\, dx = \frac{1}{2}\frac{\sin ax^2}{a}$

Assume $a \neq 0$. Let $u = ax^2$, $du = 2ax\, dx$, so that $x\, dx = du/2a$.

35. $\displaystyle\int x\sin(x^2+1)\, dx = -\frac{1}{2}\cos\left(x^2+1\right)$

Let $u = x^2+1$, $du = 2x\, dx$. Then $x\, dx = du/2$.

36. $\displaystyle\int \sec^2\frac{\theta}{2}\, d\theta = 2\tan\frac{1}{2}\theta$

Let $u = \theta/2$, $du = d\theta/2$. The result follows since $\int \sec^2 u\, du = \tan u$.

37. $\displaystyle\int \frac{d\theta}{\cos^2 3\theta} = \frac{1}{3}\tan 3\theta$

The integrand is equal to $\sec^2 3\theta$. Now let $u = 3\theta$, $du = 3d\theta$.

38. $\displaystyle\int \frac{d\theta}{\sin^2 2\theta} = -\frac{1}{2}\cot 2\theta$

The integrand is equal to $\csc^2 2\theta$. Now let $u = 2\theta$, $du = 2d\theta$, and note that $\int \csc^2 u\, du = -\cot u$.

39. $\displaystyle\int x\csc^2(x^2)\, dx = -\frac{1}{2}\cot x^2$

Let $u = x^2$, $du = 2x\, dx$, so that $x\, dx = du/2$. Note that $\int \csc^2 u\, du = -\cot u$.

40. $\displaystyle\int \tan\frac{3x+4}{5}\, dx = \frac{5}{3}\ln\left|\sec\frac{3x+4}{5}\right|$

Let $u = \frac{3x+4}{5}$, $du = 3dx/5$ and so $dx = 5du/3$. The result follows since $\int \tan u\, du = -\ln|\cos u| = \ln|\sec u|$.

41. $\displaystyle\int \frac{dx}{\tan 2x} = \frac{1}{2}\ln|\sin 2x|$

The integrand is equal to $\cot 2x$. Let $u = 2x$, $du = 2dx$. Then, $dx = du/2$, and since $\int \cot u\, du = \ln|\sin u|$, the result follows.

42. $\displaystyle\int \sqrt{1+\cos 5x}\, dx = \frac{2\sqrt{2}}{5}\sin\frac{5x}{2}$

Use the identity in Exercise 6, above. Since $\sqrt{1+\cos 5x} = \sqrt{2}\cdot\cos\left(\frac{5x}{2}\right)$ we let $u = \frac{5x}{2}$, $du = 5dx/2$. Then $dx = 2du/5$ and the conclusion follows.

43. $\displaystyle\int \csc\left(x+\frac{\pi}{2}\right)\cot\left(x+\frac{\pi}{2}\right)\, dx = -\sec x$

Trigonometry tells us that $\sin(x+\frac{\pi}{2}) = \cos x$, and $\cos(x+\frac{\pi}{2}) = -\sin x$. Thus, by definition, $\csc(x+\frac{\pi}{2})\cot(x+\frac{\pi}{2}) = -\sec x\tan x$. On the other hand, $\int \sec x\tan x\, dx = \sec x$.

44. $\displaystyle\int \cos 3x\cos 4x\, dx = \frac{1}{2}\sin x + \frac{1}{14}\sin 7x$

Use the identity $\cos A\cos B = \frac{1}{2}(\cos(A-B) + \cos(A+B))$, with $A = 4x$, $B = 3x$, and integrate the terms individually. This is also a "three-row problem" using the Table method in Integration by Parts and so you can use this alternate method as well.

45. $\displaystyle\int \sec 5\theta\tan 5\theta\, d\theta = \frac{1}{5}\sec 5\theta$

Let $u = 5\theta$, $du = 5d\theta$. Then $d\theta = du/5$ and since $\int \sec u\tan u\, du = \sec u$, we have the result.

46. $\displaystyle\int \frac{\cos x}{\sin^2 x}\, dx = -\frac{1}{\sin x}$

The integrand is equal to $\cot x\csc x$. The result is now clear since $\frac{1}{\sin x} = \csc x$.

47. $\displaystyle\int x^2\cos(x^3+1)\, dx = \frac{1}{3}\sin\left(x^3+1\right)$

Let $u = x^3+1$, $du = 3x^2\, dx$. Then $x^2\, dx = du/3$ and the answer follows.

48. $\displaystyle\int \sec\theta\ (\sec\theta + \tan\theta)\ d\theta = \sec\theta + \tan\theta$

Expand the integrand and integrate it term-by-term. Use the facts
$\int \sec^2 u\ du = \tan u$, and $\int \sec u \tan u\ du = \sec u$

49. $\displaystyle\int (\csc\theta - \cot\theta)\csc\theta\ d\theta = \csc\theta - \cot\theta = \dfrac{1}{\sin\theta} - \dfrac{\cos\theta}{\sin\theta}$

Expand the integrand and integrate it term-by-term. Use the facts
$\int \csc^2 u\ du = -\cot u$, and $\int \csc u \cot u\ du = -\csc u$. Rewrite your answer using the elementary functions sine and cosine.

50. $\displaystyle\int \cos^{-4} x \sin(2x)\ dx = \dfrac{1}{\cos^2 x}$

Write $\sin 2x = 2\sin x \cos x$ and simplify the integrand. Put the $\cos^3 x$-term in the denominator and then use the substitution $u = \cos x$,
$du = -\sin x\ dx$. Then $-2\int u^{-3}\ du = u^{-2}$ and the result follows.

51. $\displaystyle\int \dfrac{\tan^2\sqrt{x}}{\sqrt{x}}\ dx = 2\tan\sqrt{x} - 2\sqrt{x}$

Let $u = \sqrt{x}$, $du = \dfrac{1}{2\sqrt{x}}\ dx$, which gives $2\sqrt{x}\ du = dx$, or $dx = 2u\ du$. The integral becomes
$\displaystyle\int \dfrac{2u\ \tan^2 u}{u}\ du = \int 2\tan^2 u\ du = \int 2(\sec^2 u - 1)\ du = 2\tan u - 2u$, and the result follows.

52. $\displaystyle\int \dfrac{1 + \sin 2x}{\cos^2 2x}\ dx = \dfrac{1}{2\cos 2x} + \dfrac{1}{2}\dfrac{\sin 2x}{\cos 2x}$

Note that the integrand is equal to $\sec^2 2x + \sec 2x \tan 2x$. Let $u = 2x$, $du = 2dx$, or $dx = du/2$. Use the facts $\int \sec^2 u\ du = \tan u$, and
$\int \sec u \tan u\ du = \sec u$. Now reduce your answer to elementary sine and cosine functions.

53. $\displaystyle\int \dfrac{dx}{\cos 3x} = \dfrac{1}{3}\ln|\sec 3x + \tan 3x|$

Let $u = 3x$, $du = 3dx$, $dx = du/3$, and use the result from Example 368, with $x = u$.

54. $\displaystyle\int \dfrac{dx}{\sin(3x + 2)} = \dfrac{1}{3}\ln|\csc(3x + 2) - \cot(3x + 2)|$

Note that the integrand is equal to $\csc(3x + 2)$. Now let $u = 3x + 2$, $du = 3dx$, $dx = du/3$. The integral looks like
$(1/3)\int \csc u\ du = (1/3)\ln|\csc u - \cot u|$ and the result follows. This last integral is obtained using the method described in Example 368, but applied to these functions. See also Table 8.9.

55. $\displaystyle\int \dfrac{1 + \sin x}{\cos x}\ dx = \ln|\sec x + \tan x| - \ln|\cos x|$

Break up the integrand into two parts and integrate term-by-term. Note that $-\ln|\cos x| = \ln|\sec x|$ so that the final answer may be written in the form
$\ln|\sec x + \tan x| + \ln|\sec x| = \ln\left|\sec^2 x + \tan x\ \sec x\right|$.

56. $\displaystyle\int (1 + \sec\theta)^2\ d\theta = \theta + 2\ln|\sec\theta + \tan\theta| + \tan\theta$

Expand the integrand and integrate term-by-term.

57. $\displaystyle\int \dfrac{\csc^2 x\ dx}{1 + 2\cot x} = -\dfrac{1}{2}\ln|1 + 2\cot x|$

Let $u = 1 + 2\cot x$, $du = -2\csc^2 x\ dx$. So, $\csc^2\ dx = -\dfrac{du}{2}$. The integral now becomes $(-1/2)\displaystyle\int \dfrac{du}{u} = -(1/2)\ln|u|$.

58. $\displaystyle\int e^x\ \sec e^x\ dx = \ln\left|\sec\left(e^x\right) + \tan\left(e^x\right)\right|$

Let $u = e^x$, $du = e^x\ dx$, and use Example 368.

59. $\displaystyle\int \dfrac{dx}{x\ln x} = \ln|\ln x|$

Let $u = \ln x$, $du = \dfrac{dx}{x}$. The integral looks like $\int \dfrac{du}{u} = \ln|u|$ and the result follows.

60. $\displaystyle\int \dfrac{dt}{\sqrt{2 - t^2}} = \text{Arcsin}\dfrac{1}{2}\sqrt{2}t$

The integrand contains a square root of a difference of squares of the form $\sqrt{a^2 - u^2}$ where $a = \sqrt{2}$, and $u = t$. Let $t = \sqrt{2}\sin\theta$, $dt = \sqrt{2}\cos\theta\ d\theta$. Since $\sqrt{2 - t^2} = \sqrt{2}\cos\theta$, the integral looks like
$\int d\theta = \theta = \text{Arcsin}\dfrac{t}{\sqrt{2}}$.

61. $\displaystyle\int \frac{dx}{\sqrt{3-4x^2}} = \frac{1}{2}\text{Arcsin}\,\frac{2}{3}\sqrt{3}\,x$

The integrand contains a square root of a difference of squares of the form $\sqrt{a^2-u^2}$ where $a=\sqrt{3}$, and $u=2x$. Let $2x=\sqrt{3}\sin\theta$, $2dx=\sqrt{3}\cos\theta\,d\theta$. Since $\sqrt{3-4x^2}=\sqrt{3}\cos\theta$, the integral looks like $\int (1/2)d\theta = \frac{\theta}{2} = \frac{1}{2}\text{Arcsin}\,\frac{2x}{\sqrt{3}}$, which is equivalent to the answer.

62. $\displaystyle\int \frac{(2x+3)\,dx}{\sqrt{4-x^2}} = -2\sqrt{4-x^2} + 3\text{Arcsin}\,\frac{1}{2}x$

Break up the integrand into two parts so that the integral looks like
$$\int \frac{2x\,dx}{\sqrt{4-x^2}} + \int \frac{3}{\sqrt{4-x^2}}\,dx.$$

Let $u=4-x^2$, $du=-2x\,dx$ in the first integral and $x=2\sin\theta$, $dx=2\cos\theta\,d\theta$ in the second integral. Then $\sqrt{4-x^2}=2\cos\theta$ and the second integral is an Arcsine. The first is a simple substitution.

63. $\displaystyle\int \frac{dx}{x^2+5} = \frac{1}{5}\sqrt{5}\,\text{Arctan}\,\frac{1}{5}x\sqrt{5}$

This integrand contains a sum of two squares. So let, $x=\sqrt{5}\tan\theta$, $dx=\sqrt{5}\sec^2\theta\,d\theta$. The integral becomes
$$\int \frac{\sqrt{5}\sec^2\theta\,d\theta}{5\sec^2\theta} = \frac{\sqrt{5}}{5}\int d\theta \text{ and the result follows since } \theta=\text{Arctan}\,\frac{x}{\sqrt{5}}, \text{ and } \frac{1}{\sqrt{5}}=\frac{\sqrt{5}}{5}.$$

64. $\displaystyle\int \frac{dx}{4x^2+3} = \frac{1}{6}\sqrt{3}\,\text{Arctan}\,\frac{2}{3}\sqrt{3}\,x$

The integrand contains a sum of two squares, a^2+u^2 where $a=\sqrt{3}$ and $u=2x$. So let $2x=\sqrt{3}\tan\theta$, $2\,dx=\sqrt{3}\sec^2\theta\,d\theta$. The integral becomes
$$\int \frac{(1/2)\sqrt{3}\sec^2\theta\,d\theta}{3\sec^2\theta} = \frac{\sqrt{3}}{6}\int d\theta \text{ and the result follows since } \theta=\text{Arctan}\,\frac{2x}{\sqrt{3}}.$$

65. $\displaystyle\int \frac{dx}{x\sqrt{x^2-4}} = \frac{1}{2}\text{Arcsec}\,\frac{x}{2}$

The integrand contains a square root of a difference of two squares, $\sqrt{u^2-a^2}$ where $a=2$ and $u=x$. So let $x>2$ and $x=2\sec\theta$, $dx=2\sec\theta\,\tan\theta\,d\theta$. Moreover, $\sqrt{x^2-4}=2\tan\theta$. The integral becomes
$$\int \frac{2\sec\theta\,\tan\theta\,d\theta}{(2\sec\theta)(2\tan\theta)} = \frac{1}{2}\int d\theta \text{ and the result follows since } \theta=\text{Arcsec}\,\frac{x}{2}.$$

66. $\displaystyle\int \frac{dx}{x\sqrt{4x^2-9}} = \frac{1}{3}\text{Arcsec}\,\frac{2x}{3}$

The integrand contains a square root of a difference of two squares, $\sqrt{u^2-a^2}$ where $a=3$ and $u=2x$. So let $x>0$ and set $2x=3\sec\theta$, $2dx=3\sec\theta\,\tan\theta\,d\theta$. Moreover, $\sqrt{4x^2-9}=3\tan\theta$. The integral becomes
$$\int \frac{(3/2)\sec\theta\,\cdot\tan\theta\,d\theta}{(3/2)\sec\theta\cdot 3\tan\theta} = \frac{1}{3}\int d\theta \text{ and the result follows since } \theta=\text{Arcsec}\,\frac{2x}{3}.$$

67. $\displaystyle\int \frac{dx}{\sqrt{x^2+4}} = \ln\left|\frac{\sqrt{4+x^2}}{2} + \frac{x}{2}\right|$

$= \ln\left|\sqrt{4+x^2}+x\right|$, where the "missing" constants are absorbed by the constant of integration, C.

The integrand contains a square root of a sum of two squares, $\sqrt{u^2+a^2}$ where $a=2$ and $u=x$. Set $x=2\tan\theta$, $dx=2\sec^2\theta\,d\theta$. Moreover, $\sqrt{x^2+4}=2\sec\theta$. The integral becomes
$$\int \frac{2\sec^2\theta\,d\theta}{(2\sec\theta)} = \int \sec\theta\,d\theta \text{ and the result follows from Example 368.}$$

68. $\displaystyle\int \frac{dx}{\sqrt{4x^2+3}} = \frac{1}{2}\ln\left|\frac{\sqrt{4x^2+3}}{\sqrt{3}} + \frac{2x}{\sqrt{3}}\right|$

$= \ln\left|\sqrt{4x^2+3}+2x\right|$, where the "missing" constants are absorbed by the constant of integration, C.

The integrand contains a square root of a sum of two squares, $\sqrt{u^2+a^2}$ where $a=\sqrt{3}$ and $u=2x$. Set $2x=\sqrt{3}\tan\theta$, $2\,dx=\sqrt{3}\sec^2\theta\,d\theta$. Moreover, $\sqrt{4x^2+3}=\sqrt{3}\sec\theta$. The integral becomes
$$\int \frac{(\sqrt{3}/2)\sec^2\theta\,d\theta}{\sqrt{3}\sec\theta} = (1/2)\int \sec\theta\,d\theta \text{ and the result follows from Example 368, once again.}$$

69. $\displaystyle\int \frac{dx}{\sqrt{x^2 - 16}} = \ln\left|\frac{x}{4} + \frac{\sqrt{x^2 - 16}}{4}\right|$

$= \ln\left|x + \sqrt{x^2 - 16}\right|$, where the "missing" constants are absorbed by the constant of integration, C.

The integrand contains a square root of a difference of two squares, $\sqrt{u^2 - a^2}$ where $a = 4$ and $u = x$.

Set $x = 4\sec\theta$, $dx = 4\sec\theta\,\tan\theta\,d\theta$. Moreover, $\sqrt{x^2 - 16} = 4\tan\theta$. The integral becomes

$\displaystyle\int \frac{4\sec\theta\,\tan\theta\,d\theta}{4\tan\theta} = \int \sec\theta\,d\theta$ and the result follows from Example 368.

70. $\displaystyle\int \frac{e^x}{1 + e^{2x}}\,dx = \operatorname{Arctan}\left(e^x\right)$

Use a substitution here: Let $u = e^x$, $du = e^x\,dx$. The integral now looks like $\displaystyle\int \frac{1}{1 + u^2}\,du = \operatorname{Arctan} u$,

where $u = e^x$.

71. $\displaystyle\int \frac{1}{x\sqrt{4x^2 - 1}}\,dx = \operatorname{Arcsec} 2x$

The integrand contains a square root of a difference of two squares, $\sqrt{u^2 - a^2}$ where $a = 1$ and $u = 2x$.

So let $x > 0$ and set $2x = \sec\theta$, $2dx = \sec\theta\,\tan\theta\,d\theta$. Moreover, $\sqrt{4x^2 - 1} = \tan\theta$. The integral becomes

$\displaystyle\int \frac{(1/2)\sec\theta\cdot\tan\theta\,d\theta}{(1/2)\sec\theta\cdot\tan\theta} = \int d\theta$ and the result follows since $\theta = \operatorname{Arcsec} 2x$.

72. $\displaystyle\int \frac{dx}{\sqrt{4x^2 - 9}} = \frac{1}{2}\ln\left|\frac{2x}{3} + \frac{\sqrt{4x^2 - 9}}{3}\right| = \ln\left|2x + \sqrt{4x^2 - 9}\right|$, where the "missing" constants are

absorbed by the constant of integration, C.

The integrand contains a square root of a difference of two squares, $\sqrt{u^2 - a^2}$ where $a = 3$ and $u = 2x$.

So let $x > 0$ and set $2x = 3\sec\theta$, $2\,dx = 3\sec\theta\,\tan\theta\,d\theta$. Moreover, $\sqrt{4x^2 - 9} = 3\tan\theta$. The integral

becomes

$\displaystyle\int \frac{(3/2)\sec\theta\cdot\tan\theta\,d\theta}{3\tan\theta} = (1/2)\int \sec\theta\,d\theta$ and the result follows since $\int \sec\theta\,d\theta = \ln|\sec\theta + \tan\theta|$.

73. $\displaystyle\int e^{-3x}\,dx = -\frac{1}{3}e^{-3x}$

Let $u = -3x$, $du = -3\,dx$. Then $dx = -du/3$.

74. $\displaystyle\int \frac{dx}{e^{2x}} = -\frac{1}{2}e^{-2x}$

Write the integrand as e^{-2x} and let $u = -2x$, $du = -2\,dx$.

75. $\displaystyle\int (e^x - e^{-x})^2\,dx = \frac{1}{2}e^{2x} - 2x - \frac{1}{2}e^{-2x}$

Expand the expression and integrate term-by-term using the two preceding exercises.

76. $\displaystyle\int xe^{-x^2}\,dx = -\frac{1}{2}e^{-x^2}$

Let $u = -x^2$, $du = -2x\,dx$ so that $x\,dx = -du/2$.

77. $\displaystyle\int \frac{\sin\theta\,d\theta}{\sqrt{1 - \cos\theta}} = 2\sqrt{1 - \cos\theta}$

Let $u = 1 - \cos\theta$, $du = \sin\theta\,d\theta$. We now have an easily integrable form.

78. $\displaystyle\int \frac{\cos\theta\,d\theta}{\sqrt{2 - \sin^2\theta}} = \operatorname{Arcsin}\left(\frac{1}{2}\sqrt{2}\sin\theta\right)$

Write $\theta = x$. Let $u = \sin x$, $du = \cos x\,dx$. The integral takes the form

$\displaystyle\int \frac{du}{\sqrt{2 - u^2}}$. Now set $u = \sqrt{2}\sin\theta$. (This is why we changed the name of the original variable to "x",

so that we wouldn't get it confused with THIS θ). Then $du = \sqrt{2}\cos\theta\,d\theta$ and $\sqrt{2 - u^2} = \sqrt{2}\cos\theta$ and the rest of the integration is straightforward. (Note: If you want, you could set $u = \sin\theta$ immediately and proceed as above without first having to let $\theta = x$ etc.)

79. $\displaystyle\int \frac{e^{2x}\,dx}{1 + e^{2x}} = \frac{1}{2}\ln\left(1 + e^{2x}\right)$

Let $u = 1 + e^{2x}$, $du = 2e^{2x}\,dx$. Now, the integral gives a natural logarithm

80. $\displaystyle\int \frac{e^x \, dx}{1 + e^{2x}} = \text{Arctan}\left(e^x\right)$

Let $u = e^x$, $du = e^x \, dx$. Now, the integral is of the form

$\displaystyle\int \frac{du}{1 + u^2}$ and this gives an Arctangent.

81. $\displaystyle\int \frac{\cos\theta \, d\theta}{2 + \sin^2\theta} = \frac{1}{2}\sqrt{2}\,\text{Arctan}\left(\frac{1}{2}\sqrt{2}\sin\theta\right)$

Write $\theta = x$. Let $u = \sin x$, $du = \cos x \, dx$. The integral takes the form

$\displaystyle\int \frac{du}{2 + u^2}$. Now set $u = \sqrt{2}\tan\theta$. (This is why we changed the name of the original variable to "x", so that we wouldn't get it confused with THIS θ). Then $du = \sqrt{2}\sec^2\theta \, d\theta$ and $2 + u^2 = 2\sec^2\theta$ and the rest of the integration is straightforward. (Note: If you want, you could set $u = \sin\theta$ immediately and proceed as above without first having to let $\theta = x$ etc.)

82. $\displaystyle\int \sin^3 x \cos x \, dx = \frac{1}{4}\sin^4 x$

Let $u = \sin x$, $du = \cos x \, dx$.

83. $\displaystyle\int \cos^4 5x \sin 5x \, dx = -\frac{1}{25}\cos^5 5x$

Let $u = \cos 5x$, $du = -5\sin 5x \, dx$ or $\sin 5x = -du/5$. The rest is straightforward.

84. $\displaystyle\int (\cos\theta + \sin\theta)^2 \, d\theta = \theta - \cos^2\theta$

or, this can also be rewritten as $\theta + \sin^2\theta$

Expand and use the identities $\cos^2\theta + \sin^2\theta = 1$, along with $\sin 2\theta = 2\sin\theta \cos\theta$. Then use the substitution $u = 2x$, or if you prefer, let $u = \sin\theta$, etc.

85. $\displaystyle\int \sin^3 x \, dx = -\frac{1}{3}\sin^2 x \cos x - \frac{2}{3}\cos x$

This is the case m is even ($m = 0$) and n is odd ($n = 3$) in the text.

86. $\displaystyle\int \cos^3 2x \, dx = \frac{1}{6}\cos^2 2x \sin 2x + \frac{1}{3}\sin 2x$

Let $u = 2x$. The new integral is in the case where m is odd ($m = 3$) and n is even ($n = 0$) in the text.

87. $\displaystyle\int \sin^3 x \cos^2 x \, dx = -\frac{1}{5}\sin^2 x \cos^3 x - \frac{2}{15}\cos^3 x$

This is the case m is even ($m = 2$) and n is odd ($n = 3$) in the text. To get the polynomial in $\cos x$ simply use the identities $\sin^2 x = 1 - \cos^2 x$ whenever you see the $\sin^2 x$−term and expand and simplify.

88. $\displaystyle\int \cos^5 x \, dx = \frac{1}{5}\cos^4 x \sin x + \frac{4}{15}\cos^2 x \sin x + \frac{8}{15}\sin x$

This is the case m is odd ($m = 5$) and n is even ($n = 0$) in the text. To get the polynomial in $\sin x$ simply use the identities $\cos^2 x = 1 - \sin^2 x$ whenever you see a $\cos^2 x$−term and then expand and simplify.

89. $\displaystyle\int \sin^3 4\theta \cos^3 4\theta \, d\theta = -\frac{1}{24}\sin^2 4\theta \cos^4 4\theta - \frac{1}{48}\cos^4 4\theta$

Let $u = 4\theta$. Then the new integral is in the case where m is odd ($m = 3$) and n is odd ($n = 3$) in the text.

90. $\displaystyle\int \frac{\cos^2 x \, dx}{\sin x} = \cos x + \ln|\csc x - \cot x|$

Write $\cos^2 x = 1 - \sin^2 x$, break up the integrand into two parts, and use the fact that $\displaystyle\int \csc x \, dx = \ln|\csc x - \cot x|$.

91. $\displaystyle\int \frac{\cos^3 x \, dx}{\sin x} = \frac{1}{2}\cos^2 x + \ln|\sin x|$

Write $\cos^2 x = 1 - \sin^2 x$, break up the integrand into two parts. In one, use the fact that $\displaystyle\int \cot x \, dx = \ln|\sin x|$. In the other, use the substitution $u = \sin x$ in the other.

92. $\displaystyle\int \tan^2 x \sec^2 x \, dx = \frac{1}{3}\tan^3 x$

Let $u = \tan x$, $du = \sec^2 x \, dx$.

93. $\displaystyle\int \sec^2 x \tan^3 x \, dx = \frac{1}{4}\tan^4 x$

Let $u = \tan x$, $du = \sec^2 x \, dx$.

94. $\displaystyle\int \frac{\sin x \; dx}{\cos^3 x} = \frac{1}{2\cos^2 x}$

Let $u = \cos x, \; du = -\sin x \; dx$.

95. $\displaystyle\int \frac{\sin^2 x \; dx}{\cos^4 x} = \frac{1}{3}\tan^3 x$

The integrand is equal to $\tan^2 x \; \sec^2 x$. Now let $u = \tan x$.

96. $\displaystyle\int \sec^4 x \; dx = \frac{1}{3}\tan x \; \sec^2 x + \frac{2}{3}\tan x$

This is the case $m = 4, \; n = 0$ in the text. Note that $sec^2 x = 1 + \tan^2 x$. So, this answer is equivalent to $\tan x + \frac{\tan^3 x}{3}$ with the addition of a constant.

97. $\displaystyle\int \tan^2 x \; dx = \tan x \; - \; x$

The integrand is equal to $1 - \sec^2 x$. Now break up the integrand into two parts and integrate term-by-term.

98. $\displaystyle\int (1 + \cot \theta)^2 \; d\theta = -\cot \theta - \ln\left(1 + \cot^2 \theta\right)$

Expand the integrand, use the identity $1 + \cot^2 \theta = \csc^2 \theta$ and integrate using the facts that $\int \csc^2 x \; dx = -\cot x$, and $\int \cot x \; dx = \ln|\sin x|$. Note that the second term may be simplified further using the fact that
$\ln\left(1 + \cot^2 \theta\right) = \ln \csc^2 \theta = -\ln \sin^2 \theta = -2\ln \sin \theta$.

99. $\displaystyle\int \sec^4 x \tan^3 x \; dx = \frac{1}{6}\tan^4 x \; \sec^2 x + \frac{1}{12}\tan^4 x$

This is the case $m = 4, \; n = 3$ in the text.

100. $\displaystyle\int \csc^6 x \; dx = -\frac{1}{5}\csc^4 x \; \cot x - \frac{4}{15}\csc^2 x \; \cot x - \frac{8}{15}\cot x$

Use the same ideas as in the case $m = 6, \; n = 0$ in the secant/tangent case.

101. $\displaystyle\int \tan^3 x \; dx = \frac{1}{2}\tan^2 x - \frac{1}{2}\ln\left(1 + \tan^2 x\right)$

This is the case $m = 0, \; n = 3$ in the text.

102. $\displaystyle\int \frac{\cos^2 t \; dt}{\sin^6 t} = -\frac{1}{5}\csc^2 t \; \cot^3 t - \frac{2}{15}\cot^3 t$

The integrand is equal to $\cot^2 x \; \csc^4 x$, and this corresponds to the case $m = 4, \; n = 2$ in the secant/tangent case.

103. $\displaystyle\int \tan \theta \csc \theta \; d\theta = \ln|\sec \theta + \tan \theta|$

The integrand is really $\sec \theta$ in disguise!

104. $\displaystyle\int \cos^2 4x \; dx = \frac{1}{8}\cos 4x \sin 4x + \frac{1}{2}x$

Use the identity $\cos^2 \square = \frac{1+\cos 2\square}{2}$, with $\square = 4x$. Then use a simple substitution $u = 8x$, and simplify your answer using the identity $\sin 8x = \sin(2 \cdot 4x) = 2\sin 4x \; \cos 4x$.

105. $\displaystyle\int (1 + \cos \theta)^2 \; d\theta = \frac{3}{2}\theta + 2\sin \theta + \frac{1}{2}\cos \theta \sin \theta$

Expand the integrand, use the identity $\cos^2 \theta = \frac{1+\cos 2\theta}{2}$ and integrate term-by-term.

106. $\displaystyle\int (1 - \sin x)^3 \; dx = \frac{5}{2}x + \frac{11}{3}\cos x - \frac{3}{2}\cos x \sin x + \frac{1}{3}\sin^2 x \cos x$

Expand the integrand, and integrate term-by-term using the identity $\sin^2 \theta = \frac{1-\cos 2\theta}{2}$, and the case $m = 0, \; n = 3$ in the text.
Recall that $(1 - \square)^3 = 1 - 3\square + 3\square^2 - \square^3$

107. $\displaystyle\int \sin^4 x \; dx = -\frac{1}{4}\sin^3 x \cos x - \frac{3}{8}\cos x \sin x + \frac{3}{8}x$

This is the case $m = 0, \; n = 4$ in the text.

108. $\displaystyle\int \sin^2 2x \cos^2 2x \; dx = -\frac{1}{8}\sin 2x \cos^3 2x + \frac{1}{16}\cos 2x \sin 2x + \frac{1}{8}x$

Let $u = 2x$ first. Then the new integral corresponds to the case $m = 2, \; n = 2$ in the text.

109. $\displaystyle\int \sin^4 \theta \cos^2 \theta \; d\theta = -\frac{1}{6}\sin^3 \theta \cos^3 \theta - \frac{1}{8}\sin \theta \cos^3 \theta + \frac{1}{16}\cos \theta \sin \theta + \frac{1}{16}\theta$

This is the case $m = 2, \; n = 4$ in the text.

110. $\displaystyle\int \cos^6 x \ dx = \frac{1}{6}\cos^5 x \sin x + \frac{5}{24}\sin x \cos^3 x + \frac{5}{16}\cos x \sin x + \frac{5}{16}x$

This is the case $m = 6$, $n = 0$ in the text.

111. $\displaystyle\int \cos x \sin 2x \ dx = -\frac{1}{6}\cos 3x - \frac{1}{2}\cos x$

You can use either Table integration in a three-row problem or the identity
$\cos A \sin B = \frac{1}{2}\sin(A + B) - \frac{1}{2}\sin(A - B)$ to find this integral.

112. $\displaystyle\int \sin x \cos 3x \ dx = -\frac{1}{8}\cos 4x + \frac{1}{4}\cos 2x$

You can use either Table integration in a three-row problem or the identity
$\cos A \sin B = \frac{1}{2}\sin(A + B) - \frac{1}{2}\sin(A - B)$ to find this integral.

113. $\displaystyle\int \sin 2x \sin 3x \ dx = \frac{1}{2}\sin x - \frac{1}{10}\sin 5x$

You can use either Table integration in a three-row problem or the identity
$\sin A \sin B = \frac{1}{2}\cos(A - B) - \frac{1}{2}\cos(A + B)$ to find this integral.

114. $\displaystyle\int \cos 2x \cos 4x \ dx = \frac{1}{4}\sin 2x + \frac{1}{12}\sin 6x$

You can use either Table integration in a three-row problem or the identity
$\cos A \cos B = \frac{1}{2}\cos(A - B) + \frac{1}{2}\cos(A + B)$ to find this integral.

115. $\displaystyle\int \sin^2 2x \cos 3x \ dx = \frac{1}{6}\sin 3x - \frac{1}{4}\sin x - \frac{1}{28}\sin 7x$

Use the identity $\sin^2 \square = \frac{1 - \cos 2\square}{2}$ with $\square = 2x$. Break up the integrand into two parts, and integrate using the substitution $u = 4x$ and the identity
$\cos A \cos B = \frac{1}{2}\cos(A - B) + \frac{1}{2}\cos(A + B)$ to find the other integral.

116. $\displaystyle\int \sec x \csc x \ dx = \ln|\tan x|$

There are two **VERY** different ways of doing this one:

In the first proof we note the trigonometric identity (and this isn't obvious!),

$\dfrac{\sec^2 x}{\tan x} = \dfrac{1}{\sin x \cos x} = \sec x \csc x,$

so the result follows after using the substitution $u = \tan x$, $du = \sec^2 x \ dx$.

In the second proof we note that (and this isn't obvious either!)

$\dfrac{1}{\sin x \cos x} = \dfrac{2}{\sin 2x} = 2 \csc 2x.$

Now use the substitution $u = 2x$, $du = 2dx$ and this new integral becomes

$2 \cdot \dfrac{1}{2}\displaystyle\int \csc u \ du = \ln|\csc u - \cot u|$. The answer is equivalent to

$\ln|\csc 2x - \cot 2x| + C$, because of the identity $1 - \cos 2x = 2\sin^2 x$.

117. $\displaystyle\int \dfrac{dx}{1 - \cos x} = -\dfrac{1}{\tan \frac{1}{2}x} = -\cot \dfrac{x}{2}.$

Use the identity $1 - \cos 2\square = 2\sin^2 \square$, with $\square = \frac{x}{2}$. Then $\frac{1}{1 - \cos x} = \frac{1}{2}\csc^2 \frac{x}{2}$. Let $u = x/2$, $du = dx/2$ and use the integral
$\int \csc^2 u \ du = -\cot u$ and simplify.

118. $\displaystyle\int \dfrac{dx}{\sqrt{2 + 2x - x^2}} = \mathrm{Arcsin}\,\dfrac{1}{3}\sqrt{3}\,(x - 1)$

First, complete the square to find $2 + 2x - x^2 = 3 - (x - 1)^2$. Next, let $a = \sqrt{3}$, $u = x - 1$. This integrand has a term of the form $\sqrt{a^2 - u^2}$. So we use the trigonometric substitution
$u = x - 1 = \sqrt{3}\sin\theta$, $dx = \sqrt{3}\cos\theta \ d\theta$.
Furthermore, $\sqrt{2 + 2x - x^2} = \sqrt{3}\cos\theta$. So, the integral now takes the form

$\displaystyle\int \dfrac{\sqrt{3}\cos\theta \ d\theta}{\sqrt{3}\cos\theta} = \int d\theta = \theta$

where $\theta = \mathrm{Arcsin}\,\dfrac{x - 1}{\sqrt{3}}$ which is equivalent to the stated answer.

119. $\displaystyle\int \dfrac{dx}{\sqrt{1 + 4x - 4x^2}} = \dfrac{1}{2}\mathrm{Arcsin}\,\sqrt{2}\left(x - \dfrac{1}{2}\right)$

First, complete the square to find $1 + 4x - 4x^2 = 2 - (2x - 1)^2$. Next, let $a = \sqrt{2}$, $u = 2x - 1$. This integrand has a term of the form $\sqrt{a^2 - u^2}$. So we use the trigonometric substitution

$$u = 2x - 1 = \sqrt{2}\sin\theta, \; 2dx = \sqrt{2}\cos\theta \; d\theta$$

or, $dx = \dfrac{\sqrt{2}}{2}\cos\theta \; d\theta$.

Furthermore, $\sqrt{1 + 4x - 4x^2} = \sqrt{2}\cos\theta$. So, the integral now takes the form

$$\frac{1}{2}\int \frac{\sqrt{2}\cos\theta \; d\theta}{\sqrt{2}\cos\theta} = \frac{1}{2}\int d\theta = \frac{\theta}{2}$$

where $\theta = \text{Arcsin}\,\dfrac{2x-1}{\sqrt{2}}$ which is equivalent to the stated answer.

120. $\displaystyle\int \frac{dx}{\sqrt{2 + 6x - 3x^2}} = \frac{1}{3}\sqrt{3}\,\text{Arcsin}\,\frac{1}{5}\sqrt{15}\,(x - 1)$

This one is a little tricky: First, complete the square to find $2 + 6x - 3x^2 = 5 - 3(x - 1)^2$. But this is not exactly a difference of squares, yet! So we rewrite this as

$$5 - 3(x - 1)^2 = 5 - (\sqrt{3}x - \sqrt{3})^2,$$

and this is a difference of squares. Now let $a = \sqrt{5}$, $u = \sqrt{3}x - \sqrt{3}$. We see that the integrand has a term of the form $\sqrt{a^2 - u^2}$. So we use the trigonometric substitution
$u = \sqrt{3}x - \sqrt{3} = \sqrt{5}\sin\theta$,
$\sqrt{3}\,dx = \sqrt{5}\cos\theta \; d\theta$

or, $dx = \dfrac{\sqrt{5}}{\sqrt{3}}\cos\theta \; d\theta$.

Furthermore, $\sqrt{2 + 6x - 3x^2} = \sqrt{5}\cos\theta$. So, the integral now takes the form

$$\int \frac{\frac{\sqrt{5}}{\sqrt{3}}\cos\theta \; d\theta}{\sqrt{5}\cos\theta} = \frac{1}{\sqrt{3}}\int d\theta = \frac{\theta}{\sqrt{3}}$$

where $\theta = \text{Arcsin}\,\dfrac{\sqrt{3}x - \sqrt{3}}{\sqrt{5}}$ which is equivalent to the stated answer.

121. $\displaystyle\int \frac{dx}{\sqrt{x^2 + 6x + 13}} = \ln\left|\frac{\sqrt{x^2 + 6x + 13}}{2} + \frac{x + 3}{2}\right|$

First, complete the square to find $x^2 + 6x + 13 = (x + 3)^2 + 4$. Next, let $a = 2$, $u = x + 3$. This integrand has a term of the form $\sqrt{a^2 + u^2}$. So we use the trigonometric substitution

$u = x + 3 = 2\tan\theta$,
$dx = 2\sec^2\theta \; d\theta$.

Furthermore, $\sqrt{x^2 + 6x + 13} = 2\sec\theta$. So, the integral now takes the form

$$\int \frac{2\sec^2\theta \; d\theta}{2\sec\theta} = \int \sec\theta \; d\theta = \ln|\sec\theta + \tan\theta|,$$

where $\sec\theta = \text{Arcsec}\,\dfrac{\sqrt{x^2 + 6x + 13}}{2}$
and $\tan\theta = \dfrac{x+3}{2}$ which is equivalent to the stated answer.

122. $\displaystyle\int \frac{dx}{2x^2 - 4x + 6} = \frac{1}{4}\sqrt{2}\,\text{Arctan}\,\frac{1}{8}(4x - 4)\sqrt{2}$

First, complete the square to find $2x^2 - 4x + 6 = 2(x - 1)^2 + 4$. The integral now looks like:

$$\int \frac{1}{2x^2 - 4x + 6}\,dx = \int \frac{1}{2(x - 1)^2 + 4}\,dx = \frac{1}{2}\int \frac{1}{(x - 1)^2 + 2}\,dx.$$

Next, let $a = \sqrt{2}$, $u = x - 1$. The previous integrand has a term of the form $a^2 + u^2$. So we use the trigonometric substitution

$u = x - 1 = \sqrt{2}\tan\theta$,
$dx = \sqrt{2}\sec^2\theta \; d\theta$.

Furthermore, $2x^2 - 4x + 6 = 2\sec^2\theta$. So, the original integral now takes the form

$$\frac{1}{2}\int \frac{\sqrt{2}\sec^2\theta \; d\theta}{2\sec^2\theta} = \frac{\sqrt{2}}{4}\theta = \frac{\sqrt{2}}{4}\text{Arctan}\,\frac{x - 1}{\sqrt{2}},$$

which is equivalent to the stated answer.

123. $\displaystyle\int \frac{dx}{(1 - x)\sqrt{x^2 - 2x - 3}} = -\frac{1}{2}\text{Arcsec}\,\frac{x - 1}{2}$

First we complete the square so that $x^2 - 2x - 3 = (x - 1)^2 - 4$. A trigonometric substitution is hard here: Let's try another approach...

Let $u = x - 1, du = dx$. Then the integral becomes (note the minus sign)

$$-\int \frac{du}{u\sqrt{u^2 - 4}}.$$

Now we incorporate the number 4 into the square by factoring it out of the expression, thus:

$$u\sqrt{u^2 - 4} = 2u\sqrt{\left(\frac{u}{2}\right)^2 - 1}.$$

Now we use the substitution $v = \frac{u}{2}$, $2dv = du$. The integral in u now becomes

$$-\int \frac{2\,dv}{4v\sqrt{v^2 - 1}} = -\frac{1}{2}\int \frac{dv}{v\sqrt{v^2 - 1}} = -\frac{1}{2}\text{Arcsec}\,v,$$

according to Table 6.7 with $\square = v$. The answer follows after back-substitution.

124. $\displaystyle\int \frac{(2x + 3)\,dx}{x^2 + 2x - 3} = \frac{3}{4}\ln|x + 3| + \frac{5}{4}\ln|x - 1|$

Use partial fractions. The factors of the denominator are $(x + 3)(x - 1)$. You need to find two constants.

125. $\displaystyle\int \frac{(x + 1)\,dx}{x^2 + 2x - 3} = \frac{1}{2}\ln\left|x^2 + 2x - 3\right|$

Let $u = x^2 + 2x - 3$, $du = (2x + 2)\,dx$ so that
$du = 2(x + 1)\,dx$. Now the integral in u gives a natural logarithm.

Alternately, use partial fractions. The factors of the denominator are $(x + 3)(x - 1)$. You need to find the two constants.

126. $\displaystyle\int \frac{(x - 1)\,dx}{4x^2 - 4x + 2} = \frac{1}{8}\ln\left|4x^2 - 4x + 2\right| - \frac{1}{4}\text{Arctan}\,(2x - 1)$

The denominator is a Type II factor (it is irreducible) since $b^2 - 4ac = (-4)^2 - 4(4)(2) < 0$. So the expression is already in its partial fraction decomposition. So, the partial fractions method gives nothing. So, complete the square in the denominator. This gives an integral of the form

$$\int \frac{(x - 1)\,dx}{4x^2 - 4x + 2} = \int \frac{(x - 1)\,dx}{(2x - 1)^2 + 1},$$

which can be evaluated using the trigonometric substitution,

$u = 2x - 1$, $du = 2dx$ or $dx = du/2$. Solving for x we get
$x = \frac{u+1}{2}$, so $x - 1 = \frac{u-1}{2}$. The u-integral looks like

$$\frac{1}{2}\int \frac{u - 1}{1 + u^2}\,du.$$

Break this integral into two parts and use the substitution

$$v = 1 + u^2, \quad dv = 2u\,du, \quad u\,du = dv/2$$

in the first, while the second one yields an Arctangent.

127. $\displaystyle\int \frac{x\,dx}{\sqrt{x^2 - 2x + 2}} = \sqrt{x^2 - 2x + 2} + \ln\left|\sqrt{x^2 - 2x + 2} + x - 1\right|$

Completing the square we see that $x^2 - 2x + 2 = (x - 1)^2 + 1$. Next, we set

$x - 1 = \tan\theta, \quad dx = \sec^2\theta\,d\theta$
$x = 1 + \tan\theta,$
$\sqrt{x^2 - 2x + 2} = \sqrt{(x - 1)^2 + 1} = \sec\theta.$

The integral becomes

$$\int \frac{x\,dx}{\sqrt{x^2 - 2x + 2}} = \int \frac{(1 + \tan\theta)\sec^2\theta}{\sec\theta}\,d\theta$$

and this simplifies to

$$\int (\sec\theta + \sec\theta\tan\theta)\,d\theta = \ln|\sec\theta + \tan\theta| + \sec\theta.$$

Finally, use the back-substitutions $\sec\theta = \sqrt{x^2 - 2x + 2}$ and $\tan\theta = x - 1$.

128. $\displaystyle\int \frac{(4x + 1)\,dx}{\sqrt{1 + 4x - 4x^2}} = -\sqrt{1 + 4x - 4x^2} + \frac{3}{2}\text{Arcsin}\,\sqrt{2}\left(x - \frac{1}{2}\right)$

Completing the square we see that $1 + 4x - 4x^2 = 2 - (2x - 1)^2$. The integrand has a term of the form
$\sqrt{a^2 - u^2}$ where $a = \sqrt{2}$, $u = 2x - 1$. So, we set

$2x - 1 = \sqrt{2}\sin\theta, \quad 2dx = \sqrt{2}\cos\theta\,d\theta$
$x = \frac{1 + \sqrt{2}\sin\theta}{2},$

$$4x + 1 = 3 + 2\sqrt{2}\sin\theta,$$
$$\sqrt{1 + 4x - 4x^2} = \sqrt{2}\cos\theta.$$

The integral becomes

$$\int \frac{(4x + 1)\,dx}{\sqrt{1 + 4x - 4x^2}} = \int \left(\frac{3 + 2\sqrt{2}\sin\theta}{\sqrt{2}\cos\theta}\right)\frac{\sqrt{2}}{2}\cos\theta\,d\theta$$

which simplifies to

$$\frac{1}{2}\int (3 + 2\sqrt{2}\sin\theta)\,d\theta = \frac{3}{2}\theta - \sqrt{2}\cos\theta.$$

Finally, use the back-substitutions $\theta = \text{Arcsin}\frac{2x-1}{\sqrt{2}}$ and $\cos\theta = \frac{\sqrt{1+4x-4x^2}}{\sqrt{2}}$, to get it in a form equivalent to the stated answer.

129. $\int \dfrac{(3x - 2)\,dx}{\sqrt{x^2 + 2x + 3}} = 3\sqrt{x^2 + 2x + 3} - 5\ln\left|\dfrac{\sqrt{x^2 + 2x + 3}}{\sqrt{2}} + \dfrac{x + 1}{\sqrt{2}}\right|$

Completing the square we see that $x^2 + 2x + 3 = 2 + (x + 1)^2$. The integrand has a term of the form $\sqrt{a^2 + u^2}$ where $a = \sqrt{2}$, $u = x + 1$. So, we set

$$x + 1 = \sqrt{2}\tan\theta, \quad dx = \sqrt{2}\sec^2\theta\,d\theta$$
$$x = \sqrt{2}\tan\theta - 1,$$
$$3x - 2 = 3\sqrt{2}\tan\theta - 5 = 3\sqrt{2}\tan\theta - 5,$$
$$\sqrt{x^2 + 2x + 3} = \sqrt{2}\sec\theta.$$

The integral becomes

$$\int \frac{(3x - 2)\,dx}{\sqrt{x^2 + 2x + 3}} = \int \left(\frac{3\sqrt{2}\tan\theta - 5}{\sqrt{2}\sec\theta}\right)\sqrt{2}\sec^2\theta\,d\theta$$

which simplifies to

$$3\sqrt{2}\int \sec\theta\tan\theta\,d\theta - 5\int \sec\theta\,d\theta = 3\sqrt{2}\sec\theta - 5\ln|\sec\theta + \tan\theta|.$$

Finally, use the back-substitutions $\sec\theta = \dfrac{\sqrt{x^2+2x+3}}{\sqrt{2}}$, and $\tan\theta = \dfrac{x+1}{\sqrt{2}}$, to get it in a form equivalent to the stated answer.

130. $\int \dfrac{e^x\,dx}{e^{2x} + 2e^x + 3} = \dfrac{1}{2}\sqrt{2}\,\text{Arctan}\dfrac{1}{4}\left(2e^x + 2\right)\sqrt{2}$

Let $u = e^x$, $du = e^x\,dx$. The integral is now a rational function in u on which we can use partial fractions. The denominator is irreducible, since $b^2 - 4ac = 4 - 4(1)(3) < 0$. You need to find two constants.

131. $\int \dfrac{x^2\,dx}{x^2 + x - 6} = x - \dfrac{9}{5}\ln|x + 3| + \dfrac{4}{5}\ln|x - 2|$

Use long division first, then use partial fractions. The factors of the denominator are $x^2 + x - 6 = (x + 3)(x - 2)$. You need to find two constants.

132. $\int \dfrac{(x + 2)\,dx}{x^2 + x} = 2\ln|x| - \ln|1 + x|$

Use partial fractions. The factors of the denominator are $x^2 + x = x(x + 1)$. You need to find two constants.

133. $\int \dfrac{(x^3 + x^2)\,dx}{x^2 - 3x + 2} = \dfrac{1}{2}x^2 + 4x - 2\ln|x - 1| + 12\ln|x - 2|$

Use long division first. Then use partial fractions. The factors of the denominator are $x^2 - 3x + 2 = (x - 1)(x - 2)$. You need to find two constants.

134. $\int \dfrac{dx}{x^3 - x} = -\ln|x| + \dfrac{1}{2}\ln|x - 1| + \dfrac{1}{2}\ln|1 + x|$

Use partial fractions. The factors of the denominator are $x^3 - x = x(x^2 - 1) = x(x - 1)(x + 1)$. You need to find three constants.

135. $\int \dfrac{(x - 3)\,dx}{x^3 + 3x^2 + 2x} = -\dfrac{3}{2}\ln|x| - \dfrac{5}{2}\ln|x + 2| + 4\ln|1 + x|$

Use partial fractions. The factors of the denominator are $x^3 + 3x^2 + 2x = x(x^2 + 3x + 2) = x(x + 1)(x + 2)$. You need to find three constants.

136. $\int \dfrac{(x^3 + 1)\,dx}{x^3 - x^2} = x + \dfrac{1}{x} - \ln|x| + 2\ln|x - 1|$

Use partial fractions. The factors of the denominator are $x^3 - x^2 = x^2(x - 1)$. You need to find three constants.

137. $\int \dfrac{x\,dx}{(x+1)^2} = \dfrac{1}{1+x} + \ln|1+x|$

Use partial fractions.

138. $\int \dfrac{(x+2)\,dx}{x^2-4x+4} = -\dfrac{4}{x-2} + \ln|x-2|$

Use partial fractions. The factors of the denominator are $x^2-4x+4 = (x-2)^2$. You need to find two constants.

139. $\int \dfrac{(3x+2)\,dx}{x^3-2x^2+x} = 2\ln|x| - \dfrac{5}{x-1} - 2\ln|x-1|$

Use partial fractions. Note that $x^3 - 2x^2 + x = x(x^2 - 2x + 1) = x(x-1)^2$. There are four constants to be found here!

140. $\int \dfrac{8\,dx}{x^4-2x^3} = \dfrac{2}{x^2} + \dfrac{2}{x} - \ln|x| + \ln|x-2|$

Use partial fractions. Note that $x^4 - 2x^3 = x^3(x-2)$. There are four constants to be found here!

141. $\int \dfrac{dx}{(x^2-1)^2} = -\dfrac{1}{4\,(x-1)} - \dfrac{1}{4}\ln|x-1| - \dfrac{1}{4\,(1+x)} + \dfrac{1}{4}\ln|1+x|$

Use partial fractions. Note that $(x^2-1)^2 = (x-1)^2(x+1)^2$.

142. $\int \dfrac{(1-x^3)\,dx}{x(x^2+1)} = -x + \ln|x| - \dfrac{1}{2}\ln\left(x^2+1\right) + \operatorname{Arctan} x$

Use long division first, then use partial fractions.

143. $\int \dfrac{(x-1)\,dx}{(x+1)(x^2+1)} = -\ln|1+x| + \dfrac{1}{2}\ln\left(x^2+1\right)$

Use partial fractions.

144. $\int \dfrac{4x\,dx}{x^4-1} = \ln|x-1| + \ln|1+x| - \ln\left(x^2+1\right)$

Note that $x^4 - 1 = (x^2-1)(x^2+1) = (x-1)(x+1)(x^2+1)$. Use partial fractions.

145. $\int \dfrac{3(x+1)\,dx}{x^3-1} = 2\ln|x-1| - \ln\left(x^2+x+1\right)$

Note that $x^3 - 1 = (x-1)(x^2+x+1)$. Use partial fractions.

146. $\int \dfrac{(x^4+x)\,dx}{x^4-4} = \dfrac{1}{4}\ln|x-2| - \dfrac{1}{12}\ln|x+2| - \dfrac{1}{12}\ln(x^2+2) + \dfrac{\sqrt{2}}{3}\operatorname{Arctan}\dfrac{x\sqrt{2}}{2}$

Use long division first, then use partial fractions.

147. $\int \dfrac{x^2\,dx}{(x^2+1)(x^2+2)} = -\operatorname{Arctan} x + \sqrt{2}\operatorname{Arctan}\dfrac{1}{2}\sqrt{2}x$

The factors are $(x^2+2)(x^2+1)$, both irreducible. Four constants need to be found. This is where the Arctangents come from!

148. $\int \dfrac{3\,dx}{x^4+5x^2+4} = -\dfrac{1}{2}\operatorname{Arctan}\dfrac{1}{2}x + \operatorname{Arctan} x$

The factors are $(x^2+4)(x^2+1)$, both irreducible. Four constants need to be found. This is where the Arctangents come from!

149. $\int \dfrac{(x-1)\,dx}{(x^2+1)(x^2-2x+3)} = -\dfrac{1}{2}\operatorname{Arctan} x + \dfrac{1}{4}\sqrt{2}\operatorname{Arctan}\dfrac{1}{4}(2x-2)\sqrt{2}$

Use partial fractions. Watch out, as both factors in the denominator are Type II.

150. $\int \dfrac{x^3\,dx}{(x^2+4)^2} = \dfrac{2}{x^2+4} + \dfrac{1}{2}\ln\left(x^2+4\right)$

Use partial fractions.

151. $\int \dfrac{(x^4+1)\,dx}{x(x^2+1)^2} = \ln|x| + \dfrac{1}{x^2+1}$

Use partial fractions.

152. $\int \dfrac{(x^2+1)\,dx}{(x^2-2x+3)^2} = -\dfrac{1}{x^2-2x+3} + \dfrac{1}{2}\sqrt{2}\operatorname{Arctan}\dfrac{1}{4}(2x-2)\sqrt{2}$

Use partial fractions. Note that $(x^2-2x+3)^2$ is irreducible (Type II). Now you have to find the four constants!

153. $\int \dfrac{x\,dx}{\sqrt{x+1}} = -2\sqrt{x+1} + \dfrac{2}{3}\left(\sqrt{x+1}\right)^3$

Let $u = x+1$, $du = dx$. Then $x = u - 1$, and the integral becomes easy.

154. $\displaystyle\int x\sqrt{x-a}\;dx = \frac{2}{5}\left(\sqrt{x-a}\right)^5 + \frac{2}{3}\left(\sqrt{x-a}\right)^3 a$

Let $u = x - a$, $du = dx$. Then $x = u + a$, and the integral becomes easy.

155. $\displaystyle\int \frac{\sqrt{x+2}}{x+3}\;dx = 2\sqrt{x+2} - 2\mathrm{Arctan}\sqrt{x+2}$

Let $u = \sqrt{x+2}$, $u^2 = x + 2$. Then $2u\;du = dx$ and $x = u^2 - 2$ which means that $x + 3 = u^2 + 1$. The integral takes the form $\int \frac{2u^2\;du}{1+u^2}$. This one can be evaluated using a long division and two simple integrations.

156. $\displaystyle\int \frac{dx}{x\sqrt{x-1}} = 2\mathrm{Arctan}\sqrt{x-1}$

Let $u = \sqrt{x-1}$, $u^2 = x - 1$. Then $2u\;du = dx$ and so $x = 1 + u^2$. The integral takes the form $\int \frac{2u\;du}{u(1+u^2)}$ which is an arctangent function...

157. $\displaystyle\int \frac{dx}{x\sqrt{a^2-x^2}} = \frac{1}{a}\ln\left|\frac{a}{x} - \frac{\sqrt{a^2-x^2}}{x}\right|.$

Let $x = a\sin\theta$, $dx = a\cos\theta\;d\theta$. Then $\sqrt{a^2-x^2} = a\cos\theta$. After some simplification we find $a^{-1}\int \csc\theta\;d\theta = a^{-1}\ln|\csc\theta - \cot\theta|$. Finally, $\csc\theta = \frac{a}{x}$, $\cot\theta = \frac{\sqrt{a^2-x^2}}{x}$.

158. $\displaystyle\int \frac{dx}{x^2\sqrt{a^2-x^2}} = -\frac{1}{a^2 x}\sqrt{a^2-x^2}$

Let $x = a\sin\theta$, $dx = a\cos\theta\;d\theta$. Then $sqrt{a}^2 - x^2 = a\cos\theta$. After some simplification we find $a^{-2}\int \csc^2\theta\;d\theta = -a^{-2}\cot\theta$.

159. $\displaystyle\int x^3\sqrt{x^2+a^2}\;dx = \frac{1}{5}x^2\left(\sqrt{x^2+a^2}\right)^3 - \frac{2}{15}a^2\left(\sqrt{x^2+a^2}\right)^3$

Let $x = a\tan\theta$, $dx = a\sec^2\theta\;d\theta$. Then $\sqrt{x^2+a^2} = a\sec\theta$. After some simplification you're left with an integral with an integrand equal to $\sec^2\theta\,\tan^3\theta$. Use Example 372.

160. $\displaystyle\int \frac{dx}{x^2\sqrt{x^2+a^2}} = -\frac{1}{a^2 x}\sqrt{x^2+a^2}$

Let $x = a\tan\theta$, $dx = a\sec^2\theta\;d\theta$. Then $x^2 + a^2 = a^2\sec^2\theta$. After some simplification you're left with an integral with an integrand equal to $\csc\theta\,\cot\theta$. Its value is a cosecant function. Finally, use the fact that, in this case, $\csc\theta = \frac{\sqrt{x^2+a^2}}{x}$.

161. $\displaystyle\int \frac{dx}{\sqrt{x^2+a^2}} = \ln\left|x + \sqrt{x^2+a^2}\right|$

Let $x = a\tan\theta$, $dx = a\sec^2\theta\;d\theta$. Then $x^2 + a^2 = a^2\sec^2\theta$. After some simplification you're left with an integral of the form in Example 368.

162. $\displaystyle\int \frac{x^2\;dx}{\sqrt{x^2+a^2}} = \frac{1}{2}x\sqrt{x^2+a^2} - \frac{1}{2}a^2\ln\left|x + \sqrt{x^2+a^2}\right|$

Let $x = a\tan\theta$, $dx = a\sec^2\theta\;d\theta$. Then $x^2 + a^2 = a^2\sec^2\theta$. After some simplification you're left with an integral of the form in Example 370.

163. $\displaystyle\int \frac{x^2\;dx}{(x^2+a^2)^2} = -\frac{1}{2}\frac{x}{x^2+a^2} + \frac{1}{2a}\mathrm{Arctan}\frac{x}{a}$

Let $x = a\tan\theta$, $dx = a\sec^2\theta\;d\theta$. Then $x^2 + a^2 = a^2\sec^2\theta$. After some simplification you're left with the integral of the square of a sine function...

164. $\displaystyle\int x\cos x\;dx = \cos x + x\sin x$

Use Table integration

165. $\displaystyle\int x\sin x\;dx = \sin x - x\cos x$

Use Table integration

166. $\displaystyle\int x\sec^2 x\;dx = x\tan x + \ln|\cos x|$

Use Integration by Parts: Let $u = x$, $dv = \sec^2 x\;dx$. No need to use Table integration here.

167. $\int x \sec x \tan x \, dx = x \sec x - \ln|\sec x + \tan x|$

Use Integration by Parts: Let $u = x$, $dv = \sec x \tan x \, dx$. No need to use Table integration here.

168. $\int x^2 e^x \, dx = x^2 e^x - 2xe^x + 2e^x$

Use Table integration

169. $\int x^4 \ln x \, dx = \frac{1}{5} x^5 \ln x - \frac{1}{25} x^5$

Use Integration by Parts: Let $u = \ln x$, $dv = x^4 \, dx$. No need to use Table integration here.

170. $\int x^3 e^{x^2} \, dx = \frac{1}{2} x^2 e^{x^2} - \frac{1}{2} e^{x^2}$

Write the integrand as $x^3 e^{x^2} = x^2 \cdot x e^{x^2}$. Then use Integration by Parts with $u = x^2$, $dv = x e^{x^2} \, dx$. Use the substitution $v = x^2$ in the remaining integral.

171. $\int \sin^{-1} x \, dx = x\,\text{Arcsin}\, x + \sqrt{\left(1 - x^2\right)}$

Use Integration by Parts: Let $u = \text{Arctan}\, x$, $dv = dx$, followed by the substitution $u = 1 + x^2$, etc.

172. $\int \tan^{-1} x \, dx = x\,\text{Arctan}\, x - \frac{1}{2} \ln\left(x^2 + 1\right)$

Use Integration by Parts: Let $u = \text{Arctan}\, x$, $dv = dx$, followed by the substitution $u = 1 + x^2$, etc.

173. $\int (x-1)^2 \sin x \, dx = \cos x - 2\sin x + 2x\cos x - x^2 \cos x + 2x \sin x$

Use Table integration

174. $\int \sqrt{x^2 - a^2} \, dx = \frac{1}{2} x \sqrt{x^2 - a^2} - \frac{1}{2} a^2 \ln\left|x + \sqrt{x^2 - a^2}\right|$

Let $x = a\sec\theta$, $dx = a\sec\theta\,\tan\theta\,d\theta$. Then $\sqrt{x^2 - a^2} = a\tan\theta$, etc.

175. $\int \sqrt{x^2 + a^2} \, dx = \frac{1}{2} x \sqrt{x^2 + a^2} + \frac{1}{2} a^2 \ln\left|x + \sqrt{x^2 + a^2}\right|$

Let $x = a\tan\theta$, $dx = a\sec^2\theta\,d\theta$. Then $\sqrt{x^2 + a^2} = a\sec\theta$, etc.

176. $\int \frac{x^2 \, dx}{\sqrt{x^2 - a^2}} = \frac{1}{2} x \sqrt{x^2 - a^2} + \frac{1}{2} a^2 \ln\left|x + \sqrt{x^2 - a^2}\right|$

Let $x = a\sec\theta$, $dx = a\sec\theta\,\tan\theta\,d\theta$. Then $\sqrt{x^2 - a^2} = a\tan\theta$, etc.

177. $\int e^{2x} \sin 3x \, dx = -\frac{3}{13} e^{2x} \cos 3x + \frac{2}{13} e^{2x} \sin 3x$

Use Table integration

178. $\int e^{-x} \cos x \, dx = -\frac{1}{2} e^{-x} \cos x + \frac{1}{2} e^{-x} \sin x$

Use Table integration

179. $\int \sin 3x \cos 2x \, dx = -\frac{1}{10} \cos 5x - \frac{1}{2} \cos x$

Use a trig.. identity ... the one for $\sin A \cos B$, with $A = 3x$, $B = 2x$.

180. $\int_0^{\frac{\pi}{8}} \cos^3(2x) \sin(2x) \, dx = \frac{3}{32}$

Let $u = 2x$ first, $du = 2dx$, and follow this by the substitution $v = \cos u$, $dv = -\sin u \, du$ which allows for an easy calculation of an antiderivative.

181. $\int_1^4 \frac{2^{\sqrt{x}}}{2\sqrt{x}} \, dx = \frac{2}{\ln 2}$

Let $u = \sqrt{x}$. The result follows easily.

182. $\int_0^\infty x^3 e^{-2x} \, dx = \frac{3}{8}$

Use Table integration to find an antiderivative and then use L'Hospital's Rule (three times!).

183. $\displaystyle\int_{-\infty}^{+\infty} e^{-|x|} \, dx = 2$

Divide this integral into two parts, one where $x \geq 0$ (so that $|x| = x$), and one where $x < 0$ (so that $|x| = -x$). Then

$\displaystyle\int_{-\infty}^{+\infty} e^{-|x|} \, dx = \int_{-\infty}^{0} e^{x} \, dx + \int_{0}^{\infty} e^{-x} \, dx$ and the integrals are defined by a limit.

184. $\displaystyle\int_{0}^{\infty} \frac{4x}{1 + x^4} \, dx = \pi$

Let $u = x^2$, $du = 2x \, dx$. The integral becomes an Arctangent.

185. $\displaystyle\int_{-1}^{1} x^2 \cos(n\pi x) \, dx = \frac{4 \cos n\pi}{n^2 \pi^2}$, when $n \geq 1$, is an integer. Use Table integration.

186. $\displaystyle\frac{1}{2} \int_{-2}^{2} x^2 \sin\left(\frac{n\pi x}{2}\right) \, dx = 0$, when $n \geq 1$, is an integer. Use Table integration.

187. $\displaystyle\frac{1}{L} \int_{-L}^{L} (1 - x) \sin\left(\frac{n\pi x}{L}\right) \, dx = 2L \frac{\cos n\pi}{n\pi}$,
when $n \geq 1$, $L \neq 0$. Use Table integration.

188. $\displaystyle\int_{0}^{2} (x^3 + 1) \cos\left(\frac{n\pi x}{2}\right) \, dx = 6 \frac{8n^2\pi^2 \cos n\pi - 16 \cos n\pi + 16}{n^4 \pi^4}$,
when $n \geq 1$, is an integer. Use Table integration.

189. $\displaystyle\int_{-1}^{1} (2x + 1) \cos(n\pi x) \, dx = \frac{2}{n\pi} \sin n\pi = 0$,
when $n \geq 1$, is an integer. Use Table integration.

190. $\displaystyle\frac{1}{L} \int_{-L}^{L} \sin x \, \cos\left(\frac{n\pi x}{L}\right) \, dx = 0$,
when $n \geq 1$, is an integer and $L \neq 0$. Use Table integration.

191. Total demand over 10 years is

$$\int_{0}^{10} 500\left(20 + t \, e^{-0.1t}\right) \, dt = \int_{0}^{10} 10000 \, dt + 500 \int_{0}^{10} t \, e^{-0.1t} \, dt.$$

Now integrating by parts

$$\int t \, e^{-0.1t} \, dt = -10t \, e^{-0.1t} + 10 \int e^{-0.1t} \, dt = -10t \, e^{-0.1t} + 10\left(-10e^{-0.1t}\right).$$

Thus total demand $= \left[10,000t + 500\{-10t \, e^{-0.1t} + 10(-10e^{-0.1t})\}\right]_{0}^{10} = \left[10,000t - 5000te^{-0.1t} - 50,000e^{-0.1t}\right]_{0}^{10} =$
$100,000 - 50,000e^{-1} - 50,000e^{-1} - (0 - 0 - 50,000) = 150,000 - 100,000e^{-1} = 113212.1 \approx 113212$
units.

192. (a) Use partial fractions.
$$\frac{1}{y(y - 10)} = \frac{A}{y} + \frac{B}{10 - y} = \frac{A(10 - y) + By}{y(10 - y)}$$

If $y = 0$, then $10A = 1$, so $A = \frac{1}{10}$. If $y = 10$, then $10B = 1$, and $B = \frac{1}{10}$. Therefore,

$$\int \frac{1}{y(y - 10)} dy = \frac{1}{10} \int \frac{dy}{y} + \frac{1}{10} \int \frac{dy}{10 - y} dy$$

$$= \frac{1}{10} \, ln|y| - \frac{1}{10} \, ln|10 - y| + C = \frac{1}{10} \, ln\left|\frac{y}{10 - y}\right| + C$$

Thus
$$t = \frac{25}{10} \, ln\left|\frac{y}{10 - y}\right| + C$$

When $t = 0$, $y = 1$, so $0 = 2.5ln\frac{1}{9} + C = 2.5(ln\ 1 - ln\ 9) + C = -2.5ln\ 9 + C$. Thus $C = 2.5ln\ 9$
and
$$t = 2.5ln\left|\frac{y}{10 - y}\right| + 2.5ln\ 9 = 2.5ln\left|\frac{9y}{10 - y}\right|$$

(b) When $y = 4$, $t = 2.5ln\ \frac{4 \times 9}{6} = 4.479$ hours.

(c) From (a), $\frac{t}{2.5} = ln\ \frac{9y}{10 - y}$, so $e^{\frac{t}{2.5}} = \frac{9y}{10 - y}$, and $(10 - y)e^{0.4t} = 9y$, so $10e^{0.4t} = 9y + ye^{0.4t} = y(9 + e^{0.4t})$. Thus

$$y = \frac{10e^{0.4t}}{9 + e^{0.4t}} = \frac{10}{1 + e^{-0.4t}}$$

(d) At $t = 10$, $y = \frac{10}{1 + 9e^{-4}} = 8.58$ gm.

Chapter 8

Solutions

8.1

8.2   Exercise Sets 42, 43

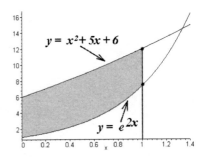

1. Vertical slice area $= (0 - (x^2 - 1))\, dx = (1 - x^2)\, dx$.

2. Horizontal slice area $\sqrt{y + 1}\, dy$.

3. Vertical slice area $= ((x^2 + 5x + 6) - (e^{2x}))\, dx = (x^2 + 5x + 6 - e^{2x})\, dx$. Note that e^{2x} is smaller than $x^2 + 5x + 6$ on this interval. See the figure in the margin, on the left.

4. Sketch the region bounded by these curves. You should get a region like the one below:

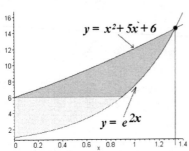

Now, using Newton's Method with $x_0 = 1.5$ as an initial estimate, $n = 3$, and $f(x) = x^2 + 5x + 6 - e^{2x}$, we obtain the approximate value of the zero of f as 1.3358. The common value of these curves at this point is given by $e^{2(1.3358)} \approx 14.46$. This represents the point of intersection of the curves $x^2 + 5x + 6$ and e^{2x}, in the interval $[0, 2]$. Beyond $x = 2$ we see that these curves get further apart so they cannot intersect once again. Since we are dealing with horizontal slices we need to write down the inverse function of each of these functions. For example, the inverse function of $y = x^2 + 5x + 6$ is given by solving for x in terms of y using the quadratic formula. This gives

$$ x = \frac{-5 \pm \sqrt{1 + 4y}}{2}. $$

Since $x \geq 0$ here, we must choose the $+$-sign. On the other hand, the inverse function of the function whose values are $y = e^{2x}$ is simply given by $x = (\ln y)/2$. So, the area of a typical horizontal slice in the darker region above is given by

$$ \left(\frac{\ln y}{2} - \frac{-5 + \sqrt{1 + 4y}}{2} \right)\, dy, $$

and this formula is valid provided $6 \leq y \leq 14.46$.

If the horizontal slice is in the lighter area above, then its area is given by

$$ \left(\frac{\ln y}{2} - 0 \right)\, dy = \left(\frac{\ln y}{2} \right)\, dy, $$

and this formula is valid whenever $0 \leq y \leq 6$.

As a check, note that both slice formulae agree when $y = 6$.

5. The horizontal line $y = 5$ intersects with the graph of $y = e^{2x}$ at the point $P \equiv (\frac{\ln 5}{2}, 5)$, approximately $(0.8047, 5)$. Draw a vertical line through P. The area of a typical vertical slice on the left of this line is

$$((x^2 + 5x + 6) - 5)\ dx \equiv (x^2 + 5x + 1)\ dx.$$

On the right of this line we have

$$(x^2 + 5x + 6 - e^{2x})\ dx$$

instead.

hugeExercise Set 43

1. Area $= \displaystyle\int_{-1}^{1} (1 - x^2)\ dx = \dfrac{4}{3}$.

2. Area $= \displaystyle\int_{-2}^{2} (4 - x^2)\ dx = \left(4x - \dfrac{x^3}{3}\right)\Big|_{-2}^{2} = \dfrac{32}{3}$.

3. Area $= \displaystyle\int_{0}^{1} (x^2 + 5x + 6 - e^{2x})dx = \left(\dfrac{x^3}{3} + \dfrac{5}{2}x^2 + 6x - \dfrac{e^{2x}}{2}\right)\Big|_{0}^{1} = \dfrac{28}{3} - \dfrac{e^2}{2}$
   ≈ 5.63881.

4. Area $= \displaystyle\int_{0}^{1.3358} (x^2 + 5x + 6 - e^{2x})\ dx \approx 6.539$.

5. Area $= \displaystyle\int_{0}^{1} ye^y\, dy = \left(ye^y - e^y\right)\Big|_{0}^{1} = 1$.

6. $\pi^2 - 4$. This curve lies above the $x-$axis because $\sin x \geq 0$ for $0 \leq x \leq \pi$. It follows that $x^2 \sin x \geq 0$ for $0 \leq x \leq \pi$, and so the area is given by the definite integral

$$\text{Area} = \int_{0}^{\pi} x^2 \sin x\ dx = \pi^2 - 4,$$

where the Table method of Integration by Parts is used to evaluate it. In particular, we note that an antiderivative is given by

$$\int^{x} t^2 \sin t\ dt = -x^2 \cos x + 2x \sin x + 2 \cos x.$$

7. Area $= \displaystyle\int_{0}^{\pi} \cos^2 x \sin x\ dx = -\dfrac{\cos^3 x}{3}\Big|_{0}^{\pi} = \dfrac{2}{3}$.

8. Using the Table method of Integration by Parts (since this is a three-row problem), we find

$$\int \sin 3x \cdot \cos 5x\ dx = \dfrac{5}{16} \sin 5x \cdot \sin 3x + \dfrac{3}{16} \cos 3x \cdot \cos 5x + C.$$

Alternatively, this integral can be computed as follows:

$$\int \sin 3x \cdot \cos 5x\ dx = \int \dfrac{1}{2}(\sin 8x - \sin 2x)\ dx = -\dfrac{1}{16} \cos 8x + \dfrac{1}{4} \cos 2x + C.$$

(Don't be fooled by its different look! This is the same answer as the above.) Notice that, for x in the interval $[\pi/10, 3\pi/10]$, $3x$ is in $[3\pi/10, 9\pi/10]$ and hence $\sin 3x$ is positive. However, for the same range of x, $5x$ is in $[\pi/2, 3\pi/2]$ and hence $\cos 3x$ is negative or zero. Hence the area of the region is the absolute value of

$$\int_{\pi/10}^{3\pi/10} \sin 3x \cdot \cos 5x\ dx = \left(\dfrac{5}{16} \sin 5x \cdot \sin 3x + \dfrac{3}{16} \cos 3x \cdot \cos 5x\right)\Big|_{\pi/10}^{3\pi/10}$$

$$= -\dfrac{5}{16}\left(\sin \dfrac{9}{10}\pi + \sin \dfrac{3}{10}\pi\right) = -\dfrac{5\sqrt{5}}{32} \approx -0.35.$$

Here we use the facts that $\cos \frac{\pi}{2} = 0$, $\cos \frac{3\pi}{2} = 0$, $\sin \frac{\pi}{2} = 1$ and $\sin \frac{3\pi}{2} = -1$. It turns out that $\sin \frac{9}{10}\pi + \sin \frac{3}{10}\pi = \frac{\sqrt{5}}{2}$, which is very hard to prove!

9. $\dfrac{9}{2}$. Refer to the graph below:

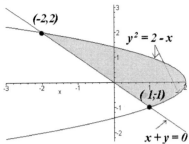

The points of intersection of these two graphs are given by setting $y = -x$ into the expression $x + y^2 = 2$ and solving for x. This gives the two points, $x = 1$ and $x = -2$. Note that if we use vertical slices we will need two integrals. Solving for x in terms of y gives $x = -y$ and $x = 2 - y^2$ and the limits of integration are then $y = -1$ and $y = 2$. The coordinates of the endpoints of a typical horizontal slice are given by $(-y, y)$ and $(2 - y^2, y)$. So, the corresponding integral is given by

$$\text{Area} = \int_{-1}^{2} (2 - y^2 + y) \, dy = \frac{9}{2}.$$

10. The required area is

$$\int_{-2}^{2} (y^2 - (y - 5)) \, dy = \left(\frac{y^3}{3} - \frac{y^2}{2} + 5y \right) \Big|_{-2}^{2} = \frac{76}{3}.$$

11. 4 units. Note the symmetry: Since, f is an *even function*, (see Chapter 5), its graph over the interval $[-\pi, \pi]$ is symmetric with respect to the y-axis and so, since f is "V"-shaped and positive, the area is given by

$$\text{Area} = 2 \times (area \ to \ the \ right \ of \ x = 0),$$

and this gives

$$\text{Area} = 2 \int_{0}^{\pi} (\sin x) \, dx = 4 \ units.$$

12. $4\sqrt{2}$. The graph on the right represents the two curves over the interval $[\frac{\pi}{4}, \frac{9\pi}{4}]$:
Using the symmetry in the graph we see that

$$\text{Area} = 2 \int_{\frac{\pi}{4}}^{\frac{5\pi}{4}} (\sin x - \cos x) \, dx = 4\sqrt{2},$$

since $\cos \dfrac{5\pi}{4} = -\dfrac{\sqrt{2}}{2}$, $\sin \dfrac{5\pi}{4} = -\dfrac{\sqrt{2}}{2}$.

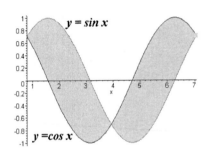

8.3   Exercise Set 44

1. Using a vertical slice: $\int_{0}^{1} \pi x^2 \, dx$;

   using a horizontal slice $\int_{0}^{1} (1 - y) \cdot 2\pi y \, dy$.

2. Using a vertical slice: $\int_{0}^{1} (x - x^2) \cdot 2\pi x \, dx$;

   using a horizontal slice: $\int_{0}^{1} \pi (y - y^2) \, dy$.

3. Using a vertical slice: $\int_{0}^{1} 3\pi \, x^2 \, dx$; (we do not use horizontal slices because this method is too complicated for the present problem.)

4. Using a vertical slice: $\int_{0}^{2} 2x \cdot 2\pi x \, dx$;

   using a horizontal slice: $\int_{0}^{1} \pi (2^2 - (y/2)^2) \, dy$.

5. Using a vertical slice: $\int_{0}^{1} (2x - x) \cdot 2\pi x \, dx = \int_{0}^{1} 2\pi x^2 \, dx$.

   Using a horizontal slice:
   $$\frac{3\pi}{4} \int_{0}^{1} y^2 \, dy + \int_{1}^{2} \pi \left(1 - \frac{y^2}{4} \right) \, dy.$$

6. $\pi/3$; $\pi/6$; 8π; $\frac{32}{3}\pi$; $\frac{2}{3}\pi$.

8.4   Exercise Set 45

1. 2. Since $y' = 0$, it follows that $L = \int_0^2 \sqrt{1}\ dx = 2$.

2. $4\sqrt{2}$. Since $y' = 1$, it follows that $L = \int_0^4 \sqrt{1+1}\ dx = 4\sqrt{2}$.

3. $2\sqrt{5}$. Here $y' = 2$, and so $L = \int_{-1}^1 \sqrt{1+4}\ dx = 2\sqrt{5}$.

4. $2\sqrt{2}$. Now $x'(y) = 1$. So, $L = \int_0^2 \sqrt{2}\ dy = 3\sqrt{2}$.

5. $3\sqrt{2}$. This is the same as $y = x + 3$, so $y' = 1$, and it follows that $L = \int_{-2}^1 \sqrt{2}\ dx = 3\sqrt{2}$.

6. $\dfrac{52}{3}$. Now $y'(x) = \sqrt{x}$ and so (if we set $u = 1 + x$, $du = dx$) we see that $L = \int_0^8 \sqrt{1+x}\ dx = \dfrac{52}{3}$.

7. $\dfrac{1}{2}\sqrt{5} + \dfrac{1}{4}\ln\left(\sqrt{5}+2\right)$. In this case, $L = \int_0^1 \sqrt{1+4x^2}\ dx$. Use the substitution $2x = \tan\theta$, $2\ dx = \sec^2\theta\ d\theta$, and the usual identity to obtain an

    antiderivative in the form $\dfrac{1}{2}\int \sec^3\theta\ d\theta$. Now, see Example 369 for this integral. We have, $\dfrac{1}{2}\int \sec^3\theta\ d\theta = \dfrac{1}{4}\left(\tan\theta\sec\theta + \ln|\sec\theta + \tan\theta|\right)$. But $\tan\theta = 2x$, and so $\sec\theta = \sqrt{1+4x^2}$. Thus, $L = \int_0^1 \sqrt{1+4x^2}\ dx = $

    $\dfrac{1}{4}\left(2x\sqrt{1+4x^2} + \ln|\sqrt{1+4x^2} + 2x|\right)\Big|_0^1 = \dfrac{1}{4}\cdot\left(2\sqrt{5} + \ln(2+\sqrt{5})\right)$, and the rest follows.

8. $\sqrt{65} + \dfrac{1}{8}\ln\left(8+\sqrt{65}\right)$. Use the method of Example 7 above. The arc length is given by $L = \int_0^2 \sqrt{1+16x^2}\ dx$.

    Now use the substitution $4x = \tan\theta$, $4\ dx = \sec^2\theta\ d\theta$, and an antiderivative will look like $\dfrac{1}{4}\int \sec^3\theta\ d\theta$.

    Finally, we see that

    $$L = \int_0^2 \sqrt{1+16x^2}\ dx = \dfrac{1}{8}\left(4x\sqrt{1+16x^2} + \ln|\sqrt{1+16x^2} + 4x|\right)\Big|_0^2 = \dfrac{1}{8}\cdot\left(8\sqrt{65} + \ln(8+\sqrt{65})\right),$$

    and the result follows.

9. $\dfrac{1}{2}\sqrt{17} + \dfrac{1}{8}\ln(4+\sqrt{17})$. See Exercise 8, above. We know that $L = \int_0^1 \sqrt{1+16x^2}\ dx$. Use the substitution $4x = \tan\theta$, $4\ dx = \sec^2\theta\ d\theta$, and the usual identity to obtain an antiderivative in the form

    $\dfrac{1}{4}\int \sec^3\theta\ d\theta$. Reverting back to the original variables, we get,

    $$L = \int_0^1 \sqrt{1+16x^2}\ dx = \dfrac{1}{8}\left(4x\sqrt{1+16x^2} + \ln|\sqrt{1+16x^2} + 4x|\right)\Big|_0^1 = \dfrac{1}{8}\cdot\left(4\sqrt{17} + \ln(4+\sqrt{17})\right) = $$
    $\dfrac{1}{2}\sqrt{17} + \dfrac{1}{8}\ln(4+\sqrt{17})$.

10. $\dfrac{181}{9}$. Note that $1 + y'(x)^2 = 1 + \left(x^6 - \dfrac{1}{2} + \dfrac{1}{16x^6}\right) = \left(x^3 + \dfrac{1}{4x^3}\right)^2$.

    It follows that the expression for the arc length is given by $L = \int_1^3 \left(x^3 + \dfrac{1}{4x^3}\right)\ dx$, giving the stated result.

11. 4π. Here, $x'(t) = -2\sin t$, $y'(t) = 2\cos t$ so that the length of the arc is given by $L = \int_0^{2\pi} \sqrt{4\sin^2 t + 4\cos^2 t}\ dt = \int_0^{2\pi} \sqrt{4\cdot 1}\ dt = 2\cdot 2\pi = 4\pi$.

12. 2π. Now, $x'(t) = -\sin t$, $y'(t) = -\cos t$ so that the length of the arc is given by $L = \int_0^{2\pi} \sqrt{\sin^2 t + \cos^2 t}\ dt = \int_0^{2\pi} \sqrt{1}\ dt = 1\cdot 2\pi = 2\pi$.

13. $\sqrt{2}$. In this example, $x'(t) = 1$, $y'(t) = -1$ so that the length of the arc is given by $L = \int_0^1 \sqrt{1+1}\,dt =$

$$\int_0^1 \sqrt{2}\,dt = \sqrt{2}.$$

14. $\frac{3}{2}$. Use the Fundamental Theorem of Calculus to show that $y'(x) = \sqrt{x^2 - 1}$. Then, $\sqrt{1 + (y'(x))^2} =$

$\sqrt{x^2} = x$. So, $L = \int_1^2 x\,dx = \frac{3}{2}$.

15. $\sqrt{2}$. Once again, use the Fundamental Theorem of Calculus to show

that $y'(x) = \sqrt{\cos 2x}$. Then, $\sqrt{1 + (y'(x))^2} = \sqrt{1 + \cos 2x} = \sqrt{2\cos^2 x}$, by a trig. identity (which

one?). So, $L = \int_0^{\pi/2} \sqrt{2\cos^2 x}\,dx = \sqrt{2}\int_0^{\pi/2} \cos x\,dx = \sqrt{2}$.

16. 10.602. See Example 465 except that we solve for x in terms of $y > 0$ (because the given interval is a $y-$interval). The length L is then given by doubling the basic integral over half the curve, that is,

$$L = 2\int_{-1}^1 \sqrt{\frac{4 - 3y^2}{4(1 - y^2)}}\,dy \approx \int_{-0.99}^{0.99} \sqrt{\frac{4 - 3y^2}{4(1 - y^2)}}\,dy \approx 5.3010.$$

17. 3.3428. The length L is given by an integral of the form $L = \int_1^4 \frac{\sqrt{1 + x^2}}{x}\,dx$.

We use a trigonometric substitution $x = \tan\theta$, $dx = \sec^2\theta\,d\theta$. Then, $\sqrt{1 + x^2} = \sec\theta$ and an antiderivative is given by

$$\int \frac{\sec^3\theta}{\tan\theta}\,d\theta = \int \frac{\sec\theta}{\tan\theta}\left(1 + \tan^2\theta\right)\,d\theta = \int \frac{\sec\theta}{\tan\theta}\,d\theta + \int \sec\theta\,\tan\theta\,d\theta =$$

$$\int \csc\theta\,d\theta + \sec\theta = \ln|\csc\theta - \cot\theta| + \sec\theta.$$

Since $x = \tan\theta$ it follows that $\csc\theta = \frac{\sec\theta}{\tan\theta} = \frac{\sqrt{1+x^2}}{x}$, $\cot\theta = \frac{1}{x}$. So an antiderivative is given

by $\int \frac{\sqrt{1+x^2}}{x}\,dx = \ln\left|\frac{\sqrt{1+x^2}}{x} - \frac{1}{x}\right| + \sqrt{1+x^2}$. Finally, we see that $L = \int_1^4 \frac{\sqrt{1+x^2}}{x}\,dx =$

$$\left(\ln\left|\frac{\sqrt{1+x^2}}{x} - \frac{1}{x}\right| + \sqrt{1+x^2}\right)\Bigg|_1^4$$

$$= \left(\ln\left|\frac{\sqrt{17}}{4} - \frac{1}{4}\right| + \sqrt{17}\right) - \left(\ln\left|\sqrt{2} - 1\right| + \sqrt{2}\right) = \sqrt{17} - \sqrt{2} + \ln\left|\frac{\sqrt{17} - 1}{4}\right| - \ln\left|\sqrt{2} - 1\right| \approx 3.3428.$$

18. $\ln(1 + \sqrt{2}) \approx 0.8813$. Here, $y'(x) = \tan x$ and so $\sqrt{1 + y'(x)^2} = \sqrt{1 + \tan^2 x} = \sqrt{\sec^2 x} = \sec x$. So, the arc length is given by

$$\int_0^{\pi/4} \sec x\,dx = \ln|\sec x + \tan x|\Bigg|_0^{\pi/4} = \ln(\sqrt{2} + 1) - \ln(1 + 0) = \ln(1 + \sqrt{2}).$$

19. $\frac{1}{2}\sqrt{5} - \frac{1}{4}\ln(\sqrt{5} - 2)$. See Exercise 7, above for the evaluation of the integral. Note that $-\frac{1}{4}\ln(\sqrt{5} - 2) = \frac{1}{4}\ln(\sqrt{5} + 2)$.

20. Follow the hints.

8.5 Exercise Set 46

1. 3.75. Set m_1 at $x_1 = 0$ and m_2 at $x_2 = 5$. Then $\overline{x} = \frac{m_1 x_1 + m_2 x_2}{m_1 + m_2} = 3.75$.

2. 1.33. Set m_1 at $x_1 = 0$, m_2 at $x_2 = 1$ and m_3 at $x_3 = 2$. Then $\overline{x} = 1.33$.

3. $(\overline{x}.\overline{y}) = \left(\frac{5}{12}, \frac{1}{3}\right)$. Note that $\overline{x} = \frac{\sum m_i x_i}{\sum m_i}$ and $\overline{y} = \frac{\sum m_i y_i}{\sum m_i}$ where (x_i, y_i)

   are the coordinates of m_i. In this case, $\overline{x} = \frac{4 \cdot 0 + 5 \cdot 1}{12} = \frac{5}{12}$. Similarly, $\overline{y} = \frac{4 \cdot 1 + 0}{12} = \frac{1}{3}$. Note that even though the system of masses is at the vertices of an isosceles triangle, the center of mas is not along the bisector of the right-angle (which is the line of symmetry). This doesn't contradict the Symmetry Principle since the masses are not all the same!

4. $(\overline{x}.\overline{y}) = \left(1, \frac{\sqrt{3}}{3}\right)$. As before, $\overline{x} = \frac{\sum m_i x_i}{\sum m_i}$ and $\overline{y} = \frac{\sum m_i y_i}{\sum m_i}$ where (x_i, y_i)

are the coordinates of m_i. Here, $\overline{x} = \dfrac{0 + 6 + 3}{9} = 1$. Similarly, $\overline{y} = \dfrac{0 + 0 + 3\sqrt{3}}{9} = \dfrac{\sqrt{3}}{3}$. In this exercise the masses are all the same and the triangle is equilateral, so (by the Symmetry Principle) the center of mass must lie along the line of symmetry (which it does), that is, it must lie on the line $x = 1$ which bisects the base of the triangle.

5. $\left(0, \dfrac{4R}{3\pi}\right)$. The total mass $m = \dfrac{\pi R^2 \delta}{2}$ since we are dealing with one-half the area of a circle and δ is constant. This use of geometry saves us from actually *calculating* the mass integral which looks like $\displaystyle\int_{-R}^{R} \sqrt{R^2 - x^2}\, \delta\, dx$. Next, the moment about the $y-$axis is given by $M_y = \displaystyle\int_{-R}^{R} \overline{x}_{slice}\, \delta\, dA = \delta \displaystyle\int_{-R}^{R} x\sqrt{R^2 - x^2}\, dx$. Now, let $x = R\cos\theta$, etc. But even simpler is the remark that the integrand, $x\sqrt{R^2 - x^2}$, is an *odd function* defined over a symmetric interval and so its integral must be zero. Either way, this gives $M_x = \delta \displaystyle\int_{-R}^{R} x\sqrt{R^2 - x^2}\, dx = 0$ and so $\overline{x} = 0$, *i.e.*, the center of mass lies along the axis of symmetry (which is the $y-$axis, since δ is constant).

Similarly we find the moment about the $x-$axis, $M_x = \displaystyle\int_{-R}^{R} \overline{y}_{slice}\, \delta\, dA = \dfrac{\delta}{2} \displaystyle\int_{-R}^{R} \left(R^2 - x^2\right)\, dx = \dfrac{\delta}{2}\dfrac{4R^3}{3} = \dfrac{2R^3\delta}{3}$. It follows that the $y-$coordinate, $\overline{y}$, of the center of mass is given by $\overline{y} = \dfrac{M_x}{m} = \dfrac{2R^3\delta}{3} \cdot \dfrac{2}{\pi R^2 \delta} = \dfrac{4R}{3\pi}$.

6. $\left(\dfrac{b}{2}, \dfrac{h}{2}\right)$. Use of geometry shows us that the total mass is its area times its density, that is, $m = bh\delta$. Next, $\overline{x} = \displaystyle\int_0^b \overline{x}_{slice}\, \delta\, dA = \dfrac{1}{bh\delta} \displaystyle\int_0^b xh\delta\, dx = \dfrac{b}{2}$. Similarly, $\overline{y} = \displaystyle\int_0^b \overline{y}_{slice}\, \delta\, dA = \dfrac{1}{bh\delta} \displaystyle\int_0^b \dfrac{h}{2}h\delta\, dx = \dfrac{h}{2}$.

7. $\left(0, \dfrac{2}{3}\right)$. The region is an inverted triangle with a vertex at the origin and opposite side equal to 2 units. Its total mass is its area times its density, which, in this case, is δ. So, $m = \delta$. Let $f(x) = 1$ and $g(x) = 1 - |x|$, over $[-1, 1]$. Note that the region can be described by means of these two graphs. Also, $f(x) \geq g(x)$ and so we can use the formulae already derived for the center of mass. So, $\overline{x} = \dfrac{1}{\delta} \displaystyle\int_{-1}^{1} \overline{x}_{slice}\, \delta\, dA = \dfrac{1}{\delta} \displaystyle\int_{-1}^{1} x\left(1 - |x|\right)\delta\, dx = \dfrac{1}{\delta} \displaystyle\int_{-1}^{0} x\left(1 + x\right)\delta\, dx + \dfrac{1}{\delta} \displaystyle\int_{0}^{1} x\left(1 - x\right)\delta\, dx = 0$.

Next, $\overline{y} = \dfrac{1}{\delta} \displaystyle\int_{-1}^{1} \overline{y}_{slice}\, \delta\, dA = \dfrac{1}{\delta} \displaystyle\int_{-1}^{1} \left(\dfrac{1 + |x|}{2}\right)\left(1 - |x|\right)\delta\, dx = \dfrac{1}{2\delta} \displaystyle\int_{-1}^{1} \left(1 - x^2\right)\delta\, dx = \dfrac{2}{3}$.

8. $\left(-\dfrac{1}{12}, \dfrac{1}{3}\right)$. The total mass is $m = \displaystyle\int_{-1}^{1} \delta(x)\, dx = \displaystyle\int_{-1}^{1} (1 - x)\, dx = 2$. Next, $\overline{x} = \dfrac{1}{2} \displaystyle\int_{-1}^{1} \overline{x}_{slice}\, \delta\, dA = \dfrac{1}{2} \displaystyle\int_{-1}^{1} x\left(1 - |x|\right)(1 - x)\, dx = \dfrac{1}{2} \displaystyle\int_{-1}^{0} x\left(1 + x\right)(1 - x)\, dx + \dfrac{1}{2} \displaystyle\int_{0}^{1} x\left(1 - x\right)(1 - x)\, dx = \left(\dfrac{1}{2}\right) \cdot \left(\dfrac{-1}{6}\right) = -\dfrac{1}{12}$.

Similarly, $\overline{y} = \dfrac{1}{2} \displaystyle\int_{-1}^{1} \overline{y}_{slice}\, \delta\, dA = \dfrac{1}{2} \displaystyle\int_{-1}^{1} \left(\dfrac{1 + |x|}{2}\right)\left(1 - |x|\right)(1 - x)\, dx = \dfrac{1}{4} \displaystyle\int_{-1}^{1} \left(1 - x^2\right)(1 - x)\, dx = \dfrac{1}{3}$.

9. $\left(\dfrac{3}{5}, \dfrac{3}{8}\right)$. The total mass, $m = \delta \displaystyle\int_0^1 \sqrt{x}\, dx = \dfrac{2\delta}{3}$. So, $\overline{x} = \dfrac{3}{2\delta} \displaystyle\int_0^1 \overline{x}_{slice}\, \delta\, dA = \dfrac{3}{2} \displaystyle\int_0^1 x\sqrt{x}\, dx = \dfrac{3}{2} \displaystyle\int_0^1 x^{3/2}\, dx = \dfrac{3}{5}$.

Furthermore, $\overline{y} = \dfrac{3}{2\delta} \displaystyle\int_0^1 \overline{y}_{slice}\, \delta\, dA = \dfrac{3}{2} \displaystyle\int_0^1 \dfrac{\sqrt{x}}{2}\sqrt{x}\, dx = \dfrac{3}{4} \displaystyle\int_0^1 x\, dx = \dfrac{3}{8}$.

10. $\left(\dfrac{3}{2}, \dfrac{3}{10}\right)$. The total mass, $m = \delta \displaystyle\int_0^2 \dfrac{x^2}{4}\, dx = \dfrac{2\delta}{3}$. So, $\overline{x} = \dfrac{3}{2\delta} \displaystyle\int_0^2 \overline{x}_{slice}\, \delta\, dA = \dfrac{3}{2\delta} \displaystyle\int_0^2 x\delta\dfrac{x^2}{4}\, dx = \dfrac{3}{8} \displaystyle\int_0^2 x^3\, dx = \dfrac{3}{2}$.

Similarly,

$$\overline{y} = \frac{3}{2\delta} \int_0^2 \overline{y}_{slice}\ \delta\ dA = \frac{3}{2\delta} \int_0^2 \delta\ \frac{x^2}{8}\ \frac{x^2}{4}\ dx = \frac{3}{2\cdot 32} \int_0^2 x^4\ dx = \frac{3}{10}.$$

11. $\left(\frac{1}{2}, \frac{\pi}{4}\right)$. The graph of this function is positive on $[0,1]$. The total mass, $m = \delta \int_0^1 2\ \sin(\pi x)\ dx =$

$$2\delta \left(-\frac{\cos(\pi x)}{\pi}\right)\Big|_0^1 = \frac{4\delta}{\pi}.\ \text{So,}$$

$$\overline{x} = \frac{\pi}{4\delta} \int_0^1 \overline{x}_{slice}\ \delta\ dA = \frac{\pi}{4\delta} \int_0^1 x\ 2\sin(\pi x)\ \delta\ dx$$

$$= \frac{\pi}{2} \int_0^1 x\ \sin(\pi x)\ dx = \frac{1}{2}.$$

Similarly,

$$\overline{y} = \frac{\pi}{4\delta} \int_0^1 \overline{y}_{slice}\ \delta\ dA = \frac{\pi}{4\delta} \int_0^1 \frac{2\sin(\pi x)}{2}\ \delta\ 2\sin(\pi x)\ dx = \frac{\pi}{2} \int_0^1 \sin^2(\pi x)\ dx = \frac{\pi}{2} \int_0^1 \frac{1-\cos(2\pi x)}{2}\ dx =$$

$\frac{\pi}{4}$. Note the symmetry about the line $x = 1/2$ so that the center of mass must lie along this line.

12. $\left(\frac{2(e^2-1)}{1+e^2}, \frac{3e^4+1}{8(1+e^2)}\right)$. The total mass is $m = \int_0^2 x\ \delta\ e^x\ dx = \delta \int_0^2 x\ e^x\ dx = (e^2+1)\delta$. Next,

$$\overline{x} = \frac{1}{1+e^2} \int_0^2 x^2\ e^x\ dx = \frac{2e^2-2}{1+e^2}.\ \text{Finally, one more application of}$$

Integration by Parts (or the Table Method)

$$\overline{y} = \frac{1}{2(1+e^2)} \int_0^2 x\ e^{2x}\ dx = \frac{3e^4+1}{8(1+e^2)}.$$

13. $\left(0, \frac{11}{3\sqrt{3}+2\pi}\right)$. Since $\delta = 2$, the total mass is $m = \int_{-1}^1 \sqrt{4-x^2}\ \delta\ dx = 2 \int_{-1}^1 \sqrt{4-x^2}\ dx =$

$2\sqrt{3} + \frac{4\pi}{3}$, where we used the trig. substitution $x = 2\sin\theta$, etc.

The geometric area is not so easy to calculate in this case, so we return to the integral definition. Now, because of symmetry about the line $x = 0$ and since δ is constant, we must have
$\overline{x} = 0$.

Furthermore,

$$\overline{y} = \frac{3}{6\sqrt{3}+4\pi} \int_{-1}^1 \frac{\sqrt{4-x^2}}{2}\ \sqrt{4-x^2}\ 2\ dx = \frac{3}{6\sqrt{3}+4\pi} \int_{-1}^1 (4-x^2)\ dx = \frac{3}{6\sqrt{3}+4\pi}\cdot\frac{22}{3} =$$

$\frac{11}{3\sqrt{3}+2\pi}.$

14. $\left(\frac{6}{5}, -\frac{2}{5}\right)$, see the solved example. The total mass is

$$m = \int_0^2 (6x-3x^2)\ 2x\ dx = 8.\ \text{Next,}\ \overline{x} = \frac{1}{8} \int_0^2 x\ (6x-3x^2)\ 2x\ dx = \frac{6}{5}.\ \text{Similarly,}$$

$$\overline{y} = \frac{1}{8} \int_0^2 \frac{x^2-2x}{2}\ (6x-3x^2)\ 2x\ dx = -\frac{2}{5}.$$

8.6 Chapter Exercises

1. $\frac{\pi}{3} = \int_0^1 \pi\ y^2\ dy = \int_0^1 2\pi\ x(1-x)\ dx.$

2. $\frac{\pi}{3} = \int_0^1 \pi\ x^2\ dx = \int_0^1 2\pi\ y(1-y)\ dy.$

3. $\frac{\pi}{3} = \int_0^1 \pi\ y^2\ dy = \int_0^{1/2} \pi\ (1-4x^2)\ dx.$

4. $\frac{4\pi}{3} = \int_0^1 4\pi\ x^2\ dx = \int_0^2 \pi\ \left(1-\frac{y^2}{4}\right)\ dy.$

5. $\frac{16\pi}{3}$ (you'll need two terms if you use horizontal slices here).

$$\frac{16\pi}{3} = \int_0^2 2\pi\ x^2\ dx$$

$$= \frac{3\pi}{4} \int_0^2 y^2 \, dy + \pi \int_2^4 \left(4 - \frac{y^2}{4}\right) \, dy.$$

6. $\dfrac{8\pi}{5} = 4\pi \displaystyle\int_0^1 y^{3/2} \, dy = \int_{-1}^1 \left(1 - x^4\right) \, dx.$

7. $\dfrac{\pi^2}{2} = \pi \displaystyle\int_0^\pi \sin^2 x \, dx = 4\pi \int_0^1 y \, \text{Arcsin} \, y \, dy.$

8. $\pi^2 - 2\pi = 2\pi \displaystyle\int_0^{\pi/2} x \cos x \, dx = \pi \int_0^1 \text{Arccos}^2 y \, dy.$ This last integral is very hard to evaluate! Try the substitution $y = \cos u$, $dy = -\sin u \, du$. Then use the Table method and then back-substitute. The first intergal in x is evaluated using the Table method.

9. $\dfrac{\pi}{4}(e^2 - 1) = \pi \displaystyle\int_0^1 x^2 e^{2x} \, dx.$ You can't use horizontal slices here because it is almost impossible to solve for x in terms of y in the expression for $y = xe^x$. Use the Table method to evaluate the integral.

10. $2\pi \left(1 - \dfrac{5}{e^2}\right) = 2\pi \displaystyle\int_0^2 x^2 e^{-x} \, dx.$ Use the Table method to evaluate the integral.

11. $\dfrac{3\pi}{10} = \pi \displaystyle\int_0^1 \left(x - x^4\right) \, dx = 2\pi \int_0^1 \left(y^{3/2} - y^3\right) \, dy.$

12. $\dfrac{4223\pi}{5670} = \pi \displaystyle\int_0^{1/3} \left(1 - (x^3 - 3x + 1)^2\right) \, dx + \pi \int_{1/3}^1 \left(1 - x^6\right) \, dx.$

Chapter 9

Solutions

9.1 Exercise Set 47

1. $y(x) = 3e^x$ means $y'(x) = 3e^x$ and $y''(x) = 3e^x$. So, all these derivatives are equal which means that

$$(1-x)y''(x) + xy'(x) - y(x) = 3e^x((1-x) + x - 1) = 3e^x(0) = 0.$$

2. From $y = 2e^x - 0.652e^{-x}$ we have

$$y' = 2e^x + 0.652e^{-x} \quad \text{and} \quad y'' = 2e^x - 0.652e^{-x}.$$

Clearly $y'' = y$. So $y'' - y = 0$.

3. From $y = 2\sin x$ we have $y' = 2\cos x$ and $y'' = -2\sin x$. Next,
$y'''(x) = -2\cos x$, and finally $y^{(4)}(x) = 2\sin x = y(x)$.

Alternately, note that $y'' = -y$. Taking the second derivative of both sides of this last identity, we have
$y^{(4)} = -y''$. But $-y'' = -(-y) = y$. So $y^{(4)} = y$, or $y^{(4)} - y = 0$.

4. $y(x) = ce^{3x} - e^{2x}$, $y'(x) = 3ce^{3x} - 2e^{2x}$, so

$$
\begin{aligned}
y'(x) - 3y(x) &= (3ce^{3x} - 2e^{2x}) - 3(ce^{3x} - e^{2x}) \\
&= 3ce^{3x} - 2e^{2x} - 3ce^{3x} + 3e^{2x} = e^{2x}.
\end{aligned}
$$

5. Differentiating $y = c_1 x^2 + c_2 x + c_3$ three times, we see that $y' = 2c_1 x + c_2$, $y'' = 2c_1$ and $y''' = 0$ which is what we wanted to show.

6. No. Even though the function $y = e^x - e^{-x}$ satisfies the equation
$y'' - y = 0$, its derivative $y' = e^x + e^{-x}$ is equal to $e^0 + e^{-0} = 2$ at $x = 0$. So the initial condition $y'(0) = 1$ fails for this function.

7. No, because this function does not satisfy the initial condition, $y(0) = 1$. In this case, $y(0) = 2$, so it cannot be a solution of the stated initial value problem. On the other hand, $y(x) = e^x + e^{-x}$, $y'(x) = e^x - e^{-x}$ and so, $y'(x) \neq y(x)$, so again it isn't a solution (because it doesn't even satisfy the equation).

8. From $y = e^{2x} - e^{-2x}$ we have $y' = 2e^{2x} + 2e^{-2x}$ and hence $y'(0) = 2e^0 + 2e^0 = 4$, violating the second initial condition $y'(0) = 2$.

9. No. The value of the function $\sin x + \cos x$ is 1 at $x = 0$. So the initial condition $y(0) = 0$ is not satisfied.

10. No, because although $y(x) = x^2$ does satisfy the equation, (since $y'''(x) = 0$) and it does satisfy $y(0) = 0$ and $y'(0) = 0$ it is NOT the case that $y''(0) = 3$, since, in fact, $y''(0) = 2$.

11. From $y = (c_1 + c_2 x)e^x$ we have $y' = (c_1 + c_2 x)e^x + c_2 e^x$. Hence the intial condtions $y(0) = 1$ and $y'(0) = 0$ gives $c_1 = 1$ and $c_2 + c_1 = 0$, from which it is easy to get $c_1 = 0$ and $c_2 = -1$. So the solution satisfying the required initial conditions is $y = (1-x)e^x$.

12. The initial condtion $y(1) = -1$ gives $\frac{1}{1-C} = -1$, from which we obtain $C = 2$. Thus the answer is
$y(t) = \dfrac{t}{1-2t}$.

13. The general solution is given by $y(x) = x^4 + c_1 x^2/2 + c_2 x + c_3$. But $y(0) = 0$ means that $c_3 = 0$. Next,
$y'(0) = 0$, means that $c_2 = 0$ and finally $y''(0) = 0$ means that $c_1 = 0$. Combining all this we get that the solution of the initial value problem is given by $y(x) = x^4$.

14. $y = -4e^{t^2} + 2$.

15. $y = -5e^{-1} - 1 + (1 + 2e^{-1})x + (x+2)e^{-x}$.

9.2   Exercise Set 48

1. Let $f(x) = (1 - x^2)^{-1}$ and $g(y) = 4 + y^2$. We separate the variables and use Table 9.1, with $a = 0$, $y(a) = 1$, to find

    $$\int_1^{y(x)} \frac{1}{u^2 + 4} \, du = \int_0^x \frac{1}{1 - t^2} \, dt,$$

    as the form of the required solution. Now use the trigonometric substitution $u = 2 \tan \theta$ on the left and partial fractions on the right to find the special antiderivatives,

    $$\frac{1}{2}\text{Arctan} \frac{y(x)}{2} - \frac{1}{2}\text{Arctan} \frac{1}{2} = \frac{1}{2} \ln \left| \frac{1 - x}{1 + x} \right|$$

    as the required solution. We don't need to solve for $y(x)$.

2. $e^y = x^2 e^x - 2xe^x + 2e^x + e^{-1} - 2$, or $y = \ln((x^2 - 2x + 2)e^x + e^{-1} - 2)$.

3. We can rewrite the equation as $\frac{y'}{y} = 1 + \frac{1}{x}$. Taking integrals, we have $\ln|y| = x + \ln|x| + C$, which gives the general solution $|y| = |x|e^{x+C}$. So it looks like: $y = |x|e^{x+C}$ or $y = -|x|e^{x+C}$, depending on whether $y(x) > 0$ or $y(x) < 0$, respectively. Now, since $y(1) = 1 > 0$ we must use the form $y = |x|e^{x+C}$ of the general solution (otherwise $y(1)$ cannot be equal to 1). This gives $1 = e^{1+C}$ from which we get $C = -1$. So the required solution is $y = xe^{x-1}$.

4. Let $f(x) = \cos x$ and $g(y) = y^3$. We separate the variables and use Table 9.1, with $a = 0$, $y(a) = -2$, to find

    $$\int_{-2}^{y(x)} \frac{1}{u^3} \, du = \int_0^x \cos t \, dt,$$

    as the form of the required solution. Both sides are easily integrated to give

    $$\left(-\frac{1}{2u^2} \right) \Big|_{-2}^{y(x)} = \sin x,$$

    $$-\frac{1}{2y(x)^2} + \frac{1}{8} = \sin x.$$

    as the required solution. We don't need to solve for $y(x)$.

5. $y = e^{\frac{1}{2}e^{x^2}}$. Let $x^2 = u$ in the integral on the right.

6. $y = \left(\frac{2}{3}x + 2 \right)^3$.

7. Let $f(x) = x \sin x^2$ and $g(y) = 1$. We separate the variables and use Table 9.1, with $a = \sqrt{\pi}$, $y(a) = 0$, to find (using the **FTC**)

    $$y(x) - y(\sqrt{\pi}) = \int_{\sqrt{\pi}}^x t \sin t^2 \, dt,$$

    as the form of the required solution. The right-side needs a substitution only, namely, $u = t^2$, etc. Then,

    $$y(x) - y(\sqrt{\pi}) = \int_{\sqrt{\pi}}^x t \sin t^2 \, dt,$$

    $$= \frac{1}{2} \int_\pi^{x^2} \sin u \, du,$$

    $$= \frac{1}{2} \left((- \cos x^2) - (- \cos \pi) \right),$$

    $$y(x) = \frac{1}{2} \left((- \cos x^2) - 1 \right),$$

    $$= -\frac{1}{2} \left(1 + \cos x^2 \right),$$

    as the required solution.

8. $y = 6x$. Since $x \neq 0$, near the intial condition, we can divide both sides of the diffferential equation $xy' = 6x$ by x, and find $y'(x) = 6$ and the result follows.

9.3   Exercise Set 49

1. Let t be in hours, $N(t) = N(0)e^{kt}$. We are given $N(0) = 6000$ and $N(2.5) = 18000$. We need to find a formula for $N(t)$ and then find the value of $N(5)$. We set $t = 2.5$ into the general Growth Law above and find $N(2.5) = N(0)e^{2.5k}$, or $18000 = 6000e^{2.5k}$ from which we get $3 = e^{2.5k}$ or $k = (\ln 3)/2.5$. Substituting this value back into the original equation $N(t) = N(0)e^{kt}$ and simplifying, we find $N(t) = 6000 \, 3^{\frac{t}{2.5}}$ as the virus population after t hours. Thus, after $t = 5$ hours we have, $N(5) = 6000 \, 3^{\frac{5}{2.5}} = 54,000$ viruses.

2. Here we may apply the half-life formula $N(t) = N(0)/e^{t/T}$ to get $20 = 50/2^{t/1600}$ which gives $2^{t/1600} = 2.5$. Taking natural logarithm on both sides and rearranging the identity, we have

$$t = 1600 \frac{\ln 2.5}{\ln 2} \approx 2115.$$

So it takes about 2115 years for the original sample of 50 micrograms to be reduced to 20 micrograms.

3. a) Divide both sides of the differential equation by $T_0 - T$. Then the left-side depends only on $T(t)$ while the right side is a constant. So the equation is separable since it takes the form

$$T'(t) = f(t)g(T),$$

where $f(t) = c$ and $g(T) = T_0 - T$. Now use Table 10.1 in the form

$$\int_{T(0)}^{T(t)} \frac{du}{T_0 - u} = \int_0^t c \, dt.$$

Integration shows that $- \ln |T_0 - u| \Big|_{u=T(0)}^{u=T(t)} = ct$ from which we can derive that

$$T(t) = T_0 + (T(0) - T_0)e^{-ct}.$$

b) Here we have $T_0 = 20$, $T_0 = 90$ and $T(4) = 80$. So, letting $t = 4$ in the above identity, we have $80 = 20 + (90 - 20)e^{-4c}$. So $e^{-4c} = 6/7$. Now we have to find t such that $T(t) = 70$. Applying the same identity again, we have $70 = 20 + (90 - 20)e^{-ct}$, or

$$5/7 = e^{-ct} = \left(e^{-4c}\right)^{t/4} = (6/7)^{t/4}.$$

Taking the natural logarithm on both sides and rearranging, we have

$$t = 4 \frac{\ln 5 - \ln 7}{\ln 6 - \ln 7} \approx 8.731.$$

Thus it takes about nine minutes to reach a drinkable temperature.

4. We assume a Law of Growth, $N(t) = N(0)e^{kt}$. After 5,700 years there will be exactly one-half of the original amount, $N(0)$, which translates into $N(5700) = N(0)/2$. Thus, $N(0)/2 = N(0)e^{5700k}$, and the $N(0)$ cancel out (they always do!). So, $1/2 = e^{5700k}$ which means that $k = -(\ln 2)/5700$. This gives the value of k.

Next, if 90% decays then only 10% remains, right? But we want a value of t such that $N(t) = (0.1)N(0)$ (which translates as "90% of the original amount has decayed"). But whatever this value of t may be, it is also given by $(0.1)N(0) = N(t) = N(0)\left(e^{(-\ln 2)}\right)^{\frac{t}{5700}} = \frac{1}{2^{\frac{t}{5700}}}$. So, $(0.1) = \frac{1}{2^{\frac{t}{5700}}}$ which, when solved for t, gives $t = 5700 \frac{\ln 10}{\ln 2} \approx 18,935$ years.

5. a) Denote by $N(t)$ the number of bacteria at time t. Then we can write $T(t) = 4000e^{kt}$ where k is the rate of growth per bacteria. By assumption, $T(0.5) = 12000$ and so $12000 = 4000e^{0.5k}$, which gives $e^{0.5k} = 3$, or $0.5k = \ln 3$, that is $k = 2\ln 3 = \ln 9$. Thus

$$N(t) = 4000e^{(\ln 9)t} = 4000 \cdot 9^t.$$

b) After 20 minutes, the population of the bacteria is

$$N(1/3) = 4000 \times 9^{1/3} \approx 8320.$$

c) Suppose that $N(t) = 50000$. Then $50000 = 4000 \times 9^t$ and hence $9^t = 12.5$. So

$$t = \frac{\ln 12.5}{\ln 9} \approx 1.15.$$

Thus the bacteria population reach 50000 in an hour and 9 minutes.

6. Since the population satisfies a Law of Growth we can write $P(t) = P(0)e^{kt}$, where t is in years. We are given that $P(0) = 6 \times 10^8$ and that 300 years "later" (from A.D. 1650) the population was 2.8×10^9, that is, $P(300) = 2.8 \times 10^9$. We want a value of t such that $P(t) = 25 \times 10^9$. So, $2.8 \times 10^9 = P(300) = P(0)e^{300k} = 6 \times 10^8 \, e^{300k}$ and we can solve for k giving $0.467 \times 10 = e^{300k}$, or $k = \frac{\ln 4.67}{300} \approx 0.00513$. Thus, $P(t) = (6 \times 10^8)e^{0.00513t}$ is the Law of Growth, at time t in years. But we want $P(t) = 25 \times 10^9$ so this means that $25 \times 10^9 = (6 \times 10^8)e^{0.00513t}$ and we can solve for t, using logarithms. This gives, $41.667 = e^{0.00513t}$ or $t = \frac{\ln 41.667}{0.00513} \approx 727$ years. Thus, the population of the earth will reach 25 billion around the year $1650 + 727 = 2377$.

7. The differential equation for this learning model is $P' = c(1 - P)$ which is of the form $P' = f(t)g(P)$ where $f(t) = c$ and $g(P) = 1 - P$. Using Table 10.1 we see that the general solution is given by evaluating the integrals

$$\int_{P(0)}^{P(t)} \frac{du}{1 - u} = \int_0^t c \, dt$$

$$- \ln |1 - u| \Big|_{u=P(0)}^{u=P(t)} = ct$$

$$\ln |1 - P(t)| = -ct \quad \text{(since } P(0) = 0\text{)},$$

$$P(t) = 1 - e^{-ct}.$$

b) By assumption, we have $P(3) = 0.4$ and hence $0.4 = 1 - e^{-3c}$, which gives $e^{-3c} = 0.6$. Now suppose $P(t) = 0.95$, that is $1 - e^{-ct} = 0.95$, which can be rewritten as $(e^{-3c})^{t/3} = 0.05$, or $0.6^{t/3} = 0.05$. Taking natural logarithm on both sides and rearranging, we have

$$t = 3 \frac{\ln 0.05}{\ln 0.6} \approx 17.6.$$

Thus the student has to do at least 18 exercises in order to achieve a 0.95 (or 95 percent) chance of mastering the subject.

8. As suggested, we use the "integrating factor" $e^{kt/m}$ and let $z(t) = v(t)e^{kt/m}$. Then, by the product rule,

$$z'(t) = v'(t)e^{kt/m} + v(t) \cdot \frac{k}{m}e^{kt/m} = \left(v'(t) + \frac{k}{m}v(t) \right) e^{kt/m} = ge^{kt/m},$$

in view of the fact that the equation $mv' = mg - kv$ can be rewritten as $v' + \frac{k}{m}v = g$. Integrating, we have

$$z(t) = z(0) + \int_0^t ge^{ks/m}\, ds = v(0) + \frac{mg}{k}\left(e^{kt/m} - 1 \right),$$

where $v(0)$ is just the initial speed v_o. Thus

$$v(t) = z(t) \cdot e^{-kt/m} = \frac{mg}{k}\left(1 - e^{-kt/m} \right) + v_o e^{-kt/k}.$$

9. In this case we assume a Law of Decay of the usual form $N(t) = N(0)e^{kt}$. We can use the Half-Life Formula and find $N(t) = N(0)/2^{t/T}$ where T is the half-life of the radionuclide. In this case, $T = 29.1$, so the amount left at time t is given by $N(t) = N(0)/2^{t/29.1}$. The initial sample of 5 g means that $N(0) = 5$. If we want to find out when 90% of the sample has decayed, then there is only 10% of it left, that is we want to find t such that $N(t) = (0.1)N(0) = (0.1)(5) = 0.5$. This means that $0.5 = 5/2^{t/29.1}$, or using logarithms, $t = \frac{\ln 100}{\ln 2} \times 29.1 \approx 193.33$ years.

Chapter 10

Solutions to Problems in the Appendices

10.1   APPENDIX A - Exercise Set 50

1. 2

2. $\dfrac{1}{25}$

3. $2^6 = 64$

4. 12

5. 45

6. $4x^2 - y^2$

7. x^2

8. $\dfrac{2}{25}$

9. $x^2 y^3$

10. $1 - r^4$

11. $a^3 b^5$

12. $8a^9$

13. $\dfrac{1}{x^{\frac{7}{12}}}$

14. 64

15. 6

16. $\dfrac{x^{12}}{27}$

17. 3

18. 8

19. 3^{n+1}

20. 2

21. Expand the right side, collect terms and compare the coefficients. You'll find that $1 = -a^2$ which is an impossibility since the right side is always negative or zero and the left side is positive.

22. See Example 502 where you set $r = x^2$.

23. $1 + x^2 + x^4 + x^6$; see the previous exercise.

24. Expand the left-side and simplify.

25. Use the Power Laws and simplify

26. Since $a^{r+s} = a^r a^s$ we can set $s = -r$. Then $a^0 = a^r a^{-r}$ and since $a^0 = 1$ we get $1 = a^r a^{-r}$ and the result follows.

27. See the Introduction to this section for a similar argument.

28. Let $x = 2$, $y = 3$. Then $2^8 \neq 2^6$.

29. Replace r by $-r$ in Example 502 and then set $r = \dfrac{x}{2}$ and simplify.

30. Write x as $x = \dfrac{a^{\frac{1}{2}} + a^{-\frac{1}{2}}}{2}$. Square both sides of this equality, use the Powers Laws, and then subtract 1 from the result. Simplify.

10.2   APPENDIX B - Exercise Set 51

1. $\dfrac{2}{3}$

2. $\dfrac{2}{3}$

3. 3

4. $y = 3x - 10$

5. $y = x - 1$

6. $y = -2x - 5$

7. $y = \dfrac{4}{3}x - 10$

8. $y = -\dfrac{3}{2}x + 3$

9. $y = -\dfrac{2}{3}x + \dfrac{1}{3}$

10. $\left(-\frac{1}{3}, \frac{2}{3}\right)$

11. There is no intersection whatsoever since the lines are parallel or have the same slope ($= 1$)

12. There is no intersection point either since the lines are parallel or have the same slope ($= 1$)

13.   a) $y = x - 2$

   b) The altitude has length $\sqrt{32} = 4\sqrt{2}$. First, we find the equation of the line through $(4, -6)$ having slope -1 as it must be perpendicular to the line through $(2, 0)$ and $(6, 4)$ (*i.e.*, $y = x - 2$). This line is given by $y = -x - 2$. The find the point of intersection of this line with $y = x - 2$. We get the point $(0, -2)$. The base of the triangle has length given by the distance formula in the exercise applied to the points A and B. Its value is $\sqrt{32}$. The altitude has height given by the same distance formula, namely, the distance between the points C$(4, -6)$ and $(0, -2)$; its value is $\sqrt{32}$ as well. The rest follows.

   c) Area $= (1/2)\sqrt{(32)}\sqrt{(32)} = 16$

14. $y = x$

15. $y = -x + 4$

Credits

The design, graphics, and caricatures in this book were created and manipulated by the author. Layout and front cover design by the author. The original cover on the Modules showed a ghosted image of the original front page of Leibniz's pioneering paper on the Calculus, dated 1684, and written in Latin. The present manuscript shows a colour photograph (by the author) of a path in the Taronga Zoo in Sydney, Australia.

My most sincere thanks are extended to my colleague, Dr. Che Kao Fong, and to Genevieve Hay, M.Sc., M.B.A., for proofreading the manuscript and for their invaluable assistance in the arduous task of compiling the solutions to many of the exercises. Many thanks are also extended to my colleague Dr. Lazer Resnick for finding a number of typographical and other errors, and to R. Takac and G. Hay for their assistance in producing some of the graphics in Chapter 4.

The present Millennium Edition contains typographical revisions and corrections to the January 4, 1999 printing. Many thanks to the following individuals who have found errors and or typographical corrections in all past editions: Dr. Lazer Resnick (Physics), Stephen Burchill, Ian Rosso, Heather Leaman, Reza Rahimy, Michelle Bamji, Amy Cameron, Mina Boghdady, Jan Hiscock, Omar Nada, Glen Robitaille, Hamid Boland.

Many thanks to Ann Woodside for her help in compiling material for business applications in the August, 2000 edition and to Dr. Lazer Resnick for finding additional typographical errors and omissions.

The first 2001 edition owes most of its (typographical) revisions to my colleagues: Dr. Sam Melkonian, Mr. Sam Dubé, Dr. Elena Devdariani, and to the following students: Michael Lombardi, Mr. Mortezavi, Derek Voisin, Shane McDowell, Anderson Wong, Javed Bagha and Nick Argent among others whose names may have been omitted inadvertently.

The Millennium Series in Calculus

The *Millennium Series in Calculus* represents a collection of Calculus texts written by the author and intended to cover the usual sequence of three one- or two-term Calculus courses in North-American universities. The topics in these courses are covered in a modular format with Modules 1 and 2 covering the material for a first one-term course, while Modules 3 and 4 will address the remaining two multivariable courses with series. A module in differential equations is anticipated for a future date.

Module 1 Differential Calculus, Summer, 1998
ISBN 0-9698889-1-0

Module 2 Integral Calculus, Fall, 1998
ISBN 0-9698889-2-9

Calculus, Combined Edition (Modules 1 and 2 together), Fall, 1999
ISBN 0-9698889-3-7

Solutions Manual to Accompany Calculus, Fall, 1999
ISBN 0-9698889-4-5

About the Author

Angelo B. Mingarelli received his B.Sc. (*Hons*) in Mathematics from Loyola College in Montreal, with the mention, *summa cum laude*. After being awarded an NRC 1967 Science Scholarship, he pursued his graduate studies at the University of Toronto where he received his Master's and Doctorate in Mathematics, the latter with a disseration on the spectral theory of differential and integral operators under the supervision of Professor F.V. Atkinson. His teaching career began at The Pennsylvania State University, in University Park, followed by a tenured appointment at the University of Ottawa where he was an NSERC University Research Fellow for many years. While there he was nominated for the University-wide award of *Teacher of the Year* in 1987. After his move to Carleton University in Ottawa, he received *Faculty of Science Awards for Excellence in Teaching* on two occasions (in 1992, and again in 1996). These were complemented recently by a *Teaching Achievement Award for 1998-1999* offered by the University in recognition of Excellence in teaching and teaching development. His interests include research in analysis and differential equations and mathematical education.

Index